lone

Eastern USA

Trisha Ping, Ali Lemer, Charles Rawlings-Way, Regis St Louis, Mara Vorhees, Isabel Albiston, Mark Baker, Amy C Balfour, Robert Balkovich, Ray Bartlett, Jade Bremner, Gregor Clark, Ashley Harrell, Adam Karlin, Brian Kluepfel, Vesna Maric, Virginia Maxwell, Hugh McNaughtan, MaSovaida Morgan, Lorna Parkes, Kevin Raub, Simon Richmond, Benedict Walker, Greg Ward, Karla Zimmerman

PLAN YOUR TRIP

Welcome to Eastern USA 4

Eastern USA Map 6

Eastern USA's Top Experiences 8

Need to Know 22

What's New 24

Accommodations 26

Month by Month 28

Itineraries 33

Road Trips & Scenic Drives 38

Outdoor Activities 46

Eat & Drink Like a Local 50

Family Travel 54

Regions at a Glance 57

ON THE ROAD

NEW YORK, NEW JERSEY & PENNSYLVANIA 60

New York City 61

New York State 121

Long Island 121

Hudson Valley 127

Catskills 131

Finger Lakes 134

The Adirondacks 136

Thousand Islands 140

New Jersey 145

Hoboken 145

Princeton 146

Jersey Shore 147

Pennsylvania 152

Philadelphia 152

Pennsylvania Dutch Country 163

Pittsburgh 165

NEW ENGLAND 170

Massachusetts 171

Boston 174

Cape Cod 194

Pioneer Valley 203

The Berkshires 205

Rhode Island 208

Providence 209

Newport 211

East Bay 213

Connecticut 213

Hartford 214

Connecticut Coast 216

Vermont 221

New Hampshire 232

Lakes Region 234

White Mountains 236

Hanover 240

Maine 240

Ogunquit 241

Portland 241

WASHINGTON, DC & THE CAPITAL REGION 250

Washington, DC 251

Maryland 280

Baltimore............... 280

Annapolis.............. 286

Ocean City............. 289

Delaware 293

Wilmington & Brandywine Valley 295

Dover 296

Virginia.............. 298

Historic Triangle........ 304

Norfolk................ 307

Virginia Beach 308

The Piedmont.......... 308

Shenandoah Valley 314

Blue Ridge Highlands & Southwest Virginia.......319

West Virginia..........322

Eastern Panhandle 323

Monongahela National Forest......... 325

New River & Greenbrier Valley 327

THE SOUTH........332

North Carolina 333

The Triangle 342

COVID-19

We have re-checked every business in this book before publication to ensure that it is still open after the COVID-19 outbreak. However, the economic and social impacts of COVID-19 will continue to be felt long after the outbreak has been contained, and many businesses, services and events referenced in this guide may experience ongoing restrictions. Some businesses may be temporarily closed, have changed their opening hours and services, or require bookings; some unfortunately could have closed permanently. We suggest you check with venues before visiting for the latest information.

Contents

Charlotte 346
Great Smoky Mountains National Park 354
South Carolina 355
Charleston............. 356
Lowcountry............361
Myrtle Beach 363
Greenville & the Upcountry 365
Tennessee 366
Memphis 366
Nashville 373
Kentucky 386
Louisville 387
Bluegrass Country...... 390
Georgia.............. 394
Atlanta 394
Alabama..............413
Birmingham 414
Montgomery...........416
Selma..................417
Mobile 418
Mississippi 419
Oxford 419
Mississippi Delta 420
Jackson 422
Natchez 423
Gulf Coast 425
Arkansas 425
Little Rock............. 425
Hot Springs............ 427
Tri-Peaks Region 428
Ozark Mountains 430
Louisiana 432
New Orleans 433
St Francisville 447
Cajun Country 447
Cajun Wetlands 449
FLORIDA 452
Miami 453
Fort Lauderdale 470
Palm Beach............474
The Everglades..........477
Florida Keys 482
Space Coast 488
Daytona Beach......... 490
St Augustine...........491
Jacksonville............ 493
Amelia Island 495
Tampa 496
St Petersburg 499
Sarasota 500
Sanibel & Captiva Islands..........501
Naples 502
Orlando 504
Tallahassee 511
Pensacola 513
GREAT LAKES......516
Illinois 517
Chicago 517
Indiana...............552
Indianapolis 552
Ohio 560
Cleveland..............561
Erie Lakeshore & Islands............... 564
Ohio Amish Country 565
Columbus 566
Yellow Springs 567
Dayton 568
Cincinnati 568
Michigan 571
Detroit 571
Dearborn..............578
Ann Arbor 579
Gold Coast.............582
Straits of Mackinac 587
Upper Peninsula.........588
Wisconsin 591
Milwaukee............. 591
Minnesota 601
Minneapolis.............602
St Paul 607

UNDERSTAND

History 616
The Way of Life....... 626
Arts & Architecture 630
Music 633
Landscapes & Wildlife............ 636

SURVIVAL GUIDE

Directory A–Z 642
Transportation 649
Index................ 659
Map Legend.......... 669

SPECIAL FEATURES

Road Trips & Scenic Drives 38
Family Travel.......... 54
Central Park in 3D..... 84
National Mall in 3D ...260
National Parks 331

Right: Acadia National Park (p247), Maine

JOSEPH SOHM/SHUTTERSTOCK ©

WELCOME TO

Eastern USA

In an increasingly globalized world, I love how you can find so many unique pockets of culture amid the 29 states of Eastern USA. Truth be told, each could be a country of its own, from tiny Rhode Island with its yacht-loving harbors and polo fields to the Cajun fiddle halls and alligator-filled cypress swamps of Louisiana. In between you have Appalachian peaks, oceanlike freshwater lakes, and countless miles of coastline studded with sandy beaches and barrier islands – not to mention grand cityscapes where you can cross continents just by heading to another part of town.

By Regis St Louis, Writer
@regisstlouis @ regisstlouis
For more about our writers, see p672

Eastern USA

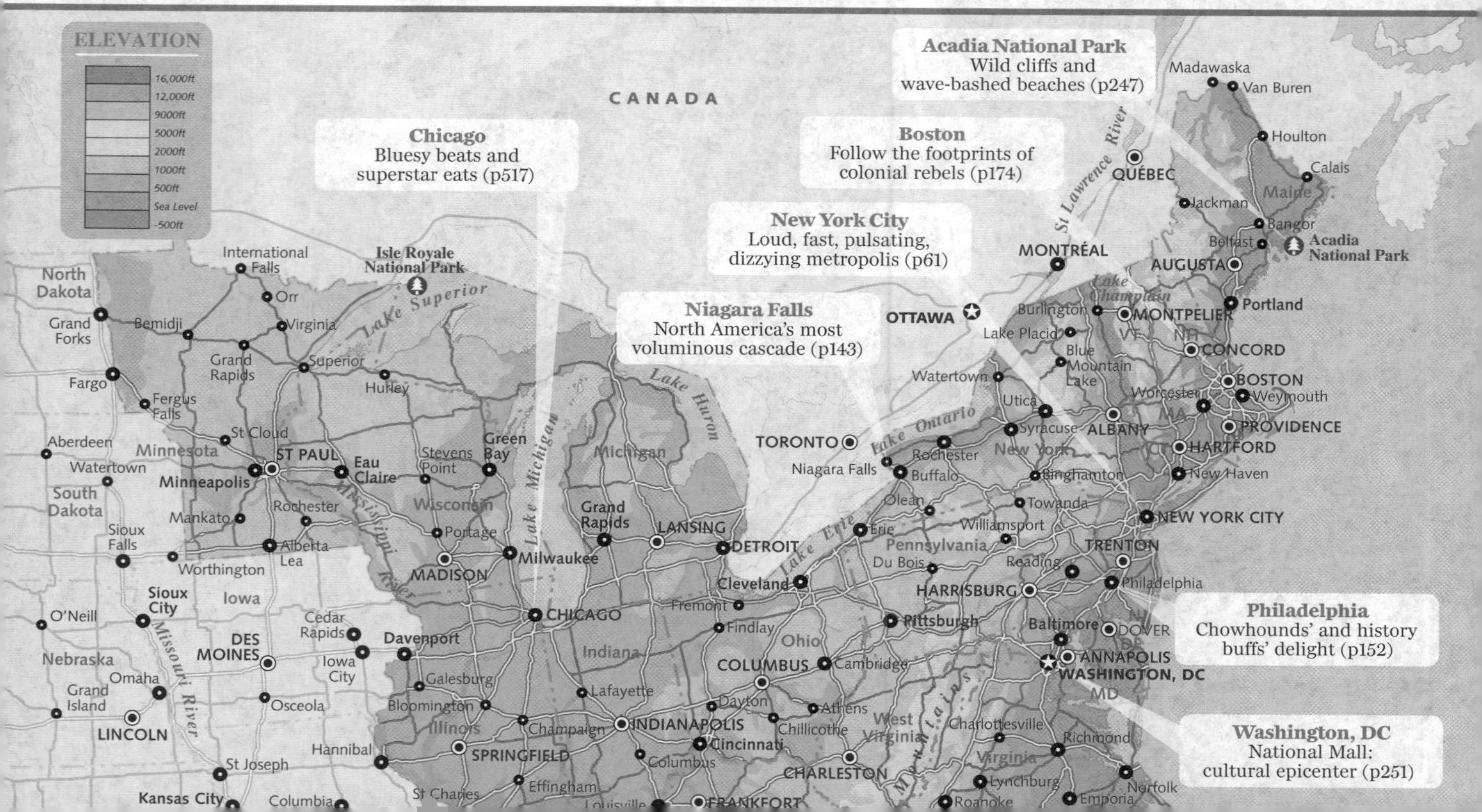

0 — 500 km
0 — 300 miles

ELEVATION

16,000ft
12,000ft
9000ft
5000ft
2000ft
1000ft
500ft
Sea Level
-500ft

Acadia National Park
Wild cliffs and
wave-bashed beaches (p247)

Chicago
Bluesy beats and
superstar eats (p517)

Boston
Follow the footprints of
colonial rebels (p174)

New York City
Loud, fast, pulsating,
dizzying metropolis (p61)

Niagara Falls
North America's most
voluminous cascade (p143)

Philadelphia
Chowhounds' and history
buffs' delight (p152)

Washington, DC
National Mall:
cultural epicenter (p251)

CANADA
Madawaska
Van Buren
Houlton
Calais
Maine
Jackman
Bangor
Belfast
Acadia National Park
AUGUSTA
Portland
QUÉBEC
St Lawrence River
MONTRÉAL
OTTAWA
Lake Champlain
Burlington
MONTPELIER
VT
NH
CONCORD
Lake Placid
Blue Mountain Lake
Watertown
BOSTON
Weymouth
Worcester
MA
PROVIDENCE
Utica
Syracuse
ALBANY
HARTFORD
CT
New Haven
Lake Ontario
TORONTO
Rochester
New York
Binghamton
Niagara Falls
Buffalo
Olean
Towanda
NEW YORK CITY
Williamsport
Erie
Lake Erie
Pennsylvania
TRENTON
Reading
Du Bois
Philadelphia
HARRISBURG
Pittsburgh
Baltimore
DOVER
ANNAPOLIS
WASHINGTON, DC
MD
Cleveland
Fremont
Findlay
Ohio
COLUMBUS
Cambridge
Dayton
Athens
Chillicothe
West Virginia
Mountains
Charlottesville
Richmond
Virginia
CHARLESTON
Lynchburg
Norfolk
Roanoke
Emporia
Cincinnati
Columbus
FRANKFORT
Louisville
INDIANAPOLIS
Indiana
Lafayette
Champaign
SPRINGFIELD
Effingham
St Charles
Illinois
Bloomington
Galesburg
Hannibal
Columbia
Kansas City
St Joseph
LINCOLN
Omaha
Grand Island
Nebraska
Missouri River
O'Neill
Sioux City
Iowa
DES MOINES
Osceola
Cedar Rapids
Iowa City
Davenport
CHICAGO
Lake Michigan
Milwaukee
MADISON
Mississippi River
Portage
Wisconsin
Stevens Point
Green Bay
Eau Claire
Grand Rapids
LANSING
DETROIT
Michigan
Lake Huron
Lake Superior
Isle Royale National Park
Hurley
Superior
Virginia
Orr
International Falls
Grand Rapids
Bemidji
North Dakota
Grand Forks
Fargo
Fergus Falls
St Cloud
Minnesota
ST PAUL
Minneapolis
Rochester
Mankato
Albert Lea
Worthington
Aberdeen
Watertown
South Dakota
Sioux Falls

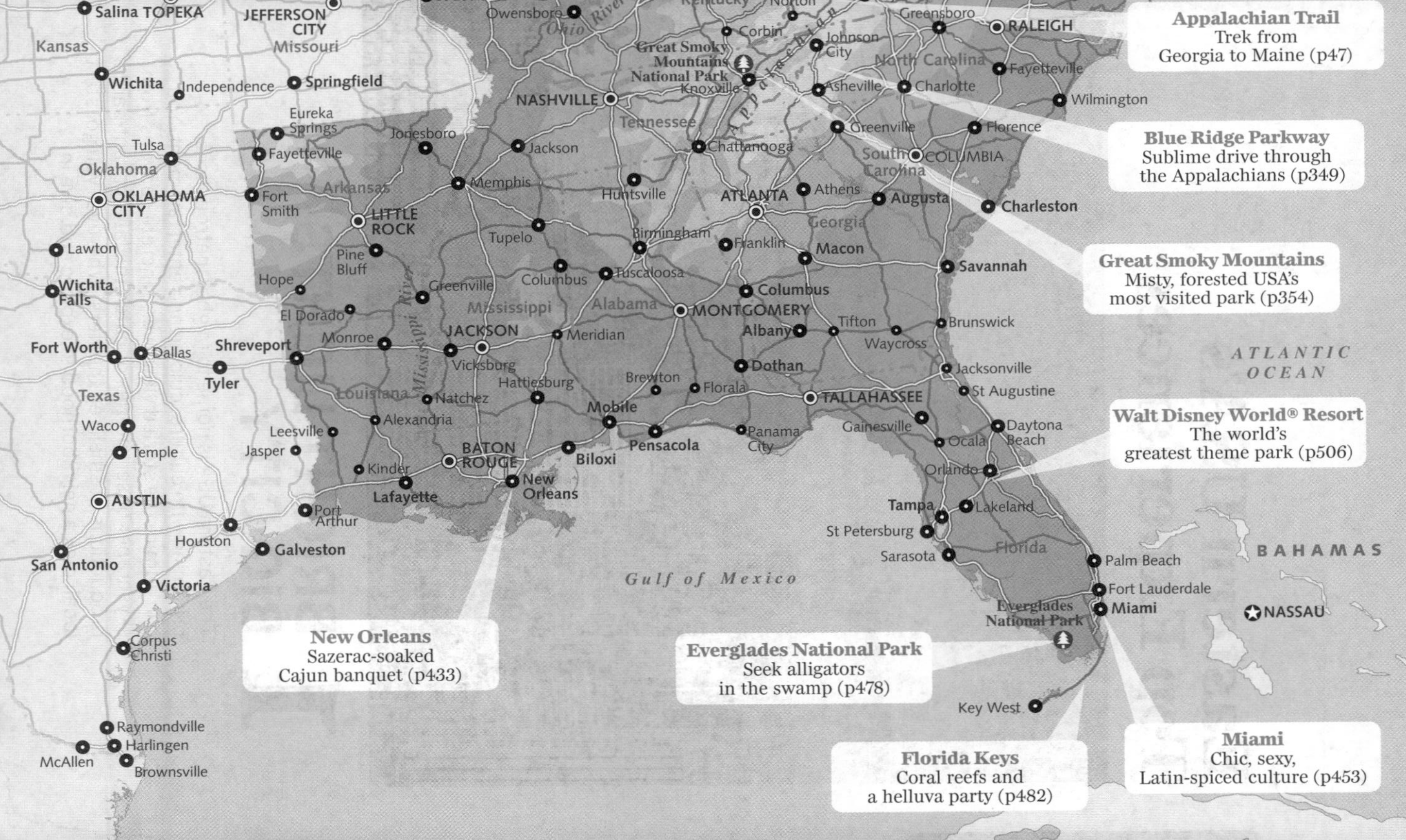

Appalachian Trail
Trek from
Georgia to Maine (p47)
Blue Ridge Parkway
Sublime drive through
the Appalachians (p349)
Great Smoky Mountains
Misty, forested USA's
most visited park (p354)
Walt Disney World® Resort
The world's
greatest theme park (p506)
New Orleans
Sazerac-soaked
Cajun banquet (p433)
Everglades National Park
Seek alligators
in the swamp (p478)
Florida Keys
Coral reefs and
a helluva party (p482)
Miami
Chic, sexy,
Latin-spiced culture (p453)
ATLANTIC OCEAN
Gulf of Mexico
BAHAMAS
NASSAU
Salina
TOPEKA
JEFFERSON CITY
Kansas
Missouri
Wichita
Independence
Springfield
Eureka Springs
Tulsa
Fayetteville
Oklahoma
OKLAHOMA CITY
Fort Smith
Arkansas
LITTLE ROCK
Lawton
Pine Bluff
Wichita Falls
Hope
El Dorado
Fort Worth
Dallas
Shreveport
Tyler
Texas
Waco
Temple
AUSTIN
Leesville
Jasper
Houston
Port Arthur
Galveston
San Antonio
Victoria
Corpus Christi
Raymondville
Harlingen
McAllen
Brownsville
Owensboro
Ohio River
Kentucky
Norton
Corbin
Johnson City
Great Smoky Mountains National Park
Knoxville
Greensboro
RALEIGH
North Carolina
Fayetteville
Wilmington
NASHVILLE
Tennessee
Asheville
Charlotte
Greenville
Florence
Jonesboro
Jackson
Chattanooga
South Carolina
COLUMBIA
Memphis
Huntsville
ATLANTA
Athens
Augusta
Charleston
Georgia
Tupelo
Birmingham
Franklin
Macon
Savannah
Columbus
Tuscaloosa
Columbus
Greenville
Mississippi
Alabama
MONTGOMERY
Tifton
Brunswick
Mississippi River
Monroe
JACKSON
Meridian
Albany
Waycross
Vicksburg
Dothan
Jacksonville
Hattiesburg
Brewton
Florala
St Augustine
Louisiana
Natchez
TALLAHASSEE
Alexandria
Mobile
Gainesville
Daytona Beach
Panama City
Pensacola
Ocala
BATON ROUGE
Biloxi
Kinder
New Orleans
Orlando
Lafayette
Tampa
Lakeland
St Petersburg
Sarasota
Florida
Palm Beach
Fort Lauderdale
Miami
Everglades National Park
Key West

Eastern USA's Top Experiences

1 BRIGHT LIGHTS, BIG CITY

The Eastern USA is home to mighty metropolises brimming with culture, cuisine and entertainment. You can admire the storied view over concrete canyons from skyscraper observatories or catch the latest avant-garde productions at small rep theaters. Wherever you go, start local: pick a neighborhood to explore and dive in.

New York

Home to immigrants from every corner of the globe, New York City (pictured opposite and right) is loud, fast, pulsing with energy and always evolving. Whether you come for the day or stay for a lifetime, it's never enough. A staggering number of museums, parks and ethnic neighborhoods are scattered through the five boroughs. p61

Chicago

The Windy City will blow you away with its architecture, lakefront beaches and indie theater. But its real lure is its blend of high culture and earthy pleasures – like dressing its Picasso sculpture in local sports-team gear. p517

Washington, DC

You could spend weeks exploring the free museums of the Smithsonian, though there are also iconic monuments (pictured above), ethnic restaurants and blossom-filled parks. Afterwards, head to nearby Baltimore to visit one of America's most astonishing art collections. p251

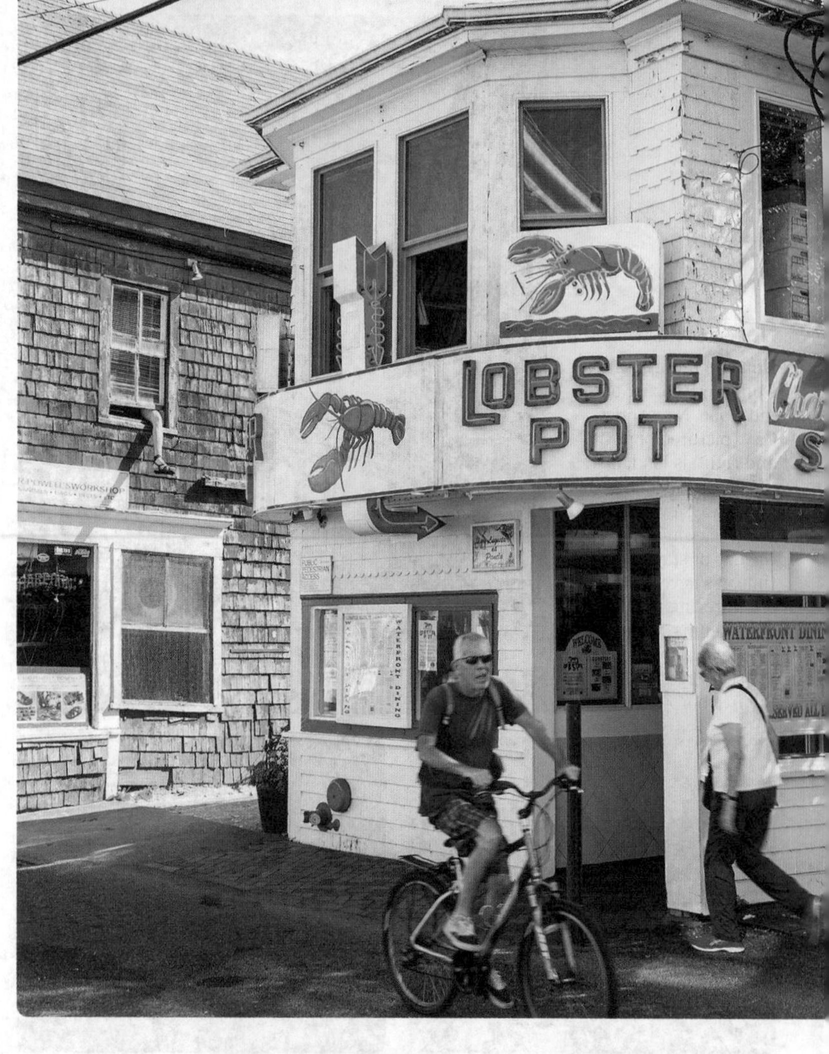

2 BEACHES & ISLANDS

Amid thousands of miles of shorelines, you'll find islands, seaside towns and some of America's loveliest beaches. There will be plenty of surprises, from herds of wild horses descended from shipwreck survivors to remote national parks reached only by boat. Wherever you roam, it's hard not to feel like you've left the modern world behind as you head out to a place where nature rules supreme in a salt-tinged realm of sea, sand and sky.

TRAVELER1116/GETTY IMAGES ©

COLIN D YOUNG/SHUTTERSTOCK ©

KARENFOLEYPHOTOGRAPHY/GETTY IMAGES ©

Cape Cod

Massive sand dunes, picturesque lighthouses and cool forests invite endless exploring on the Massachusetts cape. After a day on the shore, treat yourself to an oyster feast in Wellfleet or a bit of nightlife in Provincetown. p194

Above left: lobster restaurant, Provincetown (p198)

Gulf Islands

Throw a dart at a map of Florida and you'll likely land near a pristine stretch of shoreline. The Panhandle beaches, however, outshine the rest. With snow-white sands backed by nature reserves, the Gulf Islands National Seashore (pictured top right) is a coastal treasure. p514

Outer Banks

On North Carolina's underdeveloped shoreline you can spy wild Spanish mustangs on Corolla, explore the history of flight at Kitty Hawk, and look for the ghost of Blackbeard on isolated Ocracoke Island. p333

Above: hang-gliding at Jockey's Ridge State Park (p337)

3 AMERICAN RHYTHMS

From the soulful blues born in the Mississippi Delta to the bluegrass of Appalachia and Detroit's Motown sound – plus jazz, funk, hip-hop, country, and rock and roll – America has invented sounds integral to modern music. You can walk in the footsteps of musical legends on visits to Sun Studio in Memphis (where BB King, Johnny Cash and Elvis Presley recorded) and hear tomorrow's future stars in concert halls, honky-tonks and music clubs across the region.

New Orleans Jazz

Music flows deep in the soul of New Orleans. Major music festivals are well worth planning a trip around, though no matter when you visit, you'll always find plenty on offer at jazz clubs and backyard bars across town. p433

Above: Mardi Gras (p439)
Top right: Bacchanal (p442)

KRIS DAVIDSON/LONELY PLANET ©

CHICK WAGNER/SHUTTERSTOCK ©

Crooked Road

Old-time mountain music lives on in the vintage music halls sprinkled around a remote corner of Virginia. You can pay homage to bluegrass legends at the Carter Family Fold, browse for custom-made fiddles in Galax or join the weekly jamboree in Floyd. p321

Bottom left: fiddle-maker, Floyd

Chicago Blues

In Chicago no genre is as iconic as the blues – the electric blues, to be exact. Hear it in clubs around town, such as Buddy Guy's Legends (pictured below), or Rosa's Lounge, where it's a bit more down and dirty. p543

MYLES NEW/LONELY PLANET ©

MARC LACHAPELLE/500PX ©

4 MOUNTAIN HIGH

Coursing through 14 states, the Appalachians are among the oldest mountains on earth. It's easy to reconnect with nature when hiking forested slopes past gurgling streams and old-growth poplars up to lofty summits overlooking the wilderness-covered horizon. Hiking and camping immerse you in the region's natural wonders, though you can also go on wildlife watching excursions, hit the slopes in winter or just bunk for the night in a cabin, with age-old forests right outside your door.

TONY BARBER/GETTY IMAGES ©

RUSH JAGOE/LONELY PLANET ©

SEBASTIEN LEMYRE/GETTY IMAGES ©

Acadia National Park

Maine's unspoiled wilderness offers craggy coastal mountains, towering sea cliffs and surf-pounded beaches. You can overnight in historic inns overlooking the water or pitch a tent in well-placed campgrounds. p247

Top right: pitcher plant flower

Great Smoky Mountains

Don't miss out on Eastern USA's most magnificent park (pictured above left), with its cascades and jaw-dropping viewpoints. Take a stunning scenic drive or hike through misty mountain trails while on the lookout for deer, birds and black bears. p354

White Mountains

New England's ultimate destination for adventurers (pictured above), with 1200 miles of hiking trails and 48 peaks over 4000ft. Franconia Notch is a perfect starting place, with myriad walking routes, waterfalls and an aerial tramway up Cannon Mountain. p236

5 BEHIND THE WHEEL

The open road awaits. As you hop into the driver's seat (preferably in a car with low or no emissions) and hit the highway, you can chart a course through some of North America's most striking landscapes. Appalachian mountains, the sultry swamplands of the South and the scenic country lanes of New England are a few fine starting points for the great American road trip. Veer off the interstate often to discover the bucolic 'blue highways' of lore.

Blue Ridge Parkway

Snaking from North Carolina to Virginia, this high-elevation pavement (pictured below left) offers grand views at every bend in the road. You can stop at scenic overlooks, hike through Appalachian woodlands and overnight in old-fashioned inns. p320

MATT MUNRO/LONELY PLANET ©

VT 100

In autumn, Vermont is the star of the foliage show. Drive along historic VT 100 (pictured top right) to ogle the gaudy colors on the slopes of Mt Snow and blanketing the Mad River Valley. p226

Florida Keys

With a name like 'Overseas Highway' who can resist? The 126-mile trip takes you from Florida City to Key West (pictured right), passing mangrove-fringed islands, scenic bridges and arts-loving towns. p482

6 FOOD, GLORIOUS FOOD

DANIEL GRILL/TETRA IMAGES/GETTY IMAGES ©

S. HOSS/SHUTTERSTOCK ©

MIA2YOU/SHUTTERSTOCK ©

Whatever your reasons for visiting, food is likely to play a starring role during your travels. This the land of Maine lobster shacks, bagels and lox in Manhattan delis, smoked barbecue in Memphis roadhouses and decadent Creole cooking in New Orleans. You also won't go thirsty in a region of abundant vineyards, craft breweries and home-grown bourbon (and myriad other spirits), not to mention southern-style sweet tea and much-loved local coffee roasters all across the Eastern USA.

Lowcountry Cuisine

No trip to the South is complete without gorging on the fresh, seafood-centric, African-influenced cuisine of the coastal lowlands. Charleston is the gateway to feasting on crab, fish, shrimp and oysters. p359

Maine Lobster

Forget ambrosia: surely the succulent cold-water crustacean (pictured above) is the real food of the gods. Head to Maine to feast on freshly steamed lobster (best dunked in butter) at summertime lobster pounds. p247

Philadelphia

Teeming food halls like the Reading Terminal Market showcase Philly's bounty, with stalls offering everything from steaming Pennsylvania Dutch–style dumplings to spicy Thai curries. p152

7 SMALL-TOWN CULTURE

Some of the best places to discover the soul of the country are in small towns sprinkled from northern Maine to southwestern Louisiana. In diverse communities, you'll hear the region's colorful accents, discover local specialities and experience unsung attractions overlooked by most travelers. Small-town pride runs deep, and you needn't limit your travels to the city to discover one-of-a-kind museums, creative craft-makers and farm-to-table restaurants.

WENDYOLSENPHOTOGRAPHY/GETTY IMAGES ©

DENISTANGNEYJR/GETTY IMAGES ©

Asheville

Perhaps North Carolina's prettiest mountain town, Asheville charms with its 1930s downtown, craft beer culture and easy access to some of the state's best outdoor adventures (pictured top left). p351

Woodstock

The bohemian, arts-loving town (pictured above) north of NYC puts you in the heart of the peaks of the Catskills. Browse crafts, sip locally roasted coffee and visit hidden sculpture gardens. p133

Route 66

The Mother Road begins in Chicago, and the first 300-mile stretch through Illinois offers time-warped touring amid small-town diners and kitschy roadside sculptures. p551

Above: Gemini Giant

8 REMEMBERING THE PAST

NAGEL PHOTOGRAPHY/SHUTTERSTOCK ©

JIAWANGKUN/SHUTTERSTOCK ©

Ancient mound cities, the signing of the Declaration of Independence, Revolutionary War battlefields, the first airplane flight, the continuing struggle for Civil Rights – The eastern US is the epicenter of the country's most tragic and triumphant moments. Pay homage to American visionaries and delve into the complexities of the past at the region's many museums and historical sites, and ponder the way century-old events continue to influence the present.

Martin Luther King Jr National Historic Site

The giant of the Civil Rights movement was born and raised in Atlanta's Sweet Auburn neighborhood, and the well-preserved places where he lived, prayed and later preached serve as powerful inspiration. p398

Top left: Tomb of Martin Luther King Jr and Coretta Scott King

Williamsburg

Step back into the 1700s in the well-preserved town of Williamsburg, Virginia (pictured bottom left), the largest living-history museum on the planet. You can even taste traditional recipes and sip 200-year-old cocktails at on-site taverns. p304

St Augustine

Wander the cobblestone streets, stare over the ramparts at 300-year-old forts and seek the fountain of youth at this Spanish colonial town in Florida, founded in the 1500s. p491

9 WATERY WILDERNESS

You can stroll the boardwalk though a 'river of grass' in search of great blue herons, or hop in a canoe and paddle off into the great Northwoods. America's backcountry encompasses wildlife-filled wetlands, lake islands and some of the largest freshwater bodies of water on the planet. Adventure comes in many forms from camping along forest-backed shores in Michigan's Upper Peninsula to alligator-spotting in the cypress swamps of southern Louisiana.

Everglades

Mottled by tree-covered islands, cypress domes and mangroves, the Everglades (pictured below left) are home to abundant wildlife, from great blue herons to toothy alligators and crocodiles. p478

FEDERICO ROBERTAZZI/GETTY IMAGES ©

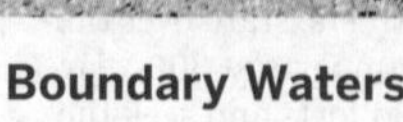

Boundary Waters

Amid one million acres of wilderness, pine forest-covered islands and countless lakes (pictured top right) set the stage for one of the world's great canoeing and camping adventures. p612

Isle Royale

Pitch a tent by the water or overnight in a historic lodge and enjoy the unadulterated sights and sounds of nature on the world's fourth largest lake island (pictured right). p590

10 UNCOMMON ADVENTURES

GUILLERMO OLAIZOLA/SHUTTERSTOCK ©

WILDNERDPIX/SHUTTERSTOCK ©

STEVENSCHREMP/GETTY IMAGES ©

Across 29 states, you'll find near limitless opportunities for adventure. You can raft world-class rapids, go sailing off rocky coastlines, bike along former rail lines, hike up mountain peaks, dive (or snorkel) over coral reefs, and paddle through steamy, primordial swamps. America's love for the outdoors doesn't end when the snows arrive. Wintry days bring snowshoeing through tranquil forests and skiing down steep slopes. The biggest challenge is deciding where to begin.

River Action

One of America's newest national parks, the New River Gorge is gateway to some outstanding white-water rafting as well as ziplining, rappelling and treetop walks. p327

Underwater Allure

At John Pennekamp Coral Reef State Park in Florida you can see reefs and their denizens by glass-bottom boat or get a deeper look on snorkeling and diving excursions. p482

Cycle the Canal

A multiday bike adventure takes you from western Maryland to Washington, DC on a 185-mile route that hugs the C&O Canal (pictured above). Bike outfits in Cumberland rent gear and provide shuttle service. p292

Need to Know

For more information, see Survival Guide (p641)

Currency
US dollar ($)

Language
English, Spanish

Visas
Visitors from the UK, Canada, Australia, New Zealand, Japan and many EU countries do not need visas for stays of fewer than 90 days, with ESTA approval. For other nations, see http://travel.state.gov.

Money
ATMs are widely available. Credits cards are accepted at most hotels, restaurants and shops.

Cell Phones
Foreign phones operating on tri- or quad-band frequencies will work here. Or purchase inexpensive cell (mobile) phones with a pay-as-you-go plan when here.

Time
Eastern Time Zone (GMT minus five hours): NYC, New England, Florida; Central Time Zone (GMT minus six hours): Chicago, Nashville, New Orleans.

When to Go

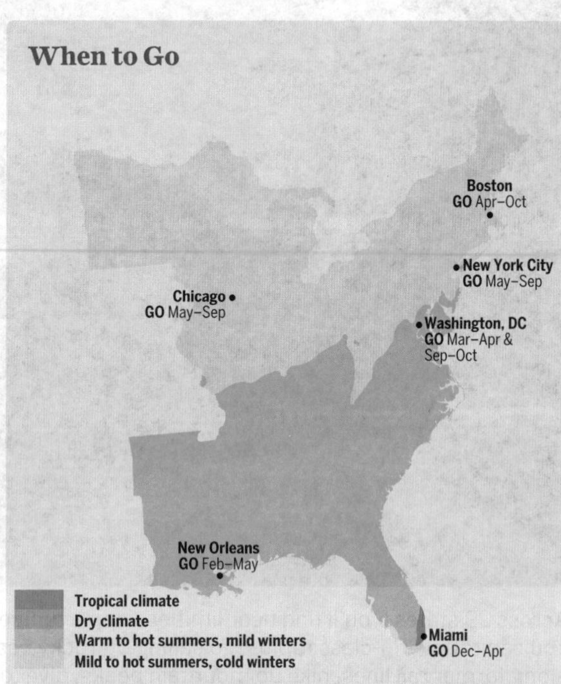

High Season
(Jun–Aug)

- Warm, sunny days across the region.
- Accommodation prices peak (30% up on average).
- Big outdoor music festivals abound: Milwaukee's Summerfest, Newport's Folk Fest, Chicago's Lollapalooza etc.

Shoulder Season
(Apr–May, Sep–Oct)

- Milder temperatures; can be rainy.
- Wildflowers bloom, especially in May.
- Fall foliage areas (ie New England, Blue Ridge Parkway) remain busy.

Low Season
(Nov–Mar)

- Short, wintry days, with snowfall in New England and the Great Lakes.
- Lowest prices for accommodations (aside from ski resorts and warmer getaway destinations such as Florida).
- Attractions keep shorter hours or close for the winter.

Useful Websites

Lonely Planet (www.lonelyplanet.com/usa/eastern-usa) Destination information, hotel reviews and more.

Eater (www.eater.com) Foodie insight into two-dozen American cities.

National Park Service (www.nps.gov) Gateway to America's greatest natural treasures, its national parks.

New York Times Travel (www.nytimes.com/section/travel) Travel news, practical advice and engaging features.

Roadside America (www.roadsideamerica.com) For all things weird and wacky.

Thrillist (www.thrillist.com) Food, drink, travel and entertainment, from New York.

Important Numbers

To call a number within the USA, dial 1, followed by the area code and the seven-digit number.

USA country code	☎1
International access code	☎011
Emergency	☎911
Directory assistance	☎411
International directory assistance	☎00

Exchange Rates

Australia	A$1	$0.74
Canada	C$1	$0.79
Euro zone	€1	$1.10
Japan	¥100	$0.82
New Zealand	NZ$1	$0.69
UK	UK£1	$1.32

For current exchange rates see www.xe.com.

Daily Costs

Budget: Less than $100

- Dorm bed: $20–40
- Campsite: $15–30
- Room in a budget motel: $60–80
- Lunch from a cafe or food truck: $6–10
- Travel on public transit: $2–4

Midrange: $150–250

- Room in a midrange hotel: $80–200
- Dinner in a popular restaurant: $20–40
- Car hire per day: from $30

Top End: More than $250

- Room in a top hotel/resort: from $250
- Dinner in a top restaurant: $60–100
- Big night out (plays, concerts, clubs): $60–200

Opening Hours

Typical opening hours are as follows:

Banks 8:30am to 4:30pm Monday to Friday (and possibly 9am to noon Saturday)

Bars 5pm to midnight Sunday to Thursday, to 2am Friday and Saturday

Nightclubs 10pm to 3am Thursday to Saturday

Post offices 9am to 5pm Monday to Friday

Shopping malls 9am to 9pm

Stores 9am to 6pm Monday to Saturday, noon to 5pm Sunday

Supermarkets 8am to 8pm (some open 24 hours)

Arriving in Eastern USA

JFK International (New York) From JFK take the AirTrain to Jamaica Station and then LIRR to Penn Station ($12 to $16; 35 minutes). A flat-rate taxi to Manhattan costs $52, plus toll and tip (45 to 90 minutes).

O'Hare International (Chicago) The CTA Blue Line train ($5) runs 24/7. Trains depart every 10 minutes or so; they reach downtown in 40 minutes. Airport Express shuttle vans cost $32 to $34 (around one hour); taxis cost around $55 (30 minutes or so).

Miami International SuperShuttle to South Beach costs $22 (50 to 90 minutes), a taxi to Miami Beach costs $36 (40 to 60 minutes) or take the Metrorail to downtown (Government Center) for $2.25 (15 minutes).

Getting Around

Car Driving is the main way to access the region. In big cities (New York, Chicago) it can be a hassle, though, with traffic gridlock and hefty parking fees (upward of $40 per day). Car rentals are available in every town and airport.

Train Outside the Boston–Washington, DC, corridor, train travel is mostly for scenic journeys. Amtrak (www.amtrak.com) is the national carrier.

Bus Short-haul carriers such as Megabus (www.megabus.com/us) are popular for getting between main cities (eg New York to DC) – this is typically the cheapest way to travel. Tickets must be purchased online in advance.

For much more on **getting around**, see p651

What's New

After too many months of staying mostly at home, Americans are eagerly heading out and about once again. New national parks are luring more visitors outdoors, though there's also budding excitement about exploring the lesser-known forgotten places often right in their backyard.

Best in Travel

Two American destinations made Lonely Planet's Best in Travel list in 2022, and they're both in the Eastern US. West Virginia (awarded second place in the top 10 regions) is a still-uncrowded region with unspoiled mountains and unmistakable heritage, where the leisurely tempo of Southern small towns converges with the adrenaline sports that attract adventurers from across the continent. Atlanta (awarded fourth place in the top 10 cities) is a thriving, shining cultural jewel in the heart of the American South with passion and activism in its soul. The birthplace of Martin Luther King Jr was a major battleground state during the United States' 2020 presidential election.

Electric Road Trip

Car rental companies have been slow to make the transition from gas-guzzlers to electric vehicles. Hertz, however, has shaken things up by signing a deal in late 2021 for an order of 100,000 Teslas, and plans to convert 20% of its fleet to electric by the end of 2022. Look for Tesla Model 3 compact sedans in major markets across the US.

Little Island

In 2021 New York saw the completion of new green space in the Hudson River. The $260 million Little Island opened in the Hudson River. Connected via gangways to Manhattan's west side, the 2.4-acre expanse is a verdant oasis of lush lawns, gently sloping hills, forestlike fringes and an impressive variety of weather-hardy plants, including 35 species of trees. Fully acces-

LOCAL KNOWLEDGE

WHAT'S HAPPENING IN EASTERN USA

Regis St Louis, Lonely Planet Writer

Climate change is on everyone's lips these days, with increasing numbers of Americans in agreement that the human-caused climate crisis is real (a recent Pew survey found that 59% of Americans rated global warming as very important to them as an issue, up from 49% in 2018). The evidence is hard to deny, with the prevalence of more powerful storms and hurricanes, cataclysmic forest fires that were once unthinkable and record-breaking droughts and heat waves across the country.

So far, more than 500 local governments have adopted climate action plans to help reduce carbon emissions. Though some have made only token efforts to reach meaningful sustainability goals, around 25 cities (including NYC, Boston, Minneapolis and Washington, DC) have adopted major green building, energy and transportation policies and launched ambitious climate programs: adding bike lanes, integrating renewable power, deploying electric vehicles and ensuring businesses are more energy efficient among many other initiatives.

sible pathways wind around the park and loop up to various viewpoints. There's also a 687-seat amphitheater hosting concerts, plays, dance performances, storytelling and other events. (www.littleisland.org)

Return of the Wolves

Isle Royale, an island and national park in Lake Superior, has long been home to moose and wolves. Owing to climate change and diseases unwittingly introduced by pets (now banned) in the past, the wolf population plummeted to just two members in 2018. With a soaring moose population and destruction of key habitats, the park decided to release over a dozen new wolves on the island. As of 2022, the results are promising. New wolf pups have been born on the island, and the moose population has stabilized.

Glamping on the Rise

During the pandemic, when foreign travel was largely inaccessible to most Americans, new glamping spots provided the opportunity to discover wilderness lurking within easy reach. Hideaway Co, a glamping experience launched in 2020, allows guests to experience the allure of the outdoors without having to forego luxury amenities. Guests overnight in comfy beds in large white canvas Stout Tents, and rotating chefs from renowned restaurants serve meals (bespoke cocktails are also on hand). The location changes each year, but is usually in Western Maryland, near rushing rivers and mountainous state parks.

Airport Renaissance

Some of the busiest airports in the US have received a much-needed upgrade in recent years. New York's LaGuardia and JFK both saw big renovations (with a price tag of over $100 million). Nearby Newark Airport saw even larger transformations with the opening of a new terminal and improved rail service links as part of a long-term $2.7 billion redevelopment program.

Train Travel

There are more reasons to ride the rails, with new sightseeing tours and premium service, while new high-speed routes are on the horizon. Amtrak is upgrading its trains and adding touches like freshly prepared meals (rather than prepackaged) on some routes. High-speed service is now available on Florida-based Brightline, which runs from Miami to West Palm Beach and will eventually reach Orlando.

New National Parks

Over the last few years, the US has named several iconic destinations as national parks. The Gateway Arch in St Louis and the Indiana Dunes on the southern shores of Lake Michigan have both been elevated to national status along with New River Gorge, a region of mountains and rushing white water (both the backdrop to myriad outdoor adventures) in West Virginia.

LISTEN, WATCH & FOLLOW

For inspiration, visit www.lonelyplanet.com/usa/eastern-usa/articles.

This American Life Long-running NPR program and podcast featuring in-depth reporting on culture and society.

Code Switch Podcast featuring conversations about race and culture hosted by journalists of color.

Insta @usinterior Stunning images from the USA's federal lands.

Bitter Southerner (www.bittersoutherner.com) Perspectives on life and culture in the Southern USA today.

twitter.com/humansofny Powerful stories of people from NYC and beyond that celebrate our shared humanity.

FAST FACTS

Food trend Kelp and other plant-based ingredients

Number of US presidents born in the Eastern United States 39

Miles of coastline 3700

Population 201 million

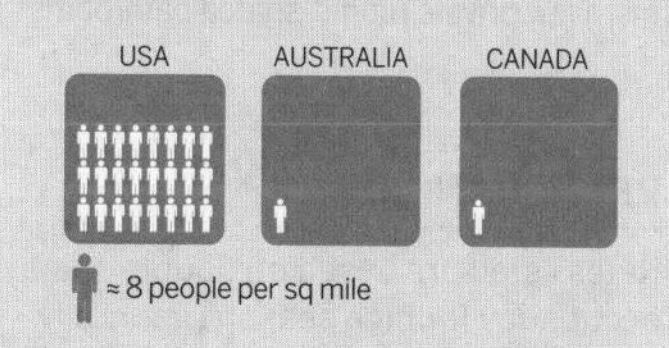

Accommodations

Find more accommodation reviews throughout the On the Road chapters (from p59).

Types of Accommodations

B&Bs & Inns Range from small comfy houses with shared bathrooms to romantic historic homes with private bathrooms. Reservations essential.

Camping Typically there are three types of campsites: primitive (free to $10 per night; no facilities); basic ($10 to $20; toilets, drinking water and fire pits); or developed ($20 to $50; more amenities such as showers and RV sites with hookups). Camping is usually limited to 14 days and can be reserved up to six months in advance.

Hostels Most hostels have gender-segregated dorms, a few private rooms, shared bathrooms and a communal kitchen. Dorm-bed fees range from $25 to $45 (though in NYC, a dorm bed can cost upward of $75).

Hotels Hotels in all categories typically include cable TV, in-room wi-fi, private bathrooms and a simple continental breakfast.

Motels Distinguishable from hotels by having rooms that open onto a parking lot, motels tend to cluster around interstate exits and along main routes into town.

Resorts Found mainly in Florida, resorts can include all manner of facilities, such as fitness and sports, pools, spas, restaurants and bars.

PRICE RANGES

Rates listed are based on double occupancy for high season (generally May to September, with the exception of Florida and ski resorts), and do not include taxes, which can add 10% to 15% or more. When booking, ask for the rate including taxes.

$ less than $150

$$ $150–250

$$$ more than $250

For New York City, Boston, Chicago and Washington, DC, the rate is as follows:

$ less than $200

$$ $200–350

$$$ more than $350

Best Places to Stay

Best on a Budget

Traveling on a budget is easy in the Eastern USA, even in – maybe especially in – the largest cities. As in most countries, campsites and hostels remain the best options for those keeping a tight rein on their finances, but hotels and B&Bs can also offer impressive value.

Best budget accommodations:

- Carlton Arms (p93), New York City
- Crash Pad (p383), Chattanooga, TN
- HI Washington DC Hostel (p269), Washington, DC

Best for Families

While homesharing websites remain popular choices for families, hotels and resorts are upping the ante by providing amenities such as board games, milk and cookies, and spacious suites to lure parents and little ones. And of course, pools provide hours of fun.

Best accommodations for families:

- Hotel Beacon (p95), New York City
- Yogi Bear's Jellystone Park Camp-Resort (p315), Shenandoah Valley
- Tranquilo (p472), Fort Lauderdale
- Trapp Family Lodge (p228), Stowe

Best for Solo Travelers

Solo travel in the Eastern USA is only as lonely as you want it to be. From big cities to small towns, locals are usually friendly and curious about visitors. Hostels offer the best chances to meet other travelers, and the best prices, but B&Bs are also welcoming to solo travelers, with engaging hosts to give you the lay of the land.

Small hotels and pod hotels also have single rooms at typically low rates.

Best accommodations for solo travelers:

- SoBe Hostel (p466), Miami
- Found Hotel (p534), Chicago
- Freehand New York (p93), New York City
- Apple Hostels (p158), Philadelphia

ALENA VEASEY/SHUTTERSTOCK ©

Freehand New York (p93)

Booking

For all but the cheapest places and the slowest seasons, reservations are advised. In high-season tourist hot spots and on holiday weekends, hotels can book up months ahead.

Lonely Planet (lonelyplanet.com) Find independent reviews, as well as recommendations on the best places to stay.

BedandBreakfast.com (www.bedandbreakfast.com) The largest B&B booking site in the world features thousands of properties in the Eastern USA.

Hostelling International USA (www.hiusa.org) National network of hostels; free membership required to get the best rate.

Recreation.gov (www.recreation.gov) Make reservations to camp in national parks and other federal lands.

Reserve America (https://www.reserveamerica.com) Make reservations for state park and other campsites.

Internet Access

Most properties offer in-room wi-fi. It's usually free in budget and midrange lodgings, while top-end hotels often charge a fee (typically $10 to $20 per day).

Month by Month

TOP EVENTS

Mardi Gras, February or March

National Cherry Blossom Festival, March-April

Bonnaroo Music & Arts Festival, June

Independence Day, July

Art Basel Miami Beach, December

January

The New Year starts off with a shiver as snowfall blankets large swaths of the northern regions. Ski resorts kick into high gear, while sun-lovers seek refuge in warmer climes (especially Florida).

Mummers Parade

Philadelphia's biggest event is this brilliant parade (www.mummers.com) on New Year's Day, for which local clubs spend months creating costumes and mobile scenery in order to win top honors. String bands and clowns add to the general good cheer.

Chinese New Year

In late January or early February, you'll find colorful celebrations and feasting anywhere there's a Chinatown. NYC and Chicago each ring in the occasion with a parade, floats, firecrackers, bands and plenty of merriment.

St Paul Winter Carnival

Is it cold in Minnesota in late January? You betcha. That doesn't stop denizens from bundling up in parkas and snow boots to partake in 10 days of ice sculptures, ice skating and ice fishing (www.wintercarnival.com).

February

Unless they're indulging in winter sports or hiding out in Florida, most Americans dread February for its long, dark nights and chilly days. For foreign visitors, this can be the cheapest time to travel, with ultra-discount rates for flights and hotels.

Savannah Black Heritage Festival

Every year during Black History Month, this multidisciplinary festival (www.facebook.com/savblackheritagefestival) features events that range from cultural educational programs, ethnic cuisine demonstrations and craft fairs to historic tours, visual arts exhibitions and dance and spoken-word performances.

Groundhog Day

Made world famous by the 1993 film, the little town of Punxsutawney, PA, has long held the nation's attention at sunrise on 2 February, when marmot maven Punxsutawney Phil makes his predictions about the coming of winter's end.

Mix NYC Experimental Film Festival

New York City's longest running queer film festival (www.mixnyc.org) is a stalwart on the global LGBTIQ+ film festival circuit and a must-attend for avant-garde and experimental film buffs.

North Carolina Jazz Festival

Since 1980, this volunteer-run not-for-profit festival (www.ncjazzfestival.com) has been warming winter hearts with the magic of world-renowned jazz musicians, over three days in February.

Top: Mummers Parade (p158), Philadelphia
Bottom: National Cherry Blossom Festival (p269), Washington, DC

Mardi Gras

Held in late February or early March, Mardi Gras is the finale of Carnival. New Orleans' celebrations (www.mardigrasneworleans.com) are legendary, with colorful parades, masquerade balls and plenty of feasting leading up to the big day.

March

The first blossoms of spring arrive – at least in the Southern USA. In New England's mountains, it's still ski season. Meanwhile, the Spring Break masses descend on Florida.

National Cherry Blossom Festival

The brilliant blooms of Japanese cherry blossoms around DC's Tidal Basin are celebrated with concerts, parades, *taiko* drumming, kite-flying and loads of other events during the three-week fest (www.nationalcherryblossomfestival.org). More than 1.5 million people go each year, so don't forget to book ahead.

Maple Syrup Tasting

Vermont's maple-syrup producers invite the public to their 'sugarhouses' to see the sweet stuff being made during the Vermont Maple Open House Weekend (www.vermontmaple.org) in late March. Maine producers do the same on the last Sunday of the month.

Baseball Spring Training

Throughout March, Florida hosts Major League Baseball's spring training

'Grapefruit League' (www.floridagrapefruitleague.com): 15 pro baseball teams train and play exhibition games, drawing fans to the Orlando, Tampa Bay and southeast areas.

St Patrick's Day

On the 17th, the patron saint of Ireland is honored with brass bands and ever-flowing pints of Guinness. Huge parades occur in NYC, Boston and Chicago (which goes all-out by dyeing the Chicago River green).

April

The weather is warming up, but April can still be unpredictable, with chilly weather mixed with a few teasingly warm days up north. Down south, it's a fine time to travel.

Boston Marathon

At the country's oldest marathon (www.baa.org), tens of thousands of spectators watch runners cross the finish line at Copley Sq on Patriots' Day, a Massachusetts holiday held on the third Monday of April.

☆ New Orleans Jazz & Heritage Festival

The Big Easy hosts the country's best jazz jam (www.nojazzfest.com) for 10 days in late April with top-notch horn blowers and ivory ticklers. Almost better than the music is the food: soft-shell crab po'boys, Cajun rice with pork sausage and white-chocolate bread pudding.

☆ Tribeca Film Festival

Robert De Niro co-organizes this NYC soiree (www.tribecafilm.com) showcasing documentaries and narrative features, held during 12 days in late April. It has quickly risen in stature since its 2002 inception.

May

May is true spring and one of the loveliest times to travel in the region, with blooming wildflowers and generally mild, sunny weather. Summer crowds and high prices stay at bay until Memorial Day (the last Monday in May).

☆ North Charleston Arts Festival

Now in its fourth decade, this five-day South Carolina festival (www.northcharlestonartsfest.com) has grown from humble beginnings to be one of the most comprehensive arts festivals on the eastern seaboard.

☆ Kentucky Derby

On the first Saturday of the month, a who's who of upper-crust America puts on their seersucker suits and most flamboyant hats and descends on Louisville for the horse race (www.kentuckyderby.com) known as the 'greatest two minutes in sports.'

☆ Movement

Billed as the world's largest electronic music festival (www.movement.us), Movement packs Detroit's Hart Plaza over Memorial Day weekend. You'll find both up-and-comers and the big names in the biz, such as Snoop Dog, Skrillex and Felix da Housecat, at the dance-loving extravaganza.

June

Summer is here. Americans spend more time at outdoor cafes and restaurants, and head to the shore or to national parks. School is out; vacationers fill the highways and resorts, bringing higher prices.

☆ Chicago Blues Festival

It's the globe's biggest free blues fest (www.chicagobluesfestival.us), with three days of the electrified music that made Chicago famous. More than a half-million people unfurl blankets in front of the multiple stages that take over Grant Park in early June.

☆ CMA Music Festival

Legions of country-music fans unite in Nashville for boot-stomping fun and concerts featuring the genre's top crooners. More than 400 artists perform at stages in Riverfront Park and Nissan Stadium (www.cmafest.com).

☆ Bonnaroo Music & Arts Festival

Set in Tennessee's heartland on a 700-acre farm, this sprawling music fest (www.bonnaroo.com) showcases big-name rock, soul, country and more over four days in mid-June.

Mermaid Parade

In Brooklyn, NYC, Coney Island celebrates summer's steamy arrival with a kitsch-loving parade (www.coneyisland.com), complete with skimpily attired mermaids and horn-blowing mermen.

Summerfest

Milwaukee lets loose with a heckuva music fest (www.summerfest.com) for 11 days in late June/early July, with hundreds of big-name rock, blues, jazz, country and alternative bands swarming 10 lakefront stages. Local beer, brats and cheese accompany the proceedings.

July

With summer in full swing, Americans break out the backyard barbecues or head for the beach. The prices are high and the crowds can be fierce, but it's one of the liveliest times to visit.

Independence Day

The nation celebrates its birthday with a fireworks-filled bang on the 4th. In Philadelphia, descendants of the Declaration of Independence signatories ring the Liberty Bell. NYC, Nashville and Washington, DC, are also great spots to enjoy the fun.

Newport Folk Festival

Newport, RI, a summer haunt of the well-heeled, hosts this high-energy music fest (www.newportfolk.org) in late July. Top folk artists take to the storied stage, best remembered as the venue where Bob Dylan went electric.

Eastern Music Festival

For half a century, North Carolina's musical treasure (www.easternmusicfestival.org) has been educating and entertaining through its month-long series of workshops and performances.

August

Expect blasting heat in August, with temperatures and humidity less bearable the further south you go. You'll find people-packed beaches, high prices and empty cities on weekends, when residents escape to the nearest waterfront.

Lollapalooza

This massive rock fest (www.lollapalooza.com) in Chicago is a raucous event, with 170 bands – including many A-listers – spread over eight stages in Grant Park the first weekend in August.

Maine Lobster Festival

If you love lobster like Maine loves lobster, indulge in this five-day feeding frenzy (www.mainelobsterfestival.com) held in Rockland in early August. King Neptune and the Sea Goddess oversee a week full of events and, of course, as much crustacean as you can eat.

September

With the end of summer, cooler days arrive, making for pleasant outings region-wide. The kids are back in school, and concert halls, gallery spaces and performing-arts venues kick off a new season.

Fraley Festival of Traditional Music

What began as a family reunion in the 1970s has become an annual three-day celebration (www.fraleyfestival.com) of traditional southern music in Kentucky. Held at the Carter Caves State Resort Park.

Music Midtown

Atlanta's biggest and best music festival (www.musicmidtown.com), this two-day Piedmont Park extravaganza attracts the biggest names in music over the course of a long weekend.

New York Film Festival

One of several big film fests in NYC, this one features world premieres from across the globe, plus Q&As with indie and mainstream directors alike. Lincoln Center (www.filmlinc.org) plays host.

New Orleans Fried Chicken Festival

The inaugural Fried Chicken Festival (www.friedchickenfestival.com) in 2016 drew crowds of up to 40,000 – come join the hordes for a three-day weekend dedicated to the juicy, golden-fried bird.

Together Festival

Boston's burgeoning and aptly named week-long Together Festival (www.togetherboston.com) is all about how music, art and technology converge in this historic yet high-tech city, home to Harvard, Cambridge and cutting-edge MIT.

October

Temperatures are falling as fall brings fiery colors to northern climes. It's high season where the leaves are most brilliant (New England); elsewhere expect lower prices and smaller crowds.

Fantasy Fest

Key West's answer to Mardi Gras brings more than 100,000 revelers to the subtropical enclave during the week leading up to Halloween. Expect parades, colorful floats, costume parties, the selecting of a conch king and queen and plenty of alcohol-fueled merriment (www.fantasyfest.com).

Halloween

It's not just for kids: adults celebrate Halloween in costume, too. In New York City, you can don a costume and join the Halloween parade up Sixth Ave. Chicago does a cultural take with skeleton-rich Day of the Dead events that take place at the National Museum of Mexican Art. In Salem, MA, the Haunted Happenings Halloween builds on the city's witchy history.

November

No matter where you go, this is generally low season, with cold winds discouraging visitors. Prices are lower (although airfares skyrocket around Thanksgiving). There's much happening culturally in the main cities.

Thanksgiving

On the fourth Thursday of November, Americans gather with family and friends over daylong feasts of roast turkey, sweet potatoes, cranberry sauce, wine, pumpkin pie and loads of other dishes. New York City hosts a huge parade. Plymouth, MA, where the Pilgrims landed, hosts events as well.

December

Winter arrives, though skiing conditions in the Eastern USA usually aren't ideal until January. Christmas lights and holiday fairs make the region come alive during the festive season.

Art Basel Miami Beach

This massive arts fest (www.artbasel.com/miami-beach) has four days of cutting-edge art, film, architecture and design. More than 250 major galleries from across the globe come to the event, with works by some 2000 artists, plus much hobnobbing by a glitterati crowd.

New Year's Eve

Americans are of two minds when it comes to ringing in the New Year. Some join festive crowds to celebrate; others plot a getaway to escape the mayhem. Whichever you choose, plan well in advance. Expect high prices (especially in NYC).

Itineraries

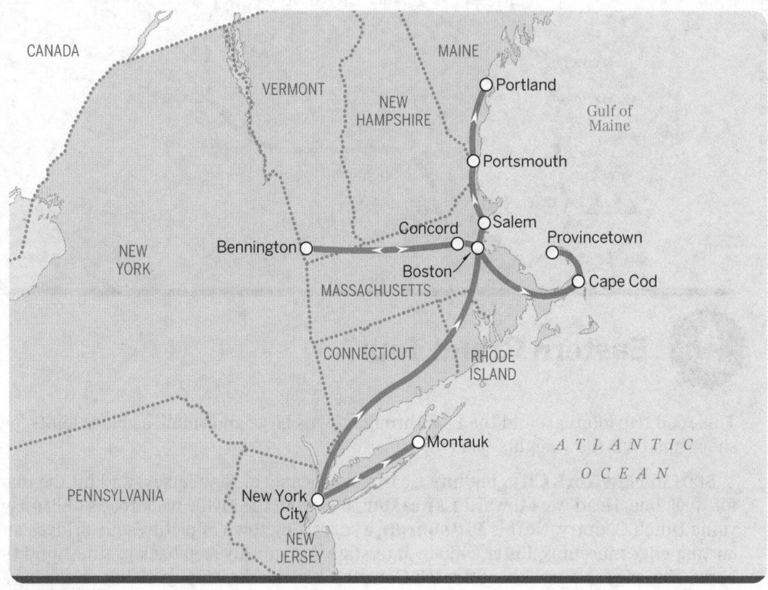

2 WEEKS Up the Coast

Get your big-city fill in the biggest city of all, then mosey into New England for small-town pleasures.

The great dynamo of art, fashion and culture, **New York City** is America at its most urbane. Spend three days blending touristy must-dos – Top of the Rock viewpoint, Upper East Side art museums, Central Park rambling – with vibrant nightlife and dining adventures, perhaps in the East Village. After big-city culture, catch your breath at the pretty beaches and enticing charms of **Montauk** on Long Island. Back in NYC, catch the train to **Boston** for two days, visiting historic sights, dining in the North End and pub-hopping in Cambridge. Rent a car and drive to **Cape Cod**, with its idyllic dunes, forests and pretty shores. Leave time for **Provincetown**, the Cape's liveliest settlement. Then set off for a three-day jaunt taking in New England's back roads, covered bridges, picturesque towns and beautiful scenery, staying at heritage B&Bs en route. Highlights include **Salem** and **Concord** in Massachusetts; **Bennington** in Vermont; and **Portsmouth** in New Hampshire. If time allows, head onward to Maine for lobster feasts amid beautifully rugged coastlines – **Portland** is a fine place to start.

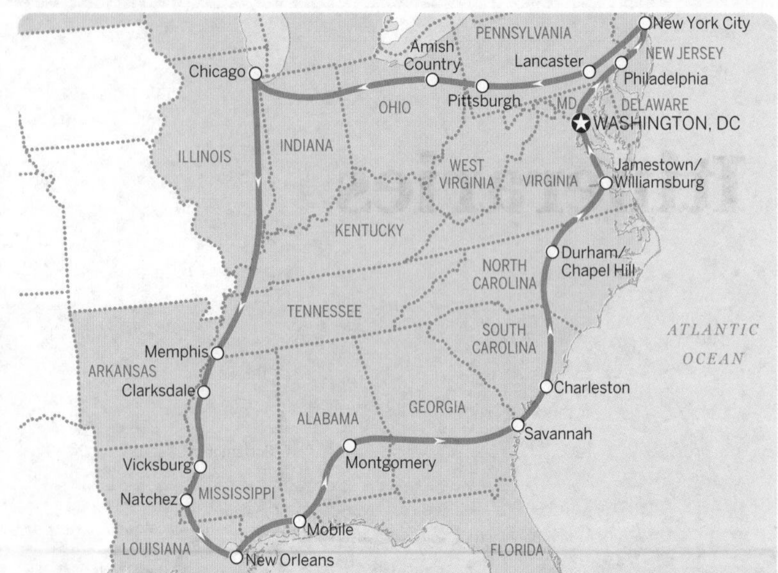

Eastern Grand Tour

This road trip loops around the East through towns large and small, as blues joints, pie shops and civil-rights sights flash by.

Start in **New York City** (but hire a car more cheaply in New Jersey) and hit the road for week one. Head west toward **Lancaster** to explore the idyllic back roads of Pennsylvania Dutch Country. Next is **Pittsburgh**, a surprising town of picturesque bridges and cutting-edge museums. Enter Ohio by interstate, but quickly step back in time amid the horses, buggies and byways of **Amish Country**. See the skyscrapers rising on the horizon? That's big-shouldered **Chicago**. Hang out for a few days to marvel at famous artworks and steely architecture, and chow through the city's celebrated restaurant scene.

For week two, motor south from Chicago on old Route 66, at least for a few time-warped, pie-filled miles. **Memphis** is the next destination, a draw for Elvis fans, barbecue connoisseurs, civil-rights students and blues-music buffs alike. Follow the Great River Rd south from here through juke-jointed **Clarksdale**, the Civil War battlegrounds of **Vicksburg** and the antebellum mansions of **Natchez**. It's not far now to **New Orleans**, where you can hear live jazz, consult with a voodoo priestess and spoon into thick, spicy-rich gumbo.

Begin journeying back east for week three. Wheel along the Gulf Coast to the azalea-lined boulevards of **Mobile**, then inland to **Montgomery**, to see the world-renowned Memorial for Peace and Justice, a tribute to the victims of lynching. Fall under the spell of live oaks in **Savannah** and pastel architecture and decadent food in **Charleston**. Take your pick of **Durham** or **Chapel Hill**, side-by-side university towns offering groovy nightlife.

Begin week four brushing up on your history in Virginia. Visit **Jamestown**, where Pocahontas helped the New World's first English settlement survive, then wander through the 18th century at nearby **Williamsburg**. A pair of big cities completes the route: **Washington, DC**, is a museum free-for-all, while **Philadelphia** fires up the Liberty Bell, Ben Franklin and the mighty, meaty cheesesteak. Finally, it's back to the neon lights of NYC.

Top: Sun Studio (p367), Memphis

Bottom: Amish Country (p565)

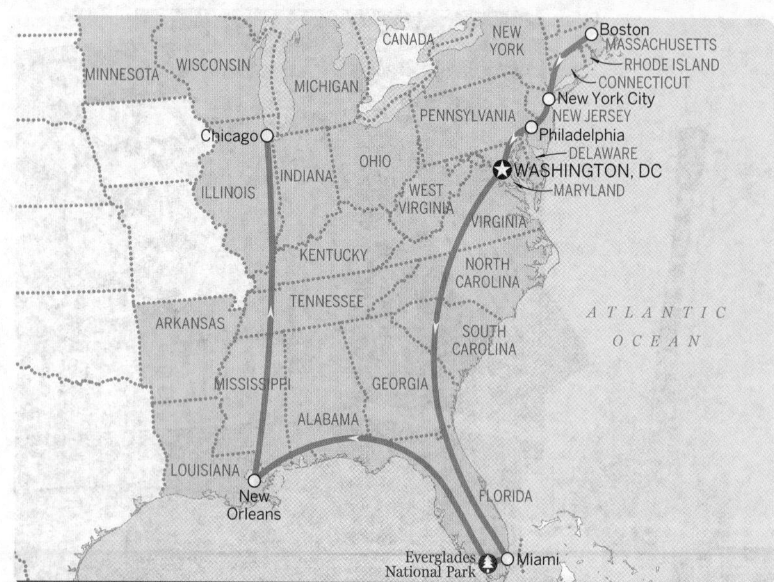

Bright Lights, Big Cities

For big, brawny, bold metropolises, the East is your place. These are the cities that never sleep.

Begin with a few days in history-rich **Boston**. Walk the Freedom Trail past Paul Revere's house. Hang out in Harvard Sq's cafes and bookshops, and chow down in North End trattorias and oyster houses. Then catch the train to **New York City**. With four days, you can indulge in iconic Manhattan and beyond. Stroll Central Park, walk the canyons of Wall St, go bohemian in Greenwich Village and catch a ferry to the Statue of Liberty. For a more local scene, join residents on the High Line, in Nolita's stylish shops and in Queens' creative microbreweries and galleries.

Next hop on board a train to **Philadelphia**, which is practically down the block from NYC. Philly was the birthplace of American independence, and has the Liberty Bell and Declaration of Independence artifacts to prove it. Spend a few days touring the historic sites and indulging in foodie delights like the Italian Market. Don't leave the Northeast without spending a few days in **Washington, DC**, a quick trip by bus or train. Beyond the staggering number of free museums and monuments – the Air and Space Museum and Lincoln Memorial among them – the US capital has rich dining and drinking scenes in Logan Circle, Shaw and along U St. Who knows what politico might be swirling a whisky next to you?

It's a long haul to **Miami** (flying is the easy way to go), so allocate four days to get your money's worth exploring the exotic museums and galleries, the art deco district, Little Havana and sexy, sultry South Beach. For a change of pace, day-trip to the **Everglades** and commune with alligators. Keep the Southern thing going in jazz-loving **New Orleans**, with a soundtrack of smokin'-hot funk/brass bands and the sizzle of Cajun and Creole food. Three days of heavy eating with locals in Uptown, the Central Business District, Marigny and the Bywater should do it.

Last, but not least, **Chicago** leaps up; the *City of New Orleans* train is a scenic way to arrive. Bike to the beach, see mod art in Millennium Park and plug into the blues.

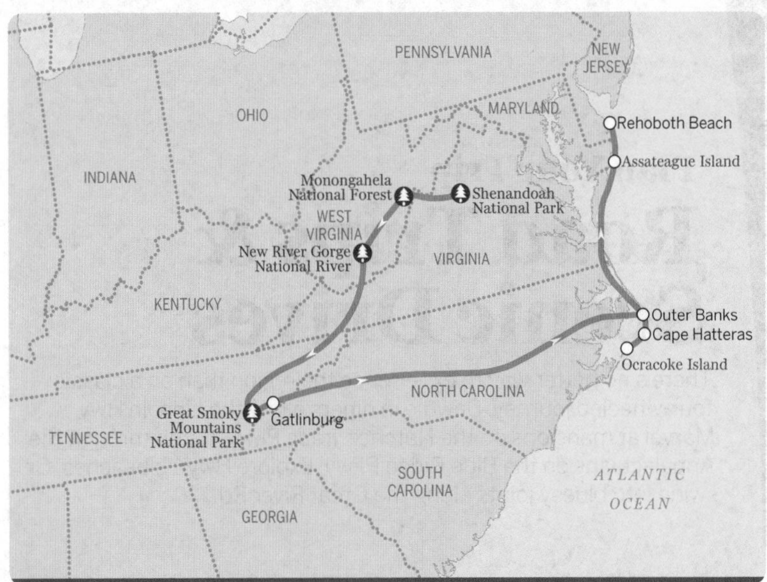

The Great Outdoors

This trip is for those who like their nature ancient and wild. Timbered mountains, raging rivers and sheltered islands are all on tap.

Shenandoah National Park rolls out the welcome mat: this sliver of gorgeousness straddles the Blue Ridge Mountains, so-named for their color when glimpsed in the hazy cerulean distance. Besides scenic drives, hiking is the big to-do here. Five hundred miles of paths – including 100 miles of the Appalachian Trail – wind by spring wildflowers, summer waterfalls and fiery autumn leaves. More activities await a few hours west at **Monongahela National Forest**, where you can strap on ropes for Seneca Rocks or a bicycle helmet for the Greenbrier River Trail. Adventure-sports enthusiasts will find their wet-and-wild bliss nearby at **New River Gorge National River**. Outfitters provide white-water rafting gear for the infamous Class V rapids.

Next up: **Great Smoky Mountains National Park**. Though it's the USA's most popular patch of parkland, you can leave most of the crowds behind if you're willing to hike or paddle – studies have shown that 95% of tourists here never venture more than 100 yards from their cars! After a day spent in the wilderness surrounded by lush, heather-colored peaks, there's nothing quite like arriving in **Gatlinburg**, the park's kitschy base. Prepare for fudge shops, *Ripley's Believe It or Not* oddities and moonshine distilleries.

So goes the first week. Now it's time to fuel up for the twisty drive through the mountains and across to the coast, where the **Outer Banks** pay off big. Laid-back beach towns full of locally owned ice-cream shops and mom-and-pop motels dot the windswept barrier islands. Check out **Cape Hatteras**, with its unspoiled dunes, marshes and woodlands, or catch the ferry to remote **Ocracoke Island**, where the wild ponies run. Speaking of which: more wild horses roam **Assateague Island**, which floats to the north between Virginia and Maryland. It too offers brilliant, secluded beaches and a landscape ripe for birding, kayaking, crabbing and fishing. Still craving surf and sand? Family-friendly, gay-friendly **Rehoboth Beach** bestows traditional gingerbread houses, kiddie amusements and a big ol' boardwalk along the oceanfront.

Plan Your Trip

Road Trips & Scenic Drives

There's no better way to experience the region than on a classic four-wheeled journey. Dawdle in diners along the Lincoln Hwy. Marvel at mansions on the Natchez Trace Pkwy. Climb through the Appalachians on the Blue Ridge Pkwy. Explore Hwy 1's beaches. Or swing into bluesy joints along the Great River Rd.

Best Experiences

Best Beaches

See dazzling coastal scenery on Florida Hwy 1.

Best Oddball Sights

Discover goofball roadside attractions on Route 66 and the Lincoln Hwy.

Best Scenery

Watch dramatic sunsets over the Appalachian Mountains on the Blue Ridge Pkwy.

Best Music

Listen to blues at a Memphis juke joint on the Great River Rd, or crazy fiddling at a Galax mountain music hall on the Blue Ridge Pkwy.

Best Food

Fork into Nashville's fried chicken and biscuits on the Natchez Trace Pkwy, or New Orleans' famed Creole fare on the Great River Rd.

Best History

Explore the Civil War supersight of Gettysburg on the Lincoln Hwy, or 450-year-old St Augustine on Florida Hwy 1.

Blue Ridge Parkway

Snaking through the Appalachian Mountains of Virginia and North Carolina, the parkway immerses road trippers in glorious highlands scenery, with plenty of pull-offs for vista-gaping, hiking and Southern hospitality.

Why Go

Although it skirts dozens of small towns and a few metropolitan areas, the Blue Ridge Pkwy feels far removed from modern-day America. Here, rustic log cabins with creaky rocking chairs on the front porches still dot the hillsides, while signs for folk-art shops and live-bluegrass-music joints entice travelers onto meandering side roads. Log-cabin diners dish up heaping piles of buckwheat pancakes with blackberry preserves and a side of country ham.

When you need to work off all that good Southern cooking, more than 100 hiking trails can be accessed along the Blue Ridge Pkwy, from gentle nature walks to rough-and-ready tramps along the legendary Appalachian Trail. Go canoeing, kayaking or inner-tubing along rushing rivers, or dangle a fishing line over the side of a row-boat on petite lakes.

ADVANCE PLANNING

- Join an automobile club (p653) that provides 24-hour emergency roadside assistance and discounts on lodging and attractions.
- Some international automobile associations have reciprocal agreements with US clubs, so check first and bring your member card from home.
- International travelers might want to review the USA's road rules (p654) and common road hazards (p654).
- Make sure your vehicle has a spare tire, tool kit (eg jack, jumper cables, ice scraper, tire pressure gauge) and emergency equipment (eg flashers).
- Bring good maps, especially if you're touring off-road or away from highways. Don't rely solely on GPS – in remote areas it may not work.
- Always carry your driver's license and proof of insurance (p654).

The Route

This bucolic byway connects Virginia's Shenandoah National Park with Great Smoky Mountains National Park, spanning the North Carolina–Tennessee border. Towns along the way include Boone and Asheville in North Carolina and Galax and Roanoke in Virginia, with Charlottesville, VA, also a short drive away. Bigger cities within range of the parkway include Washington, DC (140 miles), and Richmond, VA (95 miles).

Many road trippers also add Skyline Drive (p316) onto their Blue Ridge route. The bendy, 105-mile Skyline connects to the parkway's northern end and ups the scenic ante by doling out mind-blowing mountain vistas on its ramble through Shenandoah National Park. One caveat: you will have to pay a $25 fee to travel the road – this is not a toll, but rather the park's admission charge.

When to Go

April through October, when visitor facilities are open (many close during winter) is best. May is best for wildflowers. Leaf-peepers pour in during October. Expect big crowds if you go during the summer or early fall.

Resources

Blue Ridge Parkway (www.blueridgeparkway.org) Maps, activities and places to stay along the way. Also offers the free *Blue Ridge Parkway Travel Planner* to download.

Hiking the Blue Ridge Parkway (Randy Johnson; 2010) This book offers in-depth trail descriptions, topographic maps and other essential info for hikes both short and long.

Skyline Drive (www.visitskylinedrive.org) Lodging, hiking and wildlife along the picturesque addendum to the parkway.

Time & Mileage

Time At least two days, but allow five days to do it right. It's slow going on the steep, curvy roads, plus you'll want to make a pit-stop for hiking, eating and sightseeing.

Mileage 469 miles

Start/End Front Royal, VA/Cherokee, NC

Great River Road

This epic roadway edges the Mississippi River from its headwaters in northern Minnesota's pine forests all the way south to its endpoint in New Orleans. For a look at America across cultural divides – North/South, urban/rural, Baptist/bohemian – this is the road trip to make.

Why Go

The sweeping scenery awes as you meander alongside America's longest river, from the rolling plains of the north down to the sun-baked cotton fields of the Mississippi Delta. Wind-hewn bluffs, dense forests, flower-filled meadows and steamy swamps are all part of the backdrop – along with smokestacks, riverboat casinos and urban sprawl: this is the good, the bad and the ugly of life on the Mississippi.

DEE BROWNING/SHUTTERSTOCK ©

Top: Green Parrot bar, end of Florida Hwy 1 (p44)
Bottom: Bridge at the start of the Natchez Trace Pkway (p43)

Road Trips & Scenic Drives

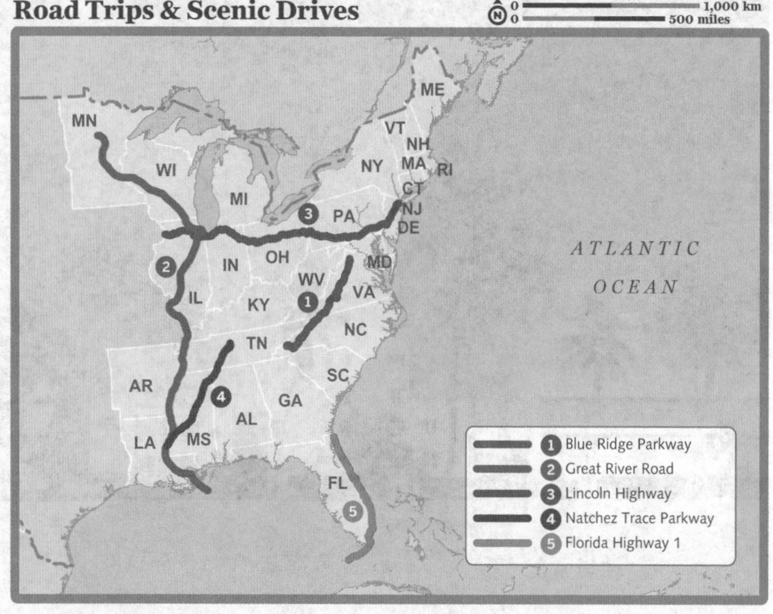

The Route

Despite the name, the Great River Rd is not a single highway, but a series of linked federal, state and county roads that follow the Mississippi River as it flows through 10 different states. The one constant, wherever you are, is the green paddle-wheel sign that marks the way.

Small towns provide a glimpse into varying facets of American culture: there's Brainerd, MN, as seen in the Coen brothers' film *Fargo*; La Crosse, WI, where the world's largest six-pack pops its top; and Nauvoo, IL, a pilgrimage site for Mormons, complete with gleaming white temple.

The southern section of the route traces American musical history, from rock and roll in Memphis to blues in the Mississippi Delta to jazz in New Orleans. You won't go hungry either, with retro diners, Southern barbecue joints and smokehouses, and Cajun taverns and dance halls in Louisiana.

Major urban areas that provide easy access to the route include New Orleans, Memphis, St Louis and Minneapolis.

When to Go

May to October is best, for snow-free weather in the northern states.

Resources

Mississippi River Travel (www.experiencemississippiriver.com) Great resource for history, outdoor recreation and live music in all 10 Great River Rd states.

National Scenic Byways (www.fhwa.dot.gov/byways/byways/2279) Turn-by-turn directions.

Time & Mileage

Time Six days to drive the road from north to south; 10 days enables a more comfortable, realistic pace.

Mileage About 2000 miles

Start/End Itasca State Park, MN/New Orleans, LA

Lincoln Highway

America's first transcontinental roadway – begun in 1913 and paved to completion by 1925 – rambles from New York City to San Francisco. Its 1000-mile eastern portion traces a distinctive path through the nation's heartland, leaving giant coffee-pot statues, fried-chicken diners, jellybean murals and other Americana in its wake.

South Beach (p453), Miami

Why Go

The Lincoln Hwy is authentic road-tripping, sans much of the hype and commercialization of other famous byways. The eastern portion navigates some prominent cities – NYC and Philadelphia among them – but it also steers well off the tourist path in genuine back-road style. You'll tick off seven states along the way: New York, New Jersey, Pennsylvania, West Virginia, Ohio, Indiana and Illinois.

The Route

Between New York City and Fulton, IL, the eastern portion of this rambling route cuts across the Mid-Atlantic and Great Lakes regions. Note that the Lincoln Hwy doesn't appear on most maps, because it's no longer an official road, but rather a patchwork of federal and state highways.

The journey begins at Times Sq, where the bright lights of Broadway provide an epic send-off. From there it's on to New Jersey and Princeton, the natty Ivy League university town. Pennsylvania rolls up next, offering the Liberty Bell and Independence Hall in Philadelphia; quilts and clip-clopping horses in the Amish communities near Lancaster; the Civil War super-site of Gettysburg; and river-tastic, pop art–rich Pittsburgh. Cornfields and haunted prisons flash by in Ohio. Indiana's pit stops include more Amish areas and the town of South Bend, home to the football-crazed university of Notre Dame. In Illinois the route swipes Chicago's suburbs, then sets a course through small farming communities pressed flat against the horizon. After that the Lincoln Hwy heads over the Mississippi River and onward west to San Francisco.

Cities that provide easy access to the road include New York City, Philadelphia, Pittsburgh and Chicago.

When to Go

April through October is best, when the weather is snow-free and attractions are open (many shut down between November and March).

Resources

Lincoln Highway Association (www.lincolnhighwayassoc.org) Lots of free info online. It also sells turn-by-turn directions that are the definitive source for navigating the road.

Greetings from the Lincoln Highway: A Road Trip Celebration of America's First Coast-to-Coast Highway (Brian Butko; 2013) Photos, maps and stories to keep you company along the way.

The Lincoln Highway (Michael Wallis; 2007) Coffee-table book filled with gorgeous photos and the lowdown on route hot spots.

Time & Mileage

Time Two-and-a-half days without stopping much, but four or five days lets you soak up the highway's essence.

Mileage About 1000 miles

Start/End NYC/Fulton, IL

Natchez Trace Parkway

With emerald mounds, jade swamps, hiking trails, opulent mansions, riverside saloons and layer upon layer of American history, the Natchez Trace Pkwy is the richest drive in the South.

Why Go

Think about this as you set out: you'll be following the same path as a who's who of historic figures, including Andrew Jackson (7th president of the USA and face of the $20 bill), James Audubon (naturalist and painter), Meriwether Lewis (famous explorer who died on the Trace in 1809), Ulysses S Grant (18th president of the USA) and – wait for it – a young Elvis Presley. The drive meanders past various cultural and historic sites that let you learn more about each man.

The Route

Nashville is the easiest place to access the parkway, and for music fans and wannabe songwriters all over the world, a trip to the city is the ultimate pilgrimage, with boot-stomping honky-tonks, the Country Music Hall of Fame and friendly neighborhoods to explore. There's also good eatin' at local meat-and-threes (cafeteria-style restaurants), the ultimate way to indulge in everything from barbecue pork and meatloaf to turnip greens and corn pudding.

About 10 miles beyond Nashville, the road swings by one of the Civil War's bloodiest battlefields at Franklin, where 20,000 Confederates and 17,000 Union soldiers fought on November 30, 1864. Further along are Confederate grave sites for unknown soldiers. Several centuries-old indigenous burial mounds likewise rise up along the way. Emerald Mound, near Natchez, is one of the nation's largest, and the massive grassy pyramid still buzzes with ancient energy.

Other highlights en route include the town of Tupelo – where you can visit the humble house where Elvis grew up, learned to play the guitar and dreamed big – and tree-shaded, milky-green Cypress Swamp, filled with alligators. Natchez itself is a living architectural museum, boasting mansions with sweeping spiral staircases, chandeliers and thick columns, and humble historic taverns.

When to Go

April to June and September to November are best. Summer can be hotter than hot.

Resources

Natchez Trace Parkway (www.nps.gov/natr) Park-service website that provides road construction updates, plus information on local activities and historic sites.

DOWNLOADS: BLUEGRASS SOUNDS

- 'Blue Moon of Kentucky' – Bill Monroe and the Blue Grass Boys
- 'Foggy Mountain Breakdown' – Earl Scruggs
- 'I'm Going Away' – Elizabeth Cotten
- 'Bombshell' – Sierra Hull
- 'Windy Mountain' – Lonesome Pine Fiddlers
- 'Flame of Love' – Jim and Jesse
- 'I'm a Man of Constant Sorrow' – Stanley Brothers
- 'Every Time You Say Goodbye' – Alison Krauss and Union Station
- 'I'll Wash Your Love from My Heart' – Hazel Dickens and Alice Gerrard

Natchez Trace Compact (www.scenictrace.com) State tourism bureaus of Tennessee, Alabama and Mississippi band together to offer route itineraries, maps and event info.

Time & Mileage

Time Three days, though you could do it in two. Travel times aren't exactly speedy on the two-lane road.

Mileage 444 miles

Start/End Nashville, TN/Natchez, MS

Florida Highway 1

The coast-hugging thoroughfare features miles and miles of beaches interspersed with fascinating historical sights, from the USA's oldest city to sobering slavery exhibits to NASA rockets. Glittering Miami provides the big finale.

Why Go

For quintessential Florida sights and experiences, Hwy 1 spanning the Atlantic shoreline is it: Palm Beach's mansions, Fort Lauderdale's yachts and Miami's domino-clacking Cuban enclave of Little Havana all pop up along the way. Pristine, windswept beaches harboring endangered birds and manatees? They're here (at Canaveral National Seashore). Beaches known for hard-partying nightlife and NASCAR racing? Also here (at Daytona). Delicious seafood shacks and pastel-hued waterfront hotels are everywhere.

The Route

Begin in Florida's northeastern tip at Amelia Island, an upper-class beach-resort town since the 1890s. From there the road drifts south, past cultural parks and plantations where you can see how enslaved people lived. Pull over in venerable St Augustine, founded in 1565, to seek out Ponce de León's fountain of youth and the Pirate Museum. Lighthouses, unspoiled strands of sand and surfing hot spots flash by.

Moving on you'll come to the Kennedy Space Center, where shuttles used to launch into the stratosphere. After that, art-filled We amyatthereadyy@gmail.com st Palm Beach appears among a slew of well-heeled towns. Hwy 1 then saves the best for last: Miami. The sexy city offers eye candy galore, from mural-splashed neighborhoods to the world's largest art deco district to the young and glamorous locals preening around South Beach.

But let's back up a bit and cover a few basics. The road is actually called Hwy

OTHER GREAT ROAD TRIPS

ROUTE	STATE	START/END	SIGHTS & ACTIVITIES	BEST TIMES
Rte 28	NY	Stony Hollow/Arkville	Catskills Mountains, lakes, rivers; hiking, leaf-peeping, tubing	May-Sep
Old King's Hwy	MA	Sandwich/Orleans	Historic districts, period homes, coastal scenery	Apr-Oct
Hwy 13	WI	Bayfield/Superior	Lakeside beaches, forests, farmlands; nature walks	May-Sep
Hwy 61	MN	Duluth/Canadian border	State parks, waterfalls, quaint towns; hiking	May-Sep
VT 100	VT	Stamford/Newport	Rolling pastures, green mountains; hiking, skiing	Jun-Sep
Kancamagus Hwy	VT	Conway/Lincoln	Craggy mountains, streams, waterfalls; camping, hiking, swimming	May-Sep
Hwy 12	NC	Corolla/Sealevel	Beaches, lighthouses, Wright brothers launching site; surfing, ferry rides	Apr-Oct
Overseas Hwy	FL	Key Largo/Key West	Beaches, protected coral reefs, plates of conch fritters, key lime pie; people-watching, diving	Dec-Apr

ROUTE 66

For a classic American road trip, nothing beats good ol' Route 66. Nicknamed the 'Mother Road' by novelist John Steinbeck, this string of small-town main streets and country byways first connected big-shouldered Chicago with the waving palm trees of Los Angeles in 1926.

Most of the Mother Road unfurls through the western part of the country, but Illinois' 300-mile portion offers classic, time-warped moseying. Fork into thick slabs of pie in neon-lit diners; snap photos of roadside attractions like the Gemini Giant, a sky-high fiberglass spaceman; and motor on past drive-in movie theaters, mom-and-pop motels and other Americana.

Road trippers with a couple of extra weeks to spare can keep on truckin' all the way to the Pacific. The route's remaining 2100 miles wind by singular sensations such as frozen custard stands in Missouri, a totem-pole park in Oklahoma, a barbed-wire museum in Texas, the Grand Canyon in Arizona, and wild and crazy Santa Monica Pier in California.

For more detail, check out www.roadtripusa.com/route-66.

A1A (not to be confused with US 1, the larger, faster version that runs parallel). A1A is not continuous – there are a few towns where you have to detour onto other roads before picking up the A1A again. Should you want more road-tripping after Miami, hop on US 1, which becomes the scenic but congested Overseas Hwy at Key Largo and dips south to Key West – a fine way to keep the party going.

When to Go

March and April means spring break mayhem in Florida. Set out in temperate May or September if you can.

Resources

Florida Scenic Highways (www.floridascenichighways.com) Info for specially designated parts of the highway near St Augustine and Fort Lauderdale.

Highway A1A: Florida at the Edge (Herbert L Hiller; 2007) Part travel guide, part history about the cities and towns along the way.

Time & Mileage

Time Six days to take in the sights.

Mileage 475 miles

Start/End Amelia Island/Miami

Plan Your Trip

Outdoor Activities

Smoky mountains, wave-bashed beaches, coral reefs, river-cut gorges: the Eastern USA has no shortage of spectacular settings for a bit of adventure. No matter what your weakness – hiking, cycling, kayaking, rafting, surfing, diving or skiing – you'll find world-class places to commune with the great outdoors.

Best Outdoors

Best Hiking

Appalachian Trail, Shenandoah National Park, VA; Great Smoky Mountains National Park, NC and TN; Adirondacks, NY; Sleeping Bear Dunes, MI

Best Cycling

Chequamegon National Forest, WI (off-road); Cape Cod Rail Trail, MA (paved); Minneapolis, MN (city riding); Pisgah National Forest, NC (mountain biking)

Best Paddling

Boundary Waters, MN (canoeing); New River Gorge, VA (white-water rafting); Apostle Islands, WI (kayaking); Pictured Rocks, MI (kayaking)

Best Surfing

Cocoa Beach, FL; Long Island, NY; Coast Guard Beach, MA

Best Diving

Florida Keys, FL (coral garden); Cape Hatteras, NC (Civil War shipwrecks); Dry Tortugas, FL (sea turtles); Crystal River, FL (manatees)

Hiking & Trekking

Almost anywhere you go, great hiking and backpacking are within easy striking distance. National parks are ideal for short and long hikes. Beyond them, you'll find troves of state-maintained footpaths. There's no limit to the terrain you can explore, from the dogwood-choked Wild Azalea Trail (www.townofwoodworth.com/azalea-trail) in Louisiana to the multistate North Country National Scenic Trail (www.nps.gov/noco), winding across rugged landscapes from New York to Minnesota.

Resources

Survive Outdoors (www.surviveoutdoors.com) Dispenses safety and first-aid tips, plus helpful photos of dangerous critters.

Wilderness Survival (Gregory Davenport; 2006) Easily the best book on surviving nearly every contingency.

American Hiking Society (www.americanhiking.org) Links to 'volunteer vacations' building trails.

Backpacker (www.backpacker.com) Premier national magazine for backpackers, from novices to experts.

National Park Service (www.nps.gov) The federal government agency responsible for the management and conservancy of all national park resources, including hiking trails and campsites.

Cycling

Cycling's popularity increases by the day. The nation's biggest cities, led by New York and Chicago, are constantly adding more cycle lanes, and a growing number of greenways and rails-to-trails projects have started striping the East's picturesque countryside. Minneapolis (MN), Cambridge (MA) and Washington (DC) also rate as among the most bike-friendly cities in the Eastern USA.

Several abandoned rail lines across the region have been converted into paved cycling paths, offering gentle rides through quaint villages, over bridges and alongside verdant pastures. Massachusetts' Cape Cod Rail Trail (p195) is a popular one.

Mountain bikers should steer for Wisconsin's Chequamegon and Nicolet National Forests (p600), revered for badass trails and the grueling Fat Tire Festival (www.cheqfattire.com) in September.

Resources

Bicycling (www.bicycling.com) This magazine has information on city rides, off-road trails and much in between.

Rails-to-Trails Conservancy (www.railstotrails.org) Publishes free trail reviews at www.traillink.com.

Kayaking & Canoeing

Paddlers will find their bliss in the Eastern USA. Rentals and instruction are yours for the asking. Lake Superior is a kayaking hot spot, from gliding through arches and sea caves in Wisconsin's Apostle Islands National Lakeshore (p600) to paddling by the wildly colored cliffs of Michigan's Pictured Rocks National Lakeshore (p588). In New England, Maine's Penobscot Bay offers bioluminescent night paddles along its pine-fringed coast.

Canoeing is downright legendary here, including the 12,000 miles of wet and wild routes in Minnesota's Boundary Waters (p612). In the Southern USA, memorable paddles include the primordial **Okefenokee National Wildlife Refuge** (☎912-496-7836; http://okeswamp.com/; 2700 Suwannee Canal Rd, Folkston; private vehicle $5, on foot or bicycle $1; ⏲30min before sunrise to 7:30pm Mar-Oct, to 5pm Nov-Feb; P) in Georgia and the 27,000 acres of swampy old growth forest at Congaree National Park (p364) in South Carolina.

Florida's Everglades National Park (p478), one of America's great natural treasures, is a once-in-a-lifetime destination for hitting the water – paddle past basking alligators and herons as you work your way through the vast network of mangrove canals and peaceful lakes that make up the park, which encompasses a whopping 1.5 million acres.

Resources

American Canoe Association (www.americancanoe.org) Has a water-trails database for canoeing and kayaking, as well as information on local paddling clubs and courses (including stand-up paddleboarding).

White-Water Rafting

East of the Mississippi, West Virginia has an arsenal of famous white water. First, there's the New River Gorge (p327), which, despite its name, is one of the oldest rivers in the world. Slicing from North Carolina into West Virginia, it cuts a deep gorge, known as the Grand Canyon of the East, producing frothy rapids in its wake.

THE APPALACHIAN TRAIL

Completed in 1937, the country's longest footpath spans more than 2100 miles, crossing two national parks, traversing eight national forests and hitting 14 states from Georgia to Maine. Misty mountains, deep woods, flowery pastures and bear sightings are the rewards. Each year, roughly 3500 hardy souls attempt to hike the entire trail – only one in four makes it all the way through. But don't let that discourage you. It's estimated that two to three million people trek a portion of the Appalachian Trail annually, thanks to easy-to-access day hikes up and down its length. See www.appalachiantrail.org for more information.

Then there's the Gauley (p328), arguably among the world's finest white water. Revered for its ultra-steep and turbulent chutes, the venerable Appalachian river is a watery roller coaster, dropping more than 668ft and churning up 100-plus rapids in a mere 28 miles. Six more rivers, all in the same neighborhood, offer training grounds for less-experienced river rats.

In May and September, kayakers flock to **Jamaica State Park** (☎802-874-4600; www.vtstateparks.com/jamaica.html; 48 Salmon Hole Lane, Jamaica; day use adult/child $4/2, campsites $20-22, lean-tos $27-29; ⏰early May–mid-Oct) in Vermont for white-water fun (class II to IV) during biannual releases from Ball Mountain Dam.

In the South there are also a variety of white-water rafting experiences. **White-Water Express** (☎706-321-4720; www.whitewaterexpress.com; 1000 Bay Ave; from $38.50; ⏰9am-6pm) in Columbus, GA, is the longest urban white-water rafting experience, with thrilling constructed rapids up to class V. In North Carolina, the **Nantahala Outdoor Center** (NOC; ☎828-785-4972; www.noc.com; 13077 Hwy 19 W; duckie rental per day $35-40, guided Nantathala River trips from $54; ⏰8am-8pm Jun & Jul, reduced hours Aug-May) is the perfect place for family groups to share the exhilaration.

Resources

American Whitewater (www.americanwhitewater.org) Works to preserve America's wild rivers; has links to local rafting clubs.

Surfing

The Atlantic states harbor some terrific and unexpected surfing spots – especially if you're after more moderate swells. The warmest waters are off Florida's Gulf Coast. Top spots to hang 10:

Cocoa Beach (p488) Small crowds and mellow waves make this Florida beach a paradise for beginners and longboarders.

Long Island (p122) More than a dozen surfing areas dot the region, from Montauk's oft-packed Ditch Plains to Nassau County's Long Beach, with its 3-mile stretch of curling waves.

Coast Guard Beach (Ocean View Dr) Part of the Cape Cod National Seashore, MA, this family-friendly beach is known for its consistent shortboard/longboard swell all summer long.

Resources

Surfer (www.surfer.com) Has travel reports covering the eastern seaboard and just about every break in the USA.

USA Surfing (www.usasurfing.org) The national governing body for the sport of surfing.

Diving

Florida has the lion's share of great diving, with more than 1000 miles of coastline subdivided into 20 unique undersea areas. There are hundreds of sites and countless dive shops offering equipment and guided

TIPS FOR VISITING NATIONAL PARKS

- Park entrance fees vary, from nothing at all to $30 per vehicle.
- The 'America the Beautiful' annual pass ($80; https://store.usgs.gov/pass), which allows admission for four adults and all children under 16 years to all federal recreational lands for 12 calendar months, is sold at park entrances and visitor centers.
- Lifetime senior-citizen passes ($10) are also available for US citizens over 62 years.
- Park lodges and campgrounds book up far in advance; for summer vacations, reserve six months to one year ahead.
- Some parks offer first-come, first-served campgrounds – for these, try to arrive between 10am and noon, when other campers may be checking out.
- For overnight backpacking and some day hikes, you'll need a wilderness permit; the number of permits is often subject to quotas, so apply far in advance (up to six months before your trip, depending on park regulations).

excursions. South of West Palm Beach, you'll find clear waters and fantastic year-round diving with ample reefs. In the Panhandle you can scuba in the calm and balmy waters of the Gulf of Mexico; off Pensacola (p513) there are fabulous wreck dives (www.floridapanhandledivetrail.com), and you can dive with manatees near **Crystal River** (☎352-563-2088; www.fws.gov/crystalriver; 1502 SE Kings Bay Dr; ⊙8am-5:30pm Mon-Fri).

The Florida Keys are the crown jewel. Expect a brilliant mix of marine habitats, North America's only living coral garden and the occasional shipwreck. Key Largo is home to the John Pennekamp Coral Reef State Park (p482) and more than 200 miles of underwater idyll. The expansive reefs around **Dry Tortugas National Park** (☎305-242-7700; www.nps.gov/drto) swarm with barracuda, sea turtles and a couple of hundred sunken ships.

Other popular places to submerge in the eastern waters include North Carolina's Cape Hatteras National Seashore (p336), where you can explore Civil War wrecks and encounter tiger sand sharks, and Lake Ouachita (www.lakeouachita.org), Arkansas' largest lake, known for its pristine mountain waters and 16-mile water-based trail.

Resources

Scuba Diving (www.scubadiving.com) Provides the latest on diving destinations in the USA and abroad.

PADI (www.padi.com) Professional Association of Diving Instructors: the world's leading scuba diver training organization.

Skiing & Winter Sports

Vermont's first-rate Stowe Mountain (p226) offers sweet slopes – freeze your tail off on the lifts, but thaw out nicely après-ski in timbered bars with local brews. In Lake Placid (p139), NY, you can luge or bobsled at old Olympic facilities. Snowmobiles rev in northern Wisconsin, Michigan and Minnesota; there are more than 6500 groomed trails in Michigan alone. Eagle River, WI, known as the Snowmobile Capital of the World, rolls out 500 miles of trails and holds the World Championship Derby in front of 30,000 spectators each January. In Minnesota, Voyageurs National Park (p613) hosts lots of wintry action on its frozen waterways – people come to cross-country ski or snowmobile on specially marked trails.

ALEC HARRIGAN/SHUTTERSTOCK ©

Skiing in Stowe (p226), Vermont

Resources

SkiMag (www.skimag.com) Provides lodging info, downloadable trail maps and more.

Ski Central (www.skicentral.com) A one-stop shop for all things ski and snow in North America.

Plan Your Trip

Eat & Drink Like a Local

The cuisine of the Eastern USA mixes myriad cultures, and each region has evolved its own unique flavor palette. From seafood in Maine to slow-cooked brisket in Mississippi, you're in for a treat. Tipplers will find the Eastern USA to be the country's most spirited side. A booming microbrewery industry has brought artful beers to every corner of the region; New York, Michigan, Georgia and Virginia give wine drinkers vintages to appreciate; and Kentucky pours on the bourbon.

Lip-Smacking Festivals

Crawfish Festival

If you're in Breaux Bridge, LA, during the first week of May, don't miss the gluttony of music, dancing and Cajun food at this delicious crustacean celebration (www.bbcrawfest.com).

Kentucky Bourbon Festival

Historic downtown Bardstown, KY, the 'Bourbon Capital of the World,' comes alive for this festival (www.kybourbonfestival.com), held for five days in mid-September.

Maine Lobster Festival

Lobster fanatics won't want to miss this five-day festival (www.mainelobsterfestival.com) in Rockland, ME, which also includes plenty of live music, parades, an art show and a fun run.

World's Largest Brat Fest

More than 209,000 bratwursts go down the hatch in Madison, WI, in late May (www.bratfest.com); carnival rides and bands provide the backdrop.

Local Flavors

NYC: Foodie Heaven

They say that you could eat at a different restaurant every night of your life in New York City and not exhaust the possibilities. Considering that there are more than 20,000 restaurants in the five boroughs, with scores of new ones opening each year, it's true. The city's diverse neighborhoods serve up authentic Italian food and thin-crust pizza, all manner of Asian food, French haute cuisine and classic Jewish deli food, from bagels to piled-high pastrami on rye. More exotic cuisines are found here as well, from Ethiopian to Scandinavian.

Don't let NYC's image as expensive get to you: compared to other world cities, eating here can be a bargain, especially if you limit your cocktail intake.

New England: Clambakes & Lobster Boils

New England claims to have the nation's best seafood, and who's to argue? The North Atlantic Ocean offers up clams, mussels, oysters and huge lobsters, along with shad, bluefish and cod. The bounty gets stirred into a mighty fine chowder (soup), for which every seafood shack up the coast has its own secret recipe, put to the test during summertime chowder fests and cook-offs. The clambake is another tradition, where shellfish are buried in a pit fire with foil-wrapped corn, chicken and sausages. Fried clam fritters and lobster rolls (lobster meat with mayonnaise in a bread bun) are served throughout the region.

Vermont makes excellent cheeses, Massachusetts harvests cranberries (a Thanksgiving staple), and New England's forests drip sweet maple syrup. Still hungry? Connecticut is famed for its thin-crust New Haven–style pizza (best topped with white clams); Boston specializes in baked beans and brown bread; and Rhode Islanders pour coffee syrup into milk and embrace traditional cornmeal johnnycakes.

Mid-Atlantic: Cheesesteaks, Crabcakes & Scrapple

From New York down through Virginia, the Mid-Atlantic states share a long coastline and a cornucopia of apple, pear and berry farms. New Jersey wins prizes for tomatoes and New York's Long Island for potatoes. Chesapeake Bay's blue crabs make diners swoon, as do Pennsylvania Dutch Country's heaped plates of chicken pot pie, noodles and meatloaf-like scrapple. In Philadelphia, you can gorge on 'Philly cheesesteaks,' made with thin strips of sautéed beef, onions and melted cheese on a bun. Virginia serves its salt-cured 'country style' ham with biscuits. New York's Finger Lakes, Hudson Valley and Long Island uncork highly regarded wines to accompany the region's well-set table.

The South: Barbecue, Biscuits & Gumbo

No region is prouder of its food culture than the South, which has a long history of mingling Anglo, French, African, Spanish and Native American foods. Slow-cooked barbecue is one of the top stokers of regional pride; there are as many meaty and saucy variations as there are towns in the South. Southern fried chicken and catfish pop out of the pan crisp on the outside and moist inside. Fluffy hot biscuits, cornbread, sweet potatoes, collard greens, and grits (ground corn cooked to a cereal-like consistency) accompany Southern plates, all butter-smothered. Treasured dessert recipes tend to produce big layer cakes or pies made with pecans, bananas or citrus. Sweet iced tea (nonalcoholic), a cool mint-julep cocktail (with bourbon) or wine from the Dahlonega Plateau in Georgia help wash it down.

For the region's crème de la crème, pull up a chair at Louisiana's tables. The state stands out for its two main cuisines: Cajun food is found in the bayou country and marries native spices like sassafras and chili peppers to provincial French cooking. Creole food is centered in New Orleans, where zesty dishes like shrimp rémoulade, crabmeat ravigote and gumbo (a soupy stew of chicken, shellfish and/or sausage, and okra) have eaters dabbing their brows.

WEIRD REGIONAL FOODS

Scrapple (Pennsylvania) Pork and cornmeal meatloaf.

Lutefisk (Minnesota) Aged, gelatinous whitefish.

Pimento Cheese (Southern USA) Sharp cheddar cheese, mayo and pimentos, blended into a chunky paste.

Horseshoe sandwich (Illinois) Hamburger and fries on toast covered in cheese sauce.

The Great Lakes: Burgers, Bacon & Beer

Folks from the Great Lakes love their food. Portions are huge – this is farm country, after all, where people need sustenance to get their work done. The region is tops for serving American classics like pot roast, meatloaf, steak and pork chops; add walleye, perch and other freshwater fish to menus in towns near the Great Lakes. Count on a nice cold beer to complement the wares. Chicago stands tall as the region's best place to pile a plate, with hole-in-the-wall ethnic eateries cooking alongside many of the country's most acclaimed restaurants, although up-and-coming foodie destination Minneapolis is giving it a run for its money. Another great place to sample Midwestern foods is at a county fair, which offers everything from bratwurst to fried dough to grilled corn on the cob. Elsewhere at diners and family restaurants, you'll taste the varied influences of Eastern European, Scandinavian, Latino and Asian immigrants.

Price Ranges

The following price ranges refer to a main dish. Unless otherwise stated, drinks, appetizers, desserts, taxes and tips are not included.

$ less than $15

$$ $15–25

$$$ more than $25

Top Vegetarian Options

Green Elephant (p243) Portland, ME.

Moosewood Restaurant (p135), Ithaca, NY.

Zenith (p167), Pittsburgh, PA.

Butcher's Daughter (p97), New York City.

Detroit Vegan Soul (p576) Detroit, MI.

Harvest Time

January The ice wine grape harvest takes place around the Finger Lakes, NY, and in northern Michigan. Sweet dessert drinks ensue.

March In Vermont and Maine, it's sugaring season, when fresh maple syrup flows. Down South, crawfish ramps up: Louisiana harvests around 110 million pounds of the critters between now and May.

May Georgia's peach harvest begins mid-month and goes until mid-August. To the north, Chesapeake Bay blue crabs hit the market through September.

July Early in the month Michigan goes wild, picking tart cherries and hosting fruity festivities like the International Cherry Pit Spitting Championship in Eau Claire.

August The action shifts to New England: the coast's lobster shacks and clambakes are in full swing, while Maine's wild blueberries get heaped into pies.

September & October It's prime time to pick apples in New York and Michigan (the nation's second- and third-largest producers). Cider houses pour their wares. Meanwhile, it's cranberry season in Massachusetts and Wisconsin.

MEALS OF A LIFETIME

Rose's Luxury (p271) Southern comfort food by candlelight in an industrial setting in Washington, DC.

Ulele (p498) Alligator beans, okra fries, pompano fish and guava pie in a former water-pumping station in Tampa, FL.

Goosefoot (p539) This Michelin-starred BYOB restaurant serves a cutting-edge, modern American tasting menu that never fails to surprise.

Clancy's (☎504-895-1111; www.clancysneworleans.com; 6100 Annunciation St; mains lunch $17-20, dinner $28-40; ⊙11:30am-1:30pm Thu & Fri, 5:30-10pm Mon-Sat) Dress up and pull up a seat at this zesty neighborhood restaurant serving up Creole specialties in New Orleans.

Eleven Madison Park (p101) Inimitable poster-child for sustainable cooking – one of only six NYC three-Michelin-starred restaurants.

Pye Boat Noodle (☎718-685-2329; 35-13 Broadway, btwn 35th & 36th Sts, Astoria; mains $11-13; ⊙11:30am-10:30pm, to 11pm Fri & Sat; 🌶; Ⓢ N/W to Broadway, M, R to Steinway St) Top NYC Thai restaurant serves up fedora-wearing waitstaff, boat noodles, papaya salad and pink seafood soup!

Habits & Customs

For breakfast, Americans love their eggs and bacon, waffles and hash browns, and big glasses of orange juice. Most of all, they love a steaming cup of coffee. After a mid-morning snack break, the lunch hour of most American workers affords time enough for just a sandwich, quick burger or hearty salad. While you may spot (rarely) diners drinking a glass of wine or beer with their noontime meal, the days of the 'three-martini lunch' are long gone. Early in the evening, people settle in to a more substantial weeknight dinner, which, given the workload of most Americans, is often takeout, delivery pizza or prepackaged food.

Americans tend to eat dinner early, usually between 6pm and 8pm. In smaller towns, it may be hard to find anywhere to eat after 8:30pm or so. Dinner parties usually begin around 6:30pm or 7pm, with cocktails followed by a meal. If invited to dinner, it's polite to be prompt: ideally, you should plan to arrive within 15 minutes of the designated time. Americans are notoriously informal in their dining manners, although they will usually wait until everyone is served before eating.

Cooking Classes

Many cooking schools offer courses for enthusiastic amateur chefs.

Chopping Block (☎312-644-6360; www.thechoppingblock.com; 222 Merchandise Mart Plaza, Suite 107, River North; 2½hr class $55-95) Master knife skills or learn to make deep-dish pizza at this Chicago spot.

Zingerman's Bakehouse (☎734-761-7255; www.bakewithzing.com; 3723 Plaza Dr) Take a 'bake-cation' to make bread or pastries in Michigan's Ann Arbor.

League of Kitchens (www.leagueofkitchens.com; 2½/4½hr course $125/175) In NYC, let new Americans teach you the culinary arts of their home country (shaping Uzbek dumplings, frying Trini roti) from the kitchens of their own homes.

DANIEL GRILL/GETTY IMAGES ©

Clams and lobsters (p50), Maine

Cook (☎215-735-2665; http://audreyclairecook.com; 253 S 20 St, Rittenhouse; lunch/dinner classes from $85/160; 🚌12, 17) Book well ahead for these Philadelphia classes featuring leading, up-and-coming and under-the-radar local chefs.

Chef Darin's Kitchen Table (☎912-662-6882; www.chefdarinskitchentable.com; 2514 Abercorn St, Suite 40; 4hr class per person from $75; ⏰11am-6pm Tue-Fri, 10am-6pm Sat) Learn the basics of Lowcountry cuisine in Savannah.

Soft-Drink Speak

In many parts of the South, a 'coke' means any kind of flavored, carbonated soft drink, so you may have to specify – if you say 'I'll have a Coke,' the waiter might ask, 'What kind?' In the nation's heartland, the generic term is 'pop,' while New England uses 'soda.'

Plan Your Trip

Family Travel

Family travel is fun in the Eastern USA, which boasts a diverse range of scenery and activities to suit all ages. As a bonus, most of it is accessible by car, which means you don't have to break your back carrying luggage and strollers.

Keeping Costs Down

Accommodations

In motels and hotels, children under 17 or 18 years old are usually free when sharing a room with their parents. The many campgrounds in the Eastern USA are a fun and affordable way for families to see the country. Homesharing websites are also widely available in the USA and popular with families.

Transport

Most public transportation offers reduced fares for children. Children under the age of two can fly for free. Driving is the cheapest way to travel and often the easiest for families.

Eating

Many restaurants have children's menus with significantly lower prices – always inquire about options. For moderately healthy, affordable meals on the go, hit up the grocery store for some Uncrustables (frozen peanut butter sandwiches) and fruit.

Activities

Most sights and museums offer free admission for children five years and under, and reduced admission for children under 12 years.

Children Will Love...

Outdoor Adventures

Everglades, FL (p478) Keep your eyes peeled for gators as you explore the swamps.

New River Gorge, WV (p327) Ramp up the adrenaline with white-water rafting.

Provincetown, MA (p198) Spot humpbacks spouting on a whale-watch tour.

Mammoth Cave National Park, KY (p394) Take a jaunt through the underground chambers.

Great Smoky Mountains National Park, TN/NC (p354) Plenty of short hikes for shorter legs.

Dining Fun

Ulele, FL (p498) Kids can frolic and feed the fish while their grown-ups drink and dine.

Dacha Beer Garden, DC (p276) Anything goes in this family-friendly beer garden.

Smorgasburg, NYC (p105) This is Brooklyn's biggest food market, with a scrumptious world-ranging lineup.

Courtyard Brewery, New Orleans (p444) A rolling roster of food trucks and plenty of play space.

Theme Parks & Zoos

Walt Disney World® Resort, FL (p506) Immerse your kids in the mightiest attraction of all, with four action-packed parks spread across 20,000 acres.

Bronx Zoo, NYC (p88) Take the subway to one of the USA's biggest and best zoos.

Wisconsin Dells, WI (p596) Choose a water park – or 20 – and splash it up.

Cedar Point, OH (p564) Ride some of the planet's wildest roller coasters, then play at the mile-long beachfront and water park.

Traveling in Time

Williamsburg, VA (p304) Don 18th-century garb and mingle with costumed interpreters in the history-rich triangle where America began.

Fort Mackinac, MI (p588) Plug your ears as soldiers in 19th-century costumes fire muskets and cannons.

Freedom Trail, Boston, MA (p191) Go on a walking tour with a Ben Franklin look-alike.

St Augustine, FL (p491) Hop on a horse-drawn carriage through the streets of this historic city.

Rainy-Day Activities

National Air & Space Museum, DC (p251) Inspire budding aviators with rockets, spacecraft, biplanes and ride simulators.

American Museum of Natural History, NYC (p79) Discover the planetarium, the dinosaur skeletons and 30 million other artifacts.

Museum of Science & Industry, Chicago (p529) Geek out at the biggest science center in the western hemisphere: mock tornadoes await.

Children's Museum of Indianapolis, IN (p553) Let 'em loose at the world's largest kids museum, with five floors of fun dinosaur-laden galleries.

Region by Region

New York, New Jersey & Pennsylvania

This region has tons of beaches, bike paths and outdoor activities in stunning natural areas like Delaware Water Gap (p147) and the Catskills (p131). Kids will love the all-ages fun of the Silverball Museum Arcade (p148), the interactive displays at the Museum of the American Revolution (p153), the traditional culture of Pennsylvania Dutch Country (p163) and the raw energy of New York City (p61).

New England

Roadside stands pepper rural New England, offering kid-friendly fare like fish sticks, burgers and ice cream. Also family-friendly are the many beaches, from the calm waters of Martha's Vineyard (p202) to the superb stretch of shore at Ogunquit Beach (p241). Plus there are museums aplenty for rainy days and Acadia National Park (p247) for rugged adventures.

Washington, DC & the Capital Region

The Mid-Atlantic features fun distractions for all ages: bucket-and-spade adventures on Delaware beaches, the massive National Aquarium (p281) in Baltimore, historic sites like Mount Vernon (p299), and white-water thrills on the New River Gorge (p327). The highlight, of course, is DC (p251), with its miles of museums and monuments.

The South

The Great Smoky Mountains (p354) are a wonderful family destination, as are nearby theme parks Anakeesta (p385) and Dollywood (p385). Atlanta holds the Center for Puppetry Arts (p395), Charlotte has simulators at the NASCAR Hall of Fame (p347), Huntsville hosts the US Space & Rocket Center (p415) and New Orleans (p433) is fabulous for music-minded families.

Florida

From Walt Disney World® Resort (p506) to Everglades National Park (p478) to the calm waters and white beaches of the Panhandle (p511) – the Sunshine State makes it so easy for families to have a good time that many return year after sandy year.

Great Lakes

Chicago has ferocious dinosaurs at the Field Museum of Natural History (p523), and lively Navy Pier (p523); Indianapolis boasts the world's largest kids' museum (p553); and outside of Detroit, Greenfield Village (p578) and the Henry Ford Museum (p579) hold hours of entertainment. Skiing in Minnesota, ice cream in Wisconsin's Door County or biking across Mackinac Island (p587) are also sure to please.

Good to Know

Look out for the [family icon] icon for family-friendly suggestions throughout this guide.

Accommodations Cots and roll-away beds are usually available in hotels and resorts. Children are often not welcome at smaller B&Bs and inns.

Baby items Baby food, formula and disposable diapers (nappies) are widely available in supermarkets across the country.

Breastfeeding All large airports are required to have lactation rooms. Breastfeeding in public is legal and generally accepted, although many American women will choose to use nursing covers.

Changing facilities Many public toilets have a baby-changing table, and gender-neutral 'family' facilities appear in airports.

Driving Seat belts or age-appropriate child safety seats are compulsory. Most rental car companies offer car-seat rentals, but be sure to inquire about availability at the time of booking.

Eating out High chairs or booster seats are usually available, but it pays to inquire ahead of time. At upscale restaurants, children are typically tolerated with more grace early in the evening.

Medical services Medical facilities in America are of a high standard, albeit pricey. Be sure to purchase travel insurance.

Toilets If traveling by car, rest areas are your best bets for bathroom breaks, although a gas station or fast-food restaurant will do in a pinch.

Travel documentation Single parents or guardians traveling with anyone under 18 years should carry proof of legal custody or a notarized letter from the non-accompanying parent(s) authorizing the trip. This isn't required, but it can help avoid potential problems entering the USA.

Useful Resources

Lonely Planet Kids (www.lonelyplanetkids.com) Loads of activities and great travel blog content.

City Trails New York (www.shop.lonelyplanet.com) Discover New York's best-kept secrets, amazing stories and loads of other cool stuff. Ages eight to 12.

Family Travel Files (www.thefamilytravelfiles.com) Ready-made vacation ideas, destination profiles and travel tips.

Parents Magazine (www.parents.com) Monthly magazine that includes travel tips and advice.

Kids' Corner

Say What?

Y'all	The plural form of 'you' in the South.
Yinz	The plural form of 'you' in parts of Ohio and Pennsylvania.
Pike	Another word for road.

Did You Know?

- The Great Lakes hold 20% of the world's fresh water.
- The East contains all 13 of the original colonies.

Have You Tried?

Bison burger
A buffalo-meat hamburger

Regions at a Glance

New York City is the hub of the Eastern USA. More than eight million inhabitants live in this megacity, a world center for fashion, food, arts and finance. The crowd thins out in neighboring New Jersey and Pennsylvania, where beaches, mountains and literal horse-and-buggy hamlets join the landscape. New England arches north to rocky shores, clapboard fishing villages and Ivy League universities.

The Mid-Atlantic begins the march south through voluptuous valleys and a slew of historic sites. By the time you reach the true South, the pace has slowed, pecan pie tempts on the table and bluesy tunes drift from juke joints. Surreal Florida brings on mermaids, manatees, Mickey Mouse and Miami, while the sensible Great Lakes region prefers bratwursts and beer with its natural attractions.

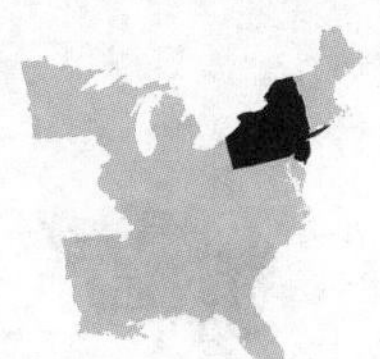

New York, New Jersey & Pennsylvania

Arts
History
Outdoors

Culture Spot

Home to the Met, MoMA and Broadway – and that's just New York City. Buffalo, Philadelphia and Pittsburgh also have world-renowned cultural institutions and renowned live-music scenes.

A Living Past

From Gilded Age mansions in the Hudson Valley to numerous sites dedicated to formative moments in the nation's founding, the region provides an interactive education.

Wild Worlds

The outdoors lurks just beyond the city's gaze, with hiking in the Adirondack wilderness and Catskill Mountains, rafting down the Delaware River, and ocean frolics along the Jersey Shore and Hamptons.

p60

New England

Seafood
History
Outdoors

Land of Lobsters

New England is justifiably famous for its fresh seafood: seaside eateries pepper the coast, where you can suck oysters, crack lobster claws and spoon into clam chowder.

Legends of the Past

From the Native Americans to the Pilgrims' landing, to Paul Revere's revolutionary ride and Boston's Black Heritage Trail, New England is home to American history.

Fall Foliage

The brilliance of fall in these parts is legendary. Changing leaves put on a fiery display all around New England, from the Litchfield Hills in Connecticut all the way up to the White Mountains in New Hampshire and Maine.

p170

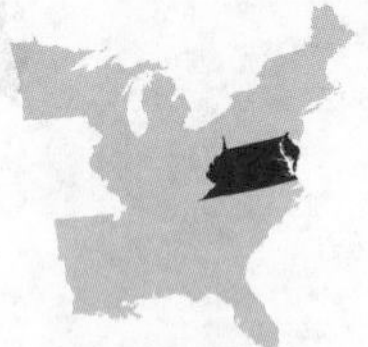

Washington, DC & the Capital Region

Arts
History
Food

Museums & Music

Washington, DC, has a superb collection of museums and galleries. You'll also find mountain music on Virginia's Crooked Road and famous theaters and edgy art in Baltimore.

Times Past

For historical lore, Jamestown, Williamsburg and Yorktown offer windows into Colonial America, while Civil War battlefields litter the Virginia countryside.

Culinary Delights

Feasts await: Maryland blue crabs, oysters and seafood platters; international restaurants in DC; and farm-to-table dining rooms in Baltimore, Charlottesville, Staunton and Rehoboth.

p250

The South

Food
Music
Charm

Barbecue & Biscuits

Slow-cooked barbecue, fried catfish, butter-smothered biscuits, cornbread, grits and spicy Cajun-Creole dishes – the South knows how to fill up a plate.

Musical Moments

Nowhere on earth has a soundtrack as influential as the South. Head to music hot spots for the authentic experience: country in Nashville, blues in Memphis, hip-hop in Atlanta and big-band jazz in New Orleans.

Pretty Cities

Picture-book towns such as Charleston and Savannah have long captivated visitors with their historic tree-lined streets and antebellum architecture. Other charmers include Chapel Hill, Oxford, Chattanooga and Natchez.

p332

Florida

Beaches
Outdoors
History

Shades of Sand

You'll find an array of sandy shores from steamy South Beach to upscale Palm Beach, island allure on Sanibel and Captiva, and Panhandle rowdiness in Pensacola.

Outdoor Adventures

From the world-class theme parks of Orlando and Tampa, to getting swampy with egrets, eagles and alligators, or snorkeling with Florida manatees.

Historical Bounty

Florida has a complicated soul: the home of Miami's colorful art deco district and Little Havana also holds some of the nation's most historical but little-known attractions in St Augustine and the rich island heritage of Key West.

p452

Great Lakes

Food
Music
Culture

Heartland Cuisine

From James Beard Award–winning restaurants in Chicago and Minneapolis to fresh-from-the-dairy milkshakes in Michigan, the region's produce, wines and brews captivate the palate.

Rock & Blues

Home to the Rock and Roll Hall of Fame, blowout fests like Lollapalooza and Summerfest, a cacophony of thrashing clubs and the blues bastion of Chicago, the Great Lakes knows how to turn up the volume.

Quirky Sights

A big ball of twine, a mustard museum, a cow-doo throwing contest: these gems of Americana appear along the region's back roads and in the backyards of passionate folks with imagination to spare.

p516

On the Road

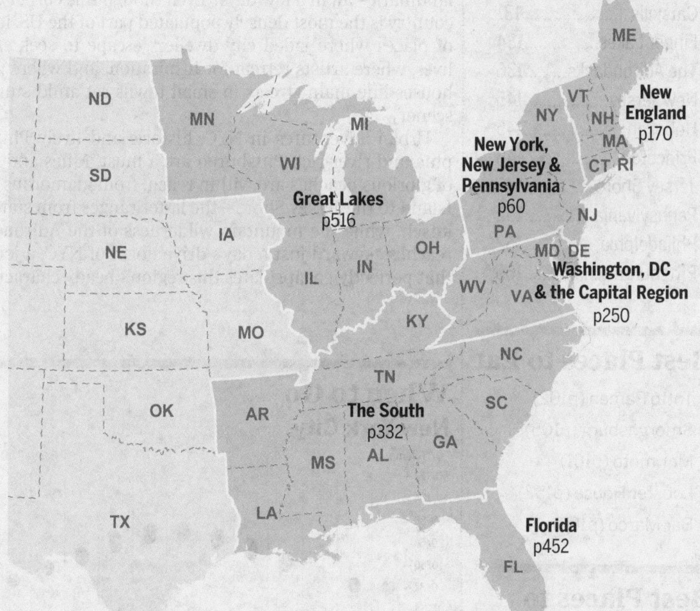
ND
MN
MI
WI
SD
Great Lakes
p516
IA
NE
OH
IN
IL
KS
MO
KY
WV
VA
ME
VT
NH
New England
p170
NY
MA
New York,
New Jersey &
Pennsylvania
p60
CT
RI
NJ
PA
MD
DE
Washington, DC
& the Capital Region
p250
NC
TN
SC
OK
AR
The South
p332
GA
AL
MS
LA
TX
Florida
p452
FL

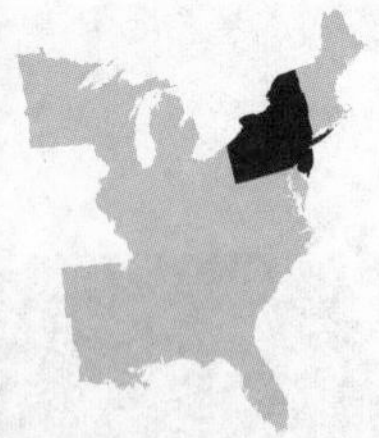

New York, New Jersey & Pennsylvania

Includes ➡

New York City.................61
Long Island.................121
Hudson Valley.............127
Catskills.....................131
Finger Lakes................134
The Adirondacks.........136
New Jersey..................145
Hoboken......................145
Princeton....................146
Jersey Shore...............147
Pennsylvania...............152
Philadelphia................152
Pittsburgh...................165

Best Places to Eat

- ➡ Totto Ramen (p102)
- ➡ Smorgasburg (p105)
- ➡ Morimoto (p161)
- ➡ Lobster House (p152)
- ➡ Bar Marco (p167)

Best Places to Sleep

- ➡ Yotel (p93)
- ➡ Scribner's Catskill Lodge (p133)
- ➡ White Pine Camp (p139)
- ➡ Priory Hotel (p167)
- ➡ Asbury Hotel (p148)

Why Go?

Where else could you visit an Amish family's farm, camp on a mountaintop, read the Declaration of Independence and view New York, New York from the 86th floor of an art-deco landmark – all in a few days? Even though this corner of the country is the most densely populated part of the US, it's full of places where jaded city dwellers escape to seek simple lives, where artists retreat for inspiration, and where pretty houses line main streets in small towns set amid stunning scenery.

Urban adventures in NYC, historic and lively Philadelphia and river-rich Pittsburgh are a must. Miles and miles of glorious beaches are within reach, from glamorous Long Island to the Jersey Shore – the latter ranges from stately to kitsch, while the mountain wilderness of the Adirondacks reaches skyward just a day's drive north of NYC, a journey that perfectly encapsulates this region's heady character.

When to Go

New York City

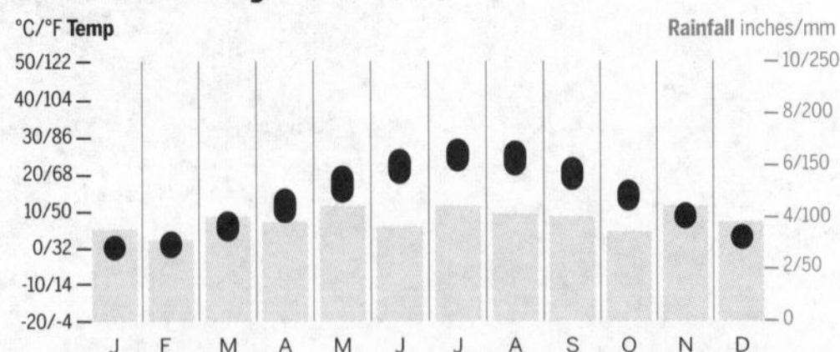

Feb Winter-sports buffs head to the mountains of the Adirondacks, Catskills and Poconos.

Late May–early Sep Memorial Day through Labor Day is for beaches from Montauk to Cape May.

Oct–Nov Autumn in NYC brings cool temps, fruit harvests, the marathon and gearing up for holiday season.

NEW YORK CITY

Epicenter of the arts. Architectural darling. Dining and shopping capital. Trendsetter. New York City wears many crowns, and spreads an irresistible feast for all.

Sights

New York City has a fabled spread of attractions, with dozens of world-class sites sprinkled across the urban landscape. If you want to tick off the marquee attractions, Midtown is a fine place to start. This is where you'll find iconic buildings with panoramic roof decks (Empire State Building, Rockefeller Center), hallowed architecture (Chrysler Building, St Patrick's Cathedral, Grand Central Station) and the city's best modern-art museum (MoMA).

Of course, if it's art you're after, then you could spend days exploring the fabled galleries of the Upper East Side – aka the 'Museum Mile'. The Met and the Guggenheim are just the beginning. The UES also makes a fine gateway to Central Park.

Downtown there are plenty of highlights, though with less density. Chelsea and the Meatpacking District have some stars (the Whitney, the High Line, Chelsea Market), as does Lower Manhattan (notably the ferries to the Statue of Liberty and Ellis Island).

Financial District & Lower Manhattan

★Statue of Liberty MONUMENT

(Map p64; 212-363-3200, tickets 877-523-9849; www.nps.gov/stli; Liberty Island; adult/child incl Ellis Island $18.50/9, incl crown $21.50/12; 8:30am-5:30pm, hours vary by season; to Liberty Island, S 1 to South Ferry, 4/5 to Bowling Green, then ferry) Reserve your tickets online well in advance (up to six months ahead) to access Lady Liberty's crown for breathtaking city and harbor views. If you miss out on crown tickets, you may have better luck with tickets for the pedestal, which also offers commanding views. If you don't score either, don't fret: all ferry tickets to Liberty Island offer basic access to the grounds, including **guided ranger tours** or self-guided audio tours. Book tickets at www.statuecruises.com to avoid long queues.

Conceived as early as 1865 by French intellectual Édouard Laboulaye as a monument to the republican principles shared by France and the USA, the Statue of Liberty is still a symbol of the ideals of opportunity and freedom. French sculptor Frédéric-Auguste Bartholdi traveled to New York in 1871 to select the site, then spent more than 10 years in Paris designing and making the 151ft-tall figure known in full as *Liberty Enlightening the World*. It was then shipped to New York, erected on a small island in the harbor (then known as Bedloe's Island) and unveiled in 1886. Structurally, it consists of an iron skeleton (designed by Gustave Eiffel) with a copper skin attached to it by stiff but flexible metal bars.

The 146-stair slog up to the statue's crown is arduous and should not be undertaken by anyone with significant health conditions that might impair their ability to complete the climb. Access to the torch has been prohibited since 1916.

Liberty Island is usually visited in conjunction with nearby Ellis Island. **Ferries** (Map p66; 877-523-9849; www.statuecruises.com; Battery Park, Lower Manhattan; adult/child from $18.50/9; departures 8:30am-5pm, shorter hours winter; S 4/5 to Bowling Green, R/W to Whitehall St, 1 to South Ferry) leave from Battery Park; South Ferry and Bowling Green are the closest subway stations. (Ferry tickets include admission to both sights.)

★Ellis Island LANDMARK

(Map p64; 212-363-3200, tickets 877-523-9849; www.nps.gov/elis; Ellis Island; ferry incl Liberty Island adult/child $18.50/9; 8:30am-6pm, hours vary by season; to Ellis Island, S 1 to South Ferry, 4/5 to Bowling Green, then ferry) Ellis Island is America's most famous and historically important gateway. Between 1892 and 1924 more than 12 million immigrants passed through this processing station; more than 100 million current Americans are their descendants. Today, the island's **Immigration Museum** delivers a poignant tribute to the immigrant experience: narratives from historians, immigrants themselves and other sources animate a fascinating collection of personal objects, official documents, photographs and film footage. Purchase your tickets online in advance (at www.statuecruises.com) to avoid soul-crushingly long queues.

★One World Observatory VIEWPOINT

(Map p66; 212-602-4000; www.oneworldobservatory.com; 285 Fulton St, cnr West & Vesey Sts, Lower Manhattan; adult/child $35/29; 9am-9pm Sep-Apr, from 8am May-Aug; S E to World Trade Center, 2/3 to Park Pl, A/C, J/Z, 4/5 to Fulton St, R/W to Cortlandt St) Spanning levels 100 to 102 of the tallest building in the Western Hemisphere, One World Observatory offers dazzling panoramic views from its sky-high perch. On a clear day you'll be able to see all

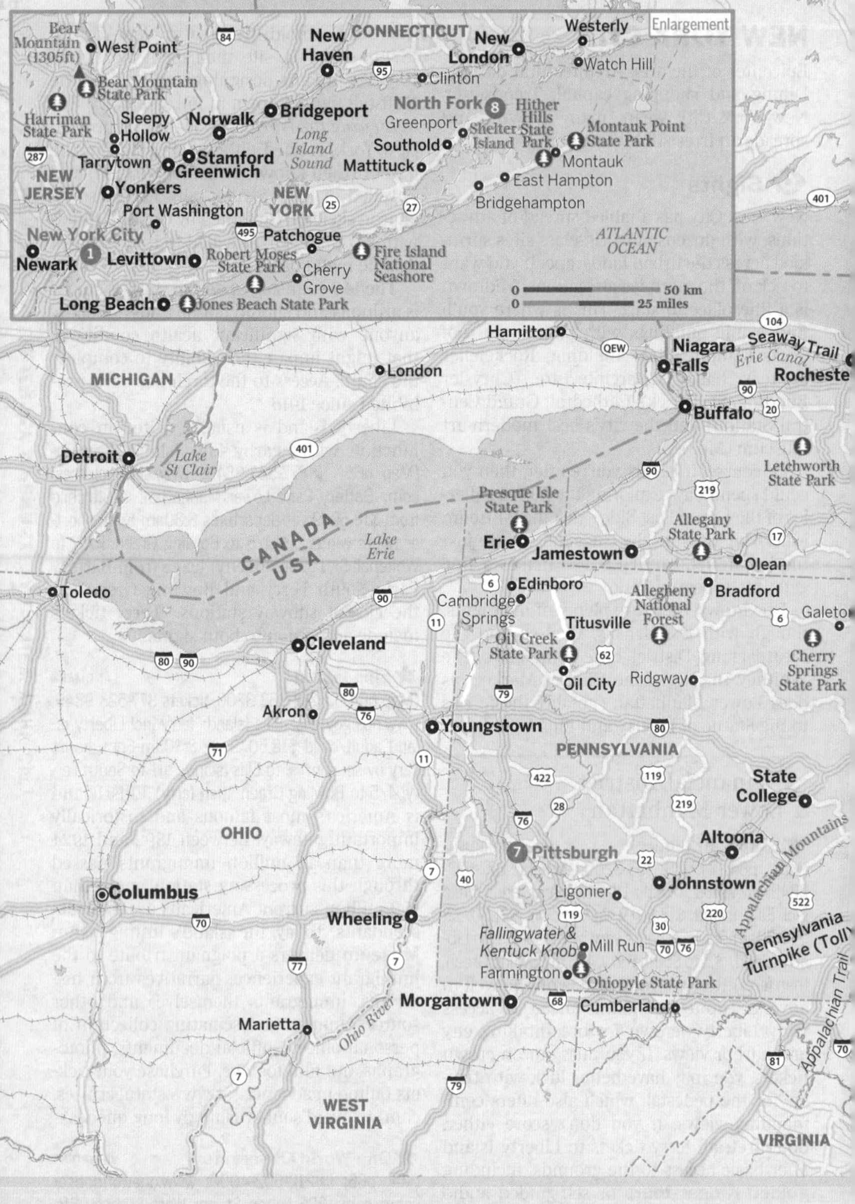

New York, New Jersey & Pennsylvania Highlights

1. **New York City** (p61) Diving into a kaleidoscope of world-class sights and international cultures in this great cosmopolis.
2. **Jersey Shore** (p147) Enjoying the kitsch, kettle corn, coastline and calm.
3. **Philadelphia** (p152) Exploring colonial American history and quirky local flavor.
4. **Catskills** (p131) Hiking the densely forested paths.
5. **Adirondacks** (p136) Paddling a canoe in the shadow of majestic mountains.

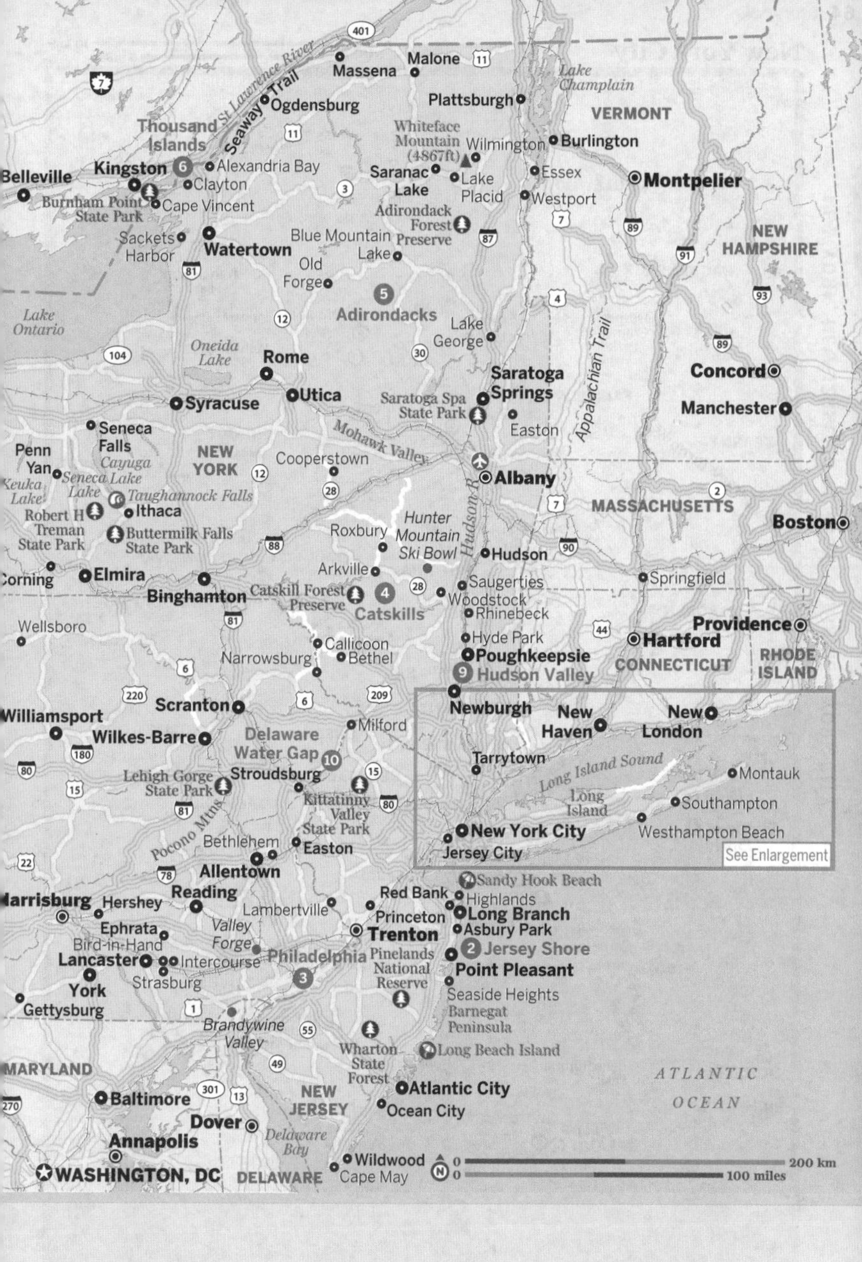

6 Thousand Islands (p140) Camping along the shores of the St Lawrence River.

7 Pittsburgh (p165) Admiring great modern art in an old industry town.

8 North Fork (p126) Tippling the whites and reds of Long Island.

9 Hudson Valley (p127) Savoring local cuisine, contemporary art and historic houses.

10 Delaware Water Gap (p147) Floating gently past bucolic scenery (or whitewater rafting after a wet spring).

New York City

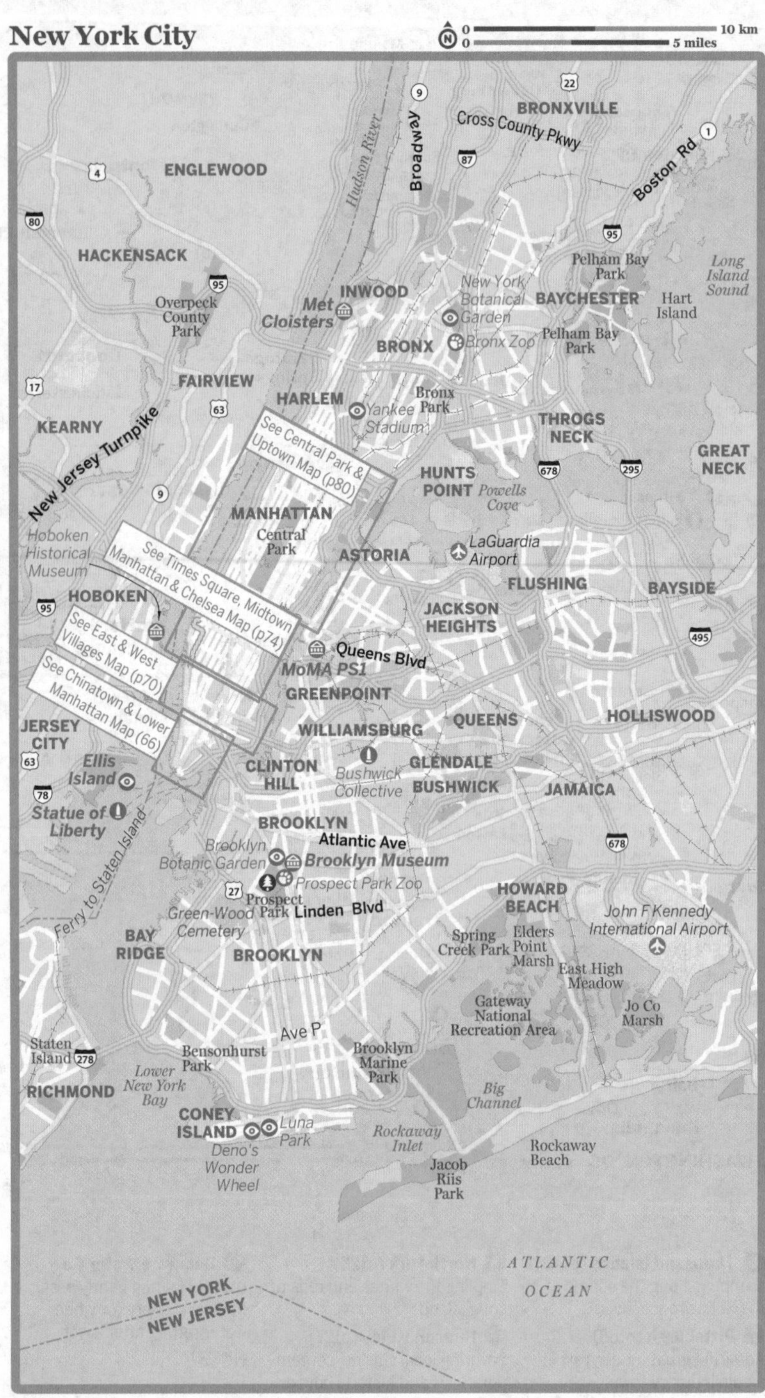

five boroughs and some surrounding states, revealed after an introductory video abruptly disappears to allow the dazzling view in through immense picture windows. Not surprisingly, it's a hugely popular attraction. Purchase tickets online in advance, choosing the date and time of your visit.

★National September 11 Memorial MONUMENT

(Map p66; www.911memorial.org; 180 Greenwich St, Lower Manhattan; 7:30am-9pm; S E to World Trade Center, 2/3 to Park Pl, R/W to Cortlandt St) FREE The focal point of the National September 11 Memorial is **Reflecting Absence**, two imposing reflecting pools that occupy the actual footprints of the ill-fated Twin Towers. From their rim, a steady cascade of water pours 30ft down toward a central void. Bronze panels frame the pools, inscribed with the names of the nearly 3000 people who died in the terrorist attacks of September 11, 2001, and in the World Trade Center car bombing on February 26, 1993.

★National September 11 Memorial Museum MUSEUM

(Map p66; 212-312-8800; www.911memorial.org/museum; 180 Greenwich St, Lower Manhattan; memorial free, museum adult/child $26/15, 5-8pm Tue free; 9am-8pm Sun-Thu, to 9pm Fri & Sat, last entry 2hr before close; S E to World Trade Center, 2/3 to Park Pl, R/W to Cortlandt St) Just beyond the reflective pools of the September 11 Memorial is the National September 11 Memorial Museum, incorporating part of the site and the few remnants of the towers. Architecturally intriguing and deeply moving, its collection of artifacts, video, photographs and audio create a dignified, reflective exploration of the day of the tragedy, the events that preceded it (including the World Trade Center car bombing of 1993), and the stories of grief, resilience and hope that followed.

Trinity Church CHURCH

(Map p66; 212-602-0800; www.trinitywallstreet.org; 75 Broadway, at Wall St, Lower Manhattan; 7am-6pm, churchyard closes 6pm summer, dusk in winter; S 1, R/W to Rector St, 2/3, 4/5 to Wall St) New York City's tallest building upon consecration in 1846, Trinity Church features a 280ft-high bell tower and a richly colored stained-glass window over the altar. Famous residents of its serene cemetery include Founding Father and first secretary of the Treasury (and now Broadway superstar) Alexander Hamilton, while its excellent musical program includes organ-recital series Pipes at One (1pm Friday), and evening choral performances including new works co-commissioned by Trinity and an annual December rendition of Handel's *Messiah*.

SoHo & Chinatown

★Chinatown AREA

(Map p66; www.explorechinatown.com; south of Broome St & east of Broadway; S N/Q/R/W, J/Z, 6 to Canal St; B/D to Grand St; F to East Broadway) A walk through Manhattan's most colorful, cramped neighborhood is never the same, no matter how many times you hit the pavement. Peek inside temples and exotic storefronts. Catch the whiff of ripe persimmons, hear the clacking of mah-jongg tiles on makeshift tables, eye dangling duck roasts in store windows and shop for anything from rice-paper lanterns and 'faux-lex' watches to tire irons and a pound of pressed nutmeg. America's largest congregation of Chinese immigrants is your oyster.

The area has its own tourist information kiosk with local volunteers giving out free maps, at the intersection of Walker, Baxter and Canal Sts (11am to 5pm).

Little Italy AREA

(Map p70; S N/Q/R/W, J/Z, 6 to Canal St; B/D to Grand St) This once-strong Italian neighborhood (film director Martin Scorsese grew up on Elizabeth St) saw an exodus in the mid-20th century when many of its residents moved to more suburban neighborhoods in Brooklyn and beyond. Today, it's mostly concentrated on Mulberry St between Broome and Canal Sts, a stretch packed with checkerboard tablecloths and (mainly mediocre) Italian fare. If you're visiting in late September, be sure to check out the raucous **San Gennaro Festival** (www.sangennaro.nyc; Sep), which honors the patron saint of Naples. For a more authentic insight into an Italian community in New York, head to Arthur Ave in the Bronx.

West Village, Chelsea & Meatpacking District

★High Line PARK

(Map p70; 212-500-6035; www.thehighline.org; Gansevoort St, Meatpacking District; 7am-11pm Jun-Sep, to 10pm Apr, May, Oct & Nov, to 7pm Dec-Mar; M14 crosstown along 14th St, M23 along 23rd St, S A/C/E, L to 8th Ave-14th St, 1, C/E to 23rd St, 7 to 34th St-Hudson Yards) It's hard to believe that the 1½-mile-long High Line – a shining example of brilliant urban renewal – was

Chinatown & Lower Manhattan

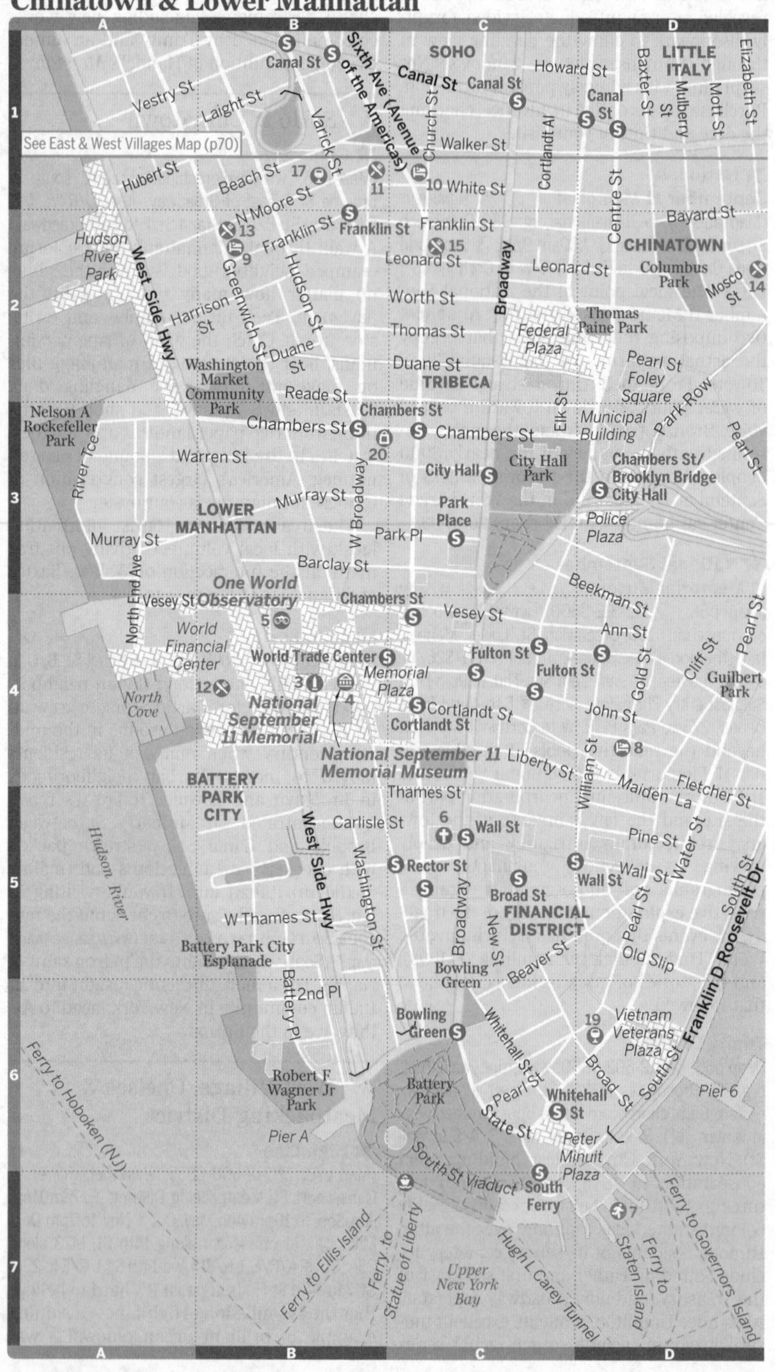

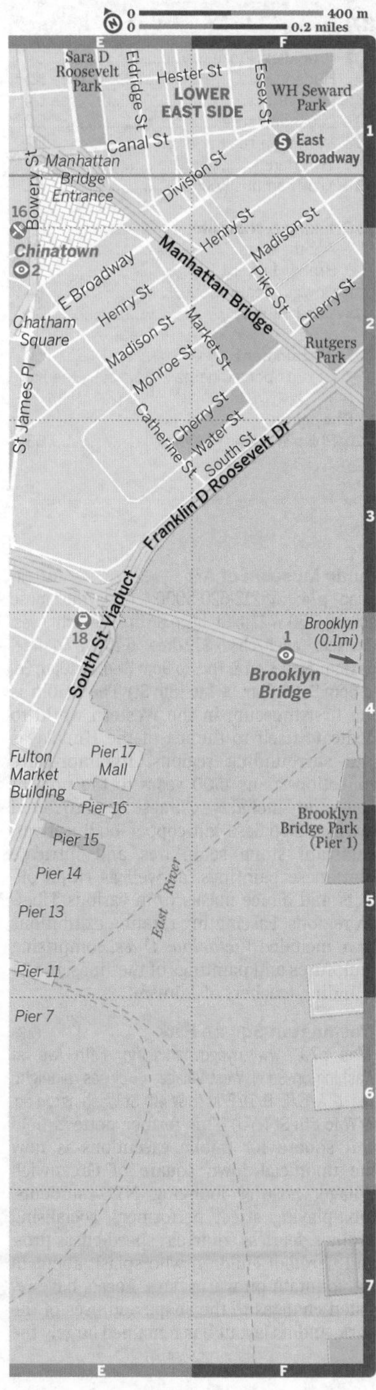

once a dingy freight line that anchored a rather unsavory district of slaughterhouses. Today, this eye-catching attraction is one of New York's best-loved green spaces, drawing visitors who come to stroll, sit and picnic 30ft above the city – while enjoying fabulous views of Manhattan's ever-changing urban landscape. Its final extension, which loops around the Hudson Yards, ends at 34th St.

The attractions are numerous, and include stunning vistas of the Hudson River, public art installations commissioned especially for the park, wide lounge chairs for soaking up some sun, willowy stretches of native-inspired landscaping (including a mini sumac forest), food and drink vendors, and a thoroughly unique perspective on the neighborhood streets below – especially at various overlooks, where bleacher-like seating faces huge panes of glass that frame the traffic, buildings and pedestrians below as living works of art. There's also André Balazs' luxury hotel, the Standard (p92), which straddles the park, as well as the sparkling Whitney Museum, which anchors the southern end.

★Whitney Museum of American Art MUSEUM

(Map p70; ☎212-570-3600; www.whitney.org; 99 Gansevoort St, at Washington St, Meatpacking District; adult/child $25/free, 7-10pm Fri pay-what-you-wish; ⏰10:30am-6pm Mon, Wed, Thu & Sun, to 10pm Fri & Sat; S A/C/E, L to 8th Ave-14th St) After years of construction, the Whitney's downtown location opened to much fanfare in 2015. Anchoring the southern reaches of the High Line, this stunning building – designed by Renzo Piano – provides 63,000 sq ft of space for the museum's unparalleled collection of American art. Inside the light-filled galleries you'll find works by all the greats, including Edward Hopper, Jasper Johns, Georgia O'Keeffe and Mark Rothko. Unlike at many museums, special emphasis is placed on the work of living artists.

★Chelsea Market MARKET

(Map p74; ☎212-652-2110; www.chelseamarket.com; 75 Ninth Ave, btwn W 15th & W 16th Sts, Chelsea; ⏰7am-2am Mon-Sat, 8am-10pm Sun; S A/C/E, L to 8th Ave-14th St) In a shining example of redevelopment and preservation, the Chelsea Market has transformed a former factory into a shopping concourse that caters to foodies. More than two-dozen food vendors ply their temptations, including Mokbar (ramen with Korean accents); Takumi (mixing Japanese and Mexican ingredients); Very Fresh Noodles (hand-pulled

Chinatown & Lower Manhattan

Top Sights
1 Brooklyn Bridge....F4
2 Chinatown....E2
3 National September 11 Memorial....B4
4 National September 11 Memorial Museum....B4
5 One World Observatory....B4

Sights
6 Trinity Church....C5

Activities, Courses & Tours
7 Staten Island Ferry....D7

Sleeping
8 Gild Hall....D4
9 Greenwich Hotel....B2
10 Roxy Hotel....C1

Eating
11 Bâtard....B1
12 Brookfield Place....B4
Hudson Eats....(see 12)
Le District....(see 12)
13 Locanda Verde....B2
14 Nom Wah Tea Parlor....D2
15 Two Hands....C2
16 Xi'an Famous Foods....E2

Drinking & Nightlife
Apothéke....(see 14)
17 Brandy Library....B1
18 Cowgirl SeaHorse....E4
19 Dead Rabbit....D6

Entertainment
Roxy Tribeca Cinema....(see 10)

Shopping
20 Philip Williams Posters....B3

northern Chinese noodles); Bar Suzette (crepes); Num Pang (Cambodian sandwiches); Ninth St Espresso (perfect lattes); Doughnuttery (piping-hot mini-doughnuts); and Fat Witch Bakery (brownies and other decadent sugar hits).

Also worth visiting is one of the market's long-time tenants The Lobster Place (overstuffed lobster rolls and killer sushi). Once you've had your fill make sure to check out Imports from Marrakesh (specializing in Moroccan art and design); Artists and Fleas (a small market chockablock with local artists selling their wares, open 10am to 9pm Monday to Saturday and to 8pm Sunday); and Bowery Kitchen Supply (a dizzying array of cooking odds and ends).

Hudson River Park PARK
(Map p70; 9am-5pm Mon-Fri 212-627-2020; www.hudsonriverpark.org; West Village; 6am-1am; ; M23 crosstown bus, S 1 to Christopher St, C/E to 23rd St) The High Line (p65) may be all the rage these days, but one block away from that famous elevated park stretches a 5-mile-long recreational space that has transformed the city over the past decade. Covering 550 acres (400 of which are on the water) and running from Battery Park at Manhattan's southern tip to 59th St in Midtown, Hudson River Park is Manhattan's wondrous backyard. The long riverside path is a great spot for cycling, running and strolling.

Rubin Museum of Art GALLERY
(Map p74; 212-620-5000; http://rubinmuseum.org; 150 W 17th St, btwn Sixth & Seventh Aves, Chelsea; adult/child $19/free, 6-10pm Fri free; 11am-5pm Mon & Thu, to 9pm Wed, to 10pm Fri, to 6pm Sat & Sun; S 1 to 18th St) The Rubin is the first museum in the Western world to dedicate itself to the art of the Himalayas and surrounding regions. Its impressive collection spans 1500 years to the present day, and includes Chinese embroidered textiles, Nepalese gilt-copper bodhisattvas, Pakistani stone sculptures and intricate Bhutanese paintings, as well as ritual objects and dance masks from various Tibetan regions. Fascinating rotating exhibitions have included *Victorious Ones*, comprising sculptures and paintings of the Jinas, the 24 founding teachers of Jainism.

Washington Square Park PARK
(Map p70; www.nycgovparks.org; Fifth Ave, at Washington Sq N, West Village; closes midnight; ; S A/C/E, B/D/F/M to W 4th St-Washington Sq, R/W to 8th St-NYU) This former potter's field and square for public executions is now the unofficial town square of Greenwich Village, hosting lounging NYU students, tuba-playing street performers, socialising canines, fearless squirrels, speed-chess pros, and barefoot children who splash about in the fountain on warm days. Locals have resisted changes to the shape and uses of the park, and its layout has remained largely the

same since the 1800s. Check out the Washington Square Park Conservancy (www.washingtonsquareparkconservancy.org) for news and events.

Paula Cooper Gallery GALLERY

(Map p74; 212-255-1105; www.paulacoopergallery.com; 534 W 21st St, btwn Tenth & Eleventh Aves, Chelsea; 10am-6pm Tue-Sat; S 1, C/E to 23rd St) An icon of the art world, Paula was one of the first to move from SoHo to Chelsea in 1996 (she was also one of SoHo's pioneers, opening the first gallery south of Houston St back in 1968). She continues to push boundaries, as she did for her exhibition *The Clock,* when the gallery stayed open 24 hours a day on weekends.

Gagosian GALLERY

(Map p74; 212-741-1717; www.gagosian.com; 555 W 24th St, at Eleventh Ave, Chelsea; 10am-6pm Mon-Sat; S 1, C/E to 23rd St) International works dot the walls at the Gagosian. The ever-revolving exhibits feature the work of greats such as Jeff Koons, Andy Warhol and Jean-Michel Basquiat. Gagosian has five New York locations, and 10 more in San Francisco, London, Rome and other cities.

Stonewall National Monument NATIONAL PARK

(Map p70; www.nps.gov/ston; W 4th St, btwn Christopher & Grove Sts, West Village; 9am-dusk; S 1 to Christopher St-Sheridan Sq, A/C/E, B/D/F/M to W 4th St-Washington Sq) In 2016 President Barack Obama declared Christopher Park, a small fenced-in triangle with benches and some greenery in the heart of the West Village, a national park and on it the first national monument dedicated to LGBTQ history. It's well worth stopping here to reflect on the Stonewall uprising of 1969, when LGBTQ citizens fought back against discriminatory policing of their communities – many consider the event the birth of the modern LGBTQ-rights movement in the US.

East Village & Lower East Side

★Lower East Side Tenement Museum MUSEUM

(Map p70; 877-975-3786; www.tenement.org; 103 Orchard St, btwn Broome & Delancey Sts, Lower East Side; tours adult/student & senior $29/24; visitor center 10am-6:30pm Fri-Wed, to 8:30pm Thu; S B/D to Grand St, F, J/M/Z to Delancey-Essex Sts) This museum allows visitors to briefly inhabit the Lower East Side's heartbreaking, hardscrabble but unexpectedly inspiring heritage. Two remarkably preserved (and minimally restored) 19th-century tenements are the focus of various tours, including the impossibly cramped home and garment shop of the Levines, a family from Poland, and two immigrant dwellings from the Great Depressions of 1873 and 1929. Visits to the tenement building are available only as part of scheduled guided tours, with many departures each day.

In addition to the 'Hard Times' tour that features the homes of two immigrant families, the museum also runs various other tours, including 'Sweatshop Workers,' which illuminates life for garment workers and the balance between work, family life and religion, and 'Irish Outsiders', which visits the restored home of Irish immigrants who dealt with the death of a child in the 1800s. You can have a more interactive experience with 'Meet Victoria Confino,' which gives a firsthand glimpse of life in a tenement as related by a 14-year-old Italian immigrant (played by a costumed interpreter) – it's the only tour recommended for children between five and eight years, but there's really nothing to stop them going on any of the tours.

There are also neighborhood **walking tours**, **food tours** and special **evening tours** exploring the life of the Rogarshevsky family (encountered on the sweatshop tour) on Thursday. New tours are added occasionally, so be sure to check the website.

The visitor center – which has an excellent gift shop – shows a video detailing the difficult life endured by the people who once lived in the surrounding buildings, which initially had no plumbing or electricity. Reserve tickets online – popular tours sell out in advance.

★New Museum of Contemporary Art MUSEUM

(Map p70; 212-219-1222; www.newmuseum.org; 235 Bowery, btwn Stanton & Rivington Sts, Lower East Side; adult/child $18/free, 7-9pm Thu by donation; 11am-6pm Tue, Wed & Fri-Sun, to 9pm Thu; S F to 2nd Ave, R/W to Prince St, J/Z to Bowery, 6 to Spring St) The New Museum of Contemporary Art is a sight to behold: a seven-story stack of ethereal, off-kilter white boxes (designed by Tokyo-based architects Kazuyo Sejima and Ryue Nishizawa of SANAA and New York firm

East & West Villages

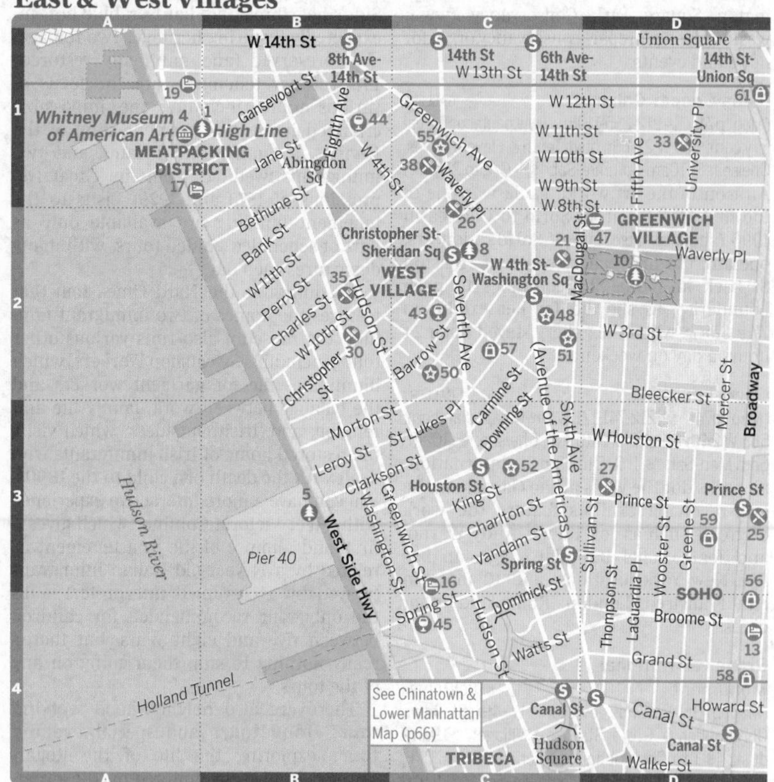

Gensler) rearing above its medium-rise neighborhood. It was a long-awaited breath of fresh air along what was a completely gritty Bowery strip when it arrived back in 2007 – since the museum's opening, many glossy new constructions have joined it, quickly transforming this once down-and-out avenue.

Tompkins Square Park PARK

(Map p70; www.nycgovparks.org; btwn E 7th & E 10th Sts & Aves A & B, East Village; 6am-midnight; S 6 to Astor Pl) This 10.5-acre park is like a friendly town square for locals, who gather for chess at concrete tables, picnics on the lawn, and spontaneous guitar or drum jams on various grassy knolls. It's also the site of basketball courts, a fun-to-watch dog run (a fenced-in area where humans can unleash their canines), a mini public swimming pool for kids, frequent summer concerts and an always lively playground.

Union Square, Flatiron District & Gramercy

★Flatiron Building HISTORIC BUILDING

(Map p74; Broadway, cnr Fifth Ave & 23rd St, Flatiron District; S N/R, F/M, 6 to 23rd St) Designed by Daniel Burnham and built in 1902, the 20-story Flatiron Building has a narrow triangular footprint that resembles the prow of a massive ship. It also features a traditional beaux-arts limestone and terra-cotta facade, built over a steel frame, that gets more complex and beautiful the longer you stare at it. It is best viewed from the traffic island north of 23rd St between Broadway and Fifth Ave, where there's public seating and a beer and wine kiosk that enables admirers to linger.

Madison Square Park PARK

(Map p74; 212-520-7600; www.madisonsquarepark.org; E 23rd to 26th Sts, btwn Fifth & Madison Aves, Flatiron District; 6am-11pm; ; S R/W, F/M, 6 to 23rd St) This park defined

the northern reaches of Manhattan until the island's population exploded after the Civil War. These days it's a much-welcome oasis from Manhattan's relentless pace, with a popular children's playground, dog-run area and the Shake Shack (p100) burger joint. It's also one of the city's most cultured parks, with specially commissioned art installations and (in the warmer months) activities ranging from literary discussions to live-music gigs. See the website for more information.

★Union Square SQUARE

(Map p74; www.unionsquarenyc.org; 17th St, btwn Broadway & Park Ave S, Union Sq; S 4/5/6, N/Q/R, L to 14th St-Union Sq) Union Square is like the Noah's Ark of New York, rescuing at least two of every kind from the curling seas of concrete. In fact, one would be hard pressed to find a more eclectic cross-section of locals gathered in one public place: suited businessfolk gulping fresh air during their lunch breaks, dreadlocked musicians tapping beats on their tabla, skateboarders flipping tricks on the southeastern stairs, old-timers pouring over chess boards, and throngs of protesting masses chanting fervently for various causes.

Union Square Greenmarket MARKET

(Map p74; ☎212-788-7476; www.grownyc.org/unionsquaregreenmarket; E 17th St, btwn Broadway & Park Ave S, Union Sq; 8am-6pm Mon, Wed, Fri & Sat; S 4/5/6, N/Q/R/W, L to 14th St-Union Sq) Don't be surprised if you spot some of New York's top chefs prodding the produce here: Union Square's greenmarket is arguably the city's most famous. Whet your appetite trawling the stalls, which peddle anything and everything from upstate fruit and vegetables to artisanal breads, cheeses and cider.

Midtown

★Empire State Building HISTORIC BUILDING

(Map p74; www.esbnyc.com; 350 Fifth Ave, at W 34th St; 86th-fl observation deck adult/child $38/32, incl 102nd-fl observation deck $58/52;

East & West Villages

Top Sights
1 High Line ... B1
2 Lower East Side Tenement Museum ... F3
3 New Museum of Contemporary Art ... E3
4 Whitney Museum of American Art ... A1

Sights
5 Hudson River Park ... B3
6 Little Italy ... E4
7 Sara D Roosevelt Park ... E3
8 Stonewall National Monument ... C2
9 Tompkins Square Park ... F1
10 Washington Square Park ... D2

Activities, Courses & Tours
11 Great Jones Spa ... E2

Sleeping
12 Bowery Hotel ... E2
13 Broome ... D4
14 Crosby Street Hotel ... E3
15 East Village Hotel ... F1
16 Hotel Hugo ... C3
17 Jane Hotel ... A1
18 Ludlow ... F3
19 Standard ... A1
20 Standard East Village ... E2

Eating
21 Blue Hill ... C2
22 Butcher's Daughter ... E3
23 Clinton Street Baking Company ... G3
24 Crif Dogs ... F1
25 Dean & DeLuca ... D3
26 Dominique Ansel Kitchen ... C2
27 Dutch ... D3
28 Il Buco Alimentari & Vineria ... E2
29 Ivan Ramen ... F3
30 JeJu Noodle Bar ... B2
31 Mamoun's ... E2
32 Momofuku Noodle Bar ... F1
33 Nix ... D1
34 Prince Street Pizza ... E3
35 RedFarm ... B2
36 Russ & Daughters Cafe ... F3
37 Supermoon Bakehouse ... F3
38 Taïm ... C1
39 Uncle Boons ... E3
40 Veselka ... E1

Drinking & Nightlife
41 Bar Goto ... F3
42 Berlin ... F2
43 Buvette ... C2
44 Cubbyhole ... B1
45 Ear Inn ... C4
46 Rue B ... F1
47 Stumptown Coffee Roasters ... D2
Top of the Standard ... (see 19)

Entertainment
48 Blue Note ... C2
49 Bowery Ballroom ... E3
50 Cherry Lane Theatre ... C2
51 Comedy Cellar ... C2
52 Film Forum ... C3
53 Metrograph ... F4
54 Public Theater ... E2
55 Village Vanguard ... C1

Shopping
56 Galeria Melissa ... D4
57 Murray's Cheese ... C2
58 Pearl River Mart ... D4
59 Rag & Bone ... D3
60 Russ & Daughters ... F3
61 Strand Book Store ... D1

⌚8am-2am, last elevators up 1:15am; Ⓢ6 to 33rd St, B/D/F/M, N/Q/R/W to 34th St-Herald Sq) This limestone classic was built in just 410 days – using seven million hours of labor during the Great Depression – and the views from its 86th-floor outdoor deck and 102nd-floor indoor deck are heavenly. Alas, the queues to the top are notorious. Getting here very early or very late will help you avoid delays – as will buying your tickets online ahead of time (the extra $2 convenience fee is well worth the hassle it will save).

As one would expect, the views from both decks are especially spectacular at sunset. For a little of that 'Arthur's Theme' magic, head to the 86th floor between 9pm and 1am Thursday to Saturday, when the twinkling sea of lights is accompanied by a soundtrack of live saxophone (requests are welcome).

Located on the site of the original Waldorf-Astoria Hotel, the 1454ft-high (to the top of the antenna) behemoth opened in 1931 after the laying of 10 million bricks, installation of 6400 windows and setting of 328,000 sq ft of marble. The construction of the building is now expertly explained in the mezzanine **'Dare to Dream' exhibition** above the W 34th St entrance. The famous **antenna** was originally meant to be a mooring mast for zeppelins, but the Hindenberg disaster slammed the brakes on that plan. Later an aircraft did (accidentally) meet up with the building: a B-25 bomber crashed into the 79th floor on a foggy day in 1945, killing 14 people.

Since 1976, the building's top 30 floors have been floodlit in a spectrum of colors each night, reflecting seasonal and holiday hues. Famous combos include orange, white and green for St Patrick's Day; blue and white for Chanukah; white, red and green for Christmas; and the rainbow colors for Gay Pride weekend in June. For a full rundown of the color schemes, check the website.

A tour app is available in English, Spanish, French, German, Italian, Mandarin, Portuguese, Japanese and Korean.

New York Public Library HISTORIC BUILDING
(Stephen A Schwarzman Building; Map p74; ☎917-275-6975; www.nypl.org; 476 Fifth Ave, at W 42nd St; ⏲8am-8pm Mon & Thu, to 9pm Tue & Wed, to 6pm Fri, 10am-6pm Sat, 10am-5pm Sun, guided tours 11am & 2pm Mon-Sat, 2pm Sun; Ⓢ B/D/F/M to 42nd St-Bryant Park, 7 to 5th Ave) FREE Loyally guarded by 'Patience' and 'Fortitude' (the marble lions overlooking Fifth Ave), this beaux-arts show-off is one of NYC's best free attractions. When dedicated in 1911, New York's flagship library ranked as the largest marble structure ever built in the US, and to this day its restored **Rose Main Reading Room** steals the breath away with its lavish coffered ceiling. And it's not just for show: anybody who's working can use it, making it surely the most glamorous co-working space in the world.

★**Museum of Modern Art** MUSEUM
(MoMA; Map p74; ☎212-708-9400; www.moma.org; enter at 18 W 54th St, btwn Fifth & Sixth Aves; adult/child under 17yr $25/free, 4-8pm Fri free; ⏲10:30am-5:30pm Sat-Thu, to 8pm Fri; 👪; Ⓢ E/M to 5th Ave-53rd St; F to 57th St) Superstar of the modern-art scene, MoMA's galleries scintillate with heavyweights: Van Gogh, Matisse, Picasso, Warhol, Lichtenstein, Rothko, Pollock and Bourgeois. Since its founding in 1929, the museum has amassed almost 200,000 artworks, documenting the emerging creative ideas and movements of the late 19th century through to those that dominate today. For art buffs, it's Valhalla. For the uninitiated, it's a thrilling crash course in all that is beautiful and addictive about art.

MoMA's permanent collection spans four levels. Works are on rotation so it's hard to say exactly what you'll find on display, but Van Gogh's phenomenally popular *The Starry Night* is usually a sure bet. Other highlights of the collection include Picasso's *Les Demoiselles d'Avignon* and Henri Rousseau's *The Sleeping Gypsy*, not to mention iconic American works like Warhol's *Campbell's Soup Cans* and *Gold Marilyn Monroe*, Lichtenstein's equally poptastic *Girl with Ball*, and Hopper's haunting *House by the Railroad*. Audioguides are free, available on a device from the museum or via the app.

A massive redesign in 2019 added another 50,000 sq ft of gallery space, as well as new performance and multimedia spaces and free galleries at street level.

When gallery fatigue sets in, recharge in MoMA's **Abby Aldrich Rockefeller Sculpture Garden**, dotted with works by dexterous greats like Matisse, Miró and Picasso. Or try to catch a film at one of the gallery's theaters; same-day tickets are free with admission (see moma.org/film).

★**Times Square** AREA
(Map p74; www.timessquarenyc.org; Broadway, at Seventh Ave; Ⓢ N/Q/R/W, S, 1/2/3, 7 to Times Sq-42nd St) Love it or hate it, the intersection of Broadway and Seventh Ave (aka Times Square) pumps out the NYC of the global imagination – yellow cabs, golden arches, soaring skyscrapers and razzle-dazzle Broadway marquees. It's right here that Al Jolson 'made it' in the 1927 film *The Jazz Singer*, photojournalist Alfred Eisenstaedt famously captured a lip-locked sailor and nurse on V-J Day in 1945, and Alicia Keys and Jay-Z waxed lyrically about the concrete jungle.

For several decades, the dream here was a sordid, wet one. The economic crash of the early 1970s led to a mass exodus of corporations from Times Square. Billboard niches went dark, stores shut and once-grand hotels were converted into SRO (single-room occupancy) dives, attracting the poor and the destitute. What was once an area bathed in light and showbiz glitz became a dirty den of drug dealers and crime. While the adjoining **Theater District** survived, its respectable playhouses shared the streets with porn cinemas, strip clubs and adult bookstores.

That all changed with tough-talking mayor Rudolph Giuliani, who in the 1990s forced out the skin flicks, boosted police numbers and lured in a wave of 'respectable' retail chains, restaurants and attractions. By the new millennium, Times Square had gone from X-rated to G-rated, drawing around 50 million visitors annually. On any given night, with the square flooded with light from wall-to-wall LCD screens and the sidewalks packed with people, it can feel like all of them are there at once.

★**Rockefeller Center** HISTORIC BUILDING
(Map p74; ☎212-588-8601; www.rockefellercenter.com; Fifth to Sixth Aves, btwn W 48th & 51st Sts; Ⓢ B/D/F/M to 47th-50th Sts-Rockefeller

Times Square, Midtown Manhattan & Chelsea

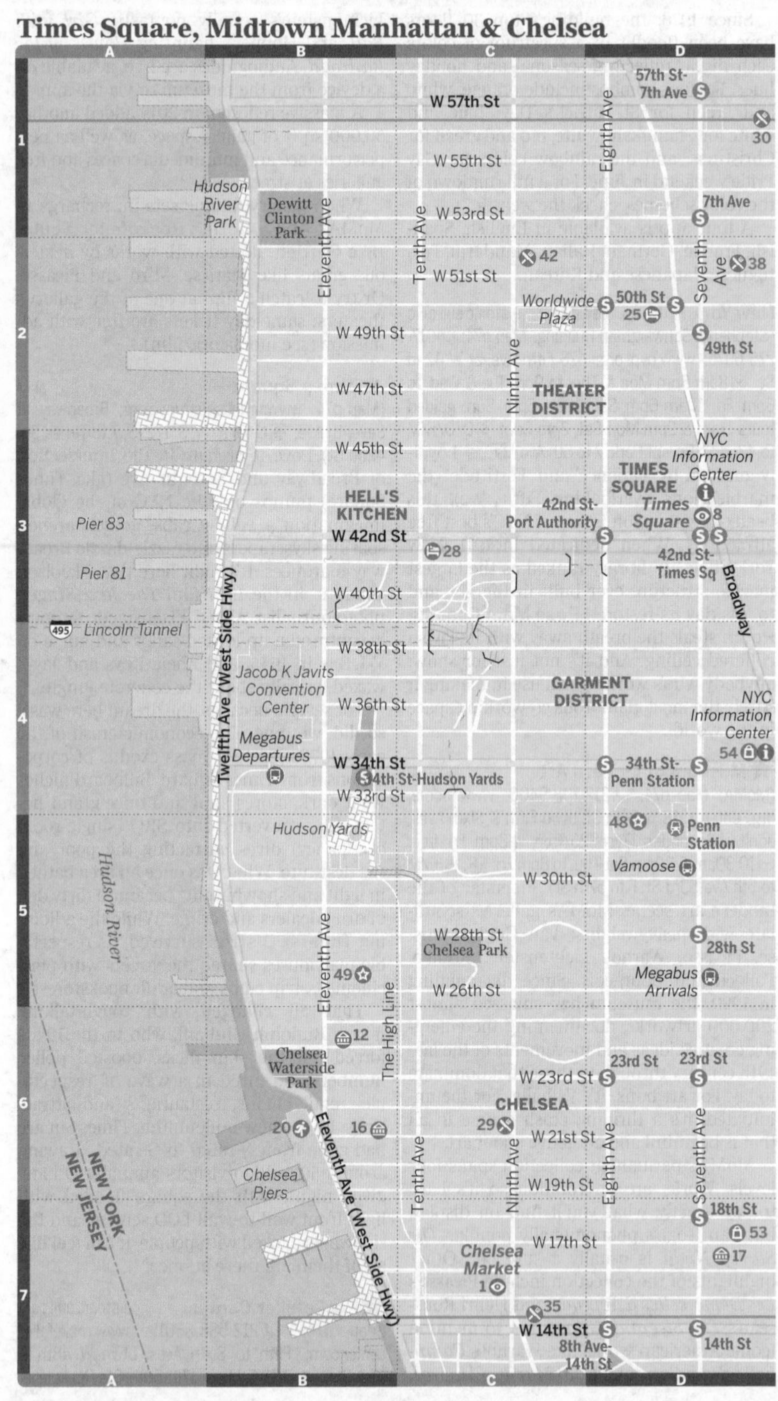

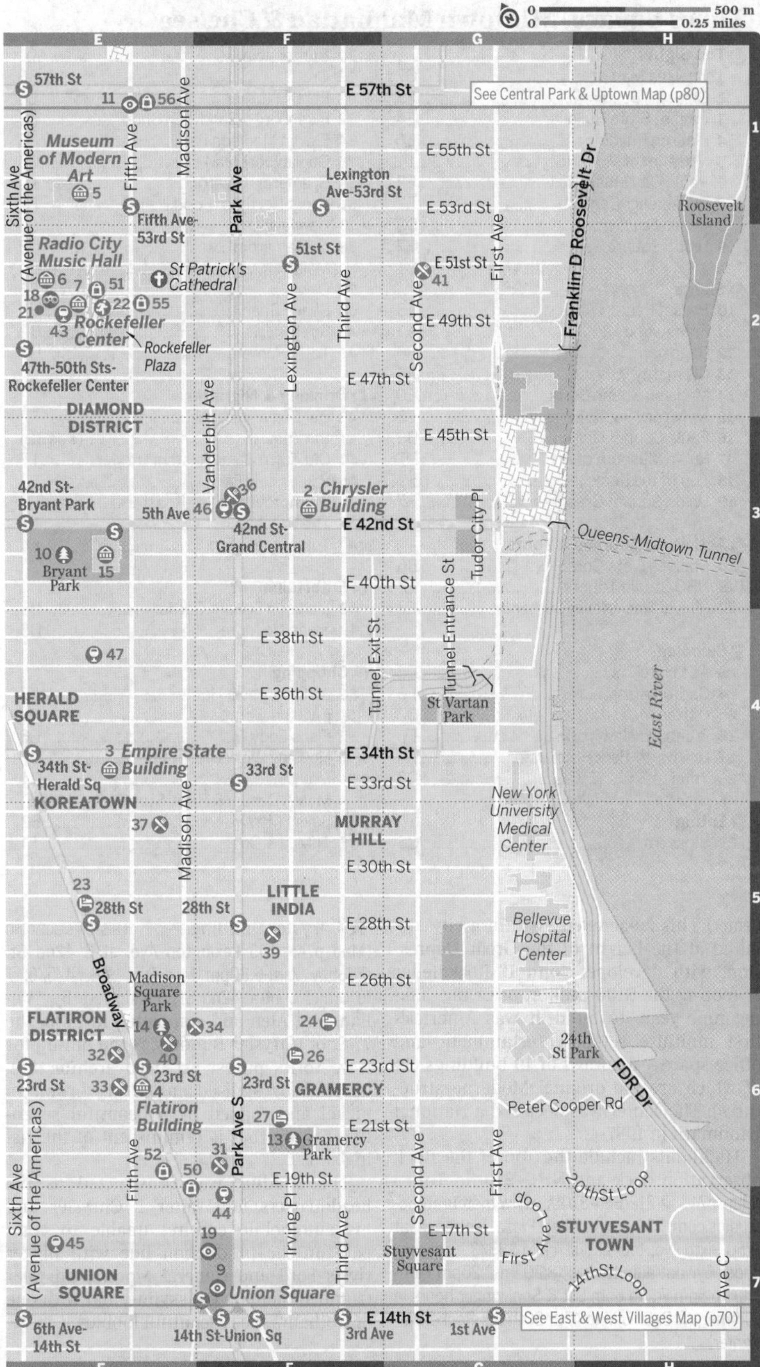
0 500 m
0 0.25 miles
See Central Park & Uptown Map (p80)
57th St
E 57th St
Museum of Modern Art
Radio City Music Hall
St Patrick's Cathedral
Rockefeller Center
Rockefeller Plaza
47th-50th Sts-Rockefeller Center
Fifth Ave-53rd St
Lexington Ave-53rd St
51st St
E 55th St
E 53rd St
E 51st St
E 49th St
E 47th St
E 45th St
DIAMOND DISTRICT
Sixth Ave (Avenue of the Americas)
Fifth Ave
Madison Ave
Park Ave
Vanderbilt Ave
Lexington Ave
Third Ave
Second Ave
First Ave
Franklin D Roosevelt Dr
Roosevelt Island
42nd St-Bryant Park
5th Ave
42nd St-Grand Central
Chrysler Building
E 42nd St
Tudor City Pl
Queens-Midtown Tunnel
Bryant Park
E 40th St
E 38th St
E 36th St
Tunnel Exit St
Tunnel Entrance St
St Vartan Park
East River
HERALD SQUARE
34th St-Herald Sq
Empire State Building
E 34th St
33rd St
E 33rd St
KOREATOWN
MURRAY HILL
New York University Medical Center
E 30th St
LITTLE INDIA
28th St
E 28th St
Bellevue Hospital Center
Broadway
Madison Square Park
E 26th St
FLATIRON DISTRICT
24th St Park
FDR Dr
23rd St
E 23rd St
GRAMERCY
Flatiron Building
Peter Cooper Rd
Park Ave S
E 21st St
Gramercy Park
E 19th St
Irving Pl
20th St Loop
First Ave Loop
STUYVESANT TOWN
E 17th St
Stuyvesant Square
14th St Loop
UNION SQUARE
Union Square
Ave C
6th Ave-14th St
14th St-Union Sq
E 14th St
3rd Ave
1st Ave
See East & West Villages Map (p70)
NEW YORK, NEW JERSEY & PENNSYLVANIA NEW YORK CITY

Times Square, Midtown Manhattan & Chelsea

Top Sights
1 Chelsea Market ... C7
2 Chrysler Building ... F3
3 Empire State Building ... E4
4 Flatiron Building ... E6
5 Museum of Modern Art ... E1
6 Radio City Music Hall ... E2
7 Rockefeller Center ... E2
8 Times Square ... D3
9 Union Square ... F7

Sights
10 Bryant Park ... E3
11 Fifth Avenue ... E1
12 Gagosian ... B6
13 Gramercy Park ... F6
14 Madison Square Park ... E6
15 New York Public Library ... E3
16 Paula Cooper Gallery ... B6
17 Rubin Museum of Art ... D7
18 Top of the Rock ... E2
19 Union Square Greenmarket ... F7

Activities, Courses & Tours
20 Chelsea Piers Complex ... B6
21 NBC Studio Tours ... E2
22 Rink at Rockefeller Center ... E2

Sleeping
23 Ace Hotel ... E5
24 Carlton Arms ... F6
25 Citizen M ... D2
26 Freehand New York ... F6
27 Gramercy Park Hotel ... F6
28 Yotel ... C3

Eating
29 Blossom ... C6
30 Burger Joint ... D1
31 Craft ... F6
32 Eataly ... E6
33 Eisenberg's Sandwich Shop ... E6
34 Eleven Madison Park ... E6
35 Gansevoort Market ... C7
Gramercy Tavern ... (see 31)
36 Great Northern Food Hall ... F3
37 Hangawi ... E5
38 Le Bernardin ... D2
Maialino ... (see 27)
39 O-ya ... F5
40 Shake Shack ... E6
41 Smith ... G2
42 Totto Ramen ... C2

Drinking & Nightlife
43 Bar SixtyFive ... E2
Birreria ... (see 32)
44 Old Town Bar & Restaurant ... F7
45 Raines Law Room ... E7
Stumptown Coffee Roasters ... (see 23)
46 The Campbell ... F3
47 Top of the Strand ... E4

Entertainment
48 Madison Square Garden ... D5
49 Sleep No More ... B5

Shopping
50 ABC Carpet & Home ... E7
51 FAO Schwarz ... E2
52 Fishs Eddy ... E6
53 Housing Works Thrift Shop ... D7
54 Macy's ... D4
MoMA Design & Book Store ... (see 5)
55 Saks Fifth Ave ... E2
56 Tiffany & Co ... E1

Center) This 22-acre 'city within a city' debuted at the height of the Great Depression, with developer John D Rockefeller Jr footing the $100 million price tag. Taking nine years to build, it was America's first multiuse retail, entertainment and office space – a sprawl of 19 buildings (14 of which are the original Moderne structures). The center was declared a National Landmark in 1987.

Highlights include the Top of the Rock observation deck and **NBC Studio Tours** (Map p74; ☎212-664-3700; www.thetouratnbcstudios.com; 30 Rockefeller Plaza, entrance at 1250 Sixth Ave; tours adult/child $33/29, children under 6yr not admitted; ⊙8:20am-2:20pm Mon-Thu, to 5pm Fri, to 6pm Sat & Sun, longer hours in summer; S B/D/F/M to 47th-50th Sts-Rockefeller Center).

★ **Chrysler Building** HISTORIC BUILDING
(Map p74; 405 Lexington Ave, at E 42nd St; ⊙lobby 7am-6:30pm Mon-Fri; S S, 4/5/6, 7 to Grand Central-42nd St) Designed by William Van Alen and completed in 1930, the 77-floor Chrysler Building is the pin-up for New York's purest art deco architecture, guarded by stylised eagles of chromium nickel and topped by a beautiful seven-tiered spire that is reminiscent of the rising sun.

The building was constructed as the headquarters for Walter P Chrysler and his automobile empire; unable to compete on the production line with bigger rivals Ford and General Motors, Chrysler trumped them on the skyline, and with one of Gotham's most beautiful lobbies.

Fifth Avenue AREA
(Map p74; Fifth Ave, btwn 42nd & 59th Sts; S E, M to 5th Ave-53rd St, N/R/W to 5th Ave-59th St) Immortalized in film and song, Fifth Ave first developed its high-class reputation in the early 20th century, when it was known for its 'country' air and open spaces. The series of mansions called **Millionaire's Row** extended right up to 130th St, though most of those above 59th St faced subsequent demolition or conversion to the cultural institutions now constituting Museum Mile. Despite a proliferation of ubiquitous chains, the avenue's Midtown stretch still glitters with upmarket establishments, among them **Tiffany & Co** (Map p74; 212-755-8000; www.tiffany.com; 727 Fifth Ave, at E 57th St; 10am-7pm Mon-Sat, noon-6pm Sun; S F to 57th St; N/R/W to 5th Ave-59th St).

New York home of Donald Trump and family, the **Trump Tower**, at Fifth Ave and 56th St, has become a sight in and of itself and was a popular spot for protestors.

Far more interesting for architecture fans is the succession of lovely beaux-arts and art deco facades, many of them washed in burnished gold, that have been preserved for retail occupants. The section between W 45th and 50th Streets is particularly good: notable facades include the **French Building** at 551 (1926–27), the **Scribner Building** at 597 (1912–13), and the **British Empire Building** at 620 (1932; part of the Rockefeller Center).

★**Radio City Music Hall** HISTORIC BUILDING
(Map p74; www.radiocity.com; 1260 Sixth Ave, at W 51st St; tours adult/child $30/26; tours 9:30am-5pm; ; S B/D/F/M to 47th-50th Sts-Rockefeller Center) This spectacular Moderne movie palace was the brainchild of vaudeville producer Samuel Lionel 'Roxy' Rothafel. Never one for understatement, Roxy launched his venue on December 23, 1932, with an over-the-top extravaganza that included camp dance troupe the Roxyettes (mercifully renamed the Rockettes). Guided tours (75 minutes) of the sumptuous interiors include the glorious auditorium, Witold Gordon's classically inspired mural *History of Cosmetics* in the Women's Downstairs Lounge, and the VIP Roxy Suite, where luminaries such as Elton John and Alfred Hitchcock have been entertained.

St Patrick's Cathedral CATHEDRAL
(Map p74; 212-753-2261; www.saintpatrickscathedral.org; Fifth Ave, btwn E 50th & 51st Sts; 6:30am-8:45pm; S B/D/F/M to 47th-50th Sts-Rockefeller Center, E/M to 5th Ave-53rd St) Still shining after a $200 million restoration in 2015, America's largest Catholic cathedral graces Fifth Ave with Gothic Revival splendor. Built at a cost of nearly $2 million during the Civil War, the building did not originally include the two front spires; those were added in 1888. Step inside to appreciate the Louis Tiffany–designed altar, gleaming below a 7000-pipe church organ, and Charles Connick's stunning Rose Window above the Fifth Ave entrance. Occasional walk-in guided tours are available; check the website for details.

A **basement crypt** behind the altar contains the coffins of every New York cardinal and the remains of Pierre Toussaint, a champion of the poor and the first African American up for sainthood.

Bryant Park PARK
(Map p74; 212-768-4242; www.bryantpark.org; 42nd St, btwn Fifth & Sixth Aves; 7am-midnight Mon-Fri, to 11pm Sat & Sun Jun-Sep, shorter hours Oct-May; S B/D/F/M to 42nd St-Bryant Park, 7 to 5th Ave) European coffee kiosks, alfresco chess games, summer film screenings and winter ice skating: it's hard to believe that this leafy oasis was a crime-ridden hellscape known as 'Needle Park' in the '70s. Nestled behind the beaux-arts New York Public Library building, it's a whimsical spot for a little time-out from the Midtown madness.

Fancy taking a beginner Italian language, yoga or juggling class, joining a painting workshop or signing up for a birding tour? There's a daily smorgasbord of quirky activities here.

Top of the Rock VIEWPOINT
(Map p74; 212-698-2000, toll free 877-692-7625; www.topoftherocknyc.com; 30 Rockefeller Plaza, entrance on W 50th St, btwn Fifth & Sixth Aves; adult/child $36/30, sunrise/sunset combo $54/43; 8am-midnight, last elevator at 11pm; S B/D/F/M to 47th-50th Sts-Rockefeller Center) Designed in homage to ocean liners and opened in 1933, this 70th-floor open-air observation deck sits atop the **GE Building**, the tallest skyscraper at the Rockefeller Center. Top of the Rock beats the Empire State Building on several levels: it's less crowded, has wider observation decks (both outdoor and indoor) and offers a view of the Empire State Building itself. Before ascending, a fascinating 2nd-floor exhibition gives an insight into the legendary philanthropist behind the art deco complex.

If you don't have under-21s in tow, note that similar views can be had from the Rockefeller's 65th-floor **Bar SixtyFive** (Map p74; ☎212-632-5000; www.rainbowroom.com/bar-sixty-five; 30 Rockefeller Plaza, entrance on W 49th St; ⊙5pm-midnight Mon-Fri, 4-9pm Sun, closed Sat; S B/D/F/M to 47th-50th Sts-Rockefeller Center)...and you don't need a ticket to Top of the Rock to get in.

Upper East Side

★Metropolitan Museum of Art — MUSEUM

(Map p80; ☎212-535-7710; www.metmuseum.org; 1000 Fifth Ave, at E 82nd St; 3-day pass adult/senior/child $25/$17/free, pay-as-you-wish for NY State residents; ⊙10am-5:30pm Sun-Thu, to 9pm Fri & Sat; 🚻; S 4/5/6, Q to 86th St; 6 to 77th St) The vast collection of art and antiquities contained within this palatial museum (founded in 1870) is one of the world's largest and most important, with more than two million individual objects in its permanent collection of paintings, sculptures, textiles and artifacts from around the globe – even an ancient Egyptian temple straight from the banks of the Nile. 'The Met' has 17 acres of exhibition space to explore, so plan to spend several hours here. (Wear comfy shoes.)

The 1st-floor ancient Egyptian collection is unrivaled; do not miss the **Temple of Dendur**, built around 10 BCE and relocated from Egypt in 1978. On the 2nd floor, numerous **European Paintings galleries** display stunning masterworks from the 13th through 20th centuries, while 15 incredible rooms are devoted to an extensive collection of **Islamic art and artifacts**. The **American Wing** features decorative and fine art from across US history. Other galleries are devoted to classical antiquity (with sculptures dramatically illuminated by natural daylight), Asian art, and modern and contemporary paintings and sculptures – there are simply too many to list.

Kids will most enjoy the artifact-rich Egyptian, African and Oceania galleries, as well as the collection of medieval armor and weaponry (all on the 1st floor). There's a specially designed brochure and map for kids, and events listed on the website.

If visiting from April through October, head up to the excellent **roof garden**, which features rotating sculpture installations by contemporary and 20th-century artists – though the grand city and park views are the real draw. Enjoy a sundowner cocktail from its on-site bar, the Cantor Roof Garden Bar (p110).

Self-guided **audio tours** (adult/child $7/5) are available in 10 languages; download the Met's free smartphone app for excerpts. **Guided tours** of specific galleries are free with admission. Tickets are good for three consecutive days, and also give admission to the Cloisters (p83).

★Guggenheim Museum — MUSEUM

(Map p80; ☎212-423-3500; www.guggenheim.org; 1071 Fifth Ave, at E 89th St; adult/child $25/free, cash-only pay-what-you-wish 5-8pm Sat; ⊙10am-5:30pm Wed-Fri, Sun & Mon, to 8pm Sat & 9pm Tue; 🚻; S 4/5/6, Q to 86th St) A New York icon, architect Frank Lloyd Wright's conical white spiral is probably more famous than the artworks inside, which include works by Kandinsky, Picasso, Pollock, Monet, Van Gogh and Degas; photographs by Mapplethorpe, and important surrealist works. But temporary exhibitions climbing the much-photographed central rotunda are the real draw. Other key works are often exhibited in the more recent adjoining tower (1992).

Pick up the free audioguide or download the Guggenheim app for information about the exhibits and architecture.

★Frick Collection — GALLERY

(Map p80; www.frick.org; 1 E 70th St, at Fifth Ave; adult/student $22/12, pay-what-you-wish 2-6pm Wed, 6-9pm 1st Fri of month excl Jan & Sep free; ⊙10am-6pm Tue-Sat, 11am-5pm Sun; S 6 to 68th St-Hunter College) This historic mansion was built by steel magnate Henry Clay Frick, one of the many such residences lining the section of Fifth Ave that was once called 'Millionaires' Row.

Note that the mansion is closed for renovations until 2023 – in the meantime, the Frick's spectacular art collection can be found at the Breuer building, formerly the **Met Breuer** (Map p80; 945 Madison Ave, at E 75th St). The collection features masterpieces by Titian, Vermeer, Gilbert Stuart, El Greco, Joshua Reynolds, Goya and Rembrandt. Sculpture, ceramics, antique furniture and clocks are also on display.

Jewish Museum — MUSEUM

(Map p80; ☎212-423-3200; www.thejewishmuseum.org; 1109 Fifth Ave, btwn E 92nd & 93rd Sts; adult/child $18/free, Sat free, pay-what-you-wish 5-8pm Thu; ⊙11am-5:45pm Mon-Tue & Fri, 11am-8pm Thu, 10am-5:45pm Sat-Sun; 🚻; S 6, Q to 96th St) This gem occupies a French-Gothic mansion from 1908, housing 30,000 items

CENTRAL PARK

One of the world's most renowned green spaces, **Central Park** (Map p80; www.centralparknyc.org; 59th to 110th Sts, btwn Central Park West & Fifth Ave; ⏲6am-1am; 🚸) comprises 843 acres of rolling meadows, boulder-studded outcroppings, elm-lined walkways, manicured European-style gardens, a lake and reservoir — not to mention an outdoor theater, a memorial to John Lennon, an idyllic waterside eatery at the **Loeb Boathouse** (☎212-517-2233; www.thecentralparkboathouse.com; Central Park Lake, near E 74th St; mains lunch $26-38, dinner $29-45; ⏲restaurant noon-4pm Mon-Fri, from 9:30am Sat & Sun year-round, 5:30-9:30pm Mon-Fri, from 6pm Sat & Sun Apr-Nov; S B, C to 72nd St; 6 to 77th St), and a famous statue of Alice in Wonderland. Highlights include the 15-acre **Sheep Meadow**, where thousands of people lounge and play on warm days; **Central Park Zoo** (☎212-439-6500; www.centralparkzoo.com; 64th St, at Fifth Ave; adult/child $20/15, without 4-D Theater $14/11; ⏲10am-5pm Mon-Fri, to 5:30 Sat & Sun Apr-Oct, 10am-4:30pm Nov-Mar; 🚸; S N/R to 5th Ave-59th St); and the forest-like paths of the **Ramble** (btwn 73rd & 78th Sts; S B,C to 81st St).

Like the city's subway system, the vast and majestic Central Park, a rectangle of open space in the middle of Manhattan, is a great class leveler – exactly as it was envisioned. Created in the 1860s and '70s by Frederick Law Olmsted and Calvert Vaux on the marshy northern fringe of the city, the immense park was designed as a leisure space for all New Yorkers regardless of color, class or creed. It's also an oasis from the insanity: the lush lawns, cool forests, flowering gardens, glassy bodies of water and meandering, wooded paths provide the dose of serene nature that New Yorkers crave.

Olmsted and Vaux (who also created Prospect Park, p86, in Brooklyn) were determined to keep foot and road traffic separated and cleverly designed the crosstown transverses under elevated roads to do so. That such a large expanse of prime real estate has survived intact for so long is proof that nothing eclipses the heart, soul and pride that forms the foundation of New York City's greatness.

Today, this 'people's park' is still one of the city's most popular attractions, beckoning throngs of New Yorkers with free outdoor concerts on the **Great Lawn** (btwn 79th & 85th Sts; ⏲Apr–mid-Nov; S B, C to 86th St) and top-notch drama at the annual Shakespeare in the Park (p91) productions held each summer at the open-air **Delacorte Theater** (www.publictheater.org; enter at W 81st St; S B, C to 81st St). Other recommended stops include the ornate **Bethesda Fountain** (S B, C to 72nd St), which edges the Lake, and its **Loeb Boathouse** (boating per hr $15; ⏲10am-6:45pm; 🚸; S B, C to 72nd St), where you can rent rowboats or enjoy lunch; the **Shakespeare Garden**, on the west side between 79th and 80th Sts, with its lush plantings and excellent skyline views; and the Ramble, a wooded thicket that's popular with bird-watchers. While parts of the park swarm with joggers, inline skaters, musicians and tourists on warm weekends, it's quieter on weekday afternoons, especially in the less-trodden spots above 72nd St, such as the **Harlem Meer** and the **North Meadow** (north of 97th St).

Folks flock to the park even in winter, when snowstorms inspire cross-country skiing and sledding or just a simple stroll through the white wonderland, and crowds turn out every New Year's Eve for a midnight run. The **Central Park Conservancy** (☎212-310-6600; www.centralparknyc.org/tours) offers ever-changing guided tours of the park, including ones that focus on public art, wildlife and places of interest to kids (check online for dates and times; most tours are free or $15).

of Judaica including torah shields and hanukah lamps, as well as sculpture, painting and decorative arts. It does not, however, include any historical exhibitions relating to the Jewish community in New York. Temporary exhibits are often excellent, featuring retrospectives on influential figures such as Art Spiegelman or Leonard Cohen, as well as world-class shows on luminaries like Marc Chagall and Modigliani. The landmark Lower East Side deli Russ & Daughters has a restaurant in the basement.

Upper West Side

★American Museum of Natural History MUSEUM

(Map p80; ☎212-769-5100; www.amnh.org; Central Park West, at W 79th St; suggested admission

Central Park & Uptown

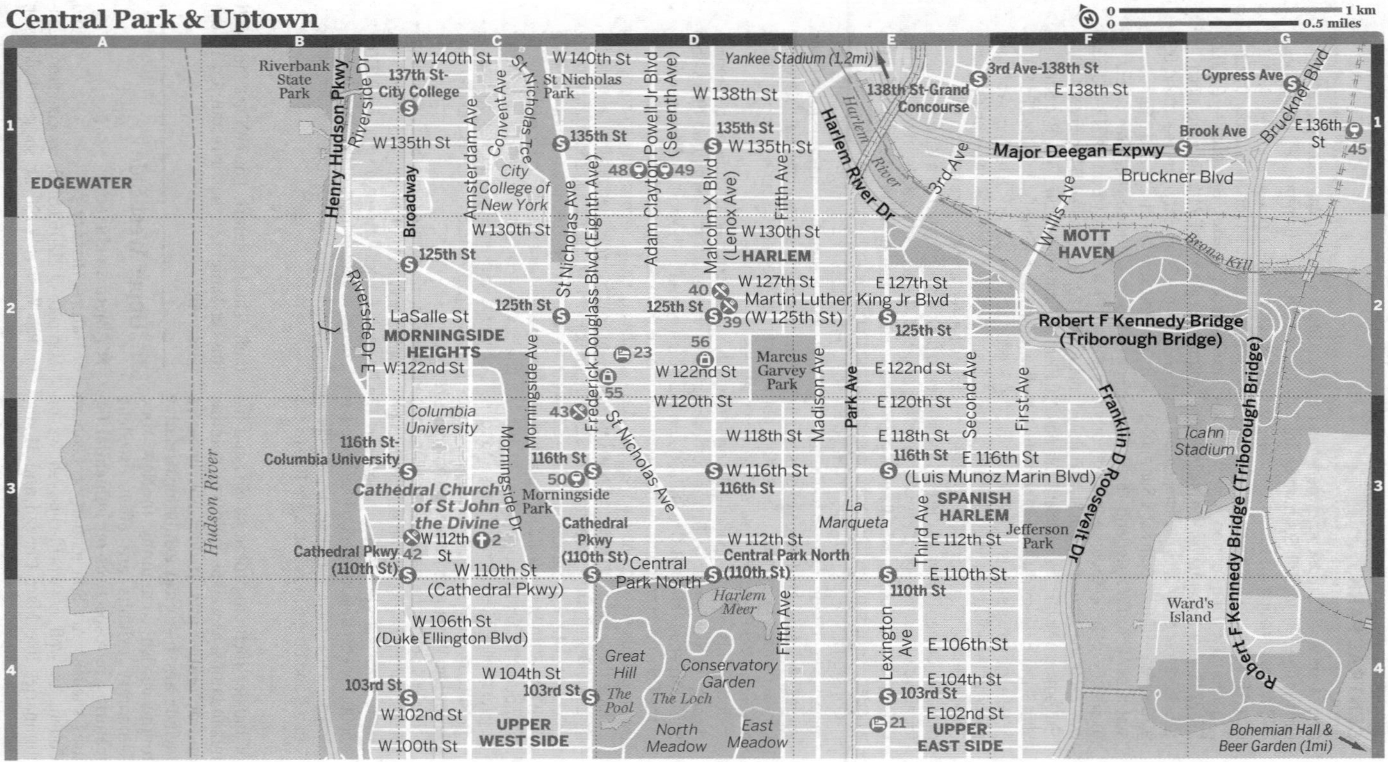

0 1 km
0 0.5 miles

A B C D E F G
1 2 3 4

EDGEWATER
Hudson River
Riverbank State Park
Henry Hudson Pkwy
Riverside Dr
Riverside Dr E
137th St-City College
W 140th St
W 135th St
Broadway
Amsterdam Ave
Convent Ave
St Nicholas Tce
City College of New York
St Nicholas Park
W 130th St
125th St
LaSalle St
MORNINGSIDE HEIGHTS
W 122nd St
Columbia University
116th St-Columbia University
Cathedral Church of St John the Divine
Morningside Dr
Morningside Ave
Morningside Park
W 112th St
Cathedral Pkwy (110th St)
W 110th St (Cathedral Pkwy)
W 106th St (Duke Ellington Blvd)
W 104th St
103rd St
W 102nd St
W 100th St
UPPER WEST SIDE
135th St
St Nicholas Ave
Frederick Douglass Blvd (Eighth Ave)
Adam Clayton Powell Jr Blvd (Seventh Ave)
Malcolm X Blvd (Lenox Ave)
116th St
Cathedral Pkwy (110th St)
Central Park North
W 120th St
HARLEM
W 127th St
Martin Luther King Jr Blvd (W 125th St)
Marcus Garvey Park
W 118th St
W 116th St
W 112th St
Central Park North (110th St)
Harlem Meer
Great Hill
The Pool
The Loch
Conservatory Garden
North Meadow
East Meadow
Fifth Ave
Madison Ave
Park Ave
La Marqueta
Yankee Stadium (1.2mi)
W 138th St
138th St-Grand Concourse
Harlem River
Harlem River Dr
3rd Ave
3rd Ave-138th St
E 138th St
E 127th St
E 122nd St
E 120th St
E 118th St
E 116th St (Luis Munoz Marin Blvd)
SPANISH HARLEM
E 112th St
E 110th St
Lexington Ave
E 106th St
E 104th St
E 102nd St
UPPER EAST SIDE
Third Ave
Second Ave
First Ave
Jefferson Park
Franklin D Roosevelt Dr
Willis Ave
MOTT HAVEN
Bronx Kill
Major Deegan Expwy
Brook Ave
Bruckner Blvd
Cypress Ave
E 136th St
Robert F Kennedy Bridge (Triborough Bridge)
Icahn Stadium
Ward's Island
Bohemian Hall & Beer Garden (1mi)
2 21 23 39 40 42 43 45 48 49 50 55 56

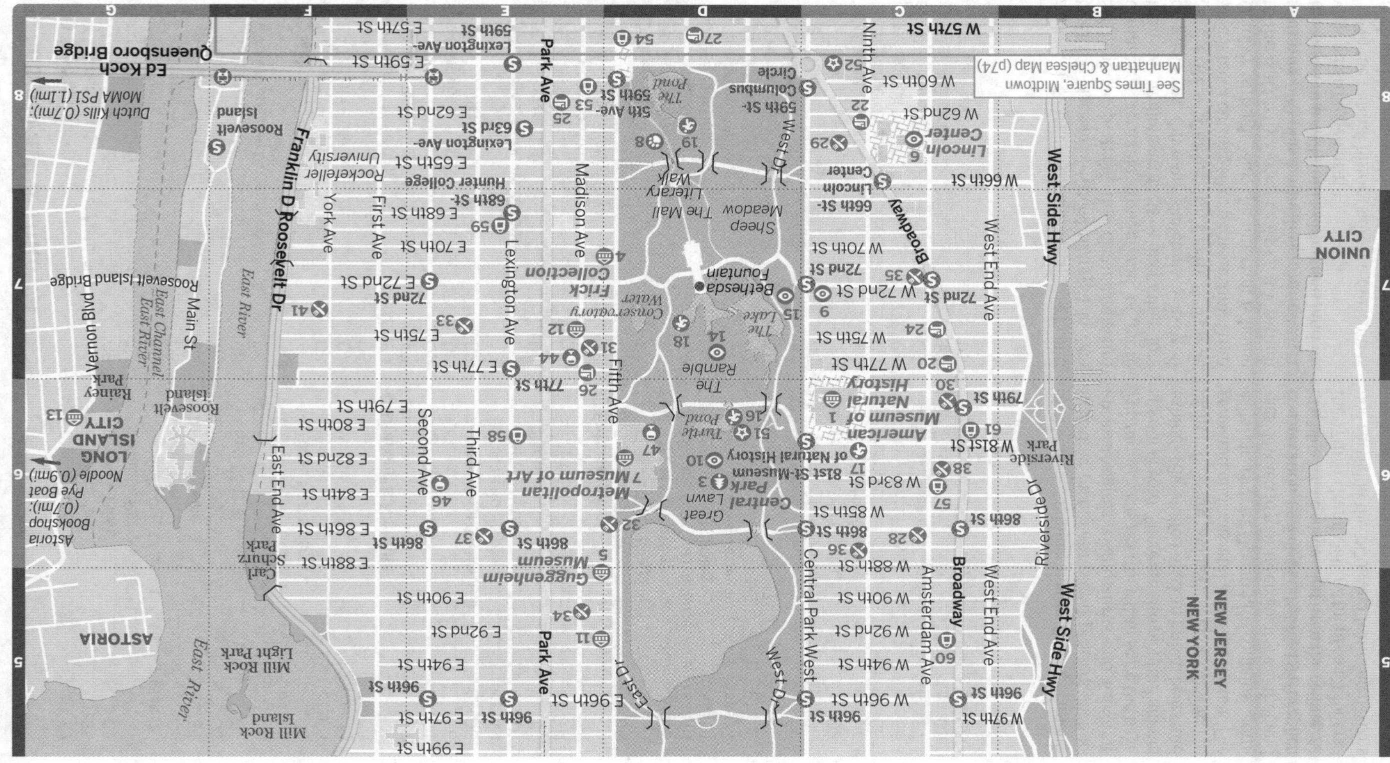
ASTORIA
LONG ISLAND CITY
Astoria Bookshop (0.7mi); Pye Boat Noodle (0.9mi)
Dutch Kills (0.7mi); MoMA PS1 (1.1mi)
Ed Koch Queensboro Bridge
Vernon Blvd
Rainey Park
Roosevelt Island Bridge
East Channel East River
Main St
Roosevelt Island
East River
Mill Rock Island
Mill Rock Light Park
Carl Schurz Park
East End Ave
Franklin D Roosevelt Dr
Rockefeller University
York Ave
First Ave
Second Ave
Third Ave
Lexington Ave
Park Ave
Madison Ave
Fifth Ave
E 99th St
E 97th St
96th St
E 96th St
E 94th St
E 92nd St
E 90th St
E 88th St
86th St
E 86th St
E 84th St
E 82nd St
E 80th St
E 79th St
77th St
E 77th St
E 75th St
72nd St
E 72nd St
E 70th St
68th St-Hunter College
E 68th St
E 65th St
Lexington Ave-63rd St
E 62nd St
E 59th St
Lexington Ave-59th St
E 57th St
5th Ave-59th St
Guggenheim Museum
Metropolitan Museum of Art
Frick Collection
Conservatory Water
East Dr
West Dr
Central Park
Great Lawn
Turtle Pond
The Ramble
The Lake
Bethesda Fountain
Sheep Meadow
The Mall
Literary Walk
The Pond
59th St-Columbus Circle
Central Park West
81st St-Museum of Natural History
American Museum of Natural History
W 96th St
W 94th St
W 92nd St
W 90th St
W 88th St
86th St
W 85th St
W 83rd St
W 81st St
79th St
W 77th St
W 75th St
72nd St
W 72nd St
W 70th St
66th St-Lincoln Center
Lincoln Center
W 66th St
W 62nd St
W 60th St
W 57th St
W 97th St
Amsterdam Ave
Broadway
West End Ave
Ninth Ave
Riverside Dr
Riverside Park
West Side Hwy
NEW YORK
NEW JERSEY
UNION CITY
See Times Square, Midtown Manhattan & Chelsea Map (p74)
A
B
C
D
E
F
G
5
6
7
8

Central Park & Uptown

Top Sights
1 American Museum of Natural History C6
2 Cathedral Church of St John the Divine C3
3 Central Park....... D6
4 Frick Collection....... D7
5 Guggenheim Museum....... E5
6 Lincoln Center C8
7 Metropolitan Museum of Art....... D6

Sights
8 Central Park Zoo D8
9 Dakota Building C7
10 Great Lawn D6
11 Jewish Museum....... E5
12 Met Breuer....... E7
13 Noguchi Museum G6
14 Ramble....... D7
15 Strawberry Fields D7

Activities, Courses & Tours
16 Belvedere Castle D6
17 Bike & Roll....... C6
18 Loeb Boathouse D7
19 Wollman Skating Rink D8

Sleeping
20 Arthouse Hotel NYC....... C7
21 Bubba & Bean Lodges....... E4
22 Empire Hotel....... C8
23 Harlem Flophouse D2
24 Hotel Beacon C7
25 Loews Regency Hotel....... E8
26 Mark....... E7
27 Quin D8

Eating
28 Barney Greengrass C6
29 Boulud Sud C8
30 Burke & Wills C6
31 Café Boulud....... E7
32 Café Sabarsky D6
33 Candle Cafe....... E7
34 Eli's Essentials....... E5
35 Gray's Papaya C7
Lakeside Restaurant at Loeb Boathouse .... (see 18)
36 Milk Bar C6
37 Papaya King E6
38 Peacefood Cafe....... C6
39 Red Rooster D2
40 Sylvia's D2
41 Tanoshi F7
42 Tom's Restaurant C3
43 Vinatería....... C3
Wright....... (see 5)

Drinking & Nightlife
44 Bemelmans Bar E7
45 Bronx Brewery G1
46 Caledonia E6
47 Cantor Roof Garden Bar D6
Empire Rooftop....... (see 22)
48 Harlem Hops D1
49 Shrine D1
50 Silvana....... C3

Entertainment
51 Delacorte Theater....... D6
Frick Collection Concerts .... (see 4)
52 Jazz at Lincoln Center C8
Metropolitan Opera House....... (see 6)
New York City Ballet....... (see 6)
New York Philharmonic .... (see 6)

Shopping
53 Barneys E8
54 Bergdorf Goodman....... D8
55 Flamekeepers Hat Club D2
56 Harlem Haberdashery D2
57 Magpie....... C6
58 Mary Arnold Toys E6
59 Shakespeare & Co E7
60 Shishi....... C5
61 Zabar's C6

adult/child $23/13; 10am-5:45pm; ; C to 81st St-Museum of Natural History; 1 to 79th St) Founded in 1869, this classic museum contains a veritable wonderland of more than 34 million artifacts – including lots of menacing dinosaur skeletons – as well as the **Rose Center for Earth & Space**, which has a cutting-edge planetarium. From October through May, the museum is home to the **Butterfly Conservatory**, a vivarium featuring 500-plus butterflies from all over the world that will flutter about and land on your outstretched arm.

On the natural history side, the museum is perhaps best known for its light and airy **Fossil Halls** containing nearly 600 specimens, including mammoth crowd pleasers such as an apatosaurus, titanosaurus and fearsome *Tyrannosaurus rex* (they'll all scare the bejesus out of you). There are also plentiful animal exhibits (the stuffed Alaskan brown bears and giant moose are popular), galleries devoted to gems and minerals, and an IMAX theater. The **Milstein Hall of Ocean Life** contains dioramas devoted to marine ecologies, weather and conservation, as well as a beloved 94ft replica of a blue whale suspended from the ceiling. At the 77th St Grand Gallery, there's a 63-foot canoe carved in the 1870s and featuring designs from different Native American peoples of the Northwest Coast.

For the astronomical set, the Rose Center is the star of the show. Every half-hour at the planetarium (check website for specific times) you can drop yourself into a cushy seat to view *Worlds Beyond Earth,* narrated by Academy Award winner Lupita Nyong'o. You'll also find an astonishing **Willamette Meteor**, a 15.5-ton hunk of metallic iron that fell to earth in present-day Oregon some 30-40,000-years ago.

Note that while you can pay what you wish for general admission (in person only), in order to see space shows, IMAX films or ticketed exhibits you'll need to pay the posted prices for admission plus one show (adult/child $28/16.50) or admission plus all shows ($33/20).

The museum broke ground in 2019 on a $383-million expansion that will include the Richard Gilder Center for Science, Education, and Innovation.

★Lincoln Center — ARTS CENTER

(Map p80; ☎212-875-5456, tours 212-875-5350; www.lincolncenter.org; Columbus Ave, btwn W 62nd & 66th Sts; tours adult/student $25/20; ⏲tours 11:30am & 1:30pm Mon-Sat, 3pm Sun; 👪; Ⓢ1, 2, 3 to 66th St-Lincoln Center, A/C or B/D to 59th St-Columbus Circle) **FREE** This stark arrangement of gleaming modernist temples houses some of Manhattan's most important performance companies: the New York Philharmonic (p113), the New York City Ballet (p112) and the Metropolitan Opera (p112). The lobby of the iconic Opera House is dressed with brightly saturated murals by painter Marc Chagall. Various other venues are tucked in and around the 16-acre campus, including a theater, two film-screening centers and the renowned **Juilliard School** for performing arts.

Strawberry Fields — MEMORIAL

(Map p80; www.centralparknyc.org; Central Park, at 72nd St on west side; ⓈC, B to 72nd St) Standing inside the park across from the famous **Dakota apartment building** (Map p80; 1 W 72nd St, at Central Park West; ⓈB, C to 72nd St), where John Lennon was fatally shot in 1980, is this poignant, tear-shaped garden – a memorial to the slain star. It contains a grove of stately elms and a tiled mosaic that says, simply, 'Imagine.'

The spot is officially designated a quiet zone but you wouldn't know it from the multitude of tour guides and buskers who come to vocalize here.

Harlem & Upper Manhattan

★Met Cloisters — MUSEUM

(Map p64; ☎212-923-3700; www.metmuseum.org/cloisters; 99 Margaret Corbin Dr, Fort Tryon Park; 3-day pass adult/senior/child $25/17/free, pay-as-you-wish for residents of NY State & students from CT, NY and NJ; ⏲10am-5:15pm Mar-Oct, to 4:45pm Nov-Feb; ⓈA to 190th St) On a hilltop overlooking the Hudson River, the Cloisters is a curious architectural jigsaw, its many parts made up of various European monasteries and other historic buildings. Built in the 1930s to house the Metropolitan Museum's medieval treasures, its frescoes, tapestries and paintings are set in galleries that sit around a romantic courtyard, connected by grand archways and topped with Moorish terra-cotta roofs. Among its many rare treasures is the beguiling tapestry series *The Hunt of the Unicorn* (1493–1505).

Also worth seeking out is the remarkably well-preserved 15th-century Annunciation Triptych (Merode Altarpiece). Then there's the stunning French 12th-century Saint-Guilhem and Bonnefant cloisters, the latter featuring plants used in medieval medicine, magic, ceremony and the arts, and with views over the Hudson River.

Your ticket gives you three-day admission to the Cloisters and the Metropolitan Museum of Art. Note that although the Dyckman St subway station looks closest to the museum, there are steep slippery steps between the station and the entrance; use 190th St station instead and walk through the park.

★Cathedral Church of St John the Divine — CATHEDRAL

(Map p80; ☎tours 212-316-7540; www.stjohndivine.org; 1047 Amsterdam Ave, at W 112th St, Morningside Heights; adult/student $10/8, highlights tour $14, vertical tour $20/18; ⏲7:30am-6pm Mon-Sat, 12:30-2:30pm Sun; ⓈB/C, 1 to 110th St-Cathedral Pkwy) New York's most impressive house of worship is a towering monument that looks like it's straight out of medieval Europe. Built in a mix of styles – with elements of Romanesque, Gothic and neo-Gothic design – St John's is packed with treasures, from gorgeous stained-glass windows to 17th-century tapestries, as well as works by contemporary artists such as Keith Haring and Tom Otterness. Despite the grandeur, the cathedral has yet to be completed; some even jokingly refer to it as 'St John the Unfinished.'

Central Park

THE LUNGS OF NEW YORK

The rectangular patch of green that occupies Manhattan's heart began life in the mid-19th century as a swampy piece of land that was carefully bulldozed into the idyllic nature-scape you see today. Since officially becoming Central Park, it has brought New Yorkers of all stripes together in interesting and unexpected ways. The park has served as a place for the rich to show off their fancy carriages (1860s), for the poor to enjoy free Sunday concerts (1880s) and for activists to hold be-ins against the Vietnam War (1960s).

Since then, legions of locals – not to mention travelers from all kinds of faraway places – have poured in to stroll, picnic, sunbathe, play ball and catch free concerts and performances of works by Shakespeare.

Duke Ellington Circle

Harlem Meer

The Blockhouse

North Woods

97th St Transverse

Fifth Ave

86th St Transverse

The Great Lawn

Central Park West

Loeb Boathouse

Perched on the shores of the lake, the historic Loeb Boathouse is one of the city's best settings for an idyllic meal. You can also rent rowboats and bicycles and ride on a Venetian gondola.

Conservatory Garden

The only formal garden in Central Park is perhaps the most tranquil part of the park. On the northern end, chrysanthemums bloom in late October. To the south, the park's largest crab apple tree grows by the Burnett Fountain.

STUDIOLASKA/SHUTTERSTOCK © FOUNTAIN SCULPTOR: BESSIE POTTER VONNOH

Jacqueline Kennedy Onassis Reservoir

This 106-acre body of water covers roughly an eighth of the park's territory. Its original purpose was to provide clean water for the city. Now it's a good spot to catch a glimpse of water birds.

LULU AND ISABELLE/SHUTTERSTOCK ©

Belvedere Castle

A so-called 'Victorian folly,' this Gothic-Romanesque castle serves no other purpose than to be a very dramatic lookout point. It was built by Central Park co-designer Calvert Vaux in 1869.

The park's varied terrain offers a wonderland of experiences. There are quiet, woodsy knolls in the north. To the south is the reservoir, crowded with joggers. There are European gardens, a zoo and various bodies of water. For maximum flamboyance, hit the Sheep Meadow on a sunny day, when all of New York shows up to lounge.

Central Park is more than just a green space. It is New York City's backyard.

FAST FACTS

➡ The landscape architects were Frederick Law Olmsted and Calvert Vaux.

➡ Construction commenced in 1858.

➡ The park covers 843 acres.

➡ Hundreds of movies have been shot on location, from Depression-era blockbuster *Gold Diggers* (1933) to monster-attack flick *Cloverfield* (2008).

Conservatory Water

This pond is popular in the warmer months, when children sail their model boats across its surface. Conservatory Water was inspired by 19th-century Parisian model-boat ponds and figured prominently in EB White's classic book, *Stuart Little.*

CHRISTOPHER PENLER/SHUTTERSTOCK ©

KRIDSADA KAMSOMBAT/SHUTTERSTOCK ©

Bethesda Fountain

This neoclassical fountain is one of New York's largest. It's capped by the *Angel of the Waters*, which is supported by four cherubim. The fountain was created by bohemian-feminist sculptor Emma Stebbins in 1868.

Metropolitan Museum of Art

Alice in Wonderland Statue

79th St Transverse

The Ramble

Delacorte Theater

The Lake

Fifth Ave

Central Park Zoo

65th St Transverse

Sheep Meadow

Columbus Circle

Strawberry Fields

A simple mosaic memorial pays tribute to musician John Lennon, who was killed across the street outside the Dakota Building. Funded by Yoko Ono, its name is inspired by the Beatles song 'Strawberry Fields Forever.'

The Mall/ Literary Walk

A Parisian-style promenade – the only straight line in the park – is flanked by statues of literati on the southern end, including Robert Burns and Shakespeare. It is lined with rare North American elms.

Brooklyn

★Brooklyn Bridge BRIDGE

(Map p66; Ⓢ4/5/6 to Brooklyn Bridge-City Hall, J/Z to Chambers St, R/W to City Hall, Ⓢ2/3 to Clark St, A/F to High St-Brooklyn Bridge Station) A New York icon, the Brooklyn Bridge was the world's first steel suspension bridge, and, at 1596ft, the longest when it opened in 1883. Although construction was fraught with disaster, the bridge became a magnificent example of urban design. Its suspended bicycle/pedestrian walkway delivers soul-stirring views of Manhattan, the East River and the Brooklyn waterfront. Though beautiful, the crossing can be challenging – if walking, stay in the pedestrian portion of the lane as cyclists move quickly.

Brooklyn Bridge Park PARK

(718-222-9939; www.brooklynbridgepark.org; East River Waterfront, btwn Atlantic Ave & John St, Brooklyn Heights/Dumbo; 6am-1am, some sections to 11pm, playgrounds to dusk; ; B63 to Pier 6/Brooklyn Bridge Park, B25 to Old Fulton St/Elizabeth Pl, East River or South Brooklyn routes to Dumbo/Pier 1, Ⓢ A/C to High St, 2/3 to Clark St, F to York St) FREE This 85-acre park is one of Brooklyn's best-loved attractions. Wrapping itself around a 1.3-mile bend on the East River, it runs from just beyond the far side of the Manhattan Bridge in Dumbo to the west end of Atlantic Ave in Brooklyn Heights. It has revitalized a once-barren stretch of shoreline, turning a series of abandoned piers into beautifully landscaped parkland with jaw-dropping views of Manhattan. There's lots to see and do here, with playgrounds, walkways and lawns galore.

Brooklyn Heights Promenade VIEWPOINT

(www.nycgovparks.org; btwn Orange & Remsen Sts, Brooklyn Heights; 24hr; Ⓢ N/R/W to Court St, 2/3 to Clark St, A/C to High St) Six of of the east-west streets of well-to-do Brooklyn Heights (such as Montague and Clark Sts) lead to the neighborhood's number-one attraction: a narrow, paved walking strip with breathtaking views of Lower Manhattan and New York Harbor that is blissfully removed from the busy Brooklyn–Queens Expwy (BQE) over which it sits. This little slice of urban beauty, fiercely defended by locals against development proposals, is a great spot for a sunset walk.

★Prospect Park PARK

(Map p64; 718-965-8951; www.prospectpark.org; Grand Army Plaza; 5am-1am; Ⓢ2/3 to Grand Army Plaza, F, G to 15th St-Prospect Park, B, Q to Prospect Park, Q to Parkside Ave) Brooklyn is blessed with a number of historic, view-laden and well-used green spaces, but its emerald is Prospect Park. The designers of the 585-acre park – Frederick Law Olmsted and Calvert Vaux – considered it an improvement on their other New York project, Central Park, and between rambling its tree-fringed walkways and sighing at ornamental bridges, you might agree. Opened in 1867, Brooklyn's lovely, faux-natural greenspace has a long meadow to the west (filled with dog-walkers, sportspeople or barbecuers, depending on the season), hilly woodlands, and a boathouse on the east side, by its expansive lake. The neoclassical arches, sculptures and columns at the major entrances were later additions.

Many visitors come to bike, run, stroll, walk their dogs or just lounge around. The park has a **zoo** (Map p64; 718-399-7339; www.prospectparkzoo.com; 450 Flatbush Ave, Prospect Park; adult/child $10/7; 10am-5pm Mon-Fri, to 5:30pm Sat & Sun Apr-Oct, to 4:30pm Nov-Mar; ; B41 to Flatbush Ave, Ⓢ B, Q to Prospect Park, 2/3 to Grand Army Plaza) and an ice-skating rink (p89), which becomes a water-play area for kids in the warm months, when boats are also available for hire. There are are also **free concerts** (718-683-5600; www.bricartsmedia.org; Prospect Park Bandshell, near Prospect Park W & 11th St, Park Slope; Jun-Aug) at the **Prospect Park Bandshell** (near the entrance at 9th St and Prospect Park W) and a year-round **farmers market** (www.grownyc.org; Grand Army Plaza, cnr Prospect Park W & Flatbush Ave, Prospect Park; 8am-4pm Sat; Ⓢ2, 3 to Grand Army Plaza) is held on Saturdays at the Grand Army Plaza entrance.

★Brooklyn Museum MUSEUM

(Map p64; 718-638-5000; www.brooklynmuseum.org; 200 Eastern Pkwy, Prospect Park; adult/child $16/free; 11am-6pm Wed & Fri-Sun, to 10pm Thu year-round, to 11pm 1st Sat of month Oct-Dec & Feb-Aug; ; Ⓢ2/3 to Eastern Pkwy-Brooklyn Museum) This encyclopedic museum, imagined as the centrepiece of the 19th-century Brooklyn Institute, occupies a five-story, 560,000-sq-ft beaux-arts building stuffed with more than 1.5 million objects – ancient Egyptian sarcophagi, 19th-century period rooms, and a cornucopia of art. This elegant, airy space is an inspiring place to explore, and a calmer alternative to Manhattan's manic museums.

The collection is augmented by thought-provoking temporary exhibitions on diverse subjects from European art retrospectives to provocative contemporary art,

WORTH A TRIP

CONEY ISLAND

Coney Island – a name synonymous in American culture with antique seaside fun and frolicking – achieved worldwide fame as a working-class amusement park and beach-resort area at the turn of the 20th century. After decades of decline, its kitschy charms have experienced a 21st-century revival. Though it's no longer the booming, peninsula-wide attraction it once was, it still draws crowds of tourists and locals alike for legendary roller-coaster rides, hot dogs and beer on the beachside boardwalk.

Luna Park (Map p64; 718-373-5862; www.lunaparknyc.com; 1000 Surf Ave, at W 10th St; Apr-Oct; D/F, N/Q to Coney Island-Stillwell Ave) is one of Coney Island's most popular amusement parks and contains one of its most legendary rides: the Cyclone ($10), a wooden roller-coaster that reaches speeds of 60mph and makes near-vertical drops. In a neighboring park is the 150ft-tall pink-and-mint-green **Deno's Wonder Wheel** (Map p64; 718-372-2592; www.denoswonderwheel.com; 1025 Riegelmann Boardwalk, at W 12th St; rides $10; from noon Jul & Aug, from noon Sat & Sun Apr-Jun, Sep & Oct; ; D/F, N/Q to Coney Island-Stillwell Ave), which has been delighting New Yorkers since 1920 as the best place to survey Coney Island from up high.

The hot dog was invented in Coney Island in 1867, and there's no better place to eat one than **Nathan's Famous** (718-333-2202; www.nathansfamous.com; 1310 Surf Ave, at Stillwell Ave; hot dogs from $4; 10am-11pm Mon-Thu, to midnight Fri, 9am-midnight Sat, to 11pm Sun; ; D/F to Coney Island-Stillwell Ave), established in 1916. When thirst strikes, head to **Ruby's** (718-975-7829; www.rubysbar.com; 1213 Riegelmann Boardwalk, btwn Stillwell Ave & W 12th St; 11am-10pm Sun-Thu, to 1am Fri & Sat Apr-Sep, weekends only Oct; D/F, N/Q to Coney Island-Stillwell Ave), a legendary dive bar right on the boardwalk.

often with a spotlight on feminist thought and LGBTIQ+ artists. Special events run until 11pm on the first Saturday of each month (except September).

Brooklyn Botanic Garden GARDENS

(Map p64; 718-623-7200; www.bbg.org; 150 Eastern Pkwy, Prospect Park; adult/student/child $15/8/free, 8am-noon Fri free, Tue-Fri Dec-Feb free; 8am-6pm Tue-Fri, from 10am Sat & Sun Mar-Oct, shorter hours rest of year; ; 2/3 to Eastern Pkwy-Brooklyn Museum, B, Q to Prospect Park) Opened in 1911 and now one of Brooklyn's most picturesque sights, this 52-acre garden is home to thousands of plants and trees and a **Japanese garden** where river turtles swim alongside a Shinto shrine. The best times to visit are late April or early May, when the blooming cherry trees (a gift from Japan) are celebrated in Sakura Matsuri, the Cherry-Blossom Festival (p89), or fall, when the deciduous trees blaze their colours.

★**Bushwick Collective** PUBLIC ART

(Map p64; www.instagram.com/thebushwickcollective; Bushwick; L to Jefferson St) FREE Further cementing Bushwick's status as Brooklyn's coolest neighborhood is this outdoor gallery of murals by some of the most talented street artists in NYC and beyond. The works change regularly, and can be found mainly along Jefferson and Troutman Sts between Cypress and Knickerbocker Aves, with others along Gardner Ave (north of Flushing Ave). Other street art can be found around the Morgan Ave L stop, particularly on Seigel and Grattan Sts.

The latter two streets are conveniently near Roberta's (p106) and **Pine Box Rock Shop** (718-366-6311; www.pineboxrockshop.com; 12 Grattan St, btwn Morgan Ave & Bogart St, East Williamsburg; 4pm-2am Mon & Tue, to 4am Wed-Fri, 2pm-4am Sat, noon-2am Sun; L to Morgan Ave) – great places to stop for a pizza or some drinks.

Though overall safe to visit, Bushwick still has occasional incidents of crime, so pay attention to your surroundings in this area, especially late at night and on weekends.

Queens

★**MoMA PS1** GALLERY

(Map p64; 718-784-2084; www.momaps1.org; 22-25 Jackson Ave, Long Island City; suggested donation adult/child $10/free, NYC residents or with MoMA ticket free, Warm Up party online/at venue $18/22; noon-6pm Thu-Mon, Warm Up parties noon-9pm Sat Jul-early Sep; G, 7 to Court Sq, E, M to Court Sq-23rd St) At MoMA's hip contemporary outpost, you'll be peering at videos through floorboards, schmoozing at DJ parties and debating the meaning of nonstatic structures while staring through a hole in the wall. Exhibits include everything from

Middle Eastern video art to industrial boilers covered in gold leaf. Many are site-specific installations – *Meeting* (1986), an installation by LA light artist James Turrell, is definitely worth seeking out, especially just before sundown.

Noguchi Museum MUSEUM
(Map p80; ☎718-204-7088; www.noguchi.org; 9-01 33rd Rd, at Vernon Blvd, Long Island City; adult/child $10/free, 1st Fri of month free; ⊙10am-5pm Wed-Fri, 11am-6pm Sat & Sun; Q103, Q104 to Vernon Blvd-33 Rd, S N/W to Broadway) Both the art and the context in which it's displayed here are the work of LA-born sculptor, designer and landscape architect Isamu Noguchi, famous for iconic lamps and coffee tables, as well as elegant, abstract stone sculptures. Artifacts are displayed in serene indoor galleries and a minimalist sculpture garden, forming a complete aesthetic vision and an oasis of calm. The 1st floor holds the permanent collection, while the upstairs gallery shows temporary exhibitions.

The Bronx

Bronx Zoo ZOO
(Map p64; ☎718-220-5100; www.bronxzoo.com; 2300 Southern Blvd; full-experience adult/child Apr-Oct $37/27, Nov-Mar $29/21, pay-as-you-wish general admission Wed; ⊙10am-5pm Mon-Fri, to 5:30pm Sat & Sun Apr-Oct, to 4:30pm Nov-Mar; S 2, 5 to West Farms Sq-E Tremont Ave) This 265-acre zoo is the country's biggest and oldest, with more than 6000 animals and re-created habitats from around the world, such as African plains and Asian rainforests. It's deservedly popular, with especially large crowds on discounted Wednesdays and weekends in good weather, and any day in July or August (try to go Monday morning). The southwest Asia Gate (four blocks north of the West Farms Sq–E Tremont Ave stop, up Boston Rd) is your easiest access point by subway.

New York Botanical Garden GARDENS
(Map p64; ☎718-817-8716; www.nybg.org; 2900 Southern Blvd; all-garden pass Mon-Fri adult/child $23/10, Sat & Sun $28/12, grounds only NYC residents $15/4, Wed & 9-10am Sat grounds admission free; ⊙10am-6pm Tue-Sun; ; Metro-North to Botanical Garden) First opened in 1891 and incorporating 50 acres of old-growth forest, the New York Botanical Garden is home to the restored Enid A Haupt Conservatory, a grand, Victorian iron-and-glass edifice that is now a New York landmark. See the website for a list of regular events, which include themed walking tours, children's book readings and film screenings.

Yankee Stadium STADIUM
(Map p64; ☎212-926-5337; www.mlb.com/yankees; 1 E 161st St, at River Ave; tours $20; S B/D, 4 to 161st St-Yankee Stadium) The Boston Red Sox like to talk about their record of nine World Series championships in the last 90 years... well, the Yankees have won a mere 27 in that period. The team's magic appeared to have moved with them across 161st St to the new Yankee Stadium, where they played their first season in 2009 – winning the World Series there in a six-game slugfest against the Phillies. The Yankees play from April to October.

Activities

Cycling

Central Park Bike Tours CYCLING
(Map p80; ☎212-541-8759; https://centralparkbiketours.com; 203 W 58th, btwn Broadway & 7th Ave; bike rentals per hr/day adult from $10.50/28, child $9/23; ⊙8am-8pm; ; S 1/2/3 to 59th/Columbus Cir) The official bike rental outfitter of NYC Parks has more than 3000 bikes in 12 locations around the city (you can't miss their green-shirted touts around the edge of the park). This outlet is one of two along 58th St just south of the park. Two-hour guided tours of the park ($30) are also offered. Helmut and bike locks are included in the rates. Reserve rentals online to guarantee a bike in summer.

Health & Fitness

Chelsea Piers Complex HEALTH & FITNESS
(Map p74; ☎212-336-6666; www.chelseapiers.com; Pier 62, at W 23rd St, Chelsea; ⊙5:30am-11pm Mon-Fri, 8am-9pm Sat & Sun; ; M23 to 12th Ave-W 23 St, S 1, C/E to 23rd St) This massive waterfront sports center caters to the athlete in everyone. You can hit endless golf balls at the four-level driving range, skate on an indoor ice rink or rack up strikes in a jazzy bowling alley. There's basketball at Hoop City, a sailing school for kids, batting cages, a huge gym and covered swimming pool, and indoor rock climbing.

Great Jones Spa SPA
(Map p70; ☎212-505-3185; www.gjspa.com; 29 Great Jones St, btwn Lafayette St & Bowery, NoHo; ⊙9am-10pm; S 6 to Bleecker St; B/D/F/M to Broadway-Lafayette St) Don't skimp on the services at this downtown feng shui–designed place, whose offerings include blood-orange salt scrubs and stem-cell facials. If you spend over $100 per person (not difficult: hour-

long massages/facials start at $150/135), you get access to the water lounge with thermal hot tub, sauna, steam room and cold plunge pool (swimwear required). There's even a three-story indoor waterfall.

Ice Skating

Wollman Skating Rink SKATING

(Map p80; ☎212-439-6900; www.wollmanskatingrink.com; Central Park, btwn E 62nd & 63rd Sts; adult Mon-Thu $12, Fri-Sun $19, child $6, skate rentals $10; ⏰10am-2:30pm Mon & Tue, to 10pm Wed & Thu, to 11pm Fri & Sat, to 9pm Sun late Oct-early Apr; 👪; Ⓢ F to 57 St; N/R/W to 5th Ave-59th St) This rink is much larger than the Rockefeller Center skating rink, and not only does it allow all-day skating, its position at the southeastern edge of Central Park offers magical views. There's locker rental for $5 and a spectator fee of $5. Cash only.

Rink at Rockefeller Center ICE SKATING

(Map p74; ☎212-332-7654; www.therinkatrockcenter.com; Rockefeller Center, Fifth Ave, btwn W 49th & 50th Sts; adult $25-33, child $15, skate rental $13; ⏰8:30am-midnight mid-Oct–Apr; 👪; Ⓢ B/D/F/M to 47th-50th Sts-Rockefeller Center) From mid-October to April, Rockefeller Plaza is home to New York's most famous ice-skating rink. Carved out of a recessed oval with the 70-story art deco Rockefeller Center towering above, plus a massive Christmas tree during the holiday season, it's incomparably magical. It's also undeniably small and crowded. Opt for the first skating period of the day (8:30am) to avoid a long wait. Sessions last 90 minutes. Come summer, the rink becomes a cafe.

Outdoor Activities

LeFrak Center at Lakeside BOATING

(☎718-462-0010; www.lakesideprospectpark.com; 171 East Dr, near Ocean & Parkside Aves, Prospect Park; skating $7.25-10, skate rental $7, boat rental per hour $16-36, bike rental per hour $13-38; ⏰hours vary; 👪; Ⓢ Q to Parkside Ave) The most significant addition to Prospect Park (p86) since its creation, the LeFrak is a 26-acre ecofriendly playground. In winter there's ice-skating, in summer there's roller-skating and a sprinkler-filled water-play area for kids to splash about in. Pedal boats and kayaks are also available (usually late March to mid-October), and a variety of bikes can be rented to tour the park.

Belvedere Castle BIRDWATCHING

(Map p80; ☎646-790-4833; www.centralparknyc.org; Central Park, at W 79th St; ⏰9am-7pm mid-Jun–mid-Aug, 10am-5pm mid-Aug–mid-Jun; 👪; Ⓢ 1/2/3, B, C to 72nd St) For a DIY birding expedition with kids, borrow a 'Discovery Kit' at Belvedere Castle in Central Park, which comes with binoculars, a bird book, colored pencils and paper – a perfect way to get the kids excited about birds. Picture ID is required.

Tours

★ Staten Island Ferry CRUISE

(Map p66; www.siferry.com; Whitehall Terminal, 4 Whitehall St, at South St, Lower Manhattan; ⏰24hr; Ⓢ 1 to South Ferry, R/W to Whitehall St, 4/5 to Bowling Green) FREE Staten Islanders know these hulking orange ferries as commuter vehicles, while Manhattanites think of them as their secret, romantic vessels for a spring-day escape. Yet many tourists are also wise to the charms of the Staten Island Ferry, whose 25-minute, 5.2-mile journey between Lower Manhattan and the Staten Island neighborhood of St George is one of NYC's finest free adventures.

Museum Hack WALKING

(☎347-282-5001; www.museumhack.com; 2hr tour from $59) For a fascinating, alternative perspective of the Met, sign up for a tour with Museum Hack. Knowledgeable but delightfully irreverent guides take on topics like 'Badass Bitches' (a look at paradigm-shifting feminist artists) and lead night tours that include wine. Museum Hack also runs tours in the Museum of Natural History, with an 'Un-Highlights Tour' of museum curiosities.

Children under 16 years cannot be accommodated on regular tours but private family-friendly tours can be arranged.

Festivals & Events

Tribeca Film Festival FILM

(☎212-941-2400; www.tribecafilm.com; ⏰Apr-May) Founded in 2003 by Robert De Niro and Jane Rosenthal, the Tribeca Film Festival is now a major star of the indie movie circuit. Gaggles of celebs come to walk the red carpets each spring, while New Yorkers snap up tickets to screenings and talks. Vote for the Audience Award by downloading the festival app, which also details the programme lineup and accompanying talks.

Cherry-Blossom Festival CULTURAL

(☎718-623-7200; www.bbg.org; Brooklyn Botanic Garden, Prospect Park; ⏰late Apr/early May) Known in Japanese as Sakura Matsuri, this tradition celebrates the pink, puffy flowering of myriad varieties of cherry tree in the Brooklyn Botanic Garden (p87), in particular

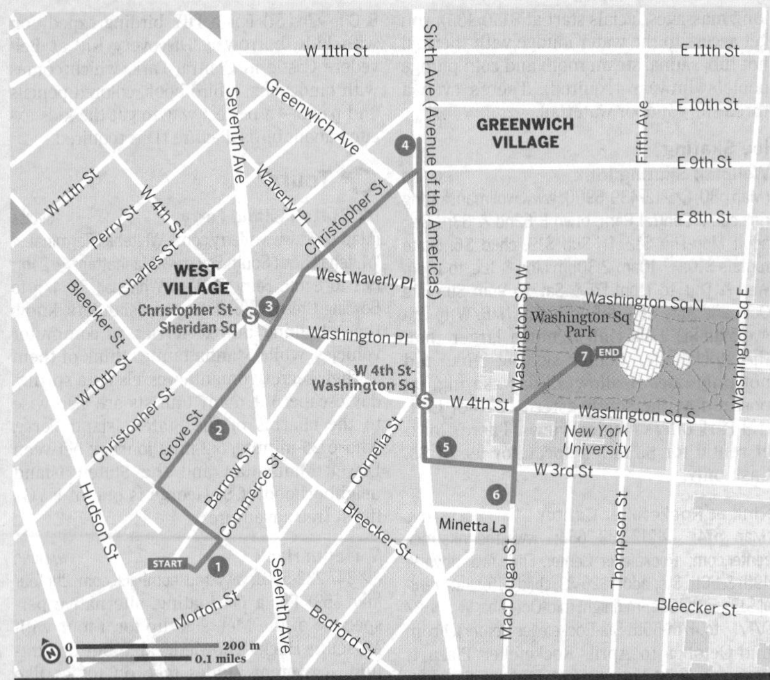

Walking Tour Greenwich Village

START COMMERCE ST
END WASHINGTON SQUARE PARK
LENGTH 1.2 MILES; ONE HOUR

Greenwich Village's brick-lined byways break Manhattan's signature grid pattern, striking off on intriguing tangents that beg to be explored on foot. Start at ❶ **Cherry Lane Theatre** (www.cherrylanetheater.org; 38 Commerce St), hidden in the crook of handsome, residential Commerce St. Established in 1924, the Cherry is the city's longest continuously running off-Broadway establishment, and has hosted many famous playwrights and thespians.

Make a left on Bedford and turn right into Grove St (number 90, on the corner, may be familiar as the apartment building in *Friends*) to reach your first pit stop, ❷ **Buvette** (p108). Literally 'snack bar,' this dreamy Francophile wine bar is ideal for people-watching over the rim of a flat white or a glass of Côtes du Rhône, depending on the hour.

Continue along Grove St. The next stop is Christopher Park, home to the ❸ **Stonewall National Monument** (p69). On the north side of the green is the legendary Stonewall Inn, where in 1969 LGBTQ men and women rioted against routine police harassment, sparking what came to be known as the Gay Rights Movement.

Follow Christopher St to Sixth Ave to find the ❹ **Jefferson Market Library** just north. Built as a courthouse in 1885, this gracious red-brick building rises from a tranquil garden of the same name, complete with flowering trees, lawns and a koi pond.

Head south again through Sixth Ave's flurry of foot traffic, then turn left onto West 3rd St, looking for legendary jazz venue ❺ **Blue Note** (www.bluenote.net; 131 W 3rd St) on your left. Sarah Vaughan, Lionel Hampton and other immortals have performed here; try to time your visit for jazz brunch on Sunday (11:30am or 1:30pm).

Turn right onto MacDougal St to reach the ❻ **Comedy Cellar** (www.comedycellar.com; 117 MacDougal St), where the likes of Jerry Seinfeld and Amy Schumer have performed, then double back, heading north on MacDougal to end your stroll in ❼ **Washington Square Park** (p68), the village's unofficial town square.

the many-petaled Kwanzan along its famous esplanade. Entry to a full day's program of entertainment, against a photogenic canopy provided by cherry, apricot and almond blooms, costs $30 (under-12s can accompany adults for free).

It's worth booking in advance. If you can't make the festival, check the map on the website for the most florescent times and places anytime from late March through mid-May.

SummerStage PERFORMING ARTS
(www.cityparksfoundation.org/summerstage; Rumsey Playfield, Central Park, access via Fifth Ave & 69th St; May-Oct; ; 6 to 68th St-Hunter College) Every summer Central Park hosts dozens of outdoor concerts known as SummerStage, showcasing indie rock, jazz, modern dance, rockabilly, African, zydeco and much more. Most performances are free and the festival draws big crowds, so start queuing up early or you may have to listen to the music outside (not always a bad place, especially with a picnic blanket on the grass).

Shakespeare in the Park THEATER
(www.publictheater.org/Free-Shakespeare-in-the-Park; Central Park; Jun-Aug; A/B/C to 81st St) The much-loved Shakespeare in the Park pays tribute to the Bard, with free performances in the open-air Delacorte Theater (p79) in Central Park. It's a magical experience. The catch? You'll have to wait hours in line to score tickets, or win them in the online lottery. It's managed by the Public Theater (p112).

BAM Next Wave Festival PERFORMING ARTS
(www.bam.org; tickets from $32; Oct-Dec) Running for around 12 weeks from October to mid-December at the Brooklyn Academy of Music (p113), this arts festival offers the city's edgiest, most comprehensive survey of avant-garde music, theater, opera and dance.

Thanksgiving Day Parade PARADE
(www.macys.com; 4th Thu Nov) This famous cold-weather event, for hardy viewers only, parades its famous floats and balloons (watch your head) from 77th St to Herald Sq along Central Park W, Central Park S and then Sixth Ave. The parade culminates in live performances, from high-school marching bands to A-list stars.

For a close-up preview, join the throngs who gather at the southwest corner of Central Park to watch the balloons being inflated the night before.

Rockefeller Center Christmas Tree Lighting LIGHT SHOW
(www.rockefellercenter.com; Rockefeller Plaza; Dec; B/D/F/M to 47th-50th Sts-Rockefeller Center) At this traditional mob-scene event, people flock around the massive spruce tree to watch it come aglow with energy-efficient bulbs before it's taken down and recycled into lumber. It's a green Christmas!

The lighting happens in late November or early December and the tree is taken down early in the new year. Expect huge crowds for days around this event.

Sleeping

Expect high prices and small spaces. Room rates waver by availability, not by any high-season or low-season rules. You'll pay dearly during holidays. Accommodations fill up quickly, especially in summer and December, and range from cookie-cutter chains to stylish boutiques.

You'll find better-value hotels in Brooklyn and Queens; Long Island City has an increasing number of bargain designer hotel options with killer Manhattan views. A few B&Bs and hostels are scattered throughout the city.

Financial District & Lower Manhattan

★ **Roxy Hotel** HOTEL $$
(Map p66; 212-519-6600; www.roxyhotelnyc.com; 2 Sixth Ave, at White St, Tribeca; standard/superior/deluxe r from $349/359/409; ; 1 to Franklin St, A/C/E to Canal St) The reimagined Tribeca Grand offers mid-century glamor, luxurious living, cinema, music, drinking and dining in one foxy package. Its 201 rooms, decked out with modern fittings in a retro brown-and-gold palette, surround a spacious central atrium with multiple bars, a boutique **art-house cinema** (212-519-6820; www.roxycinematribeca.com; tickets $12) and jazz cellar Django.

Regular events here such as the annual New Year's Surrealist Ball heighten the fun.

Gild Hall BOUTIQUE HOTEL $$
(Map p66; 212-232-7700; www.thompsonhotels.com/hotels/gild-hall; 15 Gold St, at Platt St, Lower Manhattan; superior/deluxe from $249/289; ; 2/3 to Fulton St) Boutique and brilliant, Gild Hall's entryway leads to a split-level, book- and sofa-stuffed lobby exuding a style best characterised as 'Wall St meets hunting lodge.' Rooms fuse Euro

elegance and American comfort with high tin ceilings, Sferra linens and well-stocked minibars. King-size beds sport leather headboards, which work perfectly in their warmly hued, minimalist surroundings.

★Greenwich Hotel BOUTIQUE HOTEL $$$
(Map p66; ☎212-941-8900; www.thegreenwichhotel.com; 377 Greenwich St, btwn N Moore & Franklin Sts, Tribeca; r from $650; ; S1 to Franklin St, A/C/E to Canal St) From the plush drawing room (complete with crackling fire and deep armchairs) to the lantern-lit pool inside a reconstructed 18th-century Japanese farmhouse, nothing about Robert De Niro's Greenwich Hotel is generic. Each of the 88 individually designed rooms features aged-wood floors, and bathrooms with opulent Carrara marble or Moroccan tiling. French windows open onto Tuscan-inspired inner courtyards in some rooms.

SoHo & Chinatown

Hotel Hugo BOUTIQUE HOTEL $$
(Map p70; ☎212-608-4848; www.hotelhugony.com; 525 Greenwich St, btwn Vandam & Spring Sts, SoHo; r from $240; ; S1 to Houston St/Canal St, C/E to Spring St) It might not have the bells and whistles of some other SoHo hotels, but Hotel Hugo is a quiet little champion in this pricey 'hood. Rooms subtly channel industrial style, there's a goldmine rooftop terrace bar and suave restaurant-cafe. It's a 10- to 15-minute walk from central SoHo but that's A-OK when prices can be as low as $340 a night even in peak season.

★Broome BOUTIQUE HOTEL $$$
(Map p70; ☎212-431-2929; www.thebroomenyc.com; 431 Broome St, at Crosby St, SoHo; r from $399; ; SR/W to Prince St; 6 to Spring St) Occupying a handsomely restored, 19th-century building, the Broome feels far more intimate than most NYC hotels. Its 14 rooms are the epitome of simple, muted elegance, each with locally sourced fittings.

There's a hidden surprise here, too: a tranquil open-air internal patio with Parisian-style seating for relaxing with a coffee (which is complimentary, as is the farm-to-table breakfast). The service here is personable.

Crosby Street Hotel BOUTIQUE HOTEL $$$
(Map p70; ☎212-226-6400; www.firmdalehotels.com; 79 Crosby St, btwn Spring & Prince Sts, SoHo; r from $725; ; S6 to Spring St; N/R to Prince St) The team behind this hotel, converted from a former parking lot, have torn up the rule book in terms of interior design, and the results are sublime. Guest rooms all have oversized headboards with matching mannequins, but that's where the uniformity ends. Some are starkly black and white while others are as floral as an English garden; all are plush, refined and subtly playful.

West Village, Chelsea & Meatpacking District

Jane Hotel HOTEL $
(Map p70; ☎212-924-6700; www.thejanenyc.com; 113 Jane St, at West St, West Village; r with shared/private bath $135/295; P; SA/C/E, L to 8th Ave-14th St, 1 to Christopher St-Sheridan Sq) The Jane's 50-sq-ft rooms are undeniably snug, but if you have the sea in your blood, check into this renovated red-brick gem, built for mariners in 1908 (*Titanic* survivors stayed here in 1912).

The lobby is all pale-green antique tiles, stag's heads, peacocks and liveried bellboys, while the gorgeous ballroom-bar looks like it belongs in a five-star hotel.

Standard BOUTIQUE HOTEL $$$
(Map p70; ☎212-645-4646; www.standardhotels.com; 848 Washington St, at W 13th St, Meatpacking District; r from $383; ; SA/C/E, L to 8th Ave-14th St) Straddling the High Line, this unique hotel welcomes guests with an upside-down sign, a canary-yellow revolving door and a giant gumball machine in the lobby, signalling the offbeat design within. Each of the 338 rooms has sweeping views of Manhattan and the Hudson and is filled with cascading sunlight, making the glossy, wood-framed beds and marbled bathrooms glow.

The amenities are first rate, with a buzzing German beer garden and brasserie at street level, an ice rink in winter, and a plush nightclub on the top floor. The location is also unbeatable, with the best of NYC right outside. There's a hyper-modern **sister hotel** (Map p70; ☎212-475-5700; 25 Cooper Sq/Third Ave, btwn E 5th & E 6th Sts; r $400; ; SR/W to 8th St-NYU, 4/6 to Bleecker St, 4/6 to Astor Pl) in the East Village.

East Village & Lower East Side

Ludlow HOTEL $$
(Map p70; ☎212-432-1818; www.ludlowhotel.com; 180 Ludlow St, btwn E Houston & Stanton

Sts, Lower East Side; d from $325; ❄📶; Ⓢ F to 2nd Ave) This 175-room boutique hotel oozes New York style. Rooms are beautifully designed, and come with unique features such as huge golden-hued ceiling lights, nightstands made of petrified tree trunks, mosaic-tiled bathrooms and small balconies (although the cheapest rooms here are quite small).

There's a gorgeous lobby bar and patio here, plus an acclaimed French bistro, **Dirty French**, open for breakfast, lunch and dinner.

East Village Hotel HOTEL **$$**
(Map p70; ☎917-635-7757; www.eastvillagehotel.com; 147 First Ave, at E 9th St, East Village; d $250-300; ❄📶; Ⓢ 6 to Astor Pl) In a vibrant location, this place has clean, simple rooms (a little larger than most in NYC) with exposed brick walls, comfy mattresses, wall-mounted flat-screen TVs, irons, hairdryers and small kitchenettes.

Street noise is an issue here (light sleepers, beware), and it's in an old building, so you'll have to walk your luggage up a few flights.

Bowery Hotel BOUTIQUE HOTEL **$$$**
(Map p70; ☎212-505-9100; www.theboweryhotel.com; 335 Bowery, btwn E 2nd & E 3rd Sts, East Village; r from $435; ❄@📶; Ⓢ F to 2nd Ave, 6 to Bleecker St) Pick up your red-tasselled gold room key in the hushed timber-lined lobby, admiring the antique velvet chairs and faded Persian rugs. Walk over mosaic-tiled floors to your room with its huge factory windows and quality bed. Push aside the bowler-hatted 'bowery boy' teddy you'll find there, settle in and watch a movie on your 42in plasma TV.

Union Square, Flatiron District & Gramercy

Carlton Arms HOTEL **$**
(Map p74; ☎212-679-0680; www.carltonarms.com; 160 E 25th St, at Third Ave, Gramercy; s/d with shared bath $90/130, with private bath $130/160; ❄📶; Ⓢ 6 to 23rd St or 28th St) At this divey art hotel, every inch of the interior is a canvas scrawled with artists' musings. Murals crawl up the five flights of stairs and into each of the uniquely decorated guest rooms, ranging from fantastical to downright horrifying (the helpful staff will let you pick your room). Rooms with shared bathrooms still have a small sink.

★ **Freehand New York** BOUTIQUE HOTEL **$$**
(Map p74; ☎212-475-1920; www.freehandhotels.com/new-york; 23 Lexington Ave, btwn E 23rd & E 24th Sts, Gramercy; d, tr & q from $220; ❄📶; Ⓢ 6 to 23rd St) Budget-conscious style hunters will feel right at home at Freehand, hailed a New York hotel game-changer thanks to its combination of sensible pricing, group-friendly (bunk) and solo room options, and design-led common areas. The aesthetic is mid-century modern, while rooms also feature unobtrusive art murals and frills such as slippers, robes, Argan toiletries and free fruit. Note: prices can double in summer.

Gramercy Park Hotel BOUTIQUE HOTEL **$$$**
(Map p74; ☎212-920-3300; www.gramercyparkhotel.com; 2 Lexington Ave, at 21st St, Gramercy; r from $330, ste from $1000; ❄📶; Ⓢ 6, R/W to 23rd St) More than $50 million in contemporary art decorates the lounge of this stylish hotel, setting a tone of quiet opulence. Dark-wood paneling and sumptuous sofas greet guests in the lobby, with an open fire in winter, and the signature rose-and-jade color scheme is rich and alluring.

Some rooms overlook the **park** (E 20th St, btwn Park & Third Aves), and guests have private access.

Midtown

Yotel HOTEL **$$**
(Map p74; ☎646-449-7700; www.yotel.com; 570 Tenth Ave, at 41st St, Midtown West; r from $190; ❄📶; Ⓢ A/C/E to 42nd St-Port Authority Bus Terminal; 1/2/3, N/Q/R, S, 7 to Times Sq-42nd St) Part futuristic spaceport, part *Austin Powers* set, this uber-cool 713-room hotel bases its rooms on airplane classes: premium cabin (economy), first cabins (business) and suites (first) – some come with terraces and outdoor tubs. Yotel's design trademarks include adjustable beds and color-changing mood walls. Small but cleverly configured, all cabins feature floor-to-ceiling windows with killer views, USB ports and device-streaming tech.

Hidden away on the 1st-floor, the main hotel landing area feels like a city within a city, with an espresso bar, full-service restaurant, covered terrace bar with heaters – even an Off-Broadway entertainment space called the Green Room (ask staff about buying tickets for shows). The highlight is the city's largest outdoor hotel terrace, with stunning skyscraper backdrop (naturally).

The only downside to staying here is the grungy location, though you're still situated just a short walk from Times Square and Broadway.

Citizen M HOTEL **$$**
(Map p74; ☎212-461-3638; www.citizenm.com; 218 W 50th St, btwn Broadway & Eighth Ave, Midtown West; r from $300; ❄📶; S1, C/E to 50th St) A few steps from Times Square, Citizen M is a true millennial. Communal areas are upbeat, contemporary and buzzing, and rooms are space-agey and compact. A tablet in each controls lighting, blinds and room temperature, and the plush mattresses, free movies and soothing rain showers keep guests purring.

On-site perks include gym, a 24-hour canteen and flash rooftop bar with terrace on three sides.

Quin HOTEL **$$$**
(Map p80; ☎212-245-7846; www.thequinhotel.com; 101 W 57th St, at Sixth Ave, Midtown West; d from $449; ❄📶; SF to 57th St; N/Q/R/W to 57th St-7th Ave) The Quin is an opulent, modern hotel with the bones of a grand old dame. In the 1920s it was the Buckingham, a storied hotel that hosted artists and musicians like Georgia O'Keefe and Marc Chagall.

Today it keeps the artistic connection alive with rotating in-house exhibitions – the hotel lounge has a 15ft video wall showcasing art installations. Rooms here are exceedingly comfortable and elegantly restrained.

Highlights include the custom-made, king-sized Duxiana beds and marble bathrooms. Rooms can be linked together for families and those on the 17th floor all benefit from fabulous terraces. Seek out the wall of guitars, hidden on the 2nd floor, painted by artists who have exhibited at the hotel.

Ace Hotel BOUTIQUE HOTEL **$$$**
(Map p74; ☎212-679-2222; www.acehotel.com/newyork; 20 W 29th St, btwn Broadway & Fifth Ave, Midtown West; r from $399; ❄📶; SR/W to 28th St) A hit with cashed-up creatives, the Ace's standard and deluxe rooms recall upscale bachelor pads – plaid bedspreads, quirky wall stencils, leather furnishings and fridges. Some even have Gibson guitars and turntables.

For cool kids with more 'cred' than 'coins,' there are 'mini' and 'bunk' rooms (with bunk beds), both of which can slip under $200 in winter.

Upper East Side

Bubba & Bean Lodges B&B **$**
(Map p80; ☎917-345-7914; www.bblodges.com; 1598 Lexington Ave, btwn E 101st & 102nd Sts; d $110-190, tr $120-230, q $130-260; ❄📶; S6 to 103rd St) Owners Jonathan and Clement are well known for turning a Manhattan town house into an excellent home-away-from-home, but an unusually high rate of property-initiated last-minute cancellations coupled with their refusal to show us a room means you should tread cautiously here. Five simply furnished guest rooms feature crisp, white walls, hardwood floors and navy linens, providing the place with a modern, youthful feel.

All units in this three-floor walk-up have private baths and also come with equipped kitchenettes.

★**Mark** DESIGN HOTEL **$$$**
(Map p80; ☎212-744-4300; www.themarkhotel.com; 25 E 77th St, at Madison Ave; d/ste from $895/1275; ❄📶; S6 to 77th St) French designer Jacques Grange left his artful mark on the Mark, with bold geometric shapes and rich, playful forms that greet visitors in the lobby (the zebra-striped marble floor, which also features in the room bathrooms, is pure eye candy).

Upstairs, lavishly renovated rooms and multi-bedroom suites are equally stylish with custom-made furnishings and luxury local linen.

Loews Regency Hotel HOTEL **$$$**
(Map p80; ☎212-759-4100; www.loewshotels.com/regency-hotel; 540 Park Ave, btwn E 61st & 62nd Sts; d $300-600, ste $500-4000; ❄@📶; SN/R, 4/5/6 to Lexington Ave/59 St, F, Q to Lexington Ave-63rd St) This fabled hotel is prime territory for Park Ave shoppers. Guests even get 15% off at nearby Bloomingdales (25% during the holidays!).

Inside, the hotel is designed to feel like an Upper East Side apartment block. Its 379 rooms – standard clock in huge at 325 to 375 sq ft – come with roomy desks and elegant marble bathrooms that have pro-style hair-dryers – some rooms also have balconies.

Upper West Side

★**Arthouse Hotel NYC** BOUTIQUE HOTEL **$$**
(Map p80; ☎212-362-1100; www.arthousehotelnyc.com; 2178 Broadway, at 77th St; d/ste from $250/350; ❄@📶; S1 to 77th St) This art-focused boutique hotel mixes vintage fur-

nishings with contemporary industrial design. The dapper lounge and bar areas on the ground floor are stylish spaces to decamp after a day spent exploring. Above, 291 airy rooms benefit from lots of natural light and restrained decor.

Flickers of mid-century design are complemented by contemporary amenities like coffeemakers, flat-screen TVs and marble bathrooms.

Hotel Beacon HOTEL **$$**

(Map p80; ☎212-787-1100, reservations 800-572-4969; www.beaconhotel.com; 2130 Broadway, btwn 74th & 75th Sts; d from $250; ; S1/2/3 to 72nd St) Adjacent to the Beacon Theatre, this family favorite offers a winning mix of attentive service, comfortable rooms and convenient location. The Beacon has 278 rooms (some are multi-bedroom suites) decorated in muted shades of Pottery Barn green. The units are well-maintained and quite roomy; all come with coffeemakers and kitchenettes.

Amenities here include a bar, gym, outsourced cycling classes and self-service laundry.

Empire Hotel HOTEL **$$$**

(Map p80; ☎212-265-7400; www.empirehotelnyc.com; 44 W 63rd St, at Broadway; r from $340; ; S1 to 66th St-Lincoln Center) The bones are all that remain of the original Empire, just across the street from Lincoln Center, with wholesale renovations dressing them in earthy tones and contemporary stylings complete with canopied pool deck, huge Empire Rooftop bar (p110) and sexy two-story lobby lounge with sweeping staircase and floor-to-ceiling drapes.

Its 420 rooms feature brightly hued walls with plush dark-leather furnishings.

Harlem & Upper Manhattan

Harlem Flophouse GUESTHOUSE **$**

(Map p80; ☎347-632-1960; www.harlemflophouse.com; 242 W 123rd St, btwn Adam Clayton Powell Jr & Frederick Douglass Blvds, Harlem; d with shared bath $99-150; ; SA/B/C/D, 2/3 to 125th St) Rekindle Harlem's Jazz Age in this atmospheric 1890s town house, its four nostalgic rooms decked out with brass beds and vintage radios (set to a local jazz station). It feels like a delicious step back in time, which also means shared bathrooms, no air-con and no TVs. One of the downstairs lounges doubles as a music room that sometimes hosts intimate concerts.

Last but not least is friendly house-cat Phoebe, who completes the homely, welcoming vibe. For longer stays, the owner also rents out a spacious basement suite (per night $175) with double and single bed plus an ensuite bathroom – contact directly to enquire.

Brooklyn

Wythe Hotel BOUTIQUE HOTEL **$$**

(☎718-460-8000; www.wythehotel.com; 80 Wythe Ave, at N 11th St, Williamsburg; d from $329; ; SL to Bedford Ave, G to Nassau Ave) Set in a converted 1901 factory, the red-brick Wythe (pronounced 'white') Hotel brings a dash of high design to Williamsburg. Exposed brick and 13ft timber ceilings allow the building's history to breathe. Meanwhile beds fashioned from reclaimed wood and a faintly nautical theme conspire with nostalgic paisley, leather and custom-made wallpaper to create a space that feels rough-hewn but elegant.

McCarren Hotel & Pool BOUTIQUE HOTEL **$$**

(☎718-218-7500; www.mccarrenhotel.com; 160 N 12th St, btwn Bedford Ave & Berry St, Williamsburg; d from $286; ; SL to Bedford Ave, G to Nassau Ave) The tropical-style pool area, where patrons armed with cocktails drape themselves across loungers, is the prime draw of this swish, mural-clad hotel. Rooms (most with balconies) are attired like a hip friend's lounge – velvety sofas, vinyl, the odd guitar – while a rooftop vegan restaurant and jazz bar mean you can kick off your evening onsite. Note: the pool's summer only.

A gym is available for guest use.

NU Hotel HOTEL **$$**

(Map p66; ☎718-852-8585; www.nuhotelbrooklyn.com; 85 Smith St, at Atlantic Ave, Boerum Hill; d incl breakfast from $209; P@; SF, G to Bergen St) Brooklyn-themed adornments, upcycled teak furnishings and occasionally eyebrow-raising artwork bestow an artful industrial flair on rooms at NU. The location, on the border of Boerum Hill and Downtown, is handy and free bikes are a convenient perk.

Groups of four can consider the 'Bunkbed' suite, with a queen and twin bunks, while art-lovers will appreciate the mural-washed 'NU Perspective' rooms.

EVEN Hotel BOUTIQUE HOTEL **$$**

(Map p66; ☎718-552-3800; www.evenhotels.com; 46 Nevins St, at Schermerhorn St, Downtown Brooklyn; r from $256; ; S2/3, 4/5 to Nevins

St, A/C, G to Hoyt-Schermerhorn) This wellness-concept hotel caters to the fitness-minded, with 'workout zones' (with personal yoga mat, foam roller, yoga block and stability ball) inside the 202 rooms, a 24-hour gym, organic food and fresh-squeezed OJ in the cafe, and free laundry service. Central location in Downtown Brooklyn is super convenient for subway stops.

Williamsburg Hotel BOUTIQUE HOTEL $$$
(718-362-8100; www.thewilliamsburghotel.com; 96 Wythe Ave, at N 10th St, Williamsburg; d from $396; ; L to Bedford Ave) Just two blocks from the water, this eight-story, industrial-chic hotel is blessed with spectacular river and Manhattan views. It's worth paying extra for one of the 'terrace' rooms on the northern side, which give you an unbroken view of the Empire State Building, the Chrysler Building and the Upper East Side from your artificial-grass-carpeted balcony (some have swing chairs).

Floor-to-ceiling windows and glassed-in showers with bright subway tiles make the smallish rooms feel more open. Minibars, leather headboards, safes and essential-oil amenities by local maker Apotheke all come standard. There's a rooftop bar in the shape of a classic NYC water tower (open 6pm to 4am Wednesday to Saturday) and an outdoor rooftop swimming pool, plus free pushbikes for cruising Williamsburg stress-free.

Eating

From inspired iterations of world cuisine to quintessentially local nibbles, New York City's dining scene is infinite, all-consuming and a proud testament to its kaleidoscope of citizens.

Even if you're not an obsessive foodie hitting ethnic enclaves or the newest cult-chef openings, an outstanding meal is always only a block away.

Financial District & Lower Manhattan

Hudson Eats FOOD HALL $
(Map p66; 212-978-1698; https://bfplny.com/directory/food; Brookfield Place, 225 Liberty St, at West St, Lower Manhattan; dishes from $7; 8am-9pm Mon-Sat, to 7pm Sun; ; E to World Trade Center, 2/3 to Park Pl, R/W to Cortlandt St, 4/5 to Fulton St, A/C to Chambers St) Sleekly renovated office and retail complex Brookfield Place is home to Hudson Eats, a shiny, upmarket food hall. Decked out with terrazzo floors, marble countertops and floor-to-ceiling windows with expansive views of Jersey City and the Hudson River, it has a string of respected, chef-driven eateries, including Blue Ribbon Sushi, Fuku, Northern Tiger and Dos Toros Taqueria.

Two Hands AUSTRALIAN $$
(Map p66; www.twohandsnyc.com; 251 Church St, btwn Franklin & Leonard Sts, Tribeca; lunch & brunch mains $14-19; 8am-5pm; ; 1 to Franklin St, N/Q/R/W, 6 to Canal St) An interior of whitewashed brick gives this modern 'Australian-style' cafe-restaurant an airy feel – and the local crowds love it.

The menu offers light breakfast and lunch dishes such as a fully loaded açai bowl with berries and granola or a chicken sandwich with feta cream and olive tapenade. The coffee on offer here is top-notch, and there's happy hour from 2pm to 5pm.

Brookfield Place FOOD HALL $$
(Map p66; 212-978-1673; www.brookfieldplaceny.com; 230 Vesey St, at West St, Lower Manhattan; ; E to World Trade Center, 2/3 to Park Pl, R/W to Cortlandt St, 4/5 to Fulton St, A/C to Chambers St) This polished, high-end office and retail complex offers two fabulous food halls. Francophile foodies should hit Le District, a charming and mouthwatering marketplace with several stand-alone restaurants and counters selling everything from stinky cheese to steak-*frites*.

Situated one floor above is Hudson Eats, a fashionable enclave of upmarket fast bites, from sushi and tacos to salads and burgers.

Le District FOOD HALL $$$
(Map p66; 212-981-8588; www.ledistrict.com; Brookfield Place, 225 Liberty St, at West St, Lower Manhattan; market mains $12-30, Beaubourg dinner mains $19-36; Beaubourg 8am-10pm Mon, to 11pm Tue & Wed, to midnight Thu & Fri, 10am-midnight Sat, to 10pm Sun, other hours vary; ; E to World Trade Center, 2/3 to Park Pl, R/W to Cortlandt St, 4/5 to Fulton St, A/C to Chambers St) Paris on the Hudson reigns at this sprawling French food emporium selling everything from high-gloss pastries and pretty *tartines* to stinky cheese and savory steak-*frites*. Main restaurant Beaubourg does bistro classics such as coq au vin, but for a quick sit-down feed, head to the Market District counter for frites or the Cafe District for a savory crepe. The Garden District offers fresh produce, groceries

and a salad bar that's perfect for putting together an impromptu alfresco lunch by the river.

Opening hours vary at each of the restaurants and between the Market, Cafe and Garden District areas; check the website for specific times.

★Locanda Verde ITALIAN $$$
(Map p66; ☎212-925-3797; www.locandaverdenyc.com; 377 Greenwich St, at N Moore St, Tribeca; mains lunch $25-32, dinner $38-54; ⏰7am-11pm Mon-Thu, to 11:30pm Fri, 8am-11:30pm Sat, to 11pm Sun; Ⓢ1 to Franklin St, A/C/E to Canal St) Curbside at the Greenwich Hotel (p92) you'll find this Italian fine diner by Andrew Carmellini, where velvet curtains part onto a scene of loosened button-downs, black dresses and slick bar staff. It's a place to see and be seen, but the food – perhaps Sicilian cod with chickpeas, *orecchiette* with duck sausage and kale, or truffle ravioli – is the main event. Booking ahead is recommended.

Bâtard EUROPEAN $$$
(Map p66; ☎212-219-2777; www.batardtribeca.com; 239 W Broadway, btwn Walker & White Sts, Tribeca; 2/3/4 courses $65/89/99; ⏰5:30-10pm Mon-Wed, to 10:30pm Thu-Sat; Ⓢ1 to Franklin St, A/C/E to Canal St) Austrian chef Markus Glocker heads this warm, Michelin-starred hot spot, where a pared-back interior puts the focus squarely on the food. Glocker's dishes are precise examples of classical French and Italian cooking: the prix-fixe menus hold rich delights such as striped bass with chanterelle mushrooms, or tagliatelle with roast lamb loin, olives and pecorino.

Service is gracious and the Francophile wine list is particularly strong on the wines of Burgundy. On Monday, bring your own bottle and pay no corkage.

SoHo & Chinatown

★Nom Wah Tea Parlor CHINESE $
(Map p66; ☎212-962-6047; www.nomwah.com; 13 Doyers St, Chinatown; dim sum from $3.75; ⏰10:30am-10pm Sun-Wed, to 11pm Fri & Sat; ⓈJ/Z to Chambers St; 4/5/6 to Brooklyn Bridge-City Hall) Hidden down a narrow lane, 1920s Nom Wah Tea Parlor might look like an old-school American diner, but it's actually the oldest dim-sum place in town. Grab a table or seat at one of the red banquettes or counter stools and simply tick off what you want on the paper menu provided. Roast pork buns, Shanghainese soup dumplings, shrimp siu mai...it's all finger-licking good.

Prince Street Pizza PIZZA $
(Map p70; ☎212-966-4100; 27 Prince St, btwn Mott & Elizabeth Sts, Nolita; pizza slices from $3.20; ⏰11:45am-11pm Sun-Thu, to 2am Fri & Sat; ⓈR/W to Prince St; 6 to Spring St) It's a miracle the oven door hasn't come off its hinges at this classic standing-room-only slice joint, its brick walls hung with shots of celebrity fans like Rebel Wilson, Usher and Kate Hudson. The sauces, mozzarella and ricotta are made in-house and New Yorkers go wild for the pepperoni square variety.

The pizza is decent, but not dazzling enough to justify waiting in the perpetual queues.

Xi'an Famous Foods CHINESE $
(Map p66; www.xianfoods.com; 45 Bayard St, btwn Elizabeth St & Bowery, Chinatown; dishes $4.70-12; ⏰11:30am-9pm Sun-Thu, to 9:30pm Fri & Sat; ⓈN/Q/R/W, J/Z, 6 to Canal St, B/D to Grand St) Food bloggers hyperventilate at the mere mention of this small chain's hand-pulled noodles. The burgers are also menu stars: tender lamb sautéed with ground cumin and toasted chili seeds, or melt-in-the-mouth stewed pork.

There are 11 other locations throughout the city.

Butcher's Daughter VEGETARIAN $$
(Map p70; ☎212-219-3434; www.thebutchersdaughter.com; 19 Kenmare St, at Elizabeth St, Nolita; salads & sandwiches $13-16, dinner mains $15-18; ⏰8am-10pm; ✎; ⓈJ to Bowery; 6 to Spring St) The butcher's daughter certainly has rebelled, peddling nothing but fresh herbivorous fare in her whitewashed cafe. While healthy it is, boring it's not: everything from the soaked organic muesli to the spicy kale Caesar salad with almond Parmesan or the dinnertime Butcher's burger (vegetable and black-bean patty with cashew cheddar cheese) is devilishly delish.

★Uncle Boons THAI $$
(Map p70; ☎646-370-6650; www.uncleboons.com; 7 Spring St, btwn Elizabeth St & Bowery, Nolita; small plates $13-16, large plates $22-32; ⏰5:30-11pm Sun-Thu, to midnight Fri & Sat; 📶; ⓈJ/Z to Bowery; 6 to Spring St) Michelin-star Thai is served up in a fun, tongue-in-cheek combo of retro wood-paneled dining room with Thai film posters and old family snaps.

Spanning the old and the new, dishes on offer here are tangy, rich and creative.

Standouts include the *kob woonsen* (garlic and soy marinated frogs legs), *koong* (grilled baby octopus) and *kaduuk* (roasted bone marrow satay).

★Dutch AMERICAN **$$$**
(Map p70; ☎212-677-6200; www.thedutchnyc.com; 131 Sullivan St, at Prince St, SoHo; mains lunch $18-38, dinner $27-68; ⏰11:30am-3pm & 5:30-10:30pm Mon-Thu, to 11:30pm Fri, 10am-3pm & 5:30-11:30pm Sat, to 10:30pm Sun; Ⓢ C/E to Spring St; R/W to Prince St; 1 to Houston St) Whether perched at the bar or dining snugly in the back room, you can always expect smart, farm-to-table comfort grub at this see-and-be-seen stalwart. Flavors traverse the globe, from wagyu steak tartare with béarnaise aioli ($22) to grilled lamb chops with jerk sauce and roti pancake ($46).

Reservations are recommended, especially for dinner and all day on weekends.

Il Buco Alimentari & Vineria ITALIAN **$$$**
(Map p70; ☎212-837-2622; www.ilbucovineria.com; 53 Great Jones St, btwn Bowery & Lafayette St, NoHo; mains lunch $14-34, dinner $34-70; ⏰8am-11pm Mon-Thu, to midnight Fri, 9am-midnight Sat, to 11pm Sun; 📶; Ⓢ 6 to Bleecker St; B/D/F/M to Broadway-Lafayette St) Whether it's espresso at the front bar, cheese from the deli or long-and-lazy Italian feasting in the sunken dining room, Il Buco's trendier spin-off delivers the goods. Brickwork and giant industrial lamps set a hip and rustic tone, echoed in the menu. The lunchtime paninis are huge, decadent and divine: try the porchetta with fried eggs, salsa verde and arugula ($18).

West Village, Chelsea & Meatpacking District

Dominique Ansel Kitchen BAKERY **$**
(Map p70; ☎212-242-5111; www.dominiqueanselkitchen.com; 137 Seventh Ave, btwn Charles & W 10th Sts, West Village; pastries $6-8, sandwiches $14-15; ⏰9am-9m; Ⓢ 1 to Christopher St-Sheridan Sq) The much-garlanded creator of the cronut owns this small, sunlit bakery, where you can nibble on perfectly flaky croissants, brownies finished with smoked sage, lemon-yuzu butter tarts and many other heavenly treats (but no cronuts). There's also light savory fare, such as sausage, kale and lentil soup and an extra-large croque monsieur, served with salad.

Taïm ISRAELI **$**
(Map p70; ☎212-691-1287; www.taimfalafel.com; 222 Waverly Pl, btwn Perry & W 11th Sts, West Village; sandwiches $8.50; ⏰11am-10pm; 🖉; Ⓢ 1 to Christopher St-Sheridan Sq, 2/3 to 14th St, A/C/E, L to 8th Ave-14th St) This tiny joint whips up some of the best falafel in the city. You can order it Green (traditional style) or Harissa (with Tunisian spices) – whichever you choose, you'll get it stuffed into pita with tahini, salad and pickles, on a platter with sides such as Moroccan carrots and marinated beets, or over Israeli salad.

Blossom VEGAN **$$**
(Map p74; ☎212-627-1144; www.blossomnyc.com; 187 Ninth Ave, btwn 21st & 22nd Sts, Chelsea; mains lunch $18-19, dinner $22-24; ⏰noon-2:45pm & 5-9:30pm Mon-Thu, noon-2:45pm & 5-10pm Fri & Sat, noon-2:45pm & 5-9pm Sun; 🖉; Ⓢ 1, C/E to 23rd St) Cozily occupying a historic Chelsea town house, this beacon to hungry vegans is a peaceful, romantic dining spot that offers imaginative, all-kosher tofu, seitan and vegetable creations, some raw. Brunch dishes like tofu Benedict and Florentine impersonate animal proteins deliciously, while superb dinner mains such as risotto with shiitake, cremini and king-trumpet mushrooms and miso-cashew cream need no affectations.

Desserts such as vegan tiramisu and 'cheesecake' are so voluptuous you'll swear they're filled with butter and cream.

JeJu Noodle Bar NOODLES **$$**
(Map p70; ☎646-666-0947; http://jejunoodlebar.com; 679 Greenwich St, at Christopher St, West Village; noodles $18-19; ⏰5-10pm Sun-Wed, to 11pm Thu-Sat; 🚌M8 to Greenwich St-Christopher St, Ⓢ 1 to Christopher St-Sheridan Sq) With classic ramen continuing to rampage across the world's tables, perhaps it's time to explore its variations – such as the Korean *ramyun* served at this welcoming restaurant on Christopher St's quieter western stretch. Start with *toro ssam bap* (fatty tuna, toasted seaweed, *tobiko* rice and scrambled egg) before slurping down a *so ramyun* – brisket and noodles in veal broth.

★RedFarm FUSION **$$$**
(Map p70; ☎212-792-9700; www.redfarmnyc.com; 529 Hudson St, btwn W 10th & Charles Sts, West Village; mains $28-52, dumplings $15-17; ⏰dinner 5-11:45pm Mon-Sat, to 11pm Sun, brunch 11am-2:30pm Sat & Sun; Ⓢ 1 to Christopher St-Sheridan Sq, A/C/E, B/D/F/M to W 4th St-Washington Sq) Experience Chinese cooking as unique, delectable artistry in this small, buzzing space. Diced tuna and eggplant bruschetta, juicy rib steak (marinated in papaya,

ginger and soy) and pastrami egg rolls are among the many stunning, genre-defying dishes. Other hits include lobster sautéed with egg and chopped pork, cheeseburger spring rolls, and black-truffle chicken-soup dumplings.

★Blue Hill AMERICAN $$$

(Map p70; ☎212-539-1776; www.bluehillfarm.com; 75 Washington Pl, btwn Sixth Ave & Washington Sq W, West Village; prix-fixe menu $95-108; ⏲5-11pm Mon-Sat, to 10pm Sun; Ⓢ A/C/E, B/D/F/M to W 4th St-Washington Sq) A place for Slow Food junkies with deep pockets, Blue Hill was an early crusader in the farm-to-table movement. Gifted chef-patron Dan Barber, who hails from a farm family in the Berkshires, MA, uses regional harvests to create his widely praised fare.

Expect judiciously seasoned, perfectly ripe vegetables that highlight proteins such as Maine diver scallops or Blue Hill Farm grass-fed beef. The space itself, set just below street level in a former speakeasy on a quaint village block, is sophisticated and serene. Reservations and 'elegant casual' dress are recommended, and cell phones and photography are forbidden in the dining room.

East Village & Lower East Side

Supermoon Bakehouse BAKERY $

(Map p70; www.supermoonbakehouse.com; 120 Rivington St, at Essex St, Lower East Side; pastries $4-9.5; ⏲8am-10pm Mon-Thu, to 11am Fri, 9am-11pm Sat, to 10pm Sun; Ⓢ F to Delancey St) This super-friendly Aussie-owned bakery, where the bakers can be seen doing their thing behind glass, produces perhaps Manhattan's most imaginative and remarkable baked croissants, both sweet and savory, from the hot apple pie or matcha-blueberry to the ham-and-cheese or the Reuben. Varying flavors of soft-serve ice cream and doughnuts round out the offerings.

Mamoun's MIDDLE EASTERN $

(Map p70; ☎646-870-5785; www.mamouns.com; 30 St Marks Pl, btwn Second & Third Aves, East Village; sandwiches $5-9, plates $9-13; ⏲11am-1am Mon-Thu, to 4am Fri & Sat, to midnight Sun; ✎; Ⓢ 6 to Astor Pl, L to 3rd Ave) This former grab-and-go outpost of the beloved NYC falafel chain has expanded its St Marks storefront with more seating inside and out. Late on weekends a line of inebriated bar-hoppers ends the night with a juicy shawarma covered in Mamoun's famous hot sauce. If you don't do lamb, perhaps a falafel wrap or a sustaining bowl of *fool mudammas* (stewed beans)?

★Ivan Ramen RAMEN $$

(Map p70; ☎646-678-3859; www.ivanramen.com; 25 Clinton St, btwn Stanton & E Houston Sts, East Village; mains $15-21; ⏲12:30-10pm Sun-Thu, to 11pm Fri & Sat; Ⓢ F, J/M/Z to Delancey-Essex Sts, F to 2nd Ave) After creating two thriving ramen spots in Tokyo, Long Islander Ivan Orkin brought his talents back home. Few can agree about NYC's best ramen, but this intimate shop, where solo ramen heads sit at the bar watching their bowls take shape, is on every short list. The *tsukumen* (dipping-style) ramen with pickled collard greens and shoyu-glazed pork belly is unbeatable.

Russ & Daughters Cafe JEWISH $$

(Map p70; ☎212-475-4880; www.russanddaughterscafe.com; 127 Orchard St, btwn Delancey & Rivington Sts, Lower East Side; mains $18-23; ⏲9am-10pm Mon-Fri, from 8am Sat & Sun; Ⓢ F, J/M/Z to Delancey-Essex Sts) Sit down and feast on shiny boiled bagels and perhaps the best lox in the city in all the comfort of an old-school diner, in this extension of the storied Jewish delicatessen Russ & Daughters (p116), just up Orchard St. Aside from thick, smoky fish, there are potato latkes, borscht, eggs plenty of ways, and even chopped liver, if you must.

★Clinton Street Baking Company AMERICAN $$

(Map p70; ☎646-602-6263; www.clintonstreetbaking.com; 4 Clinton St, btwn Stanton & E Houston Sts, Lower East Side; mains $12-18; ⏲8am-3:30pm & 5:30-10pm Mon-Fri, 9am-4:30pm Sat & Sun; Ⓢ F, J/M/Z to Delancey-Essex Sts, F to 2nd Ave) Mom-and-pop shop extraordinaire Clinton Street Baking Company takes the cake in so many categories – best pancakes, best muffins, best po'boys (Southern-style sandwiches), best biscuits etc – that you're pretty much guaranteed a stellar meal no matter what time you stop by. In the evening you can opt for 'breakfast for dinner' (pancakes, eggs Benedict), fish tacos or buttermilk fried chicken.

Weekend brunch can see hordes of locals lining up for an hour or more, so do your brunching during the week.

★Veselka UKRAINIAN $$

(Map p70; ☎212-228-9682; www.veselka.com; 144 Second Ave, at E 9th St, East Village; mains $13-19; ⏲24hr; Ⓢ 6 to Astor Pl, L to 3rd Ave)

TO MARKET, TO MARKET

Don't let the concrete streets and buildings fool you – New York City has a thriving greens scene that comes in many shapes and sizes. At the top of your list should be the Chelsea Market (p67), which is packed with gourmet goodies of all kinds – both shops (where you can assemble picnics) and food stands (where you can eat on-site). Many other food halls have opened in recent years, including **Gansevoort Market** (Map p74; 646-449-8400; www.gansmarket.com; 353 W 14th St, btwn Eighth & Ninth Aves, Meatpacking District; mains $10-15; 7am-9pm; ; A/C/E, L to 8th Ave-14th St) in the Meatpacking District and a trio of food halls at Brookfield Place (p96), in Lower Manhattan. Across the river, there's the DeKalb Market Hall (p105) in downtown Brooklyn.

Many neighborhoods in NYC have their own Greenmarket. One of the biggest is the Union Square Greenmarket (p71), open four days a week throughout the year. Check Grow NYC (www.grownyc.org/greenmarket) for a list of the other 50-plus markets around the city.

Out in Brooklyn, the best weekend markets for noshers (rather than cook-at-home types) are Smorgasburg (p105), with over 100 craft-food vendors, and the Brooklyn Flea Market (p119), which has several dozen stalls.

Also popular are high-end market-cum-grocers like Eataly (p109) and **Dean & DeLuca** (Map p70; 212-226-6800; www.deananddeluca.com; 560 Broadway, at Prince St, SoHo; pastries from $4, sandwiches $12; 7am-9pm Mon-Fri, 8am-9pm Sat & Sun; N/R to Prince St; 6 to Spring St), where fresh produce and ready-made fare are given the five-star treatment. Whole Foods is another big draw, particularly its ecofriendly, locavore-focused **Brooklyn outpost** (718-907-3622; www.wholefoodsmarket.com; 214 3rd St, btwn Third Ave & Gowanus Canal, Gowanus; 8am-11pm; ; R to Union; F, G to 4th Ave-9th St).

This beloved vestige of the area's Ukrainian past has been serving up handmade *pierogi* (cheese, potato or meat dumplings), borscht and goulash since 1954. The cluttered spread of tables is available to loungers and carb-loaders all night long, though it's a great, warming pit stop any time of day, and a haunt for writers, actors and East Village characters.

Momofuku Noodle Bar NOODLES $$

(Map p70; 212-777-7773; https://momofukunoodlebar.com; 171 First Ave, btwn E 10th & E 11th Sts, East Village; mains $17-27; lunch noon-4:30pm Mon-Fri, to 4pm Sat & Sun, dinner 5:30-11pm Sun-Thu, to midnight Fri & Sat; ; L to 1st Ave, 6 to Astor Pl) With just a handful of tables and a no-reservations policy, this bustling phenomenon may require you to wait. But you won't regret it: spicy short-rib ramen; ginger noodles with pickled shiitake; cold noodles with Sichuan sausage and Thai basil – it's all amazing. The ever-changing menu includes buns (perhaps brisket and horseradish), snacks (smoked chicken wings) and desserts.

The open kitchen creates quite a bit of steam, but the devoted crowd remains unfazed.

Momofuku is part of David Chang's crazy-popular, now global, restaurant empire (www.momofuku.com). NYC outposts include two-Michelin-starred **Momofuku Ko**, which serves up pricey tasting menus ($225) and has a prohibitive, we-dare-you-to-try reservations scheme; **Momofuku Ssäm Bar**, which features large and small meat-heavy dishes; chicken joint Fuku; and another Noodle Bar in Columbus Circle.

Union Square, Flatiron District & Gramercy

Shake Shack BURGERS $

(Map p74; 646-889-6600; www.shakeshack.com; Madison Square Park, cnr E 23rd St & Madison Ave, Flatiron District; burgers $4.20-9.50; 7:30am-11pm Mon-Fri, from 8:30am Sat & Sun; R/W, F/M, 6 to 23rd St) The flagship of chef Danny Meyer's gourmet burger chain (this is where it all started – in a hot-dog cart), Shake Shack whips up hyper-fresh burgers, hand-cut fries and a rotating lineup of frozen custards. Veg-heads can dip into the crisp portobello burger. Lines are long – but worth it – and you can eat while people-watching at tables and benches in the park.

Its breakfast menu is all about egg-based fillings stuffed into its trademark potato buns: a bit like a posh McDonald's, and cheap.

Eisenberg's Sandwich Shop SANDWICHES $
(Map p74; ☎212-675-5096; www.eisenbergsnyc.com; 174 Fifth Ave, btwn W 22nd & 23rd St, Flatiron District; sandwiches $4-14; ⏰7:30am-6pm Mon-Fri, 9am-5pm Sat, 10am-3pm Sun; 📶; Ⓢ R/W to 23rd St) This old-school diner – an anomaly on this mostly upscale stretch of real estate – is a comfy, quiet spot for traditional Jewish-diner fare like chopped liver, pastrami and whitefish salad. Grab a stool at the long bar and rub elbows with an eclectic mix of customers who know meatloaf isn't a joke dish.

★Eleven Madison Park AMERICAN $$$
(Map p74; ☎212-889-0905; www.elevenmadisonpark.com; 11 Madison Ave, btwn 24th & 25th Sts, Flatiron District; tasting menu $315; ⏰5:30-10pm Mon-Wed, to 10:30pm Thu, noon-1pm & 5:30-10:30pm Fri-Sun; Ⓢ R/W, 6 to 23rd St) Eleven Madison Park consistently bags a spot on top restaurant lists. Frankly, we're not surprised: this revamped poster child of modern, sustainable American cooking is also one of only five NYC restaurants sporting three Michelin stars. Insane attention to detail, intense creativity and whimsy are all trademarks of chef Daniel Humm's approach.

After a revamp, it's now more accessible than ever thanks to the addition of dining tables in the bar. Here, an abbreviated tasting menu (five rather than 10 courses, for $175) can be had, or select mains (around $50) from the core tasting menu. Reservations – for both the main dining room and bar tables – open on the first of the month for the following month. Dress to impress.

Maialino ITALIAN $$$
(Map p74; ☎212-777-2410; www.maialinonyc.com; Gramercy Park Hotel, 2 Lexington Ave, at 21st St, Gramercy; mains $24-58; ⏰7:30-10am, noon-2pm & 5:30-10:30pm Mon-Thu, to 11pm Fri, 10am-2pm & 5:30-11pm Sat, to 10:30pm Sun; Ⓢ 6, R/W to 23rd St) Fans reserve tables up to four weeks in advance at this Danny Meyer classic, but the best seats in the house are at the walk-in bar, with sociable, knowledgeable staffers. Wherever you're plonked, take your taste buds on a Roman holiday. Maialino's lip-smacking, rustic Italian fare is created using produce from the nearby Union Square Greenmarket (p71).

A solid wine list on offer and good-value $48 prix-fixe lunch (Monday to Friday) seals the deal.

Gramercy Tavern AMERICAN $$$
(Map p74; ☎212-477-0777; www.gramercytavern.com; 42 E 20th St, btwn Broadway & Park Ave S, Flatiron District; tavern mains $34-36, dining room 3-course menu $134, tasting menus $164-184; ⏰tavern 11:30am-11pm Sun-Thu, to midnight Fri & Sat, lunch 11:30am-2pm, dinner 5-9:45pm Sun-Thu, to 10:30pm Fri & Sat; 📶✍; Ⓢ R/W, 6 to 23rd St) 🌿 Seasonal, local ingredients drive this perennial favorite, a vibrant, country-chic institution aglow with copper sconces, murals and dramatic floral arrangements. Choose from two spaces: the walk-in-only tavern and its à la carte menu, or the swankier dining room and its fancier prix-fixe and degustation feasts. Regardless of where you sit, you'll find service is excellent.

New Yorkers really *love* this place: book ahead.

★Craft AMERICAN $$$
(Map p74; ☎212-780-0880; www.craftrestaurant.com; 43 E 19th St, btwn Broadway & Park Ave S, Union Sq; mains $33-69; ⏰5:30-10pm Mon-Thu, to 11pm Fri, 5-11pm Sat, to 9pm Sun; 📶; Ⓢ 4/5/6, N/Q/R/W, L to 14th St-Union Sq) 🌿 Humming, high-end Craft flies the flag for small, family-owned farms and food producers, their bounty transformed into pure, polished dishes. Whether nibbling on flawlessly charred braised octopus, juicy roasted quail or pumpkin mezzaluna pasta with sage, brown butter and Parmesan, expect every ingredient to sing with flavor. Book ahead Wednesday to Saturday or head in by 6pm or after 9:30pm.

Midtown

Great Northern Food Hall FOOD HALL $
(Map p74; www.greatnorthernfood.com; Grand Central Terminal, Vanderbilt Hall, 89 E 42nd St; sandwiches $7-12; ⏰7am-11pm Mon-Fri, 8am-8pm Sat & Sun; 📶; Ⓢ S, 4/5/6, 7 to Grand Central-42nd St, 🚆 Metro North to Grand Central-42nd St) Ensconced in the beautiful beaux-arts Vanderbilt Hall, this airy food hall has upped the ante for food in New York's grandest station terminal. Pull up a stool beneath the glamorous chandelier and enjoy a glass of wine, Danish beer or artisan coffee. Gourmet bites on offer mesh Nordic flair with New York produce. Hours differ for individual kiosks.

The hall is the brainchild of Claus Meyer, the New Nordic rock star who co-founded Noma in Copenhagen. The fare is mostly soups, salads, hot sandwiches and *smorresbord* (Danish open-faced sandwiches) such as curried herring with egg yolk or roast beef with pickled onions. The hall also serves breakfast (8am to 11am weekdays, 10am to 4pm weekends) and brunch.

★Totto Ramen JAPANESE $

(Map p74; ☎212-582-0052; www.tottoramen.com; 366 W 52nd St, btwn Eighth & Ninth Aves; ramen $12-18; ⏰noon-4:30pm & 5:30pm-midnight Mon-Sat, 4-11pm Sun; Ⓢ C/E to 50th St) There might be another two branches in Midtown, but purists know that neither beats the tiny 20-seat original. Write your name and number of guests on the clipboard and wait your turn. Your reward: extraordinary ramen.

Go for the butter-soft *char siu* (pork), which sings in dishes like miso ramen (with fermented soybean paste, egg, scallion, bean sprouts, onion and homemade chili paste).

Burger Joint BURGERS $

(Map p74; ☎212-708-7414; www.burgerjointny.com; Le Parker Meridien, 119 W 56th St, btwn Sixth & Seventh Aves; burgers $9-17; ⏰11am-11:30pm Sun-Thu, to midnight Fri & Sat; Ⓢ F to 57th St) With only a small neon burger as your clue, this speakeasy-style burger hut lurks behind the lobby curtain in the Parker New York hotel. Though it might not be as secret as it once was (you'll see the queues), it still delivers the same winning formula of graffiti-strewn walls, retro booths and attitude-loaded staff slapping up beef 'n' patty brilliance.

★Smith AMERICAN $$

(Map p74; ☎212-644-2700; http://thesmithrestaurant.com; 956 Second Ave, at 51st St, Midtown East; mains $22-33; ⏰7:30am-midnight Mon-Thu, to 1am Fri, 9am-1am Sat, to midnight Sun; 📶; Ⓢ 6, E/M to 51st St) This chic, bustling brasserie has an industrial-chic interior, sociable bar and well-executed grub. Much of the food is made from scratch, the seasonal menus a mix of nostalgic American and Italian inspiration (we're talking hot potato chips with blue-cheese fondue, chicken pot pie with cheddar-chive biscuit, and Sicilian baked eggs with artichokes, spinach and spicy tomato sauce).

Hangawi KOREAN $$

(Map p74; ☎212-213-0077; www.hangawirestaurant.com; 12 E 32nd St, btwn Fifth & Madison Aves; mains lunch $13-14, dinner $18-30; ⏰noon-2:30pm & 5:30-10:15pm Mon-Thu, to 10:30pm Fri, 1-10:30pm Sat, 5-9:30pm Sun; 🌿; Ⓢ B/D/F/M, N/Q/R/W to 34th St-Herald Sq) Meat-free Korean is the draw at high-achieving Hangawi. Leave your shoes at the entrance and slip into a soothing, Zen-like space of meditative music, soft low seating and clean, complex dishes. Dishes include pumpkin noodles, spicy kimchi pancakes and a seductively smooth tofu claypot in ginger sauce. At lunch time there's a four-course prix-fixe deal for $25.

★O-ya SUSHI $$$

(Map p74; ☎212-204-0200; https://o-ya.restaurant/o-ya-nyc; 120 E 28th St; nigiri $6-25; ⏰5:30-10pm Mon-Sat; Ⓢ 4/6 to 28th St) With the cheapest nigiri pairs at close to $15, this is not a spot you'll come to every day. But if you're looking for a special night out and sushi's in the game plan, come here for exquisite flavors, fish so tender it melts like butter on the tongue, and preparations that are so artful you almost apologize for eating them.

Le Bernardin SEAFOOD $$$

(Map p74; ☎212-554-1515; www.le-bernardin.com; 155 W 51st St, btwn Sixth & Seventh Aves; prix-fixe lunch/dinner $90/160, tasting menus $170-225; ⏰noon-2:30pm & 5:15-10:30pm Mon-Thu, to 11pm Fri, 5:15-11pm Sat; Ⓢ 1 to 50th St; B/D, E to 7th Ave) The interiors may have been subtly sexed-up for a 'younger clientele' (the stunning storm-themed triptych is by Brooklyn artist Ran Ortner), but triple-Michelin-starred Le Bernardin remains a luxe, fine-dining holy grail. At the helm is French-born celebrity chef Éric Ripert, whose deceptively simple-looking seafood often borders on the transcendental. Life is short, and you only live (er, eat!) once.

The menu works simply: three lunch courses for $90 or four dinner courses for $160, with ample choices per course, and two tastings menus for those with more time and money. The dishes themselves are divided into three categories (Almost Raw, Barely Touched, Lightly Cooked), and most shine with delicious complexity. Book at least three weeks ahead for dinner and two weeks ahead for lunch.

Upper East Side

Eli's Essentials AMERICAN $

(Map p80; ☎646-755-3999; www.elizabar.com/Elis-Essentials-.aspx; 1270 Madison Ave, at E 91st St; buffet per lb $16.95, sandwiches from $7.50; ⏰7am-11pm; 📶🌿; Ⓢ 6 to 96th St) The youngest son of the founders of Zabar's (p119) delicatessen is building a mini empire on the Upper East Side, and this update on New York's traditional Jewish deli is perfect for a pit stop near Fifth Ave's Museum Mile. As well as lox bagels and Eli's signature egg brioche roll, there's a buffet with fried chicken, mac 'n' cheese and salads.

★Papaya King HOT DOGS $

(Map p80; www.papayaking.com; 179 E 86th St, at Third Ave; hot dogs $3-4.50; ⌚8am-midnight Sun-Thu, to 1am Fri & Sat; Ⓢ4/5/6, Q to 86th St) The original hot-dog-and-papaya-juice shop, from 1932, over 40 years before crosstown rival **Gray's Papaya** (Map p80; ☎212-799-0243; 2090 Broadway, at 72nd St, entrance on Amsterdam Ave; hot dogs $2.50; ⌚24hr; Ⓢ1/2/3, B, C to 72nd St) opened, Papaya King has lured many a New Yorker to its neon-lit corner for a cheap and tasty snack of hot dogs and fresh-squeezed papaya juice. (Why papaya? The informative wall signs will explain all.)

Try the Homerun, with sauerkraut and New York onion relish.

Wright AMERICAN $$

(Map p80; ☎212-423-3665; www.guggenheim.org; Guggenheim Museum, 1071 Fifth Ave, at E 89th St; mains $23-28; ⌚11:30am-3:30pm Mon-Fri, from 11am Sat & Sun; 📶; Ⓢ4/5/6, Q to 86th St) The Wright restaurant at the Guggenheim, serving such dishes as kohlrabi fritters, house-made pasta and seared salmon (the menu changes regularly), is somewhat overshadowed by its gleaming-white, modernist design aesthetic. Four intricately woven canvas collages by Sarah Crowner were installed in early 2017. On weekends it serves brunch.

Café Sabarsky AUSTRIAN $$

(Map p80; www.neuegalerie.org/cafes/sabarsky; 1048 Fifth Ave, at E 86th St; mains $19-32; ⌚9am-6pm Mon & Wed, to 9pm Thu-Sun; Ⓢ4/5/6 to 86th St) The lines can get long at this popular cafe evoking an opulent, turn-of-the-century Vienna coffeehouse. The Austrian specialties, courtesy of Michelin-starred chef Kurt Gutenbrunner, include crepes with smoked trout, goulash soup and roasted bratwurst – all beautifully presented. There's also a mouthwatering list of specialty sweets, including a divine Sacher torte (dark chocolate cake with apricot confiture).

If the wait feels too long, you can find the same menu downstairs at Café Fledermaus, which sports a more modern look and is often used when Sabarsky is full.

Candle Cafe VEGAN $$

(Map p80; ☎212-472-0970; www.candlecafe.com; 1307 Third Ave, btwn E 74th & 75th Sts; mains $16-22; ⌚11:30am-10pm Mon-Fri, from 11am Sat, 11am-9:30pm Sun; 🌱; ⓈQ to 72nd St-2nd Ave) The moneyed yoga set piles into this minimalist vegan cafe serving a long list of sandwiches, salads, comfort food and market-driven specials. The specialty here is the housemade seitan.

There is a juice bar, gluten-free menu and organic cocktails.

★Café Boulud FRENCH $$$

(Map p80; ☎212-772-2600; www.cafeboulud.com/nyc; 20 E 76th St, btwn Fifth & Madison Aves; breakfats $13-29, mains $39-52; ⌚7-10:30am, noon-2:30pm & 5:30-10:30pm Mon-Fri, 8-10:30am, 11:30am-2:30pm & 5:30-10:30pm Sat, 8-10:30am, 11:30am-3pm & 5-10pm Sun; 🌱; Ⓢ6 to 77th St) This long-standing Michelin-starred bistro by Daniel Boulud attracts a rather staid crowd with its globe-trotting French-Vietnamese cuisine. Seasonal menus include classics like bass 'en paupiette', as well as fare such as duck with sour cherry and baby fennel.

Tanoshi SUSHI $$$

(Map p80; www.tanoshisushinyc.com; 1372 York Ave, btwn E 73rd & 74th Sts; chef's sushi selection $95-100; ⌚seatings 6pm, 7:30pm & 9pm Tue-Sat; ⓈQ to 72nd St) It's not easy to snag one of the 22 stools at Tanoshi, a wildly popular, pocket-sized sushi spot. The setting may be humble here, but the flavors are simply magnificent.

Only sushi is on offer and only *omakase* (chef's selection) – which might include Hokkaido scallops, kelp-cured flake or mouthwatering *uni* (sea urchin). BYO beer, sake or whatnot.

Reserve well in advance via website only.

Upper West Side

Milk Bar BAKERY $

(Map p80; www.milkbarstore.com; 561 Columbus Ave, at 87th St; cookies $2.75; ⌚9am-11pm Sun-Thu, to midnight Fri & Sat; 📶; ⓈC, B to 86th St) Conceived by a Momofuku dessert chef with a soft spot for junk food, the big draw at Milk Bar is the delicious, chewy cookies. A popular teeth-rotter is the Compost Cookie: pretzels, potato chips, coffee, oats, graham crackers, butterscotch and chocolate chips. Elsewhere, things are equally inventive, with options like cereal milk soft-serve and pickled strawberry jam and corn cookie milkshakes.

Peacefood Cafe VEGAN $
(Map p80; 212-362-2266; www.peacefoodcafe.com; 460 Amsterdam Ave, at 82nd St; mains $11-18; 10am-10pm; ; 1 to 79th St) This bright and airy vegan haven dishes up a popular fried seitan panini (served on homemade focaccia and topped with cashew cheese, arugula, tomatoes and pesto), as well as pizzas, roasted-vegetable plates and an excellent quinoa salad. There are daily raw specials, energy-fueling juices and rich desserts, plus a more substantial dinner menu served 5pm to 10pm.

Barney Greengrass DELI $$
(Map p80; 212-724-4707; www.barneygreengrass.com; 541 Amsterdam Ave, at 86th St; mains $5.25-28, fish platters $37-67; deli 8am-6pm Tue-Sun, cafe 8:30am-4pm Tue-Fri, to 5pm Sat-Sun; 1 to 86th St) The self-proclaimed 'King of Sturgeon,' Barney Greengrass serves up the same heaping dishes of eggs and salty lox, luxuriant caviar and melt-in-your-mouth chocolate babkas that first made it famous when it opened over a century ago. Fuel up in the morning at casual tables amid the crowded produce counters, or take lunch at the serviced cafe in an adjoining room.

In addition to an array of Jewish delicacies – seriously, try the smoked sturgeon – you can, of course, get a commendable New York bagel.

Boulud Sud MEDITERRANEAN $$$
(Map p80; 212-595-1313; www.bouludsud.com; 20 W 64th St, btwn Broadway & Central Park W; 3-course prix fixe 5-7pm Mon-Sat $65, mains lunch $25-35, dinner $31-63; 11:30am-2:30pm & 5-11pm Mon-Fri, 11am-3pm & 5-11pm Sat, to 10pm Sun; ; 1 to 66th St-Lincoln Center) Pear-wood paneling and a yellow-grey palette lend a 1960s *Mad Men* feel to Daniel Boulud's restaurant championing cuisines from the Mediterranean and North Africa. Dishes such as Moroccan tagines, spicy green shakshouka and Sardinian lemon saffron linguini emphasize seafood, vegetables and regional spices. Look out for specials, like the express lunch ($26), pre-theater menu ($65) and happy pasta hour (50% off).

★**Burke & Wills** AUSTRALIAN $$$
(Map p80; 646-823-9251; www.burkeandwillsny.com; 226 W 79th St, btwn Broadway & Amsterdam Ave; mains $21-38; bar from 4pm, dinner 5:30-11pm, brunch 11am-3pm Sat & Sun; ; 1 to 79th St) About as far as you could get from an outback watering hole, this sophisticated bistro and bar brings modern Australian cuisine to the Upper West Side. That means platters of oysters ($35 per dozen), barramundi with broccolini and yuzu cream and even a kangaroo burger in brioche (if you're so inclined). Popular and dimly lit: good for couples.

Harlem & Upper Manhattan

Tom's Restaurant DINER $
(Map p80; 212-864-6137; www.tomsrestaurant.net; 2880 Broadway, at 112th St; mains $10-15, sandwiches $6-9; 7am-1am Tue-Thu, 24hr Fri-Mon; ; 1 to 110th St) The exterior of Tom's may look familiar if you're a fan of the TV series *Seinfeld,* but the interiors are all New York Greek diner. As in, *busy.* Reminisce about those Kramer scenes while chomping on classic burgers, gyros, bagels or gut-warming homemade soups. Breakfast is served all day, and Tom's is open 24 hours Friday to Saturday. Cash only.

Sylvia's SOUTHERN US $$
(Map p80; 212-996-0660; www.sylviasrestaurant.com; 328 Malcolm X Blvd, btwn 126th & 127th Sts, Harlem; mains $14-27; 8am-10:30pm Mon-Sat, 11am-8pm Sun; 2/3 to 125th St) Founded by Sylvia Woods back in 1962, this Harlem icon has been dazzling Harlemites and visitors (including a few presidents) with its lip-smackingly good down-home Southern cooking – succulent fried chicken, baked mac 'n' cheese and cornmeal-dusted catfish, plus requisite sides like collard greens. Come on Sundays for the gospel brunch, and book ahead to avoid the overwhelming scrum for a table.

Vinatería EUROPEAN $$
(Map p80; 212-662-8462; www.vinaterianyc.com; 2211 Frederick Douglass Blvd, btwn 119th & 120th Sts; mains $19-29; 5-10pm Mon, to 11pm Tue-Thu, to midnight Fri, 10:30am-midnight Sat, to 10pm Sun; A/C, B to 116th St) This classy Michelin-recommended neighborhood restaurant shows a new side to Harlem, taking inspiration from Italy and Spain with flavor-packed dishes such as spicy veal meatballs bedded in parmigiano polenta and grilled octopus with roasted poblano peppers and fennel pollen. Pasta is made in-house, and the black seafood spaghetti is a signature dish.

★**Red Rooster** AMERICAN $$$
(Map p80; 212-792-9001; www.redroosterharlem.com; 310 Malcolm X Blvd, btwn W 125th & 126th Sts, Harlem; mains lunch $20-25, dinner

$25-40; ⏲11:30am-3pm & 4:30-10:30pm Mon-Thu, to 11:30pm Fri, 10am-3pm & 4:30-11:30pm Sat, to 10pm Sun; Ⓢ2/3 to 125th St) Transatlantic superchef Marcus Samuelsson laces upscale comfort food with a world of flavors at his effortlessly cool brasserie. Mac 'n' cheese joins forces with lobster, blackened catfish pairs with pickled mango, and Swedish meatballs salute Samuelsson's home country.

The DJ-led bar atmosphere is as good, if not better, than the food: roll in after midnight on weekends and you'll find it's still buzzing.

Brooklyn

DeKalb Market Hall FOOD HALL $
(www.dekalbmarkethall.com; City Point, 445 Albee Sq W, at DeKalb Ave, Downtown Brooklyn; mains $12-15; ⏲7am-10pm; 📶; ⓈB, Q/R to DeKalb Ave; 2/3 to Hoyt St; A/C, G to Hoyt-Schermerhorn) One of Downtown Brooklyn's best options for a quick feed is this popular basement food hall in the City Point retail center. Choose from nearly 40 vendors from across the culinary spectrum: pastrami sandwiches, arepas, tacos, Berlin-style doner, hand-pulled noodles, pierogi, rice bowls, sushi, rotisserie chicken, crepes – you name it.

Crif Dogs HOT DOGS $
(☎718-302-3200; www.crifdogs.com; 555 Driggs Ave, at N 7th St, Williamsburg; hot dogs $4.50-6.50; ⏲noon-2am Sun-Thu, to 4am Fri & Sat; 🖉; ⓈL to Bedford Ave) Many a late-night Billyburg excursion ends up at this laid-back hot-dog joint, with no-nonsense beef-and-pork and veggie weiners done how you like, with two-dozen toppings to choose from. Get a draft beer and a side of tater tots, order your dog with pineapple, sauerkraut or Swiss cheese, and keep the party going. The **original** (Map p70; ☎212-614-2728; 113 St Marks Pl, btwn Ave A & First Ave, East Village; hot dogs from $4; ⏲noon-2am Sun-Thu, to 4am Fri & Sat; ⓈL to 1st Ave) is in the East Village.

Dough BAKERY $
(☎347-533-7544; www.doughdoughnuts.com; 448 Lafayette Ave, cnr Franklin Ave, Bedford-Stuyvesant; doughnuts around $3; ⏲6am-9pm; 📶; ⓈG to Classon Ave) Situated on the border of Clinton Hill and Bed-Stuy, this tiny, out-of-the-way bakery takes the business of doughnuts seriously – making light, chewy 'nuts in frequent small batches to ensure peak freshness. The brioche-style dough is twice-proved, fried, then rolled in a changing array of glazes and toppings, including salted chocolate caramel, passionfruit, dulche de leche and even hibiscus.

Ample Hills Creamery ICE CREAM $
(☎347-240-3926; www.amplehills.com; 623 Vanderbilt Ave, at St Marks Ave, Prospect Heights; ice cream from $4.50; ⏲noon-10pm Sun-Thu, to 11pm Fri & Sat; ⓈB, Q to 7th Ave, 2/3 to Grand Army Plaza) Taking its name from Walt Whitman's 'Crossing Brooklyn Ferry,' Ample Hills makes superb ice cream from organic ingredients. Each Ample Hills outlet has one location-specific flavor; in Prospect Heights it's the salty-sweet 'Commodore', studded with homemade honeycomb and potato chips coated in chocolate. Everything is made from scratch with fresh, hormone-free milk and cream at their factory in Red Hook.

★Smorgasburg MARKET $
(www.smorgasburg.com; mains from $10; ⏲Williamsburg 11am-6pm Sat, Prospect Park 11am-6pm Sun; 👪) The largest foodie event in Brooklyn (perhaps the US) brings together more than 100 vendors selling an incredible array of goodness. Seize stuffed calamari or Afghan comfort food; queue for hipster inventions like ramen burgers and pizza cupcakes; or wash down Colombian *arepas* (cornbread sandwiches) with lavender lemonade. Note that sites are exposed (bring sunblock in summer, rain-proof gear in poor weather).

Locations can change, so check the website. Most vendors accept cards.

★Fette Sau BARBECUE $$
(☎718-963-3404; www.fettesaubbq.com; 354 Metropolitan Ave, btwn Havemeyer & Roebling Sts, Williamsburg; meats per half-pound $12-15, sides $4-8; ⏲5-11pm Mon, from noon Tue-Sun; ⓈL to Bedford Ave) The atmosphere is unfussy, but the reverence for smoky meat is indubitable at the 'Fat Pig,' Brooklyn's best house of barbecue. The cement floor and inside-outside feel echo the garage that once operated from this space, while shared trestles and an 'order by the pound' system put lovers of brisket, pulled pork, smoked chicken and ancho-chili-spiced sausage further at ease.

Completing the package are sides of German-style potato salad, pickles and garlic broccoli, and a stout wooden bar serving craft beers and a great range of bourbon, whiskey and cocktails.

Roberta's PIZZA $$

(☎718-417-1118; www.robertaspizza.com; 261 Moore St, near Bogart St, East Williamsburg; pizzas $17-21; ⏰11am-midnight Mon-Fri, from 10am Sat & Sun; 🖉; Ⓢ L to Morgan Ave) This hiply renovated warehouse restaurant in one of Brooklyn's booming food enclaves makes some of the best pizza in NYC. Service is relaxed, but the brick-oven pies are serious: chewy, fresh and topped with knowing combinations of outstanding ingredients. The classic margherita is sublime; more adventurous palates can opt for near-legendary options like 'beastmaster' (gorgonzola, pork sausage and jalapeño).

Juliana's PIZZA $$

(☎718-596-6700; www.julianaspizza.com; 19 Old Fulton St, btwn Water & Front Sts, Brooklyn Heights; pizzas $26-29; ⏰11:30am-10pm, closed 3:15-4pm; 🖉; Ⓢ A/C to High St) Legendary pizza maestro Patsy Grimaldi has returned to Brooklyn, offering delicious, thin-crust perfection in both classic and creative combos – like the No 1, with mozzarella, *scamorza affumicata* (an Italian smoked cow's cheese), pancetta, scallions and white truffles in olive oil. Note that Juliana's closes for 45 minutes every afternoon to stoke the coal-fired pizza oven.

Modern Love VEGAN $$

(☎929-298-0626; www.modernlovebrooklyn.com; 317 Union Ave, at S 1st St, East Williamsburg; mains brunch $16-18, dinner $18-24; ⏰5:30-10pm Tue-Thu, to 11pm Fri, 10am-2:30pm & 5-11pm Sat, 10am-2:30pm & 5-10pm Sun; 🖉; Ⓢ G to Metropolitan Ave, L to Lorimer St) Celebrated chef Isa Chandra Moskowitz's 'swanky vegan comfort food' has been received with open, watering mouths in Williamsburg. The restaurant is a lovely date spot with sultry lighting and immaculate service, while dishes include 'mac 'n' shews' (with creamy cashew cheese), truffled poutine and a lip-smacking Korean BBQ bowl with glazed tofu and kimchi. It's always buzzing, so consider booking.

Buttermilk Channel AMERICAN $$

(☎718-852-8490; www.buttermilkchannelnyc.com; 524 Court St, at Huntington St, Carroll Gardens; mains brunch $13-18, lunch $14-22, dinner $24-30; ⏰11:30am-3pm & 5-10pm Mon-Thu, 11:30am-3pm & 5-11:30pm Fri, 10am-3pm & 5-11:30pm Sat, 10am-3pm & 5-10pm Sun; Ⓢ F, G to Smith-9th Sts) Taking comfort food to rare heights, Buttermilk Channel is a bustling, friendly place beloved of locals. Brunch is dominated by French toast and syrup-drowned pancakes, while buttermilk-fried chicken and duck meatloaf feature on the dinner menu, always complemented by a head-lightening array of cocktails. Named for the tidal strait between Brooklyn and Governors Island, its weekend brunch draws large crowds.

Reservations aren't taken, so leave a number and the host will text you when a table opens up. Monday nights feature a three-course dinner ($40) that's great value.

★Finch AMERICAN $$$

(☎718-218-4444; www.thefinchnyc.com; 212 Greene Ave, btwn Cambridge Pl & Grand Ave, Clinton Hill; mains $28-40; ⏰6-10pm Mon & Wed-Fri, 5:30-10pm Sat, 5:30-9pm Sun; 🚌B52 to Greene Ave/Grand Ave, Ⓢ G to Classon Ave, G or C to Clinton-Washington) This quiet, residential brownstone block seems an unlikely setting for a Michelin-starred restaurant, but the Finch is the real deal, serving modern American cuisine in a stylishly unadorned setting. The menu is perfect for sharing, with cooked-to-perfection mains like bluefish with tomato panzanella and pork belly with peaches. The ample wine list and sophisticated cocktails induce dilemmas, but it's hard to go wrong.

★Olmsted AMERICAN $$$

(☎718-552-2610; www.olmstednyc.com; 659 Vanderbilt Ave, btwn Prospect Pl & Park Pl, Prospect Heights; small plates $14-17, large plates $23-24; ⏰dinner 5:30-10pm Mon-Thu, 5-10:30pm Fri & Sat, 5-9:30pm Sun, brunch 11:30am-2:30pm Fri, 11am-3pm Sat & Sun; Ⓢ B, Q to 7th Ave) 🍃 Chef-owner Greg Baxtrom, alumnus of a string of hot kitchens, cooks such outstanding, seasonally inspired food that even Manhattanites cross the river to eat here. Much of the menu comes from the restaurant's backyard garden – which doubles as a lovely spot for cocktails or dessert. Whether it's pork belly with dandelion, carrot crepe or scallops with chanterelles, a sensational meal is almost guaranteed. Reservations recommended; Mondays are for walk-ins only.

Miss Ada MEDITERRANEAN $$$

(☎917-909-1023; www.missadanyc.com; 184 DeKalb Ave, at Carlton Ave, Fort Greene; mains $18-27; ⏰5:30-10:30pm Tue-Thu, to 11:30pm Fri & Sat, 11am-2:30pm & 5:30-10:30pm Sun; 🖉; Ⓢ G to Fulton St or Clinton/Washington Aves, B, Q/R to DeKalb Ave) Chef-owner Tomer Blechman presents dishes inspired by Mediterranean flavors and recipes from his native Israel: octopus with eggplant, za'atar-seasoned salmon, and shakshuka (eggs baked in spicy tomato with goat's cheese). Many are flavored with herbs grown in the backyard, which features canopied dining in warmer months. And Miss Ada? A misdirection: *misada* is Hebrew for restaurant. Reserve far in advance.

 Drinking & Nightlife

You'll find all species of thirst-quenching venues here, from terminally hip cocktail lounges and historic dive bars to specialty taprooms and Third Wave coffee shops. Then there's the legendary club scene, spanning everything from celebrity staples to gritty, indie hangouts.

Head downtown or to Brooklyn for the parts of the city that, as they say, truly never sleep.

 Financial District & Lower Manhattan

Dead Rabbit BAR

(Map p66; ☎646-422-7906; www.deadrabbitnyc.com; 30 Water St, btwn Broad St & Coenties Slip, Financial District; ⌚Taproom 11am-4am Mon-Fri, 10am-3am Sat & Sun, Parlor 11am-3pm & 5pm-2am Mon-Sat, noon-midnight Sun; Ⓢ R/W to Whitehall St, 1 to South Ferry) Named for a feared 19th-century Irish American gang, this three-story drinking den is regularly voted one of the world's best bars. Hit the sawdust-sprinkled Taproom for specialty beers, historic punches and pop-inns (lightly soured ale spiked with different flavors). On the next floor there's the cozy Parlor, serving meticulously researched cocktails, and above that the reservation-only Occasional Room, 'for whiskey explorers.'

Be warned: the Wall St crowd packs the place after work.

Brandy Library COCKTAIL BAR

(Map p66; ☎212-226-5545; www.brandylibrary.com; 25 N Moore St, btwn Varick & Hudson Sts, Tribeca; ⌚5pm-1am Sun-Wed, 4pm-2am Thu, 4pm-4am Fri & Sat; Ⓢ1 to Franklin St) This brandy-hued bastion of brown spirits is the place to go for top-shelf cognac, whiskey and brandy. Settle into handsome club chairs facing floor-to-ceiling, bottle-lined shelves and sip your tipple of choice, paired with nibbles such as Gruyère-cheese puffs, hand-cut steak tartare and foie gras. Saturday nights are generally quieter than weeknights, making it a civilized spot for a weekend tête-à-tête.

Cowgirl SeaHorse BAR

(Map p66; ☎212-608-7873; www.cowgirlseahorse.com; 259 Front St, at Dover St, Lower Manhattan; ⌚11am-2am Mon-Fri, 10am-1am Sat & Sun; Ⓢ A/C, J/Z, 2/3, 4/5 to Fulton St) In an ocean of more serious bars and restaurants, Cowgirl SeaHorse is a party ship. Its ranch-meets-sea theme (wagon wheels and seahorses on the walls) and southern home cooking (blackened fish, oyster po'boy sliders, shrimp and grits etc) make it irresistibly fun. Live music on Monday, happy hour every day except Saturday and great frozen margaritas don't hurt, either.

 SoHo & Chinatown

★Apothéke COCKTAIL BAR

(Map p66; ☎212-406-0400; www.apothekenyc.com; 9 Doyers St, Chinatown; ⌚6:30pm-2am Mon-Sat, from 8pm Sun; Ⓢ J/Z to Chambers St; 4/5/6 to Brooklyn Bridge-City Hall) It takes a little effort to track down this former opium-den-turned-apothecary bar on Doyers St (look for the illustration of a beaker hanging above the doorway). Inside, skilled barkeeps work like careful chemists, using local, seasonal produce from Greenmarkets to produce intense, flavorful 'prescriptions.' The pineapple-cilantro spiced Sitting Buddha is one of the best drinks on the menu.

The menu is just as much fun as sipping the drinks, divided into sections including 'aphrodisiacs', 'pain killers' and 'stress relievers.' On Wednesdays there is a special Prohibition-based theme, and on Sundays it's Belle Époque, with a focus on absinthe.

Ear Inn PUB

(Map p70; ☎212-226-9060; www.earinn.com; 326 Spring St, btwn Washington & Greenwich Sts, SoHo; ⌚bar 11:30am-4am, kitchen to 2am; 📶; Ⓢ C/E to Spring St) Want to see what SoHo was like before the trendsetters and fashionistas? Come to the creaking old Ear Inn, proudly billed as one of the oldest drinking establishments in NYC. The house it occupies was built in the late 18th century for James Brown, an African aide to George Washington. Drinks are cheap and the crowd's eclectic.

Regulars come for late-night dinners at barebones wooden tables with paper table cloths, crammed between walls drowning in old ad signs and Americana. Every Sunday, a corner of the bar is cleared for popular jazz ensembles (8pm to around 11:30pm).

West Village, Chelsea & Meatpacking District

Buvette WINE BAR
(Map p70; 212-255-3590; www.ilovebuvette.com; 42 Grove St, btwn Bedford & Bleecker Sts, West Village; small plates $12-18; 7am-2am; S 1 to Christopher St-Sheridan Sq, A/C/E, B/D/F/M to W 4th St-Washington Sq) Buzzing with the animated conversation of locals, courting couples and theater types, this devotedly Francophile wine bar and restaurant makes a great rest stop amid a West Village backstreet wander. Enjoy a cocktail or a glass of wine, or settle in for a meal. Brunch dishes such as croque monsieurs are replaced by tartines and small plates at dinner.

Buvette also has outposts in Tokyo and Paris.

Cubbyhole LGBTIQ+
(Map p70; 212-243-9041; www.cubbyholebar.com; 281 W 12th St, at W 4th St, West Village; 4pm-4am Mon-Fri, from 2pm Sat & Sun; S A/C/E, L to 8th Ave-14th St) This West Village dive bills itself as 'lesbian, gay and straight friendly since 1994.' While the crowd's mostly ladies, it welcomes anyone looking for a drink in good company beneath a ceiling festooned with lanterns, toys and other ephemera. It's got a great jukebox, friendly bartenders and plenty of regulars who prefer to hang and chat rather than hook up and leave.

Happy hour is 4pm to 7pm Monday to Saturday. There are also daily drink specials, so be sure to check the website.

Top of the Standard BAR
(Map p70; 212-645-7600; www.standardhotels.com; Standard, 848 Washington St, at W 13th St, Meatpacking District; 4pm-midnight Sun-Tue, to 9pm Wed-Sat; S A/C/E, L to 8th Ave-14th St) Afternoon tea and drinks morph into evening cocktails in this splendid perch atop the ever-so stylish Standard hotel (p92). Small plates ($16 to $18), such as English-pea risotto or Moroccan shrimp with pickled raisins and Greek yogurt, are on hand to address any pangs of hunger, while live jazz and fabulous views complete the picture of sophistication.

East Village & Lower East Side

Bar Goto COCKTAIL BAR
(Map p70; 212-475-4411; www.bargoto.com; 245 Eldridge St, btwn E Houston & Stanton Sts, Lower East Side; 5pm-midnight Tue-Thu & Sun, to 2am Fri & Sat; S F to 2nd Ave) Maverick mixologist Kenta Goto has cocktail connoisseurs spellbound at his eponymous, intimate hot spot. Expect meticulous, elegant drinks that draw on Goto's Japanese heritage (the Umami Mary, with vodka, shiitake, dashi, miso, lemon, tomato and Clamato, is inspired), paired with authentic Japanese comfort bites, such as *okonomiyaki* (savory cabbage pancakes).

Berlin CLUB
(Map p70; reservations 347-586-7247; www.berlinundera.com; 25 Ave A, btwn E 1st & E 2nd Sts, East Village; occasional cover $5; 8pm-2am Sun-Thu, to 4am Fri & Sat; S F to 2nd Ave) This brick-vaulted cavern beneath Ave A does its best to hide – access is through an unmarked door around the corner on the side of bar that seems to occupy its (Berlin's) address, then steep stairs lead down into a dim, riotous indie lair. Once you're in, enjoy a night of rock, funk, disco, house and other party tunes in close proximity to your fellow revelers. The fun, bohemian crowd mixes with little pretension, and you might see a vestige of the East Village as it was in its days of full-blown hedonism.

Rue B BAR
(Map p70; 212-358-1700; www.rueb-nyc.com; 188 Ave B, btwn E 11th & E 12th Sts, East Village; 6pm-4am; S L to 1st Ave) There's live jazz (and the odd rockabilly group) nightly from 9pm to midnight ($10 cover) at this tiny, amber-lit drinking den on a bar-dappled stretch of Ave B. A celebratory crowd packs the small space – so mind the tight corners, lest the trombonist end up in your lap. Photos and posters of jazz greats and NYC icons enhance the ambience.

If you fancy getting a head start, draft beer, wine and cocktails are half price from opening until 8pm every night. If you overdo it, basic bar snacks may be the answer.

Union Square, Flatiron District & Gramercy

Old Town Bar & Restaurant BAR
(Map p74; 212-529-6732; www.oldtownbar.com; 45 E 18th St, btwn Broadway & Park Ave S, Union Sq; 11:30am-1am Mon-Fri, noon-1am Sat, 3pm-midnight Sun; ; S 4/5/6, N/Q/R/W, L to 14th St- Union Sq) It still looks like 1892 in here, with the mahogany bar, original tile floors and tin ceilings – the Old Town is an old-

world drinking-man's classic. It's frequently used as an old-school shooting location for movies and TV (and even Madonna's 'Bad Girl' video).

Most people settle into one of the snug wooden booths for beers and a burger (from $12.50).

Raines Law Room COCKTAIL BAR

(Map p74; www.raineslawroom.com; 48 W 17th St, btwn Fifth & Sixth Aves, Flatiron District; 5pm-2am Mon-Thu, to 3am Fri & Sat, to 1am Sun; S F/M to 14th St, L to 6th Ave, 1 to 18th St) A sea of velvet drapes and overstuffed leather lounge chairs, the perfect amount of exposed brick, expertly crafted cocktails using hard-to-find spirits – these folks are as serious as a mortgage payment when it comes to amplified atmosphere. There's no sign from the street; look for the '48' above the door and ring the bell to gain entry.

Reservations (recommended) are only accepted Sunday to Tuesday. Whatever the night, style up for a taste of a far more sumptuous era.

Birreria ROOFTOP BAR

(Map p74; 212-937-8910; www.eataly.com; 200 Fifth Ave, at W 23rd St, Flatiron District; 11:30am-11pm; S F/M, R/W, 6 to 23rd St) The crown jewel of Italian food emporium **Eataly** (Map p74; 212-229-2560; www.eataly.com; 200 Fifth Ave, at W 23rd St, Flatiron District; 7am-11pm; ; S R/W, F/M, 6 to 23rd St) is this covered rooftop garden tucked betwixt the Flatiron's corporate towers. The theme is refreshed each season, meaning you might find a Mediterranean beach escape one month and an alpine country retreat the next, but the setting is unfailingly impressive and food and drink always matches up to the gourmet goodies below.

The sneaky access elevator is located near the checkouts on the 23rd St side of the store.

Midtown

★The Campbell COCKTAIL BAR

(Map p74; 212-297-1781; www.thecampbellnyc.com; D Hall, Grand Central Terminal; noon-2am; S S, 4/5/6, 7 to Grand Central-42nd St) In 1923 this hidden-away hall was the office of American financier John W Campbell. It later became a signalman's office, a jail and a gun storage before falling into obscurity. In 2017 it was restored to its original grandeur, complete with the stunning hand-painted ceiling and Campbell's original safe in the fireplace. Come for cocktails and you'll feel like you're waiting for Rockefeller or Carnegie to join you.

Try to book ahead Thursday to Sunday. It's a little tricky to find: take the elevator in the corridor next to the oyster bar.

Top of the Strand COCKTAIL BAR

(Map p74; 646-368-6426; www.topofthestrand.com; Marriott Vacation Club Pulse, 33 W 37th St, btwn Fifth & Sixth Aves, Midtown East; 5pm-midnight Sun & Mon, to 1am Tue-Sat; ; S B/D/F/M, N/Q/R to 34th St) For that 'Oh my God, I'm in New York' feeling, head to the Marriott Vacation Club Pulse (formerly the Strand) hotel's rooftop bar, order a martini (extra dirty) and drop your jaw (discreetly).

Sporting comfy cabana-style seating, a refreshingly mixed-age crowd and a retractable glass roof, its view of the Empire State Building is simply unforgettable.

Stumptown Coffee Roasters COFFEE

(Map p74; 855-711-3385; www.stumptowncoffee.com; 18 W 29th St, btwn Broadway & Fifth Ave; 6am-8pm Mon-Fri, from 7am Sat & Sun; S R/W to 28th St) Hipster baristas in fedora hats brewing killer coffee? No, you're not in Williamsburg, you're at the Manhattan outpost of Portland's cult-status coffee roaster. The queue is a small price to pay for proper espresso, so count your blessings. It's standing-room only, though weary punters might find a seat in the adjacent Ace Hotel lobby.

There's a second branch situated in **Greenwich Village** (Map p70; 855-711-3385; 30 W 8th St, at MacDougal St, West Village; 7am-8pm; S A/C/E, B/D/F/M to W 4th St-Washington Sq).

Upper East Side

★Bemelmans Bar LOUNGE

(Map p80; 212-744-1600; www.thecarlyle.com; Carlyle Hotel, 35 E 76th St, at Madison Ave; noon-1:30am; ; S 6 to 77th St) Sink into a chocolate-leather banquette and take in the glorious, old-school elegance at this atmospheric bar – the sort of place where the waiters wear white jackets and serve martinis, a pianist tinkles on a baby grand and the ceiling is 24-carat gold leaf. The walls are covered in charming murals by the bar's namesake Ludwig Bemelmans, famed creator of the *Madeline* books.

Cantor Roof Garden Bar ROOFTOP BAR
(Map p80; www.metmuseum.org/visit/dining; Metropolitan Museum, 1000 Fifth Ave, 5th fl, at E 82nd St; 11am-4:30pm Sun-Thu, to 8:15pm Fri & Sat mid-Apr–Oct; ; S 4/5/6 to 86th St) The sort of setting you can't get enough of (even if you are a jaded local). Located atop the Met, this rooftop bar sits right above Central Park's tree canopy, allowing for splendid views of the park and the city skyline all around. Sunset is when you'll find fools in love...then again, it could all be those martinis.

Access is via the elevator in the European sculpture and decorative arts galleries.

Caledonia BAR
(Map p80; www.caledoniabar.com; 1609 Second Ave, btwn E 83rd & 84th Sts; 5pm-2am Mon-Thu, 4pm-4am Fri-Sat 4pm-1am Sun, happy hour to 7pm Mon-Fri; S Q, 4/5/6 to 86th St) The name of this unpretentious, dimly lit bar is a dead giveaway: it's devoted to Scotch whisky, with more than 100 single malts to choose from (be they Highlands, Islands, Islay, Lowlands or Speyside), as well as some blends and even a few from the US, Ireland and Japan. The bartenders know their stuff and will be happy to make recommendations.

Upper West Side

Empire Rooftop ROOFTOP BAR
(Map p80; 212-265-2600; www.empirehotelnyc.com; 44 W 63 St, at Broadway; 3pm-1am Mon-Wed, to 2am Thu & Fri, 11am-2am Sat, to 1am Sun; ; S 1 to 66th St-Lincoln Center) Sprawled across the top of the Empire Hotel, this stylish rooftop bar is one of New York's most expansive drinking spaces in the sky at 8000 sq ft. A bright, glass-roofed wing strewn with palms and sofas is perfect for winter and has a retractable roof for summer, and there's a handful of outdoor terraces.

Harlem & Upper Manhattan

★ **Shrine** BAR
(Map p80; www.shrinenyc.com; 2271 Adam Clayton Powell Jr Blvd, btwn 133rd & 134th Sts, Harlem; 4pm-4am; S 2/3 to 135th St) Don't fret that it looks like a dive from outside: friendly, unpretentious Shrine is one of the best places in Harlem (if not New York) to hear live bands without a cover charge. Musicians take to its small stage every day of the week with blues, reggae, Afro-beat, funk, and indie rock. Beer is cheap and the crowd is as eclectic as the music.

Silvana BAR
(Map p80; www.silvana-nyc.com; 300 W 116th St, Harlem; upstairs 7am-4am, downstairs from 4pm; S 2/3 to 116th St) This appealing Middle Eastern cafe and shop whips up tasty hummus and falafel plates; the real draw, though, is the hidden downstairs club, which draws a friendly, easygoing local crowd with good cocktails and live bands (kicking off around 6pm) followed by DJs. The lineup is anything-goes, with jazz, Cuban *son*, reggae and Balkan gypsy punk all in the rotation.

Harlem Hops CRAFT BEER
(Map p80; 646-998-3444; www.harlemhops.com; 2268 Adam Clayton Powell Jr Blvd, btwn 133th & 134th Sts, Harlem; 4pm-midnight Sun-Thu, to 2am Fri & Sat; ; S 2/3 to 135th St) Harlem's only 100% African American–owned beer bar has its home 'hood emblazoned on the ceiling in neon lights, and bratwurst and meat pies on the menu. Order a $15 beer paddle of four 5oz pours, pair with a habanero beef pie with African spices, and settle in.

Brooklyn

★ **Maison Premiere** COCKTAIL BAR
(347-335-0446; www.maisonpremiere.com; 298 Bedford Ave, btwn S 1st & Grand Sts, Williamsburg; 2pm-2am Sun-Wed, to 4am Thu-Sat; S L to Bedford Ave) Perched on a stool in Maison Premiere, it's hard not to be seduced by this New Orleans–style oyster and cocktail bar, from antique pictures and soft lighting to suspender-wearing staff. Contemplate a small plate ($13 to $19) – perhaps shrimp cocktail or littleneck clams – and enjoy the maracas sound of cocktail shakers preparing another round of Spring Pimm's and gimlets.

June WINE BAR
(917-909-0434; www.junebk.com; 231 Court St, btwn Warren & Baltic Sts, Cobble Hill; happy hour 5-7pm Mon-Fri, brunch 11am-4pm Sat & Sun, dinner 5:30pm-midnight Sun-Thu, to 1am Fri & Sat; S F, G to Bergen St) Seductive use of curved, polished wood, leadlighting and inviting niches make June a delightful place to linger over interesting natural wines from Europe, America and Australia. Dishes such as chicken with fennel and pea leaves, littleneck clams with celery root, and carrot and olive-oil cake prove that the food's no afterthought (snacks from $11). The doors to a lovely terrace are flung open when it's warm.

★ **Montero Bar & Grill** BAR
(☎646-729-4129; 73 Atlantic Ave, at Hicks St, Brooklyn Heights; ⏲noon-4am; Ⓢ4/5 to Borough Hall) Montero's is the real deal: an anachronistic, neon-fronted, Pabst-peddling longshoreman's bar that's weathered every change thrown at this corner of Brooklyn since WWII. Its eclectic decor recalls the maritime types who once drank here.

Lavender Lake PUB
(☎347-799-2154; www.lavenderlake.com; 383 Carroll St, btwn Bond St & Gowanus Canal, Gowanus; ⏲4pm-midnight Mon-Thu, 2pm-1am Fri, noon-2am Sat, to 10pm Sun; ⓈF, G to Carroll St, R to Union St) Named after the colorfully polluted Gowanus Canal, this popular local haunt is set in a former stable. Lavender Lake serves carefully selected craft beers and deceptively named cocktails with unorthodox ingredients like hibiscus mezcal and strawberry-infused tequila. The lumber-decked garden is a brilliant spot in summer. Weekday happy hour runs from 4pm to 7pm (and all day on Mondays). Bar food staples like nachos, burgers and a couple of plant-based options are on the menu (mains $12 to $17).

★ **House of Yes** CLUB
(www.houseofyes.org; 2 Wyckoff Ave, at Jefferson St, Bushwick; tickets free-$60; ⏲usually 7pm-4am Wed-Sat; ⓈL to Jefferson St) Anything goes at this hedonistic warehouse venue, with two stages, three bars and a covered outdoor area that offers some of the most creative themed performance and dance nights in Brooklyn. You might see aerial-silk acrobats, punk bands, burlesque shows, drag shows or performance artists, or DJs as revered as Jellybean Benítez spinning disco, soul, house and other delights.

Leave the baseball caps and sneakers at home – costumes or other funky outfits will get you priority admission most nights, and on Friday and Saturday they're required for entry. (An on-site pop-up costume shop will let you throw something together – ecofriendly glitter included – if you've arrived unprepared.) This is an inclusive, open-minded and joyous crowd.

Amplifying the feel-good factor, the venue has gone green with water refill stations, biodegradable straws on request and more.

Spuyten Duyvil BAR
(☎718-963-4140; www.spuytenduyvilnyc.com; 359 Metropolitan Ave, btwn Havemeyer & Roebling Sts, Williamsburg; ⏲5pm-2am Mon-Fri, noon-3am Sat, to 2am Sun; ⓈL to Lorimer St, G to Metropolitan Ave) This low-key, beer-centric Williamsburg bar looks as though it was pieced together from a rummage sale, with crimson-painted pressed-tin ceilings, book shelves and a vintage bike mounted on the walls, and mismatched thrift-store furniture. The selection of beer (Belgian especially) is staggering, with knowledgeable bar staff primed to steer you to Danish beers or Normandy ciders.

If you get peckish working through the blackboard of 'rare and obscure' beers, plates of imported cheese and charcuterie (from $8) can provide ballast. There's a large, leafy backyard that's open in good weather.

Partners COFFEE
(☎347-586-0063; www.partnerscoffee.com; 125 N 6th St, btwn Bedford Ave & Berry St, Williamsburg; ⏲6:30am-7pm; ; ⓈL to Bedford Ave) The flagship of a small chain roaster bringing aromatic pour-overs, smooth flat whites and punchy *cortados* (espresso with a dash of milk) to the streets of Billyburg. Even if it does follow all the unspoken rules of Williamsburg cafe design (bare brick and wood, retro miscellany on display...) it's an enjoyable place to hang.

Queens

Bohemian Hall & Beer Garden BEER GARDEN
(☎718-274-4925; www.bohemianhall.com; 29-19 24th Ave, btwn 29th & 31st Sts, Astoria; ⏲5pm-1am Mon-Thu, to 3am Fri, noon-3am Sat, to midnight Sun; ⓈN/W to Astoria Blvd) This Czech community center kicked off NYC's beer-garden craze, and nothing quite matches it for space and heaving drinking crowds, which pack every picnic table under the towering trees in summer. There's Czech food such as schnitzels and goulash (mains $10 to $20), but the focus is on cold and foamy Czech beers, augmented by local craft brews.

★ **Dutch Kills** COCKTAIL BAR
(www.dutchkillsbar.com; 27-24 Jackson Ave, btwn Queens & Dutch Kills Sts, Long Island City; ⏲5pm-2am Sun-Thu, to 3am Fri & Sat; ⓈE/M/R to Queens Plaza, G to Court Sq) Named for the area where Dutch settlers first established themselves around Newtown Creek, this moodily lit bar is all about atmosphere and amazing craft cocktails. Enter through the nondescript door beneath a blinking neon 'bar' sign on an old industrial building, and whistle up an expertly mixed Headless Horseman, or another of the house classic cocktails ($15).

The Bronx

★Bronx Brewery BREWERY

(Map p80; ☎718-402-1000; www.thebronxbrewery.com; 856 E 136th St, btwn Willow & Walnut Aves; ⊙3-7pm Mon-Wed, to 8pm Thu & Fri, noon-8pm Sat, noon-7pm Sun; Ⓢ6 to Cypress Ave) This buzzing South Bronx microbrewery comes with a small, graffiti-scrawled taproom, where you can pony up to the bar and choose from a changing lineup of eight or so quality brews on draft. There's also a backyard (open weekends in the summer) and creative events, including Brewers Dinners – local chefs preparing multi-course feasts paired with beers – and open mic nights.

☆ Entertainment

Actors, musicians, dancers and artists flock to the bright lights of the Big Apple, hoping to finally get that big break. The result? Audiences are spoiled by the continual influx of supremely talented, dedicated, boundary-pushing performers. Like the song goes: if you can make it here, you can make it anywhere.

Opera & Ballet

Metropolitan Opera House OPERA

(Map p80; ☎tickets 212-362-6000, tours 212-769-7028; www.metopera.org; Lincoln Center, Columbus Ave at W 64th St; tickets $25-480; ⊙box office 10am-10pm Mon-Sat, noon-6pm Sun; Ⓢ1 to 66th St-Lincoln Center) New York's premier opera company is the place to see classics such as *La Boheme*, *Madame Butterfly* and *Macbeth*. It also hosts premieres and revivals of more contemporary works, such as John Adams' *The Death of Klinghoffer*. The season runs from September to May. Tickets start at $25 and can get close to $500.

Note that the box seats can be a bargain, but unless you're in boxes right over the stage, the views are dreadful: seeing the stage requires sitting with your head cocked over a handrail – a literal pain in the neck.

For last-minute ticket-buyers there are other deals. You can get bargain-priced standing-room tickets (from $20 to $30) from 10am on the day of the performance. (You won't see much, but you'll hear everything.) Monday through Friday at noon and Saturdays at 2pm, a number of rush tickets are put on sale for starving-artist types – just $25 for a seat; these are available online only. Matinee tickets go on sale four hours before curtain.

Don't miss the gift shop, which is full of operatic knickknacks (like binoculars), and an extensive collection of classical music – many from past Met performances.

For a behind-the-scenes look, the **Met Opera Guild** (www.metguild.org) runs guided tours ($30) weekdays at 3pm and Sundays at 10:30am and 1:30pm during the performance season.

New York City Ballet DANCE

(Map p80; ☎212-496-0600; www.nycballet.com; Lincoln Center, Columbus Ave at W 63rd St; tickets $39 to $204; ⊙box office 10am-7:30pm Mon, to 8:30pm Tue-Sat, 4:30am-7:30pm Sun; 🚸; Ⓢ1 to 66th St-Lincoln Center) This prestigious company was first directed by renowned Russian-born choreographer George Balanchine in the 1940s. Today, it's the largest ballet organization in the US, performing 23 weeks a year at Lincoln Center's David H Koch Theater. Rush tickets for those under 30 years are $30. During the holidays the troupe is best known for its annual production of *The Nutcracker* (tickets go on sale in September: book early).

There are also select one-hour Family Saturday performances, appropriate for young audiences ($22 per ticket, on sale first week of August).

Film & Theater

Public Theater LIVE PERFORMANCE

(Map p70; ☎212-539-8500, tickets 212-967-7555; www.publictheater.org; 425 Lafayette St, btwn Astor Pl & 4th St, NoHo; Ⓢ6 to Astor Pl; R/W to 8th St-NYU) This legendary theater was founded as the Shakespeare Workshop back in 1954 and has launched some of New York's big hits, including *Hamilton* back in 2015. Today, you'll find a lineup of innovative programming as well as reimagined classics from the past, with Shakespeare in heavy rotation. Speaking of the bard, the Public also stages star-studded Shakespeare in the Park (p91) performances during the summer.

★St Ann's Warehouse THEATER

(☎718-254-8779; www.stannswarehouse.org; 45 Water St, at Old Dock St, Dumbo; 🚌B25 to Water/Main Sts, ⓈA/C to High St, F to York St) This handsome red-brick building, a Civil War-era tobacco warehouse, is the first permanent home of avant-garde performance company St Ann's. The 'warehouse' – a high-tech, flexible 320-seat theater – is ideal for staging genre-bending theater, music, dance and puppet performances.

Past shows and screenings of note include Lou Reed and John Cale's *Songs for Drella*, Charlie Kaufman and the Coen Brothers' *Theater of the New Ear*, and the Donmar Warehouse and Phyllida Lloyd's all-female Shakespeare Trilogy.

★Sleep No More THEATER
(Map p74; ☎ box office 212-904-1880; www.sleepnomorenyc.com; 530 W 27th St, btwn Tenth & Eleventh Aves, Chelsea; tickets from $100; ⊙ sessions begin 4-7pm; Ⓢ 1, C/E to 23rd St) One of the most immersive theater experiences ever conceived, *Sleep No More* is a loose, noir retelling of *Macbeth* set inside a series of Chelsea warehouses that have been redesigned to look like the 1930s-era 'McKittrick Hotel' (a nod to Hitchcock's *Vertigo*); the hopping jazz bar, Manderley, is another Hitchcock reference, this time to his adaptation of Daphne du Maurier's *Rebecca*.

First staged in London, it's a choose-your-own-adventure kind of experience, where audience members are free to wander the elaborate rooms (ballroom, graveyard, taxidermy shop, lunatic asylum) and follow or interact with the actors, who perform a variety of scenes that can run from the bizarre to the risqué. Be prepared: you must check in everything when you arrive (jackets, bag, cell phone), and you must wear a mask, à la *Eyes Wide Shut*.

★Metrograph CINEMA
(Map p70; ☎ 212-660-0312; www.metrograph.com; 7 Ludlow St, btwn Canal & Hester Sts, Lower East Side; tickets $15; ⊙ 11am-midnight Sun-Wed, to 2am Fri & Sat; 📶; Ⓢ F to East Broadway, B/D to Grand St) The Lower East Side hasn't gentrified this far yet, giving the owners of this true movie mecca the chance to acquire a building adequate for their vision. It has two screens, both a state-of-the-art digital projector and an old 35mm reel-to-reel. The expertly curated films often form series on subjects such as Japanese animation studio Ghibli or provocateur Gasper Noé.

Film Forum CINEMA
(Map p70; ☎ 212-727-8110; www.filmforum.com; 209 W Houston St, btwn Varick St & Sixth Ave, SoHo; adult/child $15/9; ⊙ noon-midnight; Ⓢ 1 to Houston St) This nonprofit cinema shows an astounding array of independent films, revivals and career retrospectives from greats such as Orson Welles. Showings often include director talks or other film-themed discussions for the hardcore cinephiles.

In 2018, the cinema upgraded its theaters to improve the seating, leg room and sight lines, and expanded to add a fourth screen.

Live Music

New York Philharmonic CLASSICAL MUSIC
(Map p80; ☎ 212-875-5656; www.nyphil.org; Lincoln Center, Columbus Ave at W 65th St; tickets $29-125; 👪; Ⓢ 1 to 66 St-Lincoln Center) The oldest professional orchestra in the US (dating to 1842) holds its season every year at David Geffen Hall. The orchestra plays a mix of classics (Tchaikovsky, Mahler, Haydn) and contemporary works, as well as concerts geared toward children.

If you're on a budget, check out the open rehearsals held several times a month (starting at 9:45am) on the day of the concert for only $22. In addition, students with a valid school ID can pick up rush tickets for $21.50 to $23.50 online before some events; check the website for options.

★Jazz at Lincoln Center JAZZ
(Map p80; ☎ Dizzy's Club Coca-Cola reservations 212-258-9595, Rose Theater & Appel Room tickets 212-721-6500; www.jazz.org; Time Warner Center, 10 Columbus Circle, Broadway at W 59th St; Ⓢ A/C, B/D, 1 to 59th St-Columbus Circle) Perched atop the Time Warner Center, Jazz at Lincoln Center consists of three state-of-the-art venues: the midsized Rose Theater; the panoramic, glass-backed Appel Room; and the intimate, atmospheric Dizzy's Club Coca-Cola. It's the last of these that you're most likely to visit, given its nightly shows (cover charge $5 to $45). The talent is often exceptional, as are the dazzling Central Park views.

★Brooklyn Academy of Music PERFORMING ARTS
(BAM; ☎ 718-636-4100; www.bam.org; 30 Lafayette Ave, at Ashland Pl, Fort Greene; 📶; Ⓢ B/D, N/Q/R, 2/3, 4/5 to Atlantic Ave-Barclays Center) Founded in 1861 (the year the Civil War erupted), BAM is the country's oldest performing-arts center. Spanning several venues in the Fort Greene area, the complex hosts innovative works of opera, modern dance, music, cinema and theater – everything from 'retro-modern' Mark Morris Group ballets and Laurie Anderson multimedia shows to avant-garde Shakespeare productions, comedy and kids' shows.

The 1908 Italian Renaissance–style Peter J Sharp Building houses the **Howard**

DISCOUNT BROADWAY TICKETS

The dozens of Broadway and off-Broadway theaters near Times Square run everything from blockbuster musicals to new and classic drama. Unless there's a specific show you're after, the best – and cheapest – way to score tickets in the area is at the **TKTS Booth** (www.tdf.org/tkts; Broadway, at W 47th St; ⌚3-8pm Mon & Fri, 2-8pm Tue, 10am-2pm & 3-8pm Wed, Thu & Sat, 11am-7pm Sun; S N/Q/R/W, S, 1/2/3, 7 to Times Sq-42nd St), where you can line up and get same-day discounted tickets for top Broadway and off-Broadway shows. Smartphone users can download the free TKTS app, which offers rundowns of both Broadway and off-Broadway shows, as well as real-time updates of what's available on that day. Always have a back-up choice in case your first preference sells out, and never buy from scalpers on the street.

The TKTS Booth is an attraction in its own right, with its illuminated roof of 27 ruby-red steps rising a panoramic 16ft 1in above the 47th St sidewalk.

Gilman Opera House, showing opera, dance, music and more, and the four-screen **Rose Cinemas** (tickets $15-18), showing first-run, indie and foreign films in gorgeously vintage-feel theaters; the on-site bar and restaurant, **BAM Café**, stages free jazz, R&B and pop performances on Friday and Saturday. A block away on Fulton St is the **Harvey Lichtenstein Theater** (651 Fulton St, at Rockwell Pl; S B, Q/R to DeKalb Ave, 2/3, 4/5 to Nevins St), aka 'the Harvey,' which stages cutting-edge, contemporary plays and sometimes radical interpretations of classics. Around the corner from the Sharp building is the **Fisher Building** (www.bam.org/fisher; 321 Ashland Pl, at Lafayette Ave; S B/D, N/Q/R, 2/3, 4/5 to Atlantic Ave-Barclays Center), with its more intimate 250-seat theater.

From October through December, BAM hosts its acclaimed Next Wave Festival (p91), which presents an array of international avant-garde theater and dance and artist talks. Buy tickets early.

National Sawdust LIVE PERFORMANCE

(☎646-779-8455; www.nationalsawdust.org; 80 N 6th St, at Wythe Ave, Williamsburg; ⌚10am-1am Mon-Fri, noon-11pm Sat & Sun; 👪; 🚌B32 to Wythe Ave-N 6th St, S L to Bedford Ave) Covered in wildly hued murals, this cutting-edge space for classical and new music has come a long way since its days as a sawdust factory, with artists as diverse as Pussy Riot and Yo La Tengo performing within. The angular, high-tech interior stages contemporary opera with multimedia projections, electro-acoustic big-band jazz and concerts by experimental composers, alongside less common genres.

National Sawdust's *raison d'être* is shining a light on emerging artists and helping offbeat genres and performers find their audience. Browse their events calendar to decide between Indian classical, ambient 'sound baths' or light-shows with a soundscape of synth.

Village Vanguard JAZZ

(Map p70; ☎212-255-4037; www.villagevanguard.com; 178 Seventh Ave S, btwn W 11th & Perry Sts, West Village; cover around $35; ⌚7:30pm-12:30am; S 1/2/3 to 14th St, A/C/E, L to 8th Ave-14th St) Possibly NYC's most prestigious jazz club, the Vanguard has hosted literally every major star of the past 50 years. Starting out in 1935 as a venue for beat poetry and folk music, it occasionally returns to its roots, but most of the time it's just big, bold jazz all night long. The Vanguard Jazz Orchestra has been a Monday-night mainstay since 1966.

Mind your step on the steep stairs, and close your eyes to the signs of wear and tear – acoustically, you're in one of the greatest venues in the world. There's a one-drink minimum.

★**Barbès** LIVE MUSIC

(☎347-422-0248; www.barbesbrooklyn.com; 376 9th St, at Sixth Ave, Park Slope; requested donation for live music $10; ⌚5pm-2am Mon-Thu, 2pm-4am Fri & Sat, to 2am Sun; S F, G to 7th Ave, R to 4th Ave-9th St) This compact bar and performance space, named after a neighborhood in Paris with a strong North African flavor, is owned by French musicians (and longtime Brooklyn residents). There's live music all night, every night: an impressively eclectic lineup including Balkan brass, contemporary opera, Afro-Peruvian grooves, West African funk and other diverse sounds.

Don't miss the brassy nine-piece Slavic Soul Party, which plays here most Tuesdays (from 9pm). There are also DJ nights, book readings and film screenings.

Bowery Ballroom LIVE MUSIC
(Map p70; 800-745-3000, 212-533-2111; www.boweryballroom.com; 6 Delancey St, at Bowery, Lower East Side; S J/Z to Bowery, B/D to Grand St) This terrific medium-size venue has the perfect sound and feel for well-known indie-rock acts such as The Shins, Jonathan Richman, Stephen Malkmus and Patti Smith.

Sports

Madison Square Garden LIVE PERFORMANCE
(MSG, 'the Garden'; Map p74; www.thegarden.com; 4 Pennsylvania Plaza, Seventh Ave, btwn 31st & 33rd Sts; S A/C/E, 1/2/3 to 34th St-Penn Station) NYC's major performance venue – part of the massive complex housing Penn Station – hosts big-arena performers, from Kanye West to Madonna. It's also a sports arena, with **New York Knicks** (www.nba.com/knicks) and **New York Liberty** (https://liberty.wnba.com) basketball games and **New York Rangers** (www.nhl.com/rangers) hockey games, as well as boxing and events like the Annual Westminster Kennel Club Dog Show.

Dubbed the 'Mecca of basketball' and 'the worlds most famous arena', good basketball was hard to come by in recent years while the Knicks endured years of woeful play. In 2021 they made the playoffs for the first time since 2013. The arena has been part of the decades-old redevelopment plans for the claustrophobic underground Penn Station.

Barclays Center STADIUM
(917-618-6100; www.barclayscenter.com; cnr Flatbush & Atlantic Aves, Prospect Heights; S B/D, N/Q/R, 2/3, 4/5 to Atlantic Ave-Barclays Center) The **Brooklyn Nets** in the NBA (formerly the New Jersey Nets) hold court at this high-tech stadium. Basketball aside, Barclays also stages boxing, professional wrestling, major concerts and shows by big names; Ariana Grande, Justin Bieber, KISS and Cirque de Soleil have all rocked the stadium.

The stadium, with its futuristic design – which looks like a rusting spaceship, topped by a well-kept grassy lawn, rearing above Atlantic Ave – has transformed the neighborhood, though there are regular murmurs about whether the venue has lived up to its own hype.

MCU Park BASEBALL
(718-372-5596; www.brooklyncyclones.com; 1904 Surf Ave, at W 17th St, Coney Island; tickets $10-19, all tickets Wed $10; S D/F, N/Q to Coney Island-Stillwell Ave) The minor-league baseball team **Brooklyn Cyclones**, part of the New York–Penn League and inter-borough rivals of the **Staten Island Yankees**, plays at this beachside park just off Coney Island boardwalk.

Shopping

Not surprisingly for a capital of commercialism, creativity and fashion, New York City is quite simply one of the best shopping destinations on the planet. Every niche is filled. From indie designer-driven boutiques to landmark department stores, thrift shops to haute couture, record stores to the Apple store, street-eats to gourmet groceries, it's quite easy to blow one's budget.

Financial District & Lower Manhattan

★ **Philip Williams Posters** VINTAGE
(Map p66; 212-513-0313; www.postermuseum.com; 122 Chambers St, btwn Church St & W Broadway, Lower Manhattan; 10am-7pm Mon-Sat; S A/C, 1/2/3 to Chambers St) You'll find more than 100,000 posters dating back to 1870 in this cavernous treasure trove, from oversized French advertisements for perfume and cognac to Eastern European film posters and decorative Chinese *Nianhua* posters. Prices range from $15 for small reproductions to thousands of dollars for rare, showpiece originals like an AM Cassandre. There's a second entrance at 52 Warren St.

Owner Philip Williams, looking for a way out of construction jobs, bought his first trunk of random goods – which included original letters from the Wright brothers – for $50 in 1972. He's since accumulated one of the largest inventories for sale in the world. His passion still alive, he also collects and sells poster books, advertising ephemera and art from the South.

SoHo & Chinatown

Rag & Bone FASHION & ACCESSORIES
(Map p70; 212-219-2204; www.rag-bone.com; 117-119 Mercer St, btwn Prince & Spring Sts, SoHo; 11am-8pm Mon-Sat, to 7pm Sun; S R/W to Prince St) Downtown label Rag & Bone is a hit with many of New York's coolest, sharpest dressers – both men and women. Detail-oriented pieces range from clean-cut shirts and blazers and graphic tees to monochromatic sweaters, feather-light strappy dresses, leather goods and Rag & Bone's

highly prized jeans (from $200). Accessories on offer include shoes, hats, bags and wallets.

See the website for all of Rag & Bone's New York locations.

★**Galeria Melissa** SHOES

(Map p70; ☎212-775-1950; www.melissa.com.br/us/galerias/ny; 500 Broadway, btwn Broome & Spring Sts, SoHo; ⏰10am-7pm Mon-Fri, to 8pm Sat, 11am-7pm Sun; 👪; Ⓢ6 to Spring St, R/W to Prince St) This Brazilian designer specializes in downpour-friendly plastic footwear. Recyclable, sustainable, stylish – women's and kids' shoes run the gamut from mod sandals to brogues, runners and, of course, boots.

Melissa's SoHo boutique is the only one in the USA and it's a lesson in the future of retail, with an Instagram room, a vertical rainforest plant wall, shoes displayed on plinths and prismatic mirror walls.

Pearl River Mart DEPARTMENT STORE

(Map p70; ☎212-431-4770; www.pearlriver.com; 452 Broadway, SoHo; ⏰10am-7:20pm; ⓈN/Q/R/W, J/M/Z, 6 to Canal St) A local institution since 1971, Pearl River offers a dizzying array of Asian gifts, housewares, clothing and accessories: silk men's pajamas, cheongsam dresses, blue-and-white Japanese ceramic tableware, clever kitchen gadgets, paper lanterns, origami and calligraphy kits, bamboo plants and an abundance of lucky-cat figurines. The mezzanine art gallery features free rotating shows with work from Asian American artists and photographers.

There's also a branch situated at Chelsea Market (p67).

West Village, Chelsea & Meatpacking District

★**Strand Book Store** BOOKS

(Map p70; ☎212-473-1452; www.strandbooks.com; 828 Broadway, at E 12th St, West Village; ⏰9:30am-10:30pm Mon-Sat, from 11am Sun; ⓈL, N/Q/R/W, 4/5/6 to 14th St-Union Sq) Beloved and legendary, the iconic Strand Book Store embodies downtown NYC's intellectual bona fides – a bibliophile's Oz, where generations of book lovers carrying the store's trademark tote bags happily lose themselves for hours.

In operation since 1927, the Strand sells new, used and rare titles, spreading an incredible 18 miles of books (more than 2.5 million of them) among three labyrinthine floors.

★**Murray's Cheese** FOOD & DRINKS

(Map p70; ☎212-243-3289; www.murrayscheese.com; 254 Bleecker St, btwn Morton & Leroy Sts, West Village; sandwiches $7-8; ⏰8am-9pm Mon-Sat, 9am-8pm Sun; ⓈA/C/E, B/D/F/M to W 4th St-Washington Sq, 1 to Christopher St-Sheridan Sq) Founded in 1940 by Spanish Civil War veteran Murray Greenberg, this is one of New York's best cheese shops. Former owner (now 'advisor') Rob Kaufelt is known for his talent for sniffing out the best curds from around the world: you'll find (and be able to taste) all manner of *fromage*, all aged in cheese caves on site and in Queens.

Housing Works Thrift Shop VINTAGE

(Map p74; ☎718-838-5050; www.housingworks.org; 143 W 17th St, btwn Sixth & Seventh Aves, Chelsea; ⏰10am-7pm Mon-Sat, noon-6pm Sun; Ⓢ1 to 18th St) The flagship for 13 other branches around town, this shop with its swank window displays looks more boutique than thrift, but its selections of clothes, accessories, furniture, books and records are great value.

It's the place to go to find discarded designer clothes for a bargain, and all proceeds benefit the charity serving the city's HIV-positive and AIDS-affected homeless communities.

East Village & Lower East Side

★**Russ & Daughters** FOOD

(Map p70; ☎212-475-4800; www.russanddaughters.com; 179 E Houston St, btwn Orchard & Allen Sts, Lower East Side; ⏰8am-6pm Fri-Wed, to 7pm Thu; ⓈF to 2nd Ave) Since 1914 this much-loved deli, has served up Eastern European Jewish delicacies, such as caviar, herring, sturgeon and, of course, lox. Proudly owned by four generations of the Russ family, it's a great place to load up for a picnic or stock your fridge with breakfast goodies. Foodies, history buffs and interior designers will love it.

A Russ & Daughters Cafe (p99) with sit-down service is close by on Orchard St, but it's just as pleasant to order your 'Shtetl' (or other choice of bagel or bialy sandwich) and eat in nearby **Sara D Roosevelt Park** (Map p70; E Houston St, at Chrystie St, Lower East Side; ⓈF to Delancey-Essex Sts).

Polish immigrant Joel Russ started out selling herring from a barrel on the street, but with energy and determination built his way up to a storefront deli in 1914. In 1935 he made his daughters Hattie, Ida and Anne full partners, renaming the business and becoming the first-ever American company with '& Daughters' in the name.

Union Square, Flatiron District & Gramercy

ABC Carpet & Home HOMEWARES

(Map p74; ☎212-473-3000; www.abchome.com; 888 Broadway, at E 19th St; ⏰10am-7pm Mon-Sat, noon-6pm Sun; Ⓢ4/5/6, N/Q/R/W, L to 14th St-Union Sq) A mecca for home designers and decorators brainstorming ideas, this beautifully curated, seven-level temple to good taste heaves with all sorts of furnishings, small and large. Shop for easy-to-pack knickknacks, boho textiles and jewelry, as well as statement furniture, designer lighting, ceramics and antique carpets. Come Christmas the shop is a joy to behold and it's a great place to buy decorations.

Fishs Eddy HOMEWARES

(Map p74; ☎212-420-9020; www.fishseddy.com; 889 Broadway, at E 19th St, Union Sq; ⏰10am-9pm Mon-Fri, to 8pm Sat & Sun; ⓈR/W, 6 to 23rd St) High-quality and irreverent design has made Fishs Eddy a staple in the homes of hip New Yorkers for years. Its store is a veritable landslide of mugs, plates, dish towels, carafes and anything else that belongs in a cupboard. Styles range from tasteful color blocking to delightfully outrageous patterns. The 'Brooklynese' line (Cawfee, Shuguh, Sawlt etc) makes for great souvenirs.

If you live in the US, you don't have to worry about hauling your new flatware home: staff can arrange affordable shipping for you at the store.

Midtown

★MoMA Design & Book Store GIFTS & SOUVENIRS

(Map p74; ☎212-708-9700; www.momastore.org; 11 W 53rd St, btwn Fifth & Sixth Aves; ⏰9:30am-6:30pm Sat-Thu, to 8pm Fri; ⓈE, M to 5th Ave-53rd St) The flagship store at the Museum of Modern Art (p73) is a fab spot for souvenir shopping. Besides gorgeous books (from art and architecture tomes to pop-culture readers and kids' picture books), you'll find art prints and posters and one-of-a-kind knickknacks. For furniture, lighting, homewares, jewelry, bags and arty gifts, head to the MoMA Design Store across the street.

Barneys DEPARTMENT STORE

(Map p80; ☎212-826-8900; www.barneys.com; 660 Madison Ave, at E 61st St; ⏰10am-8pm Mon-Wed & Sat, to 9pm Thu & Fri, 11am-7pm Sun; 📶; ⓈN/R/W to 5th Ave) Serious fashionistas swipe their plastic at Barneys, respected for its collections of top-tier labels like Isabel Marant Étoile, Mr & Mrs Italy and Lanvin – all spaced out adequately enough to show just how precious each collection is. If you're not armed with the big bucks, expect to find it a little intimidating.

Highlights include the basement cosmetics department, the chic Freds restaurant and Genes, a futuristic cafe with touch-screen communal tables for online shopping. You'll find other branches on Seventh Ave in downtown Manhattan and on Atlantic Ave in Brooklyn.

Bergdorf Goodman DEPARTMENT STORE

(Map p80; ☎212-753-7300; www.bergdorfgoodman.com; 754 Fifth Ave, btwn W 57th & 58th Sts; ⏰10am-9pm Mon-Fri, to 8pm Sat, 11am-8pm Sun; ⓈN/R/W to 5th Ave-59th St, F to 57th St) Not merely loved for its Christmas windows (the city's best), plush BG, at this location since 1928, leads the fashion race, led by its industry-leading fashion director Linda Fargo. A mainstay of ladies who lunch, its draws include exclusive collections and a coveted women's shoe department.

The men's store is across the street.

Macy's DEPARTMENT STORE

(Map p74; ☎212-695-4400; www.macys.com; 151 W 34th St, at Broadway; ⏰10am-10pm Mon-Sat, 11am-9pm Sun; ⓈB/D/F/M, N/Q/R/W to 34th St-Herald Sq; A/C/E to Penn Station) Occupying most of an entire city block, the country's largest department store covers most bases, with fashion, furnishings, kitchenware, sheets, cafes and hair salons. It's more 'mid-priced' than 'exclusive,' stocking mainstream labels and big-name cosmetics. The store also houses an **NYC Information Center** (☎212-484-1222; www.nycgo.com) with information desk, free city maps and 10% store discount vouchers for tourists (bring valid ID).

FAO Schwarz TOYS

(Map p74; ☎800-326-8638; www.faoschwarz.com; 30 Rockefeller Plaza; ⏰9am-10pm Mon-Sat, from 11am Sun; ⓈB/D/F/M 47-50 Sts-Rockefeller Center) New Yorkers mourned the loss of this landmark toy store (c 1862) when it closed its famed flagship on Fifth Ave in 2015 (you might remember Tom Hanks playing a giant floor keyboard here in the movie *Big*). It was resurrected in this new Rockefeller location in 2018, looking jazzier than ever. Even the keyboard has made a comeback.

It really is retail nirvana for kids, with giant spaceships to clamber over, magic show demonstrations, a colorful candy bar and loads of different zones stuffed with toys. Highlights include the 'pit crew' area where car fans can customize their racers, the clockwork stairwell and the neon-lit top-floor piano lounge. Expect to feel like a kid in a candy store, whether you're nine or 90.

Saks Fifth Ave DEPARTMENT STORE

(Map p74; 212-753-4000; www.saksfifthavenue.com; 611 Fifth Ave, at E 50th St; 10am-8:30pm Mon-Sat, 11am-7pm Sun; S B/D/F/M to 47th-50th Sts-Rockefeller Center, E, M to 5th Ave-53rd St) Graced with vintage escalators, Saks' 10-floor flagship store is home to the 'Shoe Salon,' NYC's biggest women's shoe department (complete with express elevator and zip code). Other fortes include the revamped beauty floor and men's departments, the latter home to destination grooming salon John Allan's and a sharply edited offering of fashion-forward labels. The store's January sale is legendary.

Upper East Side

Shakespeare & Co BOOKS

(Map p80; 212-772-3400; www.shakeandco.com; 939 Lexington Ave, at E 69th St; 7:30am-8pm Mon-Fri, 8am-7pm Sat, 9am-6pm Sun; ; S 6 to 68th St) No relation to the Paris seller, this popular bookstore is one of NYC's great indie options. There's a wide array of contemporary fiction and nonfiction, art and local history books, plus a small but unique collection of periodicals, while an Espresso book machine churns out print-on-demand titles. A small cafe serves coffee, tea and light meals.

Mary Arnold Toys TOYS

(Map p80; 212-744-8510; www.maryarnoldtoys.com; 1178 Lexington Ave, btwn E 80th & 81st Sts; 9am-6pm Mon-Fri, 10am-6pm Sat, to 5pm Sun; ; S 4/5/6 to 86th St) Several generations of Upper East Siders have spent large chunks of their childhood browsing the stuffed shelves of this personable local toy store, opened in 1931. Its range is extensive – stuffed animals, action figures, science kits, board games, arts and crafts, educational toys – even Lomo cameras for budding retro photographers.

Upper West Side

Shishi FASHION & ACCESSORIES

(Map p80; www.shishiboutique.com; 2488 Broadway, btwn 92nd & 93rd Sts; 11am-8pm Mon-Sat, to 7pm Sun; S 1/2/3 to 96th St) Shishi is a delightful Israeli-owned boutique stocking an ever-changing selection of stylish, affordable apparel: elegant sweaters, sleeveless shift dresses and eye-catching jewelry from Brazilian designers, among others. (All its clothes are wash-and-dry friendly too.) It's fun for browsing, and with the enthusiastic staff kitting you out in the glamorous changing area, you'll feel like you have your own personal stylist.

★ **Zabar's** FOOD

(Map p80; 212-787-2000; www.zabars.com; 2245 Broadway, at W 80th St; 8am-7:30pm Mon-Fri, to 8pm Sat, 9am-6pm Sun; S 1 to 79th St) A bastion of gourmet kosher foodie-ism, this sprawling local market has been a neighborhood fixture since the 1930s. And what a fixture it is! It features a heavenly array of cheeses, meats, olives, caviar, smoked fish, pickles, dried fruits, nuts and baked goods, including pillowy, fresh-out-of-the-oven *knishes* (Eastern European–style potato dumplings wrapped in dough; $3).

With cramped and crowded aisles, the shopping experience can feel like a bit of a scrum. Grab a number at the specialty counters upon entering – the wait can be long. Upstairs is an entire floor of oft-overlooked houseware products and next door is a sit-down cafe with frozen yoghurt, paninis and Zabar's own-blend coffee.

Magpie ARTS & CRAFTS

(Map p80; www.magpienewyork.com; 488 Amsterdam Ave, btwn 83rd & 84th Sts; 11am-7pm Mon-Sat, to 6pm Sun; S 1 to 86th St) This charming little shop carries a wide range of ecofriendly objects: elegant stationery, beeswax candles, hand-painted mugs, organic-cotton scarves, recycled-resin necklaces, hand-dyed felt journals and wooden earth puzzles are a few things that may catch your eye.

Most products are fair-trade, made of sustainable materials or locally designed and made.

Harlem & Upper Manhattan

Harlem Haberdashery FASHION & ACCESSORIES

(Map p80; 646-707-0070; www.harlemhaberdashery.com; 245 Malcolm X Blvd, btwn 122nd & 123rd Sts, Harlem; noon-8pm Mon-Sat; S 2/3 to 125th St) Keep your wardrobe fresh at this uberhip uptown boutique, which has covetable apparel in all shapes and sizes. Lovely T-shirts, high-end sneakers, dapper woven hats, bespoke denim jackets and jazzy sunglasses are among the ever-changing collections on display.

Flamekeepers Hat Club FASHION & ACCESSORIES
(Map p80; ☎ 212-531-3542; 273 W 121st St, at St Nicholas Ave, Harlem; ⏰ noon-7pm Tue & Wed, to 8pm Thu-Sat, to 6pm Sun; **S** A/C, B/D to 125th St) Polish your look at this sassy little hat shop owned by affable Harlem local Marc Williamson. His carefully curated stock is a hat-lover's dream: soft Barbisio fedoras from Italy, Selentino top hats from the Czech Republic, and woolen patchwork caps from Ireland's Hanna Hats of Donegal.

Prices here range from $55 to $1000; ask about hats that Marc has customized himself.

Brooklyn

★ Artists & Fleas MARKET
(☎ 917-488-4203; www.artistsandfleas.com; 70 N 7th St, btwn Wythe & Kent Aves, Williamsburg; ⏰ 10am-7pm Sat & Sun; **S** L to Bedford Ave) This exuberant flea market provides stripped-back vending space for more than 75 purveyors of vintage and craft wares. Clothing, records, paintings, photographs, hats, handmade jewelry, unique T-shirts and canvas bags, plus an in-store cafe and DJ – it's all here.

There are also two locations in Manhattan that are smaller but open daily, one in SoHo, the other situated inside the Chelsea Market (p67).

Brooklyn Flea MARKET
(www.brooklynflea.com; 80 Pearl St, Manhattan Bridge Archway, Anchorage Pl, at Water St, Dumbo; ⏰ 10am-6pm Sun Apr-Oct; 👪; 🚌 B67 to York/Jay Sts, **S** F to York St) Every Sunday from spring through early fall, numerous vendors sell their wares inside a giant archway under the Manhattan Bridge. There's everything from antiques to records, vintage clothes, homemade foods, quirky handicrafts, housewares and furniture. Locations can change, so check the website before you head out.

A slightly smaller indoor version runs Saturday and Sunday from 10am to 6pm in the Atlantic Center, together with the winter version of superlative food market Smorgasburg.

★ Dellapietras FOOD
(☎ 718-618-9575; 193 Atlantic Ave, btwn Court & Clinton Sts, Downtown Brooklyn; sandwiches $12; ⏰ 10am-7pm Mon-Sat, to 5pm Sun; **S** 4/5 to Borough Hall) Meet the meat – dry-aged prominently in the front window of this outstanding deli-butcher. Great cuts of meat and sausages are augmented by charcuterie and a huge range of lovingly prepared food. Fried chicken, salads, stews and amazing carvery sandwiches make this an ideal lunch stop. The porchetta, broccoli rabe and pecorino sandwich is a thing of immense pleasure.

Twisted Lily PERFUME
(☎ 347-529-4681; www.twistedlily.com; 360 Atlantic Ave, btwn Bond & Hoyt Sts, Boerum Hill; ⏰ noon-7pm Tue-Sun; **S** F, G to Hoyt-Schermerhorn) Come out smelling like a rose (or, if you'd prefer, almond, clary sage or orange blossom) from this 'fragrance boutique and apothecary' specializing in unusual scents from around the world. The attentive staff will help you shop by fragrance for personalized perfumes, scented candles, and skincare and grooming products.

Beacon's Closet VINTAGE
(☎ 718-486-0816; www.beaconscloset.com; 74 Guernsey St, btwn Nassau & Norman Aves, Greenpoint; ⏰ 11am-8pm; **S** G to Nassau Ave) This vast warehouse of vintage clothing is both a gold mine and a gauntlet. Arranged by color, its circular racks of coats, dresses, polyester tops and '90s-era T-shirts take time and determination to conquer. The committed will also find shoes of all sorts, flannels, hats, handbags, chunky jewelry and sunglasses. There are other branches in **Bushwick** (☎ 718-417-5683; 23 Bogart St, btwn Varet & Cook Sts; ⏰ 11am-8pm; **S** L to Morgan Ave), **Park Slope** (☎ 718-230-1630; 92 Fifth Ave, cnr Warren St; ⏰ noon-9pm Mon-Fri, 11am-8pm Sat & Sun; **S** 2/3 to Bergen St, B, Q to 7th Ave) and Manhattan.

Industry City DESIGN
(☎ 718-736-2516; www.industrycity.com; 220 36th St, btwn Second & Third Aves, Sunset Park; ⏰ 9am-9pm; 📶; **S** D, N, R to 36th St) These six towering warehouses by the Brooklyn waterfront have been repurposed as a 35-acre hub for shops, design studios, start-ups and nonprofits. The slick design lacks Brooklyn's characteristic grungy spirit, but it's worth stopping by for lunch at the very good food court or summer performances, held in the outdoor courtyard.

Japan Village stands out for its well-stocked supermarket, complete with take-away mochi (rice flour dumplings stuffed with sweet fillings like red bean paste) and various other Japanese groceries, plus a cafe-bakery and nearby sake shop.

Another worthwhile stop here is the outlet of venerable Manhattan chocolatier Li-Lac.

Queens

Astoria Bookshop BOOKS

(☎718-278-2665; www.astoriabookshop.com; 31-29 31st St, btwn 31st Ave & Broadway, Astoria; ⏰11am-7pm; Ⓢ N/W to Broadway) A much-loved indie bookshop with ample shelf space dedicated to local authors, Astoria is a good spot to pick up a title about the Queens dining scene or the borough's wide-ranging ethnic diversity.

A stalwart of the community, Astoria also hosts author readings, discussion groups, writing workshops and kids' storytelling (every Thursday at 11am).

The Bronx

Hit the old-school shops and market stalls around Arthur Ave for Italian larder essentials, from truffle oil and anchovies to ripe, sweet *sugo* (tomato sauce).

Information

New York City is actually one of the USA's safest cities – in 2018 homicides fell to 289, a record low not seen since the early 1950s. Overall violent-crime statistics also declined for the 28th straight year.

Still, it's always best to take a common-sense approach when exploring.

- Don't walk around alone at night in unfamiliar, sparsely populated areas.
- Be aware of pickpockets, particularly in mobbed areas like Times Square or Penn Station at rush hour.
- While it's generally safe to ride the subway after midnight, you may want to skip going underground and take a taxi instead, especially if traveling alone.

NYC Information Center (Map p74; ☎212-484-1222; www.nycgo.com; Broadway Plaza, btwn W 43rd & 44th Sts; ⏰8am-8pm; Ⓢ N/Q/R/W, S, 1/2/3, 7, A/C/E to Times Sq-42nd St) is the official NYC tourist information booth, and you'll find maps, brochures and bilingual staff here.

Getting There & Away

AIR

Fifteen miles from Midtown in southeastern Queens, **John F Kennedy International Airport** (JFK; ☎718-244-4444; www.jfkairport.com; Ⓢ A to Howard Beach, E, J/Z to Sutphin Boulevard-Archer Ave then AirTrain) has six working terminals, serves more than 59 million passengers annually and hosts flights coming and going from all corners of the globe. You can use the AirTrain (free within the airport) to move from one terminal to another.

A massive $10 billion overhaul of the airport first began in 2017 but was delayed due to the pandemic. A terminal 1 revamp is now planned to begin in 2022, with new gates scheduled to open in 2026.

Used mainly for domestic flights, **LaGuardia** (LGA; ☎718-533-3400; www.laguardiaairport.com; 🚌 M60, Q70) is smaller than JFK but only 8 miles from midtown Manhattan; it sees nearly 30 million passengers per year.

Much maligned by politicians and ordinary travelers alike over the years, the airport is now receiving a much-needed $4 billion overhaul of its terminal facilities, which is due to finish in 2022.

BUS

A number of budget bus lines operate from locations on the west side of Midtown:

Megabus (Map p74; ☎877-462-6342; https://us.megabus.com; 34th St, btwn 11th & 12th Aves; 📶; Ⓢ 7 to 34th St-Hudson Yards) Travels from New York to Boston, Washington, DC, and Toronto, among other destinations. Free (sometimes functioning) wi-fi. Departures leave from 34th St near the Jacob K Javits Convention Center and **arrivals** (Map p74; cnr Seventh Ave & 27th St; Ⓢ 1 to 28th St) drop off at 27th and 7th.

Vamoose (Map p74; ☎212-695-6766; www.vamoosebus.com; cnr Seventh Ave & 30th St; from $20; Ⓢ 1 to 28th St; A/C/E, 1/2/3 to 34th St-Penn Station) Buses head to Arlington, Virginia, and Bethesda, Maryland.

TRAIN

Penn Station (W 33rd St, btwn Seventh & Eighth Aves; Ⓢ 1/2/3, A/C/E to 34th St-Penn Station) The oft-maligned departure point for all Amtrak (www.amtrak.com) trains, including the Acela Express services to Boston and Washington, DC (note that this express service costs twice as much as a normal fare). Fares vary, based on the day of the week and the time you want to travel. There's no baggage-storage facility at Penn Station.

Long Island Rail Road (www.mta.info/lirr) Serves more than 300,000 commuters each day, with services from Penn Station to points in Brooklyn and Queens, and on Long Island. Prices are broken down by zones. A peak-hour ride from Penn Station to Jamaica Station (en route to JFK via AirTrain) costs $10.25 if you buy it at the station (or a whopping $16 on board!).

NJ Transit (www.njtransit.com) Also operates trains from Penn Station, with services to the New Jersey suburbs and the Jersey Shore.

New Jersey PATH (www.panynj.gov/path) An option for getting into NJ's northern points, such as Hoboken and Newark. Trains ($2.75) run from Penn Station along the length of Sixth Ave, with stops at 33rd, 23rd, 14th, 9th and Christopher Sts, as well as at the reopened World Trade Center site.

Metro-North Railroad (www.mta.info/mnr) The last line departing from the magnificent Grand Central Terminal, it serves Connecticut, Westchester County and the Hudson Valley.

Getting Around

Check the Metropolitan Transportation Authority website (www.mta.info) for public transportation information (buses and subway). Delays have increased as ridership has expanded.

Subway Inexpensive, somewhat efficient and operates around the clock, though navigating lines can be confusing. A single ride is $2.75 with a MetroCard.

Buses Convenient during off hours – especially when transferring between the city's eastern and western sides (most subway lines run north to south). Uses the MetroCard; same price as the subway.

Taxi Meters start at $2.50 and increase roughly $5 for every 20 blocks. See www.nyc.gov/taxi.

Bicycle The city's popular bike-share program Citi Bike (www.citibikenyc.com) provides excellent access to most parts of Manhattan.

Inter-borough ferries The New York City Ferry (www.ferry.nyc) provides handy transport between waterside stops in Manhattan, Brooklyn and Queens.

TIPPING

Tipping is *not* optional; only withhold tips in cases of outrageously bad service.

Restaurant servers 18–20%, unless a gratuity is already charged on the bill (usually only for groups of five or more)

Bartenders 15–20% per round, minimum per drink $1 for standard drinks, and $2 per specialty cocktail

Taxi drivers 10–15%, rounded up to the next dollar

Airport & hotel porters $2 per bag, minimum per cart $5

Hotel maids $2–4 per night, left in envelope or under the card provided

NEW YORK STATE

For most, any trip to the Empire State starts or finishes in its iconic metropolis: New York City. However, if you confine your travels only to the five boroughs there's a considerable amount you're missing out on.

Long Island and upstate New York – generally accepted as anywhere north of the NYC metro area – shouldn't be missed. Long Island has cozy beach towns, while upstate is a dream destination for those who cherish the great outdoors. The Hudson River valley acts as an escape route from the city, leading eager sojourners north. From Albany, the 524-mile Erie Canal cuts due west to Lake Erie, passing spectacular Niagara Falls, Buffalo and Rochester. In the east you'll find the St Lawrence River and its thousands of islands, as well as the magnificent Adirondack and Catskills mountains. Head to the middle of the state and you'll be ensconced in the serene Finger Lakes.

Resources

511 NY (www.511ny.org) Statewide traffic and transit info.

I Love NY (www.iloveny.com) Comprehensive state tourism bureau, with the iconic heart logo.

New York State Parks, Recreation & Historic Preservation (www.parks.ny.gov) Camping, lodging and general info on all state parks.

And North (www.andnorth.com) A curated online guide to upstate New York.

Escape Brooklyn (www.escapebrooklyn.com) Respected blog by clued-up Brooklynites on upstate getaways.

Lonely Planet (www.lonelyplanet.com/usa/new-york-state) Destination information, hotel reviews and more.

Long Island

Technically, the 118 miles of Long Island includes the boroughs of Brooklyn and Queens on the western edge, but in the popular imagination, 'Long Island' begins

ACCESSIBLE TRAVEL IN NYC

Much of the city is accessible with curb cuts for wheelchair users. All the major sites (like the Met museum, the Guggenheim, the National September 11 Memorial and Museum, and the Lincoln Center) are also accessible. Some, but not all, Broadway venues have provisions for theater-goers with disabilities, from listening devices to wheelchair seating; consult http://theatreaccess.nyc.

Unfortunately, only about 100 of New York's 468 subway stations are fully wheelchair accessible. In general, the bigger stations have access, such as 14th St-Union Sq, 34th St-Penn Station, 42nd St-Port Authority Terminal, 59th St-Columbus Circle, and 66th St-Lincoln Center. For a complete list of accessible subway stations, visit http://web.mta.info/accessibility/stations.htm. Also visit www.nycgo.com/accessibility.

On the plus side, all of NYC's MTA buses are wheelchair accessible, and are often a better option than negotiating cramped subway stations. Taxis suitable to travelers with mobility aids are available through Accessible Dispatch (646-599-9999; http://accessibledispatch.org); there's also an app that allows you to request the nearest available service.

Another excellent resource is the **Big Apple Greeter** (☎212-669-8159; www.bigapplegreeter.org) FREE program, which has more than 50 volunteers on staff who have various disabilities and are happy to show off their corner of the city.

Restrooms can be found in most department stores and the NYC parks website (www.nycgovparks.org/facilities/bathrooms) is a good source of info regarding bathrooms – some of them wheelchair-accessible – across the city's green spaces.

The city also provides paratransit buses for getting around town for the same price as a subway fare, though this service – called Access-a-Ride (https://access.nyc.gov/programs/access-a-ride) – isn't very practical for tourists as you'll need to attend an assessment appointment and fill in mailed paperwork before eligibility for the service can be confirmed (which can take up to 21 days). Visit the website for more info.

Download Lonely Planet's free Accessible Travel guides from https://shop.lonelyplanet.com/categories/accessible-travel.com.

only where the city ends, in a mass of traffic-clogged expressways and suburbs that every teenager aspires to leave. (Levittown, the first planned 1950s subdivision, is in central Nassau County.) But there's plenty more out on 'Lawn-guy-land' (per the local accent). Push past the central belt of 'burbs to windswept dunes, proud stands of pine, glitzy summer resorts, fresh farms and wineries, a wealth of perfect Pleasantvilles and Mayberry-esque Main Streets and whaling and fishing ports established in the 17th century. Then you'll see why loyalists prefer the nickname 'Strong Island.'

Getting There & Around

Thanks to **Long Island Rail Road** (LIRR; ☎718-217-5477; www.mta.info/lirr), which runs three lines from New York Penn Station to the furthest eastern ends of the island, it's possible to visit without a car. Additionally, the Hampton Jitney (p125) and **Hampton Luxury Liner** (☎631-537-5800; www.hamptonluxuryliner.com) buses connect Manhattan to various Hamptons villages and Montauk; the former also picks up in Brooklyn, and runs to the North Fork. With a car, however, it is easier to visit several spots on the island in one go. I-495, aka the Long Island Expwy (LIE), runs down the middle of the island – but avoid rush hour, when it's commuter hell.

The **Cross Sound Ferry** (☎631-323-2525, 860-443-5281; www.longislandferry.com; 41270 Main Rd, Orient; vehicle/bike/foot from $57/5/16.25) connects Long Island with New London, Connecticut.

South Shore

Easily accessible by public transit, South Shore beaches can get crowded, but they're a fun day out. Not nearly as much of a schlep as the Hamptons, and far more egalitarian, the beach towns along these barrier islands each have their own vibe and audience – you can get lost in the crowds or go solo on the dunes. **Long Beach** is just over the border from Queens, and its main town strip is busy with ice-cream shops, bars and eateries.

Sights

Fire Island National Seashore ISLAND
(☎631-687-4750; www.nps.gov/fiis) FREE Federally protected, this island offers sand dunes, forests, clean beaches, camping (wilderness

permits $25 obtained throughwww.recreation.gov), hiking trails, inns, restaurants, 15 hamlets and two villages. The scenery ranges from car-free areas of summer mansions and packed nightclubs to stretches of sand where you'll find nothing but pitched tents and deer.

Most of the island is accessible only by **ferry** (631-665-3600; www.fireislandferries.com; 99 Maple Ave, Bay Shore; one-way adult/child $11/6) and is free of cars – regulars haul their belongings on little wagons instead. You can drive to either end of the island (the lighthouse or the Wilderness Visitor Center) but there is no road in between. The island is edged with a dozen or so tiny hamlets, mostly residential. Party-center **Ocean Beach Village** and quieter **Ocean Bay Park** (take ferries from the Bayshore LIRR stop) have a few hotels; **Cherry Grove** and the **Pines**, via ferries from Sayville, are gay enclaves, also with hotels.

Robert Moses State Park STATE PARK
(631-669-0449; www.parks.ny.gov; 600 Robert Moses State Pkwy, Babylon, Fire Island; per car $10, golf adult/senior $11/8; dawn-dusk) Robert Moses State Park, one small part of Fire Island accessible by car, lies at the westernmost end and features wide, soft-sand beaches with mellower crowds than those at Jones Beach. It's also adjacent to the **Fire Island Lighthouse** (Fire Island National Seashore; 631-661-4876; www.fireislandlighthouse.com; Robert Moses Causeway; adult/child $8/4; 9:30am-6pm Jul & Aug, shorter hours rest of year), which you can walk to from here.

Sunken Forest FOREST
(631-597-6183; www.nps.gov/fiis; Fire Island; visitor center mid-May–mid-Oct) FREE This 300-year-old forest, a surprisingly dense stretch of trees behind the dunes, is easily accessible via a 1.5-mile boardwalk trail looping through it. It's pleasantly shady in summer, and vividly colored when the leaves change in fall. It's accessible by its own ferry stop, Sailors Haven, where there's also a visitor center, or a long walk in the winter season, after the ferry shuts down.

Ranger-guided tours available.

Sleeping & Eating

Seashore Condo Motel HOTEL $$
(631-583-5860; www.seashorecondomotel.com; Bayview Ave, Ocean Bay Park, Fire Island; week/weekend d from $200/300;) Small, wood-paneled rooms without many frills, despite the price. Take the Ocean Bay Park ferry from Bayside.

Madison Fire Island Pines BOUTIQUE HOTEL $$$
(631-597-6061; www.themadisonfi.com; 22 Atlantic Walk, Fire Island Pines, Fire Island; d from $300;) Fire Island's first 'boutique' hotel, which rivals anything Manhattan has to offer in terms of amenities, but also has killer views from its rooftop deck and a gorgeous pool.

The hotel is reached by **Sayville Ferry Service** (631-589-0810; www.sayvilleferry.com; 41 River Rd, Sayville) to Pines.

Sand Castle SEAFOOD $$$
(631-597-4174; www.fireislandsandcastle.com; 106 Lewis Walk, Cherry Grove, Fire Island; mains $24-33; 11am-11pm Mon, Tue & Thu-Sat, 9:30am-11pm Sun May-Sep;) One of Fire Island's only oceanfront (rather than bayfront) options, Sand Castle serves up satisfying appetizers (fried calamari, seafood chowder) and lots of seafood temptations (mussels, octopus carpaccio, grilled King Salmon).

Nice cocktails and people-watching, too.

Getting There & Away

You can drive to Fire Island by taking the Long Island Expwy to Exit 53 (Bayshore), 59 (Sayville) or 63 (Patchogue).

Using public transportation, take the LIRR to one of three stations with connections to the ferries: **Patchogue** (631-475-1665; www.davisparkferry.com; 80 Brightwood St, Patchogue), Bayshore or Sayville. Patchogue is walking distance from the train to the boat. You can also purchase a train-taxi combination ticket from the railroad for excursions to Sunken Forest and a train-bus combo for Jones Beach.

The LIRR (www.mtainfo.com/lirr) runs directly to Long Beach (55 minutes) from New York Penn Station. You can buy special beach combination excursion tickets from the railroad.

The Hamptons

This string of villages is a summer escape for Manhattan's wealthiest, who zip to mansions by helicopter. Mere mortals take the Hampton Jitney bus and chip in on rowdy rental houses.

Behind the glitz is a long cultural history, as noted artists and writers have lived here. Beneath the glamour, the gritty and life-risking tradition of fishing continues.

The area is small, and connected by often traffic-clogged Montauk Hwy.

Sights

EAST HAMPTON

East Hampton Town Marine Museum MUSEUM
(631-324-6850; www.easthamptonhistory.org; 301 Bluff Rd, Amagansett; $8; 10am-4pm Fri & Sat Jul & Aug) One of your last outposts before you drive on to Montauk, this small museum dedicated to the fishing and whaling industries is as interesting as its counterpart in Sag Harbor, full of old harpoons, boats half the size of their prey, and a beautiful B&W photographic tribute to the local fishers and their families.

Osborn-Jackson House MUSEUM
(631-324-6850; www.easthamptonhistory.org; 101 Main St; donation $5; 10am-4pm Mon-Fri) Check out East Hampton's colonial past with a visit to the Historical Society, including this historic home. The Society tends to five attractions around East Hampton, including several colonial farms, mansions and the marine museum.

Pollock-Krasner House ARTS CENTER
(631-324-4929; www.pkhouse.org; 830 Springs Fireplace Rd; Sat $10, guided tours Thu & Fri $15; noon-5pm Sat, guided tours noon, 2pm & 4pm Thu & Fri May-Oct) Tour the home of husband-and-wife art stars Jackson Pollock and Lee Krasner – worth it just to see the paint-spattered floor of Pollock's studio. You can simply show up on a Saturday, but reservations are required for the guided tours on Thursday and Friday.

SAG HARBOR

Sag Harbor Whaling & Historical Museum MUSEUM
(631-725-0770; www.sagharborwhalingmuseum.org; 200 Main St; adult/child $8/3; 10am-5pm May-Oct) The cool collection here includes actual artifacts from 19th-century whaling ships: sharp flensing knives, battered pots for rendering blubber, delicate scrimshaw and more. It's a bit surreal to see photos of the giant mammals in a village that's now a cute resort town. It occupies a striking 19th-century residential home that doubles as a Masonic Temple.

SOUTHAMPTON

★ **Parrish Art Museum** MUSEUM
(631-283-2118; www.parrishart.org; 279 Montauk Hwy, Water Mill; adult/child $12/free; 10am-5pm Wed-Mon, to 8pm Fri) In a sleek, long barn designed by Herzog & de Meuron, this institution spotlights local artists such as Jackson Pollock, Willem de Kooning, Chuck Close and William Merritt Chase. Special temporary exhibitions change over five times throughout the year; seven of the galleries are dedicated to permanent works that are curated from a 3000-strong collection. For more Pollock, make reservations to see his nearby studio and home.

Southampton History Museum MUSEUM
(631-283-2494; www.southamptonhistory.org; 17 Meeting House Lane; adult/child $5/free; 11am-4pm Wed-Sat Mar-Dec) Before the Hamptons was the Hamptons, there was this clutch of buildings, now nicely maintained and spread around Southampton. The main museum is Rogers Mansion, once owned by a whaling captain. You can also visit a former dry-goods store, now occupied by a local jeweler, around the corner at 80 Main St; and a 17th-century homestead, the Halsey House (adult/child $5/free, Saturday only, July to September).

Additional buildings include an 1830 one-room schoolhouse, an 1825 barn and a 19th-century paint store, among others.

St Andrew's Dune Church CHURCH
(631-283-0549; www.standrewsdunechurch.com; 12 Gin Lane; service 11am Sun Jun-Sep) The triple spires of this 19th-century red wooden church glow beautifully in the afternoon light. You can come to Sunday service if so inclined, admiring the stained glass and quaint wooden pews, or simply enjoy a stroll along the placid waterway across the street from the curious iron pot donated by an early congregant. The building was the earliest life-saving station in New York, and is well worth the short drive or walk from downtown.

Sleeping

1708 House B&B $$$
(631-287-1708; www.1708house.com; 126 Main St; d from $300, cottages from $625;) History buffs might gravitate towards this local standout, run by supreme storyteller Skip and his daughters. The deed on the house (and the old world European-style wine cellar in the basement) date to 1651. It's in central Southampton and prides itself on its turn-of-the-century charm and traditional furnishings in the 13 rooms and three cottages.

★ **Topping Rose House** BOUTIQUE HOTEL $$$
(631-537-0870; www.toppingrosehouse.com; 1 Bridgehampton-Sag Harbor Turnpike, Bridgehampton; d from $985; P) In an 1842 home, this exclusive boutique hotel boasts

22 rooms, including six suites decorated with local artists' work. A Manhattan gallery curates the rotating (for sale) art collection, and there's a spa and heated pool in addition to Jean-Georges Vongerichten's farm-to-table restaurant (mains $28 to $49), some produce for which is sourced from the one-acre garden adjoining the property.

Eating

Candy Kitchen DINER $

(2391 Montauk Hwy; mains $4.25-19; 7am-8pm) An antidote to glitz, this old school corner diner has been serving good soups, homemade ice cream and other staples since 1925. Its policy is similarly old school – cash only, please. As far as ice cream goes, give mint chip or coffee chip a go; for lunch, the souvlaki and other Greek staples are popular.

Fellingham's PUB FOOD $$

(Restaurant Sports Bar; 631-283-9417; www.fellinghamsrestaurant.com; 17 Cameron St; burgers $11-24; 11am-11pm;) This favored sports bar, rich with historical photos and memorabilia, boasts a hearty menu featuring a bacon-cheeseburger named for baseball legend Babe Ruth and a Sharapova burger with – naturally – Russian dressing. Mains are heavy on the steaks and chops. With so much local flavor, this qualifies as the 'Cheers' of Southampton.

★Dockside Bar & Grill SEAFOOD $$$

(631-725-7100; www.docksidesagharbor.com; 26 Bay St; mains $24-43; noon-4pm & 5:30-10pm Mon-Thu, noon-4pm & 5:30-10:30pm Fri, 11am-2pm & 5:30-10:30pm Sat, 11am-2pm & 5:30-10pm Sun) A local favorite inside the American Legion Hall (the original bar's still there). The seafood-heavy menu here features a prize-winning, stick-to-the-spoon chowder and luscious avocado-lobster spring rolls, among other mouthwatering delights.

The outdoor patio can be a nice place to be in the summer.

Getting There & Away

Driving the Montauk Hwy (Rte 27) to and from New York involves careful planning to avoid major congestion, and it's often at a standstill within the Hamptons itself on busy weekends. Better to take the ever-popular **Hampton Jitney** (631-283-4600; www.hamptonjitney.com) out here from Manhattan or Brooklyn – it serves the entire Hamptons with frequent comfortable buses. The LIRR (p122) is a second but often more time-consuming option.

Getting Around

The app-driven, converted turquoise **Hampton Hopper** (631-259-7076; www.hamptonhopper.com; 10am-10pm Jun-Labor Day) school buses are an economical, hassle-free way to get around the towns and operate into the bar hours. Download the app to buy daily passes from $20 (the Montauk Loop is free) and see where the buses are.

Montauk

Towards the east-pointing tip of Long Island's South Fork, you'll find the mellow town of Montauk, aka 'The End,' and the famous surfing beach **Ditch Plains**. With the surfers have come affluent hipsters and boho-chic hotels, but the area is still far less of a scene than the Hamptons, with proudly blue-collar residents and casual seafood restaurants.

Route 27, the Montauk Hwy, divides east of **Napeague State Park**, with the Montauk Hwy continuing down the center of the peninsula while Old Montauk Hwy hugs the water. The roads converge at the edge of central Montauk and Fort Pond, a small lake. Two miles east is a large inlet called **Lake Montauk**, with marinas strung along its shore.

Sights

Montauk Point State Park STATE PARK

(631-668-3781; www.parks.ny.gov; 2000 Montauk Hwy/Rte 27; per car $8; dawn-dusk) Covering the eastern tip of the South Fork is Montauk Point State Park, with its impressive **lighthouse** (631-668-2544; www.montauklighthouse.com; 2000 Montauk Hwy; adult/child $12/5; 10:30am-5:30pm Sun-Fri, to 7pm Sat mid-Jun–Aug, shorter hours mid-Apr–mid-Jun & Sep-Nov). A good place for windswept walks, surfing, surf fishing (with permit) and seal-spotting – call the park for the schedule; rangers will set up spotting scopes to better view the frisky pinnipeds.

Lost at Sea Memorial MEMORIAL

(2000 Montauk Hwy, Montauk Lighthouse; Montauk State Park parking fee $8; 10:30am-5:30pm Sun-Fri, to 7pm Sat mid-Jun–Aug, shorter hours mid-Apr–mid-Jun & Sep-Nov) Visitors to the Montauk Lighthouse may not immediately notice a smaller 15ft structure at the eastern end of the park, where the 60ft cliffs fall off into the sea, but for local fishers it's a daily reminder of their struggle against the power of the sea. The 8ft, 2600lb bronze statue set on a 7ft slab of granite is inscribed with the names of those lost to the waves, from the colonial days of New York to the present.

Sleeping

Hither Hills State Park CAMPGROUND $
(☎631-668-2554; www.parks.ny.gov; 164 Old Montauk Hwy; campsites state residents/nonresidents $35/70) These wooded dunes form a natural barrier between Montauk and the Hamptons. The 189-site campground caters for tents and RVs, and there are spots for fishing (permit required) and hiking through the dunes; online reservations ($9 fee) are a must.

The park's western border is the stunning **Walking Dunes** (Napeague Harbor Rd, Hither Hills State Park) FREE.

★**Sunrise Guesthouse** GUESTHOUSE $$$
(☎631-668-7286; www.sunrisebnb.com; 681 Old Montauk Hwy; r/ste $295/425; P ❄ 📶) A tasteful yet homey four-room B&B a mile from town, and just across the road from the beach. The breakfast is ample and delicious, served in a comfy dining area with a million-dollar view. Summer weekends require a two-night minimum stay.

Eating & Drinking

Lobster Roll SEAFOOD $$
(☎631-267-3740; www.lobsterroll.com; 1980 Montauk Hwy, Amagansett; mains $14-28; ⏰11:45am-9:30pm Mon-Sat, to 9pm Sun Jun-Sep, shorter hours May & Oct) 'Lunch' is the sign to look for on the roadside west of Montauk, marking this clam-and-lobster shack that has been in operation since 1965.

It's now become infamous as the liaison site in the Showtime television series *The Affair*.

★**Clam Bar at Napeague** SEAFOOD $$
(☎631-267-6348; www.clambarhamptons.com; 2025 Montauk Hwy, Amagansett; mains $13-29; ⏰11:30am-8pm Apr-Oct, to 6pm Nov & Dec) You won't get fresher seafood or a saltier waitstaff, and holy mackerel, those lobster rolls are good, even if you choke a bit on the price. Three decades in business – the public has spoken – with cash only, of course. Locals favor this one.

Find it on the road between Amagansett and Montauk. Winter hours are weather permitting.

Montauk Brewing Company MICROBREWERY
(☎631-668-8471; www.montaukbrewingco.com; 62 S Erie Ave; ⏰2-7pm Mon-Fri, noon-7pm Sat & Sun) 'Come as you are,' preaches the small tasting room, and Cobain's family hasn't asked for their lyrics back yet. There's a more-than-palatable rotating range of cervezas, from lagers to stouts, and an outdoor patio on which to enjoy them in the right weather. Take a mixed six-pack to go.

Montauket BAR
(☎631-668-5992; 88 Firestone Rd; ⏰noon-10pm) Experts agree: this is the best place to watch the sun go down on Long Island. An unassuming slate-blue-shingled building, full of local flavor (and people).

Getting There & Away

Montauk is the last stop on the eastbound Hampton Jitney bus ($30 to $38), as well as the Long Island Rail Road (p122). Suffolk County bus 10C ($2.25) runs to the Montauk (and the lighthouse) from East Hampton five times per day from July to September.

North Fork & Shelter Island

The North Fork is known for its bucolic farmland and vineyards (though the weekends can draw rowdy limo-loads on winery crawls). Rte 25, the main road through **Jamesport**, **Cutchogue** and **Southold**, is pretty and edged with farm stands; the less-traveled Rte 48 also has many wineries.

The largest town on the North Fork is laid-back **Greenport**, with working fishing boats, a history in whaling and a **vintage carousel** (www.villageofgreenport.org; Mitchell Park; $2; ⏰10am-9pm Jun-Aug, shorter hours rest of yr) in Mitchell Park. It's compact and easily walkable from the LIRR station.

Like a pearl in Long Island's claw, Shelter Island rests between the North and South Forks. The island is a smaller, more low-key version of the Hamptons, with a touch of maritime New England. Parking is limited; long **Crescent Beach**, for instance, has spots only by permit. If you don't mind a few hills, it's a nice place to visit by bike, and Mashomack Nature Preserve is a wildlife lover's dream.

Sights

Mashomack Nature Preserve NATURE RESERVE
(☎631-749-1001; www.nature.org/Mashomack; Rte 114, Shelter Island; suggested donation adult/

child $3/2; ⏲ 9am-5pm Jul & Aug, closed Tue Apr-Jun, Sep & Oct, shorter hours rest of year) The 2000 acres of this Shelter Island reserve, shot through with creeks and marshes, are great for kayaking, birding and hiking (no cycling allowed). Take precautions against ticks, an ever-present problem on the island.

Orient Beach State Park BEACH
(☎ 631-323-2440; www.parks.ny.gov/parks/106; 40000 Main Rd, Orient; per car $10, kayaks per hour $25; ⏲ 8am-4pm) A sandy slip of land at the end of the North Fork, where you can swim in the calm ocean water (July and August only; 10:30am to 6pm) or rent kayaks to paddle in the small bay. True believers can view four different lighthouses, including the Orient Point Lighthouse, known as 'the coffee pot' for its stout bearing. To best see the lighthouse, go up the road to Orient Point County Park, which has a half-mile trail to a white-rock beach.

Horton Point Lighthouse LIGHTHOUSE
(☎ 631-765-5500; www.southoldhistoricalsociety.org/lighthouse; 3575 Lighthouse Rd, Southold; suggested donation $5; ⏲ Memorial Day-mid-Sep 11:30am-4pm Sat-Sun, shorter hours rest of year) Perhaps a poorer sister to the famous Montauk lighthouse, Horton Point was also commissioned by President Washington, but finally built 60 years later by William Sinclair, a Scotsman, who was an engineer in Brooklyn's Navy Yard. There's a nice nature trail in the adjacent park that leads to two Long Island Sound overlooks and steps to the beach.

Sleeping & Eating

Greenporter Hotel BOUTIQUE HOTEL $$$
(☎ 631-477-0066; www.greenporterhotel.com; 326 Front St, Greenport; d incl breakfast $239-309; P ❄ ☎ ≋) An older motel redone with white walls and Ikea furniture but a few steps from the downtown Greenport action. The 30 rooms – big bathrooms, all with bathtubs – wrap around the pool and it all adds up to decent value for the area.

Love Lane Kitchen AMERICAN $$
(☎ 631-298-8989; www.lovelanekitchen.com; 240 Love Lane, Mattituck; mains lunch $14-17, dinner $17-34; ⏲ 7am-4pm Tue & Wed, 7am-4pm & 5-9:30pm Mon, Thu & Fri, 8am-4pm & 5-9:30pm Sat & Sun; ☎) At this popular place on a cute street, local meat and vegetables drive the global diner menu: burgers, of course, plus portobello panini, fish tacos and duck tagine.

★ **North Fork Table & Inn** AMERICAN $$$
(☎ 631-765-0177; www.nofoti.com; 57225 Main Rd, Southold; mains $33-45, 5-course tasting menu $125; ⏲ 5:30-9pm Mon-Thu, to 9:30pm Fri, 5-9pm, 11:30am-2pm & Sat-Sun; ☎) A favorite foodies' escape, this four-room inn (rooms from $250) has an excellent farm-to-table restaurant, run by alums of the esteemed Manhattan restaurant Gramercy Tavern. Dinner is served nightly (along with weekend brunch), but if you're hankering for a gourmand-to-go lunch ($5.50 to $21), the inn's food truck is parked outside Friday to Monday from 11:30am to 3:30pm (daily July and August).

Getting There & Away

The Hampton Jitney (p125) bus picks up passengers on Manhattan's East Side on 96th, 83rd, 77th, 69th, 59th and 40th Sts, and makes stops in 10 North Fork villages (from $21). The Hampton Luxury Liner (p122) also runs to the North Fork. The ride from Manhattan to Greenport takes about 3½ hours.

If you're driving, take the Midtown Tunnel out of Manhattan, which will take you onto I-495/Long Island Expwy. Take this until it ends at Riverhead and follow signs onto Rte 25. You can stay on Rte 25 for all points east, but note that the North Rd (Rte 48) is faster as it does not go through the town centers.

The Long Island Rail Road's (p122) line is the Ronkonkoma Branch, with trips leaving from Penn Station and Brooklyn and running all the way out to Greenport.

To get from the North Fork to the South Fork (or vice versa), take the **North Ferry** (☎ 631-749-0139; www.northferry.com; NY 114 South, Greenport; one-way car/bike/foot $12/4/2) and the **South Ferry** (☎ 631-749-1200; www.southferry.com; 135 South Ferry Rd, Shelter Island; ⏲ one way car/bike/foot $15/4/2) services, crossing Shelter Island in between. There is no direct ferry – you must take one and then the other.

Hudson Valley

Winding roads along either side of the Hudson River take you by picturesque farms, Victorian cottages, apple orchards and old-money mansions built by New York's elite. Painters of the Hudson River School romanticized these landscapes, especially the region's famous fall foliage.

The eastern side of the river is more populated thanks to the commuter train line between NYC and Albany. Several magnificent homes can be found near Tarrytown and Sleepy Hollow. The formerly industrial town of Beacon has become an outpost of contemporary art, while the galleries and antique shops of historic Hudson attract a wealthier set of weekenders.

The Hudson's west bank is experiencing a boom thanks to its cheaper real estate. Head across the river to explore several state parks, West Point military academy, and New Paltz, which offers access to superb rock climbing in the Minnewaska State Park Preserve and Mohonk Preserve.

Getting There & Away

Metro-North Railroad (www.mta.info/mnr) runs as far north as Poughkeepsie (p130) from NYC's Grand Central; NJ Transit (www.njtransit.com) runs another line through New Jersey that gives access to Harriman. Amtrak (www.amtrak.com) also stops in Rhinecliff (for Rhinebeck), Poughkeepsie and Hudson. For New Paltz, Kingston and other destinations east of the Hudson, you'll need the bus; Trailways (www.trailwaysny.com) runs to these towns.

Lower Hudson Valley

Made famous by 19th-century author Washington Irving as the location of his headless horseman tale, *The Legend of Sleepy Hollow,* Sleepy Hollow and its larger neighbor, Tarrytown, are the jumping-off points for a trio of historic estates, as well as the gourmet and farm-activity destination of Stone Barn Center for Food & Agriculture.

The blue-collar town of Beacon, beside the Hudson River, has steadily evolved into a magnet for creatives, commuters and second-homers. It's backed by Mt Beacon, the tallest summit in the Hudson Valley and one of the more rewarding hikes in the region. While the town has embraced its status as a retreat for the hip, it still proudly displays its working-class roots and is all the more attractive for it.

Sights

★Dia:Beacon GALLERY

(845-440-0100; www.diaart.org; 3 Beekman St, Beacon; adult/child $15/free; 11am-6pm Thu-Mon Apr-Oct, to 4pm Thu-Mon Nov & Dec, to 4pm Fri-Mon Jan-Mar) The 300,000-sq-ft former Nabisco box printing factory beside the Hudson River is now a storehouse for a series of stunning monumental works by the likes of Richard Serra, Dan Flavin, Louise Bourgeois and Gerhard Richter. The permanent collection is complemented by temporary shows of large-scale sculptures and installations, making this a must-see for contemporary art fans.

Guided tours (free with admission) are offered here on weekends at 12:30pm and 2pm.

Boscobel House & Gardens HISTORIC BUILDING

(845-265-3638; www.boscobel.org; 1601 Rte 9D, Garrison; house & gardens adult/child $18/9, gardens only $12/6; guided tours 10am-4pm Wed-Mon mid-Apr–Oct, to 3pm Nov & Dec) The elegant backdrop for the summer season **Hudson Valley Shakespeare Festival** (845-265-9575; www.hvshakespeare.org; 1601 Rte 9D, Garrison; tickets $10-100; Jun-Sep), Boscobel dates from 1808 and is considered to be one of the finest examples of Federal-style architecture in the state. Entry to the house, which is 8 miles south of Beacon, is by guided tour (45 minutes), running regularly throughout the day.

Stone Barns Center for Food & Agriculture FARM

(914-366-6200; www.stonebarnscenter.org; 630 Bedford Rd, Pocantico Hills; 10am-4pm Wed-Sun) Stop by this massive, ecofriendly farm for a peek into the modern agriculture movement. On warm-weather weekends (April to November; adult/child $22/free) you'll find the place teeming with visitors partaking in activities such as egg collecting, lettuce planting and meeting a flock of sheep. Other tours and workshops are available Wednesday through Friday; check their calendar online. Book in advance as they tend to fill up quickly.

There's a good shop and a small takeout cafe. For a banquet meal, book ahead for the gourmet Blue Hill at Stone Barns also located here.

Washington Irving's Sunnyside HISTORIC BUILDING

(914-591-8763, Mon-Fri 914-631-8200; www.hudsonvalley.org; 3 W Sunnyside Lane, Tarrytown; adult/child $14/8; tours 10:30am-4pm Wed-Sun May–mid-Nov) Washington Irving, famous for tales such as *The Legend of Sleepy Hollow,* built this imaginative home, which he said had more nooks and crannies than a cocked hat. Tour guides in 19th-century costume tell good stories, and the wisteria Irving planted a century ago still climbs the walls. Tickets are $2 cheaper if bought online.

The closest train station to Sunnyside is Irvington, one stop before Tarrytown.

Sleeping & Eating

★Roundhouse BOUTIQUE HOTEL $$
(☎845-765-8369; www.roundhousebeacon.com; 2 E Main St; r from $230;) Occupying a former blacksmiths and hat factory spread out over both sides of the town's Fishkill Creek, Roundhouse is a model of Beacon's renaissance as a tourist destination. Elements of the buildings' industrial past blend seamlessly with contemporary comforts in the spacious rooms, which feature designer lighting, timber headboards and alpaca-wool blankets.

Homespun Foods CAFE $
(☎845-831-5096; www.homespunfoods.com; 232 Main St, Beacon; mains $10-15; ⊙8am-5pm Sun-Tue, to 8pm Wed-Sat;) A low-key gourmet legend in these parts, Homespun offers fresh everything, including creative salads, sandwiches and a veggie meatloaf made from nuts and cheese.

★Blue Hill at Stone Barns AMERICAN $$$
(☎914-366-9600; www.bluehillfarm.com; 630 Bedford Rd, Pocantico Hills; set menu $278; ⊙5-10pm Wed-Sat, 1-7:30pm Sun) Go maximum locavore at chef Dan Barber's farm (which also supplies his Manhattan restaurant). Settle in for an eye-popping multicourse feast based on the day's harvest (allow three hours), where the service is as theatrical as the presentation. Be sure to book at least a month in advance.

Be aware that the dress code here prefers jackets and ties for gentlemen; shorts not permitted.

Getting There & Away

Metro-North Railroad (www.mta.info/mnr) commuter trains connect NYC with Beacon (one-way off-peak/peak $24/29, 1½ hours).

Tarrytown Station (www.mta.info/mnr; 1 Depot Plaza, Tarrytown) has regular train connections with NYC (one-way off-peak/peak from $11.25/14.75, 40 to 50 minutes). Irvington, one stop before Tarrytown, is the closest station to Sunnyside, while Philipse Manor, one stop after, is walkable to Philipsburg Manor.

For the most flexibility in getting around the area, hire a car.

New Paltz

New Paltz, a short drive from the west bank of the Hudson, is a college town known for its charming 'village' downtown and hippie vibe. New Paltz is also home to a campus of the State University of New York, great dining and drinking opportunities, and is the gateway to Shawangunk Ridge (aka 'The Gunks'), beloved for its hiking and rock-climbing opportunities.

Sights & Activities

Historic Huguenot Street HISTORIC SITE
(☎845-255-1660; www.huguenotstreet.org; 86 Huguenot St; guided tours adult/child $12/free; ⊙10am-5pm Thu-Tue May-Oct, 10am-5pm Sat & Sun Nov–mid-Dec) Step back in time on a stroll around this picturesque enclave of buildings remaining from a Huguenot settlement dating back to 1678. Guided tours (which depart the visitor center every half-hour starting at 10:30am; the last one is at 3:30pm) relate the history of the various people who have inhabited this site over the centuries: the native Esopus Munsee people, Dutch settlers, Hugenot families who fled religious persecution in France, and enslaved African laborers.

As well as a visitor center, the 10-acre National Historic Landmark District includes seven historic stone houses, a replica Munsee wigwam, a reconstructed 1717 Huguenot church and a 17th-century burial ground.

Mohonk Preserve PARK
(☎845-255-0919; www.mohonkpreserve.org; 3197 Rte 55, Gardiner; day pass hikers/climbers & cyclists $15/20; ⊙visitor center 9am-5pm) Some 8000 acres of land held in private trust, with trails and other services maintained with visitor fees. This is home to some of the best rock climbing on the East Coast. The grounds are open from sunrise to one hour after sunset.

Rock & Snow ADVENTURE SPORTS
(☎845-255-1311; www.rockandsnow.com; 44 Main St; ⊙9am-6pm Mon-Thu, to 8pm Fri, 8am-8pm Sat, to 7pm Sun) This long-running outfitters rents tents, and rock-climbing, ice-climbing and other equipment. It can also team you up with guides for climbing and other outdoor adventures in the Gunks.

Sleeping & Eating

New Paltz Hostel HOSTEL $
(☎845-255-6676; www.newpaltzhostel.com; 145 Main St; dm/r from $40/60;) Aligned with New Paltz's hippie vibe, this hostel in a big old house next to the bus station is popular with visiting rock climbers and hikers. There's one mixed dorm room and several

private rooms (both with private and shared bathrooms), as well as a good communal kitchen.

A full-time home to some students, it has a strict no-drugs-or-alcohol policy, as well as a 10pm curfew for the dorms.

Mohonk Mountain House RESORT $$$
(☎855-436-0832; www.mohonk.com; 1000 Mountain Rest Rd; r from $710; ❄@🛜🏊) This giant faux 'Victorian castle' perches over a dark lake, offering guests all the luxuries, from lavish meals to golf to spa services, plus a full roster of outdoor excursions, including hiking and trail rides. Rates include all meals and most activities and you can choose from rooms in the main building, cottages or the luxury Grove Lodge.

★**Huckleberry** AMERICAN $$
(☎845-633-8443; www.huckleberrynewpaltz.com; 21 Church St; mains $14-18; ⏰noon-2am Mon-Thu, to 4am Fri & Sat, 10am-2am Sun; 🛜) This cute sea-green house set back from the road offers an appealing menu of gourmet items, including grass-fed-beef burgers, fish tacos and IPA mac 'n' cheese. There are also creative cocktails, craft beers and a lovely outdoor dining and drinking area in which to enjoy it all. The kitchen stays open to midnight most nights (to 1am Friday and Saturday).

Getting There & Away

Trailways (☎800-776-7548; www.trailwaysny.com; 139 Main St) bus services connect New Paltz with NYC ($23, 1½ hours) and Saugerties ($8, one hour).

Poughkeepsie

Six miles south of Hyde Park, where you'll find US President Franklin Roosevelt's family home, is Poughkeepsie (puh-*kip*-see), the largest town in the Hudson Valley. The city is home to the prestigious Vassar College, which was women-only until 1969, as well as an IBM office – once the 'Main Plant' where notable early computers were built.

The main attraction here is the chance to walk across the Hudson River on the world's longest pedestrian bridge, although Vassar's **Frances Lehman Loeb Art Center** (☎845-437-5237; www.fllac.vassar.edu; 124 Raymond Ave; ⏰10am-5pm Tue, Wed, Fri & Sat, to 9pm Thu, 1-5pm Sun) FREE, housed in a building designed by César Pelli, is also worth a visit. While you're here, stop in for a taste of the local distilleries and brew pubs – full details can be found at **Dutchess Tourism** (☎800-445-3131; www.dutchesstourism.com; 3 Neptune Rd, Poughkeepsie; ⏰9am-5pm Tue-Fri).

Sights

Franklin D Roosevelt Home HISTORIC BUILDING
(☎845-229-5320; www.nps.gov/hofr; 4097 Albany Post Rd; adult/child $20/free, museum or house only adult/child $10/free; ⏰tours every 30min 9am-4pm) Rangers lead interesting hourlong tours around Springwood, the home of Franklin D Roosevelt (FDR) who won a record four presidential elections and led America from the Great Depression through WWII. Considering his family wealth, it's a modest abode, but can be unpleasantly crowded in summer. Intimate details have been preserved, including his desk – left as it was the day before he died – and the hand-pulled elevator he used to hoist his polio-stricken body to the 2nd floor.

The home is part of a 1520-acre estate, formerly a working farm, which also includes the simple marble tomb where FDR and Eleanor (and their dog Fala) were interred, various walking trails and the **FDR Presidential Library & Museum** (☎845-486-7770; www.fdrlibrary.org; ⏰9am-6pm Apr-Oct, to 5pm Nov-Mar), which details important achievements in FDR's presidency. Admission tickets last two days and include the Springwood tour.

Walkway Over the Hudson VIEWPOINT, PARK
(☎845-834-2867; www.walkway.org; 61 Parker Ave, Poughkeepsie; ⏰7am-sunset) This is the main eastern entrance (with parking) to what was once a railroad bridge (built in 1889) crossing the Hudson. Today it's the world's longest pedestrian bridge – 1.28 miles – and a state park. The 212ft-high span provides breathtaking views along the river.

Sleeping & Eating

Roosevelt Inn MOTEL $
(☎845-229-2443; www.rooseveltinnofhydepark.com; 4360 Albany Post Rd; r $90-210; ⏰Mar-Dec; ❄🛜) Family owned and run since 1971, this roadside motel offers a great deal, especially for its pine-paneled 'rustic' rooms. The attention paid to the property by the owners – they make yearly improvements to the rooms – elevate the Roosevelt Inn above other motels in the area. Book one of the upper-level deluxe rooms for more space.

A continental breakfast is served at the on-site coffee shop, which can be used as a common space by guests.

Eveready Diner AMERICAN $
(☎845-229-8100; www.theevereadydiner.com; 4184 Albany Post Rd/Rte 9; mains $9-21.50; ⏲6am-midnight Sun-Thu, 24hr Fri & Sat) It's difficult to resist turning off the highway to visit this giant sparkling chrome diner. There's been a diner here since the 1950s, and even though this building is from 1995 it's a classic, with an authentic interior and extensive menu of slightly elevated diner fare to match.

Getting There & Away

Metro-North runs trains from NYC's Grand Central (from $19.25, 1¾ hours) to **Poughkeepsie Station** (☎800-872-7245; www.amtrak.com; 41 Main St).

Rhinebeck

Midway up the eastern side of the Hudson, Rhinebeck has a charming main street and an affluent air. In town you'll find a plethora of fine dining options and charming boutiques. Further afield is the holistic Omega Institute, as well as the super-liberal Bard College, 8 miles north, worth dropping by for its Frank Gehry–designed performing arts center.

Sights

Staatsburgh State Historic Site HISTORIC BUILDING
(☎845-889-8851; www.parks.ny.gov; Old Post Rd, Staatsburg; adult/child $8/free; ⏲tours 11am-4pm Thu-Sun mid-Apr–Oct, noon-3pm Thu-Sun late Nov–Dec) Take a tour around this beaux-arts mansion, the home of Ogden Mills and his wife Ruth. The Mills family made its fortune by investing in banks, railroads and mines during the Gilded Age; the house boasts 79 luxurious rooms filled with brocaded Flemish tapestries, gilded plasterwork, period paintings and Oriental art. Find it 6 miles south of Rhinebeck, just off Rte 9.

Old Rhinebeck Aerodrome MUSEUM
(☎845-752-3200; www.oldrhinebeck.org; 9 Norton Rd, Red Hook; museum adult/child $12/8, air shows adult/child $25/12, flights $100; ⏲10am-5pm May-Oct, air shows 2pm Sat & Sun) This museum, located a short drive north of the center of Rhinebeck, has vintage planes and other related vehicles and artifacts that date back to 1900. On weekends you can watch an air show or take a ride in an old biplane.

Sleeping & Eating

★**Olde Rhinebeck Inn** B&B $$$
(☎845-871-1745; www.rhinebeckinn.com; 340 Wurtemberg Rd; r $225-325; ❄📶) Built by German settlers between 1738 and 1745, this expertly restored oak-beamed inn oozes comfort and authenticity. It's run by a charming woman who has decorated the four cozy rooms beautifully and serves a lush breakfast made from local produce.

Bread Alone Bakery & Cafe BAKERY $
(☎845-876-3108; www.breadalone.com/rhinebeck; 45 E Market St; sandwiches $8-10.50; ⏲cafe 7am-5pm, dining room 8am-3pm Mon-Fri, 7am-4pm Sat & Sun; 📶🌿) Superior-quality baked goods, sandwiches and salads (including vegan options) are served up at the Rhinebeck location of this popular bakery and cafe. There's also a full-service dining room with the same menu. Those looking for small-town charm will probably find the uninspired chain restaurant decor lacking, though.

Entertainment

Fisher Center for the Performing Arts ARTS CENTER
(☎845-758-7900; www.fishercenter.bard.edu; Robbins Rd, Bard College, Annandale-on-Hudson; ⏲tours 10am-4:30pm Mon-Fri) Architecture buffs will want to drop by to view this Frank Gehry–designed building, whose spectacularly modern metal waves make for a great contrast to Bard College's Gothic buildings and manicured lawns. It contains two theaters and studio spaces and hosts a program of musical concerts, dance performances and theatrical events.

Getting There & Away

Amtrak runs trains to/from NYC (from $29, 1¾ hours). **Rhinecliff Station** (☎800-872-7245; 455 Rhinecliff Rd, Rhinecliff) is 3 miles west of the center of Rhinebeck. Local taxis wait at the station to ferry people up to town (about $10).

Catskills

This beautiful mountainous region west of the Hudson Valley has been a popular getaway since the 19th century. The romantic image of mossy gorges and rounded peaks, as popularized by Hudson Valley School painters, encouraged a preservation movement: in 1894 the state constitution was amended so that thousands of acres are 'forever kept as wild forest lands.'

In the early 20th century, the Catskills became synonymous with so-called 'borscht belt' hotels, summer escapes for middle-class NYC Jews. The vast majority of these hotels have closed, although orthodox Jewish communities still thrive in many towns – as does a back-to-the-land, hippie ethos on numerous small farms. In the fall, this is the closest place to NYC with really dramatic colors in the trees.

Getting There & Around

There is some bus service, the most useful being Trailways (www.trailwaysny.com) from NYC to Woodstock (from $30, 2½ to three hours) and Phoenicia (from $32, three hours). However, if you really want to tour the area, having a car is essential.

Phoenicia & Mt Tremper

This quirky pair of hamlets (just down the highway from one another) are the perfect jumping-off point to explore the Catskills. Phoenicia is the bigger of the two, while Mt Tremper boasts a few impressive hotels. Outdoor activities are easily arranged and include hiking, cycling, floating down the creek on an inner tube or swimming in mountain pools in summer and skiing at nearby **Belleayre Mountain** (845-254-5600; www.belleayre.com; 181 Galli Curci Rd, Highmount; 1-day lift pass weekday/weekend $56/68; 9am-4pm Dec-Mar) in winter.

Fall is the prime time to visit here and is also the best season for a jaunt in an open-air carriage on the Delaware & Ulster Railroad between nearby Arkville and Roxbury.

Sights & Activities

Empire State Railway Museum MUSEUM
(845-688-7501; www.esrm.com; 70 Lower High St, Phoenicia; donations accepted; 11am-4pm Sat & Sun Jun-Oct) FREE Maintained by enthusiasts since 1960, this small museum occupies an old railway station on the largely decommissioned Delaware & Ulster line.

Delaware & Ulster Railroad RAIL
(845-586-3877; www.durr.org; 43510 Rte 28, Arkville; adult/child $18/12; Sat & Sun May-Oct) It takes around 2½ hours to travel the 24 miles between Arkville and Roxbury in open-air carriages on this touristy rail journey; the views are at their best during fall.

Belleayre Beach SWIMMING
(845-254-5202; www.belleayre.com/summer/belleayre-beach; 33 Friendship Manor Rd, Pine Hill; per person/car $5/15; 10am-6pm Mon-Fri, to 7pm Sat & Sun mid-Jun–Aug) Near the base of Belleayre Mountain ski resort, this lake is a popular and refreshing swimming spot. Boats, kayaks and paddleboards can be rented, and there's also volleyball and basketball courts and a climbing wall.

Sleeping & Eating

★**Graham & Co** MOTEL $$
(845-688-7871; www.thegrahamandco.com; 80 Rte 214, Phoenicia; r $125-250;) There's a lot going for this hipster motel an easy walk from the center of town. Rooms are whitewashed and minimalist with the cheapest ones in a 'bunkhouse' where bathrooms are shared. Other pluses include a comfy den with a fireplace, a provisions store, an outdoor pool in summer, a wigwam and lawn games!

Foxfire Mountain House BOUTIQUE HOTEL $$
(845-688-2500; www.foxfiremountainhouse.com; 72 Andrew Lane, Mt Tremper; r from $200; P) Hidden in the forest, this chic hotel channels modern '70s rugged cool in its 11 individually decorated rooms (the cheapest of which share a bathroom) and one three-bedroom cottage. The cozy restaurant (offering dinner Friday to Sunday) and bar, open to nonguests, serves French-inspired cuisine such as *steak au poivre* (peppercorn steak) and *coq au cidre* (chicken cooked in cider).

★**Phoenicia Diner** AMERICAN $
(845-688-9957; www.phoeniciadiner.com; 5681 Rte 28, Phoenicia; mains $11-15; 7am-5pm late May–Sep, 7am-5pm Mon, Thu & Fri, to 8pm Sat & Sun Oct–mid-May;) New York hipsters and local families rub shoulders at this elevated roadside diner. The appealing menu offers all-day breakfast, skillets, sandwiches and burgers – all farm-fresh and fabulous.

Peekamoose AMERICAN $$$
(845-254-6500; www.peekamooserestaurant.com; 8373 Rte 28, Big Indian; mains $24-33; 4-10pm Thu-Mon, lounge to midnight Fri & Sat) One of the finest restaurant in the Catskills, this renovated farmhouse approximately 9 miles from Phoenicia has been promoting local farm-to-table dining for more than a decade. The menu changes daily, although the braised beef short ribs are a permanent fixture.

Getting There & Away

Trailways (www.trailwaysny.com) runs buses to Phoenicia from NYC (from $32, three hours). Mt Tremper is a short drive once you're there.

Tannersville

The small town of Tannersville, which primarily services the nearby ski resort of Hunter Mountain, also offers access to the gorgeous Kaaterskill Falls. There are superb hikes and drives in the area, as well as rustically charming hotels in which to stay and enjoy the beautiful mountain scenery. Tannersville itself sports a main street lined with brightly painted shops and houses.

Sights & Activities

Kaaterskill Falls WATERFALL

For the best view of New York State's highest falls – 260ft, compared to Niagara's 167ft – without a strenuous hike, head to the **viewing platform** (Laurel House Rd, Palenville). Popular paintings by the Hudson River Valley School of painters in the mid-1800s elevated this two-tier cascade to iconic status, making it a major draw for hikers, artists and nature lovers.

There's parking just above on Rte 23A; be sure to stick to the shoulder and keep your eyes on cars coming around the bend on your walk down to the trailhead.

Hunter Mountain SKIING

(518-263-4223; www.huntermtn.com; 64 Klein Ave, Hunter; day lift pass weekday/weekend $79/89; 9am-4pm Dec-Mar) Spectacular views from the 56 trails (including some challenging black runs that are a minefield of moguls) draw crowds of snowhounds to Hunter; avoid weekends and holidays if you don't relish lines at the lifts. Snowmaking ensures that skiing continues through the season, whatever the weather.

Zipline New York ADVENTURE SPORTS

(518-263-4388; www.ziplinenewyork.com; Hunter Mountain, Rte 23A; zipline tours $89-129; Mon-Sun Jun-Aug, Thu-Sun May, Sep & Oct, Fri-Sun Nov-Apr) Throughout the year Hunter Mountain is the location of this zipline course that's not for the faint hearted. The longest of the six ziplines is 650ft and 60ft above the ground. It's best to book in advance.

Sleeping & Eating

★**Scribner's Catskill Lodge** LODGE $$

(518-628-5130; www.scribnerslodge.com; 13 Scribner Hollow Rd; r $180-375; P) Run by a super-cool staff, this 1960s motor lodge has been given a stylish contemporary makeover. Snow-white painted rooms, some of which feature gas-fired stoves, contrast with the warm tones of the long library lounge with pool table and comfy nooks.

Deer Mountain Inn BOUTIQUE HOTEL $$$

(518-589-6268; www.deermountaininn.com; 790 Rte 25; r/cottages from $250/800; restaurant 5-10pm Thu-Sun, 11:30am-2:30pm Sun; P) There are only six rooms and two cottages (sleeping up to nine guests) at this gorgeous arts-and-crafts-style property hidden within a vast mountainside estate. It's all been interior designed to the max.

Last Chance Cheese Antiques Cafe AMERICAN $$

(518-589-6424; www.lastchanceonline.com; 6009 Main St; mains $11-27; 11am-8pm Jun-Aug & Dec-Mar, to 9pm Fri-Sun only Apr, May & Sep-Nov;) A fixture on Main St since 1970, this is part roadhouse with live bands, part candy store and cheese shop, and part restaurant, serving hearty meals. Many of the antiques and whatnots that decorate the place are for sale, too.

Getting There & Away

The drive along Rte 23A to and from Tannersville is one of the most scenic in the Catskills, but take it slowly as there are several hairpin bends. It's possible to reach Tannersville from NYC (from $37, three hours) by bus with Trailways (www.trailwaysny.com), but you'll have to change services in Kingston.

Woodstock

A minor technicality: the 1969 music festival was actually held in Bethel, an hour's drive west. Nonetheless, the town of Woodstock still attracts an arty, music-loving crowd and cultivates the free spirit of that era, with rainbow tie-dye style and local grassroots everything, from radio to a respected indie film festival and a farmers market (fittingly billed as a farm festival).

Sights

Center for Photography at Woodstock ARTS CENTER

(845-679-9957; www.cpw.org; 59 Tinker St; noon-5pm) FREE Founded in 1977, this creative space gives classes, hosts lectures and mounts exhibitions that expand the strict definition of the art form, thanks to a lively artist-in-residence program.

This was formerly the Café Espresso, and Bob Dylan once had a writing studio above it – that's where he typed up the liner notes for *Another Side of Bob Dylan* in 1964 – and Janis Joplin was a regular performer.

Karma Triyana Dharmachakra BUDDHIST MONASTERY
(☎845-679-5906; www.kagyu.org; 335 Meads Mountain Rd; ⏲8:30am-5:30pm) Join stressed-out New Yorkers and others needing a spiritual break at this blissful Buddhist monastery about 3 miles north from Woodstock. Soak up the serenity in the carefully tended grounds. Inside the shrine room is a giant golden Buddha statue; as long as you take off your shoes, you're welcome to sit down and meditate. Free guided tours are given at 12:45pm on Saturday and Sunday.

Sleeping & Eating

Woodstock Inn on the Millstream INN $$
(☎845-679-8211; www.woodstock-inn-ny.com; 48 Tannery Brook Rd; r/cottages from $170/375; ❄📶) Pleasantly decorated in quiet pastels, some of the rooms at this inn surrounded by serene, flower-filled grounds, come with kitchenettes, electric fireplaces and large tubs.

Village Green B&B B&B $$
(☎845-679-0313; www.villagegreenbb.com; 12 Tinker St; r $150; ❄📶) Overlooking Woodstock's 'village green,' this B&B occupies part of a three-story 1847 mansard-roof Victorian. The decor is a bit mumsy, but the rooms are comfortable and the owner is well liked by guests.

★**Garden Cafe** VEGAN $
(☎845-679-3600; www.thegardencafewoodstock.com; 6 Old Forge Rd; mains $9-22; ⏲11:30am-9pm Mon & Wed-Fri, 10am-9pm Sat & Sun; 📶✎) All the ingredients used at this relaxed, charming cafe are organic. The food served is appealing, tasty and fresh, and includes salads, sandwiches, rice bowls and veggie lasagna. It also serves freshly made juices, smoothies, organic wines, craft beers and coffee made with a variety of nondairy milks. In nice weather you can sit outside in their large garden.

Finger Lakes

In west-central New York, the rolling hills are cut through by 11 long narrow bodies of water appropriately named the Finger Lakes. The region is an outdoor paradise, as well as the state's premier wine-growing region, with more than 120 vineyards.

At the south of Cayuga Lake, Ithaca, home to Ivy League Cornell University, is the region's gateway. At the northern tip of Seneca Lake, Geneva is a pretty and lively town, thanks to the student population at Hobart and William Smith Colleges. Here the restored 1894 Smith Opera House is a vibrant center for performing arts.

To the west, Y-shaped Keuka Lake is edged by two small state parks that keep it relatively pristine; it's a favorite for trout fishing. Base yourself at sweet little Hammondsport, on the southwestern end. Arts and crafts lovers should also schedule a stop in Corning to see the brilliant glass museum there.

Getting There & Around

Ithaca is the region's major hub with several daily bus connections to NYC (from $36, five hours). Ithaca Tompkins Regional Airport (p136) has direct flights to Detroit, Newark and Philadelphia.

Ithaca

An idyllic home for college students and first-wave hippies, Ithaca, on the southern tip of Cayuga Lake, is the largest town around the Finger Lakes. With an art-house cinema, good eats and great hiking ('Ithaca is gorges' goes the slogan, for all the surrounding canyons and waterfalls), it's both a destination in itself and a convenient halfway point between NYC and Niagara Falls.

The center of Ithaca is a pedestrian street called the Commons. On a steep hill above is Ivy League Cornell University, founded in 1865, with a small business strip at the campus' front gates, called Collegetown. The drive from Ithaca up scenic Rte 89 (west side) or Rte 90 (east side) to Seneca Falls, at the northern end of Cayuga Lake, takes about an hour.

Sights

★**Herbert F Johnson Museum of Art** MUSEUM
(☎607-255-6464; www.museum.cornell.edu; 114 Central Ave; ⏲10am-5pm Tue-Sun year-round, to 7:30pm Thu Sep-May) FREE IM Pei's brutalist building looms like a giant concrete robot above the ornate neo-Gothic surrounds of Cornell University's campus. Inside you'll find an eclectic collection ranging from medieval wood carvings to modern masters and an extensive collection of Asian art.

WORTH A TRIP

SAUGERTIES

Around 10 miles northeast of Woodstock, the town of Saugerties (www.discoversaugerties.com) dates back to the Dutch settling here in the mid-17th century. Today it's well worth making a day trip to a couple of local attractions. **Opus 40 Sculpture Park & Museum** (845-246-3400; www.opus40.org; 50 Fite Rd; adult/child $10/3; 11am-5:30pm Thu-Sun May-Oct) is where artist Harvey Fite worked for nearly four decades to coax an abandoned quarry into an immense work of land art, all sinuous walls, canyons and pools. The picturesque 1869 **Saugerties Lighthouse** (845-247-0656; www.saugertieslighthouse.com; 168 Lighthouse Dr; tour suggested donation adult/child $5/3; trail dawn-dusk), on the point where Esopus Creek joins the Hudson, can be reached by a half-mile nature trail. Classic-rock lovers may also want to search out **Big Pink** (www.bigpinkbasement.com; Parnassus Lane, West Saugerties; house $580;), the house made famous by Bob Dylan and the Band, although note it's on a private road. It's possible to stay at both the lighthouse and Big Pink, but you'll need to book well ahead.

It's worth a visit if only for the panoramic views of Ithaca and Cayuga Lake from the top floor galleries.

Cornell Botanic Gardens GARDENS
(607-255-2400; www.cornellbotanicgardens.org; 124 Comstock Knoll Dr; 9am-5pm Sun-Thu, to 6pm Fri & Sat) FREE The verdant spaces in and around campus includes a 100-acre arboretum, a botanical garden and numerous trails. Stop at the Nevin Welcome Center for maps and to find out about tours.

A great way to reach the campus is by hiking up the dramatic **Cascadilla Gorge** (College Ave Bridge), which starts near the center of town.

Robert H Treman State Park STATE PARK
(607-273-3440; www.parks.ny.gov; 105 Enfield Falls Rd; per car mid-Apr–mid-Oct $8, mid-Oct–mid-Apr free) Five-and-a-half miles southwest of Ithaca, the biggest state park in the area offers extensive trails and a very popular **swimming hole** (late June to early September). Treman's gorge trail passes a stunning 12 waterfalls: don't miss Devil's Kitchen and Lucifer Falls, a multi-tiered wonder that spills Enfield Creek over rocks for about 100ft.

Sleeping

★**William Henry Miller Inn** B&B $$
(877-256-4553; www.millerinn.com; 303 N Aurora St; r $215-270;) Gracious and grand, and only a few steps from the Commons pedestrian street, this historic home offers luxurious rooms (two with whirlpool tubs and two in a separate carriage house), gourmet breakfast and a dessert buffet.

Firelight Camps TENTED CAMP $$$
(607-229-1644; www.firelightcamps.com; 1150 Danby Rd; tents $190-330; mid-May–Oct;) Glamping comes to Ithaca at this attractive site attached to the La Tourelle Hotel and with quick access to the trails of nearby Buttermilk Falls State Park. The safari-style canvas tents rise over hardwood platforms and comfy beds. The bathhouse is separate.

There's a campfire in the evenings and yoga on Saturday mornings.

Eating & Drinking

Ithaca Bakery CAFE $
(607-273-7110; www.ithacabakery.com; 400 N Meadow St; sandwiches $5-11; 6am-8pm Sun-Thu, to 9pm Fri & Sat;) An epic selection of pastries, smoothies, sandwiches and prepared food, serving Ithacans of every stripe. Ideal for picnic goods and for vegetarians and vegans.

★**Moosewood Restaurant** VEGETARIAN $$
(607-273-9610; www.moosewoodcooks.com; 215 N Cayuga St; mains $17-28; 11:30am-8:30pm Sun-Thu, to 9pm Fri & Sat;) Established in 1973, this near-legendary veggie restaurant is run by a collective. It has a slightly upscale feel, with a full bar and global menu. It is very popular so reservations are recommended, especially during Cornell events.

Sacred Root Kava Lounge & Tea Bar TEAHOUSE
(607-272-5282; www.sacredrootkava.com; 103 S Geneva St; 3pm-midnight) Pretty much as alternative as it gets for Ithaca is this chilled basement space serving the Polynesian non-alcoholic, psychoactive beverage kava. If

that's not your bag, then there's a nice range of teas. Check online for events.

The entrance is on S Geneva St, beneath the Cornell Daily Sun building.

Getting There & Away

Ithaca Tompkins Regional Airport (ITH; ☎607-257-0456; www.flyithaca.com; 1 Culligan Dr) receives flights from Delta and United.

Greyhound (www.greyhound.com) and Shortline buses from NYC (one-way $38, five hours, daily) pull into **Ithaca Bus Station** (710 W State St).

Seneca Falls

The quiet, postindustrial town of Seneca Falls is said to have inspired visiting director Frank Capra to create Bedford Falls, the fictional small American town in his classic movie *It's a Wonderful Life*. Indeed, you can stand on a bridge crossing the town's river and just picture Jimmy Stewart doing the same. The town also has a special place in history as the location of the first American women's rights convention, where the fight for female suffrage was launched.

Sights

Women's Rights National Historical Park MUSEUM
(☎315-568-0024; www.nps.gov/wori; 136 Fall St; ⏲9am-5pm Mar-Nov, 9am-5pm Wed-Sun Dec-Feb) FREE Visit the chapel where Elizabeth Cady Stanton and friends declared in 1848 that 'all men and women are created equal,' the first step towards women's suffrage. The adjacent museum tells the story, including the complicated relationship with abolition.

National Women's Hall of Fame MUSEUM
(☎315-568-8060; www.womenofthehall.org; 76 Fall St; adult/child $5/free; ⏲10am-4pm Mar-Oct, 10am-4pm Wed-Sun Nov-Feb) The tiny National Women's Hall of Fame honors inspiring American women. Learn about some of the 256 inductees, including first lady Abigail Adams, American Red Cross founder Clara Barton and civil-rights activist Rosa Parks.

WORTH A TRIP

AURORA

Around 28 miles north of Ithaca on the eastern side of Cayuga Lake is the picturesque village of Aurora. Established in 1795, the village has over 50 buildings on the National Register of Historic Places, including parts of the campus of Wells College, founded in 1868 for the higher education of women (it's now co-ed). The **Inns of Aurora** (☎315-364-8888; www.innsofaurora.com; 391 Main St; r $200-400; P ❄ 📶), which is composed of four grand properties – the Aurora Inn (1833), EB Morgan House (1858), Rowland House (1903) and Wallcourt Hall (1909) – is a wonderful place to stay. Alternatively, stop by the Aurora Inn's lovely dining room for a meal with lakeside views and pick up a copy of the self-guided walking tour of the village.

Sleeping & Eating

Gould Hotel BOUTIQUE HOTEL $$
(☎877-788-4010; www.thegouldhotel.com; 108 Fall St; r $210-600; ❄ 📶) Originally a 1920s-era hotel, the downtown building has undergone a stylish renovation with a nod to the past – the mahogany bar comes from an old Seneca Falls saloon. The standard rooms are small, but the decor, in metallic purple and gray, is quite flash. The hotel's upscale restaurant and tavern serves local food, wine and beer.

Mac's Drive In BURGERS $
(☎315-539-3064; www.macsdrivein.net; 1166 US-20/Rte 5, Waterloo; mains $4-8; ⏲10:30am-10pm Tue-Sun Jun-Aug, Fri-Sun only Apr & May) Midway between Seneca Falls and Geneva, this classic drive-in restaurant established in 1961 (and little changed since) serves up burgers, fried chicken and fish dinners at bargain prices.

Getting There & Away

The best way to get to Seneca Falls is by car.

The Adirondacks

The Adirondack Mountains (www.visitadirondacks.com) may not compare in drama and height with mountains in the western US, but they more than make up for it in area: the range covers 9375 sq miles, from the center of New York just north of the state capital Albany, up to the Canadian border. And with 46 peaks over 4000ft high, the Adirondacks provide some of the most wild-feeling terrain in the east. Like the Catskills to the south, much of the Adirondacks' dense forest and lake lands are protected by the state constitution, and it's a fabulous location to see the color show of autumn leaves. Hiking, canoeing and backcountry camping are the most popular activities, and there's good fishing, along with powerboating on the bigger lakes.

Getting There & Around

The area's main airport is in Albany, although **Adirondack Regional Airport** (518-891-4600; www.adirondackairport.com; 96 Airport Rd) in Saranac Lake has connections via Cape Air (www.capeair.com) to Boston.

Both Greyhound (www.greyhound.com) and Trailways (www.trailwaysny.com) buses serve Albany and various towns in the Adirondacks, though a car is essential for exploring widely.

Amtrak runs from NYC to Albany (from $45, 2½ hours) and on to Ticonderoga ($70, five hours) and Westport ($70, six hours), both on Lake Champlain, with a bus connection to Lake Placid ($90.50, 9½ hours).

Albany

Built between 1965 and 1976, the architectural ensemble of government buildings in Albany's central Empire State Plaza is a sight to behold and includes the excellent New York State Museum, as well as a fine collection of modern public art. In downtown and leafy Washington Park, stately buildings and gracious brownstones speak to the state capital's wealthy past.

Albany became state capital in 1797 because of its geographic centrality to local colonies and its strategic importance in the fur trade. These days it's as much synonymous with legislative dysfunction as with political power. Its struggling economy is reflected in the number of derelict and abandoned buildings (the ones with white cross signs on a red background). Even so, the locals' friendliness and the city's usefulness as a gateway to the Adirondacks and Hudson Valley make it worth more than a casual look.

Sights

★Empire State Plaza — PUBLIC ART

(518-473-7521; www.empirestateplaza.org) FREE While the plaza's ensemble of architecture surrounding a central pool is hugely impressive, it's the splendid collection of modern American art liberally sprinkled outside, inside and underground the complex that is the true highlight here. The collection includes sculptures and massive paintings by Mark Rothko, Jackson Pollock, Alexander Calder and many other star artists.

★New York State Museum — MUSEUM

(518-474-5877; www.nysm.nysed.gov; 222 Madison Ave; 9:30am-5pm Tue-Sun) FREE There are exhibits on everything from New York's original Native Amerian residents, the state's history of activism, its architectural and engineering marvels and more in this top-class museum. A large chunk is dedicated to the history and development of New York City. The section on 9/11, including a damaged fire truck and debris from the site, is very moving. Don't miss a ride on the gorgeous antique carousel on the 4th floor.

New York State Capitol — HISTORIC BUILDING

(518-474-2418; www.hallofgovernors.ny.gov; Washington Ave; guided tours 10am, noon, 2pm & 3pm Mon-Fri, 11am & 1pm Sat) FREE Completed in 1899, this grand building is the heart of the state government. The interior features detailed stone carving, carpentry, and tile and mosaic work, with highlights being the Great Western Staircase, the Governor's Reception Room and the HH Richardson–designed Senate Chamber. Saturday tours require online reservations.

Sleeping & Eating

Washington Park Inn — BOUTIQUE HOTEL $

(518-225-4567; www.washingtonparkinn.com; 643 Madison Ave; r $130-140; P ❄ @ ☎) Rocking chairs on the covered porch and tennis rackets for guests to use on the courts in the park across the road set the relaxed tone for this appealing hotel in one of Albany's heritage buildings. Big rooms have simple and clean decoration, and food and drink is available on a serve-yourself basis around the clock from the well-stocked kitchen.

Cafe Madison — BREAKFAST $

(518-935-1094; www.cafemadisonalbany.com; 1108 Madison Ave; mains $8-14; 7:30am-2pm Mon-Thu, to 3pm Fri-Sun;) Highly popular breakfast spot, especially on the weekend, when 30-minute waits for one of the cozy booths or tables is not uncommon (you might have more luck sitting at the bar). The staff know all the regulars and the menu here includes inventive omelets, crepes, vegan options and a wide variety of specialty cocktails, such as cajun Bloody Marys.

Getting There & Away

As state capital, Albany has the full range of transport connections. **Albany International Airport** (☎518-242-2200; www.albanyairport.com; Albany Shaker Rd, Colonie) is 10 miles north of downtown.

The Amtrak **Albany-Rensselaer Station** (☎800-872 7245; www.amtrak.com; 525 East St, Rensselaer), on the east bank of the Hudson River, has connections with NYC (from $45, 2½ hours), upstate New York and beyond. Greyhound and Trailways bus services use the centrally located **bus terminal** (☎518-427-7060; 34 Hamilton St).

Lake George

Lake George covers 45 square miles of the Adirondacks and attracts thousands of visitors to its shores every summer for swimming, boating, and just sitting and staring at its shimmering waters in admiration. The town of Lake George is a major tourist center with arcades, fireworks every Thursday in July and August, and paddleboat rides. It's a chaotic good time for those looking to dive headfirst into summer-by-the-lake culture. Anyone looking for a more mellow experience will find many nearby towns that offer a less hectic atmosphere, such as upscale Bolton Landing, cozy Glens Falls and bucolic Warrensburg.

In the winter, Lake George freezes over and most of the towns surrounding it go into hibernation. Other than skiing up in North Creek you won't find many winter activities and most restaurants and hotels stay closed until early summer.

Sights & Activities

Fort William Henry Museum MUSEUM
(☎518-668-5471; www.fwhmuseum.com; 48 Canada St, Lake George; adult/child $19.50/8, ghost tours $18/8; ⏲9:30am-6pm May-Oct; 👪) Guides dressed as 18th-century British soldiers muster visitors along, with stops for battle reenactments that include firing period muskets and cannons, at this replica of the 1755 wooden fort. Check online for details of the evening ghost tours.

Hyde Collection Art Museum MUSEUM
(☎518-792-1761; www.hydecollection.org; 161 Warren St, Glens Falls; adult/child $12/free; ⏲10am-5pm Tue-Sat, noon-5pm Sun, plus 10am-5pm Mon mid-Jul–Aug) This remarkable gathering of art was amassed by local newspaper heiress Charlotte Pryun Hyde. In her rambling Florentine renaissance mansion in Glens Falls, you'll stumble across Rembrandts, Rubens, Matisses and Eakins, as well as tapestries, sculptures and turn-of-the-century furnishings.

Lake George Steamboat Cruises CRUISE
(☎518-668-5777; www.lakegeorgesteamboat.com; 57 Beach Rd, Lake George; adult/child from $17/8; ⏲May-Oct) This company has been running cruise boats on Lake George since 1917. In season take your pick from a variety of cruise options on its three vessels: the authentic steamboat *Minne Ha Ha,* the 1907-vintage *Mohican* and the flagship *Lac du Saint Sacrement.*

Sleeping & Eating

Cornerstone Victorian B&B $$
(☎518-623-3308; www.cornerstonevictorian.com; 3921 Main St, Warrensburg; r $120-200; P❄📶) There are many Victorian-themed B&Bs in New York state, but few offer a gourmet, five-course breakfast each morning. The menu changes daily and alone is worth the price of a stay, although you'll also find that the rooms are comfortable and the hospitality of the hosts, Doug and Louise, extends well beyond the breakfast table.

Morgan & Co AMERICAN $$$
(☎518-409-8060; www.morganrestaurant.com; 65 Ridge St, Glens Falls; mains $20-38; ⏲4-10pm Tue & Wed, to 11pm Thu-Sat, 10am-8pm Sun) Morgan & Co is the offspring of husband and wife Steve Butters and Rebecca Newell-Butters (who is a *Chopped* winner) and specializes in modern American cuisine with more than a few hints of international flair. Many of the dishes have a twist – swordfish Milanese, beef brisket lasagne – but the real draw here is that everything is exquisitely prepared.

The three-course prix-fixe dinner ($44) is a great deal.

Getting There & Away

Albany International Airport is 50 miles south of Lake George. Amtrak stops in Fort Edwards, about 20 minutes by car from Lake George. Greyhound and Trailways also have long-distance buses to the region. A rental car is the best way of getting around the lake area.

Lake Placid

The resort town of Lake Placid is synonymous with snow sports – it hosted the Winter Olympics in 1932 and 1980. Elite athletes

GREAT CAMPS

Far from big fields of canvas tents, the Adirondacks' 'great camps' were typically lake and mountainside compounds of grandiose log cabins built in the latter half of the 19th century, as rustic retreats for the very wealthy. A prime example is **Great Camp Sagamore** (Sagamore Institute; ☎315-354-5311; www.greatcampsagamore.org; Sagamore Rd, Raquette Lake; tours adult/student $18/10; ⏲hours vary May–mid-Oct), a former Vanderbilt vacation estate on the western side of the Adirondacks, which is now open to the public for tours, workshops and overnight stays on occasional history-oriented weekends.

Less ostentatious is **White Pine Camp** (☎518-327-3030; www.whitepinecamp.com; 432 White Pine Rd, Paul Smiths; r/cabin from $165/315; 📶), 12 miles northwest of Saranac Lake. This collection of rustically cozy cabins is set amid pine forests, wetlands and scenic Osgood Pond – a boardwalk leads out to an island on which sits a Japanese-style teahouse and an antique all-wood bowling alley. The fact that President Calvin Coolidge spent a few summer months here in 1926 is an interesting historical footnote, but the camp's charm comes through in its modest luxuries such as claw-foot tubs and wood-burning fireplaces. Naturalist walking tours are open to nonguests on select days from mid-June to September.

continue to train here; the rest of us can ride real bobsleds, speed-skate and more. Mirror Lake, which is right downtown, freezes thick enough for ice-skating, tobogganing and dogsledding. The town is also pleasant in summer, as the unofficial center of the High Peaks region of the Adirondacks and a great base for striking out on a hike or going canoeing or kayaking on one of the area's many lakes.

Sights & Activities

A major draw at Lake Placid is the opportunity to play like an Olympian (or just watch athletes train). Most activities are managed by **Whiteface Mountain** (☎518-946-2223; www.whiteface.com; 5021 Rte 86, Wilmington; full-day lift ticket adult/child from $68/44, gondola only $24/18; ⏲8:30am-4pm Dec-Apr), the ski area where the Olympic ski races were held, but located in other spots around the area. Among other activities, you can do a half-mile on the bobsled track ($75) or a modified biathlon (cross-country skiing and shooting; $55). Lake Placid Speed Skating (www.lakeplacidspeedskating.wildapricot.org) organizes speed-skating rental and tutorials ($25) at the Olympic Center. Many sports are modified for summer – bobsledding on wheels, for instance.

The **Olympic Sites Passport** ($35), available at all Whiteface-managed venues, can be a good deal, covering admission at sites (such as the tower at the ski-jump complex and the gondola ride at Whiteface Mountain) and offering discounts on some activities.

Olympic Center STADIUM

(☎518-523-3330; www.whiteface.com; 2634 Main St; tours $10, adult/child skating $10/8; ⏲10am-5pm daily, skating shows 4:30pm Fri; 👪) This is the location of the 1980 'Miracle on Ice,' when the upstart US hockey team trumped the unstoppable Soviets. In winter you can skate on the outside oval rink and year-round take a one-hour tour of the stadium. There are usually free figure-skating shows on Friday, with an additional ticketed show Saturday at 7:30pm in July and August (adult/child $11/9).

There is also a small **museum** (☎518-523-3330; www.lpom.org; 2634 Main St; adult/child $8/6; ⏲10am-5pm) here.

Whiteface Veteran's Memorial Highway SCENIC DRIVE

(www.whiteface.com; Rte 431; driver & vehicle $16, additional passengers $9; ⏲8:45am-5:30pm late May–mid-Oct) Whiteface, the state's 5th highest peak at 4867ft, is the only summit in the Adirondacks accessible by car, with a neat castle-style lookout and cafe at the top. It can be socked in with clouds, making for an unnerving drive up, but when the fog clears, the 360-degree view is awe-inspiring. Tolls are paid at Lake Steven.

Sleeping & Eating

★**Adirondack Loj** LODGE $

(☎518-523-3441; www.adk.org; 1002 Adirondack Loj Rd; dm/r from $60/170, lean-tos winter/summer from $25/45; P📶) The Adirondack Mountain Club runs this rustic retreat on the shore of pretty Heart Lake. All rooms in the lodge share communal bathrooms. Rates for rooms in the lodge include breakfast, and

WORTH A TRIP

SARANAC LAKE

Saranac Lake is not as tourist-oriented as its neighbor Lake Placid and gives a better idea of regular Adirondacks life. The town, built up in the early 20th century as a retreat for tuberculosis patients, has a lively old-fashioned main street leading towards the titular lake. Many other stretches of water pepper the surrounding forested hills, making this another great base for hiking, kayaking and canoeing.

since it's 8 miles south of Lake Placid, you'll want to arrange a trail lunch and dinner here, too.

Lake Placid Lodge HERITAGE HOTEL **$$$**
(☎518-523-2700; www.lakeplacidlodge.com; 144 Lodge Way; r $600-1600; ⊙May-Mar; P ⊖ ❄ @ ☎) Overlooking Lake Placid and channeling the rustic glamor of classic Gilded Age Adirondack lodges, this luxury hotel offers 13 gorgeously decorated rooms and cabins. The cabins are 19th-century originals, but the main hotel is a remarkable reconstruction following a devastating 2008 fire.

Liquids & Solids at the Handlebar AMERICAN **$$**
(☎518-837-5012; www.liquidsandsolids.com; 6115 Sentinel Rd; mains $15-24; ⊙4-9pm Tue-Sat, 5-9pm Sun) It's all about craft beers, creative cocktails and fresh, inventive dishes at this rustic bar and restaurant where the kielbasa sausages and other charcuterie are made in-house. Mains may include dishes such as cauliflower stroganoff or crispy confit pork.

ℹ Getting There & Away

Trailways buses serve Lake Placid. Amtrak runs once a day to Westport, with a bus connection to Lake Placid ($90.50, 9½ hours).

Adirondack Regional Airport (p137), 17 miles northwest near Saranac Lake, has connections via Cape Air (www.capeair.com) to Boston.

Thousand Islands

To downstate New Yorkers, this region is the source of the Thousand Islands salad dressing made of ketchup, mayonnaise and relish. In fact, it's a scenic wonderland along Lake Ontario and the St Lawrence River speckled with 1864 islands of all shapes and sizes either side of the US–Canada maritime border. The area was a Gilded Age playground for the rich; now it's more populist. Pros: beautiful sunsets, good-value lodging and Canada across the water. Cons: dead in winter and large mosquitoes in summer (bring repellent).

The historic port of Oswego is the region's southern gateway and makes a good base for exploring places like Sackets Harbor, where reenactors stage an annual War of 1812 Weekend. On the northern side, Clayton and Alexandria Bay both offer boat tours to the islands in the St Lawrence River, or you could camp amid glorious nature in the Wellesley Island State Park.

ℹ Getting There & Around

The main airport for the region is **Syracuse Hancock International Airport** (☎315-454-4330; www.syrairport.org; 1000 Colonel Eileen Collins Blvd, Syracuse); connections here include NYC on JetBlue and Delta; Newark, Washington, DC, and Chicago on United; and Toronto on Air Canada. Cars can be rented at the airport or in downtown Syracuse, which is connected to other parts of the state by bus and train.

Alexandria Bay

Summer on the western shores of the Lawrence River, which separate New York state from Canada, sees thousands flock to the smattering of small waterfront towns that cater to all kinds of fun in the water. Alexandria Bay (A-Bay or Alex Bay), Clayton and Cape Vincent are the best places to hunker down to experience some of the sunny frivolity. They are all a bit rundown and tacky, but fun, nonetheless, and if you need a break you can always explore the region's wineries and distilleries, or some of the many islands from which the region gets its name. There is incredible nature and unique sights like a castle to discover. Be aware, though, that in winter things more or less close down.

⊙ Sights & Activities

★**Boldt Castle** CASTLE
(☎800-847-5263; www.boldtcastle.com; Heart Island; adult/child $10/7; ⊙10am-6:30pm May, Jun & Sep, to 7:30pm Jul & Aug, 11am-5pm Oct) This Gothic gem, a replica of a German castle, was (partly) built by tycoon hotelier George C Boldt in the late 19th century. In 1904, however, midway through construction, Boldt's wife died suddenly, and the project was abandoned. Since 1977 the Thousand

Islands Bridge Authority has spent millions restoring the place to something of its planned grandeur.

Singer Castle CASTLE
(☎877-327-5475; www.singercastle.com; Dark Island; adult/child $14.50/7.50; ⌚10am-4pm mid-May–mid-Oct) This stone castle, on Dark Island in the middle of the St Lawrence River, was built in 1905 by American entrepreneur Frederick Bourne. It's full of secret passages and hidden doors and has a dungeon – all of which you'll see on a tour. Uncle Sam runs boats from Alex Bay; **Schermerhorn Harbor** (☎315-324-5966; www.schermerhornharbor.com; 71 Schermerhorn Landing, Hammond; shuttle to Singer Castle $31.25; ⌚10:30am-2:30pm late May-Aug) also visits.

Uncle Sam Boat Tour BOATING
(☎315-482-2611; www.usboattours.com; 45 James St, Alexandria Bay; adult/child $23/11.75) The main offering from the largest boat-tour operator in the area is a two-hour ride that visits both the US and Canada sides of the river (no passport required) and stops at Boldt Castle. Trips to Singer Castle, too.

Sleeping & Eating

Bonnie Castle RESORT $$
(☎800-955-4511; www.bonniecastle.com; 31 Holland St, Alexandria Bay; r/apt from $160/242;) This somewhat run-down resort, one of Alex Bay's largest and open year-round, offers a variety of rooms, some with nice views across the St Lawrence River towards Boldt Castle.

Dockside Pub AMERICAN $
(☎315-482-9849; www.thedocksidepub.com; 17 Market St, Alexandria Bay; mains $8-18; ⌚11am-midnight Mon-Thu, to 2am Fri & Sat, noon-midnight Sun;) Unpretentious pub fare – burgers, fries, pizza and some specials. Despite the name its location is inland, with no dock view.

Getting There & Away

The region is best reached by car.

Western New York

Tourism in this region revolves around Buffalo, New York State's second-largest city. After being the largest and most prosperous metropolis along the Great Lakes at the turn of the 19th century, Buffalo fell on hard times in the 20th, but is bouncing back in the 21st. Its amazing stock of heritage architecture is being restored and reinvented into hotels, museums and other businesses.

The area first developed thanks to the hydroelectric power of Niagara Falls and the Erie Canal, which linked the Great Lakes to the Atlantic Ocean. The falls are now better known as a tourist destination, with millions of visitors flocking here annually.

Rochester, about an hour northeast, shares a similar economic trajectory but has long been buoyed by its rich history of activism. The city was home to the famed suffragette Susan B Anthony and civil rights pioneer Frederick Douglass, among other 19th- and 20th-century iconoclasts.

Getting There & Around

Buffalo Niagara International Airport (p143) is a regional hub with the widest range of flights, but you can also fly into and out of Niagara Falls International Airport (p145) and the **Greater Rochester International Airport** (☎585-753-7000; www2.monroecounty.gov; 1200 Brooks Ave). Amtrak runs trains to Buffalo, Rochester and Niagra, with connections to and from NYC, Albany, Toronto, and from Buffalo to/from Chicago. Greyhound (www.greyhound.com) has bus services to all three locations. For other places in the region you are best getting there by rental car.

Buffalo

The winters may be long and cold, but Buffalo stays warm with a vibrant creative community and strong local pride. Settled by the French in 1758, the city is believed to derive its name from *beau fleuve* (beautiful river). With power from nearby Niagara Falls, it boomed in the early 1900s; Pierce-Arrow cars were made here, and it was the first American city to have electric streetlights. One of its nicknames – Queen City – was because it was the largest city along the Great Lakes.

Those rosy economic times are long over, leaving many abandoned buildings in their wake. But revival is in Buffalo's air. Masterpieces of late 19th- and early-20th-century architecture, including designs by Frank Lloyd Wright and HH Richardson, have been magnificently restored. There's a park system laid out by Frederick Law Olmsted, of NYC's Central Park fame, great museums, and a positive vibe that's impossible to ignore.

Sights & Activities

★Buffalo City Hall ARCHITECTURE
(716-852-3300; www.preservationbuffaloniagara.org; 65 Niagara Sq; tours noon Mon-Fri) FREE This 32-story art deco masterpiece, opened in 1931 and beautifully detailed inside and out, towers over downtown.

It's worth joining the free tour at noon that includes access to the mayor's office, the council chamber and the open-air observation deck.

★Martin House Complex ARCHITECTURE
(716-856-3858; www.darwinmartinhouse.org; 125 Jewett Pkwy; tour basic/extended $22/45; tours hourly 10am-3pm Wed-Mon) This 15,000-sq-ft house, completed in 1905, was designed by Frank Lloyd Wright for his friend and patron Darwin D Martin. Representing Wright's Prairie House ideal, it consists of six interconnected buildings, each meticulously restored inside and out.

Two tour options (book these online) offer different levels of detail on this elaborate project.

★Albright-Knox Art Gallery MUSEUM
(716-882-8700; www.albrightknox.org; 1285 Elmwood Ave; adult/child $16/9; 10am-5pm Tue-Sun) The gallery's superb collection, which ranges from Degas and Picasso to Ruscha, Rauschenberg and other abstract expressionists, occupies a neoclassical building planned for Buffalo's 1905 Pan American Expo.

Its temporary exhibits are particularly creative and compelling.

Graycliff Estate ARCHITECTURE
(716-947-9217; www.graycliffestate.org; 6472 Old Lake Shore Rd, Derby; 1/2hr tours $19/35) Occupying a dramatic clifftop location on Lake Erie, 16 miles south of downtown Buffalo, this 1920s vacation home was designed by Frank Lloyd Wright for the wealthy Martin family; a lengthy interior restoration was completed in 2018. You can learn a lot about Wright's overall plan on interesting tours (book in advance).

Guaranty Building ARCHITECTURE
(Prudential Building; www.hodgsonruss.com/Louis-Sullivans-Guaranty-Building.html; 140 Pearl St; interpretive center 7:15am-9pm) FREE Completed in 1896 for the Guaranty Construction company, this gorgeous piece of architecture has a facade covered in detailed terra-cotta tiles and a superb stained-glass ceiling in its lobby.

The interpretative center provides details of how groundbreaking this Adler & Sullivan–designed building was when it was built, when it was the tallest building in Buffalo.

Explore Buffalo TOURS
(716-245-3032; www.explorebuffalo.org; 1 Symphony Circle) Architectural and history tours around the Buffalo area by bus, on foot and by bicycle and kayak.

Sleeping

Hostel Buffalo Niagara HOSTEL $
(716-852-5222; www.hostelbuffalo.com; 667 Main St; dm/r $31/85;) Conveniently located in Buffalo's downtown Theater District, this hostel occupies three floors of a former school, with a basement rec room, plenty of kitchen and lounge space, a small art gallery, and spotless if institutional bathrooms.

Services include laundry facilities, free bikes and lots of info on local music, food and arts happenings.

★InnBuffalo off Elmwood GUESTHOUSE $$
(716-867-7777; www.innbuffalo.com; 619 Lafayette Ave; ste $200-350;) Ellen and Joe Lettieri have done a splendid job restoring this 1898 mansion, originally built for local brass and rubber magnate HH Hewitt. The owners are happy to share how much of the building's original grandeur was uncovered in their restorations, which is evident in the nine superbly decorated suites, some with original features such as Victorian needle-spray showers.

Hotel Henry HERITAGE HOTEL $$
(716-882-1970; www.hotelhenry.com; cnr Rockwell Rd & Cleveland Circle; r $165-277;) Occupying a grand late-19th-century 'lunatic asylum,' Hotel Henry preserves much of the stately architecture of Henry Richardson's original building. Its 88 rooms, reached off super-broad corridors, have tall ceilings and contemporary decor.

Eating

★Cole's AMERICAN $
(716-886-1449; www.colesonelmwood.com; 1104 Elmwood Ave; mains $12-15; 11am-10pm Mon-Thu, to 11pm Fri & Sat, to 9pm Sun;) Since 1934 this atmospheric restaurant and bar has been dishing up local favorites such as

beef on weck (roast beef on a caraway-seed roll) – try it with a side of spicy Buffalo chicken wings, or go for one of the juicy burgers. It's handy for lunch if you are visiting the Delaware Park area and its museums.

The spacious bar, decorated with all kinds of vintage stuff, offers scores of beers on tap.

Betty's AMERICAN $$
(☎716-362-0633; www.bettysbuffalo.com; 370 Virginia St; mains $13-26; ⏲8am-9pm Tue-Fri, 9am-9pm Sat, to 2pm Sun;) On a quiet Allentown corner, bohemian Betty's does flavorful, fresh interpretations of American comfort food such as meatloaf. Brunch is deservedly popular and there's a pleasant bar.

Plenty of vegetarian and vegan, as well as gluten- and dairy-free, options are on the menu.

Black Sheep INTERNATIONAL $$
(☎716-884-1100; www.blacksheepbuffalo.com; 367 Connecticut St; mains $17-30; ⏲5-10pm Wed-Sat, 11am-2pm Sun) Black Sheep likes to describe its style of western New York farm-to-table cuisine as 'global nomad,' which means you might find exciting, unique takes on chimichangas, pierogies and vegetable lasagna on the menu. You can also eat at the bar, which serves creative cocktails and local craft ales.

Drinking & Entertainment

★Resurgence Brewing Company MICROBREWERY
(☎716-381-9868; www.resurgencebrewing.com; 1250 Niagara St; ⏲4-10pm Tue-Thu, to 11:30pm Fri, noon-11:30pm Sat, to 5pm Sun) Housed in a former engine factory that was later to became the city's dog pound, Resurgence typifies Buffalo's skill at adaptive reuse of its infrastructure.

The beers here ($8 for a tasting flight) are excellent, with some 20 different ales on tap from fruity sweet Loganberry Wit to a porter with an amazing peanut-butter flavor.

Kleinhans Music Hall CLASSICAL MUSIC
(☎716-885-5000; www.kleinhansbuffalo.org; 3 Symphony Circle) This fine concert hall, home to the Buffalo Philharmonic Orchestra, has wonderful acoustics. The building is a National Historic Landmark and was partly designed by the famous Finnish father-and-son architecture team of Eliel and Eero Saarinen.

Getting There & Away

Buffalo Niagara International Airport (BUF; ☎716-630-6000; www.buffaloairport.com; 4200 Genesee St), about 10 miles east of downtown, is a regional hub. JetBlue Airways offers affordable round-trip fares from NYC.

NFTA (www.nfta.com), the local transit service, runs express bus 204 to the **Buffalo Metropolitan Transportation Center** (☎716-855-7300; www.nfta.com; 181 Ellicott St) downtown; Greyhound buses also pull in here. NFTA local bus 40 goes to the American side of Niagara Falls ($2, one hour); express bus 60 also goes to the area, but requires a transfer.

From Amtrak's downtown **Exchange Street Station** (☎716-856-2075; www.amtrak.com; 75 Exchange St), you can catch trains to NYC (from $67, 8½ hours), Niagara Falls (from $14, one hour), Albany (from $53, five hours) and Toronto (from $47, 4½ hours). All services also stop at **Buffalo-Depew Station** (55 Dick Rd), 8 miles east, where you can board trains to Chicago (from $61, 10½ hours).

Niagara Falls

It's a tale of two cities: Niagara Falls, New York (USA), and Niagara Falls, Ontario (Canada). Both overlook a natural wonder – 150,000 gallons of water per second, plunging more than 1000ft – and both provide a load of tourist kitsch around it. The Canadian side offers somewhat better views and a much larger town. However, the view from the New York side is still impressive and the falls surroundings are far more pleasant as they are preserved within a beautifully landscaped state park.

The town itself is also largely devoid of the commercial razzmatazz you'll find on the Canadian side; if that's what you want, it's easy to walk across the Rainbow Bridge between the two – just be sure to bring your passport.

Sights & Activities

★Cave of the Winds VIEWPOINT
(☎716-278-1730; www.niagarafallsstatepark.com; Goat Island Rd; adult/child $19/16; ⏲from 9am May-Oct, closing times vary) On the northern corner of Goat Island, don a souvenir rain poncho and sandals (provided) and take an elevator down to walkways just 25ft from the crashing water at the base of Bridal Veil Falls. (Despite the name, the platforms run in front of the falls, not into a cave.)

Old Fort Niagara MUSEUM
(☎716-745-7611; www.oldfortniagara.org; Youngstown; adult/child $13/9; ⊙9am-7pm Jul & Aug, to 5pm Sep-Jun) This 1726 French-built fortress, restored in the 1930s, defends the once very strategic point where the Niagara River flows into Lake Ontario. It has engaging displays of Native American artifacts, small weapons, furniture and clothing, as well as breathtaking views from its windblown ramparts. In summer months there are tours and demonstrations by costumed guides of what life was like here in the past. Surrounding the fort are hiking trails in Fort Niagara State Park.

Whirlpool State Park PARK
(☎716-284-4691; www.parks.ny.gov; Robert Moses State Pkwy) This park, 3 miles north of the falls, sits just above a sharp bend in the Niagara River – a bend that creates a giant whirlpool easily visible from your vantage point. Steps take you 300ft to the gorge below and mind you don't tumble into the vortex.

Rainbow Bridge BRIDGE
(www.niagarafallsbridges.com; ⊙cars/pedestrians/cyclists US$3.75/1/1) Bring your passport for the walk or drive across this bridge linking the US and Canadian sides of the falls – there are good views along the way.

★**Maid of the Mist** BOATING
(☎716-284-8897; www.maidofthemist.com; 1 Prospect St; adult/child $19.25/11.20; ⊙hours vary) The traditional way to see Niagara Falls is on this boat cruise, which has ferried visitors into the rapids right below the falls since 1846. Make sure you wear the blue poncho they give you, as the torrential spray from the falls will soak you.

Sleeping & Eating

Seneca Niagara Resort & Casino RESORT $$$
(☎877-873-6322; www.senecaniagaracasino.com; 310 4th St; r $255-405; P ⊖ ❄ @ ≈ ≋) With some 600 spacious rooms and suites, and a lively casino, this purple-and-glass-covered tower is the American town's answer to the tourist glitz across on the Canadian side of the falls. A variety of music and comedy shows are staged here, too, headlined by relatively big names.

Giacomo BOUTIQUE HOTEL $$$
(☎716-299-0200; www.thegiacomo.com; 222 1st St; r from $247; P ❄ @ ≈) A rare bit of style among the bland chain hotels and motels of Niagara, the luxe Giacomo occupies part of a gorgeous art-deco office tower, with spacious, ornately decorated rooms. Even if you're not staying here, grab a drink at the lobby bar (open from 5pm) and take it up to the 19th-floor lounge for spectacular views.

Third Street Retreat Eatery & Pub AMERICAN $
(☎716-371-0760; www.thirdstreetretreat.com; 250 Rainbow Blvd; mains $8-13; ⊙9am-3pm Wed-Sat, hours vary) The walls are decorated with old LP covers at this popular local spot serving all-day breakfasts and other comforting pub-grub dishes. There's a good selection of beers on tap or in bottles, plus a pool table and darts in an upstairs section.

DON'T MISS

NIAGARA FALLS, CANADA

The Canadian side of the falls is naturally blessed with superior views. **Horseshoe Falls**, on the western half of the river, are wider than Bridal Veil Falls on the eastern, American side, and they're especially photogenic from Queen Victoria Park. The **Journey Behind the Falls** (☎905-354-1551; www.niagaraparks.com; 6650 Niagara Pkwy; adult/child $22/14; ⊙9am-10pm, hours vary by season) gives access to a spray-soaked viewing area – similar to Cave of the Winds.

The Canadian town is also livelier, in an over-the-top touristy way. Chain hotels and restaurants dominate, but there is an HI hostel, and some older motels have the classic honeymooners' heart-shaped tubs. For more local info, visit the **Niagara Falls Tourism office** (☎905-356-6061; www.niagarafallstourism.com; 6815 Stanley Ave; ⊙9am-5pm Mon-Fri), near the base of the Skylon Tower observation deck.

Crossing the Rainbow Bridge and returning costs US$3.75/1 per car/pedestrian. Walking takes about 10 minutes; car traffic can grind to a standstill in summer or if there's a major event on in Toronto. US citizens and overseas visitors must show a passport or an enhanced driver's license at immigration at either end. Driving a rental car from the US over the border should not be a problem, but check with your rental company.

Getting There & Away

NFTA (www.nfta.com) bus 40 connects downtown Buffalo and Niagara Falls ($2, one hour); the stop in Niagara Falls is at 1st St and Rainbow Blvd. Express bus 60 goes to a terminal east of the town center; you'll have to transfer to bus 55 to reach the river. The **Amtrak train station** (☎716-285-4224; www.amtrak.com; 825 Depot Ave) is about 2 miles north of downtown; the station on the Canadian side is more central, but coming from NYC, you have to wait for Canadian customs. From Niagara Falls, daily trains go to Buffalo ($14, 50 minutes), Toronto (from $36, three hours) and NYC (from $67, nine hours). **Greyhound** (www.greyhound.com; 240 1st St) buses stop at the Quality Inn.

Flights from Florida and South Carolina are offered by Allegiant Air and Spirit Airlines to **Niagara Falls International Airport** (☎716-297-4494; www.niagarafallsairport.com; 2035 Niagara Falls Blvd).

NEW JERSEY

Everything you've seen on TV, from the McMansions of *Real Housewives of New Jersey* to the thick accents of *The Sopranos,* is at least partially true. But Jersey (natives lose the 'New') is at least as well defined by its high-tech and banking headquarters, and a quarter of it is lush farmland (hence the Garden State nickname) and pine forests. And on the 127 miles of beautiful beaches, you'll find, yes, the guidos and guidettes of *Jersey Shore,* but also many other oceanfront towns, each with a distinct character.

Stay east and you'll experience the Jersey (sub)urban jungle. Go west to find its opposite: the peaceful, refreshing landscape of the Delaware Water Gap.

Getting There & Around

Though many NJ folks love their cars, there are other transportation options.

PATH (www.panynj.gov/path) train services connect lower Manhattan to Hoboken, Jersey City and Newark. **NJ Transit** (www.njtransit.com) operates buses and trains around the state, including bus service to NYC's Port Authority and downtown Philadelphia, and trains to Penn Station, NYC. Train service has declined severely in the past decade – fair warning.

New York Waterway (www.nywaterway.com) ferries run up the Hudson River, and from the NJ Transit train station in Hoboken to the World Financial Center in Lower Manhattan.

Hoboken

The Square Mile City is among the trendiest of zip codes, with real-estate prices to match. On weekends the bars come alive, and loads of restaurants line Washington St. If you can step over the designer dogs, and navigate the mega-strollers, trolling black Uber cars with NY plates, and lines for Carlo the Cake Boss, it's a good walking town with amazing views of NYC. Get here before the chain stores do.

Sights

Hoboken Historical Museum MUSEUM
(Map p64; ☎201-656-2240; www.hobokenmuseum.org; 1301 Hudson St; adult/child $5/free; ⏰2-7pm Tue-Thu, 1-5pm Fri, noon-5pm Sat & Sun) This small museum conveys a sense of Hoboken that's hard to imagine today – a city of blue-collar Irish and Italian Catholic immigrants, toiling in the shipyards and docks. It also offers self-guided walking tours of Frank Sinatra's Hoboken haunts, and *On the Waterfront* film locales.

Eating

La Isla CUBAN $
(☎201-659-8197; www.laislarestaurant.com; 104 Washington St; breakfast $8-17, sandwiches $8-16, mains $16-28; ⏰7am-10pm Mon-Sat, 10am-9pm Sun) The most authentic Cuban choice in town since 1970, the Formica counters ring with plates spilling over with grilled Cuban sandwiches, *maduros* (fried plantains) and rice with pigeon peas – all to the soundtrack of staccato Spanish chatter and salsa, under the watchful eye of Celia Cruz portraits.

Forget the fancier 'uptown' branch – this is the real thing.

Amanda's GASTRONOMY $$
(☎201-798-0101; www.amandasrestaurant.com; 908 Washington St; mains $17-31; ⏰dinner 5-10pm Mon-Thu, to 11pm Fri & Sat, to 9pm Sun, brunch 11am-3pm Sat & Sun) For three decades the Flynn family has served first-rate fare in these conjoined, converted brownstones, each room with a different theme. An extensive wine list and monthly wine evenings make this a classy option.

The early dinner special here is great value.

Getting There & Away

NY Waterway (www.nywaterway.com) ferries run between 39th St on Manhattan's West Side and Hoboken ($9, eight minutes). There is frequent, if crowded, NJ PATH train service from lower Manhattan to Hoboken terminal. Parking is atrocious – don't even think about driving here.

Princeton

Settled by an English Quaker missionary, this tiny town is filled with lovely architecture and several noteworthy sites, number one of which is its Ivy League university. Princeton is more upper-crust than collegiate, with preppie boutiques edging central Palmer Sq. Just over a mile from campus and town, however, you can escape to the idyllic Institute Woods, a 600-acre forested retreat.

Like any good seat of learning, Princeton has a bookstore, record store, brew pub and indie cinema, all within blocks of the rabbit's warren of streets and alleys that crisscross Palmer Sq, as well as innumerable sweet shops, cafes and ice-cream specialty stores.

Sights

★Institute Woods FOREST
(www.ias.edu; 1 Einstein Dr; dawn-dusk) Walk 1½ miles down Mercer St to a bucolic slice of countryside seemingly completely removed from the jammed-up campus-area thoroughfares. Nearly 600 acres have been set aside here, and birders, joggers and dog-walkers luxuriate on the soft, loamy pathways.

It's an avian paradise here during the spring warbler migration.

Princeton University UNIVERSITY
(609-258-3000; www.princeton.edu) Built in the mid-1700s, this institution soon became one of the largest structures in the early colonies. Now it's in the top-tier Ivy League. You can stroll around on your own, or take a student-led tour.

Morven Museum & Garden MUSEUM
(609-924-8144; www.morven.org; 55 Stockton St; adult/child $10/8; 10am-4pm Wed-Sun) Stop by for fine displays of decorative arts and fully furnished period rooms; other galleries change their exhibitions periodically. The gardens, and the house itself – a perfectly coiffed colonial revival mansion originally built by Richard Stockton, a prominent lawyer in the mid-18th century and signer of the Declaration of Independence – are worth a visit in and of themselves.

Sleeping & Eating

Inn at Glencairn B&B $$
(609-497-1737; www.innatglencairn.com; 3301 Lawrenceville Rd/Rte 206; r from $220;) The best value in the Princeton area: five serene rooms in a renovated Georgian manor, a 10-minute drive from campus. The property is visited by flocks of goldfinches (the state bird) and also, legend has it, by the unquiet spirit of a British soldier from the Revolutionary War era: listen for Lord Ralston's footsteps at night.

★Mistral MEDITERRANEAN $$
(609-688-8808; www.mistralprinceton.com; 66 Witherspoon St; sharing plates $12-18, mains $17-32; 5-9pm Mon, to 9:30pm Tue, 11:30am-3pm & 5-9:30pm Wed & Thu, 11:30am-3pm & 5-10:30pm Fri & Sat, 10:30am-3pm & 4-9pm Sun) Princeton's most creative restaurant offers plates that are made to share, with flavors ranging from the Caribbean to Scandinavia.

Sit at the chef's counter for a bird's-eye view of the controlled chaos in the open-plan kitchen.

Mediterra Restaurant & Taverna MEDITERRANEAN $$$
(609-252-9680; www.mediterrarestaurant.com; 29 Hulfish St; mains $22-36; 11:30am-10pm Mon-Thu, to 11pm Fri & Sat, 11am-9pm Sun) Centrally located in Palmer Sq, Mediterra is the sort of upscale, contemporary place designed for a college town. Visiting parents, flush students and locals all crave the dishes here, which highlight locally sourced and organic ingredients, and reflect the owners' Chilean and Italian heritage. The fish and small plates are particularly good.

The daily happy hour (4pm to 6:30pm) features half-price tapas and, sometimes, live music.

Getting There & Away

Coach USA (www.coachusa.com) express buses 100 and 600 run frequently between Manhattan and Princeton ($15.70, 1½ hours). NJ Transit (www.njtransit.com) trains run frequently from New York Penn Station to Princeton Junction train station ($16, one to 1½ hours). The 'Dinky' shuttle will then run you to Princeton campus ($3, five minutes).

WORTH A TRIP

DELAWARE WATER GAP

With one foot in Pennsylvania and the other in New Jersey, the place where the Delaware River makes a tight S-curve through the ridge of the Kittatinny Mountains was, in the days before air-conditioning, a popular resort destination. In the modern era it remains an area of surpassing dramatic beauty, a slice of rugged wilderness within a day's trip of the largest urban conurbations on the North American Eastern Seaboard. The current preserved areas dates to 1965, when the **Delaware Water Gap National Recreation Area** (☎570-426-2452; www.nps.gov/dewa; 1978 River Rd, Bushkill) was established, covering land in both NJ and Pennsylvania.

Note that entrance to most of the park is free, but for some areas there is a $10 amenities fee for cars and a $2 fee for bicycles.

The Delaware Water Gap is about 70 miles west of New York City, accessible by I-80, or 100 miles north of Philadelphia via I-476. A car is by far the easiest way out here.

It's about a two-hour bus ride from NYC to the area. Coach USA (www.coachusa.com) provides bus service from the Port Authority to Milford, PA ($25.75), running seven times a day on weekdays, and at 10am, 2:30pm and 5:35pm daily.

Martz Trailways (www.martztrailways.com) runs from NYC Port Authority to Stroudsburg, PA ($39, 1½ hours, more than 12 daily).

Jersey Shore

Perhaps the most famous and revered feature of New Jersey is its sparkling shore – and heading 'down the shore' (local parlance – never 'to the beach') is an essential summer ritual. Stretching from Sandy Hook to Cape May, the coastline is dotted with resort towns both tacky and tony. It's mobbed on summer weekends (traffic is especially bad on the bridges to the barrier islands), and finding good-value accommodations is nearly as difficult as locating untattooed skin; campgrounds can be low-cost alternatives. By early fall, however, you could find yourself blissfully alone on the sand.

Getting There & Around

Sitting in bumper-to-bumper traffic on the Garden State Pkwy may turn you lobster red, so driving early in the day to summer destinations is a must.

NJ Transit (www.njtransit.com) runs special Shore Express trains (twice daily June to September), stopping in Asbury Park, Bradley Beach, Belmar, Spring Lake, Manasquan, Point Pleasant Beach and Bay Head. You can buy a beach tag along with your train ticket, and there are two northbound express trains returning in the evening.

NJ Transit buses from New York's Port Authority service Seaside Heights/Seaside Park, Island Beach State Park, Atlantic City, Wildwood and Cape May.

Greyhound (www.greyhound.com) runs special buses to Atlantic City.

Asbury Park & Ocean Grove

During decades of economic stagnation, the town of Asbury Park had nothing more to its name than the fact that state troubadour Bruce Springsteen got his start at the Stone Pony nightclub here in the mid-1970s. But since 2000, blocks of previously abandoned Victorian homes have seen such a revival that Asbury is sometimes called 'Brooklyn on the Beach.' Thousands more units are projected over the next few years, and a 17-story luxury condo complex called the Asbury Ocean Club now looms over the boardwalk, with one floor comprising a 54-room boutique hotel.

The downtown area, several blocks of Cookman and Bangs Aves, has antiques shops, hip restaurants (from vegan to French bistro) and an art-house cinema. Thirty-nine bars and counting lure trains full of young NY-based revelers to the convenient NJ transit depot, like moths to the vodka.

Immediately south of Asbury Park, Ocean Grove is a kind of time and culture warp. 'God's Square Mile at the Jersey Shore,' as it's known, was founded by Methodists in the 19th century as a revival camp, and it's still a dry town (no liquor) and the beach is closed on Sunday mornings. The Victorian architecture is so covered in gingerbread trim that you may want to eat it.

At the center, around a 6500-seat wooden auditorium with a huge pipe organ, the former revival camp is now Tent City

– a historic site with more than a hundred quaint canvas tents used as summer homes.

Sights & Activities

Historic Village at Allaire MUSEUM

(☎732-919-3500; www.allairevillage.org; 4263 Atlantic Ave, Farmingdale; parking Sat & Sun May-Sep $5; ⏱village 11am-4pm Wed-Sun Jun-Aug, Sat & Sun only Apr, May & Sep-Nov, shorter hours Dec-Mar) FREE Just a 15-minute-drive from the 21st century and Asbury Park, this quirky museum is what remains of what was once a thriving 19th-century village called Howell Works, which produced bog iron for James Allaire's New York City steam engine works. Visit shops and historic gardens, all run by folks in period costume, and bake your own bread at the 1835 bakery (11am to 4pm Wednesday to Friday, to 5pm Saturday and Sunday in summer).

Sleeping

Quaker Inn INN $$

(☎732-775-7525; www.quakerinn.com; 39 Main Ave; tw $97-155, d $123-177, f $172-214; ❄📶) A great old creaky Victorian with 28 rooms, some of which open onto wraparound porches or balconies. There's a nice common area and library to linger over your coffee, and the managers, Liz and Mark, reflect the town's charm and hospitality. Light sleepers take note: the walls are a bit thin.

★**Asbury Hotel** BOUTIQUE HOTEL $$$

(☎732-774-7100; www.theasburyhotel.com; 210 5th Ave; d $185-425; P❄📶🏊) Wow. From the performance space and lobby stocked with LP records, old books and a solarium to the rooftop bar, this hotel oozes style. Two blocks from Convention Hall and the boardwalk, you could stay inside all day, playing pool or lounging by the heated one. Weeknights are a better deal.

On the flip side: you'll get charged for coffee in a paper cup. Not cool. But it does have an ice-skating rink in winter: very cool.

Eating & Drinking

Moonstruck ITALIAN $$$

(☎732-988-0123; www.moonstrucknj.com; 517 Lake Ave; mains $28-44; ⏱5-10pm Wed-Fri, to 11pm Sat, 4:30-10pm Sun mid-Jun–Aug, shorter hours Sep–mid-Jun) With views of Wesley Lake dividing Asbury and Ocean Grove and an extensive martini menu, it's hard to find fault here. The menu is eclectic, though it leans towards Italian with a good selection of pastas; the meat and fish dishes have varied ethnic influences.

Asbury Festhalle & Biergarten BEER GARDEN

(☎732-997-8767; www.asburybiergarten.com; 527 Lake Ave; ⏱4pm-1am Mon-Fri, noon-1am Sat & Sun) Deutschland by the Sea: quaff from 38 draft ales on the rooftop beer garden or check out live music in a space as big as two barns, with classic long beer-hall tables. Snack on pretzels bigger than your face, fill up on plates of wurst (mains $15 to $28) or tipple some of the different schnapps on offer.

Entertainment

Stone Pony LIVE MUSIC

(☎732-502-0600; www.stoneponyonline.com; 913 Ocean Ave; ⏱box office noon-5pm Wed-Mon & during shows) Best known as the bar where Bruce Springsteen launched his career, the Pony has continued to be a respectable rock venue – a genuine, sweaty, feet-stick-to-the-floor club – and hosts a big outdoor festival at the beginning of summer.

Silverball Museum Arcade ARCADE

(Pinball Hall of Fame; ☎732-774-4994; www.silverballmuseum.com; 1000 Ocean Ave; per hour/half-day/day $12.50/15/25; ⏱11am-9pm Mon-Thu, to 1am Fri, 10am-1am Sat, 10am-10pm Sun) Dozens of pinball machines in mint condition, from mechanical 1950s games to modern classics such as Addams Family. Play all you like, for a single price.

Getting There & Away

NJ Transit's Asbury Park Station is at the intersection of Cookman and Main Sts and is about 45 minutes from NYC. Some late-night trains run during the summer.

Driving along the S Main St (Rte 71) from the north or south, you'll see the impressive gates that mark the entranceway to Ocean Grove's Main Ave. If you're taking the NJ Transit's Shore Express, disembark at neighboring Asbury Park and walk or taxi over to Ocean Grove. Academy buses from New York's Port Authority (www.academybus.com) go directly to Ocean Grove ($19, 1¾ hours).

Barnegat Peninsula

Locals call this 22-mile stretch 'the barrier island,' though it's technically a peninsula, connected to the mainland at **Point Pleasant Beach**. Surfers should seek out **Inlet Beach** in Manasquan, immediately north (not on the peninsula), for the Shore's most reliable year-round waves.

South of **Mantoloking** and **Lavallette**, midway down the island, a bridge from the mainland (at Toms River) deposits the hordes in **Seaside Heights**, location of the MTV reality show *Jersey Shore,* and epitome of the deliciously tacky Shore culture. It's still a sticky pleasure to lick a Kohr's orange-vanilla twist cone and stroll through the boardwalk's raucous, deeply tanned, scantily clad crowds, refueling at an above-average number of bars. Look out for the 1910 Dentzel-Looff carousel, and the 310ft Ferris wheel and German-built roller coaster added in 2017.

For a bit of quiet, escape south to residential **Seaside Park** and the wilderness of Island Beach State Park beyond.

Sights

Island Beach State Park PARK
(☎732-793-0506; www.islandbeachnj.org; Seaside Park; per car weekday/weekend Jun-Aug $12/20, Sep-May $10; ⏰8am-8pm Mon-Fri, 7am-8pm Sat & Sun Jun-Aug, 8am-dusk Sep-May) This beautiful tidal island offers fishing, wildlife (from foxes to ospreys and other shorebirds), more than 40 trees and shrubs, including pepperbush and prickly pear cactus, and a killer view of Barnegat Lighthouse, seemingly only an arm's length across the water. Of the 10 miles of relatively untouched beach, one is open for swimming; the rest makes a nice bike ride. On the bay side, the lush tidal marshes are good for kayaking.

Casino Pier AMUSEMENT PARK
(☎732-793-6488; www.casinopiernj.com; 800 Ocean Tce, Seaside Heights; rides $4-30, water park adult/child $35/29; ⏰noon-late Jun-Aug, hours vary Sep-May) The amusement pier at the northern end of the Seaside boardwalk has a few kiddie rides and more extreme thrills for the 48in-and-taller set, plus a chairlift that runs above the boardwalk. Nearby is Breakwater Beach, a water park with tall slides; hours can vary but it generally opens at 9:30am in July and August.

Sleeping & Eating

Luna-Mar Motel MOTEL $$
(☎732-793-7955; www.lunamarmotel.com; 1201 N Ocean Ave, Seaside Park; r from $160; ❄📶🏊) Directly across the road from the beach, this tidy motel has tile floors (no sandy carpets) and a heated pool. Rates include beach badges.

BEACH FEES

Many communities on the Jersey Shore charge $7 to $15 for access, issuing a badge (also called a tag) for the day. From Long Beach Island north to near Sandy Hook, all beaches have a fee; the southern Shore is mostly, but not entirely, free. If you're staying a few days, it's worthwhile investing in a weekly badge, although some hotels provide them.

Klee's PUB FOOD $$
(☎732-830-1996; www.kleesbarandgrill.com; 101 Boulevard, Seaside Heights; pizza from $8, mains $13-28; ⏰11am-10pm Sun-Thu, to 11pm Fri & Sat) Around for 40 years, this solid sports bar (with 12 screens) plates up big servings of sandwiches, burgers and other pub grub. Klee's is famous for its pizza, and its best recommendation is that it comes at family prices on Monday.

Getting There & Away

NJ Transit has a special Shore Express train (no transfer required) to Shore towns between Asbury Park and Bay Head; in the summer months it includes a beach pass. It also offers direct bus service to Seaside Heights from New York's Port Authority (bus 137; $27, 1½ hours) and Newark's Penn Station (bus 67; $17, one hour) from the end of June to Labor Day.

Atlantic City

Atlantic City (AC) may be the largest city on the Shore, but the vision of 'Vegas on the East Coast' has foundered and casinos have gone bankrupt. But the hotels can be a bargain and the lovely beach is free and often empty because most visitors are indoors playing the slots. And in contrast with many homogeneous beach enclaves, the population here is more diverse.

As for the Prohibition-era glamour depicted in the HBO series *Boardwalk Empire,* there's little trace – though you can still ride along the boardwalk on a nifty wicker rolling chair. As you do, consider that the first boardwalk was built here, and if Baltic Ave rings a bell, it's because the game Monopoly uses AC's street names. A later contribution: the Miss America pageant, though it's now held in Vegas; the Miss'd America drag pageant fills the gap.

OFF THE BEATEN TRACK

SANDY HOOK

The northernmost tip of the Jersey Shore is the **Sandy Hook Gateway National Recreation Area** (☎718-354-4606; www.nps.gov/gate; 128 S Hartshorne Dr, Highlands; parking late May-Aug $15; ⊙5am-9pm Apr-Oct) FREE, a 7-mile barrier island at the entrance to New York Harbor. From your beach blanket, you can see the NYC skyline. The wide beaches, including NJ's only legal nude beach (Gunnison), are edged by a system of bike trails, while the bay side is great for fishing, kayaking and bird-watching.

Historic Fort Hancock and the nation's oldest operational **lighthouse** (☎732-872-5970; www.nps.gov/gate; 85 Mercer Rd, Highlands; ⊙visitor center 9am-5pm, tours half-hourly 1-4:30pm) FREE give a glimpse of Sandy Hook's prior importance as a military and navigational site.

Sights

Steel Pier AMUSEMENT PARK
(☎866-386-6659; www.steelpier.com; 1000 Boardwalk; ⊙1pm-midnight Mon-Fri, noon-1am Sat & Sun mid-Jun–Aug, shorter hours May–mid-Jun, Sep & Oct) The Steel Pier, directly in front of the Taj Mahal casino, was the site of the famous high-diving horses that plunged into the Atlantic before crowds of spectators from the 1920s to the '70s. Today it's a collection of amusement rides, games of chance, candy stands and a go-kart track.

Ripley's Believe it or Not! MUSEUM
(Odditorium; ☎609-347-2001; www.ripleys.com/atlanticcity; 1441 Boardwalk; adult/child $19/12; ⊙11am-8pm Mon-Fri, 10am-9pm Sat, to 8pm Sun) Robert Ripley spent a lifetime collecting bizarre stuff, and a lot of it's here. Two-headed goat fetuses, a baling-wire Jimi Hendrix head, the world's smallest car and a roulette wheel made of 14,000 jellybeans – you'll have fun for about the cost of a movie.

Historic Pipe Organ THEATRE
(Boardwalk Hall; www.boardwalkorgans.org; 2301 Boardwalk; ⊙organ recital 12:30pm Wed May-Jul, plus 12:30pm Tue Jun-Sep, tours 10am Wed May-Jul) FREE A nonprofit institute runs tours, recitals and silent films to maintain the Boardwalk Hall's two historic – and impressive – pipe organs: the 'sonic Mount Rushmore.' The 2½-hour Curator's Tour (suggestion donation $10) relates the history of both instruments and the hall itself.

Sleeping & Eating

Tropicana Casino & Resort HOTEL $
(☎609-340-4000; www.tropicana.net; 2831 Boardwalk; r from $70; P ❄ ☎ ≋) The Trop is a sprawling city-within-a-city, including a casino, the Boogie Nights disco, a spa and high-end restaurants. We recommend the newer 'Havana' wing; try to get up above the 40th floor for spectacular views. Weekday rates can be incredibly cheap.

★ **Kelsey & Kim's Café** SOUTHERN US $$
(Kelsey's Soul Food; ☎609-350-6800; www.kelseysac.com; 201 Melrose Ave; mains $14-20; ⊙8am-9pm Mon-Thu, to 10pm Fri-Sun) In the pretty residential Uptown area, this friendly cafe does excellent Southern comfort food, from morning grits and waffles to fried whiting and barbecue brisket. BYOB makes it a deal.

Getting There & Away

The small **Atlantic City International Airport** (ACY; ☎609-573-4700; www.acairport.com; 101 Atlantic City International Airport, Egg Harbor Township) is a 20-minute drive from the town center. If you happen to be coming from Florida (where most of the flights come from), it's a great option for South Jersey or Philadelphia.

The only train service is NJ Transit from Philadelphia (one way $10.75, 1½ hours), arriving at the **train station** (☎973-491-9400; www.njtransit.com; 1 Atlantic City Expwy) next to the convention center. AC's **bus station** (☎609-345-5403; 1901 Atlantic Ave) receives NJ Transit and Greyhound services from NYC ($39, 2½ hours) and Philadelphia ($18, 1½ hours). A casino will often refund much of the fare (in chips, coins or coupons) if you get a bus, such as Greyhound's Lucky Streak service, directly to its door. When leaving AC, buses first stop at various casinos and only stop at the bus station if not already full.

Wildwood

Wildwood, and its neighboring towns of North Wildwood and Wildwood Crest, is a virtual outdoor museum of 1950s motel architecture and neon signs. The community has a relaxed atmosphere, somewhere between clean-cut fun and wild party. The beach is the widest in NJ (a proposal to ferry beach-goers across the sands on camel was once floated but voted down) and there's no admission fee. Along the 2-mile boardwalk, several massive piers have roller coasters and rides best suited to aspiring astronauts.

Sights

Doo Wop Experience MUSEUM
(☎609-523-1958; www.doowopusa.org; 4500 Ocean Ave; ⏰10am-5pm Mon, to 8pm Tue-Thu, to 9pm Fri-Sun Jun-Aug, shorter hours Apr, May, Sep & Oct) FREE The Doo Wop Preservation League runs this small museum that tells the story of Wildwood's 1950s heyday. Its 'neon-sign garden' shows off relics from no-longer-standing buildings. On Tuesday, Wednesday and Thursday nights in summer, a trolley tour (adult/child $13/7) departs from here, passing the most colorful landmarks.

Sleeping & Eating

Heart of Wildwood HOTEL $$
(☎609-522-4090; www.heartofwildwood.com; cnr Ocean & E Spencer Aves; r $70-250; P❄📶🏊) If you're here for waterslides and roller coasters, book a room at Heart of Wildwood, facing the amusement piers. It's not fancy, but gets high marks for cleanliness (the tile floors help), and from the heated rooftop pool you can watch the big wheel go round and round. Smallish suites are handy for families, with stoves, sinks and fridges.

Starlux BOUTIQUE HOTEL $$$
(☎609-522-7412; www.thestarlux.com; 305 E Rio Grande Ave; r/ste from $270/345; P📶🏊) The sea-green-and-white Starlux has the soaring profile, the lava lamps, the boomerang-decorated bedspreads and the sailboat-shaped mirrors, plus it's as clean as a whistle. Even more authentically retro are its two chrome-sided Airstream trailers (sleeping three comfortably).

Key West Cafe BREAKFAST $
(☎609-522-5006; www.keywestcafe.us; 4701 Pacific Ave; mains $7-15; ⏰7am-2pm) Basically every permutation of pancakes and eggs imaginable, all freshly prepared – oh, and lunch too. Bonus: it's open year-round. The eggs Benedict is a fave among frequent diners.

Getting There & Away

NJ Transit runs bus service to Wildwood from NYC ($46, 4½ hours) with a possible transfer in Atlantic City, and express bus service from Philadelphia's 30th St Station ($23, three hours) during summer. Driving from the Garden State Pkwy, take Rte 47 into Wildwood; from the south a more scenic route from Cape May is Rte 109, then Ocean Dr.

Cape May

Established in 1620, Cape May is a town with deep history and some 600 gorgeous Victorian buildings. Its sweeping beaches are a draw in summer, but its year-round population of about 3500 makes it a lively off-season destination, unlike most of the Jersey Shore. Whales can be spotted off the coast May to December, and migratory birds are plentiful in spring and fall: just check in at the Cape May Bird Observatory.

The state's booming wine industry is represented by six different sites here, among them trendy Willow Creek Winery. And thanks to the location on New Jersey's southern tip (it's Exit 0 from the turnpike), you can watch the sun rise or set over the water.

Sights

Cape May Point State Park STATE PARK
(☎609-884-2159; www.state.nj.us; ⏰dawn-dusk, office 8am-4pm) The 190-acre Cape May Point State Park, just off Lighthouse Ave, has 2 miles of trails, plus the famous 1859 **Cape May Lighthouse** (☎609-884-5404; www.capemaymac.org; 215 Lighthouse Ave; adult/child $10/5; ⏰10am-5pm May-Aug, shorter hours rest of year). You can climb the 199 stairs to the top for the view. Short, easy trails (0.5 to 2 miles) are great for birding and a breath of salty ocean air.

Cape May Bird Observatory BIRD SANCTUARY
(☎609-884-2736; www.njaudubon.org; ⏰9:30am-4:30pm Apr-Oct, closed Tue Nov-Mar) FREE Cape May is one of the country's top birding spots, with more than 400 species during the spring and fall migration seasons, when neotropical birds are heading south for the winter or north to breed for the summer. The mile-long loop trail here is a good introduction, and there are plenty of books, binoculars and birding bric-a-brac in the bookstore.

Sleeping

Congress Hall HOTEL $$$
(☎609-884-8421; www.caperesorts.com; 200 Congress Pl; r from $240-580; ❄📶🏊) Opened

in 1816, the enormous Congress Hall is a local landmark, now suitably modernized without wringing out all the history. It's got everything you could ask for, including a spa and bicycle rentals, but can come off as a bit highfalutin.

Eating & Drinking

Mad Batter AMERICAN $

(☎609-884-5970; www.madbatter.com; 19 Jackson St, Carroll Villa Hotel; dinner mains $30, brunch $8-13; ⏲8am-10pm; ✎) Tucked away in a white Victorian B&B, this restaurant is locally beloved for brunch – including fluffy oat pancakes and rich clam chowder. The Chesapeake Bay Benedict, stuffed with crab, is to die for. Dinner is fine but pricier.

Lobster House SEAFOOD $$

(☎609-884-8296; www.thelobsterhouse.com; 906 Schellengers Landing Rd; mains $15-30; ⏲11:30am-3pm & 4:30-10pm Mon-Sat, 11:30am-10pm Sun Apr-Dec, to 9pm Jan-Mar; P) This clubby-feeling classic on the wharf serves local oysters and scallops. No reservations means very long waits – go early or late, or have a drink on the boat-bar, the *Schooner American,* which is docked next to the restaurant.

★**Willow Creek Winery** WINERY

(☎609-770-8782; www.willowcreekwinerycapemay.com; 168 Stevens St; tastings $10-20; ⏲11am-5pm Mon-Thu, to 9:30pm Fri, to 8pm Sat, to 6pm Sun) The 'baby' of Cape May's six wineries, this former lima bean and dairy farm christened its first bottles in 2011, and produces a solid combo of reds and whites. The weekend tapas menu and sangria bar is pretty mind-blowing, and a tour around the 50 acres on an electric tram ($15) is a kick. The 'educational tasting' will smarten up your palate.

You can pick up fresh Jersey produce like sweet corn and peaches at their nearby Legates Farm.

Getting There & Away

NJ Transit buses serve Cape May from NYC ($48.50, three to five hours), with a possible transfer at Atlantic City, and a discounted round-trip express bus from Philadelphia ($25, 3½ to four hours) during the summer. For onward car travel, the **Cape May-Lewes Ferry** (☎800-643-3779; www.cmlf.com; 1200 Lincoln Blvd; car/passenger $35/10; ⏲7am-7:45pm Apr-Oct) crosses the bay in 1½ hours to Lewes, Delaware, near Rehoboth Beach.

PENNSYLVANIA

A horse and buggy trundles through the Lancaster fog before it is overtaken by a Philadelphia-bound sports car driven by a young tech entrepreneur. In Pittsburgh, children of immigrants who work as nurses in the city's burgeoning hospitals make experimental contemporary art. In Gettysburg, descendants of Union soldiers proudly fly Confederate flags. This is Pennsylvania, which contains within its 46,000 sq miles some of the Eastern seaboard's most striking landscapes, culture clashes and contradictions.

Here you'll find massive elk herds loping across forested ravines in the Pennsylvania Wilds; former steel towns embracing wine-fueled arts walks; cities populated by the descendants of America's founders living side-by-side with immigrants; Mennonites who eschew modern tech but run agribusiness empires. This is a state that never fails to fascinate, and while it's wowing you with its culture, it's feeding you great food and awesome landscapes at the same time.

Getting There & Around

Pennsylvania is home to a number of airports, several of them with international connections; the eastern end is near the giant hub of New Jersey's Newark International, with connections around the world. Trains serve many of its major cities, while buses service most towns. That said, with so much of this state's beauty lying off the beaten path, renting a car and driving around on your own is highly recommended.

The main air access points are Philadelphia International Airport (p163) and Pittsburgh International Airport (p168). Both of these cities are also major hubs for Amtrak trains and Greyhound buses.

Philadelphia

Blessed with the glamour and culture of a big city, 'Philly' as it's affectionately known, also delights visitors with its rich history and small-town charm.

Sights & Activities

★**Barnes Foundation** MUSEUM

(Map p156; ☎215-278-7200; www.barnesfoundation.org; 2025 Benjamin Franklin Pkwy, Spring Garden; adult/student/child $25/5/free; ⏲11am-5pm Wed-Mon; 🚌7, 32, 33, 38, 48, 49) In the first half of the 20th century, collector and educator Albert C Barnes amassed a remarkable trove of artwork by Cézanne, Degas, Matisse, Renoir, Van Gogh and other European stars. Alongside, he set beautiful pieces of folk art from Africa and the Americas – an artistic desegregation that was shocking at the time. Today's Barnes Foundation is a contemporary shell, inside which is a faithful reproduction of the galleries of Barnes' original mansion (still in the Philadelphia suburbs).

The art is hung according to Barnes' vision, a careful juxtaposition of colors, themes and materials. In one room, all the portraits appear to be staring at a central point. Even more remarkable: you've likely never seen any of these works before, because Barnes' will limits reproduction and lending.

The first Sunday of the month admission is free. Tickets are limited to four per person and there's a focus on family activities.

★Independence Hall HISTORIC BUILDING

(Map p160; ☎877-444-6777; www.nps.gov/inde; 520 Chestnut St, Old City; 8:30am-6pm, to 7pm late May-early Sep; S 5th St) FREE The 'birthplace of American government,' this modest early 18th-century Georgian building is where delegates from the 13 colonies met to approve the Declaration of Independence on July 4, 1776. Expect a line out the door and around the block for this one – it's the prime attraction in a city packed with history.

The entrance is via the security screening area in the east wing on the corner of Chestnut and 5th Sts. Get free advance tickets and times for the next available tour at the nearby Independence Visitor Center (p163) or reserve online (fee $1). Budget for at least an hour-long wait in peak summer months.

Independence National Historical Park PARK

(Map p160; ☎215-965-2305; www.nps.gov/inde; Old City; visitor center & most sites 9am-5pm; S 5th St) This L-shaped park, between 6th, 2nd, Walnut and Arch Sts, protects and honors the history and institutions that formed the foundation of the US government. Stroll around and you'll see storied buildings in which the seeds for the Revolutionary War were planted and the US government came into bloom. You'll also find beautiful, shaded urban lawns dotted with plenty of squirrels, pigeons and, in warmer months, costumed actors. Rangers can provide information about it all at the Independence Visitor Center (p163).

★Museum of the American Revolution MUSEUM

(Map p160; ☎215-253-6731; www.amrevmuseum.org; 101 S 3rd St; adult/student/child $21/18/13; 10am-5pm Sep-late May, 9:30am-6pm late May-Aug; S 2nd St) This impressive, multimedia-rich museum will have you virtually participating in the American Revolution; interactive dioramas and 3-D experiences take you all the way from contentment with British rule to the eventual rejection of it. Learn about the events, people, cultures and religions that participated in one of the world's most important revolutions. Lots of hands-on displays and video stories mean kids will have as much fun as adults. Note that all tickets are timed: reserve them early online.

★Philadelphia Museum of Art MUSEUM

(Map p156; ☎215-763-8100; www.philamuseum.org; 2600 Benjamin Franklin Pkwy, East Fairmount Park; adult/student/child $20/14/free; 10am-5pm Tue, Thu, Sat & Sun, to 8:45pm Wed & Fri; 32, 38, 43) The city's premier cultural institution occupies a Grecian temple-like building housing a superb collection of Asian art, Renaissance masterpieces, postimpressionist works and modern pieces by Picasso, Duchamp and Matisse among others. Especially notable are galleries filled with complete architectural ensembles, including a medieval cloister, Chinese and Indian temples and a Japanese teahouse.

There's so much to see that a ticket covers admission for two days, here and at the separate **Perelman Building** (Map p156; ☎215-763-8100; www.philamuseum.org; 2525 Pennsylvania Ave, Fairmount; incl in admission to Philadelphia Museum of Art adult/student/child $20/14/free; 10am-5pm Tue-Sun; 32, 38, 43), Rodin Museum and two historic houses **Mount Pleasant** (www.philamuseum.org; 3800 Mt Pleasant Dr, East Fairmount Park; closed to public; W Girard Ave & 33rd St) and **Cedar Grove** (☎215-763-8100; www.philamuseum.org/historichouses; 1 Cedar Grove Dr, West Fairmount Park; adult/child $8/free; tours at 11am, 1pm & 2pm Thu-Sun, also 10am & 4pm 1st Sun of month Apr-Dec; 38).

Mütter Museum MUSEUM

(Map p156; ☎215-560-8564; www.muttermuseum.org; 19 S 22nd St, Rittenhouse; adult/child $18/13; 10am-5pm; 22nd St) Maintained

NEW YORK, NEW JERSEY & PENNSYLVANIA IN...

One Week

Start off in Philadelphia (p152), birthplace of American independence. Visit Independence Hall (p153) and the Museum of the American Revolution, then spend an evening investigating the great restaurants and nightlife in up-and-coming neighborhoods like Fishtown.

Next, head to New Jersey for a bucolic night in Cape May (p151), a sleepy beach town full of Victorian charm. After a quick, scenic cruise along Ocean Dr, stop off overnight further up the Shore in Wildwood (p150), a treasure trove of iconic '50s kitsch. Land in New York City (p61) the following day and spend at least a couple of days blending touristy must-dos – such as the Top of the Rock (p77) and Central Park (p79) – with vibrant nightlife and eclectic dining.

Two Weeks

With NYC in your rearview mirror, head north along the majestic Hudson and its palisades for a night or two in Beacon (p128) or Hudson (p127), before reaching the Catskills (p131). After touring this beautiful region, head further north to the Adirondacks (p136) and its outdoor wonders, then loop back south through the Finger Lakes (p134) region with stops in wineries and waterfall-laden parks along the way. Spend a night in gorgeous college-town Ithaca (p134).

From here you can head towards the Canadian border to Buffalo (p141) and Niagara Falls (p143), or southwest to Pittsburgh (p165).

by the College of Physicians, this unique, only-in-Philadelphia attraction is a museum dedicated to rare, odd or disturbing medical conditions. Not for the squeamish, its nonetheless fascinating exhibits include a saponified body, a conjoined female fetus, incredibly realistic wax models of medical conditions and skulls by the dozen.

The College of Physicians also hosts many events in the building, including classical music concerts and lectures – check the website for details. Note there's $2 off admission on Monday and Tuesday.

★Benjamin Franklin Museum MUSEUM
(Map p160; ☎215-965-2305; www.nps.gov/inde; Market St, btwn 3rd & 4th Sts, Old City; adult/child $5/2; ⏲9am-5pm; Ⓢ2nd St) This underground museum is dedicated to Franklin's storied life as a printer (he started the nation's first newspaper), inventor (Bifocals! Lightning rods!) and political figure who signed the Declaration of Independence. The exhibition, divided into five areas, with each focusing on a particular trait of the man, is inventively laid out with interactive elements and plenty of famous Franklin quotations.

In the same courtyard, don't miss the **printing office** (Map p160; ☎215-965-2305; www.nps.gov/inde; Franklin Court, Market St btwn 3rd & 4th Sts, Old City; ⏲10am-5pm; Ⓢ2nd St) FREE, where park rangers demonstrate an 18th-century printing press similar to that used by Franklin.

Rodin Museum MUSEUM
(Map p156; ☎215-763-8100; www.rodinmuseum.org; 2151 Benjamin Franklin Pkwy, Spring Garden; suggested donation adult/student/child $10/7/free; ⏲10am-5pm Wed-Mon; 🚌7, 32, 33, 38, 48) This is the only institution outside of Paris dedicated to the French sculptor Auguste Rodin. The superb collection is based on works amassed by Jules E Mastbaum in the 1920s. There are versions of *The Thinker* and *Burghers of Calais* among its 140 sculptures from every part of Rodin's spectacular career.

Administered by the Philadelphia Museum of Art, the small museum's garden is always open and free.

Liberty Bell Center HISTORIC SITE
(Map p160; ☎215-965-2305; www.nps.gov/inde; 526 Market St, Old City; ⏲9am-5pm, to 7pm late May-early Sep; Ⓢ5th St) FREE A glass-walled building protects this icon of Philadelphia history from the elements. You can peek from outside, or join the line to file past, reading about the history and significance of the 2080lb object along the way. The line – and it can be a long one in peak summer months – starts on the building's northern end.

The gist of the story: originally called the State House Bell, it was made in 1751, to commemorate the 50th anniversary of

Pennsylvania's constitution. Mounted in Independence Hall (p153), it tolled on the first public reading of the Declaration of Independence. The crack developed in the 19th century, and the bell was retired in 1846.

One Liberty Observation Deck OBSERVATORY

(Philly From the Top; Map p156; ☎215-561-3325; www.phillyfromthetop.com; 1650 Market St, Center City; adult/child $15/10; ⏲10am-8pm Sep-Apr, to 9pm May-Aug) One way to get a bird's-eye view of the city, especially pretty after dark, is to ride the ear-popping elevator up to this 883ft-high observation deck on the 57th floor of One Liberty Place.

There are tickets allowing two visits within 48 hours, family deals and online discounts.

Shofuso Japanese House & Garden GARDENS

(☎215-878-5097; www.japanesehouse.org; Horticultural Dr, West Fairmount Park; adult/child $12/8; ⏲10am-4pm Wed-Fri, 11am-5pm Sat & Sun Apr-Oct; 🚌38) This picturesque house, built in Nagoya in 1953 to a 17th-century design, has been set in 1.2 acres of traditional Japanese gardens in Fairmount Park since 1958. Check online for various events, including tea ceremonies, that are held here (bookings and extra payment required).

The cherry trees blooming in spring are not to be missed

★City Hall NOTABLE BUILDING

(Map p156; ☎215-686-2840; www.phlvisitorcenter.com; cnr Broad & Market Sts; tower adult/student $8/4, interior & tower $15/8; ⏲tower tours every 15min 9:30am-4:15pm, interior tour 12:30pm Mon-Fri; Ⓢ City Hall & 15th St) Completed in 1901 following 30 years of construction, City Hall takes up a whole block, and at 548ft is the world's tallest structure without a steel frame. The view from the observation area immediately beneath the 27-ton bronze statue of William Penn that crowns the tower takes in most of the city; reserve tickets as space is limited. The daily interior tour is a treat, too, and will give you a greater appreciation of this grand building. In winter, the **Rothman Ice Rink** (Map p156; www.centercityphila.org/parks/dilworth-park/rothman-rink; 1 S 15th St, Center City; adult/child $5/3, skate rental $10; ⏲noon-9pm Mon-Thu, to 11pm Fri, 11am-11pm Sat, 11am-8pm Sun mid-Nov–Feb; ⓂCity Hall & 15th St) sets up in Dilworth Park on the western side of the plaza.

Eastern State Penitentiary MUSEUM

(Map p156; ☎215-236-3300; www.easternstate.org; 2027 Fairmount Ave, Fairmount; adult/child $14/10; ⏲10am-5pm; 🚌7, 32, 33, 43, 48) The modern prison didn't just happen – it was invented, and Eastern State Penitentiary was the first one, opened in 1829 and finally closed in 1971. A self-guided audio tour leads you through the eerie, echoing halls; one stop is Al Capone's famously luxurious cell. There's also info on America's current prison system, and art installations throughout. It's a popular stop, so expect crowds at peak times; tickets are cheaper online. From mid-September through Halloween, the prison hosts a terrifying haunted house.

Edgar Allan Poe National Historic Site HISTORIC SITE

(Map p156; ☎215-597-8780; www.nps.gov/edal; 532 N 7th St, Poplar; ⏲9am-5pm Fri-Sun; Ⓢ Spring Garden: Market-Frankford Line) FREE Often called the creator of the horror story, Edgar Allan Poe lived for six years in Philadelphia, in five different houses. This historic site, his only Philly home still remaining, is now a small but interesting museum, with a lot of original items and restored rooms. Don't miss the creepy brick cellar (complete with cobwebs) thought to have inspired Poe's masterwork 'The Black Cat.' A statue of a raven stands outside.

Center / Architecture + Design CENTER

(Map p156; ☎215-569-3186; www.philadelphiacfa.org; 1218 Arch St, Center City; ⏲9am-5pm Mon-Fri; Ⓢ 13th St) FREE Run by the American Institute of Architects, there's an exhibition space here with regularly changing exhibits about local architecture projects. Check their online calendar to find out about lectures and other events.

Mural Arts Tours TOURS

(Map p156; ☎215-925-3633; www.muralarts.org/tours; 118-128 N Broad St, Center City; tours $23-32; Ⓢ Race-Vine or City Hall & 15th St) The best way to appreciate the transformative nature of the Mural Arts Program across Philadelphia is to join one of its guided tours of the city's numerous outdoor murals.

Walking and trolley tours are held from April through November, while in the colder months you can join the excellent Love Letters tour, which uses the subway.

The Mural Finder Mobile, a free self-guided tour with smartphone-optimized map, is available on the website.

Philadelphia

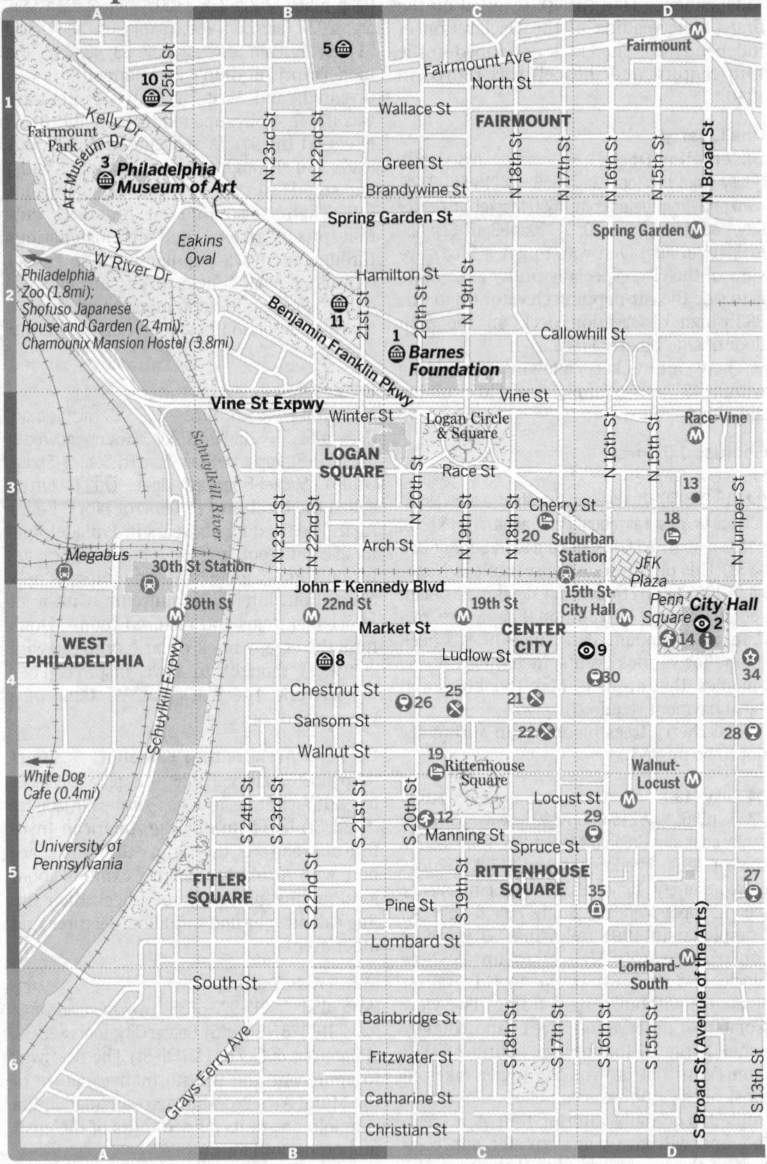

Taste of Philly Food Tour FOOD & DRINK (Map p156; ☎800-838-3006, 215-545-8007; www.tasteofphillyfoodtour.com; Reading Terminal Market, 51 N 12th St, Center City; adult/child $17/10; ⊙10am Wed & Sat; Ⓢ11th or 13th) Snack and learn Philly food lore during this 75-minute tour around Reading Terminal Market with knowledgeable food writer Carolyn Wyman. Reservations are recommended, particularly in busy holiday periods, but you can also just turn up at the meeting point at the market's Welcome Desk, by the entrance on 12th and Filbert.

Festivals & Events

Audi Feastival FOOD & DRINK

(☎610-585-7038; www.phillyfeastival.com; 140 N Columbus Blvd, Penn's Landing; per person from $300; Ⓢ2nd St) Eat, meet and greet at the city's highest-lauded food fest, held one evening every September to benefit **Fringe-Arts** (Map p160; ☎215-413-1318; www.fringearts.com; 140 N Columbus Blvd, Old City; tickets from $5; Ⓢ2nd St), the city's cultural organization that puts on the Fringe Festival.

Philadelphia

Top Sights
1 Barnes Foundation C2
2 City Hall D4
3 Philadelphia Museum of Art A1

Sights
4 Center / Architecture + Design E3
5 Eastern State Penitentiary B1
6 Edgar Allan Poe National Historic Site F1
7 Famous Franks E5
8 Mütter Museum B4
9 One Liberty Observation Deck D4
10 Perelman Building A1
11 Rodin Museum B2

Activities, Courses & Tours
12 Cook C5
13 Mural Arts Tours D3
14 Rothman Ice Rink D4
15 Taste of Philly Food Tour E3

Sleeping
16 Alexander Inn E5
17 Independent E5
18 Le Méridien D3
19 Rittenhouse Hotel C4
20 Windsor Suites C3

Eating
21 Gran Caffè L'Aquila C4
22 Luke's Lobster C4
23 Morimoto F4
24 Tom's Dim Sum E3
25 V Street C4

Drinking & Nightlife
26 1 Tippling Place C4
27 Dirty Franks D5
28 Double Knot D4
29 Monk's Cafe D5
30 R2L Restaurant D4
31 Tavern on Camac E5
32 Trestle Inn E2

Entertainment
33 PhilaMOCA E2
34 Wanamaker Organ D4

Shopping
35 Omoi Zakka Shop D5

★ Mummers Parade CARNIVAL
(www.phillymummers.com; Jan 1) Uniquely Philly: a cross between Mardi Gras and a marching band competition, the elaborate costumes, music and deep lore of the various mummer divisions and brigades make this a must-see in the bracing cold of winter. The parade starts by City Hall and moves down Broad St to finish at Washington Ave.

Fringe Festival PERFORMING ARTS
(www.fringearts.com) Running since 1996, the Fringe Festival sees 17 days in mid-September packed with performance art, events, productions and creative craziness.

Sleeping

★ Apple Hostels HOSTEL $
(Map p160; 215-922-0222; www.applehostels.com; 33 Bank St, Old St; dm/d with shared bath from $33/106; ; 2nd St) The Old City's best hostel is hidden down an alley and spans both sides of the street. The apple-green color scheme fits the name, but this Hosteling International–affiliated place is also strong on details: two spotless kitchens, lounges and a library, plus power outlets in lockers, USB ports and reading lights at every bed, free coffee and earplugs.

There are male, female and coed dorms, plus eight private rooms. The friendly staff run nightly activities such as walking tours, pasta nights and a Thursday bar crawl.

Chamounix Mansion Hostel HOSTEL $
(215-878-3676; www.philahostel.org; 3250 Chamounix Dr, West Fairmount Park; dm $22; closed Dec 15-Jan 15; P; 38 & 40) In a lovely wooded area of Fairmount Park, this handsome Hosteling International hostel is best for guests with their own transport. In its public areas, set with antiques, harp, oriental rugs and paintings, the place feels more like a B&B than a hostel; the dorms themselves are basic. There's also a great communal kitchen and free bicycles for getting around. A downside is that the building is closed (and all guests have to leave) between 11am and 4:30pm and there's a 2am curfew, not that you'd want to be wandering around this isolated part of the park at that hour.

From the bus stop on the corner of Ford and Cranston Rds it's around a 1-mile walk to the hostel, which is at the end of Chamounix Dr.

★ Alexander Inn BOUTIQUE HOTEL $$
(Map p156; 215-923-3535; www.alexanderinn.com; 301 S 12th St, Midtown Village; s/d from $135/150; ; 23, 40) Online photos

undersell this place. The impeccably kept rooms have a subdued, slightly vintage style; some have old-fashioned half-size tubs. Original architectural details – including stained-glass windows, oak moldings, marble-tiled floors – add to the atmosphere.

The included continental breakfast is convenient, and free snacks are available throughout the day.

Independent BOUTIQUE HOTEL **$$**
(Map p156; 215-772-1440; www.theindependenthotel.com; 1234 Locust St, Midtown Village; r from $160; ; S Walnut-Locust) At the heart of the 'Gayborhood' and a block from the Avenue of the Arts, the Independent is housed in a handsome brick Georgian Revival building with a four-story atrium decorated with a 30ft watercolor. The 24 wood-floored rooms are uncluttered and sunny, and the complimentary off-site gym pass, and wine and cheese served Monday through Thursday, sweeten the deal.

Le Méridien HOTEL **$$**
(Map p156; 215-422-8200; www.starwoodhotels.com; 1421 Arch St, Center City; d from $230; ; S City Hall & 15th St, Suburban) Though part of a luxury chain, the central location and tasteful appropriation of an old building to make a contemporary hotel sets Le Méridien apart. Entirely smoke-free, the rooms sport monochrome design with red accents. It's also pet-friendly and has a wide range of facilities, including a fitness and business center.

Windsor Suites HOTEL **$$**
(Map p156; 215-981-5678; www.thewindsorsuites.com; 1700 Benjamin Franklin Pkwy, Center City; ste from $150; P; S City Hall & 15th St, Suburban) The comfortable and roomy suites here come with full kitchens; some also have balconies. There are options for extended stays or monthly rentals, as well as good facilities, including a rooftop pool (May to mid-September).

Staff are friendly and the hotel allows pets to stay free (they even get their own amenities).

★Rittenhouse Hotel HOTEL **$$$**
(Map p156; 215-546-9000; www.rittenhousehotel.com; 210 W Rittenhouse Sq, Rittenhouse; d from $490; P; 9, 12, 17, 21, 42) Rooms at this five-star – excuse us, make that five-*diamond* – hotel on Rittenhouse Sq have marble baths. Of the downtown options with a half-Olympic-sized pool, this is one of the nicest. It serves a top-notch brunch and a soothing afternoon tea service with music.

On Friday and Saturday a live jazz band plays in the library bar.

Eating

Tom's Dim Sum CHINESE **$**
(Map p156; 215-923-8880; www.tomsdimsumpa.com; 59 N 11th St, Chinatown; dim sum $2-7, mains $7-14; 11am-9pm Mon-Fri, to 10pm Sat & Sun; S 11th St, Jefferson) Dim sum are served throughout the day at this casual spot. Dig into tasty buns and soup dumplings, as well as rice plates and noodles.

★Zahav MIDDLE EASTERN **$**
(Map p160; 215-625-8800; www.zahavrestaurant.com; 237 St James Pl, Old City; mains $10-14, tasting menus $48; 5-10pm Sun-Thu, to 11pm Fri & Sat; S 2nd St) Zahav means 'gold' in Hebrew and that's what you'll find here in terms of gastronomy. The menu at this sophisticated modern Israeli restaurant sees chef Michael Solomonov, winner of a James Beard Foundation Award, drawing primarily from North African, Persian and Levantine kitchens for inspiration.

Pick your own meze and grills, or go for the tasting menu, but under no circumstances bypass their luscious hummus served with a chef's selection of toppings. Book well ahead or turn up early (as soon as they open is recommended) for a spot at the bar.

Luke's Lobster SEAFOOD **$$**
(Map p156; 215-564-1415; www.lukeslobster.com; 130 S 17th St, Rittenhouse; lobster roll $17; 11am-9pm Sun-Thu, to 10pm Fri & Sat; 9, 21, 42, S City Hall & 15th St) As one diner put it: 'Lobster roll. Drop mic.' Part of a casual East Coast chain serving authentic tastes of Maine using sustainably sourced seafood. Wash down your buttered-bun lobster roll with a wild-blueberry soda.

★White Dog Cafe AMERICAN **$$**
(215-386-9224; www.whitedog.com; 3420 Sansom St, University City; dinner mains $19-42; 11:30am-9:30pm Mon-Thu, to 10pm Fri, 9:30am-10pm Sat, 9:30am-9pm Sun; ; 30, 42, S 34th St) If the dozen Boston terriers on the wall seem incongruous with the food, don't worry: this place has been serving farm-to-table since 1983. Come here for your truffles and artisan cheeses, peak summer tomatoes and plenty more. Yes, the Greyhound is the signature drink. Need you have asked?

Philadelphia – Old City

Philadelphia – Old City

Top Sights
1 Benjamin Franklin Museum C3
2 Independence Hall B4
3 Museum of the American Revolution C3

Sights
4 Franklin Court Printing Museum B3
5 Independence National Historical Park A3
6 Liberty Bell Center A3

Sleeping
7 Apple Hostels C3

Eating
8 Cuba Libre C3
9 Zahav C4

Entertainment
10 FringeArts D1

Shopping
11 Shane Confectionery D3

Cuba Libre CUBAN $$
(Map p160; ☎215-627-0666; www.cubalibrerestaurant.com; 10 S 2nd St, Old City; mains $20-32; ⏰11:30am-10pm Mon-Wed, to 11pm Thu & Fri, 10:30am-11pm Sat, 10:30am-10pm Sun; ; S 2nd St) Colonial America couldn't feel further away at this festive, multistory Cuban eatery and rum bar, part of a small chain found in several East Coast cities. The creative menu, featuring Cuba's *criollo* (home-style) cuisine, includes shrimp ceviche, Cuban sandwiches, guava-spiced BBQ and excellent mojitos. A $45 tasting menu lets you get a variety of the specialties.

★**Gran Caffè L'Aquila** ITALIAN $$
(Map p156; ☎215-568-5600; www.grancaffelaquila.com; 1716 Chestnut St, Rittenhouse; mains $16-35; ⏰7am-10pm Mon-Thu, to 11pm Fri, 8am-11pm Sat, to 10pm Sun, bar open 1hr later; 9, 21, 42, 19th St) Mamma mia, this is impressive Italian food. Not only are the flavors everything you could ask for, one of the owners is an award-winning gelato maker and the 2nd floor has its own gelato factory. Some of the main courses even have savory gelato as a garnish. Coffee is house-roasted and the dapper waitstaff are eager to please.

The three co-owners came here after their village in Italy was destroyed by a 2014 earthquake. Reservations are recommended.

Morimoto JAPANESE $$$
(Map p156; ☎215-413-9070; www.morimotorestaurant.com; 723 Chestnut St, Washington Sq West; mains $26-58; ⏰11:30am-2pm & 5-10pm Mon-Thu, to midnight Fri, 5pm-midnight Sat, 5-10pm Sun; ; S 8th St) Morimoto is high concept and heavily stylized, from a dining room that looks like a futuristic aquarium to a menu of globe-spanning influences and eclectic combinations. A meal at this *Iron Chef* regular's restaurant is a theatrical experience.

If price isn't a problem, opt for the *omakase* ($125) – the chef's special choice of dishes.

Drinking & Nightlife

1 Tippling Place BAR
(Map p156; ☎215-665-0456; www.1tpl.com; 2006 Chestnut St, Rittenhouse; ⏰5pm-2am Tue-Sun; 9, 17, 21, 42, 19th St) Whether you pull up a seat at the bar or find a cozy couch to relax on, this spot has everything you could want in a craft cocktail bar. Extra points if you can spot more than four typos on the menu. Note: this place looks closed even when it isn't, with minimal (read: zero) outdoor signage.

★**Monk's Cafe** BAR
(Map p156; ☎215-545-7005; www.monkscafe.com; 264 S 16th St, Rittenhouse; ⏰11:30am-2am, kitchen to 1am; S Walnut-Locust) Hop fans crowd this mellow wood-paneled place for Belgian and American craft beers on tap – it has one of the best selections in the city. For those needing assistance, a 'Beer Bible' is available.

There's also a reasonably priced food menu, with typical mussels-and-fries as well as a daily vegan special.

R2L Restaurant LOUNGE
(Map p156; ☎215-564-5337; www.r2lrestaurant.com; 50 S 16th St, Center City; ⏰lounge 4pm-1am Mon-Thu, to 2am Fri & Sat, to 11pm Sun; S City Hall & 15th St, Suburban) The view, the view, the view. And did we mention the view? This upscale spot serves up the nightscape of Philly along with whatever is on the menu. Craft cocktails are smooth and balanced, but even tap water would seem ritzy when you're looking out at the cosmos of lights below you.

Happy hour (4:30pm to 6:30pm Monday to Friday) offers $4 beers, $7 wines, $8 cocktails and snacks from $2.

★**Trestle Inn** BAR
(Map p156; ☎267-239-0290; www.thetrestleinn.com; 339 N 11th St, Callowhill; ⏰5pm-2am Wed-Sat; S Spring Garden: Broad Street Line) On a dark corner this classed-up old dive is notable for its friendliness and craft cocktails, which can be enjoyed in a happy hour that lasts from 5pm until 8pm. From 9pm on Thursday and 10pm on Friday and Saturday go-go dancers get their groove on under the disco ball as DJs play hits from the 1960s onward.

There's a cover charge of $5 after 10pm at the weekends.

Double Knot BAR
(Map p156; ☎215-631-3868; www.doubleknotphilly.com; 120 S 13th St, Midtown Village; ⏰8am-midnight Sun-Tue, to 1am Wed & Thu, to 2am Fri & Sat; S 13th St or Walnut-Locust) This is one of the few places in Philly that serves sake properly (poured into an overflowing cup inside a wooden *masu* container). They also make great craft cocktails and have a delicious food menu. It can get crowded, but the stylish decor and friendly service make it a fun spot to grab a bite and late-night drink.

LOCAL KNOWLEDGE

CLASSIC PHILLY FLAVOUR

If there's one thing you *must* eat while in town its a cheesesteak. Philadelphians argue over the nuances of these hot sandwiches comprised of thin-sliced, griddle-cooked beef on a chewy roll: there are pork, chicken and even vegan versions available, but die-hard fans will tell you that only the classic beef really qualifies. And don't get people started on where the best one is to be found – there's as many opinions on this as there are areas of the city.

What a visitor most needs to know is how to order. First say the kind of cheese you want – prov (provolone), American (melty yellow) or whiz (molten orange Cheez Whiz). Then 'wit' (with) or 'widdout' (without), referring to fried onions: 'Prov wit,' for example, or 'whiz widdout. And if it's a take-out place, have your money ready – cheesesteak vendors are famously in a hurry.

From 5pm they open up the basement, which hides an impressive Japanese restaurant with a sushi bar and *robatayaki* (flame-grilled cooked items).

Tavern on Camac GAY & LESBIAN

(TOC; Map p156; ☎215-545-0900; www.tavernoncamac.com; 243 S Camac St, Midtown Village; ⏰piano bar 4pm-2am, restaurant 5pm-midnight Sun, Mon, Wed & Thu, to 1am Fri & Sat, club 9pm-2am; Ⓢ Walnut-Locust) One of the longest-established gay bars in Philly has a piano bar and restaurant downstairs. Upstairs is Ascend, a small club with a dance floor; Tuesday is karaoke night, Friday and Saturday have DJs. And don't overlook Showtune Sunday.

★Dirty Franks BAR

(Map p156; ☎215-732-5010; www.dirtyfranksbar.com; 347 S 13th St, Washington Sq West; ⏰11am-2am; 🚌23, 40) In business since 1933, Franks' regulars call this bar an 'institution' with some irony, but it does have grunge style as well as housing the Off The Wall gallery. Like many Philly dives, it offers the 'citywide special': a shot of Jim Beam and a can of PBR for $2.50. Need cheaper? Try the 'DF Shelf of Shame' beer for just two bucks!

The bar's exterior is decorated with the mural **Famous Franks** (Map p156; www.muralarts.org/artworks/famous-franks; 347 S 13th St, Midtown Village; 🚌23, 40).

☆ Entertainment

PhilaMOCA PERFORMING ARTS

(Philadelphia Mausoleum of Contemporary Art; Map p156; ☎267-519-9651; www.philamoca.org; 531 N 12th St, Poplar; Ⓢ Spring Garden: Broad Street Line) A former tombstone store, then producer Diplo's studios, this eclectic space now has an equally eclectic program of cult movie nights, live-music shows, art, comedy and more.

Wanamaker Organ LIVE MUSIC

(Map p156; ☎484-684-7250; www.wanamakerorgan.com; 1300 Market St, Macy's, Center City; ⏰concerts noon Mon-Sat, plus 5:30pm Mon, Tue, Thu & Sat, 7pm Wed & Fri; Ⓢ 13th St) Back in 1909 when Macy's was Wanamaker's, owner John Wanamaker installed this enormous pipe organ hosting free concerts to delight shoppers and make them linger. The tradition lives on, with classical and pop tunes filling the department store's central atrium a couple of times a day.

It's a treat for visitors who are welcome to tour the console area (2nd floor) and meet the organist following the daily concerts.

Johnny Brenda's LIVE MUSIC

(☎215-739-9684; www.johnnybrendas.com; 1201 N Frankford Ave, Fishtown; tickets $5-20; ⏰kitchen 11am-1am, showtimes vary; Ⓢ Girard, Market-Frankford Line) One of the hubs of Philly's indie-rock scene, this is a great small venue with a balcony, plus is also home to a solid restaurant and bar with equally indie-minded beers.

Shopping

Omoi Zakka Shop STATIONERY

(Map p156; ☎215-545-0963; www.omoionline.com; 1608 Pine St, Rittenhouse; ⏰11am-7pm Mon-Sat, noon-5pm Sun; Ⓢ Lombard-South St) Get your inner Japanophile on with this shop that embraces the concept of *zakka* – stocking all things that might make life a little better. Fashion items, books, housewares, stationery and more, all with a Japan-inspired eye for cuteness or good design.

★Shane Confectionery FOOD & DRINKS

(Map p160; ☎215-922-1048; www.shanecandies.com; 110 Market St, Old City; ⏰11am-8pm Sun-

Thu, to 10pm Fri & Sat; S 2nd St) Since 1863 this wonderfully old-school candy shop has been making sweet treats, including buttercreams and slabs, from antique molds. With the shop assistants dressed in Victorian garb it's like stepping back in time. Settle down in the historic hot-chocolate kitchen in the back where you can indulge in a flight of luscious drinks for $15.

Tours ($10) of the operation are held on Friday at 6:30pm.

Information

City Hall Visitor Center (Map p156; 267-514-4757; www.phlvisitorcenter.com/attraction/city-hall-visitor-center; City Hall, Center City; 9am-5pm Mon-Fri, 11am-4pm every 3rd Sat; S City Hall & 15th St) Come here to buy tickets for tours of City Hall and its tower. Information on many other city tourist attractions also available.

Independence Visitor Center (Map p160; 800-537-7676; www.phlvisitorcenter.com; 599 Market St, Old City; 8:30am-7pm, longer hours in summer; S 5th St) This large center covers the national park and provides tourist information on Philadelphia. You can purchase tickets to many museums, book a slot for a visit to Independence Hall (necessary in peak summer months), watch a historical documentary, grab refreshments and – crucially – take a toilet break.

Getting There & Away

AIR

Philadelphia International Airport (PHL; 215-937-6937; www.phl.org; 8000 Essington Ave, Southwest Philadelphia; Airport Line), 10 miles southwest of Center City, is a hub for American Airlines, and is served by direct international flights. There are five terminals so check which one you are arriving at and departing from before you set off.

BUS

Greyhound, Peter Pan Bus Lines (www.peterpanbus.com), NJ Transit (www.njtransit.com) and the no-frills Chinatown Bus (www.chinatown-bus.org) all depart from the **Greyhound Terminal** (Map p156; 215-931-4075; www.greyhound.com; 1001 Filbert St, Chinatown; S 11th St, Jefferson) downtown, near the convention center; Greyhound goes nationwide, Peter Pan focuses on the northeast, NJ Transit gets you to New Jersey and the Chinatown bus connects to NYC.

From just west of 30th St Station, **Megabus** (Map p156; http://us.megabus.com; JFK Blvd & N 30th St, University City; S 30th St, 30th St) serves major US cities in the northeast and Toronto.

CAR & MOTORCYCLE

From the north and south, I-95 (Delaware Expwy) follows the eastern edge of the city along the Delaware River, with several exits for Center City. In the north of the city, I-276 (Pennsylvania Turnpike) runs east over the river to connect with the New Jersey Turnpike.

TRAIN

Just west of downtown across the Schuylkill, beautiful neoclassical **30th St Station** (1-800-872-7245; www.amtrak.com; 2955 Market St, University City; S 30th St) is a major hub. From here, Amtrak provides service on its Northeast Corridor line to New York City ($60 to $152, 1½ hours), Boston ($104 to $204, 5½ to 6½ hours) and Washington, DC ($59 to $128, two hours), as well as to Lancaster ($20, 1¼ hours) and Pittsburgh ($87, nine to 10 hours).

A slower but cheaper way to get to NYC is on regional SEPTA (www.septa.org) to Trenton ($9, 50 minutes), then NJ Transit (www.njtransit.com) to NYC's Penn Station ($16.75, 1½ hours). NJ Transit's Atlantic City Rail Line also connects 30th St Station with the seaside resort ($10.75, 1½ hours).

Getting Around

For timetables and further information check with **SEPTA** (215-580-7800; www.septa.org), which operates Philadelphia's transit system.

Bicycle Walk-up rates for Philly's bike-share system Indego (www.rideindego.com) is $12 for an all-day unlimited-ride pass.

Buses Convenient for quick hops across Center City and further afield.

Ferries From late May to early September the RiverLink ferry connects Penn's Landing and Camden's waterfront.

Subway & Trolley Philly has two subways and a trolley line (fare $2.50, exact change). Purchase the stored-value key card for discounted fares.

Taxi Easy to hail Downtown. Flag fall is $2.70, then $2.70 per mile or portion thereof. All licensed taxis have GPS and most accept credit cards. Rideshares are also commonly used.

Walking Downtown, it's barely 2 miles between the Delaware and Schuylkill Rivers, so you can walk most places.

Pennsylvania Dutch Country

Lancaster County and the broader space between Reading and the Susquehanna River is the center of the so-called Pennsylvania

Dutch community. The term refers to myriad religious orders and cultures of Germanic roots (*Deutsch* – mistakenly anglicized to Dutch) who have lived here since the 18th century; Amish, Mennonites and German Baptist (Brethren) are the best known. One common cultural thread: all are devoted to various degrees of low-tech plain living.

This simple life, with its picturesque horse-drawn buggies, ironically attracts busloads of visitors and has spawned an astoundingly kitschy tourist industry. Get onto the back roads and you can appreciate the quiet pastoral serenity these religious orders have preserved.

Small settlements in the area include train-mad Strasburg and pretty, red-brick Lititz. Ephrata is headquarters of Ten Thousand Villages, a massive Mennonite-run fair-trade imports store with branches all over the country.

Sights

★Railroad Museum of Pennsylvania MUSEUM

(717-687-8628; www.rrmuseumpa.org; 300 Gap Rd, Ronks; adult/child $10/8; 9am-5pm Tue-Sat, noon-5pm Sun year-round, plus 9am-5pm Mon Apr-Oct) Set over nearly 18 acres, the Railroad Museum of Pennsylvania has 100 gigantic mechanical marvels to climb around and admire. Combo tickets are available for the **Strasburg Railroad** (866-725-9666; www.strasburgrailroad.com; 301 Gap Rd, Ronks; coach class adult/child $15.50/8.50;) across the road. This place is packed with kids of all ages.

National Toy Train Museum MUSEUM

(717-687-8976; www.nttmuseum.org; 300 Paradise Lane, Ronks; adult/child $7.50/4.50; 10am-5pm May-Oct, hours vary Nov-Apr;) Let's be clear: you can have never touched a toy train in your life and still love this odd little museum. The push-button interactive dioramas are so up to date and clever (such as a 'drive-in movie' that's a live video of kids working the trains), and the walls packed with so many gleaming railcars, that you can't help but feel a bit of that childlike Christmas-morning wonder.

The **Red Caboose Motel** (717-687-5000; www.redcaboosemotel.com; 312 Paradise Lane, Ronks; d from $95; P) next door to the museum allows even nonguests to climb the silo in back for wonderful views (50¢), and kids can enjoy a small petting zoo.

Landis Valley Museum MUSEUM

(717-569-0401; www.landisvalleymuseum.org; 2451 Kissel Hill Rd, Lancaster; adult/child $12/8; 9am-5pm Wed-Sat, noon-5pm Sun year-round, plus 9am-5pm Tue Mar-Dec; P) Based on an 18th-century village, this open-air museum is the best way to get an overview of early Pennsylvania Dutch culture, and Mennonite culture in particular. Costumed staff are on hand to demonstrate tin-smithing, among other things, and there's a tavern, a gun shop and also several beautiful crafts exhibits.

Sleeping & Eating

Lancaster

Cork Factory BOUTIQUE HOTEL $$

(717-735-2075; www.corkfactoryhotel.com; 480 New Holland Ave, Suite 3000; r from $160; P) An abandoned brick behemoth of a factory now houses this hotel, one of the more stylish properties in the area. The posh rooms are outfitted with exposed brick, understated decor and a general sense of casual cool. It's a short drive from downtown.

Lancaster Brewing Co PUB FOOD $$

(717-391-6258; www.lancasterbrewing.com; 302 N Plum St; mains $10-29; 11:30am-10pm;) This brewery, established in 1995, is a local favorite. The restaurant serves hearty but sophisticated food – lamb burger with tzatziki, hummus tacos or pretzel-crusted chicken, say – and housemade sausages at tables with copper-clad tops and great views of the brewing tanks.

★Maison EUROPEAN $$$

(717-293-5060; www.maisonlancaster.com; 230 N Prince St; mains $26-32; 5-10pm Wed-Sat;) A husband-and-wife team run this homey but meticulous place downtown, giving local farm products a rustic Italian-French treatment: pork braised in milk, housemade rabbit sausage, fried squash blossoms or handmade gnocchi, depending on the season.

Getting There & Away

Lancaster lies at the heart of a squished 'H' shape made by Rte 30, Rte 283 and Rte 222. Buses head to Philly and Pittsburgh, but driving your own vehicle is the best option for sightseeing here.

Lancaster town is also served by Amtrak trains, which run frequently to Philadelphia ($20 to $29, 1¼ hours) and twice a day to Pittsburgh ($65, eight to nine hours).

Head 9 miles east from Lancaster on Rte 30 to reach Strasburg. The area is most easily accessible by car, but can also be reached via **RRTA** (Red Rose Transit Authority; 717-393-3315; www.redrosetransit.com) bus services.

Pennsylvania Wilds

North-central Pennsylvania, known as 'the Wilds,' is largely deep forest with an occasional regal building or grand mansion – remnants of the late 19th century, when lumber, coal and oil brought wealth to this now little-visited patch of the state. The cash cow of resource extraction was eventually milked dry by the turn of the 20th century, and the land fell on hard times. Since the bust, this swath of 12 counties has reverted to its wild state; much of the area is national forest or state park land.

Sights

★Cherry Springs State Park STATE PARK
(814-435-1037; www.visitpaparks.com; 4639 Cherry Springs Rd, Coudersport; 24hr) Considered one of the best places for stargazing east of the Mississippi, this mountaintop state park seems to have plenty of space, but be sure to book well ahead in July and August, when the Milky Way is almost directly overhead.

There's a $6.50 transaction fee for making overnight reservations.

Leonard Harrison State Park STATE PARK
(570-724-3061; www.visitpaparks.com; 4797 Rte 660, Wellsboro; park dawn-dusk, visitor center 10am-4:30pm Mon-Thu, to 6:30pm Fri-Sun; P) FREE This park has full views of the **Pine Creek Gorge**, aka the Grand Canyon of PA, with trails that descend 800ft down to the creek below.

A visitor center has toilets and a modest display of local fauna, and a viewing deck makes this side more accessible for people not planning to hike.

For the undeveloped side go to Colton Point State Park instead.

★Kinzua Bridge Skywalk BRIDGE
(814-778-5467; www.visitpaparks.com; 1721 Lindholm Rd, Mt Jewett; skywalk 8am-dusk, visitor center to 6pm) FREE The world's tallest railroad structure when it was built in 1882, this 301ft-high bridge was rebuilt in steel in 1900 – but then partially collapsed in 2003, when it was hit by an F1-grade tornado. The remaining piece, jutting out into the air, is now an observation deck, with an impressive and perhaps unnerving view over the ruined steel piers and the valley below.

Sleeping & Eating

Mansfield Inn MOTEL $
(570-662-2136; www.mansfieldinn.com; 26 S Main St, Mansfield; d from $60; P) There may be more charming B&Bs deeper in the PA Wilds, but this motel is hard to beat for straight-ahead value. The walls are thin, the rooms are clean and our wallets are happy.

Night & Day Coffee Cafe CAFE $
(570-662-1143; http://nightanddaycoffee.wixsite.com/cafe; 2 N Main St, Mansfield; sandwiches $5.50-8.50; 7am-7pm Mon-Fri, to 5pm Sat, 8am-5pm Sun;) Well worth detouring for, the Night & Day Coffee Cafe proudly claims to be enriching the neighborhood one latte at a time, and it's doing a good job of it. Boutique coffees, great chai and a wide selection of specialty salads and sandwiches make for a perfect breakfast or a great lunch.

Getting There & Away

Driving is your only option to reach the Pennsylvania Wilds. Allegheny National Forest is about 100 miles northwest of Pittsburgh and 90 miles southwest of Erie, NY. Route 6 makes for a scenic route that traverses much of the region, with the tiny college town of Mansfield acting as an eastern gateway.

Pittsburgh

There may be more beautiful cities than Pittsburgh, but few mix the seemingly contradictory aesthetics of filigreed beaux-arts elegance with muscular art-deco swagger. This is a city of stone and steel, with old public libraries and brick row houses beside wide bridges and towering skyscrapers. There's an old-school class to Pittsburgh's good looks, underlined by an attitude towards dining, drinking and the arts that is genuinely innovative.

Pittsburgh's surroundings also set the city apart. Situated between the Monongahela and Allegheny Rivers and the upland ridge of Mt Washington, this city has a distinctive geography; physically, it is very much defined by its mountains and rivers. While this is the main urban center for western Pennsylvania, it has avoided the economic depression of the surrounding region by investing in 'meds and eds' – hospitals and universities – buttressing its economy with expansive intellectual energy.

Sights & Activities

Points of interest in Pittsburgh are scattered in every neighborhood, but because of the hills it's difficult to walk between them. Bike, taxi or bus (or light rail in some areas) are the best ways to span suburbs. The usual ridesharing services are well represented in Pittsburgh.

★Andy Warhol Museum MUSEUM

(412-237-8300; www.warhol.org; 117 Sandusky St; adult/child $20/10, 5-10pm Fri $10/5; 10am-5pm Tue-Thu, Sat & Sun, to 10pm Fri) This six-story museum celebrates Pittsburgh's coolest native son, Andy Warhol, who moved to NYC, got a nose job and made himself famous with pop art. The exhibits start with Warhol's earliest drawings and commercial illustrations and include a simulated Velvet Underground happening, a DIY 'screen test' and pieces of Warhol's extensive knickknack collection.

Cans of inflatable Campbell's soup are for sale.

★Duquesne Incline FUNICULAR

(412-381-1665; www.duquesneincline.org; 1197 W Carson St; one-way adult/child $2.50/1.25; 5:30am-12:30am Mon-Sat, 7am-12:30am Sun) This nifty funicular and its **Monongahela Incline** (412-381-1665; www.duquesnein-cline.org; 5 Grandview Ave; one-way adult/child $2.50/1.25; 5:30am-12:30am Mon-Sat, 7am-12:30am Sun) twin down the road, both built in the late 19th century, are Pittsburgh icons, zipping up the steep slope of Mt Washington every five to 10 minutes. They provide commuters with a quick connection, and give visitors great city views, especially at night. You can make a loop, going up one, walking along aptly named Grandview Ave (about 1 mile, or take bus 40) and coming down the other.

If you ride just one, make it the Duquesne (du-*kane*). At the top, you can pay 50¢ to see the gears and cables at work.

Frick Art & Historical Center MUSEUM

(412-371-0600; www.thefrickpittsburgh.org; 7227 Reynolds St; 10am-5pm Tue-Thu, Sat & Sun, to 9pm Fri) FREE Henry Clay Frick, of New York City's Frick Collection (p78) fame, built his steel fortune in Pittsburgh. This Frick shows a small art collection (including beautiful medieval icons), plus his cars. For more art and general splendor, join a tour (adult/child $15/8) of **Clayton**, the family mansion.

Carnegie Museums MUSEUM

(412-622-3131; www.carnegiemuseums.org; 4400 Forbes Ave; adult/child both museums $20/12; 10am-5pm Mon, Wed & Fri-Sun, to 8pm Thu year-round, plus 10am-5pm Tue Jun-Aug;) Founded in 1895, these neighboring institutions are both tremendous troves of knowledge. The **Carnegie Museum of Art** has European treasures and an excellent architectural collection, while the **Carnegie Museum of Natural History** features a complete *Tyrannosaurus rex* skeleton and beautiful old dioramas. The art museum is open until 11pm on the third Thursday of the month.

Cathedral of Learning TOWER

(412-624-6001; www.tour.pitt.edu; 4200 Fifth Ave; 9am-2:30pm Mon-Sat, 11am-2:30pm Sun) FREE Soaring 42 stories, this Gothic tower at the center of the University of Pittsburgh is a city landmark. Visit to see the delightful **Nationality Rooms**, 31 classrooms themed to localities ranging from Russia to Syria to Africa to the Philippines. Self-guided audio tours (adult/child $4/2) are available daily in summer, or weekends during school term. New rooms may be added in the future.

Center for PostNatural History MUSEUM

(412-223-7698; www.postnatural.org; 4913 Penn Ave; by donation; noon-4pm Sun) FREE 'Postnatural history,' according to the artist-founder of this quirky museum, is the field of plants and animals designed by humankind. Learn all about spider-silk-making goats, selective breeding and more.

This is probably not your best first-date spot, but definitely a fun and unconventional place to learn about all things *human*-ipulated.

Wigle Whiskey DISTILLERY

(412-224-2827; www.wiglewhiskey.com; 2401 Smallman St; tours $20-25; 11am-6pm Mon, to 8pm Tue-Thu, to 10pm Fri, 10am-10pm Sat, 1-5pm Sun) This family-owned craft distillery in a brick warehouse in the Strip gives tours on Saturdays and has inexpensive sample flights ($10) of the many libations. Whiskey is a top choice, but there's also gin, vodka, bitters and even a housemade absinthe and more.

Pittsburgh Glass Center ART
(☎412-365-2145; www.pittsburghglasscenter.org; 5472 Penn Ave; ⏰10am-7pm Mon-Thu, to 4pm Fri-Sun) See a variety of glass-making techniques, and even try your hand at making something yourself in a demo. Or take an actual class; the PGC offers everything from newbie level to advanced (prices vary).

'Burgh Bits & Bites FOOD & DRINK
(☎412-901-7150; www.burghfoodtour.com; tours $43) These two-hour food tours through various neighborhoods are a fun way to discover the city's unique ethnic eats.

The Strip District tour is the most popular, but Bits & Bites also visits Bloomfield, Brookline, Lawrenceville, the South Side and more.

Pittsburgh History & Landmarks Foundation WALKING
(☎412-471-5808; www.phlf.org; tours free-$20) This group runs a free walking tour from Market Sq on Wednesday at 10am, among other excursions. Some paid, docent-led tours are also available.

Sleeping

Residence Inn by Marriott North Shore HOTEL $$
(☎412-321-2099; www.marriott.com; 574 W General Robinson St; d from $140, ste $170-320; P⊖❄@☎≋) This renovated chain-hotel option has a pool, a fitness center, free breakfasts and rooms that feel like mansions. It's also well located: a quick zip over the bridges to the downtown area, or within walking distance of some of the North Side attractions.

Note: it can be a zoo if the Steelers or the Pirates are playing.

★**Priory Hotel** INN $$
(☎412-231-3338; www.thepriory.com; 614 Pressley St; s $100-130, d $155-230, ste $180-295; P❄☎) The monks had it good when this was still a Catholic monastery: spacious rooms, high ceilings, a fireplace in the parlor. Breakfast, with its pastries and cold cuts, is reminiscent of a European hostel. It's on the North Side, in the historic-but-scruffy Deutschtown area.

The tiny Monk's Bar just off the lobby is open 5pm to 11pm daily – perfect for an evening tipple.

Omni William Penn Hotel HOTEL $$
(☎412-281-7100; www.omnihotels.com; 530 William Penn Pl; r $180-290; P⊖❄☎) Pittsburgh's stateliest old hotel, built by Henry Frick, has a cavernous lobby, with luxury suites that were remodeled in 2016. The great public spaces give it a sense of grandeur that some luxury hotels lack. Worth booking if you have the money…or can find it at a discount, which is often the case in the off-season.

Eating

E Carson St on the South Side has the highest concentration of restaurants, but the Strip District comes a close second. The North Side, Lawrenceville and the East Liberties have the most up-and-coming activity. Catering to a large Catholic population, many Pittsburgh restaurants serve fish on Friday, and fried-fish sandwiches are especially popular – despite the city's lack of coastline, they're pretty tasty, too!

Primanti Bros SANDWICHES $
(☎412-263-2142; www.primantibros.com; 46 18th St; sandwiches $6-10; ⏰24hr) The original location serves up the signature sandwiches Pittsburghers miss when they move away: hot, greasy delights stuffed with grilled meat, french fries and coleslaw.

With branches all around Pittsburgh, you're never too far away from a Primanti Bros fix.

La Prima CAFE $
(☎412-281-1922; www.laprima.com; 205 21st St; pastries $2-4; ⏰6am-4pm Mon-Wed, to 5pm Thu-Sat, 7am-4pm Sun) Great Italian coffee and pastries have people lined up out the door at peak times. The cranberry scone is their most popular sweet, but it has a range of other yummy treats (*sfogliatelle,* tarts, cookies etc).

If you speak Italian you can enjoy the weekly quote here written on the green chalkboard.

Zenith VEGAN $
(☎412-481-4833; www.zenithpgh.com; 86 S 26th St; mains $7-11; ⏰11:30am-8:30pm Thu-Sat, 11am-2:30pm Sun; ✎) All meals are vegan here, though cheese is optional. A visit is like eating in an antique shop, as everything, including the Formica tables, is for sale.

The Sunday buffet brunch ($11.50) draws a great community of regulars.

Bar Marco ITALIAN $$
(☎412-471-1900; www.barmarcopgh.com; 2216 Penn Ave; mains $8-20; ⏰dinner 5-11pm Tue-Sat,

brunch 10am-3pm Sat & Sun) A Strip District favorite, this is one of the city's more sophisticated kitchens, with an excellent brunch too. Cocktails are creative; you can also try the bartender's suggestion based on what types of drinks you enjoy.

The refreshing no-tipping policy means the staff are appropriately compensated in a fair and equitable way.

★Legume FUSION $$$
(☎412-621-2700; www.legumebistro.com; 214 N Craig St; mains $23-42; ⏲5-9pm Mon-Thu, to 9:30pm Fri & Sat) Excellent meats and fish here, with a farm-to-table mindset and a menu that changes daily. If it's available, try the stinging-nettle soup – partly because where else can you try stinging nettles, but mostly because it's out of this world.

★Paris 66 FRENCH $$$
(☎412-404-8166; www.paris66bistro.com; 6018 Centre Ave; dinner mains $20-35; ⏲11am-10pm Mon-Thu, to 11pm Fri & Sat, 10am-3pm Sun) This is top-end French at its best, in a cozy, bistro-style setting. Blink and you'll think you're in France. That said, this isn't *haute* cuisine, but rather solid food of rural France: *coq au vin,* rabbit in mustard sauce, *steak frites* and the rest.

Drinking & Entertainment

Church Brew Works MICROBREWERY
(☎412-688-8200; www.churchbrew.com; 3525 Liberty Ave; ⏲11:30am-11:15pm Mon-Thu, to 12:15am Fri & Sat, to 9:15pm Sun) There are some who put drunkenness next to godliness, and they probably invented Church Brew Works. Gleaming and shining, giant brewery vats sit in what was once the pulpit. If you think this is sacrilegious, you'll want to skip this place – although of course many a great Belgian beer was proudly brewed by highly religious monks.

Spice Island Tea House TEAHOUSE
(☎412-687-8821; www.spiceislandteahouse.com; 253 Atwood St; ⏲11:30am-8:45pm Mon-Thu, to 9:45pm Fri & Sat) If you fancy sipping a quiet cuppa (tea infusions $3.50 to $5.50) while your friend has a cocktail, this is the spot to visit.

Alongside a number of delectable teas this place also serves Southeast Asian fusion food.

★Allegheny Wine Mixer WINE BAR
(☎412-252-2337; www.alleghenywinemixer.com; 5326 Butler St; ⏲5pm-midnight Tue-Thu, to 1am Fri-Sun) All the perks of a high-end wine bar – great list, smart staff, tasty nibbles – in the comfort of a neighborhood dive.

★Elks Lodge LIVE MUSIC
(☎412-321-1834; www.elks.org; 400 Cedar Ave) Find out why Pittsburgh is known as the Paris of Appalachia at the Elks' Banjo Night (Wednesdays at 7pm; free): the stage is packed with players and the audience sings along to all the banjo classics. Also hosts a big-band night on the first, third and fifth Thursdays of the month (7:15pm; $5 cover). Located on the North Side in Deutschtown.

Information

VisitPITTSBURGH Main Branch (☎412-281-7711; www.visitpittsburgh.com; 120 Fifth Ave, Ste 2800; ⏲10am-6pm Mon-Fri, to 5pm Sat, hours vary Sun) Publishes the *Official Visitors Guide* as well as providing maps and tourist advice.

Getting There & Away

AIR

Pittsburgh International Airport (PIT; ☎412-472-3525; www.flypittsburgh.com; 1000 Airport Blvd), 18 miles west of downtown, has direct connections to Europe, Canada and major US cities via a slew of airlines.

BUS

The **Greyhound bus station** (Grant Street Transportation Center; ☎412-392-6514; www.greyhound.com; 55 11th St), at the far edge of the Strip District, has frequent buses to Philadelphia (from $31, six to seven hours), NYC (from $34, 8½ to 11 hours) and Chicago, IL (from $72, 11 to 14 hours).

CAR & MOTORCYCLE

Pittsburgh is accessible via I-76 or I-79 from the west and I-70 from the east. It's about a six-hour drive from NYC and about three hours from Buffalo.

TRAIN

Pittsburgh has a magnificent old train station – and **Amtrak** (☎800-872-7245; www.amtrak.com; 1100 Liberty Ave) drops you off in a dismal modern building behind it.

Services run daily to Philadelphia (from $68, 7½ hours), NYC (from $81, 9½ hours), Chicago (from $72, 10 hours) and Washington, DC (from $53, eight hours).

Getting Around

PortAuthority (www.portauthority.org) provides public transport around Pittsburgh, including the 28X Airport Flyer ($2.75, 40 minutes, every 30 minutes 5:10am to 12:10am) from the airport to downtown and Oakland.

A taxi from the airport costs about $43 (not including tip) to downtown. Various shuttles also make downtown runs for around $25 per person.

Driving in Pittsburgh can be frustrating – roads end with no warning or deposit you suddenly on bridges. Parking is scarce downtown. Where possible, use the extensive bus network, which includes a fast express busway (routes beginning with P).

There is also a limited light-rail system, the T, useful for the South Side. Rides on the T downtown are free; other in-city fares are $2.50, plus $1 for a transfer.

New England

Includes ➡

Massachusetts 171
Boston 174
Cape Cod 194
The Berkshires 205
Rhode Island 208
Providence 209
Newport 211
Connecticut 213
Vermont 221
New Hampshire 232
Maine 240

Best Places to Eat

- Saltie Girl (p188)
- Nudel (p206)
- Pantry (p220)
- Fore Street (p244)
- birch (p210)

Best Places to Sleep

- The Dean Hotel (p210)
- Liberty Hotel (p186)
- Inn at Shelburne Farms (p230)
- Notch Hostel (p237)
- Guest House at Field Farm (p207)

Why Go?

The history of New England is the history of America. It's the Pilgrims who came ashore at Plymouth Rock, the minutemen who fought for independence from Britain, and the abolitionists who challenged America's legacy of slavery. It's the ponderings of Ralph Waldo Emerson and the protests of Harriet Beecher Stowe. It's hundreds of years of poets and philosophers: progressive thinkers who dared to dream and dared to do. It's liberty-loving citizens not afraid to challenge the status quo, as well as generations of immigrants, who have shaped New England into the dynamic region that it is today.

For outdoor adventure, the region undulates with the rolling hills and rocky peaks of the Appalachian Mountains. Nearly 5000 miles of coastline make for unlimited opportunities for fishing, swimming, surfing and sailing. New England also boasts a bounty of epicurean delights: pancakes drenched in maple syrup, just-picked fruit and sharp cheddar cheese, and sublimely fresh seafood that is the hallmark of this region.

When to Go

Boston

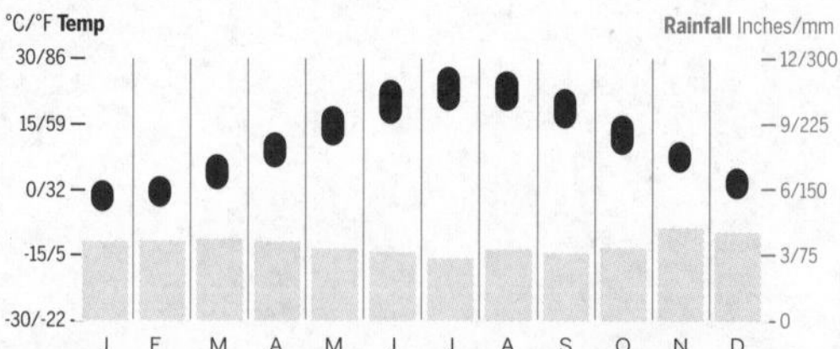

May & Jun Uncrowded sights and lightly trodden trails. Whale-watching begins.

Jul & Aug Top tourist season with summer festivals and warmer ocean weather.

Sep & Oct New England's blazing foliage peaks from mid-September to mid-October.

History

When the first European settlers arrived in the New World, they found about 100,000 Native American inhabitants, mostly Algonquians, organized into small regional tribes. The northern tribes were solely hunter-gatherers, while the southern tribes hunted and practiced slash-and-burn agriculture, growing corn, squash and beans.

In 1602 English Captain Bartholomew Gosnold landed at Cape Cod and sailed north to Maine; but it wasn't until 1614 that Captain John Smith, who charted the region's coastline for King James I, christened the land 'New England.' With the arrival of the Pilgrims at Plymouth in 1620, European settlement began in earnest. Over the next century the colonies expanded, often at the expense of the indigenous people.

Although subjects of the British Crown, New Englanders governed themselves with legislative councils and they came to view their affairs as separate from those of England. In the 1770s King George III imposed a series of taxes to pay for England's involvement in costly wars. The colonists, unrepresented in the British parliament, protested under the slogan, 'No taxation without representation.' Attempts to quash the protests eventually led to battles at Lexington and Concord, MA, setting off the War for Independence. The historic result was the birth of the USA in 1776.

Following independence, New England became an economic powerhouse, its harbors booming centers for shipbuilding and trade. New England's famed Yankee Clippers plied ports from China to South America. A thriving whaling industry brought unprecedented wealth to Nantucket and New Bedford. The USA's first water-powered cotton-spinning mill was established in Rhode Island in 1793.

No boom lasts forever. By the early 20th century many of the mills had moved south. Today, education, finance, biotechnology and tourism are linchpins of the regional economy.

ℹ Resources

Appalachian Mountain Club (www.outdoors.org) Fantastic resource for hiking, biking, camping, climbing and paddling in New England's great outdoors.

Boston.com (www.boston.com/tags/new-england-travel) Travel news, tips and itineraries from the *Boston Globe*.

Lonely Planet (www.lonelyplanet.com/usa/new-england) Destination information, hotel reviews and more.

New England Network (www.newengland.com) New England travel resources from *Yankee Magazine*.

MASSACHUSETTS

New England's most populous state, Massachusetts packs in appealing variety, from the sandy beaches of Cape Cod to college towns of the Pioneer Valley to the woodsy hills of the Berkshires. The state's rich history oozes from almost every quarter: discover the shoreline in Plymouth, where the Pilgrims first settled in the New World; explore the battlefields in Lexington and Concord, where the first shots of the American Revolution rang out; and wander the cobbled streets and old ports of Salem, Nantucket and New Bedford, where whaling and merchant boats once docked.

Modern-day Massachusetts is also diverse and dynamic. Boston is the state's undisputed cultural (and political) capital, but smaller towns such as Provincetown and Northampton also offer lively art and music scenes, out and active queer populations and plenty of opportunities to enjoy the great outdoors.

History

Massachusetts has played a leading role in American politics since the arrival of the first colonists – the Pilgrims – who landed in Plymouth in 1620.

In the 18th century, spurred by a booming maritime trade, Massachusetts colonists revolted against trade restrictions and taxes imposed by Great Britain. The independence movement grew up in Boston, where the Sons of Liberty instigated uprisings and spread propaganda about their cause. These rebellions against the crown set the stage for battles in nearby Lexington and Concord, which kicked off the War for Independence in 1775.

In the 18th and 19th centuries, the North Shore of Massachusetts was a shipbuilding center, and Salem in particular grew rich on the returns of merchant ships that sailed around the world. In the southern part of the state, the whaling industry brought unprecedented wealth to Nantucket and New Bedford, whose ports are still lined with

New England Highlights

1 Freedom Trail (p185) Following the footsteps of Colonial rabble-rousers in Boston.

2 Aquinnah Public Beach (p202) Romping in the sand and surf on one of the gorgeous beaches on Martha's Vineyard.

3 Tanglewood Music Festival (p206) Listening to world-class music under the stars in Lenox.

4 Franconia Notch (p237) Catching an aerial tram up Cannon Mountain or following the spectacular rush of water through Flume Gorge in the White Mountains.

5 Cliff Walk (p211) Sneaking a peak into the world of unabashed wealth of 19th-century capitalists in Newport.

6 Acadia National Park (p247) Savoring the scenery of New England's only national park, on Mount Desert Island.

7 Shannon's Unshelled (p246) Feasting on a succulent lobster roll on the rocky coast of Maine.

8 Burlington Waterfront (p230) Kayaking, cycling and sailing in and around Lake Champlain.

grand sea captains' homes. Other towns such as Lowell, Worcester and Springfield grew up when textile mills and other industry were built up during the 20th century.

Nowadays, the Commonwealth continues to thrive, as tourists and students are drawn to its rich history and vibrant cultural life.

Information

Massachusetts Department of Conservation and Recreation (☎617-626-1250; www.mass.gov/orgs/department-of-conservation-recreation) offers camping in 29 state parks.

Boston

Boston's history recalls revolution and transformation, and today the city is still among the country's most forward-thinking and barrier-breaking cities.

For all intents and purposes, Boston is the oldest city in America. And you can hardly walk a step over its cobblestone streets without running into some historic site. But that doesn't mean Boston has been relegated to the past.

A history of cultural patronage means that the city's art and music scenes continue to charm and challenge contemporary audiences. Cutting-edge urban planning projects are reshaping the city even now, as neighborhoods are revived and rediscovered. Historic universities and colleges still attract scientists, philosophers and writers, who shape the city's evolving culture.

Sights

Beacon Hill & Boston Common

Abutted by the Boston Common – the nation's original public park and the centerpiece of the city – and topped with the gold-domed Massachusetts State House, Beacon Hill is the neighborhood most often featured on Boston postcards. The retail and residential streets on Beacon Hill are delightfully, quintessentially Boston.

★Public Garden GARDENS

(Map p180; ☎617-723-8144; www.friendsofthepublicgarden.org; Arlington St; ⌚dawn-dusk; 👪; Ⓣ Arlington) Adjoining Boston Common, the Public Garden is a 24-acre botanical oasis of Victorian flower beds, verdant grass and weeping willow trees shading a tranquil lagoon. The old-fashioned pedal-powered **Swan Boats** (☎617-522-1966; www.swanboats.com; adult/child $4/2.50; ⌚10am-4pm Apr-Jun, to 5pm Jul & Aug) have been delighting children for generations. The most endearing spot in the Public Garden is the **Make Way for Ducklings Statue**, depicting Mrs Mallard and her eight ducklings, the main characters in the beloved book by Robert McCloskey.

★Boston Common PARK

(Map p180; btwn Tremont, Charles, Beacon & Park Sts; ⌚6am-midnight; P👪; Ⓣ Park St) America's oldest public park, Boston Common has a long and storied history, serving as a campground for British troops during the Revolutionary War and as green grass for cattle grazing until the 1830s. Nowadays, the Common is a place for picnicking and people-watching. In winter, the **Frog Pond** (☎617-635-2120; www.bostonfrogpond.com; adult/child $6/free, skate rental $12/6; ⌚10am-3:45pm Mon, to 9pm Tue-Thu & Sun, to 10pm Fri & Sat mid-Nov–mid-Mar) attracts ice-skaters, while summer draws theater lovers for **Shakespeare on the Common** (☎617-426-0863; www.commshakes.org; ⌚Jul & Aug). This is also the starting point for the Freedom Trail.

Massachusetts State House NOTABLE BUILDING

(Map p180; ☎617-727-7030; www.sec.state.ma.us; cnr Beacon & Bowdoin Sts; ⌚8:45am-5pm Mon-Fri, tours 10am-3:30pm Mon-Fri; Ⓣ Park St) FREE High atop Beacon Hill, Massachusetts' leaders and legislators attempt to turn their ideas into concrete policies and practices within the State House. John Hancock provided the land (previously part of his cow pasture) and Charles Bulfinch designed the commanding state capitol, but it was Oliver Wendell Holmes who called it 'the hub of the solar system' (thus earning Boston the nickname 'the Hub'). Free 40-minute tours cover the history, artwork, architecture and political personalities of the State House.

Downtown & Waterfront

Much of Boston's business and tourist activity takes place in this central neighborhood, which includes the Financial District. Downtown is not the thriving shopping area that it once was, especially since the closure of Filene's Department Store. But it is a bustling district crammed with modern

BOSTON IN TWO DAYS...

Day One

Spend your first day in Boston following the Freedom Trail (p184), which starts on the Boston Common and continues through downtown. There isn't time to go inside every museum, but you can admire the architecture and learn the history. Highlights include the Old South Meeting House , the Old State House and Faneuil Hall.

In the afternoon, the Freedom Trail continues into the North End, where you can visit the historic Paul Revere House, Old North Church and Copp's Hill Burying Ground. Move on to the exquisite Liberty Hotel (p186), former site of the Charles St Jail.

Day Two

Spend the morning admiring Boston's most architecturally significant collection of buildings, clustered around Copley Sq (p182). Admire the art and books at the Boston Public Library (p183), and then ogle the magnificent stained-glass windows at Trinity Church (p182).

Your afternoon is reserved for one of Boston's art museums. Unfortunately you'll have to choose between the excellent, encyclopedic collection at the Museum of Fine Arts (p183) or the smaller but no less extraordinary exhibits at the Isabella Stewart Gardner Museum (p183). Either way, you won't be disappointed.

In the evening, catch the Boston Symphony Orchestra at the acoustically magnificent Symphony Hall (p190), or for lower-brow entertainment, catch a baseball game at Fenway Park (p183) or go bar-hopping on Lansdowne St.

complexes and colonial buildings, including Faneuil Hall and Quincy Market. The Waterfront is home to the Harbor Islands ferries and the New England Aquarium.

★Old State House HISTORIC BUILDING

(Map p180; ☎617-720-1713; www.bostonhistory.org; 206 Washington St; adult/child $10/free; ⌚9am-6pm Jun-Aug, to 5pm Sep-May; Ⓣ State) Dating from 1713, the Old State House is Boston's oldest surviving public building, where the Massachusetts Assembly used to debate the issues of the day before the Revolution. The building is best known for its balcony, where the Declaration of Independence was first read to Bostonians in 1776. Inside, the Old State House contains a small museum of revolutionary memorabilia, with videos and multimedia presentations about the Boston Massacre, which took place out the front.

Old South Meeting House HISTORIC BUILDING

(Map p180; ☎617-482-6439; www.osmh.org; 310 Washington St; adult/child $6/1; ⌚9:30am-5pm Apr-Oct, 10am-4pm Nov-Mar; 👪; Ⓣ Downtown Crossing, State) 'No tax on tea!' That was the decision on December 16, 1773, when 5000 angry colonists gathered here to protest British taxes, leading to the Boston Tea Party. Download an audio of the historic pre–Tea Party meeting from the museum website, then visit the graceful meeting house to check out the exhibit on the history of the building and the protest.

Rose Kennedy Greenway PARK

(Map p180; ☎617-292-0020; www.rosekennedygreenway.org; 👪; Ⓣ Aquarium, Haymarket) Where once there was a hulking overhead highway, now winds a 27-acre strip of landscaped gardens, fountain-lined greens and public art installations. The park has something for everyone: the artist-driven Greenway Open Market (p191) for weekend shoppers, food trucks for weekday lunchers, summertime block parties for music lovers and **Trillium Garden** (☎857-449-0083; www.trilliumbrewing.com; cnr Atlantic Ave & High St; ⌚2-10pm Wed-Fri, from 11am Sat, 1-8pm Sun May-Oct; 📶; Ⓣ South Station, Aquarium) for beer drinkers. Cool off in the whimsical **Rings Fountain**, walk the calming **labyrinth**, or take a ride on the custom-designed **Greenway Carousel** (per ride $3; ⌚11am-7pm Apr-Dec).

Faneuil Hall HISTORIC BUILDING

(Map p180; ☎617-242-5642; www.nps.gov/bost; Congress St; ⌚9am-5pm; Ⓣ State, Haymarket, Government Center) FREE 'Those who cannot bear free speech had best go home,' said Wendell Phillips. 'Faneuil Hall is no place for slavish hearts.' Indeed, this public meeting place was the site of so much rabble-rousing that it earned the nickname the 'Cradle of Liberty.' After the revolution, Faneuil Hall

Boston

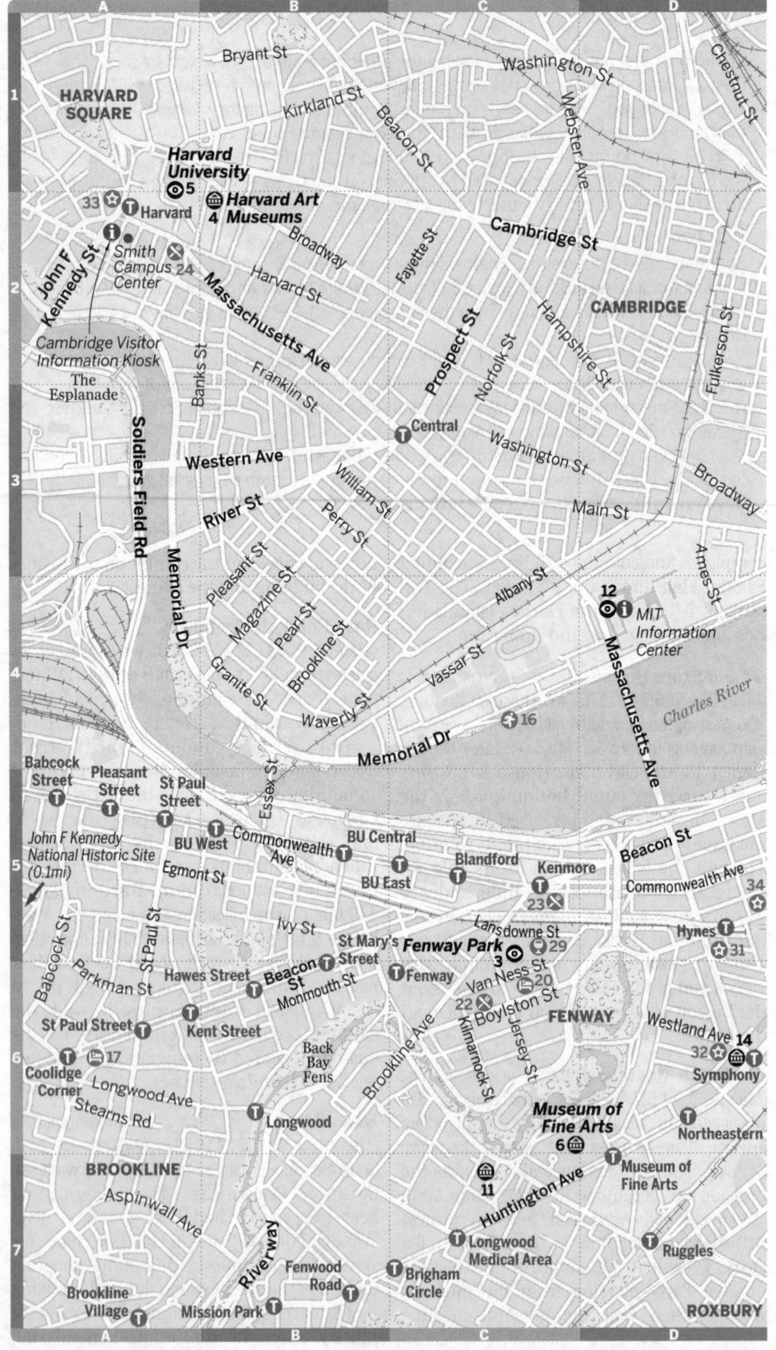
HARVARD SQUARE
Harvard University
5
Harvard Art Museums
4
33
Harvard
Smith Campus Center
24
Cambridge Visitor Information Kiosk
The Esplanade
John F Kennedy St
Bryant St
Kirkland St
Washington St
Chestnut St
Beacon St
Webster Ave
Cambridge St
Broadway
Harvard St
Fayette St
Massachusetts Ave
Prospect St
Norfolk St
Hampshire St
CAMBRIDGE
Fulkerson St
Franklin St
Banks St
Central
Washington St
Western Ave
Soldiers Field Rd
William St
River St
Perry St
Main St
Broadway
Ames St
Memorial Dr
Pleasant St
Magazine St
Pearl St
Brookline St
Albany St
12
MIT Information Center
Vassar St
Granite St
Waverly St
16
Charles River
Memorial Dr
Massachusetts Ave
Essex St
Babcock Street
Pleasant Street
St Paul Street
BU West
Commonwealth Ave
BU Central
BU East
Blandford
Kenmore
Beacon St
Commonwealth Ave
34
John F Kennedy National Historic Site (0.1mi)
Egmont St
23
Ivy St
Lansdowne St
Hynes
31
Babcock St
St Paul St
Parkman St
St Mary's Street
Fenway Park
3
29
Hawes Street
Beacon St
Monmouth St
Fenway
Van Ness St
20
22
Boylston St
FENWAY
Westland Ave
14
32
Symphony
St Paul Street
Kent Street
Brookline Ave
Kilmarnock St
Jersey St
Back Bay Fens
17
Coolidge Corner
Longwood Ave
Stearns Rd
Longwood
Museum of Fine Arts
6
Northeastern
BROOKLINE
11
Museum of Fine Arts
Huntington Ave
Aspinwall Ave
Riverway
Longwood Medical Area
Ruggles
Fenwood Road
Brigham Circle
Brookline Village
Mission Park
ROXBURY

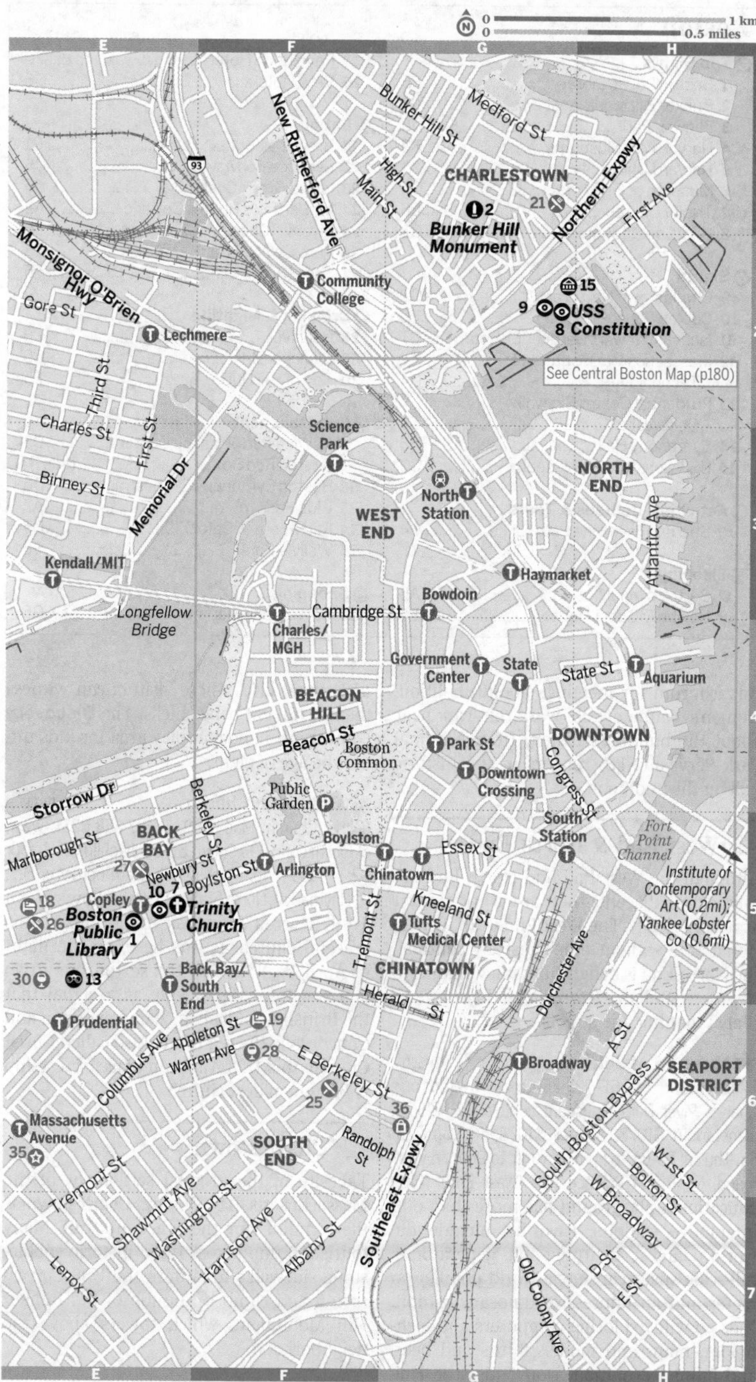

0 1 km
0 0.5 miles
Bunker Hill St
Medford St
New Rutherford Ave
High St
Main St
CHARLESTOWN
21
Northern Expwy
First Ave
2
Bunker Hill Monument
Monsignor O'Brien Hwy
Community College
15
9
USS
8 Constitution
Gore St
Lechmere
Third St
See Central Boston Map (p180)
Charles St
First St
Science Park
Memorial Dr
Binney St
NORTH END
North Station
WEST END
Atlantic Ave
Kendall/MIT
Haymarket
Bowdoin
Longfellow Bridge
Cambridge St
Charles/ MGH
Government Center
State
State St
Aquarium
BEACON HILL
DOWNTOWN
Beacon St
Boston Common
Park St
Downtown Crossing
Congress St
Public Garden
Storrow Dr
Berkeley St
BACK BAY
South Station
Fort Point Channel
Marlborough St
Boylston
Essex St
27
Newbury St
Boylston St
Arlington
Chinatown
10 7
Institute of Contemporary Art (0.2mi); Yankee Lobster Co (0.6mi)
18
Copley
Trinity Church
Kneeland St
26
Boston Public Library
1
Tremont St
Tufts Medical Center
Dorchester Ave
CHINATOWN
30
13
Back Bay/ South End
Herald St
Prudential
Appleton St
19
Columbus Ave
Warren Ave
28
E Berkeley St
A St
Broadway
SEAPORT DISTRICT
25
36
South Boston Bypass
Massachusetts Avenue
SOUTH END
Randolph St
35
Southeast Expwy
W 1st St
Tremont St
Bolton St
Shawmut Ave
W Broadway
Washington St
Harrison Ave
Albany St
Old Colony Ave
D St
Lenox St
E St

Boston

Top Sights
1 Boston Public Library E5
2 Bunker Hill Monument G1
3 Fenway Park C5
4 Harvard Art Museums B2
5 Harvard University A1
6 Museum of Fine Arts C6
7 Trinity Church E5
8 USS Constitution G2

Sights
9 Charlestown Navy Yard G2
10 Copley Square E5
11 Isabella Stewart Gardner Museum C7
12 Massachusetts Institute of Technology D4
13 Prudential Center Skywalk Observatory E5
14 Symphony Hall D6
15 USS Constitution Museum G2

Activities, Courses & Tours
16 Charles River Bike Path C4

Sleeping
17 Bertram Inn A6
18 Newbury Guest House E5
19 Revolution Hotel F6
20 Verb Hotel C6

Eating
21 Brewer's Fork G1
22 Eventide Fenway C6
23 Island Creek Oyster Bar C5
24 Mr Bartley's Burger Cottage A2
25 Myers + Chang F6
26 Puro Ceviche Bar E5
27 Saltie Girl E5

Drinking & Nightlife
28 Beehive F6
29 Bleacher Bar C5
30 Top of the Hub E5

Entertainment
31 Berklee Performance Center D5
Boston Red Sox .... (see 3)
32 Boston Symphony Orchestra D6
33 Club Passim A2
34 Red Room @ Cafe 939 .... D5
35 Wally's Café E6

Shopping
36 SoWa Open Market G6

was a forum for meetings about abolition, women's suffrage and war. You can hear about the building's history from National Park Service (NPS) rangers in the historic hall on the 2nd floor.

West End & North End

Although the West End and North End are physically adjacent, they are worlds apart atmospherically. The West End is an institutional area without much zest. By contrast, the North End is delightfully spicy, thanks to the many Italian *ristoranti* and *salumerie* (delis) that line the streets.

★Museum of Science MUSEUM
(Map p180; 617-723-2500; www.mos.org; Charles River Dam; museum adult/child $28/23, planetarium $10/8, theater $10/8; 9am-7pm Sat-Thu Jul & Aug, to 5pm Sep-Jun, to 9pm Fri year-round; P; T Science Park/West End) This educational playground has more than 600 interactive exhibits. Favorites include the world's largest lightning-bolt generator, a full-scale space capsule, a world population meter and an impressive dinosaur exhibit. Kids go wild exploring computers and technology, maps and models, birds and bees, and human evolution. Don't miss the **Hall of Human Life**, where visitors can witness the hatching of baby chicks. The **Discovery Center** is a hands-on play area for kids under the age of eight.

★Old North Church CHURCH
(Christ Church; Map p180; 617-858-8231; www.oldnorth.com; 193 Salem St; adult/child $8/4, tour $2; 10am-4pm Nov-March, 9am-6pm Apr-Oct; T Haymarket, North Station) Longfellow's poem 'Paul Revere's Ride' has immortalized this graceful church. It was here, on the night of April 18, 1775, that the sexton hung two lanterns from the steeple as a signal that the British would advance on Lexington and Concord via the sea route. Also called Christ Church, this 1723 Anglican place of worship is Boston's oldest church.

Charlestown

The site of the original settlement of the Massachusetts Bay Colony, Charlestown is the terminus for the Freedom Trail. Many tourists tramp across these historic cobblestone sidewalks to admire the USS *Constitution* and climb to the top of the Bunker Hill Monument, which towers above the neighborhood.

★Bunker Hill Monument MONUMENT

(Map p176; ☎617-242-7275; www.nps.gov/bost; Monument Sq; ⏰9am-5pm Oct-May, to 6pm Jun-Sep; 🚌93 from Haymarket, Ⓣ Community College) FREE This 220ft granite obelisk monument commemorates the turning-point battle that was fought on the surrounding hillside on June 17, 1775. Ultimately, the Redcoats prevailed, but the victory was bittersweet, as they lost more than one-third of their deployed forces, while the colonists suffered relatively few casualties. Climb the 294 steps to the top of the monument to enjoy the panorama of the city, the harbor and the North Shore.

★USS Constitution SHIP

(Map p176; ☎617-242-2543; www.navy.mil/local/constitution; Charlestown Navy Yard; ⏰10am-4pm Wed-Sun Jan-Mar, to 6pm Apr, 10am-6pm Tue-Sun May-Sep, to 5pm Oct-Dec; 👪; 🚌93 from Haymarket, ⛴Inner Harbor Ferry from Long Wharf, Ⓣ North Station) FREE 'Her sides are made of iron!' cried a crewman upon watching a shot bounce off the thick oak hull of the USS *Constitution* during the War of 1812. This bit of irony earned the legendary ship its nickname. Indeed, it has never gone down in a battle. The USS *Constitution* remains the oldest commissioned US Navy ship, dating from 1797, and it is normally taken out onto Boston Harbor every July 4 in order to maintain its commissioned status.

Make sure you bring a photo ID to go aboard. You'll learn lots, such as how the captain's son died on the ship's maiden voyage (an inauspicious start).

USS Constitution Museum MUSEUM

(Map p176; ☎617-426-1812; www.ussconstitutionmuseum.org; First Ave, Charlestown Navy Yard; suggested donation adult $10-15, child $5-10; ⏰9am-6pm Apr-Oct, 10am-5pm Nov-Mar; 👪; 🚌93 from Haymarket, ⛴Inner Harbor Ferry from Long Wharf, Ⓣ North Station) Head indoors to this museum for a play-by-play of the various battles of the USS *Constitution*, as well as its current role as the flagship of the US Navy. The exhibits on the War of 1812 and the Barbary War are especially interesting, and trace the birth of the US Navy during these relatively unknown conflicts. Upstairs, kids can experience what it was like to be a sailor on the USS *Constitution* in 1812.

Seaport District

The Seaport District is a section of South Boston that is fast developing as an attractive waterside destination, thanks to the dynamic contemporary-art museum and the explosion of new dining and entertainment options.

★Institute of Contemporary Art MUSEUM

(ICA; ☎617-478-3100; www.icaboston.org; 25 Harbor Shore Dr; adult/child $15/free, 5-9pm Thu free; ⏰10am-5pm Tue, Wed, Sat & Sun, to 9pm Thu & Fri; 👪; 🚌SL1, SL2, Ⓣ South Station) Boston has become a focal point for contemporary art in the 21st century, with the Institute of Contemporary Art leading the way. The building is a work of art in itself: a glass structure cantilevered over a waterside plaza. The vast light-filled interior allows for multimedia presentations, educational

BOSTON FOR CHILDREN

Boston is one giant history museum, and the setting for many lively and informative field trips. Cobblestone streets and costume-clad tour guides can bring to life the events that kids read about in history books, while hands-on experimentation and interactive exhibits fuse education and entertainment.

Great tours for kids:

Boston by Foot (p185) Runs 'Boston by Little Feet,' the only Freedom Trail walking tour designed especially for children aged six to 12.

Boston Duck Tours (☎617-267-3825; www.bostonducktours.com; adult/child $42/28; 👪; Ⓣ Aquarium, Science Park, Prudential) Kids of all ages are invited to drive the duck on the raging waters of the Charles River. Bonus: quacking loudly is encouraged.

Freedom Trail Foundation (Map p180; ☎617-357-8300; www.thefreedomtrail.org; adult/child $14/8; Ⓣ Park St) Tours are run by guides in period costume. Download a kid-friendly podcast or reading list for your child before setting out.

Urban AdvenTours (p185) This bike tour is great for all ages. Kids' bikes and helmets are available for rent, as are bike trailers for toddlers.

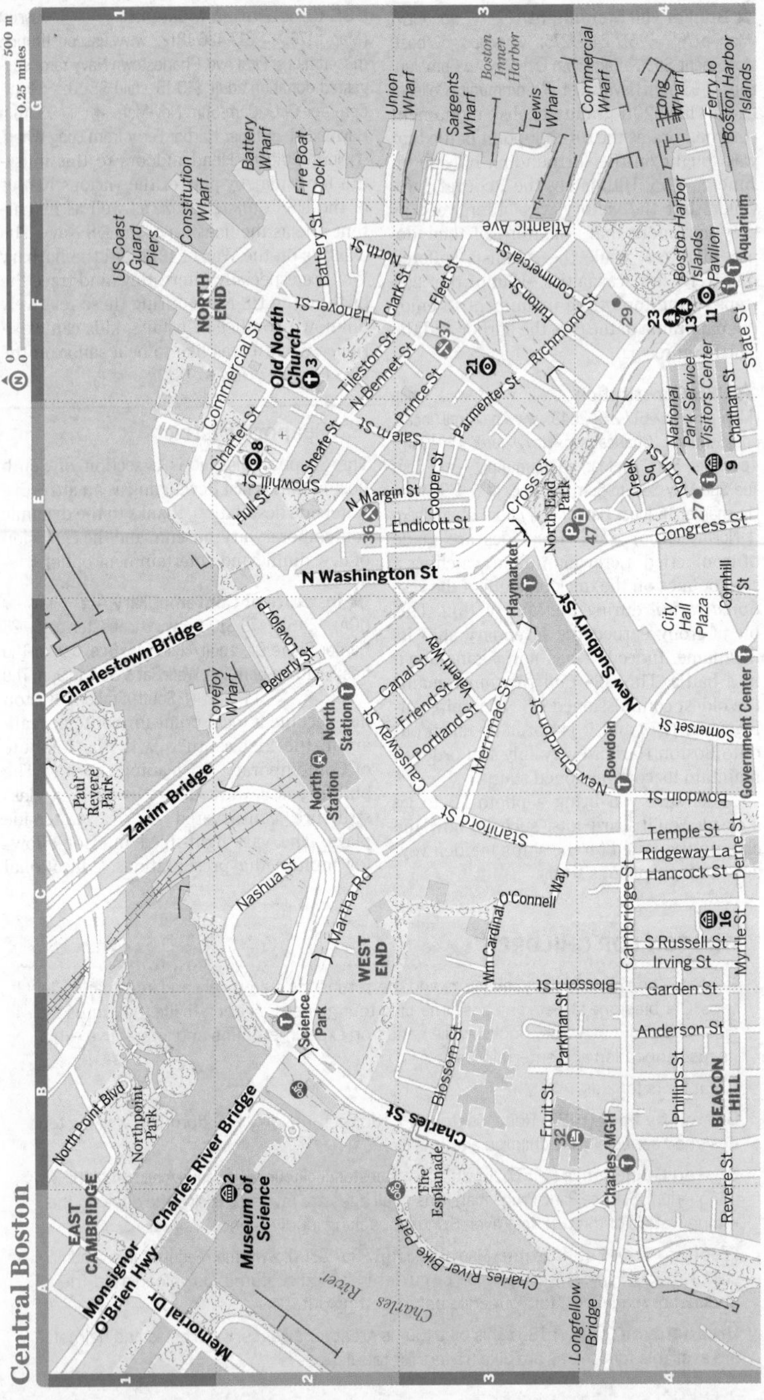
Central Boston
500 m
0.25 miles
EAST CAMBRIDGE
Monsignor O'Brien Hwy
Memorial Dr
Charles River Bridge
Museum of Science
2
North Point Blvd
Northpoint Park
Charles River
Charles River Bike Path
The Esplanade
Longfellow Bridge
Charles/MGH
Charles St
Revere St
BEACON HILL
Phillips St
Fruit St
32
Blossom St
Parkman St
Anderson St
Garden St
Blossom St
Irving St
S Russell St
Myrtle St
16
Cambridge St
Hancock St
Derne St
Ridgeway La
Temple St
Bowdoin St
Bowdoin
Government Center
Science Park
WEST END
Martha Rd
Wm Cardinal O'Connell Way
Nashua St
Staniford St
New Chardon St
Merrimac St
Somerset St
New Sudbury St
Paul Revere Park
Zakim Bridge
North Station
Causeway St
Portland St
Friend St
Canal St
Valenti Way
Lovejoy Wharf
Beverly St
Lovejoy Pl
Charlestown Bridge
N Washington St
Haymarket
City Hall Plaza
Cornhill St
Congress St
North End Park
47
Cross St
Endicott St
36
N Margin St
Cooper St
Hull St
Snowhill St
8
Charter St
Sheafe St
Salem St
Prince St
Parmenter St
Creek Sq
North St
27
9
National Park Service Visitors Center
Chatham St
State St
11
13
23
29
Richmond St
Fulton St
Commercial St
Old North Church
3
21
37
Tileston St
N Bennet St
Clark St
Fleet St
Hanover St
North St
Commercial St
NORTH END
Battery St
US Coast Guard Piers
Constitution Wharf
Battery Wharf
Fire Boat Dock
Union Wharf
Sargents Wharf
Boston Inner Harbor
Lewis Wharf
Commercial Wharf
Atlantic Ave
Long Wharf
Boston Harbor Islands Pavilion
Aquarium
Ferry to Boston Harbor Islands
A
B
C
D
E
F
G
1
2
3
4

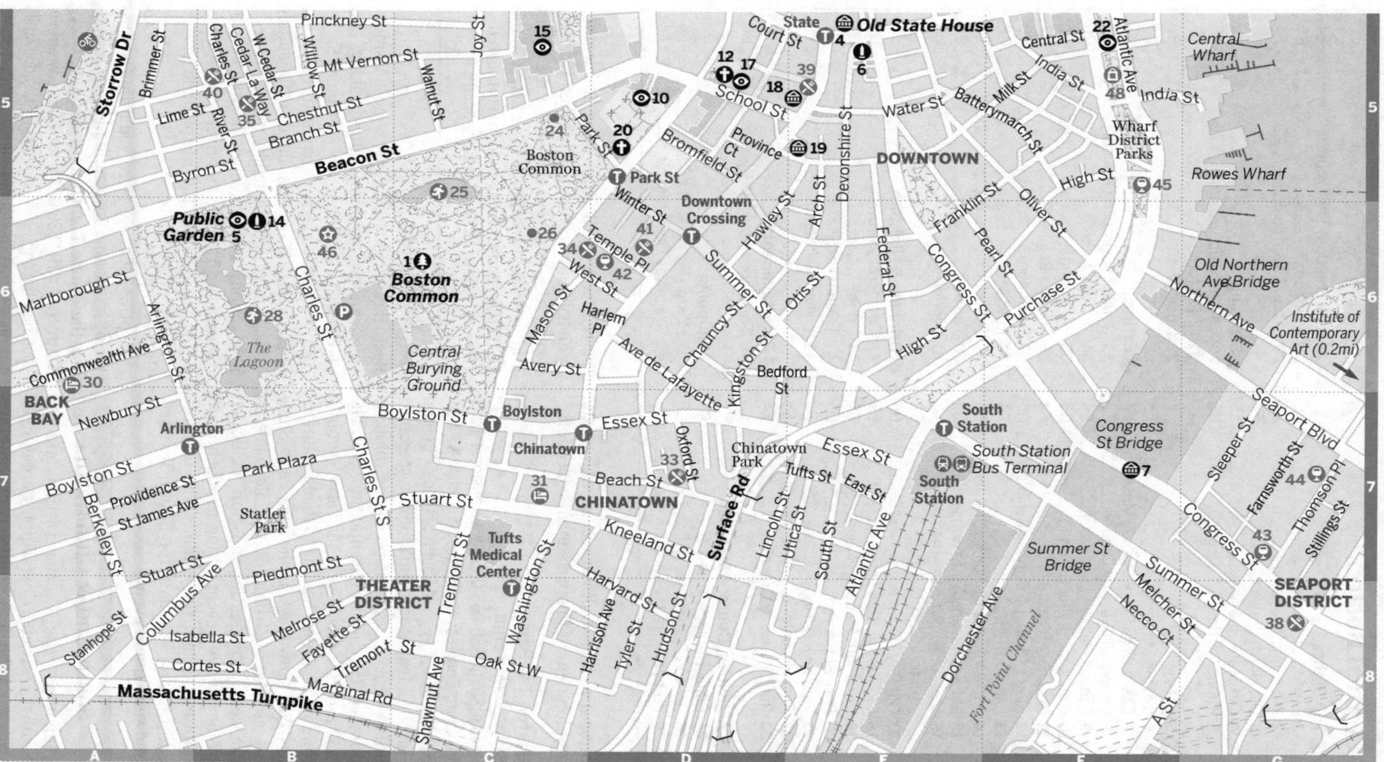
Storrow Dr
Brimmer St
Charles St
Cedar La Way
W Cedar St
Willow St
Pinckney St
Mt Vernon St
Walnut St
Joy St
Lime St
River St
Chestnut St
Branch St
Byron St
Beacon St
Public Garden
The Lagoon
Boston Common
Central Burying Ground
Charles St
Court St
State
Old State House
School St
Province Ct
Bromfield St
Park St
Winter St
Downtown Crossing
Temple Pl
West St
Mason St
Harlem Pl
Avery St
Hawley St
Arch St
Devonshire St
DOWNTOWN
Water St
Batterymarch St
Milk St
India St
Central St
Atlantic Ave
Central Wharf
Wharf District Parks
Rowes Wharf
Franklin St
Oliver St
High St
Pearl St
Federal St
Congress St
Purchase St
Summer St
Otis St
Chauncy St
Kingston St
Ave de Lafayette
Bedford St
High St
Old Northern Ave Bridge
Northern Ave
Institute of Contemporary Art (0.2mi)
Marlborough St
Arlington St
Commonwealth Ave
BACK BAY
Newbury St
Arlington
Boylston St
Boylston
Essex St
Chinatown
Oxford St
Beach St
CHINATOWN
Chinatown Park
Essex St
Tufts St
East St
South Station
South Station Bus Terminal
Congress St Bridge
Seaport Blvd
Sleeper St
Farnsworth St
Thomson Pl
Stillings St
Congress St
Boylston St
Providence St
St James Ave
Park Plaza
Statler Park
Charles St S
Stuart St
Berkeley St
Stuart St
Columbus Ave
Piedmont St
THEATER DISTRICT
Tremont St
Tufts Medical Center
Washington St
Kneeland St
Surface Rd
Lincoln St
Utica St
South St
Atlantic Ave
Summer St Bridge
Summer St
Melcher St
Necco Ct
SEAPORT DISTRICT
Stanhope St
Isabella St
Melrose St
Fayette St
Tremont St
Cortes St
Oak St W
Harrison Ave
Harvard St
Tyler St
Hudson St
Dorchester Ave
Fort Point Channel
A St
Massachusetts Turnpike
Marginal Rd
Shawmut Ave

Central Boston

Top Sights
1 Boston Common C6
2 Museum of Science A2
3 Old North Church F2
4 Old State House E5
5 Public Garden B6

Sights
6 Boston Massacre Site E5
7 Boston Tea Party Ships & Museum F7
8 Copp's Hill Burying Ground E2
9 Faneuil Hall E4
10 Granary Burying Ground D5
11 Greenway Carousel F4
12 King's Chapel & Burying Ground D5
13 Labyrinth F4
14 Make Way for Ducklings Statue B6
15 Massachusetts State House C5
16 Museum of African American History C4
17 Old City Hall D5
18 Old Corner Bookstore E5
19 Old South Meeting House E5
20 Park St Church D5
21 Paul Revere House F3
22 Rings Fountain F5
23 Rose Kennedy Greenway F4

Activities, Courses & Tours
24 Black Heritage Trail C5
25 Boston Common Frog Pond C5
26 Freedom Trail Foundation C6
27 NPS Freedom Trail Tour E4
28 Swan Boats B6
29 Urban AdvenTours F4

Sleeping
30 College Club A6
31 HI-Boston C7
32 Liberty Hotel B3

Eating
33 Gourmet Dumpling House D7
34 jm Curley C6
35 Paramount B5
36 Pizzeria Regina E2
37 Pomodoro F3
38 Row 34 .... G8
39 Spyce E5
40 Tatte B5
41 Yvonne's D6

Drinking & Nightlife
42 Democracy Brewing D6
43 Drink G7
44 Trillium Fort Point G7
45 Trillium Garden F5

Entertainment
46 Shakespeare on the Common B6

Shopping
47 Boston Public Market E4
48 Greenway Open Market F5

programs and studio space, as well as the development of the permanent collection.

Boston Tea Party Ships & Museum MUSEUM
(Map p180; 866-955-0667; www.bostonteapartyship.com; Congress St Bridge; adult/child $30/18; 10am-5pm; ; South Station) 'Boston Harbor a teapot tonight!' To protest against unfair taxes, a gang of rebellious colonists dumped 342 chests of tea into the water. The 1773 protest – the Boston Tea Party – set into motion the events leading to the Revolutionary War. Nowadays, replica Tea Party Ships are moored at Griffin's Wharf, alongside an excellent experiential museum dedicated to the catalytic event. Using re-enactments, multimedia and fun exhibits, the museum addresses all aspects of the Boston Tea Party and subsequent events.

South End & Chinatown

Chinatown, the Theater District and the Leather District are overlapping areas, filled with glitzy theaters, Chinese restaurants and the remnants of Boston's shoe and leather industry (now converted lofts and clubs). Nearby, the Victorian manses in the South End have been reclaimed by artists and the LGBTIQ+ community, who have created a vibrant restaurant and gallery scene.

Back Bay

Back Bay includes the city's most fashionable window-shopping, latte-drinking and people-watching area, on Newbury St, as well as its most elegant architecture, around Copley Sq. Its streets lined with stately brownstones and shaded by magnolia trees, it is among Boston's most prestigious addresses. For fresh air and riverside strolling, head to the Charles River Esplanade.

Copley Square PLAZA
(Map p176; Copley) Here you'll find a cluster of handsome historic buildings, including the ornate French-Romanesque **Trinity Church** (617-536-0944, ext 206; www.trinitychurchboston.org; 206 Clarendon St; adult/child $10/free; 10am-4:30pm Tue-Sat, 12:15-4:30pm

Sun Easter-Oct, reduced hours rest of year), the masterwork of architect HH Richardson. Across the street, the classic **Boston Public Library** (☎617-536-5400; www.bpl.org; 700 Boylston St; ⏰9am-9pm Mon-Thu, to 5pm Fri & Sat year-round, plus 1-5pm Sun Oct-May) was America's first municipal library. Pick up a self-guided tour brochure and wander around, noting gems such as the murals by John Singer Sargent and sculpture by Augustus Saint-Gaudens.

Prudential Center Skywalk Observatory VIEWPOINT

(Map p176; www.skywalkboston.com; 800 Boylston St; adult/child $20/14; ⏰10am-10pm Mar-Oct, to 8pm Nov-Feb; P 👪; T Prudential) Technically called the Shops at Prudential Center, this landmark Boston building is not much more than a fancy shopping mall. But it does provide a bird's-eye view of Boston from its 50th-floor Skywalk. Completely enclosed by glass, the Skywalk offers spectacular 360-degree views of Boston and Cambridge, accompanied by an entertaining audio tour (with a special version catering to kids). Alternatively, you can enjoy the same view from **Top of the Hub** (☎617-536-1775; www.topofthehub.net; ⏰11:30am-1am; 📶) for the price of a drink.

Kenmore Square & Fenway

Kenmore Sq and Fenway attract club-goers and baseball fans to the streets surrounding Fenway Park. At the other end of the neighborhood, art-lovers and culture-vultures flock to the artistic institutions along the Avenue of the Arts (Huntington Ave), including the Museum of Fine Arts and Symphony Hall.

★ **Fenway Park** STADIUM

(Map p176; ☎617-226-6666; www.redsox.com; 4 Jersey St; tours adult/child $20/14, pre-game $35-45; ⏰9am-5pm Apr-Oct, special schedule game days, 10am-5pm Nov-Mar; T Kenmore) Home of the Boston Red Sox since 1912, Fenway Park is the oldest operating baseball park in the country. As such, the park has many quirks that make for a unique experience. See them all on a ballpark tour, or come see the Sox playing in their natural habitat.

★ **Museum of Fine Arts** MUSEUM

(MFA; Map p176; ☎617-267-9300; www.mfa.org; 465 Huntington Ave; adult/child $25/free; ⏰10am-5pm Sat-Tue, to 10pm Wed-Fri; T Museum of Fine Arts, Ruggles) Founded in 1876, the Museum of Fine Arts is Boston's foremost art museum. The museum covers all parts of the globe and all eras, from the ancient world to contemporary times. The collections are strong in Asian and European art, but the uncontested highlight is the gorgeous Art of the Americas wing.

Isabella Stewart Gardner Museum MUSEUM

(Map p176; ☎617-566-1401; www.gardnermuseum.org; 25 Evans Way; adult/child $15/free; ⏰11am-5pm Wed-Mon, to 9pm Thu; T Museum of Fine Arts) Once home to Isabella Stewart Gardner, this splendid palazzo now houses her exquisite collection of art. The museum includes thousands of artistic objects, especially Italian Renaissance and Dutch Golden Age paintings. The interior courtyard, lush with seasonal plants and flowers, is an oasis of tranquility and beauty.

Cambridge

Stretched out along the north shore of the Charles River, Cambridge is a separate city with two distinguished universities, a host of historic sites, and artistic and cultural attractions galore. The streets around Harvard Square are home to restaurants, bars and clubs that rival their counterparts across the river.

★ **Harvard University** UNIVERSITY

(Map p176; ☎617-495-1000; www.harvard.edu; Massachusetts Ave; T Harvard) America's oldest college, Harvard University was founded in 1636 and remains one of the country's most prestigious universities. Alumni of the original Ivy League school include eight US presidents, and dozens of Nobel Laureates and Pulitzer Prize winners. For visitors, the university campus contains some historic buildings clustered around Harvard Yard, as well as impressive architecture and excellent museums. Free historical tours depart from the **Smith Campus Center** (☎617-495-6916; www.commonspaces.harvard.edu/smith-campus-center/about; 30 Dunster St; ⏰7am-midnight Sun-Fri, to 1am Sat); self-guided tours are also available.

★ **Harvard Art Museums** MUSEUM

(Map p176; ☎617-495-9400; www.harvardartmuseums.org; 32 Quincy St; adult/child/student $15/free/free; ⏰10am-5pm; T Harvard) The renovation and expansion of Harvard's art

City Walk Freedom Trail

START BOSTON COMMON
END BUNKER HILL MONUMENT
LENGTH 2.5 MILES; THREE HOURS

Start at 1 **Boston Common** (p174), the USA's oldest public park. On the northern side, you can't miss the gold-domed 2 **Massachusetts State House** (p174) sitting atop Beacon Hill and open for tours. Walk north on Tremont St, passing the soaring steeple of 3 **Park St Church** and the Egyptian Revival gates of the 4 **Granary Burying Ground**, final resting place of many patriots.

At School St, the columned 5 **King's Chapel** overlooks the adjacent burying ground. Turn east on School St, and take note of the plaque outside the 6 **Old City Hall** commemorating this spot as the site of the first public school. Continue down School St past the 7 **Old Corner Bookstore**. Diagonally opposite, the 8 **Old South Meeting House** (p175) saw the beginnings of the Boston Tea Party.

Further north on Washington St, the 9 **Old State House** (p175) was the seat of the colonial government. Later, it was the scene of the city's first public reading of the Declaration of Independence. Outside the Old State House a ring of cobblestones marks the 10 **Boston Massacre site**, where yet another uprising fueled the revolution. Across the intersection, historic 11 **Faneuil Hall** (p175) has served as a public meeting place and marketplace for more than 250 years. National Park Service rangers give free presentations about the site's significance.

From Faneuil Hall, follow Hanover St across the Rose Kennedy Greenway. One block east, charming North Sq is the site of the 12 **Paul Revere House**, the city's oldest wooden house. Back on Hanover St, the Paul Revere Mall offers a lovely vantage point to view the 13 **Old North Church** (p178), where two lanterns were hung to signal the British soldiers' route. From the church, head west on Hull St to 14 **Copp's Hill Burying Ground**, with grand views across the river to Charlestown.

Across the Charlestown Bridge, Constitution Rd brings you to the Charlestown Navy Yard, home of the world's oldest commissioned warship, the 15 **USS Constitution** (p179). Finally, wind your way through the historic streets of Charlestown center to the 16 **Bunker Hill Monument** (p179), site of the turning-point battle of the American Revolution.

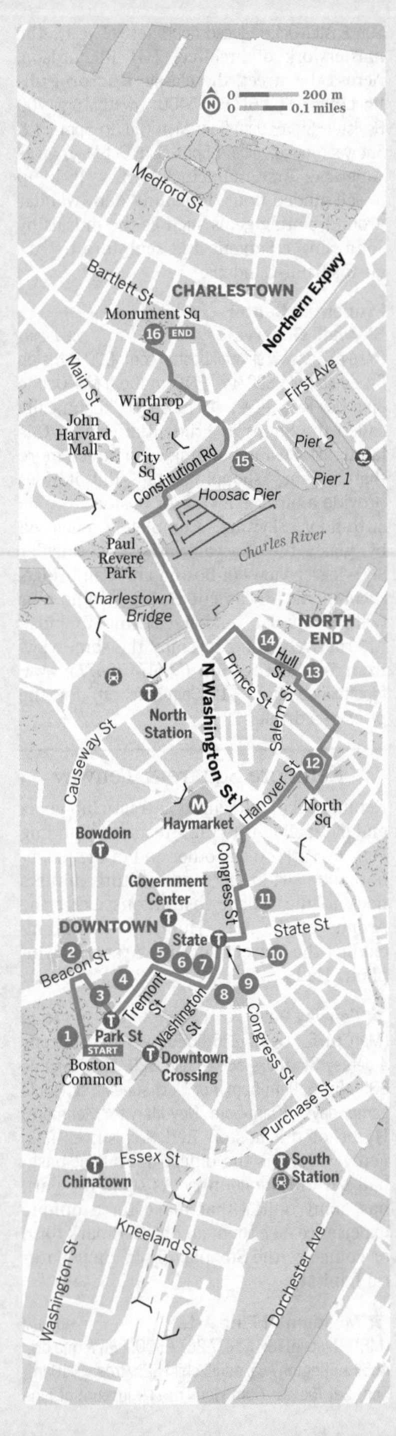

museums in 2014 allowed the university's massive 250,000-piece collection to come together under one very stylish roof, designed by architect extraordinaire Renzo Piano. The artwork spans the globe, with separate collections devoted to Asian and Islamic cultures, northern European and Germanic cultures and other Western art, especially European modernism.

Massachusetts Institute of Technology UNIVERSITY
(MIT; Map p176; ☎617-253-1000; www.mit.edu; 77 Massachusetts Ave; ⊙info session incl campus tour 10am & 2:30pm Mon-Fri; Ⓣ Kendall/MIT) The Massachusetts Institute of Technology offers a different perspective on academia. MIT has a proud history of pushing the boundaries, from its innovative architecture and oddball art to its cutting-edge technology and playful pranks. Campus tours depart from the **MIT Information Center** (☎617-253-3400; www.web.mit.edu/visitmit; 77 Massachusetts Ave, No 7-121, Rogers Bldg; ⊙9am-5pm Mon-Fri).

Activities

Considering Boston's large student population and extensive green spaces, it's no surprise to see urban outdoorsy people running along the Esplanade and cycling the Emerald Necklace. For water bugs, the Charles River and the Boston Harbor offer opportunities for kayaking, sailing and even swimming, if you don't mind the frigid temperatures.

★**Freedom Trail** WALKING
(☎617-357-8300; www.thefreedomtrail.org; Ⓣ Park St) FREE For a sampler of Boston's revolutionary sights, follow the red-brick road. It leads 2.5 miles through the center of Boston, from Boston Common (p174) to the Bunker Hill Monument (p179), and traces the events leading up to and following the War of Independence. The Freedom Trail is well marked and easy to follow on your own.

Charles River Bike Path CYCLING
(Map p176; Storrow Dr & Memorial Dr; ; Ⓣ Harvard, Kendall/MIT, Charles/MGH, Science Park) A popular cycling circuit runs along both sides of the Charles River between the Museum of Science and the Mt Auburn St Bridge in Watertown center (5 miles west of Cambridge). The round trip is 17 miles, but 10 bridges in between offer ample opportunities to shorten the trip. Rent a bike at **Cambridge Bicycle** (☎617-876-6555; www.cambridgebicycle.com; 259 Massachusetts Ave; per 24hr $35; ⊙10am-7pm Mon-Sat, noon-6pm Sun; Ⓣ Central) or **Back Bay Bicycles** (☎617-247-2336; www.papa-wheelies.com; 362 Commonwealth Ave; rental per day $55-65; ⊙10am-7pm Mon-Fri, to 6pm Sat, noon-5pm Sun; Ⓣ Hynes).

Tours

★**Urban AdvenTours** CYCLING
(Map p180; ☎617-670-0637; www.urbanadventours.com; 103 Atlantic Ave; tours from $55, rentals per 24hr $40-75; ⊙9am-8pm Apr-Oct, reduced hours rest of year; Ⓣ Aquarium) This outfit was founded by avid cyclists who believe the best views of Boston are from a bicycle. And they're right! The City View Ride tour provides a great overview of how to get around by bike, including ride-bys of some of Boston's best sites. Other specialty tours include Bikes at Night and the Emerald Necklace tour. Bicycles, helmets and water are all provided.

Boston by Foot WALKING
(☎617-367-2345; www.bostonbyfoot.com; adult/child $15/10;) This fantastic nonprofit organization offers 90-minute walking tours, with neighborhood-specific walks and specialty theme tours such as the Hub of Literary America, the Dark Side of Boston and Boston by Little Feet – a kid-friendly version of the Freedom Trail.

Black Heritage Trail WALKING
(Map p180; ☎617-742-5415; www.nps.gov/boaf; ⊙tours 1pm Mon-Sat, more frequently in summer; Ⓣ Park St) The NPS conducts excellent, informative 90-minute guided tours exploring the history of the abolitionist movement and African American settlement on Beacon Hill. Tours depart from the Robert Gould Shaw memorial on Boston Common. Alternatively, take a self-guided tour with the NPS Freedom Trail app (www.nps.gov/bost/planyourvisit/app.htm) or grab a route map from the **Museum of African American History** (Map p180; ☎617-725-0022; www.maah.org; 46 Joy St; adult/child $10/free; ⊙10am-4pm Mon-Sat; Ⓣ Park St, Bowdoin).

Free Tours By Foot WALKING
(☎617-299-0764; www.freetoursbyfoot.com/boston-tours) Take the tour then decide how much you think it's worth. Popular 90-minute walking tours cover the Freedom Trail, Harvard University, the North

End and the Beacon Hill 'crime tour.' Tour guides are passionate and entertaining. Best of all, you'll never pay more than you think you should.

Festivals & Events

★Boston Marathon SPORTS
(www.baa.org; 3rd Mon Apr) One of the country's most prestigious marathons takes runners on a 26.2-mile course ending at Copley Sq on Patriots' Day, a Massachusetts holiday on the third Monday in April.

Independence Day CULTURAL
(www.bostonpopsjuly4th.org; Jul 4) Boston hosts one of the biggest Independence Day bashes in the USA, with a free Boston Pops concert on the Esplanade and a fireworks display that's televised nationally.

Boston Tea Party Reenactment CULTURAL
(www.oldsouthmeetinghouse.org; $30; Dec) On the Sunday prior to December 16, costumed actors march from Old South Meeting House to the waterfront and toss crates of tea into the harbor. Nowadays, the ticketed event takes place on the newly rebuilt Griffin's Wharf, where the Tea Party ships are docked.

Sleeping

Boston offers a wide range of accommodations, from inviting guesthouses in historic quarters to swanky hotels with all the amenities. There is no shortage of stately homes that have been converted into B&Bs, offering an intimate atmosphere and personal service.

Considering that this city is filled with students, there are surprisingly few accommodations targeting budget travelers and backpackers.

★HI-Boston HOSTEL $
(Map p180; 617-536-9455; www.bostonhostel.org; 19 Stuart St; dm from $47, d with bath from $230; ; T Chinatown, Boylston) HI-Boston sets the standard for urban hostels, with its modern, ecofriendly facility in the historic Dill Building. Purpose-built rooms are functional and clean, as are the shared bathrooms. Community spaces are numerous, from fully equipped kitchen to ground-floor cafe, and there's a whole calendar of activities on offer. The place is large, but it books out, so reserve in advance.

Revolution Hotel HOTEL $
(Map p176; 617-848-9200; www.therevolutionhotel.com; 40 Berkeley St; d/tr/q without bath $100/125/150, d/ste from $150/250; ; T Back Bay) A beacon for budget travelers, the Revolution Hotel is a concept hotel with a cool, creative atmosphere. Rooms are compact, comfortable and affordable. The cheapest share bathrooms are spacious, private and well stocked with plush towels and high-end products.

The place exudes innovation, especially thanks to the fantastic mural that adorns the lobby.

★Newbury Guest House GUESTHOUSE $$
(Map p176; 617-670-6000, 800-437-7668; www.newburyguesthouse.com; 261 Newbury St; d from $249; ; T Hynes, Copley) Dating from 1882, these three interconnected brick and brownstone buildings offer a prime location in the heart of Newbury St. The place has preserved charming features like ceiling medallions and in-room fireplaces, but the rooms also feature clean lines, luxurious linens and modern amenities. Each morning a complimentary buffet breakfast is laid out in the attached restaurant.

College Club B&B $$
(Map p180; 617-536-9510; www.thecollegeclubofboston.com; 44 Commonwealth Ave; s without bath from $179, d $269-289; ; T Arlington) Originally a private club for female college graduates, the College Club has 11 spacious rooms with high ceilings, now open to all genders. Period details – typical of the area's Victorian brownstones – include claw-foot tubs, ornamental fireplaces and bay windows. Local designers have lent their skills to decorate the various rooms, with delightful results. Prices include a continental breakfast.

★Liberty Hotel HOTEL $$$
(Map p180; 866-961-3778, 617-224-4000; www.libertyhotel.com; 215 Charles St; r from $375; ; T Charles/MGH) It is with intended irony that the notorious Charles St Jail has been converted into the classy Liberty Hotel. Today, the 90ft ceiling soars above a spectacular lobby. All 298 guest rooms come with luxurious linens and high-tech amenities, while the 18 in the original jail wing boast floor-to-ceiling windows with amazing views of the Charles River and Beacon Hill.

Verb Hotel BOUTIQUE HOTEL $$$

(Map p176; ☎617-566-4500; www.theverbhotel.com; 1271 Boylston St; r $349-399; P ❄ 🛜 🏊 🐾; T Kenmore, Fenway) The Verb Hotel took a down-and-out HoJo property and turned it into Boston's most radical, retro, rock-and-roll hotel. The style is mid-century modern; the theme is music. Memorabilia is on display throughout the joint, with turntables in the guest rooms and a jukebox cranking out tunes in the lobby. Classy, clean-lined rooms face the swimming pool or Fenway Park.

Eating

Beacon Hill & Boston Common

★Tatte BAKERY $

(Map p180; ☎617-723-5555; www.tattebakery.com; 70 Charles St; mains $10-14; ⏲7am-8pm Mon-Fri, from 8am Sat, 8am-7pm Sun; T Charles/MGH) The aroma of buttery goodness – and the lines stretching out the door – signal your arrival at this fabulous bakery on the lower floor of the historic Charles St Meeting House. Swoon-worthy pastries (divinely cinnamon-y buns, chocolate-hazelnut twists, avocado and mushroom tartines) from $3 taste even more amazing if you're lucky enough to score a table on the sunny front patio.

Paramount CAFETERIA $$

(Map p180; ☎617-720-1152; www.paramountboston.com; 44 Charles St; mains $17-24; ⏲7am-10pm Mon-Fri, from 8am Sat & Sun; 🍷👪; T Charles/MGH) This old-fashioned cafeteria is a neighborhood favorite. A-plus diner fare includes pancakes, home fries, burgers and sandwiches, and big, hearty salads. Banana and caramel French toast is an obvious go-to for the brunch crowd. Don't sit down until you get your food! The wait may seem endless, but patrons swear it is worth it.

Downtown & Waterfront

Spyce INTERNATIONAL $

(Map p180; www.spyce.com; 241 Washington St; bowls $7.50; ⏲10:30am-10pm; 🍷👪; T State) A new concept in dining, Spyce is the brainchild of four hungry MIT grads, who teamed up with a Michelin-starred chef. The food is all prepared in a robotic kitchen – that is, self-rotating woks that are programmed for the optimal temperature and time to create consistently perfect 'bowls' of goodness. It's fast, fresh, healthy and pretty darn delicious.

★jm Curley PUB FOOD $$

(Map p180; ☎617-338-5333; www.jmcurleyboston.com; 21 Temple Pl; mains $10-20; ⏲11:30am-1am Mon-Sat, to 10pm Sun; 🍷; T Downtown Crossing) This dim, inviting bar is a perfect place to settle in for a Dark & Stormy on a dark and stormy night. The fare is bar food like you've never had before: Curley's cracka jack (caramel corn with bacon); mac 'n' cheese (served in a cast-iron skillet); and fried pickles (yes, you read that right). That's why they call it a gastropub.

Yvonne's MODERN AMERICAN $$$

(Map p180; ☎617-267-0047; www.yvonnesboston.com; 2 Winter Pl; ⏲5-11pm, bar to 2am; 🍷; T Park) Upon arrival at Yvonne's, staff will usher you discreetly through closed doors into a hidden 'modern supper club.' The spectacular space artfully blends old-school luxury with contemporary eclecticism. The menu of mostly small plates does the same, with items from tuna crudo to baked oysters to chicken and quinoa meatballs.

West End & North End

Pizzeria Regina PIZZA $

(Map p180; ☎617-227-0765; www.pizzeriaregina.com; 11½ Thacher St; pizzas $13-24; ⏲11am-11:30pm Sun-Thu, to 12:30am Fri & Sat; 🍷; T Haymarket) The queen of North End pizzerias is the legendary Pizzeria Regina, famous for brusque but endearing waitstaff and crispy, thin-crust pizza. Thanks to the slightly spicy sauce (flavored with aged Romano cheese), Regina repeatedly wins accolades for its pies, including recognition by a certain unmentionable travel website as the best pizza *in the country*. Worth the wait.

★Pomodoro ITALIAN $$

(Map p180; ☎617-367-4348; 351 Hanover St; mains $22-26; ⏲5:30-11pm; T Haymarket) Seductive Pomodoro offers a super-intimate, romantic setting (reservations are essential). The food is simple but perfectly prepared: fresh pasta, spicy tomato sauce, grilled fish and meats, and wine by the glass. If you're lucky, you might be on the receiving end of a complimentary tiramisu for dessert. Cash only.

Charlestown

★Brewer's Fork PIZZA $$
(Map p176; ☎617-337-5703; www.brewersfork.com; 7 Moulton St; small plates $8-14, pizzas $14-18; ⊙11:30am-10:30pm, to 11pm Thu-Sat, from 10:30am Sat & Sun; 🚌93 from Haymarket, ⛴Inner Harbor Ferry from Long Wharf, Ⓣ North Station) This casual hipster hangout is a local favorite thanks to its enticing menu of small plates and pizzas, not to mention the excellent, oft-changing selection of about 30 craft beers. The wood-fired oven is the star of the show, but this place also does amazing things with its cheese and charcuterie boards.

Seaport District

Yankee Lobster Co SEAFOOD $
(☎617-345-9799; www.yankeelobstercompany.com; 300 Northern Ave; mains $11-26; ⊙10am-9pm Mon-Sat, 11am-6pm Sun; 🚌SL1, SL2, Ⓣ South Station) The Zanti family has been fishing for three generations, so they definitely know their stuff. A relatively recent addition is this retail fish market, scattered with a few tables in case you want to dine in. And you do. Order something simple such as clam chowder or a lobster roll, accompany it with a cold beer, and you won't be disappointed.

★Row 34 SEAFOOD $$
(Map p180; ☎617-553-5900; www.row34.com; 383 Congress St; oysters $2-3, mains $14-32; ⊙11:30am-10pm Sun-Thu, to 11pm Fri & Sat; Ⓣ South Station) In the heart of the new Seaport District, set in a sharp, postindustrial space, this place offers a dozen types of raw oysters and clams, alongside an amazing selection of craft beers. There's also a full menu of cooked seafood, ranging from the traditional to the trendy.

South End & Chinatown

Gourmet Dumpling House CHINESE $
(Map p180; ☎617-338-6223; www.gourmetdumplinghouse.com; 52 Beach St; dumplings $5-8, mains $9-17; ⊙11am-1am; ✍; Ⓣ Chinatown) *Xiao long bao*. That's all the Chinese you need to know to take advantage of the specialty at the Gourmet Dumpling House (or GDH, as it is fondly called). They are Shanghai soup dumplings, and they are fresh, doughy and delicious. The menu offers plenty of other options, including scrumptious crispy scallion pancakes. Come early or be prepared to wait.

★Myers + Chang ASIAN $$
(Map p176; ☎617-542-5200; www.myersandchang.com; 1145 Washington St; small plates $7-17, mains $16-25; ⊙5-10pm Sun-Thu, to 11pm Fri & Sat; ✍; 🚌SL4, SL5, Ⓣ Tufts Medical Center) This superhip Asian spot blends Thai, Chinese and Vietnamese cuisines, which means delicious dumplings, spicy stir-fries and oodles of noodles. The kitchen staff do amazing things with a wok, and the menu of small plates allows you to sample a wide selection of dishes. Dim sum for dinner? This is your place.

Back Bay

★Puro Ceviche Bar LATIN AMERICAN $$
(Map p176; ☎617-266-0707; www.purocevichebar.com; 264 Newbury St; small plates $10-16; ⊙4-11pm Mon-Thu, 11am-11pm Fri-Sun; Ⓣ Hynes) This bar serves up delightfully modern yet still authentic Latin American fare in its funky downstairs digs, where exposed brick walls are covered with bold murals. Choose between six types of ceviche, six kinds of tacos and a slew of Latin-inspired small plates. Also on offer are classic cocktails and a nicely curated wine list. Attention, budget-minded travelers: there are $2 tacos on Tuesdays.

Saltie Girl SEAFOOD $$$
(Map p176; ☎617-267-0691; www.saltiegirl.com; 281 Dartmouth St; small plates $12-18, mains $18-40; ⊙11:30am-10pm; Ⓣ Copley) Here's a new concept in dining: the seafood bar. It's a delightfully intimate place to feast on tantalizing dishes that blow away all preconceived notions about seafood. From your traditional Gloucester lobster roll to tinned fish on toast to the irresistible torched salmon belly, this place is full of delightful surprises.

Kenmore Square & Fenway

★Eventide Fenway SEAFOOD $
(Map p176; ☎617-545-1060; www.eventideoysterco.com; 1321 Boylston St; mains $9-16; ⊙11am-11pm; 📶; Ⓣ Fenway) James Beard–award winners Mike Wiley and Andrew Taylor opened this counter-service version of their beloved Maine seafood restaurant. Fast, fresh and fabulous, the menu features just-shucked oysters and brown-butter lobster rolls, along

LGBTIQ+ BOSTON

Out and active gay communities are visible all around Boston, especially in the South End and Jamaica Plain. There is no shortage of entertainment options catering to LGBTIQ+ travelers. From drag shows to dyke nights, this sexually diverse community has something for everybody.

There are excellent sources of information for the gay and lesbian community.

Bay Windows (www.baywindows.com) is a weekly newspaper for LGBTIQ+ readers. The print edition is distributed throughout New England, but the website is also an excellent source of news and information.

Edge Boston (www.edgeboston.com) is the Boston branch of the nationwide network of publications offering news and entertainment for LGBTIQ+ readers. Includes a nightlife section with culture and club reviews.

with some pretty sophisticated seafood specials. Wash it down with a craft beer or a glass of rosé and the whole experience feels (and tastes) gourmet.

Island Creek Oyster Bar SEAFOOD $$$

(Map p176; ☎617-532-5300; www.islandcreekoysterbar.com; 500 Commonwealth Ave; oysters $3, mains lunch $13-21, dinner $24-36; ⏲4-11pm Mon-Fri, 11:30am-11:30pm Sat, 10:30am-11pm Sun; T Kenmore) Island Creek claims to unite farmer, chef and diner in one space – and what a space it is. It serves up the region's finest oysters, along with other local seafood, in an ethereal new-age setting. The specialty – lobster-roe noodles topped with braised short ribs and grilled lobster – lives up to the hype.

Cambridge

Mr Bartley's Burger Cottage BURGERS $

(Map p176; ☎617-354-6559; www.mrbartley.com; 1246 Massachusetts Ave; burgers $14-21; ⏲11am-9pm Tue-Sat; T Harvard) Packed with small tables and hungry college students, this burger joint has been a Harvard Square institution for more than 50 years. Bartley's offers two dozen different burgers, including topical newcomers with names such as Trump Tower and Tom Brady Triumphant; sweet-potato fries, onion rings, thick frappés and raspberry-lime rickeys complete the classic American meal.

Drinking & Nightlife

★Bleacher Bar SPORTS BAR

(Map p176; ☎617-262-2424; www.bleacherbarboston.com; 82a Lansdowne St; ⏲11am-1am Sun-Wed, to 2am Thu-Sat; T Kenmore) Tucked under the bleachers at Fenway Park, this classy bar offers a view onto center field. It's not the best place to watch the game as it gets packed, but it's a fun way to experience America's oldest ballpark, even when the Sox are not playing.

★Drink COCKTAIL BAR

(Map p180; ☎617-695-1806; www.drinkfortpoint.com; 348 Congress St; ⏲4pm-1am; 🚌SL1, SL2, T South Station) There is no cocktail menu at Drink. Instead you have a chat with the bartender, and he or she will whip something up according to your mood and taste. It takes seriously the art of mixology – and you will too, after you sample one of its concoctions. The subterranean space, with its low-lit, sexy ambience, makes a great date destination.

Trillium Fort Point MICROBREWERY

(Map p180; ☎857-449-0083; www.trilliumbrewing.com; 50 Thompson Pl; ⏲11am-11pm; T South Station) Trillium has been brewing beer in the Fort Point area for years. But it was only in 2018 that they opened this fantastic taproom, complete with bar, dining room and rooftop deck. Enjoy the full range of Trillium favorites – not only India pale ales, but also American pale ales, gose ales, wild ales and stouts.

Democracy Brewing BREWERY

(Map p180; ☎857-263-8604; www.democracybrewing.com; 35 Temple Pl; ⏲11:30am-11pm Sun-Thu, to 1am Fri & Sat; T Downtown Crossing) The beer is fresh, the fries are crispy perfection and the politics are 'woke.' Not only do they brew exceptional beer at Democracy Brewing, they also foment revolution – by supporting democratic businesses, organizing community events, and showcasing the revolutionaries and rabble-rousers from Boston's past and present.

Beehive COCKTAIL BAR
(Map p176; ☎617-423-0069; www.beehivebos ton.com; 541 Tremont St; ⊙5pm-midnight Mon-Wed, to 1am Thu, to 2am Fri, 9:30am-2am Sat, to midnight Sun; Ⓣ Back Bay) The Beehive has transformed the basement of the Boston Center for the Arts into a 1920s Paris jazz club. This place is more about the scene than the music, which is often provided by students from Berklee College of Music. But the food is good and the vibe is definitely hip.

Reservations required if you want a table.

☆ Entertainment

★ Boston Red Sox BASEBALL
(Map p176; ☎617-226-6666; www.redsox.com; 4 Jersey St; bleachers $10-45, grandstand $23-87, box $38-189; Ⓣ Kenmore) From April to September you can watch the Red Sox play at Fenway Park, the nation's oldest and most storied ballpark. Unfortunately it is also the most expensive – not that this stops the Fenway faithful from scooping up the tickets.

There are sometimes game-day tickets on sale, starting 90 minutes before the opening pitch.

★ Boston Symphony Orchestra CLASSICAL MUSIC
(BSO; ☎617-266-1200, 617-266-1492; www.bso.org; tickets $30-145) Flawless acoustics match the ambitious programs of the world-renowned Boston Symphony Orchestra. From September to April, the BSO performs in the beauteous **Symphony Hall** (Map p176; 301 Massachusetts Ave; ⊙hours vary; Ⓣ Symphony), featuring an ornamental high-relief ceiling and attracting a well-dressed crowd.

In summer months the BSO retreats to Tanglewood in Western Massachusetts.

> **CHEAP SEATS**
>
> ℹ ArtsBoston (www.artsboston.org) offers discounted tickets to theater productions through BosTix Deals (up to 25% for advance purchases online; up to 50% for same-day purchase at ArtsBoston kiosks at Quincy Market and Prudential Center).

Red Room @ Cafe 939 LIVE MUSIC
(Map p176; ☎617-747-2261; www.berklee.edu/cafe939; 939 Boylston St; tickets free-$20; ⊙box office 10am-6pm Mon-Sat; Ⓣ Hynes) Run by Berklee students, the Red Room @ Cafe 939 has emerged as one of Boston's least predictable and most enjoyable music venues. It has an excellent sound system and a baby grand piano; most importantly, it books interesting, eclectic up-and-coming musicians. Buy tickets in advance at the **Berklee Performance Center** (Map p176; ☎617-747-2261; www.berklee.edu/bpc; 136 Massachusetts Ave; tickets $10-65; ⊙box office 10am-6pm Mon-Sat; Ⓣ Hynes).

Club Passim LIVE MUSIC
(Map p176; ☎617-492-7679; www.clubpassim.org; 47 Palmer St; tickets $10-32; Ⓣ Harvard) The legendary Club Passim is a holdout from the days when folk music was a staple in Cambridge (and around the country). The club continues to book top-notch acts, single-handedly sustaining the city's folk scene.

The colorful, intimate room is hidden off a side street in Harvard Square, just as it has been since 1969.

Wally's Café JAZZ
(Map p176; ☎617-424-1408; www.wallyscafe.com; 427 Massachusetts Ave; ⊙5pm-2am; Ⓣ Massachusetts Ave) When Wally's opened in 1947, Barbadian immigrant Joseph Walcott became the first African American to own a nightclub in New England. Old-school, gritty and small, it still attracts a racially diverse crowd to hear jammin' jazz music 365 days a year. Berklee students love this place, especially the nightly jam sessions (6pm to 9pm).

Shopping

★ SoWa Open Market MARKET
(Map p176; ☎857-362-7692; www.sowabos ton.com; 460 Harrison Ave; ⊙10am-4pm Sun May-Oct; 🚌SL4, SL5, Ⓣ Tufts Medical Center) Boston's original art market, this outdoor event is a fabulous opportunity for strolling, shopping and people-watching. More than 100 vendors set up shop under white tents. It's never the same two weeks in a row, but there's always plenty of arts and crafts, as well as edgier art, jewelry, homewares, and homemade food and body products.

Boston Public Market MARKET

(BPM; Map p180; 617-973-4909; www.boston publicmarket.org; 136 Blackstone St; 8am-8pm Mon-Sat, 10am-6pm Sun; ; Haymarket) A locavore's longtime dream come true, this daily farmers market – housed in a brick-and-mortar building – gives shoppers access to fresh foodstuffs, grown, harvested and produced right here in New England. Come for seasonal produce, fresh seafood, meats and poultry from local farms, artisanal cheeses and dairy products, maple syrup and other sweets.

Don't miss the local brews found in Hopsters' Alley.

Greenway Open Market ARTS & CRAFTS

(Map p180; 800-401-6557; www.newengland openmarkets.com; Rose Kennedy Greenway; 11am-5pm Sat, plus 1st & 3rd Sun May-Oct; ; Aquarium) This weekend artist market brings out dozens of vendors to display their wares in the open air. Look for unique, handmade gifts, jewelry, bags, paintings, ceramics and other arts and crafts – most of which are locally and ethically made. Food trucks are always on hand to cater to the hungry.

Information

Boston Harbor Islands Pavilion (Map p180; 617-223-8666; www.bostonharborislands.org; cnr State St & Atlantic Ave; 9am-4:30pm mid-May–Jun & Sep-early Oct, to 6pm Jul & Aug; ; Aquarium) Ideally located on the Rose Kennedy Greenway. This information center will tell you everything you need to know to plan your visit to the Boston Harbor Islands. Don't miss the nearby *Harbor Fog* sculpture, which immerses passersby in the sounds and sensations of the harbor.

Cambridge Visitor Information Kiosk (Map p176; 617-441-2884; www.cambridge-usa.org; Harvard Sq; 9am-5pm Mon-Fri, to 1pm Sat & Sun; Harvard) Has detailed information on current Cambridge happenings and self-guided walking tours.

Greater Boston Convention & Visitors Bureau (www.bostonusa.com) Has a website packed with information on hotels, restaurants and special events, as well as LGBTIQ+, family travel and more.

Massachusetts Office of Travel & Tourism (www.massvacation.com) Information about events and activities throughout the state, including an excellent guide to green tourism.

National Park Service Visitors Center (NPS; Map p180; 617-242-5642; www.nps.gov/bost/planyourvisit/index.htm; Faneuil Hall; 9am-6pm; State) Has loads of information about the Freedom Trail sights and is the starting point for the free **NPS Freedom Trail Tour** (10am, 11am, 2pm & 3pm Jun-Sep). There is an additional NPS Visitors Center at the **Charlestown Navy Yard** (Map p176; 617-242-5601; www.nps.gov/bost; visitor center 10am-5pm Wed-Sun Jan-Apr, 9am-5pm May-Sep, 10am-5pm Oct-Dec; 93 from Haymarket, Inner Harbor Ferry from Long Wharf, North Station).

Getting There & Away

Most travelers arrive in Boston by plane, with many national and international flights in and out of **Logan International Airport** (BOS; 800-235-6426; www.massport.com/logan-airport). Two smaller regional airports – Manchester Airport in New Hampshire and Green Airport near Providence, RI – offer alternatives that are also accessible to Boston and are sometimes less expensive.

Most trains operated by Amtrak (www.amtrak.com) go in and out of **South Station** (Map p180; 617-523-1300; www.south-station.net; 700 Atlantic Ave).

Boston is the northern terminus of the Northeast Corridor, which sends frequent trains to New York City, NY (3½ to 4½ hours), Philadelphia, PA (five to six hours) and Washington, DC (6¾ to eight hours). *Lake Shore Limited* goes daily to Buffalo, NY (11 hours) and Chicago, IL (22 hours), while the *Downeaster* goes from North Station to Portland, ME (2½ hours).

Buses are most useful for regional destinations, although Greyhound (www.greyhound.com) operates services around the country. There are also a few newer companies offering cheap and efficient service to New York City (four to five hours).

Getting Around

TO/FROM THE AIRPORT

Boston Logan International Airport Take the silver line bus (free) or blue line subway ($2.25 to $2.75) to central Boston from 5:30am to 12:30am, or catch a taxi for $25 to $30.

Green Airport Take the commuter rail to South Station ($12).

Manchester Airport Book in advance for the hourly Flight Line Inc shuttle bus to Logan International Airport, or catch the infrequent Greyhound bus to South Station.

South Station Located in central Boston on the red line.

PUBLIC TRANSPORTATION

Blue Bikes Boston's bike-share program, with 1800 bikes available to borrow at 200 stations.

MBTA bus Supplements the subway system.

T (Subway) The quickest and easiest way to get to most destinations. Runs from 5:30am or 6am until 1:30am.

Around Boston

Lexington

This upscale suburb, about 18 miles from Boston's center, is a bustling village of white churches and historic taverns, with tour buses surrounding the village green. A skirmish kicked off the War of Independence. Each year on April 19, historians and patriots don their 18th-century costumes and grab their rifles for an elaborate re-enactment of the events of 1775.

While this history is celebrated and preserved, it is in stark contrast to the peaceful, even staid, community that is Lexington today. If you stray more than a few blocks from the green, you could be in Anywhere, USA, with few reminders that this is where it all started. Nonetheless, it is a pleasant enough Anywhere, USA, with restaurants and shops lining the main drag, and impressive Georgian architecture anchoring either end.

★Minute Man National Historic Park PARK

(www.nps.gov/mima; 3113 Marrett Rd; ⏲9am-5pm Apr-Oct; 👪) FREE The route that British troops followed to Concord has been designated the Minute Man National Historic Park. The visitor center at the eastern end of the park shows an informative multimedia presentation depicting Paul Revere's ride and the ensuing battles. Within the park, Battle Rd is a 5-mile wooded trail that connects the historic sites related to the battles – from Meriam's Corner, where gunfire erupted while British soldiers were retreating, to the Paul Revere capture site.

Battle Green HISTORIC SITE

(Lexington Common; Massachusetts Ave) The historic Battle Green is where the skirmish between patriots and British troops jump-started the War of Independence. The **Lexington Minuteman Statue** (crafted by Henry Hudson Kitson in 1900) stands guard at the southeastern end of Battle Green, honoring the bravery of the 77 minutemen who met the British here in 1775, and the eight who died.

★Minuteman Commuter Bikeway CYCLING

The Minuteman Commuter Bikeway follows an old railroad right of way from near the Alewife red-line subway terminus in Cambridge through Arlington to Lexington and Bedford, a total distance of about 14 miles. From Lexington center, you can also ride along Massachusetts Ave to Rte 2A, which parallels the Battle Rd trail, and eventually leads into Concord center.

ℹ Getting There & Away

MBTA (www.mbta.com) buses 62 (Bedford VA Hospital) and 76 (Hanscom Field) run from the red-line Alewife subway terminus through Lexington center at least hourly on weekdays and less frequently on Saturday; there are no buses on Sunday.

Concord

On April 18, 1775, British troops marched out of Boston, searching for arms that colonists had hidden west of the city. The following morning, they skirmished with Colonial minutemen in Lexington, then continued on to Concord, where the rivals faced off at North Bridge, in the first battle of the War of Independence.

Today, tall white church steeples rise above ancient oaks, elms and maples, giving Concord a stateliness that belies the revolutionary drama that occurred centuries ago. Indeed, it's easy to see how writers such as Ralph Waldo Emerson, Nathaniel Hawthorne, Henry David Thoreau and Louisa May Alcott found their inspiration here. Concord was also the home of famed sculptor Daniel Chester French (who went on to create the Lincoln Memorial in Washington, DC).

These days travelers can relive history in Concord. **Patriots' Day** (www.lexingtonma.gov/patriotsday) is celebrated with gusto, and many significant literary sites are open for visitors.

★Old North Bridge HISTORIC SITE

(www.nps.gov/mima; Monument St; ⏲dawn-dusk) A half-mile north of Monument Sq in Concord center, the wooden span of Old North Bridge is the site of the 'shot heard around the world' (as Emerson wrote in his poem *Concord Hymn*). This is where enraged minutemen fired on British troops, forcing them to retreat to Boston. Daniel Chester French's first statue, *Minute Man,* presides over the park from the opposite side of the bridge.

Concord Museum MUSEUM
(www.concordmuseum.org; 200 Lexington Rd; adult/child $10/5;) Southeast of Monument Sq, Concord Museum brings the town's diverse history under one roof. The museum's prized possession is one of the 'two if by sea' lanterns that hung in the steeple of the Old North Church in Boston as a signal to Paul Revere. It also has the world's largest collection of Henry David Thoreau artifacts, including his writing desk from Walden Pond.

i Getting There & Away

MBTA commuter rail trains run between Boston's North Station and Concord ('the Depot'; $9.25, 40 minutes, 12 daily) on the Fitchburg/South Acton line.

Salem

This town's very name conjures up images of diabolical witchcraft and people being burned at the stake. The famous Salem witch trials of 1692 are ingrained in the national memory. Indeed, Salem goes all out at Halloween, when the town dresses up for parades and parties, and shops sell all manner of Wiccan accessories.

These incidents obscure Salem's true claim to fame: its glory days as a center for clipper-ship trade with the Far East. Elias Hasket Derby, America's first millionaire, built Derby Wharf, which is now the center of the Salem Maritime National Historic Site. The marvelous Peabody Essex Museum displays some of the treasures that were brought home from these merchant expeditions.

Today, Salem is a middle-class commuter suburb of Boston with an enviable location on the sea. Its rich history and culture, from witches to ships to art, continue to cast a spell on visitors.

★Peabody Essex Museum MUSEUM
(978-745-9500; www.pem.org; 161 Essex St; adult/child $20/free; 10am-5pm Tue-Sun;) All of the art, artifacts and curiosities that Salem merchants brought back from the Far East were the foundation for this museum. Founded in 1799, it is the country's oldest museum in continuous operation. The building itself is impressive, with a light-filled atrium, and it's a wonderful setting for the vast collections, which focus on New England decorative arts and maritime history.

Salem Maritime National Historic Site HISTORIC SITE
(www.nps.gov/sama; 160 Derby St; 9am-5pm May-Oct, 10am-4pm Wed-Sun Nov-Apr) FREE This National Historic Site comprises the Custom House, the wharves and other buildings along Derby St that are remnants of the shipping industry that once thrived along this stretch of Salem. Of the 50 wharves that once lined Salem Harbor, only three remain, the longest of which is Derby Wharf. Check the website for a schedule of guided tours of the various buildings, or download an audio walking tour of the whole area.

i Getting There & Away

The Rockport/Newburyport line of the MBTA commuter rail runs from Boston's North Station to Salem Depot ($7.50, 30 minutes). Trains run every 30 minutes during the morning and evening rush hours, hourly during the rest of day, and less frequently at weekends.

Plymouth

Plymouth calls itself 'America's Home Town.' It was here that the Pilgrims first settled in the winter of 1620, seeking a place where they could practice their religion as they wished, without interference from government. An innocuous, weathered ball of granite – the famous Plymouth Rock – marks the spot where they supposedly first stepped ashore in this foreign land, but Plimoth Plantation provides a more informative and accurate account of their experiences. Many other museums and historic houses in the surrounding streets recall their struggles, sacrifices and triumphs.

★Plimoth Plantation MUSEUM
(508-746-1622; www.plimoth.org; 137 Warren Ave; adult/child $28/16; 9am-5pm Apr-Nov;) Three miles south of Plymouth center, Plimoth Plantation authentically re-creates the Pilgrims' settlement in its primary exhibit, entitled **1627 English Village**. Everything in the village – costumes, implements, vocabulary, artistry, recipes and crops – has been painstakingly researched and remade. Costumed interpreters, acting in character, explain the details of daily life and answer your questions as you watch them work and play.

★Mayflower II SHIP
(www.plimoth.org/what-see-do/mayflower-ii; State Pier, Water St; 👪) If Plymouth Rock tells us little about the Pilgrims, *Mayflower II* speaks volumes. Climb aboard this replica of the small ship in which the Pilgrims made the fateful voyage, where 102 people lived together for 66 days as the ship passed through stormy North Atlantic waters. Actors in period costume are on board, recounting harrowing tales from the journey.

Native Plymouth Tours WALKING
(☎774-454-7792; www.facebook.com/nativeplymouthtours; adult/child $15/10) A two-hour walking tour with a Native American guide. You'll see many typical sights, but your guide Timothy Turner will debunk myths, give unusual insights and share a completely different perspective on Plymouth (and American) history. Four-person minimum.

Getting There & Away

You can reach Plymouth from Boston by MBTA commuter rail trains, which depart from South Station three or four times a day ($11.50, 90 minutes). From the station at Cordage Park, GATRA buses connect to Plymouth center.

Cape Cod

Quaint fishing villages, kitschy tourist traps and genteel towns – the Cape has many faces. Each attracts a different crowd. Families seeking calm waters perfect for little tykes favor Cape Cod Bay on the peninsula's quieter north side. College students looking to play hard in the day and let loose after the sun goes down set out for Falmouth or Wellfleet. Provincetown is a paradise for art lovers, whale-watchers, LGBTIQ+ travelers and…well, just about everyone.

Getting There & Around

Your own wheels (two or four) make getting around easy, but there are also bus links; see the website of the **Cape Cod Regional Transit Authority** (☎800-352-7155; www.capecodrta.org; single ride/day pass $2/6) for routes and schedules, including summertime shuttles in Falmouth, Hyannis and Provincetown.

Sandwich

The Cape's oldest town (founded in 1637) makes a perfect first impression as you cross over the canal from the mainland. Head straight to the village center, where white-steepled churches, period homes and a working grist mill surround a picturesque swan pond.

Heritage Museums & Gardens MUSEUM, GARDENS
(☎508-888-3300; www.heritagemuseumsandgardens.org; 67 Grove St; adult/child $18/7; ⊙10am-5pm mid-Apr–mid-Oct; 👪) Fun for kids and adults alike, the 100-acre Heritage Museums & Gardens sports a superb vintage automobile collection in a Shaker-style round barn, an authentic 1908 carousel (rides free with admission) and unusual folk art collections. The grounds also contain one of the finest rhododendron gardens in America; from mid-May to mid-June thousands of 'rhodies' blaze with color. You'll also find ways to get your heart racing, via the **Adventure Park** (☎508-866-0199; www.heritageadventurepark.org; 2hr ticket $38-49; ⊙8am-8pm Jun & Jul, to 7:30pm mid-Aug, to 7pm late Aug, shorter hours mid-Apr–May & Sep–mid-Nov; 👪).

Information

Sandwich Visitor Center (☎508-833-9755; www.sandwichchamber.com; 520 MA 130; ⊙10am-5pm Mon-Sat, to 4pm Sun mid-May–mid-Oct, to 4pm Mon-Fri mid-Oct–mid-May) Stop in for local tips and maps.

Falmouth

Crowd-pleasing beaches, a terrific bike trail and one of the busiest downtowns outside of Provincetown make this charmer of a town worth checking out. There's also plenty for history buffs to be found here: Falmouth puffs with pride over its most cherished daughter, Katharine Lee Bates, who wrote the words to the nation's favorite patriotic hymn, *America the Beautiful*.

★Shining Sea Bikeway CYCLING
(👪) A bright star among the Cape's stellar bike trails, this 10.7-mile beaut runs along the entire west coast of Falmouth, from County Rd in North Falmouth to Woods Hole ferry terminal, offering unspoiled views of salt ponds, marsh and seascapes. Completed in 2009, the bikeway follows an abandoned railroad bed, taking you places you'd never get a glimpse of otherwise.

Maison Villatte CAFE $
(☎774-255-1855; 267 Main St; snacks $4-12; ⊙7am-5pm Tue-Sun) A pair of French bakers crowned in toques work the ovens at this buzzing bakery-cafe, creating crusty artisan

DON'T MISS

CAPE COD RAIL TRAIL

The mother of all Cape bicycle trails, the **Cape Cod Rail Trail** (CCRT; www.mass.gov/locations/cape-cod-rail-trail) runs 22 glorious paved miles through forest, past cranberry bogs and along sandy ponds ideal for a dip. This rural route, formerly used as a railroad line, is one of the finest bike trails in all of New England.

The path begins in Dennis on MA 134 and continues through **Nickerson State Park** (☎508-896-3491; www.mass.gov/dcr; 3488 MA 6A; parking $15; ⏲dawn-dusk;) in Brewster, into Orleans and across the Cape Cod National Seashore (p198), all the way to South Wellfleet.

There's a hefty dose of Ye Olde Cape Cod scenery en route and you'll have opportunities to detour into villages for lunch or sightseeing. If you have only enough time to do part of the trail, begin at Nickerson State Park and head for the National Seashore – the landscape is unbeatable.

Bicycle rentals are available at the trailheads in Dennis and Wellfleet and opposite the National Seashore's visitor center in Eastham. There's car parking at all four sites (free except for Nickerson).

breads, flaky croissants and sinful pastries. Hearty sandwiches and robust coffee make it an ideal lunch spot.

★Añejo MEXICAN **$$**
(☎508-388-7631; www.anejomexicanbistro.com; 188 Main St; mains $13-26; ⏲11:30am-late Mon-Sat, from 10:30am Sun) This buzzing bistro and tequila bar brings a little year-round heat to the Main St scene, with a big selection of margaritas and tequilas, and a menu of fab street food – enchiladas, tacos, tostadas – that spins fresh Mexican flavors Cape Cod–style, with lots of fish and local seafood.

Information

Falmouth Chamber of Commerce (☎508-548-8500; www.falmouthchamber.com; 20 Academy Lane; ⏲8:30am-4:30pm Mon-Fri, plus 10am-2pm Sat late May-Aug) In the town center, just off Main St.

Getting There & Away

Sitting at the southwest corner of the Cape, Falmouth is reached via MA 28, which becomes Main St in the town center. Buses connect the town with Boston and other Cape destinations.

Ferries to Martha's Vineyard (p203) leave from Falmouth Harbor in summer, and year-round from Woods Hole, 4.5 miles southwest of downtown.

Hyannis

Ferries, buses and planes all converge on Hyannis, the Cape's commercial hub (and part of the larger Barnstable township). So there's a good chance you will, too. Although the downtown area lacks the charm of others on Cape, the village center and harborfront have been rejuvenated, making them a pleasant place to break a journey.

In addition to being a jumping-off point for boats to Nantucket and Martha's Vineyard, Hyannis attracts Kennedy fans – JFK made his summer home here, and it was at the Kennedy compound that Teddy passed away in 2009. Hyannis Harbor, with its waterfront eateries and ferries, is a few minutes' walk from Main St.

Sights

★John F Kennedy Hyannis Museum MUSEUM
(☎508-790-3077; www.jfkhyannismuseum.org; 397 Main St; adult/child $12/6; ⏲9am-5pm Mon-Sat, from noon Sun Jun-Oct, 10am-4pm Mon-Sat, from noon Sun Nov, 10am-4pm Thu-Sat Dec-Apr, 10am-5pm Mon-Sat, noon-5pm Sun May) Hyannis has been the summer home of the Kennedy clan for generations. Back in the day, JFK spent the warmer months here – times that are beautifully documented at this museum with photographs and video from JFK's childhood to the Camelot years of his presidency. The exhibits are poignantly done, and present a theme that changes annually (previous years have covered matriarch Rose and explored the brotherly bond between Jack and Bobby).

Sleeping

HI Hyannis HOSTEL **$**
(☎508-775-7990; www.hiusa.org; 111 Ocean St; dm/d from $40/119; ⏲mid-May–mid-Oct; P@) For a million-dollar view on a backpacker's

budget, book yourself a bed at this hostel overlooking the harbor. It was built in 2010 by adding new wings to a period home and is within walking distance of the Main St scene, beaches and ferries. Now the caveat: there are only 42 beds, so book well in advance.

★**Anchor-In** HOTEL **$$$**
(☎508-775-0357; www.anchorin.com; 1 South St; r $206-316;) This family-run boutique hotel puts the chains to shame. The harbor-front location offers a fine sense of place, and the heated outdoor pool is a perfect perch from which to watch fishing boats unload their catch. The rooms are bright and smart, with water-view balconies. If you're planning a day trip to Nantucket, the ferry is just a stroll away.

Eating & Drinking

Pain D'Avignon BAKERY, BISTRO **$$**
(☎508-778-8588; www.paindavignon.com; 15 Hinckley Rd; lunch $8-17, dinner mains $19-32; ⏲7am-4pm daily, plus 5-10pm Tue-Thu & Sun, to 11pm Fri & Sat Jun-Sep, also 5-9pm Tue-Thu, to 10pm Fri & Sat Oct-May) It's not in the likeliest of locations (out by the airport, off MA 132), but seek this place out for a delectable slice of Paris. Patisserie favorites beckon in the morning, but more leisurely options like omelets and galettes (savory crepes) can be ordered. At lunch and dinner, classic French bistro fare shines: croque monsieur, quiche Lorraine, steak *frites*.

★**Naked Oyster** SEAFOOD **$$$**
(☎508-778-6500; www.nakedoyster.com; 410 Main St; lunch $11-20, dinner mains $22-38; ⏲noon-10pm Mon-Sat) Limited ingredient travel times are preferred at this upmarket joint, where the eponymous bivalves come from the restaurant's oyster farm in Barnstable Harbor. They keep fine company in the raw bar: shrimp, littlenecks, lobster. The menu borrows global flavors to dress up fresh seafood – Thai shrimp, *moules frites,* fish tacos, curried scallops – with fine results.

Cape Cod Beer BREWERY
(☎508-790-4200; www.capecodbeer.com; 1336 Phinneys Lane; ⏲10am-6pm Mon-Fri, 11am-4pm Sat) Not just a place for beer connoisseurs (although they'll be pretty happy), this brewery is a fun spot to while away some time. Free brewery tours happen daily (except Sunday) at 11am, but you can stop in for tastings ($6) any time. Check the website for events, from bring-your-pet 'yappy hour' to painting classes, live music and comedy nights.

OFF THE BEATEN TRACK

SCENIC DRIVE: MA 6A

When exploring the Cape, eschew the speedy Mid-Cape Hwy (MA 6) and follow instead the Old King's Hwy (MA 6A), which snakes along Cape Cod Bay. The longest continuous stretch of historic district in the USA, it's lined with gracious period homes, antique shops and art galleries, all of which make for good browsing en route.

Getting There & Away

Hyannis is the Cape's transportation hub. Flights go to/from Boston and Nantucket year-round, as well as Martha's Vineyard and New York in summer. Ferries go to Nantucket. And buses run to Boston and to Provincetown (calling at Cape towns en route).

The **Cape Flyer** (☎508-775-8504; www.capeflyer.com; one-way tickets $5-22; ⏲late May-Aug) is a weekend train service operating from Memorial Day to Labor Day (late May to mid-October), connecting Boston's South Station with Hyannis.

Chatham

The patriarch of Cape Cod towns, Chatham has a genteel reserve that is evident along its shady Main St: the shops are upscale and the lodgings tastefully swank. That said, there's something for everyone here – families flock to town for seal-watching and birders migrate to the wildlife refuge. And then there are all those beaches. Sitting at the 'elbow' of the Cape, Chatham has an amazing 60 miles of shoreline along the ocean, the sound and countless coves and inlets.

MA 28 leads right to Main St, where the lion's share of shops and restaurants are lined up. Chatham is a town made for strolling. You'll find free parking along Main St and in the parking lot behind the Chatham Squire restaurant (but you'll have to fight for a space in summer).

Chatham Shark Center MUSEUM
(☎508-348-5901; www.atlanticwhiteshark.org; 235 Orleans Rd, North Chatham; $5; ⏲10am-4pm Fri, Sat & Mon, from 11am Sun Jun, 10am-4pm Mon-Sat, from 11am Sun Jul & Aug, 10am-4pm Sat, from 11am Sun Sep-early Oct) Stop here for the low-

Cape Cod, Martha's Vineyard & Nantucket

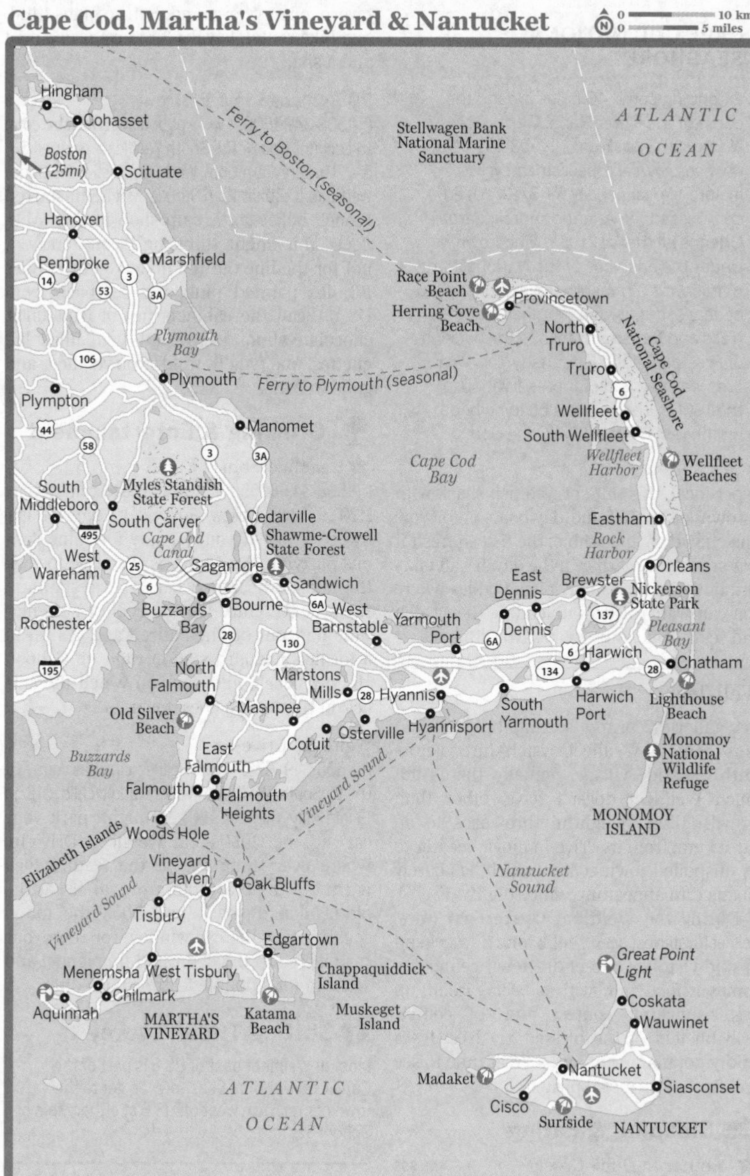

down on one of the Cape's most intriguing summer residents: the great white shark. Interactive exhibits and videos aimed at kids and adults attempt to demystify the animal given a good deal of bad PR in the Cape Cod–set movie, *Jaws*. It's under the auspices of the Atlantic White Shark Conservancy (motto: 'Awareness inspires conservation').

★ **Chatham Pier Fish Market** SEAFOOD $$
(☎ 508-945-3474; www.chathampierfishmarket.com; 45 Barcliff Ave; mains $12-24; ⏲ 10am-7pm mid-May–mid-Nov) If you like it fresh and

CAPE COD NATIONAL SEASHORE

Extending some 40 miles around the curve of the Outer Cape, **Cape Cod National Seashore** (☎508-255-3421; www.nps.gov/caco; pedestrian/cyclist/motorcycle/car per day $3/3/10/20) encompasses the Atlantic shoreline from Orleans all the way to Provincetown. Under the auspices of the National Park Service, it's a treasure trove of unspoiled beaches, dunes, salt marshes, nature trails and forests. Thanks to the backing of President John F Kennedy, this vast area was set aside for preservation in the 1960s, just before a building boom hit the rest of his native Cape Cod.

hyper-local, this salt-sprayed fish shack with its own sushi chef and day-boats is for you. The chowder's incredible, the fish so fresh it was swimming earlier in the day. It's all takeout, but there are shady picnic tables where you can watch fishers unloading their catch and seals frolicking as you savor dinner.

Wellfleet

Art galleries, primo surfing beaches and those famous Wellfleet oysters lure visitors to this seaside village. Actually, there's not much Wellfleet doesn't have, other than crowds. It's a delightful throwback to an earlier era, from its drive-in movie theater to its unspoiled town center, which has barely changed in appearance since the 1950s.

During the **Wellfleet OysterFest** (www.wellfleetoysterfest.org), held on a weekend in mid-October, the entire town center becomes a food fair, with a beer garden, an oyster-shucking contest and, of course, belly-busters of the blessed bivalves. It's a wildly popular event and a great time to see Wellfleet at its most spirited.

Sleeping & Eating

★Wagner at Duck Creek INN $$$

(☎508-942-8185; www.thewagneratduckcreek.com; 70 Main St; r $217-373; ❄📶) Energetic owners have breathed new life into this iconic inn – no small undertaking, given it encompasses 27 rooms housed in three antique timber buildings spread over lovely grounds. The result is a boutique feel, with pretty, well-equipped rooms plus an on-site tavern, open year-round. Future plans think big: bike rental, kayaks for guest use, a pool and a spa.

PB Boulangerie & Bistro BAKERY $

(☎508-349-1600; www.pbboulangeriebistro.com; 15 Lecount Hollow Rd, South Wellfleet; pastries $3-5; ⏲bakery 7am-6pm Wed-Sun, bistro 5-9:30pm Wed-Sat, 10:30am-2pm Sun) A Michelin-starred French baker setting up shop in tiny Wellfleet? You might think he'd gone crazy, if not for the line out the door. You can't miss PB: it's painted pink and set back from US 6. Scan the cabinets full of fruit tarts, chocolate-almond croissants and filled baguettes and you'll think you've died and gone to Paris.

Drinking & Entertainment

★Beachcomber BAR

(☎508-349-6055; www.thebeachcomber.com; 1120 Cahoon Hollow Rd; ⏲11:30am-1am late May-early Sep) If you're ready for some serious partying, 'Da Coma' is *the* place to rock the night away. It's a bar. It's a restaurant. It's a dance club. It's the coolest summertime hangout on the entire Cape. It's set in a former lifeguard station right on Cahoon Hollow Beach, and you can watch the surf action till the sun goes down.

Wellfleet Drive-In CINEMA

(☎508-349-7176; www.wellfleetcinemas.com; 51 US 6, South Wellfleet; tickets adult/child $12/9; ⏲late May–mid-Sep; 👪) By night, park your car at the 1950s-era Wellfleet Drive-In, where everything except the feature flick is true to the era. Grab a bite to eat at the old-fashioned snack bar, hook the mono speaker over the car window (or tune your car's stereo to the dedicated frequency) and settle in for a double feature. Cash only.

Getting There & Away

Most of Wellfleet east of US 6 is part of the Cape Cod National Seashore. To get to the town center, turn west off US 6 at either Main or School Sts.

Provincetown

This is it: Provincetown is as far as you can go on the Cape, and more than just geographically. The draw is irresistible. Fringe writers and artists began making a summer haven in Provincetown a century ago. Today this sandy outpost has morphed into the hottest LGBTIQ+ destination in the Northeast. Flamboyant street scenes, brilliant art galleries and unbridled nightlife paint the town center. But that's only half the show. Provincetown's untamed coastline and vast beaches also beg to be explored. Sail off on a whale-watching tour, cruise the night away, get lost in the dunes – it's all easy to do in Provincetown.

Summers, specifically between June and August, are when the town shines brightest, but you'll still find plenty of nature adventure opportunities and cute guys in the spring and fall. Whenever you decide to come, make sure you don't miss this unique, welcoming corner of New England.

Sights

★Provincetown Art Association & Museum MUSEUM
(PAAM; ☎508-487-1750; www.paam.org; 460 Commercial St; adult/child $10/free; ⏰11am-5pm Sat-Thu, to 10pm Fri Jun & Sep, to 8pm Mon-Thu, to 10pm Fri, to 5pm Sat & Sun Jul & Aug, noon-5pm Thu-Sun Oct-May) Founded in 1914 to celebrate the town's thriving art community, this vibrant museum showcases the works of hundreds of artists who have found their inspiration on the Lower Cape. Chief among them are Charles Hawthorne, who led the early Provincetown art movement, and Edward Hopper, who had a home and gallery in the Truro dunes.

Pilgrim Monument & Provincetown Museum MUSEUM
(☎508-487-1310; www.pilgrim-monument.org; 1 High Pole Hill Rd; adult/child $12/4; ⏰9am-5pm Apr, May & Sep-Jan, to 7pm Jun-Aug) Climb to the top of the country's tallest all-granite structure (253ft) for a sweeping view of town, the beaches and the spine of the Lower Cape. The climb is 116 steps plus 60 ramps and takes about 10 minutes at a leisurely pace. At the base of the c 1910 tower is an evocative, but quite Eurocentric, museum depicting the landing of the *Mayflower* Pilgrims and other Provincetown history.

Activities

Province Lands Bike Trail (www.nps.gov/caco), an exhilarating 7.5 miles of paved bike trails, crisscrosses the forest and undulating dunes of the Cape Cod National Seashore. As a bonus, you can cool off with a swim: the main 5.5-mile loop trail has spur trails leading to **Herring Cove Beach** (Province Lands Rd) and **Race Point Beach** (Race Point Rd). There are plenty of bike-rental places in central P-town.

Dolphin Fleet Whale Watch WILDLIFE
(☎508-240-3636, 800-826-9300; www.whalewatch.com; 307 Commercial St; adult/child $52/31; ⏰mid-Apr–Oct; 🚸) Dolphin Fleet offers as many as 10 whale-watching tours daily in peak season, each lasting three to four hours. You can expect a lot of splashy fun. Humpback whales have a flair for acrobatic breaching and come surprisingly close to the boats. The naturalists on board are informative and play a vital role in monitoring whale populations.

Sleeping

★AWOL BOUTIQUE HOTEL $$$
(☎508-413-9820; www.awolhotel.com; 59 Province Lands Rd; r $397-639; ⏰May-Oct; P❄📶🏊) Overlooking the salt marsh and away from the bustle of Provincetown's main drag is AWOL, a boutique hotel with a tropical 1960s vibe. Wood and wicker furniture is featured both in the rooms and on the large front lawn, which is set up with lounge chairs and fire pits, perfect for sipping a tiki cocktail under the moonlight.

Carpe Diem BOUTIQUE HOTEL $$$
(☎508-487-4242; www.carpediemguesthouse.com; 12-14 Johnson St; r $349-599; P❄📶) Sophisticated yet relaxed, this boutique inn blends a soothing mix of smiling Buddhas, orchid sprays and artistic decor. Each guest room is inspired by a different LGBTIQ+ literary genius; the room themed on poet Raj Rao, for example, has sumptuous embroidered fabrics draped over the modern furniture. The on-site spa includes a Finnish sauna, a hot tub and massage therapy.

EAST END GALLERY DISTRICT

With the many artists who have worked here, it's no surprise that Provincetown hosts some of the finest art galleries in the region. For the best browsing, begin at PAAM and start walking southwest along Commercial St. Over the next few blocks every second storefront harbors a gallery worth a peek.

Pick up a copy of the *Provincetown Gallery Guide* (www.provincetowngalleryguide.com), or check out its website for gallery info, a map and details of events.

Eating

★Canteen MODERN AMERICAN $
(☎508-487-3800; www.thecanteenptown.com; 225 Commercial St; mains $10-16; ⏰11am-9pm Sun-Thu, to 10pm Fri & Sat;) Cool and casual, but unmistakably gourmet – this is your optimal P-town lunch stop. Choose from classics such as lobster rolls and barbecued pulled-pork sandwiches, or innovations like cod *banh mi* and shrimp sliders. We strongly recommend you add crispy Brussels sprouts and a cold beer to your order and then take a seat at the communal picnic table on the sand.

Mews Restaurant & Cafe MODERN AMERICAN $$$
(☎508-487-1500; www.mews.com; 429 Commercial St; mains $19-44; ⏰5-10pm Mon-Sat year-round, plus 10am-2pm Sun mid-May–Sep) A fantastic water view, the hottest martini bar in town and scrumptious food add up to Provincetown's finest dining scene. There are two sections: opt to dine gourmet on lobster risotto and filet mignon downstairs, where you're right on the sand, or go casual with a juicy Angus burger from the bistro menu upstairs. Reservations recommended.

Drinking & Nightlife

Aqua Bar BAR
(☎774-593-5106; www.facebook.com/aquabarptown; 207 Commercial St; ⏰10:30am-10pm Sun-Thu, to midnight Fri & Sat May-Oct) Imagine a food court where the options include a raw bar, sushi, gelato and other international delights. Add a fully stocked bar with generous bartenders pouring the drinks. Now put the whole place in a gorgeous seaside setting, overlooking a little beach and a beautiful harbor. Now imagine this whole scene at sunset. That's Aqua Bar.

Boatslip Beach Club GAY
(☎508-487-1669; www.boatslipresort.com; 161 Commercial St; ⏰tea dances daily from 4pm Jun-early Sep, Fri-Sun mid-Sep–May) Hosts wildly popular afternoon tea dances (4pm to 7pm), often packed with gorgeous guys. DJs fire things up: visit on Thursdays for dance classics from the 1970s and '80s. There's accommodations too.

Crown & Anchor GAY & LESBIAN
(☎508-487-1430; www.onlyatthecrown.com; 247 Commercial St; ⏰hours vary) The queen of the scene, this multiwing complex has a nightclub, a video bar, a leather bar and a fun, steamy cabaret that takes it to the limit, plus loads of shows and events – from Broadway concerts to drag revues and burlesque troupes. Check the calendar (and buy tickets) online. Accommodations and restaurant on-site too.

Information

Provincetown Chamber of Commerce (☎508-487-3424; www.ptownchamber.com; 307 Commercial St; ⏰9am-5pm) The town's helpful tourist office is right at MacMillan Pier.

Getting There & Away

From the Cape Cod Canal via US 6, it takes about 1½ hours to reach Provincetown (65 miles), depending on traffic.

BOAT

From around May to October, boats connect Provincetown's MacMillan Pier with Boston and Plymouth. Schedules are geared to day-trippers, with morning arrivals into Provincetown and late-afternoon departures. No ferries carry cars, but bikes can be transported for a fee (around $16 round trip in addition to your regular ticket). Advance reservations are recommended, especially on weekends and in peak summer.

Bay State Cruise Co (☎617-748-1428; www.boston-ptown.com; round trip adult/child $95/72) Fast ferry (1½ hours) operates three times daily from Boston's World Trade Center Pier.

Boston Harbor Cruises (☎617-227-4321; www.bostonharborcruises.com; round trip adult/child $93/65) Fast-ferry service (1½ hours) from Long Wharf in Boston up to three times daily.

Plymouth-to-Provincetown Express Ferry (☎508-927-5587; www.captjohn.com; round trip adult/child $53/32) Ferry from Plymouth (1½ hours, once daily) to Provincetown's MacMillan Pier.

BUS

Plymouth & Brockton (☎508-746-0378; www.p-b.com) Bus service from Boston that runs several times daily (one way $38, three to 3½ hours) and services other Cape towns. To get all the way to Provincetown you must switch buses in Hyannis.

The Islands

Nantucket

One need not be a millionaire to visit Nantucket, but it couldn't hurt. This compact island, 30 miles south of Cape Cod, grew rich from whaling in the 19th century. In recent decades it's experienced a rebirth as a summer getaway for CEOs, society types and other well-heeled visitors from Boston and New York.

It's easy to see why. Nantucket is New England at its most rose-covered, cobble-stoned, picture-postcard perfect. Nantucket town is the biggest draw for its fine dining, lively bars and one-of-a-kind history you can experience on just about every street. Elsewhere on the island outdoor activities abound. Even in summer you'll be able to find uncrowded stretches of sandy beach. All on an island that is close enough to reach without much hassle, but still feels deliciously remote.

The town of Nantucket (called 'Town' by locals) is the island's only real population center. Once home port to the world's largest whaling fleet, the town's storied past is reflected in the gracious period buildings lining its leafy streets. It boasts the nation's largest concentration of houses built prior to 1850 and is the only place in the US where the entire town is a National Historic Landmark. It's a thoroughly enjoyable place to amble about the cobblestone streets and soak up the atmosphere.

Sights

★Nantucket Whaling Museum MUSEUM
(☎508-228-1894; www.nha.org; 13 Broad St; museum & sites/all access $20/25; ⏲9am-5pm late May–mid-Oct, 10am-4pm mid-Oct–Dec & Apr–mid-May, 10am-4pm Thu-Sun early Feb-Mar, closed Jan) One of the island's highlights, this evocative museum occupies an 1847 spermaceti (whale oil) candle factory and the excellent exhibits relive Nantucket's 19th-century heyday as the whaling center of the world. There's a worthwhile, albeit long (54 minutes), documentary on the island, incredible scrimshaw exhibits (engravings and carvings done by sailors on ivory, whalebone or baleen) and a 46ft sperm-whale skeleton rising above it all. Be sure to head to the rooftop deck for lovely views.

Sleeping

Unless you've got island friends with a spare room, a summer stay on Nantucket won't be cheap. Don't even look for a motel or a campground – tony Nantucket is all about inns, and many of those are receiving dramatic makeovers to bring them to design-magazine standard.

★HI Nantucket HOSTEL $
(Star of the Sea; ☎508-228-0433; www.hiusa.org; 31 Western Ave; dm/5-person r $42/210; ⏲mid-May–mid-Oct; @📶) Known locally as Star of the Sea, this cool hostel has a million-dollar setting just minutes from Surfside Beach. It's housed in a former lifesaving station that dates from 1873 and is listed on the National Register of Historic Places. As Nantucket's sole budget option, its 49 beds are in high demand, so book as far in advance as possible.

Barnacle Inn B&B $$$
(☎508-228-0332; www.thebarnacleinn.com; 11 Fair St; r $450, without bath $330; ⏲late Apr-early Nov; ❄📶) This is what old Nantucket is all about: folksy owners and simple, quaint accommodations that hearken back to earlier times. Rooms in this turn-of-the-19th-century inn don't have phones or TVs, but they do have good rates for Nantucket town, particularly if you opt for a shared bathroom.

Eating & Drinking

Corner Table CAFE $
(☎508-228-2665; www.nantucketculinary.com; 22 Federal St; mains $11-19; ⏲7am-9pm) 🌿 A real local gathering place, this sweet cafe has great coffee, a cabinet full of high-quality eats to have here or take away (black bean and sweet potato salad, Bolognese, mascarpone raspberry cheesecake), daily soups and sandwiches, a sofa or two, and a sustainable, community-minded ethos.

★Proprietors MODERN AMERICAN $$
(☎508-228-7747; www.proprietorsnantucket.com; 9 India St; plates $17-35; ⏲5:30pm-late Mon-Sat, 10:30am-2pm Sun Apr-Oct) 🌿 Creative, globally inspired cooking and fine cocktails go down a treat at this bar-restaurant that proudly flaunts local farm-to-table fare. Your eyes may be bigger than your belly when reading the small-plates-focused menu: the house-made charcuterie is a worthy choice, as are kimchi pancakes, roasted bone marrow and tuna crudo. Return on Sundays for the lauded brunch.

Cisco Brewers BREWERY
(☎508-325-5929; www.ciscobrewers.com; 5 Bartlett Farm Rd; tours $20; ⏲noon-7pm Mon-Thu, from 11am Fri & Sat, noon-6pm Sun year-round) Enjoy a hoppy pint of Whale's Tale pale ale at the friendliest brewery you'll likely ever see. Cisco Brewers is the 'other' Nantucket, a laid-back place where fun banter loosens

those stiff upper lips found in primmer quarters. In addition to the brewery, there's a small **distillery**, casual indoor and outdoor bars, regular food trucks and live music.

Information

Visitor Services & Information Bureau (☎508-228-0925; www.nantucket-ma.gov; 25 Federal St; ⏱9am-5pm daily mid-Apr–mid-Oct, Mon-Sat rest of year) Has everything you'll need, including public restrooms and a list of available accommodations. The folks here also maintain a summertime kiosk (⏱9am-5pm late May-early Sep) on Straight Wharf.

Getting There & Away

AIR

Nantucket Memorial Airport (☎508-325-5300; www.nantucketairport.com; 14 Airport Rd) is 3 miles southeast of Nantucket town. Cape Air (www.capeair.com) offers year-round service to Boston, Hyannis, New Bedford and Martha's Vineyard, and seasonal service to New York. Delta, American, United and JetBlue also offer seasonal services to/from New York, Newark and Washington, DC.

The airport is connected by local bus to town ($2) from mid-June to early September.

BOAT

The most common way to reach Nantucket is by the **Steamship Authority** (☎508-548-5011; www.steamshipauthority.com) and **Hy-Line Cruises** (☎508-778-2600; www.hylinecruises.com) ferries from Hyannis. The traditional ferry takes 2¼ hours, while the high-speed ferry (passengers only) takes one hour. Additional summertime ferries run to Oak Bluffs on Martha's Vineyard, New Bedford, New Jersey and New York.

Martha's Vineyard

Bathed in unique beauty, Martha's Vineyard attracts wide-eyed day-trippers, celebrity second-home owners, and urbanites seeking a restful getaway; its 15,000 year-round residents include many artists, musicians and back-to-nature types. The Vineyard remains untouched by the kind of rampant commercialism found on the mainland – there's not a single chain restaurant or cookie-cutter motel in sight. Instead you'll find cozy inns, chef-driven restaurants and a bounty of green farms and grand beaches. And there's something for every mood here – fine dining in gentrified Edgartown one day and hitting the cotton candy and carousel scene in Oak Bluffs the next.

Martha's Vineyard is the largest island in New England, extending some 23 miles at its widest. Although it sits just 7 miles off the coast of Cape Cod, Vineyarders feel themselves such a world apart that they often refer to the mainland as 'America.'

Sights & Activities

★Campgrounds & Tabernacle HISTORIC SITE
(☎508-693-0525; www.mvcma.org) Oak Bluffs started out in the mid-19th century as a summer retreat by a revivalist church, whose members enjoyed a day at the beach as much as a gospel service. They first camped out in tents, then built some 300 wooden cottages, each adorned with whimsical filigree trim.

Flying Horses Carousel HISTORIC SITE
(☎508-693-9481; www.mvpreservation.org; Oak Bluffs Ave; 1/10 rides $3/25; ⏱11am-4:30pm Sat & Sun May–mid-Jun, 10am-10pm daily mid-Jun–Aug, 11am-4:30pm Sep-early Oct; 👪) Take a nostalgic ride on this National Historic Landmark, which has been captivating kids of all ages since 1876. It's the USA's oldest continuously operating merry-go-round, and these antique horses have manes of real horse hair.

Aquinnah Public Beach BEACH
(Moshup Trail) Aquinnah Public Beach (also known as Moshup Beach) is an impressive 5 miles long. Access is free, although parking ($10 to $20) is not. From the parking lot, it's a 10-minute walk to the beach.

Sleeping

HI Martha's Vineyard HOSTEL $
(☎508-693-2665; www.hiusa.org; 525 Edgartown–West Tisbury Rd; dm/d/tr $41/119/159; ⏱mid-May–early Oct; P@📶) Reserve early for a bed at this popular, purpose-built hostel in the center of the island. It has everything you'd expect: a solid kitchen, a games room, bike delivery, no curfew and friendly staff. The public bus stops out front and it's right on the bike path. Dorms and private rooms are available.

★Summercamp HOTEL $$$
(☎508-693-6611; www.summercamphotel.com; 70 Lake Ave; r $389-579; ⏱May-Oct; ❄📶) We dare you not to smile in response to the detail of this fun place, the 2016 incarnation of an iconic 1879 hotel that borders the Tabernacle area. The nostalgic summer-camp theme extends from the Astro-

turfed games room to the canteen selling retro snacks. And there's even a twin room with bunks. Decor is fresh and inspired, location is ace.

Eating & Drinking

★ArtCliff Diner CAFE $
(☎508-693-1224; 39 Beach Rd, Vineyard Haven; mains $9-14; ⏲7am-2pm Thu-Tue) Hands down the best place in town for breakfast and lunch. Chef-owner Gina Stanley, a grad of the prestigious Culinary Institute of America, adds flair to everything she touches, from the almond-encrusted French toast to the fresh fish tacos. The eclectic menu utilizes farm-fresh island ingredients. Expect a line, but it's worth the wait.

Sweet Life Café MODERN AMERICAN $$$
(☎508-696-0200; www.sweetlifemv.com; 63 Circuit Ave; mains $32-38; ⏲5:30-10pm Wed-Sun mid-May–Oct) New American cuisine with a French accent is offered by this stylish bistro, which provides the town's finest dining. Tuna tartare, fried softshell crab and miso-glazed local cod are joined on the menu by other innovative dishes using local produce (not just seafood). Reservations advised.

★Offshore Ale Co MICROBREWERY
(☎508-693-2626; www.offshoreale.com; 30 Kennebec Ave; ⏲11:30am-8:30pm Sun-Thu, to 9:30pm Fri & Sat) Join the throngs of locals and visitors at this popular microbrewery – enjoy a pint of Hop Goddess ale, some superior pub grub (including a knockout lobster roll) and the kind of laid-back atmosphere where boats are suspended from the ceiling and peanut shells are thrown on the floor.

Information

Visitor Information Booth (☎508-693-4266; cnr Circuit & Lake Aves; ⏲9am-5pm late May–mid-Oct) The town hall staffs this convenient summertime info booth near the carousel.

Getting There & Away

AIR

Martha's Vineyard Airport (MVY; ☎508-693-7022; www.mvyairport.com; 71 Airport Rd, Vineyard Haven) is in the center of the island, about 6 miles south of Vineyard Haven, and is served by buses. It has year-round service to Boston and Nantucket and seasonal services to Hyannis, New Bedford, MA, and New York. Check Cape Air (www.capeair.com) for schedules. Delta and JetBlue also offer seasonal services from New York's JFK Airport.

BOAT

Steamship Authority (www.steamship authority.com) operates a frequent, year-round ferry service connecting Vineyard Haven with Woods Hole, south of Falmouth on the Cape (a 45-minute voyage). This is the only ferry that carries vehicles.

Oak Bluffs is a busy summertime port from mid-May to mid-October, when ferries from Hyannis, Falmouth, Woods Hole and New Bedford bring day-trippers across.

Pioneer Valley

With the exception of gritty Springfield, the Pioneer Valley offers a gentle landscape of college towns, picturesque farms and old mills that have been charmingly converted into modern use. The uber-cool burg of Northampton provides the region's top dining, nightlife and street scenes, while the other destinations offer unique museums, geological marvels and a few unexpected roadside gems.

Getting There & Away

Pioneer Valley Transit Authority (www.pvta.com) provides bus services (with bike racks) throughout the Five College area; the Northampton–Amherst route has the most frequent service.

Northampton

In a region famous for its charming college towns, you'd be hard-pressed to find anything more appealing than the crooked streets of downtown Northampton. Old redbrick buildings and lots of pedestrian traffic provide a lively backdrop for your wanderings, which will likely include cafes, rock clubs and bookstores (which explains why locals call their town 'NoHo'). Move a few steps outside of the picturesque commercial center and you'll stumble onto the bucolic grounds of Smith College. Northampton is a well-known liberal enclave in these parts. The lesbian community is famously outspoken, and rainbow flags wave wildly all over town.

Sights & Activities

Northampton is at the center of a series of interconnected, accessible walking and cycling paths. The **Norwottuck Rail Trail**

WORTH A TRIP

DR SEUSS IN SPRINGFIELD

The innovative **Amazing World of Dr Seuss** (☎413-263-6800; www.seussinspringfield.org; 21 Edwards St; adult/child $25/13; ⏰10am-5pm Mon-Sat, from 11am Sun; 👪) is dedicated to the life and work of Springfield native Theodore Geisel, aka Dr Seuss. On the 1st floor, interactive exhibits use the stories of Dr Seuss to engage children with rhyming games and storytelling. Upstairs, galleries display original artwork, a moving collection of letters from the author to his great nephew, and a reproduction of Geisel's studio. Your ticket includes admission to four other museums in Springfield.

(☎413-586-8706; www.mass.gov/locations/norwottuck-rail-trail) extends 11 miles to Hadley and Amherst, while the **Manhan Rail Trail** (www.manhanrailtrail.org) connects Northampton and Easthampton. You can rent bikes from **Northampton Bicycle** (☎413-586-3810; www.nohobike.com; 319 Pleasant St; per day from $25; ⏰9:30am-6pm Mon-Fri, 9:30am-5pm Sat, noon-5pm Sun).

Smith College COLLEGE
(☎413-584-2700; www.smith.edu; Elm St) Founded 'for the education of the intelligent gentlewoman' in 1875, Smith College is one of the largest women's colleges in the country, with 2600 students. The verdant 125-acre campus holds an eclectic architectural mix of nearly 100 buildings, set on a pretty pond. Notable alums of the college include Sylvia Plath, Julia Child and Gloria Steinem. After exploring the campus, take a stroll around Paradise Pond and snap a photo at the Japanese tea hut.

Smith College Museum of Art MUSEUM
(☎413-585-2760; www.smith.edu/artmuseum; 20 Elm St; adult/child $5/free; ⏰10am-4pm Tue, Wed, Fri & Sat, to 8pm Thu, noon-4pm Sun) This impressive campus museum boasts a 25,000-piece collection. It's particularly strong in 19th- and 20th-century European and North American paintings, including works by Degas, Winslow Homer, Picasso and James Abbott McNeill Whistler. Another highlight is the so-called 'functional art': the remarkable restrooms and the eclectic collection of benches (that you can actually sit on) – all designed and created by contemporary American artists.

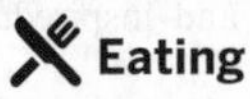

Eating

Woodstar Cafe CAFE $
(www.woodstarcafe.com; 60 Masonic St; mains $5.50-9.30; ⏰7am-6pm Mon, to 7pm Tue-Fri, 8am-7pm Sat, 8am-6pm Sun; 📶🌿) Students flock to this family-run bakery-cafe, just a stone's throw from campus, for tasty sandwiches made on the freshest of bread and named after local towns and landmarks. Save room for dessert, as the pastries – made on-site – are divine.

Local Burger BURGERS $
(www.localnorthampton.com; 16 Main St; mains $6.50-14; ⏰11:30am-10pm Sun-Thu, to 3am Fri & Sat; 👪) Locavores rave about this burger joint on Main St, where every effort is made to use locally sourced beef and produce. Burger-masters turn out eight tasty custom burgers (especially good for satisfying the late-night munchies), while the sweet-potato fries are an irresistible accompaniment. Alcoholic drinks – including spiked milkshakes – are served until midnight.

Information

Greater Northampton Chamber of Commerce
(☎413-584-1900; www.explorenorthampton.com; 99 Pleasant St; ⏰9am-5pm Mon-Fri, plus 10am-2pm Sat & Sun May-Oct) Get all your questions answered at the local chamber.

Amherst

This quintessential college town is home to the prestigious Amherst College, a pretty 'junior ivy' that borders the town green, as well as the hulking University of Massachusetts and the cozy liberal-arts Hampshire College. Start your explorations at the town green, at the intersection of MA 116 and MA 9. In the surrounding streets, you'll find a few small galleries, a bookstore or two, countless coffeehouses and a few small but worthwhile museums (several of which are associated with the colleges).

Emily Dickinson Museum MUSEUM
(☎413-542-8161; www.emilydickinsonmuseum.org; 280 Main St; guided tour adult/child $15/free; ⏰10am-5pm Wed-Mon Jun-Aug, 11am-4pm Wed-Sun Mar-May & Sep-Dec) During her lifetime, Emily Dickinson (1830–86) published only seven poems, but more than

1000 were discovered and published posthumously, and her verses on love, nature and immortality have made her one of the USA's most important poets. Dickinson spent most of her life in near seclusion in this stately home near the center of Amherst. Worthwhile guided tours (one hour) focus on the poet and her works, visiting both the Dickinson Homestead and the adjacent Evergreens.

Eric Carle Museum of Picture Book Art MUSEUM
(☎ 413-559-6300; www.carlemuseum.org; 125 W Bay Rd; adult/child $9/6; ⏲ 10am-4pm Tue-Fri, to 5pm Sat, noon-5pm Sun; 🚻) Co-founded by the author and illustrator of *The Very Hungry Caterpillar,* this superb museum celebrates book illustrations from around the world with rotating exhibits in three galleries, as well as a permanent collection. All visitors (grown-ups included) are encouraged to express their own artistic sentiments in the hands-on art studio.

The Berkshires

Few places in America combine culture and country living as deftly as the Berkshire hills, home to world-class music, dance and theater festivals – the likes of Tanglewood and Jacob's Pillow – as well as miles of hiking trails and acres of farmland.

Extending from the highest point in the state – Mt Greylock – southward to the Connecticut state line, the Berkshires have been a summer refuge for more than a century, when the rich and famous arrived to build summer 'cottages' of grand proportions. Many of these mansions survive as inns or performance venues. And still today, on summer weekends when the sidewalks are scorching in Boston and New York, crowds of city dwellers jump in their cars and head for the Berkshire breezes.

ℹ Getting There & Around

Most travelers are likely to reach this region by driving from Boston, Hartford or New York. It is possible to arrive by bus or train, but you'll want your own vehicle if you intend to visit the more rural areas. If not, the Berkshire Regional Transit Authority (www.berkshirerta.com) runs buses between major Berkshire towns. A ride costs $1.75 for short trips and $4 for longer journeys.

Great Barrington

Great Barrington's Main St used to consist of Woolworth's, hardware stores, thrift shops and a run-down diner. These have given way to artsy boutiques, antique shops, coffeehouses and restaurants. Nowadays, the town boasts the best dining scene in the region, with easy access to hiking trails and magnificent scenery in the surrounding hills.

The Housatonic River flows through the center of town just east of Main St/US 7, the central thoroughfare.

★ **Monument Mountain** HIKING
(www.thetrustees.org; US 7; parking $5; ⏲ sunrise-sunset) Less than 5 miles north of Great Barrington center on US 7 is Monument Mountain, which has hiking trails to the 1642ft summit of Squaw Peak. Turning right from the parking lot, the 3-mile circular route ascends steeply via the **Hickey trail** and runs along the cliff edge to Squaw Peak and the Devil's Pulpit lookout. From the top you'll get fabulous views all the way to Mt Greylock to the northwest and to the Catskills in New York.

Wainwright Inn B&B $$
(☎ 413-528-2062; www.wainwrightinn.com; 518 S Main St; r $140-230; ❄ 📶) Great Barrington's finest place to lay your head, this inn (c 1766) exudes historical appeal from its wraparound porches and spacious parlors to the period room decor in the nine guest rooms. Breakfast is a decadent experience. The inn is a short walk from the center of town on a busy road.

ℹ Information

Southern Berkshire Chamber of Commerce
(☎ 413-528-1510; www.southernberkshire chamber.com; 362 Main St; ⏲ 10am-6pm Thu-Mon) Maintains a kiosk at the corner of St James Pl that's well stocked with maps, restaurant menus and accommodations lists.

Stockbridge

Take a good look down Stockbridge's wide Main St. Notice anything? More specifically, notice anything missing? Not one stoplight interrupts the view; not one telephone pole blights the picture-perfect scene – it looks very much the way Norman Rockwell might have seen it.

In fact, Rockwell did see it – he lived and worked in Stockbridge during the last 25 years of his life. Nowadays, Stockbridge attracts summer and fall visitors en masse, who come to stroll the streets, inspect the shops and sit in the rockers on the porch of the historic Red Lion Inn. And they come by the busload to visit the Norman Rockwell Museum on the town's outskirts.

All that fossilized picturesqueness comes at a price. Noticeably absent from the village center is the kind of vitality that you find in the neighboring towns.

★Norman Rockwell Museum MUSEUM
(413-298-4100; www.nrm.org; 9 Glendale Rd/MA 183; adult/child $20/free; 10am-5pm May-Oct, to 4pm Nov-Apr) Born in New York City, Norman Rockwell (1894–1978) sold his first magazine cover illustration to the *Saturday Evening Post* in 1916. In the following half-century he did another 321 covers for the *Post,* as well as illustrations for books, posters and many other magazines on his way to becoming the most popular illustrator in US history.

This excellent museum has the largest collection of Rockwell's original art, as well as Rockwell's studio, which was moved here from nearby Stockbridge.

Lenox

This appealing, wealthy town is a historical anomaly: firstly, its charm was not destroyed by the industrial revolution; and then, prized for its bucolic peace, the town became a summer retreat for wealthy families with surnames such as Carnegie, Vanderbilt and Westinghouse, who had made their fortunes by building factories in other towns.

As the cultural heart of the Berkshires, Lenox's illustrious past remains tangibly present today. The superstar among its attractions is the Tanglewood Music Festival, an incredibly popular summer event drawing scores of visitors from New York City, Boston and beyond.

Festivals

Tanglewood Music Festival MUSIC
(888-266-1200; www.tanglewood.org; 297 West St/MA 183, Lenox; lawn tickets from $21; late Jun-early Sep) Dating from 1934, the Tanglewood Music Festival is among the most esteemed summertime music events in the world. Symphony, pops, chamber music, jazz and blues are performed from late June through early September. You can count on renowned cellist Yo-Yo Ma, violinist Joshua Bell and singer James Taylor to perform each summer, along with a run of world-class guest artists and famed conductors.

Sleeping

Birchwood Inn INN $$$
(413-637-2600; www.birchwood-inn.com; 7 Hubbard St; r $208-399;) A pretty hilltop inn a couple of blocks from the town center, Birchwood occupies the oldest (1767) home in Lenox. The 11 spacious rooms vary in decor: some swing with a vintage floral design, others are more country classic, but all are romantic and luxurious. Deluxe rooms feature king-size beds and wood-burning fireplaces.

Eating

Haven Cafe & Bakery CAFE $
(413-637-8948; www.havencafebakery.com; 8 Franklin St; mains $7.50-15.50; 7:30am-3pm Mon-Fri, 8am-3pm Sat & Sun;) It looks like a casual cafe, but the sophisticated food evokes a more upscale experience. For breakfast, try croissant French toast or inventive egg dishes such as salmon scramble; for lunch there are fancy salads and sandwiches – all highlighting local organic ingredients. Definitely save room for something sweet from the bakery counter.

Bagel & Brew BAGELS $
(www.facebook.com/BagelandBrew; 18 Franklin St; bagels $5-9; bagels 7am-1pm, bar 5-11pm Sat & Sun) Bagels by day, brews by night. Tasty bagel sandwiches are served for breakfast and lunch; then there's a dozen different beers on tap – most of them regional – served in the beer garden, starting around the dinner hour. The food that accompanies the brew is not bagels, but truly delicious pub grub. This place has a great vibe.

★Nudel AMERICAN $$
(413-551-7183; www.nudelrestaurant.com; 37 Church St; mains $18-26; 5-9:15pm) Nudel is a driving force in the area's sustainable food movement, with just about everything on the menu seasonally inspired and locally sourced. The back-to-basics approach rings through in inventive dishes, which change daily but never disappoint. Incredible flavors. Nudel has a loyal following, so reser-

vations are recommended. The last seating is at 9:15pm.

Information

Visit Lenox (413-637-3646; www.lenox.org; 4 Housatonic St; 10am-4pm Wed-Sat Sep-Jun, to 6pm daily Jul & Aug) This office is a clearinghouse of information on everything from inns to what's going on.

Williamstown

Small but pretty Williamstown is nestled within the heart of the Purple Valley, so named because the surrounding mountains often seem shrouded in a lavender veil at dusk. Folks congregate in the friendly town center, which is only two blocks long, while dogs and kids frolic in the ample green spaces.

Williamstown is a quintessential New England college town, its charming streets and greens dotted with the stately brick and marble buildings of Williams College. Cultural life is rich, with a pair of exceptional art museums and one of the region's most respected summer theater festivals.

Sights

★Clark Art Institute MUSEUM

(413-458-2303; www.clarkart.edu; 225 South St; adult/child $20/free; 10am-5pm Tue-Sun Sep-Jun, daily Jul & Aug) Even if you're not an avid art lover, don't miss this gem, set on 140 gorgeous acres of expansive lawns, flower-filled meadows and rolling hills. The building – with its triple-tiered reflecting pool – is a stunner. The collections are particularly strong in the impressionists, with significant works by Monet, Pissarro and Renoir. Mary Cassatt, Winslow Homer and John Singer Sargent represent contemporaneous American painting.

Williams College Museum of Art MUSEUM

(413-597-2429; https://wcma.williams.edu; 15 Lawrence Hall Dr; 10am-5pm, to 8pm Thu, closed Wed Sep-May) FREE In the center of town is this worthwhile – and free! – art museum. It has a collection of some 15,000 pieces, with substantial works by notables such as Edward Hopper *(Morning in a City)*, Winslow Homer and Grant Wood, to name only a few. The photography collection is also noteworthy. Temporary exhibitions are accompanied by academic talks. To find the museum, look for the huge bronze eyes by Louise Bourgeois, embedded in the front lawn on Main St.

> **WORTH A TRIP**
>
> **MASS MOCA IN NORTH ADAMS**
>
> Sprawling over 13 acres of downtown North Adams, **MASS MoCA** (Massachusetts Museum of Contemporary Art; 413-662-2111; www.massmoca.org; 1040 Mass MoCA Way; adult/child $20/8; 10am-6pm Sun-Wed, to 7pm Thu-Sat Jul & Aug, 11am-5pm Wed-Mon Sep-Jun) makes up one-third of the entire business district. After the Sprague Electric Company closed in 1985, some $31 million was spent to modernize the property into 'the largest gallery in the United States.' The museum encompasses 222,000 sq ft in 25 buildings, including art construction areas, performance centers and 19 galleries. Long-term exhibitions include a gallery of wall paintings by Sol LeWitt. Thought-provoking guided tours run daily at 1pm and 3pm.

Sleeping & Eating

River Bend Farm B&B B&B $$

(413-458-3121; www.riverbendfarmbb.com; 643 Simonds Rd/US 7; r $120; Apr-Oct;) Step back in time to 1770, when this Georgian Colonial was a local tavern owned by Benjamin Simonds. The house owes its painstaking restoration to hosts Judy and Dave Loomis. Four simple, comfortable doubles share two bathrooms with claw-foot tubs. Breakfast is served in the wood-paneled taproom, next to the wide stone fireplace. A truly atmospheric place to stay.

★Guest House at Field Farm INN $$$

(413-458-3135; www.thetrustees.org/field-farm; 554 Sloan Rd; r $250-350;) Located about 6 miles south of Williamstown, this one-of-a-kind inn offers an artful blend of mid-20th-century modernity and timeless mountain scenery. The six rooms are spacious and fitted with handcrafted furnishings that reflect the modernist style of the house. The sculpture-laden grounds feature miles of lightly trodden walking trails and a pair of Adirondack chairs set perfectly for unobstructed stargazing.

Pappa Charlie's Deli DELI $

(413-458-5969; 28 Spring St; sandwiches $5-7; 8am-8pm Mon-Sat, to 7pm Sun) Here's a welcoming breakfast spot where locals really do ask for 'the usual.' The stars themselves created the lunch sandwiches that bear their names. The Mary Tyler Moore is a favorite (bacon, lettuce, tomato and avocado); the actress later went vegetarian, so you can also get a version with soy bacon. Order a Politician and get anything you want.

★Mezze Bistro & Bar FUSION **$$**
(☎413-458-0123; www.mezzerestaurant.com; 777 Cold Spring Rd/US 7; mains $16-28; ⊙5-9pm Sun-Thu, to 9:30pm Fri & Sat) You don't know exactly what you're going to get at this contemporary restaurant – the menu changes frequently – but you know it's going to be good. Situated on 3 spectacular acres, Mezze's farm-to-table approach begins with an edible garden right on-site. Much of the rest of the seasonal menu, from small-batch microbrews to organic meats, is locally sourced as well.

RHODE ISLAND

Rhode Island, the smallest of the US states, isn't actually an island. Although it only takes about an hour to traverse, this little wonder packs in more than 400 miles of coastline with wonderful, white-sand swimming beaches and some of the country's finest historic architecture, galleries and museums. What's more, Rhode Islanders are about as friendly as folks come.

Hugging the rugged shoreline before heading inland, seaside resorts, quaint Colonial villages and extravagant country homes give way to lush fields of berry farms, vineyards and horse studs. Rhode Island's main cities – Providence, with working-class roots, and Newport, born of old money the likes of which most cannot conceive – are among New England's finest.

With year-round cultural attractions, festivals, events, top-notch restaurants and seriously cool bars, it's no wonder the nouveau riche continue to flock here for summer shenanigans. While visiting Rhode Island ain't cheap, it's worth every penny.

History

Ever since it was founded in 1636 by Roger Williams, a religious outcast from Boston, Providence has enjoyed an independent frame of mind. Williams' guiding principle, the one that got him ostracized from Massachusetts, was that all people should have freedom of conscience. He put his liberal beliefs into practice when settling Providence, remaining on friendly terms with the local Narragansett Native Americans after purchasing from them the land for a bold experiment in tolerance and peaceful coexistence.

Williams' principles would not last long. As Providence and Newport grew and merged into a single colony, competition and conflict with area tribes sparked several wars, leading to the decimation of the Wampanoag, Pequot, Narragansett and Nipmuck peoples. Rhode Island was also a prolific slave trader and its merchants would control much of that industry in the years after the Revolutionary War.

The city of Pawtucket birthed the American industrial revolution, with the establishment of the water-powered Slater Mill in 1790. Industrialism impacted the character of Providence and surrounds, particularly along the Blackstone River, creating urban density. As with many small East Coast cities, these urban areas went into a precipitous decline in the 1940s and '50s as manufacturing industries (textiles and costume jewelry) faltered. In the 1960s, preservation efforts salvaged the historic architectural framework of Providence and Newport. Today, Newport has flourished into one of the nation's most attractive historical centers.

Providence also rerouted its destiny to emerge as a lively and stylish city with a dynamic economy and vibrant downtown core, largely due to the work of Buddy Cianci, twice-convicted felon and twice-elected mayor (1975–84, 1991–2002). The spectacle of today's wildly popular WaterFire festival is a powerful symbol of the city's phoenix-like rebirth along the confluence of the three rivers that gave it life. Cianci died in 2016, aged 74.

ℹ Information

Rhode Island Division of Parks & Recreation (www.riparks.com) For a listing of all of Rhode Island's state beaches.

Rhode Island Tourism Division (www.visitrhodeisland.com) The official state provider of tourist information on Rhode Island.

Providence

Atop the confluence of the Providence, Moshassuck and Woonasquatucket Rivers, Rhode Island's capital city offers some of the finest urban strolling in New England: around Brown University's historic campus on 18th-century College Hill, along the landscaped Riverwalk trail, and through downtown's handsome streets and lanes with their hip cafes, art-house theaters, fusion restaurants and trendsetting bars.

Once destined to become an industrial relic, Providence's fate was spared when Buddy Cianci, its then controversial two-time mayor, rolled out a plan to revitalize the downtown core by rerouting subterranean rivers, reclaiming land and restoring historic facades. It created a city where history's treasures are not simply memorialized but rather integrated into a creative present; three centuries of architectural styles are unified in colorful urban streetscapes that are at once bold, beautiful and cooler than cool.

Providence's large student population helps keep the city's social and arts scenes cutting edge. Play it cool.

Sights

★Rhode Island State House NOTABLE BUILDING

(☎401-222-3983; www.sos.ri.gov; 82 Smith St; ⏰self-guided tours 8:30am-4:30pm Mon-Fri, guided tours 9am, 10am, 11am, 1pm & 2pm Mon-Fri; P) FREE Designed by McKim, Mead and White in 1904, the Rhode Island State House rises above the Providence skyline, easily visible from miles around. Modeled in part on St Peter's Basilica in Vatican City, it has the world's fourth-largest self-supporting marble dome and houses one of Gilbert Stuart's portraits of George Washington, which you might want to compare to a dollar bill from your wallet.

Providence Athenaeum LIBRARY

(☎401-421-6970; www.providenceathenaeum.org; 251 Benefit St; ⏰10am-7pm Mon-Thu, to 6pm Fri & Sat, 1-5pm Sun) FREE One of the most prominent buildings on Benefit St, the Greek Revival Providence Athenaeum was designed by William Strickland and completed in 1838. This is a library of the old school with plaster busts and oil paintings filling in spaces not occupied by books. Edgar Allen Poe used to court ladies here. Pick up a brochure for a self-guided Raven Tour of the building's artwork and architecture.

Brown University UNIVERSITY

(☎401-863-1000; www.brown.edu; 1 Prospect St) FREE Dominating the crest of the College Hill neighborhood on the East Side, Brown University's campus exudes Ivy League charm. **University Hall**, a 1770 brick edifice used as a barracks during the Revolutionary War, sits at its center. To explore the campus, start at the wrought-iron gates at the intersection of College St and Prospect St and make your way across the green toward Thayer St.

Benefit Street STREET

(Benefit St) Immediately east of Providence's downtown, you'll find College Hill, where you can see the city's Colonial history reflected in the 18th-century houses that line Benefit St on the East Side. These are mostly private homes, but many are open for tours one weekend in June during the annual **Festival of Historic Houses** (www.ppsri.org/programs-events/signature-events/festival-of-houses/; ⏰Jun) FREE. Benefit St is a fitting symbol of the Providence renaissance, rescued by local preservationists in the 1960s from misguided urban-renewal efforts that would have destroyed it.

★RISD Museum of Art MUSEUM

(☎401-454-6500; www.risdmuseum.org; 20 N Main St; adult/under 18yr $15/free; ⏰10am-5pm Tue-Sun, to 9pm 3rd Thu of month; P 👪) Wonderfully eclectic, the Rhode Island School of Design's art museum showcases everything from ancient Greek art to 20th-century American paintings and decorative arts from its own collection, and always has visiting exhibitions and events. Pop in before 1pm on a Sunday and admission is free. Check out the excellent website before you go.

Festivals

★WaterFire STREET CARNIVAL

(☎401-273-1155; www.waterfire.org; ⏰dates vary) FREE During summer and on a handful of dates in the cooler months, much of downtown Providence transforms into a carnivalesque festival during the popular WaterFire art installation created by Barnaby Evans in 1994. Marking the convergence of the Providence, Moshassuck and Woonasquatucket rivers, 100 flaming braziers illuminate the water, overlooked by crowds strolling over the bridges and along the riverside.

Sleeping

★The Dean Hotel BOUTIQUE HOTEL $

(☎401-455-3326; http://thedeanhotel.com; 122 Fountain St; d from $109) The Dean epitomizes all that is design in Providence. It features a beer hall, a karaoke bar, a cocktail den and a beer hall downstairs; upstairs has eight quirky, design-themed rooms that provide a stylish urban oasis from the fun and frivolity downstairs. If you're a cool kid and you know it, you belong here.

Providence Biltmore HISTORIC HOTEL $$

(☎401-421-0700; www.providencebiltmore.com; 11 Dorrance St; d from $189; P 📶) The granddaddy of Providence's hotels, the Biltmore dates from the 1920s, although its 292 oversized guest rooms and suites have been thoroughly refurbished to a high standard, stretching many stories above the old city: ask for a room on a high floor. The lobby, both intimate and regal, nicely combines dark wood, twisting staircases and chandeliers, harking back to a lost age.

Eating

Haven Brothers Diner DINER $

(☎401-603-8124; www.havenbrothersmobile.com; cnr Dorrance & Fulton Sts; meals $5-12; ⏲5pm-3am) Parked next to City Hall, this Providence institution is basically a diner on the back of a truck that has rolled into the same spot every evening for decades. Climb up a rickety ladder to get basic diner fare alongside everyone from drunks to prominent politicians and college kids pulling an all-nighter. The murder burger comes highly recommended.

birch MODERN AMERICAN $$$

(☎401-272-3105; www.birchrestaurant.com; 200 Washington St; 4-course dinner $60, beverage pairings $40; ⏲5-10pm Thu-Mon) With a background at Noma in Copenhagen and the Dorrance at the Biltmore, chef Benjamin Sukle and his wife, Heidi, now have their own place: the understated but fabulously good birch. Its intimate size and style (seating surrounds a U-shaped bar) means attention to detail is exacting in both the decor and the food, which focuses on under-utilized, hyper-seasonal produce.

Drinking

★Ogie's Trailer Park BAR

(☎401-383-8200; www.ogiestrailerpark.com; 1155 Westminster St; ⏲4pm-1am Mon-Thu, 3pm-2am Fri & Sat, noon-1am Sun) This place is just so awesome and unexpected that we almost want to keep it to ourselves. Let's just say that in terms of thematics and design, if you crossed the *Brady Bunch* with *Mad Men* with *Breaking Bad*, you'd be somewhere in the vicinity. Eat, drink and love.

The Eddy COCKTAIL BAR

(☎401-831-3339; www.eddybar.com; 95 Eddy St; ⏲4pm-1am) Providence's classiest cocktail concoctions are served at the Eddy alongside a healthy selection of on-tap and bottled beers and an impressive wine list. Dress to impress.

Information

Providence Visitor Information Center
(☎401-751-1177; www.goprovidence.com; 1 Sabin St, Rhode Island Convention Center; ⏲9am-5pm Mon-Sat)

Getting There & Away

BUS

All long-distance buses and most local routes stop at the central **Intermodal Transportation Center** (Kennedy Plaza; ⏲6am-7pm). Greyhound and Peter Pan Bus Lines have ticket counters inside and there are maps outlining local services.

Peter Pan connects Providence and Green Airport with Boston's South Station (from $9, one hour, 12 daily) and Boston's Logan International Airport (from $18, 70 minutes, 10 daily).

Greyhound buses depart for Boston (from $9, 65 minutes), New York City (from $15, 5½ to six hours) and elsewhere.

TRAIN

Amtrak trains, including high-speed Acela trains, connect Providence with Boston (from $12, 50 minutes) and New York (from $54, three to 3½ hours).

MBTA commuter rail has regular scheduled services to Boston ($12, 60 to 75 minutes).

Getting Around

Providence is small, pretty and walkable, so once you arrive it makes sense to get around on foot.

RIPTA operates two 'trolley' routes. The Green Line runs from the East Side through downtown to Federal Hill. The Gold Line runs from the Providence Marriott Downtown hotel, south to the hospital via Kennedy Plaza, and stops at the Point St Ferry Dock. Fares are $2 per ride.

Newport

Established by religious moderates, 'new port' flourished in the independent colony of Rhode Island, which declared itself a state here in 1776. Downtown, shutterbugs snap excitedly at immaculately preserved Colonial-era architecture and landmarks at seemingly every turn.

Fascinating as Newport's early history is, the real intrigue began in the late 1850s, when wealthy industrialists began building opulent summer residences along cliff-top Bellevue Ave. Impeccably styled on Italianate palazzi, French châteaux and Elizabethan manor houses, these gloriously restored mansions filled with priceless antiques and their breathtaking location must be seen to be believed. The curiosity, variety and extravagance of this spectacle is unrivaled.

Honoring its maritime roots, Newport remains a global center for yachting. Put simply, summers here sparkle: locals have excellent taste and know how to throw a shindig. There's always something going on, including a series of cross-genre festivals that are among the best in the USA.

Sights & Activities

★The Breakers HISTORIC BUILDING

(401-847-1000; www.newportmansions.org; 44 Ochre Point Ave; adult/child $24/8; 9am-5pm Apr–mid-Oct, hours vary mid-Oct–Mar; P) A 70-room Italian Renaissance megapalace inspired by 16th-century Genoese palazzi, the Breakers is the most magnificent of Newport's grandiose mansions. At the behest of Cornelius Vanderbilt II, Richard Morris Hunt did most of the design (though craftspeople from around the world perfected the decorative program). The building was completed in 1895 and sits at Ochre Point, on a grand oceanside site. The furnishings, most made expressly for the Breakers, are all original. Don't miss the **Children's Cottage** on the grounds.

★The Elms HISTORIC BUILDING

(401-847-1000; www.newportmansions.org/explore/the-elms; 367 Bellevue Ave; adult/child $17.50/8, servant life tours adult/child $18/7.50; 10am-5pm Apr–mid-Oct, hours vary mid-Oct–Mar; P) Designed by Horace Trumbauer in 1901, the Elms is a replica of Château d'Asnières, built near Paris in 1750. Here you can take a 'behind-the-scenes' tour that will have you snaking through the servants' quarters and up onto the roof. Along the way you'll learn about the activities of the army of servants and the architectural devices that kept them hidden from the view of those drinking port in the formal rooms.

Rough Point HISTORIC BUILDING

(401-849-7300; www.newportrestoration.org/roughpoint/; 680 Bellevue Ave; adult/child $25/free; 9:30am-2pm Thu-Sun Apr-early May, 9:30am-3:30pm Tue-Sun early May-early Nov; P) While the peerless position and splendor of the grounds alone are worth the price of admission, this faux-English manor house also contains heiress and philanthropist Doris Duke's impressive art holdings, including medieval tapestries, furniture owned by French emperors, Ming dynasty ceramics, and paintings by Renoir and Van Dyck.

Fort Adams State Park STATE PARK

(401-847-2400; www.riparks.com/Locations/LocationFortAdams.html; Harrison Ave; overnight parking $6; dawn-dusk) America's largest coastal fortification and the centerpiece of this gorgeous state park is **Fort Adams** (401-841-0707; www.fortadams.org; 90 Fort Adams Dr; tours adult/child $12/6; 10am-4pm late May-Oct, reduced hours Nov & Dec), which juts out into Narragansett Bay. It's the venue for the Newport jazz and folk festivals and numerous special events. A beach, picnic and fishing areas, and a boat ramp are open daily.

Cliff Walk WALKING

(www.cliffwalk.com; Memorial Blvd) For a glorious hike take the 3.5-mile Cliff Walk, which hugs the coast along the back side of Newport's mansions from Memorial Blvd to Bailey's Beach. You will not only enjoy the same dramatic ocean views that were once reserved for the Newport elite, but you'll also get to gawk at their mansions along the way.

Festivals

★Newport Music Festival MUSIC

(401-849-0700; www.newportmusic.org; tickets $25-50; mid-Jul) This internationally regarded festival offers a wide program of classical music concerts performed in the spectacular settings of some of the Newport Mansions, as well as other visually delicious and acoustically satisfying venues around town.

OFF THE BEATEN TRACK

BLOCK ISLAND

From the deck of the ferry, a cluster of mansard roofs and gingerbread houses rises picturesquely from the commercial village of Old Harbor, where little has changed since 1895, short of adding electricity and flushing toilets! If you remain after the departure of the masses on the last ferry, the scale and pace of the island will delight or derange you: some find it blissfully quiet, but others get island fever fast.

Block Island's simple pleasures center on strolling the beach, which stretches for miles to the north of Old Harbor, biking around the island's rolling farmland and getting to know the calls of the many bird species that make the island home. During off-season, when the population dwindles to a few hundred, the landscape has the spare, haunted feeling of an Andrew Wyeth painting, with stone walls demarcating centuries-old property lines and few trees interrupting the spectacular ocean vistas.

Sleeping

Many places have a two- or three-day minimum stay in summer and close between November and April. Advance reservations are essential. Peak season runs roughly from mid-June to Labor Day. Off-season prices can be far cheaper than those listed here. Camping is not allowed on the island.

The **Block Island Hospitality Center** (☎401-466-2982; www.blockislandchamber.com; 1 Water St, Old Harbor Ferry Landing; ⏰9am-5pm late May-early Sep, 10am-4pm rest of year) near the ferry dock keeps track of vacancies, and will try to help should you arrive *sans réservation*.

Getting There & Away

The island can only be reached by sea or air.

Block Island Ferry (☎401-783-7996; www.blockislandferry.com) Runs a year-round traditional car ferry and a high-speed ferry from Point Judith in Narragansett from Memorial Day to mid-October. There are additional high-speed, passenger-only ferries from Newport and Fall River, MA.

Block Island Express (☎860-444-4624; www.goblockisland.com) Operates services from New London, CT, to Old Harbor, Block Island, between May and September.

New England Airlines (www.blockislandsairline.com) Flies between Westerly State Airport, on Airport Rd off RI 78, and Block Island State Airport (12 minutes).

Newport Folk Festival MUSIC
(www.newportfolk.org; Fort Adams State Park; check website for current pricing; ⏰late Jul) Big-name stars and up-and-coming groups perform at Fort Adams State Park and other venues around town during one of the top folk festivals in the USA. Not just limited to music, this popular festival has a family-friendly, carnival-like atmosphere and features workshops, exhibitions and pop-up shops.

Newport Jazz Festival MUSIC
(www.newportjazz.org; Fort Adams State Park; tickets adult/child from $65/15; ⏰Aug) This classic festival usually takes place on an August weekend, with concerts at Fort Adams State Park and smaller gigs in venues around town. Popular shows can sell out a year in advance.

Sleeping

Newport International Hostel HOSTEL $
(William Gyles Guesthouse; ☎401-369-0243; www.newporthostel.com; 16 Howard St; dm/d from $29/79; ⏰May-Nov; 📶) Book as early as you can to get into Rhode Island's only hostel, run by an informal and knowledgeable host. The tiny guesthouse contains the fixings for a simple breakfast, plus a laundry machine and clean digs in a dormitory room.

Francis Malbone House B&B $$
(☎401-846-0392; www.malbone.com; 392 Thames St; d/ste from $149/289; P 📶) This grand brick mansion was designed by Peter Harrison and was built in 1760 for a shipping merchant. Now beautifully decorated and immaculately kept with a lush garden, it is one of Newport's finest inns. Some guest rooms have working fireplaces, as do the public

areas. Gourmet breakfast and afternoon tea are included in the tariff.

★ Attwater BOUTIQUE HOTEL $$$

(☎401-846-7444; www.theattwater.com; 22 Liberty St; r $139-659; P ❄ ☎) Newport's newest hotel has the bold attire of a midsummer beach party with turquoise, lime green and coral prints, ikat headboards and snazzily patterned geometric rugs. Picture windows and porches capture the summer light and rooms come furnished with thoughtful luxuries such as iPads, Apple TVs and beach bags.

Eating

★ Anthony's Seafood SEAFOOD $$

(☎401-846-9620; www.anthonysseafood.net; 963 Aquidneck Ave; mains $12-32; ⏲11am-8pm Mon-Sat, from noon Sun) Lauded by locals and featured on TV's *Diners, Drive-ins and Dives*, this wholesale, takeout and dine-in seafood joint tucked away from the main drag in Middletown is always hopping, testament to the quality and freshness of the seafood. It's a great place to try a quahog (also known as 'stuffies' or stuffed clams). Portions are enormous!

Fluke Wine Bar SEAFOOD $$$

(☎401-849-7778; www.flukenewport.com; 41 Bowens Wharf; mains $24-36; ⏲5-11pm May-Oct, 5-10pm Wed-Sat Nov-Apr) Fluke's Scandinavian-inspired dining room, with blond wood and picture windows, offers an accomplished seafood menu featuring roasted monkfish, seasonal striped sea bass and plump scallops. Upstairs, the Harbor View Bar overlooking the docks and the bay, serves beer and rock-and-roll cocktails, and pours from an extensive wine list. Reservations are recommended.

Information

Newport Visitor's Center (☎401-845-9131; www.discovernewport.org; 23 America's Cup Ave; ⏲9am-5pm) Offers maps, brochures, local bus information, tickets to major attractions, public restrooms and an ATM. There's free parking for 30 minutes adjacent to the center.

Getting There & Away

Peter Pan Bus Lines operates buses to Boston (from $22, 1¾ to two hours, four to five daily) from the Newport Visitor Center.

RIPTA bus 60 serves Providence ($2, one hour) almost every hour. For the West Kingston Amtrak station, take bus 64 ($2, one hour, five buses Monday to Friday, three on Saturday). Bus 14 serves TF Green airport ($2, one hour) in Warwick. Most RIPTA buses arrive and depart from the Newport Visitor Center.

East Bay

Rhode Island's jagged East Bay captures the early American story in microcosm, from the graves of early settlers in Little Compton to the farmsteads and merchant homes of whalers and farmers in Warren and Barrington, and the mansions of slave traders in Bristol.

Aside from Barrington's historic and picturesque **Tyler Point Cemetery**, set between the Warren and Barrington Rivers, and Warren's clutch of early stone and clapboard churches (built in the 18th and 19th centuries), the most interesting of the three communities is Bristol. Further south is Sakonnet, the Wampanoag's 'Place of Black Geese,' a rural landscape of pastures and woods centered on the two tiny communities of Tiverton and Little Compton.

The East Bay is proudly protected by its residents and represents a fascinating, largely unpromoted region for the discerning independent traveler interested in American history and New England's natural delights.

★ Colt State Park STATE PARK

(☎401-253-7482; www.riparks.com/Locations/LocationColt.html; Rte 114; ⏲dawn-dusk; P) FREE Bristol's Colt State Park is Rhode Island's most scenic park, with its entire western border fronting Narragansett Bay. The parks is fringed by 4 miles of cycling trails and has more than 400 shaded picnic tables (you read that correctly!) set among 464 acres of groomed fruit trees, flower beds and lush greenery.

CONNECTICUT

Known for its commuter cities, New York's neighbor is synonymous with the affluent lanes and mansions of *The Stepford Wives* and TV's *Gilmore Girls*. In old-moneyed Greenwich, the Litchfield Hills and the Quiet Corner, these representations ring true.

Many regard the state as being a mere stepping stone to the 'real' New England, from whose tourist boom Connecticut has been spared. The upside is that Connecticut retains a more 'authentic' feel. The downside is a slow decaying of former heavyweights like Hartford and New London, where visitors can ponder the price of progress and get enthused about urban renewal. New Haven, home of Yale University, is one such place rewiring itself as a vibrant cultural hub.

Rich in maritime, literary and national history, as well as the farm-to-table food movement, celebrity chefs and enough waterfalls and state parks for the most avid outdoors folk, the Nutmeg State unfolds in incredible layers the longer you stick around.

History

A number of Native American tribes (notably the Pequot and the Mohegan, whose name for the river became the name of the state) were here when the first European explorers, primarily Dutch, appeared in the early 17th century. The first English settlement was at Old Saybrook in 1635, followed a year later by the Connecticut Colony, built by Massachusetts Puritans under Thomas Hooker. A third colony was founded in 1638 in New Haven. After the Pequot War (1637), the Native Americans were no longer able to check Colonial expansion in New England, and Connecticut's English population grew. In 1686 Connecticut was brought into the Dominion of New England.

The American Revolution swept through Connecticut, leaving scars with major battles at Stonington (1775), Danbury (1777), New Haven (1779) and Groton (1781). Connecticut became the fifth state in 1788. It embarked on a period of prosperity, propelled by its whaling, shipbuilding, farming and manufacturing (firearms to bicycles to household tools) industries, which lasted well into the 19th century.

The 20th century brought world wars and the Depression but, thanks in no small part to Connecticut's munitions industries, the state was able to fight back. Everything from planes to submarines were made in the state, and when the defense industry began to decline in the 1990s, the growth of other businesses (such as insurance) helped pick up the slack. Today, two booming casinos are a key source of income for the state – $7 billion since 1997 – so much so that a third casino has been approved by legislators.

Information

Connecticut Office of Tourism (www.ctvisit.com) The official site for tourism in Connecticut.

Connecticut River Valley and Shoreline Travel Information (www.ctrivervalley.com) A privately maintained resource of tourist information relating to the Connecticut River Valley.

CTNow (www.ctnow.com) Regularly updated listings and information on what's hot, where and when.

Edible Nutmeg: Celebrating the Local Food Community of Fairfield, Litchfield, and New Haven Counties (www.ediblenutmeg.com) Quarterly gourmand's guide to the great cuisine of this part of the state.

Lonely Planet (www.lonelyplanet.com/usa/new-england/connecticut) Destination information, hotel reviews and more.

Hartford

Connecticut's capital, one of America's oldest cities, is famed for the 1794 birth of the lucrative insurance industry, conceived when a local landowner sought fire insurance. Policy documents necessitated printing presses, which spurred a boom in publishing that lured the likes of Mark Twain, Harriet Beecher Stowe and Wallace Stevens. In 1855 Samuel Colt made the mass production of the revolver commercially viable. Big business boomed in Hartford.

It's ironic that the industries responsible for the city's wealth (insurance and guns) have contributed to its slow decline: Hartford has a gritty track record for crime. Although things are improving, keep this in mind. Old money has left a truly impressive legacy of fine historic attractions worthy of any New England itinerary. Visit during spring when the darling buds burst to life or in summer when trees are green and skies are blue, and you're likely to be pleasantly surprised.

Sights

★**Wadsworth Atheneum** MUSEUM
(☎860-278-2670; https://thewadsworth.org; 600 Main St; adult/child $15/free; ⏰11am-5pm Wed-Fri, 10am-5pm Sat & Sun) In 2015 the nation's oldest public art museum completed a five-year, $33-million renovation, renewing 32 galleries and 15 public spaces. The Wadsworth houses nearly 50,000 pieces of art in a castlelike Gothic Revival building. On display are paintings by members of the

Hudson River School, including some by Hartford native Frederic Church; 19th-century impressionist works; 18th-century New England furniture; sculptures by Connecticut artist Alexander Calder; and an outstanding array of surrealist, postwar and contemporary works.

★**Mark Twain House & Museum** MUSEUM
(☎860-247-0998; www.marktwainhouse.org; 351 Farmington Ave, parking at 385 Farmington Ave; guided house tours adult/child $20/11, Living History/Ghost tours $25/12, museum only $6; ⏲9:30am-5:30pm, closed Tue Jan & Feb; P) For 17 years, encompassing the most productive period of his life, Samuel Langhorne Clemens (1835–1910) and his family lived in this striking orange-and-black brick Victorian house, which then stood in the pastoral area of the city called Nook Farm. Architect Edward Tuckerman Potter lavishly embellished it with turrets, gables and verandas, and some of the interiors were done by Louis Comfort Tiffany. Admission to the house is by guided tour only; advance ticket purchase is recommended.

Connecticut Science Center MUSEUM
(☎860-520-2160; www.ctsciencecenter.org; 250 Columbus Blvd; adult/child $24/17, movies $7/6; ⏲10am-5pm Tue-Sun; P) Designed by Argentinian architect Cesar Pelli, the Connecticut Science Center is both an exciting architectural space and an absorbing museum for adults and kids alike. Innovative, interactive exhibits and programs abound; there's a dedicated KidsZone on the 1st floor; films, stage shows and special events are on offer; and there's always a fascinating world-class visiting themed exhibition. You could easily spend a whole day here, but it's best to arrive after 2pm when the school groups clear out. Check the website for what's on.

Harriet Beecher Stowe Center MUSEUM
(☎860-522-9258; www.harrietbeecherstowecenter.org/; 77 Forest St; adult/child $16/10; ⏲9:30am-5pm Mon-Sat, noon-5pm Sun; P) Hartford was home to Harriet Beecher Stowe, author of the antislavery book *Uncle Tom's Cabin*. Upon meeting Stowe, Abraham Lincoln reputedly said, 'So this is the little lady who made this big war.' The facility centers on Stowe House, built in 1871 and restored in 2017, which reflects the author's strong ideas about decorating and domestic efficiency, as expressed in her bestseller *American Woman's Home* (nearly as popular as her famous novel).

Sleeping

Sadly it's slim pickings for decent hotels in Hartford's downtown core and prices can be steep for what you get. Better value may be found in chain offerings outside the city center, and you'll find contentment in B&Bs just a short drive away.

★**Goodwin** BOUTIQUE HOTEL $$$
(☎860-246-1881; www.goodwinhartford.com; 1 Haynes St; r from $359) This historic building reopened with a bang in 2017, redone in modern New York chic. The Queen Anne terracotta facade exudes the building's 19th-century origins while the inside oozes 21st-century cool. Convenient to the downtown scene, the Goodwin gives you no reason to leave the premises; it has its own charming bar-restaurant Porrón and Piña, managed by chef Tyler Anderson.

Silas W. Robbins House B&B $$$
(☎860-571-8733; www.silaswrobbins.com; 185 Broad St, Wethersfield; d $195-325; P) About 6 miles south of downtown Hartford in the charming historic village of Wethersfield, you'll find this beautiful and opulent 1873 French Second Empire home. Its common areas and five plush rooms, with their soaring ceilings and light-filled windows overlooking the manicured grounds, have been refurbished in the style of the period.

Eating

★**Trumbull Kitchen** MODERN AMERICAN $$
(www.maxrestaurantgroup.com/trumbull; 150 Trumbull St; mains $13-30; ⏲noon-11pm Mon-Sat, 4-10pm Sun) TK's smart-yet-casual fine-dining atmosphere awaits, with excellent service and a wonderfully executed, diverse menu, making it a great alternative to some of Hartford's upscale joints. Drop in for a cocktail and some fabulous appetizers, or save that appetite for fish, chicken, burgers and steak, freshly prepared and presented like works of art: dressed-up comfort food. The interior is flash, too.

Bear's Smokehouse BARBECUE $$
(☎860-724-3100; www.bearsbbq.com; 89 Arch St; mains $10-20; ⏲11am-9pm) Locals love this wood-smoked Kansas-style barbecue famed for brisket, baby back ribs and pulled pork. Vegetarians might want to head elsewhere,

although there are some kick-ass sides: collard greens, broccoli salad and mac 'n' cheese. Carnivores will dig the Moink balls (a little bit of 'moo' crossed with a little bit of 'oink'): bacon-wrapped meatballs with your choice of sauce.

Information

Greater Hartford Welcome Center (Greater Hartford Arts Council; ☎860-244-0253; www.letsgoarts.org; 100 Pearl St; ⏰9am-5pm Mon-Fri) The bulk of tourist services can be found at this centrally located office.

Getting There & Away

Central **Union Station** (1 Union Pl) is the city's transportation hub. Catch trains, airport shuttles, intercity buses and taxis from here.

Litchfield Hills

The rolling hills in the northwestern corner of Connecticut are sprinkled with lakes and dotted with forests and state parks. Historic Litchfield is the hub of the region, but lesser-known Bethlehem, Kent and Norfolk boast similarly illustrious lineages and are just as photogenic.

An intentional curb on development continues to preserve the area's rural character. Accommodations are limited. Volunteers staff a useful information booth on Litchfield's town green from June to November.

If you have your own car, there's no shortage of postcard-perfect country roads to explore in the Litchfield Hills. One particularly delightful stretch is from Cornwall Bridge taking CT 4 west and then CT 41 north to Salisbury. Gourmands will also find this area surprisingly rich in good food.

Among the plentiful lakes and ponds in the Litchfield Hills, Lake Waramaug, north of New Preston, stands out. Gracious inns dot its shoreline, parts of which are a state park.

Haight-Brown Vineyards WINERY
(☎860-567-4045; www.haightvineyards.com; 29 Chestnut Hill Rd; tastings from $12; ⏰noon-5pm Fri-Sun) The veranda overlooking the state's first wine-producing vineyard (established 1975) sets the mood, while chocolate and cheese pairings make it even more palatable. Chocolate Decadence rail excursions ($79, April to June) with the nearby Railroad Museum of New England up the ante. There are dog biscuits at the entrance if you care to bring a four-legged friend (they even distribute a canine-themed calendar).

★Hopkins Inn INN $$
(☎860-868-7295; www.thehopkinsinn.com; 22 Hopkins Rd, Warren; r $140-150, without bath $130, apt $160-250; P ❄ 🐾) The 19th-century Hopkins Inn boasts a well-regarded restaurant with Austrian-influenced country fare (the second-generation chef whips up a mean schnitzel and mouthwatering pastries) and a variety of lodging options, from simple rooms with shared bathrooms to lake-view apartments. Whatever the season, there's something magical about sitting on the porch gazing upon Lake Waramaug and the hills beyond.

★Community Table MODERN AMERICAN $$$
(Ct; ☎860-868-9354; http://communitytablect.com; 223 Litchfield Turnpike/US 202, Washington; brunch $22-28, mains $26-42; ⏰5-9:30pm Sat, 10am-2pm & 3:30-9pm Sun; P) The name of this Scandinavian-inspired restaurant comes from the 300-year-old black-walnut table, where you can sit down to Sunday brunch. The modern American menu is locally sourced.

Getting There & Around

The Litchfield Hills run north from Danbury and cover the northwest portion of the state, as far as the Massachusetts and New York borders, to the north and west, respectively. Highways US 7 and CT 8 are the main north–south trunk roads. You'll need a car.

Connecticut Coast

The southeastern corner of Connecticut is home to the state's number-one tourist attraction and the country's largest maritime museum, Mystic Seaport. Built on the site of a former shipbuilding yard in 1929, the museum celebrates the area's seafaring heritage, when fishers, whalers and clipper-ship engineers broke world speed records and manufactured gunboats and warships for the Civil War.

To the west of Mystic, you'll find the submarine capital of the USA, Groton, where General Dynamics built WWII subs, and, across the Thames River, New London. To the east is the historic fishing village of Stonington, extending along a narrow mile-long peninsula into the sea. It's one of the most charming seaside villages in New England, where Connecticut's only remaining commercial fleet operates and yachties come ashore in summer to enjoy the restaurants on Water St.

Getting There & Around

Car The area is served well by road, with the I-95 plowing through the middle of New London and around the outskirts of Mystic. I-395 runs northeast to Norwich and beyond.

Ferry Services run from New London to Block Island, Fisher's Island and Long Island.

Train Many Amtrak trains from New York City stop in New London (from $39, three hours) and Mystic (from $41, 3¼ hours). The return run from Boston also stops in Mystic (from $26, 80 minutes), then New London (from $29, 1½ hours).

Mystic

A skyline of masts greets you as you arrive in town on US 1. They belong to the vessels bobbing ever so slightly in the postcard-perfect harbor. There's a sense of self-satisfied calm and composure in the air – until suddenly a heart-stopping steamer whistle blows, followed by the cheerful cling of a drawbridge bell. You know you've arrived in Mystic.

From simple beginnings in the 17th century, the village of Mystic grew to become a prosperous whaling center and one of the great shipbuilding ports of the East Coast. In the mid-19th century, Mystic's shipyards launched clipper ships, gunboats and naval transport vessels, many from the George Greenman & Co Shipyard, now the site of Mystic Seaport Museum, Connecticut's largest tourist attraction. Some great food and drink spots have grown up around the tourism, including the state's hottest bakery.

Sights

★Mystic Seaport Museum MUSEUM

(860-572-0711; www.mysticseaport.org; 75 Greenmanville Ave; adult/child $29/19; 9am-5pm Apr-Oct, 10am-4pm Thu-Sun Nov-Mar; P) More than a museum, this is a re-creation of an entire New England whaling village spread over 17 acres of the former George Greenman & Co Shipyard. To re-create the past, 60 historic buildings, four tall ships and almost 500 smaller vessels are gathered along the Mystic River. Interpreters staff the site and are glad to discuss traditional crafts and trades. Most illuminating are the demonstrations on such topics as ship rescue, oystering and whaleboat launching.

Sleeping

Whaler's Inn INN $$

(860-536-1506; www.whalersinnmystic.com; 20 E Main St; d $159-299; P@) Beside Mystic's historic drawbridge, this hotel combines an 1865 Victorian with a reconstructed adults-only luxury hotel from the same era (the landmark 'Hoxie House' burned down in the 1970s) and a modern motel known as Stonington House. Seasonal packages include dinners and area attractions. Rates include continental breakfast at respected Bravo Bravo next door, a small gym and complimentary bicycles.

★Steamboat Inn INN $$$

(860-536-8300; www.steamboatinnmystic.com; 73 Steamboat Wharf; d $220-350; P) Located in the heart of downtown Mystic, the 11 rooms and suites of this historic inn have wraparound water views and luxurious amenities, (some) hot tubs, cable TV and fireplaces. Some have stunning floor-to-ceiling windows overlooking the river. Antiques lend the interior a romantic, period feel, and service is top-notch with baked goods for breakfast, complimentary bikes and boat docks.

Eating

Sift Bake Shop BAKERY $

(860-245-0541; www.siftbakeshopmystic.com; 5 Water St; desserts $4-7, sandwiches $8-10; 7am-7pm) When pastry chef Adam Young won the Food Network's Best Baker award in 2018, things blew up at this Water St location. Baguettes, ciabattas, chocolate croissants, brioche and specialties such as pumpkin cheesecake are all so good, it may be worth the (long) line. *So* good.

★Oyster Club SEAFOOD $$$

(860-415-9266; www.oysterclubct.com; 13 Water St; oysters $2-2.50, lunch mains $13-20, dinner mains $18-40; noon-3pm & 5-10pm Fri & Sat, 10am-3pm & 5-9pm Sun, 5-9pm Mon-Thu; P) Offering casual fine dining at its best, this is the place locals come to knock down oysters on the deck out back. Grilled lobster and pan-roasted monkfish or flounder feature alongside veal, steak and a drool-worthy burger. If oysters are an aphrodisiac, anything could happen at the bar after the daily happy hour (4pm to 6pm), when shucked oysters are a buck each.

Captain Daniel Packer Inne AMERICAN $$$
(☎860-536-3555; www.danielpacker.com; 32 Water St; mains $19-34; ⏲11am-4pm & 5-10pm) This 1754 historic house has a low-beam ceiling and creaky floorboards. On the lower pub level, you'll find bar denizens, live music, a good selection of tap beer and excellent pub grub: try the fish and chips. Upstairs, the dining room has river views and an imaginative American menu, including petite filet mignon with Gorgonzola sauce and walnut demi-glace. Reservations recommended.

Information

Stop in at the **Greater Mystic Chamber of Commerce** (☎860-572-9578; www.mysticchamber.org; 62 Greenmanville Ave; ⏲9am-6pm Jun-Sep, reduced hours Oct-May) or its kiosk in the train depot, or head to the **Mystic & Shoreline Tourist Information Center** (☎860-536-1641; www.mysticinfocenter.com; 27 Coogan Blvd, Olde Mistick Village; ⏲10am-5pm Mon-Sat, 11am-4pm Sun).

New London

During its golden age in the mid-19th century, New London, then home to some 200 whaling vessels, was one of the largest whaling centers in the USA and one of the wealthiest port cities. In 1858 the discovery of crude oil in Pennsylvania sent the value of whale oil plummeting and began a long period of decline for the city, from which it has never fully recovered. Even so, New London retains strong links with its seafaring past (the US Coast Guard Academy and US Naval Submarine Base are here) and its downtown is listed on the National Register of Historic Places.

Despite lacking the sanitized tourism push of nearby Mystic and Stonington, remnants of New London's glorious and opulent times are still evident throughout the city, making it one of Connecticut's most surprising destinations for those interested in history, architecture and urban sociology. Hip Bank St is a hopeful sign of rejuvenation.

★Captain Scott's Lobster Dock SEAFOOD $$
(☎860-439-1741; www.captscotts.com; 80 Hamilton St; mains $7-21; ⏲11am-9pm May-Oct; 👪) The Coast Guard knows a bit about the sea, and you'd be remiss if you didn't follow its cadets to *the* place for summer seafood. The setting's just picnic tables by the water (BYOB), but you can feast on succulent (hot or cold) lobster rolls, followed by steamers, fried whole-belly clams, scallops or lobsters, and two kinds of chowder.

On the Waterfront SEAFOOD $$
(☎860-444-2800; www.onthewaterfrontnl.com; 250 Pequot Ave; mains $15-28; ⏲noon-9pm Tue-Thu & Sun, to 10pm Fri & Sat; 👪) A spectacular lobster bisque and other delights from the deep, such as pistachio-crusted salmon and Montauk-jumbo-stuffed shrimp, are served up with water views from a multitude of windows. The bar is a popular spot with locals who don't like it rowdy. A diverse menu and friendly staff help to accommodate die-hard landlubbers and those with food intolerances.

Essex

Tree-lined Essex, established in 1635, stands as the chief town of the Connecticut River Valley region. It's worth a visit if only to gawk at the beautiful, well-preserved Federal-period houses, legacies of rum and tobacco fortunes made in the 19th century. The town has a strong following with steam train and riverboat enthusiasts, and also has lovely St John's church, a picturesque riverside park, and a handful of galleries and antique dealers.

★Essex Steam Train & Riverboat Ride TOURS
(☎860-767-0103; www.essexsteamtrain.com; 1 Railroad Ave; adult/child $20/10, incl cruise $30/20; ⏲daily May-Oct, seasonal events year-round; 👪) This wildly popular attraction features a steam locomotive and antique carriages. The journey travels 6 scenic miles to Deep River, where you can cruise to the **Goodspeed Opera House** (☎860-873-8668; www.goodspeed.org; 6 Main St; tickets $29-85, tours adult/child $5/1; ⏲performances Wed-Sun Apr-Dec) in East Haddam, before returning to Essex via train. The round-trip train ride takes about an hour; with the riverboat ride it's 2½ hours. This train also connects with Connecticut Audubon for special bird-watching trips in the fall.

Griswold Inn INN $$
(☎860-767-1776; www.griswoldinn.com; 36 Main St; d/ste from $195/240; P 📶) The 'Gris' is one of the country's oldest continually operating inns, Essex' physical and social centerpiece since 1776. The buffet-style Hunt Breakfast (11am to 1pm Sunday) is a tradition dating

from the War of 1812, when British soldiers occupying Essex demanded to be fed. Two main buildings were refurbished and connected in 2017, eliminating walks between in inclement weather.

At other times, the expansive dining room remains a favorite place to enjoy traditional New England cuisine in a historic setting. In kinder weather, the new 2200-sq-ft bluestone patio is a nice place to wine and unwind. The historic taproom has free popcorn and live music.

New Haven

Connecticut's second-largest city radiates out from pretty New Haven Green, laid by Puritan settlers in the 1600s. Around it, Yale University's over-300-year-old accessible campus offers visitors a wealth of world-class attractions, from museums and galleries to a lively concert program and walking-tour tales of secret societies.

As you admire Yale's gorgeous faux-Gothic and Victorian architecture, it's hard to fathom New Haven's struggle to shake its reputation as a dangerous, decaying seaport – but the city is successfully repositioning itself as a thriving home for the arts, architecture and the human mind.

While Yale may have put New Haven on the map, there's much to savor beyond campus. Well-aged dive bars, ethnic restaurants, barbecue shacks and cocktail lounges make the area almost as lively as Cambridge's Harvard Sq, but with better pizza and less ego.

Sights

★Yale University UNIVERSITY
(203-432-2300; www.yale.edu/visitor; 149 Elm St) FREE Each year, thousands of high-school students make pilgrimages to Yale, nursing dreams of attending the country's third-oldest university, which boasts such notable alums as Noah Webster, Naomi Wolf and Hillary Clinton, and presidents William H Taft and George W Bush. You don't need to share the students' ambitions in order to take a stroll around the campus – just pick up a map at the visitor center or join a free, one-hour guided tour.

★Yale Center for British Art MUSEUM
(203-432-2800; www.ycba.yale.edu; 1080 Chapel St; 10am-5pm Tue-Sat, noon-5pm Sun) FREE Reopened in 2016 after extensive restoration, this fabulous gallery was architect Louis Kahn's last commission and is the setting for the largest collection of British art outside the UK. Spanning three centuries from the Elizabethan era to the 19th century, and arranged thematically as well as chronologically, the collection gives an unparalleled insight into British art, life and culture. A visit is an absolute must for anyone interested in beautiful things. And yes, it's free.

Yale University Art Gallery MUSEUM
(203-432-0600; http://artgallery.yale.edu; 1111 Chapel St; 10am-5pm Tue, Wed & Fri, to 8pm Thu, 11am-5pm Sat & Sun) FREE This outstanding museum was architect Louis Kahn's first commission and houses the oldest university art collection in the country; it includes Vincent van Gogh's *The Night Café* and European masterpieces by Frans Hals, Peter Paul Rubens, Manet and Picasso. In addition there are displays of American masterworks by Winslow Homer, Edward Hopper and Jackson Pollock, silver from the 18th century, and art from Africa, Asia, and the pre- and post-Columbian Americas.

Shore Line Trolley Museum MUSEUM
(203-467-6927; www.shorelinetrolley.org; 17 River St, East Haven; adult/child $10/7; 10:30am-4:30pm daily Jul & Aug, Sat & Sun May, Jun, Sep & Oct;) For a unique take on East Haven's shoreline, take a ride on this open-sided antique trolley – the oldest continuously running suburban trolley line in the country – along 3 miles of track that takes you from River St in East Haven to Short Beach in Branford. Enjoy the museum and its beautifully maintained carriages when you're done. Bring a picnic lunch.

WORTH A TRIP

HAMMONASSET BEACH

Though not off the beaten path by any means, the two full miles of flat, sandy beach at **Hammonasset Beach State Park** (203-245-2785; www.ct.gov; 1288 Boston Post Rd, Madison; weekdays/weekends $15/22; 8am-sunset; P), 3 miles southwest of Essex, handily accommodate summer crowds. This is the ideal beach (the state's largest) at which to set up an umbrella chair, crack open a book and forget about the world. The surf is tame, making swimming superb. Restrooms and showering facilities are clean and ample, and a wooden boardwalk runs the length of the park.

Sleeping

★New Haven Hotel BOUTIQUE HOTEL $$

(☎800-644-6835; www.newhavenhotel.com; 229 George St; d from $169) This robust downtown hotel is both simply stylish and affordable. It's nice to see a private operator raising the bar. The hotel occupies a handsome mid-20th-century brick building with bright, modern common areas, while guest rooms are airy with large windows, clean lines, dark woods and sink-into-me bedding. Reasonable rates mean it's understandably popular. Book in advance.

Study at Yale HOTEL $$$

(☎203-503-3900; www.thestudyatyale.com; 1157 Chapel St; r $250-389; P ☎) The Study at Yale manages to evoke a mid-century modern sense of sophistication (call it '*Mad Men* chic') without being over the top or intimidating. There's also an in-house restaurant and cafe, to which you can stumble for snacks.

Eating

★Pantry AMERICAN $

(☎203-787-0392; 2 Mechanic St; breakfast $11-24; ⏲7am-2pm Mon-Sat, 8am-3pm Sun) The secret is already out about New Haven's ah-mazing little breakfast-lunch joint. You'll most likely have to line up then rub shoulders with a bunch of hungry students (who'd probably rather we kept this one to ourselves), but persevere if you can: you won't find a better-value, more drool-worthy breakfast for miles. Take your pick: it's *all* good.

Atticus Bookstore Café CAFE $

(☎203-776-4040; www.atticusbookstorecafe.com; 1082 Chapel St; salads & sandwiches $6-12; ⏲7am-9pm Tue-Sat, 8am-8pm Sun-Mon) On the fringe of the Yale campus, come here to get your bearings and mingle with the alumni over great coffee, artisanal sandwiches, stellar breads, soup and salad, surrounded by an immaculately presented selection of books.

Frank Pepe PIZZA $

(☎203-865-5762; www.pepespizzeria.com; 157 Wooster St; pizzas $8-29; ⏲11am-10pm; ✍👪) Pepe's lays claim to baking the 'best pizza in America,' a title it's won three times running. We'll let you be the judge, but can confirm this joint cranks out tasty pies fired in a coal oven, just as it has since 1925; only now it has locations across Connecticut (and New York), making consistency harder to master. Cash only.

★ZINC AMERICAN $$$

(☎203-624-0507; www.zincfood.com; 964 Chapel St; mains $12-28; ⏲noon-2:30pm & 5-9pm Tue-Fri, 5-10pm Sat & Mon) Whenever possible, this trendy bistro's ingredients hail from local organic sources, but the chef draws inspiration from all over, notably Asia and the Southwest. There's a constantly changing 'market menu,' but for the most rewarding experience, share several small plates, such as smoked duck nachos or *prosciutto Americano crostini.* Reservations are advised.

Drinking & Nightlife

★Ordinary COCKTAIL BAR

(☎203-907-0238; www.ordinarynewhaven.com; 990 Chapel St; ⏲4pm-midnight Mon-Thu, to 1am Fri & Sat) Ordinary is anything but. It's tall, dark and handsome, ineffably stylish and a treat for the senses. Its patrons often also fall into at least one of these categories. They come for cheese boards, charcuterie and cocktails. Put on your fancy pants and join them.

116 Crown BAR

(☎203-777-3116; www.116crown.com; 116 Crown St; ⏲5pm-1am Tue-Sun) Upscale contemporary design, DJ sets, expertly mixed cocktails and an international wine list draw the style crowd to this Ninth Sq bar. Small plates and a raw bar keep you from toppling off your stool, but style this chic doesn't come cheap.

Toad's Place LIVE MUSIC

(☎203-624-8623; www.toadsplace.com; 300 York St) Toad's is arguably New England's premier music hall, having earned its rep hosting the likes of the Rolling Stones, U2 and Bob Dylan. These days, an eclectic range of performers works the intimate stage, including They Might Be Giants and Martin & Wood.

Information

INFO New Haven (☎203-773-9494; www.infonewhaven.com; 1000 Chapel St; ⏲10am-9pm Mon-Sat, noon-5pm Sun) This downtown bureau offers maps and helpful advice.

New Haven Magazine (www.newhavenmagazine.com) Keeps its finger on the urban pulse.

Yale University Visitor Center (☎203-432-2300; http://visitorcenter.yale.edu; 149 Elm St; ⏲9am-4:30pm Mon-Fri, 11am-4pm Sat & Sun) Take a free tour or pick up a map of campus here.

Getting There & Away

BUS

Peter Pan Bus Lines (www.peterpanbus.com) connects New Haven with New York City (from $12, two hours, eight daily), Hartford (from $12, one hour, six daily) and Boston (from $11, four to five hours, seven daily), as does Greyhound (www.greyhound.com). Buses depart from inside New Haven's Union Station.

Connecticut Limousine (www.ctlimo.com) is an airport shuttle servicing Hartford's Bradley airport, New York's JFK and LaGuardia airports, and New Jersey's Newark airport. Pick-up and drop-off are at Union Station and select downtown New Haven hotels. Services to Newark attract a higher rate.

TRAIN

Metro-North (www.mta.info/mnr) trains make the run between **Union Station** (50 Union Ave) and New York City's Grand Central Terminal (peak/off-peak $23.25/17.50, two hours) almost every hour from 7am to midnight.

Shore Line East (www.shorelineeast.com) runs regional trains up the shore of Long Island Sound to Old Saybrook (45 minutes) and New London (70 minutes), and Commuter Connection buses that shuttle passengers from Union Station (in the evenings) and from State St Station (in the mornings) to New Haven Green.

Amtrak trains run express from New York City's Penn Station to New Haven (from $32, 1¾ hours).

VERMONT

Whether seen under blankets of snow, patchworks of blazing fall leaves or the exuberant greens of spring and summer, Vermont's blend of bucolic farmland, mountains and picturesque small villages make it one of America's most appealing states. Hikers, bikers, skiers and kayakers will find four-season bliss on the expansive waters of Lake Champlain, the award-winning Kingdom Trails Network, the 300-mile Long and Catamount Trails, and the fabled slopes of Killington, Stowe and Mad River Glen.

Foodies will love it: small farmers have made Vermont a locavore paradise, complemented by America's densest collection of craft brewers. But most of all, what sets Vermont apart is its independent spirit: the only state with a socialist senator and the only one without a McDonald's in its capital city, Vermont remains a haven for quirky creativity, a champion of grassroots government and a bastion of 'small is beautiful' thinking, unlike anywhere else in America.

History

Frenchman Samuel de Champlain explored Vermont in 1609, becoming the first European to visit these lands long inhabited by the native Abenaki.

Vermont played a key role in the American Revolution in 1775 when Ethan Allen led a local militia, the Green Mountain Boys, to Fort Ticonderoga, capturing it from the British. In 1777 Vermont declared independence as the Vermont Republic, adopting the first New World constitution to abolish slavery and establish a public school system. In 1791 Vermont was admitted to the USA as the 14th state.

The state's independent streak is as long and deep as a vein of Vermont marble. Long a land of dairy farmers, Vermont is still largely agricultural and has the lowest population of any New England state.

Information

Vermont Chamber of Commerce (www.visitvt.com) Distributes a wealth of information about the state.

Vermont Division of Tourism (www.vermontvacation.com) Maintains a fabulous Welcome Center on I-91 near the Massachusetts state line, one on VT 4A near the New York state line, and three others along I-89 between White River Junction and the Canadian border. Produces a free, detailed road map and camping guide.

Vermont Public Radio (www.vpr.net) Vermont's statewide public radio station features superb local programming, including *Vermont Edition* (weekdays at noon) for coverage of Vermont current events, and the quirky, information-packed *Eye on the Sky* weather forecast.

Vermont Ski Areas Association (www.skivermont.com) Helpful information for planning ski trips, as well as summer adventures at Vermont ski resorts.

Southern Vermont

White churches and inns surround village greens throughout historic southern Vermont, a region that's home to several towns that predate the American Revolution. In summer the roads between the three 'cities' of Brattleboro, Bennington and Manchester roll over green hills; in winter, they wind their way toward the ski slopes of Mt Snow, southern Vermont's cold-weather playground. For hikers, the Appalachian and Long Trails pass through the Green Mountain National Forest here, offering a colorful hiking experience during the fall foliage season.

Brattleboro

Perched at the confluence of the Connecticut and West Rivers, Brattleboro is a little gem that reveals its facets to those who stroll the streets and prowl its dozens of independent shops and eateries. An energetic mix of aging hippies and the latest crop of pierced and tattooed hipsters fuels the town's sophisticated eclecticism, keeping the downtown scene percolating and skewing its politics decidedly leftward.

Whetstone Brook runs through the south end of town, where a wooden stockade dubbed Fort Dummer was built in 1724, becoming the first European settlement in Vermont (theretofore largely a wilderness populated exclusively by the native Abenaki people).

At Brattleboro's old Town Hall, celebrated thinkers and entertainers, including Oliver Wendell Holmes, Horace Greeley and Mark Twain, held forth on civic and political matters. Rudyard Kipling married a Brattleboro woman in 1892, and while living here he wrote *The Jungle Book*.

While most of Brattleboro's action is found in the downtown commercial district, the surrounding hillsides are speckled with farms, cheese makers and artisans, all awaiting discovery on a pleasant back-road ramble.

Sleeping & Eating

Latchis Hotel HOTEL $$
(802-254-6300; www.latchishotel.com; 50 Main St; r $100-210, ste $190-240;) You can't beat the location of these 30 reasonably priced rooms and suites, in the center of downtown and adjacent to the historic theater of the same name. The hotel's art-deco overtones are refreshing, and wonderfully surprising for New England.

★**Inn on Putney Road** B&B $$$
(802-536-4780; www.vermontbandbinn.com; 192 Putney Rd; r $169-309; @) Designed to resemble a miniature château, this sweet 1930s-vintage B&B north of town has a glorious landscaped yard, five cozy, beautifully appointed rooms and one luxurious suite with fireplace. Overlooking the West River estuary, it offers opportunities for walking, biking and boating right on its doorstep, and plenty of rainy-day activities, including billiards, board games, DVDs and a guest library.

Whetstone Station PUB FOOD $$
(802-490-2354; www.whetstonestation.com; 36 Bridge St; beer garden mains $4-13, restaurant mains $12-22; 11:30am-10pm Sun-Wed, to 11pm Thu-Sat) This place is beloved for its dozen-plus craft brews on tap and excellent pub fare, but the real showstopper is its outstanding roof deck Bier Garten, with bird's-eye views of the Connecticut River and occasional live music. It's the ideal spot for a beer and a bite at sundown.

★**TJ Buckley's** AMERICAN $$$
(802-257-4922; www.tjbuckleysuptowndining.com; 132 Elliot St; mains incl salad $45; 5:30-9pm Thu-Sun year-round, plus Wed mid-Jun–early Oct) Chef-owner Michael Fuller founded this exceptional, upscale little eatery in an authentic 1925 Worcester dining car more than 30 years ago. Ever since, he's been offering a verbal menu of four seasonally changing items, sourced largely from local farms. Locals rave that the food here is Brattleboro's best. The diner seats just 18 souls, so reserve ahead. No credit cards.

Information

Brattleboro Chamber of Commerce (802-254-4565; www.brattleborochamber.org; 180 Main St; 9am-5pm Mon-Fri) Dependable year-round source of tourist info, with a seasonal **info booth** (80 Putney Rd; Sat & Sun late May–mid-Oct) on the green north of downtown.

Getting There & Away

Greyhound (www.greyhound.com) runs one bus daily to New York City (from $32, 5¾ hours) via Northampton, MA ($12, one hour) and Hartford, CT ($21, three hours). For the best fares, buy tickets in advance on Greyhound's website.

Amtrak's scenic daily *Vermonter* train (www.amtrak.com/vermonter-train) connects Brattleboro with points north and south, including Montpelier ($30, 2¾ hours), Burlington/Essex Junction ($34, 3½ hours), New York City ($67, 5½ hours) and Washington, DC ($99, nine hours). See Amtrak's website for details.

Bennington

Bennington is a mix of historic Vermont village (Old Bennington), workaday town (Bennington proper) and college town (North Bennington). It is also home to the

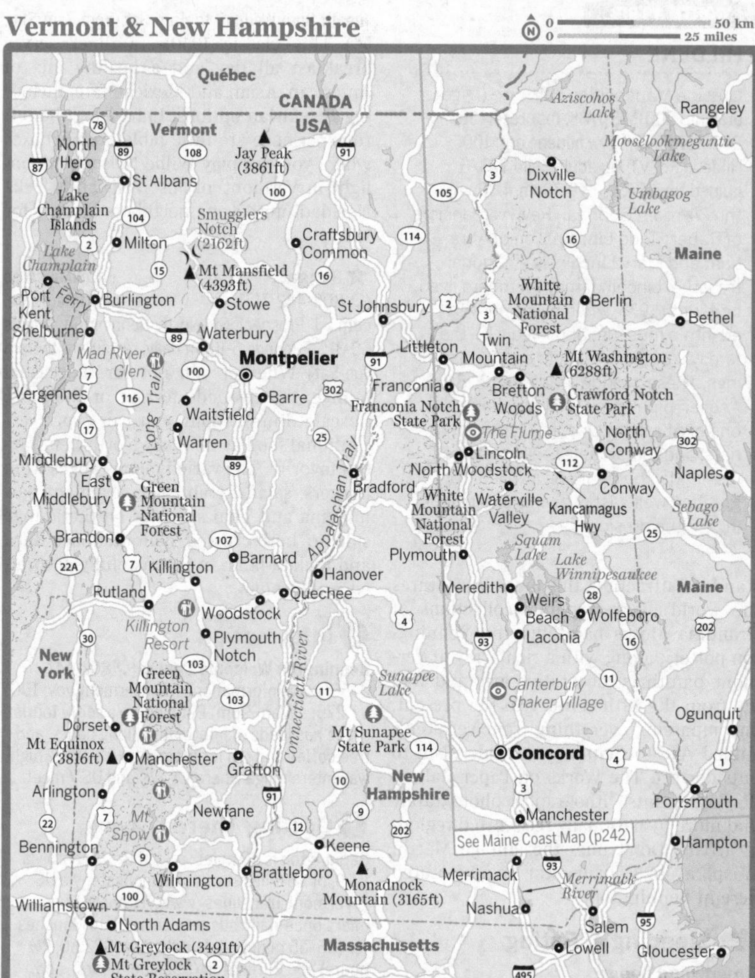

Bennington Battle Monument (☎802-447-0550; www.benningtonbattlemonument.com; 15 Monument Circle, Old Bennington; adult/child $5/1; ⏲9am-5pm late Apr-Oct), which commemorates the crucial Battle of Bennington during the American Revolution. Had Colonel Seth Warner and the local 'Green Mountain Boys' not helped weaken British defenses during this battle, the colonies might well have been split.

The charming hilltop site of Colonial Old Bennington is studded with 80 Georgian and Federal houses (dating from 1761 – the year Bennington was founded – to 1830). The poet Robert Frost is buried here and a museum in his old homestead pays eloquent tribute.

As Bennington is within the bounds of the Green Mountain National Forest, there are many hiking trails nearby, including the grandparents of them all: the Appalachian and Long Trails.

⊙ Sights

Bennington Museum MUSEUM
(☎802-447-1571; www.benningtonmuseum.org; 75 Main St; adult/child $10/free; ⏲10am-5pm daily Jun-Oct, Thu-Tue Nov-May) Bennington's

WORTH A TRIP

HILDENE

Outside Manchester, **Hildene** (☎general info 800-578-1788, tour reservations 802-367-7968; www.hildene.org; 1005 Hildene Rd/VT 7A; adult/child $23/6, guided tour $7.50; ⏰9:30am-4:30pm), the 24-room Georgian Revival mansion of Robert Todd Lincoln, son of Abraham and Mary Lincoln, is a national treasure. Lincoln family members lived here until 1975, when it was converted into a museum and filled with the family's personal effects and furnishings. These include a vintage 1908 Aeolian pipe organ (still functioning), one of Abraham Lincoln's famous top hats, and remarkable brass casts of his hands, the right one swollen from greeting well-wishers while campaigning for the presidency.

standout attraction, this museum features the world's largest public collections of Grandma Moses paintings and Bennington pottery, along with a rich array of Vermont paintings, decorative arts and folk art from the 18th century to the present, encompassing everything from Vermont's Gilded Age to Bennington modernism to outsider art. The Works on Paper Gallery displays prints, lithographs, photography and more by nationally recognized regional artists. Don't miss the vintage Martin Wasp, a 1925 luxury car manufactured here in Bennington.

Sleeping & Eating

Greenwood Lodge & Campsites HOSTEL, CAMPGROUND $
(☎802-442-2547; www.campvermont.com/greenwood; 311 Greenwood Dr, Woodford; 2-person tent/RV sites $30/39, dm $35-38, r $79; ⏰mid-May–late Oct;) Nestled in the Green Mountains in Woodford, this 120-acre space with three ponds is home to one of Vermont's best-sited hostels. Accommodations include 17 budget beds and 40 campsites. You'll find it 8 miles east of Bennington, just off VT 9 near the Prospect Mountain ski area. Facilities include hot showers and a games room.

Blue Benn Diner DINER $
(☎802-442-5140; 314 North St; mains breakfast $4-10, lunch & dinner $6-11; ⏰6am-5pm Mon & Tue, to 8pm Wed-Fri, to 4pm Sat, from 7am Sun;) This classic 1950s-era diner serves breakfast all day and a healthy mix of American, Asian and Mexican fare, including vegetarian options. Enhancing the retro experience are little tabletop jukeboxes where you can play Willie Nelson's 'Moonlight in Vermont' or José Feliciano's 'Feliz Navidad' until your neighbors scream for mercy.

★**Pangaea** INTERNATIONAL $$
(☎802-442-7171; www.vermontfinedining.com; 1 Prospect St, North Bennington; mains $9-31; ⏰lounge 5-10pm daily, restaurant to 9pm Tue-Sat) Whether you opt for the casual lounge, the riverside terrace or the more upscale dining room, you can expect exceptional food at this cozy North Bennington favorite. The varied menu ranges from burgers, salads, crab cakes, eggplant parmigiana and Thai stir-fries on the lounge side to herb-crusted halibut, roast duck and rack of lamb in the tastefully decorated restaurant.

Information

Bennington Welcome Center (☎802-447-2456; www.informationcenter.vermont.gov; 100 VT 279; ⏰7am-9pm) Bennington's spiffy tourist office has loads of information, long hours, and free coffee and tea for motorists; it's at the highway interchange where VT 279 and US 7 meet.

Getting There & Away

Bennington is 40 miles west of Brattleboro via VT 9, or 25 miles south of Manchester via US 7. Vermont Translines (www.vttranslines.com) offers once-daily bus service north to Manchester ($6, 35 minutes), Middlebury ($22.50, 2½ hours) and Burlington ($32, four hours), and west to Albany, NY ($10, one hour).

Central Vermont

Vermont's heart features some of New England's most bucolic countryside. Cows begin to outnumber people just north of Rutland (Vermont's second-largest city, with a whopping 15,500 residents). Lovers of the outdoors make frequent pilgrimages to central Vermont, especially to the resort areas of Killington, Sugarbush and Mad River Glen, which attract countless skiers and summer hikers. For those interested in indoor pleasures, antique shops and art galleries dot the back roads.

Woodstock & Quechee

Chartered in 1761, Woodstock has been the highly dignified seat of scenic Windsor County since 1766. Many grand houses surround the oval village green, and four of Woodstock's churches can claim bells cast by Paul Revere. Senator Jacob Collamer, a friend of Abraham Lincoln's, once observed, 'The good people of Woodstock have less incentive than others to yearn for heaven.'

Today Woodstock is still very beautiful and very wealthy. Spend some time walking around the green, surrounded by Federal and Greek Revival homes and public buildings, or along the Ottauquechee River, spanned by three covered bridges. The Rockefellers and the Rothschilds own estates in the surrounding countryside, and the well-to-do come to stay at the grand Woodstock Inn & Resort.

About a five-minute drive east of Woodstock, small, twee Quechee Village is home to Quechee Gorge – Vermont's diminutive answer to the Grand Canyon – as well as some outstanding restaurants.

Sights

★Quechee Gorge CANYON

(US 4, Quechee) FREE Lurking beneath US 4, less than a mile east of Quechee Village, the gorge is a 163ft-deep scar that cuts about 3000ft along a stream that you can view from a bridge or easily access by footpaths from the road. A series of well-marked, undemanding trails, none of which should take more than an hour to cover, lead down into the gorge.

Billings Farm & Museum FARM

(☎802-457-2355; www.billingsfarm.org; 69 Old River Rd, Woodstock; adult/child $16/8; ⏰10am-5pm daily Apr-Oct, to 4pm Sat, Sun & holidays Nov-Feb; 👪) A mile north of Woodstock's village green, this historic farm founded by 19th-century railroad-magnate Frederick Billings delights children with hands-on activities related to old-fashioned farm life. Farm animals, including pretty cows descended from Britain's island of Jersey, are abundant. Family-friendly seasonal events include wagon and sleigh rides, pumpkin and apple festivals, and old-fashioned Halloween, Thanksgiving and Christmas celebrations.

Marsh-Billings-Rockefeller National Historical Park PARK

(☎802-457-3368; www.nps.gov/mabi; 54 Elm St, Woodstock; mansion tours adult/child $8/free, trails & carriage roads free; ⏰visitor center & tours 10am-5pm late May-Oct, trails & carriage roads year-round) Built around the historic home of early American conservationist George Perkins Marsh, Vermont's only national park examines the relationship between land stewardship and environmental conservation. The estate's 20 miles of trails and carriage roads are free for exploring on foot, horseback, cross-country skis or snowshoes. There's an admission fee to the mansion itself, where tours are offered every 30 minutes.

Sleeping & Eating

Shire HOTEL $$

(☎802-457-2211; www.shirewoodstock.com; 46 Pleasant St/US 4, Woodstock; r $119-259; ❄📶🐾) Within walking distance of Woodstock's town center on US 4, this recently expanded hotel has 50 comfortable rooms, the best of which come with fireplaces, Jacuzzis and/or decks with rockers looking out over the Ottauquechee River. New beds and linens offer a comfy night's sleep, and most units have river views (the ones from room 405 are especially dreamy).

★Blue Horse Inn INN $$$

(☎802-457-9999; www.thebluehorseinn.com; 3 Church St, Woodstock; d $179-359, ste $299-389; 📶🏊) In 2018, Jill and Tony Amato completely renovated and reopened this grand Federal Greek Revival inn in the heart of Woodstock. Set on 2 acres of grassy lawns sloping down to riverside Adirondack chairs, the red-brick and white-clapboard 19th-century home conceals a sprawling collection of fireplace-equipped common areas and carpeted guest rooms gazing out over the yard or downtown Woodstock.

Mon Vert Cafe CAFE $

(☎802-457-7143; www.monvertcafe.com; 28 Central St, Woodstock; breakfast $7-13, lunch $9-11; ⏰7:30am-5:30pm Mon-Thu, to 6:30pm Fri & Sat, 8am-5:30pm Sun) Pop into this cheerful two-level cafe for croissants, scones, egg sandwiches and maple lattes in the morning, or settle in on the front patio for salads and panini at lunchtime. A large map of Vermont and New Hampshire highlights the multitude of farms and food purveyors

BEST VERMONT SKIING

Mad River Glen (802-496-3551; www.madriverglen.com; VT 17, Waitsfield; lift tickets adult/child $89/72) The most rugged lift-served ski area in the East, Mad River is also one of the quirkiest. Managed by an owner cooperative, not a major ski corporation, it largely eschews artificial snowmaking, prohibits snowboarding and proudly continues to use America's last operating single chairlift, a vintage 1948 model. It's 6 miles west of Waitsfield.

Killington Resort (info 800-734-9435, reservations 800-621-6867; www.killington.com; 4763 Killington Rd; lift tickets adult/child/senior $124/95/105) Known as the 'Beast of the East,' Vermont's prime ski resort is enormous, yet runs efficiently enough to avoid overcrowding. It has five separate lodges, each with a different emphasis, as well as 29 lifts and 92 miles of trails. The ski season runs from November through early May, enhanced by America's largest snowmaking system.

Stowe Mountain Resort (802-253-3000; www.stowe.com; 5781 Mountain Rd; lift ticket adult $85-115, child $72-98) Purchased by Colorado's Vail Resorts in 2017, this venerable resort encompasses two mountains: Mt Mansfield (which has a vertical drop of 2360ft) and Spruce Peak (1550ft). It offers 116 beautiful trails, two-thirds for beginners and intermediates, and the remainder for hard-core backcountry skiers – many of whom get their adrenaline rushes from the 'front four' runs: Starr, Goat, National and Liftline.

that provide the restaurant's locally sourced ingredients.

★ Simon Pearce Restaurant MODERN AMERICAN $$$
(802-295-1470; www.simonpearce.com; 1760 Quechee Main St, Quechee; mains lunch $14-19, dinner $23-33; 11:30am-2:45pm & 5:30-9pm) Few views in Vermont compare with those from the window tables overlooking spectacular Ottauquechee Falls in Simon Pearce's dining room, suspended over the river in a converted brick mill. Local ingredients are used to fine effect in salads, cheese plates and dishes such as braised lamb shoulder or cider-brined chicken. The restaurant's stemware is hand-blown in the adjacent glass workshop.

Mangalitsa BISTRO $$$
(802-457-7467; www.mangalitsavt.com; 61 Central St; mains $26-32; 5-9pm) Launched in 2017 to universal acclaim, this sweet, chef-owned bistro was a welcome addition to Woodstock's dining scene. The ever-changing menu of small and large plates draws on seasonal ingredients such as fiddlehead ferns, house-butchered meats, whole fish and produce from local purveyors such as Fat Sheep Farm. With only 22 seats it fills up fast; book ahead.

Information

Woodstock Welcome Center (802-457-3555; www.woodstockvt.com; 3 Mechanic St, Woodstock; 9am-5pm) Woodstock's welcome center is housed in a lovely red building on a riverside backstreet, two blocks from the village green. There's also a small information booth on the village green itself. Both places can help with accommodations.

Getting There & Away

Greyhound buses (www.greyhound.com) from Boston and Amtrak trains (www.amtrak.com/vermonter-train) from New York stop at nearby White River Junction. From either station, it's a 15-mile trip to Woodstock. Vermont Translines (www.vttranslines.com) runs once-daily buses from Woodstock to Quechee ($1.50, 15 minutes), White River Junction ($3.50, 30 minutes) and Killington ($5, 40 minutes).

Mad River Valley

North of Killington, VT 100 is one of the finest stretches of road in the country: a bucolic mix of rolling hills, covered bridges, white steeples and fertile farmland. Here you'll find the Mad River Valley, where the pretty villages of Waitsfield and Warren nestle in the shadow of two major ski areas, Sugarbush and Mad River Glen.

For tantalizing valley perspectives, explore the glorious back roads on either side of VT 100. Leave the pavement behind and meander up the valley's eastern side, following Brook, E Warren, Common, North and Pony Farm Rds from Warren north to Moretown; or head west from Warren over Lincoln Gap Rd, the highest, steepest and perhaps prettiest of all the 'gap roads' that run east to west over the Green Mountains. Stop at Lincoln Gap (2424ft) for the scenic 3-mile hike up the **Long Trail** to Mt Abraham (4017ft), Vermont's fifth-highest peak.

Sleeping

★Tevere Hostel HOSTEL $
(802-496-9222; www.hosteltevere.com; 203 Powderhound Rd, Warren; dm $35-40;) One of New England's coolest hostels, Tevere spreads across two floors of an artfully renovated old farmhouse in Warren, just downhill from Sugarbush resort. Four-to seven-bed dorms with comfy mattresses and colorful walls are complemented by a lounge with a blazing woodstove and an animated bar-restaurant that hosts live music on Saturdays throughout the ski season.

Inn at Round Barn Farm INN $$$
(802-496-2276; www.theroundbarn.com; 1661 E Warren Rd, Waitsfield; r $179-359;) This place gets its name from the adjacent 1910 round barn – among the few authentic examples remaining in Vermont. The decidedly upscale inn has antique-furnished rooms with mountain views, gas fireplaces and canopy beds. All overlook the meadows and mountains. In winter guests leave their shoes at the door to preserve the hardwood floors. The country-style breakfast is huge.

Eating & Drinking

★Warren Store SANDWICHES $
(802-496-3864; www.warrenstore.com; 284 Main St, Warren; sandwiches & light meals $5-9; 7:45am-7pm) This atmospheric country store serves the area's best sandwiches along with delicious pastries and breakfasts. In summer, linger over coffee and the *New York Times* on the front porch, or eat on the deck overlooking the waterfall, then descend for a cool dip among river-sculpted rocks. Browsers will love the store's eclectic upstairs collection of clothing, toys and jewelry.

American Flatbread PIZZA $$
(802-496-8856; www.americanflatbread.com/restaurants/waitsfield-vt; 46 Lareau Rd, Waitsfield; flatbread $14-22; 5-9:30pm Thu-Sun;) For two decades, this valley mainstay on pretty Lareau Farm has been baking delicious thin-crust pizza in the wood-fired oven, topped with fresh-from-the-farm meats, cheeses and veggies and homemade tomato sauce. Stay cozy by the fireside in winter, or play Frisbee on the lawn against a gorgeous Green Mountain backdrop while waiting to eat alfresco on picnic tables in summer.

★Lawson's Finest Liquids MICROBREWERY
(802-496-4677; www.lawsonsfinest.com; 155 Carroll Rd, Waitsfield; noon-7pm) For years, Mad River locals would line up for special releases of Sean and Karen Lawson's homebrew, dispensed from a converted maple-sugar shack at their home in Warren. In late 2018, the Lawsons opened this cavernous timber-framed brewery, taproom and store in Waitsfield, with 16 beers on tap, a convivial bar and fireside seating indoors and out. Beer lovers, rejoice!

Information

Mad River Valley Visitor Information (802-496-3409; www.madrivervalley.com; cnr Main & Bridge Sts, Waitsfield; 10am-5pm Wed-Sat, to 3pm Sun) The valley's info center in downtown Waitsfield can assist with lodging and the latest skiing info.

Northern Vermont

Northern Vermont is home to the state's largest city, Burlington, and the state capital, Montpelier. Even so, this area still has all the rural charms found elsewhere in the Green Mountain State. Even within Burlington, cafe-lined streets coexist with scenic paths along Lake Champlain and the Winooski River. Further north, the pastoral Northeast Kingdom offers a full range of outdoor activities, from skiing to biking, in the heart of the mountains.

Montpelier

Montpelier (mont-*peel*-yer) would qualify as nothing more than a large village in most places. But in sparsely populated Vermont it's the state capital – the smallest in the country (and the only one without a McDonald's, in case you were wondering). Remarkably cosmopolitan for a town of 7500 residents, its two main thoroughfares – State St and Main St – make for a pleasant wander, with some nice bookstores, boutiques and eateries.

Montpelier's smaller, distinctly working-class neighbor Barre (*bear*-ee), which touts itself as the 'granite capital of the world,' is a 15-minute drive southeast of the capital.

Information

Capitol Region Visitors Center (802-828-5981; www.informationcenter.vermont.gov; 134 State St; 6am-5pm Mon-Fri, from 9am Sat & Sun) Opposite the Vermont state capitol building. Free wi-fi and comfy seating.

Getting There & Away

On weekdays, you can reach Burlington via the Montpelier LINK Express bus ($4, 1¼ hours) operated by Green Mountain Transit (www.ridegmt.com).

The daily *Vermonter* train (www.amtrak.com/vermonter-train) runs from Montpelier to points northwest and southeast, including Brattleboro ($30, 2½ hours) and Burlington ($12, 45 minutes).

Stowe

In a cozy valley where the West Branch River flows into Little River and mountains rise in all directions, the quintessential Vermont village of Stowe (settled in 1794) bustles quietly. The town's long-standing reputation as one of the east's classiest mountain resorts draws well-heeled urbanites from Boston, New York and beyond. A bounty of inns and eateries lines the thoroughfares leading up to Smugglers Notch, an enchantingly narrow rock-walled pass through the Green Mountains just below Mt Mansfield (4393ft), the highest point in Vermont. More than 200 miles of cross-country ski trails, some of the finest mountain biking and downhill skiing in the east, and world-class rock- and ice-climbing lure adrenaline junkies and active families.

Waterbury, on the interstate highway 10 miles south, is Stowe's gateway. Its attractions include some standout restaurants and the world-famous **Ben & Jerry's Ice Cream Factory** (802-882-2047; www.benjerry.com/about-us/factory-tours; 1281 VT 100, Waterbury; adult/child under 13yr $4/free; 9am-9pm Jul–mid-Aug, to 7pm mid-Aug–mid-Oct, 10am-6pm mid-Oct–late May, to 7pm late May–Jun;).

Sights & Activities

★ Alchemist Brewery BREWERY
(www.alchemistbeer.com; 100 Cottage Club Rd; 11am-7pm Tue-Sat) One of Vermont's most legendary beers, Heady Topper, was born at this microbrewery. Visitors to the state-of-the-art, solar-powered building with its silo-like tower can enjoy free tastes, observe the beer production process and purchase four-packs of Heady Topper, Focal Banger and other outstanding brews to bring home.

★ Stowe Recreation Path OUTDOORS
(www.stowerec.org/parks-facilities/rec-paths/stowe-recreation-path;) The flat to gently rolling 5.3-mile Stowe Recreation Path, which starts from the steepled Stowe Community Church in the village center, offers a fabulous four-season escape for all ages. It rambles through woods, meadows and outdoor sculpture gardens along the West Branch of Little River, with sweeping views of Mt Mansfield unfolding in the distance.

Smugglers Notch Boardwalk OUTDOORS
Opened in 2018, this boardwalk represents a revolutionary improvement in accessibility to the Smugglers Notch area, allowing visitors in strollers or wheelchairs to follow a section of the Long Trail out through a montane wetland to a viewpoint with lovely perspectives on the notch. Pull-offs along the way feature informational displays about the wetlands' ecology, flora, fauna and natural history.

Sleeping & Eating

Stowe Motel & Snowdrift MOTEL, APARTMENT $$
(802-253-7629; www.stowemotel.com; 2043 Mountain Rd; r $109-215, ste $195-265, apt $179-280;) In addition to motel-like rooms and suites – some with kitchenette and wood-burning fireplace – this sprawling 16-acre property midway between Stowe village and the slopes offers multibedroom houses and an apartment. Clinching the deal are countless amenities: a tennis court, two swimming pools, a hot tub, badminton, lawn games and free bicycles or snowshoes to use on the nearby recreation path.

Trapp Family Lodge LODGE $$$
(802-253-8511; www.trappfamily.com; 700 Trapp Hill Rd; r $175-425, ste $275-750;) This hilltop lodge 3km above town boasts Stowe's most dramatic setting. The Austrian-style chalet, built by Maria von Trapp of *Sound of Music* fame (note the family photos lining the walls), houses 96 traditional lodge rooms, many newly renovated and most with balconies affording lovely mountain vistas. Alternatively, rent one of the cozy villas or guesthouses scattered across the property.

The 2700-acre spread offers stupendous hiking, mountain biking, snowshoeing and cross-country skiing, while the family's Kaffehaus and **Bierhall** (☎802-253-5750; www.vontrappbrewing.com/bierhall.htm; 1333 Luce Hill Rd; mains $13-31; ⊙11:30am-9pm), both located nearby, add another delightful dose of Austria-in-Vermont flavor.

Doc Ponds AMERICAN **$$**

(☎802-760-6066; www.docponds.com; 294 Mountain Rd; mains $8-22; ⊙4pm-midnight Tue-Thu, from 11:30am Fri-Mon) Casual fare, from tacos to burgers to mac 'n' cheese and milkshakes, dominates the menu at this popular spot near the heart of Stowe village. Walls festooned with skateboards enhance the festive mood, as do the twin turntables spinning vintage vinyl at the entrance. Craft beer and cider specials go for $4 a pint every day.

★**Hen of the Wood** MODERN AMERICAN **$$$**

(☎802-244-7300; www.henofthewood.com; 92 Stowe St, Waterbury; small plates $12-15, mains $22-35; ⊙5-9pm Tue-Sat) Arguably the finest dining in Northern Vermont, this chef-driven restaurant, set in a historic grist mill in Waterbury, gets rave reviews for its innovative farm-to-table cuisine. The ambience is as fine as the food, which features seasonal ingredients such as wild mushrooms and densely flavored dishes such as smoked duck breast and sheep's-milk gnocchi.

Information

Barnes Camp Visitor Center (www.greenmountainclub.org; VT 108, 2 miles east of Smugglers Notch; ⊙9am-5pm Fri-Sun mid-Jun–mid-Oct) Get hiking info at this seasonal visitor center near the Long Trail's intersection with Smugglers Notch.

Green Mountain Club Visitors Center (☎802-244-7037; www.greenmountainclub.org; 4711 Waterbury-Stowe Rd/VT 100, Waterbury Center; ⊙9am-5pm daily mid-May–mid-Oct, 10am-4pm Mon-Fri rest of year) Stop by this office (5 miles south of Stowe) or check the website for details about the Long Trail and shorter day hikes in the region.

Stowe Area Association (☎802-253-7321; www.gostowe.com; 51 Main St; ⊙9am-6pm Mon-Sat, 11am-5pm Sun;) This well-organized association can help you plan your trip, including making reservations for rental cars and local accommodations.

Getting There & Away

The Amtrak *Vermonter* train stops daily at Waterbury (mornings southbound to Brattleboro and New York City, evenings northbound to Burlington). Some hotels and inns will arrange to pick up guests at the station. Otherwise, get a taxi from **Stowe Taxi** (☎802-253-9490; www.stowetaxi.com).

Burlington

Perched on the shores of Lake Champlain, Vermont's largest city would be considered tiny in most other states, but its relatively diminutive size is one of Burlington's charms. With the University of Vermont (UVM) swelling the city by 13,000 students and contributing to its vibrant cultural and social life, Burlington has a spirited, youthful vibe and more ethnic diversity than anywhere else in Vermont.

Burlington's walkable downtown, bike paths, farmers market, fabulous food co-op, and proximity to nature earn it accolades as one of America's greenest and most livable cities. The city's ongoing Great Streets Initiative (www.greatstreetsbtv.com) aims to sustain that momentum, with wider sidewalks, enhanced green spaces and reduced pollution.

Burlington makes an attractive base for exploring the rest of northwestern Vermont. Two of Vermont's crown jewels, **Shelburne Farms** (☎802-985-8686; www.shelburnefarms.org; 1611 Harbor Rd, Shelburne; adult/child mid-May–mid-Oct $8/5, rest of year free; ⊙9am-5:30pm mid-May–mid-Oct, 10am-5pm rest of year;) and the Shelburne Museum (p229), lie just 15 minutes south, while Stowe and the Green Mountains are within an hour's drive.

Sights & Activities

★**Church Street Marketplace** MARKET

(www.churchstmarketplace.com;) Burlington's pulse can often be taken along this four-block pedestrian zone running from Pearl to Main Sts. When the weather's good, buskers (licensed by the town), food and craft vendors, soapbox demagogues, restless students, curious tourists and kids climbing on rocks mingle in a vibrant human parade.

★**Shelburne Museum** MUSEUM

(☎802-985-3346; www.shelburnemuseum.org; 6000 Shelburne Rd/US 7, Shelburne; adult/child $25/14 May-Oct, $10/5 Nov-Apr; ⊙10am-5pm daily May-Dec, Wed-Sun Jan-Apr;) This extraordinary 45-acre museum, 9 miles south of

Burlington, showcases the priceless Americana collections of Electra Havemeyer Webb (1888–1960) and her parents – 150,000 objects in all. The mix of folk art, decorative arts and more is housed in 39 historic buildings, most of them moved here from other parts of New England to ensure their preservation.

Intervale Center FARM
(☎802-660-0440; www.intervale.org; 180 Intervale Rd) FREE You'd never guess it standing on a busy Burlington street corner, but one of Vermont's most idyllic green spaces is less than 2 miles from downtown. Tucked among the lazy curves of the Winooski River, Burlington's Intervale encompasses half a dozen organic farms and a delightful trail network, open 365 days a year for hiking, biking, skiing, bird-watching, paddling and more.

Waterfront WATERFRONT
A five-minute walk from downtown, Burlington's delightfully uncommercialized waterfront features a scenic, low-key promenade, a 7.5-mile bike path, a pier for Lake Champlain **boat trips** and the family-friendly **Echo aquarium** (☎802-864-1848; www.echovermont.org; 1 College St; adult/child $14.50/11.50; ⏱10am-5pm; 👪).

Sleeping

Burlington Hostel HOSTEL $
(☎802-540-3043; www.theburlingtonhostel.com; 53 Main St, 2nd fl; dm midweek/weekend $39/49; ⏱mid-Feb–Nov; ❄@📶) Hidden behind an unassuming facade just minutes from the action centers of Church St and Lake Champlain, Burlington's hostel accommodates up to 48 guests in four- to eight-bed mixed and women-only dorms. There's an invitingly open kitchen and lounge area where breakfast (coffee and waffles) is served each morning.

★**Willard Street Inn** INN $$
(☎802-651-8710; www.willardstreetinn.com; 349 S Willard St; r $155-305; 📶) Perched on a hill within easy walking distance of UVM and the Church Street Marketplace, this mansion, fusing Queen Anne and Georgian Revival styles, was built in the late 1880s. It has a fine-wood and cut-glass elegance, yet radiates a welcoming warmth. Many of the guest rooms overlook Lake Champlain.

★**Inn at Shelburne Farms** INN $$$
(☎802-985-8498; www.shelburnefarms.org/staydine; 1611 Harbor Rd, Shelburne; r $270-530, without bath $160-230, cottages & houses $270-850; ⏱early May-late Oct; 📶) One of New England's top 10 places to stay, this inn, 7 miles south of Burlington off US 7, was once the summer mansion of the wealthy Webb family. It now welcomes guests, with rooms in the gracious, welcoming country manor house by the lakefront, as well as four independent, kitchen-equipped cottages and guesthouses scattered across the property.

Hotel Vermont HOTEL $$$
(☎802-651-0080; www.hotelvt.com; 41 Cherry St; r/ste from $259/439) Burlington's newest downtown hotel, in a LEED-certified energy-efficient building halfway between Church St and Lake Champlain, pampers guests with 125 bright modern rooms filled with high-end amenities. There's a pair of excellent on-site restaurants and regular live jazz in the lobby.

Eating

Penny Cluse Cafe CAFE $
(☎802-651-8834; www.pennycluse.com; 169 Cherry St; mains $6-14; ⏱6:45am-3pm Mon-Fri, from 8am Sat & Sun) This ever-popular downtown eatery serves pancakes, biscuits and gravy, omelets and tofu scrambles, along with sandwiches, tacos, salads and delightful drinks ranging from smoothies to Bloody Marys. Don't miss its decadent Bucket-o-Spuds (home-fried potatoes with cheddar, salsa, sour cream and scallions) and *chiles rellenos* – among the best you'll find anywhere east of the Mississippi. Expect an hour's wait on weekends.

★**Revolution Kitchen** VEGAN, VEGETARIAN $$
(☎802-448-3657; www.revolutionkitchen.com; 9 Center St; mains $14-18; ⏱5-9pm Tue-Thu, to 10pm Fri & Sat; 🌱) Vegetarian fine dining? And romantic atmosphere to boot? Yep, they all come together at this cozy brick-walled restaurant that makes creative use of Vermont's abundant organic produce. Asian, Mediterranean and Latin American influences abound in house favorites such as Revolution tacos, crispy seitan piccata and the laksa noodle pot. Most items are (or can be adapted to be) vegan.

American Flatbread PIZZA $$
(☎802-861-2999; www.americanflatbread.com; 115 St Paul St; flatbreads $14-23; ⏱11:30am-3pm & 5-11:30pm Mon-Fri, 11:30am-11:30pm Sat & Sun) 🍃 Central location, great beers on tap from the in-house Zero Gravity microbrew-

ery and superb flatbread (thin-crust pizza) are reason enough to visit this bustling downtown eatery. Throw in an outdoor summer terrace in the back alleyway, and you have one of Burlington's most appealing restaurants.

Drinking & Entertainment

★Citizen Cider MICROBREWERY
(802-497-1987; www.citizencider.com; 316 Pine St; 11am-10pm Mon-Sat, to 7pm Sun) Tucked into an industrial-chic building with painted concrete floors and long wooden tables, this homegrown success story uses tankfuls of apples trucked in from Vermont orchards to make its ever-growing line of hard ciders. Taste test a flight of five for $7, including perennial favorites such as the ginger-and-lemon-peel-infused Dirty Mayor, or go for one of the inventive cider-based cocktails.

Foam Brewers MICROBREWERY
(802-399-2511; www.foambrewers.com; 112 Lake St; noon-9pm Mon-Thu, 11am-11pm Fri & Sat, to 7pm Sun) Housed in an attractive brick building with exposed post-and-beam woodwork and a dreamy terrace looking out toward Lake Champlain, Foam was founded by a group of local beer aficionados looking to unleash their improvisational spirit. The result: one of Burlington's liveliest new brewpubs, with a rotating selection of inventive craft beers and live music six nights a week.

Radio Bean BAR
(802-660-9346; www.facebook.com/radiobean; 8 N Winooski Ave; 8am-2am Mon-Fri, from 10am Sat & Sun;) This is Burlington's social hub for arts and music. Espressos, beer and wine keep things jumping at the all-day cafe, while nightly live performances (jazz, acoustic, Afro-Cuban and more) animate two stages, here and at the semi-attached **Light Club Lamp Shop** (802-660-9346; www.radiobean.com/light-club-info; 12 N Winooski Ave; 7pm-late Sun-Thu, 6pm-2am Fri & Sat). Radio Bean is also noteworthy for having co-founded the Radiator, Burlington's fabled low-power indie radio station (105.9 FM, www.bigheavyworld.com/live-stream-intro).

ArtsRiot LIVE MUSIC
(802-540-0406; www.artsriot.com; 400 Pine St; 4:30pm-late Tue-Sat) This brick-walled, exuberantly frescoed former timber warehouse in Burlington's South End is the venue for myriad events, from live music to storytelling. In the late afternoons it's a convivial bar-restaurant with early-bird specials till 5:30pm; come nightfall the door opens onto the performance space and dance floor. On Fridays in summer a host of food trucks parks out back.

Information

BTV Information Center (802-863-1889; www.vermont.org; Burlington International Airport; 4pm-midnight) This helpful office in Burlington's airport is staffed by the Lake Champlain Regional Chamber of Commerce.

Lake Champlain Regional Chamber of Commerce (877-686-5253, 802-863-3489; www.vermont.org; 60 Main St; 8:30am-4:30pm Mon-Thu, to 3pm Fri) Staffed tourist office in the heart of downtown.

Waterfront Tourism Center (off Lake St; 10am-8pm daily late May–Aug, to 6pm Sep–mid-Oct) Opens seasonally down near the lakefront.

Getting There & Away

AIR

A number of national carriers serve **Burlington International Airport** (BTV; 802-863-2874; www.btv.aero; 1200 Airport Dr, South Burlington), 3 miles east of the city center. You'll find all the major car-rental companies at the airport.

BUS

Green Mountain Transit (www.ridegmt.com) Operates a few long-distance buses to other cities in northwestern Vermont. See its website for fares and schedules.

Greyhound (www.greyhound.com) Runs multiple buses daily from Burlington International Airport to Montréal, Canada (from $18, 2½ hours) and Boston (from $28, 4½ to 5½ hours).

Megabus (877-462-6342; www.megabus.com; 119 Pearl St) Offers a once-daily bus service to Boston (from $25, four hours). Buses stop just around the corner from Burlington's **GMT Downtown Transit Center** (Green Mountain Transit; 802-864-2282; www.ridegmt.com; cnr St Paul & Cherry Sts; 6am-11pm Mon-Fri, 7am-5pm Sat).

Middlebury Routes 46 and 76

Montpelier Route 86

TRAIN

Amtrak's daily *Vermonter* train (www.amtrak.com/vermonter-train), which provides service as far south as New York City and Washington, DC, stops in Essex Junction, 5 miles from Burlington.

NEW HAMPSHIRE

Jagged mountains, serene valleys and island-dotted lakes lurk in every corner of New Hampshire. The whole rugged state begs for exploration, whether kayaking the hidden coves of the Lakes Region or trekking the upper peaks surrounding Mt Washington. Each season yields a bounty of adrenaline and activity: skiing and snowshoeing in winter, with many slopes open into spring; magnificent walks and drives through fall's fiery colors; and swimming in crisp mountain streams and berry-picking in summer.

Jewel-box colonial settlements such as Portsmouth set a sophisticated tone, while historical allure and small-town culture live on in pristine villages like Keene and Peterborough. Manchester and Concord are two urban strongholds sprucing up their main drags with indie shops and innovative eats. There's a relaxing whiff in the air, too – you're encouraged to gaze out at a loon-filled lake, recline on a scenic railway trip or chug across a waterway on a sunset cruise.

History

Named in 1629 after the English county of Hampshire, New Hampshire was one of the first American colonies to declare its independence from England in 1776. During the 19th-century industrialization boom, the state's leading city, Manchester, became such a powerhouse that its textile mills were the world's largest.

New Hampshire played a high-profile role in 1944 when President Franklin D Roosevelt gathered leaders from 44 Allied nations at remote Bretton Woods for a conference to rebuild global capitalism. It was from the Bretton Woods Conference that the World Bank and the International Monetary Fund emerged.

In 1963 New Hampshire, long famed for its anti-tax sentiments, found another way to raise revenue – by becoming the first state in the USA to have a legal lottery.

Information

New Hampshire Division of Parks & Recreation (www.nhstateparks.org) Offers information on a statewide bicycle route system and a very complete camping guide.

New Hampshire Division of Travel & Tourism Development (www.visitnh.gov) Ski conditions and fall foliage reports, among other things.

Southern New Hampshire

Manchester

Once home to the world's largest textile mill – at its peak, the Amoskeag Manufacturing Company employed 17,000 people (out of a city population of 70,000) – this riverside town retains, both historically and culturally, a bit of its blue-collar roots. Exploiting the abundant water power of the Merrimack River, and stretching along its east bank for more than a mile, the mill made the city into a manufacturing and commercial powerhouse from 1838 until its bankruptcy in the 1930s.

Nowadays, attracted by low taxes and a diverse workforce, the high-tech and financial industries have moved in, bringing city culture with them. The former mill is a prime symbol of successful redevelopment: the redbrick swath of structures houses a museum, an arts center, a college, restaurants and a growing array of local businesses. Manchester has opera, several orchestras, a growing gallery and dining scene, and the state's most important art museum.

Millyard Museum MUSEUM
(☎603-622-7531; www.manchesterhistory.org; 200 Bedford St; adult/child 12-18yr $8/4; ⏲10am-4pm Tue-Sat) A highlight in the Amoskeag Millyard Historic District, this well-executed museum spotlights the various communities that have lived and worked near Amoskeag Falls from prehistoric times forward, with a focus on the city's years as a textile manufacturing center. Stories about the different immigrant enclaves during this time are particularly fascinating.

Currier Museum of Art MUSEUM
(☎603-669-6144; www.currier.org; 150 Ash St; adult/child $15/5, incl Zimmerman House tour $25/10; ⏲11am-5pm Sun, Mon & Wed-Fri, 10am-5pm Sat; Ⓟ) Housing works by John Singer Sargent, Georgia O'Keeffe, Monet, Matisse and Picasso (among many others), this fine-arts museum is Manchester's greatest cultural gem. With advance reservation, museum guides also offer tours of the nearby **Zimmerman House**, the only Frank Lloyd Wright–designed house in New England that's open to the public.

Getting There & Away

Fast growing but still not too large, **Manchester-Boston Regional Airport** (603-624-6556; www.flymanchester.com; 1 Airport Rd;), off US 3 south of Manchester, is a civilized alternative to Boston's Logan International Airport.

Concord Coach Lines (www.concordcoachlines.com) runs frequent daily buses to Logan International Airport ($19, 1¾ hours) and South Station ($15, 1½ hours) in Boston, as well as north to Concord ($6, 30 minutes). Buses depart from the Manchester Transportation Center.

Portsmouth

Perched on the edge of the Piscataqua River, Portsmouth is one of New Hampshire's most elegant towns, with a historical center set with tree-lined streets and 18th-century Colonial buildings. Despite its venerable history as an early hub of America's maritime industry, the town exudes a youthful energy, with tourists and locals filling its many restaurants and cafes. Numerous museums and historic houses allow visitors a glimpse into the town's multilayered past, while its proximity to the coast brings both lobster feasts and periodic days of fog that blanket the waterfront.

Still true to its name, Portsmouth remains a working port town, and its economic vitality has been boosted by the naval shipyard (actually located across the river in Maine) and by the influx of high-tech companies.

Sights & Activities

★ **Strawbery Banke Museum** MUSEUM
(603-433-1100; www.strawberybanke.org; 14 Hancock St; adult/child 5-17yr $19.50/9; 10am-5pm May-Oct, special events only Nov-Apr;) Spread across a 10-acre site, the Strawbery Banke Museum is an eclectic blend of period homes that date back to the 1690s. Costumed guides recount tales that took place among the 40 buildings (10 furnished). Strawbery Banke includes **Pitt Tavern** (1766), a hotbed of American revolutionary sentiment, **Goodwin Mansion** (a grand 19th-century house from Portsmouth's most prosperous time) and **Abbott's Little Corner Store** (1943). The admission ticket is good for two consecutive days.

Isles of Shoals Steamship Co CRUISE
(603-431-5500; www.islesofshoals.com; 315 Market St; adult/child from $28/18;) From mid-June to early October this company runs an excellent tour of the harbor and the historic Isles of Shoals aboard a replica 1900s ferry. It also offers walking tours of Star Island and party cruises featuring DJs or live bands.

WORTH A TRIP

MONADNOCK STATE PARK

Visible from 50 miles in any direction, the commanding 3165ft peak of Mt Monadnock is southwestern New Hampshire's spiritual vortex. The surrounding **Mt Monadnock State Park** (603-532-8862; www.nhstateparks.org; 169 Poole Rd, Jaffrey; day use adult/child 6-11yr $5/2;) is an outdoor wonderland, complete with a visitor center, a camp store, 12 miles of ungroomed cross-country ski trails and more than 40 miles of hiking trails, about 10 miles of which reach the summit. The 3.9-mile White Dot & White Cross loop is a popular hiking route to the top.

Sleeping & Eating

Port Inn MOTEL $$$
(603-436-4378; www.portinnportsmouth.com; 505 US 1 Bypass; r $249-499, ste $499;) Wrapped neatly around a small courtyard, this welcoming and inviting motel is conveniently located off I-95, about 1.5 miles southwest of downtown. In the rooms, monochromatic pillows and throws add a dash of pizzazz to classic furnishings. Breakfast included. Pets are $25 per night.

Ale House Inn INN $$$
(603-431-7760; www.alehouseinn.com; 121 Bow St; r $234-304;) This former brick warehouse for the Portsmouth Brewing Company is Portsmouth's snazziest boutique inn, fusing contemporary design with comfort. Rooms are modern, with clean white lines, flat-screen TVs, and, in the suites, plush tan sofas. All rooms feature an in-room iPad. Rates include use of Trek cruising bikes, but sadly, free beer is no longer included.

Colby's BREAKFAST $
(603-436-3033; 105 Daniel St; mains $4-11; 7am-2pm) If you get to this 28-seat eatery after 8am on the weekend, there's going to be a wait, so give 'em your name and enjoy a cup of free coffee on the patio. Once in, egg lovers can choose from a multitude of

Benedicts and omelets, along with French toast, pancakes, huevos rancheros and daily chalkboard specials.

★ Black Trumpet Bistro INTERNATIONAL **$$**
(☎603-431-0887; www.blacktrumpetbistro.com; 29 Ceres St; mains $19-32; ⊙5-9pm Sun-Thu, to 10pm Fri & Sat) This bistro, with brick walls and a sophisticated ambience, serves unique combinations – anything from housemade sausages infused with cocoa beans to seared haddock with yuzu (an Asian citrus fruit) and miso. The full menu is also available at its wine bar upstairs, which whips up equally inventive cocktails.

Cure MODERN AMERICAN **$$**
(☎603-427-8258; www.curerestaurantportsmouth.com; 189 State St; mains $19-35; ⊙5-9pm Sun-Thu, to 10pm Fri & Sat) Constantly showered with accolades, chef Julie Cutting's refined but cozy brick-walled restaurant makes a romantic dinner spot. The menu revolves around New England cuisine 'revisited': pan-roasted duck breast, maple-glazed salmon, beef ribs slow-braised in red wine, horseradish-sour-cream mashed potatoes, crisp-skinned chicken and lobster bisque, all accompanied by seasonal vegetables and a superb cocktail list.

ℹ Information

The helpful **Greater Portsmouth Chamber of Commerce** (☎603-610-5510; www.portsmouthchamber.org; 500 Market St; ⊙9am-5pm Mon-Fri year-round, plus 10am-5pm Sat & Sun late May–mid-Oct), which runs a visitor center on the way into Portsmouth just off I-95, also operates a seasonal **information kiosk** (www.goportsmouthnh.com; Market Sq; ⊙10am-5pm late May–mid-Oct) in the city center.

ℹ Getting There & Away

Portsmouth is equidistant (about 57 miles) from Boston and Portland, ME. It takes roughly 1¼ hours to reach Portland and 1½ hours to Boston, both via I-95. Rush-hour and high-season traffic can easily double or triple this, however.

Lakes Region

The Lakes Region, with an odd mix of natural beauty and commercial tawdriness, is one of New Hampshire's most popular holiday destinations. Vast Lake Winnipesaukee, the region's centerpiece, has 183 miles of coastline, more than 300 islands and excellent salmon fishing. Catch the early morning mists off the lake and you'll understand why the Native Americans named it 'Smile of the Great Spirit.' The prettiest stretches are in the southwest between Glendale and Alton (on the shoreline Belknap Point Rd), and in the northeast corner between Wolfeboro and Moultonborough (on NH 109). To the north lie the smaller Squam and Little Squam Lakes.

The roads skirting the shores and connecting the lakeside towns pass forested mountains and a riotous spread of small-town Americana: amusement arcades, go-kart tracks, clam shacks, junk-food outlets and boat docks. Even if you're just passing through, stop for a swim, a lakeside picnic or a cruise.

ℹ Getting There & Around

The fastest way to reach the Lakes Region is via I-93. Coming from Boston and other points south, take exit 15E for Wolfeboro, exit 20 for Weirs Beach, exit 23 for Meredith or exit 24 for Holderness (Squam Lake).

For bus service to or from the Lakes Region, try Concord Coach Lines (www.concordcoachlines.com), which passes through Meredith on its twice-daily run between Boston and North Conway. Buses stop near the Memorial parking lot sign in the public lot near the northeast corner of US 3 and NH 25. This is a flag stop, and you cannot buy tickets here. Destinations include Concord ($13, one hour), Boston's South Station ($25, 2½ hours) and Logan International Airport ($30, 2¾ hours).

Weirs Beach

Called 'Aquedoctan' by its Native American settlers, Weirs Beach takes its English name from the weirs (enclosures for catching fish) that the first European settlers found along the small sand beach. Today Weirs Beach is the honky-tonk heart of Lake Winnipesaukee's childhood amusements, famous for video-game arcades and fried dough. The vacation scene is completed by a lakefront promenade, a public beach and a dock for small cruising ships. A water park and drive-in theater are also in the vicinity. Away from the din on the waterfront, you will notice evocative Victorian-era architecture – somewhat out of place in this capital of kitsch.

South of Weirs Beach lie Laconia, the largest town in the region but devoid of any real sights, and lake-hugging **Gilford**. Note that this side of the lake gets mobbed with bikers for nine days each June during Laconia Motorcycle Week (www.laconiamcweek.com), the world's oldest motorcycle rally.

★MV Sophie C CRUISE
(☎603-366-5531; www.cruisenh.com/sophie.php; 211 Lakeside Ave; adult/child 5-12yr $28/14; ⊙11am & 2pm Mon-Sat mid-Jun–early Sep) The MV *Sophie C* is a veritable floating post office. Passengers are invited to accompany this US mail boat as it delivers packages and letters to quaint ports and otherwise inaccessible island residents across four to five islands. Between mid-June and early September, its two 1½-hour runs depart six days a week from Weirs Beach.

MS Mount Washington CRUISE
(☎603-366-5531; www.cruisenh.com; 211 Lakeside Ave; adult/child 5-12yr regular cruises $32/16, Sun brunch cruises $52/26; ⊙mid-May–late Oct) The classic MS *Mount Washington* steams out of Weirs Beach daily, making a relaxing 2½-hour scenic circuit around Lake Winnipesaukee, with regular stops in Wolfeboro and occasional visits to Alton Bay, Center Harbor and/or Meredith. Special events include Sunday champagne brunch cruises, and themed cruises (sunset dinner-and-dance, an Elvis Tribute, a Lobsterfest cruise) throughout summer and early fall.

NazBar & Grill BAR
(☎603-366-4341; www.naswa.com; 1086 Weirs Blvd, Laconia; ⊙from 11am late May-early Oct) This colorful lakeside bar is recommended because it's a scene. This is Weirs Beach, after all. Watch boats pull up to the dock as you sip your cocktail beside – or in – the lake. Bar fare includes nachos, salads, wraps and burgers.

Information

Lakes Region Chamber of Commerce
(☎603-524-5531; www.lakesregionchamber.org; 383 S Main St, Laconia; ⊙9am-3pm Mon-Fri) Supplies information about the greater Laconia/Weirs Beach area.

Wolfeboro

On the eastern shore of Lake Winnipesaukee, Wolfeboro is an idyllic town where children still gather around the ice-cream stand on warm summer nights and a grassy lakeside park draws young and old to weekly concerts. Named for General Wolfe, who died vanquishing Montcalm on the Plains of Abraham in Quebec, Wolfeboro (founded in 1770) claims to be 'the oldest summer resort in America.' Whether that's true or not, it's certainly one of the most charming, with pretty lake beaches, intriguing museums, beautiful New England architecture (from Georgian through Federal, Greek Revival and Second Empire), cozy B&Bs and a worthwhile walking trail that runs along several lakes as it leads out of town.

Sights & Activities

Wright Museum MUSEUM
(☎603-569-1212; www.wrightmuseum.org; 77 Center St; adult/child 5-17yr $10/6; ⊙10am-4pm Mon-Sat, noon-4pm Sun May-Oct) For a Rosie-the-riveter and baked-apple-pie look at WWII, visit this museum's interactive exhibitions that feature music, documentary clips, posters and other American paraphernalia. There are also uniforms, equipment and military hardware (including a 42-ton Pershing tank), meticulously restored by the museum. The Tuesday-evening summer lecture series (June to mid-September) is a huge draw – speakers range from authors to war refugees.

Cotton Valley Rail Trail WALKING
(www.cottonvalleyrailtrail.org; Central Ave) This excellent multiuse rail trail starts at Wolfeboro's information office and runs for 12 miles along an old railway bed. It links the towns of Wolfeboro, Brookfield and Wakefield and passes two lakes, climbs through Cotton Valley, and winds through forests and fields around Brookfield. From Wolfeboro, the trail's first half mile is also known as the Bridge Falls Path.

Sleeping & Eating

Wolfeboro Inn INN $$$
(☎603-569-3016; www.wolfeboroinn.com; 90 N Main St; r $219-279, ste $319-359; P@🛜🐾) The town's best-known lodging is right on the lake with a private beach. One of the region's most prestigious resorts since 1812, it has 44 rooms across a main inn and a modern annex. Rooms have modern touches like new beds and contemporary furnishings: it feels less historic but oh-so-luxurious. Facilities include a restaurant and pub, **Wolfe's Tavern** (www.wolfestavern.com; dinner mains $12-31; ⊙7am-9pm Sun-Thu, to 10pm Fri & Sat).

Downtown Grille Cafe CAFE $
(☎603-569-4504; www.downtowngrillecafe.com; 33 S Main St; pastries $2-4, breakfast mains $4-9, lunch mains $8-14; ⏲7am-3pm) Order at the counter then head to the back patio for a great view of Lake Winn with your ham-and-pepper-jack panini, hot-pressed *cubano* or, our favorite, the kickin' buffalo chicken wrap with blue cheese and hot sauce. Stop by in the morning for pastries and breakfast sandwiches. Fancy coffees available, too.

Nolan's Brick Oven Bistro PIZZA $$
(☎603-515-1028; www.nolansbrickovenbistro.com; 39 N Main St; mains $10-26; ⏲11am-9pm) Delicious pizzas – cooked in the brick oven and laden with ingredients sourced from local farms – are the big draw at this popular spot a block north of the village center. But the kitchen offers a world of alternatives throughout the year, including seafood, soups, salads, wraps and even occasional sushi nights.

ℹ Information

Wolfeboro Chamber of Commerce Information Booth (☎603-569-2200; www.wolfeborochamber.com; 32 Central Ave; ⏲10am-3pm Mon-Sat, to noon Sun late May–mid-Oct, reduced hours rest of year) Located inside the old train station, this small office has the scoop on local activities.

White Mountains

Covering one-quarter of New Hampshire (and part of Maine), the vast White Mountains area is a spectacular region of soaring peaks and lush valleys, and contains New England's most rugged mountains. There are numerous activities on offer, including hiking, camping, skiing and canoeing. Much of the area – 786,000 acres – is protected from overdevelopment as part of the White Mountain National Forest (WMNF), which celebrated its centennial in 2018. Note, however, that this wondrous place is popular: six million visitors flock here annually to use its 1200 miles of hiking trails, 23 campgrounds and eight Nordic and alpine ski areas.

Connected by scenic drives and rugged trails, there are four popular areas in the White Mountains for recreation: Mt Washington Valley to the east, Crawford Notch and Bretton Woods along US 302 in the center, the Kancamagus Hwy along the southern fringe and the Franconia Range to the west and northwest.

Kancamagus Highway

One of New Hampshire's prettiest driving routes, the winding 34.5-mile Kancamagus Hwy (NH 112) between Lincoln and Conway runs right through the WMNF and over Kancamagus Pass (2855ft). Paved only in 1964, and still unspoiled by commercial development, the 'Kanc' offers easy access to US Forest Service (USFS) campgrounds, hiking trails and fantastic scenery.

The route is named for Chief Kancamagus (The Fearless One), who assumed the powers of *sagamore* (leader) of the Penacook Native American tribe around 1684. He was the final *sagamore,* succeeding his grandfather, the great Passaconaway, and his uncle Wonalancet. Kancamagus tried to maintain peace between the indigenous peoples and European explorers and settlers, but the newcomers pushed his patience past breaking point. He finally resorted to battle to rid the region of Europeans, but in 1691 he and his followers were forced to escape northward.

Sabbaday Falls WALKING
(NH 112/Kancamagus Hwy; day use $5) A 0.3-mile one-way stroll on the popular Sabbaday Brook Trail ends at Sabbaday Falls, a gorge waterfall powering through narrow granite walls into lovely pools. Stairs lead to overlooks with mesmerizing views of the flume. The trailhead is about 15 miles west of the Saco Ranger District Office, and the trail is accessible for people with disabilities.

ℹ Information

Saco Ranger District Office (☎603-447-5448; www.fs.usda.gov/detail/whitemountain/about-forest/offices; 33 Kancamagus Hwy, Conway; ⏲9am-4:30pm Mon, 8am-4:30pm Tue-Sun) You can pick up White Mountain National Forest brochures and hiking maps here, at the eastern end of the Kancamagus Hwy near Conway. Restrooms available.

North Woodstock & Lincoln

North Woodstock and its neighboring settlement Lincoln gather a mix of adventure seekers and drive-by sightseers en route to the Kancamagus Hwy (NH 112). North Woodstock has a busy but small-town feel with weathered motels and diners lining the main street and a gurgling river running parallel to it. Nearby Lincoln has less charm, but serves as the starting point for the entertaining Hobo Railroad and other family-friendly activities such as zipline tours and an aerial adventure park.

★Notch Hostel HOSTEL **$**
(☎603-348-1483; www.notchhostel.com; 324 Lost River Rd, North Woodstock; dm $30, d $75-90; P@🛜🐾) Tibetan prayer flags mark your arrival at this gorgeous hostel, the brainchild of outdoor enthusiasts (and husband-and-wife team) Serena and Justin. A class act all round, it welcomes guests with outdoor decks, a spacious kitchen, a mountain-themed library, a sauna for chilly winter nights and a cozy vibe. Lots of info for Appalachian Trail thru-hikers.

Wilderness Inn B&B **$$**
(☎603-745-3890; www.thewildernessinn.com; 57 S Main St, North Woodstock; r $115-200, cottage $200; P❄🛜) This former lumber-mill-owner's house has seven lovely guest rooms, ranging from small to suite-size, as well as a family-size cottage overlooking Lost River. Each is individually decorated with stenciled walls and cozy furnishings, and all but one have wood floors. Breakfasts (included in room rates) are marvelous and served on the sun porch when it's warm.

Woodstock Inn Station & Brewery PUB FOOD **$$**
(☎603-745-3951; www.woodstockinnnh.com; 135 Main St/US 3, North Woodstock; mains $9-26; ⊙11:30am-9pm Sun-Thu, to 10pm Fri & Sat, bar open later) Formerly a railroad station, this place tries to be everything to everyone. With more than 150 items, it can probably satisfy just about any food craving, but the pastas, sandwiches and burgers are the most interesting. The beer-sodden rear tavern is one of the most happening places in this neck of the woods. Also a nice front patio.

Information

Start your adventures at the helpful and comprehensive **White Mountains Visitor Center** (☎National Forest info 603-745-3816, visitor info 603-745-8720; www.visitwhitemountains.com; 200 Kancamagus Hwy, off I-93, exit 32, North Woodstock; ⊙visitor center 8:30am-5pm year-round, National Forest desk 9am-3:30pm mid-May–mid-Oct, Fri-Sun rest of year) in Lincoln. It's one of the best resources for information about the region. Here you'll find trail info and be able to purchase National Forest recreation passes. In North Woodstock, stop by the **Western White Mountains Chamber of Commerce** (☎603-745-6621; www.lincolnwoodstock.com; 126 Main St/US 3, North Woodstock; ⊙8am-4pm Mon-Fri) for information.

Getting There & Away

Concord Coach Lines (www.concordcoachlines.com) stops in Lincoln at **7-Eleven** (☎800-639-3317; 36 Main St) on its twice-daily run between Boston and Littleton. Destinations include Concord ($17.50, 1½ hours), Boston's South Station ($29, three hours) and Logan International Airport ($34, 3¼ hours).

Franconia Notch State Park

Franconia Notch, a narrow gorge shaped over the eons by a wild stream cutting through craggy granite, is a dramatic mountain pass. This was long the residence of the beloved Old Man of the Mountain, a natural rock formation that became the symbol of the Granite State. Sadly, the Old Man collapsed in 2003, though that does not stop tourists from coming to see the featureless cliff that remains. Despite the Old Man's absence, the attractions of Franconia Notch are many, from the dramatic hike down the Flume Gorge to the fantastic views of the Presidential Range.

The most scenic parts of the notch are protected by the narrow Franconia Notch State Park. Reduced to two lanes, I-93 (renamed the Franconia Notch Pkwy) squeezes through the gorge. Services are available in Lincoln and North Woodstock to the south and in Franconia and Littleton to the north.

Sights & Activities

Cannon Mountain Aerial Tramway CABLE CAR
(☎603-823-8800; www.cannonmt.com; 260 Tramway Dr; round trip adult/child 6-12yr $18/16; ⊙8:30am-5pm Jun–mid-Oct; P👪) This tram shoots up the side of Cannon Mountain, offering a breathtaking view of Franconia Notch. You can also hike up the mountain and take the tramway down (adult/child $13/10). At the summit, take the 1500ft walk along the **Rim Trail** to the observatory deck for gorgeous 360-degree views – on clear days you can see as far as Maine and Canada. There's a snack bar and picnic tables at the tram building. Located off I-93, exit 34B.

★Flume Gorge & the Basin HIKING
(☎603-745-8391; www.flumegorge.com; I-93, exit 34A; adult/child 6-12yr $16/14; ⊙8:30am-5pm early May-Jun & Sep–mid-Oct, to 5:30pm Jul & Aug) To see this natural wonder, take the 2-mile self-guided nature walk, which includes a 800ft boardwalk through the Flume, a natural 12ft- to 20ft-wide cleft in the granite bedrock. The granite walls tower 70ft to 90ft above you, with moss and plants growing from precarious niches and crevices. The Basin is a 15ft-deep granite pothole nearby.

Recreation Trail CYCLING, WALKING
(I-93, exit 34A) For a casual walk or bike ride, you can't do better than head out to this 8-mile paved trail that wends its way along the Pemigewasset River and through the notch. Bikes are available for rental with **Sport Thoma** (www.sportthoma.com; half-/full day $35/50) at Cannon Mountain, with a shuttle drop-off if you're only up for a one-way trip.

Information

Stop by the **Franconia Notch State Park Visitor Center** (☎603-745-8391; www.nhstateparks.org; I-93, exit 34A; ⊙8:30am-5pm mid-May–Jun & Sep-early Oct, to 5:30pm Jul & Aug, to 4:30pm mid-Oct–late Oct) for a wide range of information about the park and the region.

Bretton Woods & Crawford Notch

This beautiful 1773ft mountain pass on the western slopes of Mt Washington is deeply rooted in New Hampshire lore. In 1826 torrential rains here triggered massive mudslides, killing the Willey family in the valley below. The dramatic incident made the newspapers and fired the imaginations of painter Thomas Cole and author Nathaniel Hawthorne. Both men used the incident for inspiration, thus unwittingly putting Crawford Notch on tourist maps.

Even so, the area remained known mainly to locals and wealthy summer visitors who patronized the grand Mt Washington Hotel in Bretton Woods – until 1944, when President Roosevelt chose the hotel as the site of a conference to establish a post-WWII global economic order.

Today the hotel is as grand as ever, while a steady flow of visitors comes to hike the Presidential Range and climb Mt Washington – on foot or aboard a steam-powered locomotive on the dramatic Mt Washington Cog Railway.

Sights & Activities

★Crawford Notch State Park STATE PARK
(☎603-374-2272; www.nhstateparks.org; 1464 US 302, Hart's Location; ⊙visitor center 9:30am-5pm late May–mid-Oct, park year-round unless posted otherwise; Ⓟ) FREE This pretty park maintains an extensive system of hiking trails. From the Willey House visitor center, you can walk the easy 0.5-mile **Pond Loop Trail**, the 1-mile **Sam Willey Trail** and the **Ripley Falls Trail**, a 1-mile round-trip hike from US 302 via the **Ethan Pond Trail**. The trailhead for **Arethusa Falls**, a 1.5-mile one-way hike, is 0.5 miles south of the Dry River Campground on US 302. Serious hikers can also tackle the much longer trek up Mt Washington.

★Mt Washington Cog Railway RAIL
(☎603-278-5404; www.thecog.com; 3168 Base Station Rd; adult $72-78, child 4-12yr $41; ⊙daily Jun-Oct, Sat & Sun late Apr, May & Nov;) Purists walk and the lazy drive, but the quaintest way to reach Mt Washington's summit is via this cog railway. Since 1869 coal-fired, steam-powered locomotives have climbed a scenic 3.5-mile track up the mountainside (three hours round trip). Two of these old-fashioned trains run daily June to October. The steam trains are supplemented by faster, cleaner, biodiesel-fueled trains. Reservations recommended.

Arethusa Falls Trail HIKING
(US 302, Hart's Location) The highest waterfall in New Hampshire is your goal on this 3-mile round-trip hike in Crawford Notch. The moderately difficult trail ends at the base of the falls, which rise about 200ft. They are most photogenic in spring as snowmelt boosts the water levels. The parking area is 6 miles south of the Crawford Notch Depot.

Sleeping

★AMC Highland Center Lodge LODGE $$
(☎front desk 603-278-4453, reservations 603-466-2727; www.outdoors.org; NH 302, Bretton Woods; r incl breakfast & dinner per adult/child/teen $176/54/103, without bath $121/54/103; Ⓟ) This cozy Appalachian Mountain Club (AMC) lodge is set amid the splendor of Crawford Notch, an ideal base for hiking the trails crisscrossing the Presidential Range. The grounds are beautiful, rooms are basic but comfortable, meals are hearty and guests are outdoor enthusiasts. Discounts for AMC members. The information center,

open to the public, has loads of information about regional hiking.

Omni Mt Washington Hotel & Resort HOTEL $$$

(☎603-278-1000; www.omnihotels.com; 310 Mt Washington Hotel Rd, Bretton Woods; r/ste from $449/619; P ❄ @ ☎ ≋) Even if you're not staying here, don't miss the view of Mt Washington from a wicker chair on the veranda of this historic hotel, preferably with a cocktail in hand. Open since 1902, this grand place maintains a sense of fun – note the moose's head overlooking the lobby and the framed local wildflowers in many of the guest rooms.

Pinkham Notch

Pinkham Notch (2032ft) is a mountain-pass area known for its wild beauty, and its useful facilities for campers and hikers make it one of the most popular and crowded activity centers in the White Mountains. Wildcat Mountain and Tuckerman Ravine offer good skiing, and an excellent system of trails provides access to the natural beauties of Mt Washington and the Presidential Range, which stretches north from Crawford Notch to Mt Washington and then on to Mt Madison. For the less athletically inclined, the Mt Washington Auto Road provides easy – if white-knuckled – access to the summit, where you'll find a weather museum, a historic inn and sweeping views on clear days.

Activities

Tuckerman Ravine Trail HIKING

(361 NH 16, Pinkham Notch Visitor Center) It's not for everyone and you *must* be properly prepared, but this exhilarating hike to Mt Washington's summit, New England's highest mountain, is one for the bucket list. Highlights on the 4.2-mile trail (one way) include climbing a glacial cirque, strolling across an alpine plateau and navigating a half-mile boulder field. On clear days, summit views sweep across five states.

The mountain is renowned for its frighteningly bad weather – the average temperature on the summit is 26.5°F (-3°C). The mercury has fallen as low as -47°F (-43°C), but only risen as high as 72°F (22°C). About 256in (more than 21ft) of snow falls each year. (One year, it was 47ft.) At times the climate can mimic Antarctica's, and hurricane-force winds blow every three days or so, on average. In fact, the second-highest wind speed ever recorded was here during a storm in 1934, when gusts reached 231mph.

If you attempt to hike to the summit, pack warm, windproof clothes and shoes, even in high summer, and always consult with Appalachian Mountain Club (AMC) hut personnel. Don't be reluctant to turn back if the weather changes for the worse. Dozens of hikers who ignored such warnings and died are commemorated by trailside monuments and crosses.

Mt Washington Auto Road SCENIC DRIVE

(☎603-466-3988; www.mountwashingtonautoroad.com; NH 16; car & driver $31, extra adult/child 5-12yr $9/7, guided tours adult/child $36/16; ⏲8am-6pm mid-Jun–Aug, shorter hours May–mid-Jun & Sep-late Oct) One of New England's top adventures, the serpentine drive up the 7.6-mile Mt Washington Auto Road is not for the faint of heart. The Mt Washington Summit Rd Co operates this narrow, alpine toll road, which soars from the Pinkham Notch area to the parking lot just below the 6288ft summit. The price includes an audio-tour CD and entry to Mt Washington Observatory's **Extreme Weather Museum** (☎800-706-0432; www.mountwashington.org/visit-us; Mt Washington summit; $2, with Auto Road ticket free; ⏲hours vary depending on weather; P). 'This car climbed Mt Washington' bumper stickers are sold in the summit gift shop.

Sleeping

Joe Dodge Lodge LODGE $

(☎603-466-2727; www.outdoors.org/lodging/lodges/pinkham; 361 NH 16; r per person adult/child/teen incl breakfast & dinner from $86/39/74; P ❄ ☎) The AMC complex at Pinkham Notch incorporates this lodge, with dorms holding 100-plus beds. Rooms come in a variety of configurations and the price is per person. With the Tuckerman Ravine trailhead a few steps away, this cozy facility is a great place to overnight before hiking to the summit of Mt Washington. Reservations recommended. Discounts available for AMC members.

Glen House Hotel HOTEL $$$

(☎603-466-3420; www.glenhousehotel.com; 979 NH 16; r $249-369; P ❄ ☎ ≋ 🐾) Opening in late 2018, this classy number enjoys fresh rustic style and a location beside the Mt Washington Auto Road. The fifth hotel on the site since 1852, this incarnation embraces its location with big-window views of Mt Washington, clean-line Shaker-style furniture and whimsical touches such as a mounted moosehead made from colorful cloth.

Hanover

Hanover is the quintessential New England college town. On warm days, students toss Frisbees on the wide college green fronting Georgian ivy-covered buildings, while locals and academics mingle at the laid-back cafes, restaurants and shops lining Main St. Dartmouth College has long been the town's focal point, giving the area a vibrant connection to the arts.

Dartmouth was chartered in 1769 primarily 'for the education and instruction of Youth of the Indian Tribes.' Back then, the school was located in the forests where its prospective students lived. Although teaching 'English Youth and others' was its secondary purpose, in fact, Dartmouth College graduated few Native Americans and was soon attended almost exclusively by colonists. The college's most illustrious alumnus is Daniel Webster (1782–1852), who graduated in 1801 and went on to be a prominent lawyer, US senator, secretary of state and perhaps the USA's most esteemed orator.

Dartmouth College UNIVERSITY
(☎603-646-1110; www.dartmouth.edu) Hanover is all about Dartmouth College, so hit the campus. Join a free student-guided **campus walking tour** (☎603-646-2875; 10 N Main St, 6016 McNutt Hall) or just pick up a map at the admissions office and head off on your own.

Don't miss the **Baker-Berry Library** (☎603-646-2704; 25 N Main St; ⏲8am-2am Mon-Fri, 10am-2am Sat & Sun), splashed with the grand *Epic of American Civilization*, painted by the outspoken Mexican muralist José Clemente Orozco (1883–1949), who taught at Dartmouth in the 1930s.

★ **Hood Museum of Art** MUSEUM
(☎603-646-2808; http://hoodmuseum.dartmouth.edu; 6 E Wheelock St; ⏲10am-5pm Tue & Thu-Sat, to 9pm Wed, noon-5pm Sun) FREE Shortly after the college's founding in 1769, Dartmouth began to acquire artifacts of artistic or historical interest. Since then the collection has expanded to include nearly 70,000 items, which are housed at the Hood Museum of Art. The collection is particularly strong in American pieces, including Native American art. One of the highlights is a set of Assyrian reliefs from the Palace of Ashurnasirpal that dates to the 9th century BCE. Special exhibitions often feature contemporary artists.

Hanover Inn INN $$$
(☎603-643-4300; www.hanoverinn.com; 2 E Wheelock St; r $319-369, ste $369-569; ❄@📶🐾) Owned by Dartmouth College and situated directly opposite the college green, Hanover's loveliest guesthouse has nicely appointed rooms with elegant wood furnishings. It has a cocktail bar and a farm-to-table restaurant on-site.

ℹ Information

Hanover Area Chamber of Commerce (☎603-643-3115; www.hanoverchamber.org; 53 S Main St, Suite 208; ⏲9am-4pm Mon-Fri) also maintains a seasonal **information booth** (Dartmouth Green; ⏲mid-Jun–mid-Sep) on the village green.

MAINE

Maine offers numerous adventures, from summiting jagged peaks to kayaking cliff-lined shores. With vast forests, seaside villages and island getaways, the state invites seemingly limitless wandering.

Maine seems spoiled when it comes to nature's gifts. It has hundreds of miles of coastline, encompassing sea cliffs, sandy beaches and craggy wave-kissed shores. Offshore, there are countless islands for exploring, with scenic walks amid empty coves and misty forested shorelines, while villages nearby boast year-round populations that don't reach into the triple digits.

Inland, Maine has vast tracts of wilderness, with thick forests, alpine lakes and treeless boulder-strewn peaks. Such a magnificent landscape offers limitless adventures, and you can spend the day cycling along winding shore roads, kayaking beside curious harbor seals or hiking up above falcon nests to wondrous mountaintop overlooks.

History

Maine's past reaches back to the earliest Paleo-Indians, who left traces of a sometimes fascinating culture over the eons. The rugged, glacier-carved wilderness was a serious challenge for early European colonists, and the region has remained sparsely populated up to the present. Other key facets from Maine's history include the involvement of Mainers in the Civil War and the state's transformation from industrial workhouse to a 'Vacationland' for East Coasters.

In 1820 Maine at long last separated from Massachusetts and gained its statehood. Timber brought wealth to the interior. Fishing, shipbuilding, granite quarrying and farming were also boom industries, alongside manufacturing. Unfortunately, the boom days were not to last. By the turn of the 20th century, population growth stagnated and Maine became a backwater.

Maine's rustic, undeveloped landscape later became part of its great appeal to would-be visitors. Maine soon emerged as a summer cottage destination around the time the slogan 'Vacationland' (which still adorns Maine license plates) was coined in the 1890s. Today, tourists spend about $6 billion per year, supporting roughly 16% of the state's work force.

Information

Maine Bureau of Parks & Lands (207-287-3821; www.maine.gov/dacf/parks) Oversees 48 state parks and historic sites. Details of each park (including activities and camping) are on the website.

Maine Office of Tourism (www.visitmaine.com) Comprehensive website; can mail out maps and brochures.

Maine Tourism Association (www.mainetourism.com) Runs info centers along the principal routes into Maine: Calais, Fryeburg, Hampden, Houlton, Kittery, West Gardiner and Yarmouth. Each center is generally open 9am to 5:30pm; longer in summer (8am to 6pm).

Ogunquit

The Abenaki came up with the lovely name Ogunquit, which apparently means 'the beautiful place by the sea.' After a few minutes strolling around town, we were inclined to believe it meant, 'Family-friendly resort town with a thriving arts and LGBTIQ+ scene,' but our eastern woodland linguistic skills admittedly aren't up to snuff.

Seriously though, Ogunquit is simply a wonderful little arts colony, LGBTIQ+ vacation escape, and a spot where your kids can experience the American seaside holiday in all its quaint glory. Wide stretches of pounding surf front the Atlantic, while warm backcove waters make an idyllic setting for a swim. In summer, the 3-mile beach draws hordes of visitors from near and far, increasing the town's population exponentially.

Before its resort status, Ogunquit was a shipbuilding center in the 17th century. Later it became an important arts center when the Ogunquit art colony was founded in 1898.

Sights & Activities

Ogunquit Beach BEACH

(access from Beach St) A sublime stretch of family-friendly coastline, Ogunquit Beach is only a five-minute walk along Beach St, east of US 1. Walking to the beach is a good idea in summer as the parking lot fills up early (and it costs $4 per hour to park!). The 3-mile beach fronts Ogunquit Bay to the south; on the west side of the beach are the warmer waters of the tidal Ogunquit River.

★**Marginal Way** WALKING

(access from Shore Rd) Tracing the 'margin' of the sea, Ogunquit's famed mile-long footpath winds above the crashing gray waves, taking in grand sea vistas and rocky coves, and allowing for some excellent real-estate admiring. The neatly paved path, fine for children and slow walkers, is dotted with restful benches. It starts south of Beach St at Shore Rd and ends near **Perkins Cove** (access from Shore Rd).

Information

Gay Ogunquit (www.gayogunquit.com) Information for LGBTIQ+ visitors.

Ogunquit Chamber of Commerce (207-646-2939; www.ogunquit.org; 36 Main St/US 1; 9am-5pm Mon-Sat, 10am-4pm Sun late May-early Oct, 10am-4pm Mon-Fri rest of year) Located on US 1, a little way south of the town's center.

Portland

Seagulls scream, the smell of beer and fish fry flows through the streets like the fog off Casco Bay, and everywhere the salt wind licks your skin. Maine's largest city has capitalized on the gifts of its port history – the redbrick warehouse buildings, the narrow cobblestone streets – to become one of the hippest, most vibrant small cities in the Americas. You'll find excellent museums and galleries, abundant green space, and both a food culture and a brewing scene worthy of a town many times its size.

Maine Coast

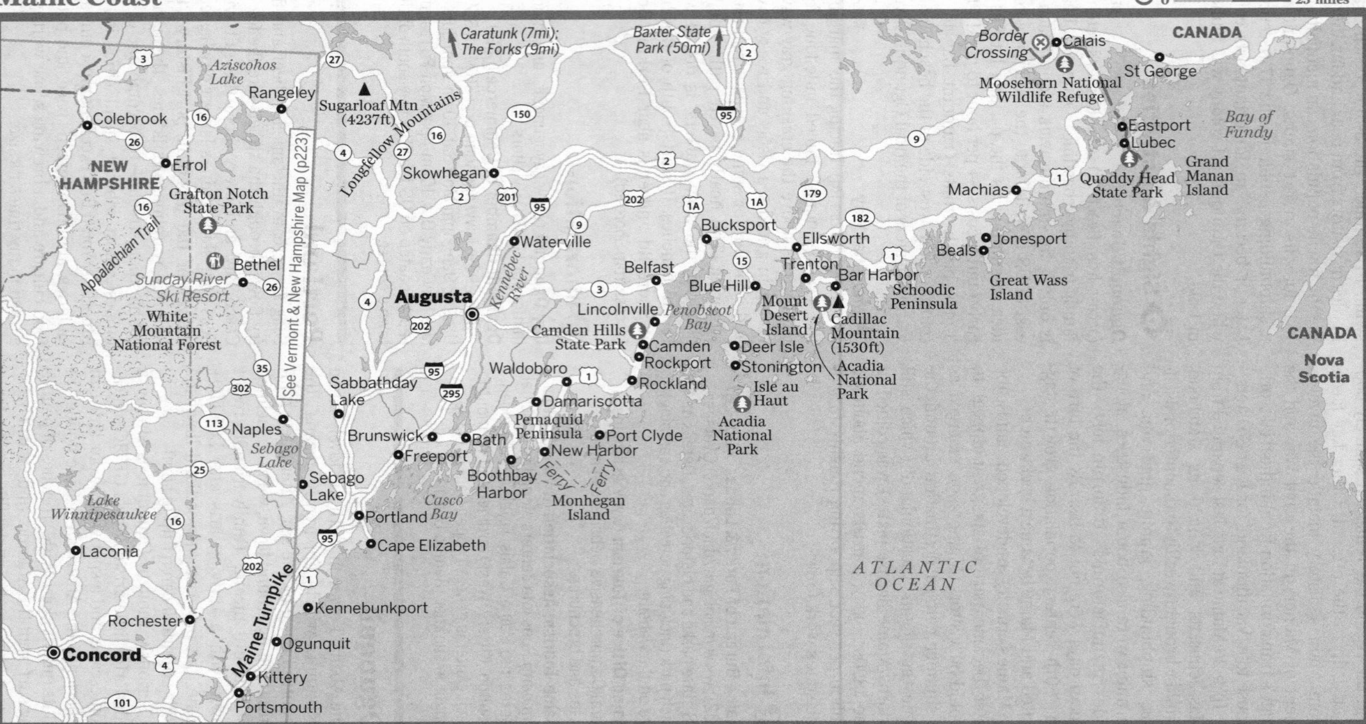
0 50 km
0 25 miles
CANADA
Border Crossing
Calais
St George
Moosehorn National Wildlife Refuge
Eastport
Lubec
Bay of Fundy
Grand Manan Island
Quoddy Head State Park
Machias
Jonesport
Beals
Great Wass Island
Schoodic Peninsula
Bar Harbor
Cadillac Mountain (1530ft)
Acadia National Park
Mount Desert Island
Trenton
Ellsworth
Bucksport
Blue Hill
Deer Isle
Stonington
Isle au Haut
Acadia National Park
Belfast
Penobscot Bay
Lincolnville
Camden Hills State Park
Camden
Rockport
Rockland
Waldoboro
Damariscotta
Pemaquid Peninsula
Port Clyde
New Harbor
Ferry
Ferry
Monhegan Island
Boothbay Harbor
Bath
Brunswick
Freeport
Casco Bay
Portland
Cape Elizabeth
Kennebunkport
Ogunquit
Kittery
Portsmouth
Maine Turnpike
Sabbathday Lake
Sebago Lake
Sebago Lake
Naples
Augusta
Kennebec River
Waterville
Skowhegan
Caratunk (7mi); The Forks (9mi)
Baxter State Park (50mi)
Longfellow Mountains
Sugarloaf Mtn (4237ft)
Rangeley
Aziscohos Lake
Colebrook
Errol
NEW HAMPSHIRE
Grafton Notch State Park
Appalachian Trail
Bethel
Sunday River Ski Resort
White Mountain National Forest
See Vermont & New Hampshire Map (p223)
Lake Winnipesaukee
Laconia
Rochester
Concord
ATLANTIC OCEAN
CANADA
Nova Scotia

Set on a peninsula, Portland's always been a city of the sea. Today, the Old Port district is the town's historic heart, with handsomely restored brick buildings filled with cafes, shops and bars. There are more hipsters than fishmongers living here these days, but there's also genuine ethnic diversity – Portland boasts a large African population – generally lacking in the rest of Maine.

Sights & Activities

★Fort Williams Park PARK
(207-767-3707; https://fortwilliams.org; 1000 Shore Rd, Cape Elizabeth; sunrise-sunset) FREE Four miles southeast of Portland on Cape Elizabeth, 90-acre Fort Williams Park is worth visiting simply for the panoramas and picnic possibilities. Stroll around the ruins of the fort, a late-19th-century artillery base, checking out the WWII bunkers and gun emplacements that still dot the rolling lawns (a German U-boat was spotted in Casco Bay in 1942). The fort actively guarded the entrance to Casco Bay until 1964.

★Portland Head Light LIGHTHOUSE
(207-799-2661; https://portlandheadlight.com; 1000 Shore Rd, Cape Elizabeth; museum adult/child $2/1; museum 10am-4pm Jun-Oct, Sat & Sun only Apr, May & Nov) Within Fort Williams Park stands the beloved, and much-photographed, Portland Head Light, the oldest of Maine's 52 functioning lighthouses. It was commissioned by President George Washington in 1791 and staffed until 1989, when machines took over. The keeper's house is now a museum, which traces the maritime and military history of the region.

Portland Museum of Art MUSEUM
(207-775-6148; www.portlandmuseum.org; 7 Congress Sq; adult/child $15/free, 4-8pm Fri free; 10am-6pm Sat-Wed, to 8pm Thu & Fri, shorter hours Oct-May) Founded in 1882, this well-respected museum houses an outstanding collection of American artists. Maine artists, including Winslow Homer, Edward Hopper, Louise Nevelson and Andrew Wyeth, are particularly well represented. You'll also find a few works by European masters, including Monet, Degas, Picasso and Renoir.

Eastern Promenade WALKING
(http://trails.org/our-trails/eastern-prom-trail) Don't leave town without having a walk or bicycle ride along this 2.1-mile trail, which offers superb, sweeping views of Casco Bay, all speckled with sailboats and rocky islets. The well-paved path has two small rises, but is otherwise flat and accessible to all levels of physical fitness. The promenade can be easily accessed throughout Portland's East End.

Sleeping

★Black Elephant Hostel HOSTEL $
(207-712-7062; www.blackelephanthostel.com; 33 Hampshire St; dm $40-60, d $65-150;) The Black Elephant is Portland's first dedicated hostel, and it's an exceptionally good one, with funky interior art, exterior murals, a central location and a range of clean and comfortable rooms. The lobby and kitchen spaces are super-colorful and inviting, and there's even a 'vampire' themed bathroom.

Press Hotel HOTEL $$$
(207-573-2425; www.thepresshotel.com; 119 Exchange St; r $220-413;) Opened in mid-2015, the Press Hotel, a creative conversion of the building that once housed the offices and printing plant of Maine's largest newspaper, has since become something of a Portland institution. The press theme shines in unique details – a wall of vintage typewriters, and old headlines on hallway wallpapers. Smart, navy-toned rooms are sexy and local art adorns walls.

Danforth Inn BOUTIQUE HOTEL $$$
(207-879-8755; www.danforthinn.com; 163 Danforth St; r $199-359, ste $699;) Staying at this ivy-shrouded West End boutique hotel feels like being a guest at an eccentric millionaire's mansion. Shoot pool in the wood-paneled games room (a former speakeasy) or climb into the rooftop cupola for views across Portland Harbor. The nine rooms are decorated with flair, in a sophisticated mix of antique and modern.

Eating

★Bayside American Cafe AMERICAN $
(207-774-0005; www.baysideamericancafe.com; 98 Portland St; mains $9-17; 7am-2pm;) This charming brunch and lunch spot is great for a rib-sticking meal to start your day. It uses steak in its corned beef and one of its eggs Benedict dishes; to go meatless, try the huevos rancheros. Staff are friendly and ingredients are often locally sourced. Reservations are accepted, otherwise expect a line.

Green Elephant VEGETARIAN, ASIAN $
(207-347-3111; http://greenelephantmaine.com; 608 Congress St; mains $12-16; 11:30am-2:30pm

& 5-9:30pm Mon-Sat, 5-9pm Sun;) Even carnivores shouldn't miss the vegetarian fare at this Zen-chic, Thai-inspired cafe (with lots of vegan and gluten-free options too). Start with the crispy spinach wontons, then move on to one of the stir-fries, pineapple brown rice, Thai ginger noodles or curry favorites like tofu tikka masala.

Central Provisions MODERN AMERICAN **$$**
(207-805-1085; www.central-provisions.com; 414 Fore St; lunch plates $4-18, dinner plates $5-30; 11am-2pm & 5-10pm Sun-Thu, to 10:30pm Fri & Sat) Snug, redbrick Central Provisions is a consistent winner in the Portland haute cuisine stakes. Angle for a seat at the bar, overlooking the line chefs in action, and choose from a masterful small-plates menu that swings from tuna crudo to suckling pig. Local oysters, fish and cheese are staples.

★**Fore Street** MODERN AMERICAN **$$$**
(207-775-2717; www.forestreet.biz; 288 Fore St; small plates $12-16, mains $26-42; 5:30-10pm Sun-Thu, to 10:30pm Fri & Sat) Fore Street is the lauded restaurant many consider to be the originator of today's food obsession in Portland. Chef-owner Sam Hayward has turned roasting into a high art: chickens turn on spits in the open kitchen as chefs slide iron kettles of mussels into the wood-burning oven. Local, seasonal eating is taken very seriously and the menu changes daily.

Drinking & Entertainment

★**Rising Tide Brewing Company** BREWERY
(207-370-2337; www.risingtidebrewing.com; 103 Fox St; tastings noon-7pm Mon-Sat, to 5pm Sun) In a pocket of town growing in stature (and with a neighboring distillery), Rising Tide is well worth investigating. Locals congregate in the car park, and food trucks visit in summer, from Wednesday to Sunday. Check the website for events (live music etc). Tours are held daily at 3pm and also on Saturday at 1pm and 5pm, and Sunday at 1pm.

Sagamore Hill BAR
(207-808-8622; www.sagamorehillmaine.com; 150 Park St; 4pm-1am) Early-20th-century elegance meets a 21st-century cocktail menu, plus lots of Teddy Roosevelt memorabilia and a ton of taxidermy at this excellent bar. The interior has an art-deco appeal that's tough not to love, especially after a Louisiana Purchase (rye, vermouth, bitters, charred thyme). Serves seasonal drinks, plus nonalcoholic mocktails.

Shopping

Maine Craft ARTS & CRAFTS
(207-808-8184; https://mainecrafts.org/center-formaine-craft/portland; 521 Congress St; 10am-6pm Sun-Wed, to 7pm Thu, to 8pm Fri & Sat) Past the clever title of this shop is an excellent retail and arts space, showcasing the best of the state's contemporary crafts and maker movement. You'll find handmade jewelry, objets d'art and general captivating creativity. Even the setting – Mechanic's Hall, a handsome 19th-century gem on the National Register of Historic Places – is superb.

Information

Ocean Gateway Information Center (207-772-5800; www.visitportland.com; 14 Ocean Gateway Pier; 9am-5pm Mon-Fri, to 4pm Sat & Sun Jun-Oct, shorter hours rest of year) Visitor information, down at the waterfront.

Getting There & Away

AIR

Portland International Jetport (PWM; 207-874-8877; www.portlandjetport.org; 1001 Westbrook St) is Maine's largest air terminal. It's served by domestic airlines, with nonstop flights to cities in the Eastern USA. Metro bus 5 takes you to the center of town for $1.50. Taxis are about $20 to downtown.

BUS

Greyhound (207-772-6588; www.greyhound.com; 950 Congress St) offers direct daily trips to Bangor and Boston, with connections on to the rest of the USA.

Concord Coach Lines (800-639-3317; https://concordcoachlines.com; 100 Thompson's Point Rd) operates daily buses between Boston (including Logan Airport; $30, two hours) and Portland, continuing on to mid-coast Maine towns. There are also services connecting Portland and the towns of Augusta ($16, one hour), Waterville ($18, 1¾ hours) and Bangor ($28, 2½ hours). Two services a day link Portland with New York City ($75, six hours).

TRAIN

The *Downeaster*, run by Amtrak, makes five trips daily between Boston and Portland ($29 to $39, 2½ hours) from **Portland Transportation Center** (100 Thompson's Point Rd).

Services extend up the midcoast all the way to Brunswick.

Midcoast Maine

On a map, rocky 'fingers' claw at Penobscot Bay, each peninsula clad in ancient forests, studded with lonely, windswept fishing villages and fog-wreathed paths through the woods. This is midcoast Maine. But it's also resort towns that cater to wealthy vacationers from the northeast and Canada, offering cheap lobster rolls, organic farm-to-table restaurants, writing retreats and tall masts creaking in harbors icebound in winter, and sun-kissed in summer. Imagine Maine, a hybrid of mountains, ocean, forests and villages, and this, too, is the midcoast.

The English first settled this region in 1607, which coincided with the Jamestown settlement in Virginia. Unlike their southerly compatriots, though, these early settlers returned to England within a year. British colonization resumed in 1620. After suffering through the long years of the French and Indian War, the area became home to a thriving shipbuilding industry, which continues today.

Getting There & Around

US 1 is the key access route for this part of the state, but note that roads along the coast flood with traffic during the summer tourist season.

Concord Coach Lines operates daily buses between Boston (including Logan International Airport) and Portland, continuing on to midcoast Maine towns (Bath, Belfast, Brunswick, Camden, Damariscotta, Lincolnville, Rockland, Searsport and Waldoboro). Greyhound buses stop in Bangor, Portland, Bath, Rockland and various other towns.

Bath

Known as the 'City of Ships,' this quaint Kennebec River town was once home to 20-plus shipyards producing more than a quarter of early America's wooden sailing vessels. In Bath's 19th-century heyday, it was one of Maine's largest cities, with a bustling downtown lined with banks and grand municipal buildings. Bath-built schooners and clipper ships sailed the seven seas and the city's name was known far and wide. Even today, the navy utilizes the shipyards at Bath Iron Works; as you leave town driving east on Rte 1, you may see warships being built along the Kennebec River.

Downtown, redbrick sidewalks and solid 19th-century buildings line quaint Front St. South of Bath stretch two scenic peninsulas well worth a detour: ME 209 takes you to **Phippsburg**, home to excellent beaches and a historic fort, while ME 127 runs south to **Georgetown**, terminating at an island-dotted cove.

★Maine Maritime Museum MUSEUM
(207-443-1316; www.mainemaritimemuseum.org; 243 Washington St; adult/child $17.50/10.50; 9:30am-5pm) There's a palpable mix of reflective nostalgia and horizon-scanning adventure at this wonderful museum, which preserves the Kennebec's long shipbuilding tradition with paintings, models and hands-on exhibits that tell the tale of 400 years of seafaring. The on-site 19th-century **Percy & Small Shipyard**, preserved by the museum, is a working wooden-boat shipyard, and there's no shortage of enthusiasts on hand to answer questions on such craft.

Boothbay Harbor

Once a beautiful little seafarers' village on a wide blue harbor, Boothbay Harbor is now an extremely popular tourist resort in the summer, when its narrow and winding streets are packed with visitors. Still, there's good reason to join the holiday masses in this picturesque place. Overlooking a pretty waterfront, large, well-kept Victorian houses crown the town's many knolls, and a wooden footbridge ambles across the harbor. From May to October, whale-watching is a major draw.

After you've strolled the waterfront along Commercial St and the business district along Todd and Townsend Aves, walk along McKown St to the top of **McKown Hill** for a fine view. Then, take the footbridge across the harbor to the town's East Side, where there are several huge dockside seafood restaurants.

Boothbay and **East Boothbay** are separate from Boothbay Harbor, the largest, busiest and prettiest of the three towns.

Topside Inn B&B $$$
(207-633-5404; www.topsideinn.com; 60 McKown St; r $239-389; May–mid-Oct; P) Atop McKown Hill, this grand gray mansion has Boothbay's best harbor views. Rooms are elegantly turned out in crisp nautical prints and beachy shades. Main-house rooms have more historic charm, but rooms in the two adjacent modern guesthouses are sunny and lovely too. Enjoy the sunset from

an Adirondack chair on the inn's sloping, manicured lawn.

★ Shannon's Unshelled SEAFOOD $

(☎ 207-446-4921; www.shannonsunshelled.biz; 11 Granary Way; mains $7-15; ⊙ from 10:30am; 🐾) If you like your lobster rolls simple, with no accoutrements but melted butter on the side, Shannon's is ideal. The meat is fresh and there's lots of it, and it comes on thick, nicely toasted bread. Shannon's closes when it runs out of lobster – sometimes late afternoon, sometimes much earlier.

Cabbage Island Clambakes SEAFOOD $$$

(☎ 207-633-7200; www.cabbageislandclambakes.com; 22 Commercial St, Pier 6; clambake incl boat tour $70; ⊙ Jul–mid-Sep) A prized Maine tradition: a scenic cruise from Boothbay Harbor to the small, family-owned Cabbage Island, where a traditional clambake provides a fabulously memorable feast for diners, who can explore the island in between courses. Chow down on chowder, steamed clams, lobster and all the fixings, plus delicious blueberry cake. Lunch cruise daily, plus an additional departure on weekends. Book ahead.

ℹ Information

Boothbay Harbor Region Chamber of Commerce (☎ 207-633-2353; www.boothbayharbor.com; 192 Townsend Ave; ⊙ 8am-5pm Mon-Fri, 9am-4pm Sat Jun-Sep) offers good info on its website; it also operates a downtown **information center** (17 Commercial St; ⊙ 9am-6pm late May-early Oct) in summer.

Rockland

This thriving port boasts a large fishing fleet and a proud year-round population that gives Rockland a vibrancy lacking in some other midcoast towns. Main St is a window into the city's sociocultural diversity, with a jumble of working-class diners, bohemian cafes and high-end restaurants alongside galleries, old-fashioned storefronts and one of the state's best art museums, the Center for Maine Contemporary Art (CMCA). Rockland is developing a reputation as an art center, partly thanks to the CMCA's relocation here in 2016.

Settled in 1769, Rockland was once an important shipbuilding center and a transportation hub for goods moving up and down the coast. Today, tall-masted sailing ships still fill the harbor, as Rockland is a center for Maine's busy windjammer cruises (along with Camden).

Rockland is also the birthplace of poet Edna St Vincent Millay (1892–1950), who grew up in neighboring Camden.

👁 Sights & Activities

★ Rockland Breakwater Lighthouse LIGHTHOUSE

(☎ 207-542-7574; www.rocklandharborlights.org; Samoset Rd; ⊙ 10am-5pm Sat & Sun late May–mid-Oct) FREE Tackle the rugged stone breakwater that stretches almost 1 mile into Rockland Harbor from Jameson Point at the harbor's northern shore. Made of granite blocks, this 'walkway', which took 18 years to build, ends at the Rockland Breakwater Lighthouse, a sweet light sitting atop a brick house, with a sweeping view of town.

While on the breakwater, watch for slippery rocks and ankle-twisting gaps between stones. Bring a sweater, and don't hike if a storm is on the horizon.

Farnsworth Art Museum MUSEUM

(☎ 207-596-6457; www.farnsworthmuseum.org; 16 Museum St; adult/child $15/free; ⊙ 10am-5pm Jun-Oct, to 8pm Wed Jul-Sep, closed Mon Nov, Dec, Apr & May, 10am-4pm Wed-Sun Jan-Mar) One of the country's best small regional museums, the Farnsworth houses a collection spanning 200 years of American art. Artists who have lived or worked in Maine are the museum's definite strength – look for works by the Wyeth family (Andrew, NC and Jamie), Edward Hopper, Louise Nevelson, Rockwell Kent and Robert Indiana. Exhibits on the Wyeth family continue in the **Wyeth Center**, in a renovated church across the garden from the main museum (open in summer).

Maine Windjammer Association CRUISE

(☎ 800-807-9463; www.sailmainecoast.com; ⊙ cruises late May–mid-Oct) Although traveling by schooner largely went out of style at the dawn of the 20th century, adventurers can still explore the rugged Maine coast the old-fashioned way: aboard fast sailing ships, or windjammers. Nine of these multimasted vessels anchor at Rockland and Camden and offer trips ranging from overnight to 11 days around Penobscot Bay and further up the coast.

Sleeping & Eating

Captain Lindsey Hotel BOUTIQUE HOTEL $$

(207-596-7950; www.lindseyhotel.com; 5 Lindsey St; r $215;) There's a sophisticated seafaring theme at this nine-room boutique hotel on a side street just steps from Main St. The building started as a sea-captain's home, but has had other incarnations; check out the 'snack vault' and the handsome oak-paneled breakfast room, or get cozy by the fire in your guest room or in the hotel library.

★**Fog Bar & Cafe** AMERICAN $$

(207-593-9371; www.facebook.com/Fogbarcafe; 328 Main St; mains $16-23; 4:30-10pm Thu-Mon) Industrial-chic aesthetic meets an experimental theater, and everything gets overlaid with maritime Maine ingredients and flourishes. The menu changes according to what's fresh and seasonal – in fall you might try saag pumpkin curry, pork belly and roasted apples or pot pies you'd fight your family for. The cocktails are great too.

Information

Penobscot Bay Regional Chamber of Commerce (207-596-0376; www.camdenrockland.com; 1 Park Dr; 9am-5pm Jun-Oct, to 4pm Mon-Fri Nov-May) Visitor center just off Main St (in the same building as the Maine Lighthouse Museum).

Getting There & Away

Cape Air (www.capeair.com) connects Rockland's **Knox County Regional Airport** (207-594-4131; www.knoxcountymaine.gov/airport; 19 Airport Rd, Owls Head), 3.5 miles south of town, and Boston's Logan International Airport. Fares are around $80 to $100 one way.

Concord Coach Lines (www.concordcoachlines.com) runs buses to and from Boston ($35, 4½ hours), Portland ($23, two hours) and various other midcoast towns, departing from the **Maine State Ferry Terminal** (517a Main St).

Downeast Maine

Without question, this is quintessential Maine: as you head further up the coast toward Canada, the peninsulas seem to narrow, jutting further into the sea. The fishing villages get smaller; the lobster pounds are closer to the water. If you make time to drive to the edge of the shore, south off US 1, let it be here.

The star of the midcoast is Mount Desert Island, home to the spectacular Acadia National Park, where the mountains meet the sea. It offers some of the best hiking in coastal Maine. Island destinations worth visiting include the vibrant summer resort town of Bar Harbor, the elegant village of Northeast Harbor and heart-of-gold Southwest Harbor.

For quiet walks and traditional coastal villages away from the tourist throngs, continue further up the coast from Bar Harbor all the way to the rugged sea cliffs near Lubec, the last town before the Canadian border.

Information

Hulls Cove Visitor Center (207-288-3338; www.nps.gov/acad; ME 3; 8:30am-4:30pm mid-Apr–Jun, Sep & Oct, 8am-6pm Jul & Aug) anchors the park's main Hulls Cove entrance, 3 miles northwest of Bar Harbor. Buy your park pass and pick up maps and info here. The 27-mile-long Park Loop Road starts near here.

When the visitor center is closed (November to mid-April), head to the **Bar Harbor Chamber of Commerce** (Acadia Welcome Center; 207-288-5103; www.visitbarharbor.com; 2 Cottage St; 8am-4pm). National park staff provide information there during winter and spring.

Acadia National Park

The only national park in all of New England, **Acadia** (207-288-3338; www.nps.gov/acad; 7-day admission per car/motorcycle $30/25, walk-ins & cyclists $15) offers unrivaled coastal beauty and activities for both leisurely hikers and adrenaline junkies. Most people spend about three days here, which is just enough to take in the park highlights. But you could easily spend a week, taking in mountaintop hikes, bike rides, scenic drives and shoreline strolls, as well as leaving time to relax on the shores of Echo Lake or Sand Beach.

The park, which incorporates both coastline and mountains, protects a remarkably diverse landscape. You can spend the morning checking out tidal pools and watching the sea crash against the cliffs down by the waterfront, then head into the interior for a walk through dense forest

PARK LOOP ROAD

Looping around the eastern half of Mount Desert Island, this 27-mile road provides a fine overview of Acadia's many natural highlights. In summer, it gets quite crowded. Go early (strike at sunrise!) or consider doing the route by bus. The free **Island Explorer** (www.exploreacadia.com) shuttle (route 4) makes the whole loop during the summer.

Start off at the Hulls Cove Visitor Center (p247), located around 3.5 miles northwest of Bar Harbor. Pick up a map, learn about any trail closures and hit the road. From the visitor center it's about 4 miles southeast to the start of the Park Loop Rd. Once you turn onto this road (one-way until just before Jordan Pond House), slow down and enjoy the view.

After about 2.5 miles, you'll turn off onto the **Wild Gardens of Acadia** (Park Loop Rd & ME 3) FREE. Here you'll see some 400 different plant species representing all of Acadia's unique biospheres. Afterwards, visit the nearby **Abbe Museum at Sieur de Monts Spring** (207-288-3519; www.abbemuseum.org; 49 Sweetwater Circel; adult/child $3/1; 10am-5pm late May-Oct), with exhibits on the island's original inhabitants. Continuing south you'll pass a few trailheads, including the start of the challenging **Precipice Trail**.

A little further along, make the turnoff to **Sand Beach**. This lovely stretch of sandy shoreline is one of Acadia's unique finds. But the water is freezing! Down the road is the **Thunder Hole**, worth a stop to see the surf crashing into a cleft in the granite. The effect is most dramatic with a strong incoming tide.

Otter Cliff, not far south of Thunder Hole, is a wall of pink granite rising from the sea. This area is popular with rock climbers. From here, follow the twists and turns for another 5 or so miles to the **Jordan Pond House** (207-276-3316; https://jordanpondhouse.com; tea & popovers $11, mains $13-29; 11am-7pm mid-May–mid-Oct). Take a break for tea and the restaurant's famous popovers (buttery, hollow muffins) served with jam. Afterwards, you can stroll around the lake, which intersects with several trails in the north and south. Another 4 miles along, you'll pass the turnoff to **Cadillac Mountain**. Drive up to the top for sublime island views.

up past a boulder-filled ridgeline with osprey and the occasional bald eagle soaring overhead. There are scenic lakes and ponds to discover too, plus plenty of fine picnic spots.

Bar Harbor

The agreeable hub for Acadia visits, Bar Harbor is crowded for the warmer months of the year with vacationers and cruise-ship passengers. Downtown is packed with souvenir stores, ice-cream shops, cafes and bars, each advertising bigger and better happy hours, early-bird specials or two-for-one deals. The quieter residential backstreets seem to have almost as many B&Bs as private homes.

Although Bar Harbor's hustle and bustle is not for everybody, it has by far the most amenities of any town around here. Even if you stay elsewhere, you'll probably wind up here to eat dinner, grab a drink or schedule a kayaking, sailing or rock-climbing tour.

Bar Harbor's busiest season is late June through August. There's a short lull just after Labor Day (early September); it gets busy again during foliage season, which lasts through mid-October. The season ends the weekend following Columbus Day with the Mount Desert Island Marathon (www.runmdi.org).

Sleeping & Eating

Acadia Inn HOTEL $$
(207-288-3500; www.acadiainn.com; 98 Eden St; r $119-229; mid-Apr–Oct; P) This traditional 95-room hotel with helpful staff sits beside a trail leading into the park. The good-sized rooms are smart and comfortable, there's a laundry and a heated pool, and the park shuttle stops here in summer. It's a good choice if you don't mind being a mile or so out of the town center.

★ **Bass Cottage Inn** INN $$$
(207-288-1234; www.basscottage.com; 14 The Field; r $280-460; mid-May–Oct) If most Bar Harbor B&Bs rate about a '5' in terms of stylishness, this Gilded Age mansion deserves an '11.' The 10 light-drenched guest rooms have an elegant summer-cottage chic, all crisp white linens and understated

botanical prints. Tinkle the ivories at the parlor's grand piano or read a novel beneath the Tiffany stained-glass ceiling of the wood-paneled sitting room.

★ Havana LATIN AMERICAN **$$$**
(☎ 207-288-2822; www.havanamaine.com; 318 Main St; mains $30-42; ⏲ 4:30-9pm Tue-Sat May-Oct, plus 9:30am-2pm Sun Jul & Aug) First things first: order a refreshing mojito or caipirinha. Then you can take your time with the menu and the epic global wine list. Havana puts a Latin spin on dishes that highlight local produce, and the kitchen output is accomplished. Signature dishes include seafood paella, braised lamb shank and a deliciously light lobster *moqueca* (Brazilian-style stew with coconut milk).

Inland Maine

Western Maine receives far fewer visitors than the coast, which thrills the outdoorsy types who love its dense forests and solitary peaks just the way they are. While much of the land is still wilderness, there are some notable settlements. The fine old town of Bethel and the mountain setting of Rangeley are relatively accessible to city dwellers in the northeast, while Bridgton's quirky offerings make it a cool weekend retreat.

In the fall, leaf-peepers make their way inland with cameras and picnic baskets. In winter, skiers and snowmobilers turn the mountains into their playground. In the warmer months, the lakes, rivers, campgrounds and hiking trails draw lovers of the great outdoors.

This is rural America at its most rustic. So bring a map and don't expect to rely on your cell phone – signals can be few and far between in these parts.

ℹ Getting Around

A car is necessary to explore this rustic, rural heartland, and there are many scenic routes to choose from. ME 302 from Portland to Bridgton and Fryeburg is a good start; you can then wend your way north to Bethel and Rangeley. Scenic overlooks abound.

Bethel

A 90-minute drive northwest of Portland, Bethel is surprisingly lively and refined for a town surrounded on all sides by deep, dark woods. Summer visitors have been coming here to escape the coastal humidity since the 1800s, and many of its fine old cottages and lodges are still operating. It's a prime spot to be in during Maine's colorful fall-foliage months and during the winter ski season.

If you head west on US 2 toward New Hampshire, be sure to admire the **Shelburne birches**, a high concentration of the white-barked trees that grow between Gilead and Shelburne.

Grafton Notch State Park STATE PARK
(☎ 207-824-2912; www.maine.gov/graftonnotch; 1941 Bear River Rd/ME 26; adult/child $4/1; ⏲ 9am-sunset) Sitting astride the Grafton Notch Scenic Byway within the Mahoosuc Range, this rugged park is a stunner. Carved by a glacier that retreated 12,000 years ago, the Notch is a four-season playground, chock-full of waterfalls, gorges, lofty viewpoints and hiking trails, including over 20 miles of the Appalachian Trail (www.appalachiantrail.org).

Peregrine falcons build nests in the cliffs, helping the park earn its spot on the **Maine Birding Trail** (www.mainebirdingtrail.com); the best viewing is May to October.

ℹ Information

Bethel Area Chamber of Commerce (☎ 800-442-5826, 207-824-2282; www.bethelmaine.com; 8 Station Pl; ⏲ 9am-5pm Mon-Fri year-round, weekend hours vary in high season; 📶) This helpful organization maintains an information office in the Bethel Station building, with loads of handouts on various sights, trails and activities.

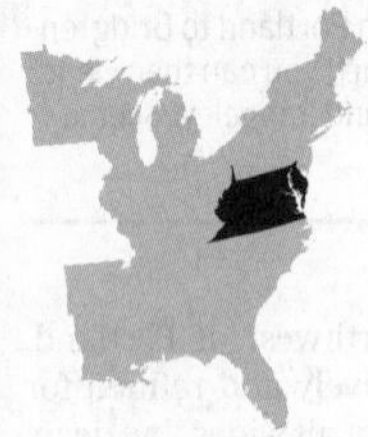

Washington, DC & the Capital Region

Includes ➡

Washington, DC 251
Maryland 280
Baltimore 280
Annapolis 286
Delaware 293
Virginia 298
Historic Triangle 304
The Piedmont 308
Shenandoah Valley 314
West Virginia 322
Monongahela National Forest 325

Best Places to Eat

- ➡ Rose's Luxury (p271)
- ➡ Woodberry Kitchen (p285)
- ➡ L'Opossum (p311)
- ➡ Public Fish & Oyster (p314)
- ➡ Faidley's (p285)

Best Places to Sleep

- ➡ Kimpton George Hotel (p269)
- ➡ Georges (p318)
- ➡ HI Richmond (p311)

Why Go?

No matter your politics, it's hard not to fall for the nation's capital. Iconic monuments and vast (and free) museums are just the beginning of the great DC experience. There's much more to discover: leafy, cobblestoned neighborhoods, sprawling markets, heady multicultural nightspots and global cuisine. And, of course, the corridors of power. Beyond the Beltway, the diverse landscapes of Maryland, Virginia, West Virginia and Delaware offer potent enticement to travel beyond the marble city.

Craggy mountains, rushing rivers, rich nature reserves (including islands where wild horses run), sparkling beaches, historic villages and the magnificent Chesapeake Bay form the backdrop to memorable adventures: sailing, hiking, rafting, camping or just sitting on a pretty stretch of shoreline, planning the next seafood feast. It's a place where traditions run deep, from the nation's birthplace to Virginia's bluegrass scene.

When to Go

Washington DC

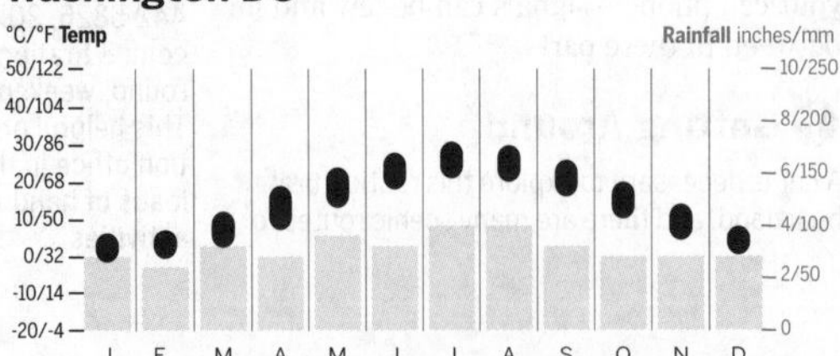

Jun–Aug Warm, sunny days across the region. Accommodation prices peak (up 30% on average).

Apr & May, Sep & Oct Milder temperatures; can be rainy. Wildflowers bloom, especially in May.

Nov–Mar Winter is high season at ski resorts, with busy ski lifts, accomodations and restaurants.

History

The modern story of America began in 1607 when a determined band of colonists built a fort on the banks of the James River, VA. Named Jamestown, this small community would become the New World's first permanent English settlement. Ever since, residents of the Mid-Atlantic have witnessed – and sparked – transformational moments in American history: wars against the British, the creation of a new nation, slavery and its abolishment, the Civil War and Reconstruction, and the labor and Civil Rights movements.

WASHINGTON, DC

The US capital is home to the corridors of power, where visionaries and demagogues roam. Along with that comes presidential monuments and war memorials, green parks and fantastic museums. Beyond the National Mall, visitors will discover tree-lined neighborhoods, vibrant immigrant populations, and a palpable dynamism percolating just beneath the surface. There's always a buzz here – no surprise, as DC attracts more talent than any city of this size deserves. Plan on jam-packed days sightseeing at museums and monuments, and lively evenings sipping local brews and chowing down in diverse restaurants.

History

Following the Revolutionary War, a balance was struck between Northern and Southern politicians, who wanted to plant a federal city somewhere between their power bases. Potential capitals such as Boston, Philadelphia and Baltimore were rejected by Southern plantation owners, for being too urban-industrial, so it was decided a new city would be carved at the midway point of the 13 colonies, along the banks of the Potomac River. Maryland and Virginia donated the land.

DC was torched by the British during the War of 1812, and ceded the south-bank slave port of Alexandria to Virginia in 1846 (when abolition talk was buzzing in the capital). Over the years, DC evolved along diverging tracks: as a marbled temple to the federal government on one side, and as an urban ghetto for northbound African Americans and overseas immigrants on the other. For decades, the city was governed by the US Congress. The city finally got its own mayor in 1973 (Walter Washington, among the first African American mayors of a major American city). Today DC residents are taxed as other American citizens, yet they lack a voting seat in Congress. DC has undergone extensive gentrification since the late 1990s. A booming economy ensures that the cost of living continues to be among the highest in the nation.

Sights

National Mall

A nation is many things: its people, its history, its politics and its amassed knowledge. Somehow, each one of these is given architectural life on the National Mall, the center of iconography of the most iconic city in America. This is where the nation's ideals are expressed in educational institutions, monuments and memorials. It's also where Americans come to protest, to rally and to watch presidents get inaugurated. A monument-studded park edged by the magnificent Smithsonian museums, this must-visit destination provides days – if not weeks – of enjoyment and edification for visitors.

★**Lincoln Memorial** MONUMENT

(☎202-426-6841; www.nps.gov/linc; 2 Lincoln Memorial Circle NW; 24hr; Circulator National Mall, M Orange, Silver, Blue Line to Foggy Bottom-GWU) Anchoring the Mall's west end is the hallowed shrine to Abraham Lincoln, who gazes across the **Reflecting Pool** beneath his neoclassical, Doric-columned abode. The words of his Gettysburg Address and Second Inaugural speech flank the huge marble statue on the north and south walls. On the steps, Martin Luther King Jr delivered his famed 'I Have a Dream' speech; look for the engraving that marks the spot (it's on the landing 18 stairs from the top).

★**National Air & Space Museum** MUSEUM

(☎202-633-2214; www.airandspace.si.edu; cnr 6th St & Independence Ave SW; 10am-5:30pm; ; Circulator National Mall, M Orange, Silver, Blue, Green, Yellow Line to L'Enfant Plaza) FREE The legendary exhibits at this hugely popular museum include the Wright brothers' flyer, Chuck Yeager's Bell X-1, Charles Lindbergh's Spirit of St Louis, Howard Hughes'

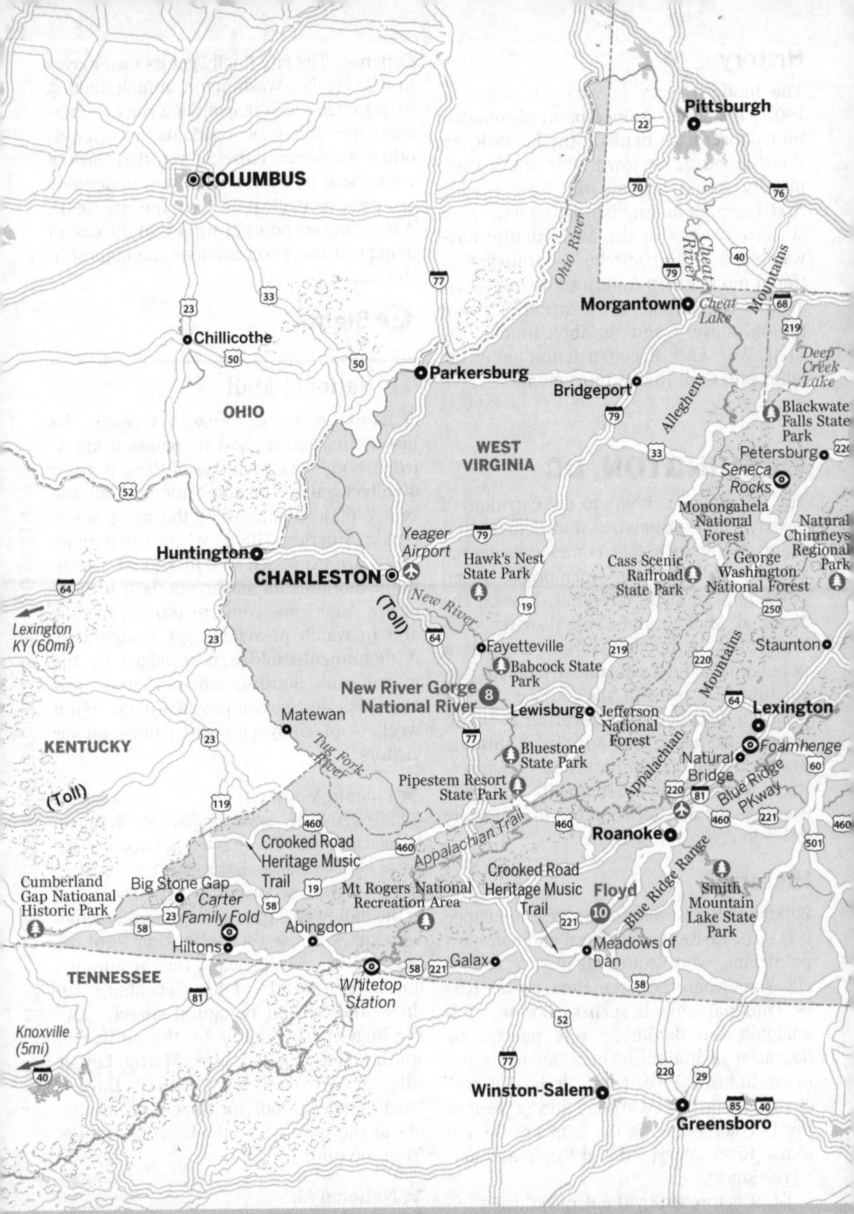

Washington, DC & the Capital Region Highlights

1. **National Air & Space Museum** (p251) Visiting Washington, DC's museums.
2. **Lincoln Memorial** (p251) Watching the sun set over the monument.
3. **Colonial Williamsburg** (p304) Tracing America's roots at this living-history museum.
4. **Annapolis** (p286) Exploring the city's historic and nautical past with a stroll through the capitol, the Naval Academy and along Main St.
5. **Shenandoah National Park** (p316) Taking a Sunday drive on Skyline Drive, followed

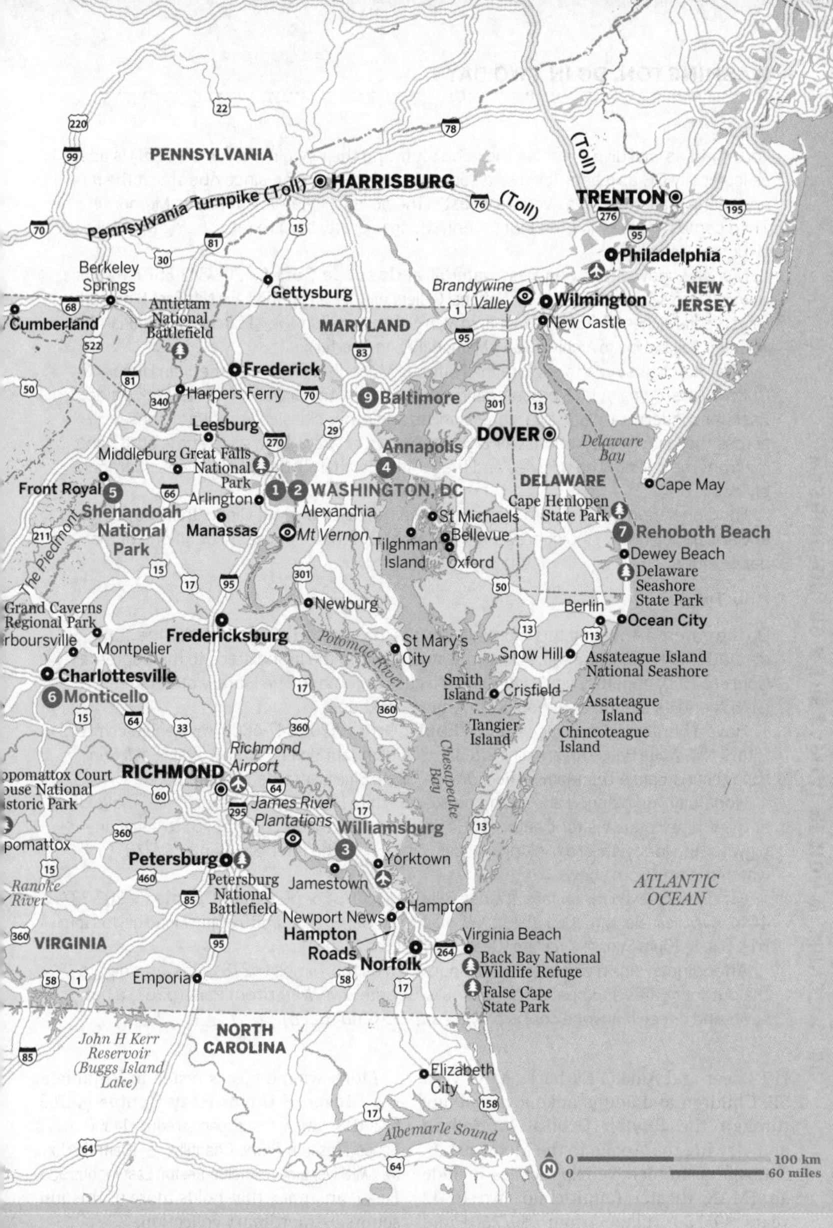

by hiking and camping under the stars.

6 Monticello (p312) Marveling at Thomas Jefferson's masterpiece.

7 Rehoboth Beach (p294) Strolling the boardwalk in this family- and gay-friendly resort.

8 New River Gorge National River (p327) Tackling the Gauley River rapids.

9 Faidley's (p285) Savoring one of the world's best crab cakes in Baltimore.

10 Floyd (p321) Feeling the beat of the old-time music at a jamboree.

WASHINGTON, DC IN TWO DAYS...

Day One

You might as well dive right into the good stuff, and the Lincoln Memorial (p251) is about as iconically DC as it gets. It's also a convenient starting point, since Abe sits at the far end of the Mall. Next up as you walk east is the powerful Vietnam Veterans Memorial. Then comes the Washington Monument, which is pretty hard to miss, being DC's tallest structure and all.

Munch sandwiches by an artsy waterfall at **Cascade Café** (☎202-842-6679; www.nga.gov/visit/cafes/cascade-cafe.html; National Gallery of Art, Constitution Ave NW, East Bldg, concourse; sandwiches $7-9.50; ⏲11am-3pm Mon-Sat, to 4pm Sun; 👪; 🚌Circulator National Mall, Ⓜ Green, Yellow Line to Archives-Navy Memorial-Penn Quarter).

After lunch, it's time to explore the National Museum of African American History & Culture (assuming you've procured a ticket) or the National Gallery of Art. Pick a side: East, for modern; or West, for Impressionists and other classics. Afterward, mosey across the lawn to the National Air & Space Museum (p251) and gape at the stuff hanging from the ceiling. The missiles and the Wright Brothers' original plane are incomparably cool.

For dinner, hop the Metro to Bistrot du Coin (p273) in Dupont Circle, then sip cocktails at Bar Charley (p277), hoist brews with locals at Board Room (p277) or hit one of the dance clubs.

Day Two

Do the government thing this morning. Start in the Capitol (p262) and tour the statue-cluttered halls. Then walk across the street and up the grand steps to the Supreme Court (p263); hopefully you'll get to hear a case argument. The Library of Congress (p263) and its 532 miles of books blow minds next door.

Have a burger amid politicos at **Old Ebbitt Grill** (☎202-347-4800; www.ebbitt.com; 675 15th St NW, White House Area; mains $18-32; ⏲7:30am-1am Mon-Fri, from 8:30am Sat & Sun, happy hour 3-6pm & 11pm-1am; Ⓜ Red, Orange, Silver, Blue Line to Metro Center).

Hopefully you planned ahead and booked a White House (p264) tour. If not, make do at the White House Visitor Center (p264). Pop into Off the Record (p276) to see if any bigwigs and lobbyists are clinking glasses. Zip over to the Kennedy Center (p278) to watch the free 6pm show.

For dinner, have French fare at Chez Billy Sud (p275) or pizza at **Il Canale** (☎202-337-4444; www.ilcanale.com; 1065 31st St NW; mains $23-32; ⏲11:30am-10:30pm Mon-Thu, to 11pm Fri & Sat, to 10pm Sun; 🚌Circulator Georgetown-Union Station).

After dinner, sink a pint in a friendly pub such as the Tombs (p278). On warm nights the outdoor cafes and boating action make Georgetown Waterfront Park (p267) a hot spot. And check if anyone cool is playing at 9:30 Club (p278).

H-1 Racer and Amelia Earhart's natty Vega 5B. Children and adults alike love walking through the **Skylab Orbital Workshop** and viewing the 'Apollo to the Moon' exhibit upstairs. Immersive experiences include an IMAX theater (adult/child two to 12 years $9/7.50), planetarium ($9/7.50) and flight simulators ($8 to $12 each).

On most days from mid-March to early September, the museum extends its hours and stays open until 7:30pm. Exhibits are being overhauled until 2025, with new exhibits such as 'Destination Moon', a comprehensive look at the history of lunar exploration, being added. Other exhibitions will be refreshed.

More avionic pieces reside in Virginia at the **Steven F Udvar-Hazy Center** (☎703-572-4118; www.airandspace.si.edu; 14390 Air & Space Museum Pkwy, Chantilly; ⏲10am-5:30pm; 👪; Ⓜ Silver Line to Wiehle-Reston East for bus 983) FREE, an annex that holds more of this museum's extraordinary collection.

★Vietnam Veterans Memorial — MONUMENT

(www.nps.gov/vive; 5 Henry Bacon Dr NW; ⏲24hr; 🚌Circulator National Mall, Ⓜ Orange, Silver, Blue Line to Foggy Bottom-GWU) Maya Lin's design for this hugely evocative memorial takes the form of a black, low-lying 'V' – an expression of the psychic scar wrought by the Vietnam War. The monument descends into the earth, with the names of the war's 58,000-plus American casualties – listed in the order they died – chiseled into the dark, reflective wall. It's a subtle but profound monument – and all the more surprising as Lin was only 21 when she designed it.

★National Gallery of Art MUSEUM
(☎202-737-4215; www.nga.gov; Constitution Ave NW, btwn 3rd & 7th Sts; ⏰10am-5pm Mon-Sat, 11am-6pm Sun; 👪; 🚌Circulator National Mall, Ⓜ Green, Yellow Line to Archives-Navy Memorial-Penn Quarter) FREE Two buildings. Hundreds of masterpieces. Infinite enjoyment. The neoclassical **West Building** showcases European art through to the early 1900s; highlights include works by da Vinci, Manet, Monet and Van Gogh. The IM Pei-designed **East Building** displays modern and contemporary art – don't miss Pollock's *Number 1, 1950 (Lavender Mist)*, Picasso's *Family of Saltimbanques* and the massive Calder mobile specially commissioned for the entrance lobby. An underground walkway connects the buildings and is made extraordinary by Leo Villareal's light sculpture, *Multiverse*.

Washington Monument MONUMENT
(www.nps.gov/wamo; 2 15th St NW; 🚌Circulator National Mall, Ⓜ Orange, Silver, Blue Line to Smithsonian) FREE Peaking at 555ft (and 5in) and composed of 36,000 blocks of stone, the Washington Monument is the district's tallest structure. Political shenanigans followed by the Civil War interrupted its construction. When work began anew, a new quarry sourced the marble; note the delineation in color where the old and new marble meet about a third of the way up. Entry is ticketed; see the website for details.

Martin Luther King Jr Memorial MONUMENT
(www.nps.gov/mlkm; 1964 Independence Ave SW; ⏰24hr; 🚌Circulator National Mall, Ⓜ Orange, Silver, Blue Line to Smithsonian) Opened in 2011, this was the first Mall memorial to honor an African American. Sculptor Lei Yixin carved the piece, which is reminiscent in concept and style to the Mt Rushmore memorial. Besides Dr King's striking, 30ft-tall image, known as the Stone of Hope, there are two blocks of granite behind him that represent the Mountain of Despair. A wall inscribed with King's powerful quotes about democracy, justice and peace flanks the piece.

★National Museum of African American History & Culture MUSEUM
(☎844-750-3012; www.nmaahc.si.edu; 1400 Constitution Ave NW; ⏰10am-5:30pm; 👪; 🚌Circulator National Mall, Ⓜ Orange, Silver, Blue Line to Smithsonian or Federal Triangle) FREE This sensational museum covers the diverse African American experience and how it helped shape the nation. Start downstairs in the sobering 'Slavery and Freedom' exhibition and work your way up to the community and culture galleries on the 3rd and 4th floors, where African American achievements in sport, music, theater and visual arts are joyfully celebrated. Artifacts, state-of-the-art interactive exhibits, site-specific artworks and fascinating interpretative panels abound in the cleverly designed and dramatically lit exhibition spaces.

National Gallery of Art Sculpture Garden GARDENS
(www.nga.gov; cnr Constitution Ave NW & 7th St NW; ⏰10am-7pm Mon-Thu & Sat, to 9:30pm Fri, 11am-7pm Sun late May-early Oct, 10am-5pm Mon-Sat, 11am-6pm Sun early Oct-late May; 👪; 🚌Circulator National Mall, Ⓜ Green, Yellow Line to Archives-Navy Memorial-Penn Quarter) FREE This 6-acre garden is studded with whimsical sculptures such as Roy Lichtenstein's *House I* (1998), a giant Claes Oldenburg typewriter eraser (1999) and Roxy Paine's *Graft* (2008–09), a stainless-steel tree. They are scattered around a fountain – a great place to dip your feet in summer.

From mid-November to mid-March the fountain is transformed into an **ice rink** (☎202-216-9397; www.nga.gov/visit/ice-rink.html; adult/child 12yr & under $9/8, skate rental $4; ⏰10am-9pm Mon-Thu, to 11pm Fri, 11am-11pm Sat, 11am-9pm Sun mid-Nov–mid-Mar), and the garden stays open a bit later.

The garden's **Pavilion Cafe** (☎202-289-3361; www.pavilioncafe.com; sandwiches $10-12, salads $11-13; ⏰10am-4pm Mon-Sat, 11am-5pm Sun, seasonal late openings) is a popular spot to grab a bite or coffee.

National Museum of Natural History MUSEUM
(☎202-663-1000; www.naturalhistory.si.edu; cnr 10th St & Constitution Ave NW; ⏰10am-5:30pm, to 7:30pm some days; 👪; 🚌Circulator National Mall, Ⓜ Orange, Silver, Blue Line to Smithsonian or Federal Triangle) FREE Arguably the most

Washington, DC

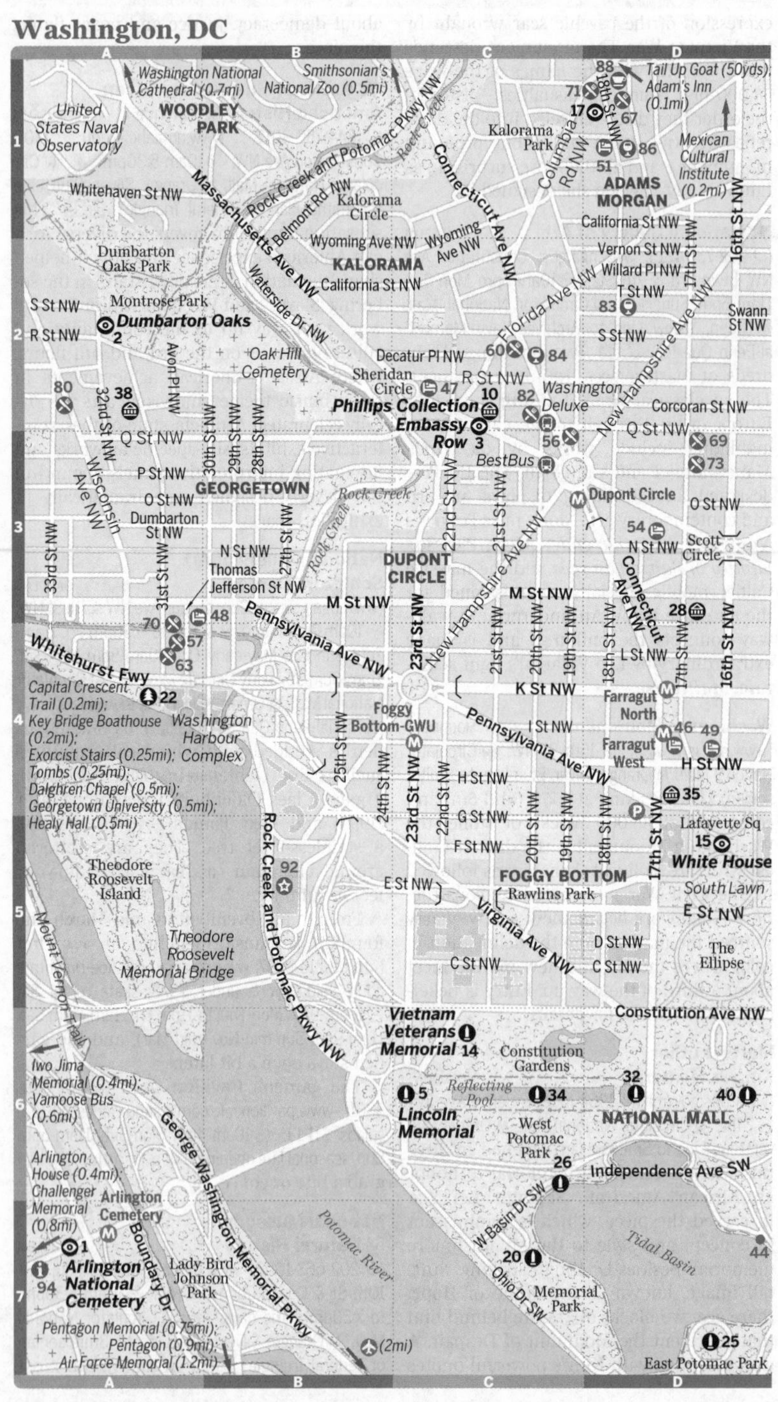

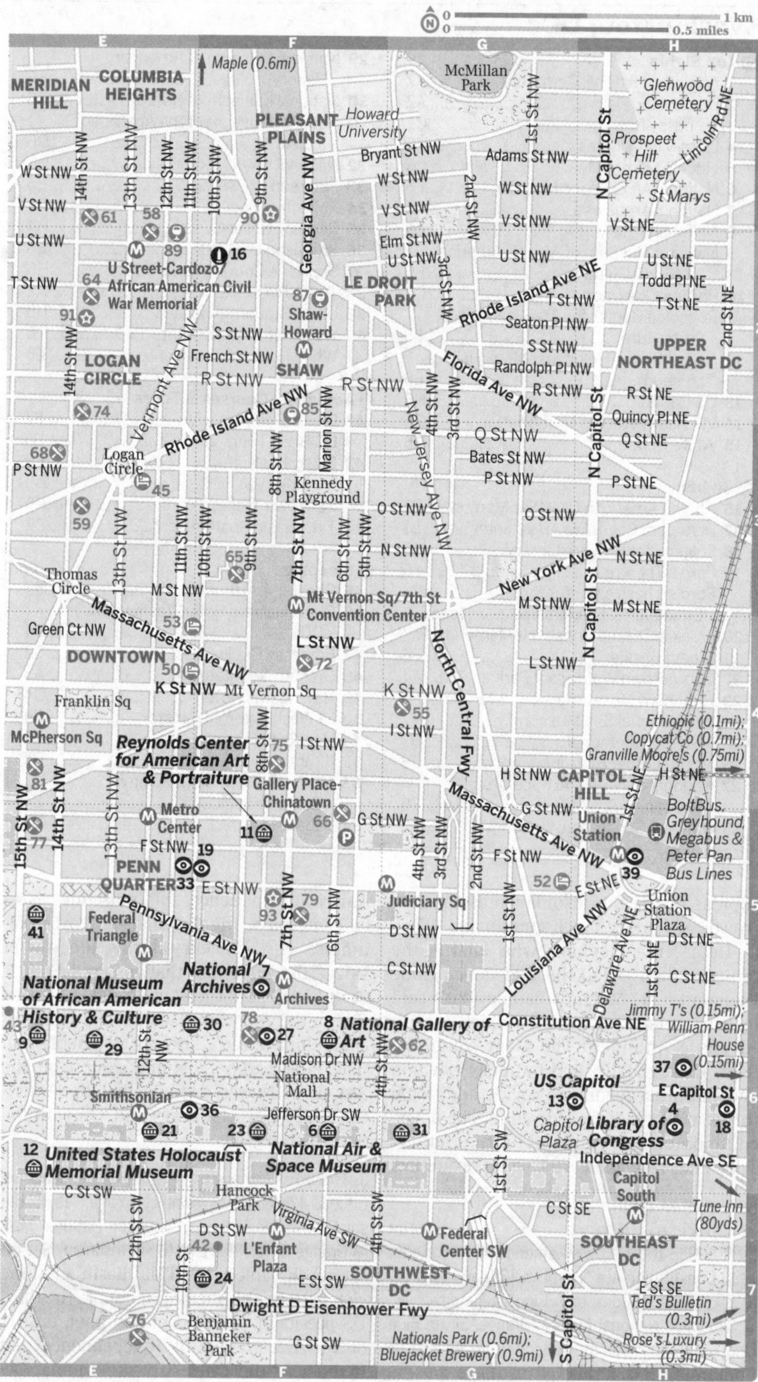

MERIDIAN HILL
COLUMBIA HEIGHTS
PLEASANT PLAINS
Howard University
McMillan Park
Glenwood Cemetery
Prospect Hill Cemetery
St Marys
LE DROIT PARK
UPPER NORTHEAST DC
LOGAN CIRCLE
SHAW
Logan Circle
Kennedy Playground
Thomas Circle
DOWNTOWN
Franklin Sq
McPherson Sq
Mt Vernon Sq
Reynolds Center for American Art & Portraiture
Gallery Place-Chinatown
Metro Center
CAPITOL HILL
Union Station
Union Station Plaza
PENN QUARTER
Federal Triangle
Judiciary Sq
National Archives
Archives
National Museum of African American History & Culture
National Gallery of Art
National Mall
Smithsonian
US Capitol
Capitol Plaza
Library of Congress
United States Holocaust Memorial Museum
National Air & Space Museum
Hancock Park
L'Enfant Plaza
Federal Center SW
Capitol South
SOUTHEAST DC
SOUTHWEST DC
Benjamin Banneker Park
U Street-Cardozo
African American Civil War Memorial
Shaw-Howard
Mt Vernon Sq/7th St Convention Center
Maple (0.6mi)
Ethiopic (0.1mi); Copycat Co (0.7mi); Granville Moore's (0.75mi)
BoltBus, Greyhound, Megabus & Peter Pan Bus Lines
Jimmy T's (0.15mi); William Penn House (0.15mi)
Tune Inn (80yds)
Ted's Bulletin (0.3mi)
Rose's Luxury (0.3mi)
Nationals Park (0.6mi); Bluejacket Brewery (0.9mi)
Rhode Island Ave NE
Rhode Island Ave NW
Florida Ave NW
Vermont Ave NW
Georgia Ave NW
New Jersey Ave NW
New York Ave NW
Massachusetts Ave NW
North Central Fwy
Pennsylvania Ave NW
Louisiana Ave NW
Delaware Ave NE
Constitution Ave NE
Madison Dr NW
Jefferson Dr SW
Independence Ave SE
Virginia Ave SW
Dwight D Eisenhower Fwy
E Capitol St
N Capitol St
S Capitol St
Lincoln Rd NE
0 1 km
0 0.5 miles

Washington, DC

Top Sights

1 Arlington National Cemetery A7
2 Dumbarton Oaks A2
3 Embassy Row C2
4 Library of Congress H6
5 Lincoln Memorial C6
6 National Air & Space Museum F6
7 National Archives F5
8 National Gallery of Art F6
9 National Museum of African American History & Culture E6
10 Phillips Collection C2
11 Reynolds Center for American Art & Portraiture F5
12 United States Holocaust Memorial Museum E6
13 US Capitol H6
14 Vietnam Veterans Memorial C6
15 White House D5

Sights

16 African American Civil War Memorial ... F2
17 District of Columbia Arts Center D1
18 Folger Shakespeare Library H6
19 Ford's Theatre F5
Ford's Theatre Center for Education & Leadership .... (see 33)
20 Franklin Delano Roosevelt Memorial ... C7
21 Freer | Sackler E6
22 Georgetown Waterfront Park A4
23 Hirshhorn Museum F6
24 International Spy Museum F7
25 Jefferson Memorial D7
26 Martin Luther King Jr Memorial C6
27 National Gallery of Art Sculpture Garden F6
28 National Geographic Museum D3
29 National Museum of American History E6
30 National Museum of Natural History ... F6
31 National Museum of the American Indian G6
32 National WWII Memorial D6
33 Petersen House E5
34 Reflecting Pool C6
35 Renwick Gallery D4
36 Smithsonian Castle E6
37 Supreme Court H6
38 Tudor Place A2
39 Union Station H5
40 Washington Monument D6
41 White House Visitor Center E5

Activities, Courses & Tours

42 Bike & Roll F7
DC Brew Tours .... (see 11)
43 DC by Foot E6
Ice Rink .... (see 27)
Old Town Trolley Tours .... (see 33)
44 Tidal Basin Boathouse D7

Sleeping

45 Chester A Arthur House E3
46 Club Quarters Hotel Washington, DC D4
47 Embassy Circle Guest House C2
48 Graham Georgetown A3
49 Hay-Adams Hotel D4
50 HI Washington DC Hostel E4
51 HighRoad Hostel D1
52 Kimpton George Hotel G5
53 Morrison-Clark Historic Inn & Restaurant E4
54 Tabard Inn D3

popular of the Smithsonian museums, so crowds are pretty much guaranteed. Wave to Henry, the elephant who guards the rotunda, then zip to the 2nd floor's Hope Diamond, a 45.52-karat bauble that's said to have cursed its owners, which included Marie Antoinette.The giant squid (1st floor, Ocean Hall), live butterfly pavilion and tarantula feedings provide additional thrills at this kid-packed venue. The beloved dinosaur hall, centered on the Nation's T-Rex, has reopened after being revamped.

National Museum of American History MUSEUM
(202-633-1000; www.americanhistory.si.edu; 1300 Constitution Ave NW, btwn 12th and 14th Sts NW; 10am-5:30pm, to 7:30pm some days; ; Circulator National Mall, M Orange, Silver, Blue Line to Smithsonian or Federal Triangle) FREE Containing all kinds of artifacts of the American experience, this museum has as its centerpiece the flag that flew over Baltimore's Fort McHenry during the War of 1812 – the same flag that inspired Francis Scott Key to pen 'The Star-Spangled Banner' (it's on the entry level). Other highlights include Julia Child's kitchen (1st floor) and 'The First Ladies' costume exhibit on the 3rd floor. Newer exhibits include 'American Enterprise' (1st floor) and 'On with the Show' (3rd floor).

Jefferson Memorial MONUMENT
(202-426-6841; www.nps.gov/thje; 13 E Basin Dr SW; 24hr; Circulator National Mall, M Orange, Silver, Blue Line to Smithsonian) Set on the south bank of the Tidal Basin amid the cherry trees, this memorial honors the third US president, political philosopher, drafter of the Declaration of Independence and founder of the University of Virginia. De-

Eating
- 55 A Baked Joint G4
- 56 Afterwords Cafe C3
- 57 Baked & Wired A4
- 58 Ben's Chili Bowl E2
- 59 Birch & Barley E3
- 60 Bistrot du Coin C2
- 61 Busboys & Poets E1
- 62 Cascade Café G6
- 63 Chez Billy Sud A4
- 64 Compass Rose E2
- 65 Dabney F3
- 66 Daikaya F5
- 67 Diner D1
- Dolcezza at the Hirshhorn .... (see 23)
- Donburi .... (see 17)
- 68 Estadio E3
- 69 Hank's Oyster Bar D3
- 70 Il Canale A4
- 71 Julia's Empanadas D1
- 72 Kinship F4
- 73 Komi D3
- 74 Le Diplomate E2
- Little Serow .... (see 73)
- 75 Matchbox Vintage Pizza Bistro F4
- 76 Municipal Fish Market E7
- 77 Old Ebbitt Grill E5
- 78 Pavilion Cafe F6
- 79 Rasika F5
- 80 Simply Banh Mi A2
- 81 Woodward Table E4
- 82 Zorba's Cafe C2

Drinking & Nightlife
- 83 Bar Charley D2
- 84 Board Room C2
- Churchkey .... (see 59)
- Columbia Room .... (see 65)
- 85 Dacha Beer Garden F2
- 86 Dan's Cafe D1
- JR's .... (see 69)
- Off the Record .... (see 49)
- 87 Right Proper Brewing Co F2
- 88 Songbyrd Record Cafe & Music House D1
- 89 U Street Music Hall E2

Entertainment
- 90 9:30 Club F1
- 91 Black Cat E2
- Folger Theatre .... (see 18)
- 92 Kennedy Center B5
- National Symphony Orchestra .... (see 92)
- 93 Shakespeare Theatre Company F5
- Washington National Opera .... (see 92)
- Woolly Mammoth Theatre Company .... (see 79)

Shopping
- Kramerbooks .... (see 56)

Information
- 94 Arlington National Cemetery Welcome Center A7
- Smithsonian Visitor Center .... (see 36)

signed by John Russell Pope in the style of the ancient Roman Pantheon, the rounded, open-air monument was initially derided by critics as 'the Jefferson Muffin.' Inside is a 19ft bronze likeness, and excerpts from Jefferson's writings are etched into the walls.

National WWII Memorial MONUMENT
(www.nps.gov/wwii; 17th St SW; 24hr; Circulator National Mall, M Orange, Silver, Blue Line to Smithsonian) Dedicated in 2004, this grandiose memorial honors the 16 million US soldiers who served in WWII. Groups of veterans regularly come here to pay their respects to the 400,000 Americans who died as a result of the conflict. The plaza's dual arches symbolize victory in the Atlantic and Pacific theaters, and the 56 surrounding pillars represent each US state and territory.

Hirshhorn Museum MUSEUM
(202-633-1000; www.hirshhorn.si.edu; cnr 7th St & Independence Ave SW; 10am-5:30pm; ; Circulator National Mall, M Orange, Silver, Blue, Green, Yellow Line to L'Enfant Plaza) FREE The Smithsonian's cylindrical art museum shows works from modernism's early days to today's most cutting-edge practitioners. Exhibitions of works drawn from the museum's extensive collection are offered alongside curated shows of work by prominent contemporary artists. Visitors can relax in the 3rd-floor sitting area, which has couches, floor-to-ceiling windows and a balcony offering Mall views. A lobby redesign by Japanese artist Hiroshi Sugimoto opened in 2018, and includes **Dolcezza at the Hirshhorn** (www.dolcezzagelato.com; gelato $4, pastries $2-7; 9am-5pm Mon-Fri, from 10am Sat & Sun;), a gelato and coffee bar.

National Mall

A DAY TOUR

Folks often call the Mall 'America's Front Yard,' and that's a pretty good analogy. It is indeed a lawn, unfurling scrubby green grass from the Capitol west to the Lincoln Memorial. It's also America's great public space, where citizens come to protest their government, go for scenic runs and connect with the nation's most cherished ideals writ large in stone, landscaping, monuments and memorials.

You can sample quite a bit in a day, but it'll be a full one that requires roughly 4 miles of walking.

Start at the 1 **Vietnam Veterans Memorial**, then head counterclockwise around the Mall, swooping in on the 2 **Lincoln Memorial**, 3 **Martin Luther King Jr Memorial** and 4 **Washington Monument**. You can also pause for the cause of the Korean War and WWII, among other monuments that dot the Mall's western portion.

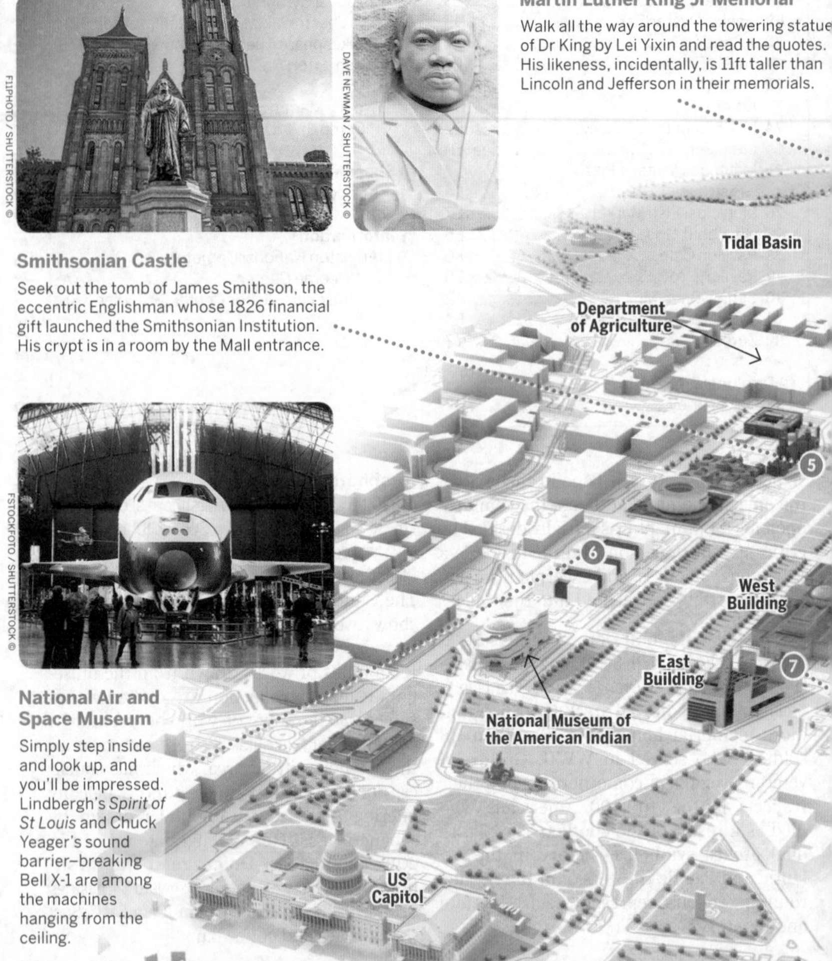

Martin Luther King Jr Memorial

Walk all the way around the towering statue of Dr King by Lei Yixin and read the quotes. His likeness, incidentally, is 11ft taller than Lincoln and Jefferson in their memorials.

Smithsonian Castle

Seek out the tomb of James Smithson, the eccentric Englishman whose 1826 financial gift launched the Smithsonian Institution. His crypt is in a room by the Mall entrance.

National Air and Space Museum

Simply step inside and look up, and you'll be impressed. Lindbergh's *Spirit of St Louis* and Chuck Yeager's sound barrier–breaking Bell X-1 are among the machines hanging from the ceiling.

Then it's onward to the museums, all fabulous and all free. Begin at the **5 Smithsonian Castle** to get your bearings – and to say thanks to the guy making all this awesomeness possible – and commence browsing through the **6 National Air & Space Museum**, **7 National Gallery of Art & National Sculpture Garden** and **8 National Museum of African American History and Culture**.

TOP TIPS

Start early, especially in summer. You'll avoid the crowds, but more importantly you'll avoid the blazing heat. Try to finish with the monuments and be in the air-conditioned museums by 10:30am. Also, consider bringing snacks, since the only food available is from scattered cart vendors and museum cafes.

Lincoln Memorial

Commune with Abe in his chair, then head down the steps to the marker where Martin Luther King Jr gave his 'Dream' speech. The view of the Reflecting Pool and Washington Monument is one of DC's best.

ADAM PARENT / SHUTTERSTOCK ©

Vietnam Veterans Memorial

Check the symbol that's beside each name. A diamond indicates 'killed, body recovered.' A plus sign indicates 'missing and unaccounted for.' There are approximately 1200 of the latter.

Washington Monument

As you approach the obelisk, look a third of the way up. See how it's slightly lighter in color at the bottom? Builders had to use different marble after the first source dried up.

National Museum of African American History and Culture

Feel the power at newest Smithsonian museum, where artifacts include Harriet Tubman's hymnal, Emmett Till's casket, a segregated lunch counter and Michael Jordan's sneakers. The building's design is based on a three-tiered Yoruban crown.

RARRARORRO/SHUTTERSTOCK © ARCHITECT: DAVID ADJAYE

National Gallery of Art & National Sculpture Garden

Beeline to Gallery 6 (West Building) and ogle the Western Hemisphere's only Leonardo da Vinci painting. Outdoors, amble amid whimsical sculptures by Miró, Calder and Lichtenstein. Also check out IM Pei's design of the East Building.

Smithsonian Castle NOTABLE BUILDING

(☎202-633-1000; www.si.edu; 1000 Jefferson Dr SW; ⏲8:30am-5:30pm; 🚌Circulator National Mall, Ⓜ Orange, Silver, Blue Line to Smithsonian) James Renwick designed this turreted, red-sandstone fairy-tale in 1855. Today the castle houses the **Smithsonian Visitor Center**, which makes a good first stop on the Mall. Inside you'll find history exhibits, multilingual touch-screen displays, a staffed information desk, free maps, a cafe and the tomb of James Smithson, the institution's founder. His crypt lies inside a little room by the main entrance off the Mall.

Freer | Sackler MUSEUM

(☎202-633-1000; www.asia.si.edu; 1050 Independence Ave SW; ⏲10am-5:30pm; 🚌Circulator National Mall, Ⓜ Orange, Silver, Blue Line to Smithsonian) FREE This is a lovely spot in which to while away a Washington afternoon. Japanese silk scrolls, smiling Buddhas, rare Islamic manuscripts and Chinese jades are exhibited in cool, quiet galleries in two museums connected by an underground tunnel. The Freer also houses works by American painter James Whistler, including five *Nocturnes*. Don't miss the extraordinarily beautiful blue-and-gold Peacock Room on its ground floor, designed by Whistler in 1876–77 as an exotic showcase for a shipping magnate's Chinese porcelain collection.

National Museum of the American Indian MUSEUM

(☎202-663-1000; www.americanindian.si.edu; cnr 4th St & Independence Ave SW; ⏲10am-5:30pm; 👪; 🚌Circulator National Mall, Ⓜ Orange, Silver, Blue, Green, Yellow Line to L'Enfant Plaza) FREE Ensconced in an architecturally notable building clad in honey-colored limestone, this museum offers cultural artifacts, videos and audio recordings related to the indigenous people of the Americas. Sadly, navigation of the exhibits is confusing on both a curatorial and physical level. The focus on didactic panels at the expense of interpretative labels for artifacts is also problematic. The 'Our Universes' gallery (on Level 4) about Native American beliefs and creation stories is one of the more interesting exhibits.

Franklin Delano Roosevelt Memorial MONUMENT

(www.nps.gov/frde; 400 W Basin Dr SW; ⏲24hr; 🚌Circulator National Mall, Ⓜ Orange, Silver, Blue Line to Smithsonian) The 7.5-acre memorial pays tribute to the longest-serving president in US history. Visitors are taken through four red-granite areas that narrate FDR's time in office, from the Depression to the New Deal to WWII. The story is told through statuary and inscriptions, punctuated with fountains and peaceful alcoves. It's especially pretty at night, when the marble shimmers in the glossy stillness of the Tidal Basin.

Capitol Hill

The city's geographic and legislative heart surprises by being mostly a row-house-lined residential neighborhood. The vast area holds top sights such as the dramatic Capitol, book-stuffed Library of Congress and heartbreaking Holocaust Memorial Museum, but creaky bookshops and cozy pubs also thrive here. The areas around Eastern Market and H St NE are locals' hubs, with good-time restaurants and nightlife.

★US Capitol LANDMARK

(☎202-226-8000; www.visitthecapitol.gov; 1st St SE & E Capitol St, Capitol Hill; ⏲8:30am-4:30pm Mon-Sat; Ⓜ Orange, Silver, Blue Line to Capitol South) FREE Since 1800, this is where the legislative branch of American government (ie Congress) has met to write the country's laws. The lower House of Representatives (435 members) and upper Senate (100) meet respectively in the south and north wings of the building. Enter via the underground visitor center below the East Front Plaza. Guided tours of the building are free, but tickets are limited and there's often a long wait. It's best to reserve online in advance (there's no fee).

The hour-long jaunt showcases the exhaustive background of a building that fairly sweats history. You'll watch a cheesy film first, then staff members lead you into the ornate halls and whispery chambers cluttered with the busts, statues and personal mementos of generations of Congress members.

To watch Congress in session, you need a separate gallery pass. US citizens must get one in advance or in person from their representative or senator; foreign visitors should take their passports to the House and Senate Appointment Desks on the upper level. Congressional committee hearings are more interesting (and substantive) if you care about what's being debated; check for a schedule, locations and to see if they're open to the public (they often are) at www.house.gov and www.senate.gov.

Security measures here are strict, including no food, liquid or bags larger than 18in by 4in.

★United States Holocaust Memorial Museum
MUSEUM

(☎202-488-0400; www.ushmm.org; 100 Raoul Wallenberg Pl SW, South DC; ⊙10am-5:20pm, extended hours Apr–mid-Jun; 🚌Circulator, Ⓜ Orange, Silver, Blue Line to Smithsonian) FREE For a deep understanding of the Holocaust – its victims, perpetrators and bystanders – this harrowing museum is a must-see. The main exhibit gives visitors the identity card of a single Holocaust victim, whose story is revealed as you take a winding route into a hellish past marked by ghettos, rail cars and death camps. It also shows the flip side of human nature, documenting the risks many citizens took to help the persecuted.

★Library of Congress
LIBRARY

(☎202-707-8000; www.loc.gov; 10 1st St SE, Capitol Hill; ⊙8:30am-4:30pm Mon-Sat; Ⓜ Orange, Silver, Blue Line to Capitol South) FREE The world's largest library – with 164 million books, manuscripts, maps, photos, films and other items – awes in both scope and design. The centerpiece is the 1897 **Jefferson Building**. Gawk at the **Great Hall**, done up in stained glass, marble and mosaics of mythical characters, then seek out the **Gutenberg Bible** (c 1455), Thomas Jefferson's round library and the reading room viewing area. Free tours of the building take place between 10:30am and 3:30pm on the half-hour.

Supreme Court
LANDMARK

(☎202-479-3000; www.supremecourt.gov; 1 1st St NE, Capitol Hill; ⊙9am-4:30pm Mon-Fri; Ⓜ Orange, Silver, Blue Line to Capitol South) FREE The highest court in the USA occupies a pseudo-Greek temple protected by 13,000lb bronze doors. Arrive early to watch arguments (periodic Monday through Wednesday from October to April). You can visit the permanent exhibits and the building's two five-story, marble-and-bronze spiral staircases year-round. On days when court is not in session you can also hear lectures (every hour on the half-hour beginning 9:30am) in the courtroom. Be sure to exit via the doors that lead to the regal front steps.

THE WHARF

The Southwest Waterfront has long been home to the fish market (p271), but the area was otherwise unremarkable – until the Wharf shot up. The huge complex of restaurants, hotels, entertainment venues, parks and piers officially opened in late 2017, and now it buzzes.

The public piers are the niftiest bits. The **Transit Pier** (950 Wharf St SW, Transit Pier; Ⓜ Orange, Silver, Blue, Yellow, Green Lines to L'Enfant Plaza or Green Line to Waterfront) has a winter ice rink, summer mini-golf course and small outdoor stage for free concerts. The Wharf water taxi departs from here, hence the name. The **District Pier** is the longest dock, jutting well out into the Washington Channel and hosting a big stage for festivals. The **Recreation Pier** makes for a fine stroll with its benches, swinging seats and boathouse for kayak and paddleboard rentals.

Loads of eateries sit waterside, including branches of **Shake Shack** (☎202-800-9930; www.shakeshack.com; 800 F St NW, Penn Quarter; mains $5-10; ⊙11am-11pm Sun-Thu, to midnight Fri & Sat; Ⓜ Red, Yellow, Green Line to Gallery Pl-Chinatown), Hank's Oyster Bar (p274), Rappahannock Oyster Bar and **Dolcezza** (☎202-299-9116; www.dolcezzagelato.com; 1704 Connecticut Ave NW, Dupont Circle; gelato $6-8; ⊙7am-10pm Mon-Thu, 7am-11pm Fri, 8am-11pm Sat, 8am-10pm Sun; 📶; Ⓜ Red Line to Dupont Circle). The **Anthem** (☎202-888-0020; www.theanthemdc.com; 901 Wharf St SW, South DC; ⊙box office noon-7pm, to 9pm show days; Ⓜ Orange, Silver, Blue, Yellow, Green Line to L'Enfant Plaza or Green Line to Waterfront) and **Pearl Street Warehouse** (☎202-380-9620; www.pearlstreetwarehouse.com; 33 Pearl St SW, South DC; ⊙4pm-midnight Mon-Wed, 8:30am-2am Thu-Sat, 9am-midnight Sun; Ⓜ Orange, Silver, Blue, Yellow, Green Line to L'Enfant Plaza or Green Line to Waterfront) are fab venues for live music. **Politics & Prose** (☎202-488-3867; www.politics-prose.com/wharf; 70 District Sq SW, South DC; ⊙10am-10pm; Ⓜ Orange, Silver, Blue, Yellow, Green Line to L'Enfant Plaza or Green Line to Waterfront) brings the books. And more is on the way, as you'll see from the ongoing construction that will add to the Wharf for the next several years.

Folger Shakespeare Library LIBRARY
(☎202-544-4600; www.folger.edu; 201 E Capitol St SE, Capitol Hill; ⏲10am-5pm Mon-Sat, noon-5pm Sun; Ⓜ Orange, Silver, Blue Line to Capitol South) FREE Bard-o-philes will be all aflutter here, as the library holds the world's largest collection of old Billy's works. Stroll through the Great Hall to see a changing exhibit of Elizabethan artifacts, paintings, etchings and manuscripts. The highlight is the chance to peek at one of the library's First Folios, the first printed collection of Shakespeare's plays, published in 1623. Pop into the on-site Elizabethan-inspired **theater** (www.folger.edu/folger-theatre; tickets from $30); it's worth returning in the evening to catch a show.

White House & Foggy Bottom

Play image association with the words 'Washington, DC,' and chances are the first thing that comes to mind is the White House. The president's pad is likely to take your breath away the first time you see it, not least because you're standing in front of a building whose image you've seen a thousand times before. The surrounding streets are equally impressive, with handsome building stock and a bustle that comes courtesy of this neighborhood's role as America's center of bureaucratic and political business (or should that be shenanigans?).

★White House LANDMARK
(☎202-208-1631, 24hr info 202-456-7041; www.whitehouse.gov; 1600 Pennsylvania Ave NW, White House Area; ⏲tours 7:30-11:30am Tue-Thu, to 1:30pm Fri & Sat; Ⓜ Orange, Silver, Blue Line to Federal Triangle or McPherson Sq) FREE The 'President's House,' built between 1792 and 1800, is an iconic, imposing building that's thrilling to see but difficult to access. Tours must be pre-arranged: Americans must apply via one of their members of Congress; non-Americans must ask their country's embassy in DC for assistance – in reality, there's only a slim chance that the embassy will be able to help source tickets. If you're lucky enough to visit, you'll see several public rooms in the main residence via self-guided tour.

White House Visitor Center MUSEUM
(☎202-208-1631; www.nps.gov/whho; 1450 Pennsylvania Ave NW, White House Area; ⏲7:30am-4pm; Ⓜ Orange, Silver, Blue Lines to Federal Triangle) FREE Getting inside the White House can be difficult, so here is your back-up plan. Housed in the splendiferous 1932 Patent Search Room of the Department of Commerce building, this center has plenty of artifacts, anecdote-packed information panels and informative multimedia exhibits, including a presentation on the history and lives of the presidential families and an interactive touchscreen tour of the White House. It's obviously not the same as seeing the real deal firsthand, but is well worth visiting regardless.

Renwick Gallery MUSEUM
(☎202-633-7970; www.renwick.americanart.si.edu; 1661 Pennsylvania Ave NW, White House Area; ⏲10am-5:30pm; Ⓜ Orange, Silver, Blue Line to Farragut West) FREE Part of the Smithsonian group, the Renwick Gallery is located in a stately 1859 mansion on the same block of Pennsylvania as the White House.

It's emerged as a showcase for modern and contemporary artists who use innovative techniques and materials, redefining what 'craft' is and taking contemporary arts and crafts in daring new directions.

Downtown & Penn Quarter

Penn Quarter forms around Pennsylvania Ave as it runs between the White House and the Capitol. Downtown extends north beyond it. Major sights include the National Archives, a trove of eye-popping documents; the Reynolds Center for American Art & Portraiture, hanging big-name works; and Ford's Theatre, where Abraham Lincoln was assassinated. This is also DC's entertainment district and convention hub, so the place bustles day and night. Heaps of hot bars and restaurants provide sustenance.

★National Archives LANDMARK
(☎866-272-6272; www.archives.gov/museum; 701 Constitution Ave NW, Penn Quarter; ⏲10am-5:30pm; Ⓜ Green, Yellow Line to Archives-Navy Memorial-Penn Quarter) FREE It's hard not to feel a little in awe of the big three documents in the Archives: the Declaration of Independence, the Constitution and the Bill of Rights. Taken together, it becomes clear just how radical the American experiment was. The archival bric-a-brac of the **Public Vaults** makes a flashy rejoin-

der to the main exhibit. You can reserve tickets (www.recreation.gov) for $1.50 and use the fast-track entrance on Constitution Ave (especially recommended in spring and summer).

Ford's Theatre Center for Education & Leadership MUSEUM
(202-347-4833; www.fords.org; 511 10th St NW, Penn Quarter; 9am-4:30pm; M Red, Orange, Silver, Blue Line to Metro Center) FREE Across the street from the famous theater where Abraham Lincoln was shot, the center holds a gift shop on its 1st floor, as well as a 34ft tower of Lincoln books (it's actually an aluminum sculpture) – a testament to how much has been written about the 16th president.

The 2nd, 3rd and 4th floors have excellent exhibits covering the aftermath of his assassination.

Tickets, available at Ford's Theatre box office, are free and include the historic theater and **Petersen House** (516 10th St NW, Penn Quarter; 9am-4:30pm; M Red, Orange, Silver, Blue Line to Metro Center).

★ **Reynolds Center for American Art & Portraiture** MUSEUM
(202-633-1000; www.americanart.si.edu; cnr 8th & F Sts NW, Penn Quarter; 11:30am-7pm; M Red, Yellow, Green Line to Gallery Pl-Chinatown) FREE The Reynolds Center is one of DC's finest museums. This Smithsonian venue combines the National Portrait Gallery and the American Art Museum into one whopping collection of American art that's unmatched anywhere in the world. Keep an eye out for famed works by Edward Hopper, Georgia O'Keeffe, Andy Warhol, Winslow Homer and loads more celebrated artists.

International Spy Museum MUSEUM
(202-393-7798; www.spymuseum.org; 700 L'Enfant Plaza SW, South DC; ; M Orange, Silver, Blue, Yellow, Green Line to L'Enfant Plaza) One of DC's most popular museums, the International Spy Museum delivers fun and interactive exhibits portraying the flashy and over-the-top world of intelligence gathering.

Highlights include an immersive exhibit exploring communist Berlin, a Situation Room experience of the capture of Osama bin Laden, and an exploration of potential future cyber threats against international security.

Logan Circle, U Street & Columbia Heights

The U St Corridor is the heart of this vast area and a fine spot to begin your explorations. A stroll here rewards with African American historic sights, soul food restaurants, mural-splashed alleys and red-hot music clubs. Spend an afternoon checking it out, or better yet, devote an evening to the nightlife scene.

U St becomes part of the larger Shaw district, which is one of DC's hottest 'hoods. But it's not annoyingly trendy. Instead, the breweries, bars and cafes that seem to pop up weekly are local places, where neighbors come to sip among neighbors. Logan Circle is next door and also booming. Walk down 14th St NW and it's stacked with dapper bars and bistros. An evening spent eating and drinking in the area is a must.

To the north, Columbia Heights is an enclave that mixes Latinx immigrants and hipsters. There are no real sights, but the cheap ethnic food and unassuming punk dive bars can occupy many an evening.

Further on, Northeast DC is a sprawl of leafy streets that hold uncommon sights. Nature lovers have a couple of groovy, free landscapes to explore, while those who like going off the beaten path can play in on-the-rise quarters such as distillery-rich Ivy City and arty, beery Brookland. You won't find many tourists out this way; it takes wheels or a lengthy public-transportation trip to reach most places.

African American Civil War Memorial MONUMENT
(www.afroamcivilwar.org; cnr U St NW & Vermont Ave NW, U Street; 24hr; M Green, Yellow Line to U St/African-American Civil War Memorial/Cardozo) Standing at the center of a granite plaza, this bronze memorial, *Spirit of Freedom*, depicting rifle-bearing troops is DC's first major art piece by Black sculptor Ed Hamilton. The statue is surrounded on three sides by the Wall of Honor, listing the names of 209,145 African American troops who fought in the Union Army, as well as the 7000 white soldiers who served alongside them.

To look up individual names and find their location on the memorial, check the website's 'Colored Troops Search.' To reach the plaza, depart the Metro station via the

10th St exit (follow the 'memorial' signs as you leave the train).

Mexican Cultural Institute CULTURAL CENTER
(202-728-1628; www.instituteofmexicodc.org; 2829 16th St NW, Columbia Heights; 10am-6pm Mon-Fri, noon-4pm Sat; M Green, Yellow Lines to Columbia Heights) FREE The Mexican Cultural Institute looks locked up and imposing, but don't be deterred. The gilded beaux-arts mansion is open to the public and hosts excellent art and cultural exhibitions related to Mexico. You might see a show on Diego Rivera's art, Mayan religious artifacts or Octavio Paz' writings. Ring the doorbell for entry.

Dupont Circle & Kalorama

Dupont offers flashy new restaurants, hip bars, cafe society and cool bookstores. It's also the heart of the city's LGBTIQ+ community. It used to be where turn-of-the-20th-century millionaires lived. Today those mansions hold DC's greatest concentration of embassies. Kalorama sits in the northwest corner and ups the regal quotient.

★Embassy Row ARCHITECTURE
(www.embassy.org; Massachusetts Ave NW, btwn Observatory & Dupont Circles NW, Dupont Circle; M Red Line to Dupont Circle) Want to take a trip around the world? Stroll northwest along Massachusetts Ave from Dupont Circle (the actual traffic circle) and you pass more than 40 embassies housed in mansions that range from elegant to imposing to discreet. Tunisia, Chile, Turkmenistan, Togo, Haiti – flags flutter above heavy doors and mark the nations inside, while dark-windowed sedans ease out of driveways ferrying diplomats to and fro.

The district has another 130 embassies sprinkled throughout, but this is the main vein.

National Geographic Museum MUSEUM
(202-857-7700; www.nationalgeographic.org/dc; 1145 17th St NW, Dupont Circle; adult/child $15/10; 10am-6pm; M Red Line to Farragut North) The museum at National Geographic Society headquarters can't compete with the Smithsonian's more extensive offerings, but it can be worth a stop, depending on what's showing. Exhibits are drawn from the society's well-documented expeditions to the far corners of the earth, and they change periodically.

★Phillips Collection MUSEUM
(202-387-2151; www.phillipscollection.org; 1600 21st St NW, Dupont Circle; Tue-Fri free, Sat & Sun $10, ticketed exhibitions $12; 10am-5pm Tue, Wed, Fri & Sat, to 8:30pm Thu, noon-6:30pm Sun; Circulator Dupont Circle-Georgetown-Rosslyn, M Red Line to Dupont Circle) The country's first modern-art museum (opened in 1921) houses a small but exquisite collection of European and American works. Renoir's *Luncheon of the Boating Party* is a highlight, along with pieces by Gauguin, Van Gogh, Matisse, Picasso and many other greats. The intimate rooms, set in a restored mansion and adjacent former apartment building, put you unusually close to the artworks. Download the free app or dial 202-595-1839 for audio tours through the works.

Adams Morgan

Adams Morgan has long been Washington's fun, nightlife-driven party zone. It's also a global village of sorts. The result today is a raucous mash-up centered on 18th St NW. Vintage boutiques, record shops and ethnic eats poke up between thumping bars and a growing number of stylish spots for gastronomes.

District of Columbia Arts Center ARTS CENTER
(DCAC; 202-462-7833; www.dcartscenter.org; 2438 18th St NW; 2-7pm Wed-Sun; M Red Line to Woodley Park-Zoo/Adams Morgan) FREE The grassroots DCAC offers emerging artists a space to showcase their work. The 800-sq-ft gallery features rotating visual-arts exhibits, while plays, improv, avant-garde musicals and other theatrical productions take place in the 42-seat theater. The gallery is free and worth popping into to see what's showing.

Georgetown

Georgetown is DC's most aristocratic neighborhood, home to elite university students, ivory-tower academics and diplomats. Chi-chi brand-name shops, dark-wood pubs, snug cafes and upscale restaurants line the streets. Lovely parks and gardens color the edges, while sweet cycling trails roll out along the waterways.

★Dumbarton Oaks GARDENS, MUSEUM
(202-339-6400; www.doaks.org; 1703 32nd St NW; museum free, gardens adult/child $10/5;

museum 11:30am-5:30pm Tue-Sun, gardens 2-6pm; Circulator Georgetown-Union Station) The mansion's 27 acres of enchanting formal gardens are straight out of a storybook. The springtime blooms – including heaps of cherry blossoms – are stunning. The mansion itself is worth a walk-through to see exquisite Byzantine and pre-Columbian art (including El Greco's *The Visitation*) and the fascinating library of rare books that date as far back as 1491. From November to mid-March the gardens are free (and they close at 5pm). Enter them at R and 31st Sts NW.

Georgetown Waterfront Park PARK
(www.georgetownwaterfrontpark.org; Water St NW/K St, btwn 31st St NW & Key Bridge; ; Circulator Georgetown-Union Station) This park is a favorite with couples on first dates, families on an evening stroll and power players showing off their yachts. Benches dot the way, where you can sit and watch the rowing teams out on the Potomac River. Alfresco restaurants cluster at nearby Washington Harbour. They ring a terraced plaza filled with fountains (which become an ice rink in winter). The docks are also here for ferries that ply the Potomac to Alexandria, VA, and Capitol Hill's Wharf.

Georgetown University UNIVERSITY
(202-687-0100; www.georgetown.edu; cnr 37th & O Sts NW; Circulator Georgetown-Union Station) Georgetown is one of the nation's top universities, with a student body that's equally hard-working and hard-partying. Founded in 1789, it was America's first Roman Catholic university. Notable Hoya (derived from the Latin *hoya saxa*, 'what rocks') alumni include Bill Clinton, as well as many international royals and heads of state. Near the campus' east gate, medieval-looking **Healy Hall** impresses with its tall, Hogwarts-esque clock tower. Pretty **Dalghren Chapel** and its quiet courtyard hide behind it.

Exorcist Stairs FILM LOCATION
(3600 Prospect St NW; Circulator Georgetown-Union Station) The steep set of stairs dropping down to M St is a popular track for joggers, but more famously it's the spot where demonically possessed Father Karras tumbles to his death in horror-film classic *The Exorcist* (1973). Come on foggy nights, when the stone steps really are creepy as hell.

Tudor Place MUSEUM
(202-965-0400; www.tudorplace.org; 1644 31st St NW; 1hr house tour adult/child $10/3, self-guided garden tour $3; 10am-4pm Tue-Sat, from noon Sun, closed Jan; Circulator Georgetown-Union Station) This 1816 neoclassical mansion was owned by Thomas Peter and Martha Custis Peter, the granddaughter of Martha Washington, and lived in by six generations of her family. Today the manor functions as a small museum, featuring family furnishings and artwork (including some from Mt Vernon), which give a good insight into American decorative arts. The grand, 5-acre gardens bloom with roses, lilies, poplar trees and exotic palms.

Upper Northwest DC

★ Washington National Cathedral CHURCH
(202-537-6200; www.cathedral.org; 3101 Wisconsin Ave NW, Cathedral Heights; adult/child 5-17yr $12/8, Sun free; 10am-5pm Mon-Fri, to 4pm Sat, 12:45-4pm Sun; N2, N3, N4, N6 from Dupont Circle) Constructed between 1907 and 1990, this huge neo-Gothic cathedral blends the spiritual with the profane in its architecture. Most of its richly colored stained-glass windows celebrate religious themes, although the 'Scientists and Technicians' window with its embedded lunar rock is an exception. The famed exterior gargoyles depict everything from Darth Vader to a Missouri bear. Specialty tours are available so check online for details.

The excellent **Open City** (202-965-7670; www.opencitycathedraldc.com; brunch dishes $4-11, sandwiches $8-10; 7am-6pm;) cafe is in the cathedral's grounds, occupying the historic baptistery building.

Smithsonian's National Zoo ZOO
(202-633-4888; www.nationalzoo.si.edu; 3001 Connecticut Ave NW, Woodley Park; 9am-6pm mid-Mar–Sep, to 4pm Oct–mid-Mar, grounds 8am-7pm mid-Mar–Sep, to 5pm Oct–mid-Mar; M Red Line to Cleveland Park or Woodley Park) FREE Home to more than 2700 animals and more than 390 species in natural habitats, the National Zoo is famed for its giant pandas, Mei Xiang, Tian Tian and Bei Bei. Other highlights include the African lion pride, Asian elephants, and orangutans swinging 50ft overhead from steel cables and interconnected towers (aka the 'O Line').

Activities

Hiking & Cycling

Capital Bikeshare — CYCLING

(877-430-2453; www.capitalbikeshare.com; per 1/3 days $8/17) It has a network of 4300-plus bicycles scattered at 500-odd stations around the region. Purchase a pass at a kiosk (one day or three days) on the spot. Insert a credit card, get your ride code, then unlock a bike. The first 30 minutes are free; after that, rates rise fast if you don't dock the bike.

Capital Crescent Trail — CYCLING

(www.cctrail.org; Water St; Circulator Georgetown-Union Station) Stretching between Georgetown and Bethesda, MD, the constantly evolving Capital Crescent Trail is a fabulous (and very popular) jogging and biking route. Built on an abandoned railroad bed, the 7-mile trail is paved and is a great leisurely day trip. It has beautiful lookouts over the Potomac River, and winds through woodsy areas and upscale neighborhoods.

Boating

Tidal Basin Boathouse — BOATING

(202-337-9642; www.boatingindc.com/boathouses/tidal-basin; 1501 Maine Ave SW; 2-/4-person boat per hour $18/30, swan boat per hour $34; 10am-6pm mid-Mar–Sep; Circulator National Mall, M Orange, Silver, Blue Line to Smithsonian) Rents paddleboats to take out on the Tidal Basin. Make sure you bring a camera as there are great views from the water.

Key Bridge Boathouse — WATER SPORTS

(202-337-9642; www.boatingindc.com/boathouses/key-bridge-boathouse; 3500 Water St NW; hours vary mid-Apr–Oct; Circulator Georgetown-Union Station) Located beneath the Key Bridge, the boathouse rents canoes, kayaks and stand up paddleboards (prices start at $16 per hour). In summer it also offers guided, 90-minute kayak trips ($45 per person) that glide past the Lincoln Memorial as the sun sets. If you have a bike, the boathouse is a mere few steps from the Capital Crescent Trail.

Tours

DC by Foot — WALKING

(202-370-1830; www.freetoursbyfoot.com/washington-dc-tours) Guides for this pay-what-you-want walking tour offer engaging stories and historical details on different jaunts covering the National Mall, Lincoln's assassination, Capitol Hill's ghosts and many more. Most takers pay around $10 to $15 per person. Reserve in advance to guarantee a spot.

DC Metro Food Tours — WALKING

(202-851-2268; www.dcmetrofoodtours.com; per person $56-67) These walkabouts explore the culinary riches of various neighborhoods, stopping for multiple bites along the way. Offerings include Capitol Hill, U St, Little Ethiopia, Georgetown and Old Town Alexandria, VA. Most last from three to 3½ hours. Departure points vary.

DC Brew Tours — BUS

(202-759-8687; www.citybrewtours.com/dc; 801 F St NW, Penn Quarter; tours $70-99; M Red, Yellow, Green Line to Gallery Pl-Chinatown) Visit three to four breweries by van. Routes vary but could include DC Brau, Atlas, Hellbender and Port City, among others. Three- to five-hour jaunts feature tastings of 15-plus beers and a light meal. The 3½-hour tour forgoes the meal and pares down the brewery tally. Departure is from outside the Reynolds Center. Tours go daily, at various times.

Bike & Roll — CYCLING

(202-842-2453; www.bikeandrolldc.com; 955 L'Enfant Plaza SW, South DC; tours adult/child from $44/34; 9am-8pm, reduced hours spring & fall, closed early Jan–mid-Mar; M Orange, Silver, Blue, Yellow, Green Line to L'Enfant Plaza) This branch of the bike-rental company (from $16 per two hours) is the one closest to the Mall. In addition to bike rental, it also provides tours. Three-hour jaunts wheel by the main sights of Capitol Hill and the National Mall. The evening rides to the monuments are particularly good.

Old Town Trolley Tours — BUS

(202-832-9800; www.trolleytours.com; 1000 E St NW, Penn Quarter; adult/child $47/30; Circulator National Mall, M Red, Orange, Silver, Blue Line to Metro Center) This open-sided bus offers hop-on, hop-off exploring of some 25 major sights around the Mall, Arlington and Downtown DC. The company also offers a 'monuments by moonlight' tour and the DC Ducks tour, via an amphibious vehicle that plunges into the Potomac. Buy tickets at the Washington Welcome Center (1000 E St NW), at Union Station or online.

Festivals & Events

Independence Day CULTURAL
(Jul 4) Huge crowds gather along Constitution Ave to watch marching bands parade and hear the Declaration of Independence read from the National Archives steps. Later the National Symphony Orchestra plays a concert on the Capitol's West Lawn, followed by mega-fireworks over the National Mall.

National Cherry Blossom Festival CULTURAL
(www.nationalcherryblossomfestival.org; late Mar–mid-Apr) The star of DC's annual calendar celebrates spring's arrival with a kite festival, evening walks by lantern light, cultural fairs and a parade. The three-week event also commemorates Japan's gift of 3000 cherry trees in 1912. It's DC at its prettiest.

Smithsonian Folklife Festival CULTURAL
(www.festival.si.edu; late Jun-early Jul; ; Circulator National Mall, Orange, Silver, Blue Line to Smithsonian) This fun family event, held over 10 days in late June and early July, celebrates international and US cultures. The fest features folk music, dance, crafts, storytelling and ethnic fare, and it highlights a diverse mix of countries and regions.

It takes place on the National Mall between 12th and 14th Sts.

Sleeping

Capitol Hill

William Penn House HOSTEL $
(202-543-5560; www.williampennhouse.org; 515 E Capitol St SE; dm $50-65; ; Orange, Silver, Blue Line to Capitol South or Eastern Market) This friendly Quaker-run guesthouse with garden offers clean, well-maintained dorms, though it could use more bathrooms. There are 30 beds in total, including two 10-bed dorms, two four-bed dorms and one two-bed room. The facility doesn't require religious observance, but there is a religious theme throughout, and it prefers guests who are active in progressive causes. Rates include continental breakfast.

★ **Kimpton George Hotel** HOTEL $$
(202-347-4200; www.hotelgeorge.com; 15 E St NW; d $210-245; ; Red Line to Union Station) Nods to namesake George Washington are pervasive at this hotel, which is the hippest lodging on the Hill. Rooms exude a cool, creamy-white Zen and feature large bathrooms, Colonial-inspired work desks, fun presidential pop art and wallpaper adorned with Washington's cursive-written inaugural address. The handy location puts you between Union Station and the Capitol.

White House & Foggy Bottom

Club Quarters Hotel Washington, DC HOTEL $
(202-463-6400; www.clubquarters.com/washington-dc; 839 17th St NW, White House Area; d $110-250; ; Orange, Silver, Blue Line to Farragut West) Club Quarters is a favorite with business travelers on the go. Rooms are small and many don't have views, lacking any semblance of charm or quirk, but the bed is comfortable, the desk workable, the wi-fi fast enough and the coffee maker well stocked. Oh, and the prices are reasonable in an area where they're usually sky-high.

★ **Hay-Adams Hotel** HERITAGE HOTEL $$$
(202-638-6600; www.hayadams.com; 800 16th St NW, White House Area; d from $400; ; Orange, Silver, Blue Line to McPherson Sq) One of the city's great heritage hotels, the Hay is a beautiful old building where 'nothing is overlooked but the White House.' The property has the best rooms of the old-school luxury genre in the city, sporting elegant decor, top-quality fittings, hugely comfortable beds and luxe bathrooms.

The facilities available here include a gym, restaurant and popular basement bar (p276).

Downtown & Penn Quarter

★ **HI Washington DC Hostel** HOSTEL $
(202-737-2333; www.hiwashingtondc.org; 1009 11th St NW, Downtown; dm $33-55, d $110-130; ; Red, Orange, Silver, Blue Line to Metro Center) Top of the budget picks, this large, friendly hostel attracts a laid-back international crowd and has loads of amenities: lounge rooms, a pool table, a 60in TV for movie nights, free tours of various neighborhoods and historic sites, and also has free continental breakfast and free wi-fi.

Morrison-Clark Historic Inn & Restaurant HISTORIC HOTEL $$
(202-898-1200; www.morrisonclark.com; 1011 L St NW, Downtown; d $180-330; ; M Green, Yellow Line to Mt Vernon Sq/7th St-Convention Center) Listed on the Register of Historic Places and helmed by a doting staff, the 114-room Morrison-Clark comprises two 1864 Victorian residences filled with fine antiques, tear-drop chandeliers and gilded mirrors, and a newer wing with Asian-influenced decor set in the repurposed Chinese church next door. It may sound odd, but the overall effect is lovely and dignified.

Logan Circle, U Street & Columbia Heights

Chester A Arthur House B&B $
(877-893-3233; www.chesterarthurhouse.com; 23 Logan Circle NW, Logan Circle; r $125-165; ; M Green, Yellow Line to U Street/African-American Civil War Memorial/Cardozo) Snooze in one of four rooms in this beautiful Logan Circle row house, located a stumble from the restaurant boom along P and 14th Sts. The 1883 abode is stuffed with crystal chandeliers, antique oil paintings, oriental rugs and a mahogany paneled staircase, plus ephemera from the hosts' global expeditions.

Dupont Circle & Kalorama

Embassy Circle Guest House B&B $$
(202-232-7744; www.dcinns.com; 2224 R St NW, Dupont Circle; r $200-350; ; M Red Line to Dupont Circle) Embassies surround this 1902 French-country-style home, which sits a few blocks from Dupont's nightlife hubbub. The 11 big-windowed rooms are decked out with Persian carpets and original art; they don't have TVs, though they do have wi-fi. Staff feed you well throughout the day, with a hot organic breakfast, afternoon cookies and an evening wine-and-beer soirée.

Tabard Inn BOUTIQUE HOTEL $$
(202-785-1277; www.tabardinn.com; 1739 N St NW, Dupont Circle; r $200-270, without bath $125-170; ; M Red Line to Dupont Circle) Named for *The Canterbury Tales* inn, the Tabard spreads across three Victorian-era row houses. The 40 rooms are hard to generalize: all come with vintage quirks such as iron bed frames and old armoires, though little accents distinguish them – a Matisse-like painted headboard here, Amish-looking quilts there. There are no TVs, and wi-fi can be dodgy, but the of-yore atmosphere prevails.

Adams Morgan

Adam's Inn B&B $
(202-745-3600; www.adamsinn.com; 1746 Lanier Pl NW; r $119-199, without bath $99-160; ; M Red Line to Woodley Park-Zoo/Adams Morgan) Tucked on a shady residential street, this 27-room inn is known for its personalized service, fluffy linens and handy location just a few blocks from 18th St's global smorgasbord. Inviting, homey rooms sprawl through two adjacent townhouses and a carriage house. The common areas have a nice garden patio, and there's a general sense of sherry-scented chintz.

HighRoad Hostel HOSTEL $
(202-735-3622; www.highroadhostels.com; 1804 Belmont Rd NW; dm $35-60; ; M Red Line to Woodley Park-Zoo/Adams Morgan) HighRoad's Victorian row-house exterior belies its modern interior. The dorms come in various configurations, from four to 14 beds – some mixed, others gender-specific. There are private rooms too, a couple with en-suite bathrooms. All have stark white walls, gray metal bunks and black lockers. Nighthawks will groove on nearby 18th St's bounty.

There's a fancy (though small) community kitchen and common room with a fireplace, a chandelier and a jumbo, Netflix-wired TV.

Free movie nights, pasta dinners, outings to local bars and other group activities take place several times a week.

Georgetown

Graham Georgetown BOUTIQUE HOTEL $$
(202-337-0900; www.thegrahamgeorgetown.com; 1075 Thomas Jefferson St NW; r $275-375; ; Circulator Georgetown-Union Station) Set smack in Georgetown's heart, the Graham occupies the intersection between stately tradition and modernist hip. Good-sized rooms have tasteful silver, cream and chocolate decor with pops of ruby and geometric accents. Even the most basic rooms have linens by Liddell Ireland and L'Occitane bath amenities, which means you'll be as fresh, clean and beautiful as the surrounding Georgetown glitterati.

Eating

A homegrown foodie revolution has transformed the once-buttoned-up DC dining scene. Driving it is the bounty of farms at the city's doorstep, along with the booming local economy and influx of worldly younger residents. Small, independent, local-chef-helmed spots now lead the way. And they're doing such a fine job that Michelin deemed the city worthy of its stars.

Capitol Hill

Capitol Hill has long been an outpost for the DC burger bar, the type of unpretentious spot where you roll up your sleeves and knock back a side of beer with your patty. Hip, upscale eateries have colonized the neighborhood, especially along Pennsylvania Ave, Barracks Row (ie 8th St SE, near the Marine Barracks) and around the Navy Yard and Wharf. H St NE, east of Union Station, has seen lots of action. The formerly beat-up area continues to transform with scads of fun, offbeat restaurants and bars stretching from 4th to 14th Sts NE.

Municipal Fish Market SEAFOOD $

(www.wharfdc.com; 1100 Maine Ave SW, South DC; mains $7-13; 8am-9pm; M Orange, Silver, Blue, Yellow, Green Line to L'Enfant Plaza) This open-air fish market has long been adored for its no-nonsense vendors selling fish, crabs, oysters and other seafood so fresh it's still flopping. And now it has received a refresh in conjunction with the adjacent District Wharf. You'll find more seating, a plaza and pier for entertainment, and the restoration of its 100-plus-year-old oyster shed into Rappahannock Oyster Bar.

Jimmy T's DINER $

(202-546-3646; 501 E Capitol St SE; mains $6-10; 6:30am-3pm Tue, Fri & Sat, to 4pm Wed, to 6pm Thu, 8am-3pm Sun; M Orange, Silver, Blue Line to Eastern Market) Jimmy's is a neighborhood joint of the old school, where folks come in with their dogs, cram in to read the *Post,* have a burger or a coffee or an omelet (breakfast all day, by the way) and basically be themselves. If you're hungover on Sunday and in Cap Hill, come here for a greasy cure. Cash only.

Ted's Bulletin AMERICAN $$

(202-544-8337; www.tedsbulletincapitolhill.com; 505 8th St SE; mains $14-24; 7am-10pm Sun-Thu, to 11pm Fri & Sat; M Orange, Silver, Blue Line to Eastern Market) Plop into a booth in the art-deco-meets-diner ambience, and loosen the belt. Nana's biscuits and sausage gravy for breakfast, meatloaf with ketchup glaze for dinner and other hipster spins on comfort foods hit the table. You've got to admire a place that lets you substitute pop tarts for toast. Breakfast is available all day and pulls big crowds on weekends.

Ethiopic ETHIOPIAN $$

(202-675-2066; www.ethiopicrestaurant.com; 401 H St NE; mains $14-20; 5-10pm Tue-Thu, from noon Fri-Sun; M Red Line to Union Station) In a city with no shortage of Ethiopian joints, Ethiopic stands above the rest thanks to its warm, stylish ambience. Top marks go to the various *wats* (stews) and the signature *tibs* (sautéed meat and veg), derived from tender lamb mixed with herbs and hot spices. Vegans get lots of love here too.

★**Rose's Luxury** AMERICAN $$$

(202-580-8889; www.rosesluxury.com; 717 8th St SE; small plates $14-16, family plates $33-36; 5-10pm Mon-Sat; M Orange, Silver, Blue Line to Eastern Market) Michelin-starred Rose's is one of DC's most buzzed-about eateries. Crowds fork into worldly Southern comfort food as twinkling lights glow overhead and candles flicker around the industrial-chic,

LOCAL KNOWLEDGE

EAT STREETS

14th St NW (Logan Circle) DC's most happening road: an explosion of hot-chef bites and bars.

18th St NW (Adams Morgan) Korean, Indian, Thai, Ethiopian, Japanese and Latin mash-up, plus late-night snacks.

8th St SE (Capitol Hill) Known as Barracks Row, it's the locals' favorite for welcoming comfort-food spots.

H St NE (Capitol Hill) Hip strip of pie cafes, noodle shops and gastropubs.

Upshur St (Petworth) Block of cozy, casual *Bon Appetit*–beloved restaurants and cocktail bars.

11th St NW (Columbia Heights) Ever-growing scene of hipster cafes, edgy gastropubs and all-the-rage foodie nooks.

LOCAL KNOWLEDGE

FOOD TRUCKIN'

More than 150 food trucks roll in DC, and the White House neighborhood welcomes the mother lode. They congregate at locations including L St (corner of 20th), Farragut Sq, K St, Franklin Sq, the State Department and George Washington University on weekdays between 11:30am and 1:30pm. Follow the locals' lead, and enjoy a fast and delicious meal for under $15 – maybe a lobster roll poached in butter, a veggie empanada or a bowl of Lao drunken noodles.

half-finished room. Rose's doesn't take reservations, but ordering your meal at the upstairs bar can save time (and the cocktails are delicious).

Downtown & Penn Quarter

★A Baked Joint CAFE $

(☎202-408-6985; www.abakedjoint.com; 440 K St NW, Downtown; mains $5-11; ⏰7am-6pm Mon-Wed, to 10pm Thu & Fri, 8am-6pm Sat & Sun; Ⓜ Red, Yellow, Green Line to Gallery Pl-Chinatown) Order at the counter then take your luscious, heaped-on-housemade-bread sandwich – perhaps the smoked salmon and scallion cream cheese on an open-faced baguette, or the fried green tomatoes on buttered griddled sourdough – to a bench or table in the big, open room. Natural light streams in the floor-to-ceiling windows.

Not hungry? It's also a great place for a well-made latte.

Daikaya JAPANESE $

(☎202-589-1600; www.daikaya.com; 705 6th St NW, Penn Quarter; mains $12-14; ⏰11am-10pm Sun-Tue, to 10:30pm Wed & Thu, to midnight Fri & Sat; Ⓜ Red, Yellow, Green Line to Gallery Pl-Chinatown) Daikaya offers two options. Our favorite is downstairs, which is a casual ramen-noodle shop, where locals swarm in and slurp with friends in the slick wooden booths. Upstairs it's a sake-pouring Japanese *izakaya* (tavern), with rice-bowl lunches and small, fishy plates. Note the upstairs closes between lunch and dinner (ie between 2pm and 5pm).

Matchbox Vintage Pizza Bistro PIZZA $

(☎202-289-4441; www.matchboxrestaurants.com; 713 H St NW, Downtown; 10in pizzas $13-20; ⏰11am-10:30pm Mon-Thu, to 11:30pm Fri, 10am-11:30pm Sat, 10am-10:30pm Sun; Ⓜ Red, Yellow, Green Line to Gallery Pl-Chinatown) The pizza here has a devout following of gastronomes and the restaurant's warm, exposed-brick interior is typically packed. What's so good about it? Fresh ingredients, a thin, blistered crust baked by angels, and more fresh ingredients. Oh, and the beer list rocks, with Belgian ales and hopped-up craft brews flowing from the taps.

Reserve ahead to avoid a wait.

Rasika INDIAN $$

(☎202-637-1222; www.rasikarestaurant.com; 633 D St NW, Penn Quarter; mains $19-28; ⏰11:30am-2:30pm Mon-Fri, 5:30-10:30pm Mon-Thu, 5-11pm Fri & Sat; 🖉; Ⓜ Green, Yellow Line to Archives-Navy Memorial-Penn Quarter) Rasika is as cutting edge as Indian food gets. The room resembles a Jaipur palace decorated by modernist art-gallery curators. Top marks go to the *murgh mussalam*, a plate of juicy tandoori chicken with cashews and quail eggs; and the deceptively simple *dal* (lentils), with just the right kiss of sharp fenugreek. Vegetarians will feel a lot of love here.

Kinship AMERICAN $$$

(☎202-737-7700; www.kinshipdc.com; 1015 7th St NW, Downtown; mains $16-35; ⏰5:30-10pm; Ⓜ Yellow, Green Line to Mt Vernon Sq/7th St-Convention Center) Round up your friends and enjoy a convivial night at this Michelin-starred restaurant by James Beard Award–winning chef Eric Ziebold. Pick and choose across the menu's five categories echoing the chef's passions: ingredients (crispy Jerusalem artichokes, *yuzukoshō* broth), history (classics), craft (using culinary techniques), indulgence (caviar, white truffles) and 'For the Table.'

★Dabney AMERICAN $$$

(☎202-450-1015; www.thedabney.com; 122 Blagden Alley NW, Downtown; small plates $14-25; ⏰5:30-10pm Tue-Thu, 5-11pm Fri & Sat, 5-10pm Sun; Ⓜ Green, Yellow Line to Mt Vernon Sq/7th St-Convention Center) Chef Jeremiah Langhorne studied historic cookbooks, discovering recipes that used local ingredients and lesser-explored flavors in his quest to resuscitate mid-Atlantic cuisine lost to the ages. Most of the dishes are even cooked over a wood-burning hearth, as in George Washington's time. Langhorne gives it all a modern twist – enough to earn him a Michelin star.

Logan Circle, U Street & Columbia Heights

★Ben's Chili Bowl AMERICAN $

(202-667-0058; www.benschilibowl.com; 1213 U St NW, U Street; mains $6-10; 6am-2am Mon-Thu, to 4am Fri, 7am-4am Sat, 11am-midnight Sun; M Green, Yellow Line to U Street/African-American Civil War Memorial/Cardozo) Ben's is a DC institution. The main stock in trade is half-smokes, DC's meatier, smokier version of the hot dog, usually slathered with mustard, onions and the namesake chili. For 60-plus years presidents, rock stars and Supreme Court justices have come to indulge in the humble diner, but despite the hype, Ben's remains a true neighborhood establishment. Cash only.

★Compass Rose INTERNATIONAL $$

(202-506-4765; www.compassrosedc.com; 1346 T St NW, U Street; small plates $8-16; 5pm-2am Mon-Thu, to 3am Fri & Sat, 11am-2am Sun; M Green, Yellow Line to U Street/African-American Civil War Memorial/Cardozo) Compass Rose feels like a secret garden, set in a discreet townhouse a whisker from 14th St's buzz. The exposed brick walls and sky-blue ceiling give it a casually romantic air. The menu is a mash-up of global comfort foods, so dinner might entail Jamaican curried lamb, Argentinian asado (rib eye with chimichurri) and Georgian *khachapuri* (buttery, cheese-filled bread).

Estadio SPANISH $$

(202-319-1404; www.estadio-dc.com; 1520 14th St NW, Logan Circle; tapas $7-17; 5-10pm Mon-Thu, 11:30am-2pm & 5-11pm Fri, 11am-2pm & 5-11pm Sat, 11am-2pm & 5-9pm Sun; M Red Line to Dupont Circle) Estadio buzzes with a low-lit, date-night vibe. The tapas menu is as deep as an ocean trench. There are four variations of *ibérico* ham and a delicious foie gras, scrambled egg and truffle open-faced sandwich. Wash it down with some traditional *calimocho* (red wine and cola). No reservations after 6pm, which usually means a wait at the bar.

Busboys & Poets CAFE $$

(202-387-7638; www.busboysandpoets.com; 2021 14th St NW, U Street; mains $16-22; 7am-midnight Mon-Thu, to 1am Fri, 8am-1am Sat, 8am-midnight Sun; M Green, Yellow Line to U Street/African-American Civil War Memorial/Cardozo) Busboys & Poets is one of U Street's linchpins. Locals pack the place for coffee, boozy brunches, books and a progressive vibe that makes San Francisco feel conservative. The lengthy, vegetarian-friendly menu spans sandwiches, pizzas and Southern fare such as shrimp and grits. Tuesday night's open-mike poetry reading ($5 admission, from 9pm to 11pm) draws big crowds.

Le Diplomate FRENCH $$$

(202-332-3333; www.lediplomatedc.com; 1601 14th St NW, Logan Circle; mains $20-35; 5-11pm Mon-Thu, to midnight Fri, 9:30am-midnight Sat, 9:30am-11pm Sun; M Green, Yellow Line to U Street/African-American Civil War Memorial/Cardozo) This charming French bistro is one of the hottest tables in town. DC celebrities galore cozy up in the leather banquettes and at the sidewalk tables. They come for an authentic slice of Paris, from the coq au vin (wine-braised chicken) and aromatic baguettes to the vintage curios and nudie photos decorating the bathrooms. Make reservations.

Dupont Circle & Kalorama

Zorba's Cafe GREEK $

(202-387-8555; www.zorbascafe.com; 1612 20th St NW, Dupont Circle; mains $13-15; 11am-11:30pm Mon-Sat, to 10:30pm Sun; M Red Line to Dupont Circle) Generous portions of moussaka and souvlaki, as well as pitchers of Rolling Rock beer, make family-run Zorba's Cafe one of DC's best bargain haunts. On warm days the outdoor patio packs with locals. With the bouzouki music playing in the background, you can almost imagine you're in the Greek islands.

Afterwords Cafe AMERICAN $$

(202-387-3825; www.kramers.com; 1517 Connecticut Ave NW, Dupont Circle; mains $18-22; 7:30am-1am Sun-Thu, to 3am Fri & Sat; M Red Line to Dupont Circle) Attached to Kramerbooks, this buzzing spot is not your average bookstore cafe. The packed indoor tables, wee bar and outdoor patio overflow with good cheer. The menu features tasty bistro fare and an ample beer selection, making it a prime spot for happy hour, brunch and late nights on weekends (open until 3am, baby!).

Browsing the stacks before stuffing the gut is many locals' favorite way to spend a Washington weekend.

★Bistrot du Coin FRENCH $$

(202-234-6969; www.bistrotducoin.com; 1738 Connecticut Ave NW, Dupont Circle; mains $20-30; 11:30am-midnight Mon-Wed, 11:30am-1am Thu &

Fri, noon-1am Sat, noon-midnight Sun; Ⓜ Red Line to Dupont Circle) The lively and much-loved Bistrot du Coin is a neighborhood favorite for roll-up-your sleeves, working-class French fare. The kitchen sends out consistently good onion soup, classic *steak-frites* (grilled steak and French fries), cassoulet, open-face sandwiches and 11 varieties of its famous *moules* (mussels). Regional wines from around the motherland accompany the food by the glass, carafe and bottle.

★Little Serow THAI $$$
(www.littleserow.com; 1511 17th St NW, Dupont Circle; prix-fixe menu $54; ⏲5:30-10pm Tue-Thu, to 10:30pm Fri & Sat; Ⓜ Red Line to Dupont Circle) Set in a cavern-like green basement, Little Serow has no phone, no reservations and no sign on the door, and it only seats groups of four or fewer (larger parties will be separated). Despite all this, people line up around the block. What for? Superlative northern Thai cuisine. The single-option menu, consisting of six or so hot-spiced courses, changes weekly.

Komi FUSION $$$
(☎202-332-9200; www.komirestaurant.com; 1509 17th St NW, Dupont Circle; set menu $165; ⏲5:30-10pm Tue-Sat; Ⓜ Red Line to Dupont Circle) There is an admirable simplicity to Komi's changing menu, rooted in Greece and influenced by everything – but primarily genius. Its Michelin star proves that. Dinner comprises 12 or so dishes; say suckling pig, scallops and truffles, or roasted baby goat. Komi's cozy space doesn't take groups larger than four. Call a month before your desired dining date for required reservations.

Hank's Oyster Bar SEAFOOD $$$
(☎202-462-4265; www.hanksoysterbar.com; 1624 Q St NW, Dupont Circle; mains $28-36; ⏲11:30am-1am Mon-Thu, 11:30am-2am Fri, 11am-2am Sat, 11am-1am Sun; Ⓜ Red Line to Dupont Circle) DC has several oyster bars, but mini-chain Hank's is our favorite, mixing power-player muscle with a casual, beachy ambience. As you'd expect, the oyster menu is extensive and excellent; there are always at least four varieties on hand, along with lobster rolls, fried clams and witty cocktails. It's best to reserve ahead.

Hank's pre-theater menu (three courses for $32, offered between 5:30pm and 6:30pm) earns big praise.

Adams Morgan

Diner AMERICAN $
(☎202-232-8800; www.dinerdc.com; 2453 18th St NW; mains $9-18; ⏲24hr; 🍷👪; Ⓜ Red Line to Woodley Park-Zoo/Adams Morgan) The Diner serves hearty comfort food, any time of the day or night. It's ideal for wee-hour breakfast scarf-downs, weekend Bloody Mary brunches (if you don't mind crowds) or any time you want unfussy, well-prepared American fare. Omelets, fat buttermilk pancakes, mac 'n' cheese, veggie tacos and burgers hit the tables with aplomb. It's a good spot for kids, too.

★Donburi JAPANESE $
(☎202-629-1047; www.donburidc.com; 2438 18th St NW; mains $11-13; ⏲11am-10pm; Ⓜ Red Line to Woodley Park-Zoo/Adams Morgan) Hole-in-the-wall Donburi has 14 seats at a wooden counter where you get a front-row view of the slicing, dicing chefs. *Donburi* means 'bowl' in Japanese, and that's what arrives steaming hot and filled with, say, panko-coated shrimp atop rice, blended with the house's sweet-and-savory sauce. It's a simple, authentic meal. There's often a line, but it moves quickly. No reservations.

Donburi has another venue in Dupont Circle that's larger, but the Adams Morgan location is the atmospheric original.

Julia's Empanadas LATIN AMERICAN $
(☎202-328-6232; www.juliasempanadas.com; 2452 18th St NW; empanadas from $5; ⏲10am-midnight Mon-Wed, to 4am Thu-Sat, to 8pm Sun; Ⓜ Red Line to Woodley Park-Zoo/Adams Morgan) A frequent winner in DC's 'best late-night eats' polls, Julia's stuffs its dough bombs with chorizo, Jamaican beef curry, spinach and more. Flavors peak if you've been drinking. The little chain has a handful of takeout shops around town.

★Tail Up Goat MEDITERRANEAN $$
(☎202-986-9600; www.tailupgoat.com; 1827 Adams Mill Rd NW; mains $18-27; ⏲5:30-10pm Mon-Thu, 5-10pm Fri & Sat, 11am-1pm & 5-10pm Sun; Ⓜ Red Line to Woodley Park-Zoo/Adams Morgan) With its pale-blue walls, light wood decor and lantern-like lights dangling overhead, Tail Up Goat exudes a warm, island-y vibe. The lamb ribs are the specialty – crispy and lusciously fatty, served with date-molasses juice. The housemade breads and spreads star on the menu too – say, flaxseed sour-

dough with beets. No wonder Michelin gave it a star.

Georgetown

★Simply Banh Mi VIETNAMESE $

(☎202-333-5726; www.simplybanhmidc.com; 1624 Wisconsin Ave NW; mains $7-10; ⏱11am-7pm Sun, Tue & Wed, to 9pm Thu-Sat; ; Circulator Georgetown-Union Station) There's nothing fancy about the small, below-street-level space, and the compact menu sticks mostly to sandwiches and bubble tea. But the brother-sister owners know how to take a crusty baguette, stuff it with delicious lemongrass pork or other meat (or tofu), and make your day. They're super-attentive to quality and to customer needs (vegan, gluten-free etc).

Baked & Wired BAKERY $

(☎703-663-8727; www.bakedandwired.com; 1052 Thomas Jefferson St NW; baked goods $3-8; ⏱7am-8pm Mon-Thu, to 9pm Fri, 8am-9pm Sat, 8am-8pm Sun; Circulator Georgetown-Union Station) This cheery cafe whips up beautifully made coffees, bacon cheddar buttermilk biscuits and enormous cupcakes (like the banana and peanut-butter-frosted Elvis impersonator). It's a fine spot to join university students and cyclists coming off the nearby trails for a sugar buzz. When the weather permits, patrons take their treats outside to the adjacent grassy area by the C&O Canal. Inside, head to the right for coffee drinks and stay left for the sweet treats.

Chez Billy Sud FRENCH $$$

(☎202-965-2606; www.chezbillysud.com; 1039 31st St NW; mains $25-38; ⏱5-10pm Mon, 11:30am-2pm & 5-10pm Tue-Thu, 11:30am-2pm & 5-11pm Fri, 11am-2pm & 5-11pm Sat, 11am-2pm & 5-10pm Sun; Circulator Georgetown-Union Station) An endearing little bistro tucked away on a residential block, Billy's mint-green walls, gilt mirrors and wee marble bar exude laid-back elegance. Mustachioed servers bring baskets of warm bread to the white-linen-clothed tables, along with crispy moulard duck leg, Maine mussels with pastis, and plump cream puffs.

Drinking & Nightlife

When Andrew Jackson swore the oath of office in 1829, the self-proclaimed populist dispensed with pomp and circumstance and, quite literally, threw a raging kegger. Folks got so gone they started looting art from the White House. The historical lesson: DC loves a drink, and these days it enjoys said tipples in many incarnations besides executive-mansion-trashing throwdowns.

Capitol Hill

★Copycat Co COCKTAIL BAR

(☎202-241-1952; www.copycatcompany.com; 1110 H St NE, Capitol Hill; ⏱5pm-2am Sun-Thu, to 3am Fri & Sat; M Red Line to Union Station then streetcar) When you walk into Copycat it feels like a Chinese fast-food restaurant. That's because it is (sort of) on the 1st floor, where Chinese street-food nibbles are available. The fizzy drinks and egg-white-topped cocktails fill glasses upstairs, in the dimly lit, speakeasy-meets-opium-den-vibed bar. Staff are unassuming and gracious in helping newbies figure out what they want from the lengthy menu.

Bluejacket Brewery BREWERY

(☎202-524-4862; www.bluejacketdc.com; 300 Tingey St SE, South DC; ⏱11am-1am Sun-Thu, to 2am Fri & Sat; ; M Green Line to Navy Yard-Ballpark) Beer-lovers' heads will explode in Bluejacket. Pull up a stool at the mod-industrial bar, gaze at the silvery tanks bubbling up the ambitious brews, then make the hard decision about which of the 20 tap beers you want to try. A dry-hopped kolsch? Sweet-spiced stout? A cask-aged farmhouse ale? Four-ounce tasting pours help with decision-making.

Granville Moore's PUB

(☎202-399-2546; www.granvillemoores.com; 1238 H St NE, Capitol Hill; ⏱5-10pm Mon-Thu, to 11pm Fri, 11am-11pm Sat, 11am-10pm Sun; M Red Line to Union Station then streetcar) Besides being one of DC's best places to grab *frites* and steak au poivre, Granville Moore's has an extensive Belgian-beer menu that should satisfy any fan of low-country boozing. With its raw, wooden fixtures and walls that look like they're made from daub and mud, the interior resembles a medieval barracks. The fireside setting is ideal come winter.

Tune Inn BAR

(☎202-543-2725; 331 Pennsylvania Ave SE, Capitol Hill; ⏱8am-2am Sun-Thu, to 3am Fri & Sat; M Orange, Silver, Blue Line to Capitol South or Eastern Market) Tune Inn has been helping the thirsty since 1947. Mounted deer heads

BEER

The city is serious about beer. It even brews much of its own delicious stuff. That trend started in 2009, when DC Brau became the District's first brewery to launch in more than 50 years. Several more beer makers followed. As you drink around town, keep an eye out for local concoctions from 3 Stars, Atlas Brew Works, Hellbender and Lost Rhino (from northern Virginia).

stare from the wall and watch over old-timers knocking back Budweisers at the bar. Meanwhile, Hill staffers, off-duty cops and other locals scarf greasy-spoon grub and all-day breakfasts in the vinyl-backed booths.

How do you know when you're in a first-rate dive? When your beer-and-shot combo glows under the dim light of an antler chandelier.

White House & Foggy Bottom

★ Off the Record BAR

(☎ 202-638-6600; www.hayadams.com/dining/off-the-record; 800 16th St NW, Hay-Adams Hotel, White House Area; ⏲ 11:30am-midnight Sun-Thu, to 12:30am Fri & Sat; Ⓜ Orange, Silver, Blue Line to McPherson Sq) Table seating, an open fire in winter and a discreet basement location in one of the city's most prestigious hotels (p269), right across from the White House – it's no wonder DC's important people submerge to be seen and not heard (as the tagline goes) here. Experienced bartenders swirl martinis and manhattans for the suit-wearing crowd. Enter through the hotel lobby.

Downtown & Penn Quarter

Columbia Room COCKTAIL BAR

(☎ 202-316-9396; www.columbiaroomdc.com; 124 Blagden Alley NW, Downtown; ⏲ 5pm-12:30am Tue-Thu, to 1:30am Fri & Sat; Ⓜ Green, Yellow Line to Mt Vernon Sq/7th St-Convention Center) Serious mixology goes on at Columbia Room, the kind of place that sources spring water from Scotland, and uses pickled cherry blossom and barley tea among its ingredients. But it's done in a refreshingly nonsnooty environment. Choose from three areas: the festive Punch Garden on the outdoor roof deck, the comfy, leather-chair-dotted Spirits Library, or the 14-seat, prix-fixe Tasting Room.

Logan Circle, U Street & Columbia Heights

★ Right Proper Brewing Co BREWERY

(☎ 202-607-2337; www.rightproperbrewery.com; 624 T St NW, Logan Circle; ⏲ 5-11pm Mon-Thu, 11:30am-midnight Fri & Sat, 11:30am-10pm Sun; Ⓜ Green, Yellow Line to Shaw-Howard U) Right Proper Brewing makes sublime ales in a building that shares a wall with the joint where Duke Ellington used to play pool. It's the Shaw district's neighborhood clubhouse, a big, sunny space filled with folks gabbing at reclaimed wood tables. The tap line-up changes regularly as the brewers work their magic, but crisp farmhouse ales are an oft-flowing specialty.

Dacha Beer Garden BEER GARDEN

(☎ 202-350-9888; www.dachadc.com; 1600 7th St NW, Shaw; ⏲ 4-10:30pm Mon, Tue & Thu, 3pm-midnight Fri, 8am-midnight Sat, noon-10:30pm Sun, reduced hours winter; 👪 🐾; Ⓜ Green, Yellow Line to Shaw-Howard U) Happiness reigns in Dacha's freewheeling beer garden. Kids and dogs bound around the picnic tables, while adults hoist glass boots filled with German brews. When the weather gets nippy, staff bring blankets and stoke the firepit. And it all takes place under the sultry gaze of Elizabeth Taylor (or a mural of her, which sprawls across the back wall).

Churchkey BAR

(☎ 202-567-2576; www.churchkeydc.com; 1337 14th St NW, Logan Circle; ⏲ 4pm-1am Mon-Thu, to 2am Fri, 11:30am-2am Sat, 11:30am-1am Sun; Ⓜ Orange, Silver, Blue Line to McPherson Sq) Coppery, mod-industrial Churchkey glows with hipness. Fifty beers flow from the taps, plus five brain-walloping, cask-aged ales. If none of those please you, another 500 types of brew are available by bottle (including gluten-free suds). Churchkey is the upstairs counterpart to **Birch & Barley** (☎ 202-567-2576; www.birchandbarley.com; mains $17-29; ⏲ 5:30-10pm Tue-Thu, to 11pm Fri, 11am-3pm & 5:30-11pm Sat, 11am-3pm & 5-9pm Sun), a popular nouveau comfort-food restaurant, and you can order much of its menu at the bar.

U Street Music Hall CLUB

(☎ 202-588-1889; www.ustreetmusichall.com; 1115 U St NW, U Street; tickets $10-25; ⏲ hours vary;

Ⓜ Green, Yellow Line to U Street/African-American Civil War Memorial/Cardozo) Two local DJs own and operate the basement club; it looks like a no-frills rock bar, but it has a pro sound system, a cork-cushioned dance floor and other accoutrements of a serious dance club. Alternative bands also thrash a couple of nights per week to keep it fresh. Shows start between 7pm and 10pm.

Dupont Circle & Kalorama

★ Bar Charley BAR

(☎ 202-627-2183; www.barcharley.com; 1825 18th St NW, Dupont Circle; ⏲ 5pm-12:30am Mon-Thu, 4pm-1:30am Fri, 10am-1:30am Sat, 10am-midnight Sun; Ⓜ Red Line to Dupont Circle) Bar Charley draws a mixed crowd from the neighborhood – young, old, gay and straight. They come for groovy cocktails sloshing in vintage glassware and ceramic tiki mugs, served at very reasonable prices by DC standards. Try the gin and gingery Suffering Bastard. The beer list isn't huge, but it's thoughtfully chosen with some wild ales. Around 60 wines available too.

★ Board Room BAR

(☎ 202-518-7666; www.boardroomdc.com; 1737 Connecticut Ave NW, Dupont Circle; ⏲ 4pm-2am Mon-Thu, 4pm-3am Fri, noon-3am Sat, noon-2am Sun; Ⓜ Red Line to Dupont Circle) Grab a table, pull up a stool and crush your opponent at Hungry Hungry Hippos. Or cozy up to a serious game of Scrabble. Board Room lets you flash back to childhood via stacks of board games (Battleship, Risk, Operation) – name it, and it's available to rent for $2.

Around 20 beers flow from the taps and are available by pitcher to stoke the festivities.

JR's GAY

(☎ 202-328-0090; www.jrsbar-dc.com; 1519 17th St NW, Dupont Circle; ⏲ 4pm-2am Mon-Thu, 4pm-3am Fri, 1pm-3am Sat, 1pm-2am Sun; Ⓜ Red Line to Dupont Circle) Button-down shirts are de rigueur at this gay hangout frequented by the 20- and 30-something, work-hard-and-play-hard set. Some DC residents claim that the crowd here epitomizes the conservative nature of the capital's gay scene, but even if you love to hate it, as many do, JR's knows how to rock a happy hour and is teeming more often than not.

Adams Morgan

★ Dan's Cafe BAR

(☎ 202-265-0299; 2315 18th St NW; ⏲ 7pm-2am Tue-Thu, to 3am Fri & Sat; Ⓜ Red Line to Woodley Park-Zoo/Adams Morgan) This is one of DC's great dive bars. The interior looks sort of like an evil Elks Club, all unironically old-school 'art,' cheap paneling and dim lights barely illuminating the unapologetic slumminess. It's famed for its whopping, mix-it-yourself drinks, where you get a ketchup-type squirt bottle of booze, a can of soda and bucket of ice for $20. Cash only.

Songbyrd Record Cafe & Music House CAFE

(☎ 202-450-2917; www.songbyrddc.com; 2475-2477 18th St NW; mains $10-14; ⏲ 8am-2am Sun-Thu, to 3am Fri & Sat, cafe to 10pm; 📶; Ⓜ Red Line to Woodley Park-Zoo/Adams Morgan) By

LGBTIQ+ DC

DC is one of the most gay-friendly cities in the USA. It has an admirable track record of progressivism and a bit of a scene to boot. The rainbow stereotype here consists of well-dressed professionals and activists working in politics on LGBTIQ+ issues such as gay marriage (legal in DC since 2010). The community concentrates in Dupont Circle, but U Street, Shaw, Capitol Hill and Logan Circle also have lots of gay-friendly businesses.

Capital Area Gay & Lesbian Chamber of Commerce (www.caglcc.org) Sponsors lots of networking events around town.

LGBT DC (https://washington.org/lgbtq) The DC tourism office's portal, with events, neighborhood breakdowns and a travel resource guide.

Metro Weekly (www.metroweekly.com) Free weekly news magazine. Aimed at a younger demographic than its rival, the *Washington Blade*.

Washington Blade (www.washingtonblade.com) Free weekly gay newspaper. Covers politics and has lots of business and nightlife listings.

day hang out in the retro cafe, drinking excellent coffee, munching sandwiches and browsing the soul and indie LPs for sale. You can even cut your own record in the vintage recording booth ($15). By night the party moves to the DJ-spinning bar, where beer and cocktails flow alongside burgers and tacos, and indie bands rock the basement club.

Georgetown

Tombs PUB

(202-337-6668; www.tombs.com; 1226 36th St NW; 11:30am-1:30am Mon-Thu, to 2:30am Fri, 11am-2:30am Sat, 9:30am-1:30am Sun; Circulator Georgetown-Union Station) Every college of a certain pedigree has 'that' bar – the one where faculty and students alike sip pints under athletic regalia of the old school. The Tombs is Georgetown's contribution to the genre. If it looks familiar, think back to the '80s: the subterranean pub was one of the settings for the classic film *St Elmo's Fire*. The close-set tables buzz on various Tuesdays for Trivia Night shenanigans.

Check the website for the schedule.

☆ Entertainment

Live Music

★Black Cat LIVE MUSIC

(202-667-4490; www.blackcatdc.com; 1811 14th St NW, U Street; tickets $10-25; M Green, Yellow Line to U Street/African-American Civil War Memorial/Cardozo) The Black Cat is the go-to venue for music that's loud and grungy with a punk edge. The White Stripes, Arcade Fire and Foo Fighters have all thrashed here. The big action takes place on the Mainstage. The legendary Backstage and Red Room bar are being reimagined on the club's 2nd story; check the website for updates.

9:30 Club LIVE MUSIC

(202-265-0930; www.930.com; 815 V St NW, U Street; tickets $20-35; M Green, Yellow Line to U Street/African-American Civil War Memorial/Cardozo) The 9:30, which can pack 1200 people into a surprisingly compact venue, is the granddaddy of the live-music scene in DC. Pretty much every big name that comes through town ends up on this stage at some point.

Headliners usually begin between 10:30pm and 11:30pm.

Performing Arts

★Kennedy Center PERFORMING ARTS

(202-467-4600; www.kennedy-center.org; 2700 F St NW, Foggy Bottom; box office 10am-9pm Mon-Sat, noon-9pm Sun; M Orange, Silver, Blue Line to Foggy Bottom-GWU) Overlooking the Potomac River, the magnificent Kennedy Center hosts a staggering array of performances – more than 2000 each year in venues including the Concert Hall, home to the **National Symphony** (www.kennedy-center.org/nso), and Opera House, home to the **National Opera** (www.kennedy-center.org/wno). Free performances are staged on the Millennium Stage daily at 6pm as part of the center's 'Performing Arts for Everyone' initiative.

Shakespeare Theatre Company THEATER

(202-547-1122; www.shakespearetheatre.org; 450 7th St NW, Lansburgh Theatre, Penn Quarter; average ticket $85; M Green, Yellow Line to Archives-Navy Memorial-Penn Quarter) The nation's foremost Shakespeare company presents masterful works by the Bard, as well as plays by George Bernard Shaw, Oscar Wilde, Eugene O'Neill and other greats. The season spans about a half-dozen productions annually, plus a free summer Shakespeare series on-site for two weeks in late August. The company also performs at the nearby Sidney Harman Hall, 610 F St NW.

★Woolly Mammoth Theatre Company THEATER

(202-393-3939; www.woollymammoth.net; 641 D St NW, Penn Quarter; average ticket $67; M Green, Yellow Line to Archives-Navy Memorial-Penn Quarter) Woolly Mammoth is the edgiest of DC's experimental groups. For most shows, $20 'stampede' seats are available at the box office two hours before performances. They're limited in number, and sold first-come, first-served, so get there early.

Sports

★Nationals Park STADIUM

(202-675-6287; www.mlb.com/nationals; 1500 S Capitol St SE, South DC; M Green Line to Navy Yard-Ballpark) The major-league Washington Nationals play baseball at this spiffy stadium beside the Anacostia River. Don't miss the mid-fourth-inning 'Presidents' Race' – an odd foot race between giant-headed caricatures of George Washington, Abraham Lincoln, Thomas Jefferson and Teddy Roosevelt.

Hip bars and eateries and playful green spaces surround the ballpark, and more keep coming as the area gentrifies.

Information

Cultural Tourism DC (www.culturaltourismdc.org) Neighborhood-oriented events and DIY tours.

Destination DC (www.washington.org) Official tourism site packed with sightseeing and event info.

Lonely Planet (www.lonelyplanet.com/usa/washington-dc) Destination information, hotel reviews and more.

Washingtonian (www.washingtonian.com) Features on dining, entertainment and local luminaries.

Getting There & Away

AIR

Dulles International Airport (IAD; ☎703-572-2700, 703-572-8296; www.flydulles.com) is located in the Virginia suburbs 26 miles west of Washington, DC. It has free wi-fi, several currency exchanges and restaurants throughout the terminals. Famed architect Eero Saarinen designed the swooping main building. The Metro Silver Line now reaches Dulles International Airport, providing a transfer-free ride at long last.

Ronald Reagan Washington National Airport (DCA; www.flyreagan.com) is 4.5 miles south of downtown in Arlington, VA. It has free wi-fi, several eateries and a currency exchange (National Hall, Concourse Level).

Baltimore/Washington International Thurgood Marshall Airport (BWI; ☎410-859-7111; www.bwiairport.com; 7035 Elm Rd; 📶) is 30 miles northeast of DC in Maryland.

BUS

Cheap bus services to and from Washington, DC, abound. Most charge $25 to $30 for a one-way trip to NYC (it takes four to five hours). Many companies use Union Station as their hub; other pickup locations are scattered around town, but are always accessible by Metro. Tickets usually need to be bought online, but can sometimes be purchased on the bus itself if there are still seats available.

BestBus (☎202-332-2691; www.bestbus.com; cnr 20th St & Massachusetts Ave NW, Dupont Circle; 📶; Ⓜ Red Line to Dupont Circle) Several trips to/from NYC daily. The main bus stop is by Dupont Circle; there's another at Union Station.

Greyhound (☎202-589-5141; www.greyhound.com; 50 Massachusetts Ave NE, Capitol Hill; 📶; Ⓜ Red Line to Union Station) Provides nationwide service. The terminal is at Union Station.

Megabus (☎877-462-6342; http://us.megabus.com; 50 Massachusetts Ave NE, Capitol Hill; 📶; Ⓜ Red Line to Union Station) Offers the most trips to NYC (around 15 to 20 per day), as well as other East Coast cities; arrives at/departs from Union Station. Buses run behind schedule fairly often.

Peter Pan Bus Lines (☎800-343-9999; www.peterpanbus.com; 50 Massachusetts Ave NE, Capitol Hill; 📶; Ⓜ Red Line to Union Station) Travels throughout northeastern USA; has its terminal at Union Station.

Vamoose Bus (☎212-695-6766; www.vamoosebus.com; 1801 N Lynn St; $60) Service between NYC and Arlington, VA (the stop is near the Rosslyn Metro station).

Washington Deluxe (☎866-287-6932; www.washny.com; 1610 Connecticut Ave NW, Dupont Circle; 📶; Ⓜ Red Line to Dupont Circle) Good express service to/from NYC. There are stops located at both Dupont Circle and Union Station.

TRAIN

Magnificent, beaux-arts **Union Station** (☎202-289-1908; www.unionstationdc.com; 50 Massachusetts Ave NE, Capitol Hill; ⏲24hr, ticketed passengers only midnight-5am; Ⓜ Red Line to Union Station) is the city's rail hub. There's a handy Metro station (Red Line) here for transport onward in the city.

Amtrak (www.amtrak.com) arrives at least once per hour from major East Coast cities. Its Northeast Regional trains are cheaper but slower (about 3½ hours between NYC and Washington, DC).

Amtrak's Acela Express trains are more expensive but faster (2¾ hours between NYC and DC; 6½ hours between Boston and DC). The express trains also have bigger seats and other business-class amenities.

MARC trains (www.mta.maryland.gov) arrive frequently from downtown Baltimore (one hour) and other Maryland towns, as well as Harpers Ferry, WV.

Getting Around

The Metro is the main way to move around the city. Buy a rechargeable SmarTrip card at any Metro station. You must use the card to enter *and* exit station turnstiles.

Bicycle Capital Bikeshare stations are everywhere; a day pass costs $8.

DC Circulator bus Useful for the Mall, Georgetown, Adams Morgan and other areas with limited Metro service. Fare is $1.

Metro Fast, frequent, ubiquitous (except during weekend track maintenance). It operates between 5am (from 7am weekends) and 11:30pm (1am on Friday and Saturday). Fares are from $2 to $6 depending on distance traveled. A day pass costs $14.75.

Taxi Relatively easy to find (less so at night), but costly. Ridesharing companies are used more in the District.

MARYLAND

The nickname 'America in Miniature' perfectly captures Maryland: this small state possesses all of the best bits of the country, from the Appalachian Mountains in the west to sandy white beaches in the east. A blend of northern street smarts and Southern down-home appeal gives this border state an appealing identity crisis.

Its main city, Baltimore, is a sharp, demanding port town; the Eastern Shore jumbles art-and-antique-minded city escapees and working fishermen; and the DC suburbs are packed with government and office workers seeking green space, and those seeking more affordable rents.

Yet it all somehow works – scrumptious blue crabs, Natty Boh beer and lovely Chesapeake country being the glue that binds it all.

This is also an extremely diverse and progressive state, and was one of the first in the USA to legalize gay marriage.

History

George Calvert established Maryland as a refuge for persecuted English Catholics in 1634 when he purchased St Mary's City from the local Piscataway tribe, with whom he initially tried to coexist. Puritan refugees drove both Piscataway and Catholics from control and shifted power to Annapolis; their harassment of Catholics produced the Tolerance Act, a flawed but progressive law that allowed freedom of any (Christian) worship in Maryland – a North American first.

A commitment to diversity has always characterized this state, despite a mixed record on slavery. Although state loyalties were split during the Civil War, a Confederate invasion was halted here in 1862 at Antietam. Following the war, Maryland harnessed its Black, white and immigrant work force, splitting the economy between Baltimore's industry and shipping, and the later need for services in Washington, DC.

Today the answer to 'What makes a Marylander?' is 'all of the above': the state mixes rich, poor, foreign-born, urban sophisticates and rural villages like few other states do.

Baltimore

Once among the most important port towns in America, Baltimore – or 'Bawlmer' to locals – is a city of contradictions. It remains a defiant, working-class city tied to its nautical past, but in recent years has earned acclaim for impressive, up-to-the-minute entrepreneurial ventures, from new boutique hotels and edgy exhibits at world-class museums to forgotten neighborhoods now bustling with trendy food courts and farm-to-table restaurants. Traditionalists shouldn't worry, though – local culture and hometown sports, from lacrosse to baseball, remain part of the appeal.

For travelers, a visit to B'more (another nickname) should include one trip to the waterfront, whether it's the Disney-fied Inner Harbor, the cobblestoned streets of portside Fells Point or the shores of Fort McHenry, birthplace of America's national anthem, 'The Star-Spangled Banner.' As you'll discover, there's an intense, sincere friendliness here, which is why Baltimore lives up to its final, most accurate nickname: 'Charm City.'

Sights

Harborplace & Inner Harbor

This is where most tourists start and, unfortunately, end their Baltimore sightseeing. The Inner Harbor is a big, gleaming waterfront-renewal project of shiny glass, air-conditioned malls and flashy bars that manages to capture the maritime heart of this city, albeit in a safe-for-the-whole-family kinda way.

The neighborhood is home to an amazing aquarium and several impressive historic ships, but these worthy sights are just the tip of Baltimore's iceberg.

WORTH A TRIP

SCENIC DRIVE: MARITIME MARYLAND

Maryland and the Chesapeake Bay have always been inextricable, but there are some places where the old-fashioned way of life on the bay seems to have changed little over the passing centuries.

About 150 miles south of Baltimore, at the edge of the Eastern Shore, is **Crisfield**, the top working water town in Maryland. Stop by the **chamber of commerce** (☎410-968-2500; www.crisfieldchamber.com; 906 W Main St, Crisfield; ⏰9am-5pm Mon-Fri, 11am-4pm Sat & Sun Apr-Nov, 10am-4pm Mon-Fri Dec-Mar) for an introduction to regional attractions then delve into the region's history at the **J Millard Tawes Historical Museum** (☎410-968-2501; www.crisfieldheritagefoundation.org/museum; 3 9th St, Crisfield; adult/child $3/1; ⏰10am-4pm Mon-Sat Jun-Aug, 11am-4pm Sat Sep-late Nov, closed rest of the year; P), nearby. Any seafood you eat will be first-rate, but for a true Shore experience, **Watermen's Inn** (☎410-968-2119; www.crisfield.com/watermens; 901 W Main St, Crisfield; sandwiches $8-17, mains $18-28; ⏰3-8pm Thu, to 9pm Fri & Sat, noon-8pm Sun) is legendary; you can feast on local catch from an ever-changing menu in an unpretentious setting. You can find local waterfolk at their favorite hangout, **Gordon's Confectionery** (☎410-968-0566; www.facebook.com/gordons1924; 831 W Main St, Crisfield; mains $2-9; ⏰4am-8:30pm), having 4am coffee before shipping off to check and set traps.

From here you can leave your car and take a boat to **Smith Island** (www.smithisland.org), the only offshore settlement in the state. Settled by fisherfolk from the English West Country some 400 years ago, the island's tiny population still speak with what linguists reckon is the closest thing to a 17th-century Cornish accent.

We'll be frank: this is more of a dying fishing town than a charming tourist attraction, although there are B&Bs and restaurants. But it's also a last link to the state's past, so if you approach Smith Island as such, you may appreciate the limited amenities on offer. These notably include paddling through miles of some of the most pristine marshland on the eastern seaboard. Ferries travel daily between Crisfield and Smith Island year-round but call ahead to confirm departure times. Check the website for details about lodging, restaurants and ferries.

National Aquarium AQUARIUM
(☎410-576-3800; www.aqua.org; 501 E Pratt St, Piers 3 & 4; adult/child $40/30; ⏰9am-5pm Sun-Thu, to 8pm Fri, to 6pm Sat, varies seasonally; 👪) Standing seven stories high and capped by a glass pyramid, this is widely considered to be America's best aquarium, with almost 20,000 creatures from more than 700 species, a rooftop rainforest, a multistory shark tank and a vast re-creation of an Indo-Pacific reef that is home to blacktip reef sharks, a green sea turtle and stingrays. There's also a reconstruction of the Umbrawarra Gorge in Australia's Northern Territory, complete with 35ft waterfall, rocky cliffs and free-roaming birds and lizards.

The largest exhibit contains seven bottlenose dolphins kept in captivity, though at time of writing the aquarium was planning to retire them to an oceanside sanctuary by 2023 (freeing them to the wild is not an option, since they lack survival skills). These dolphins no longer perform in shows. Kids will love the 4-D Immersion Theater (admission costs an additional $5), and there are loads of unique, behind-the-scenes tours, as well as aquarium sleepovers. Go on weekdays (right at opening time) if you want to beat the crowds.

Downtown & Little Italy

You can easily walk from downtown Baltimore to Little Italy, but follow the delineated path: there's a rough housing project along the way.

National Great Blacks in Wax Museum MUSEUM
(☎410-563-3404; www.greatblacksinwax.org; 1601 E North Ave; adult/student/child $15/14/12; ⏰9am-5pm Tue-Sat, from noon Sun, longer hours Jul & Aug) This simple but thought-provoking African American history museum has exhibits spotlighting Frederick Douglass, Jackie Robinson, Dr Martin Luther King Jr and Barack Obama, as well as lesser-known figures such as explorer Matthew Henson. It

BALTIMORE FOR CHILDREN

Most attractions are centered on the Inner Harbor, including the National Aquarium (p281), perfect for pint-size visitors as well as preteens and teenagers. Kids can run wild o'er the ramparts of historic Fort McHenry National Monument & Historic Shrine, too, while older children will appreciate the history.

Maryland Science Center (☎410-685-2370; www.mdsci.org; 601 Light St; adult/child $25/19; ⏲10am-5pm Mon-Fri, to 6pm Sat, 11am-5pm Sun, longer hours in summer) is an awesome attraction featuring a three-story atrium, tons of interactive exhibits on dinosaurs, outer space and the human body, and the requisite IMAX theater (adult/child $14/11 for feature films). This one works well for the whole family.

Two blocks north is the converted fish market of **Port Discovery** (☎410-727-8120; www.portdiscovery.org; 35 Market Pl; $16; ⏲10am-5pm Tue-Sat, noon-5pm Sun, plus Mon Jun-Aug; 👪), which has a tree house, an Egypt-inspired archaeology site and an artist's studio. It's geared to younger kids, so you can wear them out here – especially if they spend time climbing and sliding in the multilevel tree house.

At **Maryland Zoo in Baltimore** (☎410-396-7102; www.marylandzoo.org; 1 Safari Pl, Druid Hill Park; adult/child $22/18; ⏲10am-4pm daily Mar-Dec, Fri-Mon only Jan & Feb; P 👪), lily-pad-hopping adventures with Wade the Bog Turtle and grooming live animals are all in a day's play. Older kids may enjoy the zookeeper chats – and the reptiles!

Many public toilets in Baltimore have a baby-changing table. Items such as baby food, formula and disposable diapers are widely available in supermarkets.

Sidewalks are often crowded downtown during the day, especially north of the Inner Harbor, and you may not feel comfortable pushing a stroller through the busy mix. Sidewalks are wider than normal near Inner Harbor attractions such as the National Aquarium and the **Historic Ships** (☎410-539-1797; www.historicships.org; 301 E Pratt St, Piers 1, 3 & 5; adult/student/child from $15/13/7; ⏲10am-5pm, hours vary seasonally; 👪) – although strollers won't do well on the claustrophobic submarine, one of the historic ships.

also covers slavery, the Jim Crow era and African leaders – all told in surreal but informative fashion through Madame Tussaud–style wax figures. Unflinching exhibits about the horrors of slave ships and lynchings are graphic and may not be suitable for younger children.

For a compelling first-person introduction to the museum, listen to NPR's *This American Life* Episode 627: 'Suitable for Children,' which aired in October 2017 and is archived online (www.thisamericanlife.org).

Mt Vernon

★Walters Art Museum MUSEUM

(☎410-547-9000; www.thewalters.org; 600 N Charles St; ⏲10am-5pm Wed & Fri-Sun, to 9pm Thu) FREE The magnificent Chamber of Art & Wonders re-creates the library of an imagined 17th-century scholar, one with a taste for the exotic. The abutting Hall of Arms & Armor displays the most impressive collection of medieval weaponry you'll see this side of *Game of Thrones*. In sum, don't pass up this excellent, eclectic museum. It spans more than 55 centuries, from ancient to contemporary, with top-notch displays of Asian treasures, rare and ornate manuscripts and books, and a comprehensive French paintings collection.

Washington Monument MONUMENT

(☎410-962-5070; www.mvpconservancy.org; 699 Washington Pl; adult/child $6/4; ⏲10am-5pm Wed-Sun) For the best views of Baltimore, climb the 227 marble steps of the 178ft-tall Doric column dedicated to America's founding father, George Washington. The monument was designed by Robert Mills, who also created DC's Washington Monument, and is looking better than ever following a $6-million restoration project. The ground floor contains a museum about Washington's life. To climb the monument, buy a ticket on-site or reserve online. Spaces are limited. The 1st-floor gallery is free.

Claustrophobes beware – the climb is narrow, steep and surrounded by brick, with only one window before reaching the enclosed viewpoints at the top.

Maryland Historical Society MUSEUM
(☎410-685-3750; www.mdhs.org; 201 W Monument St; adult/child $9/6; ⏲10am-5pm Wed-Sat, from noon Sun) With more than 350,000 objects and seven million books and documents, this is among the world's largest collections of Americana. Highlights include one of two surviving Revolutionary War officer's uniforms, photographs from the Civil Rights movement in Baltimore, and Francis Scott Key's original manuscript of 'The Star-Spangled Banner' (displayed at the top of the hour). The 10ft-tall replica mastodon – the original was preserved by artist and Maryland native Charles Wilson Peale – is impressive. A few original bones are displayed.

There are often excellent temporary exhibits that explore the role of Baltimore residents in historic events.

Federal Hill & Around

On a bluff overlooking the harbor, Federal Hill Park lends its name to the comfortable neighborhood that's set around **Cross St Market** (www.southbaltimore.com; 1065 S Cross St, btwn Light & Charles Sts; ⏲7am-7pm) and comes alive after sundown.

★**American Visionary Art Museum** MUSEUM
(AVAM; ☎410-244-1900; www.avam.org; 800 Key Hwy; adult/child $16/10; ⏲10am-6pm Tue-Sun) Housing a jaw-dropping collection of self-taught (or 'outsider' art), AVAM is a celebration of unbridled creativity utterly free of arts-scene pretension. Across two buildings and two sculpture parks, you'll find broken-mirror collages, homemade robots and flying apparatuses, elaborate sculptural works made of needlepoint, and gigantic model ships painstakingly created from matchsticks. The whimsical automatons in the Cabaret Mechanical Theater are worth a closer look. And don't miss the famous Flatulence Post and its, er, 'fart art' in the Basement Gallery.

Fort McHenry National Monument & Historic Shrine HISTORIC SITE
(☎410-962-4290; www.nps.gov/fomc; 2400 E Fort Ave; adult/child $15/free; ⏲9am-5pm; P) On September 13 and 14, 1814, this star-shaped fort successfully repelled a British navy attack during the Battle of Baltimore. After a long night of bombs bursting in the air, shipbound prisoner Francis Scott Key saw, 'by dawn's early light,' the tattered flag still waving. Inspired, he penned 'The Star-Spangled Banner,' which was set to the tune of a popular drinking song.

Fell's Point & Canton

Once the center of Baltimore's shipbuilding industry, the historic cobblestoned neighborhood of Fells Point is now a gentrified mix of 18th-century homes and restaurants, bars and shops. The neighborhood has been the setting for several films and TV series, most notably *Homicide: Life on the Street*. Further east, the slightly more sophisticated streets of Canton fan out, with its grassy square surrounded by great restaurants and bars.

North Baltimore

The 'Hon' expression of affection – an often-imitated but never-quite-duplicated 'Bawlmerese' peculiarity – originated in **Hampden**, an area straddling the line between working class and hipster-creative class. Spend a lazy afternoon browsing kitsch, antiques and vintage clothing along the Avenue (aka W 36th St). To get to Hampden, take I-83 N, merge onto Falls Rd (northbound) and take a right onto the Avenue.

The prestigious **Johns Hopkins University** (☎410-516-8000; www.jhu.edu; 3400 N Charles St) is nearby. South of Johns Hopkins, just east of I-83, new restaurants and housing developments mark rapidly gentrifying **Remington**, a walkable neighborhood with a demographic similar to that of Hampden.

★**Evergreen Museum** MUSEUM
(☎410-516-0341; http://museums.jhu.edu; 4545 N Charles St; adult/child $8/5; ⏲11am-4pm Tue-Fri, from noon Sat & Sun; P) Well worth the 7-mile drive north from the Inner Harbor, this grand 19th-century mansion provides a fascinating glimpse into upper-class Baltimore life of the 1800s. The house is packed with fine art and masterpieces of the decorative arts – including paintings by Modigliani, glass by Louis Comfort Tiffany and exquisite Asian porcelain – not to mention the astounding rare book collection, numbering some 32,000 volumes. Visits are by guided tour offered on the hour until 3pm.

Even more impressive than the collection is the compelling story of the Garrett family. Patriarch John W Garrett was president of the B&O Railroad and he purchased the home in 1878 for his son T Harrison. The Garretts were world travelers – T Harrison's son John W, who inherited the house in 1920, was an active diplomat for some years. They were also astute philanthropists, as well as lovers of the arts, if not always successful performers in their own right – though that didn't stop the younger John W's wife, Alice, from taking the stage (her own, which you'll see in the intimate theater below the house).

Festivals & Events

Preakness Stakes SPORTS

(410-542-9400; www.preakness.com; 5201 Park Heights Ave; May) Held the third Saturday in May at Pimlico, this long-running thoroughbred horse race is the second of three races comprising the Triple Crown, occurring between the Kentucky Derby and Belmont Stakes.

Artscape ART

(www.artscape.org; 140 W Mt Royal Ave, Patricia & Arthur Modell Performing Arts Center; mid-Jul) FREE America's largest free arts festival, lasting three days, features art displays, live music and theater and dance performances.

Sleeping

Stylish, affordable B&Bs are mostly found in the downtown 'burbs of Canton, Fells Point and Federal Hill. New boutique hotels are bringing fresh, hip style to downtown, Mt Vernon and Fells Point.

In Fells Point, you can typically park for free between 8pm and 10am in spots covered by parking kiosks, though read parking signage carefully for variations and remember to move your car or pay ahead in the morning.

HI Baltimore Hostel HOSTEL $

(410-576-8880; www.hiusa.org/baltimore; 17 W Mulberry St, Mt Vernon; dm $23-25, d $70; P ❄ @) Located in a beautifully restored 1857 mansion, the HI Baltimore has dorms with six, eight, 10 and 12 beds, as well as private doubles. Helpful management, a nice location between Mt Vernon and downtown, and a filigreed classical-chic look make this one of the region's best hostels. The front desk is open 24 hours. Breakfast is included. Parking is $8 per night.

★ **Sagamore Pendry** BOUTIQUE HOTEL $$$

(443-552-1400; www.pendryhotels.com; 1715 Thames St, Fells Point; d from $250; P) Hunkered commandingly on the historic Recreation (Rec) Pier, this luxury property is a game changer, bringing a big dose of charm and panache to Baltimore's favorite party neighborhood. With local art on the walls, nautical and equestrian touches in the common areas, and an 18th-century cannon on display (unearthed during construction), the hotel embraces Charm City's culture and history.

Eating

Baltimore is an ethnically rich town that sits on top of the greatest seafood repository in the world. The city also straddles the fault line between the down-home South and cutting-edge innovation of the urban North, meaning you'll find Southern comfort-food favorites such as biscuits and gravy at mom-and-pop diners, and fusion creations such as sushi burritos at glossy food halls.

Handlebar Cafe AMERICAN $

(443-438-7065; www.handlebarcafe.com; 511 S Caroline St, Fells Point; mains $7-18; 11am-2am Tue-Fri, 8am-2am Sat, 8am-2pm Sun) Owned by X-Games champ Marla Streb, this friendly bike shop and bistro – adorned with mountain bikes and gear-themed decor – serves breakfast, burritos and wood-fired pizzas behind its big garage door. Craft beer, live music and an indoor sprint series too. The vibe is so darn cool even the clumsiest goof in town will be considering a career in trick dirt biking.

Artifact Coffee CAFE $

(410-235-1881; www.artifactcoffee.com; 1500 Union Ave, Woodberry; sandwiches $9-15; 7am-7pm Mon-Fri, from 8am Sat & Sun;) From the folks behind Woodberry Kitchen, Artifact serves the city's best coffee, along with tasty light meals, such as egg muffins, spinach salads, vegetarian banh mi and pastrami sandwiches. It's inside a former mill space, handsomely repurposed from its industrial past. It's a two-minute stroll from the Woodberry light-rail station.

Ekiben FUSION $

(410-558-1914; www.ekibenbaltimore.com; 1622 Eastern Ave, Fells Point; mains $9-12; 11am-10pm Mon-Thu, to 11pm Fri & Sat) The 'neighborhood bird' at this Asian fusion box of deliciousness is a sight to behold, and then devour: a giant piece of curry-fried chicken practically leaping from the pillowy embrace of a soft steamed bun. Buns and bowls are the draw at this tiny spot. With just a few tables and stools, it's best for takeout.

Lexington Market MARKET $
(www.lexingtonmarket.com; 400 W Lexington St, Mt Vernon; ⏲6am-6pm Mon-Sat) Around since 1782, Mt Vernon's Lexington Market is one of Baltimore's true old-school food markets. It's a bit shabby on the outside, but the food is great. Don't miss the crab cakes at **Faidley's** (☎410-727-4898; www.faidleyscrabcakes.com; 203 N Paca St; lump crab cakes $15; ⏲9:30am-5:30pm Mon-Sat) seafood stall, because my goodness, they are amazing – maybe the best in the city.

★**Thames St Oyster House** SEAFOOD $$
(☎443-449-7726; www.thamesstreetoysterhouse.com; 1728 Thames St, Fells Point; sandwiches $12-28, mains $18-29; ⏲5-9:30pm Sun-Thu, to 10:30pm Fri & Sat, plus 11:30am-2:30pm Wed-Sun) A Fells Point icon, this vintage dining and drinking hall serves some of Baltimore's best seafood. Dine in the polished upstairs dining room with waterfront views, take a seat in the backyard, or plunk down at the bar in front (which stays open till midnight) and watch the drink-makers and oyster-shuckers in action. The lobster rolls are recommended too.

★**Helmand** AFGHANI $$
(☎410-752-0311; www.helmand.com; 806 N Charles St, Mt Vernon; mains $14-20; ⏲5-10pm Sun-Thu, to 11pm Fri & Sat) The Helmand is a longtime favorite for its *kaddo borawni* (pumpkin in yogurt-garlic sauce), vegetable platters and flavorful beef-and-lamb meatballs, followed by cardamom ice cream. If you've never tried Afghan cuisine, this is a great place to do so.

★**Woodberry Kitchen** AMERICAN $$$
(☎410-464-8000; www.woodberrykitchen.com; 2010 Clipper Park Rd, Woodberry; mains brunch $17-26, dinner $23-33; ⏲5-9pm Sun & Tue-Thu, to 10pm Fri & Sat, plus 10am-2pm Sat & Sun) The Woodberry takes everything the Chesapeake region has to offer, plops it into a former flour mill and creates culinary magic. The menu is a playful romp through the best of regional produce, seafood and meats, from Maryland catfish with Heritage grits to Tilghman Island crab cakes, and hearty vegetable dishes made with produce plucked from nearby farms. Reserve ahead.

Food Market MODERN AMERICAN $$$
(☎410-366-0606; www.thefoodmarketbaltimore.com; 1017 W 36th St, Hampden; mains dinner $17-40, brunch $14-22; ⏲5-10pm Mon-Thu, 9am-11pm Fri & Sat, 9am-10pm Sun) Award-winning local chef Chad Gauss elevates American comfort fare to high art in dishes such as bread-and-butter-crusted sea bass with black-truffle vinaigrette, and spaghetti and crab meatballs in sherry *fra diavolo*. It's located on Hampden's lively restaurant- and shop-lined main drag.

Drinking & Nightlife

On weekends, Fells Point and Canton turn into temples of alcoholic excess that would make a Roman emperor blush. Mt Vernon and North Baltimore are a little more civilized, but any one of Baltimore's neighborhoods houses a cozy local pub. Closing time is generally 2am.

Brewer's Art PUB
(☎410-547-6925; www.thebrewersart.com; 1106 N Charles St, Mt Vernon; ⏲4pm-1:45am Mon-Fri, from noon Sat, from 2pm Sun) In a vintage early-20th-century mansion, Brewer's Art serves well-crafted Belgian-style microbrews to a laid-back Mt Vernon crowd. There's tasty pub fare (mac 'n' cheese, cheeseburgers) in the bar, and upscale American cuisine in the elegant back dining room. Head to the subterranean drinking den for a more raucous crowd. During happy hour (4pm to 7pm) house drafts are just $4.

Cannon Room COCKTAIL BAR
(☎443-552-1300; www.pendryhotels.com; 1715 Thames St, Fells Point; ⏲5pm-midnight Sun-Thu, to 1am Fri & Sat) The curved roof of this 20-seat whiskey bar, which is tucked in the deep recesses of the Sagamore Pendry, was designed to resemble an oversized whiskey barrel. Look down to see the namesake cannon, which basks in the spotlight beneath a glass-panel floorboard. The cannon dates from the 1700s and was discovered during construction.

Clavel BAR
(☎443-900-8983; www.barclavel.com; 225 W 23rd St, Remington; ⏲5pm-1am Mon-Sat, 10am-3pm Sun) Celebrating agave is the stated mission at this sultry gathering spot, where mescal flights and a mescal library are on the menu. Complement that flight with a few of chef Carlos Raba's traditional Mexican tacos, expertly simmered and seasoned with moles,

chiles and salsa. They may be the best in town.

☆ Entertainment

Baltimoreans *love* sports. The town plays hard and parties even harder, with tailgating parties in parking lots and games showing on numerous televisions in bars and restaurants.

★Oriole Park at Camden Yards STADIUM
(☎888-848-2473; www.orioles.com; 333 W Camden St, Downtown; tours adult/child $9/6) The Baltimore Orioles play here, arguably the best ballpark in America, from April through September. Daily tours of the stadium are offered April through November.

M&T Bank Stadium STADIUM
(☎410-261-7283; www.baltimoreravens.com; 1101 Russell St, Downtown) The Baltimore Ravens play football here from September to January.

ℹ Information

Baltimore Area Visitor Center (☎877-225-8466; www.baltimore.org; 401 Light St, Inner Harbor; ⏰10am-5pm, closed Mon Jan & Feb; 📶) Located on the Inner Harbor. Sells the Harbor Pass (adult/child $75/57), which gives admission to four major area attractions (select from a total of five options).

University of Maryland Medical Center (☎ER 410-328-9595, general 410-328-8667; www.umm.edu; 22 S Greene St, University of Maryland-Baltimore) Has a 24-hour emergency room.

ℹ Getting There & Away

The Baltimore/Washington International Thurgood Marshall Airport (p279) is 10 miles south of downtown via I-295.

Departing from a terminal 2 miles southwest of Inner Harbor, **Greyhound** (☎410-752-7682; www.greyhound.com; 2110 Haines St) has numerous buses from Washington, DC ($10 to $23, roughly every 45 minutes, one hour), and from New York ($15 to $54, 15 per day, four hours). **Peter Pan Bus Lines** (☎800-343-9999; www.peterpanbus.com; 2110 Haines St, Carroll-Camden) also heads to New York ($20, 10 daily, 3½ hours) from the Greyhound station. FlixBus (www.flixbus.com) services to/from NYC ($20 to $30, three to seven daily) depart from a streetside location across from the Wells Fargo bank on New Ponca St.

MARC operates weekday commuter trains between **Penn Station** (https://mta.maryland.gov/marc-train; 1500 N Charles St, Charles North) and Washington's Union Station ($8, about one hour), on the Penn Line. The Brunswick Line runs from Union Station to Frederick and Harpers Ferry, WV. Amtrak trains serve the East Coast and beyond.

Supershuttle (www.supershuttle.com) provides a BWI van service to the Inner Harbor from $17.

ℹ Getting Around

The light rail (http://mta.maryland.gov/light-rail) runs from BWI airport to Lexington Market, Mt Vernon and Penn Station, every 10 to 15 minutes. MARC trains run hourly on weekdays (and six to nine times daily on weekends) between Penn Station and BWI for $5. Check Maryland Transit Administration (https://mta.maryland.gov) for all local transportation schedules and fares.

Baltimore Water Taxi (☎410-563-3900; www.baltimorewatertaxi.com; Inner Harbor; daily pass adult/child $16/9; ⏰11am-10pm Mon-Thu, from 10am Fri-Sun May-Aug, shorter hours Sep-Apr) docks at all harborside attractions and neighborhoods.

The free green-and-purple **Charm City Circulator** (☎410-545-1956; www.charmcitycirculator.com) shuttles travel four routes, three of them to tourist spots in neighborhoods in the downtown area. The Purple Route connects the Inner Harbor, Mt Vernon and Federal Hill. The Green Route runs through Fells Point. The Banner Route runs from the Inner Harbor to Fort McHenry.

Annapolis

Annapolis is as charming as state capitals get. The Colonial architecture, cobblestones, flickering lamps and brick row houses are worthy of Victorian author Charles Dickens, but the effect isn't artificial: this city has preserved, rather than created, its heritage.

Perched on Chesapeake Bay, Annapolis revolves around the city's rich maritime traditions. It's home to the US Naval Academy, whose 'middies' (midshipmen students) stroll through town in their starched white uniforms. Sailing is not just a hobby here but a way of life, and the city docks are crammed with vessels of all shapes and sizes. With its historic sights, water adventures and great dining and shopping, Annapolis is worthy of more than a day trip – try for at least two if you can.

Sights

US Naval Academy UNIVERSITY

(visitor center 410-293-8687; www.usnabsd.com/for-visitors; Randall St, btwn Prince George & King George Sts) The undergraduate college of the US Navy is one of the most selective universities in America. The Armel-Leftwich Visitor Center (p289) is the place to book 75-minute tours and immerse yourself in all things Academy-related. Come for the formation weekdays at 12:05pm sharp, when the 4000 students conduct a 20-minute military marching display in the yard. Photo ID is required for entry. If you've got a thing for American naval history, revel in the well-done **Naval Academy Museum** (410-293-2108; www.usna.edu/museum; 118 Maryland Ave; 9am-5pm Mon-Sat, from 11am Sun) FREE.

The visitor entrance for pedestrians is located at Gate 1 on Prince George St (at Craig St), within easy walking distance of the historic downtown.

Maryland State House HISTORIC BUILDING

(410-260-6445; http://msa.maryland.gov/msa/mdstatehouse/html/home.html; 99 State Circle; 9am-5pm) FREE The country's oldest state capitol in continuous legislative use, the grand 1772 State House also served as national capital from 1783 to 1784. Notably, General George Washington returned his commission here as Commander-in-Chief of the Continental Army in 1783 after the Revolutionary War, ensuring that governmental power would be shared with Congress. The exhibits and portraits here are impressive and include Washington's copy of his speech resigning his commission. Pick up a self-guided tour map on the 1st floor.

The upside-down giant acorn atop the building's dome stands for wisdom. The Maryland Senate is in session from January to April.

Photo ID is required at the entrance, where you'll pass through metal detectors.

Hammond Harwood House MUSEUM

(410-263-4683; www.hammondharwoodhouse.org; 19 Maryland Ave; adult/child $10/5; noon-5pm Wed-Mon Apr-Dec) Of the many historical homes in town, the Hammond Harwood House, dating from 1774, is the one to visit. It has a superb collection of decorative arts, including 18th-century furniture, paintings and ephemera, and is one of the finest existing British Colonial homes in America. Knowledgeable guides help bring the past to life on 50-minute house tours (held at the top of the hour).

Even if you don't have time for a tour, take a moment to stroll past. Thomas Jefferson called the ornate front door the 'most beautiful door in America.' We think it is rather nice too.

Kunta Kinte–Alex Haley Memorial MONUMENT

(City Dock, off Market Space) Beside City Dock, the Kunta Kinte–Alex Haley Memorial marks the spot where Kunta Kinte – ancestor of *Roots* author Alex Haley – was brought in chains from Africa. The statues here depict Haley sharing the story of his ancestor with three children.

Sleeping

Inns and B&Bs fill the historic downtown. Several hotels line West St, which runs west from Church Circle. National hotel chains cluster near exits 22 and 23 off US 50/301.

ScotLaur Inn GUESTHOUSE $

(410-268-5665; www.scotlaurinn.com; 165 Main St; d $120-150; P) The folks from Chick & Ruth's Delly offer 10 rooms above the restaurant, each with wrought-iron beds, floral wallpaper and private bath. The quarters are small but have a cozy and familial atmosphere (the guesthouse is named after the owners' children Scott and Lauren, whose photos adorn the hallways). Breakfast included. Two-night minimum stay on weekends.

Historic Inns of Annapolis HOTEL $$

(410-263-2641; www.historicinnsofannapolis.com; 58 State Circle; d from $150; P) The Historic Inns comprise three different boutique guesthouses, each set in a heritage building in the heart of old Annapolis: the Maryland Inn, the Governor Calvert House and the Robert Johnson House. Common areas are packed with period details, and the best rooms boast antiques, fireplaces and attractive views (the cheapest can be small). Check in at Governor Calvert House.

Eating

With the Chesapeake Bay at its doorstep, Annapolis has superb seafood. The openings of several farm-to-table-minded restaurants

MARYLAND BLUE CRABS

Eating at a crab shack, where the dress code stops at shorts and flip-flops, is the quintessential Chesapeake Bay experience. Folks in these parts take their crabs seriously, and can spend hours debating the intricacies of how to crack a crab, the proper way to prepare crabs and where to find the best ones. There is one thing Marylanders can agree on: they must be blue crabs (scientific name: *Callinectes sapidus*, or 'beautiful swimmers'). Sadly, blue crab numbers have suffered with the continuing pollution of the Chesapeake Bay, and many crabs you eat here are imported from elsewhere.

Steamed crabs are prepared very simply, using beer and Old Bay seasoning. One of the best crab shacks in the state is near Annapolis at **Jimmy Cantler's Riverside Inn** (☎410-757-1311; www.cantlers.com; 458 Forest Beach Rd; mains $12-29; ⏲11am-10pm Sun-Thu, to 11pm Fri & Sat), located 4 miles northeast of the Maryland State House, across the Severn River Bridge; here, eating a steamed crab has been elevated to an art form – a hands-on, messy endeavor, normally accompanied by corn on the cob and ice-cold beer. Another fine spot is across the bay at **Red Roost** (☎410-546-5443; www.theredroost.com; 2670 Clara Rd, Whitehaven; mains $18-35; ⏲5:30-9pm Mon-Thu, to 10pm Fri, noon-10pm Sat, to 9pm Sun mid-Mar–Oct).

have added depth to the dining scene along Main St and near the dock.

Chick & Ruth's Delly DINER $
(☎410-269-6737; www.chickandruths.com; 165 Main St; mains breakfast & lunch $8-15, dinner $10-20; ⏲6:30am-11:30pm Sun-Thu, to 12:30am Fri & Sat; 👪) A cornerstone of Annapolis, the-squeeze-'em-in-tight Delly bursts with affable quirkiness and a big menu, heavy on sandwiches and breakfast fare. Patriots can relive grade-school days reciting the Pledge of Allegiance at 8:30am weekdays and 9:30am Saturday and Sunday. Breakfast is served all day.

Vida Taco Bar MEXICAN $
(☎443-837-6521; www.vidatacobar.com; 200 Main St; tacos $4-6; ⏲5-10pm Tue-Thu, noon-11pm Fri & Sat, noon-9pm Sun) The crowd is stylish – and getting its drink on – at this convivial spot serving fantastic street tacos and strong margaritas.

★**Vin 909** AMERICAN $$
(☎410-990-1846; www.vin909.com; 909 Bay Ridge Ave; small plates $12-21; ⏲5:30-10pm Wed & Thu, to 11pm Fri, 5-11pm Sat, 5-10pm Sun, plus noon-3pm Wed-Sat, shorter hours in winter) Perched on a little wooded hill and boasting an intimate yet enjoyably casual ambience, Vin is the best thing happening in Annapolis for food. Farm-sourced goodness features in the form of duck confit, dry-aged Angus-beef sliders and homemade pizzas with toppings such as wild-boar meatballs or honey-braised squash with applewood bacon.

There's a great wine selection, including more than three dozen wines by the glass. No reservations are accepted, so arrive early to beat the often lengthy waits.

Boatyard Bar & Grill SEAFOOD $$
(☎410-216-6206; www.boatyardbarandgrill.com; 400 4th St, Eastport; mains $10-27; ⏲7:30am-midnight Mon-Fri, from 8am Sat & Sun; 👪) This bright, nautically themed restaurant with a big central bar is a festive and welcoming spot for crab cakes, fish and chips, oysters, fish tacos and other seafood. Happy hour (3pm to 7pm Monday to Friday) draws in the crowds with $3 drafts and 99¢ oysters.

🍷 Drinking & Entertainment

Fox's Den PUB
(☎443-808-8991; www.foxsden.com; 179 B Main St; ⏲5pm-midnight Mon, Wed & Thu, to 1am Fri, 4pm-1am Sat, 4pm-midnight Sun) Head underground for microbrews and craft cocktails, all served in a snug gastropub in the thick of the Main St action. Things are hopping on Monday when the brick-oven pizzas are $10.

Rams Head On Stage LIVE MUSIC
(☎410-268-4545; www.ramsheadonstage.com; 33 West St; tickets $15-115) Settle in at tables to watch performances by well-known bands and musicians, from Dave Davies to Lee Ann Womack to Keller Williams. Small bites ($8 to $16), wine, cocktails and beer are served. The venue is next door to **Rams Head Tavern** (☎410-268-4545; www.ramsheadtavern.com; 33 West St; mains lunch & din-

ner $10-30, brunch $10-16; ⌚11am-2am Mon-Sat, from 10am Sun), which has a separate menu.

Information

There's a **visitor center** (☎410-280-0445; www.visitannapolis.org; 26 West St; ⌚9am-5pm) in town and a seasonal information booth at City Dock (9am to 5pm March to October). For information about tours and sights at the Naval Academy, stop by the expansive **Armel-Leftwich Visitor Center** (☎410-293-8687; www.usnabsd.com/for-visitors; 52 King George St, Gate 1, City Dock entrance; tours adult/child $12/10; ⌚9am-5pm Mar-Dec, to 4pm Jan & Feb) on the Yard near the waterfront.

Getting There & Away

Annapolis is 26 miles from Baltimore and 30 miles from Washington, DC. Check https://mta.maryland.gov for light rail and bus route options connecting Baltimore/Washington International Thurgood Marshall Airport (p279) and Baltimore with Annapolis.

Greyhound (☎800-231-2222; www.greyhound.com; 275 Harry S Truman Pkwy) runs buses to Washington, DC ($8 to $10, daily), from a pickup and drop-off stop 5 miles west of the historic downtown.

Eastern Shore

Just across the Chesapeake Bay Bridge, nondescript suburbs give way to unbroken miles of bird-dotted wetlands, serene waterscapes, endless cornfields, sandy beaches and friendly villages. The Eastern Shore retains its charm despite the growing influx of gentrifiers and day-trippers. This area revolves around the water: working waterfront communities still survive off Chesapeake Bay and its tributaries, and boating, fishing, crabbing and hunting are integral to local life. Come here to explore nature by trail, boat or bicycle, to read on the beach, to delve into regional history and, of course, to enjoy the delicious seafood.

Activities

Rebecca T Ruark CRUISE

(☎text 410-829-3976; www.skipjack.org; Dogwood Harbor, off US 33; 2hr cruise adult/child $30/15; ⌚11am-1pm & 5-7pm daily May-Oct) For old-fashioned fun, hop aboard this 1886 skipjack, a traditional oyster-dredging boat, for a sunset sail. It's the oldest one on the Chesapeake Bay and is now a historic landmark. Cash or check only.

Lady Patty Classic Yacht Charters BOATING

(☎410-886-1127; www.ladypatty.com; 6176 Tilghman Island Rd, Tilghman Island; cruises adult/child from $47/26; ⌚tours Wed-Mon May-Oct) Runs two-hour sails on the Chesapeake on a 1935 racing yacht. Think teak, bronze and wind-driven prowess – these trips are for the pure thrill of sailing.

Eating

★**Blacksmith Bar & Restaurant** AMERICAN $$

(☎410-973-2102; www.blacksmithberlin.com; 104 Pitts St, Berlin; mains lunch $11-22, dinner $19-29; ⌚11:30am-9:30pm Mon-Sat) Folks across the Eastern Shore recommend this cozy and congenial spot, which began life as a blacksmith shop and now serves hearty portions of delicious farm-to-table comfort food. Servers soon feel like friends – in a non-annoying way – while the low ceiling and thick walls evoke a warm roadside tavern. The jumbo lump crab cakes with herbed potatoes are divine.

Getting There & Around

The region is best explored by car. Baltimore is 70 miles from Easton and 150 miles from Ocean City. Berlin is 23 miles east of Salisbury and 9 miles west of Ocean City, along the route between these two larger towns. Greyhound stops in Easton and Salisbury.

Ocean City

Two words describe 'the OC' from June through August: party central. This is where you'll experience the American seaside resort in its wildest glory. Some might call it tacky. Others might call it, well, fun. Here you can take a spin on nausea-inducing thrill rides, buy a T-shirt with obscene slogans and drink to excess at cheesy theme bars.

The center of action is the 2.5-mile-long boardwalk, which stretches from the inlet to 27th St. The beach is attractive, but you'll have to contend with heavy traffic and noisy crowds; the beaches north of the boardwalk are much quieter. How busy is it? They say Ocean City welcomes eight million visitors annually, with most of them arriving in summer – in a town with a year-round population of just over 7000!

Sights

Ocean City Life-Saving Station Museum MUSEUM
(☎410-289-4991; www.ocmuseum.org; 813 S Atlantic Ave; adult/child $5/3; ⏲10am-5pm May-Oct, 10am-4pm Sat & Sun Nov-Apr) This small but engaging museum sits inside an 1891 life-saving station at the southern end of the boardwalk. Here, the station keeper and six to eight 'surfmen' lived and responded to emergency calls from ships in distress. Exhibits include stories about nearby shipwrecks and a display spotlighting rescue gear, including a 26ft-long rescue boat, which would look rather small and fragile in a storm!

Boardwalk history and regional surfing – check out that 1920s pine surfboard – are also covered.

Trimpers Rides AMUSEMENT PARK
(☎410-289-8617; www.trimpersrides.com; S 1st St & Boardwalk; unlimited afternoon rides $28; ⏲1pm-midnight Mon-Fri, from noon Sat & Sun, hours vary seasonally) If you really want to engage in tacky seaside fun to the fullest possible extent, hit up Trimpers Rides, one of the oldest of old-school amusement parks. Have some fries with vinegar, play the games and enjoy people-watching here.

Tickets are 75¢ each, with a varying number required per ride.

Sleeping

Hotels and motels line the boardwalk and the streets running parallel to the ocean. These lodgings are a mix of national chains and independently owned accommodations. From June through August they're ready to pack in guests – and prices can skyrocket. For a quieter stay, try a B&B or spend the night in Berlin, 8 miles south. Many smaller properties close in the winter.

King Charles Hotel GUESTHOUSE $$
(☎410-289-6141; www.kingcharleshotel.com; 1209 N Baltimore Ave, cnr 12th St; d $120-200, q $125-210; ⏲May-Oct; P ❄ 📶) This place could be a quaint summer cottage, except it happens to be a short stroll to the heart of the boardwalk action. It has aging but clean rooms with small porches attached, and it's quiet (ie it's not a party hotel).

Eating & Drinking

Surf 'n' turf and all-you-can-eat deals are the order of the day.

Liquid Assets MODERN AMERICAN $$
(☎410-524-7037; https://la94.com; 9301 Coastal Hwy, cnr 94th St; mains $14-38; ⏲11:30am-11pm Sun-Thu, to midnight Fri & Sat) Like a diamond in the rough, this bistro and wine shop is hidden in a strip mall in north OC. The menu is a refreshing mix of innovative seafood, grilled meats and re-

WORTH A TRIP

ASSATEAGUE ISLAND

The Assateague Island seashore, a perfectly barren landscape of sand dunes and beautiful, secluded beaches, is just 8 miles south but a world away from Ocean City. This undeveloped barrier island is populated by a herd of wild horses, made famous in the book *Misty of Chincoteague*.

The 37-mile-long island is divided into three sections: **Assateague State Park** (☎410-641-2918; http://dnr.maryland.gov; 6915 Stephen Decatur Hwy; Jun-Aug $6, Sep-May $5; ⏲day-use areas 7am-sunset, campground late Apr-Oct; P 👪) in Maryland; federally administered **Assateague Island National Seashore** (☎410-641-1441; www.nps.gov/asis; 7206 National Seashore Lane, Berlin; adult/vehicle access per week $10/20; ⏲visitor center 9am-5pm daily Mar-Dec, Thu-Mon Jan & Feb; P); and **Chincoteague National Wildlife Refuge** (☎757-336-6122; www.fws.gov; 8231 Beach Rd, Chincoteague Island; vehicle pass $20; ⏲5am-10pm May-Sep, 6am-6pm Nov-Mar, to 8pm Apr & Oct; P 👪) in Virginia. For an overview, check out the Plan your Visit section of the National Park Service website (www.nps.gov/asis) or pick up the *Assateague Island National Seashore* pamphlet, which has a helpful map.

As well as swimming and sunbathing, recreational activities include birding, hiking, kayaking, canoeing, camping, crabbing and fishing. There are no food or drink services on the Maryland side of the island in the off-season. Don't forget insect repellent: the mosquitoes and biting horseflies can be ferocious!

gional classics. The small bar area is a convivial place to be early in the evening, and the pan-steamed mussels are a hit with the drinking crowd.

Seacrets BAR
(☎410-524-4900; www.seacrets.com; 117 49th St; ⊙11am-2am, hours vary seasonally) This is a Jamaican-themed, rum-soaked bar straight out of MTV's *Spring Break*. You can drift around on a big raft while sipping a drink and people-watching at OC's most famous meat market. When it comes to the wildest beach-party bar, this is the one against which all other claimants must be judged.

Getting There & Around

Ocean City is 140 miles southeast of Baltimore via Hwy 10 and US 50. **Greyhound** (☎800-231-222; www.greyhound.com; 101 S Division St, S Division St Transit Ctr) stops 30 miles west of Ocean City in Salisbury, where you can transfer to a local shuttle running to the southern end of the boardwalk.

The **Coastal Hwy Beach Bus** (www.ococean.com/explore-oc/getting-around-oc; day pass $3; ⊙24hr Apr-early Nov, hours vary rest of the year) travels up and down the length of the beach around the clock year-round. There's also a **tram** (☎410-289-5311; www.ococean.com/explore-oc/getting-around-oc; per ride $4, day pass $8; ⊙11am-midnight Jun-Aug, hours vary Sep) that runs along the boardwalk from June through September. For details about off-season transit and schedules, visit www.shoretransit.org.

Western Maryland

The western spine of Maryland is mountain country. The Appalachian peaks soar to 3000ft above sea level, and the surrounding valleys are packed with rugged scenery and Civil War battlefields. This is Maryland's playground, where hiking, cycling, skiing, rock climbing and white-water rafting draw the outdoor-loving crowd. Two long-distance hiking and biking trails are particularly noteworthy: the Great Allegheny Passage and the C&O Canal towpath, both offering an invigorating mix of history, scenery and adventure.

Passionate local chefs are embracing the region's bounty, and you'll find fantastic farm-to-table fare in the larger towns. There are plenty of welcoming microbreweries too.

When trip planning, remember that the narrow Maryland panhandle is bordered by Virginia, West Virginia and Pennsylvania. If you're exploring Civil War battlefields or looking for larger towns for an overnight stay, check for options that may be just a few miles over state lines.

Getting There & Around

Towns in western Maryland may look close to each other on a map, but narrow and twisting mountain roads can extend driving times. The main interstates running east–west are I-70 and I-68, with I-81 traveling north–south through the region.

MARC trains (https://mta.maryland.gov) from Union Station in Washington, DC, stop in **Frederick** (☎866-743-3682; 100 S East St) and **Brunswick** (100 S Maple St, Brunswick), while Amtrak serves Cumberland (p292) on the Capitol Limited route, which also connects with DC. Greyhound stops in both Cumberland and Frederick.

For flights, consider Washington Dulles International Airport (p298) or Baltimore/Washington International Thurgood Marshall Airport (p279).

Frederick & Mt Airy

Central Frederick is, well, perfect. Its historic, pedestrian-friendly center of red-brick row houses is filled with a diverse array of restaurants and shops. The engaged, cultured arts community is anchored by the excellent Weinberg Center for the Arts. The meandering Carroll Creek runs through it all, flanked by a lovely park with art and gardens. Unlike other communities in the region with historic districts, this is a mid-size city, an important commuter base for thousands of federal government employees and a biotechnology hub in its own right. For travelers, Frederick makes a great central base for exploring Brunswick, Mt Airy and the regional Civil War battlefields.

Sights

Antietam National Battlefield HISTORIC SITE
(☎301-432-5124; www.nps.gov/anti; 5831 Dunker Church Rd, Sharpsburg; 3-day pass per person/vehicle $7/15; ⊙grounds sunrise-sunset, visitor center 9am-5pm) The site of the bloodiest day in American history is now, ironically, supremely peaceful, quiet and haunting – and uncluttered, save for plaques and statues.

On September 17, 1862, General Robert E Lee's first invasion of the north was stalled here in a tactical stalemate that left more than 23,000 dead, wounded or missing – more casualties than America had suffered in all its previous wars combined. Check out the exhibits in the visitor center then walk or drive the grounds.

Poignantly, many of the battlefield graves are inscribed with German and Irish names, a roll call of immigrants who died fighting for their new homeland.

The visitor center shows a short film (playing on the hour and half-hour) about the events that transpired here. It also sells books and materials, including self-guided driving and walking tours of the battlefield.

Antietam is 25 miles west of Frederick and just 5 miles northeast of Shepherdstown, WV.

National Museum of Civil War Medicine MUSEUM

(☎301-695-1864; www.civilwarmed.org; 48 E Patrick St; adult/student/child $9.50/7/free; ⏲10am-5pm Mon-Sat, from 11am Sun) The National Museum of Civil War Medicine gives a fascinating, and sometimes gruesome, look at the health conditions soldiers and doctors faced during the war, as well as important medical advances that resulted from the conflict.

Sleeping & Eating

Hollerstown Hill B&B B&B $

(☎301-228-3630; www.hollerstownhill.com; 4 Clarke Pl; r $130-170; P❄📶) The elegant, friendly Hollerstown has four pattern-heavy rooms, two resident dogs, a doll collection and a fancy billiards room. This lovely Victorian sits right in the middle of the historic downtown area of Frederick, so you're within easy walking distance of all the goodness.

No children under 16.

Brewer's Alley PUB FOOD $$

(☎301-631-0089; www.brewers-alley.com; 124 N Market St; mains $11-26; ⏲11:30am-11:30pm Sun-Tue, to midnight Wed & Thu, to 2:30am Fri & Sat; 📶) This bouncy brewpub is one of our favorite places in Frederick for several reasons. First, the beer: house-brewed, plenty of variety, delicious. Second, the burgers: enormous, half-pound monstrosities of staggeringly yummy proportions. Third, the rest of the menu: excellent Chesapeake seafood plus Frederick County farm produce and meats. The small patio is pleasant on sunny days.

Entertainment

Weinberg Center for the Arts THEATER

(☎301-600-2828; www.weinbergcenter.org; 20 W Patrick St) Check the calendar for the schedule of classic and silent movies, live music ranging from banjo to funk and an intriguing speaker series – featuring the likes of autism spokesperson and professor Temple Grandin, and actor Mark Ruffalo – supported by an engaged and cultured arts community.

Information

Frederick Visitor Center (☎301-600-4047; www.visitfrederick.org/visit/visitor-center; 151 S East St; ⏲9am-5:30pm)

Getting There & Away

Frederick is accessible via Greyhound and MARC trains (Monday to Friday only) at the transit center (p291) located one block north of the visitor center. The MARC train Brunswick Line connects Frederick with Harpers Ferry, WV, Silver Spring, MD, and Washington, DC.

Cumberland

At the Potomac River, the frontier outpost of Fort Cumberland (not to be confused with the Cumberland Gap between Virginia and Kentucky) was the pioneer gateway across the Alleghenies to Pittsburgh and the Ohio River. With the completion of the C&O Canal and the arrival of the railroad in the 1800s, the city became a commercial hub, transporting goods and natural resources down the river to Georgetown.

Cumberland today has expanded into the outdoor recreation trade to guide visitors into the region's rivers, forests and mountains. The heart of the outdoor scene is Canal Pl, where two long-distance hike-and-bike paths meet: the C&O Canal towpath and the Great Allegheny Passage. Their junction point is just a few steps from the depot for the popular scenic railroad. Canal Pl is also just a short stroll from the pedestrian-friendly streets of downtown.

Sights & Activities

C&O Canal National Historic Park NATIONAL PARK

(www.nps.gov/choh; 13 Canal St, Western Maryland Railway Station; ⏲sunrise-sunset) FREE A marvel of engineering, the C&O Canal was designed to stretch alongside the Potomac River from the Chesapeake Bay to the Ohio River. Construction on the canal began in 1828 but was halted here in 1850 by the Appalachian Mountains. The park's protected 184.5-mile corridor includes a 12ft-wide towpath, now a hiking and bicycling trail, which stretches from here to Georgetown in DC. The **Cumberland Visitor Center** (☎301-722-8226; ⌚9am-5pm; P), also located here, has displays chronicling the importance of river trade in eastern seaboard history.

Great Allegheny Passage – Cumberland CYCLING
(www.gaptrail.org; Canal Pl) From its trailhead in Pittsburgh, this biking-and-hiking trail runs 150 scenic miles to its terminus in Cumberland. Here it meets the 184.5-mile C&O Canal towpath. This trail is free of cars.

Cumberland Trail Connection CYCLING
(☎301-777-8724; www.ctcbikes.com; 14 Howard St, Canal Pl; per half-day/day/week from $20/35/175; ⌚8am-7pm Apr-Oct, 10am-5pm Tue-Sun Nov-Mar) Conveniently located near the start of the C&O Canal towpath, this outfit rents bicycles (cruisers, touring bikes and mountain bikes), and also arranges shuttle service anywhere from Pittsburgh to DC. Does bike repair, too. Check the website for a basic map of the towpath.

Sleeping & Eating

Fairfield Inn & Suites HOTEL $$
(☎301-722-0340; www.marriott.com; 21 N Wineow St; r $154; P ❄ @ ☎ 🏊) This modern and recently renovated property bordering the C&O Canal towpath is a prime spot for cyclists. The included continental buffet breakfast will energize you for your ride. It's also an easy walk to the **Western Maryland Scenic Railroad** (☎800-872-4650; www.wmsr.com; 13 Canal St; adult/child $56/40; ⌚11:30am Thu-Sun, 6pm Sat mid-Apr–Oct, hours & trips vary seasonally) depot as well as downtown. Rooms come with a microwave and mini-fridge.

Queen City Creamery & Deli DINER $
(☎301-777-0011; www.queencitycreamery.com; 108 W Harrison St; sandwiches $8-10, 1 scoop custard $3; ⌚7am-9pm Mon-Thu, to 10pm Fri, 8am-10pm Sat, 8am-9pm Sun, hours vary seasonally) This retro soda fountain is like a 1940s time warp, with creamy shakes and homemade frozen custard, thick sandwiches and belly-filling breakfasts.

Getting There & Away

The **Amtrak station** (☎800-872-7245; www.amtrak.com; 201 E Harrison St) is close to downtown. Cumberland is on the daily Capitol Limited route that links Washington, DC, and Chicago. Pittsburgh is 100 miles northwest of the city. Greyhound buses also stop at the station. From the eastern part of Maryland, Cumberland can be reached by following I-70 west to I-68 west.

DELAWARE

Tiny Delaware, the nation's second-smallest state (96 miles long and less than 35 miles across at its widest point) is overshadowed by its neighbors – and often overlooked by visitors to the region. And that's too bad, because Delaware has a lot more on offer than just tax-free shopping and chicken farms.

Long, white sandy beaches, cute colonial villages, a cozy countryside and small-town charm characterize the state that happily calls itself the 'Small Wonder.' It's also the home state of President Joe Biden.

History

In colonial days, Delaware was the subject of an aggressive land feud between Dutch, Swedish and British settlers. The first two imported classically northern European middle-class concepts, the third a plantation-based aristocracy – which is partly why Delaware remains a typically mid-Atlantic cultural hybrid today.

The little state's big moment came on December 7, 1787, when Delaware became the first colony to ratify the US Constitution, thus becoming the first state in the Union. It remained in that union throughout the Civil War, despite supporting slavery. During this period, as throughout much of the state's history, the economy drew on its chemical industry. DuPont, the world's second-largest chemical company, was founded here in 1802 as a gunpowder factory by French immigrant Eleuthère Irénée du Pont. Low taxes drew other firms (particularly credit-card companies) in the 20th century, boosting the state's prosperity.

Getting There & Around

The coastal cities are 120 miles from both Washington, DC, and Baltimore. Wilmington is in the northern reaches of the state, 75 miles northeast of Baltimore via I-95 and 30 miles south of Philadelphia via I-95 – and just a few miles from the Pennsylvania state line. Amtrak runs nine routes through Wilmington. The closest major airport to Wilmington is Philadelphia International Airport (p163).

Delaware Coast

With beach towns for every personality along with gorgeous coastal views, Delaware's 28 miles of sandy Atlantic beaches are the best reason to linger here. They're also quick and easy to reach for city folk from Washington, DC, Baltimore and NYC looking to escape the grind.

Head to Lewes for the walkable downtown, filled with history and great restaurants. Gay-friendly Rehoboth also works well for families and those looking for upscale distractions, from pampering spas to fine cocktails. Just south of Rehoboth, wild Dewey is the place to get your beach party on while Bethany is made for slow days on the sand.

Running south all the way to the Maryland border, pretty beaches and state parks stretch between the towns and connect the ocean and the bays. Cycling the parks and kayaking the salt marshes are top outdoor activities.

Most businesses and services are open year-round. Off-season (outside of June to August), price bargains abound.

Lewes

In 1631, the Dutch gave this whaling settlement the pretty name of Zwaanendael (Valley of the Swans), before promptly getting massacred by local Nanticokes. The name was changed to Lewes (*loo*-iss) when William Penn gained control of the area. Today it's an attractive seaside gem with a mix of English and Dutch architecture – and loads of great restaurants. Pretty Cape Henlopen State Park is only 2.5 miles from downtown.

Cape Henlopen State Park STATE PARK
(☎302-645-8983; www.destateparks.com/beaches/cape-henlopen; 15099 Cape Henlopen Dr; Mar-Nov per vehicle $10, Dec-Feb free; ⏱8am-sunset; P) One mile east of Lewes, more than 4000 acres of dune bluffs, pine forests and wetlands are preserved at this lovely state park that's popular with bird-watchers, beachgoers and campers. There's also a 3.5-mile paved loop cycling trail. You can see clear to Cape May from the observation tower. **North Shores beach** draws many gay and lesbian couples. Campsites ($35 to $44) and cabins ($120) are also available. The admission fee is cash only.

Hotel Rodney HOTEL $$
(☎302-645-6466; www.hotelrodneydelaware.com; 142 2nd St; r $150-260, ste $270-330; P ❄ @) This charming boutique hotel features exquisite bedding and restored antique furniture, but it also has plenty of modern touches that keep it all feeling very fresh.

Getting There & Away

Cape May–Lewes Ferry (☎800-643-3779; www.capemaylewesferry.com; 43 Cape Henlopen Dr; round-trip per car $50, adult/child 6-13yr $18/9) runs daily ferries (1½ hours) across Delaware Bay to New Jersey from the terminal, 1 mile from downtown Lewes. For foot passengers, a seasonal shuttle bus ($5) operates between the ferry terminal and Lewes. Reservations recommended. The town sits on the coast just off the Coastal Hwy/Rte 1.

Rehoboth Beach

As the closest stretch of sand to Washington, DC (121 miles), Rehoboth Beach is often dubbed 'the Nation's Summer Capital.' It is both a family-friendly and gay-friendly destination. To escape the chaos of busy Rehoboth Ave (and the heavily built-up outskirts), wander into the side streets downtown. There you'll find a mix of gingerbread houses, tree-lined streets, posh restaurants and kiddie amusements, plus a wide beach fronted by a mile-long boardwalk.

Sleeping

★Cottages at Indian River Marina COTTAGE $$$
(☎302-227-3071; www.destateparks.com/reservations/cottages; 39415 Inlet Rd; per week peak/shoulder/off-season $1900/1250/850, 2 days off-season $200-300; P ❄) These cottages, located in Delaware Seashore State Park 6 miles south of Dewey Beach, are some of our favorite local vacation rentals. Not for the decor per se, but for the patios and unadulterated views across the pristine beach to the water. Each cottage has two bedrooms and a loft.

While they must be rented out by the week during the summer, they're available in two-day increments off-season.

Avenue Inn & Spa SPA HOTEL $$$

(800-433-5870; www.avenueinn.com; 33 Wilmington Ave; d $275-400;) Rooms sport a crisp and unfussy beach style at this relaxing property just one block from the boardwalk. Complimentary perks such as afternoon wine and cheese followed by fresh cookies in the evening contribute to the hospitable vibe. Spa services include deep-tissue massage, organic facials and an Earl Grey 'teatox' body treatment.

Eating & Drinking

Chesapeake & Maine GASTROPUB $$

(302-226-3600; www.dogfish.com; 316 Rehoboth Ave; mains $18-29; 3-10pm) The bar at Chesapeake & Maine sparkles with style and top-notch service. Beer-making powerhouse Dogfish Head owns the place, and the acclaimed cocktails here are mixed with spirits produced by Dogfish Head Distilling Co. The raw bar and the seafood dishes are sourced from Chesapeake Bay and coastal Maine.

Blue Hen AMERICAN $$

(302-278-7842; www.thebluehenrehoboth.com; 33 Wilmington Ave; mains $14-32; noon-late Thu-Mon) From the same team behind the lauded Henlopen City Oyster House, the Blue Hen earned a Best New Restaurant semi-finalist nomination from the James Beard Foundation shortly after it opened in 2017. Inside the eatery's farmhouse-chic digs, chef Julia Robinson whips up gourmet comfort fare, including deviled eggs with chicken cracklins and lobster pot pie.

The cocktail game is strong at the stylish bar, where communal tables keep the vibe festive. There's a firepit out front. The Blue Hen, named after the state bird of Delaware, sits inside Avenue Inn & Spa.

★Henlopen City Oyster House SEAFOOD $$$

(302-260-9193; www.hcoysterhouse.com; 50 Wilmington Ave; sandwiches $12-24, mains $28-38; dinner from 5pm) Seafood lovers won't want to miss this elegant but inviting spot, where an enticing raw bar and mouthwatering seafood dishes draw crowds (arrive early; no reservations). Good microbrews, cocktails and wine selections round out the appeal. The menu changes every day. Happy hours runs from 3pm to 5pm; lunch is served in the off-season.

★Dogfish Head Brewings & Eats PUB

(302-226-2739; www.dogfish.com; 320 Rehoboth Ave; mains $12-25; 11am-11pm Sun-Thu, to 1am Fri & Sat, to 3pm Sun) There's a long list of beers available at this iconic brewery, which also serves tasty pizzas, burgers, crab cakes and other pub fare. They all go perfectly with the award-winning IPAs. Kids menu available with $6 meals. Dogfish is a regional draw.

Getting There & Away

BestBus (www.bestbus.com) offers services from DC ($40, 2½ hours) and NYC ($49, 4½ hours) to Rehoboth, running Friday to Sunday in summertime only (late May through early September). Also stops in Dewey Beach.

The Jolly Trolley (www.jollytrolley.com) connects Rehoboth and Dewey beaches, and makes frequent stops along the way. A round-trip costs $5, and the trolley runs from 8am to 2am June through August. Cash only.

Wilmington & Brandywine Valley

A unique cultural milieu (African Americans, Jews and Caribbeans) and an energetic arts scene make this city worth a visit. Wilmington is also a good launchpad for exploring the scenic Brandywine Valley, 6 miles north, and its many historic homes, gardens and mills. Much of the current grandeur traces back to the Du Pont family, whose legacy began with a gunpowder mill on the banks of the Brandywine River.

The 1.3-mile downtown riverfront along the Christina River is a nice place for a patio meal and a stroll. And no description of Wilmington is complete without mentioning hometown politician President Joe Biden.

Sights

Delaware Art Museum MUSEUM

(302-571-9590; www.delart.org; 2301 Kentmere Pkwy; adult/child 7-18yr $12/6, 4-8pm Thu & Sun free; 10am-4pm Wed & Fri-Sun, to 8pm Thu; P) Exhibits work of the local Brandywine School, including Edward Hopper, John Sloan and three generations of Wyeths. The museum's fantastic collection of original works by illustrator Howard Pyle, a native of Wilmington, is showcased in six galleries.

Winterthur HISTORIC SITE
(☎302-888-4600; www.winterthur.org; 5105 Kennett Pike/Rte 52; adult/child 2-11yr $20/6; ⌚10am-5pm Tue-Sun Mar-Dec, closed Jan & Feb) Six miles northwest of Wilmington is the 175-room country estate of industrialist Henry Francis du Pont and his collection of antiques and American arts, one of the world's largest. Nice gardens too.

Brandywine Creek State Park STATE PARK
(☎302-577-3534; www.destateparks.com/BrandywineCreek; 41 Adams Dam Rd; Mar-Nov per vehicle $8, Dec-Feb free; ⌚8am-sunset, nature center 8am-4pm Mon-Fri; P) This state park is the gem of the area. A green space this size would be impressive anywhere, but is doubly so considering how close it is to prodigious urban development. Nature trails and shallow streams wend through the park. Come here to watch the annual hawk migrations, flying north in the spring (March to May) and south in the fall (September to November).

Sleeping & Eating

Holiday Inn Express HOTEL $$
(☎302-479-7900; www.ihg.com; 300 Rocky Run Pkwy; d $150, ste $180-230; P❄@☎) This good-value option sits inside a nondescript hotel building – reminiscent of most midlevel national chains – 5 miles north of downtown Wilmington. Decor is well loved but also well kept, and rooms come with a mini-fridge and microwave. Hot breakfast buffet included. Not far from Brandywine Valley attractions.

★**Hotel du Pont** HOTEL $$$
(☎302-594-3100; www.hoteldupont.com; 42 W 11th St, cnr Market & 11th Sts; r $440-460, ste $900; P❄☎) Under new ownership since 2017 after 100 years as a Du Pont–owned property, there is only one word to describe this revamped hotel: opulent. The premier hotel in the state, the Du Pont is luxurious and classy enough to satisfy its namesake (one of America's most successful industrialist families). The spot exudes an art-deco majesty that Jay Gatsby would have embraced.

Iron Hill Brewery PUB FOOD $$
(☎302-472-2739; www.ironhillbrewery.com; 620 Justison St; mains $17-27; ⌚11:30am-11pm Mon-Fri, 11am-midnight Sat, 11am-11pm Sun) The spacious and airy multilevel Iron Hill Brewery is set in a converted brick warehouse on the riverfront. Satisfying microbrews pair nicely with the hearty pub fare.

Getting There & Away

Just off I-95, Wilmington is midway between Washington, DC, and New York City, about two hours from either city. **Greyhound** (☎302-655-6111; www.greyhound.com; 101 N French St) stops downtown. Amtrak trains leave from the **Joseph R Biden Jr Railroad Station** (☎800-872-7245; www.amtrak.com; 100 S French St) and connect Wilmington with DC (1½ hours), Baltimore (45 minutes) and New York (two hours).

Dover

Dover's city center is quite attractive; the row-house-lined streets are peppered with restaurants and shops, while broadleaf trees spread their branches over pretty little lanes. Most museums and historic sites are downtown near the capitol, with a couple just south of downtown off Rte 1. Dover Air Force Base is 4 miles south of downtown.

Sights

Old State House MUSEUM
(☎302-744-5054; http://history.delaware.gov/museums; 25 The Green; ⌚9am-4:30pm Mon-Sat, 1:30-4:30pm Sun) FREE Take a moment to enjoy the short docent-led tour of this small but interesting former state capitol building. Built in 1791 and since restored, the Old State House contains art galleries and in-depth exhibits about the First State's history and politics.

We learnt here that every state house in the USA has a portrait of George Washington!

First State Heritage Park Welcome Center & Galleries MUSEUM
(☎302-744-5055; www.destateparks.com/heritagepark; 121 Martin Luther King Blvd N; ⌚8am-4:30pm Mon-Fri, 9am-4:30pm Sat; P) FREE Delve into the history of Delaware at First State Heritage Park, which also serves as a welcome center for the city of Dover, the state of Delaware and the adjacent state house. This so-called 'park without boundaries' includes 19 historic sites within a few blocks of one another. Start out at the Welcome Center & Galleries, which has exhibitions exploring Delaware's history. You can pick up more info about other key

attractions nearby along with a walking map.

John Dickinson Plantation MUSEUM
(☎302-739-3277; http://history.delaware.gov/museums; 340 Kitts Hummock Rd; ⏰10am-4:30pm Tue-Sat year-round, plus 1:30-4:30pm Sun Apr-Sep; P) FREE A restored 18th-century home of the founding father of the same name, also known as the Penman of the Revolution for his eloquent written arguments for independence. Dickinson is perhaps not as well known as some colonial statesmen because he did not sign the Declaration of Independence. He was a cautious and contemplative man, they say, but he did sign the Constitution. On-site Colonial-era demonstrations – weaving, knitting, fabric dyeing – are held on Saturday.

Air Mobility Command Museum MUSEUM
(☎302-677-5938; www.amcmuseum.org; 1301 Heritage Rd; ⏰9am-4pm Tue-Sun; P) FREE If you're into aviation, you'll enjoy this museum; the nearby airfield holds more than 30 restored vintage cargo and freight planes, including C-130s, a Vietnam War–era C-7 and a WWII-era 'Flying Boxcar.' Guided tours avaliable.

Dover Air Force Base (AFB) is a visible symbol of American military muscle and a poignant reminder of the cost of war. This is the location of the Department of Defense's largest mortuary, and traditionally the first stop on native soil for the remains of American service members killed overseas.

Bombay Hook National Wildlife Refuge WILDLIFE RESERVE
(☎302-653-9345; www.fws.gov/refuge/Bombay_Hook; 2591 Whitehall Neck Rd, Smyrna; per vehicle/pedestrian or cyclist $4/2; ⏰sunrise-sunset, visitor center 8am-4pm Mon-Fri, plus Sat & Sun spring & fall; P) Hundreds of thousands of waterfowl use this protected wetland as a stopping point along their migration routes. A 12-mile wildlife driving trail, running through 16,251 acres of saltwater marsh, cordgrass and tidal mud flats, manages to encapsulate all of the soft beauty of the DelMarVa peninsula in one perfectly preserved ecosystem. There are also short walking trails and observation towers. On the scenic drive, keep watch for quick-moving red foxes. Admission is cash only.

Sleeping

Dover may be somewhat small but it's also the state capital and the home of Dover Air Force Base, so there are plenty of lodging options. Nationally known and indie-owned hotels and motels line Dupont Hwy/Rte 13, plus there is one inn downtown near the capitol.

Home2 Suites HOTEL $$
(☎302-674-3300; http://home2suites3.hilton.com; 222 S Dupont Hwy; ste $152-180; P❄📶🏊🐾) This all-suites hotel is a short drive – or a half-mile walk – from downtown. Good for multiday stays, the suites are modern, spacious and have full kitchenettes. There's also a combo laundry-fitness area. Hot breakfast included.

Eating & Drinking

Restaurant 55 BURGERS $
(☎302-535-8102; www.myrestaurant55.com; 2461 S State St; mains $10-15; ⏰11am-2pm Tue-Fri, 4-9pm Tue-Thu, 4-10pm Fri, noon-10pm Sat, noon-8pm Sun) An all-ages crowd muscles in for the black-and-bleu burger and other gourmet patties at this hopping restaurant not far from Dover Air Force Base. Regional craft beer from Dogfish Head, Dewey Beer and Evolution keeps the grown-ups happy.

Flavors of India INDIAN $$
(☎302-677-0121; www.flavorofindiade.com; 348 N Dupont Hwy; mains $12-19; ⏰11am-10pm Mon-Sat, to 9pm Sun; P🌶👪) To say this place is an unexpected delight would be an understatement. First: it's in a Super 8 Motel off the highway. Second: it's great. The standards – vindaloos and kormas and tikka masalas – are all wonderful. The goat *palakwala* (goat curry with a spinach base)? Amazing. It's also by far the best vegetarian option in the area.

Governor's Cafe COFFEE
(☎302-747-7531; www.governorscafe.de; 144 Kings Hwy SW; ⏰7:30am-10pm Mon-Fri, 10am-11pm Sat, 10am-6pm Sun) In a rambling 1850s house across the street from the Governor's Mansion, this inviting place is a talented multi-tasker. Pop in early to grab a coffee and a pastry to go. Come by in the afternoon to nibble cheese and read on the porch. Sip a cocktail in the cozy bar after work. Or tuck in at night for wine and a civilized meal.

Getting There & Away

Dover is 50 miles south of Wilmington via Rte 1. US 301 connects Dover and Baltimore, which is 85 miles west. DART Bus 301 (one-way fare $6) runs between Wilmington and the **Dover Transit Center** (www.dartfirststate.com; S Queen St), which is a half-mile from downtown Dover. **Greyhound** (800-231-2222; www.greyhound.com; 654 N Dupont Hwy) buses stop 2 miles north of downtown.

VIRGINIA

The Commonwealth of Virginia is steeped in history and tradition. It's the birthplace of America, where English settlers established the first permanent colony in the New World in 1607. Since that time, the state has played a lead role in nearly every major American drama, from the Revolutionary and Civil wars to the Civil Rights movement and the attacks of September 11, 2001.

Virginia's natural beauty is as diverse as its history and people. Chesapeake Bay and the wide sandy beaches kiss the Atlantic Ocean. Pine forests, marshes and rolling green hills form the soft curves of the central Piedmont region, while the rolling Blue Ridge mountains and stunning Shenandoah Valley line its back.

There's loads for the visitor to enjoy, including world-class tourist attractions such as Colonial Williamsburg, a wealth of outdoor activities, a foot-tapping mountain-music scene and an ever-growing network of wine, beer and spirit trails to follow.

History

Humans have occupied Virginia for at least 5000 years. Several thousand Native Americans were already here in May 1607 when Captain James Smith and his crew sailed up Chesapeake Bay and founded Jamestown, the first permanent English colony in the New World. Named for Queen Elizabeth I – aka the 'Virgin Queen' – the territory originally occupied most of America's eastern seaboard. By 1610 most of the colonists had died from starvation in their quest for gold, until John Rolfe (husband of Pocahontas) discovered Virginia's real riches: tobacco.

A feudal aristocracy grew out of tobacco farming, and many gentry scions became Founding Fathers, including native son George Washington. In the 19th century, the slave-based plantation system grew both in size and incompatibility with the industrializing North; Virginia seceded in 1861 and became the epicenter of the Civil War. Following its defeat, the state walked a tense cultural tightrope, accruing a layered identity that included older aristocrats, a rural and urban working class, waves of immigrants and, today, the burgeoning tech-heavy suburbs of DC. The state revels in its history, yet still wants to pioneer the American experiment; thus, while Virginia reluctantly desegregated in the 1960s, today it houses one of the most ethnically diverse populations of the New South.

Getting There & Around

The largest regional airports include **Washington Dulles International Airport** (IAD; www.metwashairports.com;) in Northern Virginia, **Richmond International Airport** (RIC; 804-226-3000; www.flyrichmond.com; 1 Richard E Byrd Terminal Dr;) in Richmond, **Norfolk International Airport** (NIA; 757-857-3351; www.norfolkairport.com; 2200 Norview Ave;) in Norfolk, and **Roanoke-Blacksburg Regional Airport** (540-362-1999; www.roanokeairport.com; 5202 Aviation Dr NW) in Southwest Virginia. American, United and Delta serve Charlottesville Albemarle Airport (p314) in the Piedmont region.

Amtrak stops in Richmond at Main St Station (p312) and Staples Mill Rd Station (p312). There are also train stations or platforms in Charlottesville (p314), Staunton (p317), Roanoke (p320), **Williamsburg** (757-229-8750; http://gowata.org/; 468 N Boundary St, cnr Boundary & Lafayette Sts; 7:30am-10pm) and **Newport News**. In and around Northern Virginia, Amtrak stops in Fredericksburg (p303) and near Manassas National Battlefield Park (p301).

Northern Virginia

Arlington

Sitting just across the Potomac River from DC, Arlington is best known as the home of the Arlington National Cemetery and the Pentagon. Other than these two – admittedly major – draws, there's not much to attract the average visitor. The once-vibrant music and club strip on Wilson Blvd has been decimated in recent times as buildings are torn down to make way for sleek new high-rise apartment and office towers.

★Arlington National Cemetery CEMETERY
(☎877-907-8585; www.arlingtoncemetery.mil; Memorial Ave; ⏲8am-7pm Apr-Sep, to 5pm Oct-Mar; Ⓜ Blue Line to Arlington Cemetery) FREE Arlington is the somber final resting place for more than 400,000 military personnel and their dependents. The 624-acre grounds contain the dead of every war the USA has fought since the Revolution. Highlights include the Tomb of the Unknown Soldier, with its elaborate changing-of-the-guard ceremony (every hour on the hour October through March; every half-hour April through September), and the grave of John F Kennedy and his family, marked by an eternal flame.

Departing from the Welcome Center, hop-on, hop-off **bus tours** (☎800-844-7601; www.arlingtontours.com; adult/child $15/7.25; ⏲8:30am-6pm Apr-Sep, to 4pm Oct-Mar) are an easy way to visit the cemetery's main sights. Other points of interest include the **Shuttle Challenger Memorial** (off Memorial Dr); the **USS Maine Memorial** (off McPherson Dr), marked by the battleship's huge mast; the controversial **Confederate Memorial** (off McPherson Dr) that honors war dead from the Civil War's breakaway states; and the tomb of DC city planner **Pierre L'Enfant** (off Sherman Dr).

The **Iwo Jima Memorial** (Marine Corps War Memorial; Ord & Weitzel Dr), displaying the famous raising of the flag over Mt Suribachi, is on the cemetery's northern fringes and is included in the bus tour.

Much of the cemetery was built on the grounds of **Arlington House** (☎703-235-1530; www.nps.gov/arho; Sherman Dr; ⏲10am-4pm) FREE, the former home of Robert E Lee and his wife Mary Anna Custis Lee, a descendant of Martha Washington. When Lee left to lead Virginia's army in the Civil War, Union troops confiscated the property to bury their dead.

★Pentagon NOTABLE BUILDING
(https://pentagontours.osd.mil; Arlington; ⏲memorial 24hr, tours by appointment 10am-4pm Mon-Thu, noon-4pm Fri; Ⓜ Blue, Yellow Line to Pentagon) South of Arlington Cemetery is the Pentagon, the largest office building in the world and the headquarters of the US Department of Defense, the Army, Navy and Air Force. Outside the building is the **Pentagon Memorial** (https://pentagonmemorial.org; ⏲24hr) FREE; 184 illuminated benches honor each person killed in the September 11, 2001, terrorist attack on the Pentagon. To get inside the building, you'll have to book a free guided one-hour tour on the website and provide appropriate photo ID. Make reservations 14 to 90 days in advance.

Nearby, you can spot the three soaring arcs of the **Air Force Memorial** (☎703-462-4093; www.airforcememorial.org; 1 Air Force Memorial Dr; ⏲9am-9pm Apr-Sep, 8am-8pm Oct-Mar) FREE.

Getting There & Away

From DC, use the Arlington Cemetery station (Blue Line) to get to the cemetery and the Pentagon station (Blue and Yellow Lines) to visit Pentagon sites.

Alexandria

The charming town of Alexandria is 5 miles and 250 years away from Washington. Once a salty port, Alexandria – known as 'Old Town' to locals – is today a posh collection of red-brick homes, cobblestone streets, gas lamps and a waterfront promenade near the Potomac River. It's often described as one of the best-preserved historical districts in the nation. Boutiques, outdoor cafes and bars pack the main thoroughfare, making the town a fine afternoon or evening jaunt. Two miles north of Old Town, the residential Del Ray neighborhood is a pleasant place to stroll, especially along the eatery-lined Mt Vernon Ave. Alexandria is also a jumping-off spot for excursions to Mount Vernon.

Sights

★Mount Vernon HISTORIC SITE
(☎703-780-2000; www.mountvernon.org; 3200 Mount Vernon Memorial Hwy; adult/child 6-11yr $20/12; ⏲9am-5pm Apr-Oct, to 4pm Nov-Mar) One of America's most visited historic sites, Mount Vernon was the beloved home of George and Martha Washington, who lived here from the time of their marriage in 1759 until George's death in 1799. Regular guided tours of the furnished main house give a fascinating insight into the Washingtons' daily life, and self-guided tours of the outbuildings and gardens estate offer plenty of opportunities to interact with actors offering first-person narratives of working and living on the 18th-century plantation.

From April to October, the Mount Vernon entrance ticket also includes entry to Washington's nearby **distillery and gristmill** (☎703-780-2000; 5514 Mount Vernon Memorial Hwy; $6, with Mount Vernon ticket free; ⏰10am-5pm Apr-Oct); a free shuttle travels between these and the estate.

To avoid inevitable queues at the entrance to Mount Vernon, purchase your ticket online ahead of your visit (you'll save money too!). A number of tours and performances are offered daily, including the popular one-hour 'Enslaved People of Mount Vernon' tour ($10). Some tours sell out, so it's best to book these online ahead of your visit. Audioguide tours of the estate cost $7 and can be shared within a group.

Be sure to allow at least one hour to browse the object-rich exhibits and view the immersive 4D 'Revolutionary War Experience' spectacular in the Donald W Reynolds Museum & Education Center. Kids will love the 'Hands on History' activity room here, too.

Mount Vernon is 16 miles south of DC, off the Mount Vernon Memorial Hwy. By public transportation, take the Metro (Yellow Line) to Huntington, then switch to Fairfax Connector bus 101. **Grayline** (☎202-779-9894; www.graylinedc.com; adult/child 3-11yr $105/40; ⏰8:30am-5:30pm Tue, Thu & Sat late Jan-Dec) and **USA Guided Tours** (☎202-733 7376; www.usaguidedtours.com; adult/child 3-12yr incl Mount Vernon $79/69; ⏰10am) run bus tours from DC.

Several companies offer seasonal boat trips to Mount Vernon; **Potomac Riverboat Company** (☎703-684-0580; www.potomacriverboatco.com; return adult/child incl Mount Vernon from $50/30; ⏰Apr-Oct) has boats that depart from the Alexandria City Marina and **Spirit Cruises** (☎866-302-2469; www.spiritcruises.com; return adult/child 6-11yr incl Mount Vernon $51/46; ⏰Mar-Oct) has the *Spirit of Mount Vernon*, which departs from the SW Waterfront in DC.

Alternatively, it's possible to ride a bike along the Potomac River from DC (18 miles from Roosevelt Island).

★ Pope-Leighey House ARCHITECTURE
(☎703-570-6902; www.woodlawnpopeleighey.org; 9000 Richmond Hwy; adult/student $12/7.50, incl Woodlawn $20/11; ⏰11am-4pm Fri-Mon Apr-late Nov) Between 1937 and 1959, famed architect Frank Lloyd Wright designed a series of small-scale houses that he called 'Usonian.' Modest in scale but rich in innovation and detail, these site-specific single-story dwellings were constructed using native materials, had flat roofs and clerestory windows, and made the most of natural light, air and the surrounding landscape. This example dates from 1940. Young guides (often architects) conduct tours and impart lots of information about the house and its architect.

The house was originally constructed in Falls Church but was relocated to the Woodlawn estate after the house was threatened with demolition as part of an expansion of Hwy 66. It's now sited in a grassy knoll a short walk from the plantation mansion, which is located near George Washington's Distillery & Gristmill. To get here by public transport, take the Metro to Huntington station and then board Richmond Hwy Express Bus No 171; alight at Jeff Todd Way.

Freedom House Museum MUSEUM
(☎708-746-4702; www.alexandriava.gov/FreedomHouse; 1315 Duke St; suggested donation $5; ⏰1-5pm Fri & Sat; Ⓜ Blue, Yellow Line to King St-Old Town) This demure Federal-style row house holds a tragic story. At a time when Alexandria was the nation's second-largest slave center (after New Orleans), a flourishing slave-trading business occupied this building and adjoining space. A well-presented basement museum, developed by the Northern Virginia Urban League, powerfully tells the stories of the thousands of enslaved people who passed through. Personal video narratives and artifacts are on view in a heartbreaking setting.

Up to 150 slaves were kept in the holding pen outside (since torn down). Among those likely held here was Solomon Northup, a free Black man who in 1841 was kidnapped from Washington and sold into bondage in the south. His story was portrayed in the film *Twelve Years a Slave*. There's no admission, but donations are encouraged. The museum isn't signed; look for the Franklin and Armfield Slave Office information panel.

George Washington Masonic National Memorial MONUMENT
(☎703-683-2007; www.gwmemorial.org; 101 Callahan Dr at King St; adult/child under 13yr $18/free; ⏰9am-5pm; Ⓜ Blue, Yellow Line to King St-Old Town) Alexandria's most prominent landmark features a fine view from the observation deck of its 333ft tower. Modeled after

OFF THE BEATEN TRACK

MANASSAS NATIONAL BATTLEFIELD SITE

The site of two major Confederate victories early in the Civil War, **Manassas National Battlefield Park** (☎703-361-1339; www.nps.gov/mana; 6511 Sudley Rd, off I-66; ⊙park dawn-dusk, visitor center 8:30am-5pm) today is a curving green hillscape, sectioned into fuzzy fields of tall grass and wildflowers by split-rail wood fences. Start your tour at the Henry Hill Visitor Center to watch the orientation film and pick up park and trail maps. Guided tours are offered daily in summer; check the park website for times (which vary seasonally).

The history? On July 21, 1861, Union and Confederate soldiers clashed in the first major land battle of the Civil War. Expecting a quick victory, DC residents flocked here to picnic and watch the First Battle of Bull Run (known in the South as First Manassas). The surprise Southern victory erased any hopes of a quick end to the war. Union and Confederate soldiers again met on the same ground for the larger Second Battle of Manassas in August 1862; again the South was victorious.

Daily Amtrak (www.amtrak.com) and Virginia Railway Express (www.vre.org) trains make the 50- to 70-minute journey between DC's Union Station and the historic Old Town Manassas Railroad Station; from there it's a 6-mile taxi ride to the park. There are several restaurants and bars around the Manassas train station, but the rest of the city is a mess of strip malls and suburban sprawl.

Egypt's Lighthouse of Alexandria, it honors the first president (who was initiated into the Masons in Fredericksburg in 1752 and later became Worshipful Master of Alexandria Lodge No 22). After paying admission, you can explore exhibits on the 1st and 2nd floors, but to visit the tower and see Washington-family artifacts, you must take a 60-minute guided tour.

Tours depart at 9:30am, 11am, 1pm, 2:30pm and 4pm. If you ask one too many questions about masonic symbolism and the *National Treasure* movies, a trapdoor will open and drop you into the parking lot. We jest; it's all quite welcoming and fascinating.

Torpedo Factory Art Center ARTS CENTER
(☎703-746-4570; www.torpedofactory.org; 105 N Union St; ⊙10am-6pm Fri-Wed, to 9pm Thu; Ⓜ Blue, Yellow Line to King St-Old Town) FREE What do you do with a former munitions dump and arms factory? How about turning it into one of the best art spaces in the region? Three floors of artist studios and galleries are on offer in Old Town Alexandria, as well as the opportunity to buy paintings, sculptures, glass works, textiles and jewelry direct from their creators – all 165 of them. Take the trolley from King St station.

Sleeping & Eating

Most accommodation options are located on King St, and are on the pricey side. You'll have to travel outside the neighborhood to find cheaper options.

Lorien Hotel & Spa HOTEL $$
(☎703-894-3434; www.lorienhotelandspa.com; 1600 King St; r $200-400; P ⊖ ❄ ☎ 🐾; Ⓜ Blue, Yellow Line to King St-Old Town) Hidden behind King St shopfronts, this is Alexandria's best accommodation option. Renovated rooms are comfortable and well sized, but it's the added extras here that matter: a communal wine hour in the early evening, complimentary morning coffee in the foyer, spa treatments (massages $115 to $250), a gym and a steam room. Meals can be enjoyed in the attached Brabo Tasting Room.

Stomping Ground BREAKFAST $
(☎703-567-6616; www.stompdelray.com; 2309 Mt Vernon Ave; mains $10-12; ⊙7am-3pm Tue-Sat, 9am-3pm Sun; Ⓜ Blue, Yellow Line to Braddock Rd/King St-Old Town) Did somebody say biscuit? Oh yes they did. And make that a homemade buttermilk biscuit piled with fillings of your choice (Benton's bacon, eggs, veggie frittata, avocado and many more) and with gouda grits on the side. Or just stop by this stylish Del Ray spot for coffee and to work on your laptop. Order and collect at the counter.

Brabo Tasting Room INTERNATIONAL $$
(☎703-894-5252; www.braborestaurant.com; 1600 King St; sandwiches & small plates $14-17; ⊙7am-11pm Mon-Thu, to midnight Fri, 8am-midnight Sat, 8am-10pm Sun; Ⓜ Blue, Yellow Line to King St-Old Town) The inviting and sunlit

Brabo Tasting Room serves its signature mussels, tasty wood-fired tarts and gourmet sandwiches with a good beer and wine selection. In the morning, stop by for brioche French toast and Bloody Marys. Brabo Brasserie, next door, is the high-end counterpart serving seasonal fare (mains $29 to $44).

Take a trolley from King St station.

Drinking & Entertainment

Head to King St for good bar-hopping with a crowd of folks who seem to be perpetually enrolled in the University of Virginia, Virginia Tech or George Mason University. There is a growing trend here for intimate speakeasies handcrafting cocktails.

★Captain Gregory's COCKTAIL BAR

(☎571-659-4934; www.captaingregorys.com; 804 N Henry St; ⏲5:30-10:15pm Wed, Thu & Sun, to 11:45pm Fri & Sat; Ⓜ Blue, Yellow Line to Braddock Rd) This nautical-themed speakeasy is hidden inside a Sugar Shack doughnut shop, which explains the decadent gourmet doughnuts on the menu. As for drinks, from Anais Needs a Vacay to Moaning Myrtles Morning Tea, the names are as diverse as the ingredients. Think flavored liqueurs, infused spirits and a range of fruit and spices. The cocktail menu changes frequently.

Reservation recommended.

Birchmere LIVE MUSIC

(☎703-549-7500; www.birchmere.com; 3701 Mt Vernon Ave; tickets $25-100; ⏲box office 5-9pm, shows 7:30pm; Ⓜ Blue, Yellow Line to Pentagon City) This 50-year-old place, hailing itself as 'America's Legendary Music Hall,' hosts a wide range of fare, from old-time folk musicians to country, blues and R&B stars. The lineup also features the odd burlesque show, indie rock bands and the occasional one-person comedy act.

The talent that graces the stage is reason enough to come, but the venue is pretty great too: it sort of looks like a warehouse that collided with an army of LSD-affected muralists. Located north of Old Town Alexandria, off Glebe Rd. Take bus 10A from Pentagon City station.

Getting There & Away

To get to Alexandria from downtown DC, take the Metro (Blue and Yellow Lines) to the King St-Old Town station. A free **trolley** (www.dashbus.com/ride-dash/king-street-trolley; ⏲11am-10:30pm Sun-Wed, 10:30am-midnight Thu-Sat, longer hours Jun-Aug; Ⓜ Blue, Yellow Line to King St-Old Town) makes the 1-mile journey from the Metro station to the waterfront and then back again.

Seasonal **water taxis** (☎703-684-0580; www.potomacriverboatco.com; one-way adult/child from $10/7; ⏲Mar-Sep) travel between Alexandria's wharf and the Wharf District in DC (25 minutes). There's also a seasonal service between Georgetown and Alexandria. Tour boats travel to/from the Mount Vernon estate during the summer season, too.

Fredericksburg

Fredericksburg is a pretty town with a downtown area that's almost a cliché of small-town Americana. George Washington grew up here, and the Civil War exploded in the streets and surrounding fields. Today the historic district surrounding William St provides opportunities for atmospheric ambles, with Colonial-era architecture to admire, intimate museums to visit and plenty of eating and drinking options to sample.

Sights

Ellwood Manor HISTORIC SITE

(☎540-786-2880; www.fowb.org; 36380 Constitution Hwy, Rte 20, Locust Grove; ⏲10am-5pm early Jun-Aug, Sat & Sun only Apr-early Jun & Aug-Nov) FREE This fascinating home sits on the grounds of the Wilderness Battlefield. Perhaps best known as the burial site for Confederate general Stonewall Jackson's amputated arm – there's a marker – the manor (c 1790) here once anchored a 5000-acre estate and has undergone a full interior restoration in recent times.

Step inside to learn the interesting history of the house on a docent-led guided tour.

Fredericksburg & Spotsylvania National Military Park HISTORIC SITE

(☎540-693-3200; www.nps.gov/frsp; 1013 Lafayette Blvd; ⏲Fredericksburg & Chancellorsville visitor centers 9am-5pm, hours vary at other exhibit areas) FREE More than 13,000 Americans were killed during the Civil War in four battles fought in a 17-mile radius covered by this park: Fredericksburg, Chancellorsville, the Wilderness and Spotsylvania Courthouse. Today the park is maintained by the National Park Service. Check its website for the locations of vari-

SCENIC DRIVE: VIRGINIA'S HORSE COUNTRY

About 40 miles west of Washington, DC, suburban sprawl gives way to endless green farms, vineyards, quaint villages and palatial estates and ponies. This is 'Horse Country,' where wealthy Washingtonians pursue their equestrian pastimes.

The following route is the most scenic drive to Shenandoah National Park (p316). From DC, take Rte 50 West to **Middleburg**, a too-cute-for-words town of taverns, antique shops and boutiques. The **National Sporting Museum** (☎540-687-6542; www.nationalsporting.org; 102 The Plains Rd, Middleburg; museum adult/child 13-18yr $10/8, Wed free; ⊙10am-5pm Wed-Sun) is a museum and research center devoted to horse and field sports such as foxhunting, dressage, steeplechase and polo. About 20 miles northeast of Middleburg is **Leesburg**, another town with a Colonial feel and historic sites. Stop in **Morven Park** (☎703-777-2414; www.morvenpark.org; 17195 Southern Planter Lane; grounds free, mansion tours adult/child 6-12yr $10/5; ⊙grounds 8am-5pm daily, mansion noon-5pm Thu-Mon Mar-Dec) for a tour of a staggering Virginia home on 1000 acres. For more Colonial grandeur, visit **Oatlands Historic House & Gardens** (☎703-777-3174; www.oatlands.org; 20850 Oatlands Plantation Lane, Leesburg; adult/child 6-16yr $15/10, grounds only $10; ⊙10am-5pm Apr-Dec, closed Jan-Mar), outside of town.

The area has some wonderful accommodation and dining options. Of these, the historic **Red Fox Tavern** (☎540-687-6301; www.redfox.com/tavern; 2 E Washington St; mains $32-52; ⊙8-10am & 5-9pm Mon-Fri, 11am-2pm & 5-9pm Sat, 11am-2pm & 5-8pm Sun) in Middleburg is notable, as is **Goodstone Inn & Restaurant** (☎540-687-3333, 877-219-4663; www.goodstone.com; 36205 Snake Hill Rd; d/ste from $385/435; P ⊖ 📶 ≋) just outside town.

Further down the road at the foothills of the Blue Ridge Mountains is **Sperryville**. Its many galleries and shops make it a must-stop for antique-lovers. Continue 9 miles west to reach the Thornton Gap entrance of Skyline Dr in Shenandoah National Park.

ous visitor centers, and for staffing, which may be seasonal.

Orientation films (adult/child under 10 years $2/free) are screened at the Fredericksburg and Chancellorsville visitor centers every 30 minutes, and audioguides can be hired.

James Monroe Museum & Memorial Library HISTORIC SITE
(☎540-654-1043; http://jamesmonroemuseum.umw.edu; 908 Charles St; adult/child 6-17yr $6/2; ⊙10am-5pm Mon-Sat, from 1pm Sun, to 4pm Dec-Feb) The museum's namesake was the nation's fifth president. US history buffs will delight in the small and eclectic collection of Monroe memorabilia, including the desk on which he wrote the famous Monroe Doctrine. His diplomatic court suit, worn at the coronation of Napoleon and dating from 1785 or so, is also on display.

Sleeping

There are several inns and B&Bs located in and around the downtown historic district, as well as a good Marriott hotel. Other chains have hotels on the Jefferson David Hwy (US1) on the edge of town.

Richard Johnston Inn B&B $$
(☎540-899-7606; www.therichardjohnstoninn.com; 711 Caroline St; d $150-225; P ❄ 📶 🐾) In an 18th-century brick mansion, this cozy B&B scores points for its downtown location, handsome communal areas and rear garden. Room rates drop midweek. The same friendly team operates the 1890 Caroline House annexe a short distance away, which offers three larger rooms ($225 to $300); its Sawyer Scott Suite is particularly nice. Breakfast (included) can be vegan or gluten-free by arrangement.

Getting There & Away

Virginia Railway Express (www.vre.org; $12.15, 1½ hours) and Amtrak (www.amtrak.com; from $28, 1½ hours) trains depart from the **Fredericksburg train station** (200 Lafayette Blvd) with service to DC. Greyhound has buses to/from DC ($10 to $24, 1½ hours, four or five per day) and Richmond ($14 to $30, one hour, four per day). The **Greyhound station** (☎540-373-2103; www.greyhound.com; 1400 Jefferson Davis Hwy; ⊙ticket office 7am-2pm & 4-7:30pm Mon-Fri, 7am-noon Sat & Sun) is roughly 2 miles west of the historic district. Fredericksburg borders I-95 midway between Washington, DC, and Richmond, VA. It's about

55 miles north to DC and 60 miles south to Richmond.

Historic Triangle

This is America's birthplace. Nowhere else in the country has such a small area played such a pivotal role in the course of the nation's history. The nation's roots were planted in Jamestown, the first permanent English settlement in the New World; the flames of the American Revolution were fanned at the Colonial capital of Williamsburg; and America finally won its independence from Britain at Yorktown. You'll need at least two days to do the Triangle any justice.

Getting There & Around

The Historic Triangle surrounds I-64. The largest regional airport is Norfolk International Airport (p298) followed by **Newport News/Williamsburg International Airport** (PHF; www.flyphf.com). Williamsburg is serviced by Amtrak (www.amtrak.com), and local WATA buses (www.gowata.org) link it with Jamestown ($1.50).

Williamsburg

If you visit only one historic town in Virginia, make it Williamsburg – home to Colonial Williamsburg, one of the largest, most comprehensive living-history museums in the world. If any place is going to get kids into history, this is it, but it's plenty of fun for adults too. The actual town of Williamsburg, Virginia's capital from 1699 to 1780, is a stately place that can sometimes verge on being twee. Fortunately, the campus of the College of William & Mary adds a decent dash of youth culture.

Sights

★Colonial Williamsburg HISTORIC SITE
(888-965-7254; www.colonialwilliamsburg.org; adult/child 6-12yr day $41/21, multiday $51/26; 8:45am-5pm) The restored capital of England's largest colony in the New World is a must-see attraction for visitors of all ages. This is not some phony, fenced-in theme park: Colonial Williamsburg is a living, breathing, working history museum with a painstakingly researched environment that brilliantly evokes 1700s America. It contains 88 original 18th-century buildings and several hundred faithful reproductions, as well as an impressive museum complex. Townsfolk and 'interpreters' in period dress go about their colonial jobs, emulating daily life.

Laudably, the park doesn't gloss over America's less glorious moments. Today's re-enactors debate and question slavery (52% of the population of 18th-century Williamsburg were slaves), women's suffrage, the rights of indigenous Americans and whether or not it is even moral to engage in revolution.

Walking around the historic district and patronizing the shops and taverns is free, but entry to building tours and most exhibits is restricted to ticket holders. Expect crowds, lines and overtired children, especially in summer. There are a number of taverns and a bakery where visitors can eat, and there's also a bakery in the Art Museums complex.

To park and to purchase tickets, follow signs to the **visitor center** (757-220-7645, 888-965-7254; 101 Visitor Center Dr; 8:45am-9pm), found north of the historic district between Hwy 132 and Colonial Pkwy. A program detailing the day's events will be given to you with your ticket, which helps when planning your time at the site.

Parking at the visitor center is free; shuttle buses run frequently between it and the historic district, or you can walk along the tree-lined footpath. You can also buy tickets at the **Merchants Square information booth** (W Duke of Gloucester St; 9am-5pm).

★Art Museums MUSEUM
(www.colonialwilliamsburg.com/art-museums; Francis St; adult/child 6-12yr $13/6.50, with Colonial Williamsburg admission free; 10am-7pm Mar-Dec, to 5pm Jan & Feb) Entered through Colonial Williamsburg's former public hospital, this complex is home to two equally splendid museums: the **DeWitt Wallace Decorative Arts Museum** and the **Abby Aldrich Rockefeller Folk Art Museum**. The decorative arts museum is home to the world's largest collection of Southern furniture and one of the largest collections of British ceramics outside England. The folk art museum has one of the largest collections of American folk art in the world – portraits, quilts, toys, musical instruments and much more.

College of William & Mary HISTORIC BUILDING
(www.wm.edu; 200 Stadium Dr) Chartered in 1693, the College of William & Mary is the second-oldest college in the country and retains the oldest academic building in

continued use in the USA, the **Sir Christopher Wren Building**. The school's alumni include Thomas Jefferson, James Monroe and comedian Jon Stewart. A free campus audio tour and interactive map are available online.

Sleeping & Eating

Williamsburg White House B&B $$
(757-229-8580; www.awilliamsburgwhitehouse.com; 718 Jamestown Rd; r $150-200; P) This romantic, beautifully furnished B&B is located across from the College of William & Mary campus, just a few blocks' walk from Colonial Williamsburg. It's a favorite spot of visiting politicos and bigwigs. Guests love the lavish breakfast and the afternoon drinks and nibbles served in the Diplomatic Reception Room. Book ahead, as there are only six rooms.

Colonial Williamsburg Historic Lodging – Colonial Houses GUESTHOUSE $$
(844-280-4578; www.colonialwilliamsburg.com; 136 E Francis St; d from $150, cabin $300-350;) For true 18th-century immersion, guests can stay in one of 26 original Colonial houses inside the historic district. Accommodations range in size and style, though the best have period furnishings, canopy beds and wood-burning fireplaces.

Cheese Shop DELI $
(757-220-0298; www.cheeseshopwilliamsburg.com; 410 W Duke of Gloucester St, Merchants Square; sandwiches $5.50-8; 10am-8pm Mon-Sat, 11am-6pm Sun) This gourmet deli showcases some flavorful sandwiches and antipasti, plus baguettes, pastries, ready-made meals, wine, beer and wonderful cheeses. Order a sandwich and a glass of wine – at different counters – then enjoy your meal and the people-watching from the patio.

★ Fat Canary MODERN AMERICAN $$$
(757-229-3333; www.fatcanarywilliamsburg.com; 410 W Duke of Gloucester St, Merchants Square; mains $29-42; 5-9:30pm, closed Mon Jan & Feb) The best restaurant in the historic triangle, this friendly and stylish place offers top-notch service, excellent wines and a menu of Modern American cuisine with Asian and Italian accents. We love the fact that local produce is a focus, that orders of half serves are possible and that the list of wine by the glass features interesting choices.

Jamestown

On May 14, 1607, a group of 104 English men and boys settled on this swampy island, bearing a charter from the Virginia Company of London to search for gold and other riches. Instead they found starvation and disease. By January 1608, only about 40 colonists were still alive and had resorted to cannibalism to survive. The colony pulled through the 'Starving Time' with the leadership of Captain James Smith and help from Powhatan, a local Native American leader. In 1619, the elected House of Burgesses convened, forming the first democratic government in the Americas. Today two sites share the story of this early settlement.

★ Historic Jamestowne HISTORIC SITE
(757-856-1250; www.historicjamestowne.org; 1368 Colonial Pkwy; adult/child under 16yr $20/free; 9am-5pm) Run by the NPS, this fascinating place is the original Jamestown site, established in 1607 and home of the first permanent English settlement in North America. The settlement's ruins were rediscovered in 1994; visitors can take a free guided tour of the excavations (daily 11am, also 2pm on weekends and between April and September). On arrival, view the orientation film and then head to the Archaearium, an archaeology museum with more than 4000 artifacts and a 'World of Pocahontas, Unearthed' exhibit.

Entry is discounted to $10 for visitors with a ticket receipt for Yorktown Battlefield, and to $5 if you have a National Parks pass. There's a cafe on-site.

Jamestown Settlement HISTORIC SITE
(888-593-4682; www.historyisfun.org; 2110 Jamestown Rd; adult/child 6-12yr $17.50/8.25, incl American Revolutionary Museum at Yorktown $26/12.50; 9am-5pm, to 6pm mid-Jun–mid-Aug; P) Popular with kids, the state-run Jamestown Settlement reconstructs the 1607 James Fort; a Native American village; and full-scale replicas of the first ships that brought the settlers to Jamestown, along with living-history fun. Multimedia exhibits and costumed interpreters bring the 17th century to life. This one can get uncomfortably busy with elementary-school field trips, so arrive early during the school year.

JAMES RIVER PLANTATIONS

The grand homes of Virginia's slaveholding aristocracy were a clear sign of the era's class divisions. A string of them line scenic Hwy 5 on the northern side of the river, though only a few are open to the public.

For cyclists, the new Virginia Capital Trail (p310) linking Richmond and Williamsburg travels beside Rte 5, near the Shirley and Berkeley Plantations.

Berkeley Plantation (☎804-829-6018; www.berkeleyplantation.com; 12602 Harrison Landing Rd, Charles City; adult/child 6-16yr $12.50/7; ⏰9:30am-4:30pm, shorter hours Jan & Feb) Dating from 1726, this plantation on the James River was the birthplace and home of Benjamin Harrison V, a signatory of the Declaration of Independence, and of his son William Henry Harrison, the ninth US president. It was also the site of the first official Thanksgiving (in 1619) and the first place where bourbon whiskey was distilled (1620). Lively guided tours of its brick Georgian-style house offer plenty of anecdotes.

Shirley Plantation (☎800-829-5121; www.shirleyplantation.com; 501 Shirley Plantation Rd, Charles City; grounds adult/child 7-16yr $11/6, guided tour incl admission $20/7.50; ⏰9:30am-4pm early Mar-Dec) Built on the banks of the James River, this is Virginia's oldest plantation (1613). It retains an original row of brick service and trade houses – tool barn, ice house, laundry etc – leading up to the big house, which dates from 1738. Established by Edward Hill I, the plantation was subsequently owned by descendants of Robert 'King' Carter and is still home to members of the Hill-Carter family. Guided tours of the downstairs reception rooms are held on the hour.

Yorktown

On October 19, 1781, British General Cornwallis surrendered to George Washington here, effectively ending the American Revolution. Overpowered by massive American guns on land and cut off from the sea by the French, the British were in a hopeless position. Although Washington anticipated a much longer siege, the devastating barrage quickly overwhelmed Cornwallis, who surrendered within days.

The actual town of Yorktown (www.visityorktown.org) is a pleasant waterfront village overlooking the York River, with a sandy beach, a scattering of shops, and a few restaurants and pubs.

Sights

American Revolution Museum at Yorktown MUSEUM

(☎757-887-1776; www.historyisfun.org; 200 Water St; adult/child 6-12yr $15/7.50, incl Jamestown Settlement $26/12.50; ⏰9am-5pm, to 6pm mid-July–mid-Aug; P 🚻) Formerly the Yorktown Victory Center, this expanded exhibition space and living history museum vividly describes the build-up to the Revolutionary War, the war itself and daily life on the home front. The award-winning introductory film *Liberty Fever* sets the stage for the rest of the museum. Lots of significant artifacts are here too, including an early printing of the Declaration of Independence. At the re-created military encampment outside, costumed Continental soldiers share details about life in a Revolutionary War camp.

Yorktown Battlefield HISTORIC SITE

(☎757-898-2410; www.nps.gov/york; 1000 Colonial Pkwy; adult/child under 16yr $10/free; ⏰9am-5pm; P 🚻) Yorktown Battlefield, run by the NPS, is the site of the last major battle of the American Revolution. Start your tour at the visitor center and check out the orientation film and the display of Washington's original tent, then drive the 7-mile Battlefield Rd Tour, which takes you past the major highlights. Don't miss a walk through the last British defensive sites, Redoubts 9 and 10, reached via Ballard St. Entry is free if you have a ticket receipt for Historic Jamestowne (p305).

Sleeping & Eating

★**Hornsby House Inn** B&B $$

(☎757-369-0200; www.hornsbyhouseinn.com; 702 Main St; r $160-260; P 📶) Close to Yorktown's beach and eateries, this house was built by the current owner's grandfather in 1933 and retains its old-fashioned ambience. That's not to say that it's dated or dowdy, because nothing could be further from the truth – we love the elegant ground-floor lounge and the five large, light and elegantly furnished rooms (most accessed by stairs).

Yorktown Pub SEAFOOD **$$**

(☎757-886-9964; www.yorktownpub.com; 540 Water St; sandwiches $6-14, mains $17-27; ⏲11am-midnight Sun-Thu, to 2am Fri & Sat) Most of the local action in Yorktown occurs at this pub by the beach. Serving good pub grub (including loads of local seafood) and staging live music on Friday and Saturday nights, it's as popular in winter as it is in the warmer weather due to the open fire and warm welcome offered by the staff.

Getting There & Away

There is no public transportation to Yorktown, so you'll need a car to visit. A free trolley loops between historic sites and the village every 20 to 35 minutes (11am to 5pm mid-March to December; longer hours June to August).

Norfolk

It's home to the world's largest naval base, so it's not surprising that Norfolk has long had a reputation as a rowdy port town filled with drunken sailors. However, in recent years the city has worked hard to clean up its image through development and by focusing on its burgeoning arts scene, which is spearheaded by the impressive Chrysler Museum of Art. The downtown Ghent District is where most of the town's cultural and entertainment action occurs, and the nearby Waterside District, a dining and entertainment complex on the Elizabeth River, is worth a visit.

Sights

★Chrysler Museum of Art MUSEUM

(☎757-664-6200; www.chrysler.org; 1 Memorial Pl; ⏲10am-5pm Tue-Sat, noon-5pm Sun) FREE A glorious setting for an eclectic collection of artifacts from ancient Egypt to the present day, including works by Henri Matisse, Albert Bierstadt, Georgia O'Keeffe, Jackson Pollock and Andy Warhol, and an expansive collection of glass objects spanning 3000 years. Don't miss the collection of Tiffany blown glass.

Naval Station Norfolk MUSEUM

(☎757-444-7955; www.cnic.navy.mil/norfolksta; 9079 Hampton Blvd, near Gate 5; adult/child 3-11yr $10/5; ⏲hours vary) The world's largest navy base, and one of the busiest airfields in the country. Hampton-based company Tidewater Touring works with the base to offer 45-minute bus tours conducted by naval personnel; tours must be booked in advance (hours vary). Photo ID is required for adults.

Nauticus MUSEUM

(☎757-664-1000; www.nauticus.org; 1 Waterside Dr; adult/child 4-12yr $16/11.50; ⏲10am-5pm Mon-Sat Jun-Aug, 10am-5pm Tue-Sat, noon-5pm Sun Sep-May) This massive, interactive, maritime-themed museum has exhibits on undersea exploration, aquatic life of the Chesapeake Bay and US Naval lore. The museum's highlight is clambering around the decks and inner corridors of the USS *Wisconsin*. Built in 1943, it was the largest (887ft long) and last battleship built by the US Navy.

Sleeping

For waterfront digs, there are tons of budget to midrange options lining Ocean View Ave (which actually borders the bay).

Main Hotel HOTEL **$$$**

(☎757-763-6200; www.hilton.com; 100 E Main St; d from $230; P ❄ 🛜 ≋) The rooms are swanky at this member of the Hilton family, which is located near the Nauticus Center. Rooms with a river view cost more, but you may not need to book one – just settle in for a drink and river view at the rooftop lounge, Grain, one of the hotel's three dining and drinking establishments. It's popular – book well in advance.

Eating & Drinking

Press 626 Wine Bar MODERN AMERICAN **$$**

(☎757-282-6234; www.press626.com; 626 W Olney Rd; sandwiches $10-14, mains $22-26; ⏲11am-11pm Mon-Fri, 5-11pm Sat, 10:30am-2:30pm Sun; 🌶) Embracing the Slow Food movement, this charming place in the Ghent district has a small but well-judged menu, with something to suit most tastes and budgets. The cheese and charcuterie plates are particularly good. Its wine selection is global and interesting, and its popular program of events includes wine seminars.

Smartmouth Brewing Company BREWERY

(☎757-624-3939; www.smartmouthbrewing.com; 1309 Raleigh Ave; ⏲4:30-9pm Wed & Thu, 4:30-10pm Fri, noon-10pm Sat, noon-6pm Sun; 🐾) In the Chelsea arts district, this indoor-outdoor tasting room and brewery has an inviting neighborhood feel, plus there's usually a food truck handy to supply sustenance. If you like *Hefeweizen* (wheat beer), give the seasonal Sommer Fling a try (April to December). There are free brewery tours every hour between 1pm and 4pm on Saturday.

Getting There & Away

The region is served by Norfolk International Airport (p298), 7 miles northeast of downtown Norfolk. **Greyhound** (757-625-7500; www.greyhound.com; 701 Monticello Ave) buses serve Virginia Beach (from $6, 40 minutes), Richmond (from $17, two to 2½ hours), and Washington, DC ($20, 5¼ hours).

Virginia Beach

With 35 miles of sandy beaches, a 3-mile concrete oceanfront boardwalk and nearby outdoor activities, it's no surprise that Virginia Beach is a prime tourist destination. The city has worked hard to shed its reputation as a rowdy 'Redneck Riviera,' and hey, the beach *is* wider and cleaner now and there are fewer louts. Beach aside, you'll find some lovely parks and nature sites beyond the crowded high-rises lining the shore. Expect thick crowds, heavy traffic and high prices if visiting in the summer.

Sights

Virginia Aquarium & Marine Science Center AQUARIUM
(757-385-3474; www.virginiaaquarium.com; 717 General Booth Blvd; adult/child 3-11yr $25/20; 9am-5pm) If you want to see an aquarium done right, come here. In various habitats, you can see a great array of aquatic life, including sea turtles, river otters and Komodo dragons.

If you and the kids have extra energy to burn after viewing the aquarium, you can watch a 3-D nature documentary on the largest cinema screen in the state ($8), set off on a 'Whales and Wildlife' boat trip (adult/child three to 11 years $30/25) or try out the ropes course and zipline in the Adventure Park (adult/child seven to 11 years $56/47), tucked in the woods between aquarium buildings.

Sleeping & Eating

First Landing State Park CAMPGROUND $
(800-933-7275; www.dcr.virginia.gov; Cape Henry; tent & RV sites $30-46, 2-bedroom cabins $156-173; early Mar-early Dec; P) You couldn't ask for a prettier campground than the one at this bay-front state park, though the cabins have no water view.

Hilton Virginia Beach Oceanfront HOTEL $$
(757-213-3000; www.hiltonvb.com; 3001 Atlantic Ave; r from $230; P @) One of the premier places to stay on the beach, this 21-story hotel offers spacious and comfortable oceanfront rooms with large balconies that open out to the beach and Neptune Park below. Facilities include a fitness center and two pools: an outdoor rooftop infinity pool and an indoor alternative. In summer, rooms are cheaper midweek than on weekends.

Esoteric AMERICAN $$
(757-822-6008; www.esotericvb.com; 501 Virginia Beach Blvd; sandwiches & small plates $12-19, mains $22-30; 4-10pm Mon-Thu, to midnight Fri, 3pm-midnight Sat, 10am-3pm Sun) The menu at this joint lives up to its name, including everything from hummus to dolmades, tacos to gnocchi. At lunch, the gourmet sandwiches and craft beer are a winning combination. The husband-and-wife team grow some of their produce in the attached garden, and embrace local food producers as collaborators. Bravo!

Getting There & Away

Greyhound (757-422-2998; www.greyhound.com; 971 Virginia Beach Blvd) runs daily buses to Richmond (from $16, 3½ hours), which also stop in Norfolk and Hampton; transfer in Richmond for services to Washington, DC, Wilmington, NYC and beyond. Buses depart from Circle D Food Mart, 1 mile west of the boardwalk.

Hampton Roads Transit runs the Virginia Beach Wave trolley ($2), which plies Atlantic Ave in summer.

The Piedmont

Nestled between the Blue Ridge Mountains and the coastal plain, this central tract of Virginia is a mix of forest and gently sloping hills with well-drained, mineral-rich soil – perfect conditions in which to cultivate grapes. More than 100 wineries are located here, alongside rural villages, grand colonial estates, microbreweries, cideries and distilleries. The history-rich cities of Charlottesville and Richmond are popular bases for exploring the region.

WORTH A TRIP

VIRGINIA'S VINEYARDS

Home to more than 200 vineyards, Virginia has a rising presence in the wine world. Good places to begin an investigation of the local scene lie just outside of DC in Loudon County, and designated wine trails continue throughout the state. For maps, wine routes and loads of other viticultural info, visit www.virginiawine.org.

It's a hard task to nominate only a few wineries as highlights, but here's our best shot.

Loudoun County

Bluemont Vineyard (540-554-8439; www.bluemontvineyard.com; 18755 Foggy Bottom Rd, Bluemont; tastings $15; 11am-7pm;)

Breaux Vineyards (540-668-6299; www.breauxvineyards.com; 36888 Breaux Vineyards Lane, Hillsboro; tastings $15; 11am-6pm mid-Mar–Oct, to 5pm Nov-early Mar;)

Sunset Hills Vineyard (540-882-4560; www.sunsethillsvineyard.com; 38295 Fremont Overlook Lane, Purcellville; tastings $12; noon-5pm Mon-Thu, to 8pm Fri, 11am-6pm Sat & Sun; P)

Tarara Vineyard (703-771-7100; www.tarara.com; 13648 Tarara Lane; tastings $15-20; 11am-5pm Mon-Thu, to 6pm Fri-Sun, closed Tue & Wed Nov-Mar;)

Also see www.loudounfarms.org/craft-beverages/wine-trail and www.visitloudoun.org/things-to-do/wine-country.

Blue Ridge Parkway

Chateau Morrisette (540-593-2865; www.thedogs.com; 287 Winery Rd, Mile 171.5, off Blue Ridge Pkwy; tastings incl glass $10; 10am-5pm Mon-Thu, to 6pm Fri & Sat, 11am-5pm Sun, closed Jan-Mar)

The Piedmont

Barboursville Vineyards (540-832-3824; www.bbvwine.com; 17655 Winery Rd; tastings $10; tasting room 10am-5pm Mon-Sat, from 11am Sun)

Grace Estate (434-823-1486; www.graceestatewinery.com; 5273 Mount Juliet Farm, Crozet; tastings $9; 11am-5:30pm Wed, Thu & Sun, to 9pm Fri & Sat)

King Family Vineyards (434-823-7800; www.kingfamilyvineyards.com; 6550 Roseland Farm, Crozet; tastings $10, tour $20; 10am-5:30pm Thu-Tue, to 8:30pm Wed;)

Pippin Hill (434-202-8063; www.pippinhillfarm.com; 5022 Plank Rd, North Garden; tastings $10; 11am-5pm Tue-Sun)

Also see www.americaswinecountry.com and https://monticellowinetrail.com.

Getting There & Around

The Piedmont region is flanked by I-81 and I-64. The area is best explored by car. Charlottesville anchors the region and has an airport (p314), Amtrak station and Greyhound station. On Friday you'll likely join a few UVA students hopping the train to Washington, DC.

Richmond

Richmond has woken up from a very long nap – and we like it. The capital of the commonwealth of Virginia since 1780, and the capital of the Confederacy during the Civil War, it's long been an old-fashioned city clinging too tightly to its Southern roots. But an influx of new and creative young residents is energizing and modernizing the community.

Today the 'River City' shares a buzzing food-and-drink scene and an active arts community. The rough-and-tumble James River has also grabbed more of the spotlight, drawing outdoor adventurers to its rapids and trails. Richmond is also an undeniably handsome town that is easy to stroll, full of redbrick row houses, stately drives and leafy parks.

Sights

★Virginia State Capitol NOTABLE BUILDING

(☎804-698-1788; www.virginiacapitol.gov; 1000 Bank St, Capitol Sq, Court End; ⏱9am-5pm Mon-Sat, from 1pm Sun) FREE Designed by Thomas Jefferson, the capitol building was completed in 1788 and houses the oldest legislative body in the Western Hemisphere – the Virginia General Assembly, established in 1619. Free one-hour guided tours of the historic building are available between 10am and 4pm Monday to Saturday, and between 1pm and 4pm on Sunday; self-guided tours are also available. Temporary exhibits are shown in the underground galleries near the visitor entrance.

★Virginia Museum of Fine Arts MUSEUM

(VMFA; ☎804-340-1400; www.vmfa.museum; 200 N Blvd, Museum District; ⏱10am-5pm Sat-Wed, to 9pm Thu & Fri) FREE Richmond is a cultured city, and this splendid art museum is the cornerstone of the local arts scene. Highlights of its eclectic, world-class collection include the Sydney and Frances Lewis Art Nouveau and Art Deco Galleries, which include furniture and decorative arts by designers including Eileen Gray, Josef Hoffmann and Charles Rennie Mackintosh. Other galleries house one of the largest Fabergé egg collections on display outside Russia, and American works by O'Keeffe, Hopper, Henri, Whistler, Sargent and other big names.

★Poe Museum MUSEUM

(☎804-648-5523; www.poemuseum.org; 1914-16 E Main St, Shockoe Bottom; adult/child 7-17yr $8/6; ⏱10am-5pm Tue-Sat, from 11am Sun) Contains the world's largest collection of manuscripts and memorabilia of poet and horror-writer Edgar Allan Poe, who lived and worked in Richmond. Exhibits include the first printing of 'The Raven,' Poe's vest, his pen knife and a work chair with the back cut off – they say his boss at the *Southern Literary Messenger* wanted Poe to sit up straight. Pesky know-it-all. Stop by on the fourth Thursday of the month for the Poe-themed Unhappy Hour (6pm to 9pm April to October; $8).

Historic Tredegar MUSEUM

(☎804-649-1861; https://acwm.org; 500 Tredegar St, Gambles Hill; adult/child 6-17yr $15/8; ⏱9am-5pm) Part of the multisite American Civil War Museum, this fascinating exhibit – housed inside an 1861 iron works that at its height employed 800 free and slave laborers – explores the causes and course of the Civil War from the Union, Confederate and African American perspectives.

The new museum building set into the hillside incorporates ruins from the historic Tredegar Iron Works.

St John's Episcopal Church CHURCH

(☎804-648-5015; www.historicstjohnschurch.org; 2401 E Broad St, Church Hill; tours adult/child 7-18yr $8/6; ⏱10am-4pm Mon-Sat, from 1pm Sun) It was here that firebrand Patrick Henry uttered his famous battle cry – 'Give me Liberty, or give me Death!' – during the rebellious 1775 Second Virginia Convention. The short but informative tour is given by guides dressed in period costume and traces the history of the church and of the famous speech. Above the pulpit, the rare 1741 sounding board and its sunburst are worth a closer look. Henry's speech is re-enacted at 1:15pm on Sunday in summer.

Hollywood Cemetery CEMETERY

(☎804-648-8501, tour reservations 804-649-0711; www.hollywoodcemetery.org; 412 S Cherry St; ⏱8am-6pm Mar-Oct, to 5pm Nov-Feb) FREE Perched above the James River rapids, this tranquil cemetery contains the gravesites of two US presidents (James Monroe and John Tyler), the only Confederate president (Jefferson Davis) and 18,000 Confederate soldiers. Guided walking tours are conducted at 10am Monday through Saturday from April to October, plus Saturday (10am) and Sunday (2pm) in November (adult/child under 13 years $15/free). For a self-guided walk, check the virtual tour offered on the website. The entrance is at the corner of Albemarle and Cherry Streets.

Activities

Virginia Capital Trail CYCLING

(www.virginiacapitaltrail.org) Open to cyclists and pedestrians, this 52-mile paved trail, completed in 2015, links Richmond with Jamestown and outer Williamsburg, passing several plantations along the way. Check the helpful website for a map showing parking areas, restrooms, bike shops, restaurants and lodging. There are loads of historic sights and markers along the way. The trail starts at the junction of S 17th and Dock Sts.

Sleeping

★HI Richmond HOSTEL $

(☎804-729-5410; www.hiusa.org; 7 N 2nd St; dm $29-31, r $85-110, nonmembers add $3;) Inside the 1940s Otis Elevator Co building, this stylish and ecofriendly downtown option is one of the best hostels that you'll ever encounter. Rooms and dorms are clean and bright, with lockers and charging stations; linen and towels are supplied. Communal facilities – free washing machines and dryers, lounge with pool table and TV, large and well-equipped kitchen – are excellent.

Quirk Hotel BOUTIQUE HOTEL $$$

(☎804-340-6040; www.destinationhotels.com/quirk-hotel; 201 W Broad St, Monroe Ward; d from $180, ste from $430;) From the moment you stroll into the big-windowed lobby, which houses a glam bar and restaurant, this downtown boutique choice impresses. The high ceilings and maple floors in rooms are a direct link to the building's past life as a luxury department store. Beds, bathrooms and amenities are excellent. The hotel's popular rooftop bar is open late April to late October.

Eating & Drinking

★Sugar & Twine CAFE $

(☎804-204-1755; www.sugartwine.com; 2928 W Cary St, Carytown; pastries $2-3, sandwiches $5-6; ⊙7am-8pm Mon-Sat, to 6pm Sun;) Let's face it: contemporary coffee culture hasn't made inroads in Virginia yet. Fortunately, stylish cafes like this one are in the vanguard. We like everything about Sugar & Twine: the excellent espresso coffee, delicious pastries, tasty sandwiches (some vegan and veggie; gluten-free bread available), free wi-fi and friendly staff.

Kuba Kuba CUBAN $

(☎804-355-8817; www.kubakuba.info; 1601 Park Ave, Fan District; sandwiches $8-10, mains $13-20; ⊙9am-9:30pm Mon-Thu, to 10pm Fri & Sat, to 8pm Sun;) Kuba Kuba feels like a bodega straight out of Old Havana, with mouthwatering roast pork dishes, Spanish-style omelets and panini offered at rock-bottom prices. Finish with a dessert and good espresso coffee.

Perly's DELI $

(☎804-912-1560; www.perlysrichmond.com; 111 E Grace St, Monroe Ward; brunch dishes $7-14, sandwiches $9-13; ⊙8am-9pm Mon-Sat, to 3pm Sun) Generations of locals have enjoyed Yiddish specialties at Perly's, which dates from 1962, and we think you should too. Choose from treats including corned-beef hash, cinnamon babka, knish and latkes at brunch (until 3pm daily) and opt for one of the sandwiches at lunch. There's booth and bar seating, and a friendly retro vibe.

Mama J's AMERICAN $

(☎804-225-7449; www.mamajskitchen.com; 415 N 1st St, Jackson Ward; sandwiches $5-10, mains $8-16; ⊙11am-9pm Sun-Thu, to 10pm Fri & Sat) The fried catfish may not look fancy, but it sure tastes like heaven. Set in the historic African American neighborhood of Jackson Ward, Mama J's serves delicious fried chicken and legendary fried catfish, along with collard greens, mac 'n' cheese, candied yams and other fixings. The service is friendly and the lines are long. Come early to beat the crowds.

★L'Opossum AMERICAN, FRENCH $$$

(☎804-918-6028; www.lopossum.com; 626 China St, Oregon Hill; mains $22-36; ⊙5pm-midnight Tue-Sat) We're not exactly sure what's going on at this gastronomic laboratory, but it works. The name of the place is terrible. And dishes come with names that are self-consciously hip and verging on offensive ('Vegan Orgy on Texan Beach'). So what ties it together? The culinary prowess of award-winning chef David Shannon and his attentive and talented staff. Make a reservation or get here early to snag a seat at the bar.

Saison BAR

(☎804-269-3689; www.saisonrva.com; 23 W Marshall St, Jackson Ward; ⊙5pm-2am) This hipster hole-in-the-wall is a peculiar mash-up of wine bar, cafe and restaurant. Creative cocktails, craft beer and local wines are on offer, as is a menu of small plates (many vegetarian), burgers and more gourmet fare. We recommend heading here for drinks rather than meals.

The kitchen closes at 10pm Sunday to Thursday and 11pm Friday and Saturday.

Capital Ale House BAR

(☎804-780-2537; www.capitalalehouse.com; 623 E Main St, Court End; ⊙11am-1:30am Mon-Fri, from 10am Sat & Sun) Popular with political wonks from the nearby state capitol, this downtown pub has a superb beer selection (more than 70 on tap and 100 bottled) and decent pub grub. Regular live gigs are staged in the music hall.

Getting There & Away

Amtrak trains stop at the **Staples Mill Rd station** (7519 Staples Mill Rd), 7 miles north of town (accessible to downtown via bus 27). More-convenient but less-frequent trains stop downtown at the **Main St Station** (1500 E Main St). Richmond is serviced by the Northeast Regional, Carolinian, Palmetto, Silver Star and Silver Meteor lines, all of which link the city frequently with Washington, DC (tickets from $38, 2¼ to 2½ hours).

Greyhound and Trailways bus services stop at the **bus station** (804-254-5910; 2910 N Arthur Ashe Blvd, The Diamond; 24hr).

Getting Around

The **RVA Bike Share** (www.rvabikes.com) program has a number of bike stations across the city. A one-way, 45-minute pass costs $1.75 and a day pass costs $6. Download the app from the website for station locations.

Greater Richmond Transit Company (www.ridegrtc.com) runs local buses. Tickets cost $1.50 and exact change is needed. The bus rapid transit line called the GRTC Pulse (often abbreviated as the Pulse) links Willow Lawn with Rockett's Landing via Broad St and Main St.

Street car parking costs $1.25 per hour.

Charlottesville

Set in the shadow of the Blue Ridge Mountains, Charlottesville is regularly ranked as one of the country's best places to live. This culturally rich town is home to the architecturally resplendent University of Virginia (UVA), which attracts Southern aristocracy and artsy lefties in equal proportions. The UVA grounds, Main St and the pedestrian downtown mall area overflow with students, professors and visiting tourists, endowing 'C-ville' with a lively, cultured and diverse atmosphere.

Sights

★Monticello HISTORIC SITE

(434-984-9800; www.monticello.org; 931 Thomas Jefferson Pkwy; adult $23-30, youth 12-18yr $17, child 5-11yr $10; 8:30am-6pm Mon-Fri, to 7pm Sat & Sun, hours vary seasonally) The house at Monticello is an architectural masterpiece designed and inhabited by Thomas Jefferson, founding father and third US president, who spent 40 years building his dream home. It was finally completed in 1809. Today it is the only home in America designated a Unesco World Heritage Site. The centerpiece of a plantation that once covered 5000 acres, it can be visited on guided tours (ground floor only), while its grounds and outbuildings can be explored on themed and self-guided tours.

The 45-minute 'Slavery at Monticello' walking tour (included in ticket price) is the highlight of any trip. Guides don't gloss over the complicated past of the man who declared that 'all men are created equal' in the Declaration of Independence, while owning slaves and likely fathering children with slave Sally Hemings. Jefferson and his other family are buried in a small wooded plot near the home.

Two tours per day visit the upstairs rooms of the house ($49 to $65, child under five years free); these are popular so must be booked in advance.

A high-tech exhibition center delves deeper into Jefferson's world – including exhibits on architecture, enlightenment through education, and the complicated idea of liberty. Frequent shuttles run from the visitor center to the hilltop house, or you can walk along a wooded footpath.

Monticello is about 4.5 miles northwest of downtown Charlottesville.

University of Virginia UNIVERSITY

(434-924-0311; www.virginia.edu; University Ave, Charlottesville) Thomas Jefferson founded the University of Virginia, and designed what he called an 'Academical Village' embodying the spirit of communal living and learning. At the heart of this 'village' is the **Lawn**, a large gently sloping grassed field fringed by columned pavilions, student rooms, the Standford White–designed **Old Cabell Hall** (1898) and Jefferson's famous **Rotunda** (434-924-7969; www.rotunda.virginia.edu; 1826 University Ave; 9am-5pm), modelled on Rome's Pantheon. Together, the original neoclassical and Palladian-style university buildings and Jefferson's Monticello comprise a Unesco World Heritage Site.

Free, student-led **guided tours** (www.uvaguides.org) of the original university and lawn depart daily from the Rotunda at 10am, 11am and 2pm during the school year (September to April).

Sleeping

Fairhaven GUESTHOUSE $

(434-933-2471; www.fairhavencville.com; 413 Fairway Ave; r $55-90; P) This friendly and welcoming guesthouse is a great deal if you don't mind sharing facilities (there's just

WORTH A TRIP

MONTPELIER

Thomas Jefferson gets all the attention in these parts, but it's well worth branching out and visiting James Madison's **Montpelier** (☎540-672-2728; www.montpelier.org; 11350 Constitution Hwy, Montpelier Station; adult/child 6-14yr $22/9; ⏰9am-5pm Apr-Oct, 10am-4pm Nov-Mar), a spectacular estate 25 miles northeast of Charlottesville (off Hwy 20). Madison was a brilliant but shy man, who devoted himself to his books; he was almost single-handedly responsible for developing and writing the US Constitution. Guided tours shed a light on the life and times of James as well as his gifted and charismatic wife Dolley, plus other residents of the estate.

Carefully reconstructed cabins show what life was like for Madison's slaves. There's an archeology lab, where on-site archeologists can explain recent findings. Hiking trails lead through the forests beyond the estate – the ambitious can even walk 4 miles to the **Market at Grelen** (☎540-672-7268; www.themarketatgrelen.com; 15091 Yager Rd, Somerset; sandwiches $8-9; ⏰cafe 11:30am-2:30pm Mon-Fri, to 3:30pm Sat & Sun, shop 10am-4pm Wed-Sat, closed late Dec-Feb), a charming lunch spot and garden center, where you can pick your own berries on the rolling, 600-acre grounds.

one bathroom for the three rooms). Each room has wood floors, comfy beds and a cheerful color scheme, and guests can use the kitchen, living room and backyard. It's about a 1-mile walk to the pedestrian mall.

★South Street Inn B&B $$
(☎434-979-0200; www.southstreetinn.com; 200 W South St; r $193-234, ste $283-291; P❄📶) Having gone through previous incarnations as a girls' finishing school, a boarding house and a brothel, this elegant 1856 building, with its picture-perfect front porch, now houses a heritage-style B&B with 11 well-sized and beautifully presented rooms. There are extra rooms in an attached cottage. Breakfast is served in the library, as is complimentary wine and cheese every evening.

Residence Inn by Marriott HOTEL $$
(☎434-220-0075; www.marriott.com; 315 W Main St; studio $175-265, 1-bed apt $205-400, 2-bed apt $298-500; P⊖❄📶🏊🐾) We're not usually chain-hotel fans, but this excellent place deserves serious praise. Its location couldn't be better, and its clean, comfortable and well-equipped studios and apartments make a great base for a Charlottesville stay. Facilities include a pool, bar, gym and coin-operated laundry, and there's even a free shuttle service within a 10-mile radius (including the airport).

Eating

★Bodo's Bagels BAGELS $
(☎434-293-6021; www.bodosbagels.com; 1609 University Ave; bagels $0.80, sandwiches $3-4; ⏰7am-8pm Mon-Fri, 8am-4pm Sat & Sun) Students and university staff are regulars at this Charlottesville institution, lured by its wonderful bagels and its location on UVA Corner. Choose from a large array of options (plain, slathered with butter or cream cheese, topped with egg). Also offers sandwiches. Eat in or order to go.

Mudhouse Coffee Roasters CAFE $
(☎434-984-6833; www.mudhouse.com; 213 W Main St; pastry $3; ⏰7am-10pm Mon-Sat, to 8pm Sun; 📶) Its mantra is 'Beautiful coffee. Thoughtfully sourced. Carefully roasted.' and we can attest to the fact that this cafe on the pedestrian mall practices what it preaches. Excellent coffee (espresso and drip) and delicious pastries are enjoyed in stylish surrounds or at tables on the mall.

Citizen Burger AMERICAN $
(☎434-979-9944; www.citizenburgerbar.com; 212 E Main St; burgers $7-21; ⏰11:30am-10:30pm Sun-Thu, to 11:30pm Fri & Sat; 🍸) 🌿 The ethos at this hugely popular burger joint on the pedestrian mall is commendably local and sustainable (organically raised, grass-fed cows, Virginia-made cheeses and beers). Don't miss the truffle fries. The bar stays open after meal service finishes.

★Oakhart Social MODERN AMERICAN $$
(☎434-995-5449; www.oakhartsocial.com; 511 W Main St; small plates $8-22, pizza $15; ⏰5pm-midnight Tue-Sun, to 2am Fri & Sat) Seasonally inspired small plates and wood-fired pizzas emerge from the kitchen of this hipster haunt at a great rate, keeping its loyal crew of regulars fed and happy. On warm nights, the front patio is a perfect cocktail-sipping

VIRGINIA'S BREW RIDGE TRAIL

A string of craft breweries stretches west from Charlottesville to Crozet and along Hwy 151, which ribbons along the base of the Blue Ridge Mountains below the Blue Ridge Pkwy. Part of the **Brew Ridge Trail** (www.brewridgetrail.com), these breweries produce fine craft beer; many also offer mountain views and great food. On pretty days you'll find the patios loaded with beer connoisseurs and outdoor adventurers. **Hop On Virginia** (www.virginiahopontours.com) shuttles between many of the breweries.

spot, and the bar is a great spot for solo diners.

★ **Public Fish & Oyster** SEAFOOD $$$
(☎434-995-5542; www.publicfo.com; 513 W Main St; mains $19-26; ⏱4-9pm Sun & Mon, to 9:30pm Tue-Thu, to 10pm Fri & Sat) This bright and inviting space will catch your eye, but it's the skillfully seasoned seafood dishes that will keep you inside ordering plate after plate of freshly shucked oysters, mussels and other maritime delights. If you're a raw-oyster virgin, this is the place to change that story. The twice-cooked Belgian fries with sea salt are fantastic. Great service too.

Getting There & Away

Amtrak (www.amtrak.com; 810 W Main St; ⏱ticket office 6am-9:30pm) trains connect Charlottesville with Washington, DC (from $27, 2¾ hours, two daily). From the **Greyhound/Trailways Terminal** (☎434-295-5131; www.greyhound.com; 310 W Main St; ⏱ticket office 8am-10pm) buses run to Richmond (from $16, 1¼ hours, four daily), Roanoke (from $27, 2½ hours, four daily) and Washington, DC (from $19, three hours, four daily).

Charlottesville Albemarle Airport (CHO; ☎434-973-8342; www.gocho.com; 100 Bowen Loop), 10 miles north of downtown, offers nonstop flights along the East Coast and to Chicago.

Getting Around

A free trolley (look for a T sign) connects the **Downtown Transit Station** (☎434-970-3649; www.charlottesville.org; 615 E Water St; ⏱7am-8pm Mon-Sat, 9am-5pm Sun) near Sprint Pavilion with UVA via W Main St. It runs every 15 minutes between 6:30am and 11:30pm Monday to Saturday and from 8am to 5:40pm on Sunday.

Appomattox

The small and somnolent town of Appomattox has one major claim to fame: this is where general Robert E Lee surrendered the Army of Northern Virginia to general Ulysses S Grant, in effect ending the Civil War. These days, Civil War enthusiasts and history buffs head here to visit the Appomattox Court House National Historic Park and American Civil War Museum, and to shop in a scattering of downtown antique shops specializing in Civil War memorabilia. The latter are open on weekends only.

Sights

★ **Appomattox Court House National Historic Park** PARK
(☎434-352-8987; www.nps.gov/apco; 111 National Park Dr; ⏱9am-5pm) FREE At the McLean House in the town of Appomattox Court House, General Robert E Lee surrendered to General Ulysses S Grant, effectively ending the Civil War. The park comprises more than two-dozen restored buildings; a number are open to visitors, and set with original and period furnishings from 1865.

Highlights include the parlor of the **McLean House**, where Lee and Grant met; the **Clover Hill Tavern**, used by Union soldiers to print 30,000 parole passes for Confederate soldiers; and the dry goods–filled **Meeks General Store**.

American Civil War Museum – Appomattox MUSEUM
(☎434-352 5791; https://acwm.org; 159 Horseshoe Rd; adult/child 6-17yr $12/6; ⏱10am-5pm; P) Artifacts, photographs, documents and audiovisual presentations tell the story of the lead-up to the end of the Civil War and the start of America becoming a reunified nation. The museum's pride and joy is the uniform coat and sword that Robert E Lee wore to the surrender.

Shenandoah Valley

Local lore says Shenandoah was named for a Native American word meaning 'Daughter of the Stars.' True or not, there's no question this is God's country, and one of the most beautiful places in America. The 200-mile-long valley and its Blue Ridge Mountains are packed with picturesque small towns, wineries, microbreweries, preserved battlefields and caverns. This was once the western border of Colonial America, settled by Scots-Irish frontiersmen who were Highland Clearance refugees.

Outdoor activities such as hiking, cycling, camping, fishing, horseback riding and canoeing abound, and hitting the road on the famed Skyline Drive is an unforgettable experience, particularly in the fall when the palette of the forest canopy ranges from russet red to copper-tinged orange.

Getting There & Around

The best way to explore is by car. The I-81 and I-64 are the primary interstates here. The largest airport is Roanoke-Blacksburg Regional Airport (p298). Amtrak stops at the **train station** (www.amtrak.com; 1 Middlebrook Ave) in Staunton and the **Virginia Breeze** (800-827-3490; www.catchthevabreeze.com; tickets $15-50) bus service to/from Washington, DC, stops at Arlington, Front Royal, Staunton and Lexington.

Front Royal & Luray

There's a frontier flavour to this town nestled in the Shenandoah next to the northernmost tip of Skyline Dr. The streets are often deserted, and there aren't many top-drawer tourist attractions. It's a popular destination for outdoor enthusiasts, though, with hiking, horse riding, river rafting and canoeing opportunities aplenty. Stop here for gas and provisions before setting off along Skyline Dr.

Sights

★Luray Caverns CAVE
(540-743-6551; www.luraycaverns.com; 970 US Hwy 211 W, Luray; adult/child 6-12yr $28/15; 9am-7pm daily mid-Jun–Aug, to 6pm Sep-Nov & Apr–mid-Jun, to 4pm Mon-Fri, to 5pm Sat & Sun Dec-Mar) If you can only fit one cavern into your Shenandoah itinerary, head 25 miles south from Front Royal to the world-class Luray Caverns and hear the 'Stalacpipe Organ' – hyped as the largest musical instrument on earth. Tours can feel like a cattle call on busy weekends, but the stunning underground formations make up for all the elbow-bumping.

To save time at the entrance, buy your ticket online ahead of time, then join the entry line. Also here is a **Ropes Adventure Park** (adult/child $11/6) and a **Garden Maze** ($10/6).

Sleeping & Eating

Yogi Bear's Jellystone Park Camp-Resort CAMPGROUND $
(540-300-1697; www.campluray.com; 2250 Hwy 211 E, Luray; campsite from $40, cabins from $74; late Mar-late Nov; P) Miniature golf courses, a huge splash pad and playground, jumping pillows, four waterslides and paddleboats await at this bizarrely monikered campground. It's a paradise for kids, but could well be nightmarish for those not traveling in family groups.

Facilities here include a camp store, cafe, dog park, laundry and clean ablutions blocks.

★Hotel Laurance BOUTIQUE HOTEL $$
(540-742-7060; www.hotellaurance.com; 2 S Court St; ste $225-265;) Owner Melinda Kramer has done a splendid job of transforming this handsome but once-dilapidated 1830s building into Luray's only boutique hotel. Most of the 12 suites have an equipped kitchen; all are stylishly decorated and have comfortable beds. The only disappointment is the lack of staff to greet guests on arrival.

Weekend bookings require a two- or three-night stay.

Element FUSION $$
(540-636-1695; www.elementonmain.com; 317 E Main St; mains lunch $8-16, dinner $16-32; 11am-3pm & 5-9pm Tue-Sat) When it comes to local popularity, this friendly Front Royal eatery wins hands down. Serving good-quality bistro fare, it offers sandwiches, soups and salads at lunch, with more substantial dishes including pastas, steaks and fish-and-chips for dinner.

Getting There & Away

Front Royal is located 70 miles east of Washington, DC. The Virginia Breeze bus service from DC stops at Front Royal and continues to Harrisonburg, Staunton, Lexington, Christiansburg and Blacksburg before returning along the same route.

Staunton

This small-town beauty has much going for it, including a historic and walkable town center, a fantastic foodie scene, great microbreweries, regular live music downtown and a first-rate theater.

DON'T MISS

SHENANDOAH NATIONAL PARK

One of the most spectacular national parks in the country, **Shenandoah National Park** (☎540-999-3500; www.nps.gov/shen; Skyline Dr; 1-week pass per car $30; ⊙year-round) is a showcase of natural color and beauty: in spring and summer the wildflowers explode, in fall the leaves burn bright red and orange, and in winter a cold, starkly beautiful hibernation period sets in. White-tailed deer are a common sight and, if you're lucky, you might spot a black bear, bobcat or wild turkey. The park lies just 75 miles west of Washington, DC.

Your first stop should be the **Dickey Ridge Visitor Center** (Mile 4.6, Skyline Dr; ⊙9am-5pm Apr-Nov), close to the northern end of Skyline Dr, or the **Harry F Byrd Visitor Center** (Mile 51, Skyline Dr; ⊙9am-5pm Apr-Nov). Both places have exhibits on flora and fauna, as well as maps and information about hiking trails and activities.

The surrounds are mighty easy on the eyes, set against a backdrop of the dreamy Blue Ridge Mountains, ancient granite and metamorphic formations that are more than one billion years old. The park itself was founded in 1935 as a retreat for East Coast urban populations. It is an accessible day-trip destination from DC, but you should aim to stay longer if you can. The 500 miles of hiking trails, 75 scenic overlooks, 30 fishing streams, seven picnic areas and four campgrounds are sure to keep you entertained.

Skyline Dr is the breathtaking road that follows the main ridge of the Blue Ridge Mountains and winds 105 miles through the center of the park. It begins in Front Royal at the western end of I-66, and ends in the southern part of the range at Rockfish Gap near I-64. Mile markers at the side of the road provide a reference. Miles and miles of blazed trails wander through the park.

The most famous trail in the park is a 101-mile stretch of the **Appalachian Trail** (AT), a 2175-mile route crossing through 14 states. Access the trail from Skyline Dr, which roughly runs parallel. Aside from the AT, Shenandoah has more than 400 miles of hiking trails in the park. Options for shorter hikes include **Compton Peak** (Mile 10.4; 2.4 miles return; easy to moderate), **Traces** (Mile 22.2; 1.7 miles return; easy), **Overall Run** (Mile 22.2; 6 miles return; moderate) and **White Oak Canyon** (Mile 42.6; 4.6 miles return; strenuous). **Hawksbill Mountain Summit** (Mile 46.7; 2.1 miles return; moderate) is the park's highest peak.

Getting There & Around

You'll really need your own wheels to explore the length and breadth of the park, which can be easily accessed from several exits off I-81. The Virginia Breeze (p315) bus service to/from Washington, DC, stops at Front Royal and Staunton near the main park entrances/exits. Amtrak (p314) runs train services between DC and Staunton.

There is a **gas station** (☎540-999-2211; Mile 51.2, Skyline Dr; ⊙8am-8pm) at Big Meadows Wayside.

Add to this an abundance of outdoor activities nearby and you may find yourself looking into local real estate when you get here.

Sights

The pedestrian-friendly, handsome town center boasts more than 200 buildings designed by noted Victorian architect TJ Collins.

There's an artsy yet unpretentious bohemian vibe thanks to the presence of Mary Baldwin, a small liberal arts university.

Woodrow Wilson Presidential Library HISTORIC SITE

(☎540-885-0897; www.woodrowwilson.org; 18 N Coalter St; adult/student/child 6-12yr $14/7/5; ⊙9am-5pm Mon-Sat, from noon Sun Mar-Oct, to 4pm Nov-Feb) History buffs should check out the Woodrow Wilson Presidential Library near downtown. Stop by and tour the hilltop Greek Revival house where Wilson grew up, which has been faithfully restored to its original 1856 appearance. 'Behind the Scenes' guided tours ($40) at 2pm Tuesday and Thursday; 'Wilson and Slavery' tours

($25) at 11:30am first and third Friday of the month.

Sleeping & Eating

Frederick House B&B $$
(☎540-885-4220; www.frederickhouse.com; 28 N New St; d/ste from $156/180; P ❄ 📶 🐾) Genial owners Ross and Brooke Williams work hard to ensure that guests at their downtown guesthouse are happy. Rooms are scattered throughout five historical residences with 23 varied rooms and suites – all with private bathrooms and some with air-con. The nicest rooms are in Patrick House (request room 26). Breakfast is included.

Chicano Boy MEXICAN $
(☎540-569-2105; www.chicanoboytaco.com; 240 N Central Ave, Suite 6; tacos/burritos $10/12; ⏲11am-9pm Tue-Sun; 🖉 👪) It's hard to beat the value offered by this taquería's $8.50 lunch deal, which delivers a drink, a dip and two tacos. Prices don't rise much at dinner, when tacos – including the Carnitas (pork with pico and cilantro) and vegetarian (sweet potato and black bean) – run out the door. Eat in or take out.

★**Shack** AMERICAN $$
(☎540-490-1961; www.theshackva.com; 105 S Coalter St; mains brunch $12-15, dinner $13-30; ⏲5-9pm Wed-Sat, 10:30am-2pm Sun; 🖉) It may be cooked and served in a small and unadorned space (hence the name), but the dishes served here are among the best in the state. Chef Ian Boden, a two-time James Beard semi-finalist, makes the most of seasonal local produce in his menu, which is inspired by his mountain roots and Eastern European Jewish heritage. Good wine list.

Drinking & Entertainment

Yelping Dog WINE BAR
(☎540-885-2275; www.yelpingdogwine.com; 9 E Beverly St; ⏲11am-9pm Tue-Thu, to 10pm Fri & Sat, noon-6pm Sun) An inviting wine bar in the thick of the downtown action, the Yelping Dog has its priorities right: wine, cheese and charcuterie. It also serves craft beer. If you're on the fence about ordering one of the gourmet grilled cheese sandwiches ($9 to $10), go ahead and fall off. They're delicious. Live music some Saturday nights.

★**Blackfriars Playhouse** THEATER
(☎540-851-1733; www.americanshakespearecenter.com; 10 S Market St; tickets $29-49) Don't leave Staunton without catching a show at the Blackfriars Playhouse, where actors from the American Shakespeare Center perform in a re-creation of Shakespeare's original indoor theater. The acting is up close and engaged, and brave guests can grab a seat on the side of the stage.

Getting There & Away

Staunton sits beside I-81, not far from the junction with I-64 E. Amtrak trains stop here three times per week on their way to/from Charlottesville and Washington, DC.

Lexington

The fighting spirit of the South is visually encapsulated by the sight of cadets from the Virginia Military Institute (VMI) strutting their stuff at Friday's full dress parade. The institute is one of Lexington's two major historic institutions, the other being Washington & Lee University (W&L). Two Civil War generals, Robert E Lee and Stonewall Jackson, lived here and are buried in town, and Lexington has long been a favorite stop for Civil War enthusiasts. Today you're as likely to see hikers, cyclists and paddlers using Lexington as a launchpad for adventures in the nearby Blue Ridge Mountains, where the Blue Ridge Pkwy and the Appalachian Trail overlook the valley, as well as on the James River. The opening of new hotels, bars and restaurants has re-energized the city in recent years – it's a great Shenandoah base.

Sights & Activities

Virginia Military Institute UNIVERSITY
(VMI; www.vmi.edu; Letcher Ave) You'll either be impressed or put off by the extreme discipline of the cadets at Virginia Military Institute, the only university to have sent its entire graduating class into combat (plaques to student war dead are touching and ubiquitous). The **VMI Museum** (☎540-464-7334; www.vmi.edu/museum; 415 Letcher Ave; $5; ⏲9am-5pm) houses the stuffed carcass of Stonewall Jackson's horse among its 15,000 artifacts and the **George C Marshall Museum** (☎540-463-2083; www.marshallfoundation.org/museum; VMI Parade; adult/student/child under 13yr $5/2/free; ⏲11am-4pm Tue-Sat)

honors the creator of the Marshall Plan for post-WWII European reconstruction.

Contact the museum for a free 45-minute cadet-guided tour of the campus, offered at noon during term time. A full-dress parade takes place most Fridays at 4pm during the school year.

Washington & Lee University UNIVERSITY
(540-458-8400; www.wlu.edu; 204 West Washington St) Named for George Washington and Robert E Lee, this pretty and preppy liberal arts college was founded in 1749. George Washington saved the young school in 1796 with a gift of $20,000. Confederate general Robert E Lee served as president after the Civil War in the hope of unifying the country through education. Visitors today can stroll along the striking redbrick Colonnade and visit **Lee Chapel & Museum** (540-458-8768; www.wlu.edu/lee-chapel-and-museum; donation adult/child $4/2; 9am-4pm Mon-Sat, 1-4pm Sun Nov-Mar, to 5pm Apr-Oct).

Note that doors on the garage stall of the university president's house will likely be open. While president of the school, Lee left the door ajar for his wandering horse Traveller. Today, tradition keeps them open in case Traveller's ghost wanders home.

Natural Bridge State Park BRIDGE
(540-291-1326; www.dcr.virginia.gov; 6477 S Lee Hwy; adult/child 6-12yr $8/6; 8am-9pm) We're going to let Thomas Jefferson write the review of the main feature in this state park, which he described in his book *Notes on Virginia*: 'It is impossible for the emotions arising from the sublime to be felt beyond what they are here: so beautiful an arch, so elevated, so light, and springing as it were up to heaven...' As well as the 215ft-high limestone bridge here described, the park has 6 miles of hiking trails through forests and meadows.

Dinosaur Kingdom II AMUSEMENT PARK
(540-464-2253; www.dinosaurkingdomii.com; 5781 S Lee Hwy; adult/child 3-12yr $12/8; 11am-5pm Sat & Sun May & Sep-early Nov, 10am-6pm Jun-Aug;) One of the wackiest attractions yet from artist and creative wunderkind Mark Cline, this kitschy theme park transports visitors to an alternate reality: a forested kingdom where Union soldiers are attempting to use life-size dinosaurs as weapons of mass destruction against Confederate forces during the Civil War. Even President Lincoln is here, trying to lasso a flying pteranodon. The Styrofoam and fiberglass creations are lifelike enough to amaze younger kids, and the offbeat historic juxtapositions will entertain even the grouchiest of adults. The park is about 12 miles south of Lexington on S Lee Hwy/Rte 11.

Upper James River Water Trail CANOEING
(https://upperjamesriverwatertrail.com; Botetourt) This 74-mile paddling trail follows the James River as it flows through the foothills of the Blue Ridge Mountains toward Richmond and the coast. The trail is divided into various sections taking between one and seven hours to traverse by canoe or kayak.

Twin River Outfitters CANOEING; TUBING
(540-254-8012; https://canoevirginia.net; 640 Lowe St, Buchanan; paddling trips from $34; 9am-5pm Apr-Oct) Scan for eagles and deer as you paddle or tube down the James River on the Upper James River Water Trail with this popular outfitter, owned by twin brothers. Mileage and travel times vary, as does difficulty. A shuttle ride is included in the price.

Sleeping & Eating

Georges BOUTIQUE HOTEL $$$
(540-463-2500; www.thegeorges.com; 11 N Main St; d $185-240, ste from $335;) Set in two historic buildings on opposite sides of Main St, Georges has 18 classy rooms featuring high-end furnishings and luxury linens. The great location, friendly service and delicious breakfast (included in the room rate) make it Lexington's best accommodation option, and put it in the running for the accolade of best in the Shenandoah, too.

Pure Eats AMERICAN $
(540-462-6000; www.pure-eats.com; 107 N Main St; burgers $7-12, doughnuts $1.25; 8am-8pm) In a former filling station, Pure Eats doles out delicious house-made doughnuts and egg-and-cheese biscuits in the morning; later in the day, burgers are the popular choice. Also sells local craft brews, milkshakes made with local milk and ice cream from a local creamery.

★**Red Hen** FRENCH $$$
(540-464-4401; www.redhenlex.com; 11 E Washington St; mains $22-28; 5-9pm Tue-Sat;) Reserve well ahead for a memorable meal at Red Hen, an intimate restaurant occupying

an 1890 building just off Main St. The limited menu features a creative, French-focused menu showcasing fine local produce. Great cocktails too.

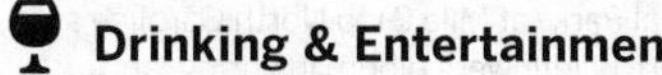

Drinking & Entertainment

Taps BAR

(540-463-2500; www.thegeorges.com; 11 N Main St, Georges; 3-11pm Mon-Thu, 11am-11pm Fri & Sat) This cozy place in Georges doubles as Lexington's living room, with students, professors and other locals hanging out on the fancy couches or at the small bar. Come here for craft beer, fine cocktails and local gossip. There's also a short pub-grub menu (sandwiches $12 to $13).

Hull's Drive-in CINEMA

(540-463-2621; www.hullsdrivein.com; 2367 N Lee Hwy/US 11; adult/child 5-11yr $7/3; gates open 6:30pm Fri & Sat Mar-Oct;) For old-fashioned amusement, catch a movie at this 1950s drive-in movie theater, set 5.5 miles north of Lexington. Movies start 20 minutes after sunset. Concession stand sells burgers, popcorn and sno-cones.

Getting There & Away

Lexington sits at the junction of I-81 and I-64. The closest airport is Roanoke-Blacksburg Regional Airport (p298), which is 55 miles south. The Virginia Breeze (p315) bus service from DC travels here daily via Front Royal, Harrisonburg and Staunton and continues to Christianburg and Blacksburg before returning along the same route.

Blue Ridge Highlands & Southwest Virginia

The Blue Ridge Highlands and the Roanoke Valley are two of the most attractive regions in the state, with farm-dotted valleys unfurling between the Blue Ridge and Allegheny Mountains. The Blue Ridge Pkwy and Appalachian Trail roll across the mountains here, which are home to scenic rivers, streams and lakes. Old-time mountain music can be heard regularly, and wineries and craft breweries offer tastings in small towns and on mountain slopes. The most rugged part of the region – and the state – is the southwestern tip of Virginia, where mountain music was born. Turn onto any side road and you'll plunge into dark strands of dogwood and fir, and see fast streams and white waterfalls. You might even hear banjos twanging and feet stomping in the distance.

Getting There & Around

To explore the byways and country roads, you will need a car. The primary interstate here is I-81, running north–south through the western edge of the state. The Blue Ridge Pkwy runs parallel to I-81, but it is much slower going.

Roanoke is served by Amtrak, with daily services linking it to New York (from $75, 9½ hours) and Washington, DC (from $37, five hours). The major airport in the region is the Roanoke-Blacksburg Regional Airport (p298).

Roanoke

Illuminated by the giant star atop Mill Mountain, Roanoke is the largest city in the Roanoke Valley and is the self-proclaimed 'Capital of the Blue Ridge.' Close to the Blue Ridge Pkwy and the Appalachian Trail, it's a convenient base camp for exploring the great outdoors. An expanding greenway system, a burgeoning arts scene and a slowly growing portfolio of farm-to-table restaurants have energized the city in recent years, flipping Roanoke from sleepy to almost hip.

Sights & Activities

★ O. Winston Link Museum MUSEUM

(540-982-5465; http://roanokehistory.org; 101 Shenandoah Ave NE; adult/child 3-11yr $6/5; 10am-5pm Tue-Sat) Trainspotters aren't the only ones who will find this museum fascinating. It is home to a large collection of photographs, sound recordings and film by O Winston Link (1914–2001), a New Yorker who in the 1950s spent nine months recording the last years of steam power on the Norfolk and Western Railway. The gelatin silver prints of Link's B&W photographs are hugely atmospheric – many were shot at night, a rarity at the time – and are very dramatic.

Center in the Square MUSEUM

(540-342-5700; www.centerinthesquare.org; 1 Market Sq; 10am-5pm Mon, to 8pm Tue-Sat, 1-6pm Sun) The city's cultural heartbeat, where you'll find three museums, a butterfly garden, aquariums and a theater. The museums cover African American culture, pinball and science. The atrium aquariums and green rooftop can be visited free of charge; admission fees apply for other attractions.

BLUE RIDGE PARKWAY

Where Skyline Dr (p316) ends, the Blue Ridge Pkwy (www.nps.gov/blri) picks up. Managed by the national park service, this pretty-as-a-picture drive stretches from the southern Appalachian ridge in Shenandoah National Park (at Mile 0) to North Carolina's Great Smoky Mountains National Park (at Mile 469). Wildflowers bloom in spring, and fall colors are spectacular, but watch out for foggy days; the lack of guardrails can make for hairy driving. There are a dozen visitor centers scattered over the parkway, and any of them make a good kick-off point for your trip. You won't find one stoplight on the entire drive, but we can almost guarantee you'll see deer. A helpful website is www.blueridge parkway.org.

Along the Blue Ridge Pkwy there are trails to the tops of three peaks clustered at the **Peaks of Otter** (Mile 85.6, Blue Ridge Pkwy; [icon]) : Sharp Top, Flat Top and Harkening Hill. Seasonal shuttles run within a quarter-mile of Sharp Top, or you can take the challenging 3-mile round-trip hike. The 360-degree view of the Blue Ridge Mountains from the rocky summit is fantastic. A short trail leads to the nearby Johnson Farm, which grew apples for the local inn before the arrival of the parkway.

Taubman Museum of Art MUSEUM
(☎540-342-5760; www.taubmanmuseum.org; 110 Salem Ave SE; ⏲10am-5pm Wed-Sat, noon-5pm Sun, 10am-9pm 1st Fri of month; P) FREE The jewel in Roanoke's cultural crown, this impressive museum is set in a sculptural steel-and-glass edifice. Inside, you'll find a small permanent collection strong in 19th- and 20th-century American works including Norman Rockwell's crowd-pleasing *Framed* (1946) and Winslow Homer's *Woodchopper in the Adirondacks* (c 1870). Four temporary exhibition galleries host everything from craft to video to installation art.

Sleeping & Eating

Hotel Roanoke HOTEL $$$
(☎540-985-5900; www.hotelroanoke.com; 110 Shenandoah Ave NW; r from $120; P@ 🛜 🏊) This Tudor-style grand dame has presided over this city at the base of the Blue Ridge Mountains for more than a century. Now part of the Hilton Group, it's in desperate need of refurbishment. Rooms are only adequate; service can be lackadaisical. A covered elevated walkway links the hotel with the downtown precinct.

Lucky MODERN AMERICAN $$
(☎540-982-1249; www.eatatlucky.com; 18 Kirk Ave SW; mains $19-40; ⏲5-9pm Mon-Wed, to 10pm Thu-Sat) Lucky has excellent cocktails (try 'The Cube') and a seasonally inspired menu of small plates (hickory-smoked porchetta, roasted oysters) and heartier mains (buttermilk fried chicken, morel and asparagus gnocchi). It also operates the equally wonderful Italian restaurant Fortunato (www.fortunatoroanoke.com) a few doors down, where the wood-fired pizzas are the stuff of dreams and poems.

Getting There & Away

Amtrak operates daily services between Roanoke and New York (from $75, 9½ hours) on the Northeast Regional line. These leave from the downtown **train station** (55 Norfolk Avenue SW) and travel via Washington, DC (from $37, five hours).

The airport (p298) is 5 miles north of downtown and serves the Roanoke and Shenandoah Valley regions. Smart Way (www.smartwaybus.com) buses link Roanoke and Blacksburg, with a stop at the airport ($4) along the way; there is no service on Sunday. If you're driving, I-81 and I-581 link to the city. The Blue Ridge Pkwy is just 5 miles from downtown.

Abingdon

One of the most photogenic towns in Virginia, Abingdon retains fine Federal and Victorian architecture in its historic district. The long-running regional theater in the center of town is a statewide draw, as is the magnificent Virginia Creeper Trail. Popular with cyclists and hikers, this leafy path down from the mountains unfurls along an old railroad bed.

Virginia Creeper Trail CYCLING, HIKING
(www.vacreepertrail.com) This 33.4-mile cycling and hiking trail on an old railroad corridor rolls through the Mount Rogers National Recreation Area, connecting lofty Whitetop with Damascus and eventually Abingdon. Local bike companies rent out bikes and provide shuttle services.

Barter Theatre THEATER
(☎276-628-3991; www.bartertheatre.com; 127 W Main St; ⏰box office 9am-5pm Tue-Sat, from 1pm Sun) Founded during the Depression, Barter Theatre earned its name from audiences trading food for performances. Actors Gregory Peck and Ernest Borgnine cut their teeth on Barter's stage.

Getting There & Away

Abingdon borders I-81 near the Virginia–Tennessee border. The city is 366 miles southwest of Washington, DC, and about 180 miles northwest of Charlotte, NC. Close regional airports include Asheville Regional Airport in Asheville, NC, and Roanoke-Blacksburg Regional Airport (p298) in Roanoke.

Floyd

Tucked in the foothills of the Blue Ridge Mountains close to the Blue Ridge Pkwy, tiny, cute-as-a-postcard Floyd isn't much more than an intersection between Hwy 8 and Hwy 221. In fact, the whole county only has one stoplight. But life explodes on Friday nights during the Friday Night Jamboree at the Floyd Country Store and the surrounding sidewalks when folks from far and wide converge for a night of live old-time music and communal good cheer.

Sleeping & Eating

Hotel Floyd HOTEL $
(☎540-745-6080; www.hotelfloyd.com; 300 Rick Lewis Way; r $100-140, ste $150-180; P ❄ @ 📶 🐾) There may not be much style on show at this place, but who cares? Rooms are large, impeccably clean and very comfortable. Service is friendly, breakfast is included in the room rate and Main St is only a short walk away. It's cheap, too. All of this makes it deservedly popular, so book ahead.

Dogtown Roadhouse PIZZA $
(☎540-745-6836; www.dogtownroadhouse.com; 302 S Locust St; pizzas $10-18; ⏰4-10pm Wed & Thu, noon-midnight Fri & Sat, noon-10pm Sun) You might see a local farmer walk in with produce for the toppings at this lively pizzeria, which serves wood-fired pies including the Appalachian (apple butter base, sausage, caramelized onion, cheddar and goat cheeses). Lagers, stouts, porters and ciders are on tap, and there's live rock on Friday and Saturday nights from 8pm.

Pine Tavern AMERICAN $
(☎540-745-4482; www.thepinetavern.com; 611 Floyd Hwy N; per person $15-17; ⏰4:30-9pm Fri, from noon Sat, 11am-8pm Sun; P 👪) One taste of the buttermilk biscuits, fried chicken and country ham at this all-you-can-eat family-style restaurant and your mouth won't stop salivating. We thoroughly approve of the way they pile on dumplings, pinto beans, green beans and mashed potatoes. There's occasional live music in the outside pavilion during spring and summer.

Getting There & Away

Floyd is 20 miles southeast of I-81 and is best reached by car. The closest major airport is Roanoke-Blacksburg Regional Airport (p298), about 50 miles north.

DON'T MISS

THE CROOKED ROAD

When Scots–Irish fiddle-and-reel joined with African American banjo-and-percussion, American mountain or 'old-time' music was born, spawning such genres as country and bluegrass. The latter genre still dominates the Blue Ridge, and Virginia's Heritage Music Trail, the 330-mile-long Crooked Road (www.myswva.org/tcr), takes you through nine sites associated with that history, along with some eye-stretching mountain scenery. It's well worth taking a detour and joining the music-loving fans of all ages who kick up their heels (many arrive with tap shoes) at these festive jamborees. During a live show you'll witness elders connecting to deep cultural roots and a new generation of musicians keeping that heritage alive and evolving.

Top venues include the Blue Ridge Music Center (p322) near Galax, the **Floyd Country Store** (☎540-745-4563; www.floydcountrystore.com; 206 S Locust St; ⏰10am-5pm Mon-Thu & Sat, to 10:30pm Fri, 11am-9pm Sun) on Friday nights and the **Carter Family Fold** (☎276-386-6054; www.carterfamilyfold.org; 3449 AP Carter Hwy/SR 614, Hiltons; adult $10-15, child 6-11yr $2; ⏰7:30pm Sat; 👪) in Hiltons on Saturday nights.

Galax

Galax claims to be the world capital of mountain music, although it feels like anywhere-else-ville outside of the immediate downtown area, which is on the National Register of Historic Places. The town is an important stop on the 330-mile-long Crooked Road (p321) music trail, and is close to the Blue Ridge Pkwy.

Sleeping

Fiddlers Roost CABIN $$
(☎276-236-1212; www.fiddlersroostcabins.com; 485 Fishers Peak Rd; cabins $120-300; P) These eight cabins resemble Lincoln Logs playsets. The interiors are decorated in 'quilt' chic; they may not win a place in *Wallpaper* magazine, but they're cozy and have gas fireplaces, kitchens, TVs and DVD players. Breakfast is included with all but Cabin on the Blue. Two-night minimum stay on weekends.

Drinking & Entertainment

Creek Bottom Brews MICROBREWERY
(☎276-236-2337; www.cbbrews.com; 307 N Meadow St; sandwiches $8-11, pizza $16; ⊙11am-9pm Tue-Thu, to 10pm Fri & Sat) Has a changing lineup of its own craft brews, which go nicely with the brick-oven pizza and smoked chicken wings fired up on-site. Try the Hellgrammite Brown Ale. The brewery is hidden behind a corrugated iron fence next to Pronets.

★**Blue Ridge Music Center** LIVE MUSIC
(☎276-236-5309; www.blueridgemusiccenter.net; 700 Foothills Rd/Mile 213, Blue Ridge Pkwy; ⊙10am-5pm late May-late Oct, 10am-5pm Thu-Mon early May-late May) An arts and music hub for the region that offers programming that focuses on local musicians carrying on the traditions of Appalachian music. Headline performances are mostly on weekends, but local musicians give free concerts on the breezeway of the visitor center most days from noon to 4pm. Bring a lawn chair and sit yourself down for an afternoon or evening performance. There's a free 'Roots of American Music' exhibit on-site, too.

Rex Theater LIVE MUSIC
(☎276-236-0329; www.rextheatergalax.com; 113 E Grayson St) A musty, red-curtained belle of yore. Frequent bluegrass acts cross its stage, but the easiest one to catch is the Friday-night live WBRF 98.1 show 'Blue Ridge Backroads' (admission $5), which pulls in crowds from across the mountains.

ℹ Getting There & Away

The best way to get to Galax is by car. The town borders US 58 about 10 miles southwest of I-77. Roanoke-Blacksburg Regional Airport (p298) is 90 miles northeast via I-77 north and I-81 N. The city is about 10 miles from the Blue Ridge Pkwy.

WEST VIRGINIA

Ready for rugged East Coast adventuring with a gorgeous mountain backdrop? Then set your car toward wild and wonderful West Virginia, a state often overlooked by both American and foreign travelers. It doesn't help that the state can't seem to shake its negative stereotypes. That's too bad, because West Virginia is one of the prettiest states in the Union. With its line of unbroken green mountains, raging white-water rivers and snowcapped ski resorts, this is an outdoor-lovers' paradise.

In a state created by secessionists, the people here still think of themselves as hard-scrabble sons of miners, and that perception isn't entirely off. But the Mountain State is also gentrifying and, occasionally, that's a good thing: the arts are flourishing in the valleys, where some towns offer a welcome break from the state's constantly evolving outdoor activities. Charleston is the capital and the state's largest city – and its population is under 50,000.

History

Virginia was once the biggest state in America, divided between the plantation aristocracy of the Tidewater and the mountains of what is now West Virginia. The latter were settled by tough farmers who staked out independent freeholds across the Appalachians. Always resentful of their Eastern brethren and their reliance on cheap (ie slave) labor, the mountaineers of West Virginia declared their independence from Virginia when the latter tried to break off from America during the Civil War.

Yet the scrappy, independent-at-all-costs stereotype was challenged in the late-19th and early-20th centuries, when miners here formed into cooperative unions and fought employers in some of the bloodiest battles in American labor history. That mix of chip-on-the-shoulder resentment toward authority and look-out-for-your-neighbor community values continues to characterize West Virginia today.

Information

West Virginia Division of Tourism (www.wvtourism.com) operates welcome centers at interstate borders and in **Harpers Ferry** (866-435-5698, 304-535-2627; www.discoveritallwv.com; 37 Washington Ct; 9am-5pm). Check the Division of Tourism website for info on the state's myriad adventure-tourism opportunities.

Getting There & Around

West Virginia's Eastern Panhandle begins about 60 miles northwest of Washington, DC, and it's a fairly easy drive from the busy metropolitan area – but expect traffic.

Amtrak and MARC trains stop at the station (p324) in Harpers Ferry. Charleston has a small airport (p328).

For the national forest and the southern reaches of the state, you will need a car to explore and will likely be accessing most mountain towns and parks on two-lane roads. So although the mileage looks short, the distance will take longer to cover than on the interstate. Cell phone coverage can be very spotty on mountain roads, so check your directions – and maybe write them down – before starting your trip.

Eastern Panhandle

The most accessible part of West Virginia has always been a mountain getaway for DC types – the region is just 70 miles west of the capital-area sprawl. Here, Civil War–era history, soothing hot springs, leafy scenery and outdoor recreation on trails and rivers work together for visitors, offering an easy package of experiences than can be enjoyed on one long weekend.

One tricky part of travel in the panhandle is the practically overlapping proximity of three states – West Virginia, Virginia and Maryland – with Pennsylvania lying in wait just north. When planning, get out your maps to make sure you've spotted all attractions in the multistate region.

Harpers Ferry

History lives on in this attractive town, set with steep cobblestoned streets, and framed by the Shenandoah Mountains and the confluence of the rushing Potomac and Shenandoah Rivers. The lower town functions as an open-air museum, with more than a dozen buildings that you can explore to get a taste of 19th-century, small-town life. Exhibits narrate the town's role at the forefront of westward expansion, American industry and, most famously, the slavery debate – in 1859 old John Brown tried to spark a slave uprising here and was hanged for his efforts; the incident rubbed friction between North and South into the fires of Civil War.

The upper town is dotted with cafes and B&Bs. Harpers Ferry sits beside the Appalachian Trail across the Potomac from the C&O Canal bike path, so there are lots of outdoorsy types filling the coffee houses and hostels. The town is touristy for sure, but it has a fun and energetic vibe.

Sights & Activities

Harpers Ferry National Historic Park PARK

(304-535-6029; www.nps.gov/hafe; 171 Shoreline Dr; per person on foot or bicycle $7, vehicle $15; trails sunrise-sunset, visitor center 9am-5pm; P) Historic buildings and museums are accessible to those with passes, which can be found, along with parking and shuttles, north of town at the **Harpers Ferry National Historic Park Visitor Center** off Hwy 340. Parking is incredibly limited in Harpers Ferry proper so plan to park at the visitor center and catch the frequent shuttle. It's a short and scenic ride.

John Brown Museum MUSEUM

(www.nps.gov/hafe; Shenandoah St; 9am-5pm) FREE Across from Arsenal Sq and one of the park's museums, this three-room gallery gives a fine overview (through videos and period relics) of the events surrounding John Brown's famous raid.

African American History Museum MUSEUM

(www.nps.gov/hafe; High St; 9am-5pm) FREE Part of the national park, this worthwhile, interactive exhibit has narrated stories of hardships and hard-won victories by African Americans from the times of enslavement through the Civil Rights era. Across the street is the Storer College exhibit, which gives an overview of the groundbreaking educational center and Niagara movement that formed in its wake.

C&O Canal National Historic Park CYCLING, HIKING
(☎301-739-4200; www.nps.gov/choh) The 184.5-mile towpath passes along the Potomac River on the Maryland side. From the historic downtown you can reach it via the Appalachian Trail across the Potomac Bridge. Check www.nps.gov/hafe for additional access points to the towpath and a list of bike-rental companies.

River Riders ADVENTURE SPORTS
(☎304-535-2663; www.riverriders.com; 408 Alstadts Hill Rd; tubing/kayaking/rafting per person from $29/59/79; ⊙8am-6pm Jun-Aug, hours vary rest of year) The go-to place for rafting, canoeing, tubing, kayaking and multiday cycling trips, plus cycle rental (two hours is $34 per person). There's even a 1200ft zipline.

Sleeping & Eating

HI-Harpers Ferry Hostel HOSTEL $
(☎301-834-7652; www.hiusa.org; 19123 Sandy Hook Rd, Knoxville; dm $25; ⊙mid-Apr–mid-Nov; P❄@📶) This friendly hostel has plenty of amenities, including a kitchen, laundry and lounge area with games and books. It's popular with cyclists on the C&O Canal towpath and hikers on the Appalachian Trail, both nearby. Breakfast is included. It's 2 miles from downtown Harpers Ferry, on the Maryland side of the Potomac River.

Jackson Rose B&B $$
(☎304-535-1528; www.thejacksonrose.com; 1167 W Washington St; r weekday/weekend $135/150, closed Jan & Feb; P❄📶) This marvelous 18th-century brick residence with stately gardens has three attractive guest rooms, including a room where Stonewall Jackson lodged briefly during the Civil War. Antique furnishings and vintage curios are sprinkled about the house, and the cooked breakfast is excellent. It's a 600m walk downhill to the historic district. No children under 12.

Beans in the Belfry AMERICAN $
(☎301-834-7178; www.beansinthebelfry.com; 122 W Potomac St, Brunswick; sandwiches $7; ⊙8am-9pm Mon-Thu, to 10pm Fri & Sat, to 7pm Sun; 📶👪) This converted redbrick church about 6 miles east of Harpers Ferry, WV, shelters mismatched couches and kitsch-laden walls. The menu features coffee and light fare (chili, sandwiches, quiche), and there's a tiny stage where live folk, blues and bluegrass bands strike up several nights a week. Sunday jazz brunch ($18) is a hit. A cool spot and worth the drive.

Information

Appalachian Trail Conservancy (ATC; ☎304-535-6331; www.appalachiantrail.org; 799 Washington St, cnr Washington & Jackson Sts; ⊙9am-5pm) The 2160-mile Appalachian Trail is headquartered here at this tremendous resource for hikers, which offers a chance for conversation, information, trail updates and restrooms. Less-ambitious travelers will appreciate the helpful Harpers Ferry map with a summary of several area day hikes, including the 1.5-mile loop around Harpers Ferry that begins here.

Getting There & Away

Amtrak trains run from the **Harpers Ferry Station** (Potomac St) to Washington's Union Station (from $14, 70 minutes, daily) on the Capitol Limited route. MARC trains (http://mta.maryland.gov) run to Washington's Union Station several times per day (Monday to Friday) on the Brunswick Line.

Berkeley Springs

America's first spa town (George Washington relaxed here) is an odd jumble of spiritualism, artistic expression and pampering spa centers. Farmers in pickups sporting Confederate flags, and acupuncturists in tie-dye smocks regard each other with bemusement on the roads of Bath (still the official name).

Berkeley Springs State Park SPA
(☎304-258-2711; www.berkeleyspringssp.com; 2 S Washington St; 30min bath $27, 1hr massage $99-129; ⊙9am-6pm) Don't let the locker-room appearance deter you from the Berkeley Springs State Park's Roman Baths – it's the cheapest spa deal in town. Fill your water bottle with some of the magic stuff at the fountain outside the door – it's mineral-filled and it's free! In the summer, kids will enjoy the spring-fed (but chlorinated) outdoor swimming pool (adult/child under 12 years $5/3) in the middle of the green.

Country Inn of Berkeley Springs HOTEL $$
(☎304-258-1200; www.thecountryinnwv.com; 110 S Washington St; r/ste from $120/170; P❄📶) The Country Inn, right next to the park, offers luxurious treatments and comfortable but not overly fancy rooms. You'll also find lodging package deals. There's a good restaurant on hand.

★Tari's FUSION $$$
(☎304-258-1196; www.tariscafe.com; 33 N Washington St; mains lunch $10-15, dinner $21-30; ⏰11am-9pm Mon-Sat, to 8pm Sun;) Tari's is a very Berkeley Springs sort of spot, with fresh local food and good vegetarian options served in a laid-back atmosphere with all the right hints of good karma abounding. Dig into the jumbo lake crab cakes with a side of fries at dinner.

Getting There & Away

Berkeley Springs is 40 miles west of I-95. It's about 90 minutes from the Washington, DC, metro area.

Monongahela National Forest

Almost the entire eastern half of West Virginia is marked green parkland on the map, and most of that goodness falls under the auspices of this stunning national forest. Established in 1920 with just 7200 acres, the forest today covers more than 900,000 acres across 10 counties. The region, also known as the Potomac Highlands, is the adventure capital of the state. Within its boundaries are wild rivers, striking rock formations and the highest peak in the state, Spruce Knob. More than 850 miles of trails include the nearly 330-mile **Allegheny Trail** and the 78-mile rails-to-trails **Greenbrier River Trail** (☎304-799-4087; www.wvstateparks.com; off WV 66, Cass). The surreal landscapes at Seneca Rocks attract rock climbers.

The towns of Thomas and Davis, in the northern reaches of the region, are good base camps for Canaan Valley and Dolly Sods. Seneca Rocks is centrally located within the forest region. Snowshoe Mountain Resort is a good launchpad in the south.

Sights

★Seneca Rocks NATURAL FEATURE
(☎304-567-2827; www.fs.usda.gov/mnf; Hwy 28/55; ⏰sunrise-sunset; P) A striking rock formation rising 900ft above a fork of the Potomac River, Seneca Rocks is one of the most recognizable natural features in the state. Rock climbers have scaled the sandstone walls here since the mid-1930s. Today there are more than 370 mapped climbing routes. Hikers can walk 1.5 miles to an observation platform near the top of the formation.

Dolly Sods Wilderness FOREST
(☎304-636-1800; www.fs.usda.gov; Fire Road 19, Davis; P) FREE Red spruce trees, windswept boulders, valley views and boggy forests set a striking scene in the northern reaches of this remote but popular wilderness atop the Allegheny Plateau. The alpine landscape evokes the mountain scenery of northern Canada, and with 47 miles of trails crisscrossing its 17,371 acres, Dolly Sods is a prime spot for a day-long or weekend adventure. You can build your own loop hike from the Beaver Dam or Bear Rocks trailheads.

There are 11 primitive first-come first-served sites at the Red Creek Campground (campsites $11 per night).

Blackwater Falls State Park STATE PARK
(☎304-259-5216; www.blackwaterfalls.com; 1584 Blackwater Lodge Rd; P) FREE The falls tumble into an 8-mile gorge lined by red spruce, hickory and hemlock trees. With more than 24 miles of trails, there are loads of hiking options; look for the **Pendleton Point Overlook**, which perches over the deepest, widest point of the Canaan Valley. There's an inviting lodge here as well as cabins and campsites ($23 to $26 per night).

Activities

★NROCKS Outdoor Adventures CLIMBING
(☎877-435-4842; www.nrocks.com; 141 Nelson Gap Rd, Circleville; $125) The thrills begin the moment you clip into your harness for this rugged *via ferrata* adventure, a fixed-anchor guided rock climb that scrambles up and over a double-fin rock formation. One highlight is the crossing of a suspension bridge 150ft above a canyon. Guides are upbeat and fun but professional, and tours last from 3½ to five hours.

Highland Scenic Highway SCENIC DRIVE
(☎304-846-2695, 304-799-4334; www.fs.usda.gov/mnf; Hwy 150) This 43-mile National Scenic Byway unfurls across the leafy heights of the Allegheny Highlands and Plateau, passing four overlooks with expansive mountain and valley views. It's an exhilarating drive that soars toward the sky, rising from 2235ft to more than 4500ft. The highway rolls north on Rte 39/55 from Richwood to the **Cranberry Nature**

Center (☎304-653-4826; www.fs.usda.gov/mnf; cnr Hwys 150 & 39/55; ⊙9am-4:30pm Thu-Mon mid-Apr–mid-Oct; P 🚻). From there, hop onto the 22-mile parkway section on Hwy 150.

Picnic tables and restrooms are located at each overlook. Note that the parkway section is not maintained in winter and is typically closed December through March. More than 150 miles of trail can be accessed from the highway.

Snowshoe Mountain Resort SKIING
(☎877-441-4386; www.snowshoemtn.com; 10 Snowshoe Dr; lift tickets adult/child 13-17yr/child 6-12yr from $79/70/66; 🚻) The largest ski resort in the region, Snowshoe attracts skiers and snowboarders from across the country with 59 trails across three ski areas. Twelve trails are open for night skiing. In summer, mountain bikers hurtle down wooded terrain on more than 35 trails. You can visit Snowshoe and enjoy the facilities without staying overnight. Lodging options range from large cabins with expansive mountain views to condos just steps from the slopes. In the central village, the Junction restaurant is open year-round. There's also a play area on the resort lake.

Sleeping

In the national forest, there are 23 campgrounds across six different districts, so pick your region and go from there. There's also dispersed camping in two districts and cabins in the Greenbrier District. For more creature comforts, you'll find half a dozen or so hotels in Elkins. Ski resorts Snowshoe and Canaan Valley have a range of options, from simple cabins to plush hotel rooms.

Seneca Shadows Campground CAMPGROUND $
(☎877-444-6777; www.recreation.gov; US 33/WV 28; campsites $22-35; ⊙Apr-Oct; P) Flanked by mountains and sitting 1 mile east of rock-climbing spot Seneca Rocks (p325), this leafy campground has picnic tables, firepits and flush toilets. Many sites have a view of the rocks.

Billy Motel MOTEL $
(☎304-851-6125; www.thebillymotel.com; 1080 William Ave, Davis; r $100; P ❄ 📶) The 10 rooms pop with bright colors and fresh modern style inside this classic motor court. The cozy lobby has a fireplace and a lounge bar, which serves cocktails from Tuesday to Saturday.

Cooper House Bed & Cocktail B&B $
(☎304-851-4553; www.cooperhousebandc.com; 114 East Ave, Thomas; r $100-120; ❄ 📶) Proprietor Joy Malinowski brings the spark to this creaky but inviting house. There's a fun communal vibe, but don't worry, the four bedrooms each have their own bathroom. Guests can enjoy a cocktail in the common area.

Allegheny Springs LODGE $$
(☎877-441-4386; http://alleghenyspringssnowshoe.usotels.co; 10 Snowshoe Dr, The Village, Snowshoe Mountain Resort; apt $143-176; P ❄ 📶 🏊) Well hello there, lobby lounge. Comfy chairs, a big stone hearth – we like your rugged style. Studios and condo units in this flagship property are in the thick of the mountaintop action and steps from the slopes and several restaurants. For the glossiest digs, reserve a condo unit in the Brigham Collection.

Eating & Drinking

Hellbender Burritos MEXICAN $
(☎304-259-5557; www.hellbenderburritos.com; 457 William Ave, Davis; mains $7-10; ⊙11:30am-9pm Wed, Thu & Sun, to 10pm Fri & Sat) 🌿 They stuff the big burritos here Mountain State style – think blue-cheese dressing, Fritos, homemade pulled pork and other stuff that may not be Mexican but sure tastes good. There's even a PB&J burrito for the kiddies. Lots of vegetarian options too. Grab a table upstairs or head down to the bar.

Mountain State Brewing Co MICROBREWERY
(☎304-463-4500; www.mountainstatebrewing.com; 1 Nelson Blvd, Thomas; ⊙6pm-midnight Thu & Fri, 3pm-midnight Sat, 1-7pm Sun) The $6 flight of eight beers may be the best deal going in the state. And staff might even throw in a sample of sangria, because heck, why not? On a cold night the Coal Miner's Daughter Oatmeal Stout hits the spot. The wood-hewn tasting room feels like a camp lodge in the deep woods.

Stumptown Ales MICROBREWERY
(☎304-259-5570; www.stumptownales.com; 390 William Ave, Davis; ⊙5-9pm Mon-Wed, 5-10pm Thu & Fri, noon-10pm Sat, 1-7pm Sun) The saws on the wall and the 21ft-long, red-oak bar give

a nod to the region's logging past. And the tasty hop-forward beers give a kick to the taste buds at this welcoming taproom.

Getting There & Away

To explore this remote and rugged region, you will need a car. Thomas is 68 miles southeast of Morgantown. Snowshoe is 230 miles from Washington, DC.

New River & Greenbrier Valley

This part of the state has carved out a viable stake as the adventure-sports capital of the eastern seaboard, with wild white-water rafting, terrific mountain biking, lots of leafy trails, and inviting small towns holding it all together. Home to mineral springs and five golf courses, the swanky Greenbrier resort brings big spenders to the region.

Getting There & Around

Fayetteville is 22 miles north of Beckley off I-64. Amtrak stops along the New River Valley on the Cardinal route, which runs between Washington, DC, and Chicago. Stops include **White Sulphur Springs** (315 W Main St) and the Prince Depot (p328), outside Beckley. The best way to explore the region is by car.

New River Gorge

The New River is actually one of the oldest in the world, and the primeval forest gorge it runs through is one of the most breathtaking in the Appalachians. In 2021 the area became one of the US's newest national parks and was renamed the New River Gorge National Park & Preserve. The region is an adventure mecca, with world-class white-water runs and challenging single-track trails. Rim and gorge hiking trails offer beautiful views.

The graceful New River Gorge Bridge sits 876ft above the river and is the third-highest bridge in the US. It carries traffic on US 19. One of four NPS visitor centers, the **Canyon Rim Visitor Center** (☎304-574-2115; www.nps.gov/neri; 162 Visitor Center Rd, Lansing; 9am-5pm) just south of the bridge has information about scenic drives, river outfitters and other outdoor adventures.

DON'T MISS

GREENBRIER RESORT & BUNKER TOUR

Travelers have enjoyed the mineral springs at **Greenbrier** (☎855-453-4858; www.greenbrier.com; 300 W Main St, White Sulphur Springs; d $280-360; P) since the 1770s. The resort itself has impressed presidents and celebrities since the 1830s. Today, this striking white, luxury property holds more than 710 rooms and suites. Common areas pop with the bright designs of famed decorator Dorothy Draper.

Don't miss the **Bunker Tour** (☎844-223-3173; www.greenbrier.com/activities/activity-collection/bunker-tours; adult/child 10-18yr $39/20; 9:30am-3:30pm), which explores a nuclear-war hideaway built for Congress during the Cold War.

There is no lodging in the park. The only camping available is free primitive camping near the river, with no drinking water or hookups. Many outdoor outfitters offer a mix of campsites and cabins near the river that are a convenient choice before an early-morning rafting trip. For more traditional lodging options head to Fayetteville (p328) or the lodge at Hawks Nest State Park.

Sights

New River Gorge Bridge BRIDGE
(www.nps.gov/neri; Hwy 19; P) FREE Completed in 1977, the New River Gorge Bridge is the third-highest bridge in the US and the longest single-arch bridge in the Western Hemisphere. Made from 22,000 tons of structural steel, it rises 876ft above the New River and stretches 3030ft across the gorge. For the best view of the span, head to the overlooks behind the Canyon Rim Visitor Center or join a Bridgewalk tour.

Hawks Nest State Park STATE PARK
(☎304-658-5212; www.hawksnestsp.com; 49 Hawks Nest Park Rd; tram & jet boat tour adult/child $29/14; P) There are hiking trails, a nature center and an aerial tram, which runs from the lodge down to the river's edge for jet boat tours of the river and views of the New River Gorge Bridge (May to October). The

layout of the lodge is a little confusing, but the comfy rooms (double $109 to $134) offer fabulous views over the gorge. Book early for the fall foliage display.

Hawks Nest Overlook VIEWPOINT
(www.wvstateparks.com; Hwy 60; P) FREE An 80yd paved trail leads to a lofty view of the New River. The photogenic rock wall surrounding the overlook was built by the Civilian Conservation Corps in the 1930s. It's worth the short walk from the parking lot to get there. The viewpoint is a quarter-mile south of the main lodge at Hawks Nest State Park.

Mystery Hole MUSEUM
(304-658-9101; www.mysteryhole.com; 16724 Midland Trail, Ansted; adult/child $7/6; 10:30am-5:30pm Thu-Mon Jun-Aug, Fri-Sun May, Sat & Sun only Sep & Oct; P) See gravity and the known limits of tackiness defied at the Mystery Hole, one of the great attractions of roadside America. Everything inside this madhouse *tilts at an angle!* It's 1 mile west of Hawks Nest State Park.

Activities

★Bridgewalk WALKING
(304-574-1300; www.bridgewalk.com; 57 Fayette Mine Rd; $72; 9am-4pm) Wow. The bird's-eye view of the New River from the catwalk running below the river's namesake bridge is amazing. And it's eerie to hear traffic rattling by overhead. If you're not afraid of heights – you're 851ft above the river – this is a recommended bucket-list adventure. The tours, which last two to three hours, are guided and very informative. Expect to walk 1.25 miles.

Long Point Trail HIKING
(www.nps.gov/neri/planyourvisit/fayetteville_trails.htm; Newtown Rd, off Gatewood Rd) At just over 3 miles for the round trip, this trail leads to a rocky outcrop with big views of the New River Gorge and the New River Gorge Bridge. This is a great short hike and the outcrop is perfect for a picnic.

Adventures on the Gorge ADVENTURE
(855-379-8738; www.adventuresonthegorge.com; 219 Chestnutburg Rd, Lansing; guided rafting trips per person from $109) How many experiences does this reputable outfit offer? Well, their catalog is 63 pages long and covers everything from white-water rafting on the New and Gauley Rivers to ziplining, rappelling, rock climbing and more. It has a wide array of cabins (including some with Jacuzzis), plus campsites and several restaurants, including Smokey's Cast Iron Grill (open for breakfast and dinner May to October; mains $14 to $36) near the rim of the gorge.

Cantrell Ultimate Rafting RAFTING
(304-877-8235; www.cantrellultimaterafting.com; 49 Cantrell Dr; rafting from $89) Among the many state-licensed rafting outfitters in the area, Cantrell Ultimate Rafting stands out for its white-water rafting trips.

Getting There & Away

The **Yeager Airport** (304-344-8033; https://yeagerairport.com; 100 Airport Rd) in Charleston is located 70 miles northwest. Amtrak stops at three places in the NPS region on the Cardinal route, which runs between Chicago, Washington, DC, and New York City. One of these stops is the **Prince Depot** (800-872-7245; 5034 Stanaford Rd, Prince), which is 23 miles south of Fayetteville near Beckley. Greyhound (www.greyhound.com) stops in Beckley at 360 Prince St.

Fayetteville

Packed tight with good restaurants and watering holes, pint-size Fayetteville acts as a jumping-off point for New River thrill-seekers. Definitely plan to stop here for a meal if you're adventuring in the area. It's an artsy mountain enclave as well.

Sights & Activities

Beckley Exhibition Coal Mine MINE
(304-256-1747; www.beckley.org/general-information-coal-mine; 513 Ewart Ave, Beckley; adult/child $22/12.50; 10am-6pm Apr-Oct) This mine in Beckley, 22 miles south of Fayetteville, is a museum about the region's coal heritage. Visitors can ride a train 1500ft into a former coal mine, check out exhibits about mining life and explore the camp town village. Don't like enclosed places? You can see everything except the mine for $11. If you do go in the mine, bring a jacket; it's cold underground!

New River Bikes CYCLING
(304-574-2453; www.newriverbikes.com; 221 N Court St; bike hire per day $35, tours $79-110; 10am-6pm Mon, Tue, Thu & Fri, to 4pm Sat)

Mountain biking is superb on the graded loops of the Arrowhead Trails.

You can hire wheels or take a guided trip through this outfit in Fayetteville.

Sleeping & Eating

River Rock Retreat Hostel HOSTEL $

(304-574-0394; www.riverrockretreatandhostel.com; cnr Lansing-Edmond & Fayette Station Rds; dm $30; P ❄) Less than 1 mile north of the New River Gorge Bridge, this is a well-run hostel with basic, clean rooms and plenty of common space. No host on-site, but owner Joy Marr is a wealth of local information.

★ **Secret Sandwich Society** AMERICAN $

(304-574-4777; www.secretsandwichsociety.com; 103 Keller Ave; mains $10-15; 11am-10pm) If you're a connoisseur of sandwiches, or just super hungry, this easygoing spot is a must. The eatery has sandwiches slathered in tasty toppings, delicious burgers, hearty salads and a changing lineup of local microbrews. Eat on the pleasant deck for a fine breeze.

Pies & Pints PIZZA $$

(304-574-2200; www.piesandpints.net; 219 W Maple Ave; pizzas $10-25; 11am-10pm Sun-Thu, to 11pm Fri & Sat) Oooh baby. Let's talk about the Gouda Chicken. Topped with gourmet cheese, chipotle crema, apple-smoked bacon and grilled yard bird, this decadent pizza is darn near heaven. The flagship location of the popular West Virginia and Ohio pizza-and-craft-beer mini-chain, this is a place where folks come to celebrate after a good time in the great outdoors.

From ales and IPAs to sours, the craft-beer list is impressive, with selections both local and national.

Getting There & Away

You will need a car to check out regional attractions.

Amtrak (www.amtrak.com) stops on Wednesday, Friday and Sunday at the Prince Depot, 23 miles south of Fayetteville on the Cardinal route linking NYC, Washington, DC, and Chicago. It's a fairly remote stop and there are no rental-car companies on-site. You will need to arrange for pickup by a friend or a taxi.

BLUESKY2U/SHUTTERSTOCK ©

1. Bar Harbor (p248), Acadia National Park **2.** Mammoth Cave National Park (p394) **3.** Great Smoky Mountains National Park (p354) **4.** Shenandoah National Park (p316)

ZACK FRANK/SHUTTERSTOCK ©

National Parks

Although their size may not compare to their western counterparts, the diverse range of climates, activities and natural beauty in the Eastern USA's national parks easily rival anything the other half of the country can serve up. As a bonus, many are easily accessible from major cities – make it a day trip!

Great Smoky Mountains National Park

Receiving more visitors than any other US national park, this southern Appalachian woodland pocket protects thickly forested ridges where black bears, white-tailed deer, antlered elk, wild turkeys and more than 1500 kinds of flowering plants find sanctuary. (p354)

Acadia National Park

Catch the first sunrise of the new year atop Cadillac Mountain, the highest point on the USA's eastern seaboard. Or come in summer to play on end-of-the-world islands tossed along this craggy, wind-whipped North Atlantic coastline. (p247)

Shenandoah National Park

Waterfalls and woodland paths await in this pastoral preserve, just 75 miles from the nation's capital. Don't miss Skyline Drive, a National Scenic Byway that winds past more than 70 scenic overlooks in its 100-plus miles. (p316)

Everglades National Park

Home to snaggle-toothed alligators and crocodiles, stealthy panthers, pink flamingos and mellow manatees, the Everglades' endless 'rivers of grass' are a wildlife watcher's delight – and have an ecosystem unlike any other on earth. (p478)

Mammoth Cave National Park

With hidden underground rivers and more than 400 miles of explored terrain, the world's longest cave system shows off sci-fi-looking stalactites and stalagmites up close. (p394)

The South

Includes ➡

North Carolina 333
South Carolina 355
Tennessee 366
Memphis 366
Nashville 373
Kentucky 386
Louisville 387
Georgia 394
Atlanta 394
Alabama 413
Mississippi 419
Arkansas 425
Louisiana 432
New Orleans 433

Best Places to Eat

- ➡ Bacchanal (p442)
- ➡ Hattie B's (p379)
- ➡ Edmund's Oast (p359)

Best Places to Sleep

- ➡ 21c Museum Hotel Louisville (p389)
- ➡ Park View Historic Hotel (p441)
- ➡ Bunn House (p352)
- ➡ Urban Oasis B&B (p400)

Why Go?

The South falls from the granite, forested fists of Kentucky and Tennessee into craggy hill country and thick woods. This rugged landscape slowly changes as the waters of its rivers – including North America's greatest, the Mississippi – saturate the land into boggy, black-water blankets and sun-seared marsh, all thinning into the salty membrane of the Atlantic Ocean and Gulf of Mexico.

Arguably the first region of the USA to be considered its own distinct place, the South is defined by its cuisine, landscape, accent, literature, music and, undergirding all of the above, history – one that is long and beautiful in places, brutal and bloody in others.

Yet while Southerners consider themselves tied to this land and water, they are also the inhabitants of cities deeply in tune with the American experience, from the sweat-drenched noir of Charleston and New Orleans to the accept-all-comers diversity of Atlanta and Nashville.

When to Go

New Orleans

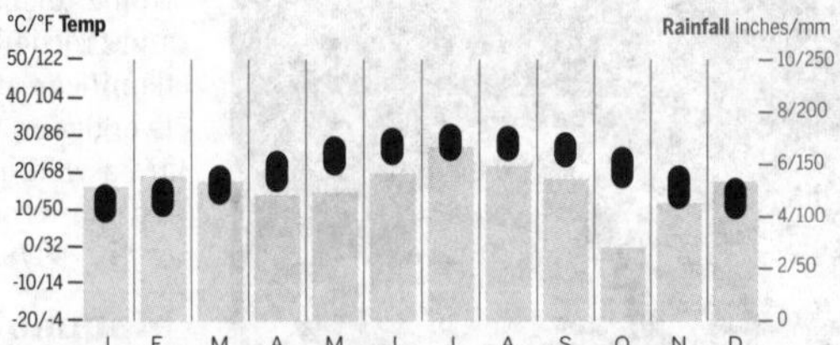

Nov–Feb Winter is generally mild in the South, and Christmas is a capital-E Event.

Apr–Jun Spring is lush and warm, abloom with fragrant jasmine, gardenia and tuberose.

Jul–Sep Summer is steamy, often unpleasantly so, and locals hit the beaches.

NORTH CAROLINA

The rural, conservative Old South and the urban, liberal-leaning New South jostle for precedence in the fast-growing Tar Heel State, home to hipsters, hog farmers and high-tech wunderkinds. From the mighty mountains in the west to the ethereal islands lining the Atlantic coast, all kinds of cultures and communities manage to coexist.

The locals are joined, especially in summer, by visitors from around the world. Many are drawn by the limitless opportunities for adventures, including hiking the woods, rafting the rivers and cruising the Blue Ridge Parkway in a convertible. Others come to savor the dynamic cities of Raleigh, Charlotte and Wilmington, with their top-class museums and restaurants – and astonishing number of craft breweries.

So grab yourself a barbecue platter and a local brew, and watch the Duke Blue Devils battle the North Carolina Tar Heels in the college-basketball league.

History

The tides of history have flowed back and forth across North Carolina. For Native Americans, the fragile coastline fringed the periphery of their world; for European colonizers, it marked the point from which they steadily pushed the original inhabitants westwards. Once it became part of the United States, North Carolina's fortunes became entwined with the plantation South, and it eventually seceded to join the Confederacy. Since then, the state has continued to identify with the South, while industrializing and entering the global economy.

North Carolina Coast

The coastline of North Carolina stretches more than 300 miles. Remarkably, it remains underdeveloped and the beach is often visible from coastal roads. Yes, the wall of cottages stretching south from Corolla to Kitty Hawk can seem endless, but for the most part the state's shores remain free of flashy, highly commercialized resort areas. Instead you'll find rugged, windswept barrier islands, Colonial villages once frequented by pirates, and laid-back beach towns full of locally owned ice-cream shops and mom-and-pop motels. Even the most touristy beaches have a small-town vibe.

For solitude, head to the isolated Outer Banks (OBX), where fishermen and women still make their living hauling in shrimp, and the older locals speak in an archaic British-tinged brogue. Further south, groovy Wilmington is known as a center of film and TV production, and its surrounding beaches are popular with local spring breakers and tourists.

Getting There & Away

The closest commercial airports to the Outer Banks are Norfolk International Airport (p298), 82 miles north of the Outer Banks, in Virginia, and North Carolina's Raleigh-Durham International Airport (p345), 192 miles west. Ferries link more isolated Ocracoke Island in the Outer Banks with Hatteras Island and Cedar Island as well as Swan Quarter on the mainland.

If you are only heading to the Crystal Coast, Coastal Carolina Regional Airport, serviced by commercial flights from Charlotte and Atlanta, is your closest bet.

Wilmington has its own **Wilmington International Airport** (ILM; ☎910-341-4125; www.flyilm.com; 1740 Airport Blvd).

Outer Banks

The Outer Banks are fragile ribbons of sand tracing the coastline for more than 100 miles, separated from the mainland by sounds and waterways. From north to south, barrier islands Bodie (pronounced 'body'), Roanoke, Hatteras and Ocracoke, essentially large sandbars, are linked by bridges and ferries. The far-northern communities **Corolla** (kur-all-ah), **Duck** and **Southern Shores** are former duck-hunting grounds for the wealthy, and are quiet and upscale. Nearly contiguous Bodie Island towns **Kitty Hawk**, **Kill Devil Hills** and **Nags Head** are developed and more populated, with fried-fish joints, drive-through beer shops, motels, and sandals and sunblock stores. **Roanoke Island**, west of Bodie, offers Colonial history and the quaint waterfront town **Manteo**. Further south, **Hatteras Island** is a protected national seashore with tiny villages and a wild, windswept beauty. At Outer Banks' southern end, find old salts, shuck oysters and weave hammocks on **Ocracoke Island**, accessible only by ferry.

Sights

Corolla, the northernmost town on Hwy 158, is famed for its wild horses. Descendants of Colonial Spanish mustangs, the horses

The South Highlights

❶ **New Orleans** (p433) Losing yourself in the magic of America's strangest, most celebratory city.

❷ **Great Smoky Mountains National Park** (p354) Hiking and camping amid some of the South's most magnificent scenery.

❸ **Nashville** (p373) Stomping your boots in honky-tonks along Lower Broadway.

❹ **Outer Banks** (p333) Driving windswept NC 12 the length of North Carolina.

❺ **Charleston** (p356) Touring antebellum homes and dining on Lowcountry fare.

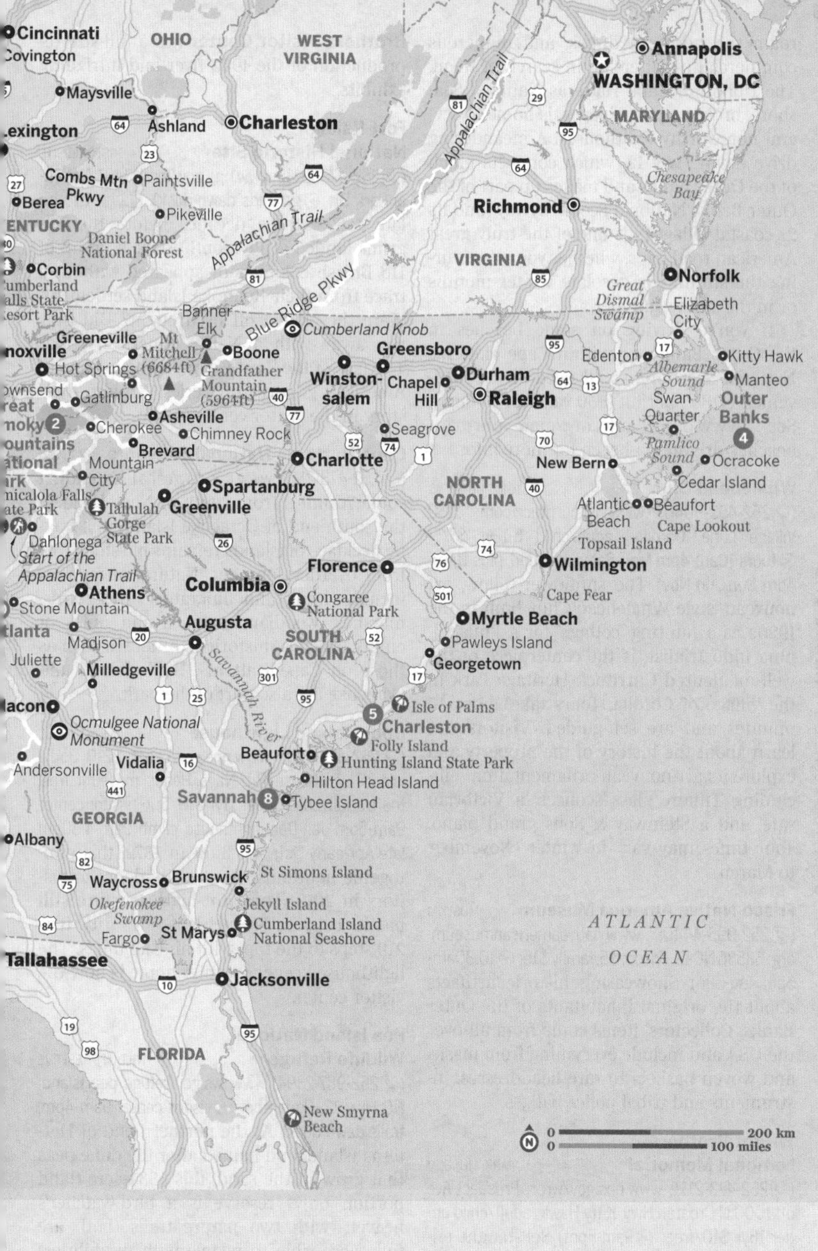

6 **Birmingham Civil Rights Institute** (p414) Learning the story of segregation and the Civil Rights movement.

7 **Ozark Mountains** (p430) Exploring the caverns, mountains, rivers, forests and folk music of Arkansas' Ozarks.

8 **Savannah** (p408) Falling for the hauntings, murderous tales and Southern hospitality of Georgia's living romance novel.

9 **Oxford** (p419) Enjoying great food and a vibrant town square.

10 **Atlanta** (p394) Embracing the energy of the most diverse city in the South.

roam the northern dunes, and numerous commercial outfitters go in search of them. The ribbon of Cape Hatteras National Seashore, broken up by villages, is home to several noteworthy lighthouses. A meandering drive down Hwy 12, which connects much of the Outer Banks and makes up part of the Outer Banks National Scenic Byway (and its 21 coastal villages), is one of the truly great American road trips, whether you come during the stunningly desolate winter months or in the sunny summer.

If you're driving on some beaches in the Outer Banks, or within Cape Hatteras National Seashore, you'll need an off-road-vehicle (ORV) permit ($50 valid for 10 days). See www.outerbanks.org/plan-your-trip/beaches/driving-on-beach for more info.

Whalehead Club HISTORIC BUILDING

(252-453-9040; www.visitcurrituck.com; 1160 Village Lane, Corolla; adult/child 6-12yr $7/5; tours 10am-4pm Mon-Sat year-round, plus 11am-4pm Sun Jun-Nov) The sunflower-yellow, art nouveau–style Whalehead Club, built in the 1920s as a hunting 'cottage' for a Philadelphia industrialist, is the centerpiece of the well-manicured Currituck Heritage Park in the village of Corolla. Tours take about 45 minutes and are self-guided. Visitors can learn about the history of the property and explore its art-nouveau ornamentation – including Tiffany glass sconces, a Victorian safe, and a Steinway & Sons grand piano. Tour times may vary in winter (November to March).

Frisco Native America Museum MUSEUM

(252-995-4440; www.nativeamericanmuseum.org; 53536 NC 12, Frisco; $5, family $15; 10:30am-5pm Tue-Sun) Showcasing historic artifacts about the original inhabitants of the Outer Banks. Collectors' items come from all over the USA and include everything from masks and woven baskets to rare headdresses, instruments and tribal police badges.

Wright Brothers National Memorial PARK, MUSEUM

(252-473-2111; www.nps.gov/wrbr; Prospect Ave off 1000 N Croatan Hwy, Kitty Hawk; adult/child under 16yr $10/free; 9am-5pm) Self-taught engineers Wilbur and Orville Wright launched the world's first successful airplane flight on December 17, 1903 (it lasted 12 seconds). A boulder marks the take-off spot. Climb a nearby hill, where the brothers conducted earlier glider experiments, for fantastic views of sea and sound. The on-site **Wright Brothers Visitor Center** has a full-size reproduction of the 1903 flyer and intriguing exhibits.

Fort Raleigh National Historic Site HISTORIC SITE

(252-473-2111; www.nps.gov/fora; 1401 National Park Dr; grounds dawn-dusk) FREE In the late 1580s, three decades before the Pilgrims landed at Plymouth Rock, a group of 116 British colonists disappeared without a trace from their Roanoke Island settlement. Were they killed off by drought? Did they run away with a Native American tribe? The fate of the 'Lost Colony' remains one of America's greatest mysteries. Explore their story in the visitor center (p338).

Cape Hatteras National Seashore ISLAND

(252-473-2111; www.nps.gov/caha) Extending some 70 miles from south of Nags Head to the south end of Ocracoke Island, this fragile necklace of islands remains blissfully free from overdevelopment. Natural attractions include local and migratory waterbirds, marshes, woodlands, dunes and miles of empty beaches; historic lighthouses such as those on Cape Hatteras, Bodie Island and Ocracoke are also part of the park.

Bodie Island Lighthouse LIGHTHOUSE

(252-473-2111; www.nps.gov/caha; 8210 Bodie Island Lighthouse Rd, Nags Head; museum free, tours adult/child under 11yr $10/5; visitor center 9am-5pm Jan-Dec, lighthouse climb 9am-4:30pm late Apr-early Oct;) Built in 1872, this photogenic lighthouse opened its doors to visitors in 2013. The 170ft-high structure still has its original Fresnel lens – a rarity. It is 219 steps to the top, with nine landings. The lighthouse keeper's former home is now the visitor center.

Pea Island National Wildlife Refuge WILDLIFE RESERVE

(252-987-2394; www.fws.gov/refuge/pea_island; NC Hwy 12, Rodanthe; visitor center 9am-4pm, trails dawn-dusk) At the northern end of Hatteras Island, and named after the dune peas that grow in the sand, this 5834-acre (land portion only) reserve is a bird-watcher's heaven, with two nature trails (both are fully accessible to people with disabilities) and 13 miles of unspoiled beach for the 365 recorded species here. Viewer scopes inside the visitor center overlook an adjacent pond. Check the online calendar for details about guided bird walks, turtle talks and canoe tours.

THE SOUTH IN...

One Week

Fly into New Orleans (p433) and stretch your legs with a walking tour in the legendary French Quarter, before devoting your remaining time to celebrating jazz history and partying the night away in a zydeco joint. Then wind your way upward through the languid Delta, stopping in Clarksdale (p421) for a sultry evening of blues at the juke joints before alighting in Memphis (p366) to walk in the footsteps of the King at Graceland (p367). From here, head down the Music Hwy to Nashville (p373) to see Elvis' gold Cadillac at the Country Music Hall of Fame & Museum (p375) and practice your line dancing at the honky-tonks (country-music clubs) of the District.

Two Weeks

From Nashville, head east to hike amid the craggy peaks and waterfalls of Great Smoky Mountains National Park (p354) before a revitalizing overnight in the arty mountain town of Asheville (p351) and a tour of the scandalously opulent Biltmore Estate, America's largest private home. Plow straight through to the Atlantic coast to loll on the sandy barrier islands of the isolated **Outer Banks** (p333), then head down the coast to finish up in Charleston (p356), with decadent food and postcard-pretty architecture.

Cape Hatteras Lighthouse LIGHTHOUSE
(☎252-473-2111; www.nps.gov/caha; 46379 Lighthouse Rd, Buxton; climbing tours adult/child under 12yr $8/4; ⊙visitor center 9am-5pm, lighthouse to 4:30pm late Apr-early Oct) At 193ft (or 198ft to the lighting rod), this striking black-and-white-striped edifice is one of North Carolina's most iconic images. The first version of the Hatteras Lighthouse was lit in October of 1803, a modest 90ft tall back then, with a lamp powered by whale oil, and a sandstone structure. Climb the 248 steps inside the current structure, then check out the interesting exhibits about local history in the **Museum of the Sea**, located in the lighthouse keeper's former home.

Graveyard of the Atlantic Museum MUSEUM
(☎252-986-0720; www.graveyardoftheatlantic.com; 59200 Museum Dr, Hattaras; ⊙10am-5pm Mon-Sat Apr-Sep, to 4pm Oct-Mar) FREE Exhibits about shipwrecks, piracy and salvaged cargo are highlights at this maritime museum at the end of the road. There have been more than 2000 shipwrecks off the coast of the Outer Banks. According to one exhibit, in 2006 a container washed ashore near Frisco, releasing thousands of Doritos bags. One local told us that residents were enjoying Doritos casseroles for months! Donations appreciated.

Activities

Kitty Hawk Kites ADVENTURE SPORTS
(☎252-441-6800; www.kittyhawk.com; 3933 S Croatan Hwy, Jockey's Ridge Crossing, Nags Head; bikes per day $15, kayaks per 2hr $39, stand-up paddleboards per hour/day $29/59; ⊙9am-6pm) In business more than 30 years, Kitty Hawk Kites has several locations along the OBX coast. It offers beginners' kiteboarding lessons (five hours, $400) in Rodanthe and hang-gliding lessons at Jockey's Ridge State Park (from $109). Also rents out kayaks, sailboats, stand-up paddleboards, bikes and in-line skates (at Kitty Hawk Surf Co in the same shopping complex).

Corolla Outback Adventures TOURS
(☎252-453-4484; www.corollaoutback.com; 1150 Ocean Trail, Corolla; 2hr tour adult/child under 13yr $50/25) Tour operator Jay Bender, whose family started Corolla's first guide service, knows his local history and his local horses. Tours bounce you down the beach and through the dunes to see the wild mustangs that roam the northern Outer Banks.

Sleeping

Cape Hatteras KOA Resort CAMPGROUND $
(☎252-987-2307; www.koa.com/campgrounds/cape-hatteras; 25094 NC Hwy 12, Rodanthe; tent sites with hookup & water from $84, RV sites with hookup from $84, 4-person cabins from $112; P ⓦ ≋) Beachfront campground open all year, with lots of facilities (including a hot tub) and sites for RVs and tents, plus cabin accommodation. Kayak and paddleboard rental are available on-site. There's a cafe, a Wednesday outdoor cinema, and Monday-night bingo during high season (May to September). Tent and RV sites accommodate up to six people.

Shutters on the Banks HOTEL $$
(☎252-441-5581; www.shuttersonthebanks.com; 405 S Virginia Dare Trail, Kill Devil Hills; r with/without ocean view from $225/185, honeymoon ste from $499; P❄📶🏊) Centrally located in Kill Devil Hills, this welcoming 88-room beachfront hotel exudes a snappy, colorful style with pastel tones and beach art on the walls. The inviting rooms come with plantation windows and colorful art as well as flat-screen TV, refrigerator and microwave. Some rooms come with a full kitchen.

Sanderling Resort & Spa RESORT $$$
(☎855-412-7866; www.sanderling-resort.com; 1461 Duck Rd, Duck; r $320-710; P❄📶🏊) Remodeled rooms have given this posh place a stylish feel. Decor is impeccably tasteful, and the attached balconies are an inviting place to enjoy the ocean sounds and breezes. Plus, the resort offers sunrise yoga on the beach. Open year-round. Standard-room deals from $179 in low season.

Eating & Drinking

John's Drive-In SEAFOOD, ICE CREAM $
(www.johnsdrivein.com; 3716 N Virginia Dare Trail, Kitty Hawk; mains $6-12, ice cream from $3.25; ⏲11am-5pm Thu-Sun, to 3pm Mon & Tue May-Oct) A Kitty Hawk institution for perfectly fried boats (trays) of shrimp or crab cakes, to be eaten at outdoor picnic tables and washed down with one of many possible milkshake combinations – like M&M, peanut butter, Oreo, mint chocolate chip, pineapple and cherry, to name but a few. Some folks just come for a burger and some soft-serve ice cream.

★**Kill Devil Grill** SEAFOOD, AMERICAN $$
(☎252-449-8181; www.thekilldevilgrill.com; 2008 S Virginia Dare Trail, Kill Devil Hills; lunch $9-14, dinner $11-24; ⏲11:30am-10pm Tue-Sat) Yowza, this place is good. It's also historic – the entrance is a 1939 dining car that's listed in the National Register of Historic Places. Pub grub and seafood arrive with tasty flair, and portions are generous. Check out the specials, and things like prime ribs or sea scallops, where the kitchen can really shine. Often closed between December and January.

★**Blue Moon Beach Grill** SEAFOOD, SANDWICHES $$
(☎252-261-2583; www.bluemoonbeachgrill.com; 4104 S Virginia Dare Trail, Nags Head; mains $12-29; ⏲11:30am-9pm) Would it be wrong to write an ode to a side of french fries? Because Lord Almighty, the lightly spiced fries at this casual hot spot are the stuff of sonnets and monologues. And we haven't even mentioned the BLT with seared mahi-mahi, applewood bacon, local Currituck tomatoes and a jalapeño rémoulade for slathering.

Information

The best sources of information are at the main visitor centers, and there are plenty of them. Many smaller centers open seasonally. Also useful is www.outerbanks.org.

Aycock Brown Welcome Center (Outer Banks Visitor Bureau; ☎877-629-4386; www.outerbanks.org; 5230 N Croatian Hwy, Kitty Hawk; ⏲8am-5pm Mon-Fri) On the bypass in Kitty Hawk; has maps and information.

Fort Raleigh National Historic Site Visitor Center (Lindsay Warren Vistor Center; ☎252-475-9001; www.nps.gov/fora; 1401 National Park Dr; ⏲9am-5pm)

Hatteras Island Visitor Center (☎252-475-9000; www.nps.gov/caha; 46368 Lighthouse Rd, Buxton; ⏲9am-5pm) Beside Cape Hatteras Lighthouse.

Ocracoke Island Visitor Center (☎252-475-9701; www.nps.gov/caha; 38 Irvin Garrish Hwy; ⏲9am-5pm) Near the southern ferry dock.

Sarah Owen Welcome Center (☎877-629-4386; www.outerbanks.org; 1 Visitors Center Circle; ⏲9am-5pm) Just east of Virginia Dare Memorial Bridge on the Hwy 64 Bypass on Roanoke Island.

Whalebone Welcome Center (☎877-629-4386; www.outerbanks.org; 2 NC Hwy 12, Nags Head; ⏲8:30am-5pm Mar-Dec) At the intersection of Hwy 64 and Hwy 12 in Nags Head.

Getting There & Away

No public transportation exists to or on the Outer Banks.

If driving, try to avoid arriving or departing on weekends in summer, when traffic can be maddening. The **Outer Banks Visitors Bureau** (www.outerbanks.org) offers a comprehensive guide to driving to OBX, including tips and alternate routes to avoid spending your vacation stuck in your vehicle. In winter, the roads are empty.

FERRY

The **North Carolina Ferry System** (www.ferry.ncdot.gov) operates several routes, including the free one-hour Hatteras–Ocracoke car ferry, which fluctuates between hourly and half-hourly, with 36 departures from 5am to midnight from Hatteras in high season; reservations aren't accepted. North Carolina ferries also run between Ocracoke and Cedar Islands (one way car/motorcycle $15/10, 2¼ hours) and between Ocracoke Island and Swan Quarter on the mainland ($15/10, 2¾ hours) every three hours or so; reservations are recommended in summer for these two routes. Pedestrians may use the ferries for $1 per one-way trip. Cyclists can use the ferries for $3 per one-way trip. There's also a high-speed passenger-only ferry between Hatteras and Ocracoke Village (one way $2, 70 minutes).

Ocracoke Island

Ocracoke Village is a funky little community that moves at a slower pace. With the exception of the village, the National Park Service owns the island. The older residents still speak in the 17th-century British dialect known as 'Hoi Toide' (their pronunciation of 'high tide') and refer to non-islanders as 'dingbatters'. Edward Teach, aka Blackbeard the pirate, used to hide out in the area and was killed here in 1718. You can camp by Pony Pen, filled with the descendants of wild ponies abandoned by explorers hundreds of years ago, have a fish sandwich in a local pub, cycle around the village's narrow streets or nestle into holes in the sand dunes along 16 miles of coastline and catch some rays.

Many people come to Ocracoke on a day trip from Hatteras, but with its preserved culture and laid-back vibe, it's a nice place to spend a night or two. There are a handful of B&Bs, several motels, a park-service campground near the beach and rental cottages.

Sights & Activities

Ocracoke Beach BEACH
(Irvin Garrish Hwy; P) Dolphins are commonly spotted on Ocracoke's gorgeous, undeveloped 16-mile stretch of sandy beach. Swimmers should be aware of rip currents. Find parking and toilet facilities at this access point on the right-hand side of Irvin Garrish Hwy when traveling north out of town.

Ocracoke Lighthouse LIGHTHOUSE
(www.nps.gov/caha; Lighthouse Rd) Built in 1823, this is the oldest lighthouse still operating in North Carolina, though it cannot be climbed. The walls are 5ft thick and the non-rotating light at the top sits only 75ft above sea level. It can be seen as far as 14 miles away.

Portsmouth Island ATV Tours HISTORY
(252-928-4484; www.portsmouthislandatv.com; 396 Irvin Garrish Hwy; tours $90, max 6 people; 2 trips per day 8am-noon & 1-5pm Apr-Oct) Runs two fascinating daily tours to the nearby island of Portsmouth, a 20-minute boat ride from Ocracoke, where you'll find an Outer Banks ghost town that was abandoned in the 1970s. Guided ATV tours focus on shelling, bird-watching and swimming, in addition to the historic village.

Ride the Wind KAYAKING
(252-928-6311; www.surfocracoke.com; 486 Irvin Garrish Hwy; 2-2½hr kayaking tours adult/child under 13yr $45/18, group surf lessons from $75; 10am-7pm Mon-Sat, to 6pm Sun) Want to get on the water? Take a kayaking tour with Ride the Wind. The sunset tours are easy on the arms, and it also offers sunrise, midday yoga and tai chi tours, and surf lessons, and rents surfboards ($22 per day), bodyboards ($12 per day), skimboards ($19 per day), SUPs ($19 per hour) and kayaks ($14 per hour).

Sleeping & Eating

Ocracoke Campgrounds CAMPGROUND $
(877-444-6777, 252-928-6671; www.recreation.gov; 4352 Irvin Garrish Hwy; tent sites $28; Apr-late Nov; P) Good value for money for

OCRACOKE'S PENNED PONIES

Legend has it the Ocracoke Island 'wild' ponies are descended from feral Spanish mustangs abandoned by shipwrecked explorers in the 16th or 17th century, when it was common to unload livestock to lighten the load and get back out to sea after running aground. Known as 'banker' ponies, these horses are unique in the equine world – they harbor a different number of vertebrae and ribs as well as a distinct shape, posture, color, size and weight compared with those of other horses. But what's more fascinating about Ocracoke's ponies is they were eventually broken and tamed by a troop of Boy Scouts in the 1950s – you can see photos at the **Pony Island Restaurant** (252-928-5701; 51 Ocean View Rd; breakfast dishes $5-14; 7:30-11:30am Apr-Oct). They were eventually pastured in a 'pony pen' in 1959 to prevent overgrazing and protect them from the dangers of NC Hwy 12, which was under construction. They're cared for by the National Park Service at the **Ocracoke Pony Pen** (www.nps.gov/caha; Irvin Garrish Hwy) at Pony Pen Beach. You can view them from an observation deck.

small groups, Ocracoke Campgrounds offers more than 100 sites on sand on the island. Flush toilets, drinking water, showers and grills are available. Electric hookups are not available. There's a maximum of six people per site.

Pam's Pelican B&B B&B $$
(☎252-928-1661; www.pamspelican.com; 1021 Irvin Garrish Hwy; r $175-220;) This wildly popular B&B has just four rooms, reached via a series of colorful corridors, in a typical island home loaded with artsy knick-knacks. Rates include use of bikes (and rides to the beach if you're so inclined) and there is sometimes live music streamed from the front-yard gazebo in high season. Guests have access to the 2nd-floor patio.

★**Eduardo's Taco Stand** MEXICAN $
(☎252-928-0234; www.facebook.com/amadowoch; 950 Irvin Garrish Hwy; mains $4-13; 8am-3pm & 5-8pm Mon-Sat, 8am-3pm Sun;) There's a long list of tacos, burritos and fresh and spicy salsas at this sensational taco stand. If you're over fried clams and crab cakes, dishes such as prime rib-eye tacos with salsa *de xoconostle* (sour prickly pears) hit the spot, as do the fish with creamy chipotle apple slaw or poblano chowder with shrimp or clams. Full veggie menu, too.

Getting There & Away

The village is at the southern end of 16-mile-long Ocracoke Island and is accessed from Hatteras via the free **Hatteras–Ocracoke ferry** (www.ncdot.gov/ferry; first come, first served). The ferry lands at the northeastern end of the island. Other options are via the $15 Cedar Island–Ocracoke or Swan Quarter–Ocracoke ferries (which land at the southern dock; reservations accepted). Pedestrians/cyclists can board the ferries for $1/3.

Crystal Coast

The southern Outer Banks are collectively called the 'Crystal Coast.' Less rugged than the northern beaches, they include several historic coastal towns, sparsely populated islands and vacation-friendly beaches.

An industrial and commercial stretch of Hwy 70 goes through **Morehead City**, with plenty of chain hotels and restaurants. The **Bogue Banks**, across the Sound from Morehead City via the Atlantic Beach Causeway, have several well-trafficked beach communities – try Atlantic Beach if you like the smell of coconut suntan oil and doughnuts.

Just north, postcard-pretty **Beaufort** (bow-fort), the third-oldest town in the state, has a charming boardwalk and lots of B&Bs. Blackbeard himself is said to have lived in the Hammock House off Front St. You can't go inside, but some claim you can still hear the screams of the pirate's murdered wife at night.

Sights & Activities

Fort Macon State Park FORT
(☎252-726-3775; www.ncparks.gov/fort-macon-state-park; 2303 E Fort Macon Rd, Atlantic Beach; 9am-5:30pm;) FREE This remarkable five-sided fort, with 26 vaulted rooms, is one of North Carolina's most visited attractions. Completed in 1834, it was the site of the Battle of Fort Macon fought in 1862. Exhibits inside the fort's walls and tunnels document the daily lives of soldiers stationed there. Constructed from brick and stone, the fort changed hands twice during the Civil War. Visitors can walk around the exterior and climb the stairs of the grassy structure for 360-degree views.

North Carolina Maritime Museum MUSEUM
(☎252-504-7740; www.ncmaritimemuseumbeaufort.com; 315 Front St, Beaufort; 9am-5pm Mon-Fri, 10am-5pm Sat, 1-5pm Sun) FREE The pirate Blackbeard was a frequent visitor to the Beaufort area in the early 1700s. In 1996, the wreckage of his flagship, the *Queen Anne's Revenge,* was discovered at the bottom of Beaufort Inlet. You'll see plates, bottles and other artifacts from the ship in this small but engaging museum, which also spotlights the seafood industry as well as maritime rescue operations.

Olympus Dive Center DIVING
(☎252-726-9432; www.olympusdiving.com; 713 Shepard St, Morehead City; half-day dives from $70; 6am-8pm) Not only are North Carolina's warm, clear waters home to a variety of marine life, they also contain more than 2000 sunken ships, which date back as far as 1526. This excellent dive outfit takes qualified divers to see them at depths of 60ft to 140ft (18m to 42m). Divers in this area make new discoveries every day.

Sleeping & Eating

Hampton Inn Morehead City HOTEL $$
(☎252-240-2300; www.hamptoninn3.hilton.com; 4035 Arendell St, Morehead City; r from $175;

) Yep, it's part of a national chain, but the helpful staff and the views of Bogue Sound make this Hampton Inn a nice choice – plus it's in a convenient location near to Hwy 70, helpful for those driving the coast.

Rates drop significantly on weeknights in summer.

★ Inn on Turner B&B **$$**
(919-271-6144; www.innonturner.com; 217 Turner St; r $200-250;) Impeccably tasteful aqua-toned coastal contemporary decor – no gaudy antiques here – dominates this four-room B&B occupying a historic 1866 wooden cream-colored home two blocks back from the water. Innkeepers Kim and Jon are pillars of small-town Southern hospitality, despite not being from the South, and never having slept in a B&B before they opened this one in 2015.

El's Drive-In SEAFOOD **$**
(252-726-3002; www.elsdrivein.com; 3706 Arendell St, Morehead City; mains $2-15; 10:30am-10pm Sun-Thu, to 11pm Fri & Sat) The food is brought right to your car at this old-school drive-in and legendary seafood spot, open since 1959. It serves fish fillets, po'boys and hot dogs. Our recommendation? The fried shrimp burger with ketchup and slaw plus a side of fries. Cash only.

Beaufort Grocery MODERN AMERICAN **$$$**
(252-728-3899; www.beaufortgrocery.com; 117 Queen St; mains $25-42; 11:30am-2:30pm & 5:30-9:30pm Wed-Mon;) You'd never guess by the simple, unassuming nature of the decor, but chef Charles Park is a James Beard winner, and the food shines, whether that be smoked sea-salt tuna with chili yogurt, duck two ways with sweet-potato caramel or sage-wrapped chicken saltimbocca over tagliatelle. We didn't hear a bad thing about the place – and weren't disappointed.

Wilmington

Wilmington is pretty darn fun, and it's worth carving out a day or two for a visit if you're driving the coast. This seaside charmer may not have the name recognition of Charleston and Savannah, but eastern North Carolina's largest city has historic neighborhoods, azalea-choked gardens and cute cafes aplenty. All that, plus reasonable hotel prices. At night the historic riverfront downtown becomes the playground for local college students, craft-beer enthusiasts, tourists and the occasional Hollywood type – there are so many movie studios here the town has earned the nickname 'Wilmywood.' You saw *Dawson's Creek*, right?

Sights & Activities

Battleship North Carolina HISTORIC SITE
(910-399-9100; www.battleshipnc.com; 1 Battleship Rd; self-guided tours adult/child 6-11yr/under 5yr $14/6/free, full-guided tours adult/child under 5yr $17.50/free; 8am-5pm Sep-May, to 8pm Jun-Aug;) Self-guided tours take you through the decks of this 45,000-ton megaship, which earned 15 battle stars in the Pacific theater in WWII before it was decommissioned in 1947. Sights include the bake shop and galley, the print shop, the engine room, the powder magazine and the communications center. Note that there are several steep stairways leading to lower decks. Take the Cape Fear Bridge from downtown to get here. Full guided tours run on Saturdays and Sundays at 9am.

Airlie Gardens GARDENS
(910-798-7700; www.airliegardens.org; 300 Airlie Rd; adult/child 4-12yr $9/3; 9am-5pm Apr-Dec, 9am-5pm Tue-Sun Jan-Mar) In spring, wander past thousands of bright azaleas at this 67-acre wonderland, also home to bewitching formal flowerbeds, seasonal gardens, pine trees, lakes and trails. The Airlie Oak dates from 1545.

Museum of the Bizarre MUSEUM
(910-399-2641; www.museumbizarre.com; 201 S Water St; adult/child under 3yr $3/free; 11am-8pm;) Pickled specimens, occult memorabilia, a taxidermied two-headed lamb, a bigfoot imprint and plenty of other oddities are on show at this truly peculiar place. It came about after a Wilmington-based collector of strange artifacts was convinced by his wife to move all the weird stuff out of the house and into a museum. We're glad he did.

Sleeping & Eating

Best Western Plus Coastline Inn HOTEL **$$**
(910-763-2800; www.bestwestern.com; 503 Nutt St; r $89-199, ste $129-279;) We're not sure what we like best: the gorgeous views of the Cape Fear River, the wooden boardwalk or the short walk to downtown fun. Standard rooms aren't huge or too fancy, but every room has a river view. Pet fee is $30 per day.

★**CW Worth House** B&B $$
(☎910-762-8562; www.worthhouse.com; 412 S 3rd St; r $160-200; ❄@📶) One of our favorite B&Bs in North Carolina, this turreted 1893 Queen Anne home is dotted with antiques and Victorian touches, but still manages to feel laid-back and cozy. Breakfasts are top-notch. The B&B is within a few blocks of downtown.

Dixie Grill DINER $
(☎910-762-7280; www.thedixiegrillwilmington.wordpress.com; 116 Market St; breakfast mains $5-9, lunch mains $9-10; ⊙8am-3pm Mon-Sat, to 2pm Sun; ✎👪) A top breakfast spot in central Wilmington. This retro setting, with lime-green booths and a bar area for solo diners, serves apple-sage sausage patties, eggs all ways, and Southern classics including baked biscuits with onion gravy and all the trimmings. For lunch the menu is filled with burgers, sandwiches and salads.

★**PinPoint** SOUTHERN US $$$
(☎910-769-2972; www.pinpointrestaurant.com; 114 Market St; mains $24-38; ⊙5:30-9:30pm Mon-Thu, to 10pm Fri & Sat, 10:30am-2pm & 5:30-9pm Sun; 📶) PinPoint was declared by *Southern Living* magazine as one of the South's best new restaurants – and they weren't lyin'! Chef Dean Neff was Hugh Acheson's kitchen compadre in Athens, Georgia's excellent Five & Ten, and he's sailing solo and shining in Wilmington, where he has a personal relationship with his farmers and fishers.

Drinking & Entertainment

★**Satellite Lounge** BAR
(☎910-399-2796; www.facebook.com/satellitebarandlounge; 120 Greenfield St; ⊙4pm-2am Mon-Sat, from 2pm Sun; 📶) If you want to belly up to North Carolina's most stunning bar, you'll need to head in the opposite direction of Wilmington's historic downtown and into its up-and-coming South Front district. A gorgeously restored tavern highlights the space, which includes near-professional-level cornhole lanes, a fire pit and an outdoor cinema. It's also a bikers' favorite.

Dead Crow Comedy Room COMEDY
(☎910-399-1492; www.deadcrowcomedy.com; 265 N Front St; $15-18; ⊙from 7pm Tue-Thu, from 6pm Fri & Sat) Dark, cramped, underground and in the heart of downtown, just like a comedy club should be. Stop in for improv, open-mic nights and touring comedians, plus comedy bingo. Bar service and full menu available.

ℹ Information

Visitor information center (☎877-406-2356, 910-341-4030; www.wilmingtonandbeaches.com; 505 Nutt St; ⊙8:30am-5pm Mon-Fri, 9am-4pm Sat, 1-4pm Sun) In an 1800s freight warehouse; has a walking-tour map of downtown.

ℹ Getting There & Around

American Airlines and Delta Airlines serve Wilmington International Airport (p333) from Atlanta, Charlotte, New York and Philadelphia. It's 5 miles northeast of downtown. The **Greyhound** (☎910-791-8040; www.greyhound.com; 505 Cando St) station is an inconvenient 5 miles east of downtown.

The downtown area is easy to cover on foot, but a **free trolley** (www.wavetransit.com/free-downtown-trolley-schedule; ⊙7:10am-8:50pm Mon-Fri, 10:30am-8:50pm Sat, 10:30am-5:30pm Sun) runs through the historic district from morning through evening.

The Triangle

The cities of Raleigh, Durham and Chapel Hill form a rough triangle in the central Piedmont region. Three top research universities – Duke, University of North Carolina and North Carolina State – are located here, as is the 7000-acre computer and biotech-office campus known as Research Triangle Park. Swarming with egghead computer programmers, bearded peace activists and hip young families, each town has its own unique personality, despite being only a few miles apart. In March, everyone – we mean *everyone* – goes crazy for college basketball.

ℹ Getting There & Around

Raleigh-Durham International Airport (p345), a 15-mile ride northwest of downtown Raleigh, receives nonstop flights from 49 locations, including London, Paris and Cancun.

Raleigh's **Greyhound station** (☎919-834-8275; 2210 Capital Blvd) is inconveniently located 3 miles northeast of downtown. For a better downtown stop, try Durham's **Greyhound station** (☎919-687-4800; 515 W Pettigrew St) in the Durham Station Transportation Center (p345), across the street from the **Amtrak station** (601 W Main St).

GoTriangle (www.gotriangle.org) operates a regional bus system that connects Raleigh, Durham and Chapel Hill. Bus 100 runs from downtown Raleigh to the airport, and continues to the Regional Transit Center near Research Triangle Park, from where connecting buses run to Durham and Chapel Hill. The adult single fare is $2.25.

Raleigh

Founded in 1792 as a new capital for North Carolina, and named for Sir Walter Raleigh – whose image crops up in all sorts of unlikely places around the city – Raleigh remains a somewhat staid government town with major sprawl issues. Downtown is undeniably handsome, though, and is home to some top-notch (and free!) museums and galleries, while the food and music scenes are on a definite upswing.

Sights

★North Carolina Museum of Art MUSEUM
(☎919-839-6262; www.ncartmuseum.org; 2110 Blue Ridge Rd; ⏲10am-5pm Tue-Thu, Sat & Sun, to 9pm Fri, park dawn-dusk; P) FREE Expanded in 2010 with the completion of the stunning, glass-and-steel West Building, this superb museum stands 6 miles west of downtown. Ranging far and wide, from ancient Egypt to modern Africa, its permanent collection includes works credited to Giotto and Botticelli – albeit with 'assistance' – and even a 17th-century 'Golf Player' etched by Rembrandt. The museum also holds around 20 jet-black Rodin bronzes, and a gallery celebrating alumni of the pioneering Black Mountain College near Asheville, including Robert Rauschenberg.

North Carolina Museum of History MUSEUM
(☎919-814-7000; www.ncmuseumofhistory.org; 5 E Edenton St; ⏲9am-5pm Mon-Sat, from noon Sun) FREE For a comprehensive, evenhanded and engaging look at the story of North Carolina, immerse yourself in the state history museum. Starting with a 3000-year-old dugout canoe, it continues through to the Civil Rights era by way of the European arrival and the Revolutionary and Civil wars. Look out for the cannon retrieved from the 1718 wreck of Blackbeard's ship, *Queen Anne's Revenge*, and the Woolworth's lunch counter that witnessed a sit-in in 1960.

North Carolina Museum of Natural Sciences MUSEUM
(☎919-707-9800; www.naturalsciences.org; 11 W Jones St; ⏲9am-5pm Mon-Sat, from noon Sun) FREE Whale skeletons hang from the ceiling. Butterflies flutter past your shoulder. Emerald tree boas make you shiver. And be warned: if you arrive after 10am on a school day, swarms of elementary-school children rampage all over the place. Skywalks lead to a glossy extension, the Nature Research Center, where you can watch scientists at work on their projects (and displays make it clear they're in no doubt as to the reality of climate change).

Sleeping & Eating

Umstead Hotel & Spa SPA HOTEL $$$
(☎919-447-4000; www.theumstead.com; 100 Woodland Pond Dr; r/ste from $329/455; P ❄ @ 📶 🏊 🐾) Set in a wooded suburban office park, 10 miles west of downtown, and backing onto a small lake, the Umstead is targeted squarely at visiting biotech CEOs. As well as simple but sumptuous rooms – deep-soak bathtubs, twin vanities – it has a Zen-like spa complete with meditation courtyard. There's a dog playground, and a pet fee of $200 per stay.

★La Farm Bakery BAKERY $
(☎919-657-0657; www.lafarmbakery.com; 4248 NW Cary Pkwy, Cary; dishes $8-11; ⏲7am-8pm; 📶) This much-loved French bakery is hard to find, halfway to Chapel Hill and inconspicuous even once you spot the right strip mall. Its breads and pastries are truly out of this world, though – whether you grab a classic baguette or apple challah, or linger over a miso pork and kimchi brioche or a fig and prosciutto tartine.

Beasley's Chicken & Honey SOUTHERN US $
(☎919-322-0127; www.ac-restaurants.com/beasleys; 237 S Wilmington St; mains $8-13; ⏲11:30am-10pm Sun-Wed, to midnight Thu-Sat) You'll need to loosen your belt after a meal at this crispy venture from James Beard Award–winning chef Ashley Christensen. Inside her airy downtown canteen, fried chicken is the star – on a biscuit, with waffles, in a potpie. The sides are decadent too – the creamed collard greens make a perfect introduction for nervous neophytes.

Bida Manda LAOTIAN $$
(☎919-829-9999; www.bidamanda.com; 222 S Blount St; lunch mains $11-22, dinner mains $18-30;

11:30am-2pm & 5-10pm Mon-Thu, 11:30am-2pm & 5pm-midnight Fri, 5pm-midnight Sat;) The food at this artfully decorated establishment – one of very few Laotian restaurants in the US – looks as gorgeous as the space itself. Enhanced with Thai, Vietnamese and Chinese flavors, it tastes wonderful too.

From pumpkin curry to lemongrass sausage or crispy pork-belly soup, everything's bold and very satisfying. The little shot of Laos-style coffee is a nice touch, too.

Information

Really just a small counter adjoining the Convention Center, the **Raleigh Visitor Information Center** (919-834-5900; www.visitraleigh.com; 500 Fayetteville St; 9am-5pm Mon-Sat) is stocked with maps and local information that you can pick up even when it's closed.

Durham

Home a century ago to the world's largest tobacco company – American Tobacco – Durham remains at heart a working-class Southern city. Its fortunes collapsed in the 1960s, however, along with the cigarette industry, and Durham's recent revival owes much to the presence of the prestigious Duke University. The city's downtown has been comprehensively rebuilt, and transformed into a hot spot for gourmands and artists, gays and lesbians. The changing winds were epitomized in 2017, when protesters toppled the Confederate monument that had stood outside the former county courthouse since 1924.

Sights

★Historic Stagville Plantation

PLANTATION

(919-620-0120; www.stagville.org; 5828 Old Oxford Hwy; 9am-5pm Tue-Sat, tours 11am, 1pm & 3pm; P) FREE Exceptional in prioritizing the 1000 or so 'enslaved persons' who worked here above the families that claimed their ownership, Stagville Plantation ranks among North Carolina's most important historic sites. What survives today, 10 miles north of downtown, is just a fragment of the huge plantation where the state's largest enslaved population lived in scattered groups. The fascinating guided tours drive in convoy to an emotive cluster of slave homes, along with a massive barn, a mile from the main house.

★Duke Lemur Center

ZOO

(919-401-7240; www.lemur.duke.edu; 3705 Erwin Rd; adult/child under 8yr $12/9; 9am-4pm, by appointment;) The secret is out – Durham's coolest attraction has to be this research and conservation center, home to the largest collection of lemurs outside their native Madagascar. No one could fail to melt at the sight of these big-eyed fuzzy creatures. Visits are by guided tour only, and must be reserved well in advance.

Duke University

UNIVERSITY

(www.duke.edu; Chapel Dr) Although it can trace its history back to 1838, Duke University became a university, and took its current name, in 1926, thanks to a major endowment from the Duke cigarette family. Spreading across the Georgian-style East Campus and the neo-Gothic West Campus, 1 and 2 miles respectively west of downtown, it has just over 15,000 students.

American Tobacco Campus

HISTORIC SITE

(www.americantobaccocampus.com; 300 Blackwell St) The massive former American Tobacco factory has been transformed into a million-square-foot cavalcade of restaurants, bars and entertainment venues. Still dominated by the towering 'Lucky Strike' chimney, but now centering on gardens traversed by artificial cascades, it's a lively combination of thriving mall and urban park. On the south side of downtown, it's just steps across the tracks from Main St.

Sleeping & Eating

★The Durham

BOUTIQUE HOTEL $$

(919-768-8830; www.thedurham.com; 315 E Chapel Hill St; r from $180; P) When the suave, 53-room Durham turned a former bank building – a marvel of midcentury modernist might – into a supremely retro, fiercely local haven in 2015, it marked the moment when the city's revitalized downtown finally got an independent hipster sleep. Raleigh Denim bedspreads, music programming by Durham-based Merge Records – it's go local or go home.

Arrowhead Inn

B&B $$

(919-477-8430; www.arrowheadinn.com; 106 Mason Rd; r $159, cottages/cabins $279/309;) Set in an imposing white clapboard home dating back to 1775, this plush B&B is 9 miles north of downtown. Every antique-furnished room in the main house has its own fireplace, and several have private spa baths; there's a separate cottage and cabin in the grounds. Rates include a sumptuous breakfast.

Dame's Chicken & Waffles CHICKEN $
(919-682-9235; www.dameschickenwaffles.com; 530 Foster St; mains $10-16; 10am-4pm Mon & Sun, to 9pm Tue-Thu, to 10pm Fri & Sat) While it can't claim to have invented chicken and waffles – it's been a 'thing' for a couple of centuries – Dame's has raised the ultimate comfort food to a fine art. Its relocation to these larger premises should mean customers won't have to wait before enjoying crispy Southern fried chicken atop, yes, fluffy, syrup-drenched, breakfast-style waffles.

★ **Mateo** TAPAS $$
(919-530-8700; www.mateotapas.com; 109 W Chapel Hill St; small plates $8-15; 11:30am-2:30pm & 5-10:30pm Tue-Thu, 11:30am-2:30pm & 5pm-midnight Fri, 5pm-midnight Sat, 5-9:30pm Sun) A poster child for Durham's remarkable comeback, this James Beard–nominated 'bar de tapas' is downtown's culinary anchor. Many dishes come with a Southern bent, and particular revelations include the *pan com tomate* with Manchego cheese; the brussels sprouts with pine nuts, raisins and saffron yogurt; and the fried egg and cheese (in which the 'whites' are fried farmer's cheese!).

Drinking & Entertainment

★ **Cocoa Cinnamon** COFFEE
(www.cocoacinnamon.com; 420 W Geer St; 7am-10pm Mon-Fri, from 8am Sat & Sun;) If a local says you *must* order a hot chocolate at Cocoa Cinnamon, ask them to be more specific. This former service station, on downtown's northern fringes, offers so many cocoas (along with teas and single-source coffee) that newbies may be paralyzed by the sheer chocolaty awesomeness.

Fullsteam Brewery BREWERY
(919-682-2337; www.fullsteam.ag; 726 Rigsbee Ave; 4pm-midnight Mon-Thu, 11am-1am Fri & Sat, noon-10pm Sun;) Calling itself a 'plow-to-pint' brewery, Fullsteam has gained national attention for pushing the boundaries of beer with wild, Southernized concoctions. Going out of its way to support local farmers, neighborhood foragers and agricultural entrepreneurs, it uses Carolinian ingredients wherever possible. The excellent taproom features ping-pong, arcade games, cafeteria-style seating and killer T-shirts, and there's live music Sunday evenings.

Durham Bulls Athletic Park STADIUM
(box office 919-956-2855; www.dbulls.com; 409 Blackwell St; tickets $9-26) While away a quintessentially American afternoon of beer and watching the Durham Bulls minor-league baseball team, as seen in the 1988 Kevin Costner movie *Bull Durham*. They play between April and early September.

Information

Set in a former bank building downtown, the **Durham Visitor Info Center** (919-687-0288; www.durham-nc.com; 212 W Main St; 9am-5pm Mon, to 6pm Tue-Fri, 11am-7pm Sat, noon-4pm Sun, closed Sun Nov-Mar) offers information, maps and interactive displays.

Getting There & Away

Raleigh-Durham International Airport (RDU; 919-840-2123; www.rdu.com; 1000 Trade Dr, Morrisville) is 13 miles southeast of downtown Durham – a ride that costs around $20 in an off-peak Uber. Greyhound (p342) sits across the street from Amtrak (p342), in the **Durham Station Transportation Center** (919-485-7433; www.godurhamtransit.org; 515 W Pettigrew St; 8am-midnight Mon-Sat, 7am-9pm Sun), which is also the main downtown interchange for Durham's local bus network.

Chapel Hill & Carrboro

While smaller and homier than Raleigh and Durham, its Triangle cohorts, Chapel Hill is a pretty college town that bubbles with life and energy. That's largely due to the 30,000 students – and Tar Heels basketball team – of its University of North Carolina, founded in 1789 as the nation's first state university. While commercialization has increasingly cost Chapel Hill's short downtown strip some of its former charm, its near-neighbor Carrboro remains as appealing as ever. Between the two, they boast some great restaurants and bars, and continue to nurture a dynamic indie rock scene.

Sights

University of North Carolina UNIVERSITY
(www.unc.edu) The imposing buildings of America's oldest public university center on a quad lined with flowering pear trees. Pick up a map either at the university's **visitor center** (919-962-1630; www.unc.edu/visitors; 250 E Franklin St; 9am-5pm Mon-Fri) or the **Chapel Hill Visitor Center** (919-245-4320; www.visitchapelhill.org; 501 W Franklin St; 8:30am-5pm Mon-Fri, 10am-3pm Sat).

Carolina Basketball Museum MUSEUM
(☎919-962-6000; www.goheels.com; 450 Skipper Bowles Dr, Ernie Williamson Athletics Center; ⊙10am-4pm Mon-Fri, 9am-1pm Sat, hours vary on game days; P) FREE Regardless of allegiances, any basketball fan will appreciate this small but well-done temple to Tar Heel hoops. The numbers say it all – six national championships, 20 final-four appearances, 31 Atlantic Coast Conference (ACC) regular-season championships and 47 NBA first-round draft picks. Memorabilia, trophies and video footage abound, including Michael Jordan's original signed national letter of intent and other recruiting documents.

Sleeping & Eating

Carolina Inn HOTEL $$$
(☎919-933-2001; www.carolinainn.com; 211 Pittsboro St; r from $250; P ❄ 📶) Even if you're not a Tar Heel, this lovely on-campus inn will win you over with its hospitality and historic touches. The charm starts in the snappy lobby and continues through hallways lined with photos of alumni and championship teams. Classic decor – inspired by Southern antiques – feels fresh in the 185 bright rooms.

Neal's Deli DELI $
(☎919-967-2185; www.nealsdeli.com; 100 E Main St, Carrboro; breakfast dishes $3.50-7, lunch dishes $6-9.50; ⊙8am-4pm Tue-Sun; 📶) Start your day by digging into a delicious buttermilk breakfast biscuit at this tiny deli in downtown Carrboro. The egg, cheese and bacon is some kind of good. For lunch, Neal's serves sandwiches and subs, including chicken salad, pastrami and a three-cheese pimento with a splash of bourbon.

★**Lantern** ASIAN $$$
(☎919-969-8846; www.lanternrestaurant.com; 423 W Franklin St; mains $25-32; ⊙5:30-10pm Mon-Sat) A strong contender for best dining spot in the entire Triangle, this modern, dinner-only, Asian-fusion spot is very much a farm-to-table affair, with all ingredients sourced from North Carolina. Thank chef Andrea Reusing, a James Beard Award winner, for triumphs such as crispy whole black bass with hot chili, fresh turmeric, dill, fried shallots and roasted peanuts.

Drinking & Entertainment

★**Glasshalfull** WINE BAR
(☎919-967-9784; www.glasshalfull.net; 106 S Greensboro St, Carrboro; ⊙11:30am-2:30pm & 5-9:30pm Mon-Fri, 5-10pm Sat) OK, so the name doesn't quite roll off the tongue, but everything else about this Carrboro wine bar – sorry, 'wine-centric restaurant' – oozes sleek sophistication. The food is exquisite, with pan-seared scallops or duck confit for dinner, but it's the majestic array of international wines in the adjoining shop, also sold at the bar, that really draws in the crowds.

Beer Study CRAFT BEER
(☎919-240-5423; www.facebook.com/BeerStudyNC; 106 N Graham St; ⊙noon-midnight; 📶) Half bar, half bottle shop, and a refreshingly grungy alternative to Chapel Hill's smattering of breweries, this place offers 18 taps of local and regional craft beer and more than 500 bottles. City ordinances impose plastic cups on dog-friendly establishments, but that's a small price to pay for pup. Pints cost $4, and you can buy burgers next door.

Dean Smith Center STADIUM
(☎919-962-2296; www.goheels.com; 300 Skipper Bowles Dr; ⊙box office 8am-4:30pm Mon-Fri) There are no tours of the Tar Heels' home, but basketball fans can visit the 2nd and 3rd floors during business hours. It's named for legendary coach Dean Smith, who retired with 879 career wins and two national titles.

Cat's Cradle LIVE MUSIC
(☎919-967-9053; www.catscradle.com; 300 E Main St, Carrboro) Everyone from Nirvana to Arcade Fire has played the Cradle, which has been hosting the cream of the indie-music world for four decades. Most shows are all-ages.

Getting There & Away

Raleigh-Durham International Airport (p345) is 18 miles east of Chapel Hill, a journey that costs around $25 in an off-peak Uber.

Charlotte

North Carolina's largest city, Charlotte sprawls 15 miles in every direction from its compact, high-rise core. Futuristic skyscrapers pepper downtown Charlotte, which is officially known as 'Uptown,' supposedly because it sits on a barely visible ridge, but really because the council decided that sounds cooler. Uptown holds several fine museums plus the high-octane NASCAR Hall of Fame, while more museums and historic sites are scattered further afield. Hotels and restaurants are also concentrated Uptown, though funkier neighborhoods within easy reach include Plaza Midwood, just east, with its boutiques and restaurants, and hip NoDa, along North Davidson St, where former textile mills hold breweries and cafes.

Named after the wife of George III – hence its nickname, the Queen City – Charlotte boomed when gold was discovered nearby, and later prospered from cotton and textiles. Having pioneered interstate banking in the 1980s, it's now the third-largest banking center in the US.

Sights & Activities

NASCAR Hall of Fame MUSEUM
(☎704-654-4400; www.nascarhall.com; 400 E Martin Luther King Jr Blvd; adult/child 4-12yr $25/18; ⏰10am-6pm) The race-car simulator ($5) at this rip-roaring Uptown museum hurtles you onto the track and into a 15-car race that feels surprisingly real. Elsewhere, learn the history of an American-born sport whose roots lie in moonshine running, check out six generations of race cars on 'Glory Road,' and test your pit-crew skills.

Levine Museum of the New South MUSEUM
(www.museumofthenewsouth.org; 200 E 7th St; adult/child 6-18yr $10/6; ⏰10am-5pm Mon-Fri, to 4pm Sat, noon-5pm Sun; P) Tracing the story of the 'New South' that emerged from the ashes of the Civil War, this committed museum explores the years of Reconstruction, Jim Crow and the Civil Rights movement. Haunting Dorothea Lange photos illuminate the Depression era on North Carolina's plantations, while changing exhibits highlight issues such as the 2016 shooting of Keith Lamont Scott by police.

Mint Museum Randolph MUSEUM
(☎704-337-2000; www.mintmuseum.org; 2730 Randolph Rd; adult/child 5-17yr $15/6, 5-9pm Wed free; ⏰11am-6pm Tue & Thu-Sat, to 9pm Wed, 1-5pm Sun; P) The US Mint opened its first-ever outpost in Uptown Charlotte in 1837, using gold mined from the mountains nearby. Transported 3 miles southeast a century later, the building now holds treasures ranging from ceramic masterpieces from Britain and North Carolina to stunning modern American decorative glasswork. Best of all are the wonderful pre-Columbian artifacts created by the Aztecs and Maya.

SOUTHERN FAVORITES

Fundamentally, in food as in so much else, North Carolina's heart lies in the South. Classic Southern favorites such as fried chicken, fried green tomatoes, shrimp and grits, biscuits (including extra-large 'catheads') and gravy, collard greens and okra, and mac and cheese, feature on menus across the state, and that's what the locals are eating at home.

★US National Whitewater Center ADVENTURE SPORTS
(☎704-391-3900; www.usnwc.org; 5000 Whitewater Center Pkwy; all-sport day pass adult/child under 10yr $59/49, individual activities $25, 3hr canopy tour $89; ⏰dawn-dusk) A beyond-awesome hybrid of nature center and water park, this 1300-acre facility is home to the largest artificial white-water river in the world. You can paddle its rapids – which serve as training grounds for Olympic canoeists and kayakers – as part of a guided trip, or enjoy a range of other adventure activities.

Sleeping & Eating

Duke Mansion INN $$
(☎704-714-4400; www.dukemansion.com; 400 Hermitage Rd; r $140-360; P❄📶) The century-old former home of the Duke family, including legendary heiress Doris Duke, is now a delightful B&B inn. Set in wooded gardens in the attractive Myers Park neighborhood, a couple of miles south of Uptown, it holds 20 light-filled rooms. Many still have their original tiled bathrooms, and some upstairs open onto their own screened sections of porch.

★Ivey's Hotel BOUTIQUE HOTEL $$$
(☎704-228-1111; www.theiveyshotel.com; 127 N Tryon St; r $299-499; P@📶🐾) The Ivey's 42 Parisian-inspired rooms – all on the 2nd floor of a 1924 department-store building – are steeped in history (the 400-year-old oak-wood floors were sourced from a French winery) but have modern flair (55in Sony TVs, Bose soundbars). The balcony executive corner suites, awash in natural-light-sucking windows and exposed brick, are divine.

Optimist Hall FOOD HALL $
(www.optimisthall.com; 1115 N Brevard St; dishes $5-15; ⏰7am-9pm Mon-Fri, 8am-10pm Sat,

8am-9pm Sun) This sprawling new food hall and retail space, in a former textile mill, is set to revitalize the neighborhood of Optimist Park. Look for beloved local vendors such as The Dumpling Lady (Asian dumplings) and Fonta Flora Brewery.

★**Soul Gastrolounge Tapas** SUSHI, SANDWICHES **$$**
(☎704-348-1848; www.soulgastrolounge.com; 1500 Central Ave; small plates $7-20, sushi $4-14, sandwiches $9-15; ⏲5pm-2am) This sultry but welcoming Plaza Midwood speakeasy serves a globally inspired selection of small plates. Choices are wide-ranging, from skewers and sushi rolls to Cuban and Vietnamese sandwiches, but the kitchen takes care to infuse each little gem with unique, satisfying flavors. The dancing tuna rolls, with jalapeños and two spicy mayos, are highly recommended if you like heat.

Asbury SOUTHERN US **$$$**
(☎704-342-1193; www.theasbury.com; 235 N Tryon St; sandwiches $8-14, mains $20-38; ⏲5-10pm Mon, from 11am Tue-Fri, from 9am Sat & Sun) Uptown's finest dining is to be had in the Dunhill Hotel's restaurant, opening straight onto Tryon St. Rooted in Carolinian classics, but given a contemporary makeover, chef Matthew Krenz' cuisine ranges from sorghum-glazed duck with walnut and garlic gremolata to simpler staples, served anytime, such as mac, cheese and country ham.

Drinking & Nightlife

NoDa Brewing Company MICROBREWERY
(☎704-900-6851; www.nodabrewing.com; 2921 N Tryon St; ⏲4-9pm Mon-Thu, 2-10pm Fri, noon-10pm Sat, noon-7pm Sun; 📶) Charlotte's best craft-beer playground is hidden behind NoDa's easy-to-overlook North End brewery. We went up on a Friday night and it looked abandoned. At the back, however, we found a packed playhouse of brews (pints $4 to $7) and boccie ball, plus cornhole, Frisbee golf, a fire pit, a massive patio and Charlotte's top food truck, Tin Kitchen.

ℹ Information

Visitor Info Center (☎800-231-4636; www.charlottesgotalot.com; 501 S College St, Charlotte Convention Center; ⏲9am-5pm Mon-Sat) Charlotte's main visitor center is in Uptown. As well as offering maps and a visitors' guide, it sells regional gifts and souvenirs.

ℹ Getting There & Around

Charlotte Douglas International Airport (CLT; ☎704-359-4013; www.cltairport.com; 5501 Josh Birmingham Pkwy), 7 miles west of Uptown, is an American Airlines hub that welcomes nonstop flights from continental Europe and the UK. Both the **Greyhound** (☎704-372-0456; www.greyhound.com; 601 W Trade St) and **Amtrak** (www.amtrak.com; 1914 N Tryon St) stations are handy to Uptown.

Charlotte's public transport system, known as CATS (Charlotte Area Transit System), encompasses city buses; a streetcar line known as the CityLYNX Gold Line; and the LYNX Blue Line light-rail line, extended in 2018 to reach the UNC campus, 9 miles northeast of Uptown. One-way fares range $2.20 to $4.40. The **Charlotte Transportation Center** (☎704-336-7433; www.ridetransit.org; 310 E Trade St), the system's Uptown interchange, can be accessed from Brevard St between 4th and Trade St.

Charlotte also operates a shared-bike network called Charlotte B-cycle (https://charlotte.bcycle.com).

North Carolina Mountains

Towering along the skyline of western North Carolina, the mighty Appalachian Mountains hold several distinct subranges, among which the Great Smoky, Blue Ridge, Pisgah and Black Mountain ranges are especially dramatic. Carpeted in blue-green hemlock, pine and oak trees – logged a century ago but now preserved and protected – these cool hills are home to cougars, deer, black bears, wild turkeys and great horned owls. For adventurous travelers, the potential for hiking, camping, climbing and rafting expeditions is all but endless, while yet another photo opportunity lies around every bend.

The Cherokee who hunted on these forested slopes were later joined by 18th-century Scots-Irish immigrants looking for a better life. Lofty towns such as Blowing Rock enticed the sickly, lured by the fresh mountain air. Today, scenic drives, leafy trails and roaring rivers draw visitors from around the world.

ℹ Getting There & Around

Asheville Regional Airport (p353) is the gateway to the North Carolina mountains, with nonstop flights to/from Atlanta, Charlotte, Chicago and Newark, among others. Asheville also has a Greyhound (p354) station.

DON'T MISS

SCENIC DRIVE: BLUE RIDGE PARKWAY

You won't find a single stoplight or billboard along the entire Blue Ridge Pkwy, which traverses the southern Appalachians from Virginia's Shenandoah National Park at Mile 0 to North Carolina's Great Smoky Mountains National Park at Mile 469.

Commissioned by President Franklin D Roosevelt as a Great Depression–era public-works project, it's one of America's classic drives. North Carolina's piece of the parkway sweeps and swoops for 262 sinuous miles of sublime mountain vistas. The fall colors, at their finest in October, are out of this world.

The **National Park Service** (☎828-348-3400; www.nps.gov/blri; Mile 384; ⏰9am-5pm) runs campgrounds and visitor centers. Note that restrooms and gas stations are few and far between, and the speed limit never rises above 45mph. For more details about stops, visit www.blueridgeparkway.org.

Parkway highlights and campgrounds include the following, from the Virginia border south:

Cumberland Knob (Mile 217.5) NPS visitor center; easy walk to the knob.

Doughton Park (Mile 241.1) Trails and camping.

Blowing Rock (Mile 291.8) Small town named for a craggy, commercialized cliff that offers great views, occasional updrafts and a Native American love story.

Moses H Cone Memorial Park (Mile 294.1) A lovely old estate with carriage trails and a craft shop.

Julian Price Memorial Park (Mile 296.9) Camping.

Grandfather Mountain (Mile 305.1) Hugely popular for its mile-high pedestrian 'swinging bridge.' Also has a nature center and a small wildlife reserve.

Linville Falls (Mile 316.4) Short hiking trails to stunning falls; campsites.

Little Switzerland (Mile 334) Old-style mountain resort.

Mt Mitchell State Park (Mile 355.5) Highest peak east of the Mississippi (6684ft); hiking and camping.

Craggy Gardens (Mile 364) Hiking trails explode with rhododendron blossoms in summer.

Folk Art Center (Mile 382) High-end Appalachian crafts for sale.

Blue Ridge Parkway Visitor Center (Mile 384) Inspiring film, interactive map, trail information.

Mt Pisgah (Mile 408.8) Hiking, camping, restaurant, inn.

Graveyard Fields (Mile 418) Short hiking trails to waterfalls.

High Country

The northwestern corner of North Carolina, flanking the Blue Ridge Pkwy as it sets off across the state from Virginia, is known as the High Country. Of the main towns, Boone is a lively college community that's home to Appalachian State University (ASU), while Blowing Rock and Banner Elk are quaint tourist centers near the winter ski areas.

BLOWING ROCK

A stately and idyllic mountain village, tiny Blowing Rock beckons from its perch at 4000ft above sea level, the only full-service town directly on the Blue Ridge Pkwy. It's easy to be seduced by its postcard-perfect Main St, lined with antique shops, kitschy boutiques, potters, silversmiths, sweet shops, lively taverns and excellent restaurants. There are even a couple of bucolic, duck-filled lakes to drive home the storybook nature of it all. The only thing that spoils the illusion is the sheer difficulty of finding a place to park in high season.

Sights & Activities

Grandfather Mountain MOUNTAIN
(☎800-468-7325; www.grandfather.com; 2050 Blowing Rock Hwy, Linville; adult/child 4-12yr $22/9; ⏰8am-7pm Jun-Aug, 9am-6pm Apr, May, Sep & Oct, 9am-5pm Nov-Mar; P ♿) The highest of the

Blue Ridge Mountains, Grandfather Mountain looms north of the parkway 20 miles southwest of Blowing Rock. As a visitor destination, it's famous for the Mile High Swinging Bridge, the centerpiece of a private attraction that also includes hiking trails plus a small museum and wildlife reserve. Don't let a fear of heights scare you away; though the bridge is a mile above sea level, it spans a less fearsome chasm that's just 80ft deep.

River & Earth Adventures ADVENTURE
(828-355-9797; www.raftcavehike.com; 6201 Castle Ford Rd, Todd; half-/full-day rafting $60/100;) Eco-conscious operators offering everything from family-friendly caving trips to rafting class V rapids at Watauga Gorge – plus organic lunches! Canoe ($65), kayak ($35 to $65) and tube ($20) rentals are offered too.

Sleeping & Eating

Cliff Dwellers Inn MOTEL $
(828-414-9596; www.cliffdwellers.com; 116 Lakeview Terrace; r/apt from $124/144;) From its perch above town, this aptly named motel entices guests with good service, reasonable prices, stylish rooms and balconies with sweeping vistas.

Green Park Inn HISTORIC HOTEL $$
(828-414-9230; www.greenparkinn.com; 9239 Valley Blvd; r $94-299; P) This grand white clapboard hotel, 1 mile south of downtown, opened its doors in 1891, and was renovated in 2010 to hold 88 plush rooms and a grill restaurant. The eastern continental divide runs straight through the bar, and Margaret Mitchell stayed here while writing *Gone with the Wind*.

★**Bistro Roca** AMERICAN $$
(828-295-4008; www.bistroroca.com; 143 Wonderland Trail; lunch mains $9-16, dinner mains $10-32; 11am-3pm & 5-10pm Wed-Mon;) This cozy, lodge-like bistro, in a Prohibition-era building just off Main St, serves upscale New American cuisine – lobster or pork-belly mac and cheese, kicked-up habanero burgers, mountain-trout *banh mi* sandwiches – with an emphasis on local everything. Check out the walls of the atmospheric Antlers Bar, North Carolina's longest continually operating bar, plastered with fantastic B&W pet photos.

Getting There & Away

Blowing Rock is 8 miles south of Boone via Hwy 321, or more like 25 miles if you detour along the Blue Ridge Pkwy. The nearest commercial airport is Charlotte Douglas International Airport (p348), 87 miles southeast.

BOONE

Boone is a fun and lively mountain town where the predominantly youthful inhabitants – many of them students at bustling Appalachian State University – share a hankering for the outdoors. Renowned for its bluegrass musicians and Appalachian storytellers, the town is named after pioneer and explorer Daniel Boone, who often camped in the area. Downtown Boone features a fine assortment of low-rise brick-broad, Colonial Revival, art-deco and streamline-modern buildings. Those that line King St in particular now tend to house charming boutiques, cafes, and crafts galleries.

Every summer since 1952, local history has been presented in a dramatization called *Horn in the West*, performed in an outdoor amphitheater above town.

Accommodations in Boone traditionally consisted of standard chain hotels, but the **Horton** (828-832-8060; www.thehorton.com; 611 W King St; r from $189;), downtown's first boutique hotel, opened in 2018. You can also find the occasional historic B&B, rental farmhouse or cozy log cabin around town and in the surrounding countryside.

Folk Art Center CULTURAL CENTER
(828-298-7928; www.southernhighlandguild.org; Mile 382, Blue Ridge Pkwy; 9am-6pm Apr-Dec, to 5pm Jan-Mar; P) FREE Part gallery, part store, and wholly dedicated to Southern craftsmanship, the superb Folk Art Center stands directly off the Blue Ridge Pkwy, 6 miles east of downtown Asheville. Handcrafted Appalachian chairs hanging above its lobby make an impressive appetizer for the Southern Highland Craft Guild's permanent collection, a treasury of pottery, baskets, quilts and woodcarvings that's displayed on the 2nd floor.

Lovill House Inn B&B $$
(828-264-4204; www.lovillhouseinn.com; 404 Old Bristol Rd; r from $179;) Boone's finest B&B is a splendid 19th-century farmhouse, a mile west of downtown and surrounded by woods. With its snug rooms, white clapboard walls, and wraparound porch decked out with rocking chairs, it's all wonderfully restful; the breakfast is worth getting up for, though.

Wild Craft Eatery LATIN AMERICAN $
(☎828-262-5000; www.facebook.com/wildcrafteatery; 506 W King St; mains lunch $7-12, dinner $10-15; ⏰11am-10pm Wed-Mon; 🌿) Colorful, quirky downtown cafe, with an outdoor deck on King St, and an emphasis on local ingredients. There's a definite Latin flavor to the menu, with tacos and tamales aplenty, but it also offers Thai noodles and shepherd's pie. Not everything's vegetarian, but most of the standout dishes are, including the Cuzco Cakes, made with smoked quinoa, Gouda and yams.

Getting There & Away

The closest commercial airport to Boone is Charlotte Douglas International Airport (p348), 94 miles southeast.

Asheville

The undisputed 'capital' of the North Carolina mountains, Asheville is both a major tourist destination and one of the coolest small cities in the South. Cradled in a sweeping curve of the Blue Ridge Pkwy, it offers easy access to outdoor adventures of all kinds, while downtown's historic art-deco buildings hold stylish New Southern restaurants, decadent chocolate shops, and the homegrown microbreweries that explain the nickname 'Beer City.'

Despite rapid gentrification, Asheville remains recognizably an overgrown mountain town that holds tight to its traditional roots. It's also a rare liberal enclave in the conservative countryside, home to a sizable population of artists and hard-core hippies. Alternative Asheville life is largely lived in neighborhoods such as the waterfront River Arts District and, across the French Broad River, West Asheville. Remarkably enough, the French Broad River is the world's third-oldest river, its course laid before life on Earth even began.

Sights & Activities

Biltmore Estate HOUSE
(☎800-411-3812; www.biltmore.com; 1 Approach Rd; adult/child 10-16yr $75/37.50; ⏰house 9am-4:30pm, with seasonal variations; P) The largest privately owned home in the US, Biltmore House was completed in 1895 for shipping and railroad heir George Washington Vanderbilt II, and modeled after three châteaux that he'd seen in France's Loire Valley. It's extraordinarily expensive to visit, but there's a lot to see; allow several hours to explore the entire 8000-acre estate. Self-guided tours of the house itself take in 39 points of interest, including our favorite, the two-lane bowling alley.

Chimney Rock Park PARK
(☎828-625-9611; www.chimneyrockpark.com; Hwy 74A; adult/child 5-15yr $17/8; ⏰8:30am-7pm mid-Mar–Oct, 8:30am-6pm Nov & Dec, 10am-6pm Jan-mid-Mar; P) The stupendous 315ft monolith known as Chimney Rock towers above the slender, forested valley of the Rocky Broad River, a gorgeous 28-mile drive southeast of Asheville. Protruding in naked splendor from soaring granite walls, its flat top bears the fluttering American flag. Climb there via the 499 steps of the Outcropping Trail, or simply ride the elevator deep inside the rock.

BREW-ed BREWERY
(☎828-278-9255; www.brew-ed.com; adults $37-50, nondrinkers $20) Beer-focused historical walking tours, led by Cicerone-certified beer geeks and sampling at two or three different downtown breweries, on Thursdays (5:30pm), Fridays (2pm), Saturdays (11:30am and 2pm) and Sundays (1pm).

Smoky Mountain Adventure Center OUTDOORS
(☎828-505-4446; www.smacasheville.com; 173 Amboy Rd; ⏰8am-8pm Mon, to 10pm Tue-Sat, 10am-8pm Sun) One-stop adventure shopping, across the French Broad River 3 miles southwest of downtown. On-site there's an indoor climbing wall, as well as yoga and tai chi classes. They can also arrange bikes for the Blue Ridge Pkwy, inner-tubes and paddleboards for the river, plus guided rock climbing, backpacking, day hiking, ice climbing and mountaineering trips.

Sleeping

★ **Sweet Peas Hostel** HOSTEL $
(☎828-285-8488; www.sweetpeashostel.com; 23 Rankin Ave; dm/pod $32/40, r with/without bath $105/75; ❄@📶) This spick-and-span, well-run, contemporary hostel occupies an unbeatable downtown location. The loft-like open-plan space, with its exposed brick walls, steel bunks and blond-wood sleeping 'pods', can get noisy, but at least there's a 10% discount at the Lexington Ave Brewery downstairs. They also warn you if an event coincides with your planned dates.

Campfire Lodgings CAMPGROUND $$
(☎828-658-8012; www.campfirelodgings.com; 116 Appalachian Village Rd; tent sites $35-40, RV sites $50-70, yurts $115-135, cabins $160; P ❄) All yurts should have flat-screen TVs, don't you think? Sleep like the world's most stylish Mongolian nomad in a furnished multiroom tent, half a mile up a wooded hillside on an unpaved but passable road, 6 miles north of town. Cabins and tent sites are also available. RV sites, higher up, enjoy stunning valley views and the only wi-fi access.

Omni Grove Park Inn HISTORIC HOTEL $$$
(☎828-252-2711; www.omnihotels.com; 290 Macon Ave; r $189-434; P ❄ @) Commanding sweeping Blue Ridge views, this titanic Arts and Crafts–style stone lodge harks back to a bygone era of mountain glamor. Each of the 36ft-wide lobby fireplaces can hold a standing grown man, and has its own elevator to the chimney. Beyond the spectacular public spaces, though, the guest rooms can seem small by modern standards.

Aloft Asheville Downtown HOTEL $$$
(☎828-232-2838; www.aloftashevilledowntown.com; 51 Biltmore Ave; r from $289; P ❄ @) With a giant chalkboard in the lobby, groovy young staff and an outdoor clothing store on the 1st floor, this place looks like the inner circle of hipster. The only thing missing is a wool-cap-wearing bearded guy drinking a hoppy microbrew – oh wait, over there. We jest. Once settled, you'll find the staff knowledgeable and the rooms colorful and spacious.

★**Bunn House** BOUTIQUE HOTEL $$$
(☎828-333-8700; www.bunnhouse.com; 15 Clayton St; d $249-424; P ❄) The six rooms and suites in this meticulously restored 1905 home, in a residential neighborhood half a mile north of downtown, are awash with exposed brick and dark hardwoods. The small rooftop terrace boasts Blue Ridge vistas, while the heated bathroom floors and subway-tiled steam showers are glorious on chilly mountain mornings.

Eating

Asheville is a true foodie haven. Downtown and South Slope are bursting with enticing options, including simple (but oh-so-hip!) Southern-fried cafes, ethnic diners and elaborate Modern American and Appalachian kitchens. Farm-to-table is the rule; local, organic and sustainable are mantras. With more alternatives down in the River Arts District and over in West Asheville, you won't starve in these mountains.

★**12 Bones** BARBECUE $
(☎828-253-4499; www.12bones.com; 5 Foundy St; dishes $5.50-22.50; ⏲11am-4pm Mon-Fri) How good is the barbecue at 12 Bones? Good enough to lure the vacationing Barack and Michelle Obama back to the River Arts District, a few years back. Expect a long wait, though, before you get to enjoy the slow-cooked, smoky and tender meats, or succulent sides from jalapeño-cheese grits to smoked potato salad.

Chai Pani INDIAN $
(☎828-254-4003; www.chaipaniasheville.com; 22 Battery Park Ave; snacks $8-10, meals $10-13; ⏲11:30am-3:30pm & 5:30-9:30pm;) Literally 'tea and water,' *chai pani* refers more generally to inexpensive snacks. Hence the ever-changing array of irresistible street food at this popular, no-reservations downtown restaurant. Fill up on crunchy *bhel puri* (chickpea noodles and puffed rice) or live it larger with a lamb burger, fish roll or chicken or vegetarian *thali* (a full meal on a metal tray).

White Duck Taco Shop MEXICAN $
(☎828-232-9191; www.whiteducktacoshop.com; 12 Biltmore Ave; tacos $3.45-5.25; ⏲11:30am-9pm) The chalkboard menu at this downtown taco shop will give you fits. Every single one of these hefty soft tacos sounds like a must-have flavor bomb: spicy buffalo chicken with blue-cheese sauce, crispy pork belly, mole-roasted duck – even shrimp and grits! The margaritas are mighty fine too.

★**Cúrate** TAPAS $$
(☎828-239-2946; www.curatetapasbar.com; 13 Biltmore Ave; small plates $6-18; ⏲11:30am-10:30pm Tue-Fri, 10am-11pm Sat, 10am-10:30pm Sun) Owned by hip Ashevillian chef Katie Button and her Catalan husband Félix, this convivial downtown hangout celebrates the simple charms and sensual flavors of Spanish tapas, while adding an occasional Southern twist. Standout dishes run long and wide: *pan con tomate* (grilled bread with tomato), lightly fried eggplant drizzled with honey and rosemary, and a knockout squid-ink 'paella' with vermicelli.

Smoky Park Supper Club AMERICAN $$
(☎828-350-0315; www.smokypark.com; 350 Riverside Dr; mains $13-36; ⏲5-9pm Tue-Thu, 4-10pm

BEER CITY USA

If ever a city was transformed by the craft-beer movement, it's Asheville. A sleepy mountain city when its first brewery, Highland Brewing, opened in 1994, Asheville has become a true destination city for booze-bent hopheads. It now holds almost 30 breweries, catering to a population of around 90,000 locals; were it not for the half-million tourists who join them each year, that would be a lot of beer per person!

Inevitably, big-name national breweries have been flocking to Asheville too. Both New Belgium and Sierra Nevada, respectively from California and Colorado, have opened major brewing and taproom facilities here. Strolling from brewery to beerhouse in the pub-packed South Slope district – which, yes, slopes south from downtown – it's easy to see why Asheville has been nicknamed Beer City.

If you're ready to tackle the taps in Asheville, be sure to try a few of our favorite taprooms:

Burial (www.burialbeer.com; 40 Collier Ave; ⏲2-10pm Mon-Thu, from noon Fri-Sun; 📶) Never mind its menacing logo; this friendly joint whips up some of Asheville's finest and most experimental Belgian-leaning styles (farmhouse saisons, strong dubbels and tripels).

Funkatorium (☎828-552-3203; www.wickedweedbrewing.com/locations/funkatorium; 147 Coxe Ave; ⏲2-10pm Mon-Thu, noon-midnight Fri & Sat, 11am-10pm Sun; 📶) Wicked Weed's all-sour taproom is a temple of tart and funk.

Wedge Brewing (☎828-505-2792; www.wedgebrewing.com; 37 Paynes Way; ⏲noon-10pm; 📶) Our favorite microbrewery ambience – a festive, come-one, come-all outdoor space, rife with dogs, kids on tricycles, swooning couples and outdoorsy types.

Wicked Weed (☎828-575-9599; www.wickedweedbrewing.com; 91 Biltmore Ave; ⏲11:30am-11pm Mon-Thu, to 1am Fri & Sat, noon-11pm Sun; 📶) A former gas station turned craft-brew wonderland – with 58 taps!

Fri & Sat, 10:30am-9pm Sun; 📶) An anchor of cool in the River Arts District, the largest container-constructed restaurant in the USA is more than the sum of its parts – 19 shipping containers to be exact. Choose between such wood-fired delights as garlic- and lemon-roasted half chicken, cast-iron-seared Carolina fish, or, for vegetarians, roasted local apples stuffed with kale, walnuts and smoked cheddar.

Drinking & Entertainment

★Battery Park Book Exchange & Champagne Bar WINE BAR
(☎828-252-0020; www.batteryparkbookexchange.com; 1 Page Ave; ⏲11am-9pm Mon-Thu, to 10pm Fri & Sat, noon-7pm Sun) A charming champagne bar, sprawling through several opulent vintage-furnished rooms of a glorious old downtown shopping arcade, with every nook and cranny lined with shelves of neatly cataloged secondhand books covering every imaginable topic. Seriously, who could resist that as a combination? Other wines are also available, along with coffee, cakes, cheese and charcuterie.

Orange Peel LIVE MUSIC
(☎828-398-1837; www.theorangepeel.net; 101 Biltmore Ave; tickets $10-35; ⏲shows from 8pm) Asheville's premier live-music venue, downtown's Orange Peel Social Aid & Pleasure Club has been a showcase for big-name indie and punk bands since 2002. A warehouse-sized place, it seats – well, stands – a thousand-strong crowd.

Information

Asheville's main **visitor center** (☎828-258-6129; www.exploreasheville.com; 36 Montford Ave; ⏲8:30am-5:30pm Mon-Fri, 9am-5pm Sat & Sun), alongside I-240 exit 4C, sells Biltmore Estate admission tickets at a $10 discount. Downtown holds a satellite **visitor pavilion** (☎828-258-6129; www.exploreasheville.com; 80 Court Pl; ⏲9am-5pm), with restrooms, beside Pack Sq Park.

Getting There & Around

Asheville Regional Airport (AVL; ☎828-684-2226; www.flyavl.com; 61 Terminal Dr, Fletcher), 16 miles south of Asheville, is served by a handful of nonstop flights, with destinations including Atlanta, Charlotte, Chicago and

New York. **Greyhound** (☎828-253-8451; 2 Tunnel Rd) is 1 mile northeast of downtown.

Although there's very little free parking downtown, public garages are free for the first hour and only cost $1 per hour thereafter. The handy Passport app (https://passportinc.com) facilitates paying for Asheville's parking meters and paid lots.

The 18 local bus routes run by Asheville Transit (ART) typically operate between 5:30am and 10:30pm Monday through Saturday, and shorter hours Sunday. Tickets cost $1, and there are free bike racks. Route S3 connects the **downtown ART station** (☎828-253-5691; www.ashevilletransit.com; 49 Coxe Ave; ⏲6am-9:30pm Mon-Fri, from 7am Sat, 8:30am-5.30pm Sun) with Asheville Regional Airport 10 times daily.

Great Smoky Mountains National Park

Get back to nature among mist-shrouded peaks, shimmering waterfalls and lush forests in the great American wilderness.

Sights

★Great Smoky Mountains National Park NATIONAL PARK
(www.nps.gov/grsm) FREE The 816-sq-mile Great Smoky Mountains National Park is the country's most visited park and, while the main arteries and attractions can get crowded, it's easy to leave the masses behind. There are scores of memorable hikes along 850 miles of trails, with thundering waterfalls and cliff-top views among the highlights. Unlike most national parks, Great Smoky charges no admission fee.

Stop by a visitor center to pick up a park map and the free *Smokies Guide*. The remains of the 19th-century settlement at **Cades Cove** (www.nps.gov/grsm/planyourvisit/cadescove.htm; Cades Cove Loop Rd; P) are one of the park's most popular sights, as evidenced by the teeth-grinding summer traffic jams on the 11-mile loop road (it closes to vehicles on Wednesday and Saturday morning from late May through late September, making it perfect for a bike ride). **Mt LeConte** offers terrific hiking, as well as the park's only non-camping accommodations, LeConte Lodge. Although the only way to get to the lodge's rustic, electricity-free cabins is via five uphill hiking trails varying in length from 5.5 miles (Alum Cave Bluffs trail, off Newfound Gap Rd) to 8.9 miles (Trillium Gap Trail), it's so popular you need to reserve up to a year in advance.

You can drive right up to the dizzying heights of **Clingmans Dome** (off Clingmans Dome Rd), the third-highest mountain east of the Mississippi, with its futuristic observation tower.

Other popular hikes include trails to **Laurel Falls** (off Fighting Creek Gap Rd), **Rainbow Falls** (off Cherokee Orchard Rd) and **Gregorys Bald**. For something less trafficked, check out the Lakeshore Trail in the southwest part of the park, Mt Sterling in the east, or **Baskins Creek** near Gatlinburg. There are also ample opportunities for multiday backpacking adventures, with dozens of backcountry campsites (reserve online through the park website). Some 71 miles of the Appalachian Trail also traverse the park.

Activities

Whether you have an irrepressible urge to climb a mountain or just want to get some fresh air, hiking in Great Smoky Mountains National Park is the single best way to experience the sublime beauty of this area. Even if you're only here for a short visit, be sure to include at least one hike in your itinerary. Trails range from flat, easy and short paths to longer, more strenuous endeavors. Many are excellent for families and there's even one wheelchair-accessible trail. No matter what your physical ability or endurance level, there's a hike out there for you.

Foothills Parkway SCENIC DRIVE
This scenic drive runs along the western edge of the park between Chilhowee and – thanks to the completion of the 'missing link' in November 2018 – Wears Valley. There are numerous spots to pull off and admire the view, as well as a lookout tower (and weather monitoring station) you can climb at the aptly named **Look Rock** (Foothills Pkwy).

Sleeping & Eating

You'll have to book on October 1 to reserve a spot for the following season in the **LeConte Lodge** (☎865-429-5704; www.lecontelodge.com; cabins incl breakfast & dinner adult/ child 4-12yr $152/88; ⏲mid-Mar–mid-Nov); the hilltop inn, reachable only by a long uphill hike, books solid within a few days. Outside the park, Gatlinburg has the most sleeping options of any gateway town.

The National Park Service maintains developed campgrounds at nine locations in the park. Each campground has restrooms with cold running water and flush toilets, but there are no showers or electrical or water hookups in the park. Each individual campsite has a fire grate and picnic table. Many sites can be reserved in advance, and several campgrounds (Cataloochee, Abrams Creek, Big Creek and Balsam Mountain) require advance reservations. Reserve through www.recreation.gov.

Campgrounds book up in the busy summer season, so plan ahead. Cades Cove and Smokemont campgrounds are open year-round; others are open March to October.

Backcountry camping is an excellent option, which is only chargeable up to five nights ($4 per night; after that, it's free). A permit is required. You can make reservations online at http://smokiespermits.nps.gov, and get permits at the ranger stations or visitor centers.

Nuts and berries notwithstanding, there's nothing to eat in Great Smoky Mountains National Park, save for items from vending machines at Sugarlands Visitor Center and the meager offerings sold at the **Cades Cove Campground store** (☎865-448-9034; www.cadescovetrading.com; 10035 Campground Dr; ⏰9am-9pm late May-Oct, to 5pm Mar-May, Nov & late Dec). If you make the hike up to LeConte Lodge, you can purchase cookies, drinks and sack lunches (which means a bagel with cream cheese, beef summer sausage, trail mix and fruit leather). Dinner is included for those staying overnight.

Luckily, there are lots of restaurant options in the surrounding towns.

ℹ Tourist Information

Cades Cove Visitor Center (☎865-436-7318; www.nps.gov/grsm; Cades Cove Loop Rd; ⏰9am-7pm Apr-Aug, closes earlier Sep-Mar) Halfway up Cades Cove Loop Rd, 24 miles off Hwy 441 from the Gatlinburg entrance.

Clingmans Dome Visitor Station (☎865-436-1200; Clingmans Dome Rd; ⏰10am-6pm Apr-Oct, 9:30am-5pm Nov) Small, very busy center at the start of the paved path up to the Clingmans Dome lookout.

Oconaluftee Visitor Center (☎828-497-1904; www.nps.gov/grsm; 1194 Newfound Gap Rd, North Cherokee; ⏰8am-7pm Jun-Aug, to 6pm Apr, May, Sep & Oct, to 5pm Mar & Nov, to 4:30pm Dec-Feb; 🛜) At the park's southern entrance near Cherokee.

Sugarlands Visitor Center (☎865-436-1291; www.nps.gov/grsm; 107 Park Headquarters Rd; ⏰8am-7:30pm Jun-Aug, hours vary Sep-May; 🛜) At the park's northern entrance near Gatlinburg.

ℹ Getting There & Away

The closest airports to the national park are McGhee Tyson Airport (p385) near Knoxville (40 miles northwest of Sugarlands Visitor Center) and Asheville Regional Airport (p353), 58 miles east of the Oconaluftee Visitor Center. Further afield you'll find Chattanooga Metropolitan Airport (p384), 140 miles southwest of the park, Charlotte Douglas International Airport (p348), 170 miles east, and Hartsfield-Jackson International Airport (p404) in Atlanta, 175 miles south of the park.

After you fly in, you'll need a car as there's no public transportation to the park. There's a wide variety of car-rental outfits at each of the airports.

SOUTH CAROLINA

Moss-draped oaks. Stately mansions. Wide beaches. Rolling mountains. And an ornery streak as old as the state itself. Ah yes, South Carolina, where the accents are thicker and the traditions more dear. From its Revolutionary War patriots to its 1860s secessionist government to its outspoken legislators, the Palmetto State has never shied away from a fight.

Most travelers stick to the coast, with its splendid antebellum cities and palm-tree-studded beaches. But the interior has a wealth of sleepy old towns, wild and undeveloped state parks and spooky black-water swamps. Along the sea islands you hear the sweet songs of the Gullah, a culture and language created by former slaves who held on to many West African traditions through the ravages of time.

From well-bred, gardenia-scented Charleston to up-and-coming Greenville to bright, tacky Myrtle Beach, South Carolina is always a fascinating destination.

History

South Carolina is one fiery state, as its contentious and bloody history rarely fails to demonstrate. Over the last 350 years, its settlers have squared off against natural disasters, Native American residents, the British, and – when the state became the first to secede from the Union in 1860 – countrymen to the north. Race relations may have improved since the days of slavery, but poverty, inequality and discrimination have proven difficult to eradicate. Occasionally these issues still flare up, with devastating consequences.

Information

South Carolina Department of Parks, Recreation & Tourism (803-734-0124; www.discoversouthcarolina.com) Can mail you the state's official vacation guide on request. The state's nine highway welcome centers offer free wi-fi (ask inside for the passwords).

Charleston

The zenith of old-world charm, Charleston whisks you into the nation's tumultuous past and nourishes your mind, heart and stomach in roughly equal measure.

History

In strolling the tidy, peaceful streets of Charleston today, it's sometimes difficult to imagine the terrors that came before: the earthquakes, the fires, the hurricanes, slavery, the Revolutionary War and the Civil War, just to name a few. The city has managed to survive it all, and to rebuild stronger each time. Today Charleston is a living museum, and its battle scars teach important lessons. Perhaps that is exactly the reason so many people feel compelled to visit.

Sights

The quarter south of Beaufain and Hasell Sts has the bulk of the antebellum mansions, shops, bars and cafes. At the southernmost tip of the peninsula are the antebellum mansions of the Battery. A loose path, the **Gateway Walk**, winds through several church grounds and graveyards between St John's Lutheran Church and **St Philip's Church** (www.stphilipschurchsc.org; 146 Church St).

Historic District

Old Exchange & Provost Dungeon HISTORIC BUILDING

(843-727-2165; www.oldexchange.org; 122 E Bay St; adult/child 7-12yr $10/5; 9am-5pm;) Kids love the creepy dungeon, used as a prison for American patriots held by the British during the Revolutionary War. The cramped space sits beneath a stately Georgian Palladian customs house completed in 1771. Costumed guides lead the dungeon tours. Exhibits about the city are displayed on the upper floors.

★Old Slave Mart Museum MUSEUM

(843-958-6467; www.oldslavemart.org; 6 Chalmers St; adult/child 5-17yr $8/5; 9am-5pm Mon-Sat) Formerly called Ryan's Mart, this building once housed an open-air market that auctioned African American men, women and children in the mid-1800s, the largest of 40 or so similar auction houses. South Carolina's shameful past is unraveled in text-heavy exhibits illuminating the slave experience; the few artifacts, such as leg shackles, are especially chilling.

Gibbes Museum of Art GALLERY

(843-722-2706; www.gibbesmuseum.org; 135 Meeting St; adult/child $12/6; 10am-5pm Tue & Thu-Sat, to 8pm Wed, 1-5pm Sun) Houses a decent collection of American and Southern works. The contemporary collection includes works by local artists, with Lowcountry life as a highlight. A 2016 renovation added a new museum store and cafe as well as 30% more gallery space.

Battery & White Point Garden GARDENS

(cnr East Battery & Murray Blvd; 9am-sunset) The Battery is the southern tip of the Charleston Peninsula, buffered by a seawall. Stroll past cannons and statues of military heroes in the gardens, then walk the promenade and look for Fort Sumter.

Rainbow Row AREA

(83 E Bay St) With its 13 candy-colored houses, this stretch of Georgian row houses is one of the most photographed areas in Charleston. The structures date back to 1730, when they served as merchant stores on the wharf, a sketchy part of town at the time. Starting in the 1920s the buildings were restored and painted over in pastels. People dug it, and soon much of the rest of Charleston was getting a similar makeover.

Historic Homes

★Aiken-Rhett House HISTORIC BUILDING

(843-723-1159; www.historiccharleston.org; 48 Elizabeth St; adult/child 6-16yr $12/5; 10am-5pm, last tour 4:15pm) The only surviving urban town-house complex, this 1820 abode gives a fascinating glimpse into antebellum life on a 45-minute self-guided audio tour. The role of slaves is emphasized, and visitors wander into their dorm-style quarters behind the house before moving on to the lifestyle of the rich and famous.

The Historic Charleston Foundation manages the property 'preserved as found,' conserving but not restoring it. There have been few alterations and you get it as is, peeling Parisian wallpaper and all.

Joseph Manigault House HISTORIC BUILDING
(843-722-2996; www.charlestonmuseum.org; 350 Meeting St; adult/child 13-17yr/child 3-12yr $12/10/5; 10am-5pm Mon-Sat, noon-5pm Sun, last tour 4:30pm) This three-story Federal-style house from 1803 was once the showpiece of a French Huguenot rice planter. There's a tiny neoclassical gate temple in the garden and the house is full of 19th-century furnishings from the collection of the Charleston Museum, which runs the site.

Nathaniel Russell House HISTORIC BUILDING
(843-724-8481; www.historiccharleston.org; 51 Meeting St; adult/child 6-16yr $12/5; 10am-5pm, last tour 4pm) A spectacular, self-supporting spiral staircase is the highlight at this 1808 Federal-style house, built by a Rhode Islander, known in Charleston as 'King of the Yankees.' A meticulous ongoing restoration honors the home to the finest details, such as the 1000 sheets of 22-karat gold leaf in the withdrawing room. Twenty layers of wall paint were peeled back to uncover the original colors, and handmade, fitted, contoured rugs were imported from the UK, as originally done by the Russells.

Marion Square

Marion Sq (843-724-7327; www.nps.gov/nr/travel/charleston/mar.htm; 329 Meeting St; 24hr) was formerly home to the state weapons arsenal. This 10-acre park is Charleston's living room, with various monuments and an excellent **farmers market** (www.charlestonfarmersmarket.com; 8am-2pm Sat mid-Apr–Nov) on Saturdays.

Charleston Museum MUSEUM
(843-722-2996; www.charlestonmuseum.org; 360 Meeting St; adult/child 3-17yr/child 3-12yr $12/10/5; 9am-5pm Mon-Sat, from noon Sun) Founded in 1773, this is the country's oldest museum. It's helpful and informative if you're looking for historical background before strolling through the Historic District. Exhibits spotlight various periods of Charleston's long and storied history.

Aquarium Wharf

Aquarium Wharf surrounds pretty Liberty Sq and is a great place to stroll and watch the tugboats guiding ships into the fourth-largest container port in the USA. The wharf is home to the **South Carolina Aquarium** (843-577-3474; www.scaquarium.org; 100 Aquarium Wharf; adult/child $30/23; 9am-5pm;) and is one of two embarkation points for tours to Fort Sumter; the other is at Patriot's Point.

★Fort Sumter National Monument HISTORIC SITE
(843-883-3123; www.nps.gov/fosu) The first shots of the Civil War rang out at Fort Sumter, on a pentagon-shaped island in the harbor. A Confederate stronghold, this fort was shelled to bits by Union forces from 1863 to 1865. A few original guns and fortifications give a feel for the momentous history here.

The only way to get here is by **boat tour** (boat tour 843-722-2628, park 843-883-3123; www.fortsumtertours.com; 340 Concord St; adult/child 4-11yr $23/15), which departs from 340 Concord St and from Patriot's Point in Mt Pleasant at varying times depending on the season (check the website). The monument also includes **Fort Moultrie** (843-883-3123; www.nps.gov/fosu; 1214 Middle St, Sullivan's Island; adult/child $7/free; 9am-5pm).

Ashley River Plantations

Three significant plantations line the Ashley River about a 20-minute drive from downtown Charleston. All offer talks and tours concerning the role of slavery (though another, McLeod Plantation (p361), located on the northern shores of James Island, is the best for an eye-opening and highly important experience on that topic).

Of the three on the Ashley River, **Drayton Hall** (843-769-2600; www.draytonhall.org; 3380 Ashley River Rd; adult/child $32/25, grounds only $12; 9am-3:30pm Mon-Sat, from 10:30am Sun, last tour 3pm) is the best for history buffs, as it features the oldest plantation house open to the public in America. **Magnolia Plantation** (843-571-1266; www.magnoliaplantation.com; 3550 Ashley River Rd; adult/child 6-10yr $20/10, tours $8; 8am-5:30pm Mar-Oct, to 4:30pm Nov-Feb) has great tours and wild gardens, with a Disney vibe. **Middleton Place** (843-556-6020; www.middletonplace.org; 4300 Ashley River Rd; gardens adult/child 6-13yr $28/10, house-museum tour extra $15, carriage tour $18; 9am-5pm) has the country's oldest, most elegant gardens and a fancy restaurant and hotel. You'll be hard-pressed to find the time to visit all three of these in one day, but you could squeeze in two (allow at least a couple of hours for each). Ashley River Rd is also known as SC 61, which can be reached from downtown Charleston via Hwy 17.

GULLAH CULTURE

Starting in the 16th century, African slaves were transported from the region known as the Rice Coast (Sierra Leone, Senegal, Gambia and Angola) to a landscape of remote islands that was shockingly similar – swampy coastlines and tropical vegetation, plus hot, humid summers. These new African Americans were able to retain many of their homeland traditions after the fall of slavery and well into the 20th century. The resulting culture of Gullah (also known as Geechee in Georgia) has its own language, an English-based Creole with many African words and sentence structures, and many traditions, including fantastic storytelling, art, music and crafts. The Gullah culture is celebrated annually with the energetic **Gullah Festival** (www.theoriginalgullahfestival.org; ⏲ late May) in Beaufort.

St Helena Island, to the east of Beaufort, has the highest concentration of Gullah people in the state, and is the best place for a traveler to obtain an education on the culture – the Penn Center (p363) has a museum that's a great starting place. You'll also notice plenty of Gullah restaurants around the island, and their menus are heavy with shrimp, fish, okra, rice, tomatoes and cabbage. Basically, Gullah cuisine consists of whatever the state's early African American residents could find, catch or grow. There's also a distinctly African influence in the cooking style.

Gullah art, too, has stood the test of time. In Beaufort and St Helena there are several folk art galleries with many brightly colored paintings influenced by the vibrance of similar works in West Africa. Sweetgrass baskets are another mainstay; these charming, coiled baskets are prevalent in Africa and are most easily procured on the streets and in the markets of Charleston.

Also popular, **Boone Hall Plantation** (☎843-884-4371; www.boonehallplantation.com; 1235 Long Point Rd; adult/child 6-12yr $24/12; ⏲8:30am-6:30pm Mon-Sat, noon-5pm Sun early Mar-Aug, shorter hours Sep-Jan) in Mt Pleasant is where many celebrities get married, and is a very pretty spot for tourists and families. It's 11 miles from downtown Charleston on Hwy 17N.

Tours

Charleston is chock-full of worthwhile walking, horse-carriage, bus and boat tours, and you can ask at the visitor center for the gamut. If you don't feel like wading through giant stacks of brochures, though, our top recs include: Charleston Footprints for a historical walking tour in South of Broad, Culinary Tours of Charleston for food tours, **Charleston Brews Cruise** (☎843-860-9847; www.charlestonbrewscruise.com; 375 Meeting St; drinker/nondrinker $75/25; ⏲tours 1:30pm Sun & Tue-Thu, 12:30pm Fri & Sat) for brewery tours and **Bulldog Tours** (☎843-722-8687; www.bulldogtours.com; 18 Anson St; ghost tour adult/child $29/19) for anything.

Charleston Footprints WALKING
(☎843-478-4718; www.charlestonfootprints.com; 2hr tour $20) An excellent walking tour of historical Charleston sights led by a knowledgeable and theatrical local. Tours begin at the Shops of Historic Charleston Foundation.

Culinary Tours of Charleston FOOD & DRINK
(☎843-727-1100; www.culinarytoursofcharleston.com; 18 Anson St; 2½-hr tour from $65) Sample grits, pralines and barbecue on food-centric walking tours of restaurants and markets. Also available: dessert tours and a celebrity-chef experience.

Adventure Harbor Tours BOATING
(☎843-442-9455; www.adventureharbortours.com; 56 Ashley Point Dr, Charleston; adult/child 3-12yr $55/30) Runs harbor cruises, sunset cruises and fun trips to uninhabited Morris Island – great for shelling.

Festivals & Events

Spoleto USA PERFORMING ARTS
(☎843-722-2764; www.spoletousa.org; ⏲late May-early Jun) This 17-day performing-arts festival is South Carolina's biggest event, with operas, dramas and concerts staged across the city.

Lowcountry Oyster Festival FOOD & DRINK
(www.lowcountryhospitalityassociation.com/oyster-fest/; 1235 Longpoint Rd, Boone Hall Plantation, Mt Pleasant; ⏲Jan) Oyster lovers in Mt Pleasant feast on 80,000lb of the salty bivalves at this festival (oyster buckets are

$12 to $16). There's also oyster shucking and eating contests, live music, local food and a whole lotta beer.

MOJA Arts Festival PERFORMING ARTS
(843-724-7305; www.mojafestival.com; late Sep-early Oct) Spirited poetry readings and gospel concerts mark this two-week celebration of African American and Caribbean culture.

Sleeping

Not So Hostel HOSTEL $
(843-722-8383; www.notsohostel.com; 156 Spring St; dm $30, r $72-106;) Housed mainly in a wonderful 1840 dwelling complete with atmospheric blue porches and an odd, twin-matching architecture setup, Charleston's one hostel is creaky and inviting. A couple of eight-bed co-ed dorms, various four-bed male and female dorms, and nice but cramped private rooms (some with private baths) are spread over three buildings, with guest kitchens throughout. Green initiatives abound.

1837 Bed & Breakfast B&B $$
(843-723-7166; www.1837bb.com; 126 Wentworth St; r $139-295;) Close to the College of Charleston, this B&B may bring to mind the home of your eccentric, antique-loving aunt. The 1837 has nine charmingly overdecorated rooms, including three in the old brick carriage house. And, no, you're not drunk – those warped porches are lopsided as hell and full of history.

Indigo Inn BOUTIQUE HOTEL $$
(843-577-5900; www.indigoinn.com; 1 Maiden Lane; r $209-359;) This snazzy 40-room inn enjoys a prime location in the middle of the Historic District and has an oasis-like private courtyard, where guests can enjoy free wine and cheese by the fountain. Decor gives a nod to the 18th century and is a tad frilly, but the beds are comfy and renovated bathrooms have been modernized. Pets are $40 per night.

★ **Ansonborough Inn** HOTEL $$
(800-723-1655; www.ansonboroughinn.com; 21 Hasell St; r from $180-340;) Droll neo-Victorian touches such as the closet-sized British pub and the formal portraits of dogs add a sense of fun to this intimate Historic District hotel, which also manages to feel like an antique sailing ship. Huge guest rooms mix old and new, with worn leather couches, high ceilings and flat-screen TVs.

★ **Wentworth Mansion** HISTORIC HOTEL $$$
(843-853-1886; www.wentworthmansion.com; 149 Wentworth St; r $400-755;) Routinely named a top stay in the country, this Gilded Age mansion would be the ideal setting for an elaborate Clue dinner party – and who wouldn't die for a glimpse of these Tiffany stained-glass windows, Italian crystal chandeliers and hand-carved mahogany moldings? An enclosed cupola on the roof offers breathtaking cityscapes, and the service here redefines Southern hospitality.

Eating

Charleston is one of America's finest eating cities, and there are enough fabulous restaurants here for a town three times its size. The 'classic' Charleston establishments stick to fancy seafood with a French flair, while many of the trendy up-and-comers are reinventing Southern cuisine with a focus on the area's copious local bounty, from oysters to heirloom rice to heritage pork.

★ **Gaulart & Maliclet** FRENCH $
(843-577-9797; www.fastandfrenchcharleston.com; 98 Broad St; breakfast $5-13, lunch & dinner mains $13-22; 8am-8pm Mon-Wed, to 10pm Thu-Sat) Ooh la la. Locals crowd around the shared tables at this tiny spot, known as 'Fast & French,' to nibble on Gallic cheeses and sausages, fondues or nightly specials ($21 to $24) that include bread, soup, a main dish and wine.

Xiao Bao Biscuit ASIAN $
(www.xiaobaobiscuit.com; 224 Rutledge Ave; lunch mains $13, dinner mains $14-18; 11:30am-2pm & 5:30-10pm Mon-Sat) Housed in a former gas station, with exposed brick walls and concrete floor, this casual but stylish eatery hits the hipster high marks. But the food? Now we're talking. The short but palate-kicking menu spotlights simple pan-Asian fare enhanced by local ingredients and spicy flavors. For something different and memorable, try the *okonomiyaki* – a Japanese cabbage pancake – with egg and bacon.

★ **Edmund's Oast** PUB FOOD $$
(843-727-1145; www.edmundsoast.com; 1081 Morrison Dr; mains $14-29; 4:30-10pm Mon-Thu, to 11pm Fri & Sat, 10am-10pm Sun;) Occupying

a gutted former hardware store in gentrifying NoMo is Charleston's highest-brow brewpub. Grub on offer here includes Southern faves such as salt chicken skins, hanger steaks and hot-and-sour tilefish. The drink pairings: 64 taps (eight devoted to cocktails, meads and sherries, and a dozen proprietary craft beers, among other craft offerings). Pints are $6 to $9.

167 Raw SEAFOOD **$$**
(☎843-579-4997; www.167raw.com/charleston; 289 E Bay St; oysters each $2.75, mains $14-27; ⏱11am-10pm Mon-Sat) There are no reservations at this tiny hole-in-the-wall that unassumingly serves up the city's best seafood. People wait in lines down the block for the delicious lobster roll, and the tuna burger and sea-scallop po'boy are also off-the-charts toothsome. Oysters arrive fresh daily from Nantucket (where the restaurant runs its very own oyster farm), and the service is truly on point.

Fleet Landing SEAFOOD **$$**
(☎843-722-8100; www.fleetlanding.net; 186 Concord St; lunch mains $9-24, dinner $13-26; ⏱11am-3:30pm daily, 5-10pm Sun-Thu, 5-11pm Fri & Sat; 📶) Come here for the perfect Charleston lunch: a river view, a cup of she-crab soup with a splash of sherry, and a big bowl of shrimp and grits. Housed in a former naval degaussing building on a pier, it's a convenient and scenic spot to enjoy fresh fish, a fried seafood platter or a burger after a morning of downtown exploring.

Ordinary SEAFOOD **$$**
(☎843-414-7060; www.eattheordinary.com; 544 King St; dishes $10-33; ⏱5-10:30pm Tue-Sun) Inside a cavernous 1927 bank building, this buzzy seafood hall and oyster bar feels like the best party in town. The menu is short, but the savory fare is prepared with finesse – from the oyster sliders to the lobster rolls to the nightly fish dishes.

★FIG SOUTHERN US **$$$**
(☎843-805-5900; www.eatatfig.com; 232 Meeting St; mains $30-46; ⏱5-10:30pm Mon-Thu, to 11pm Fri & Sat; 📶) 🌿 FIG is a longtime foodie favorite, and it's easy to see why: welcoming staff, efficient but unrushed service and top-notch, sustainably sourced nouvelle Southern fare from James Beard Award–winner Mike Lata. The six nightly changing dishes embrace what's fresh from the sea and local farms and mills. FIG stands for Food is Good. And the gourmets agree.

Drinking & Nightlife

Proof COCKTAIL BAR
(☎843-793-1422; www.charlestonproof.com; 437 King St; ⏱4pm-2am Mon-Fri, from 6pm Sat & Sun) It may be snug in here, but the cocktails ($10 to $13) sure are first class – the mixologist is some kind of visionary. Case in point: the 'knuckleball' has Old Grand-Dad, a spicy cola reduction, orange bitters and pickled boiled peanuts.

Edmund's Oast Brewing Co BREWERY
(☎843-718-3224; www.edmundsoast.com/brewing-co; 1505 King St Ext; ⏱11am-10pm) Edmund's Oast in NoMo has this baby brewing cousin just down the street, set in a 20,000-sq-ft facility with 26 boozy beverages on tap and two hangover-prevention chambers (a wood-fired brick oven and a Polish smokehouse). Brews are ambitious and, at times, downright medieval: Domesday is brewed with yarrow, mugwort, lavender and marshmallow flower.

Revelry Brewery MICROBREWERY
(www.revelrybrewingco.com; 10 Conroy St; ⏱4-10pm Mon-Thu, noon-midnight Fri & Sat, noon-10pm Sun) Probably the hippest of the Northern Peninsula breweries. It's hard to beat knocking back a few artfully crafted cold ones on Revelry's fairy-lit and fire-pit-heated rooftop, which affords expansive views all the way to the cable-stayed Ravenel Bridge.

The downstairs bar, seemingly owned by the brewery's black Lab, is a mere 5ft from the tanks.

Shopping

Shops of Historic Charleston Foundation GIFTS & SOUVENIRS
(☎843-724-8484; www.historiccharleston.org; 108 Meeting St; ⏱9am-6pm Mon-Sat, noon-5pm Sun) This place showcases jewelry, home furnishings and furniture inspired by the city's historic homes, much of which is based on Blue Canton porcelain.

Blue Bicycle Books BOOKS
(☎843-722-2666; www.bluebicyclebooks.com; 420 King St; ⏱10am-7:30pm Mon-Sat, 1-6pm Sun) Excellent new-and-used bookstore with a great selection on Southern history and culture.

Information

Charleston Visitor Center (843-724-7174; www.charlestoncvb.com; 375 Meeting St; 8:30am-5:30pm Apr-Oct, to 5pm Nov-Mar) Find help with accommodations and tours or watch a half-hour video on Charleston history in this spacious renovated warehouse.

North Charleston Visitor Center (800-774-0006; www.charlestoncvb.com; 4975b Centre Point Dr; 10am-5pm Mon-Sat, from 1pm Sun) Has brochures, maps and staff who can help you plan your trip.

Getting There & Around

The vast majority of travelers arrive in Charleston in their own vehicles, but other visitors get here via planes, trains and buses.

Bicycle A great way to get around, with plenty of city bike-share stations, rental shops and racks.

Boat A ferry service makes four stops around Charleston Harbor.

Bus City buses cost $2 a ride, and there's also a free streetcar that makes loops from the visitor center.

Car & Motorcycle There are car-rental companies at the airport. Note that parking can be difficult downtown.

Taxi Ridesharing apps are usually cheaper and easier than calling or finding taxis.

Lowcountry

The southern half of the South Carolina coast is a tangle of islands cut off from the mainland by inlets and tidal marshes. Here, descendants of West African slaves known as the Gullah maintain small communities in the face of resort and golf-course development. The landscape ranges from tidy stretches of shimmery, oyster-gray sand to wild, moss-shrouded maritime forests.

The southernmost stretch of South Carolina's coast is popular with a mostly upscale set of golfers and B&B aficionados, but the area has quirky charms aplenty for everyone.

Charleston County Sea Islands

A dozen islands within an hour's drive of Charleston make up the Charleston County Sea Islands. Around 10 miles by road southeast of Charleston on the Mt Pleasant side, **Sullivan's Island** and **Isle of Palms** beckon day-trippers for sand-lounging and reveling on blue-sky days. Around 4 miles in the other direction brings you to **James Island**, one of the most urban of Charleston's barrier sea islands. A further 9 miles south of Charleston, **Folly Beach** is good for a day of sun and sand. The other end of the island is popular with surfers.

Upscale rental homes, golf courses and the swanky Sanctuary resort mark **Kiawah Island**, 26 miles southwest of Charleston, where you'll find those lucky enough to stay here cruising on their bikes along one of the most gorgeous beaches in the South. Nearby **Edisto Island** (*ed*-is-tow) is a homespun family vacation spot without a single traffic light.

WORTH A TRIP

MCLEOD PLANTATION

Part of a visit to Charleston is reckoning with the large role that slavery played in the development of the city. A tour at the **McLeod Plantation** (843-795-4386; www.ccprc.com/1447/McLeod-Plantation-Historic-Site; 325 Country Club Dr; adult/child $15/6; 9am-4pm Tue-Sun) on James Island lends keen insight into what the lives of enslaved people were like on an upper-middle-class plantation, where the planters were constantly trying to keep up with the Middletons, the Draytons and the Pinckneys. It's a crucial sight for understanding antebellum and Reconstruction Era South Carolina.

Sights

Kiawah Beachwater Park BEACH

(www.ccprc.com; 8 Beachwalker Dr, Kiawah Island; parking $5-15; 9am-8pm May-Sep, shorter hours rest of year) This idyllic stretch of sun-toasted sand at the southern end of Kiawah Island has been called one of the top 10 beaches in the USA and is the only publicly accessible beach on Kiawah.

Take a bike with you – the compact sand is perfect for a ride along the 10-mile barrier island.

Sleeping & Eating

James Island County Park CAMPGROUND $

(843-795-4386; www.ccprc.com; 871 Riverland Dr, James Island; tent sites from $33, 8-person cottages from $169;) A great budget option, this 643-acre park southwest of downtown Charleston has meadows, a marsh and a dog park. You can rent bikes ($10 per day)

DON'T MISS

FIREFLY DISTILLERY

The world's first hand-crafted sweet-tea-flavored vodka came from **Firefly Distillery** (843-557-1405; www.fireflyspirits.com; 6775 Bears Bluff Rd; 11am-5pm Tue-Sat), tucked into the forest on Wadmalaw Island. Sampling this classic, which is made with tea grown on the nearby **Charleston Tea Plantation** (843-559-0383; www.charlestonteaplantation.com; 6617 Maybank Hwy; trolley tour adult/child under 13yr $14/6; 10am-4pm Mon-Sat, from noon Sun), distilled four times and blended with sugarcane from Louisiana, is what brings most people to the door. Tastings are $6.

and kayaks ($5.50 per hour), go for a run or frolic with your pup. The park offers shuttle services to downtown and Folly Beach ($10). Reservations are highly recommended. There are 124 campsites and 10 marsh-adjacent rental cottages.

★Bowens Island Restaurant SEAFOOD $
(www.bowensisland.biz; 1870 Bowens Island Rd, Folly Island; mains $10-35; 5-9:30pm Tue-Sat) Down a long dirt road through Lowcountry marshland near Folly Beach, this unpainted wooden shack is one of the South's most venerable seafood dives – grab an oyster knife and start shucking! Cool beer and friendly locals give the place its soul.

Obstinate Daughter AMERICAN $$
(843-416-5020; www.theobstinatedaughter.com; 2063 Middle St, Sullivan's Island; pizzas $15-19, mains $20-31; 11am-10pm Mon-Fri, from 10am Sat & Sun;) Sullivan's Island wasn't on the region's culinary map till this place showed up and made serious waves. The chef-owner, who also received high praise for **Wild Olive** (843-737-4177; www.wildoliverestaurant.com; 2867 Maybank Hwy, Johns Island; pastas $13-22, mains $20-37; 5:30-10pm Sun-Thu, to 11:30pm Fri & Sat, bar from 4pm; P), has demonstrated considerable range here, refocusing on light and playful plates of fresh veggies, pasta, seafood and unusual ingredients. Raw oysters are flown in from top locales, and vegetarians will leave exuberant.

Information

Kiawah Island Visitor Center (800-774-0006; www.charlestoncvb.com; 4475 Betsy Kerrison Pkwy; 9am-3pm) Has maps, tourist info and helps with accommodations and tours in the Charleston area.

Getting There & Away

Charleston's barrier sea islands are all accessed via a series of byways and bridges from the city, though not always with a connection from one to another. You'll need to take the long way round if you want to go from Sullivan's Island to Kiawah or Edisto Islands, for example. Coming from the south, Edisto (via SC 174), Kiawah and Johns (via SC 17) can be accessed without going through Charleston. From the north coast, SC 17 also reaches Sullivan's and Isle of Palms without going through the city.

Beaufort & Hilton Head

On Port Royal Island, darling colonial Beaufort (byoo-furt) is the second-oldest city in South Carolina, and perhaps the nation's greatest educator on the turbulent post-Civil War period. In 2017 President Obama established four Reconstruction Era National Monuments within the county, and in pockets of the city and neighboring islands Gullah culture still thrives.

The streets of this fair city are lined with gorgeous antebellum homes, restored 18th-century mansions and twisting magnolias that drip with Spanish moss. Unsurprisingly, Beaufort is often used as a backdrop for Hollywood films, and is best explored either on foot or from the perch of a horse and buggy.

The riverfront downtown has plenty of linger-worthy cafes and galleries, and the Southern hospitality here is at its finest. Expect to be invited by perfect strangers to hop on a boat and drink beer at everybody's favorite sandbar in the middle of Port Royal Sound.

Across Port Royal Sound, tiny Hilton Head Island is South Carolina's largest barrier island and one of America's top golf spots. There are dozens of courses, many enclosed in posh private residential communities. The island was the first eco-planned destination in the USA. Founder Charles Fraser believed a resort should blend with nature, so subdued colors, strict zoning laws (no building over five stories high, signage must be low and lit from below) and a distinct lack of streetlights characterize the environment here. But while summer traffic and miles of stoplights can stifle an appreciation of the beauty of the island, you can find some lush nature preserves, wide, white beaches hard-packed enough for bike riding, and a whole lot of dolphins.

Sights

Parris Island Museum MUSEUM
(843-228-2951; www.parrisislandmuseum.com; 111 Panama St; 10am-4:30pm) FREE This fascinating museum covering Marine Corps history contains antique uniforms and weaponry, but is most engaging for its exhibits chronicling the grueling, intense and scary (that CS gas-chamber exercise!) 13-week Marine basic training, which takes place here and at a second facility in San Diego, California. It's far worse than in *An Officer and a Gentleman!*

Penn Center MUSEUM
(843-838-2432; www.penncenter.com; 16 Penn Center Circle W, St Helena Island; $7; 9am-4pm Tue-Sat) Once the home of one of the nation's first schools for freed slaves, the Penn Center has a small museum that covers Gullah culture and traces the history of Penn School. Two sites on the property became part of the National Reconstruction Era Site in 2017: Darrah Hall, the school building, and Brick Baptist Church, which was originally constructed by slaves who were not allowed to worship inside. Freed slaves took control of it in 1861.

Hunting Island State Park STATE PARK
(843-838-2011; www.southcarolinaparks.com/huntingisland; 2555 Sea Island Pkwy; adult/child 6-15yr $5/3; park 6am-6pm, to 9pm Mar-Sep, visitor center 9am-5pm Mon-Fri, from 11am Sat & Sun, nature center 9am-5pm Tue-Sat, daily Jun-Aug) Lush and inviting Hunting Island State Park impresses visitors with acres of spooky maritime forest, tidal lagoons and a bone-white beach littered with seashells and the occasional shark tooth. The Vietnam War scenes from *Forrest Gump* were filmed in the marsh, a nature-lover's dream. **Campgrounds** (office 843-838-2011, reservations 866-345-7275; RV sites $24-45, cabins from $249; 6am-9pm early Mar-early Nov, to 6pm rest of year) fill quickly in summer. Climb the **lighthouse** ($2) for sweeping coastal views. Much of the park was affected by Hurricanes Matthew and Irma, but has largely recovered.

Sleeping & Eating

City Loft Hotel BOUTIQUE HOTEL $$
(843-379-5638; www.cityloftHotel.com; 301 Carteret St; r/ste $169/209; P) The chic City Loft Hotel adds a refreshing dash of modern style to a town heavy on historic homes and stately oak trees. Enjoy flat-screen TVs in the bedroom and bathroom, artisan-tile showers and memory-foam beds. Other perks include a gym, complimentary bicycle use and an on-site coffee shop ($5 voucher included in rates).

Cuthbert House Inn B&B $$$
(843-521-1315; www.cuthberthouseinn.com; 1203 Bay St; r $190-325; P) The most romantic of Beaufort's B&Bs, this sumptuously grand white-columned mansion is straight out of *Gone with the Wind*. Antique furnishings are found throughout, but monochromatic walls add a fresh, modern feel. Some rooms have a river view (three have fireplaces). On his march through the South in 1865, General William T Sherman slept at the house.

Lowcountry Produce SOUTHERN US $
(843-322-1900; www.lowcountryproduce.com; 302 Carteret St; breakfast $9-15, sandwiches $10-18; 8am-3pm) A fantastic cafe and market for picnic rations such as pies, house-made relishes, local cheeses and all kinds of Lowcountry-spun awesomeness (including a bizarre but wildly popular cream-cheese lasagna). Or eat in and indulge in an Oooey Gooey, a grilled pimento-cheese sandwich with bacon and garlic-pepper jelly (one hot mess!), or a tasty crab-cake sandwich with brussels-sprout slaw.

Information

Beaufort Tourist Information Center (843-525-8500; www.beaufortsc.org; 713 Craven St; 9am-5pm Mon-Sat) Inside the Beaufort History Museum, offering maps, brochures and advice.

Myrtle Beach

The towering SkyWheel spins fantastically beside the sea in downtown Myrtle Beach, anchoring a 60-mile swath of sun-bleached excess known as the Grand Strand. This stretch of coastline is now infamously overdeveloped and littered with innumerable mini-golf courses, pancake houses, beach resorts and T-shirt shops – an alarming

WORTH A TRIP

FIREFLIES & SPANISH MOSS: CONGAREE NATIONAL PARK

Inky-black water, dyed with tannic acid leached from decaying plant matter. Bone-white cypress stumps like the femurs of long-dead giants. Spanish moss as dry and gray as witches' hair. **Congaree National Park** (☎803-776-4396; www.nps.gov/cong; 100 National Park Rd, Hopkins) protects the largest contiguous, old-growth bottomland forest in the eastern US, and there's nothing like canoeing through its unearthly swamp to make you feel like you've stepped into a Southern Gothic novel.

The park stretches over nearly 27,000 acres, offering excellent camping and ranger-led canoe trips and hikes.

Casual day-trippers can wander the 2.4-mile elevated boardwalk. Look carefully at the Blue Sky mural in the visitor center – the scene seems to change as you move. From mid-May through mid-June, the *Photinus carolinus*, a rare species of firefly, blink in unison, turning the forest floor into a twinkling light show. The phenomenon only occurs in a handful of spots around the world. Columbia-based **River Runner Outdoor Center** (☎803-771-0353; www.shopriverrunner.com; 905 Gervais St) can get you on the water.

The park is just a 30-minute drive from downtown Columbia.

departure from its beginnings as a laid-back summer retreat for working-class Southerners.

Love it or hate it, Myrtle Beach offers one all-American vacation. Enormous outlet malls, water parks and daiquiri bars compete for attention, bikini-clad teenagers play video games and eat hot dogs in smoky arcades, and Midwestern families roast like chickens on the white sand. North Myrtle Beach, actually a separate town, is slightly lower-key, with a thriving culture based on the 'shag' – a jitterbug-like dance invented here in the 1940s.

It isn't for nature lovers, but it's a rowdy good time and certainly a hit with the kiddos.

Sights & Activities

SkyWheel AMUSEMENT PARK
(☎843-839-9200; www.myrtlebeachskywheel.com; 1110 N Ocean Blvd; adult/child 3-11yr $14/9; ⊙11am-midnight, varying shorter hours in low season) The 187ft-high SkyWheel overlooks the 1.2-mile coastal boardwalk. One ticket includes four revolutions in an enclosed glass gondola; the whole thing lasts about 10 to 15 minutes. At night the wheel is bewitching, with more than a million dazzling colored lights.

★**Brookgreen Gardens** GARDENS
(☎843-235-6000; www.brookgreen.org; 1931 Brookgreen Garden Dr, Murrells Inlet; adult/child 4-12yr $18/10; ⊙9:30am-5pm) These magical gardens, 16 miles south of Myrtle Beach on Hwy 17S, are home to the largest collection of American sculpture in the country, set amid more than 9000 acres of rice-plantation-turned-subtropical-garden paradise. Seasonal blooms are listed on the website.

Sleeping & Eating

Myrtle Beach State Park CAMPGROUND $
(☎843-238-5325; www.southcarolinaparks.com/myrtle-beach; 4401 S Kings Hwy; tent & RV sites from $32, cabins $156-250; P) Sleep beneath the pines or rent a cabin, all just steps from the shore. During summer, cabins must be rented on a weekly basis, and there's a two-night minimum the rest of the year. Reserve months in advance.

The state park is 3 miles south of central Myrtle Beach and includes a nice beach, a fishing pier and swaths of protected maritime forest.

Hampton Inn Broadway at the Beach HOTEL $$$
(☎843-916-0600; www.myrtlebroadway.hamptoninn.com; 1140 Celebrity Circle; r/ste from $249/389; @) The bright, renovated rooms overlooking the lake and Broadway at the Beach are a great choice at this hotel. If you're traveling with preteens, you may feel more comfortable letting them roam the adjacent shops and attractions rather than the boardwalk, particularly at night.

Prosser's BBQ SOUTHERN US $$
(☎843-357-6146; www.prossersbbq.com; 3750 Hwy 17 Business, Murrells Inlet; buffet breakfast $8, lunch $11-12, dinner $14-16; ⊙6:30-10:30am & 11am-2pm daily, plus 4-8pm Tue-Sat) It's weird to come to Murrells Inlet's 'restaurant row'

and not spring for seafood, but who are we to judge? The gut-busting lunch buffet here is down-home delicious. It includes fried fish and chicken, sweet-potato souffle, mac 'n' cheese, green beans and vinegary pulled pork.

★Wicked Tuna SEAFOOD **$$$**
(☎843-651-9987; www.thewickedtuna.com; 4123 Hwy 17 Business, Murrells Inlet; mains $26-48, sandwiches $14-24; ⏰11am-10pm; 📶) Murrells Inlet is full of kitschy seafooders and, at first glance, the Wicked Tuna looks no different. Guess again! You are in for a real treat at this trip-worthy spot overlooking the beautiful inlet – it employs six fishing boats that go out for three- to six-day stints and bring back upward of 600lb of fresh fish each.

Drinking & Entertainment

American Tap House CRAFT BEER
(☎843-712-2301; www.americantaphouse.com; 1320 Celebrity Circle; ⏰11am-2am; 📶) If you prefer your craft-beer experience to come supersized, you'll find 53 taps of national options (pints $5.50 to $9) at this chef-driven gastropub at Broadway at the Beach.

★Fat Harold's Beach Club DANCE
(☎843-249-5779; www.fatharolds.com; 212 Main St; ⏰4pm-2am Mon & Tue, from 11am Wed-Sun) Folks groove to doo-wop, old-time R&B and beach music at this North Myrtle institution, which calls itself 'Home of the Shag.' The dance, that is. Free shag lessons are offered at 7pm every Tuesday. On Monday they're $10 per person.

Information

Myrtle Beach Visitor Information (☎843-626-7444; www.visitmyrtlebeach.com; 1200 N Oak St; ⏰8:30am-5pm) Has maps and brochures.

Getting There & Around

The traffic coming and going on Hwy 17 Business/Kings Hwy can be infuriating. To avoid 'the Strand' altogether, stay on the Hwy 17 bypass, or take Hwy 31/Carolina Bays Pkwy, which parallels Hwy 17 between Hwy 501 and Hwy 9.

Myrtle Beach International Airport (☎843-448-1580; www.flymyrtlebeach.com; 1100 Jetport Rd) is located within the city limits, as is the **Greyhound station** (☎843-448-2472; www.greyhound.com; 511 7th Ave N) – the airport receives direct flights from more than 30 domestic destinations.

Greenville & the Upcountry

Cherokee Indians once roamed the state's mountain foothills, which they called the 'Great Blue Hills of God.' The region today is known as the Upcountry. Geographically, it's the spot where the Blue Ridge Mountains drop dramatically to meet the Piedmont.

The region is anchored by Greenville, home to one of the most photogenic downtowns in the South. The Reedy River twists through the city center, and its dramatic falls tumble beneath Main St at Falls Park (www.fallspark.com).

Falls Park's fabulous **Liberty Bridge** (www.fallspark.com/175/The-Liberty-Bridge; Falls Park on the Reedy) is a must-cross.

Sights & Activities

★Table Rock State Park STATE PARK
(☎864-878-9813; www.southcarolinaparks.com; 158 Ellison Lane, Pickens; adult/child 6-15yr $5/3; ⏰7am-7pm Sun-Thu, to 9pm Fri & Sat, extended hours mid-May–early Nov) The Upcountry's marquee natural attraction is Table Rock Mountain, a 3124ft-high mountain with a striking granite face. The 7.2-mile round-trip hike to its summit is a popular local challenge. For overnight stays, there is the **Table Rock State Park Campground & Cabins** (campsites $16-21, cabins $155-181; ❄).

BMW Performance Center SPORTS
(☎864-968-3000; www.bmwperformancecenter.com; 1155 Hwy 101 S, Greer; 1-/2-day school from $849/1699; ⏰8:30am-8pm Mon-Fri) Your need for speed is quenched at America's only BMW performance-driving academy. Delve into fast and furious behind-the-wheel experiences over the course of one- or two-day classes with various vehicles, including the high-performance M series, or drive a Mini in stunt-driving school – *The Italian Job* will have nothing on you.

Sleeping

★Swamp Rabbit Inn B&B **$$**
(☎864-345-7990; www.swamprabbitinn.com; 1 Logan St; r $135-200; P❄📶) This fun six-room inn occupies a '50s-era former boarding house downtown. It feels like a hostel but features colorfully decked-out private rooms that are as cozy and quirky as any in the

South. Wonderful common spaces include a modern guest kitchen and wooden patio with barbecue.

Westin Poinsett HOTEL **$$$**
(864-421-9700; www.westinpoinsettgreenville.com; 120 S Main St; r $210-330;) This grand hotel, which originally opened in 1925, is in the heart of downtown Greenville, just steps from the Reedy River Falls. Past guests include Amelia Earhart, Cornelius Vanderbilt and Bobby Kennedy. The modern, comfortably furnished rooms have high-end mattresses and recently renovated bathrooms.

Eating & Drinking

Stax Omega Diner & Bakery DINER **$**
(864-297-6639; www.staxs.net; 72 Orchard Park Dr; breakfast $9-15, lunch & dinner $12-16; 6:30am-9pm;) Nobody quite does breakfast excess like the USA, and this bustling family-owned diner 4 miles east of downtown Greenville is everything fantastic about that. It's massive – capacity 500! – and it does it all really well: omelets, pancakes, French toast, eggs Benedict, scrambles – the list goes on and on... and on...

Soby's SOUTHERN US **$$**
(864-232-7007; http://sobys.com; 207 S Main St; mains $22-32; 5-9:30pm Mon-Thu, to 10:30pm Fri & Sat, 10am-1:30pm & 5-9pm Sun;) Book yourself one of the intimate, brick-walled banquettes at this downtown Greenville bastion of New Southern cuisine that also caters to wine lovers (the 5000-bottle list has been awarded a *Wine Spectator* Award of Excellence 20 years running). The oft-changing menu is steeped in the wares of local farmers, foragers and ranchers.

Getting There & Away

Greenville–Spartanburg International Airport (864-877-7426; www.gspairport.com; 2000 GSP Dr, Greer) is 13 miles east of the city, nearly halfway between Greenville and Spartanburg.

The **Greyhound bus station** (864-235-4741; www.greyhound.com; 9 Hendrix Dr) is also out that way, 7 miles southeast of downtown.

The **Amtrak train station** (800-872-7245; www.amtrak.com; 1120 W Washington St) is more conveniently located, just west of downtown.

TENNESSEE

Most states have one official state song. Tennessee has 10! And there's a reason for that: Tennessee has music deep within its soul. Here, the folk music of the Scots-Irish in the eastern mountains combined with the bluesy rhythms of the African Americans in the western Delta to give birth to the modern country music that makes Nashville famous.

The state's three geographic regions, East, Middle and West Tennessee, are represented by the three stars on the Tennessee flag. Each has its own unique beauty: the heather-colored peaks of the Great Smoky Mountains; the lush green valleys of the central plateau around Nashville; and the hot, sultry lowlands near Memphis.

In Tennessee you can hike shady mountain trails in the morning, and by evening whoop it up in a Nashville honky-tonk or on the blues-infused sidewalks of Beale St.

Information

Department of Tourist Development (615-741-2159; www.tnvacation.com) Has welcome centers at the state borders.

Tennessee State Parks (https://tnstateparks.com) Check out this well-organized website for camping, hiking and fishing info for Tennessee's more than 50 state parks.

Memphis

Memphis doesn't just attract tourists; it draws pilgrims. Music-lovers lose themselves to the throb of blues guitar on Beale St. Barbecue connoisseurs descend to stuff themselves silly on smoky pulled pork and dry-rubbed ribs. Elvis fanatics fly in to pay their respects at Graceland. You could spend days hopping from one museum or historic site to another, stopping only for barbecue, and leave happy.

Memphis has long been marked by a certain baroque, ruined quality both sad and beguiling. But the city these days feels re-energized. Neighborhoods once downtrodden and abandoned – South Main, Binghampton, Crosstown and others – are being reinvented with kitschy boutiques, hipster lofts, daring restaurants, welcoming microbreweries and design-minded revamps of old buildings, all dripping with Memphis' wild river-town spirit. Poverty is still prevalent, and some neighborhoods are considered unsafe at night, but the vibe overall here is one of optimism and local pride.

Sights

The pedestrian-only stretch of Beale St is a 24-hour carnival zone, where you'll find deep-fried funnel cakes, to-go beer counters, and music, music, music. Locals don't hang out here much, except after Memphis Grizzlies basketball games at FedEx Forum, but visitors tend to get a kick out of it.

★**National Civil Rights Museum** MUSEUM
(Map p370; ☎901-521-9699; www.civilrightsmuseum.org; 450 Mulberry St; adult/child 5-17yr $16/13; ⏰9am-5pm Wed-Sun; P) Housed partly inside the Lorraine Motel, where Martin Luther King Jr was fatally shot on April 4, 1968, is the gut-wrenching National Civil Rights Museum. Its immersive and compelling exhibits chronicle the struggle for African American freedom and equality from the earliest days of slavery in America. Both Dr King's cultural contribution and his assassination serve as prisms for looking at the Civil Rights movement, its precursors and its continuing impact on American life.

★**Graceland** HISTORIC BUILDING
(Map p368; ☎901-332-3322; www.graceland.com; 3717 Elvis Presley Blvd/US 51; house only adult/13-18yr/7-12yr $41/37/21, with airplanes $46/42/26, with Elvis Presley's Memphis $61/55/31, expanded tours adult/child under 7yr from $99/free; ⏰9am-5pm Mon-Sat, to 4pm Sun Mar-Oct, shorter hours Nov-Feb; P) If you only make one stop in Memphis, it should be here: the sublimely kitschy, gloriously bizarre home of the King of Rock and Roll. Though born in Mississippi, Elvis Presley was a true son of Memphis, raised in the Lauderdale Courts public-housing projects, inspired by blues clubs on Beale St, and discovered at Sun Studio. In the spring of 1957, the already-famous 22-year-old spent $100,000 on a colonial-style mansion, named Graceland by its previous owners.

★**Sun Studio** HISTORIC SITE
(Map p368; ☎901-521-0664; www.sunstudio.com; 706 Union Ave; adult/child 5-11yr $14/free; ⏰10am-6pm) This dusty storefront is ground zero for American rock and roll. Starting in the early 1950s, Sun's Sam Phillips recorded blues artists such as Howlin' Wolf, BB King and Ike Turner, followed by the rockabilly dynasty of Jerry Lee Lewis, Johnny Cash, Roy Orbison and, of course, the King himself (who started here in 1953). Tours last 45 minutes.

JACK LIVES HERE

The irony of the **Jack Daniel's Distillery** (☎931-759-6357; www.jackdaniels.com; 133 Lynchburg Hwy, Lynchburg; tours $15-100; ⏰9am-4:30pm; P) being in a 'dry county' is lost on no one – local liquor laws dictate that no hard stuff can be sold within county lines. But don't fret: while at least one of its five tours is dry, the serious excursions, ranging from the 90-minute Flight of Jack Daniel's to the three-hour Taste of Lynchburg – which includes a fine meal at **Miss Mary Bobo's Boarding House** (☎931-759-7394; www.jackdaniels.com; 295 Main St, Lynchburg; menu adult/child 3-10yr $25/9; ⏰11am-2pm Mon-Sat) – include plenty of whiskey.

★**Stax Museum of American Soul Music** MUSEUM
(Map p368; ☎901-942-7685; www.staxmuseum.com; 926 E McLemore Ave; adult/child 9-12yr $13/10; ⏰10am-5pm Tue-Sun; P) Wanna get funky? Head directly to Soulsville, USA, where this 17,000-sq-ft museum sits on the site of the old Stax recording studio. This venerable spot was soul music's epicenter in the 1960s, when Otis Redding, Booker T and the MGs, and Wilson Pickett recorded here.

Memphis Rock 'n' Soul Museum MUSEUM
(Map p370; ☎901-205-2526; www.memphisrocknsoul.org; 191 Beale St; adult/child 5-17yr $13/10; ⏰9:30am-7pm) This Smithsonian museum, next to FedEx Forum, examines how African American and white music mingled in the Mississippi Delta to create the modern rock and soul sound.

Memphis Pyramid LANDMARK
(Map p368; ☎901-291-8200; https://stores.basspro.com; 1 Bass Pro Dr; Sky High $10; ⏰store 8am-10pm Mon-Sat, to 7pm Sun, Sky High 9am-10pm Mon-Sat, to 7pm Sun; P) Don't laugh, but the most striking building in Memphis, a 32-story pyramid completed in 1991, is now home to an enormous Bass Pro Shop. Even if you don't need fishing gear or hiking boots, pop in to see the artificial swamp and the aquariums, or test your skill at the shooting range.

Greater Memphis

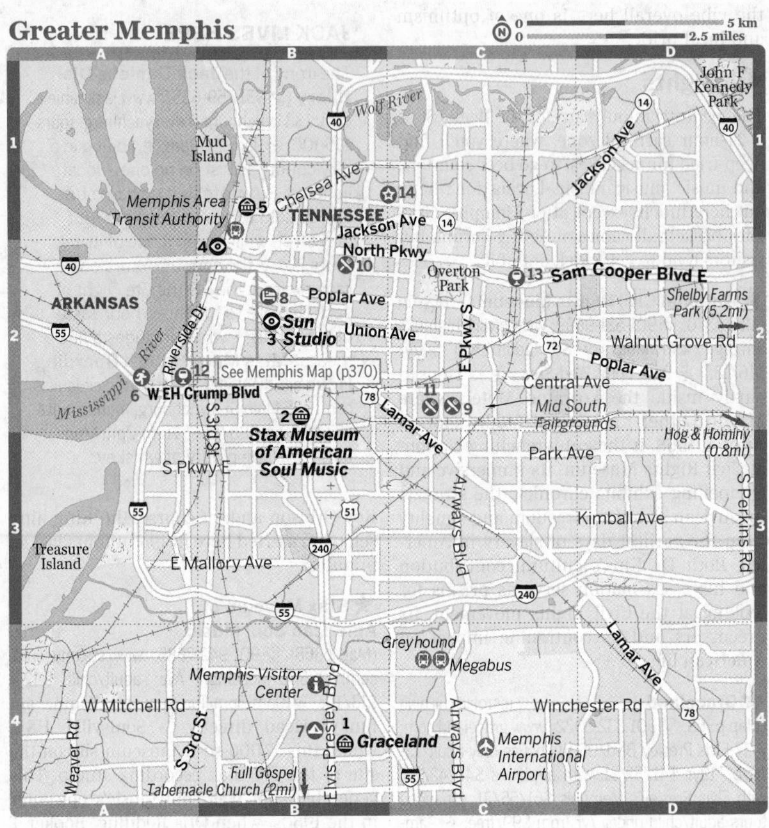

Greater Memphis

Top Sights
1 Graceland B4
2 Stax Museum of American Soul Music B2
3 Sun Studio B2

Sights
4 Memphis Pyramid B2
5 Slave Haven Underground Railroad Museum/Burkle Estate B1

Activities, Courses & Tours
6 Big River Crossing A2

Sleeping
7 Graceland RV Park & Campground B4
Guest House at Graceland .... (see 1)

8 James Lee House B2

Eating
9 Alchemy C2
Bar DKDC .... (see 9)
10 Crosstown Concourse B2
Imagine Vegan Cafe .... (see 9)
11 Sweet Grass C2

Drinking & Nightlife
12 Loflin Yard A2
13 Wiseacre Brewing Co C2

Entertainment
14 Wild Bill's C1
Young Avenue Deli .... (see 11)

Most fun is the Sky High, a central clear-walled elevator rising 28 stories to a glass observation deck with big views of downtown and the river.

Slave Haven Underground Railroad Museum/Burkle Estate MUSEUM
(Map p368; ☎901-527-3427; www.slavehavenundergroundrailroadmuseum.org; 826 N 2nd St;

adult/child 4-17yr $12/11; ⏲10am-4pm Mon-Sat, to 5pm Jun-Aug; P) This unimposing clapboard house is thought to have been a way station for runaway slaves on the Underground Railroad, complete with trapdoors, cellar entry and cubbyholes. Guided tours share details about the Railroad and include a chilling stop in the dark cellar, which would have served as a final hideout before a dash to a boat on the Mississippi River.

Full Gospel Tabernacle Church CHURCH
(787 Hale Rd; ⏲services 11am) On Sunday, put on your 'smell goods' and head to services in South Memphis, where soul-music legend turned reverend Al Green presides over a powerful choir. Visitors are welcome; it's a fascinating cultural experience. Services may last several hours, so sit in the back if you're not sure you can stay the entire time.

Activities

★Shelby Farms Park OUTDOORS
(☎901-222-7275; www.shelbyfarmspark.org; 6903 Great View Dr N; ⏲dawn-dusk;) With a children's playground, a zipline and fishing, as well as buffalo (yes, really) roaming their own 50-acre range, 4500-acre Shelby Farms is a wonderful multipurpose urban park. It's crisscrossed by 40 miles of hiking and biking trails (two-hour rentals from $28), and the 10.65-mile Shelby Farms greenline path connects the park with midtown Memphis.

Big River Crossing OUTDOORS
(Map p368; www.bigrivercrossing.com; ⏲6am-10pm) FREE In 2016 Memphis turned its historic Mississippi-traversing Harahan Bridge, out of service since 1949, into the country's longest active rail/bicycle/pedestrian bridge. Together with the Delta Regional River Park and Big River Trail, Big River Crossing makes up a 10-mile multi-modal corridor that connects the main streets of Memphis and West Memphis (AR). It's a great spot for a run, walk or cycle.

There's a light show along the span on the hour from sunset until 10pm.

Festivals & Events

Peabody Ducks PARADE
(Map p370; www.peabodymemphis.com; 149 Union Ave; ⏲11am & 5pm;) FREE A tradition dating from the 1930s begins every day at 11am sharp when five ducks file from the Peabody Hotel's gilded elevator, waddle across the red-carpeted lobby, and ensconce themselves in the marble lobby fountain for a day of happy splashing. The ducks make the reverse march at 5pm, when they retire to their penthouse accompanied by their red-coated Duckmaster.

Elvis Week CULTURAL
(☎901-332-3322, 800-238-2000; www.graceland.com/elvisweek; Graceland, Elvis Presley Blvd; ⏲mid-Aug) The King's passing and his life are celebrated across Memphis during Elvis Week, when tens of thousands of shiny-eyed pilgrims descend for nine days of festivities. *This* is Weird America. Attend a *Viva Las Vegas* or *Aloha From Hawaii* screening, a dance party, Elvis discussion panels, and an Elvis gospel brunch.

Beale Street Music Festival MUSIC
(www.memphisinmay.org; Tom Lee Park; 1/3-day passes $55/$115; ⏲1st weekend May) You've heard of Coachella, New Orleans Jazz Fest and Bonnaroo (p381), but Memphis' Beale Street Music Festival gets very little attention, despite the fact that it offers one of the country's best lineups of old-school blues masters, up-and-coming rockers, and gloriously past-their-prime pop and hip-hop artists.

Sleeping

Graceland RV Park & Campground CAMPGROUND $
(Map p368; ☎901-396-7125; www.graceland.com/rv-park-campground; 3691 Elvis Presley Blvd; tent sites/cabins from $25/52; P) Keep Lisa Marie in business when you camp out or sleep in the no-frills log cabins (with shared bathrooms) next to Graceland. Pool open June through September.

Talbot Heirs GUESTHOUSE $$
(Map p370; ☎901-527-9772; www.talbotheirs.com; 99 S 2nd St; ste $170-225; P@) Inconspicuously located on the 2nd floor of a busy downtown street, this unique, cheerful guesthouse is one of Memphis' best-kept secrets. Spacious suites, all with recently modernized bathrooms, are more like hip studio apartments than hotel rooms, with Asian rugs, funky local artwork and kitchens stocked with (included!) snacks.

Peabody Hotel HOTEL $$
(Map p370; ☎901-529-4000; www.peabodymemphis.com; 149 Union Ave; r/ste from $225/629; P) Memphis' most storied hotel

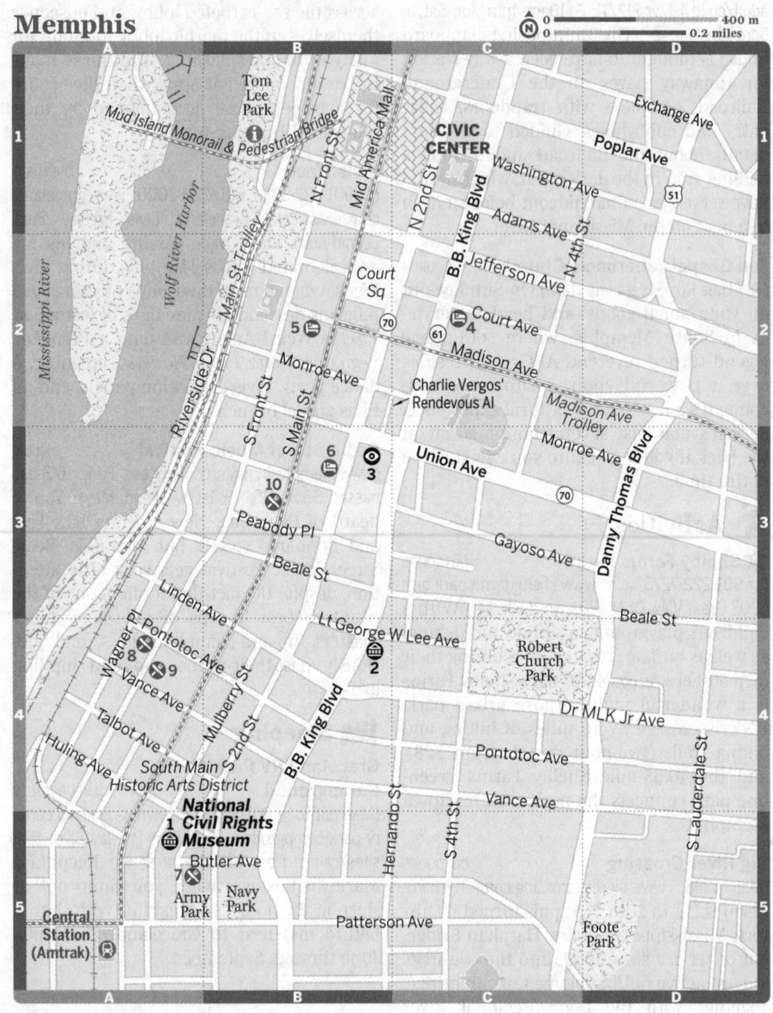

THE SOUTH MEMPHIS

Memphis

Top Sights

1 National Civil Rights Museum A5

Sights

2 Memphis Rock 'n' Soul Museum B4
3 Peabody Ducks B3

Sleeping

4 Hotel Indigo Memphis Downtown C2
5 Hu. Hotel B2
Peabody Hotel ....(see 3)
6 Talbot Heirs B3

Eating

7 Central BBQ A5
8 Gray Canary A4
9 Gus's World Famous Fried Chicken A4
10 Majestic Grille B3

Drinking & Nightlife

Old Dominick Distillery .... (see 8)

has been catering to a who's who of Southern gentry since the 1860s. The current incarnation, a 13-story Renaissance Revival–style building, dates to the 1920s and remains a social center, with a spa, shops, restaurants, an atmospheric lobby bar and 464 guest rooms in soothing turquoise tones.

Hotel Indigo Memphis Downtown HOTEL $$
(Map p370; ☎901-527-2215; www.ihg.com; 22 N BB King Blvd; r $163-180; P@🛜🏊) The brand-new Indigo gives a nod to the Memphis music industry with mid-century style. From the vintage radios in the lobby to the wall-size photos of microphones and musical accoutrements, the hotel exudes an energizing sense of fun. Three floors overlook the hip central pool.

Hu. Hotel BOUTIQUE HOTEL $$$
(Map p370; ☎901-333-1200; www.huhotelmemphis.com; 79 Madison Ave; r/ste from $249/349; P❄@🛜🏊🐾) Formerly the Madison, this sleek treat offers swanky but inviting boutique sleeps. Modern, stylish rooms have nice touches like high ceilings and private bars. The rooftop bar is one of the best places in town to watch a sunset. Check in at the lobby coffee shop.

★**James Lee House** B&B $$$
(Map p368; ☎901-359-6750; www.jamesleehouse.com; 690 Adams Ave; r $250-450; P❄@🛜) Dating in parts to 1848 and 1872, this exquisite Victorian mansion in the city's historic Victorian Village at the edge of downtown is one of Memphis' most refined sleeps. The building sat abandoned for 56 years before it underwent a glorious $2-million renovation guided by the owner's keen eye for detail and design.

Guest House at Graceland BOUTIQUE HOTEL $$$
(Map p368; ☎901-443-3000, 800-238-2000; www.guesthousegraceland.com; 3600 Elvis Presley Blvd; r/ste from $229/379; P❄@🛜🏊🐾) Intimate in name only, the Guest House, Graceland's new flagship, is a 450-room hunk of burning hotel. Stylish slate-gray standard rooms are spacious, with Dreamcatcher beds, three-sided display clocks, work-station desks and 55in flat-screen TVs. Suites, whose designs were coordinated by Priscilla Presley, all evoke themes from Elvis' life (one features a red-draped TV on the ceiling above the bed!).

Eating

Locals come to blows over which of the city's chopped-pork sandwiches or dry-rubbed ribs are the best. Barbecue joints are scattered across the city; the ugliest exteriors often yield the tastiest goods. Hip young locals head to the South Main Historic Arts District, Midtown's Cooper-Young or Overton Square neighborhoods, all fashionable dining enclaves.

★**Central BBQ** BARBECUE $
(Map p370; ☎901-672-7760; www.cbqmemphis.com; 147 E Butler Ave; plates $11-28, sandwiches from $5; ⏲11am-9pm) The downtown location of this iconic Memphis barbecue joint is the perfect side dish to an afternoon at the National Civil Rights Museum (p367). The transcendent pulled pork – almost always voted the city's best – can and should be doused in a number of sauces so good you'll want to drink them by the pint.

Crosstown Concourse FOOD HALL $
(Map p368; https://crosstownconcourse.com; 1350 Concourse Ave; ⏲hours vary) It's not your typical food hall – you won't find rows of kiosks – but there's an international array of casual eateries in the city's newest hot spot. Built in 1927 as a massive retail and distribution center for Sears, and then sitting vacant for two decades, Crosstown Concourse now holds a mix of indie restaurants, shops and businesses, and even a school.

Gus's World Famous Fried Chicken FAST FOOD $
(Map p370; ☎901-527-4877; www.gusfriedchicken.com; 310 S Front St; plates $7-12; ⏲11am-9pm Sun-Thu, to 10pm Fri & Sat) Fried-chicken connoisseurs across the globe twitch in their sleep as they dream about the gossamer-light offerings at this downtown concrete bunker, with a fun, neon-lit interior and a vintage jukebox. On busy nights waits can top an hour.

Imagine Vegan Cafe VEGAN $
(Map p368; ☎901-654-3455; www.imaginevegancafe.com; 2158 Young Ave; most mains $6-14; ⏲11am-9pm; 🛜📝) 🌿 Vegans and veggies face an uphill battle in Memphis (hell, all over the South…), but this inventive Cooper-Young cafe swims alone in a sea of pulled pork and fried chicken, pulling off all the iconic Southern staples without even changing their names (don't worry – everything is vegan!).

Bar DKDC INTERNATIONAL **$**
(Map p368; ☎901-272-0830; www.bardkdc.com; 964 S Cooper St; dishes $8-14; ⏰5pm-3am) Cheap and flavorful – and at times global – street food is the calling at this ever-evolving Cooper-Young staple, which serves up everything from *muffulettas* (classic New Orleans sandwiches) to Vietnamese *banh mi* rolls to Thai chicken dumplings. The space has eclectic decor, a chalkboard wine and beer list, and friendly bartenders.

★**Gray Canary** SEAFOOD **$$**
(Map p370; ☎901-249-2932; www.thegraycanary.com; 301 S Front St; small plates $6-18, mains $24-56; ⏰5-10pm Tue-Thu, to 11pm Fri & Sat, 3-9pm Sun) Served in a simmering hug of chili-garlic butter, spinach and Parmesan, the grilled oysters are an oh-so-delicious introduction to this newcomer, where tip-top service, chic digs and simple but exquisite seafood dishes merge for a perfect evening out. The front bar ensures a festive mood with winning craft cocktails and more than two dozen wines by the glass.

Alchemy TAPAS **$$**
(Map p368; ☎901-726-4444; www.alchemymemphis.com; 940 S Cooper St; tapas $7-18, mains $17-21; ⏰4pm-2am Mon, Fri & Sat, to 11pm Tue-Thu, 10:30am-2:30pm & 4-10pm Sun) A flash spot in the Cooper-Young district, serving tasty Southern tapas like truffled deviled eggs with smoked salmon, shrimp and grits with smoked Gouda and tasso-ham gravy, and poached-pear salad with candied pecans and blue cheese. The kitchen stays open until midnight on weekends. Good selection of cocktails, bourbons and local beers, too, at the well-run bar.

Hog & Hominy SOUTHERN, ITALIAN **$$**
(☎901-207-7396; www.hogandhominy.com; 707 W Brookhaven Circle; pizza $14-17; ⏰11am-2pm & 5-10pm Mon-Wed, to midnight Thu-Sat, 11am-11pm Sun; 📶) The chef-driven, Southern-rooted Italian at this Brookhaven Circle hot spot has grabbed the nation's attention, winning best new this and best new that from publications ranging from *GQ* to *Food & Wine* since it opened in 2011. Small plates and perfect brick-oven pizza are the mainstays, along with seasonal cocktails, craft beers and bocce.

Majestic Grille EUROPEAN **$$$**
(Map p370; ☎901-522-8555; www.majesticgrille.com; 145 S Main St; mains lunch $8-36, dinner $12-51; ⏰11am-10pm Mon-Thu, to 10pm Fri, 11am-2:30pm & 4-11pm Sat, 10am-2pm & 4-9pm Sun; 📶) Set in an old silent-movie theater near Beale St, with pre-talkie black-and-whites strobing in the handsome dark-wood dining room, Majestic serves classic continental fare, from roasted half chickens to seared tuna and grilled pork tenderloin, and four varieties of hand-cut filet mignon.

Sweet Grass SOUTHERN US **$$$**
(Map p368; ☎901-278-0278; www.sweetgrassmemphis.com; 937 S Cooper St; small plates $14-23, mains $25-41; ⏰5-9pm Mon-Thu, to 11pm Sat, 10:30am-2pm & 5-11pm Sun; 📶) Contemporary Lowcountry cuisine (the seafood-heavy cooking of the South Carolina and Georgia coasts) wins rave reviews at this casual Midtown restaurant, split between a more rambunctious bar side called **Next Door** (go for the fried-egg sandwich!) and a more refined bistro side with a more sophisticated menu, a raw bar and some unforgettable shrimp and grits.

Drinking & Entertainment

Beale St is party central but caters nearly 100% to tourists. The East Memphis neighborhoods of Cooper-Young and Overton Square are where locals go, and these offer the best concentration of hip bars and restaurants. Both are about 4 miles east of downtown. Last call is 3am. The city's first distillery, **Old Dominick** (Map p370; ☎901-260-1250; www.olddominick.com; 305 S Front St; tours $12; ⏰noon-7pm Thu, to 8pm Fri & Sat, to 5pm Sun), opened in 2017.

★**Loflin Yard** BEER GARDEN
(Map p368; ☎901-290-1140; www.loflinyard.com; 7 W Carolina Ave; ⏰4-11pm Wed & Thu, to 1am Fri, 11:30am-1am Sat, 11:30am-10pm Sun; 📶) A massive, countrified adult-play oasis in downtown Memphis, this buzzy spot sits on nearly an acre of junkyard-aesthetic beer garden anchored by the old Loflin Safe & Lock Co and wrapping around the trickling canal remains of Gayoso Bayou. Besides the space itself, the seasonal and oak-barrel-aged cocktails steal the show, though the mostly smoked offerings (chicken wings, brisket) compete.

★**Wiseacre Brewing Co** MICROBREWERY
(Map p368; www.wiseacrebrew.com; 2783 Broad Ave; ⏰4-10pm Mon-Thu, 1-10pm Fri & Sat; 📶) A favorite Memphis taproom, Wiseacre is in the warehouse district of Binghampton, 5 miles east of downtown. Sample year-

round and seasonal craft brews on the deck, which features a wraparound porch hugging two enormous, near-100-year-old concrete wheat silos, and swarms with people and pets.

Young Avenue Deli LIVE MUSIC
(Map p368; ☎901-278-0034; www.youngavenuedeli.com; 2119 Young Ave; ⊙11am-3am;) This Midtown favorite has food, pool and occasional live music that caters to a laid-back young crowd hyped up on 36 taps of draft craft and another 130 can and bottle options.

★**Wild Bill's** BLUES
(Map p368; www.wildbillsmemphis.com; 1580 Vollintine Ave; ⊙5-11pm Thu, 8pm-3am Fri & Sat, 4pm-midnight Sun) Don't even think of showing up at this gritty, hole-in-the-wall juke joint before midnight. Order a 40oz beer and a basket of wings, then sit back to watch some of the greatest blues acts in Memphis (from 11pm Friday and Saturday only). Expect some stares from the locals; it's worth it for the kick-ass, ultra-authentic jams.

Information

Memphis Visitor Center (Map p368; ☎888-633-9099; www.memphistravel.com; 3205 Elvis Presley Blvd; ⊙9am-6pm Apr-Sep, to 5pm Oct-Mar) City information center near the exit for Graceland.

Tennessee State Visitor Center (Map p370; ☎901-543-6757; www.tnvacation.com; 119 N Riverside Dr; ⊙7am-11pm) Brochures for the whole state. Near Mud Island.

Getting There & Around

Memphis International Airport (MEM; Map p368; ☎901-922-8000; www.flymemphis.com; 2491 Winchester Rd;) is around 10.5 miles southeast of Beale St via I-55; taxis to downtown cost between $23 and $25. Rideshare options are also available. The **Memphis Area Transit Authority** (MATA; Map p368; www.matatransit.com; 444 N Main St; fares $1.75) operates local buses; buses 2 and 4 go to the Airways Transit Center, where you can pick up the airport shuttle bus. The shuttle-bus stop is near Terminal C.

The station serving **Greyhound** (Map p368; ☎901-395-8770; www.greyhound.com; 3033 Airways Blvd;) and **Megabus** (Map p368; https://us.megabus.com; 3033 Airways Blvd;) is located at MATA's Airways Transit Center near Memphis International Airport. The **Amtrak Central Station** (www.amtrak.com; 545 S Main St) is right downtown.

Nashville

Nashville is on a roll that just won't stop. Country-music stars are slapping their names on brand-new honky-tonks. Boutique hotels seem to open monthly. Bachelors and bachelorettes are arriving in hordes to party. And acclaimed chefs are going far beyond the meat-and-three, though biscuits and hot chicken are doing just fine.

But don't fret about all the change. For country fans and wannabe songwriters all over the world, a trip to Nashville is still the ultimate pilgrimage. Since the 1920s the city has been attracting musicians who have taken the country genre from the 'hillbilly music' of the early 20th century to the slick 'Nashville sound' of the 1960s to the punk-tinged alt-country of the 1990s to the heartfelt indie troubadours of today. Nashville's musical attractions range from the Country Music Hall of Fame to the revered Grand Ole Opry to Jack White's niche record label.

Sights

Nashville sits on a rise beside the Cumberland River, with the state capitol situated at the highest point. The city's most engaging museums are downtown, but you'll find cultural attractions aplenty in and around the universities. Further afield, plantations, battlefields and forts draw Civil War enthusiasts and history fans. The city teems with inviting parks. Several are connected by paved greenways. South of downtown, the zoo and science center are nice distractions for the kids.

Downtown & the Gulch

Lower Broadway is downtown's country heart, thumping with shops, restaurants and honky-tonks. South of Lower Broadway is **SoBro**, revitalized by the Music City Center and the Country Music Hall of Fame. **Printers Alley**, just west of 2nd Ave N, is a narrow cobblestoned lane known for its nightlife. Along the Cumberland River, **Riverfront Park** and, across the pedestrian bridge, **Cumberland Park** are landscaped promenades, home to a greenway, a dog park and a new amphitheater. **The Gulch**, once industrial, has gone glossy with hip restaurants and upscale shops, while microbreweries cluster in the **Brewery District**.

Nashville

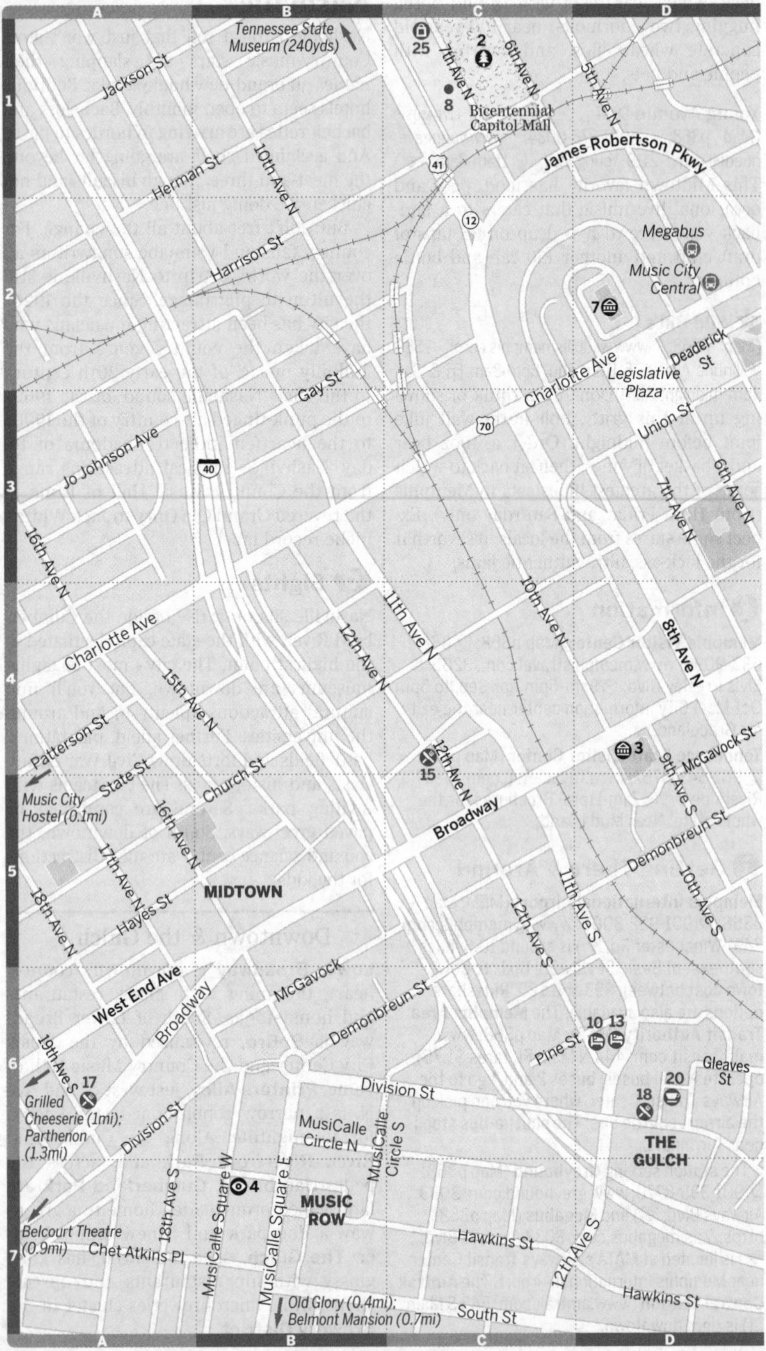

A B C D

1 2 3 4 5 6 7

Tennessee State Museum (240yds)
25
2
8
7th Ave N
6th Ave N
5th Ave N
Bicentennial Capitol Mall
Jackson St
Herman St
10th Ave N
41
James Robertson Pkwy
12
Harrison St
Megabus
Music City Central
7
Gay St
Deaderick St
Charlotte Ave
Legislative Plaza
Union St
70
Jo Johnson Ave
40
6th Ave N
7th Ave N
16th Ave N
10th Ave N
11th Ave N
Charlotte Ave
12th Ave N
8th Ave N
15th Ave N
Patterson St
3
McGavock St
15
12th Ave N
9th Ave S
Music City Hostel (0.1mi)
State St
Church St
Broadway
16th Ave N
Demonbreun St
17th Ave N
MIDTOWN
10th Ave S
18th Ave N
Hayes St
11th Ave S
12th Ave S
West End Ave
McGavock
Broadway
Demonbreun St
10
13
Pine St
19th Ave S
17
Gleaves St
20
Grilled Cheeserie (1mi); Parthenon (1.3mi)
Division St
Division St
18
MusiCalle Circle N
MusiCalle Circle S
THE GULCH
4
18th Ave S
MusiCalle Square W
MusiCalle Square E
MUSIC ROW
Belcourt Theatre (0.9mi)
Chet Atkins Pl
Hawkins St
12th Ave S
Old Glory (0.4mi); Belmont Mansion (0.7mi)
South St
Hawkins St

A B C D

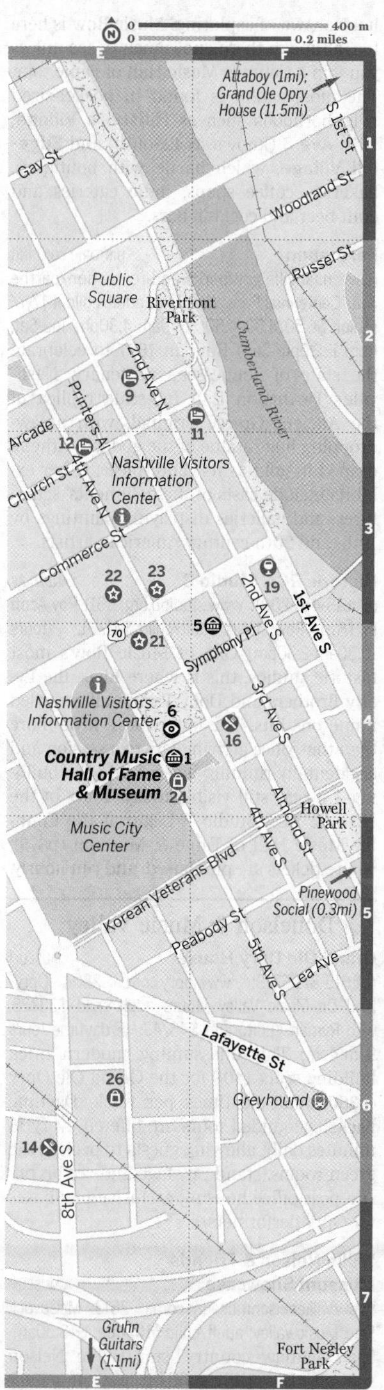

Nashville

Top Sights

1 Country Music Hall of Fame & Museum E4

Sights

2 Bicentennial Capitol Mall C1
3 Frist Center for the Visual Arts D4
4 Historic RCA Studio B B7
5 Johnny Cash Museum & Store F4
6 Music City Walk of Fame Park E4
7 Tennessee State Capitol D2

Activities, Courses & Tours

8 NashTrash C1

Sleeping

9 21c Museum Hotel E2
10 404 .... D6
11 Nashville Downtown Hostel F2
12 Noelle E3
13 Thompson Nashville D6

Eating

14 Arnold's E6
15 Chauhan Ale & Masala House C4
16 Etch F4
17 Hattie B's A6
18 Otaku Ramen D6

Drinking & Nightlife

19 Acme Feed & Seed F3
20 Barista Parlor D6

Entertainment

21 Robert's Western World E4
22 Ryman Auditorium E3
Station Inn .... (see 10)
23 Tootsie's Orchid Lounge E3

Shopping

24 Hatch Show Print E4
25 Nashville Farmers Market C1
26 Third Man Records E6

★Country Music Hall of Fame & Museum MUSEUM

(www.countrymusichalloffame.org; 222 5th Ave S; adult/child $26/16, with audio tour $28/19, with Studio B 1hr tour $41/31; ⌚9am-5pm) This monumental museum, reflecting the near-biblical importance of country music to Nashville's soul, is a must-see whether you're a country music fan or not.

Gaze at Carl Perkins' blue suede shoes, Elvis' gold Cadillac (actually white) and gold piano (actually gold), and Hank Williams' Western-cut suit with musical note appliqués.

Johnny Cash Museum & Store MUSEUM
(www.johnnycashmuseum.com; 119 3rd Ave S; adult/child $22/18; ⊙9am-7pm) Nashville's museum dedicated to 'The Man in Black' is smallish but houses the most comprehensive collection of Johnny Cash artifacts and memorabilia in the world, officially endorsed by the Cash family.

Frist Center for the Visual Arts GALLERY
(www.fristartmuseum.org; 919 Broadway; adult/senior/child $15/10/free, military discounts available; ⊙10am-5:30pm Mon-Wed & Sat, to 9pm Thu & Fri, 1-5:30pm Sun; P) A top-notch post office turned art museum and complex, hosting traveling exhibitions of everything from American folk art to Picasso, and as off-the-wall as auto shows and fashion displays.

Tennessee State Museum MUSEUM
(www.tnmuseum.org; 1000 Rosa L Parks Blvd, Bicentennial Mall; ⊙10am-5pm Tue, Wed, Fri & Sat, to 8pm Thu, 1-5pm Sun;) FREE This engaging museum, which moved into spiffy new digs in 2018, offers a worthy, balanced look at the state's past, with Native American handicrafts, interactive exhibits and quirky historical artifacts such as President Andrew Jackson's inaugural hat and a dress worn by First Lady Sarah Childress Polk. There's also a hands-on Children's Gallery and space for changing exhibits.

Tennessee State Capitol HISTORIC BUILDING
(615-741-0830; www.capitol.tn.gov; Charlotte Ave; ⊙tours 9am-3pm Mon-Fri) FREE This 1845–59 Greek Revival building was built from local limestone and marble by slaves and prison inmates working alongside European artisans. Around the back, steep stairs lead down to the **Bicentennial Capitol Mall** (615-741-5280; 600 James Robertson Parkway) FREE, whose outdoor walls are covered with historical facts about Tennessee's history, and the wonderful daily **Farmers Market** (615-880-2001; www.nashvillefarmersmarket.org; 900 Rosa L Parks Blvd; ⊙8am-6pm Sun-Thu, to 8pm Fri & Sat except farm sheds).

Midtown, Music Row & 12South

This area is anchored by Belmont and Vanderbilt Universities. Centennial Park, home to the Parthenon, and the 1853 **Belmont Mansion** (615-460-5459; www.belmontmansion.com; 1900 Belmont Blvd, Hillsboro; adult/youth 13-18yr/child 6-12yr $15/7/5; ⊙10am-4pm Mon-Sat, from 11am Sun; P) are top picks for an hour or two of exploring. Music Row is here too, although there's not much to see unless you join a Country Music Hall of Fame tour. The most action is found in pocket-sized neighborhoods such as **Hillsboro Village**, **12th Ave S** (known as 12South) and **Edgehill Village**, which bustle with boutiques, bakeries, coffee shops, indie eateries and craft beer and cocktail bars.

Parthenon HISTORIC BUILDING
(www.nashville.gov/parks-and-recreation/parthenon; Centennial Park, West End; adult/child 4-17yr/senior $6.50/4.50/4.50; ⊙9am-4:30pm Tue-Sat, from 12:30pm Sun) Built in 1897 to celebrate the state of Tennessee's centenary, Nashville's Parthenon is a full-scale replica of the Ancient Greece original, with a jaw-dropping huge statue of the goddess Athena draped in gold as its centerpiece. Other exhibits include casts of the pediments' sculptures, and galleries displaying paintings by 19th- and 20th-century American artists.

Historic RCA Studio B LANDMARK
(615-416-2001; www.studiob.org; 1611 Roy Acuff Pl, Music Row; tours adult/child $41/31; ⊙tours 10:30am-2:30pm) One of Music Row's most historic studios, this is where Elvis, the Everly Brothers and Dolly Parton all recorded numerous hits. The latter did a little more than that, once arriving late to a session and accidentally running her car into the building – a scar still visible today. Tours of the Historic RCA Studio B begin at the Country Music Hall of Fame & Museum (p375), where tickets are purchased, and run hourly.

Donelson & Music Valley

Grand Ole Opry House MUSEUM
(615-871-6779; www.opry.com; 2804 Opryland Dr, Music Valley; tours adult/child $33/28, with Ryman Auditorium $48/43; ⊙daytime tours 9am-4pm) This unassuming modern brick building seats 4400 for the Grand Ole Opry (p380) multiple times per week. Daytime backstage guided tours are offered every 15 minutes daily, allowing guests to peek in the green rooms, stand on stage and see an on-site post office housing exclusive mailboxes for Opry performers.

Willie Nelson & Friends Museum Showcase MUSEUM
(www.willienelsonmuseum.com; 2613 McGavock Pike, Music Valley; adult/child $10/free; ⊙8:30am-9pm) 'Outlaw country' star Willie Nelson sold all his worldly goods to pay off a $16.7

million tax debt in the early 1990s. You can see them at this quirky museum, not far from the Grand Ole Opry.

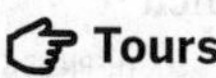

Tours

★NashTrash BUS
(615-226-7300; www.nashtrash.com; 900 Rosa L Parks Blvd; tours $35-38) The big-haired 'Jugg Sisters' lead a campy frolic through the risqué side of Nashville history, while guests sip BYO booze on the big pink bus. Book ahead as tours can sell out weeks in advance. Meet the bus at the southeast end of the Nashville Farmers Market.

Joyride SHUTTLE
(615-285-9835; www.joyrideus.com/nashville; complimentary shuttle but tips accepted, tours from $45) Tricked-out golf carts offer complimentary point-to-point shuttle service across Nashville. Rides are free, but drivers make their money on tips. For a fee the service also offers sightseeing tours, brewery tours and a bar golf crawl.

Tommy's Tours BUS
(615-335-2863; www.tommystours.com; tours $45) Wisecracking local Tommy Garmon leads highly entertaining three-hour tours of country-music sights. Cash or check only.

Festivals & Events

CMA Music Festival MUSIC
(www.cmafest.com; Jun) This four-day country-music extravaganza draws tens of thousands of fans to town.

Tennessee State Fair FAIR
(615-800-3675; www.tnstatefair.org; 500 Wedgewood Ave, Wedgewood-Houston; early Sep) Held yearly since 1869, the Tennessee State Fair is a classic American tradition to celebrate the harvest. Kids spend all year raising animals and perfecting their crafting skills to be judged in the many competitions. Spectators can enjoy pig races, mule-pulls, cake bake-offs and fun games – Hula-Hoop competition anyone? There are nightly concerts, carnival rides and plenty of fried food.

Sleeping

Downtown & the Gulch

★Nashville Downtown Hostel HOSTEL $
(615-497-1208; www.nashvilledowntownhostel.com; 177 1st Ave N; dm $32-45, r $100-250; P) Well located, only a block from Lower Broadway, and up to the minute in style and function. The common space in the basement, with its rather regal exposed stone walls and beamed rafters, is your all-hours mingle den. Dorm rooms are on the 3rd and 4th floors, and have lovely wood floors, exposed timber columns, silver-beamed ceilings and four, six or eight bunks.

WORTH A TRIP

FRANKLIN

The town of Franklin, 17 miles south of Nashville, has a charming downtown filled with boutiques, antique stores and lively eateries. Here one of the Civil War's bloodiest battles was fought. On November 30, 1864, during the Battle of Franklin, some 37,000 men (20,000 Confederates and 17,000 Union soldiers) fought over a 2-mile stretch on Franklin's outskirts. Nashville's sprawl has turned much of that battlefield into suburbs, but several historic sites spotlight the turbulent conflict. The rural community of **Arrington**, home to a popular vineyard, is 10 miles southeast of downtown.

21c Museum Hotel BOUTIQUE HOTEL $$$
(615-610-6400; www.21cMuseumHotels.com; 221 2nd Ave N; r from $299; P) The South's hippest hotel-museum-hybrid chain has settled into a rehabilitated historic Gray & Dudley Building. In addition to its 124 trademark modern, art-forward rooms – five of which have access to rooftop terraces with Cumberland River views – there's a dedicated spa, six galleries and a hip restaurant that spills out into the adjoining alleyway.

★Noelle BOUTIQUE HOTEL $$$
(615-649-5000; www.noelle-nashville.com; 200 4th Ave N; r from $280) Nashville's best sleep conjures 1930s glamor through a modern lens, and its lobby bar, Trade Room, stuns with original brass detailing and Tennessee pink marble. The rooftop bar, Rare Bird, offers panoramic downtown views from 5pm when the weather cooperates. Rooms are a minimalist take on mid-century modern style in blue, white and gray, with beautiful rustic hardwood floors.

404 BOUTIQUE HOTEL $$$
(615-242-7404; www.the404nashville.com; 404 12th Ave S; r $309-399;) Guests let themselves into Nashville's hippest – and smallest – hotel. Beyond the ebonized cedar frontage, industrial grays under violet lighting lead to four rooms in the minimalist space, most featuring painstakingly hip loft spaces. Local photography by Caroline Allison adds a splash of color here.

There's also a highly regarded restaurant in a shipping container, and parking is included.

Thompson Nashville BOUTIQUE HOTEL $$$
(615-262-6000; www.thompsonhotels.com; 401 11th Ave S; r from $349;) A bastion of finely polished, mid-century modern cool, the Thompson Nashville is the Gulch's see-and-be-seen seat of style, whether that be agonizing over which of the Third Man Records–curated vinyl collection to spin in the lobby, or where to sit at the immensely hip, open-air rooftop bar, **LA Jackson**.

Midtown, Music Row & 12South

Music City Hostel HOSTEL $
(615-497-1208; www.musiccityhostel.com; 1809 Patterson St, Midtown; dm $33-46, d $110-126, tr $128-156;) These squat brick bungalows are humble, but Nashville's West End hostel is lively and welcoming, with a common kitchen, an outdoor grill, a fire pit and some fun touches: the brightly painted doors are covered in artwork by guests passing through. The crowd is young and international, and many hoppin' West End bars are within walking distance.

Donelson & Music Valley

Gaylord Opryland Resort RESORT $$
(615-889-1000; www.marriott.com; 2800 Opryland Dr, Music Valley; r from $200;) This whopping 2888-room hotel is a universe unto itself, the largest non-casino resort in the USA. Why would you set foot outdoors when you can ride a flatboat along an artificial river, eat sushi beneath faux waterfalls in an indoor garden, or sip whisky in an antebellum-style mansion, all *inside* the hotel's three massive glass atriums?

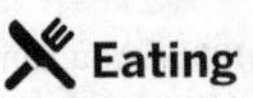

Eating

Downtown & the Gulch

Arnold's SOUTHERN US $
(www.arnoldscountrykitchen.com; 605 8th Ave S, The Gulch; mains from $10.74; 10:30am-2:45pm Mon-Fri) Grab a tray and line up with college students, garbage collectors and country-music stars at Arnold's, king of the meat-and-three ($10.74). That line is often out the door. Slabs of drippy roast beef are the house specialty, along with fried chicken on Mondays, fried green tomatoes, cornbread two ways, and big gooey wedges of chocolate meringue pie.

Otaku Ramen RAMEN $
(615-942-8281; www.otakuramen.com; 1104 Division St, The Gulch; ramen dishes $13-16; 11am-2:30pm Mon-Fri, 5-10pm Tue-Thu & Sun, noon-10pm Sat & Sun) Angle for a seat overlooking the open kitchen at this spare but stylish ramen joint. Behind the counter, efficient cooks stuff duck confit into pillowy buns, sizzle tender morsels in hot skillets and load custom noodles and regionally sourced pork into ramen bowls. Slurping is expected. One hour of free parking in the lot across the street and next door.

Chauhan Ale & Masala House INDIAN $$
(615-242-8426; www.chauhannashville.com; 123 12th Ave N, The Gulch; mains $12-28; 11am-2pm & 5-10pm Sun-Thu, to 11pm Fri & Sat;) Namaste and Nashville collide at celebrity chef Maneet Chauhan's Gulch eatery that showcases inventive Indian fusion on a global scale. Typical Desi fare meets Mexican, Canadian, British and American Southern influences. Dishes such as chili paneer bhurjee relleno, tandoori chicken poutine and a tiffin-inspired meat-and-three pair gorgeously with Indian spice-infused microbrews and creative cocktails.

★**Etch** MODERN AMERICAN $$$
(615-522-0685; www.etchrestaurant.com; 303 Demonbreun St; mains $23-39; 11am-2pm & 4:30-10pm Mon-Fri, 4:30-10:30pm Sat;) Well-known Nashville chef Deb Paquette's Etch serves some of the city's most inventive cuisine – comfort food whose flavors and textures have been manipulated into tantalizing combinations, surpassing expectations at every bite. Octopus and shrimp bruschetta, roasted cauliflower with truffled pea pesto, lamb loin with ginger grits,

venison with walnut pomegranate sauce – all masterpieces. Reservations are essential here.

Midtown, Music Row & 12South

★Hattie B's CHICKEN $

(615-678-4794; www.hattieb.com; 112 19th Ave S, Midtown; quarter/half plates from $8.50/12; 11am-10pm Mon-Thu, to midnight Fri & Sat, to 4pm Sun) When it comes to hot chicken supremacy, based on sheer numbers, Hattie B's reigns supreme in Nashville. The ultra-popular fried chicken spot serves up moist, high-quality birds, which come devilishly fried to levels that top out at 'Shut the Cluck Up!' hot, and it means business (nose-runnin', head-itchin' 'Damn Hot' was our limit). Get in line.

Grilled Cheeserie AMERICAN $

(www.grilledcheeserie.com; 2003 Belcourt Ave, Hillsboro Village; sandwiches $8-9; 11am-9pm;) Hurry up and wait for gussied up, gourmet versions of an American classic: the grilled cheese sandwich. It's done up here in versions so satisfying, you'll forget a simpler sandwich ever existed. Go for pimiento mac 'n' cheese and dip it in the creamy tomato soup, a match made in foodie heaven. Follow with an outrageous gourmet milkshake.

★Epice LEBANESE $$

(615-720-6765; www.epicenashville.com; 2902 12th Ave S, 12South; lunch mains $12-15, dinner mains $23-33; 11am-9:30pm Tue-Thu, to 10pm Fri & Sat, to 9pm Sun) For an inviting and delicious respite from exploring the shops of 12South, pop into this bright and sparkling Lebanese bistro. The highlight at lunch? The sandwiches, which are served with a hearty peasant salad and potatoes roasted with cilantro. Sandwich choices include lamb, sirloin and grilled salmon. At dinner, the sandwiches graduate to rack of lamb, tenderloin skewers and fish fillets.

Edley's Bar-B-Que BARBECUE $$

(615-953-2951; www.edleysbbq.com; 2706 12th Ave S, 12South; mains $10-23.50; 11am-10pm Sun-Fri, from 8am Sat;) This barbecue joint, with its simple, down-home decor and some seriously great aromas wafting from the kitchen, is a Nashville staple. The pork platter is the obvious choice, though the brisket sandwich isn't a bad pick either. The meat will melt in your mouth and the peppery-sweet sauce will satisfy the pickiest of barbecue connoisseurs.

East Nashville

★Wild Cow VEGETARIAN $

(615-262-2717; www.thewildcow.com; 1896 Eastland Ave; mains $8-12; 11am-9pm Mon, Wed, Thu & Sun, to 10pm Fri & Sat;) Looking for a fresh and flavor-packed meal in East Nashville? Then hit up this small but inviting vegetarian eatery, where photos of happy livestock beam down on a mostly organic line-up of sandwiches, wraps, tacos and salads. The peanut tempeh tacos, with kale, avocado and peanut-marinaded tempeh, are superb. Nice staff and significant charitable donations round out the appeal.

Pepperfire Hot Chicken SOUTHERN US $

(615-582-4824; www.pepperfirehotchicken.com; 1000 Gallatin Ave, Suite C; mains $10-13; 11am-9pm Mon-Wed, to 10pm Thu-Sat) Since 2010, East Nashville's Pepperfire has been slinging spicy bird to heat seekers who appreciate a creative twist on classic hot chicken. A thin, crispy batter with a distinctive spice blend lends a rich, complex smokiness that sets Pepperfire's chicken apart. Tasty sides include crinkle fries, fried okra and mac and cheese. And there's cold, local beer to ease the heat.

Drinking & Nightlife

★Barista Parlor COFFEE

(www.baristaparlor.com; 610 Magazine St; 7am-6pm;) Nashville's best artisan coffeehouse (coffee $3-7) has enlisted an old stereo shop in the Gulch for its downtown location, and its retro aesthetic is a great backdrop for socializing or getting some work done. The exquisite espresso – courtesy of an $18,000 hand-built Slayer coffee machine – is every bit as memorable as in its original East Nashville location.

★Old Glory COCKTAIL BAR

(615-679-0509; http://oldglorynashville.com; 1200 Villa Pl, Edgehill Village; 5pm-1am Sun-Thu, to 2am Fri, noon-2am Sat) A towering smokestack rises like an altar in a corner of this steampunk speakeasy. Tucked off an alley in Edgehill Village, the space was a laundromat boiler room in the 1930s. Today the exposed brick, industrial piping, lofty ceiling and curved staircase are the backdrop for the city's most stunning cocktail bar – if you can find it!

Attaboy COCKTAIL BAR

(http://attaboy.us; 8 McFerrin Ave; ⏲5pm-3am) New York City's famed Attaboy is one of the bars credited with the entire modern craft-cocktail movement – its cocktails are accorded near mythological status by connoisseurs. The minimalist speakeasy-style East Nashville iteration of this tipple lab concocts flat-rate ($15), off-the-cuff creations, chilled with block ice. There's no menu – drinks are personalized.

Pinewood Social BAR

(☎615-751-8111; http://pinewoodsocial.com; 33 Peabody St; ⏲7am-1am Mon-Fri, from 9am Sat & Sun; 📶) You could spend days at Pinewood Social and never run low on things to do. There are couches to hang at and play board games, a large circular bar with finely crafted cocktails, and coffee from Crema, a Nashville favorite. Lounge by the plunge pool or play bocce on the outdoor patio. Oh, and there's a bowling alley, too.

Acme Feed & Seed BAR

(www.theacmenashville.com; 101 Broadway; ⏲11am-11pm Mon-Thu, to 2am Fri & Sat, 10am-11pm Sun; 📶) This ambitious, four-floor takeover of an old 1875 farm supply warehouse has finally given Nashvillians a reason to go downtown even when family is *not* visiting. The 1st floor is devoted to lightning-fast, but elevated, pub grub, with 27 beer taps and live music that's defiantly un-country most nights (Southern rock, indie, roots etc). This place is always buzzing.

☆ Entertainment

Nashville's opportunities for hearing live music are unparalleled. As well as the big venues, many talented country, folk, bluegrass, Southern-rock and blues performers play smoky honky-tonks, college bars, coffee shops and organic cafes for tips. Cover charges are rare. The singer-songwriter is just as respected as the stadium superstar, so look for well-attended songwriter nights at smaller venues.

★Station Inn LIVE MUSIC

(☎615-255-3307; www.stationinn.com; 402 12th Ave S; cover $10-20; ⏲open mic 7pm, live bands 9pm) Sit at one of the small cocktail tables, squeezed together on the worn wood floor in this beer-only dive, and behold the lightning fingers of bluegrass savants, illuminated by stage lights and neon signs. We are talking stand-up bass, banjo, mandolin, fiddle and a modicum of yodeling.

Ryman Auditorium CONCERT VENUE

(☎615-889-3060; www.ryman.com; 116 5th Ave N) The so-called 'Mother Church of Country Music' has hosted a laundry list of performers, from Martha Graham to Elvis, and from Katharine Hepburn to Bob Dylan. The Ryman's excellent acoustics, historic charm and large seating capacity have kept it the premier venue in town, with big names frequently passing through. The *Grand Ole Opry* country music stage show returns here for winter runs.

Bluebird Cafe LIVE MUSIC

(☎615-383-1461; www.bluebirdcafe.com; 4104 Hillsboro Pike, Green Hills; cover free-$30) It's in a strip mall in suburban South Nashville, but don't let that fool you: some of the best original singer-songwriters in country music have graced this tiny stage. Steve Earle, Emmylou Harris and the Cowboy Junkies have all played the Bluebird, which is the setting for the popular CMT television series, *Nashville*. Try your luck at the Monday open-mic nights.

Grand Ole Opry LIVE MUSIC

(☎615-871-6779; www.opry.com; 2804 Opryland Dr, Music Valley; tickets $40-110; ⏲Tue, Fri & Sat Feb-Oct, plus Wed Jun-Oct; 👪) Though you'll find a variety of country shows throughout the week, *the* performance to see is the *Grand Ole Opry,* a lavish tribute to classic Nashville country music, every Tuesday, Friday and Saturday night from February through October, with Wednesday shows added in summer. Performances return to the Ryman Auditorium from November through January.

Tootsie's Orchid Lounge HONKY-TONK

(☎615-726-7937; www.tootsies.net; 422 Broadway; ⏲10am-2:30am) The most venerated of the downtown honky-tonks, with music on three levels at any given moment, Tootsie's is a blessed dive oozing boot-stomping, hillbilly, beer-soaked grace. In the 1960s, club owner and den mother 'Tootsie' Bess nurtured Willie Nelson, Kris Kristofferson and Waylon Jennings when they were on the rise.

Robert's Western World LIVE MUSIC

(www.robertswesternworld.com; 416 Broadway; ⏲11am-2am Mon-Sat, from noon Sun) A dozen bars wouldn't get you halfway down Lower Broadway, and this is a cut above all the other joints. It pulls out all the stops for folks making a country music pilgrimage, and you can even get a burger or a fried bologna sandwich at the grill. Music starts at opening and goes all night.

★Belcourt Theatre CINEMA
(☎615-383-9140; www.belcourt.org; 2102 Belcourt Ave, Hillsboro Village) A true Nashville gem, this nonprofit cinema showcases the best of independent, documentary, world, repertory and classic cinema 365 days a year. It's also one of the only movie houses chosen to be part of the Sundance Film Festival USA program. Alongside the usual cola and popcorn offerings, there's full bar service.

Shopping

★Hatch Show Print ART
(☎615-577-7710; www.hatchshowprint.com; 224 5th Ave S; ⏲9:30am-6pm) One of the oldest letterpress print shops in the USA, Hatch has been using old-school, hand-cut blocks to print its bright, iconic posters since vaudeville. The company has produced graphic ads and posters for almost every country star and now has a permanent place inside the Country Music Hall of Fame.

★Third Man Records MUSIC
(www.thirdmanrecords.com; 623 7th Ave S; ⏲10am-6pm) In a still-industrial slice of downtown you'll find Jack White's boutique record label, shop and novelty lounge, complete with its own lathe and live venue. It sells mostly Third Man recordings on vinyl and CD, collectible T-shirts, stickers, headphones and Pro-Ject record players. You'll also find White's entire catalog of recordings, and you can record yourself on vinyl ($20).

Gruhn Guitars MUSICAL INSTRUMENTS
(www.guitars.com; 2120 8th Ave S, Melrose; ⏲10am-6pm Mon-Sat) This renowned vintage-instrument store has been serving the Nashville community since 1970. The expert staff and amazing inventory attract musicians of all kinds; at any minute, some unassuming virtuoso may just walk in, grab a guitar, mandolin or banjo off the wall and jam.

Information

Metro Nashville's parks and community centers have free wi-fi, as do many hotels, restaurants and coffee shops.

DON'T MISS

BONNAROO MUSIC FESTIVAL

One of America's premier music festivals, **Bonnaroo** (www.bonnaroo.com; Manchester; ⏲mid-Jun) is the only large-scale 24/7 event in the country. Set on a 700-acre farm in Manchester, 60 miles southeast of Nashville, Bonnaroo combines camping, comedy, food, beverage and arts components, which lends it a communal feel. But it's the music that rules, spread over four blissfully raging days.

Nashville Visitors Information Center (☎615-259-4747; www.visitmusiccity.com; 501 Broadway, Bridgestone Arena; ⏲8am-5:30pm Mon-Sat, 10am-5pm Sun) Pick up free city maps here at the glass tower.

Nashville Visitors Information Center (www.visitmusiccity.com; 150 4th Ave N; ⏲8am-5pm Mon-Thu, to 4pm Fri) In the Regions Bank Building lobby.

INTERNET RESOURCES

Nashville Public Radio (www.nashvillepublicradio.org) News, music and NPR programming on 90.3 WPLN FM.

Nashville Scene (www.nashvillescene.com) Free alternative weekly with entertainment listings.

Tennessean (www.tennessean.com) Nashville's daily newspaper.

Getting There & Away

Nashville is located in Middle Tennessee at the junction of three interstates: I-40, I-65 and I-24. **Nashville International Airport** (BNA; ☎615-275-1675; www.flynashville.com; One Terminal Dr), 8 miles east of downtown, offers direct flights to more than 60 US cities, as well as Calgary, Cancun, the Bahamas and the Dominican Republic.

Greyhound (☎615-255-3556; www.greyhound.com; 709 5th Ave S) and **Megabus** (www.megabus.com; 5th Ave N, btwn Gay St & Charlotte Ave; 📶) are both located downtown and offer interstate bus services.

Getting Around

TO/FROM THE AIRPORT

It takes about 35 to 45 minutes to get downtown on MTA bus 18 ($1.70), which runs from the airport. Express 18 takes about 20 minutes. The airport bus stop is on level 1 in the Ground Transportation area.

Shuttles can be found on the Ground Transportation level (Level 1). The rate to downtown is about $30. A list of shuttle companies is provided on the airport website.

Taxis charge a flat rate of $25 for a ride to downtown or Opryland. A taxi to Vanderbilt/West End costs about $27. A trip to Franklin runs $55 to $60.

BICYCLE

Nashville's public bike-share scheme, **Nashville B-Cycle** (https://nashville.bcycle.com; ⊙ check-out hours 5am-10pm), offers more than 30 stations throughout the city. After purchasing a 24-hour membership for $5, your first hour is free; after that your credit card will be charged $1.50 per half-hour. Weekly, monthly and annual plans are also available. Maps can be found online.

Greenways run through the larger parks and connect a few of them – you can find B-Cycle stations at Shelby Bottoms Nature Center near the **Shelby Bottoms Greenway** (www.nashville.gov/parks-and-recreation; 1900 Davidson St, Main Trailhead parking lot; ⊙ dawn-dusk) and at the **Music City Walk of Fame Park** (☎ 866-584-6874; www.visitmusiccity.com/walkoffame; Demonbreun St, btwn 4th Ave S & 5th Ave S). B-Cycles are heavy, however, and may not be comfortable for longer cross-city rides. **Bike the Greenway** (☎ 615-920-1388; www.bikethegreenway.net; Two Rivers Park Trailhead, Music Valley; 2/4hr rental $30/45; ⊙ by reservation) offers rentals.

BUS

Now rebranding itself We Go, the MTA (www.nashvillemta.org) operates city bus services, based downtown at **Music City Central** (400 Charlotte Ave), including the free Music City Circuit, whose two routes hit the majority of Nashville attractions.

Eastern Tennessee

Dolly Parton, East Tennessee's most famous native, loves her home region so much that she's made a career out of singing about girls who leave the honeysuckle-scented embrace of the Smoky Mountains for the false glitter of the city. They're always sorry.

Largely a rural region of small towns, rolling hills and river valleys, the eastern third of the state is noteworthy for its friendly folks and pastoral charm. The lush southern Appalachian Mountains are great for hiking, camping and rafting. Pretty waterfalls are a regional specialty. Nearby Great Smoky Mountains National Park lures millions every year, but the crowds are easily ditched in East Tennessee's Cherokee National Forest.

The region's two main urban areas, Knoxville and Chattanooga, are easygoing riverside cities with lively student populations, great restaurants, fun craft breweries and outdoor adventures galore. For a blast of all things tacky and wacky, Gatlinburg and Pigeon Forge await.

Chattanooga

Chattanooga has charisma to spare. With world-class rock climbing, hiking, cycling and water-sports opportunities, it's one of the South's best cities for outdoorsy types. It's gorgeous, too: just check out those views from the Bluff View Art District! It's also remarkably eco-forward, with free electric buses, miles of well-used waterfront trails, and pedestrian bridges crossing the Tennessee River. All this makes it hard to credit its reputation in the 1960s as America's dirtiest city.

The city was a major railway hub throughout the 19th and 20th centuries, hence the 'Chattanooga Choo-Choo,' which was originally a reference to the Cincinnati Southern Railroad's passenger service from Cincinnati to Chattanooga, and later the title of a 1941 Glen Miller tune. The eminently walkable downtown is a maze of historic stone and brick buildings featuring tasty gourmet kitchens, craft breweries and distilleries. Burgeoning neighborhoods keep the vibe compelling. It's easy to love the 'Noog!

Sights & Activities

★ Songbirds MUSEUM

(☎ 423-531-2473; www.songbirdsguitars.com; Chattanooga Choo Choo Hotel, 35 Station St; adult/child under 13yr $16/free, all access $39; ⊙ 10am-6pm Mon-Wed, to 8pm Thu-Sat, noon-6pm Sun) This astonishing guitar collection – the largest assemblage of vintage and rare guitars anywhere – is Chattanooga's newest world-class attraction. More than 500 guitars, many arranged in time-line fashion from the 1950 Fender Broadcasters (the first mass-produced solid-body electric guitar) to the 1970s, grace this small space, including rock-star axes from Chuck Berry, BB King, Bo Diddley, Roy Orbison and Robby Krieger of the Doors, among others.

Hunter Museum of American Art GALLERY
(☎423-267-0968; www.huntermuseum.org; 10 Bluff View; adult/child under 18yr $15/free; ⏲10am-5pm Mon, Tue, Fri & Sat, to 8pm Thu, noon-5pm Wed & Sun; P) Set high on the river bluffs, this striking edifice of melted steel and glass – fronted by an early-20th-century mansion – is easily the most singular architectural achievement in Tennessee. Oh, and its 19th- and 20th-century art collection is fantastic. Permanent exhibits are free the first Thursday of the month between 4pm and 8pm, but special exhibits will cost $5.

Coolidge Park PARK
(www.chattanoogafun.com; 150 River St; P 👪) A good place to start a riverfront stroll, Coolidge Park has a play fountain, a carousel ($1 per ride), well-used playing fields, and a 50ft climbing wall attached to one of the columns supporting the **Walnut Street Bridge** (1 Walnut St; P), one of the world's largest pedestrian bridges.

★**Lookout Mountain** NATURAL FEATURE
(☎800-825-8366; www.lookoutmountain.com; 827 East Brow Rd; combo ticket adult/child 3-12yr $57/32; ⏲hours vary; P 👪) Some of Chattanooga's oldest and best-loved attractions are 6 miles outside the city at Lookout Mountain. Combination admission includes the **Incline Railway**, which chugs up a steep slope to the mountaintop; the stunning **Ruby Falls** (1720 S Scenic Hwy), the world's longest underground waterfall; and **Rock City** (1400 Patten Rd), a lofty garden marked by dramatic rock formations and a clifftop overlook with views across seven states. You can also purchase a ticket for each of the three attractions individually.

Tennessee Aquarium AQUARIUM
(☎800-262-0695; www.tnaqua.org; 1 Broad St; adult/child 3-12yr $35/22, incl IMAX $43/30; ⏲10am-6pm; P 👪) Occupying two side-by-side but separate buildings, this well-done aquarium is a fun and educational rainy-day destination. The River Journey building spotlights the inhabitants and ecology of the Tennessee River as it flows from the Appalachian Mountains to the Mississippi Delta. Exhibits in the Ocean Journey building showcase saltwater marine life – including piranhas! Crowd-pleasers include river otters, penguins, and leaping lemurs, which swung their way into the aquarium from Madagascar in 2017.

Sleeping & Eating

★**Crash Pad** HOSTEL $
(☎423-648-8393; www.crashpadchattanooga.com; 29 Johnson St; dm $38, d $89-99, tr $119; P ❄ @ 📶) 🍃 The South's best hostel, run by climbers, is a sustainable den of coolness in Southside, the 'Noog's hippest downtown neighborhood. Co-ed dorms overachieve: built-in lights, power outlets, fans and privacy curtains for each bed. Private rooms feature exposed concrete and bedside tables built into the bed frames. Access throughout is via hi-tech fobs, and linens, padlocks and breakfast supplies are included.

★**Moxy Chattanooga Downtown** HOTEL $$
(☎423-664-1180; www.moxy-hotels.marriott.com; 1220 King St; r $169-179; P ❄ 📶 🐾) Guests check in at the bar at this sharp, sassy hotel, where a kaleidoscope of bright colors and unique design details make for a compelling stay. Geared to younger travelers (but still appealing to young-at-heart visitors), the Moxy encourages communing, with numerous lounge areas tucked here and there. Rooms are on the small side, and spare, but comfortable.

Flying Squirrel AMERICAN $
(☎423-602-5980; www.flyingsquirrelbar.com; 55 Johnson St; mains $9-19; ⏲5pm-midnight Tue-Thu, to 2am Fri & Sat, 10:30am-3pm Sun; 📶) A neighbor to Crash Pad (same owners), Flying Squirrel is at its heart a very cool bar (21 and over only, except for Sunday brunch), but its locally sourced small-plate takes on fusion comfort food make for mighty fine pub grub – pork-belly fried rice, fried-chicken *bao* (Chinese steamed buns) and chocolate-hazelnut cheesecake, to name a few.

St John's Meeting Place AMERICAN $$
(☎423-266-4571; www.stjohnsmeetingplace.com; 1274 Market St; mains $12-35; ⏲5-9:30pm Mon-Thu, to 10pm Fri & Sat) The culinary anchor of Chattanooga's Southside is widely considered the city's best night out. It's Johnny Cash black (black-granite floor, black-glass chandeliers, black banquettes), lending it an unorthodox but mod elegance. The farm-to-table cuisine features the likes of duck tacos with jalapeño crema, braised-lamb sliders, and wild Alaskan halibut with wasabi-avocado mousse.

Drinking & Nightlife

Plus Coffee COFFEE

(☎423-521-2098; www.pluscoffee.co; 3800 St Elmo Ave; ⊙7am-6pm Mon-Fri, 8am-6pm Sat & Sun; 📶) It's easy to drive right by this delightfully minimalist coffeehouse in the up-and-coming neighborhood of St Elmo at the foot of the Incline Railway (p383) – the sign disappears somewhat into the historic brick building on which it sits. Reclaimed-wood tables and vintage furniture dot the loft-like space, and the menu is simple: brew, pour over and espresso.

Hutton & Smith Brewing MICROBREWERY

(☎423-760-3600; www.huttonandsmithbrewing.com; 431 E ML King Blvd; ⊙4-10pm Mon-Thu, noon-midnight Fri & Sat, noon-6pm Sun; 📶) One of the anchors of the newly hip MLK district, this 20-tap microbrewery ironically added a garage door so that it appears that its taproom is housed in a former mechanic's shop (or some such hipster industrial-building flip), but alas it wasn't anything special previously. Nevertheless, the beer – namely the Good Schist APA, coffee IPA and On-Sight Alt – pleases. Welcoming staff.

Information

Located in an outdoor public breezeway beside **High Point Climbing** (☎423-602-7625; www.highpointclimbing.com; 219 Broad St; day pass adult/child under 11yr $18/16; ⊙6am-10pm Mon, Wed & Fri, 10am-10pm Tue, Thu & Sat, 10am-8pm Sun; 👪), the **visitor center** (☎800-322-3344; www.chattanoogafun.com; 215 Broad St; ⊙10am-5pm) is easy to miss.

Getting There & Around

Chattanooga's modest **airport** (CHA; ☎423-855-2202; www.chattairport.com; 1001 Airport Rd) is 9 miles east of the city. The **Greyhound station** (☎423-892-1277; 960 Airport Rd) is just down the road from the airport.

For access to most downtown sites, ride the free **Downtown Electric Shuttle** (☎423-629-1473; www.gocarta.org) that plies the center and the North Shore. The visitor center has a route map.

Bike Chattanooga (www.bikechattanooga.com; daily pass $8) is Chattanooga's city-sponsored bike-share program. Bikes are lined and locked up at 41 stations throughout the city and riders can purchase access passes (starting at $8 for 24 hours) by credit card at any of the station kiosks. Rides under an hour are free.

Knoxville

Dubbed a 'scruffy little city' by the *Wall Street Journal* before the 1982 World's Fair, Knoxville is strutting its stuff these days as an increasingly prominent and polished destination for outdoor, gastronomy and craft-beer enthusiasts. Knoxville is also home to the University of Tennessee and its rabid college-football fan base.

Knoxville is a handy base for visiting Great Smoky Mountains National Park. Sugarlands Visitor Center is just 29 miles away, and Knoxville is a far more enticing spot to eat and drink than other cities near the park. For hikers and mountain bikers, the city's ever-expanding Urban Wilderness is becoming its own reason to visit.

Sights & Activities

Women's Basketball Hall of Fame MUSEUM

(☎865-633-9000; www.wbhof.com; 700 Hall of Fame Dr; adult/child 6-15yr $8/6; ⊙10am-5pm Mon-Sat May-Aug, 11am-5pm Tue-Fri, 10am-5pm Sat Sep-Apr; P 👪) You can't miss the massive orange basketball that marks the Women's Basketball Hall of Fame, a nifty look at the sport from the time when women were forced to play in full-length dresses. Interactive features include a half-time locker-room talk by legendary University of Tennessee coach Pat Summitt and a dribbling course to test your skills.

Ijams Nature Center OUTDOORS

(☎865-577-4717; www.ijams.org; 2915 Island Home Ave; ⊙visitor center 9am-5pm Mon-Sat, from 11am Sun, grounds 8am-sunset; 👪🐾) A one-stop shop for enjoying nature in Knoxville, 300-acre Ijams (pronounced 'eye-ams') is the de facto headquarters for the sprawling Urban Wilderness. Here you can stroll the scenic **River Boardwalk Trail** beside the Tennessee River, enjoy a canopy adventure tour (with a zipline), rent bikes ($20 per half day) and let the kids roam free in the nature-themed playground.

Sleeping & Eating

★Oliver Hotel BOUTIQUE HOTEL **$$**

(☎865-521-0500; www.theoliverhotel.com; 407 Union Ave; r $175-210, ste $295-330; P ❄ @ 📶) Knoxville's first boutique hotel boasts 28 modern, stylish rooms with fun subway-tiled showers (with rain-style shower heads), luxe linens, plush throwback furniture and carpets, and gorgeous hand-crafted coffee tables. The **Peter Kern Library bar** (⌚4pm-midnight Mon-Fri, 11am-2am Sat & Sun) draws craft-cocktail enthusiasts by night. The restaurant, **Oliver Royale** (mains lunch $10-18, dinner $16-34), is highly recommended.

★**Balter Beerworks** GASTROPUB $
(☎865-999-5015; www.balterbeerworks.com; 100 S Broadway; mains lunch $10-16, dinner $12-17; ⌚11am-11pm Mon-Thu, to midnight Fri, 10am-midnight Sat, 10am-10pm Sun) From the communal tables on the patio to the standing-room-only bar to the buzzing dining room, this joint – a former gas station – exudes a welcoming vibe. The pub fare is delicious, and options range from the Gouda-topped burger with sriracha sauce to cheesy shrimp and grits with andouille sausage. The easy-drinking house beer is brewed on-site.

★**JC Holdway** AMERICAN $$
(☎865-312-9050; www.jcholdway.com; 501 Union Ave; most mains $20-26; ⌚5:30-9:30pm Tue-Thu, to 10pm Fri & Sat; 📶) You'll want to reserve ahead for the privilege of noshing on James Beard Award–winning chef Joseph Lenn's modern Appalachian comfort cuisine. Lenn, who spent nearly a decade as executive chef at famed Blackberry Farm before returning home to Knoxville in 2016, does a ridiculously perfect wood-grilled pork with sweet-potato puree, and anything with smoked meat from Benton's Farm.

Information

Besides providing tourism info, including a free downtown walking-tour brochure, the **visitor center** (Visit Knoxville; ☎800-727-8045; www.visitknoxville.com; 301 S Gay St; ⌚8:30am-5pm Mon-Fri, 9am-5pm Sat, noon-4pm Sun) welcomes bands from across the Americana genre for WDVX's **Blue Plate Special**, a free concert series at noon Monday to Saturday.

Getting There & Around

Knoxville's **McGhee Tyson Airport** (☎865-342-3000; www.flyknoxville.com; 2055 Alcoa Hwy, Alcoa), 15 miles south of town, is served by around 20 nonstop domestic flights. The **Greyhound bus station** (☎865-524-0369; 100 E Magnolia Ave) is only about 1 mile north of downtown, making it a convenient option for ground travelers.

Gatlinburg & Pigeon Forge

Wildly kitschy and family-friendly Gatlinburg hunkers at the entrance to Great Smoky Mountains National Park, waiting to stun hikers with the scent of fudge, cotton candy and pancakes, and various odd museums and campy attractions. Boisterous new tasting rooms are drawing thirsty crowds to a slew of moonshine distilleries along Parkway, the main drag through town that rolls right into the national park. It's a wild ride of all that's good and bad about the USA at the same time, wrapped up in a gaudy explosion of magic shows and whiskey.

If you tire of all the flash and bling, you can find a handful of quality cultural and natural attractions within – or very close to – the busy downtown.

Around eight miles north of Gatlinburg, popular Pigeon Forge offers loads of amusement in a city packed tight with hotels, restaurants and family-friendly attractions.

Sights & Activities

★**Dollywood** AMUSEMENT PARK
(☎800-365-5996; www.dollywood.com; 2700 Dollywood Parks Blvd; adult/child 4-9yr $74/61; ⌚mid-Mar–Dec, hours vary seasonally; P 👪) Dollywood is a self-created ode to the patron saint of East Tennessee: the big-haired, big-bosomed and big-hearted country singer Dolly Parton. A clean and friendly place, the park features Appalachian-themed rides and attractions, the Splash Country water park, mountain crafts, restaurants serving Southern-fried food, and the **DreamMore Resort** (☎865-365-1900; www.dollywood.com/resort; 2525 DreamMore Way; r/ste from $359/379; P ❄ 📶 🏊).

Highlights include nationally acclaimed roller-coasters, live-music shows and the Chasing Rainbows Museum, which traces Dolly's fascinating life – her hometown is nearby Sevierville.

Gatlinburg SkyLift CABLE CAR
(☎865-436-4307; www.gatlinburgskylift.com; 765 Parkway; adult/child $16/13; ⌚9am-11pm Jun-Aug, hours vary rest of year) This ski-resort chairlift swoops you high into the Smokies, providing stellar views. The lofty SkyDeck and the 680ft-long SkyBridge, the longest suspension bridge in North America, opened at the top of the lift in 2019.

Anakeesta AMUSEMENT PARK
(☎865-325-2400; www.anakeesta.com; 576 Parkway; adult/child under 12yr $22/18; ⌚9am-10pm Jul–mid-Aug, shorter hours rest of year, closed Tue-Thu Jan & Feb; P 👪) A 'chondola' whisks visitors from downtown Gatlinburg

to this playground in the sky, where views of the Great Smokies are superb. Once atop Anakeesta Mountain you can bounce across 16 elevated bridges on the tree-canopy walk, hold tight on dueling ziplines (adult/child $30/26), ride the mountain coaster, let the kids explore Treehouse Village, or settle into a rocking chair and appreciate the view. Burgers and beer are available at the **Clifftop Grill** (mains $10 to $12).

★Ole Smoky Moonshine DISTILLERY
(☎865-436-6995; www.olesmoky.com; 903 Parkway; tasting $5; ⊙10am-10pm Sun-Thu, to 11pm Fri & Sat) Nicknamed The Holler, this stone-and-wood moonshine distillery – Tennessee's first licensed moonshine maker – appears at first glance to have a Disney flair, but it's the real deal. Gathering around the hilarious bartenders, sampling eight to 10 flavors of hooch and taking in the colorful commentary is Gatlinburg's best time.

★Titanic Museum MUSEUM
(☎417-334-9500; www.titanicpigeonforge.com; 2134 Parkway; adult/child 5-11yr $27/14; ⊙9am-10pm Jul & early Aug, closes earlier rest of year; P) On April 15, 1912, the steamship *Titanic* sank on her maiden voyage after colliding with an iceberg. The ship's history and the stories of many of her passengers are shared through artifacts, black-and-white photographs, personal histories and thoughtful interactive displays. Highlights include an actual deck chair from the ship, a replica of the grand staircase, and a haunting musical tribute to the ship's young musicians, who chose to stay onboard and play, possibly to keep passengers calm. All perished.

Sleeping & Eating

Bearskin Lodge LODGE $$
(☎877-795-7546; www.thebearskinlodge.com; 840 River Rd; r/ste from $139/164; P❄🛜🏊) Near the entrance to Great Smoky Mountains National Park (p354), this shingled riverside lodge is blessed with timber accents and a bit more panache than other Gatlinburg comers. All of the 96 spacious rooms have flat-screen TVs, and some have gas fireplaces and private balconies jutting over the river. There's an outdoor pool and a lazy river.

Buckhorn Inn INN $$
(☎865-436-4668; www.buckhorninn.com; 2140 Tudor Mountain Rd; r $125-205, cottages $185, 2-bedroom guesthouses from $240; P❄@🛜) A few minutes' drive and several light years away from the kitsch and crowds of downtown Gatlinburg, the tranquil Buckhorn has nine elegant rooms, seven private cottages and three guesthouses on a property that's a well-manicured private haven. If the unbroken views of Mt LeConte don't relax you enough, have a wander through the fieldstone meditation labyrinth.

Three Jimmys AMERICAN $
(☎865-325-1210; www.threejimmys.com; 1359 E Parkway; mains $10-26; ⊙11am-1am; 🛜) Escape the tourist hordes on the main drag and grab a bite at this locals' favorite with friendly waitstaff ('Here's your menu, baby...') and a long list of everything: barbecue, turkey Reubens, burgers, champagne chicken, steaks, a great spinach salad and so on. Hours vary seasonally. Good bar as well, with a dozen or so beers on tap.

Information

Pop into the **Gatlinburg Welcome Center** (☎865-277-8947; www.gatlinburg.com; 1011 Banner Rd; ⊙8:30am-7pm Jun-Oct, to 5:30pm Nov-May) for official information and maps – including a handy $1 waterfalls map – for both Gatlinburg and Great Smoky Mountains National Park.

Getting There & Around

The vast majority of visitors arrive in Gatlinburg by car. The nearest airport is Knoxville's McGhee Tyson Airport (p385), 41 miles away, and there's no regular intercity bus service.

Traffic and parking are serious issues in Gatlinburg. The **Gatlinburg Trolley** (www.gatlinburgtrolley.org; ⊙8:30am-midnight May-Oct, hours vary rest of year) serves downtown, and the trolley's tan line ($2 round trip) goes into the national park from June through October, with stops at Sugarlands Visitor Center, Laurel Falls and Elkmont Campground. Parking lots around town generally charge $10 for the day. If you get to Gatlinburg very early, you may snag free on-street parking on River Rd.

KENTUCKY

Horses thunder around racetracks, bourbon pours from distilleries and banjos twang in Kentucky, a geographical and cultural crossroads that's part North, part South, part genteel and part country cousin. Every corner is easy on the eye, but there are few sights more beautiful than the rolling limestone hills around Lexington, where long-legged steeds nibble under poplar trees on multimillion-dollar farms that you can visit. Bourbon distilleries also speckle the countryside, prime for scenic road tripping to swirl and sniff a dram at the source. It's like an offbeat version of California's Napa Valley, but with fewer crowds and headier alcohol. Caving, rock climbing and hiking prevail in the unspoiled parks and forests. And while big cities Louisville and Lexington have farm-to-table restaurants, cocktail bars and all of the other hipster requirements, most of Kentucky is made up of small towns with quiet scenes.

Information

Kentucky State Parks (502-564-2172; www.parks.ky.gov) Offers info on hiking, caving, fishing, camping and more in Kentucky's 52 state parks. So-called 'Resort Parks' have lodges. 'Recreation Parks' are for roughin' it. All are free.

Kentucky Tourism (www.kentuckytourism.com) Go online to request a detailed booklet on the state's attractions.

Louisville

Louisville (or Loo-a-vul, as the locals say) is handsome, underrated and undeniably cool. Think of it as a hipster with good Southern manners. A fun and artsy town built on bourbon and American sport icons (it's home to the Kentucky Derby, and was the birthplace of Muhammad Ali and the Louisville Slugger baseball bat), it has evolved into one of the South's most foodie-centric cities, a lovely spot to eat and museum-hop between rounds of pursuing North America's best bourbon old-fashioned cocktail.

Sights & Activities

Churchill Downs HORSE RACING
(502-636-4400; www.churchilldowns.com; 700 Central Ave) Churchill Downs is the landmark racetrack that hosts the epic Kentucky Derby (p389) in May. But there's plenty of action besides that: warm-ups and other thoroughbred races take place from late April to late June and again in September and throughout November. Tickets start at $5. You also can go on a guided tour of the grounds year-round via the onsite Kentucky Derby Museum.

Kentucky Derby Museum MUSEUM
(502-637-1111; www.derbymuseum.org; 704 Central Ave; adult/child $15/8; 8am-5pm Mon-Sat, 11am-5pm Sun mid-Mar–Nov, 9am-5pm Mon-Sat, 11am-5pm Sun Dec–mid-Mar) On the Churchill Downs racetrack grounds, the museum has exhibits on derby history, including a peek into the life of jockeys and a roundup of the most illustrious horses. Highlights include a 360-degree HD film about the race that lets you feel the horses thundering by, the 30-minute walking tour of the grandstands (which includes some engaging yarns), the eye-popping derby hat collection and sipping mint juleps in the museum cafe.

★**Muhammad Ali Center** MUSEUM
(502-584-9254; www.alicenter.org; 144 N 6th St; adult/child $14/9; 9:30am-5pm Tue-Sat, noon-5pm Sun) This must-see museum tells the tale of the city's most famous native: a local boxer nicknamed the Louisville Lip or, simply, The Greatest. Highlights among the interactive exhibits include a ring where you shadowbox with Ali, and a punching bag to practice your rhythm. Videos of his famous fights and street poetry captivate, but it's the way they're put in context with the Vietnam War and civil rights issues that Ali fought for that give the place its power.

★**Louisville Slugger Museum & Factory** MUSEUM
(877-775-8443; www.sluggermuseum.com; 800 W Main St; adult/child $15/8; 9am-5pm Mon-Sat, 11am-5pm Sun) See how baseball's most famous bat is made. Hillerich & Bradsby Co have been manufacturing the Louisville Slugger here since 1884. Admission includes a plant tour and a hall of baseball memorabilia that features Babe Ruth's 1927 record-setting bat and Hank Aaron's 700th home run bat. The displays will blow the minds of diehard fans. A take-home mini-slugger bat is included with the entrance fee.

Speed Art Museum MUSEUM
(502-634-2700; www.speedmuseum.org; 2035 S 3rd St; adult/child $15/10, free Sun; 10am-5pm Wed, Thu & Sat, 10am-8pm Fri, noon-5pm Sun) Built in 1927 and revamped to the tune of $60 million in recent years, Kentucky's most important art museum – unaffiliated but on the University of Louisville campus – is a beautiful juxtaposition of classic and

THE BOURBON TRAIL

Silky, caramel-colored bourbon whiskey was likely first distilled in Bourbon County, north of Lexington, around 1789. Today 95% of the world's bourbon is made in Kentucky, thanks to the state's pure, limestone-filtered water. Bourbon must contain at least 51% corn, and be stored in charred oak barrels for a minimum of two years. While connoisseurs drink it straight or with water, you must try a mint julep, the archetypal Southern drink made with bourbon, simple syrup and crushed mint.

The **Oscar Getz Museum of Whiskey History** (☎502-348-2999; www.oscargetzwhiskeymuseum.com; 114 N 5th St; ⊙10am-5pm Mon-Fri, 10am-4pm Sat, noon-4pm Sun May-Oct, 10am-4pm Tue-Sat, noon-4pm Sun Nov-Apr) FREE in Bardstown tells the bourbon story with old moonshine stills and other artifacts.

Most of Kentucky's traditional distilleries, which are centered on Bardstown and Frankfort, offer tours and tastings. Several new craft distilleries also have joined the pack. Plan on taking in about three sites per day. The official Bourbon Trail website (www.kybourbontrail.com) has details. Note that it doesn't include every distillery.

Distilleries near Bardstown include the following:

Maker's Mark (p393) This restored Victorian distillery is like a bourbon theme park, with an old gristmill and a gift shop where you can seal your own bottle in molten red wax. Tours depart on a rolling basis.

Willet (☎502-348-0899; www.kentuckybourbonwhiskey.com; 1869 Loretto Rd; tours $18-22; ⊙9:30am-5:30pm Mon-Sat) A family-owned distillery making small-batch bourbon in its own patented style. It's a gorgeous 120-acre property and a crowd favorite. Tours go on the hour.

Jim Beam American Stillhouse (☎502-543-9877; www.jimbeam.com; 526 Happy Hollow Rd, Clermont; 90min tours $14; ⊙9am-5:30pm Mon-Sat, noon-4:30pm Sun) It makes the country's best-selling bourbon. Watch a film about the Beam family, take the 90-minute tour through the factory and warehouses, and then converge on the distillery's high-tech tasting room to sample the wares. Tours depart every half-hour.

Limestone Branch (☎270-699-9004; www.limestonebranch.com; 1280 Veterans Memorial Hwy, Lebanon; 1hr tours $8; ⊙10am-5:30pm Mon-Thu, 10am-6pm Fri & Sat, 1-5:30pm Sun) Laid-back micro-distillery with a great backstory and venue like a western lodge.

Distilleries near Frankfort include:

Castle & Key (☎502-395-9070; www.castleandkey.com; 4445 McCracken Pike; tours $20-30; ⊙9:30am-5pm Wed-Sat, 10:30am-5pm Sun, closed Wed Jan & Feb) Craft distillery in a fairy-tale setting, complete with turreted stone castle and lush gardens. The distiller makes gin and vodka; her bourbon is still aging. Intimate, small-group tours; reservations advised.

Woodford Reserve (☎859-879-1812; www.woodfordreserve.com; 7855 McCracken Pike, Versailles; 1hr tours weekday/weekend $15/20; ⊙9am-5pm Mon-Sat, noon-4:30pm Sun, reduced hrs Jan & Feb) The prettiest of the lot, restored to its 1800s glory. The distillery still uses old-fashioned copper pots. Tours are hourly on the hour.

Buffalo Trace (☎800-654-8471; www.buffalotracedistillery.com; 1001 Wilkinson Blvd; ⊙9am-5:30pm Mon-Sat, noon-5pm Sun) FREE The nation's oldest continuously operating distillery has free tours and tastings – a rarity these days. Tours go at least hourly.

If you'd rather not drive, sit back with your whiskey snifter on a tour with **Mint Julep Experiences** (☎502-583-1433; www.mintjuleptours.com; 140 N 4th St, Ste 326; full-day tours $129-159).

contemporary. It's highlighted by Spencer Finch's (of National September 11 Memorial Museum fame) Grand Atrium walled with fretted glass and Thai architect Kulapat Yantrasast's striking stacked concrete exterior. Collection highlights include Chuck Close's Barack Obama tapestry and Rembrandt's *Portrait of a 40-Year-Old Woman.*

Festivals & Events

★Kentucky Derby SPORTS

(☎502-636-4400; www.kentuckyderby.com; 700 Central Ave) On the first Saturday in May, a who's who of upper-crust USA puts on their seersucker suits and most flamboyant hats and descends for the 'greatest two minutes in sports': the Kentucky Derby, the longest-running continuous sporting event in North America, when 20 horses thunder around the track at Churchill Downs for the race of a lifetime.

First Friday Hop ART

(www.firstfridayhop.com; Main & Market Sts; ⊙7am-7pm, 1st Fri of month) More than 50 galleries, boutiques and restaurants participate in this monthly event that takes place downtown and in NuLu along Main and Market Sts. The LouLift bus provides free transportation.

Tours

★Waverly Hills Sanatorium TOURS

(☎502-933-2142; www.therealwaverlyhills.com; 4400 Paralee Lane; 2/6hr tours $25/75; ⊙Fri & Sat Mar-Aug) Towering over Louisville like a mad king's castle, the abandoned Waverly Hills Sanatorium once housed victims of an early-20th-century tuberculosis epidemic. When patients died, workers dumped their bodies down a chute into the basement. No wonder the place is said to be one of the USA's most haunted buildings. Search for spooks with a nighttime ghost-hunting tour; the genuinely fearless can even spend the night!

Big Four Bridge WALKING, CYCLING

(www.louisvillewaterfront.com; East River Rd; ⊙24hr) Built between 1888 and 1895, the Big Four Bridge, which spans the Ohio River and reaches the Indiana shore, has been closed to vehicular traffic since 1969 but was reopened in 2013 as a pedestrian and cycling path offering excellent city and river views.

Sleeping

Bed and Bike APARTMENT $

(www.bedandbike.com; 822 E Market St; apt $100-160; ❄📶) The owners of Parkside Bikes rent out several apartments on the second floor of their building, from studios to two-bedroom units. They're all brightly furnished in urban-cool style, and you have access to two bicycles to ride around town. The heart of NuLu location is superb, with a slew of eating and drinking options on your doorstep.

Rocking Horse B&B B&B $$

(☎502-583-0408; www.rockinghorse-bb.com; 1022 S 3rd St; r $125-250; P❄📶) Near the University of Louisville on a stretch of 3rd St once known as Millionaire's Row, this 1888 Richardsonian Romanesque mansion is chock-full of astounding historic detail. The six guest rooms are decorated with Victorian antiques and splendid original stained glass. Guests can eat their two-course breakfast in the English country garden and sip complimentary port in the parlor.

★21c Museum Hotel Louisville DESIGN HOTEL $$$

(☎502-217-6300; www.21cmuseumhotels.com; 700 W Main St; r $209-329; P❄📶🐾) This contemporary art museum–hotel features edgy design details: video screens project your distorted image and falling language on the wall as you wait for the elevator; water-blurred, see-through glass urinal walls line the men's rooms. Rooms, though not as interesting as the five contemporary art galleries that double as common areas, have high ceilings and lots of natural light.

Eating

Gralehaus AMERICAN $

(☎502-454-7075; www.gralehaus.com; 1001 Baxter Ave; mains $8-13; ⊙8am-4pm; 📶) There's breakfast all day at this snug eatery housed in a historic early-20th-century home, and you should indeed indulge in its chef-centric takes on traditional Southern comforts (think locally sourced biscuits and duck gravy, lamb and grits). It's typically crowded, but seats seem to open up when you need them. Gralehaus links to Holy Grale pub across the back courtyard.

Garage Bar PUB FOOD $

(☎502-749-7100; www.garageonmarket.com; 700 E Market St; mains $13-16; ⊙5-10pm Mon-Thu, 11am-11pm Fri & Sat, 11am-10pm Sun; 📶) The best thing to do on a warm afternoon in Louisville is to make your way to this uber-hip converted NuLu service station (accented by two kissing Camaros) and order a round of basil gimlets and the ham and cheese platter (a tasting of three in each category, all locally made, served with fresh bread and preserves; $28).

Silver Dollar SOUTHERN US $$
(☎502-259-9540; www.whiskeybythedrink.com; 1761 Frankfort Ave; mains $15-27; ⊙5pm-2am Mon-Fri, from 10am Sat & Sun; 📶) Gastronomically noncommittal – we'll call the cuisine California-inspired New Southern – but unrepentantly bourbon obsessed, the Silver Dollar will dazzle your taste buds. Feast on chicken and waffles, beer can hen (roasted game hen served on an Old Milwaukee beer can) or fantastic *chilaquiles;* chase it with one of a 'poop ton' of bourbons (240 to be exact).

Decca AMERICAN $$$
(☎502-749-8128; www.deccarestaurant.com; 812 E Market St; mains $28-31; ⊙5:30-10pm Mon-Sat; 📶) A beautiful space with a cork-and-wood floor, fountain-strewn patio and gorgeous Laguiole cutlery opened by a chef from San Francisco (albeit a Southerner by birth). Kentuckians were skeptical, but Annie Pettry wooed and won. The emphasis of the delectable, seasonally changing menu is wood-fired roasts.

★**Proof on Main** AMERICAN $$$
(☎502-217-6360; www.proofonmain.com; 702 W Main St; mains $29-40; ⊙7am-2pm & 5:30-10pm Mon-Thu, to 11pm Fri, 7am-2:30pm & 5:30-11pm Sat, to 10pm Sun; 📶) Arguably Louisville's best restaurant. The cocktails are incredible, the wine and bourbon 'library' (they're known to pour from exclusive and rare barrels of Woodford Reserve and Van Winkle) is long and satisfying, and exquisite dishes range from gourmet grilled cheese to a deliciously messy bison burger or a high-minded take on 'hot' fried chicken.

Drinking & Nightlife

★**Holy Grale** PUB
(☎502-459-9939; www.holygralelouisville.com; 1034 Bardstown Rd; ⊙4pm-midnight Mon-Thu, 4pm-1am Fri, noon-1am Sat, noon-midnight Sun; 📶) One of Louisville's best bars is housed in an old church, with a menu of funked-up pub grub (gourmet Belgian *frites,* green curry mussels, short rib poutine; mains $6 to $14) and a buzzworthy beer list focusing on rare German, Danish, Belgian and Japanese brews (on tap). The most intense beers (up to 13% alcohol) can be found in the choir loft. Hallelujah!

Mr Lee's COCKTAIL BAR
(☎502-450-5368; www.mrleeslounge.com; 935 Goss Ave; ⊙5pm-2am Wed-Sat, 6pm-1am Sun) Germantown's craft cocktail anchor is this satisfyingly retro establishment that serves a small but serious list of tipples. The semi-circular red leather bar gives way to a long mid-century-modern–styled, candlelit line of intimate tables and banquettes that are perfect for settling in for a boozy evening. It's even carpeted!

Monnik Beer Co MICROBREWERY
(☎502-742-6564; www.monnikbeer.com; 1036 E Burnett Ave; ⊙11am-10pm Sun-Tue, to midnight Wed & Thu, to 1am Fri & Sat; 📶) Megapopular Monnik is in up-and-coming Schnitzelburg. There are 20 taps – the IPA stands out – in this restrained hipster environment where the beer isn't the only thing that's fabulous. The beer cheese with spent grain bread is so good you should need a prescription for it; and the seared grass-fed burgers are perfect. Bottoms up!

Information

Visitor Center (☎502-379-6109; www.gotolouisville.com; 301 S 4th St; ⊙10am-5pm Mon-Sat, noon-5pm Sun) Stuffed with brochures and has helpful staff. You can also pick up or redeem Bourbon Trail passports here.

Getting There & Around

Louisville Muhammad Ali International Airport (p393) is 5 miles south of town on I-65. Get there by cab, Lyft or Uber ($20 to $25) or local bus 2 ($1.75, exact change required). The **Greyhound** (☎502-561-2807; www.greyhound.com; 720 W Muhammad Ali Blvd) station is just west of downtown.

TARC (www.ridetarc.org) operates the free LouLift buses that cover most of the city's attractions and coolest restaurants. The Silver Line travels on 4th St and goes to Churchill Downs, while the Red Line runs along Main and Market Sts in NuLu and downtown.

Louvelo (www.louvelo.com) is Louisville's bikeshare program, with 321 lime-green bikes at stations around town. Cost is $3.50 for a one-off 30-minute ride, or $7.50 for unlimited hour-long rides for a 24hr period.

Uber and Lyft are both handy for getting around the city.

Bluegrass Country

Drive through Bluegrass Country on a sunny day and you'll spy horses grazing in the brilliant-green hills dotted with ponds, poplar trees and handsome estate houses.

These once-wild woodlands and meadows have been a center of horse breeding for more than 250 years. The region's natural limestone deposits – you'll see limestone bluffs rise majestically from out of nowhere – are said to produce especially nutritious grass. In spring the pastures bloom with tiny azure buds, hence the 'Bluegrass' name. Steer your wheels to Old Frankfort Pike (aka KY 1681), a byway between Frankfort and Lexington, and experience the landscape in all its glory.

Lexington

Cities don't get more genteel than Lexington, home of million-dollar houses and multimillion-dollar horses. Once the wealthiest and most cultured city west of the Allegheny Mountains, it was called 'the Athens of the West.' It's home to the University of Kentucky and is the heart of the thoroughbred industry. Pretty Victorian neighborhoods, garden-clad historic properties and small distilleries speckle the compact downtown. Brewery buffs and horse racing fans will find plenty to keep them occupied.

Sights

Kentucky Horse Park PARK
(www.kyhorsepark.com; 4089 Iron Works Pkwy; summer adult/child $20/10, winter adult/child $12/6, horseback riding Apr-Oct $25; 9am-5pm Apr-Oct, closed Mon & Tue Nov-Mar;) This educational theme park and equestrian sports center sits on 1200 acres just north of Lexington. Horses representing 50 different breeds live in the park and participate in special live shows.

Ashland HISTORIC BUILDING
(859-266-8581; www.henryclay.org; 120 Sycamore Rd; adult/child $15/7; 10am-4pm Tue-Sat, 1-4pm Sun Apr-Nov, closed Sun Mar & Dec, closed Jan & Feb) Part historic home and part public park with storybook gardens, Ashland was the Italianate estate of famed statesman and great compromiser Henry Clay (1777–1852), who was one of Kentucky's favorite sons.

Lexington Art League at Loudoun House GALLERY
(859-254-7024; www.lexingtonartleague.org; 209 Castlewood Dr; 10am-4pm Tue-Thu, 10am-8pm Fri, 1-4pm Sat & Sun) FREE Art and architecture buffs won't want to miss this edgy, contemporary visual arts gallery housed in a freestanding American Gothic Revival mansion in the NoLi neighborhood, one of only five such structures left in the USA. The cutting-edge exhibitions, around six per year, are quite provocative by Lexington standards. Playful modern sculptures dot the grounds.

THOROUGHBREDS

For insight into the famed racehorses reared in these parts, sign up for an excursion with **Thoroughbred Heritage Horse Farm Tours** (859-260-8687; www.seethechampions.com; 3hr tours adult/child $38/28; 8:30am & 12:30pm). These narrated tours by van typically take you to Keeneland track for a walkabout, as well as to a thoroughbred farm or two. Destinations vary depending on racing schedules. Pick up is from various hotels around Lexington.

If you prefer to go on your own, you can visit the **Thoroughbred Center** (859-293-1853; www.thoroughbred-center.com; 3380 Paris Pike; adult/child $15/8; tours 9am Mon-Sat Apr-Oct, Mon-Fri 9am Nov-Mar). There you can see working racehorses up close during 90-minute tours of the stables, practice tracks and paddock

Sleeping

Lyndon House B&B $$
(859-420-2683; www.lyndonhouse.com; 507 N Broadway; r $199-279;) A detail-oriented ordained-minister-turned-foodie is your host at this discerning and spacious downtown B&B in a historic mansion dating from 1885. Anton takes hospitality seriously, particularly when it comes to breakfast. The seven rooms feature period furnishings and all the mod-cons, and you're steps from a long list of restaurants and breweries.

★**21c Museum Hotel Lexington** DESIGN HOTEL $$$
(859-899-6800; www.21cmuseumhotels.com; 167 W Main St; r $209-329;) This downtown design hotel is marked by twisted sidewalk lampposts – hand-blown in Venice – outside its entrance. A Louisville transplant that's now in several states, it's more like a museum you can sleep in, with

four contemporary art galleries throughout the hotel (as well as permanent local art on each floor).

Eating & Drinking

★Blue Door Smokehouse BARBECUE $
(☎859-252-4227; www.bluedoorsmokehouse.com; 226 Walton Ave; mains $9-16; ⏲11am-3pm Mon-Thu, to 8pm Fri & Sat) Follow your nose to this small smokehouse marked by a bright blue door where the buttery-tender brisket is the meat to beat. Arrive early to get a juicy plateful, because they run out as the day progresses. Back-up plan: pulled pork, baby.

Stella's Kentucky Deli DELI $
(☎859-255-3354; www.stellaskentuckydeli.com; 143 Jefferson St; sandwiches $6-10; ⏲9am-4pm; 📶✎) 🍃 This don't-miss deli has more than 30 years under its apron, but the latest owners have upped the cool quotient and concentrated on delicious provisions from local farmers. Great sandwiches, soups and salads, along with seasonal brews, are served in a colorful historic home with a reclaimed tin roof and sociable bar.

★Carson's Food & Drink AMERICAN $$$
(☎859-309-3039; www.carsonsfoodanddrink.com; 362 E Main St; brunch $11-17, mains $20-36; ⏲11:30am-10pm Mon-Thu, 11:30am-11pm Fri, 10am-11pm Sat, 10am-10pm Sun; 📶) Prohibition-era cocktails ($8 to $10) and bloody Marys (garnished with bacon, shrimp, celery, olives, pepper jack cheese and pepperoncini) make for great chasers at this rustic upscale spot that serves a meat-heavy menu of decadent contemporary comfort food. The béarnaise truffle fries with soft-shell crab are divine; and there's a BBQ pork belly and beer-cheese burger.

★Country Boy Brewing MICROBREWERY
(☎859-554-6200; www.countryboybrewing.com; 436 Chair Ave; ⏲11am-midnight Mon-Sat, to 10pm Sun) True to its name, Country Boy – all trucker hats, taxidermy and camouflage – delivers great beer in an authentically Kentuckian venue. Up to 24 taps are devoted to the brewery's experimental concoctions, brewed with a rural Mikkeller-like approach (oak-aged sours with strawberries, jalapeño smoked porters, barrel-aged DIPAs).

Guest beers are frequent, too.

★Chocolate Holler COFFEE
(☎859-523-3619; www.facebook.com/chocolatehollerky; 400 Old Vine St, Ste 104; ⏲7:30am-10pm Mon-Fri, 10am-10pm Sat, noon-7pm Sun) Why isn't this concept on every street corner? A bar devoted to drinking chocolate! Baristas can help you choose from the seven types on offer, maybe the chili-spiked one from Mexico or the strong dark one from Tanzania. Can't decide? Get a flight of three ($8).

Entertainment

★Keeneland HORSE RACING
(☎859-254-3412; www.keeneland.com; 4201 Versailles Rd; general admission $5; ⏲races Apr & Oct) Second only to Churchill Downs in terms of quality of competition, Keeneland's races run in April and October, when you can also glimpse champions train from sunrise to 10am. Frequent horse auctions lure sheikhs, sultans, hedge-fund princes and those who love (or serve) them.

The Burl LIVE MUSIC
(www.theburlky.com; 375 Thompson Rd; cover $10-20; ⏲4pm-2:30am Mon & Wed-Sun) Across the railroad tracks from the Distillery District campus inside a finely restored 1928 train depot, the Burl has transformed Lexington's live music scene, which finally has a consistent home for local and regional acts.

Information

Visitor Center (VisitLEX; ☎859-233-7299; www.visitlex.com; 215 W Main St; ⏲9am-5pm Mon-Fri, from 10am Sat) Pick up maps and area driving tour information. Knowledgeable staff can help with just about anything. Located in the Historic Lexington Courthouse.

Getting There & Around

Blue Grass Airport (LEX; ☎859-425-3100; www.bluegrassairport.com; 4000 Terminal Dr) is 6 miles west of downtown, offering nonstop flights to 18 domestic destinations. **Greyhound** (☎859-299-0428; 477 NW New Circle Rd) is 2 miles northeast of downtown.

Lextran (☎859-253-4636; www.lextran.com; 150 E Vine St; ⏲6am-6pm Mon-Fri, 8am-4pm Sat & Sun) runs local buses (all fares $1). Bus 6 goes to the Greyhound station, bus 21 goes to the airport and Keeneland.

The city is testing a dockless bikeshare program with Spin (www.spin.pm). Use the app to find and unlock the orange bikes; cost is $1 per 30 minutes. Uber and Lyft both have decent networks in town.

Central Kentucky

Central Kentucky is the state's most celebrated region. The key reason: it's bourbon country! Kentucky's world-renowned homegrown spirit pays the bills, keeps the population buzzed and even flavors the local cuisine. Small and scenic Bardstown is the epicenter of big-name distilleries. More bucolic hooch makers cluster around Frankfort, the picture-postcard capital. Hip Louisville provides your urban fix with buzzy restaurants and exceptional museums (and bourbon, of course). Not to mention it hosts the world's most famous horse race. Lexington likewise knows its ponies. The refined city is the global hub for the horse-breeding industry, plus it brews a mean beer. Add in Berea's arts, Bowling Green's Corvettes and Mammoth Cave's eerie underworld and you've got the best of Kentucky.

Shaker Village of Pleasant Hill MUSEUM
(☎800-734-5611; www.shakervillageky.org; 3501 Lexington Rd, Harrodsburg; adult/child $14/7, riverboat rides $10/5; ⏰10am-5pm Mon-Thu & Sun, to 8pm Fri & Sat) This area was home to a community of the Shaker religious sect until the early 1900s. Tour dozens of impeccably restored buildings, set amid buttercup meadows and winding stone paths. There's an inn and restaurant, and a gift shop selling the Shakers' famous handicrafts. Hour-long riverboat rides show off the stunning limestone cliffs that rise up along the Kentucky River.

Shaker Village Inn INN $$
(☎859-734-5611; www.shakervillageky.org; 3501 Lexington Rd, Harrodsburg; r $125-195; P 📶) The main building is set in Harrodsburg's old trustee office, with its elaborate double-helix stairwell. Rooms are large, lovely and full of light, with high ceilings, wood furnishings and two rockers to read/snooze in. Rooms in 12 other heritage buildings follow suit. There are 72 rooms in total.

ℹ Getting There & Around

Louisville Muhammad Ali International Airport (SDF; ☎502-367-4636; www.flylouisville.com; 600 Terminal Dr) – international in name only – is Kentucky's biggest airport, receiving direct domestic flights from Atlanta, Charlotte, Chicago, Minneapolis, New York and Washington, DC, among others.

The Bluegrass Pkwy runs from I-65 in the west to US 60 in the east, passing through some of the most luscious pasturelands in Kentucky.

WORTH A TRIP

MAKER'S MARK

Touring **Maker's Mark** (☎270-865-2099; www.makersmark.com; 3350 Burks Spring Rd, Loretto; 1hr tours $14; ⏰9:30am-5pm Mon-Thu, 9:30am-7pm Fri & Sat, 11:30am-5pm Sun May-Oct, to 5pm daily Nov-Apr) is like visiting a historic theme park, in a good way. You'll see the old gristmill, the 1840s master distiller's house and the old-fashioned firehouse. Watch oatmeal-esque sour mash ferment in huge cypress vats, see whiskey being double-distilled in copper pots and peek at bourbon barrels aging in wooden warehouses. Tours depart on a rolling basis; the last one is 90 minutes before closing time. At the gift shop you can stamp your own bottle with the iconic red-wax seal.

The tasting included with the tour is generous. Longer specialty tours are also available, but require advance booking. Star Hill Provisions, the restaurant on-site, lets you soak up any bourbon overindulgence with tasty Southern fare.

Bardstown and the heart of bourbon country are located 40 miles southeast of Louisville, with Mammoth Cave National Park another 70 miles or so south. Lexington lies about 78 miles east of Louisville. Renting your own ride is undoubtedly the best way to take it all in.

Daniel Boone National Forest

Rugged ravines and gravity-defying sandstone cliffs fill massive Daniel Boone National Forest in the Appalachian foothills of eastern Kentucky. Highlights include the wild crags of Red River Gorge in the northern portion and Cumberland Falls, aka the Niagara of the South, in the southern expanse. Hiking, rock climbing, camping, boating and fishing are the big to-dos.

Cumberland Falls State Resort Park STATE PARK
(☎606-528-4121; www.parks.ky.gov; 7351 Hwy 90, Corbin) FREE Cumberland Falls is one of the few places in the world to see a moonbow, a rainbow that forms in the water's mist at night. The park website has dates for when the phenomenon occurs each month. A one-mile round-trip trail takes you to the falls, a 125ft-wide curtain of water that's pretty dramatic anytime.

Natural Bridge State Resort Park STATE PARK

(☎606-663-2214; www.parks.ky.gov; 2135 Natural Bridge Rd, Slade) FREE This state park borders Red River Gorge and is notable for its 65ft-high, 78ft-long sandstone arch. The grounds offer 20 miles of mostly short hiking trails; the most popular is the Original Trail to the arch's base (0.75 miles one way). If you don't want to walk, you can ride the sky lift over the bridge (adult/child $15/12 return).

Red River Outdoors CLIMBING

(☎859-230-3567; www.redriveroutdoors.com; 415 Natural Bridge Rd, Slade; half/full-day climb from $65/90) Offers guided climbing trips for both beginners and experienced climbers, as well as cabin rentals ($110 to $145) on the ridgeline and occasional yoga retreats.

Mammoth Cave National Park

With the longest cave system on earth, this **national park** (☎270-758-2180; www.nps.gov/maca; 1 Mammoth Cave Pkwy; park entry free, tours adult $8-60, child $6-24; ⏲8am-6:30pm mid-Mar–mid-Aug, 8am-6pm mid-Aug–Oct, 8:30am-4:30pm Nov–mid-Mar) has some 400 miles of surveyed passageways. Mammoth is at least three times longer than any other known cave, with vast interior cathedrals, bottomless pits and strange, undulating rock formations. Excellent ranger-guided tours explore the subterranean expanse. Book ahead if possible (at www.recreation.gov). Tours do sell out, especially in summer and on weekends.

In addition to the caves, the park contains 85 miles of trails – all for hiking, 60 miles for horseback riding and 25 miles for mountain biking. There are also three campgrounds (sites from $20). Reservations for camping (www.recreation.gov) and lodging (www.mammothcavelodge.com) can be made online.

GEORGIA

The largest state east of the Mississippi River is a labyrinth of geographic and cultural extremes: right-leaning Republican politics in the countryside rubs against liberal idealism in Atlanta and Savannah; small, conservative towns merge with sprawling, progressive, financially flush cities; northern mountains rise to the clouds and produce roaring rivers; and coastal marshlands teem with fiddler crabs and swaying cordgrass. Georgia's southern beaches and islands are a treat, and so are its kitchens, bars and yes, its contradictions.

Atlanta, Georgia's culturally rich and multifaceted capital, best illustrates the paradox: on one side it's a bastion of African American enlightenment, a hip-hop hotbed, a film and tech industry upstart and LGBTIQ+ epicenter; on the other, Old South wealth and Fortune 500 investment marry in a city that is an international financial workhorse steeped in conservative Southern values. Together, a sexy metropolis emerges – it's way past *Gone with the Wind*.

Information

Statewide tourism information is available through the Georgia Department of Economic Development (800-847-4842, www.exploregeorgia.org).

For information on camping and activities in state parks, contact Georgia Department of National Resources (800-864-7275, www.gastateparks.org).

Atlanta

With more than six million residents in the metro and outlying areas, Atlanta continues to experience explosive growth thanks to domestic transplants and international immigrants alike. Beyond the big-ticket Downtown attractions you will find a constellation of superlative restaurants, a palpable Hollywood influence (Atlanta is a hugely popular film-production center) and iconic African American history. That last point can't be overstated: any nationwide African American intellectual, political and artistic movement you can mention either had its genesis in Atlanta, or found a center of gravity here.

Sights & Activities

Downtown

Atlanta's Downtown packs a whole lot of world-class museums and attractions into an unbelievably condensed area, something few US cities can boast.

★Center for Civil & Human Rights MUSEUM

(☎678-999-8990; www.civilandhumanrights.org; 100 Ivan Allen Jr Blvd; adult/student & senior/

ATLANTA FOR CHILDREN

Atlanta knows how to keep children entertained, delighted and educated. Many of the city's top attractions are both kid- and adult-friendly (bonus!), such as the World of Coca-Cola and **Georgia Aquarium** (☎404-581-4000; www.georgiaaquarium.com; 225 Baker St; adult/child $40/34; ⏰10am-9pm Mon-Fri, from 9am Sat & Sun), while others are some of the Southeast's top child-driven attractions, for example the **Center for Puppetry Arts** (☎tickets 404-873-3391; www.puppet.org; 1401 Spring St NW; museum $12.50, guided tours $16.50; ⏰9am-5pm Tue-Fri, from 10am Sat, from noon Sun) and **Fernbank Museum of Natural History** (☎404-929-6300; www.fernbankmuseum.org; 767 Clifton Rd; adult/child $20/18; ⏰10am-5pm; P).

child $20/18/16; ⏰10am-5pm Mon-Sat, from noon Sun) This striking 2014 addition to Atlanta's **Centennial Olympic Park** (www.centennialpark.com; 265 Park Ave NW; ⏰7am-11pm) is a sobering $68-million memorial to the American Civil Rights and global human-rights movements. Beautifully designed and thoughtfully executed, the indisputable highlight centers on an absolutely harrowing interactive mock Woolworth's lunch-counter sit-in simulation that will leave you speechless and move some to tears.

College Football Hall of Fame MUSEUM
(www.cfbhall.com; 250 Marietta St; adult/senior/child $22/19/18; ⏰10am-5pm Sun-Fri, 9am-6pm Sat; P 👪) It is impossible to overstate the importance of college football to American culture. This museum, relocated from Indiana in 2014 and revamped into this three-story, 94,256-sq-ft gridiron sanctuary, is a supremely cool and suitable shrine.

World of Coca-Cola MUSEUM
(☎404-676-5151; www.woccatlanta.com; 121 Baker St; adult/senior/child $17/15/13; ⏰10am-5pm Mon-Fri, from 9am Sat & Sun) This self-congratulatory museum might prove entertaining to fans of fizzy beverages and rampant commercialization. The climactic moment comes when guests sample Coke products from around the world – a taste-bud-twisting good time. But there are also Andy Warhol pieces on view, a 4-D film, company history and promotional materials aplenty.

CNN Center TOURS
(☎404-827-2300; http://tours.cnn.com; 1 CNN Center, cnr Marietta St & Centennial Olympic Park Dr; adult/senior/child $15/14/12, VIP tour $33; ⏰9am-5pm, VIP tours 9:30am, 11:30am, 1:30pm & 3:30pm Mon-Sat) The 55-minute behind-the-scenes tour through the headquarters of the international, 24-hour news giant is a good time for fans. Although visitors don't get very close to Wolf Blitzer (or his cronies), the 9am and noon time slots offer the best bets for seeing anchors live on air. A VIP tour gets you access to live newsrooms, control rooms and production studios.

Midtown

Midtown is like a hipper version of Downtown, with plenty of great bars, restaurants and cultural venues.

★**High Museum of Art** MUSEUM
(☎404-733-4400; www.high.org; 1280 Peachtree St NE; adult/child under 5yr $14.50/free; ⏰10am-5pm Tue-Thu & Sat, to 9pm Fri, noon-5pm Sun) Atlanta's modern High Museum was the first to exhibit art from Paris' Louvre and is a destination as much for its architecture as its world-class exhibits. The striking whitewashed multilevel building houses a permanent collection of eye-catching late-19th-century furniture, early American modern canvases from the likes of George Morris and Albert Gallatin, and postwar work from Mark Rothko.

Atlanta Botanical Garden GARDENS
(☎404-876-5859; www.atlantabotanicalgarden.org; 1345 Piedmont Ave NE; adult/child $22/19; ⏰9am-7pm Tue-Sun Apr-Oct, to 5pm Nov-Mar; P) In the northwest corner of Piedmont Park, this stunning 30-acre botanical garden has a Japanese garden, winding paths and the amazing Fuqua Orchid Center.

Margaret Mitchell House & Museum MUSEUM
(☎404-249-7015; www.atlantahistorycenter.com; 979 Crescent Ave NE; adult/student/child $13/10/5.50; ⏰10am-5:30pm Mon-Sat, from noon Sun) Operated by the Atlanta History Center, this home has been converted into a shrine to

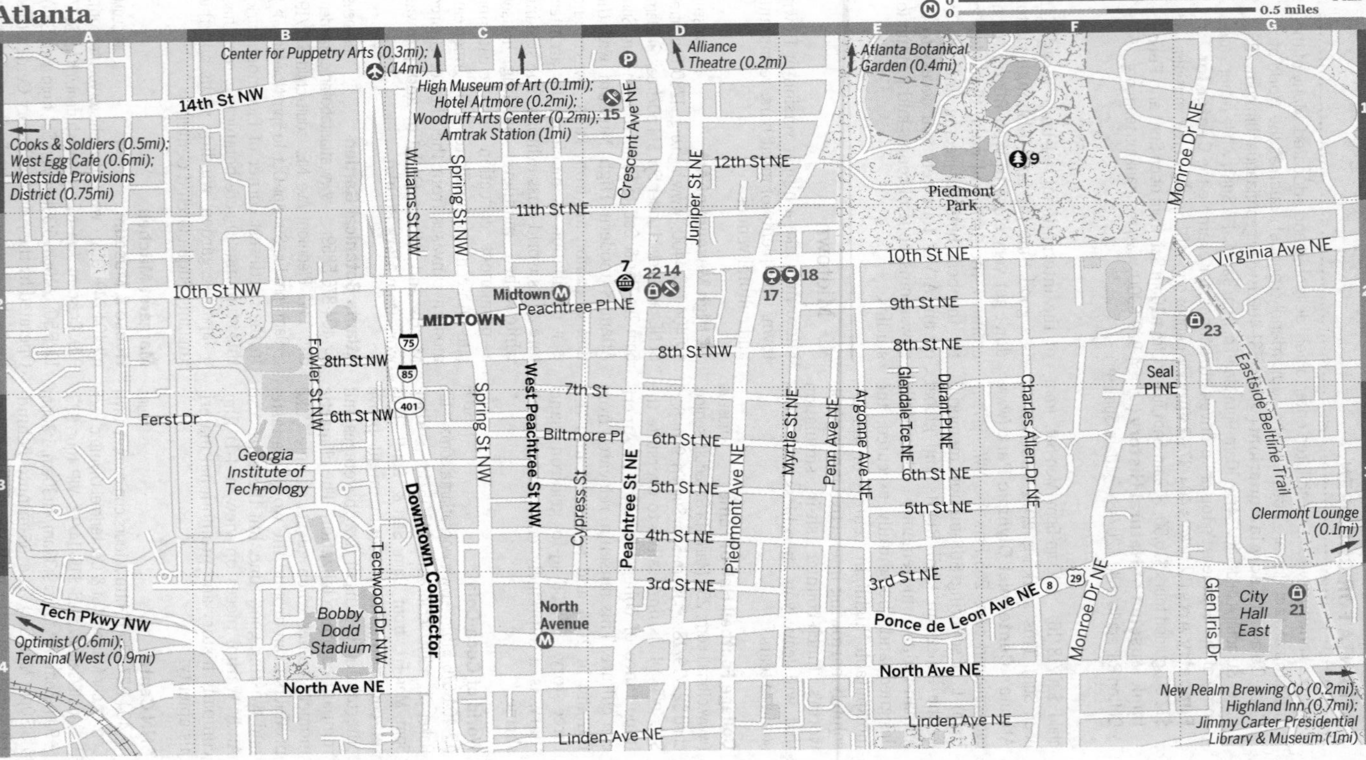

Atlanta
0 1 km
0 0.5 miles
Center for Puppetry Arts (0.3mi); (14mi)
High Museum of Art (0.1mi); Hotel Artmore (0.2mi); Woodruff Arts Center (0.2mi); Amtrak Station (1mi)
Alliance Theatre (0.2mi)
Atlanta Botanical Garden (0.4mi)
Cooks & Soldiers (0.5mi); West Egg Cafe (0.6mi); Westside Provisions District (0.75mi)
14th St NW
12th St NE
11th St NE
10th St NE
10th St NW
Virginia Ave NE
Piedmont Park
Monroe Dr NE
Williams St NW
Spring St NW
Crescent Ave NE
Juniper St NE
Midtown
Peachtree Pl NE
MIDTOWN
9th St NE
8th St NE
8th St NW
Fowler St NW
7th St
West Peachtree St NW
Seal Pl NE
Eastside Beltline Trail
Ferst Dr
6th St NW
Biltmore Pl
6th St NE
Myrtle St NE
Penn Ave NE
Argonne Ave NE
Glendale Tce NE
Durant Pl NE
Charles Allen Dr NE
Georgia Institute of Technology
Downtown Connector
Cypress St
Peachtree St NE
5th St NE
Piedmont Ave NE
4th St NE
Techwood Dr NW
Clermont Lounge (0.1mi)
3rd St NE
Ponce de Leon Ave NE
Glen Iris Dr
City Hall East
Tech Pkwy NW
Bobby Dodd Stadium
North Avenue
Optimist (0.6mi); Terminal West (0.9mi)
North Ave NE
Linden Ave NE
New Realm Brewing Co (0.2mi); Highland Inn (0.7mi); Jimmy Carter Presidential Library & Museum (1mi)

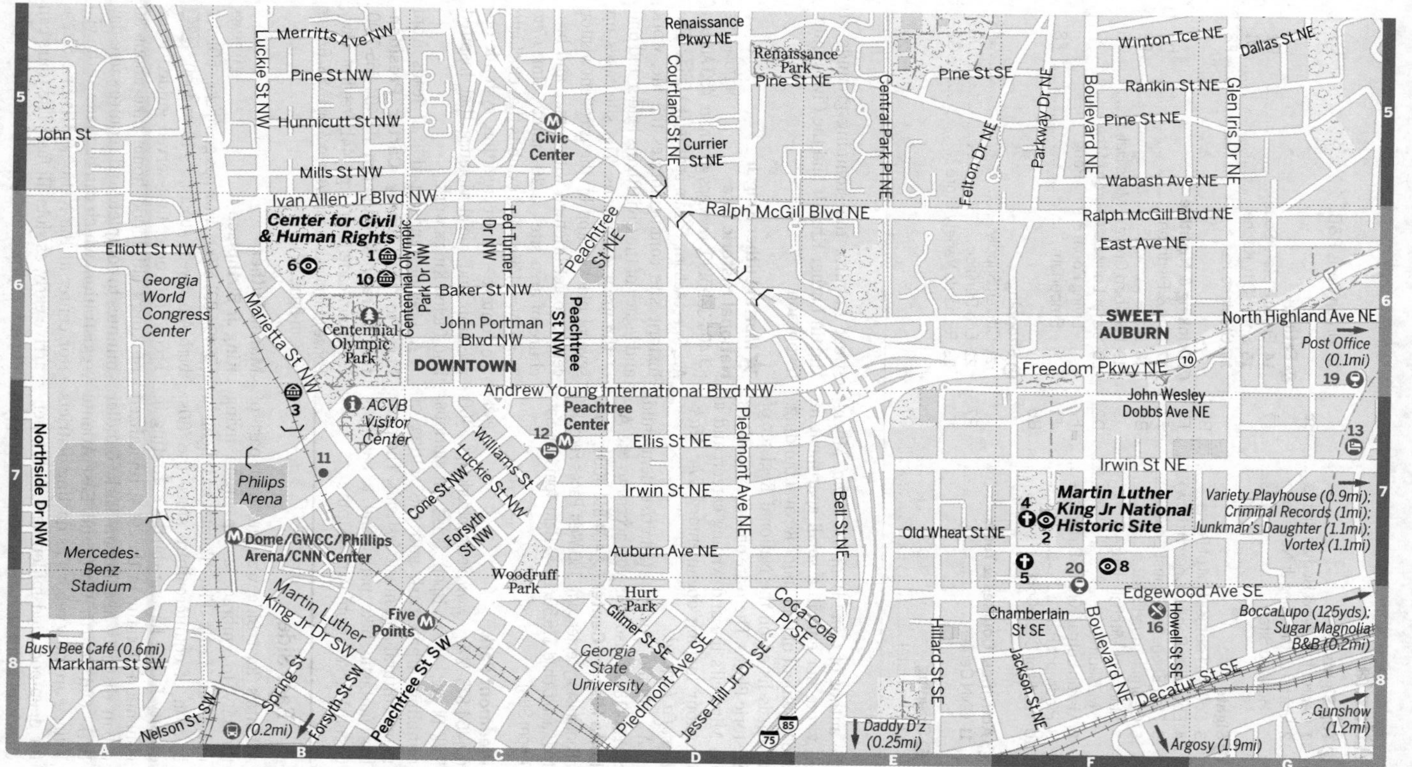
Merritts Ave NW
Luckie St NW
Pine St NW
Hunnicutt St NW
John St
Civic Center
Mills St NW
Renaissance Pkwy NE
Courtland St NE
Currier St NE
Renaissance Park
Pine St NE
Central Park Pl NE
Pine St SE
Felton Dr NE
Parkway Dr NE
Boulevard NE
Winton Tce NE
Dallas St NE
Rankin St NE
Pine St NE
Glen Iris Dr NE
Wabash Ave NE
Ivan Allen Jr Blvd NW
Center for Civil & Human Rights
1
6
10
Elliott St NW
Centennial Olympic Park Dr NW
Ted Turner Dr NW
Peachtree St NE
Ralph McGill Blvd NE
Ralph McGill Blvd NE
East Ave NE
Georgia World Congress Center
Marietta St NW
Centennial Olympic Park
Baker St NW
John Portman Blvd NW
Peachtree St NW
DOWNTOWN
SWEET AUBURN
North Highland Ave NE
Post Office (0.1mi)
19
Freedom Pkwy NE
10
3
ACVB Visitor Center
Andrew Young International Blvd NW
Peachtree Center
12
John Wesley Dobbs Ave NE
13
Northside Dr NW
11
Philips Arena
Williams St
Cone St NW
Luckie St NW
Ellis St NE
Piedmont Ave NE
Irwin St NE
Irwin St NE
Bell St NE
Martin Luther King Jr National Historic Site
4
2
Variety Playhouse (0.9mi); Criminal Records (1mi); Junkman's Daughter (1.1mi); Vortex (1.1mi)
Forsyth St NW
Old Wheat St NE
Mercedes-Benz Stadium
Dome/GWCC/Phillips Arena/CNN Center
Auburn Ave NE
5
20
8
Woodruff Park
Hurt Park
Coca Cola Pl SE
Edgewood Ave SE
Martin Luther King Jr Dr SW
Five Points
Gilmer St SE
Chamberlain St SE
Boulevard NE
16
Howell St SE
BoccaLupo (125yds); Sugar Magnolia B&B (0.2mi)
Busy Bee Café (0.6mi)
Markham St SW
Georgia State University
Hillard St SE
Jackson St NE
Decatur St SE
Spring St
Forsyth St SW
Peachtree St SW
Piedmont Ave SE
Jesse Hill Jr Dr SE
Nelson St SW
(0.2mi)
85
75
Daddy D'z (0.25mi)
Argosy (1.9mi)
Gunshow (1.2mi)

Atlanta

Top Sights

1 Center for Civil & Human Rights B6
2 Martin Luther King Jr National Historic Site F7

Sights

3 College Football Hall of Fame B7
4 Ebenezer Baptist Church (New) F7
5 First Ebenezer Baptist Church F7
6 Georgia Aquarium B6
7 Margaret Mitchell House & Museum D2
8 Martin Luther King Jr Birthplace F7
9 Piedmont Park F1
10 World of Coca-Cola B6

Activities, Courses & Tours

11 CNN Center B7

Sleeping

12 Ellis Hotel C7
13 Urban Oasis B&B G7

Eating

14 Empire State South D2
15 South City Kitchen D1
16 Staplehouse F8

Drinking & Nightlife

17 10th & Piedmont D2
18 Blake's E2
19 Ladybird Grove & Mess Hall G6
20 Sister Louisa's Church of the Living Room & Ping Pong Emporium F8

Shopping

21 Citizen Supply G4
22 Eco Denizen D2
23 Richards Variety Store G2

the author of *Gone With the Wind*. Mitchell wrote her epic in a small apartment in the basement of this Tudor Revival building, which is listed on the National Register of Historic Places. There are on-site exhibitions on Mitchell's life and writing career, and a two-hour looping documentary, *The Making of a Legend*.

A combo ticket (adult/student/child $21.50/18/9) also gets you access to the **Atlanta History Center** (404-814-4000; www.atlantahistorycenter.com; 130 West Paces Ferry Rd NW; adult/child $16.50/11; 11am-4pm Mon-Sat, 1-4pm Sun).

Piedmont Park PARK
(404-875-7275; www.piedmontpark.org; 400 Park Dr NE; 6am-11pm) FREE A glorious, rambling urban park and the setting of many cultural and music festivals. The park has fantastic bike paths and a Saturday Green Market (from 9am to 1pm).

East Side

Atlanta's East Side was the first part of the city to embrace a hip urban living upheaval: Little Five Points has been a bastion of counterculture since the '80s; quality foodie havens started sprouting in bohemian Decatur in the '90s; revitalized urban districts like Inman Park, Candler Park, Old Fourth Ward and East Atlanta Village are now reborn as darling districts for deep-pocketed millennials with a penchant for craft. It's all in stark contrast to Sweet Auburn, the stomping grounds of Martin Luther King Jr and the Civil Rights revolution.

★ **Martin Luther King Jr National Historic Site** HISTORIC SITE
(404-331-5190; www.nps.gov/malu; 450 Auburn Ave, Sweet Auburn; 9am-5pm; P) FREE The historic site commemorates the life, work and legacy of the Civil Rights leader and one of the great Americans. The site takes up several blocks. Stop by the excellent visitor center to get oriented with a map and brochure of area sites, a 20-minute film, *New Time, New Voice*, and exhibits that elucidate the context – the segregation, systemic oppression and racial violence that inspired and fueled King's work.

A 1.5-mile landscaped trail leads from here to the **Jimmy Carter Presidential Library & Museum** (404-865-7100; www.jimmycarterlibrary.org; 441 Freedom Pkwy, Poncey-Highland; adult/senior/child $8/6/free; 8am-5pm; P).

Martin Luther King Jr Birthplace LANDMARK
(404-331-5190; www.nps.gov/malu; 501 Auburn Ave, Sweet Auburn; 10am-4pm) FREE Free, first-come, first-served guided tours of King's childhood home take about 30 minutes to complete and require same-day registration, which can be made at the visitor center at the National Historic Site – arrive early, as slots fill fast. The tours can depart anytime between 10am and 4pm,

but you are free to visit the rest of the park at your leisure before your designated tour time.

First Ebenezer Baptist Church CHURCH
(☎404-331-5190; www.nps.gov/malu; 407 Auburn Ave NE, Sweet Auburn; ⊙9am-5pm) FREE Martin Luther King Jr, his father and grandfather were all pastors here, and King Jr's mother was the choir director. Sadly she was murdered here by a deranged gunman while she sat at the organ in 1974. A multimillion-dollar restoration, completed in 2011, brought the church back to the 1960–68 period when King Jr served as co-pastor with his father. Today looped recordings of King's speeches play in the church building.

Sunday services are now held at the new **Ebenezer Church** (☎404-688-7300; www.historicebenezer.org; 101 Jackson St NE, Sweet Auburn; ⊙service 9am & 11:30am Sun) across the street.

Westside

This largely industrial swath is home to the Westside Provisions District in West Midtown, a booming shopping and dining complex. Here, and along the BeltLine's soon-to-explode Westside Trail, are the focal points of this burgeoning destination entertainment district, which has been prime fodder for breweries and film studios.

Festivals & Events

Atlanta Jazz Festival MUSIC
(☎404-546-7246; www.atlanta.net/events/atlanta-jazz-festival; Piedmont Park; ⊙May) FREE One of the largest free jazz festivals in the country has attracted big names such as Miles Davis, Dizzy Gillespie and Nina Simone over its 40-year history. The month-long event culminates in live concerts in Piedmont Park on Memorial Day weekend.

Sleeping

Atlanta remains short on independent boutique options, long on chains. Rates at Downtown hotels tend to fluctuate wildly depending on whether there is a large convention in town. The least expensive option is to stay in one of the many chain hotels along the MARTA line outside Downtown and take the train into the city for sightseeing.

Highland Inn INN $
(☎404-874-5756; www.thehighlandinn.com; 644 N Highland Ave, Virginia-Highland; s/d from $73/103; P ❄ 📶) This European-style, 65-room independent inn, built in 1927, has appealed to touring musicians over the years. Rooms aren't huge, but it has a great location in the Virginia-Highland area and is as affordably comfortable as being Downtown. It's one of the few accommodations in town with single rooms.

Ellis Hotel BOUTIQUE HOTEL $$
(☎404-523-5155; www.ellishotel.com; 176 Peachtree St NW; r $159-249; P ❄ 📶 🐾) With business-chic rooms warmly dressed in blue and gray hues and ostrich-skin headboards, the Ellis is contemporary and subtly boutique. You can sleep inside a magnetic field in the Wellness Room; or pick a room on the pet-friendly floor, women-only floor or 'Fresh Air' floor (with private access and special cleaning rules for allergy sufferers).

Hotel Artmore BOUTIQUE HOTEL $$
(☎404-876-6100; www.artmorehotel.com; 1302 W Peachtree St; r $150-320; P ❄ @ 📶) This 1924 Spanish-Mediterranean architectural landmark has been completely revamped into an artistic boutique hotel that's become an urban sanctuary for those who appreciate their trendiness with a dollop of discretion. It wins all sorts of accolades: excellent service, a wonderful courtyard

MARTIN LUTHER KING JR: A CIVIL RIGHTS GIANT

Martin Luther King Jr, the quintessential figure of the Civil Rights movement and arguably America's greatest leader, was born and raised in Atlanta, the son of a preacher and choir leader. His lineage was significant not only because he followed his father to the pulpit of Ebenezer Baptist Church, but also because his political speeches rang out with a preacher's inflections. King remains one of the most respected figures of the 20th century and is Atlanta's quintessential African American hero, his legacy emblazoned across the city's historic Sweet Auburn district, home to the Martin Luther King Jr National Historic Site.

with fire pit and a superb location across the street from Arts Center MARTA station.

Sugar Magnolia B&B B&B $$
(404-222-0226; www.sugarmagnoliabb.com; 804 Edgewood Ave NE, Inman Park; r $165-205;) This lovely four-room inn occupies an impeccable 1892 Queen Anne Victorian mansion in Inman Park. Five original working fireplaces, a supremely relaxing back porch and firepit are highlights, as is Debbie, hostess with the mostest who whips up Belgian waffles and Dutch baby pancakes for breakfast. Our favorite room is the blue-curtained Royal Suite with a massive terrace and a tiled bathroom.

★**Urban Oasis B&B** B&B $$
(770-714-8618; www.urbanoasisbandb.com; 130a Krog St NE, Inman Park; r $155-215;) Hidden inside a gated and repurposed 1950s cotton-sorting warehouse, this retro-modern loft B&B is urban dwelling at its best. Enter into a huge and funky common area with natural light streaming through massive windows and make your way to one of three rooms, all discerningly appointed with Haywood Wakefield mid-century modern furnishings. In 2019, Urban Oasis featured on MTV's *Real World* reality series.

Eating

After New Orleans, Atlanta is the best city in the South to eat, and the food culture here is nothing short of obsessive. The Westside Provisions District, Krog Street Market and Ponce City Market are all newish and hip mixed-use residential and restaurant complexes sprinkled among Atlanta's continually transitioning urban neighborhoods.

Downtown & Midtown

★**BoccaLupo** ITALIAN $$
(404-577-2332; www.boccalupoatl.com; 753 Edgewood Ave NE, Inman Park; mains $17-19; 5:30-10pm Tue-Thu, to 11pm Fri & Sat;) There is so much to love about this candlelit Italian Southern comfort-food haunt led by Mario Batali–trained chef Bruce Logue, but perhaps none more than his Southern-fried-chicken parma with creamy collards and *strano* pasta. It's hands down a top-five Atlanta dish. This Southern soul food with Italian tweak is made with a lotta love and not to be missed.

Daddy D'z BARBECUE $$
(404-222-0206; www.daddydz.com; 264 Memorial Dr SE; sandwiches $8-14, plates $14-24; 11am-10pm Mon-Thu, to 11pm Fri & Sat, noon-9pm Sun;) A juke joint of a barbecue shack, consistently voted one of the top in town, with a central location. From the graffiti murals on the red, white and blue exterior, to the all-powerful smoky essence, to the reclaimed booths on the covered patio, there is soul to spare. Order the succulent ribs with corn bread, and you'll leave smiling.

Empire State South SOUTHERN US $$$
(404-541-1105; www.empirestatesouth.com; 999 Peachtree St NE; mains lunch $13-22, dinner $28-39; 7am-10pm Mon-Fri, from 4pm Sat;) This rustic-hip Midtown bistro serves imaginative New Southern fare and it does not disappoint, be it at breakfast ($8 to $11) or throughout the day. It makes its own bagels, the attention to coffee detail approaches Pacific Northwest levels, and it mixes fried chicken, bacon marmalade *and* pimento cheese on a biscuit!

South City Kitchen SOUTHERN US $$$
(404-873-7358; www.southcitykitchen.com; 1144 Crescent Ave NE; mains lunch $11-25, dinner $18-41; 11am-3:30pm & 5-10pm Mon-Fri, from 10am Sat & Sun;) An upscale, long-standing Southern kitchen featuring tasty updated and elaborated staples like buttermilk-fried chicken served with sautéed collards and red-bliss potatoes, catfish Reubens and shrimp and Geechee Boy grits with tasso ham and smoked tomato-poblano gravy. Start with goat's-cheese-stuffed fried green tomatoes, a Southern specialty *before* the movie.

East Side

★**Octopus Bar** FUSION $$
(404-627-9911; www.octopusbaratl.com; 560 Gresham Ave SE, East Atlanta; dishes $8-22; 10:30pm-2:30am Tue-Sat) Leave your hang-ups at the hotel – this is punk-rock dining – and get to know what's good at this unsigned indoor-outdoor patio dive nuanced with graffitied-up walls and ethereal electronica. No reservations, so line up early, and chow down on a Maine lobster roll (drawn butter, tomalley mayo), shoyu ramen (farm egg) or

many other innovative executions of fusion excellence.

Leon's Full Service FUSION $$
(☎ 404-687-0500; www.leonsfullservice.com; 131 E Ponce de Leon Ave; mains lunch $10-21, $16-35; ⏰ 5pm-midnight Mon, from 11:30am Tue-Thu & Sun, to 2am Fri & Sat; 📶) Leon's can come across as a bit pretentious, but the gorgeous concrete bar and open floor plan spilling out of a former service station and on to a groovy heated deck with floating beams remains cooler than thou and fully packed at all times. You may find prosciutto-wrapped trout and braised short ribs on the changing menu.

Vortex BURGERS $$
(☎ 404-688-1828; www.thevortexbarandgrill.com; 438 Moreland Ave NE, Little Five Points; burgers $10-15; ⏰ 11am-midnight Sun-Thu, to 2am Fri & Sat) An age-21-and-up joint cluttered with Americana memorabilia, the godfather of Atlanta burger joints is where alterna-hipsters mingle alongside Texas tourists and Morehouse College steppers. Burgers range from impressive to outlandish but are always some of the most heralded and heart-stopping in Atlanta. The 20ft-tall skull facade is a Little Five Points landmark of pre–Olympic Games outrageousness.

★ **Gunshow** MODERN AMERICAN $$$
(☎ 404-380-1886; www.gunshowatl.com; 924 Garrett St SE, Glenwood Park; small plates $10-18; ⏰ 6-9pm Tue-Sat; 📶) Celebrity chef Kevin Gillespie's innovative and unorthodox Gunshow is an explosively good night out. Guests choose between a dozen or so smallish dishes, dreamed up by chefs in the open kitchen, who then hawk their blood, sweat and culinary tears dim-sum-style tableside.

Staplehouse AMERICAN $$$
(☎ 404-524-5005; www.staplehouse.com; 541 Edgewood Ave SE; small plates $8-30, tasting menu $105; ⏰ 5:30-10pm Sun & Tue-Thu, to 11pm Fri & Sat; P 📶) 🍃 The hottest table in Atlanta and the darling du jour of Southern foodies, Staplehouse dishes up innovative, seasonal New American cuisine. Small to medium plates including chicken-liver tart with burnt honey and blood orange are served with such artful precision you kinda feel bad about eating them (except they're delicious, so not *that* bad). The seasonal menu changes often.

Westside

★ **Busy Bee Café** SOUTHERN US $
(☎ 404-525-9212; www.thebusybeecafe.com; 810 Martin Luther King Jr Dr NW; mains $14-19; ⏰ 11am-7pm Mon-Sat, from noon Sun) Politicians, police officers, urbanites and hungry miscreants, along with celebrities (it's had pop-ins by MLK Jr, Obama and OutKast), all converge over the city's best fried chicken paired with soul-food sides such as collard greens, candied yams, fried okra and mac 'n' cheese. This Westside classic has been steeped in hospitality and honest-to-goodness food since 1947.

West Egg Cafe DINER $
(☎ 404-872-3973; www.westeggcafe.com; 1100 Howell Mill Rd, Westside Provisions District; mains $8-15; ⏰ 7am-4pm Mon-Fri, 8am-5pm Sat & Sun; P 📶 👪) Belly up to the marble breakfast counter or grab a table and dive into black-bean cakes and eggs, turkey-sausage Benedict, pimento-cheese and bacon omelet, or a fried green tomato BLT. It's all reimagined versions of old-school classics, served in a stylish and spare dining room.

★ **Cooks & Soldiers** BASQUE $$
(☎ 404-996-2623; www.cooksandsoldiers.com; 691 14th St NW; small plates $6-18; ⏰ 5-10pm Sun-Wed, to 11pm Thu, to midnight Fri & Sat; 📶 🍸) A game-changing Westside choice, this Basque-inspired hot spot specializes in *pintxos* (Basque-style tapas) and wood-fired *asadas* (grills) designed to share. Both the food and cocktails are outstanding. Highlights include the house gin and tonics, coal-roasted mushrooms with goat's cheese, crème fraîche and black truffle, and an $84 wood-grilled bone-in rib eye that clocks in at an obviously shareable 2.2lbs (1kg)!

★ **Optimist** SEAFOOD $$$
(☎ 404-477-6260; www.theoptimistrestaurant.com; 914 Howell Mill Rd; mains $32-50; ⏰ 11:30am-2:30pm & 5-10pm Mon-Fri, 5-11pm Sat, 5-10pm Sun; 📶) 🍃 In a short space, we could never do this Westside sustainable-seafood mecca justice. In a word, astonishing! Start with crispy calamari with salsa *matcha* and almonds then move on to a duck-fat-poached swordfish or a daring whole grilled octopus with *aji amarillo* and poblano peppers, and finish with a scoop of house-made salted-caramel ice cream.

Drinking & Nightlife

Atlanta has a busy bar scene, ranging from neighborhood dives to hipster hangouts that want to pass for neighborhood dives to straight-up opulent night haunts for the wealthy and beautiful. Wherever you go, you may notice that this city has one of the most racially integrated social scenes in the country, and that's reason enough to raise a glass.

★ Sister Louisa's Church of the Living Room & Ping Pong Emporium BAR
(☎ 404-522-8275; www.facebook.com/SisterLouisasChurch; 466 Edgewood Ave, Edgewood; ⏰ 5pm-3am Mon-Sat, to midnight Sun; 📶) This cradle of Edgewood's bar revival fosters a church theme, but it's nothing like Westminster Abbey. Sacrilegious art peppers every patch of free wall space, the kind of offensive stuff that starts wars in some parts. Praise the resistance to fancy craft cocktails and join the congregation, chuckling at the artistry or staring at mesmerizing table-tennis matches.

★ Argosy PUB
(☎ 404-577-0407; www.argosy-east.com; 470 Flat Shoals Ave SE; ⏰ 5pm-2:30am Mon-Fri, noon-2:30am Sat, to midnight Sun; 📶) This East Atlanta gastropub nails it with an extensive list of rare craft beers (35 taps), elevated bar food – house-cut Kennebec potato fries, miso quinoa burger, wood-fired pizzas – and a vibe that invites you to stay for the rest of the evening. The multi-angled bar snakes its way through a rustic-chic space and living-room-style lounge areas.

Ladybird Grove & Mess Hall BAR
(☎ 404-458-6838; www.ladybirdatlanta.com; 684 John Wesley Dobbs Ave NE; ⏰ 11am-late Tue-Sun) With an enviable location (and enormous patio) overlooking the BeltLine, Ladybird offers its patrons one of the best drinking views in Atlanta. Complement that cocktail or draft beer with some of the classy pub grub on offer from the kitchen. Last call depends on how busy the bar is.

Brick Store Pub BAR
(☎ 404-687-0990; www.brickstorepub.com; 125 E Court Sq, Decatur; draft beers $5-12; ⏰ 11am-1am Mon-Wed, to 2am Thu-Sat, noon-1am Sun) Beer hounds geek out on Atlanta's best craft-beer selection at this pub in Decatur, with some 30 meticulously chosen drafts (including those in the more intimate Belgian beer bar upstairs). Nearly 300 beers by the bottle are served from a 15,000-bottle vault, drawing a fun, young crowd every night.

Kimball House COCKTAIL BAR
(☎ 404-378-3502; www.kimball-house.com; 303 E Howard Ave, Decatur; ⏰ 5pm-midnight Sun-Thu, to 1am Fri & Sat; 📶) Housed in an atmospheric period dining room in a restored train depot slightly off the grid in Decatur, Kimball House harbors a vaguely saloon-like feel under overhead belt-driven fans. It specializes in craft cocktails (around $13), absinthe and a long list of flown-in-fresh oysters.

★ New Realm Brewing Co MICROBREWERY
(☎ 404-968-2778; www.newrealmbrewing.com; 550 Somerset Tce NE, No 101; ⏰ 4-10pm Mon-Thu, to midnight Fri & Sat, 11am-10pm Sun; 📶) Ex-Stone Brewing Co brewmaster Mitch Steele wrote the book on IPAs. His latest venture, a 20,000-sq-ft restaurant and brewery along the BeltLine's Eastside Trail, is a coup for Southern hopheads. Eight taps (four direct from serving tanks behind the bar) harbor triple IPAs and small-batch brews guzzled by a fun crowd ogling the Atlanta skyline from the upstairs terrace.

☆ Entertainment

Clermont Lounge DANCE
(www.clermontlounge.net; 789 Ponce de Leon Ave NE, Poncey-Highland; ⏰ 3pm-4am) The Clermont is a strip club, the oldest in Atlanta. But not *just* a strip club. It's a bedrock of the Atlanta scene that welcomes dancers of all ages, races and body types. In short, it's a strip club built for strippers, although the audience – and *everyone* comes here at some point – has a grand time as well.

Terminal West LIVE MUSIC
(☎ 404-876-5566; www.terminalwestatl.com; 887 W Marietta St, Westside; ⏰ box office 11am-5pm Tue-Fri) One of Atlanta's best live-music venues, this concert space is located inside a beautifully revamped 100-year-old iron and steel foundry on the Westside.

Woodruff Arts Center ARTS CENTER
(☎ 404-733-4200; www.woodruffcenter.org; 1280 Peachtree St NE; ⏰ box office noon-6pm Tue-Sat, to 5pm Sun) This arts complex contains within its campus the High Museum (p395), the Atlanta Symphony Orchestra and the **Alliance Theatre** (☎ 404-733-4650; www.allianceteatre.org).

LGBTIQ+ ATLANTA

Atlanta is one of the few places in Georgia with a noticeable and active gay and lesbian population, probably second only to San Francisco in terms of visibility and population nationwide. Midtown is the center of gay life; the epicenter is around Piedmont Park and the intersection of 10th St and Piedmont Ave, where you can check out **Blake's** (404-892-5786; www.blakesontheparkatlanta.com; 227 10th St NE; 3pm-3am Mon-Fri, 1pm-3am Sat, 1pm-1am Sun), Atlanta's classic gay bar, or **10th & Piedmont** (www.10thandpiedmont.com; 991 Piedmont Ave NE; 10am-3pm & 5-10pm Mon-Thu, to 11pm Fri, 10am-4pm & 5-11pm Sat, 10am-6pm Sun), good for food and late-night shenanigans. The town of Decatur, east of downtown Atlanta, has a significant lesbian community. For news and information, grab a copy of the weekly *Peach ATL* (www.peachatl.com), monthly *Goliath Atlanta* (www.goliathatlanta.com) or visit www.gayatlanta.com.

Atlanta Pride Festival (www.atlantapride.org) is a massive annual celebration of the city's gay and lesbian community. It's held in October in and around Piedmont Park.

Variety Playhouse LIVE MUSIC
(404-524-7354; www.variety-playhouse.com; 1099 Euclid Ave NE, Little Five Points; box office noon-6pm Mon-Fri) A historic, smartly booked and well-run concert venue built in 1940 and fully renovated in 2015. It hosts a variety of touring artists and is one of the main anchors of the Little Five Points scene.

Shopping

★Criminal Records MUSIC
(404-215-9511; www.criminalatl.com; 1154 Euclid Ave, Little Five Points; 11am-9pm Mon-Sat, noon-7pm Sun) This throwback record store is stacked wall to wall with a library's worth of new pop, soul, jazz and metal, on CD or vinyl. It has a fun music-related book section, and a great collection of comic books and graphic novels. Basically, a certain kind of music-lover and genre-loving geek could live here.

Junkman's Daughter VINTAGE
(404-577-3188; www.thejunkmansdaughter.com; 464 Moreland Ave NE, Little Five Points; 11am-7pm Mon-Fri, to 8pm Sat, noon-7pm Sun) A defiant and fiercely independent cradle of counterculture since 1982, this 10,000-sq-ft alternative superstore stocks racks of vintage, ornery bumper stickers, kitschy toys and tchotchkes, *Star Wars* lunch boxes, incense, wigs, offensive coffee mugs and a whole lot more. It put Little Five Points on the map.

Citizen Supply CLOTHING
(www.citizensupply.com; 675 Ponce de Leon Ave NE, Ponce City Market; 10am-9pm Mon-Sat, noon-8pm Sun) This fiercely curated all-under-one-roof flagship shop stocks a dizzying array of top-quality – some say hipster – brands of products you didn't know you wanted until you saw them: foresty pomades from Mail Room Barber Co, Edison electric bikes, Bradley Mountain canvas and leather bags, **Wander North Georgia** (www.wandernorthgeorgia.com; 33 N Main St; 11am-5pm Mon-Thu, to 6pm Fri & Sat, noon-5pm Sun) T-shirts, Atlanta-centric art, Loyal Stricklin leather-bound Aviator mugs and a whole lot more.

Richards Variety Store GIFTS & SOUVENIRS
(www.richardsvarietystore.com; 931 Monroe Dr NE; 10am-8pm Mon-Sat, 11am-6pm Sun) There is almost nothing this massive, good-time emporium doesn't have. Hebrew alphabet kits? Ouija boards? Paper pinhole cameras? 3-D White House puzzles? Stuffed penguins? You'll tap into your inner child as you rummage sections devoted to toys, puzzles, housewares, books, art, gadgets – the aisles go on and on. There is *something* in here you didn't know you needed!

Eco Denizen GIFTS & SOUVENIRS
(www.ecodenizen.net; 999 Peachtree St NE; 11am-8pm Mon-Sat, noon-6pm Sun) This eco-driven mom-and-pop-run gift shop is full of coveted stuff: vegan wallets from Matt & Nat, Tokens & Icons wine openers fashioned from recycled Major League Baseball bats and professional tennis rackets, and local art such as Houston Llew's glass-on-copper pop-art pieces.

Information

EMERGENCY & MEDICAL SERVICES

Atlanta Medical Center (404-265-4000; www.atlantamedcenter.com; 303 Parkway Dr NE; 24hr) A tertiary-care hospital considered Atlanta's best since 1901.

ATLANTA BELTLINE

With an 8:1 return on investment and a transformative way of moving through the city, Atlanta is wallowing in the afterglow of its best idea in decades: the Atlanta BeltLine, a 22-mile rail corridor encircling the city that's being repurposed as a multiuse trail. In all fairness, it was the idea of former Georgia Tech student Ryan Gravel, but the city's adaptation of his master's thesis – the most comprehensive transportation and economic development effort ever undertaken in Atlanta and among the largest, most wide-ranging urban-redevelopment programs currently under way in the US – has spawned a payout that would send a Las Vegas casino into crisis mode: some $4.1 billion in economic development from an initial city investment of $500 million – and a lot more on the way where that came from.

Grady Memorial Hospital (☎404-616-1000; www.gradyhealth.org; 80 Jesse Hill Jr Drive SE) Home to the Marcus Trauma Center, Atlanta's only nationally verified Level 1 trauma center.

MEDIA

Atlanta (www.atlantamagazine.com) A monthly general-interest magazine covering local issues, arts and dining.

Atlanta Daily World (www.atlantadailyworld.com) The nation's oldest continuously running African American newspaper (since 1928).

Atlanta Journal-Constitution (www.ajc.com) Atlanta's major daily newspaper, with a good travel section on Sunday.

Creative Loafing (www.creativeloafing.com) For hip tips on music, arts and theater, this free alternative weekly comes out every Wednesday.

TOURIST INFORMATION

Atlanta Convention & Visitors Bureau (www.atlanta.net) Maps, information about attractions, restaurants, outdoor recreation and accommodations; operates visitor centers at Centennial Olympic Park (☎404-577-2148; 65 Upper Alabama St, Underground Atlanta; ⏰10am-6pm Mon-Sat, noon-6pm Sun) and Hartsfield-Jackson Atlanta International Airport (☎404-305-8426; 6000 N Terminal Pkwy, North Terminal; ⏰9am-9pm Mon-Fri, to 6pm Sat, noon-6pm Sun).

Getting There & Away

Atlanta straddles the intersection of three interstates: I-20, I-75 and I-85. **Hartsfield-Jackson International Airport** (ATL, Atlanta; ☎800-897-1910; www.atl.com), 9.5 miles south of Downtown, is the world's busiest airport by passenger traffic. The easiest way into the city from the airport is MARTA, the city's rail system. **Greyhound** (☎404-584-1728; www.greyhound.com; 232 Forsyth St) and **Amtrak** (www.amtrak.com/stations/atl; 1688 Peachtree St NW) both serve the city as well.

Getting Around

Despite its sprawling layout and debilitating traffic, Atlanta is fairly easy to navigate both with your own set of wheels or on public transportation.

The city is well served by the MARTA bus and rail system and a Downtown tram.

And once the groundbreaking Atlanta BeltLine completes its loop by 2030, Atlanta's multiuse trail system will be one of the most progressive in North America, if not the world.

North Georgia

Elevation seekers should head to North Georgia, which sits at the southern end of the great Appalachian Range. Those mountains, and their surrounding foothills and upcountry, provide superb mountain scenery, as well as some decent wines and frothing rivers. Fall colors emerge late here, peaking in October.

A few days are warranted here to see sites such as the 1200ft-deep Tallulah Gorge, and the mountain scenery and hiking trails at Vogel State Park and Unicoi State Park.

Dahlonega

In 1828 Dahlonega was the site of the first gold rush in the USA (locals are known as 'Nuggets'). These days the boom is in tourism, as it's an easy day excursion when coming from Atlanta and a fantastic mountain destination.

Not only is Dahlonega a hotbed of outdoor activities, but downtown in Courthouse Sq is an attractive mélange of wine-tasting rooms, gourmet emporiums, great food, countrified shops and foothill charm. Wine tasting in the surrounding vineyards is on the rise too.

There's a vaguely artistic vibe permeating throughout town (especially when it comes to music), often fueled by students at the University of North Georgia, located off the square.

Tack on Amicalola Falls State Park just 18 miles west and you have a pretty irresistible bundle of mountain fun.

Sights & Activities

Amicalola Falls WATERFALL
(706-344-1500; www.amicalolafallslodge.com/ga-state-park; 418 Amicalola Falls State Park Rd, Dawsonville; per vehicle $5; 7am-10pm, visitor center 9am-5pm Sun-Wed, to 7pm Thu-Sat;) The tallest cascading waterfall in the Southeast is a spectacular sight. It tumbles 729ft through protected North Georgia mountain scenery within Amicalola Falls State Park. You can also watch it fall right underfoot from the viewpoint bridge on the West Ridge Trail.

★ **Wolf Mountain Vineyards** WINERY
(706-867-9862; www.wolfmountainvineyards.com; 180 Wolf Mountain Trail; tastings $20, mains $15, brunch $35; tastings 11am-5pm Thu-Sat, 12:30-5pm Sun, cafe noon-3pm Thu-Sat, brunch 12:30pm & 2:30pm Sun) Wolf lures a hip and trendy 30-something crowd to its gorgeous, 30-acre winery that frames epic sunsets over Springer Mountain from its tasting-room terrace. Top wines like its *méthode champenoise* 100% chardonnay Blanc de Blanc and crisp and fresh Plentitude (an unoaked chardonnay/Viognier blend) are the way to go.

Reservations required for cafe and brunch.

Sleeping & Eating

Barefoot Hills HOTEL $
(770-312-7342; www.barefoothills.com; 7693 Hwy 19 N; dm from $35, r $85-155, cabins $140-195;) On Hwy 19 N, 7 miles or so north of town, this revamped option could be known as the Boutique Hotel Formerly Known as Hiker Hostel. New owners upgraded this former backpackers in 2017, transitioning the converted log cabin to a near boutique-level hotel – but maintaining a hiker focus with bunk beds in another location, a supply store and shuttles to trailheads.

★ **Spirits Tavern** BURGERS $
(706-482-0580; www.spirits-tavern.com; 19 E Main St; burgers $12-15; 11am-11pm Sun-Thu, to 1am Fri, to midnight Sat;) This full bar dishes up surprisingly creative burgers made from Angus beef or free-range, hormone-free turkey and veggies, including gooey mac 'n' cheese, Greek and Cajun versions. With eight taps and a seasonally changing list of serious cocktails, it's also the best 'bar' in town.

Picnic Cafe & Dessertery CAFE $
(706-864-1095; www.thepicniccafe.wixsite.com/picniccafe; 30 Public Sq; sandwiches $8.49; 7:30am-7pm Sun-Wed, to 8pm Thu-Sat;) Owned by Dahlonega mayor Sam Norten and the absolute best spot around to mingle with town characters and university students engrossed in local gossip. Picnic does simple and quick biscuit sandwiches for breakfast, and sandwiches such as honey-ham salad, pimento cheese and sweet Georgia peach chicken salad for lunch.

Information

Dahlonega-Lumpkin County Visitors Center (706-864-3711; www.dahlonega.org; 13 S Park St; 9am-5:30pm Mon-Fri, 10am-5pm Sat & Sun) has plenty of information on area sights and activities, including hiking, canoeing, kayaking, rafting and mountain biking.

Getting There & Away

Dahlonega is about 70 miles north of Atlanta; the quickest way here is via Hwy 19. There is no public bus service, but folks traveling from Atlanta often take a Metropolitan Atlanta Rapid Transit Authority (MARTA) train to North Springs station in Atlanta and catch an Uber from there ($55 to $75).

The nearest Amtrak station is in Gainesville, 21 miles south.

Athens

A beery, artsy and laid-back college town, Athens has an extremely popular football team (the University of Georgia Bulldogs), a world-famous music scene, a bona fide restaurant culture and surprisingly diverse nightlife. The university – UGA – drives the culture of Athens and ensures an ever-replenishing supply of young bar-hoppers and concert-goers, some of whom stick around long after graduation and become known as 'townies.'

The pleasant, walkable downtown offers a plethora of funky choices for eating, drinking and shopping.

Sights

★Georgia Museum of Art MUSEUM
(☎706-542-4662; www.georgiamuseum.org; 90 Carlton St; ⌚10am-5pm Tue, Wed, Fri & Sat, to 9pm Thu, 1-5pm Sun) FREE A smart, modern gallery where brainy, arty types set up in the wired lobby for personal study, while art hounds gawk at modern sculpture in the courtyard garden as well as the tremendous collection from American realists of the 1930s.

State Botanical Garden of Georgia GARDENS
(☎706-542-1244; www.botgarden.uga.edu; 2450 S Milledge Ave; ⌚8am-7pm) FREE Truly gorgeous, with winding outdoor paths and a sociohistorical edge, Athens' gardens are a gift for a city of this size. Signs provide smart context for its amazing collection of plants, which includes rare and threatened species. There are nearly 5 miles of top-notch woodland walking trails too.

Sleeping & Eating

★Graduate Athens INN $$
(☎706-549-7020; www.graduateathens.com; 295 E Dougherty St; r $155-259, ste $280-500; P@🛜🏊) This wonderfully designed boutique hotel, the first of a college-campus chain, is drowning in sexy retro hipness, from potted plants inside old-school, Dewey decimal card-catalog filing cabinets in the lobby to the sweet Crosley turntables and classic video games in the suites.

Hotel Indigo BOUTIQUE HOTEL $$
(☎706-546-0430; www.indigoathens.com; 500 College Ave; r/ste from $192/313; P@🛜🏊🐾) Rooms are spacious, loftlike pods of cool at this ecochic boutique hotel. Part of the Indigo chain, it's a Leadership in Energy and Environmental Design (LEED) gold-certified sustainable standout. Green elements include regenerative elevators and priority parking for hybrid vehicles; 30% of the building was constructed from recycled content.

Pouch PIES $
(☎706-395-6696; www.pouchpies.com; 151 E Broad St; pies $5.50; ⌚11am-9pm Mon-Sat; 🖉) In the South, 'pie' usually means something sweet, buttery and served after dinner. For the South African owners of Pouch, 'pie' means savory pastries from around the world: Aussie pies with beef and gravy, Portuguese pies with piripiri white-wine sauce, chorizo and spicy chicken, and even a local offering with pulled pork and peach BBQ sauce!

White Tiger BARBECUE $
(☎706-353-6847; www.whitetigergourmet.com; 217 Hiawassee Ave; mains $7.50-11; ⌚11am-3pm Mon-Wed, 11am-3pm & 6-8pm Thu-Sat, 10am-2pm Sun; 🛜🖉👪) The 100-year-old structure doesn't invite confidence, but this off-the-beaten-path local favorite does killer wood-smoked pulled-pork sandwiches – add pimento cheese (and send us a thank-you note!) – plus burgers and even barbecue-smoked tofu and a whole lot more for vegetarians. Chef Ken Manring honed his skills in much higher-brow kitchens before settling in Athens.

★Home.made from Scratch SOUTHERN US $$
(☎706-206-9216; www.homemadeathens.com; 1072 Baxter St; mains lunch $10-13, dinner $18-24; ⌚11am-2pm & 5-9pm Tue-Sat, 10am-2pm Sun; 🛜) Home.made is upping the game when it comes to nouveau Southern cuisine. The menu constantly changes based on ingredient availability, but whatever these folks source is always turned into something creative, delicious, rooted in local flavors and often playfully over the top. At lunch, don't miss the fried chicken and pimento-cheese sandwich with a side upgrade to tomato pie.

Five & Ten AMERICAN $$$
(☎706-546-7300; www.fiveandten.com; 1073 S Milledge Ave; mains $22-48; ⌚5:30-10pm Sun-Thu, to 11pm Fri & Sat, 10:30am-2:30pm Sun; 🖉) Sustainably driven, James Beard Award–winning Five & Ten ranks among the South's best restaurants. Its menu is earthy and slightly gamey: Georgia quail with pickled *yacón* and white-miso aioli, and Frogmore stew (stewed corn, sausage and potato). Vegetarians should try baked Crescenza cheese with confit parsnips and blue collard greens or pasta ribbons with grilled tomato sauce, jalapeños and Parmesan.

Drinking & Entertainment

★Creature Comforts Brewing Co MICROBREWERY
(www.creaturecomfortsbeer.com; 271 W Hancock Ave; pints $6-8; ⌚5-10pm Tue-Thu, 3-10pm Fri, 1-10pm Sat, 1-6pm Sun; 🛜) Athens' best craft beer emerges from 33 taps at this cutting-edge, dog-friendly former tire shop which excels at staples – Indian Pale Ales

NATURE & ADVENTURE IN NORTH GEORGIA

The 1000ft-deep **Tallulah Gorge** (706-754-7981; www.gastateparks.org/tallulahgorge; 338 Jane Hurt Yarn Dr, Tallulah Falls; per vehicle $5; 8am-sunset; P) carves a dark scar across the wooded hills of North Georgia. Walk over the *Indiana Jones*–worthy suspension bridge, and be on the lookout (literally) for rim trails to overlooks. Or get a first-come, first-served permit to hike to the gorge floor – only 100 are given out each day (arrive early, they're usually gone in the morning) and not offered on water-release dates (check schedule online).

Located at the base of the evocatively named Blood Mountain, **Vogel State Park** (706-745-2628; www.gastateparks.org/vogel; 405 Vogel State Park Rd; per vehicle $5; 7am-10pm; P) is one of Georgia's oldest parks, and constitutes a quilt of wooded mountains surrounding a 22-acre lake. There's a multitude of trails to pick from, catering to beginners and advanced hikers. Many of the on-site facilities were built by the Civilian Conservation Corp; a seasonal museum tells the story of these work teams, who both built the park and rescued the local economy during the Great Depression.

At adventure-oriented **Unicoi State Park** (706-878-2201; www.unicoilodge.com; 1788 Hwy 356; per vehicle $5; 7am-10pm; P) visitors can rent kayaks ($10 per hour), take paddleboard lessons ($25), hike some 12 miles of trails, mountain bike, or take a zipline safari through the local forest canopy ($59).

(IPAs), amber ales – but isn't afraid to play around with suds (tart blonde ale aged in wine barrels, mixed fermentation ale aged in bourbon barrels with blackberries). Local ingredients often form the backbone of the memorable brews.

Trapeze Pub CRAFT BEER
(www.trappezepub.com; 269 N Hull St; 11am-midnight;) Downtown's best craft-beer bar installed itself well before the suds revolution. You'll find dozens of taps spanning regional, national and international brews, and another 100 or so at any given time in bottles. Soak it up with its Belgian-style fries ($4), the best in town.

Old Pal BAR
(www.theoldpal.com; 1320 Prince Ave; 4pm-2am Mon-Sat;) This is Normaltown's thinking-person's bar, devoted to seasonal craft cocktails ($9) and a thoughtfully curated bourbon list. It's a beautiful, dark space that has been showered with local preservation awards.

40 Watt Club LIVE MUSIC
(706-549-7871; www.40watt.com; 285 W Washington St; $5-25; 8pm-2am Thu-Sat) Athens' most storied joint has lounges, a tiki bar and $2.50 PBRs. The venue has welcomed indie rock to its stage since REM, the B-52's and Widespread Panic owned this town and today this is still where the big hitters play when they come to town. It has recently embraced comedy as well.

Information

Athens Welcome Center (706-353-1820; www.athenswelcomecenter.com; 280 E Dougherty St; 10am-5pm Mon-Sat, noon-5pm Sun) This visitor center, in a historic antebellum house at the corner of Thomas St, provides maps and information on local tours.

Getting There & Away

This college town is about 70 miles east of Atlanta. There's no main highway that leads here, so traffic can be an issue on secondary state and county roads. The local **Greyhound station** (706-549-2255; www.greyhound.com; 4020 Atlanta Hwy, Bogart) is actually about 6 miles west of downtown Athens. Buses leave for Atlanta (from $15, 1½ hours, twice daily) and Savannah (from $59, 7 hours, twice daily).

Groome Transportation (706-612-1155; https://groometransportation.com; 3190 Atlanta Hwy, Suite 22) operates 23 shuttles per day year-round between Athens and Hartsfield–Jackson Atlanta International Airport ($41, 2½ hours). Shuttles leave from the UGA Georgia Center (1197 S Lumpkin St) and its Athens office 35 minutes later between 2:05am and 9:25pm.

Coastal Georgia

Driving through South Georgia's expansive wide-open pastures, cotton fields and fruit farms is a chance to see the 'Peach State' in all its glory. Surprisingly, South Georgia actually produces more blueberries and peanuts than it does peaches, and there's plenty of opportunity to experience local produce grown in these fertile parts.

Come for the region's simple, warm country-style hospitality, excellent barbecue and a number of underrated natural sights. Kayak along the untamed waters of Okefenokee's alligator-ravaged swamp, and trek around Providence Canyon's remarkable orange, red and purple formations. Meanwhile, visitors from around the world flock to Plains, the birthplace of former US President Jimmy Carter, and the sleepy historic town of Senoia, dubbed the 'Hollywood of the South' (it doubles as Woodbury and Alexandria in the wildly popular zombie series *The Walking Dead*).

Savannah

Rife with elegant townhouses, antebellum mansions, green public squares, pristine tidal freshwater marshes and mammoth oak trees bedecked in moss, Savannah is a beautiful and culturally rich city.

Sights & Activities

★ Wormsloe Historic Site HISTORIC SITE
(☎912-353-3023; www.gastateparks.org/wormsloe; 7601 Skidaway Rd; adult/senior/child 6-17yr/child 1-5yr $10/9/4.50/2; ⏲9am-5pm; P) A short drive from downtown, on the beautiful Isle of Hope, this is one of the most photographed sites in town. As soon as you enter, you feel as if you've been roused from the last snatch of an arboreal dream as you gaze at a corridor of mossy, ancient oaks that runs for 1.5 miles, known as the Avenue of the Oaks.

★ Forsyth Park PARK
FREE The Central Park of Savannah is a sprawling rectangular green space, anchored by a beautiful fountain that forms a quintessential photo op.

Mercer-Williams House HISTORIC BUILDING
(☎912-236-6352; www.mercerhouse.com; 429 Bull St; adult/student $12.50/8; ⏲10:30am-4pm Mon-Sat, from noon Sun) Although Jim Williams, the Savannah art dealer portrayed by Kevin Spacey in the film version of *Midnight in the Garden of Good and Evil*, died back in 1990, his infamous mansion didn't become a museum until 2004.

You're not allowed to visit the upstairs here, where Williams' family still lives, but the downstairs is an interior decorator's fantasy.

★ Laurel Grove Cemetery CEMETERY
(2101 Kollock St; ⏲8am-5pm) Originally part of a plantation, this segregated cemetery has major historical significance to Savannah. From the mid-19th century, whites – including Confederate veterans of the Civil War – were buried in the north section (which has a separate entrance); the south section contains graves of thousands of African Americans, both once-enslaved and free. Laurel Grove South is one of the largest African American cemeteries in the South and many influential figures from the community, including from during the Civil Rights Movement, are interred here.

Telfair Academy MUSEUM
(☎912-790-8800; www.telfair.org/visit/telfair; 121 Barnard St; adult/student/child $20/15/5; ⏲noon-5pm Sun & Mon, from 10am Tue-Sat) Considered Savannah's top art museum, the historic Telfair family mansion is filled with 19th-century American art and silver and a smattering of European pieces. The home itself is gorgeous and sunrise-hued – an artifact in its own right that wows visitors to this day.

SCAD Museum of Art MUSEUM
(☎912-525-7191; www.scadmoa.org; 601 Turner Blvd; adult/child under 14yr $10/free; ⏲10am-5pm Tue, Wed, Fri & Sat, to 8pm Thu, noon-5pm Sun) Architecturally striking (but what else would you expect from this school of design?), this brick, steel, concrete and glass longhouse delivers your contemporary-art fix. There are groovy, creative sitting areas inside and out, and a number of rotating and visiting exhibitions that showcase some of the most impressive talents within the contemporary-art world.

Jepson Center for the Arts GALLERY
(JCA; ☎912-790-8800; www.telfair.org/visit/jepson; 207 W York St; adult/student/child $20/15/5; ⏲noon-5pm Sun & Mon, from 10am Tue-Sat; 👪) Designed by the great Moshe Safdie, and looking pretty darn space-age by Savannah's standards, the JCA – rather appropriately, given its architecture – focuses on 20th- and 21st-century art. Be on the lookout for wandering scads of SCAD students (ha!) and temporary exhibitions covering topics from race to art in virtual-reality video games.

Savannah Bike Tours CYCLING
(☎912-704-4043; www.savannahbiketours.com; 41 Habersham St; tours $30; ⏲varies by season)

This outfit offers two-hour bike tours over easy flat terrain on its fleet of cruisers. Call ahead or check the website for current tour times.

Sleeping

Thunderbird Inn MOTEL $

(☎912-232-2661; www.thethunderbirdinn.com; 611 W Oglethorpe Ave; r $125-175; P ❄ 📶 🐾) 'A tad Palm Springs, a touch Vegas' best describes this vintage-chic 1964 motel that wins its own popularity contest – a 'Hippest hotel in Savannah' proclamation greets guests in the '60s-soundtracked lobby. In a land of stuffy B&Bs, this groovy place is an oasis, made all the better by local SCAD student art.

★**Beachview Bed & Breakfast** B&B $$

(☎912-786-5500; www.beachviewbbtybee.com; 1701 Butler Ave, Tybee Island; r $180-320; P 📶 🐾) The tastefully themed rooms in this stately home feature bright, breezy decor, clawfoot tubs and comfortable beds, all within walking distance of Tybee's south-end beachfront. Breakfast is farm-to-table, and Wendy, the on-site manager and owner's daughter, is as chipper and helpful as they come.

Kimpton Brice BOUTIQUE HOTEL $$$

(☎912-238-1200; www.bricehotel.com; 601 E Bay St; r from $260; ❄ 📶 🏊) Kimpton is known for its design-conscious hotels, so you'd figure it would bring its A game to one of the country's leading design cities. The Kimpton Brice does not disappoint in this, or any other, regard. Modern rooms have playful swatches of color, while the hotel's entrance and lobby feels like it could accommodate a cool club.

Kehoe House B&B $$$

(☎912-232-1020; www.kehoehouse.com; 123 Habersham St; r $250-400; ❄ 📶) This romantic, upscale Renaissance Revival B&B dates from 1892. Twins are said to have died in a chimney here, making it one of America's most haunted hotels (if you're skittish, steer clear of rooms 201 and 203). Ghosts aside, it's a beautifully appointed worthwhile splurge on picturesque Columbia Sq.

Mansion on Forsyth Park BOUTIQUE HOTEL $$$

(☎912-238-5158; www.mansiononforsythpark.com; 700 Drayton St; r weekday/weekend from $220/320; P ❄ @ 📶 🏊) A choice location and chic design highlight the luxe accommodations on offer at the 18,000-sq-ft Mansion – the sexy bathrooms alone are practically worth the money. The best part of the hotel-spa is the amazing local and international art that crowds its walls and hallways – over 400 pieces in all.

Eating

Sweet Spice JAMAICAN $

(☎912-335-8146; www.sweetspicesavannah.net; 5515 Waters Ave; mains $10-17; ⏲11am-8pm Mon-Thu, to 9pm Fri & Sat) This easygoing Jamaican spot, about 4.5 miles southeast of downtown, is a welcome break from all the American and Southern fare you get around here. A large platter of curry goat or jerk chicken costs just a smidge more than a fast-food meal and it's utterly delicious. It will also keep you filled up for a long time.

★**Wyld** SEAFOOD $$

(Wyld Dock Bar; ☎912-692-1219; www.thewylddockbar.com; 2740 Livingston Ave; mains $13-22; ⏲noon-9pm Tue-Thu & Sun, to 10pm Fri & Sat) Hidden along an estuary of the Savannah marshlands, this laid-back, local favorite features a seasonal, New American menu with a heavy seafood emphasis. It's also an ace spot to catch live music, chill in a hammock, rally around a firepit, play bocce ball or drop a fishing line off the dock.

★**Husk Savannah** SOUTHERN US $$$

(☎912-349-2600; www.husksavannah.com; 12 W Oglethorpe Ave; mains $25-36; ⏲11:30am-2pm & 5:30-9pm Mon & Tue, to 10pm Wed-Fri, 10am-2pm & 5:30-11pm Sat, to 9pm Sun) After acclaimed success with Charleston, Nashville and Greenville locations, celebrity-chef Sean Brock brings Husk's hyperlocal, agriculturally driven Southern food sorcery to Savannah. This outpost is the only one boasting a raw seafood bar and is the biggest of all, set in a historic, three-story space that hosts 200 people. Like all locations, the daily menu depends on what's locally available.

Local11Ten MODERN AMERICAN $$$

(☎912-790-9000; www.local11ten.com; 1110 Bull St; mains $27-42; ⏲5:30-10pm; 🍷) Upscale, sustainable, local and fresh: these elements help create an elegant, well-run restaurant that's one of Savannah's best. Start with a blue-crab soufflé, then move on to the seared sea scallops in chive-lemon beurre blanc or the honey and brown-sugar-rubbed pork chop and a salted-caramel pot de crème to finish. Wait. Scratch that. The menu already changed.

Drinking & Entertainment

River and Congress Sts, with Savannah's plastic-cup, open-container laws, are the bar-hopping nightlife corridors, but the scene is more than spring-break bacchanalia. There are some smart watering holes downtown, from speakeasy-style hidden haunts and upscale cocktail bars to quirky, geek-themed hangouts. The club scene is lacking and paltry at best, but solid DJs spin at several bars if you're looking to cut a rug.

Foxy Loxy Cafe CAFE
(📞912-401-0543; www.foxyloxycafe.com; 1919 Bull St; ⏰7am-11pm Mon-Sat, 8am-6pm Sun) Buzzing cafe and art-print gallery full of students and creatives set in an old Victorian house. The courtyard out back is the loveliest in this area. It has tasty tacos for when you get peckish, and freshly baked kolaches (fruit pastries) that are positively addictive. There's Sunday brunch, weekday happy hour, and monthly vinyl nights and poetry slams to boot.

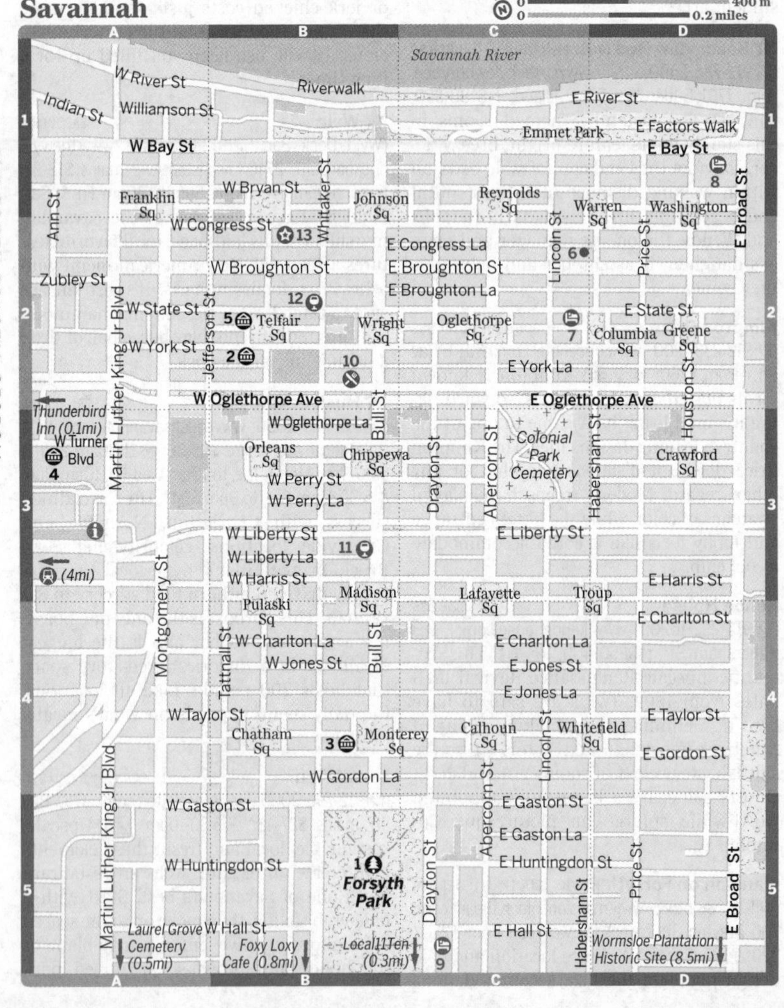

★El-Rocko Lounge
COCKTAIL BAR

(☎912-495-5808; www.elrockolounge.com; 117 Whitaker St; ⊙5pm-3am Mon-Sat) One step in the door and you feel the '70s-inspired swank, but then realize the vibe – in true Savannah fashion – is absolutely chill. Friendly barkeeps mix fancy cocktails while DJs keep the energy high and dance moves steady with diverse jams on vinyl. The crowd is superhip and delightfully unpretentious, and the owner is as rad as they come.

Artillery
COCKTAIL BAR

(www.artillerybar.com; 307 Bull St; ⊙4pm-midnight Mon-Sat) Talented mixologists craft novel, quality cocktails in this opulent space where elements of 19th-century eclecticism and romanticism meld with modern design touches. To drink here, abide by the house rules: no hats, sandals, tank tops, noisy phones, or shots. The signature Artillery Punch – a concoction of rye whiskey, gin, brandy and rum – packs a powerful punch. Sip slowly.

Jinx
LIVE MUSIC

(☎912-236-2281; www.thejinx912.com; 127 W Congress St; ⊙4pm-3am Tue-Sat) A good slice of odd-duck Savannah nightlife, the Jinx is popular with students, townies, musicians, and basically anyone else who has a thing for dive-y watering holes with live music – from rock to punk to alt-country to hip-hop – and funky stuff decorating the walls.

ℹ Information

Candler Hospital (☎912-819-4100; www.sjchs.org; 5353 Reynolds St; ⊙24hr) About 4 miles south of downtown, the Candler Hospital provides good 24/7 care and service. There's another campus at 11075 Mercy Blvd.

Savannah Visitors Center (☎912-944-0455; www.savannahvisit.com; 301 Martin Luther King Jr Blvd; ⊙9am-5:30pm) Excellent resources and services are available in this center, based in a restored 1860s train station. Many privately operated city tours start here. There is also a small, interactive tourist-info kiosk in the visitor center at Forsyth Park.

ℹ Getting There & Around

For a city of its size, Savannah is quite well connected and easy to access by bus or train, and even easier by plane or car. Within the downtown area, Savannah is very foot-friendly. Areas south of Midtown are best accessed by car or bus.

Brunswick & the Golden Isles

With its large shrimp-boat fleet and downtown historic district shaded by lush live oaks, Brunswick has charms you might miss when sailing by on I-95 or the Golden Isle Pkwy (Hwy 17). The town dates from 1733, and it feels very different from its neighbors. There were several plantations nearby, and a large African American population worked on the farms as slaves. Brunswick is not as tourism-oriented as other parts of the coast, and visitors may find multicultural Brunswick, with its West Indian flavors and rich local art scene, a refreshing change of pace.

Hostel in the Forest
HOSTEL $

(☎912-264-9738; www.foresthostel.com; 3901 Hwy 82; d $30, plus lifetime membership for first time visitors $10; P🐾) 🌿 The only budget base in the area is this set of bare-bones octagonal cedar huts and tree houses (sans air or heat) on an ecofriendly, sustainable campus. You must pay a lifetime member fee to stay, and a vegetarian dinner is included. As

Savannah

⊙ Top Sights
1 Forsyth Park B5

⊙ Sights
2 Jepson Center for the Arts B2
3 Mercer-Williams House B4
4 SCAD Museum of Art A3
5 Telfair Academy B2

Activities, Courses & Tours
6 Savannah Bike Tours C2

Sleeping
7 Kehoe House C2
8 Kimpton Brice D1
9 Mansion on Forsyth Park C5

Eating
10 Husk Savannah B2

Drinking & Nightlife
11 Artillery B3
12 El-Rocko Lounge B2

Entertainment
13 Jinx B2

you might guess, the hostel is in the woods, about 10 miles outside Brunswick. Phone reservations only.

Getting There & Around

Brunswick is located off Hwy 17. **Greyhound** (☎800-231-2222; 2990 Hwy 17 S) buses stop at the Flying J gas station, 10 miles west of town. Destinations include Savannah (from $12, two hours, twice daily) and Jacksonville ($12, 70 minutes, twice daily). You can catch onward buses from either city.

ST SIMONS ISLAND

St Simons Island is the largest and most developed of the Golden Isles. There are pretty beaches galore, majestic live oaks, and different neighborhoods to explore – spanning retail parks to cute villages. However, the sheer natural beauty of St Simons isn't as easy to access compared to other nearby islands, given the presence of heavy residential and resort development. For example, the island of Little St Simons is an all-natural jewel, but it's only accessible to guests staying at the exclusive Lodge on Little St Simons. That said, golf fans will be in their element – it has some fine courses.

Sleeping & Eating

St Simons Inn By The Lighthouse INN $$
(☎912-638-1101; www.saintsimonsinn.com; 609 Beachview Dr; r $179-290; P ❄ 📶 🏊) This cute and comfortable good-value inn is accented with white wooden shutters and a general sense of seaside breeziness. It's well located next to the downtown drag and a short pedal from East Beach. Continental breakfast included.

Lodge on Little St Simons Island LODGE $$$
(☎888-733-5774; www.littlestsimonsisland.com; ferry dock 1000 Hampton River Club Marina Dr, hotel Little St Simons Island; d all inclusive $600-750; ❄ 📶) This isolated historic lodge sits on pristine and private Little St Simons. Stays include accommodations, boat transfers to and from the island, three prepared meals daily, beverages (including soft drinks, beer and wine), all activities (including naturalist-led excursions) and use of recreation equipment. Rooms here have a rustic, cabin vibe, with modern amenities.

It's only accessible by boat. Prebooking is essential.

Southern Soul BBQ BARBECUE $
(☎912-638-7685; www.southernsoulbbq.com; 2020 Demere Rd; mains $8-17; ⏲11am-9pm Mon-Sat, to 4pm Sun; P 👪) Housed inside a former gas station at the side of a roundabout, Southern Soul BBQ serves succulent slow oak-smoked pulled pork, burnt-tipped brisket, full slab of sticky ribs, and daily specials such as jerk chicken burritos. There's a number of wonderful house-made sauces – sweet and firey BBQ, tangy mustard and big vinegar pepper – which 'cue fans can slather over their meat.

★**Halyards** SEAFOOD $$$
(☎912-638-9100; www.halyardsrestaurant.com; 55 Cinema Lane; mains $20-38; ⏲5-9pm Mon-Thu, to 10pm Fri-Sun; 📶) 🍃 Chef Dave Snyder's classy, sustainable, seasonal seafood consistently hogs best-of-everything awards on St Simons, and for good reason. The menu changes with the seasons, but may include dishes like sautéed black grouper with broccoli, leek and mascarpone *farrotto*, and roasted tomato butter. Ask for the Chef's Highlights for something extraspecial.

JEKYLL ISLAND

An exclusive refuge for millionaires in the late 19th and early 20th centuries, Jekyll is a 4000-year-old barrier island with 10 miles of beaches. Today it's an unusual clash of wilderness, preserved historic buildings, modern hotels and a massive campground. It's an easily navigable place – you can get around by car, horse or bicycle.

Sights & Activities

Georgia Sea Turtle Center WILDLIFE RESERVE
(☎912-635-4444; www.georgiaseaturtlecenter.org; 214 Stable Rd; adult/child 4-12yr/child under 3yr $10/7.50/free, tours from $27; ⏲9am-5pm; P 👪) This endearing attraction is a conservation center and turtle hospital where patients are on view for the public. Behind the Scenes tours (3pm on Wednesday, Friday and Saturday) and Sunrise Turtle Walks (around 7am on Saturday and Sunday) are also available, among other programs.

★**4-H Tidelands Nature Center** MUSEUM
(☎912-635-5032; www.tidelands4h.org; 100 S Riverview Dr; $5; ⏲9am-4pm Mon-Fri, 10am-2pm Sat & Sun; P 👪) 🍃 Run by a staff of

peppy University of Georgia science students, the Tidelands is a kid-friendly nature center with some neat display cases on local ecology and resident wildlife, including a baby alligator, loggerhead turtle and snakes. Your children can lift, look inside and open various interactive exhibits and even feel or hold certain animals in the touch tanks.

The center also conducts highly recommended two- and three-hour **tours** (www.tidelands4h.org/tours.html; single/tandem kayak 2hr tour $60/116, 3hr tour $70/135) of the salt marshes; on any given day, you may paddle past wood storks, great blue herons, pelicans and dolphins. This is by far the best local means of accessing the understated beauty of the barrier-island salt marshes. Canoe rentals (per hour/day $20/40) and aqua bikes are also available.

Sleeping & Eating

Villas By The Sea VILLA **$$**
(912-635-2521; www.villasbythesearesort.com; 1175 N Beachview Dr; r/condos from $140/260; P ❄ ☎ ≋) A nice choice on the north coast, close to the best beaches. Rooms are spacious and the one-, two- and three-bedroom condos, set in a complex of lodge buildings sprinkled over a garden, aren't fancy but they're plenty comfy.

Jekyll Island Club Hotel HISTORIC HOTEL **$$$**
(844-201-6871; www.jekyllclub.com; 371 Riverview Dr; d/ste from $185/290, resort fee $20; P ❄ @ ☎ ≋) From a distance, with its turrets and balconies, this hotel could be a castle. This posh and storied property is the backbone of the island, featuring a rambling array of rooms spread out over five historic structures. Each building feels plucked from a novel about Jazz Age decadence, although the current vibe is a little more Hilton Head Island country club.

The Wharf SOUTHERN US **$$**
(912-635-3612; www.jekyllwharf.com; 371 Riverview Dr; mains $12-28; 11:30am-10pm; P) The prettiest dining setting on the island is this wooden boathouse-style restaurant situated on a pier. There's indoor seating and an airy nautical-themed vibe, plus outdoor seating overlooking the water. Unpretentious seafood and Southern mains include Southern chicken, cathead biscuits, grilled ahi tuna, broiled sea scallops, and chipotle lobster mac 'n' cheese. Live music takes place weekly.

WORTH A TRIP

CUMBERLAND ISLAND NATIONAL SEASHORE

Georgia's largest and southernmost barrier island, **Cumberland Island National Seashore** (912-882-4336; www.nps.gov/cuis; $10) is an unspoiled paradise. A campers' fantasy, place for family day trips and secluded retreat for couples – it's no wonder the wealthy Carnegie family used Cumberland as a retreat (the derelict but spectacular mansion of Dungeness Ruins is free with entry to Cumberland Island) in the 1800s. The 36,415 acres consist of marsh, mudflats and tidal creeks. Plus, 17 miles of wide, sandy beach that you'll likely have to yourself. The interior has maritime forest, and mysterious jagged tree-lined pathways that would be at home in a *Game of Thrones* episode.

ALABAMA

History suffuses Alabama, a description that could be true of many states. But there are few places where the perception of said history is so emotionally fraught. The Mississippian Native American culture built great mound cities here, and Mobile is dotted with Franco-Caribbean architecture. But for many, the word Alabama is synonymous with the American Civil Rights movement.

Perhaps such a struggle, and all of the nobility and desperation it entailed, was bound for a state like this, with its Gothic plantations, hardscrabble farmland and fiercely local sense of place. From the smallest hunting town to river-bound cities, Alabama is a place all its own, and its character is hard to forget. Some visitors have a hard time looking beyond the state's past, but the troubling elements of that narrative are tied up in a passion that constantly manifests in Alabama's arts, food and culture.

Getting There & Away

While there are mid-sized domestic airports in Mobile and Montgomery, the most common air entry to Alabama is via Birmingham-Shuttlesworth International Airport (p415).

You can find Greyhound stations in major towns. Amtrak has service to Birmingham, and there is talk of reestablishing an Amtrak line across the Gulf Coast.

Birmingham

Birmingham is a confluence of leafy green space, fantastic bars and restaurants, and innovative public space projects. It's also a far more liberal town than you may expect given the political proclivities of its home state. This town may lack the name-brand recognition of musical powerhouses like New Orleans and Nashville, or business centers like Atlanta and Houston, but as mid-sized cities go, Birmingham is hard to beat.

This hilly, shady city, founded as an iron mine, is still a center for manufacturing – many Birmingham residents work at Mercedes Benz USA in Tuscaloosa. In addition, universities and colleges pepper the town, and all of this comes together to create a city with an unreservedly excellent dining and drinking scene. The past also lurks in Birmingham, once named 'Bombingham,' and the history of the Civil Rights movement is very much at your fingers.

Sights & Activities

Art-deco buildings abound in trendy **Five Points South**, where you'll find shops, restaurants and nightspots. Once-industrial **Avondale** is where the hipsters are congregating. Equally noteworthy is the upscale **Homewood** community's quaint commercial drag on 18th St S, close to the Vulcan, which looms illuminated above the city and is visible from nearly all angles, day and night.

★Birmingham Civil Rights Institute MUSEUM
(☎866-328-9696; www.bcri.org; 520 16th St N; adult/student/child $15/6/5; ⏲10am-5pm Tue-Sat) A maze of moving audio, video and photography exhibits tell the story of racial segregation and the Civil Rights movement, with a focus on activities in and around Birmingham.

There's an extensive exhibit on the **16th Street Baptist Church** (☎205-251-9402; www.16thstreetbaptist.org; cnr 16th St & 6th Ave N; $5; ⏲ministry tours 10am-3pm Tue-Fri, by appt only 10am-1pm Sat), located across the street, which was bombed in 1963; it's the beginning of the city's Civil Rights Memorial Trail.

★Sloss Furnaces FACTORY
(☎205-254-2025; www.slossfurnaces.com; 20 32nd St N; ⏲10am-4pm Tue-Sat, noon-4pm Sun; P) FREE This is one of Birmingham's can't-miss sites. From 1882 to 1971, it was a pig iron–producing blast furnace and a cornerstone of Birmingham's economy. Today, instead of a wasteland it's a National Historic Landmark, a red mass of steel and girders rusted into a Gothic monument to American industry. Quiet pathways pass cobwebbed workshops and production lines that form a photographer's dream playground. A small museum on-site explores the furnaces' history.

Vulcan Park PARK
(☎205-933-1409; www.visitvulcan.com; 1701 Valley View Dr; observation tower & museum adult/child $6/4, 6-10pm adult/child $5/4; ⏲observation tower 10am-10pm, museum 10am-6pm) Imagine Christ the Redeemer in Rio, but made of iron and depicting a beefcake Roman god of metalworking. *Vulcan* is visible from all over the city – this is the world's largest cast-iron statue – and the park he resides in offers fantastic views, along with an **observation tower**. A small on-site museum explores Birmingham history.

Birmingham Museum of Art GALLERY
(☎205-254-2565; www.artsbma.org; 2000 Rev Abraham Woods Jr Blvd; ⏲10am-5pm Tue-Sat, noon-5pm Sun) FREE This fine museum boasts an impressive collection, especially given Birmingham's status as a mid-sized city. Inside, you'll find works from Asia, Africa, Europe and the Americas. Don't miss pieces by Rodin, Botero and Dalí in the sculpture garden.

Birmingham Civil Rights Memorial Trail WALKING
(www.bcri.org; 520 16th St N) Installed in 2013 for the Civil Rights campaign's 50th anniversary, this poignant walk, stretching over seven blocks, depicts 22 scenes with plaques, statues and photography, some of it quite conceptual and moving – to wit, a gauntlet of snapping, sculpted dog statues that pedestrians must traverse. The experience peels back yet another layer of the sweat and blood behind a campaign that changed America.

Sleeping

★Elyton Hotel BOUTIQUE HOTEL $$
(☎205-731-3600; www.elytonhotel.com; 1928 1st Ave N; r $149-199, ste $349-369; P) The Elyton holds an admirable middle ground between boutique design and business-class

WORTH A TRIP

ROCKET CITY

The city of **Huntsville** stretches over the green North Alabama hills like a prosperous afterthought to all of the area's surrounding natural beauty. It's home to the world renowned **US Space & Rocket Center** (256-837-3400; www.rocketcenter.com; 1 Tranquility Base; adult/child $25/17; 9am-5pm; P), a Smithsonian-affiliated museum with a jaw-dropping collection of space artifacts, from rockets and lunar landers to space capsules and shuttle components. There's also a working, walk-through replica of the International Space Station, plus simulator rides for kids and adults (try the G Force simulator!).

When hunger strikes, head to **Betty Mae's Restaurant** (256-533-2188; http://bettymaes.restaurantsnapshot.com; 1222 Grace St NW; mains $6-10; 11am-3pm Mon-Fri, to 6pm Sun; P), a bustling eatery that does fabulous soul food (African American Southern food) and whips up some decadent red velvet cake.

Huntsville is a handy stop while road-tripping through the south: it's roughly halfway between Birmingham and Nashville.

amenities and dimensions. Over 100 rooms, decked out in a crisp white aesthetic accented with pops of color and modern art, occupy the Empire building, an early 20th-century architectural landmark.

Redmont Hotel HISTORIC HOTEL **$$**
(205-957-6828; www.redmontbirmingham.com; 2101 5th Ave N; r $150-170, ste $220;) The piano and chandelier in the lobby of this 1925 hotel lend a certain historical, old-world feel, and all deluxe rooms were renovated not too long ago, giving it a modern edge. The spacious rooftop bar doesn't hurt, either. It's walking distance to the Civil Rights sights.

Eating

★Saw's Soul Kitchen BARBECUE **$**
(205-591-1409; www.sawsbbq.com; 215 41st St S; mains $9-16; 11am-8pm Mon-Sat, to 4pm Sun;) Saw's offers some of the most mouthwatering smoked meat in the city, served in a family-friendly atmosphere. Stuffed potatoes make a nice addition to your meal, and the smoked chicken with a tangy local white sauce is divine – although with that said, bring on the ribs!

Blue Pacific at Hoover Food Mart THAI **$**
(205-978-0754; 3219 Lorna Rd, Hoover Food Mart; mains from $8; 11am-2:30pm, 5-8:30pm Tue-Sat) It may look like a convenience store but this tiny building serves up some of the best Thai food in Birmingham. As you'd expect, the place ain't fancy but the value can't be beat. Try the spicy Pad Kee Mao.

★Highlands Bar & Grill AMERICAN **$$$**
(205-939-1400; www.highlandsbarandgrill.com; 2011 11th Ave S; mains $33-44; 5:30-10pm Tue-Sat, bar from 4pm) Frank Stitt's most acclaimed restaurant, Highlands has been serving up modern Southern cuisine using French cooking techniques since 1982 in this elegant, 1920s-inspired dining room. The service is as outstanding as the food. Come dressed to impress – suit jackets are not required but you'll probably feel out of place without one.

Drinking & Nightlife

★Atomic Lounge BAR
(205-983-7887; www.theatomiclounge.com; 2113 1st Avenue N; 4pm-midnight Tue-Thu, to 2am Fri & Sat) This is the sort of bar Birmingham boasts would be the envy of New York or Los Angeles. Atomic Lounge is just funky and fun – a cross between a 1950s rec room, a Warhol painting, a mid-century design showcase and, hey, a craft cocktail bar.

Marty's PM BAR
(1813 10th Ct S; 8pm-6am daily, plus 10am-3pm Sat) Marty's plays to hipsters, cool kids and an unapologetically geeky crowd, who are all attracted to a friendly bar packed with comic book art, *Star Wars* memorabilia, role-playing-game references, DJ nights, pop-up dining events and the occasional live-music gig.

Getting There & Around

The **Birmingham-Shuttlesworth International Airport** (BHM; 205-599-0500; www.flybirmingham.com) is about 5 miles northeast of downtown.

Greyhound (☎205-252-7190; www.greyhound.com; 1801 Morris Ave) serves cities including Huntsville (1½ to 2 hours, from $19, four daily), Montgomery (1½ hours, from $20, three daily), Atlanta, GA (2½ hours, from $22, six daily), Jackson, MS (4½ hours, from $23, six daily), and New Orleans, LA (nine hours, from $67, one daily).

Amtrak (www.amtrak.com; 1801 Morris Avenue), downtown, has trains daily to New York (22 hours, from $124) and New Orleans (eight hours, from $38).

Birmingham Transit Authority (www.bjcta.org) runs local MAX buses. Adult fare is $1.25. You can also get around via the Zyp BikeShare program (www.zypbikeshare.com), which offers 24h, 3-day or 1-month passes.

Montgomery

Alabama's capital is a skein of forested streets, redbrick architecture and lonely railways, attached to a few government buildings and a cobblestoned downtown that accrues much of the area's new investment.

With a few exceptions, most of the main points of interest here are tied to the Civil Rights movement, which the city played a key role in. In 1955 Rosa Parks refused to give up her seat to a white man on a city bus, launching a bus boycott led by Martin Luther King Jr, then pastor of Montgomery's Dexter Avenue Baptist Church. This action ultimately desegregated city buses and galvanized the Civil Rights movement nationwide, helping to lay the foundation for the Selma to Montgomery protest marches of 1965.

Modern Montgomery has thoughtfully acknowledged its past while attracting a slew of young entrepreneurs, many of them African American.

Sights

★Dexter Avenue Parsonage — HISTORIC SITE

(☎334-263-3970; www.dexterkingmemorial.org/tours/parsonage-museum; 309 S Jackson St; adult/child $7.50/5.50; ⏲10am-3pm Tue-Fri, to 1pm Sat; P) The home of Martin Luther King Jr and Coretta Scott King has been frozen in time, a snapshot of a mid-century home complete with *Mad Men*–era furniture, appliances and indoor ashtrays (King was a regular smoker). The most fascinating part of the tour is King's old office, which still contains some of the books that influenced his theology, philosophy and activism. In the back, there's a garden filled with stones inscribed with Christian virtues.

★National Memorial for Peace & Justice — MEMORIAL

(National Lynching Memorial; ☎334-386-9100; www.eji.org/national-lynching-memorial; 417 Caroline St; memorial/combination with Legacy Museum ticket $5/10; ⏲9am-5pm Wed-Mon, last entrance 4:30pm) Stark and harrowing in its simplicity, this memorial stands in honor of 4400 African American victims of lynching. Great rectangular steel slabs, each the size and shape of a coffin, are inscribed with the name of a county, the dates of every documented lynching incident within that county and the name of the victim. The immensity of the space and the mute testimony of the slabs underlines the ubiquity of racial violence in American history.

Civil Rights Memorial Center — MEMORIAL

(☎334-956-8200; www.splcenter.org/civil-rights-memorial; 400 Washington Ave; memorial free, museum adult/child $2/free; ⏲memorial 24hr, museum 9am-4:30pm Mon-Fri, 10am-4pm Sat) With its circular design crafted by Maya Lin, this haunting memorial focuses on 40 martyrs of the Civil Rights movement. Some cases remain unsolved. Martin Luther King Jr was the most famous, but there were many 'faceless' deaths along the way, both white and African American. The memorial is part of the Southern Poverty Law Center, a legal foundation committed to racial equality and equal opportunity for justice under the law.

Scott & Zelda Fitzgerald Museum — MUSEUM

(☎334-264-4222; www.thefitzgeraldmuseum.org; 919 Felder Ave; adult/child donation $10/free; ⏲10am-3pm Tue-Sat, noon-5pm Sun) The writers' home from 1931 to 1932 now houses first editions, translations and original artwork by Zelda from her sad last days when she was committed to a mental health facility. Unlike many 'homes of famous people,' there's a ramshackle charm to this museum – while the space is curated, you also feel as if you've stumbled into the Fitzgeralds' attic, exemplified by loving handwritten letters from Zelda to Scott.

Sleeping & Eating

★Lattice Inn — B&B $$

(☎334-263-1414; www.thelatticeinn.com; 1414 South Hull St; r from $115;) This well-run

B&B is a long-standing favorite with Montgomery travelers. The owners are warm and accommodating, the lodgings drip with thoughtful vintage chic, and the grounds are surrounded by lovely, enormous gardens. A winner all around.

Mrs B's SOUTHERN US $

(334-264-5495; www.facebook.com/Mrsbscooking; 17 Cullman St; plates $8-13; 6am-5pm Mon-Fri, 11am-4:30pm Sun) Locals pack in at this culinary institution, where they serve true soul classics, including oxtail and liver or onions and neck bones (there's fried chicken and pork chops and the like for the less adventurous). The dining room is well-worn in a good way, and the food is cooked and served with a lot of love.

Vintage Year SOUTHERN US $$$

(334-819-7215; www.vymgm.com; 405 Cloverdale Rd; mains $15-42; 5-10pm Tue-Sat, 10:30am-2pm Sun) Fine Southern cuisine served in an elegantly romantic dining room? We're in. Dine on pistachio-crusted salmon, or Gulf shrimp pasta, or tempura fried chicken with charred asparagus. Tuesday night is burger night, with some eight variations of meat (and vegetables for the garden burger!) on a bun.

Information

Montgomery Area Visitor Center (334-262-0013; www.visitingmontgomery.com; 300 Water St; 8:30am-5pm Mon-Sat) Has tourist information and a helpful website.

Getting There & Around

Montgomery Regional Airport (MGM; 334-281-5040; www.flymgm.com; 4445 Selma Hwy) is about 15 miles from downtown and is served by daily flights from Atlanta, Charlotte and Dallas. **Greyhound** (334-286-0658; 950 W South Blvd) also serves the city, with routes to Birmingham (2½ hours, from $24) and New Orleans (6½ hours, from $41). Montgomery is about 100 miles south of Birmingham via I-65.

The **Montgomery Area Transit System** (www.montgomerytransit.com) operates city bus lines. Tickets are $2.

Selma

Selma is a quiet town located in the heart of the Alabama 'Black Belt,' a moniker once used to describe the area's dark, high-quality soil, then later the large population of African Americans enslaved to work the fruits of that same soil. It's most well known for Bloody Sunday: March 7, 1965. The media captured state troopers and deputies beating and gassing African Americans and white sympathizers near the Edmund Pettus Bridge.

Selma is a must-visit for those interested in the history of the Civil Rights movement, and is an attractive spot to linger in its own right.

Sights

Edmund Pettus Bridge LANDMARK

(Broad St & Water Ave) Few sites are as iconic to the American Civil Rights movement as the Pettus Bridge. On March 7, 1965, a crowd prepared to march to Montgomery to demonstrate against the murder of a local Black activist by police during a demonstration for voting rights. As those activists gathered into a crowd, the news cameras of the media were trained on the bridge and a line of state troopers and their dogs, who proceeded to lay into the nonviolent marchers.

Selma Interpretive Center MUSEUM

(334-877-1983; www.nps.gov/semo; 2 Broad St; 9am-4:30pm Mon-Sat) FREE This museum, near the north side of the Pettus Bridge, has a small interpretive center that fleshes out the history and narrative of the Jim Crow South, and the subsequent struggle against legalized segregation.

Lowndes County Interpretive Center MUSEUM

(334-877-1983; www.nps.gov/semo; 7002 US Hwy 80; 9am-4:30pm Mon-Sat; P) FREE Marking the rough halfway point on the marching route between Selma and Montgomery, this center presents small, solid exhibitions that delve into the history of Jim Crow and the Civil Rights movement.

Sleeping & Eating

At the time of writing, the historic **St James Hotel** was under renovation. The town is otherwise served by the usual midrange American hotel chains.

Lannie's BBQ (334-874-4478; 2115 Minter Ave; mains $5-12; 9am-9pm Mon-Sat; P) is a little shack that cranks out some of the finest smoked meat around.

Getting There & Away

There's a **Greyhound** (800-231-2222) station at 434 Broad St (US 80). But you really need a car to get around. Tuscaloosa is about 75 miles

WORTH A TRIP

OLD CAHAWBA ARCHAEOLOGICAL PARK

Around 14 miles southwest of Selma, this eerie **ghost town** (☎334-872-8058.; https://ahc.alabama.gov/properties/cahawba/cahawba.aspx; 9518 Cahaba Rd, Orrvile; adult/child $2/1; ⏲9am-5pm; Ⓟ), faded by time and jungly overgrowth, was once the capital of Alabama. By the 20th century, Cahawba was abandoned, and today its remains constitute an important archaeological site. It's best to explore the area on a guided tour (call and reserve at least two weeks in advance) or by bicycle – the site is flat and crossed by paved trails, and a limited number of bicycles are freely available on a first-come basis.

Within the grounds of the ghost town are ruins, a nature trail, a visitor center (noon-5pm Thu-Mon) with self-guided tour maps, and a general sense of decay. Historical re-enactments and activities like haunted history tours are pretty common; check the website for updated information.

to the north on US 80, and Montgomery is 50 miles to the east.

Mobile

Wedged between Mississippi and Florida, the only real Alabama coastal city is Mobile (mo-*beel*), a busy industrial seaport with a smattering of green space, shady boulevards and four historic districts. It's ablaze with azaleas in early spring, and festivities are held throughout February for **Mardi Gras** (www.mobilemardigras.com; ⏲late Feb/early Mar), which has been celebrated here for nearly 200 years (longer than in New Orleans).

Mobile's sights can be covered in a day; otherwise the town makes for an interesting diversion between Pensacola and New Orleans.

Sights

USS Alabama MUSEUM

(☎251-433-2703; www.ussalabama.com; 2703 Battleship Pkwy; adult/child $15/6; ⏲8am-6pm Apr-Sep, to 5pm Oct-Mar; Ⓟ) The battleship *Alabama* is a 690ft behemoth famous for escaping nine major WWII battles unscathed – the 'Lucky A' never lost any of its sailors while they served aboard ship. It's a worthwhile self-guided tour just to experience its awesome size and might; at the end of the day, this ship is an engineering marvel.

Gulf Coast Exploreum MUSEUM

(☎251-208-6893; www.exploreum.com; 65 Government St; adult/student/child $13/11/6, with IMAX $17/15/10; ⏲9am-4pm Tue-Thu, to 5pm Fri & Sat, noon-5pm Sun Sep-May, 10am-5pm Mon-Sat, noon-5pm Sun Jun-Aug; 👪) This science center contains some 150 interactive exhibits and displays in three galleries, an IMAX theater and live demonstrations in its chemistry and biology labs. The exhibits are mainly aimed at kids, and make a good time killer for those with children.

Sleeping & Eating

Malaga Inn BOUTIQUE HOTEL $$

(☎800-235-1586, 251-438-4701; www.malagainn.com; 359 Church St; r $79-165, ste $235; Ⓟ📶🏊) Graced with a pretty courtyard and general historic vibe, the Malaga, which occupies a 19th-century building, is a good deal for central Mobile. Courtyard rooms have classy hardwood floors and understated sheets, while the historic rooms have a tasteful, Victorian-era vibe. Wrought-iron balconies make you feel like you're in a New Orleans-style production of *Romeo & Juliet*.

★**Meat Boss** BARBECUE $

(☎251-591-4842; http://meatboss.com; 5401 Cottage Hill Rd; mains $7-11) If the name hasn't done it, we'll explain the appeal of Meat Boss: fresh barbecue, and lots of it, served slow-smoked and glistening. Order meat, add sides from banana pudding to potato salad – and have a great meal.

Mary's Southern Cooking AMERICAN $

(☎251-476-2232; 3011 SpringHill Ave; mains $6-12; ⏲11am-6pm; 👪) Mary's serves up soul food with a smile. Daily specials run the gamut from beef tips to pig's feet to chicken pot pie, served alongside groaning portions of sides, including collard greens, rice and gravy and mashed potatoes. Simple food, done simply very well.

Getting There & Away

There has been talk for years of reestablishing rail service through Mobile. Until then, you can arrive via **Greyhound** (☎251-478-6089; 2545 Government Blvd) or drive.

The city sits at the intersection of I-10 and I-65, about 60 miles west of Pensacola, and 150 miles east of New Orleans.

MISSISSIPPI

Flanked by the mighty Mississippi River along its entire western border, the Magnolia State encompasses many identities. You'll find palatial mansions and rural poverty; haunting cotton flats and verdant hill country; honey-dipped sand on the coast and serene farmland in the north. Often mythologized and misunderstood, this is the womb of some of the rawest history in the country. And that's why the state is worth an extended visit. The novels, music and art birthed here tell deeply personal stories. They're not always easy to hear. But there's a compelling sense of connection – even joy – in the sharing. See for yourself in a late-night blues club in the Delta. Or on a wander through the homes of the state's great novelists. Or during a quiet moment inside an artist's cabin where bright murals depict the wonders of nature here. Immersion sparks conversations and will challenge the assumptions you have.

Information

Mississippi Division of Tourism Development (601-359-3297; www.visitmississippi.org) Has a directory of visitor bureaus and thematic travel itineraries. Most are well thought-out and run quite deep.

Mississippi Wildlife, Fisheries, & Parks (800-467-2757; www.mississippistateparks.reserveamerica.com) Manages camping reservations in state parks.

Getting There & Away

There are three routes most folks take when traveling through Mississippi. I-55 and US 61 both run north–south from the state's northern to southern borders. US 61 goes through the Delta, and I-55 flows in and out of Jackson. The gorgeous Natchez Trace Pkwy runs diagonally across the state from Tupelo to Natchez. Amtrak's daily **City of New Orleans** train links Chicago and New Orleans, with stops in Memphis, TN, Greenwood and Jackson.

Oxford

Oxford both confirms and explodes any preconceptions you may have of Mississippi's most famous college town. Frat boys in Ford pickup trucks and debutante sorority sisters? Sure. But they're alongside doctoral candidates debating critical theory, and a lively arts scene. Local culture revolves around the Square (aka Courthouse Sq), where you'll find bars, restaurants, decent shopping and the regal University of Mississippi, aka Ole Miss. All around are quiet residential streets, sprinkled with antebellum homes and shaded by majestic oaks.

Sights & Activities

The gorgeous, 0.6-mile-long and rather painless **Bailey's Woods Trail** (www.museum.olemiss.edu/baileys-woods-trail; Old Taylor Rd) connects two of the town's most popular sights: Rowan Oak and the **University of Mississippi Museum** (☎662-915-7073; www.museum.olemiss.edu; University Ave at 5th St; ⏲10am-6pm Tue-Sat) FREE. **The Grove**, the shady heart of Ole Miss, is generally peaceful, except on football Saturdays, when it buzzes with one of the most unforgettable tailgating (pre-game) parties in American university sports.

Rowan Oak HISTORIC BUILDING
(☎662-234-3284; www.rowanoak.com; Old Taylor Rd; adult/child $5/free; ⏲house 10am-4pm Tue-Sat, from 1pm Sun Sep-May, 10am-6pm Tue-Sat, from 1pm Sun Jun-Aug; grounds open dawn-dusk) Literary pilgrims head here to the graceful 1840s home of William Faulkner. He authored many brilliant and dense novels set in Mississippi, and his work is celebrated in Oxford with an annual conference in July. Tours of Rowan Oak – where Faulkner lived from 1930 until his death in 1962, and which may reasonably be dubbed, to use the author's own elegant words, his 'postage stamp of native soil' – are self-guided. Admission is cash only.

Sleeping & Eating

Inn at Ole Miss HOTEL $
(☎662-234-2331; www.theinnatolemiss.com; 120 Alumni Dr; r from $119; P❄@🛜🏊) Unless it's a football weekend, in which case you'd be wise to book well ahead, you can usually find a nice room at this 180-room hotel and conference center right on the Ole Miss Grove. Although it's not super-personal, it's

comfortable, well located and walkable to downtown.

★**Big Bad Breakfast** BREAKFAST $

(☎662-236-2666; www.bigbadbreakfast.com; 719 N Lamar; mains $5-15; ⏲7am-1:30pm Mon-Fri, 8am-3pm Sat & Sun) Any place with an Elvis tapestry is gonna be good. This busy spot is no exception, serving hearty gourmet Southern breakfasts to appreciative hordes. From the egg scramble with fried Gulf oysters to the Redneck benny with country ham and sausage gravy to the brandy-spiked French toast with berries, there's something big and bad (in a good way) for everyone.

City Grocery AMERICAN $$$

(☎662-232-8080; www.citygroceryonline.com; 152 Courthouse Sq; lunch mains $11-24, dinner mains $26-32; ⏲11:30am-2:30pm Mon-Sat, 6-10pm Mon-Wed, to 10:30pm Thu-Sat, 11am-2:30pm Sun) Chef John Currence won a James Beard award and quickly set about dominating the Oxford culinary scene. City Grocery is one of his finest restaurants, offering a menu of haute Southern goodness such as blackened catfish with ham hock, stewed black-eyed peas and lard-braised hangar steak. The upstairs bar, decked out with local folk art, is a treat. Reservations recommended.

Nightlife & Entertainment

Rafter's Music & Food BAR

(☎662-234-5757; www.facebook.com/RaftersOxford; 1000 Jackson Ave E; ⏲5pm-midnight Mon-Wed, to 1am Thu, 11am-1am Fri, to midnight Sat, 10:45am-3pm Sun) Climb the stairs for the spicy bloody Marys and live bluegrass music on Sunday mornings. Gets busy on weekend nights.

Proud Larry's LIVE MUSIC

(☎662-236-0050; www.proudlarrys.com; 211 S Lamar Blvd; ⏲shows 9pm) On the Square, this iconic music venue hosts consistently good bands. It also does a nice pub-grub business at lunch and dinner before the stage lights dim.

Shopping

★**Square Books** BOOKS

(☎662-236-2262; www.squarebooks.com; 160 Courthouse Sq; ⏲9am-9pm Mon-Sat, to 6pm Sun) Square Books, one of the South's great independent bookstores, is the epicenter of Oxford's lively literary scene and a frequent stop for traveling authors. There's a cafe and balcony upstairs, along with an immense section devoted to Faulkner.

Getting There & Away

The closest interstates to Oxford are I-55 and I-22. You can get here via US 278 or MS 7; the latter is a slightly more scenic route.

Mississippi Delta

A long, low land of silent cotton plots bending under a severe sky, the Delta is a place of surreal, Gothic extremes. Here, in a feudal society of great manors and enslaved servitude, songs of labor and love eventually became American pop music. Those songs traveled from Africa via sharecropping fields, where they unfolded into the blues and ultimately into rock and roll. Tourism in this area, which still suffers some of the worst rural poverty rates in the country, largely revolves around discovering the sweat-soaked roots of this original American art form. Hwy 61 is the Delta's legendary road, traversing endless, eerie miles of flat fields, imposing agricultural and industrial facilities, one-room churches and moldering cemeteries.

Clarksdale

The scrappy epicenter of the Delta blues scene, Clarksdale is also the region's most useful base. It's within a couple of hours of all the blues sights, and big-name blues acts are regular weekend visitors. But this is still a poor Delta town, with crumbling edges and washed-out storefronts evident in ways that go beyond romantic dilapidation. It's jarring to see how many businesses find private security details a necessity after dark. On the other hand, there is a genuine warmth to the place, and most tourists in the region end up lingering for longer than they expected.

Sights

Delta Blues Museum MUSEUM

(☎662-627-6820; www.deltabluesmuseum.org; 1 Blues Alley; adult/child 6-12yr $10/8; ⏲9am-5pm Mon-Sat Mar-Oct, from 10am Nov-Feb; P) A small but well-presented collection of memorabilia is on display here. The shrine to Delta legend Muddy Waters includes the actual cabin where he grew up. Local art exhibits and a gift shop round out the display. May host live music during special events.

Quapaw Canoe Co CANOEING
(☎662-627-4070; www.island63.com; 291 Sunflower Ave; per person per day $175-400) John Ruskey and his team run trip-of-a-lifetime canoe excursions on the Lower Mississippi River and its tributaries for groups of almost every size, from solo paddlers to Boy Scout troops. Tell him where you'd like to go or let Quapaw choose your adventure. The five-day Muddy Waters Wilderness paddle is a favorite. One-day outings to multiday camping trips are available.

Sleeping & Eating

Shack Up Inn INN $
(☎662-624-8329; www.shackupinn.com; 001 Commissary Circle, off US 49; r/shack $95/100; P ❄ 📶) Located on the Hopson Plantation, these unique accommodations allow you to stay in refurbished sharecropper cabins or the creatively renovated cotton gin. The cabins have covered porches and are filled with old furniture and musical instruments. Sunsets from the porches can be gorgeous, but historical context gets a bit lost, despite all the 'authenticity.' Bar and stage inside the Gin.

Bluesberry Cafe SOUTHERN US $
(☎662-627-7008; 235 Yazoo Ave; mains $5-12; ⏲7:30am-1pm Sat & Sun, 6:30pm-midnight Mon) This isn't just a greasy spoon – there's grease on the forks, knives and napkins too. But who cares? The food – eggs, bacon, housemade sausages and big sandwiches – is cooked to order and delicious. Live blues starts at 10am on weekends and 8pm on Monday. Some blues legends may stop in and play an impromptu set. Pass the hot sauce.

Yazoo Pass CAFE $$
(☎662-627-8686; www.yazoopass.com; 207 Yazoo Ave; lunch mains $8-10, dinner $12-36; ⏲7am-9pm Mon-Sat; 📶) A contemporary space where you can enjoy fresh scones and croissants in the mornings, a salad bar, sandwiches and soups at lunch, and pan-seared ahi, filet mignon, burgers and pastas at dinner. Espresso bar too.

Entertainment

★**Red's** BLUES
(☎662-627-3166; 395 Sunflower Ave; cover $7-10; ⏲live music 9pm Fri & Sat) Clarksdale's best juke joint, with its neon-red mood lighting, plastic-bag ceiling and general soulful disintegration, is the place to see bluesmen howl. Red runs the bar, knows the acts and slings a cold beer whenever you need one.

WORTH A TRIP

THE SOUL OF THE DELTA

Stopping in the tiny Delta town of Indianola is worthwhile to visit the **BB King Museum and Delta Interpretive Center** (☎662-887-9539; https://bbkingmuseum.org; 400 2nd St; adult/child 7-17yr $15/10; ⏲10am-5pm Tue-Sat, from noon Sun & Mon, closed Mon Nov-Mar; P). While it's ostensibly dedicated to the legendary bluesman, in many ways it tackles life in the Delta as a whole. The museum is filled with interactive displays, video exhibits and an amazing array of artifacts, effectively communicating the history and legacy of the blues while shedding light on the soul of the Delta.

Getting There & Away

Clarksdale sits off US 49 and 61, 80 miles south of Memphis, and 70 miles west of Oxford. The **Greyhound** (☎662-627-7893; www.greyhound.com; 1604 N State St) station is on State St.

Vicksburg

Lovely Vicksburg sits atop a high bluff overlooking the Mississippi River. During the Civil War, Gen Ulysses S Grant besieged the city for 47 days until its surrender on July 4, 1863, at which point the North gained dominance over North America's greatest river. Although Vicksburg is most famous for a siege and a battle, many of its historic homes have survived the centuries, and today the town's historic core is considered one of the most attractive in the state.

Sights

Vicksburg National Military Park HISTORIC SITE
(☎601-636-0583; www.nps.gov/vick; 3201 Clay St; per bicycle/car $10/20; ⏲grounds dawn-dusk, visitor center 8am-5pm Apr-Oct, 8:30-4:30pm Nov-Mar; P 👪) Vicksburg controlled access to the Mississippi River, and its seizure was one of the turning points of the Civil War. A 16-mile driving tour passes historic markers explaining battle scenarios and key events from the city's long siege, when residents lived in caverns to avoid Union shells.

Plan on staying for at least 90 minutes. The USS Cairo Museum, which spotlights the ironclad gunboats used by Union forces, is worth a stop, and the salvaged USS *Cairo* is on view.

Lower Mississippi River Museum MUSEUM
(☎601-638-9900; www.lmrm.org; 910 Washington St; ⊙9am-4pm Mon-Sat, from 1pm Sun; 👪) FREE Downtown Vicksburg's pride and joy is this low-key museum, which delves into such topics as the famed 1927 flood and the Army Corps of Engineers, who have managed the river since the 18th century. Kids will enjoy climbing around the dry-docked research vessel, the MV *Mississippi IV*.

Eating & Drinking

★Walnut Hills SOUTHERN US $$
(☎601-638-4910; www.walnuthillsms.com; 1214 Adams St; mains $8-32; ⊙11am-9pm Mon & Wed-Sat, to 2pm Sun) For a dining experience that takes you back in time, head to this eatery where you can enjoy rib-sticking, down-home Southern food elbow to elbow, family-style – but there's plenty of seating for solo diners and introverts too. The corn and crab bisque is loaded with crab, and the shrimp and grits, with tasso ham, is wonderful.

Highway 61 Coffeehouse COFFEE
(☎601-638-9221; 1101 Washington St; ⊙7am-5pm Mon-Fri, from 9am Sat; 📶) 🍃 This awesome coffee shop has occasional live music on Saturday afternoons, serves Fair Trade coffee and is an energetic epicenter of artsiness, poetry readings and the like.

Getting There & Away

Vicksburg sits off I-20 and US 61, about 50 miles west of Jackson.

Jackson

Mississippi's capital and largest city mixes stately residential areas with large swaths of blight, peppered throughout with a surprisingly funky arts-cum-hipster scene in the Fondren District. The opening of the Museum of Mississippi History and the adjacent Mississippi Civil Rights Museum has boosted the appeal of downtown and drawn national acclaim – now if city officials would just do something about the terrible condition of its streets. Trust us, they're bad, especially the potholes. On the bright side, there's a slew of decent bars, good restaurants and a lot of love for live music; it's easy to have a good time in Jackson.

Sights

★Mississippi Civil Rights Museum MUSEUM
(☎601-576-6800; www.mcrm.mdah.ms.gov; 222 North St; adult/child 4-18yr $10/6; ⊙9am-5pm Tue-Sat, from 1pm Sun; 🅿) Whether it's a voice from overhead yelling at you to 'keep on moving,' graphic photos of lynchings hitting you with a gut punch, or the towering wall of mugshots of Freedom Riders stopping you in your tracks, the exhibits at this compelling museum keep you on high alert. The national Civil Rights movement is explored through the lens of the fight for racial equality in Mississippi, with eight exhibit halls tackling each of the key eras.

Plan to spend a half-day here.

Museum of Mississippi History MUSEUM
(☎601-576-6800; www.mmh.mdah.ms.gov; 222 North St; adult/child 4-18yr $10/6; ⊙9am-5pm Tue-Sat, from 1pm Sun; 🅿) In the 10-minute introductory film, the voice of God himself, Mississippian Morgan Freeman, introduces visitors to this museum. Exhibits tell the story of Mississippi and its residents, beginning in 13,000 BCE and continuing to the present.

Noteworthy displays, which are often supplemented by informative videos, cover prehistoric mound builders, the Chickasaw and Choctaw tribes and their legends, the cotton industry, the Civil War and Mississippi's rich cultural heritage – don't miss Lucille's Place, a recreated juke joint.

Eudora Welty House HISTORIC BUILDING
(☎601-353-7762; www.eudorawelty.org; 1119 Pinehurst St; adult/student/child $5/3/free; ⊙tours 9am, 11am, 1pm & 3pm Tue-Fri) Literature buffs should plan to tour the Pulitzer Prize–winning author's Tudor Revival house, where she lived for more than 75 years. It's now a true historical preservation, down to the most minute details. It's free on the 13th day of any month, assuming that's a normal operating day.

Reservations are recommended here but not required.

Sleeping & Eating

Old Capitol Inn BOUTIQUE HOTEL $

(601-359-9000; www.oldcapitolinn.com; 226 N State St; r/ste from $99/145;) This 24-room boutique hotel, located near museums and restaurants, is terrific. Rooms are comfortable and uniquely furnished, and a delicious full Southern breakfast is included. The rooftop garden offers views of downtown.

Fairview Inn INN $$$

(888-948-1908, 601-948-3429; www.fairviewinn.com; 734 Fairview St; r/ste from $199/219;) For a Colonial-estate experience, the 18-room Fairview Inn, set in a converted historic mansion, will not let you down. The antique decor is stunning rather than stuffy and tastefully deployed across each individually appointed room. It also has a full spa and a cozy cocktail bar, the Library Lounge (11am-midnight Mon-Fri, 4pm-1am Sat).

Bully's SOUTHERN US $

(601-362-0484; 3118 Livingston Rd; mains $7-10; 11am-6pm Mon-Sat) With its golden crispiness and tender meat, Bully's fried chicken is a culinary home run and worth a detour from downtown. Or pick up some chicken to go for a picnic along the Natchez Trace, five miles northwest. How good is the soul food at this low-key spot? The James Beard Foundation honored Bully's as an American Classic in 2016.

Iron Horse Grill SOUTHERN US; MEXICAN $$

(601-398-0151; www.theironhorsegrill.com; 320 W Pearl St; mains $11-32; 11am-midnight) During Friday lunch, you'd swear that all of downtown Jackson is happily digging into the delicious burgers, po'boys, tacos and seafood dishes served here. Though the space is cavernous and busy, the conscientious staff and a friendly vibe keep it feeling intimate. Free chips and salsa and live music (Thu-Sat night) round out the appeal. Get yourself here!

Drinking & Entertainment

Apothecary at Brent's Drugs COCKTAIL BAR

(www.apothecaryjackson.com; 655 Duling Ave; 5pm-1am Tue-Thu, to 2am Fri & Sat) Tucked into the back of a '50s-style soda fountain shop is a distinctly early-21st-century craft cocktail bar, complete with bartenders sporting thick-framed glasses, customers with sleeve tattoos and a fine menu of expertly mixed libations.

F Jones Corner BLUES

(601-983-1148; www.fjonescorner.com; 303 N Farish St; 10am-4am Thu-Sat) All shapes and sizes, colors and creeds descend on this down-home Farish St club when everywhere else closes. It hosts authentic Delta musicians, who have been known to play until sunrise.

Information

Convention & Visitors Bureau (601-960-1891; www.visitjackson.com; 111 E Capitol St, Suite 102; 8:30am-5pm Mon-Fri) Free information.

Getting There & Away

Since downtown sits at the junction of I-20 and I-55, it's easy to get in and out. The city's international **airport** (JAN; 601-939-5631; www.jmaa.com; 100 International Dr) is 10 miles east of downtown. **Greyhound** (601-353-6342; 300 W Capitol St) buses serve Birmingham, Memphis and New Orleans (with transfers). Amtrak's *City of New Orleans* stops at the **station** (Union Station; 300 W Capitol St).

Natchez

Sprawled across a bluff overlooking the Mississippi River, this old city is packed tight with historic buildings. But there's a sense of devil-may-care mischief these days that keeps the history from becoming oppressive. In fact, Natchez is one of the more inclusive and diverse cities in the state, despite its 668 or so antebellum homes. Historically, Natchez is the oldest post-European contact settlement on the Mississippi (beating New Orleans by two years). It is also at one end of the scenic 444-mile Natchez Trace Parkway, a popular travel corridor in the 1800s and now the state's cycling and recreational jewel. Today, the city has a boisterous party vibe on weekends, with cars parked every which way on the sidewalks and well-sauced revelers filling the watering holes, dancing to live music and gambling at the casino. During the 'pilgrimage' seasons in spring and fall, local mansions are opened to visitors.

Sights & Activities

Emerald Mound ARCHAEOLOGICAL SITE

(www.nps.gov/natr; Mile 10.3 Natchez Trace Pkwy; dawn-dusk;) FREE Just outside town, along the Trace, you'll find Emerald Mound, the grassy ruins of a Native American city that includes the second-largest pre-Columbian earthworks in the US. Using stone tools, pre-Columbian ancestors to the Natchez people graded this eight-acre mountain into a flat-topped pyramid. It is now the second-largest mound site in America. There are shady, creekside picnic spots here, and you can and should climb to the top, where you'll find a vast lawn.

Melrose HISTORIC BUILDING
(☎601-446-5790; www.nps.gov/natc; 1 Melrose-Montebello Pkwy; adult/child 6-17yr $10/5; ⏰tours 10am, 11am, 1pm, 2pm, 3pm, 4pm; P) Tours of this Greek Revival home take a fascinating, multi-perspective look at life on the city estate of a slave-owning cotton magnate. A lawyer, state legislator and businessman, John McMurran moved into the home – fronted by four Doric columns – in 1849 with his family. Today, the property is run by the National Park Service. Rangers share stories about the McMurran family inside the home; visitors can then explore the slave cabins and related exhibits out back. Cash or check only.

Sleeping & Eating

★Historic Oak Hill Inn INN $$
(☎601-446-2500; www.historicoakhill.com; 409 S Rankin St; r $140-170, ste $250; P ❄ 📶) At this B&B you can sleep in an original 1835 bed and dine on pre–Civil War porcelain under 1850 Waterford Crystal gasoliers. It's all about purist antebellum aristocratic living. Co-owner Doug Mauro defines Southern hospitality, and his Natchez knowledge runs deep. Prepared by fellow owner Donald McGlynn, an alum of Brennan's restaurant in New Orleans, breakfasts are a highlight.

Magnolia Grill SOUTHERN US $$
(☎601-446-7670; www.magnoliagrill.com; 49 Silver St; mains $10-35; ⏰11am-9pm Sun, Tue & Wed, to 10pm Fri & Sat; 👪) Down by the riverside, this attractive wooden storefront grill with exposed rafters and outdoor patio is a good place for a pork tenderloin po'boy or a fried crawfish and spinach salad.

Drinking & Entertainment

Under the Hill Saloon BAR
(☎601-446-8023; 25 Silver St; ⏰10am-late) A tremendously fun and historic bar that was once a favorite haunt of Samuel Clemens, a riverboat pilot who would go on to be known by his pen name, Mark Twain. The bar closes whenever everyone has emptied out. You might catch live music on the weekend.

Smoot's Grocery LIVE MUSIC
(☎601-653-0731; www.smootsgrocery.com; 319 N Broadway St; ⏰4pm-midnight Thu & Fri, from noon Sat, noon-8pm Sun) Smoot's Grocery, we like how you sing the blues. Housed in a well-worn former grocery close to the Mississippi, this beer hall loves live music.

It's mostly blues bands here, but you might catch swamp rock, roots music, soul or zydeco. Tuxedoed wedding guests, dance-floor divas and pool-playing good ole boys – it seems everyone's here at some point.

WORTH A TRIP

NATCHEZ TRACE PARKWAY

If you're driving through Mississippi, we highly recommend planning at least part of your trip around one of the oldest roads in North America: the Natchez Trace. This 444-mile trail follows a natural ridge line that was widely used by prehistoric animals as a grazing route; later, the area those animals trampled became a footpath and trading route utilized by Native American tribes. That route would go on to become the Natchez Trace, a major roadway into the early western interior of the young USA, that was often plagued by roving bandits.

In 1938, 444 miles of the Trace, stretching from Pasquo, TN, southwest to Natchez, MS, was designated the federally protected Natchez Trace Parkway (www.nps.gov/natr), administered by the National Park Service. It's a lovely, scenic drive that traverses a wide panoply of Southern landscapes: thick, dark forests, soggy wetlands, gentle hill country and long swaths of farmland. There are more than 50 access points to the parkway and a helpful **visitor center** (☎662-680-4027; www.nps.gov/natr; Mile 266 Natchez Trace Pkwy; ⏰9am-4:30pm; 👪🐾) outside Tupelo. There are no stoplights or stop signs to ruin your ride.

Information

The **Visitor and Welcome Center** (☎800-647-6724; www.visitnatchez.org; 640 S Canal St; ⏲8:30am-5pm Mon-Sat, 9am-4pm Sun) is a large, well-done tourist resource with exhibits of area history and a ton of information on local sites. You'll find information centers for several entities – Natchez National Historical Park, Natchez Pilgrimage Tours, the City of Natchez Visitor Information, and Mississippi Tourism – clustered here.

Getting There & Away

Natchez is located off US 61, and also forms the terminus (or beginning, depending on which way you're heading) of the Natchez Trace Pkwy. The **Greyhound** (☎601-445-5291; 127 Wood Ave) station is about 3.5 miles east of town.

Gulf Coast

The Mississippi Gulf Coast comprises a long, low series of breeze-swept dunes, patches of sea oats, lonely barrier islands, bayside art galleries and clusters of Vegas-style casinos. This is a popular retreat for families and military personnel; several important bases pepper the coast from Florida to Texas.

Charming Bay St Louis attracts federal employees, including many scientists based out at Stennis Space Center near the Louisiana border; their presence gives the town a slightly more progressive cast than you might expect from Mississippi. Yoga studios, antique stores and galleries cluster on Main St.

Ocean Springs is a peaceful getaway, with a lineup of shrimp boats in the harbor alongside recreational sailing yachts, a historic downtown core and a powdery fringe of white sand on the Gulf.

Cheap chain accommodations can be found at the I-10 exits that lead to various Gulf Coast towns. Within said towns, you may find nice B&Bs and small hotels. You'll often find the lowest-priced options at the casino hotels in Biloxi.

Getting There & Away

Biloxi is tucked between neighbor Gulfport to the west and Ocean Springs to the east. The city is 90 miles east of New Orleans and 30 miles east of Bay St Louis. Ocean Springs is 33 miles east of Bay St Louis and 60 miles west of Mobile, off I-10.

ARKANSAS

Forming the mountainous joint between the Midwest and the Deep South, Arkansas (*ar*-kan-saw) is an often-overlooked treasure of swift rushing rivers, dark leafy hollows, crenelated granite outcrops and the rugged spine of the Ozark and the Ouachita (wash-ee-tah) mountains. The entire state is blessed with exceptionally well-presented state parks and tiny, empty roads crisscrossing dense forests that let out onto breathtaking vistas and gentle pastures dotted with grazing horses. Mountain towns juke between Christian fundamentalism, hippie communes and biker bars, yet all of these divergent cultures share a love of their home state's stunning natural beauty.

Information

Arkansas State Parks (☎888-287-2757; www.arkansasstateparks.com), Arkansas' well-reputed park system, has 52 state parks. Thirty offer camping and some offer lodge and cabin accommodations. Due to popularity, reservations on weekends and holidays often require multiday stays.

Little Rock

Little Rock lives up to its name: as state capitals go, this one feels pretty petite. But this is also the center of urban life in Arkansas, and amid the leafy residential neighborhoods are friendly bars, fresh restaurants, plenty of bike trails and a tolerant vibe. Little Rock's small demographics are complemented by a wide sense of geographic space; the town is situated on the Arkansas River, and as befits this state of natural wonders, you always feel as if you're within arm's reach of lush, wooded river valleys.

Sights

William J Clinton Presidential Center MUSEUM
(☎501-374-4242; www.clintonlibrary.gov; 1200 President Clinton Ave; adult/child $10/6; ⏲9am-5pm Mon-Sat, 1-5pm Sun; P) This library houses the largest archival collection in presidential history, including 80 million pages of documents and two million photographs (although there's not a lot related to a certain intern scandal). The entire experience feels like a time travel journey to the 1990s. Peruse the full-scale replica of the Oval Office, the exhibits on all stages of

Clinton's life, or gifts from visiting dignitaries. The complex is built to environmentally friendly standards.

Riverfront Park PARK
(501-371-4770; www.littlerock.com/little-rock-destinations/riverfront-park; Ottenheimer Plaza; sunrise-sunset) FREE This park rolls pleasantly along the Arkansas River, and both pedestrians and cyclists take advantage of it. It's a truly fine integration of the river into its urban setting. The most noticeable landmark is the Clinton Presidential Park Bridge, a gorgeous pedestrian path that spans the river.

Little Rock Central High School HISTORIC SITE
(501-374-1957; www.nps.gov/chsc; 2125 Daisy L Gatson Bates Dr; 9am-4:30pm; P) FREE Little Rock's most riveting historic attraction is the site of the 1957 desegregation crisis that changed the country forever. This was where a group of African American students known as the Little Rock Nine were first denied entry to the then all-white high school despite a unanimous 1954 Supreme Court ruling forcing the integration of public schools. Images of the students being escorted to class by national guard soldiers remain some of the most iconic records of the Civil Rights movement.

Activities

Rocktown River Outfitters KAYAKING
(501-831-0548; www.rocktownriveroutfitters.com; 400 President Clinton Ave; 2hr bicycle/kayak rental from $20/35; 10am-5pm Wed & Thu, 9am-6pm Fri & Sat, 11am-6pm Sun) This outfitter can help you explore local waterways, including the **Arkansas River and Fourche Creek** (http://ar.audubon.org/fourche-creek), a major regional urban wetland. You can either opt for guided paddling tours ($45 to $65), or you can rent a kayak and get out on the water yourself. It's best to call ahead instead of just dropping in. Also rents bicycles and conducts a bicycle and brunch tour ($65).

Sleeping & Eating

Little Rock Firehouse Hostel & Museum HOSTEL $
(501-476-0294; www.firehousehostel.org; 1201 Commerce St; dm $31; P) As the name not so subtly implies, this was once a fire station. Now it's a spiffy hostel located in a gorgeous 1917 Craftsman-style building that includes a small on-site museum on early-20th-century firefighting. Dorms are clean, if very basic, and there's a good, social backpacker vibe.

★ **Capital Hotel** BOUTIQUE HOTEL $$
(501-374-7474; www.capitalhotel.com; 111 W Markham St; r $195-265, ste $315-515; P @) This 1872 former bank building with a cast-iron facade – a near-extinct architectural feature – is the top digs in Little Rock. There is a wonderful outdoor mezzanine for cocktails, and a sense of suited, cigar-chomping posh throughout. If you want to feel like a wining, dining lobbyist, you've found your spot.

★ **The Root Cafe** SOUTHERN US $
(501-414-0423; www.therootcafe.com; 1500 S Main St; mains $9-15; 7am-2:30pm Tue-Fri, 5-9pm Wed-Sat, 8am-3:30pm Sat, 9am-2pm Sun;) Little Rock boasts a genuinely innovative dining scene, and even then, the Root is where local diners look for boundary breakers. The menu is exhaustively sourced from local providers whenever possible, and the food is upscaled Arkansas cuisine: purple-hull peas and cornbread, pork carnitas, and country fried tofu with vegan gravy. The setting is rustic funky, airy and friendly.

South on Main AMERICAN $$
(501-244-9660; www.southonmain.com; 1304 S Main St; mains $16-24; 11am-2:30pm Mon-Fri, 5-10pm Tue-Sat, 10am-2pm Sun) This wonderful spot is a gastronomic pet project of *The Oxford American*, the South's seminal quarterly literary magazine. It embraces the foodways of the region with a verve and dynamism that is creative and delicious: catfish comes with cornmeal pancakes, while rabbit leg is wrapped in country ham. A great bar and frequent live music round out the awesome.

Drinking & Entertainment

★ **White Water Tavern** LIVE MUSIC
(501-375-8400; www.whitewatertavern.com; 2500 W 7th St; noon-2am Mon-Fri, 6pm-1am Sat) The White Water manages to line up some excellent acts for its small stage, with bands ranging from straight-up rockers to alt-country heroes to indie poppers to hip-hop MCs. When the music isn't playing, this is an excellent, friendly corner pub – a night out here is a quintessential Little Rock experience.

Information

Little Rock Convention Center & Tourism Bureau (501-376-4781; www.littlerock.com; 101 S Spring St; 8:30am-5pm Mon-Fri) is a good gateway into the city.

Getting There & Around

Bill & Hillary Clinton National Airport (LIT; Little Rock National Airport; 501-372-3439; www.fly-lit.com; 1 Airport Dr) lies just east of downtown. The **Greyhound station** (501-372-3007; 118 E Washington St, North Little Rock) serves Memphis, TN (from $12, 2½ hours) and New Orleans (from $80, 18 hours), among many other cities. **Union Station** (800-872-7245; 1400 W Markham St) is a stop on Amtrak's *Texas Eagle* line, which runs from Chicago ($100, 14 hours) to Los Angeles ($154, 19 hours), stopping at dozens of cities in between.

Little Rock is connected to the US highway system via I-30 and I-40. The closest large city is Memphis, about 140 miles to the east.

Central Arkansas Transit (www.cat.org) runs local buses and the **METRO Streetcar** (501-375-6717; https://rrmetro.org/services/streetcar), a free trolley that has two lines. The green makes a loop on W Markham and 3rd Sts, while the blue crosses the Main St Bridge into North Little Rock.

Taxis and ride shares serve the airport; fares should run around $10 to $15 to downtown Little Rock.

Hot Springs

Hot Springs is a gem of a mountain town, and we're not the first to notice. The healing waters the town is named for have been attracting everyone from Native Americans – for centuries – and early-20th-century health nuts, to a good chunk of the nation's organized-crime leadership. When Hot Springs was at full throttle in the 1930s, it was a hotbed of gambling, bootlegging, prostitution and opulence.

Today the appeal of Hot Springs is less the actual springs than the tourism infrastructure that commemorates them. That said, a few elaborate, restored bathhouses offering old-school spa treatments line Bathhouse Row, which sits behind shady magnolias on the east side of Central Ave. Hot Springs is an attractive town that has managed to preserve its historic center, which is always a cause for celebration.

Sights & Activities

Hot Springs National Park MUSEUM
(Fordyce Bathhouse; 501-620-6715; www.nps.gov/hosp; 369 Central Ave; Fordyce Bathhouse Visitor Center 9am-5pm) FREE On Bathhouse Row in the 1915 Fordyce bathhouse, the NPS visitor center and museum has exhibits about the park's history, first as a Native American free-trade zone, and later as a turn-of-the-20th-century European spa. Most fascinating are the amenities and standards set forth by an early-20th-century spa: the stained-glass work and Greek statues are opulent, but we could pass on the bare white walls, grout and electroshock therapy.

Hot Springs Mountain Tower VIEWPOINT
(501-881-4020; https://hotspringstower.com; 401 Hot Springs Mountain Rd; adult/child $8/4.50; 9am-9pm Jun-Aug, to 5pm Nov-Mar, hrs vary other months; P) On top of Hot Springs Mountain, the 216ft tower has spectacular views of the surrounding mountains covered with dogwood, hickory, oak and pine – lovely in the spring and fall.

Adventureworks Hot Springs ADVENTURE SPORTS
(501-262-9182; www.adventureworks.com; 1700 Shady Grove Rd; adult/child 8-17 from $65/49; 10am-4pm Mon-Sat, from 1pm Sun) This popular outfitter organizes zipline tours across the local forest canopy, where a dozen lines stretch for a mile through the treetops. Zipline options include a once-a-month full-moon zipline and a 'haunted forest' zipline. You can also attempt an aerial obstacle course that includes swinging rope bridges, Tarzan vines and other fun (from $19).

Sleeping & Eating

★Gold-Inn INN $
(501-624-9164; https://gold-inn.webflow.io; 741 Park Ave; r $88-100; P) With friendly, welcoming owners, this inn, less than a mile from Bathhouse Row, is an old road motel that has been upgraded into a mid-century boutique hotel. The rooms are impeccable, comfortable and include flat-screen TVs and comfy beds.

Lake Catherine State Park CABIN $
(https://arkansasstateparks.reserveamerica.com; 1200 Catherine Park Rd; tent camping $13-35, cabins $97-190, yurt $55; P) The lodging at this state park is excellent. The real gems are

DON'T MISS

ARCHITECTURE & GARDENS

Some 8 miles south of Hot Springs, the **Anthony Chapel** (550 Arkridge Rd S; ⏲9am-6pm; P) FREE is an architectural masterpiece. This soaring, wood-and-glass complex, built in 2006, synchronizes with and underlines the beauty of the surrounding forest. Inside, the structure is both tellingly modern and man-made, and deeply connected to its surrounding environment. The chapel is, not for nothing, one of the most popular wedding venues in the state.

The chapel lays outside of the ticketed area for **Garvan Woodland Gardens** (☎501-262-9300; www.garvangardens.org; 550 Arkridge Rd; adult/child $15/5; ⏲9am-6pm; P 👪), which feels like a forest grove caught between the mountains and an alpine lake. The grounds include the Garden of the Pine Wind (a local ravine refashioned into a Japanese rock garden), a wildflower overlook, a children's garden, bridges, pergolas, and a general surfeit of landscaped loveliness.

20 lovely Civilian Conservation Corps–built rustic cabins overlooking the lake; some come with wood fireplaces or spa tubs. You can also opt for tent camping (most sites have water and electric hookups, but some are rated as primitive), or even rent a yurt (sleeps eight).

McClard's BARBECUE $
(☎501-623-9665; www.mcclards.com; 505 Albert Pike; mains $4-15; ⏲11am-7pm Tue-Thu, to 8pm Fri & Sat) Southwest of the center, Bill Clinton's favorite boyhood barbecue is still popular for ribs, slow-cooked beans, chili and tamales. It's on the outskirts of downtown Hot Springs.

Rolando's LATIN AMERICAN $$
(☎501-318-6054; https://rolandosrestaurant.com; 210 Central Ave; mains $9-23; ⏲11am-9pm Sun-Thu, to 10pm Fri & Sat; 👪) An Ecuadoran is behind the concept of this *nuevo latino* joint, where customers enjoy a colorful dining space and solid mains like shrimp sauteed in a lime and tequila sauce, or fish tacos. Start your meal with a flaming bowl of chorizo and queso (cheese). There's a kids' menu and dishes can be ordered as small plates to share.

Drinking & Nightlife

Maxine's BAR
(☎501-321-0909; www.maxineslive.com; 700 Central Ave; ⏲5pm-3am Mon-Fri, 2pm-2am Sat, noon-midnight Sun) If you're looking for some (loud) night music, head to this infamous cathouse turned live-music venue. It hosts bands out of Austin regularly.

Superior Bathhouse Brewery and Distillery BREWERY
(☎501-624-2337; www.superiorbathhouse.com; 329 Central Ave; ⏲11am-9pm Mon-Thu, to 10pm Fri, to 11pm Sat, to 8pm Sun) It's surprising that an outdoorsy town with this many hikers and hipsters lacked a craft brewery for so long, but as the sun rises in the east, so too does Hot Springs have an indie brewery. The local suds are delicious and perfect for washing away any healthy effects of Hot Springs.

Getting There & Away

Hot Springs is located off I-30, about 60 miles southwest of Little Rock. There is no public transportation out here.

Tri-Peaks Region

The Tri-Peaks Region is the crown jewel in the gem that is the great green Arkansas River Valley, which forms one of the state's major geographic zones. In the shadow of the Tri-Peaks, you'll find four state parks and fantastic hiking, trekking and boating activities.

The area, which comprises multiple Arkansas counties, is named for the triumvirate of Mt Magazine, Mt Nebo and Petit Jean Mountain. While there is no real central base for exploring the area, you can stock up on supplies in numerous small towns, the largest of which is Russellville. We have named the closest supply town in each park's individual entry.

Sights & Activities

Each of the parks we list in the Tri-Peaks Region, with the exception of water-oriented Lake Dardanelle, contain multiple **hikes** ranging from flat, easy nature loops to difficult ascents along mountain peaks. Check with each park website for a full list of the many trails, and be sure to ask rangers about current conditions.

Mt Magazine State Park STATE PARK
(479-963-8502; www.arkansasstateparks.com/parks/mount-magazine-state-park; 577 Lodge Dr, Paris, GPS: N 35°09'52.4 W 93°38'49.7; visitor center 8am-5pm; P) FREE This stellar state park features some 14 miles of trails that wind around Arkansas' highest point. The surrounding vistas are spectacular, taking in all of the forested montane beauty of the Arkansas River Valley. If you don't have time to stop, the **Mt Magazine Scenic Byway** traverses the park and includes some drop-dead gorgeous views. If you need food or gas, the closest town is **Paris**, about 17 miles away.

Mt Nebo State Park STATE PARK
(479-229-3655; www.arkansasstateparks.com/mountnebo; 16728 W State Hwy 155, Dardanelle, GPS: N 35°13'41.0; visitor center 8am-5pm daily, to 7pm Fri & Sat Jun-Aug; P) FREE Mt Nebo and surrounds are crisscrossed by 14 miles of trails that plunge into the woodsy mountainscape. The strenuous **Nebo Springs** trail makes a loop that heads to a mossy, watery slice of outdoors loveliness. The closest town, **Dardanelle**, is 8 miles to the east.

Petit Jean State Park STATE PARK
(501-727-5441; www.petitjeanstatepark.com; 1285 Petit Jean Mountain Rd, Morrilton, GPS: N 35°07'04.3; visitor center 8am-8pm Jun & Jul, to 7pm Sep & Oct, to 5pm Nov-May & Aug; P) FREE The excellently maintained trails of this state park, the oldest in Arkansas, wind past a lush 95ft waterfall, romantic grottoes, expansive vistas and dense forests. Be on the lookout for a natural bridge spanning the Arcadian wilderness, as well as overlooks that take in huge swaths of the Arkansas River Valley. The closest town is **Morrilton** (18 miles away), although Little Rock is only about 70 miles southeast of here if you fancy a long day trip from the capital.

Lake Dardanelle State Park STATE PARK
(479-967-5516; www.arkansasstateparks.com/lakedardanelle; 100 State Park Dr (Breakwater Rd), Russellville; visitor center 8am-8pm May-Aug, to 5pm rest of year; P) FREE Miles of icy-blue water mark this 34,300-acre reservoir, which is surrounded by boat-launch ramps and flat-out pretty views. There's a big visitor center in **Russellville** that includes kid-friendly interpretive exhibits, aquariums and kayak-rental facilities.

Buffalo National River RAFTING
(870-439-2502; www.nps.gov/buff;) An under-acknowledged Arkansas gem, and perhaps the best of them all, this 135-mile river flows beneath dramatic bluffs through unspoiled Ozark forest. The upriver section tends to have most of the white water, while the lower reaches ease lazily along – perfect for an easy paddle.

The Buffalo National River has multiple **campgrounds** and three designated wilderness areas; the most accessible is through the Tyler Bend visitor center (p429), 11 miles north of Marshall on Hwy 65, where you can also pick up a list of approved outfitters for self-guided rafting or canoe trips (the best way to tour the park and see the gargantuan limestone bluffs). Or seek out Buffalo Outdoor Center (p432), which will point you in the right direction and rents out attractive cabins in the woods too.

Kayaking BOATING
(479-967-5516; www.arkansasstateparks.com; 100 State Park Dr (Breakwater Rd), Russellville; per hr/half-day/full day from $7.50/10/18) You can rent solo or tandem kayaks to explore the waters of Lake Dardanelle, or opt for a 90-minute kayak tour for an extra $12/6 per adult/child.

Sleeping & Eating

Accommodations in the four state parks range from primitive campsites to lodges. The dozens of campsites (www.arkansasstateparks.com/camping-cabins-lodging) range from those with no hookups to sites with full electricity, running water and toilets. Contact each park for details, and book through the state park website. Rates run from $12 for primitive sites to $30 or more for fully serviced areas.

There are uninspiring motels and hotels in the nearby towns.

You'll want to stock up on groceries before exploring any of the Tri-Peaks parks in-depth, with the exception of Lake Dardanelle, which is located in Russellville proper.

Information

The **Tyler Bend Visitor Center** (870-439-2502; www.nps.gov/buff; 170 Ranger Rd, St Joe; 8:30am-4:30pm) is a must visit for those who want to explore the Buffalo National River.

Getting There & Away

The Tri-Peaks Region occupies an oddly Arkansas-shaped chunk of north-central Arkansas. The four parks can only be accessed via your own vehicle. None is more than two hours from Little Rock.

The spectacular Highway 23/Pig Trail Byway, which runs from Eureka Springs to Mt Magazine State Park, runs through mountain ranges and Ozark National Forest – it's well worth your time to take this scenic drive.

Ozark Mountains

Stretching from northwest and central Arkansas into Missouri, the Ozark Mountains are an ancient range, once surrounded by sea and now well worn by time. Verdant peaks give way to misty fields and hard-dirt farms, while dramatic karst formations line sparkling lakes, rivers and capillary-thin back roads. The region derives a lot of pride from its independence and sense of place, a zeitgeist at least partially informed by multiple generations of familial roots and a long history of regional poverty. For literary company, pick up Daniel Woodrell's novel *Winter's Bone,* which was adapted into a critically acclaimed film of the same name.

Getting There & Away

The Ozarks encompass a large area, riven by numerous mountain roads, some of which are big enough to count as highways. Major roads include Hwy 62, AR 21, AR 43 and AR 66. The closest regional airport is **Northwest Arkansas Regional Airport** (XNA; ☎479-205-1000; www.flyxna.com; 1 Airport Blvd), near Bentonville. Eureka Springs is also served by **Greyhound** (☎800-451-5333; 131 E Van Buren).

Mountain View

Mountain View is a low-key tourism magnet where the main attraction is a daily showcasing of Ozark folkways, particularly regional music. It's a village filled with both culture creators and seekers. Folk-music enthusiasts rub shoulders with a local populace grounded in deeply spiritual Christianity. Folks tend to wear their religion on their sleeve, which may feel jarring to visitors from more secular backgrounds, but that faith considerably animates Mountain View's embrace of music and the arts.

The **Visitor Information Center** (☎870-269-8068; www.yourplaceinthemountains.com; 122 W Main St; ⏰9am-4:30pm Mon-Sat) promotes Mountain View as the 'Folk Music Capital of the World,' and while that may be ambitious, you can catch live music here every night of the week. This pleasant vibe stands out amidst many surrounding towns that have fallen on hard times. Mountain View, in contrast, has survived and thrived by marrying its traditions to a tourism economy, all without sacrificing its soul.

Sights & Activities

Blanchard Springs Caverns CAVE
(☎870-757-2211, tours 877-444-6777; www.fs.usda.gov; NF 54, Forest Rd, off Hwy 14; Dripstone tour adult/child$12/7, Wild Cave tour $85; ⏰varies; 🚻) The spectacular Blanchard Springs Caverns, 15 miles northwest of Mountain View, were carved by an underground river. It's a little-known, mind-blowing spot in Arkansas. Guided tours range from accessible-travel to adventurous three- to four-hour spelunking sessions. The caverns maintain seasonal hours, but usually open at 9:30am and close around sunset.

Ozark Folk Center State Park STATE PARK
(☎870-269-3851; www.ozarkfolkcenter.com; 1032 Park Ave; auditorium adult/child $12/7; ⏰10am-5pm Tue-Sat Apr-Nov, evening shows 7pm; Ⓟ) The town's top cultural attraction, just north of Mountain View, hosts ongoing craft demonstrations, a traditional herb garden and nightly live music that brings in an avid crowd. Beyond those shows, the center maintains a busy concert schedule that ropes in some of the nation's best folk and bluegrass acts.

LocoRopes OUTDOORS
(☎870-269-6566, 888-669-6717; www.locoropes.com; 1025 Park Ave; zipline from $15; ⏰10am-5pm Mar 1-Nov 30) This popular outdoors outfitter offers a ropes course, slack lining, a freefall, a climbing wall and three ziplines. Its 'loco lines' adventures ($15 to $60) pretty much combine all of the above into an absolutely thrilling aerial obstacle course and zipline experience.

Sleeping & Eating

The Inn at Mountain View B&B $
(☎870-269-4200, 800-535-1301; www.innatmountainview.com; 307 W Washington St; r $94-120, ste $145; Ⓟ📶) It's the rare property we review that hosts banjo and fiddle workshops, but then along comes the Inn at Mountain View. Besides being an active participant in the Mountain View folk-music world, the Inn

boasts 10 rooms, all appointed in a cozy-quilt grandma-chic style. Feel free to relax on the big porch and soak up the music come evening.

Tommy's Famous Pizza and BBQ PIZZA, BARBECUE $
(☎870-269-3278; www.tommysfamous.com; cnr Carpenter & W Main Sts; pizza $7-26, mains $7-13; ⊙from 3pm) The barbecue pizza here marries Tommy's stated specialties indulgently. The affable owner, a former rocker from Memphis, plays great music, has a fun vibe, and just two conditions: no attitude and no loud kids.

PJ's Rainbow Cafe AMERICAN $
(☎870-269-8633; www.facebook.com/Pjsrainbowcafe; 216 W Main St; mains $5.50-13; ⊙7am-8pm Tue-Sat, to 2pm Sun;) This country-fried cafe serves up some truly tasty diner food done with flair: think spinach-stuffed pork loin and fresh-grilled rainbow trout caught in local rivers. Cash only.

Eureka Springs

Eureka Springs, near Arkansas' northwestern corner, perches in a steep valley and is filled with Victorian buildings, crooked streets and a crunchy, New Age–aligned local population that welcomes all. This is one of the most explicitly gay-friendly towns in the Ozarks, and mixes up an odd mash of liberal politics and rainbow flags with biker-friendly Harley bars. Hiking, cycling and horseback-riding opportunities abound.

The **visitor center** (☎479- 253-8737; www.eurekaspringschamber.com; 516 Village Circle, Hwy 62 E; ⊙10am-4pm Tue-Sat) has information about lodging, activities, tours and local attractions.

Sights & Activities

Historic Loop HISTORIC SITE
(www.eurekasprings.org) FREE This 3.5-mile walking tour winds through downtown Eureka Springs and neighboring residential areas. The route is dotted with more than 300 Victorian homes, all built before 1910, each a jaw-dropper and on par with any preserved historic district in the USA. You can access the loop via the **Eureka Trolley** (☎479-253-9572; www.eurekatrolley.org; 137 W Van Buren St; day pass adult/child $6/2; ⊙10am-6pm Sun-Fri, 9am-8pm Sat May-Oct, reduced hrs other times;), or just walk it – recommended if you're fit (the streets are steep!); pick up a map or buy trolley tickets at the Visitor Center.

Thorncrown Chapel CHURCH
(☎479-253-7401; www.thorncrown.com; 12968 Hwy 62 W; ⊙9am-5pm Apr-Nov, 11am-4pm Mar & Dec; P) FREE Thorncrown Chapel is a magnificent sanctuary made of glass, with its 48ft-tall wooden skeleton holding 425 windows. There's not much between your prayers and God's green earth here. It's just outside of Eureka Springs in the woods. Donation suggested.

Lake Leatherwood City Park PARK
(☎479-253-7921; http://eurekaparks.com; 1303 Co Rd 204; ⊙24hr; P) This expansive park includes 21 miles of hiking and biking trails that crisscross the forested mountains and surround an 85-acre lake. Located about 3.5 miles from downtown Eureka Springs, this is the closest managed wild space to Eureka Springs.

Sleeping & Eating

★**Treehouse Cottages** COTTAGE $$
(☎479-253-9493; www.estreehouses.com; 3018 E Van Buren; cottage $106-189; P) Sprinkled amid 33 acres of pine forest, these cute, kitschy and spacious stilted wooden cottages are worth finding. Some rooms boast a Jacuzzi tub, a private balcony with grill at the ready, a flat-screen TV, a fireplace, or all of the above. You can also opt for an underground 'Hobbit cave,' if that's your preference, Bilbo. Two-night minimum stay.

1886 Crescent Hotel HISTORIC HOTEL $$
(☎855-725-5720; www.crescent-hotel.com; 75 Prospect Ave; r $145-220, ste $270-300; P) Of all the pretty historic buildings in Eureka Springs, the Crescent stands out: it's like *Downton Abbey* meets the Jazz Age (which happened in season 4, right?). Rooms are a well-executed synthesis of historic accents and modern comforts, and the whole vibe of the place is both elegant and fun. Rates go up on weekends.

★**Oscar's Cafe** SANDWICHES $
(☎479-981-1436; www.facebook.com/oscarsonwhitestreet; 17 White St; mains $4-9; ⊙9am-3pm Wed-Sun, to 5pm Tue;) This little cafe has a small menu, but what a menu: chicken, walnut and cranberry salad, prosciutto sandwiches and fresh quiche. This is bright, breezy cuisine, the sort of food that fills you up without weighing you down (rare in the

South), and served in the heart of Eureka Springs' cute historic district.

Stone House AMERICAN **$$$**
(479-363-6411; 89 S Main St; cheese plates $25-47; 1-10pm Thu-Sun) The Stone House has all the ingredients for a pretty perfect evening: lots of wine; a menu that focuses on cheese, bread, olives, honey and charcuterie; live music; a cute courtyard; and did we mention lots of wine? It's open until 10pm, which constitutes late-night dining in Eureka Springs.

Drinking & Entertainment

Chelsea's Corner Cafe & Bar BAR
(479-253-6723; www.chelseascafeeureka.com; 10 Mountain St; 11am-midnight) Live-music acts frequently take to the stage at this bar, which attracts a typically Eureka Springs blend of hippies and bikers. The kitchen is one of the few places in town open past 9pm, and even does pizza delivery.

Opera in the Ozarks OPERA
(479-253-8595; www.opera.org; 16311 Hwy 62 W; tickets from $20) This much-acclaimed fine-arts program has kept opera alive and loud in the mountains. A packed performance schedule and a playhouse located just outside of town is the pride of Eureka Springs.

Buffalo National River

The USA's first national river rolls for 135 glorious miles through the heart of northern Arkansas. Along the way, the rushing waters pass by ochre cliffs and granite outcroppings, while lapping at small sandy beaches that fringe deep tracts of Ozark forest.

Ponca is the best base for adventures, with a fair few outdoor outfitters here to help you set up a wilderness excursion.

Activities

Buffalo Outdoor Center ADVENTURE
(BOC; 870-861-5514; www.buffaloriver.com; 4699 AR 43; kayak/canoe per day $55/62, zipline tour $89; 8am-6pm Mar-Oct, to 5pm Nov-Feb;) Arranges paddling trips, hiking tours, fishing trips, horseback rides and a zipline tour. Reserve in advance.

Big Bluff via Centerpoint & Goat Trail HIKING
(AR 43 & Fire Tower Rd, GPS: N 36°03'50.7) Standing a dramatic 550ft tall, Big Bluff is the highest sheer rock face between the Rocky Mountains and the Appalachians. To get out here, take the Centerpoint Trail, three miles north of Ponca on AR 43 (look for the trailhead near the junction of Fire Tower Rd). Take the narrow spur route – the Goat Trail – that leads to the bluff.

This is a 2.5 mile round-trip trail, and it's pretty much uphill all the way – fair warning.

Lost Valley Canoe CANOEING
(870-861-5522; www.lostvalleycanoe.com; AR 43; kayaks per day from $55, shuttle service from $20) This knowledgeable outfitter can arrange canoe and kayak rentals, as well as shuttle pick-up services. It also rents comfortable cabins (with hot tubs!) that can sleep two for $150 ($20 for each extra guest).

Getting There & Away

Ponca sits far off any beaten tracks. You need to come by road, and it's located about 50 miles south of Eureka Springs and 80 miles east of Bentonville.

LOUISIANA

Louisiana runs deep: a French colony turned Spanish protectorate turned reluctant American purchase; a southern fringe of swampland, bayou and alligators dissolving into the Gulf of Mexico; a northern patchwork prairie of heartland farm country; and everywhere, a population tied together by a deep, unshakable appreciation for the good things in life: food and music.

New Orleans, its first city, lives and dies by these qualities, and its restaurants and music halls are second to none. But everywhere, the state shares a love for this joie de vivre. We're not dropping French for fun, by the way; while the language is not a cultural component of North Louisiana, near I-10 and below, the French language – or Louisiana's particular version of it – is a cultural touchstone.

History

The lower Mississippi River area was dominated by the Mississippian mound-building culture until around 1592 when Europeans arrived and decimated the Native Americans with the usual combination of disease, unfavorable treaties and outright hostility.

CAJUNS, CREOLES &...CREOLES

Tourists in Louisiana often use the terms 'Cajun' and 'Creole' interchangeably, but the two cultures are quite distinct. 'Creole' refers to descendants of the original European settlers of Louisiana, a blended mix of mainly French and Spanish ancestry. The Creoles tend to have urban connections to New Orleans and consider their own culture refined and urbanized.

The Cajuns can trace their lineage to the Acadians, colonists from rural France who settled Nova Scotia, New Brunswick, Prince Edward Island and parts of Quebec. After the British conquered Canada, the proud Acadians refused to kneel to the new crown and were exiled in the mid-18th century – an act known as the Grand Dérangement. Many exiles settled in South Louisiana; they knew the area was French, but the Acadians ('Cajun' is an English bastardization of the word) were often treated as country bumpkins by the Creoles. The Acadians-cum-Cajuns settled in the bayous and prairies, and to this day see themselves as a more rural, frontier-style culture.

Adding confusion to this is the practice, standard in many post-colonial French societies, of referring to mixed-race individuals as 'Creoles.' This happens in Louisiana, but there is a cultural difference between Franco-Spanish Creoles and mixed-race Creoles, even though these two communities very likely share actual blood ancestry.

The land was then passed back and forth between France, Spain and England. Under the French 'Code Noir,' slaves were kept but retained a somewhat greater degree of freedom – and thus native culture – than their counterparts in British North America.

After the American Revolution the whole area passed to the USA in the 1803 Louisiana Purchase, and Louisiana became a state in 1812. The resulting blend of American and Franco-Spanish traditions, plus the influence of Afro-Caribbean communities, gave Louisiana the unique culture it retains to this day.

Following the Civil War, Louisiana was readmitted to the Union in 1868 and the next 30 years saw political wrangling, economic stagnation and renewed discrimination against African Americans.

Hurricane Katrina (2005) and the BP Gulf Coast Oil Spill (2010) significantly damaged the local economy and infrastructure. Louisiana remains a bottom-rung state in terms of per capita income and education levels, yet it ranks high in national happiness scales.

ℹ Information

Louisiana Office of Tourism (800-677-4082; www.louisianatravel.com) Ten welcome centers dot freeways throughout the state, or contact the office directly.

Louisiana State Parks (888-677-1400; www.crt.state.la.us/louisiana-state-parks) Louisiana has 20 state parks that offer camping. Some parks also offer lodge accommodations and cabins. Reservations can be made online, by phone or on a drop-in basis if there's availability. Camping fees increase slightly from April to September.

New Orleans

New Orleans is very much of America, but extraordinarily removed from it as well. Founded by the French and administered by the Spanish (and then the French again), New Orleans is the most European city in America. But, with the *vodoun* (voodoo), weekly second-line parades, Mardi Gras Indians, jazz, brass and gumbo, it's also the most African and Caribbean city in America.

New Orleans celebrates life; while America is on deadline, this city is sipping a cocktail after a long lunch. But if you saw how people here rebuilt their homes after floods and tempests, you'd be foolish to call the locals lazy.

Tolerating everything and learning from it is the soul of this city. When New Orleans' citizens aspire to that overarching Creole ideal, where the whole is greater than the sum of its parts, we get: jazz; Nouveau Louisiana cuisine; storytellers from African *griots* (West African bards) to Seventh Ward rappers to Tennessee Williams; French townhouses a few blocks from Foghorn Leghorn mansions groaning under sweet myrtle and bougainvillea; and Mardi Gras celebrations that mix pagan mysticism with Catholic pageantry.

Just don't forget the indulgence and immersion, because that Creolization gets watered down when folks don't live life to its intellectual and epicurean hilt.

Sights

French Quarter

Also known as Vieux Carré ('voo car-*ray*'; Old Quarter) and 'the Quarter,' the French Quarter is the original city as planned by the French in the 1800s. Here lies the infamous Bourbon St, but of more interest is an elegantly aged grid of shopfronts, iron lamps and courtyard gardens. Most visitors begin exploring the city here and some never leave the area. That's not to say the Quarter isn't lovely, but it's a bit like a theme park: heavy on tourist traffic and light on locals (apart from your bartender or waiter).

★Jackson Square SQUARE
(Decatur & St Peter Sts) Sprinkled with lazing loungers, surrounded by sketch artists, fortune tellers and traveling performers, and watched over by cathedrals, offices and shops plucked from a Parisian fantasy, Jackson Sq is one of America's great town greens and the heart of the Quarter. The identical, block-long Pontalba Buildings overlook the scene, and the nearly identical Cabildo and **Presbytère** (504-568-6968; https://louisianastatemuseum.org/museum/presbytere; 751 Chartres St; adult/student/child $6/5/free; 10am-4:30pm Tue-Sun) structures flank the impressive St Louis Cathedral, which fronts the square.

★St Louis Cathedral CATHEDRAL
(504-525-9585; www.stlouiscathedral.org; Jackson Sq; donations accepted, audio guide $8; 8:30am-4pm, Mass 12:05pm Mon-Fri, 5pm Sat, 9am & 11am Sun) One of the best examples of French architecture in the country, this triple-spired 18th-century cathedral is dedicated to Louis IX, the French king sainted in 1297. It's an attractive bit of Gallic heritage in the heart of an American city. In addition to hosting Black, white and Creole Catholic congregants, St Louis has also attracted those who, in the best New Orleanian tradition, mix their influences, such as voodoo queen Marie Laveau.

★Cabildo MUSEUM
(504-568-6968; https://louisianastatemuseum.org/museum/cabildo; 701 Chartres St; adult/student/child under 6yr $9/7/free; 10am-4:30pm Tue-Sun) The former seat of government in colonial Louisiana now serves as the gateway to exploring the history of the state in general, and New Orleans in particular. It's also a magnificent building in its own right; the elegant Cabildo marries elements of Spanish Colonial architecture and French urban design better than most buildings in the city. The diverse exhibits include Native American tools, 'Wanted' posters for escaped slaves, and a gallery's worth of paintings of stone-faced old New Orleanians.

Historic New Orleans Collection MUSEUM
(THNOC; 504-523-4662; www.hnoc.org; 533 Royal St; admission free, tours $5; 9:30am-4:30pm Tue-Sat, from 10:30am Sun, tours 10am, 11am, 2pm & 3pm Tue-Sat, 11am, 2pm & 3pm Sun) A combination of preserved buildings, museums and research centers all rolled into one, the Historic New Orleans Collection is a good introduction to the history of the city. The complex is anchored by its Royal St campus, which presents a series of regularly rotating exhibits and occasional temporary exhibits. Artifacts on display include an original Jazz Fest poster, transfer documents of the Louisiana Purchase and utterly disturbing slave advertisements.

Mid-City & The Tremé

Back in the day, this was the back of beyond: the bottom of the depression that is the New Orleans geographic bowl, an area of swampy lowlands and hidden gambler dens. Today? Mid-City and its adjacent neighborhoods form one of the loveliest residential areas in the city. This semiamorphous district includes long lanes of shotgun houses, bike lanes, the gorgeous green spaces of City Park, the elegant mansions of Esplanade Ave and the slow, lovely laze of Bayou St John.

★Backstreet Cultural Museum MUSEUM
(504-657-6700; www.backstreetmuseum.org; 1116 Henriette Delille St; $10; 11am-5pm Mon-Fri, 10am-3pm Sat) Mardi Gras Indian suits grab the spotlight with dazzling flair – and finely crafted detail – in this informative museum examining the distinctive elements of African American culture in New Orleans. The museum isn't terribly big (it's the former Blandin's Funeral Home), but if you have any interest in the suits and rituals of Mardi Gras Indians, as well as second-line parades and Social Aid and Pleasure Clubs (the local African American community version of civic associations), you should stop by.

NEW ORLEANS FOR CHILDREN

New Orleans is a fairy-tale city, with its colorful beads, weekly costume parties and daily music wafting through the air. The same flights of fancy and whimsy that give this city such appeal for poets and artists also make it an imaginative wonderland for children, especially creative ones.

The **Louisiana Children's Museum** (☎504-523-1357; www.lcm.org; 420 Julia St, Warehouse District; $10; ⊙9:30am-4:30pm Tue-Sat, noon-4:30pm Sun; 👪) is a good intro to the region for toddlers, while older children and teenagers may appreciate the Ogden Museum (p438), Cabildo and Presbytère. Little ones often take a shine to the candy-colored houses in the French Quarter, Faubourg Marigny and Uptown.

The **Latter Library** (☎504-596-2625; www.nolalibrary.org; 5120 St Charles Ave, Uptown; ⊙10am-8pm Mon-Thu, to 5pm Fri & Sat, 1-5pm Sun) on St Charles Ave has a good selection of children's literature and is located in a pretty historical mansion. The city's cemeteries, especially Lafayette Cemetery No 1 (p439) in the Garden District, are authentic slices of the past and enjoyably spooky to boot.

The many **street parties** and **outdoor festivals** of New Orleans bring food stalls and, of course, great music. Children will love dancing to the beat. Seek out festivals held during the day, such as Bayou Boogaloo (www.thebayouboogaloo.com).

Mardi Gras and the **Carnival Season** are surprisingly family-friendly affairs outside of the well-known boozy debauch in the French Quarter. St Charles Ave hosts many day parades where lots of krewes roll and families set up grilling posts and tents – drinking revelers aren't welcome. Kids are set up on 'ladder seats' (www.momsminivan.com/extras/ladderseat.html) so they can get an adult-height view of the proceedings and catch throws from the floats. The crazy costumes add to the child-friendly feel of the whole affair. See www.neworleansonline.com/neworleans/mardigras/mgfamilies.html.

★City Park PARK

(☎504-482-4888; www.neworleanscitypark.com; Esplanade Ave & City Park Ave; ⊙dawn-dusk; P 👪 🐾) FREE Live oaks, Spanish moss and lazy bayous frame this masterpiece of urban planning. Three miles long and 1 mile wide, dotted with gardens, waterways and bridges and home to a captivating art museum, City Park is bigger than Central Park in NYC and it's New Orleans' prettiest green space.

Art- and nature-lovers could easily spend a day exploring the park. Anchoring the action is the stately New Orleans Museum of Art, which spotlights regional and American artists. From there, stroll past the whimsical creations in the **Sydney & Walda Besthoff Sculpture Garden** (www.noma.org/sculpture-garden; 1 Collins Diboll Circle; ⊙10am-6pm Apr-Sep, to 5pm Oct-Mar) FREE, then check out the lush **Botanical Gardens** (☎504-483-9488; www.neworleanscitypark.com/botanical-garden; adult/child/under 3 $8/4/free; ⊙10am-5pm; P). Kids in tow? Hop the rides at the **Carousel Gardens Amusement Park** (☎504-483-9402; www.neworleanscitypark.com/in-the-park/carousel-gardens; 7 Victory Ave; adult/child 36in & under $4/free, each ride $4; ⊙11am-6pm Sat & Sun Mar-May & Aug-Oct, 11am-5pm Tue-Fri, to 6pm Sat & Sun Jun & Jul) or climb the fantastical statuary inside **Storyland** (http://neworleanscitypark.com/in-the-park/storyland; 5 Victory Ave; adult/child 36in & under $4/free; ⊙10am-5pm; 👪).

Louis Armstrong Park PARK

(701 N Rampart St; ⊙sunrise-sunset) The entrance to this massive park has got to be one of the greatest gateways in the US, a picturesque arch that ought rightfully to be the final set piece in a period drama about Jazz Age New Orleans. The original Congo Sq is here, as well as a Louis Armstrong Statue and a bust of Sidney Bechet. The **Mahalia Jackson Theater** (☎504-287-0350; www.mahaliajacksontheater.com; 1419 Basin St) hosts opera and Broadway productions. The park often hosts live-music festivals throughout the year.

New Orleans Museum of Art MUSEUM

(NOMA; ☎504-658-4100; www.noma.org; 1 Collins Diboll Circle, City Park; adult/student/child 7-17yr $15/8/6; ⊙10am-6pm Tue-Fri, 10am-5pm Sat, 11am-5pm Sun) Inside City Park, this elegant museum was opened in 1911 and is well worth a visit for its special exhibitions, gorgeous marble atrium and top-floor galleries of African, Asian, Native American and

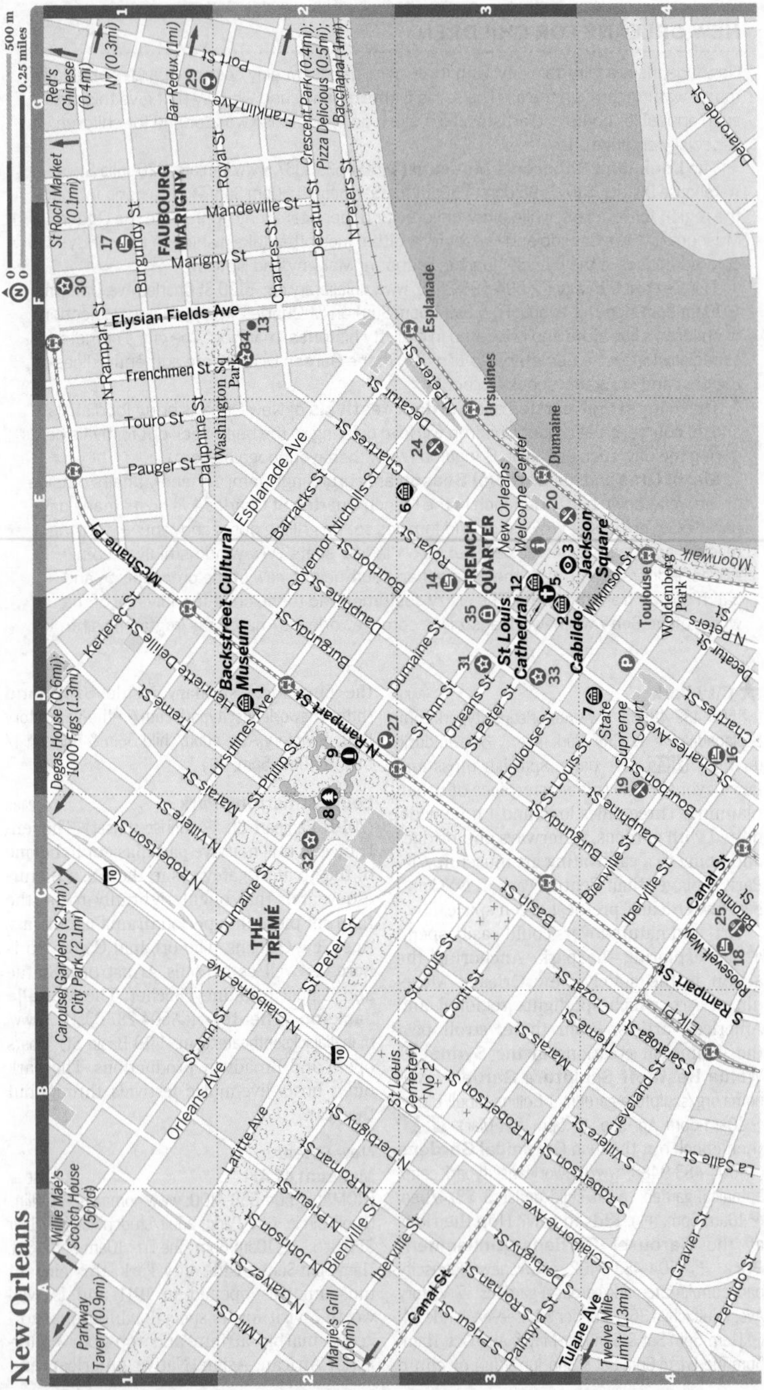

New Orleans

0 500 m
0 0.25 miles
A
B
C
D
E
F
G
1
2
3
4
Parkway Tavern (0.9mi)
Willie Mae's Scotch House (50yd)
Carousel Gardens (2.1mi); City Park (2.1mi)
Degas House (0.6mi); 1000 Figs (1.3mi)
St Roch Market (0.1mi)
Red's Chinese (0.4mi)
N7 (0.3mi)
Bar Redux (1mi)
Crescent Park (0.4mi); Pizza Delicious (0.5mi); Bacchanal (1mi)
Marjie's Grill (0.6mi)
Twelve Mile Limit (1.3mi)
FAUBOURG MARIGNY
THE TREMÉ
FRENCH QUARTER
Backstreet Cultural Museum
St Louis Cathedral
Cabildo
Jackson Square
New Orleans Welcome Center
State Supreme Court
Washington Sq Park
St Louis Cemetery No 2
Woldenberg Park
Esplanade
Ursulines
Dumaine
Toulouse
Moonwalk
N Rampart St
Elysian Fields Ave
Burgundy St
Marigny St
Mandeville St
Royal St
Franklin Ave
Port St
Chartres St
Decatur St
N Peters St
Pauger St
Touro St
Frenchmen St
Dauphine St
McShane Pl
Kerlerec St
Henriette Delille St
Tremé St
Marais St
N Villere St
N Robertson St
Ursulines Ave
St Philip St
Esplanade Ave
Barracks St
Governor Nicholls St
Bourbon St
Dumaine St
St Ann St
Orleans St
St Peter St
Toulouse St
St Louis St
Wilkinson St
Orleans Ave
Lafitte Ave
N Claiborne Ave
St Peter St
N Miro St
N Galvez St
N Johnson St
N Prieur St
N Roman St
N Derbigny St
Bienville St
Iberville St
Canal St
Conti St
Basin St
Crozat St
S Saratoga St
Elk Pl
S Rampart St
Roosevelt Way
Baronne St
St Charles Ave
Cleveland St
S Villere St
S Robertson St
S Claiborne Ave
S Derbigny St
S Roman St
S Prieur St
Palmyra St
Tulane Ave
Gravier St
La Salle St
Perdido St
Delaronde St
10
1
2
3
5
6
7
8
9
12
13
14
16
17
18
19
20
24
25
27
29
30
31
32
33
34
35

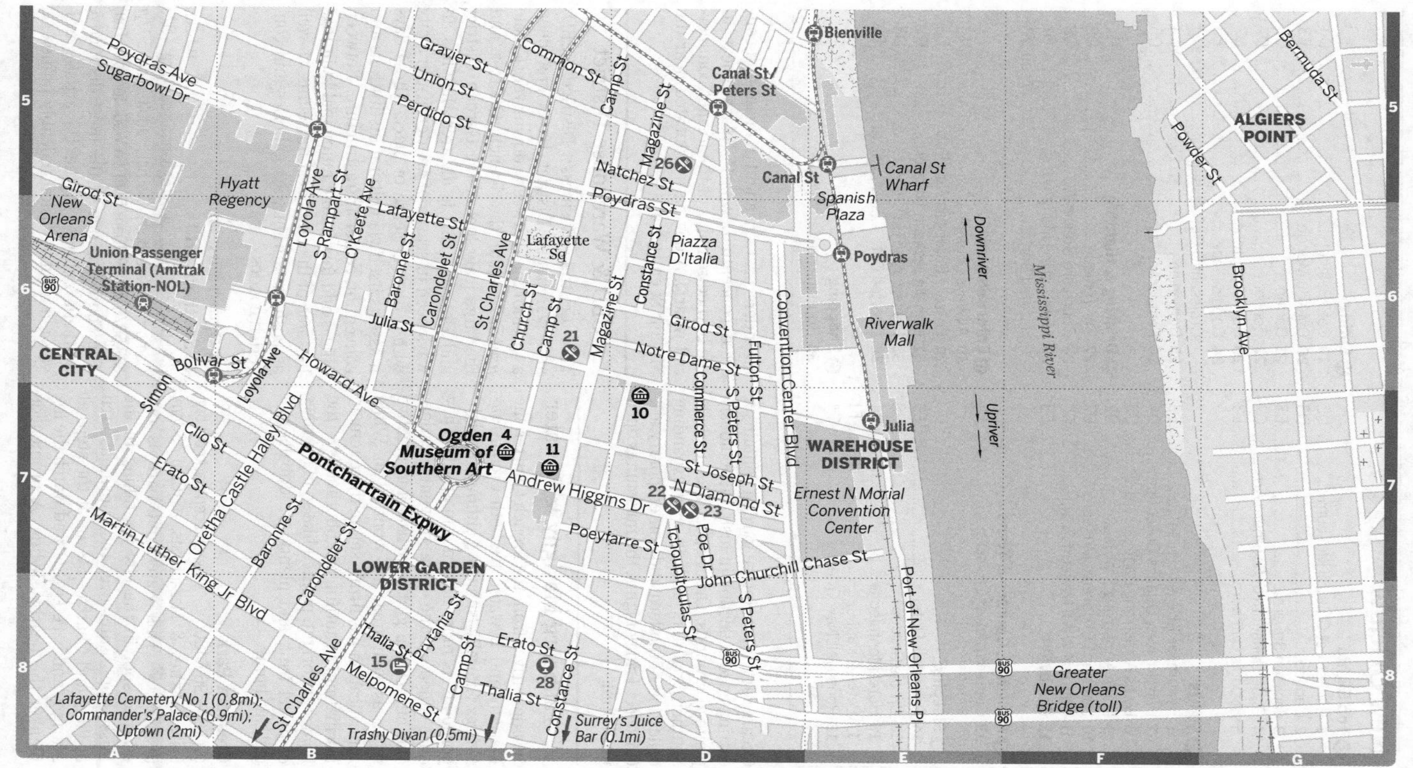

Poydras Ave
Sugarbowl Dr
Gravier St
Union St
Perdido St
Common St
Camp St
Magazine St
Canal St/ Peters St
Bienville
Canal St
Canal St Wharf
Spanish Plaza
Poydras
ALGIERS POINT
Bermuda St
Powder St
Brooklyn Ave
Mississippi River
Downriver
Upriver
Girod St
New Orleans Arena
Hyatt Regency
Union Passenger Terminal (Amtrak Station-NOL)
Loyola Ave
S Rampart St
O'Keefe Ave
Baronne St
Carondelet St
Lafayette St
St Charles Ave
Lafayette Sq
Natchez St
Poydras St
Constance St
Piazza D'Italia
Church St
Julia St
Girod St
Notre Dame St
Commerce St
S Peters St
Fulton St
Convention Center Blvd
Riverwalk Mall
Julia
WAREHOUSE DISTRICT
CENTRAL CITY
Bolivar St
Simon
Howard Ave
Clio St
Erato St
Oretha Castle Haley Blvd
Martin Luther King Jr Blvd
Pontchartrain Expwy
Ogden Museum of Southern Art
Andrew Higgins Dr
St Joseph St
N Diamond St
Ernest N Morial Convention Center
Poeyfarre St
Tchoupitoulas St
Poe Dr
John Churchill Chase St
Port of New Orleans Pl
LOWER GARDEN DISTRICT
Prytania St
Thalia St
Erato St
Camp St
Constance St
Melpomene St
Greater New Orleans Bridge (toll)
Lafayette Cemetery No 1 (0.8mi); Commander's Palace (0.9mi); Uptown (2mi)
Trashy Divan (0.5mi)
Surrey's Juice Bar (0.1mi)
4
10
11
15
21
22
23
26
28

New Orleans

Top Sights
1 Backstreet Cultural Museum D2
2 Cabildo D3
3 Jackson Square E3
4 Ogden Museum of Southern Art C7
5 St Louis Cathedral E3

Sights
6 Beauregard-Keyes House E3
7 Historic New Orleans Collection D4
8 Louis Armstrong Park C2
9 Louis Armstrong Statue D2
10 Louisiana Children's Museum D7
11 National WWII Museum C7
12 Presbytère E3

Activities, Courses & Tours
13 Confederacy of Cruisers F2

Sleeping
14 Cornstalk Hotel E3
15 Creole Gardens B8
16 Hotel Monteleone D4
17 Peter & Paul F1
18 Roosevelt New Orleans C4

Eating
19 Café Beignet D4
20 Café du Monde E3
21 Carmo C6
22 Cochon D7
23 Cochon Butcher D7
24 Coop's Place E3
Croissant D'Or Patisserie .... (see 6)
25 Domenica C4
26 Restaurant August D5

Drinking & Nightlife
27 Bar Tonique D2
28 Courtyard Brewery C8
29 Mimi's in the Marigny G1
Sazerac Bar .... (see 18)

Entertainment
30 AllWays Lounge F1
31 Fritzel's European Jazz Pub D3
32 Mahalia Jackson Theater C2
33 Preservation Hall D3
34 Spotted Cat F2

Shopping
35 Boutique du Vampyre D3

Oceanic art. Its sculpture garden contains a cutting-edge collection in lush, meticulously planned grounds. Other specialties include Southern painters and an ever-expanding collection of modern and contemporary art. On select Friday nights, the museum is open until 9pm.

Faubourg Marigny & Bywater

Just downriver from the French Quarter, the Marigny and Bywater are both Creole *faubourgs* (literally 'suburbs,' although 'neighborhoods' is more accurate in spirit). They once stood at the edge of gentrification, and attracted a glut of artists and creative types, as such areas are wont to do. While gentrification has firmly set in, these remain fascinating, beautiful neighborhoods – the homes are bright, painted like so many rows of pastel fruit, and plenty of oddballs still call this home.

Crescent Park PARK
(504-636-6400; www.crescentparknola.org; Piety, Chartres & Mazant Sts; 6am-7:30pm; P) This waterfront park is our favorite spot in the city for taking in the Mississippi. Enter over the enormous arch at Piety and Chartres Sts, or at the steps at Marigny and N Peters Sts, and watch the fog blanket the nearby skyline. A promenade meanders past an angular metal-and-concrete conceptual 'wharf' (placed next to the burned remains of the former commercial wharf). A dog park is located near the Mazant St entrance.

CBD & Warehouse District

The Central Business District (CBD) and Warehouse District have long been a membrane between downriver Creole *faubourgs* like the French Quarter and the large leafy lots of the Garden District and Uptown. This is an area that has always been in search of an identity, in a city with a distinct sense of place. These days it asserts itself via cultural institutions and convention-center infrastructure. Between offices and forgettable municipal buildings lie some of the city's best museums, as well as posh restaurants, art galleries and converted condos.

★**Ogden Museum of Southern Art** MUSEUM
(504-539-9650; www.ogdenmuseum.org; 925 Camp St, Warehouse District; adult/child 5-17yr $13.50/6.75; 10am-5pm Fri-Wed, to 8pm Thu) The South has one of the most distinctive aesthetic cultures in the US artistic universe, a creative vision indelibly influenced

by the region's complicated history and deep links to the land. Few museums explore the throughlines of Southern art like the Ogden, which boasts lovely gallery spaces, an awesome gift shop and kicking after-hours performances.

National WWII Museum MUSEUM
(☎504-528-1944; www.nationalww2museum.org; 945 Magazine St; adult/senior/child $28/24/18, films $7; ⏲9am-5pm) This extensive museum presents a fairly thorough analysis of the largest war in history. The exhibits, which are displayed across multiple grand pavilions, are enormous and immersive. The experience is designed to be both personal and awe-inducing, but with that said, the museum focuses so intently on providing the American perspective, it sometimes underplays the narrative of other Allied nations.

Garden, Lower Garden & Central City

As one proceeds south along the curve of the Mississippi River, the streets become tree-lined and the houses considerably grander. When you tire of craning back to take in multiwing mansions, you're in the Garden and Lower Garden Districts, the beginning of New Orleans' 'American Sector' (so named because it was settled after the Louisiana Purchase). This is a place of leafy, bucolic splendor and considerable wealth – and wealth disparities. Nearby Central City's main thoroughfare, Oretha Castle Haley Blvd, is undergoing a fitful but steady renaissance following years of neglect.

★**Lafayette Cemetery No 1** CEMETERY
(☎504-658-3781; Washington Ave, at Prytania St, Garden District; ⏲7am-3pm) FREE Of all the cemeteries in New Orleans, Lafayette exudes the strongest sense of subtropical Southern Gothic. The stark contrast of moldering crypts and gentle decay with the forceful fertility of the fecund greenery is incredibly jarring. It's a place filled with stories – of German and Irish immigrants, deaths by yellow fever, social societies doing right by their dead – that pulls the living into New Orleans' long, troubled past.

Tours

Confederacy of Cruisers CYCLING
(☎504-400-5468; www.confederacyofcruisers.com; 634 Elysian Fields Ave, Faubourg Marigny; tours $49-89) This company sets you up on cruiser bikes that come with fat tires and padded seats for Nola's flat, potholed roads. The 'Creole New Orleans' tour takes in the best architecture of Marigny, Bywater, Esplanade Ave and the Tremé. Confederacy also does a 'History of Drinking' tour (for those 21 and over) and a tasty culinary tour.

Festivals & Events

Mardi Gras CULTURAL
(www.mardigrasneworleans.com; ⏲Feb/early Mar) Fat Tuesday marks the orgasmic finale of the Carnival season. Expect parades, floats, insane costumes, and a day of absolute madcap revelry as the entire city throws down for an all-day party.

Jazz Fest MUSIC
(www.nojazzfest.com; entrances at Fortin St, Fair Grounds Race Course; adult/child $85/5; ⏲last weekend in Apr & first weekend in May) This world-renowned extravaganza of music, food, crafts and good living is a mainstay of the New Orleans festival calendar, attracting both international headliners and local artists. Tickets are cheaper if you order in advance.

St Joseph's Day – Super Sunday CULTURAL
(2600 Lasalle St, AL Davis Park) March 19 and its nearest Sunday bring 'gangs' of Mardi Gras Indians out into the streets in all their feathered, drumming glory. The Super Sunday parade usually begins around noon at AL Davis Park in Central City.

French Quarter Festival MUSIC
(☎504-522-5730; https://frenchquarterfest.org) During the second weekend of April, the largest free music festival in the country takes over the French Quarter.

Sleeping

Creole Gardens B&B $
(☎504-569-8700; http://creolegardens.com; 1415 Prytania St, Lower Garden District; r $89-159;) Friendly, knowledgeable hosts, a rainbow-hued property with individualized rooms and plenty of New Orleans bordello-esque vibe, and they're cool with pets? Of any size? Hey, sign us up. This is a winning B&B that's dripping with character and out-of-the-box charm (one room is called Countess Willie Piazza's Hall of Splendors).

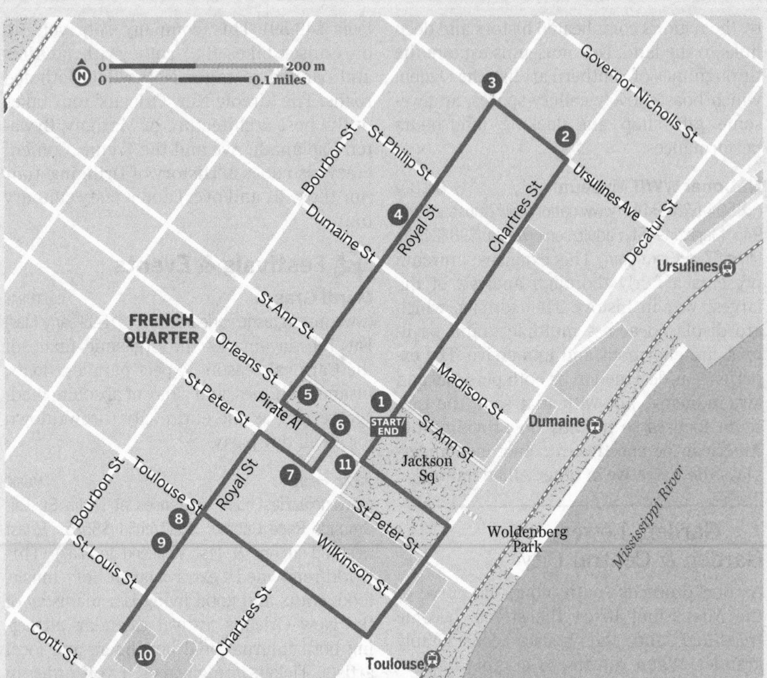

City Walk French Quarter

START JACKSON SQ
END JACKSON SQ
LENGTH 1.1 MILES; 1½ HOURS

Begin your walk at the **1 Presbytère** (p434) on Jackson Sq and head down Chartres St to the corner of Ursulines Ave. Directly across Chartres St, at No 1113, the 1826 **2 Beauregard-Keyes House** (www.bkhouse.org) combines Creole and American styles of design. Walk along Ursulines Ave to Royal St – the soda fountain at the **3 Royal Pharmacy** is a preserved relic from halcyon malt-shop days.

When it comes to quintessential New Orleans postcard images, Royal St takes the prize. Cast-iron galleries grace the buildings and a profusion of flowers garland the facades, while buoyant buskers blare their tunes from practically every street corner, often to wild acclaim. At No 915 Royal, the **4 Cornstalk Hotel** (www.cornstalkhotel.com) stands behind one of the most frequently photographed fences anywhere. At Orleans St, stately magnolia trees and lush tropical plants fill **5 St Anthony's Garden** (tough to see beyond the rows of street art) behind **6 St Louis Cathedral** (p434).

Alongside the garden, take the inviting Pirate Alley and turn right down Cabildo Alley and then right up St Peter St toward Royal St. Tennessee Williams shacked up at No 632 St Peter, the **7 Avart-Peretti House**, in 1946–47 while he wrote *A Streetcar Named Desire.*

Turn left on Royal St. At the corner of Royal and Toulouse Sts stands a pair of houses built by Jean François Merieult in the 1790s. The building known as the **8 Court of Two Lions** (now a gallery), at 541 Royal St, opens onto Toulouse St and next door is the **9 Historic New Orleans Collection** (p434) museum.

On the next block, the massive 1909 **10 State Supreme Court Building** was the setting for many scenes in director Oliver Stone's movie *JFK*.

Turn around and head right on Toulouse St to Decatur St and turn left. Cut across the road and walk the last stretch of this tour along the river. As Jackson Sq comes into view, cross back over to the Presbytère's near-identical twin, the **11 Cabildo** (p434).

★Peter & Paul BOUTIQUE HOTEL $$
(☎504-356-5200; https://hotelpeterandpaul.com; 2317 Burgundy St, Faubourg Marigny; r $110-249, ste $499; P 📶) This lovely hotel has taken over the grounds of the former Sts Peter and Paul Catholic church and school. The rooms are a study in elegant historical understatement, with muted linens, hand-painted tiles, canopied beds and highly individualized touches. The on-site church has become a performance venue – praise the higher power of your choice.

Degas House HISTORIC HOTEL $$
(☎504-821-5009; www.degashouse.com; 2306 Esplanade Ave; r $189-250, ste from $300; P ⊖ ❄ 📶) Edgar Degas, the famed French Impressionist, lived in this 1852 Italianate house when visiting his mother's family in the early 1870s. Rooms recall his time here through period furnishings and reproductions of his work. The suites have balconies and fireplaces, while the less expensive garret rooms are cramped top-floor quarters that once housed the Degas family's servants.

★Park View Historic Hotel HOTEL $$
(☎504-861-7564; http://parkviewguesthouse.com; 7004 St Charles Ave, Uptown; r $169-219; ⊖ @ 📶) The breakfasts are amazing (oh, those cheese grits) at this well-appointed three-story inn, where everyone seems glad to see you. Beside Audubon Park, this ornate wooden masterpiece was built in 1884 to impress people attending the World Cotton Exchange Exposition. The rooms and guest lounge are heavy with antiques, and the veranda overlooking the park and St Charles Ave is lovely.

★Roosevelt New Orleans HOTEL $$$
(☎504-648-1200; www.therooseveltneworleans.com; 123 Baronne St, CBD; r $200-309, ste $329-2000; P ⊖ ❄ @ 📶 ≋) The majestic, block-long lobby harks back to the early 20th century, a golden age of opulent hotels and grand retreats. Swish rooms have classical details, but the spa, restaurant **Domenica** (☎504-648-6020; www.domenicarestaurant.com; mains $15-34; ⏲11am-11pm; ✎), storied **Sazerac Bar** (☎504-648-1200; ⏲11am-midnight daily) and swanky jazz lounge are at least half the reason to stay. The rooftop pool is pretty swell too. It's an easy walk to the French Quarter.

Hotel Monteleone HOTEL $$$
(☎504-523-3341; www.hotelmonteleone.com; 214 Royal St; r $220-400; ⊖ ❄ 📶 ≋ 🐾) Perhaps the city's most venerable hotel, the Monteleone is also the Quarter's largest. Not long after it was built, preservationists put a stop to building on this scale below Iberville St. Since its inception in 1866, the hotel has lodged literary luminaries including William Faulkner, Truman Capote and Rebecca Wells. Rooms exude an old-world appeal with French toile and chandeliers.

Eating

French Quarter

Café Beignet CAFE $
(☎504-525-2611; www.cafebeignet.com; 311 Bourbon St, Musical Legends Park; breakfast $3.50-7; ⏲8am-midnight) Serves omelets, Belgian waffles, quiche and beignets. There's a low-level war among foodies over who does the better beignet – this place or **Café du Monde** (☎504-525-4544; www.cafedumonde.com; 800 Decatur St; beignets $3; ⏲24hr) – with the general consensus being that this spot uses less powdered sugar. This location has live jazz daily.

Croissant D'Or Patisserie BAKERY $
(☎504-524-4663; www.croissantdornola.com; 615-617 Ursulines Ave; mains $3-7; ⏲6am-3pm Wed-Mon) Bring a paper, order coffee and a croissant – or a tart, quiche or sandwich topped with béchamel sauce – and bliss out. Check out the tiled sign on the threshold that says 'ladies entrance' – a holdover from earlier days. While the coffee is bland, the pastries are perfect, and the shop is well-lit, friendly and clean.

★Coop's Place CAJUN $$
(☎504-525-9053; www.coopsplace.net; 1109 Decatur St; mains $10-20; ⏲11am-midnight Sun-Thu, to 1am Fri & Sat) Coop's is an authentic Cajun dive, but more rocked out. Make no mistake: it can be grotty and chaotic, the servers have attitude and the layout is annoying. But it's worth it for the food: rabbit jambalaya or chicken with shrimp and tasso (smoked ham) in a cream sauce – there's no such thing as 'too heavy' here. No patrons under 21.

Mid-City & The Tremé

★Parkway Tavern SANDWICHES $
(☎504-482-3047; www.parkwaypoorboys.com; 538 Hagan Ave, Bayou St John; po'boys $8-14; ⏲11am-10pm Wed-Mon; P 👪) Who makes the best po'boy in New Orleans? Honestly, who can say? But tell a local you think the top sandwich comes from Parkway and you will

get, at the least, a nod of respect. The roast beef in particular – a craft some would say is dying among the great po'boy makers – is messy as hell and twice as good.

★1000 Figs MIDDLE EASTERN $$

(☎504-301-0848; www.1000figs.com; 3141 Ponce de Leon St, Bayou St John; small plates $5-16; ⏰11am-9pm Mon-Sat; ✎) Although the menu isn't exclusively vegetarian, 1000 Figs serves our favorite vegetarian fare in town. The falafel, hummus, baba ghanoush and lentil soup are just *good* – freshly prepared and expertly executed. The dining space is well lit and the seating makes you feel as if you're eating in a best friend's stylish dining room.

Marjie's Grill ASIAN $$

(☎504-603-2234; www.marjiesgrill.com; 320 S Broad St, Mid-City; mains $8-26; ⏰11am-2:30pm & 5-10pm Mon-Fri, 4-10pm Sat) In one word: brilliant. Marjie's is run by chefs who were inspired by Southeast Asian street food, but rather than coming home and doing pale imitations of the real thing, they've turned an old house on Broad St into a corner in Hanoi, Luang Prabang or Chiang Mai. With that said, there's a hint of New Orleans at work.

Willie Mae's Scotch House SOUTHERN US $$

(☎504-822-9503; www.williemaesnola.com; 2401 St Ann St; fried chicken $15; ⏰10am-5pm Mon-Sat) Willie Mae's has been dubbed the best fried chicken in the world by the James Beard Foundation, the Food Network and other media, and in this case, the hype isn't far off – this is superlative fried bird. The white beans are also amazing. The drawback is everyone knows about it, so expect long lines, sometimes around the block.

Faubourg Marigny & Bywater

★Pizza Delicious ITALIAN $

(☎504-676-8482; www.pizzadelicious.com; 617 Piety St, Bywater; pizza slice from $2.25, whole pie from $15; ⏰11am-11pm Tue-Sun; ✎) The thin-crust pies here are done New York–style and taste great. The preparation is simple, but the ingredients are fresh and consistently top-notch. An easy, family-friendly ambience makes for a lovely spot for a casual dinner, and it serves good beer too if you're in the mood. Vegan pizzas are available. The outdoor area is pet-friendly.

St Roch Market MARKET $

(☎504-609-3813; www.strochmarket.com; 2381 St Claude Ave, St Roch; prices vary by vendor; ⏰7am-10pm Sun-Thu, to 11pm Fri & Sat; ✎) The St Roch Market was once the seafood and produce market for a working-class neighborhood. But after it was nearly destroyed by Hurricane Katrina, it was renovated into a shiny food court. The airy interior space now hosts 13 restaurants serving a broad range of food, including crepes, burritos, Haitian cuisine and coffee.

Red's Chinese CHINESE $

(☎504-304-6030; www.redschinese.com; 3048 St Claude Ave, Bywater; mains $5-18; ⏰noon-11pm; ✎) Red's has upped the Chinese cuisine game in New Orleans in a big way. The chefs aren't afraid to add lashings of Louisiana flavor, yet this isn't what we'd call 'fusion' cuisine. The food is grounded deeply in spicy Szechuan flavors, which pair well with the occasional dash of cayenne.

★Bacchanal AMERICAN $$

(☎504-948-9111; www.bacchanalwine.com; 600 Poland Ave, Bywater; mains $8-21, cheese from $6; ⏰11am-midnight Sun-Thu, to 1am Fri & Sat) From the outside, Bacchanal looks like a leaning Bywater shack; inside are racks of wine and stinky-but-sexy cheese. Musicians play in the garden, while cooks dispense delicious meals on paper plates from the kitchen in the back; on any given day you may try chorizo-stuffed dates or seared diver scallops that will blow your gastronomic mind.

N7 TAPAS $$

(www.n7nola.com; 1117 Montegut St, St Roch; small plates $8-23; ⏰6-10pm Mon-Thu, to 11pm Fri & Sat) Dining at N7 is deeply memorable, right down to the dining space. You walk down a potholed road to a garden littered with a vintage French junkyard theme. The food? 'Can to table' – smoked mackerel, habanero oysters etc, along with French and Japanese tapas: escargot tempura, chicken cooked in wine and pork *katsu* (breaded and fried).

CBD & Warehouse District

Cochon Butcher SANDWICHES $

(☎504-588-7675; www.cochonbutcher.com; 930 Tchoupitoulas St, Warehouse District; mains $10-14; ⏰10am-10pm Mon-Thu, to 11pm Fri & Sat, to 4pm Sun) Tucked behind the slightly more formal **Cochon** (☎504-588-2123; www.cochonrestaurant.com; 930 Tchoupitoulas St; small plates $8-14, mains $19-32; ⏰11am-10pm Mon-Thu, to 11pm Fri &

Sat), this sandwich and meat shop calls itself a 'swine bar and deli.' We call it one of our favorite sandwich shops in the city, if not the South. From the convivial lunch crowds to the savory sandwiches to the fun-loving cocktails, this welcoming place encapsulates the best of New Orleans.

★Carmo VEGETARIAN $
(☎504-875-4132; www.cafecarmo.com; 527 Julia St, Warehouse District; lunch $9-12, dinner $9-16; ⏲9am-10pm Mon-Sat;) Carmo isn't just an alternative to the fatty, carnivorous New Orleans menu – it's an excellent restaurant by any gastronomic measuring stick. Both the aesthetic and the food speak to deep tropical influences, from Southeast Asia to South America. Dishes range from pescatarian to full vegan; try Peruvian-style sashimi or Burmese tea-leaf salad and walk away happy.

★Restaurant August CREOLE $$$
(☎504-299-9777; www.restaurantaugust.com; 301 Tchoupitoulas St, CBD; lunch fixed menu $29, dinner mains $34-50; ⏲5-10pm daily, 11am-2pm Mon-Fri;) For a little romance, reserve a table at Restaurant August. This converted 19th-century tobacco warehouse, with its flickering candles and warm, soft shades, earns a nod for most aristocratic dining room in New Orleans, but somehow manages to be both intimate and lively. Delicious meals take you to another level of gastronomic perception.

Garden, Lower Garden & Central City

★Surrey's Juice Bar AMERICAN $
(☎504-524-3828; www.surreysnola.com; 1418 Magazine St, Garden District; mains $6.50-13; ⏲8am-3pm;) Surrey's makes a simple bacon-and-egg sandwich taste – and look – like the most delicious breakfast you've ever been served. And you know what? It probably *is* the best. Boudin biscuits; eggs scrambled with salmon; biscuits swimming in salty sausage gravy; and a shrimp, grits and bacon dish that should be illegal. And the juice, as you might guess, is blessedly fresh.

Commander's Palace CREOLE $$$
(☎504-899-8221; www.commanderspalace.com; 1403 Washington Ave, Garden District; dinner mains $28-46; ⏲11:30am-1pm & 6:30-10:30pm Mon-Fri, from 11am Sat, from 10am Sun) Commander's Palace is a dapper host who wows with white-linen dining rooms, decadent dishes and attentive Southern hospitality. The nouveau Creole menu shifts, running from crispy oysters with brie-cauliflower fondue to pecan-crusted gulf fish. The dress code adds to the charm: no shorts or T-shirts, and jackets preferred at dinner. It's a *very* nice place – and lots of fun.

Drinking & Nightlife

★Bar Tonique COCKTAIL BAR
(☎504-324-6045; www.bartonique.com; 820 N Rampart St; ⏲noon-2am) 'Providing shelter from sobriety since 08/08/08', Tonique is a bartender's bar. Seriously, on a Sunday night, when the weekend rush is over, we've seen no fewer than three of the city's top bartenders arrive here to unwind. This gem mixes some of the best drinks in the city, offering a spirits menu as long as a Tolstoy novel.

★Twelve Mile Limit BAR
(☎504-488-8114; www.facebook.com/twelve.mile.limit; 500 S Telemachus St, Mid-City; ⏲5pm-2am Mon-Fri, 10am-2am Sat, 10am-midnight Sun) Twelve Mile is simply a great bar. It's staffed by people who have the skill, both behind the bar and in the kitchen, to work in four-star spots, but who chose to set up shop in a neighborhood, for a neighborhood. The mixed drinks are excellent, the match of any mixologist's cocktail in Manhattan, and the vibe is super-accepting.

Mimi's in the Marigny BAR
(☎504-872-9868; www.mimismarigny.com; 2601 Royal St, Faubourg Marigny; ⏲11am-late) The name of this bar could justifiably change to 'Mimi's *is* the Marigny' – it's impossible to imagine the neighborhood without this institution. It's an attractively disheveled place, with comfy furniture, pool tables, an upstairs dance hall decorated like a Creole mansion gone punk, and dim lighting like a fantasy in sepia. The bar closes when the bartenders want it to.

Bar Redux BAR
(☎504-592-7083; www.facebook.com/BarRedux; 801 Poland Ave, Bywater; ⏲4pm-2am Sun-Thu, to 3am Fri & Sat) A friendly little bar with an outdoor courtyard that's full of offbeat local art, the sound of the nearby train tracks and lots of live performances, ranging from cabaret to theater and from comedy to music. There's a kitchen on-site slinging decent bar

LGBTIQ+ NEW ORLEANS

Louisiana is a culturally conservative state, but its largest city bucks that trend. New Orleans has always had a reputation for tolerance and remains one of the oldest gay-friendly cities in the Western hemisphere. While local gay history is not without its tragedies – in particular, the arson of the UpStairs Lounge in the French Quarter in the 1970s – there have been pioneering moments as well; the New Orleans city council passed an antidiscrimination ordinance covering the sexual orientation of city workers back in 1991.

Neighborhoods such as the French Quarter and Marigny are major destinations on the LGBTIQ+ travel circuit.

food and a warm, idiosyncratic vibe that's very Bywater.

Courtyard Brewery MICROBREWERY
(www.courtyardbrewing.com; 1020 Erato St, Lower Garden District; ⌚4:30-9:30pm Mon-Wed, 11am-10:30pm Thu-Sat, 11am-9:30pm Sun;) Beyond its home-brewed products, Courtyard also carries a few dozen beers from around the world, and hosts a regular, rotating slate of food trucks. Pets and kids are welcome and have a great time running around; their parents and owners have an even better time.

☆ Entertainment

★Preservation Hall JAZZ
(☎504-522-2841; www.preservationhall.com; 726 St Peter St; cover Sun-Thu $15, Fri & Sat $20, reserved seats $40-50; ⌚showtimes 5pm, 6pm, 8pm, 9pm & 10pm;) Preservation Hall, housed in a former art gallery dating from 1803, is one of New Orleans' most storied live-music venues. The resident performers, the Preservation Hall Jazz Band, are ludicrously talented, and regularly tour the world. 'The Hall' dates from 1961, when Barbara Reid and Grayson 'Ken' Mills formed the Society for the Preservation of New Orleans Jazz.

Spotted Cat LIVE MUSIC
(www.spottedcatmusicclub.com; 623 Frenchmen St, Faubourg Marigny; cover $5-10; ⌚2pm-2am Mon-Fri, noon-2am Sat & Sun) The Cat might just be your sexy dream of a New Orleans jazz club, a thumping sweatbox where drinks are served in plastic cups, impromptu dances break out at the drop of a feathered hat and the music is always exceptional. Fair warning, though, it can get crowded.

★AllWays Lounge THEATER, LIVE MUSIC
(☎504-218-5778; www.theallwayslounge.net; 2240 St Claude Ave; cover $5-10; ⌚6pm-2am Sun-Thu, to 4am Fri & Sat) In a city full of funky music venues, AllWays stands out as one of the funkiest. On any given night of the week you may see experimental guitar, local theater, thrash-y rock, live comedy, burlesque or a '60s-inspired shagadelic dance party. Also, the drinks are super-cheap. A cover fee applies only during shows.

★Tipitina's LIVE MUSIC
(☎504-895-8477; www.tipitinas.com; 501 Napoleon Ave, Uptown; cover $5-20; ⌚8pm-2am) 'Tips,' as locals call it, is one of New Orleans' great musical icons. The legendary Uptown nightclub, which takes its name from Professor Longhair's 1953 hit single, is the site of some of the city's most memorable shows, particularly when big names such as Dr John come home to perform. Outstanding music from local talent packs 'em in year-round.

Fritzel's European Jazz Pub JAZZ
(☎504-586-4800; www.fritzelsjazz.net; 733 Bourbon St; ⌚noon-2am) There's no cover charge at this awesome venue for live jazz, which is so small that you really can't have a bad seat. The seating is kind of rustic: benches and chairs so tightly packed that you'll be apologizing for disturbing people each time you go to the bathroom. But the music is great, so come in for a set.

Shopping

Boutique du Vampyre GIFTS & SOUVENIRS
(☎504-561-8267; www.feelthebite.com; 709 St Ann St; ⌚10am-9pm) This dungeon-esque store stocks all kinds of vampire-themed gifts. Come here for books, curses, spells, souvenirs and witty banter with the awesome clerks who oversee this curious crypt. Among the items is a deck of tarot cards with truly surreal, somewhat disturbing artwork. If your fangs have chipped, their on-call fangsmith can even shape you a new custom pair.

★**Trashy Diva** CLOTHING
(☎504-299-8777; www.trashydiva.com; 2048 Magazine St, Lower Garden District; ⏲noon-6pm Mon-Fri, from 11am Sat, 1-5pm Sun) It isn't really as scandalous as the name suggests, except by Victorian standards. Diva's specialty is sassy 1940s- and '50s-style cinched, hourglass dresses and belle-epoque undergarments – think lots of corsets, lace and such.

The shop also features Kabuki-inspired dresses with embroidered dragons, and retro tops, skirts and shawls reflecting styles plucked from just about every era.

Information

MEDIA

The Advocate (www.nola.com) Broadsheet news and arts coverage.

Gambit (www.theadvocate.com/gambit) Weekly publication that covers arts, culture and music.

The Lens (http://thelensnola.org) Investigative journalism and culture coverage; online only.

New Orleans Magazine (www.myneworleans.com/new-orleans-magazine) Monthly focus on city society.

SAFE TRAVEL

New Orleans has a high crime rate, but the majority of violent crime occurs between parties that already know each other.

- Muggings do occur. Solo travelers are targeted more often; avoid entering secluded areas alone.
- The French Quarter has a high police presence, but there are still lonely blocks near Rampart St and Esplanade Ave. Also, drunken misbehavior can happen anywhere in the Quarter.
- The CBD and Warehouse District are busy on weekdays, but some blocks are relatively deserted at night and on weekends.
- Some areas of Central City can feel lonely after dark. At night, park close to your destination on a well-traveled street.
- Be wary before entering an intersection: local drivers are notorious for running yellow and even red lights.
- Drink spikings do occur. Do not leave your drink unattended.
- If you're staying in an area and want to know what surrounding crime is like, check out www.crimemapping.com/map/la/neworleans.

TOURIST INFORMATION

New Orleans Welcome Center (☎504-568-5661; www.crt.state.la.us/tourism; 529 St Ann St; ⏲8:30am-5pm) In the heart of the French Quarter; offers maps, events listings and brochures for sights, restaurants and hotels.

Getting There & Away

The majority of travelers to New Orleans will arrive by air, landing in **Louis Armstrong New Orleans International Airport** (MSY; ☎504-303-7500; www.flymsy.com; 900 Airline Hwy, Kenner; 📶). The airport was originally named for aviator John Moisant and was known as Moisant Stock Yards, hence the airport code (MSY).

Another option is to fly into Baton Rouge (BTR), 89 miles north of the city, or Gulfport-Biloxi (GPT; ☎228-863-5951; www.flygpt.com; 14035-L Airport Rd, Gulfport), Mississippi, 77 miles east. Neither of these options is as convenient as a direct flight to New Orleans, but they may be cheaper during big events such as Mardi Gras or Jazz Fest.

Many travelers drive or bus to New Orleans, which is located at the crossroads of several major highways. Train travel to New Orleans is also easy; the city is served by major Amtrak lines.

Getting Around

Bicycle Flat New Orleans is easy to cycle – you can cross the entirety of town in 45 minutes.

Bus Services are OK, but try not to time your trip around them. Fares won't run more than $2.

Car This is the easiest way to access outer neighborhoods such as Mid-City. Parking is problematic in the French Quarter and CBD.

Streetcar Service on the charming streetcars is limited. One-way fares cost $1.25, and multi-trip passes are available.

Walk If you're just exploring the French Quarter, your feet will serve just fine.

TO/FROM THE AIRPORT

Louis Armstrong New Orleans International Airport (MSY) Located 13 miles west of New Orleans. A taxi to the CBD costs $36, or $15 per passenger for three or more passengers. Shuttles to the CBD cost $24/44 per person one way/return. The E2 bus takes you to Carrollton and Tulane Ave in Mid-City for $2. It's about a five-minute walk to the airport rental car facility from the main terminal.

Amtrak & Greyhound Adjacent to each other downtown on Loyola Ave. You can walk to the CBD or French Quarter, but don't do so at night, or if you have heavy luggage. A taxi from here to the French Quarter should cost around $10; further afield you'll be pressed to spend more than $20.

Around New Orleans

Leaving colorful New Orleans behind quickly catapults you into a world of swamps, bayous, antebellum plantation homes, laid-back small communities and miles of bedroom suburbs and strip malls.

Barataria Preserve

★Barataria Preserve PARK
(parking lot for trails 9am-5pm) FREE This section of the Jean Lafitte National Historical Park and Preserve, south of New Orleans near the town of Marrero (and Crown Point), provides the easiest access to the dense swamplands that ring New Orleans. The 8 miles of boardwalk trails are a stunning way to tread lightly through the swamp, but sadly, the area's wildlife – which does include plenty of alligators – can be tough to spot due to the proliferation of invasive water hyacinth.

Start at the **National Park Service Visitor Center** (NPS; 504-689-3690; www.nps.gov/jela; 6588 Barataria Blvd, Marrero; 9:30am-4:30pm Wed-Sun), 1 mile west of Hwy 45 off the Barataria Blvd exit, where you can pick up a map or join a guided wetland walk or canoe trip (call for more information). To rent canoes or kayaks for a tour or an independent paddle, go to **Bayou Barn** (504-689-2663; www.bayoubarn.com; 7145 Barataria Blvd, Marrero; canoe/kayak hire per person $20/25; 10am-6pm Thu-Sun) about 3 miles from the park entrance.

The North Shore

The north shore of Lake Pontchartrain is a collection of middle-to-upper-class New Orleans bedroom suburbs. Nearby, the bucolic village of Abita Springs was popular in the late 19th century for its curative waters. Today spring water still flows from a fountain in the center of the village, but more importantly for many residents, beer still bubbles from the Abita Brewery, the largest regional beer producer in Louisiana. The entirety of this region is separated from New Orleans by Lake Pontchartrain, which is spanned by the Lake Pontchartrain Causeway – at almost 24 miles long, the enormous bridge is a sight in itself.

River Road

Elaborate plantation homes dot the east and west banks of the Mississippi River between New Orleans and Baton Rouge. First indigo, then cotton and sugarcane brought great wealth to the plantation owners; today, many plantations are open to the public. Most tours focus on the lives of the owners, the restored architecture and the ornate gardens of antebellum Louisiana.

Sights

★Whitney Plantation HISTORIC SITE
(225-265-3300; www.whitneyplantation.com; 5099 Hwy 18, Wallace; adult/student/child under 6yr $23/10/free; museum 9:30am-4:30pm Wed-Mon, tours hourly 10am-3pm; P) The Whitney is the first plantation in the state to focus on slavery, and in doing so they've flipped the script on plantation tours. Whereas before the story told was that of the 'big house,' here the emphasis is given to the hundreds who died to keep the residents of the big house comfortable. There's a museum on-site that you can self-tour, but admission to the plantation is by 1½-hour guided tour only.

Laura Plantation HISTORIC SITE
(225-265-7690; www.lauraplantation.com; 2247 Hwy 18, Vacherie; adult/student 13-17yr/child $25/15/10; 10am-4pm; P) This ever-evolving and popular plantation tour teases out the distinctions between Creole, Anglo, free and enslaved African Americans via meticulous research and the written records of the Creole women who ran the place for generations. Laura is also fascinating because it was a *Creole* mansion, founded and maintained by a continental European–descended elite, as opposed to Anglo Americans; the cultural and architectural distinctions between this and other plantations is obvious and striking.

Tours are offered here in English or French.

River Road African American Museum MUSEUM
(225-474-5553; http://africanamericanmuseum.org; 406 Charles St, Donaldsonville; $10; 10am-5pm Wed-Sat; P) Learn about the region's African American history, including the truth about slave ships, the vicious toils of slavery, slave revolts, the Underground Railroad, reconstruction and Jim Crow laws.

Exhibits include antiques, artifacts, photographs and video interviews.

St Francisville

Lush St Francisville is the quintessential Southern artsy small town, a blend of historical homes, bohemian shops and outdoor activities courtesy of the nearby Tunica Hills (you read that right – hills in Louisiana). During the antebellum years (pre–Civil War) this was home to plantation millionaires, and much of the architecture these aristocrats built is still intact, forming a historic core that has magnetized tourists for over a century.

Sights & Activities

Myrtles Plantation HISTORIC BUILDING
(☎225-635-6277; www.myrtlesplantation.com; 7747 Hwy 61 N; tours adult/child $15/12, night tours $15; ⏰9am-4:30pm, evening tours 6pm, 7pm & 8pm Fri & Sat; P) Owners and docents alike perpetuate the idea that Myrtles is one of the most haunted houses in America. And hey, this place is certifiably creepy. Tours paint a vivid picture of life during the plantation era, with a hybrid focus on the history of the building on the one hand, and the spookier intrigue and ghost stories that have become synonymous with the Myrtles brand on the other.

Oakley Plantation & Audubon State Historic Site HISTORIC SITE
(☎225-635-3739; www.crt.state.la.us; 11788 Hwy 965; adult/student $10/5; ⏰9am-5pm Wed-Sun; P) Outside of St Francisville, this is where naturalist John James Audubon spent his tenure, arriving in 1821 to tutor the owner's daughter. Though his assignment lasted only four months (and his room was pretty spartan), he and his assistant finished 32 paintings of birds found in the plantation's surrounding forest.

The small West Indies–influenced house (1806) includes several original Audubon prints.

Mary Ann Brown Preserve NATURE RESERVE
(☎225-338-1040; www.nature.org; 13515 Hwy 965; ⏰sunrise-sunset; P) FREE Operated by the Nature Conservancy, the 110-acre Mary Ann Brown Preserve takes in some of the beech woodlands, dark wetlands and low, clay-soil hill country of the Tunica uplands. A 2-mile series of trails and boardwalks crosses the woods – the same trees that John James Audubon tramped around when he began work on *Birds of America*.

Sleeping

3-V Tourist Court INN $
(☎225-721-7003; www.themagnoliacafe.net; 5687 Commerce St; 1-/2-bedroom cabin $75/140; P 📶) One of the oldest motor inns in the USA – started in the 1930s and now on the National Register of Historic Places. The five units here take you back to simpler times. Rooms have period decorations and fixtures, though renovations have upgraded the beds, hardwood floors and flat-screen TVs into trendy territory.

Shadetree Inn B&B $$
(☎225-635-6116; www.shadetreeinn.com; 9704 Royal St; r $165-215; P 📶) Edging the historic district and a bird sanctuary, this super-cozy B&B has a gorgeous flower-strewn, hammock-hung courtyard and spacious but rustic upscale rooms. A deluxe continental breakfast can be served in your room, and is included along with a bottle of wine or champagne. Rates drop if you cut out breakfast and stay midweek.

Eating & Drinking

Magnolia Café CAFE $
(☎225-635-6528; www.themagnoliacafe.net; 5687 Commerce St; mains $8-16; ⏰10am-4pm daily, to 9pm Thu & Sat, to 10pm Fri) The Magnolia Café was once a health-food store and VW-bus repair shop. Today it's the nucleus of what's happening in St Francisville – it's where people go to eat, socialize and, on Friday night, dance to live music. Try the cheesy shrimp po'boy.

Birdman Coffee & Books CAFE
(☎225-635-3665; 5695 Commerce St; mains $5-8; ⏰7am-5pm Tue-Fri, 8am-2pm Sat, 8am-noon Sun; 📶) Birdman is *the* spot for strong coffee, acoustic live music several times a month, delicious baked goods and local art – both via paintings and exposure to the local arts community that makes said paintings.

Getting There & Away

St Francisville lies about 35 miles north of Baton Rouge on Hwy 61, which winds right through town.

Cajun Country

When people think of Louisiana, this – and New Orleans – is the image that comes to mind: miles of bayou, sawdust-strewn shacks, a unique take on French and lots of good food. Welcome to Cajun Country, also called Acadiana for the French settlers exiled from L'Acadie (now Nova Scotia, Canada) by the British in 1755. Cajuns are the largest French-speaking minority in the USA, and while you may not hear French spoken at the grocery store, it's still present in radio shows, church services and the singsong lilt of local English accents.

It's largely a socially conservative region, but the Cajuns also have a well-deserved reputation for hedonism. It's hard to find a bad meal here; jambalaya (a rice-based dish with tomatoes, sausage and shrimp) and crawfish étouffée are prepared slowly with pride, and if folks aren't fishing, they're probably dancing. Don't expect to sit on the sidelines...*allons danson* (let's dance).

Lafayette

The term 'undiscovered gem' gets thrown around too much in travel writing, but Lafayette really fits the bill. On Sunday this town is deader than a cemetery, but for the rest of the week there's an entirely fantastic amount of good eating to be done and lots of music venues – this is a university town so bands are rocking almost any night. One of the best free music festivals in the country is also held here. Heck, even those quiet Sundays have a saving grace: some famously delicious brunch options.

Sights

Vermilionville MUSEUM

(337-233-4077; www.vermilionville.org; 300 Fisher Rd; adult/student $10/6, 90min boat tour $12/8; 10am-4pm Tue-Sun;) This tranquil, recreated 19th-century Cajun village wends along the bayou near the airport. Friendly, enthusiastic costumed docents explain Cajun, Creole and Native American history, and local bands or dance-hall-esque events go off on Sunday (1pm to 4pm). Guided boat tours of Bayou Vermilion are also offered at 10:30am Tuesday to Saturday in spring and fall; you can combine a boat tour with a buffet lunch and a visit to Vermilionville for $31.50/27.50 per adult/child.

Acadian Village MUSEUM

(337-981-2364; www.acadianvillage.org; 200 Greenleaf Dr; adult/student $9/7; 10am-4pm Mon-Sat Jan-Oct, 5:30-9pm Dec, closed Nov;) At the understated, educational Acadian Village, you follow a brick path around a rippling bayou to restored houses, craftsman barns and a church. Old-timers sometimes still hang out here, regaling visitors with Cajun songs and stories from days gone by. The village becomes a Christmas light extravaganza in December, when it is open every evening, weather permitting.

Festivals & Events

★ Festival International de Louisiane MUSIC

(www.festivalinternational.org) At the fabulous Festival International de Louisiane, hundreds of local and international artists rock out for five days over the last weekend in April, in the largest free music festival of its caliber in the USA. Although 'Festival' avowedly celebrates Francophone music and culture, the event's remit has grown to accommodate world music in all its iterations and languages.

Sleeping & Eating

★ Blue Moon Guest House GUESTHOUSE $

(337-234-2422; www.bluemoonpresents.com; 215 E Convent St; dm $23-45, r $75-95;) This tidy home is one of Louisiana's best travel finds: an upscale hostel-like hangout within walking distance from downtown. Snag a bed and you're on the guest list for Lafayette's most popular down-home music venue, located in the backyard. The friendly owners, full kitchen and camaraderie create a unique music-meets-migration environment catering to backpackers, flashpackers and those in transition (flashbackpackers?).

Buchanan Lofts APARTMENT $$

(337-534-4922; www.buchananlofts.com; 403 S Buchanan St; r per night $190-220, per week $1000-1200;) These uberhip lofts have a Manhattan vibe, or would if they weren't so big. Doused in contemporary-cool art and design – all fruits of the friendly owner's globetrotting – the extra-spacious units come with kitchenettes and are awash with exposed brick and hardwoods.

★ French Press BREAKFAST $

(337-233-9449; www.facebook.com/frenchpresslaf; 214 E Vermillion St; mains $9-15; 7am-2pm Mon-Fri, from 9am Sat & Sun;) This French Cajun hybrid is one of the best culinary things going in Lafayette. Breakfast is mind-blowing, with a sinful Cajun Benedict (boudin instead of ham), cheddar grits (that will kill you dead) and organic granola (to offset the grits). Lunch ain't half bad either; the 'Buffalo Bill,' with fried seafood, blue cheese and hot sauce, is gorgeously decadent.

★**Johnson's Boucanière** CAJUN $

(☎337-269-8878; www.johnsonsboucaniere.com; 1111 St John St; mains $4.25-10; ⊙7am-3pm Tue-Fri, to 5:30pm Sat; 🐾) This 70-year-old smoker business turns out detour-worthy boudin (Cajun-style pork-and-rice sausage), an unstoppable smoked-pork-brisket sandwich topped with smoked sausage, smoked garlic sausage that will set your mouth to watering, pulled pork stuffed into grilled cheese biscuits (!), and dozens of other delicious variations on the theme of meat, meat and by God, more meat.

Social Southern Table SOUTHERN US $$

(☎337-456-3274; www.socialsouthern.com; 3901 Johnston St; mains $12-36; ⊙11am-10pm Tue-Sat, 10:30am-2pm Sun) The hip culinary crowd out in Acadiana pack into Social to feast on fried chicken 'n' biscuits, wild mushroom flatbreads, and local vegetables drenched in curry, among other delights. This isn't the first restaurant to elevate Southern staples, but it's doing so at a level beyond most of the competition.

☆ Entertainment

★**Blue Moon Saloon** LIVE MUSIC

(☎337-234-2422; www.bluemoonpresents.com; 215 E Convent St; cover $5-15; ⊙showtimes vary) This intimate venue on the back porch of the accompanying guesthouse is what Louisiana is all about: good music, good people and good beer. Everyone dances, eats well and gets pleasantly buzzed. What's not to love? Music tends to go off Wednesday to Saturday, usually around 8pm or 9pm.

Artmosphere LIVE MUSIC

(☎337-233-3331; www.artmosphere.vpweb.com; 902 Johnston St; ⊙11am-2am Mon-Sat, to midnight Sun) There's a deep counterculture vein running within Lafayette, a sort of bohemian backlash to the area's prevailing Christian conservatism, and this radical community finds a home (and performance venue) in Artmosphere. With walls of graffiti, hookahs, hipsters and an edgy lineup of acts, this spot feels more CBGBs than Cajun dance hall, although really, it blends both concepts.

ℹ Information

Visitors Center (☎337-232-3737; www.lafayettetravel.com; 1400 NW Evangeline Thruway; ⊙8:30am-5pm Mon-Fri, from 9am Sat & Sun) Helpful staff with French speakers.

ℹ Getting There & Away

From I-10, exit 103A, the Evangeline Thruway (Hwy 167) goes to the center of town. **Greyhound** (☎337-235-1541; www.greyhound.com; 100 Lee Ave) operates from a hub beside the central commercial district, making several runs daily to New Orleans (from $23, 3½ hours) and Baton Rouge (from $11, one hour). The **Amtrak** (www.amtrak.com; 100 Lee Ave) *Sunset Limited* service, which runs between New Orleans and Los Angeles, stops in Lafayette.

Cajun Wetlands

In 1755, the Grand Dérangement, the British expulsion of rural French settlers from Acadiana (now Nova Scotia, New Brunswick, Prince Edward Island and parts of Quebec, Canada), created a homeless population of Acadians who searched for decades for a place to settle. Some went to other British colonies, where the Catholic exiles were often rejected on religious grounds. Some returned to France, where they were denied the rights to land ownership and autonomy they had obtained in the New World.

In 1785 seven boatloads of Acadian exiles arrived in New Orleans, seeking a better life in a corner of the Western Hemisphere that was still culturally, if not politically, French (at the time Louisiana was ruled by the Spanish). By the early 19th century, 3000 to 4000 Acadians occupied the swamplands southwest of New Orleans. Native American tribes such as the Atakapas helped them learn to eke out a living based on fishing and trapping, and those practices are still near and dear to the hearts of many descendants of the Acadians, now known as the Cajuns.

For decades this was one of the poorest parts of Louisiana, an area where French-language education was repressed and infrastructure was dire. This situation largely changed thanks to an increase in Cajun political influence within Louisiana state government in the 1970s, and the presence of the oil and gas industry. While canal and pipeline dredging has been deemed a culprit in the continuing saga of Louisiana land loss, the jobs and economic revitalization that came with oil-industry jobs is undeniable. This goes some way toward explaining the enduring popularity of the oil and gas sectors in the state, culminating in

WORTH A TRIP

THE TAO OF FRED'S

Deep in the heart of Cajun country, Mamou is a typical South Louisiana small town six days of the week, worth a peek and a short stop before rolling on to nearby Eunice. But on Saturday morning, Mamou's hometown hangout, little **Fred's Lounge** (337-468-5411; 420 6th St, Mamou; 8am-2pm Sat), becomes the apotheosis of a Cajun dance hall.

This small place gets more than a little crowded on Saturdays, when the staff host a Francophone-friendly music morning, with bands, beer and dancing. Doors open around 8am and the place is usually packed by the time the music starts around 9am. Back in the day, owner Tante Sue herself would take to the stage to dispense wisdom and songs in Cajun French, all while taking pulls from a bottle of brown liquor she kept in a pistol holster. She has since passed, but something of her amazing, anarchic energy has been imbued into the very bricks of this place.

events such as – no kidding – Morgan City's annual Shrimp & Petroleum Festival.

Sights

Lake Martin BIRD SANCTUARY
(Lake Martin Rd; 24hr) FREE This lake – a mossy green dollop surrounded by thin trees and cypress trunks – serves as a wonderful, easily accessible introduction to bayou landscapes. A few walking paths, as well as a boardwalk, take visitors over the mirror-reflection sheen of the swamp, while overhead thousands of great and cattle egrets and blue herons perch in haughty indifference.

It's about 5 miles south of Breaux Bridge.

Louisiana Universities Marine Consortium NATURE CENTER
(LUMCON; 985-851-2800; www.lumcon.edu; 8124 Hwy 56, Chauvin; 8am-4pm;) FREE LUMCON? Sounds like something out of a science fiction novel, right? Well, there is science here, but it's all fact, and still fascinating. LUMCON is one of the premier research facilities dedicated to the Gulf of Mexico. At the consortium's DeFelice Marine Center, there are nature trails running through hairy tufts of grassy marsh, several small aquariums, and an observation tower offering unbeatable views of the great swaths of flat, fuzzy wetlands that make up the south Louisiana coast.

Getting There & Away

Greyhound buses stop in Thibodaux and Lafayette. Otherwise, the region is easily accessed via I-10, which cuts across Louisiana like a belt.

Cajun Prairie

Dancing cowboys? Works for us. Cajun and African American settlers in the higher, drier terrain north of Lafayette developed a culture based around animal husbandry and farming, and the 10-gallon hat still rules. In many ways, this region is a blend of both South Louisiana and East Texas.

Physically, this truly is prairie: wide expanses of green flatlands, broken up by rice and crawfish ponds. This is the heartland of zydeco music; come evening, keep your ears peeled for the accordion, fiddle and distinctive 'zzzzzzzzip' sound of the *frottoir*, a corrugated metal vest that is played as its own percussion instrument.

Eunice and **Opelousas** are the major towns in the prairie, but you'll also find interesting diversions in **Mamou** and **Ville Platte**.

Sights

Chicot State Park STATE PARK
(337-363-2403; www.crt.louisiana.gov; 3469 Chicot Park Rd, Ville Platte; $3; 6am-9pm Sun-Thu, to 10pm Fri & Sat;) A wonderful place to access the natural beauty of Cajun country. The excellent arboretum is fun for kids and informative for adults, and deserves enormous accolades for its open, airy design. Miles of trails extend into the nearby forests, cypress swamps and wetlands. If you can, stay for early evening – the sunsets over the Spanish-moss-draped trees that fringe Lake Chicot are superb.

Prairie Acadian Cultural Center MUSEUM
(337-457-8499; www.nps.gov/jela; 250 Park Ave, Eunice; 9:30am-4:30pm Wed-Fri, to 6pm Sat) FREE This NPS-run museum has exhibits on rural life and Cajun culture, and shows a variety of documentaries explaining the history of the area. It's the perfect place to begin your exploration of the Cajun Prairie. There's a full slate of events and activities on offer, including music and food demonstrations and Cajun French–language lessons – call ahead or check online for a schedule.

Sleeping & Eating

★Le Village B&B **$$**

(☎337-457-3573; www.levillagehouse.com; 121 Seale Lane, Eunice; r $125-185; P 📶) This cute spot is a typically pretty rural B&B, but where many places opt for wedding-cake frilly decor, Le Village is stocked with a tasteful collection of rustic, often Cajun-derived folk art. If you need space, there's an entire cottage available for rent. Prices drop significantly over the weekend. A two-night minimum stay is required.

Billy's Boudin & Cracklins CAJUN **$**

(☎337-942-9150; http://billysboudin.com; 904 Short Vine St, Opelousas; boudin per lb $9; ⊙7:30am-6pm Mon-Fri, 8am-5pm Sat, 8am-2pm Sun) Folks will literally drive for hours, sometimes crossing state lines, to grab some of Billy's goods. Most folks treat this as a takeout counter, but there's a seating area and some coolers where you can snag a cold drink. There's cracklin', which is amazing, and some other pork products as well.

Getting There & Away

Lafayette makes a good base for exploring the Cajun Prairie. There's a **Greyhound stop** in Opelousas (227 US-167) that has buses to Lafayette (from $14, 30 minutes) and New Orleans (from $35, three hours 40 minutes). The heart of the Cajun Prairie can best be accessed via I-49 or LA 13.

Florida

Includes ➡

Miami 453
Fort Lauderdale 470
The Everglades 477
Florida Keys 482
Atlantic Coast 488
Space Coast............... 488
Daytona Beach 490
Jacksonville 493
Tampa 496
Orlando 504
Florida Panhandle....... 511
Tallahassee 511
Pensacola 513

Best Places to Eat

- Ulele (p498)
- La Luce (p505)
- Kyu (p468)
- Cress (p511)

Best Places to Sleep

- 1 Hotel (p466)
- Hotel Palms (p494)
- Biltmore Hotel (p467)
- W Fort Lauderdale (p472)
- Hoosville Hostel (p480)

Why Go?

For countless visitors Florida is a place of promises: of eternal youth, sun, relaxation, clear skies, space, success, escape, prosperity and, for the kids, a chance to meet much-loved Disney characters in person.

No other state in America is as built on tourism, and tourism here comes in a thousand facets: cartoon mice, *Miami Vice*, country fried oysters, Spanish villas, gators kicking footballs, gators prowling golf courses, and of course, the beach. So. Much. Beach.

Don't think Florida is all marketing, though. This is one of the most genuinely fascinating states in the country. It's as if someone shook the nation and tipped it over, filling this sun-bleached peninsula with immigrants, country boys, Jews, Cubans, military bases, shopping malls and a subtropical wilderness laced with crystal ponds and sugary sand.

Florida means almost anything: amusement kingdoms, Latin and Caribbean capitals, wild wetlands, artist colonies, and wild surf beaches. This vast, flat peninsula has it all.

When to Go

Miami

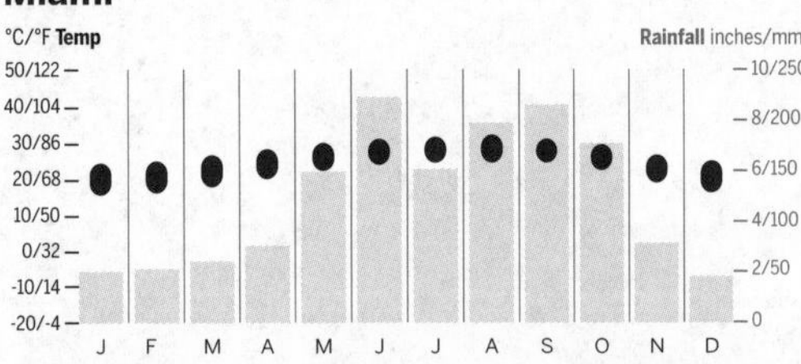

Mar–Aug Hot, humid high season sees busy theme parks; beaches peak in summer.

Oct–Dec Beach towns are quiet until winter snowbirds arrive.

Feb & Sep Shoulder season sees the region less crowded but still hot.

SOUTH FLORIDA

Once you head far enough south in Florida, you're no longer in 'the South' as a regional entity – you've slipped those bonds into South Florida, which is truly a hybrid of the USA, the Caribbean and Latin America. Miami is the area's beating urban heart and one of the few truly international cities in the country. Wealthy oceanfront communities stretch from the Palm Beaches to Fort Lauderdale, while inland, the dreamscape of the Everglades, the state's most unique, dynamic wilderness, await. And when the state's peninsula ends, it doesn't truly end, but rather stretches into the Overseas Hwy which leads across hundreds of mangrove islands to colorful Key West.

Miami

Even if there was no beach, Miami would still have undeniable allure. The gorgeous 1930s hotels lining Ocean Dr are part of the world's greatest collection of art deco buildings. Tropical motifs, whimsical nautical elements and those iconic pastel shades create a cinematic backdrop for exploring the streets of Miami Beach. Of course, you don't have to see these architectural beauties at arm's length. Lavishly restored, Miami's art deco and mid-century-modern hotels are also the playground for locals and out-of-towners alike, with sunny poolside terraces, artfully designed dining rooms and plush nightclubs.

Chalk it up to Miami's diverse population, or perhaps its love of always being on the cutting edge. Whatever the reason, creativity is one of the great hallmarks of this city. From art and design to global cuisine, Miami remains ever on the search for bold new ideas, which manifest themselves in surprising ways. You'll find brilliantly inventive chefs blending Eastern and Western cooking styles, sustainably designed buildings inspired by South Florida ecosystems and open-air galleries where museum-quality artwork covers once-derelict warehouses. The one constant in Miami is its uncanny ability to astonish.

History

It's always been the weather that's attracted Miami's two most prominent species: developers and tourists. But it wasn't the sun per se that got people moving here – it was an ice storm. The great Florida freeze of 1895 wiped out the state's citrus industry; at the same time, widowed Julia Tuttle bought out parcels of land that would become modern Miami, and Henry Flagler was building his Florida East Coast Railroad. Tuttle offered to split her land with Flagler if he extended the railway to Miami, but the train man didn't pay her any heed until north Florida froze over and Tuttle sent him an 'I told you so' message: an orange blossom clipped from her Miami garden.

The rest is a history of boom, bust, dreamers and opportunists. Generally, Miami has grown in leaps and bounds following major world events and natural disasters. Hurricanes (particularly the deadly Great Miami Hurricane of 1926) have wiped away the town, but it just keeps bouncing and building back better than before. In the late 19th and early 20th centuries, Miami earned a reputation for attracting design and city-planning mavericks such as George Merrick, who fashioned the artful Mediterranean village of Coral Gables, and James Deering, designer of the fairy-tale Vizcaya mansion.

Sights

Miami's major sights aren't concentrated in one neighborhood. The most frequently visited area is South Beach, home to hot nightlife, beautiful beaches and art deco hotels, but you'll find historic sites and museums in the Downtown area, street art in Wynwood and galleries in the Design District, old-fashioned hotels and eateries in Mid-Beach (in Miami Beach), more beaches on Key Biscayne, and peaceful neighborhood attractions in Coral Gables and Coconut Grove.

Water and income – canals, bays and bank accounts – are the geographic and social boundaries that divide Miami. Of course, the great water that divides here is Biscayne Bay, holding the city of Miami apart from its preening sibling Miami Beach (along with the fine feathers of South Beach). Don't forget, as many do, that Miami Beach is not Miami's beach, but its own distinct town.

South Beach

South Beach (SoBe) is everything Miami is known for – the sparkling beach, beautiful art-deco architecture, top-end boutiques and buzzing bars and restaurants. South Beach has its glamour, but there's more to this district than just velvet ropes and high-priced

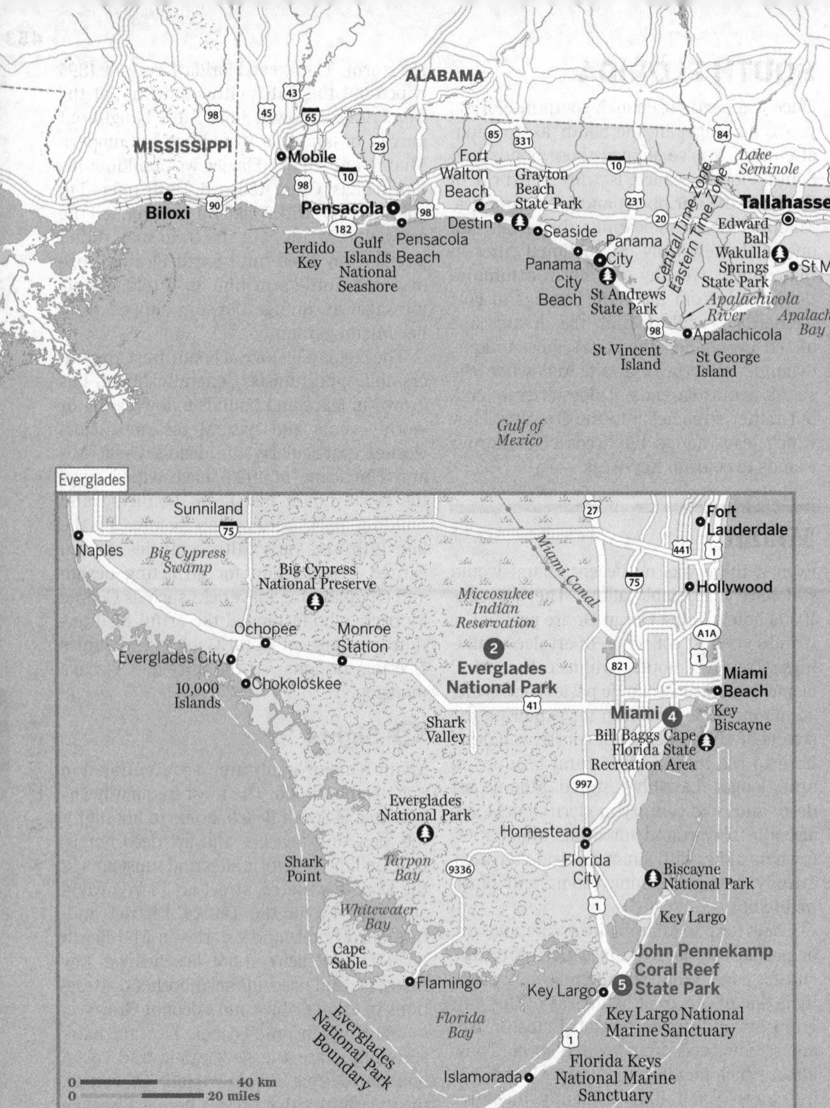

Florida Highlights

1. **Mallory Square** (p485) Joining the sunset bacchanal in Key West.
2. **Everglades National Park** (p478) Paddling among alligators and sawgrass in the Everglades.
3. **Walt Disney World® Resort** (p506) Being swept up in nostalgia and thrill rides in Orlando.
4. **Wynwood Walls** (p461) Marvelling at mural after mural in Miami.
5. **John Pennekamp Coral Reef State Park** (p482) Snorkelling the

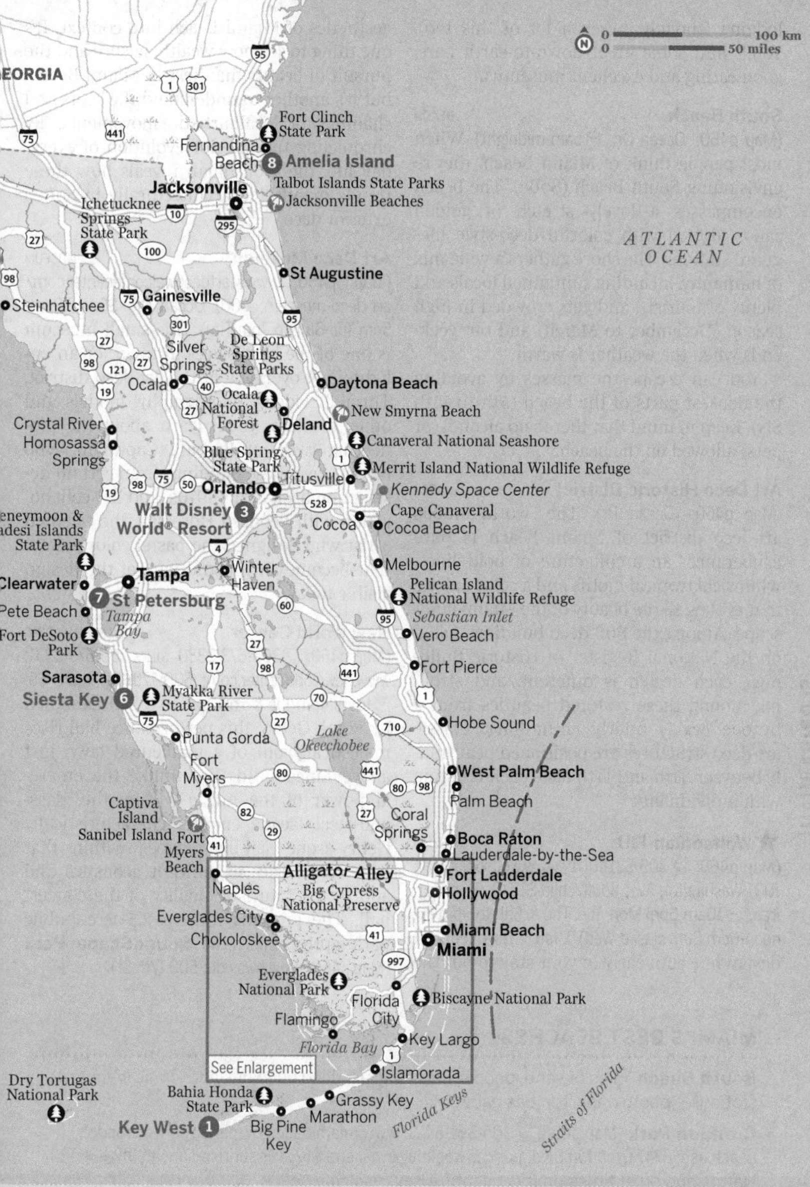

continental USA's most extensive coral reef.

6 Siesta Key (p500) Relaxing on these sugar sand beaches, in Sarasota.

7 Salvador Dali Museum (p499) Pondering the symbolism of the *Hallucinogenic Toreador* in St Petersburg.

8 Amelia Island (p495) Taking a breather among the greenery of this historic island near the Georgia border.

lodging (though there's a lot of this too). You'll find some great down-to-earth bars, good eating and excellent museums.

South Beach BEACH

(Map p460; Ocean Dr; ⏲5am-midnight) When most people think of Miami Beach, they're envisioning South Beach (SoBe). The beach encompasses a lovely stretch of golden sands, dotted with colorful deco-style lifeguard stations. The shore gathers a wide mix of humanity, including suntanned locals and plenty of tourists, and gets crowded in high season (December to March) and on weekends when the weather is warm.

You can escape the masses by avoiding the densest parts of the beach (5th to 15th Sts). Keep in mind that there's no alcohol (or pets) allowed on the beach.

Art Deco Historic District AREA

(Map p460; Ocean Dr) The world-famous art-deco district of Miami Beach is pure exuberance: an architecture of bold lines, whimsical tropical motifs and a color palette that evokes all the beauty of the Miami landscape. Among the 800 deco buildings listed on the National Register of Historic Buildings, each design is different, and strolling among these restored beauties from a bygone era is utterly enthralling. Classic art-deco structures are positioned beautifully between 11th and 14th Sts – each bursting with individuality.

★Wolfsonian-FIU MUSEUM

(Map p460; ☎305-531-1001; www.wolfsonian.org; 1001 Washington Ave; adult/child $12/8, 6-9pm Fri free; ⏲10am-6pm Mon, Tue, Thu & Sat, to 9pm Fri, noon-6pm Sun, closed Wed) Visit this excellent design museum early in your stay to put the aesthetics of Miami Beach into context. It's one thing to see how wealth, leisure and the pursuit of beauty manifest in Miami Beach, but it's another to understand the roots and shadings of local artistic movements. By chronicling the interior evolution of everyday life, the Wolfsonian reveals how these trends manifested architecturally in SoBe's exterior deco.

Art Deco Museum MUSEUM

(Map p460; www.artdecowelcomecenter.com/art-deco-museum; 1001 Ocean Dr; $5; ⏲9am-5pm Tue-Sun, to 7pm Thu) This small museum is one of the best places in town for an enlightening overview of the art-deco district. Through videos, photography, models and other displays, you'll learn about the pioneering work of Barbara Capitman, who helped save these buildings from certain destruction back in the 1970s, and her collaboration with Leonard Horowitz, the talented artist who designed the pastel color palette that become an integral part of the design visible today.

New World Center NOTABLE BUILDING

(Map p460; ☎305-673-3330, tours 305-673-3331; www.newworldcenter.com; 500 17th St; tours $5; ⏲tours 4pm Tue & Thu, 1pm Fri & Sat) Designed by Frank Gehry, this performance hall rises majestically out of a manicured lawn just above Lincoln Rd. Not unlike the ethereal power of the music within, the glass-and-steel facade encases characteristically Gehry-esque sail-like shapes within that help create the magnificent acoustics and add to the futuristic quality of the concert hall. The grounds form a 2.5-acre public park aptly known as **SoundScape Park** (Map p460; www.nws.edu; 500 17th St).

MIAMI'S BEST BEACHES

South Beach Miles of sand, people watching, art deco buildings and iconic lifeguard stations – photo opportunities galore!

Crandon Park (Map p458; ☎305-361-5421; www.miamidade.gov/parks/parks/crandon_beach.asp; 6747 Crandon Blvd; per car weekday/weekend $5/7; ⏲sunrise-sunset; P) Nature and quiet times on this beautiful Key Biscayne beach.

Haulover Beach Park (Map p458; ☎305-947-3525; www.miamidade.gov/parks/haulover.asp; 10800 Collins Ave; per car Mon-Fri $5, Sat-Sun $7; ⏲sunrise-sunset; P) In North Beach, Haulover provides privacy and tranquility for nudists and clothed bathers alike.

Bill Baggs Cape Florida State Park (p463) A picture-perfect lighthouse and miles of sand on Key Biscayne's southern end.

Boardwalk North Beach's stretch of gorgeous beach with a laid-back, real-world vibe.

MIAMI IN...

Two Days

Focus your first day on South Beach. Bookend an afternoon of sunning and swimming with a walking tour through the Art Deco Historic District and a visit to Wolfsonian-FIU, which explains it all. When the sun fades, head to Yardbird (p467) where southern comfort cooking gets a Miami foodie makeover.

Next morning, shop for Cuban music at Exquisito Restaurant (p468). Go for a stroll at Vizcaya Museum & Gardens (p462), then enjoy the tropical ambience and exceptional food at 27 Restaurant (p467) before sipping cocktails at Broken Shaker (p468).

Four Days

Follow the two-day itinerary, then head to the Everglades (p478) on day three and jump in a kayak. For your last day, immerse yourself in art and design in Wynwood (p461) and the Design District (p461), followed by a visit to the Museum of Contemporary Art North Miami (p463). In the evening, join the party at Sweet Liberty (p469).

North Beach

If you're after fewer people along a gorgeous strip of sand that more than matches South Beach, then North Beach is for you. Instead of art deco, you'll find the so-called MiMo (Miami Modern) style, of grand buildings constructed in the post-WWII boom days. Although it has fewer restaurants, bars and shops, there's good quality eating and drinking here, and a colourful and strong local community.

Boardwalk BEACH

(Map p458; www.miamibeachboardwalk.com; 21st St–46th St) Posing is what many people do best in Miami, and there are plenty of skimpily dressed hotties on the Mid-Beach boardwalk, but there are also middle-class Latinos and Jews, who walk their dogs and play with their kids here, giving the entire place a laid-back, real-world vibe that contrasts with the nonstop glamour of South Beach.

Eden Roc Renaissance HISTORIC BUILDING

(Map p458; www.nobuedenroc.com; 4525 Collins Ave) The Eden Roc was the second groundbreaking resort from Morris Lapidus, and it's a fine example of the architecture known as MiMo. It was the hangout for the 1960s Rat Pack – Sammy Davis Jr, Dean Martin, Frank Sinatra and crew. Extensive renovation has eclipsed some of Lapidus' style, but with that said, the building is still an iconic piece of Miami Beach architecture, and an exemplar of the brash beauty of Millionaire's Row.

Fontainebleau HISTORIC BUILDING

(Map p458; www.fontainebleau.com; 4441 Collins Ave) As you proceed north on Collins, the condos and apartment buildings grow in grandeur and embellishment until you enter an area nicknamed Millionaire's Row. The most fantastic jewel in this glittering crown is the Fontainebleau hotel. The pool here, which has since been renovated, features in Brian de Palma's classic *Scarface*.

Downtown Miami

Most of the sights in Downtown are on the north side of the river. While you can walk between a few highlights, it's handy to use Metromover, the free trolley, or a Citi Bike when you really need to cover some ground.

★HistoryMiami MUSEUM

(Map p458; ☎305-375-1492; www.historymiami.org; 101 W Flagler St; adult/child $10/5; ⏰10am-5pm Tue-Sat, from noon Sun; 👪) South Florida – a land of escaped slaves, guerrilla Native Americans, gangsters, land grabbers, pirates, tourists, drug dealers and alligators – has a special history, and it takes a special kind of museum to capture that narrative. This highly recommended place, located in the Miami-Dade Cultural Center, does just that, weaving together the stories of the region's successive waves of population, from Native Americans to Nicaraguans.

Pérez Art Museum Miami MUSEUM

(PAMM; Map p458; ☎305-375-3000; www.pamm.org; 1103 Biscayne Blvd; adult/senior & student $16/12, 1st Thu & 2nd Sat of month free;

Greater Miami

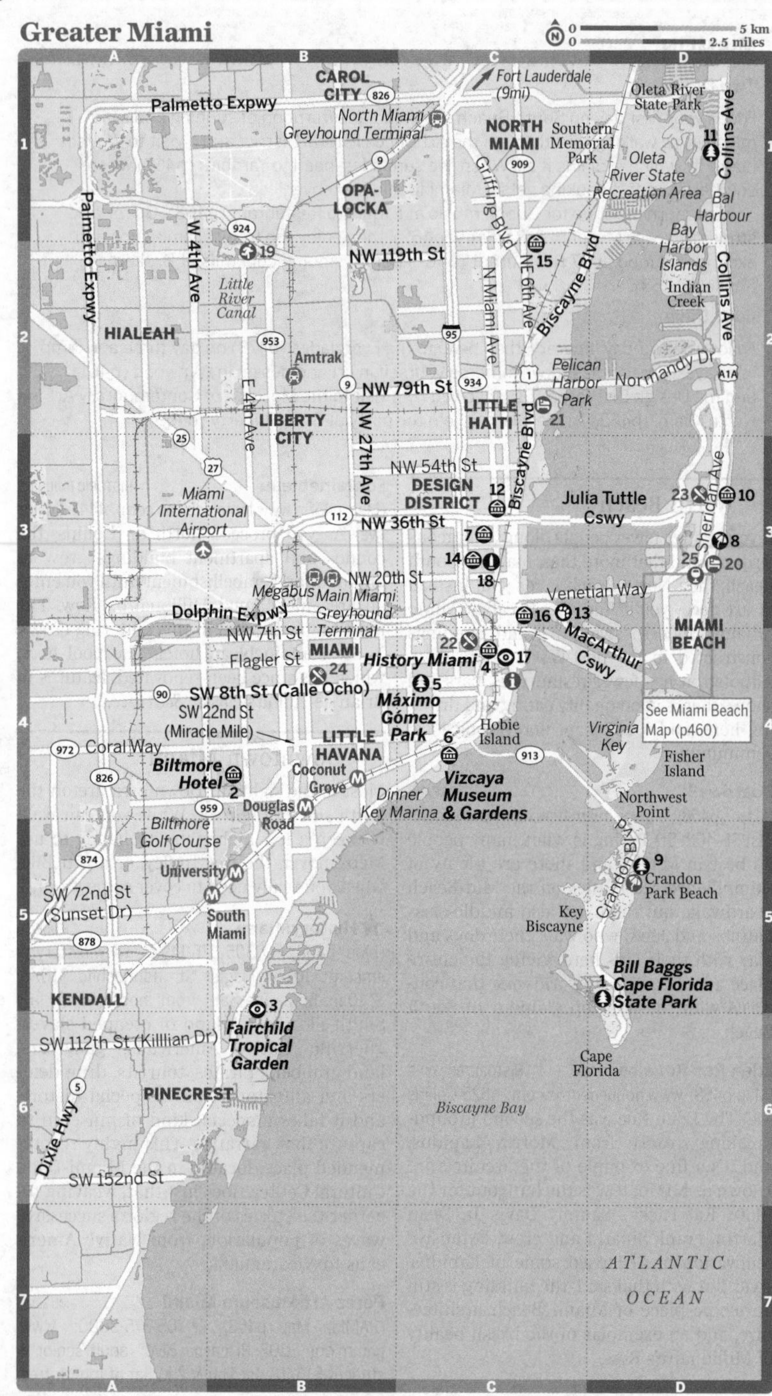

Greater Miami

Top Sights
1 Bill Baggs Cape Florida State Park ... D5
2 Biltmore Hotel ... B4
3 Fairchild Tropical Garden ... B5
4 HistoryMiami ... C4
5 Máximo Gómez Park ... C4
6 Vizcaya Museum & Gardens ... C4

Sights
7 Bakehouse Art Complex ... C3
8 Boardwalk ... D3
9 Crandon Park ... D5
Eden Roc Renaissance ... (see 10)
10 Fontainebleau ... D3
11 Haulover Beach Park ... D1
12 Institute of Contemporary Art ... C3
13 Jungle Island ... C3
Little Havana Art District ... (see 5)
14 Margulies Collection at the Warehouse ... C3
Miami Children's Museum ... (see 13)
15 Museum of Contemporary Art North Miami ... C2
Patricia & Phillip Frost Museum of Science ... (see 16)
16 Pérez Art Museum Miami ... C3
17 Void Projects ... C4
18 Wynwood Walls ... C3

Activities, Courses & Tours
19 Miami Watersports Complex ... B2

Sleeping
20 1 Hotel ... D3
Biltmore Hotel ... (see 2)
Eurostars Langford ... (see 17)
Fontainebleau ... (see 10)
Freehand Miami ... (see 8)
21 Vagabond Hotel ... C2

Eating
27 Restaurant ... (see 8)
Alter ... (see 18)
22 Casablanca ... C4
Della Test Kitchen ... (see 18)
Exquisito Restaurant ... (see 5)
Kyu ... (see 18)
Manna Life Food ... (see 17)
23 Roasters 'n Toasters ... D3
24 Versailles ... B4

Drinking & Nightlife
Ball & Chain ... (see 5)
Broken Shaker ... (see 8)
Galleria ... (see 17)
25 Sweet Liberty ... D3
Vagabond Pool Bar ... (see 21)

Entertainment
Adrienne Arsht Center for the Performing Arts ... (see 16)
Cubaocho ... (see 5)

10am-6pm Fri-Tue, to 9pm Thu, closed Wed; P) One of Miami's most impressive spaces, designed by Swiss architects Herzog & de Meuron, integrates tropical foliage, glass, concrete and wood – a melding of tropical vitality and fresh modernism that fits perfectly in Miami. PAMM stages some of the best contemporary exhibitions in the city, with established artists and impressive newcomers. The permanent collection rotates through unique pieces every few months – drawing from a treasure trove of work spanning the last 80 years. Don't miss.

Patricia & Phillip Frost Museum of Science MUSEUM
(Map p458; 305-434-9600; www.frostscience.org; 1101 Biscayne Blvd; adult/child $30/21; 9am-6pm; P) This sprawling new Downtown museum spreads across 250,000 sq ft that includes a three-level aquarium, a 250-seat, state-of-the-art planetarium and two distinct wings that delve into the wonders of science and nature. Exhibitions range from weather phenomena to creepy crawlies, feathered dinosaurs and vital-microbe displays, while Florida's fascinating Everglades and biologically rich coral reefs play starring roles. The building you now see, which cost a staggering $305 million to complete, was built with sustainability in mind and opened in 2017.

Void Projects ARTS CENTER
(Map p458; www.voidprojects.org; 60 SE 1st St; 11am-6pm) FREE If you'd like to meet local artists and see how life is lived on a smaller, more modest scale in Miami's creative pockets, visit this arts collective – run by artist Axel Void – where resident artists paint and hold exhibitions (by visiting artists) and organise free life drawing classes for the public (Thursdays from 6.30pm) and movie screenings.

Little Havana

The Cubaness of Little Havana is slightly exaggerated for visitors, though it's still an atmospheric area to explore for an afternoon, with the crack of dominoes, the scent of

Miami Beach

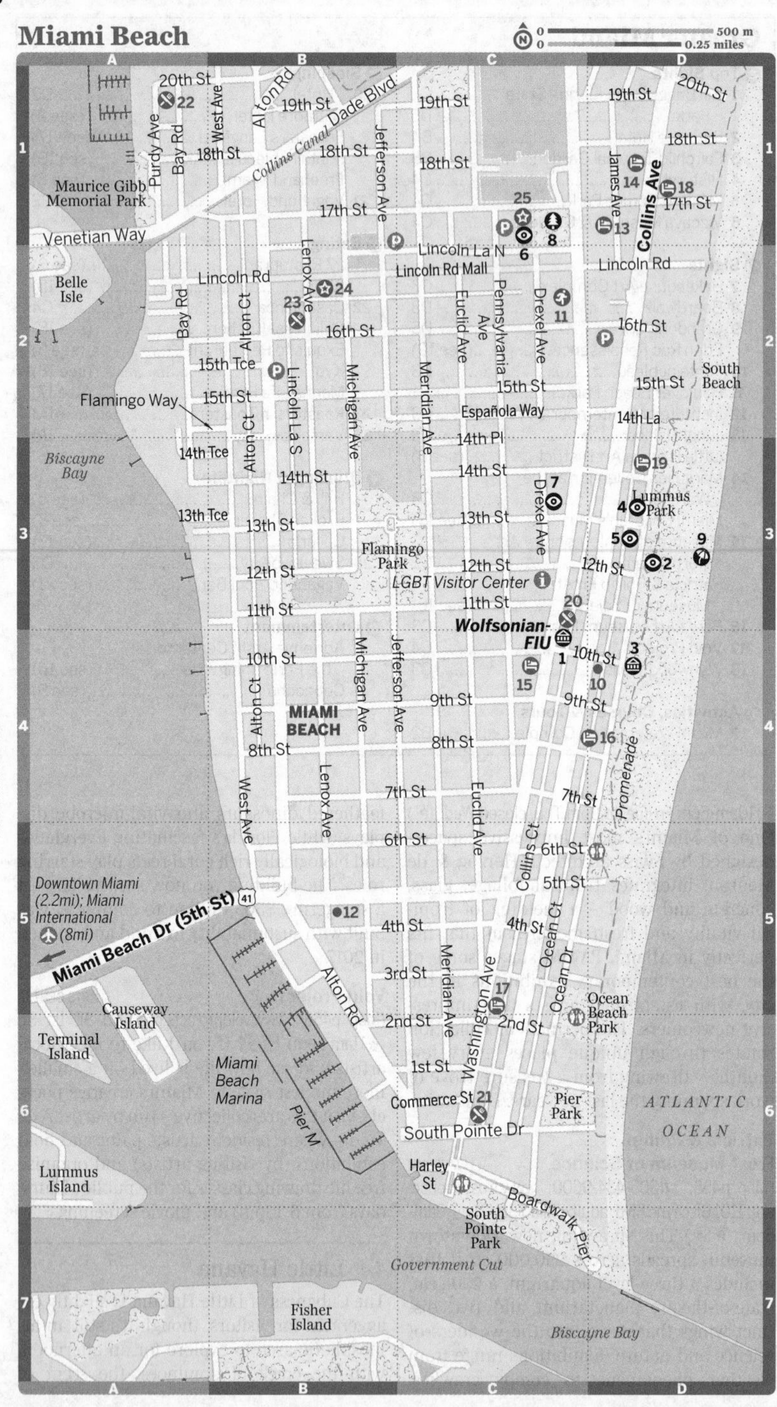

0 500 m
0 0.25 miles
20th St
19th St
18th St
17th St
Alton Rd
Dade Blvd
Collins Canal
Purdy Ave
Bay Rd
West Ave
Jefferson Ave
Maurice Gibb Memorial Park
Venetian Way
Belle Isle
Lincoln La N
Lincoln Rd Mall
Lincoln Rd
Lenox Ave
Alton Ct
Euclid Ave
Pennsylvania Ave
Drexel Ave
James Ave
Collins Ave
16th St
15th Tce
15th St
Lincoln La S
Michigan Ave
Meridian Ave
South Beach
Flamingo Way
Española Way
14th La
Biscayne Bay
14th Tce
14th Pl
14th St
13th Tce
13th St
Lummus Park
Flamingo Park
12th St
LGBT Visitor Center
11th St
Wolfsonian-FIU
10th St
9th St
MIAMI BEACH
8th St
7th St
Promenade
6th St
Collins Ct
5th St
Downtown Miami (2.2mi); Miami International (8mi)
Miami Beach Dr (5th St)
41
4th St
Ocean Ct
Ocean Dr
3rd St
Washington Ave
2nd St
Causeway Island
Terminal Island
Miami Beach Marina
Ocean Beach Park
1st St
Commerce St
Pier Park
ATLANTIC OCEAN
South Pointe Dr
Pier M
Harley St
Lummus Island
Boardwalk Pier
South Pointe Park
Government Cut
Fisher Island
Biscayne Bay

Miami Beach

Top Sights

1 Wolfsonian-FIU C4

Sights

2 Art Deco Historic District D3
3 Art Deco Museum D4
4 Cardozo Hotel D3
5 Carlyle D3
6 New World Center C1
7 Post Office C3
8 SoundScape Park C1
9 South Beach D3

Activities, Courses & Tours

10 Bike & Roll D4
11 Fritz's Skate, Bike & Surf C2
Miami Design Preservation League .... (see 3)
12 Miami Food Tours B5

Sleeping

13 Bed & Drinks D1
14 Catalina Hotel D1
15 Hotel Astor C4
16 Hotel of South Beach D4
17 SoBe Hostel C5
18 Surfcomber D1
19 Winter Haven Hotel D3

Eating

20 11th Street Diner C3
21 Joe's Stone Crab Restaurant C6
22 Pubbelly A1
23 Yardbird B2

Entertainment

24 Colony Theater B2
25 New World Symphony C1

wafting cigars and salsa spilling out of storefronts. Little Havana's main thoroughfare, Calle Ocho (SW 8th St), is the heart of the neighborhood. In many ways, this is every immigrant enclave in the USA – full of restaurants, mom-and-pop convenience shops and phonecard kiosks, except here you get intermittent tourists posing and taking selfies.

★ Máximo Gómez Park PARK
(Map p458; cnr SW 8th St & SW 15th Ave; ⏲9am-6pm) Little Havana's most evocative reminder of Cuba is Máximo Gómez Park ('Domino Park'), where the sound of elderly men trash-talking over games of dominoes is harmonized with the quick clack-clack of slapping tiles – though the tourists taking photos all the while does take away from the authenticity of the place somewhat. The heavy cigar smell and a sunrise-bright mural of the 1994 Summit of the Americas add to the atmosphere.

Little Havana Art District AREA
(Map p458; Calle Ocho, btwn SW 15th & 17th Aves) This particular stretch of Little Havana is the epicenter of the **Viernes Culturales** (Cultural Fridays; www.viernesculturales.org; ⏲7-11pm last Fri of month) celebration and has a handful of galleries and studios still in business that are worth a browse.

Wynwood & the Design District

Wynwood and the Design District are two of Miami's arts neighborhoods (though it's fair to say the edge has worn off a bit) – Wynwood is packed with galleries and lots of street art and has a lively night life, and there are some good music festivals held here every year. It's very popular with tourists who are looking for an alternative to South Beach. The Design District is a high-end shopping area, with a couple of great little art museums and a mixed bag of restaurants.

Institute of Contemporary Art MUSEUM
(Map p458; www.icamiami.org; 61 NE 41st St; ⏲11am-7pm Tue-Sun) FREE An excellent contemporary arts museum, the ICA sits in the midst of the Design District, and hosts a fantastic range of contemporary exhibitions alongside its permanent collection pieces. The building, designed in 2017 by Aranguren & Gallegos architects, is especially beautiful, with its sharp geometric lines and large windows overlooking the back garden. The metallic grey facade is simultaneously industrial and elegant

Wynwood Walls PUBLIC ART
(Map p458; www.thewynwoodwalls.com; NW 2nd Ave, btwn 25th & 26th Sts) FREE In the midst of rusted warehouses and concrete blah, there's a pastel-and-graffiti explosion of urban art. Wynwood Walls is a collection of murals and paintings laid out over an open courtyard that invariably bowls people over with its sheer color profile and unexpected location. What's on offer tends to change with the coming and going of major arts events, such as Art Basel (p465), but it's always interesting stuff.

Margulies Collection at the Warehouse GALLERY
(Map p458; ☎305-576-1051; www.marguliesware house.com; 591 NW 27th St; adult/student $10/5; ⊙11am-4pm Tue-Sat mid-Oct–Apr) Encompassing 45,000 sq ft, this vast not-for-profit exhibition space houses one of the best art collections in Wynwood – Martin Margulies' awe-inspiring 4000-piece collection includes sculptures by Isamu Noguchi, George Segal, Richard Serra and Olafur Eliasson, among many others, plus sound installations by Susan Philipsz and jaw-dropping room-sized works by Anselm Kiefer. Thought-provoking, large-format installations are the focus at the Warehouse, and you'll see works by some leading 21st-century artists here.

Bakehouse Art Complex GALLERY
(BAC; Map p458; ☎305-576-2828; www.bacfl.org; 561 NW 32nd St; ⊙noon-5pm; P) FREE One of the pivotal art destinations in Wynwood, the Bakehouse has been an arts incubator since well before the creation of the Wynwood Walls. Today this former bakery houses galleries and some 60 studios, and the range of works is quite impressive. Check the schedule for upcoming artist talks and other events.

Coral Gables

The lovely city of Coral Gables, filled with Mediterranean-style buildings, feels like a world removed from other parts of Miami. Here you'll find pretty banyan-lined streets, and a walkable village-like center, dotted with shops, cafes and restaurants. The big draws are the striking Biltmore Hotel, a lush tropical garden and one of America's loveliest swimming pools.

★Fairchild Tropical Garden GARDENS
(Map p458; ☎305-667-1651; www.fairchildgarden.org; 10901 Old Cutler Rd; adult/child/senior $25/12/18; ⊙9:30am-4:30pm; P) If you need to escape Miami's madness, consider a green day in one of the country's largest tropical botanical gardens. A butterfly grove, tropical plant conservatory and gentle vistas of marsh and keys habitats, plus frequent art installations from artists like Roy Lichtenstein, are all stunning. In addition to easy-to-follow, self-guided walking tours, a free 45-minute tram tours the entire park on the hour from 10am to 3pm (till 4pm weekends).

★Biltmore Hotel HISTORIC BUILDING
(Map p458; ☎855-311-6903; www.biltmorehotel.com; 1200 Anastasia Ave; ⊙tours 1:30pm & 2:30pm Sun; P) In the most opulent neighborhood of one of the showiest cities in the world, the Biltmore is the greatest of the grand hotels of the American Jazz Age. If this joint were a fictional character from a novel, it'd be, without question, Jay Gatsby. Al Capone had a speakeasy on-site, and the Capone Suite is said to be haunted by the spirit of Fats Walsh, who was murdered here.

Coconut Grove

Coconut Grove was once a hippie colony, but these days its demographic is middle-class, mall-going Miamians and college students. CocoWalk, the main street, has undergone massive renovations.

It's a pleasant place to explore, with intriguing shops and cafes, and a walkable village-like vibe. It's particularly appealing in the evenings, when residents fill the outdoor tables of its bars and restaurants. Coconut Grove backs onto the waterfront, with a pretty marina and some pleasant green spaces.

★Vizcaya Museum & Gardens HISTORIC BUILDING
(Map p458; ☎305-250-9133; www.vizcayamuseum.org; 3251 S Miami Ave; adult/6-12yr/student & senior $22/10/16; ⊙9.30am-4.30pm Wed-Mon; P) If you want to see something that is 'very Miami', this is it – lush, big, over the top, a patchwork of all that a rich US businessman might want to show off to his friends. Which is essentially what industrialist James Deering did in 1916, starting a Miami tradition of making a ton of money and building ridiculously grandiose digs. He employed 1000 people (then 10% of the local population) and stuffed his home with Renaissance furniture, tapestries, paintings and decorative arts.

Key Biscayne

Key Biscayne and neighboring Virginia Key are a quick and easy getaway from Downtown Miami. Once you pass those scenic causeways you'll feel like you've been transported to a far-off tropical realm, with magnificent beaches, lush nature trails in state parks and aquatic adventures aplenty. The stunning skyline views of Miami alone are worth the trip out.

MIAMI FOR CHILDREN

The best beaches for kids are in Miami Beach north of 21st St, especially at 53rd St, which has a playground and public toilets, and the dune-packed beach around 73rd St. Also head south to Matheson Hammock Park, which has calm artificial lagoons.

Miami Children's Museum (Map p458; ☎305-373-5437; www.miamichildrensmuseum.org; 980 MacArthur Causeway; $20; ⊙10am-6pm;) On Watson Island, between Downtown Miami and Miami Beach, this hands-on museum has fun music and art studios, as well as some branded 'work' experiences that make it feel a tad corporate.

Jungle Island (Map p458; ☎305-400-7000; www.jungleisland.com; 1111 Parrot Jungle Trail, off MacArthur Causeway; adult/child $50/38; ⊙10am-5pm; P) Jungle Island is packed with tropical birds, alligators, orangutans, chimps and (to the delight of Napoleon Dynamite fans) a liger – a cross between a lion and a tiger.

Zoo Miami (Metrozoo; ☎305-251-0400; www.zoomiami.org; 12400 SW 152nd St; adult/child $23/19; ⊙10am-5pm; P) Miami's tropical weather makes strolling around Zoo Miami almost feel like a day in the wild. For a quick overview (and because the zoo is so big and the sun is broiling), hop on the Safari Monorail; it departs every 20 minutes.

Monkey Jungle (☎305-235-1611; www.monkeyjungle.com; 14805 SW 216th St; adult/child/senior $30/24/28; ⊙9:30am-5pm, last entry 4pm; P) The tagline, 'Where humans are caged and monkeys run free,' tells you all you need to know – except for the fact that it's in far south Miami.

★Bill Baggs Cape Florida State Park STATE PARK
(Map p458; ☎305-361-5811; www.floridastateparks.org/capeflorida; 1200 S Crandon Blvd; per car/person $8/2; ⊙8am-sunset, lighthouse 9am-5pm; P) If you don't make it to the Florida Keys, come to this park for a taste of their unique island ecosystems. The 494-acre space is a tangled clot of tropical fauna and dark mangroves – look for the 'snorkel' roots that provide air for half-submerged mangrove trees – all interconnected by sandy trails and wooden boardwalks, and surrounded by miles of pale ocean. A concession shack rents out kayaks, bikes, in-line skates, beach chairs and umbrellas.

Greater Miami

Museum of Contemporary Art North Miami MUSEUM
(MoCA; Map p458; ☎305-893-6211; www.mocanomi.org; 770 NE 125th St; adult/student/child under 12yr $10/3/free; ⊙11am-5pm Tue-Fri & Sun, 1-9pm Sat; P) The Museum of Contemporary Art has long been a reason to hike up to North Miami – its galleries feature excellent rotating exhibitions of contemporary art by local, national and international artists, usually themed along socially engaged lines of interest. There is a pay what you wish gallery policy during Jazz@MOCA from 7pm to 10pm on the last Friday of every month, when live outdoor jazz concerts are held.

Gold Coast Railroad Museum MUSEUM
(☎305-253-0063; www.gcrm.org; 12450 SW 152nd St; adult/child 2-12yr $8/6; ⊙10am-4pm Mon-Fri, from 11am Sat & Sun; P) Primarily of interest to train buffs, this museum displays more than 30 antique railway cars, including the Ferdinand Magellan presidential car, where President Harry Truman famously brandished a newspaper with the erroneous headline 'Dewey Defeats Truman.'

Activities

Miami doesn't lack for ways to keep yourself busy. From sailing the teal waters to hiking through tropical undergrowth, yoga in the parks and (why not?) trapeze artistry above the city's head, the Magic City rewards those who want an active holiday.

Citi Bike CYCLING
(☎305-532-9494; www.citibikemiami.com; rental per 30min $4.50, 1/2/4hr $6.50/10/18, day $24) This bike-sharing program, modeled after similar initiatives in New York, London and Paris, makes getting on a bike a relative breeze. Just rock up to a solar-powered Citi Bike station (a handy map can be found on the website), insert a credit card and ride away. You can return your bike at any Citi Bike location.

City Walk Art Deco Magic

START ART DECO MUSEUM
END OCEAN'S TEN
LENGTH 1.2 MILES; TWO TO THREE HOURS

Start at the ❶ **Art Deco Museum** (p456), at the corner of Ocean Dr and 10th St (named Barbara Capitman Way here, after the Miami Design Preservation League's founder). Step in for an exhibit on art-deco style, then head out and north along Ocean Dr; between 12th and 14th Sts you'll see three examples of deco hotels: the ❷ **Leslie**, a boxy shape with eyebrows (cantilevered sunshades) wrapped around the side of the building; the ❸ **Carlyle**, featured in the film *The Birdcage* and boasting modernistic styling; and the graceful ❹ **Cardozo Hotel**, built by Henry Hohauser, owned by Gloria Estefan and featuring sleek, rounded edges.

At 14th St peek inside the sun-drenched ❺ **Winter Haven Hotel** to see its fabulous terrazzo floors, made of stone chips set in mortar that's polished when dry. Turn left and down 14th St to Washington Ave and the ❻ **US Post Office**, at 13th St. It's a curvy block of white deco in the stripped classical style. Step inside to admire the wall mural, domed ceiling and marble stamp tables.

Lunch at the ❼ **11th St Diner** (p467), a gleaming aluminum Pullman car that was imported in 1992 from Wilkes-Barre, PA. Get a window seat and gaze across the avenue to the corner of 10th St and the stunningly restored ❽ **Hotel Astor**, designed in 1936 by T Hunter Henderson. After your meal, walk half a block east from there to the imposing ❾ **Wolfsonian-FIU** (p456), an excellent design museum, formerly the Washington Storage Company. Wealthy snowbirds of the '30s stashed their pricey belongings here before heading back up north.

Continue walking on Washington Ave, turn left on 8th St and then continue north along Collins Ave to the ❿ **Hotel of South Beach**, featuring an interior and roof deck by Todd Oldham. Walk for two more blocks to Ocean Dr, where you'll spy nonstop deco beauties; at 960 Ocean Dr (the ⓫ **Ocean's Ten** restaurant) you'll see an exterior designed in 1935 by deco legend Henry Hohauser.

Bike & Roll CYCLING

(Map p460; ☎305-604-0001; www.bikemiami.com; 210 10th St; hire per 2/4hr from $10/18, day from $24, tours $40; ⊙9am-7pm) This well-run outfit offers a good selection of bikes, including single-speed cruisers, geared hybrids and speedy road bikes; all rentals include helmets, lights, locks and maps. Staff move things along quickly, so you won't have to waste time waiting to get out and riding. Bike tours are also available (daily at 10am).

Fritz's Skate, Bike & Surf SKATING

(Map p460; ☎305-532-1954; www.fritzsmiamibeach.com; 1620 Washington Ave; bike & skate rental per hour/day/5 days $10/24/69; ⊙10am-9pm Mon-Sat, to 8pm Sun) Rent your wheels from Fritz's, which offers skateboards, longboards, in-line skates, roller skates, scooters and bicycles (cruisers, mountain bikes, kids' bikes). Protective gear is included with skate rentals, and bikes come with locks. Be mindful that there's a deposit for each rental – skates $100, longboards $150 and bicycles $200.

SoBe Surf SURFING

(☎786-216-7703; www.sobesurf.com; group/private lessons from $70/100) Offers surf lessons both in Miami Beach and in Cocoa Beach, where there tends to be better waves. Instruction on Miami Beach usually happens around South Point. All bookings are done by phone or email.

Miami Watersports Complex WATER SPORTS

(MWCC; Map p458; ☎305-476-9253; www.aktionparks.com; Amelia Earhart Park, 401 E 65th St, Hialeah; ⊙11am-6pm Mar-Oct, to dusk Nov-Feb) Offers lessons in cableboarding, where the rider is pulled along by an overhead cable system. That means no boat, less pollution and less noise. A 20-minute/one-hour lesson costs $25/90, or opt for a $59 package that includes a beginner lesson, rental gear and four-hour cable pass. Call ahead to reserve a spot.

Tours

History Miami Tours TOURS

(www.historymiami.org/city-tour; tours $30-60) Historian extraordinaire Dr Paul George leads fascinating walking tours, including culturally rich strolls through Little Haiti, Little Havana, Downtown and Coral Gables at twilight, plus the occasional boat trip to Stiltsville and Key Biscayne. Tours happen once a week or so. Get the full menu and sign up online.

Miami Food Tours FOOD & DRINK

(Map p460; ☎786-361-0991; www.miamifoodtours.com; 429 Lenox Ave; South Beach tour adult/child $58/35, Wynwood tour $75/55, Swooped with Forks $129/109; ⊙tours South Beach 11am & 4:30pm daily, Wynwood 10:30am Mon-Sat) This highly rated tour explores various facets of the city – culture, history, art and of course cuisine – while making stops at restaurants and cafes along the way. It's a walking tour, though distances aren't great, and happens in South Beach and Wynwood. There is also the Swooped with Forks food tour that takes you places in a golf cart.

Miami Design Preservation League WALKING

(MDPL; Map p460; ☎305-672-2014; www.mdpl.org; 1001 Ocean Dr; guided tours adult/student $25/20; ⊙10:30am daily & 6:30pm Thu) Tells the stories and history behind the art-deco buildings in South Beach, with a lively guide from the Miami Design Preservation League. Tours last 90 minutes. Also offers tours of Jewish Miami Beach, Gay & Lesbian Miami Beach and a once-monthly tour (first Saturday at 9:30am) of the MiMo district in the North Beach area. Check website for details.

Festivals & Events

Winter Music Conference MUSIC

(www.wintermusicconference.com; ⊙Mar) Party promoters, DJs, producers and revelers come from around the globe to hear new electronic-music artists, catch up on technology and party the nights away.

Miami Spice Restaurant Month FOOD & DRINK

(www.miamiandbeaches.com/offers/temptations/miami-spice-months; ⊙Aug-Sep) Top restaurants around Miami offer three-course lunches and dinners to try to lure folks out during the heat wave. Prices hover around $25 for lunch and $40 for dinner. Reservations essential.

White Party MUSIC

(www.whiteparty.org; ⊙Nov) If you're gay and not here, there's a problem. This weeklong extravaganza draws more than 15,000 gay men and women for nonstop partying at clubs and venues all over town.

Art Basel Miami Beach ART

(www.artbasel.com/miami-beach; ⊙early Dec) One of the most important international art shows in the world, with works from more than 250 galleries and a slew of trendy parties. Even if you're not a billionaire collector, there's much to enjoy at this four-day fest, with open-air art installations around town, special exhibitions at many Miami galleries and outdoor film screenings, among other goings-on.

Sleeping

Miami has some alluring lodging options, but beware that high-season prices can be sky-high. South Beach has all the name recognition with boutique hotels set in lovely art deco buildings, but there are plenty of other options in Miami – from Downtown high-rises with sweeping views and endless amenities to historic charmers in Coral Gables and Coconut Grove and some modern – MiMo – beauties along Biscayne Boulevard.

South Beach

Bed & Drinks HOSTEL $
(Map p460; ☎305-535-7415; www.bedsndrinks.com; 1676 James Ave; dm/r $25-32/160-185) This hostel pretty shamelessly plays to the sexy, party, beautiful-people crowd – check the name – so know this before booking. The beach is a few blocks away. The rooms range from average to slightly below average. Friendly staff, a lively on-site bar and nightlife outings to clubs around town make up for the minuses.

SoBe Hostel HOSTEL $
(Map p460; ☎305-534-6669; www.sobe-hostel.com; 235 Washington Ave; dm $22-52;) On a quiet end of SoFi (the area south of 5th St, South Beach), this massive multilingual hostel has a happening common area and spartan rooms. The staff are friendly and the on-site bar (open to 5am) is a great spot to meet other travelers. Free breakfasts and dinners are included in the rates.

There are loads of activities on offer – from volleyball games to mojito-making nights, screenings of big games and bar crawls.

Catalina Hotel BOUTIQUE HOTEL $$
(Map p460; ☎305-674-1160; www.catalinahotel.com; 1732 Collins Ave; r from $220;) The Catalina is a lovely example of midrange deco style. Most appealing, besides the playfully minimalist rooms, is the vibe – the Catalina doesn't take itself too seriously, and staff and guests all seem to be having fun as a result. The back pool, concealed behind the main building's crisp white facade, is particularly attractive and fringed by a whispery grove of bamboo trees.

It was renovated to incorporate the Dorset, next door, which means that it now has two pools, a roof terrace and a reasonable Mexican restaurant.

★**1 Hotel** HOTEL $$$
(Map p458; ☎866-615-1111; www.1hotels.com; 2341 Collins Ave; r from $400;) One of the top hotels in the USA, the 1 Hotel has 400-plus gorgeous rooms that embrace both luxurious and ecofriendly features – including tree-trunk coffee tables/desks, custom hemp-blend mattresses and salvaged driftwood feature walls, plus in-room water filtration (no need for plastic bottles). The common areas are impressive, with four pools, including an adults-only rooftop infinity pool.

★**Surfcomber** HOTEL $$$
(Map p460; ☎305-532-7715; www.surfcomber.com; 1717 Collins Ave; r $250-480;) The Surfcomber has a classic art-deco exterior with strong lines and shade-providing 'eyebrows' that zigzag across the facade. But the interior is the really impressive part – rooms have undeniable appeal, with elegant lines in keeping with the art-deco aesthetic, while bursts of color keep things contemporary.

North Beach

★**Freehand Miami** BOUTIQUE HOTEL $$
(Map p458; ☎305-531-2727; www.thefreehand.com; 2727 Indian Creek Dr; dm $28-55, r $160-250;) The Freehand is the brilliant reimagining of the old Indian Creek Hotel, a classic of the Miami Beach scene. Rooms are sunny and attractively designed, with local artwork and wooden details. The vintage-filled common areas are the reason to stay here though – especially the lovely pool area and backyard that transforms into one of the best bars in town.

Dorms serve the hostel crowd, while private rooms are quite appealing. There are also bungalows for self-catering groups.

Downtown Miami

Eurostars Langford HERITAGE HOTEL $$
(Map p458; ☎305-250-0782; http://the-langford.miamiallhotels.com; 121 SE 1st St; r from $180;) Set in a beautifully restored 1925

beaux-arts high-rise, the Langford's 126 rooms blend comfort and nostalgia, with elegant fixtures and vintage details, including oak flooring and lush furniture. Thoughtful design touches abound, and there's a rooftop bar and an excellent ground-floor restaurant on-site.

Coral Gables

★ **Biltmore Hotel** HISTORIC HOTEL $$$
(Map p458; ☎855-311-6903; www.biltmorehotel.com; 1200 Anastasia Ave; r/ste from $699/730; P ❄ ☎ ≋) Though the Biltmore's standard rooms can be small, a stay here is a chance to sleep in one of the great laps of US luxury. The grounds are so palatial it would take a week to explore everything the Biltmore has to offer – sunbathe underneath enormous columns and take a dip in the largest hotel pool in continental USA.

Eating

Miami has tons of immigrants – mainly from Latin America, the Caribbean and Russia – and it's a sucker for food trends. Thus you get a good mix of cheap ethnic eateries and high-quality top-end cuisine, alongside some poor-value dross in touristy zones like Miami Beach. Downtown, Wynwood and Upper East Side have excellent offerings; for great classics, head to Coral Gables.

South Beach

11th Street Diner DINER $
(Map p460; ☎305-534-6373; www.eleventhstreetdiner.com; 1065 Washington Ave; mains $10-20; ⏲7am-midnight Sun-Wed, 24hr Thu-Sat) A gorgeous slice of Americana, this Pullman-car diner trucked down from Wilkes-Barre, PA, is where you can replicate Edward Hopper's *Nighthawks* – if that's something you've always wanted to do. The food is as classic as the architecture, with oven-roasted turkey, baby back ribs and mac 'n' cheese among the hits – plus breakfast at all hours.

★ **Yardbird** SOUTHERN US $$
(Map p460; ☎305-538-5220; www.runchickenrun.com; 1600 Lenox Ave; mains $18-38; ⏲11am-midnight Mon-Fri, from 8:30am Sat & Sun; ✎) Yardbird has earned a die-hard following for its delicious haute Southern comfort food. The kitchen churns out some nice shrimp and grits, St Louis–style pork ribs, charred okra, and biscuits with smoked brisket, but it's most famous for its supremely good plate of fried chicken, spiced watermelon and waffles with bourbon maple syrup.

★ **Pubbelly** FUSION $$
(Map p460; ☎305-532-7555; http://pubbellyglobal.com; 1424 20th St; plates $7-18; ⏲6pm-midnight Tue-Thu & Sun, to 1am Fri & Sat; ✎) A mix of Asian and Latin flavors, Pubbelly serves delicacies such as grilled miso black cod with spring onions, beef tartare rolls with mustard and truffle poached egg, and Japanese fried chicken with kimchi. Super popular and decently priced, it's a real treat on South Beach.

Joe's Stone Crab Restaurant AMERICAN $$$
(Map p460; ☎305-673-0365; www.joesstonecrab.com; 11 Washington Ave; mains lunch $14-30, dinner $19-100; ⏲11:30am-2:30pm Tue-Sat, 5-10pm Tue-Sun, to 11pm Fri & Sat) The wait is long, the prices for iconic dishes can be high, and all in all we find Miami's most famous restaurant (around since 1913!) a little overrated. Aside from stone crab (which can run to $100 for half-a-dozen jumbo claws), you'll find blackened codfish sandwiches and creamy lobster mac 'n' cheese.

North Beach

Roasters 'n Toasters DELI $
(Map p458; ☎305-531-7691; www.roastersntoasters.com; 525 Arthur Godfrey Rd; mains $10-18; ⏲6:30am-3:30pm) Given the crowds and the satisfied smiles of customers, Roasters 'n Toasters meets the demanding standards of Miami Beach's large Jewish demographic, thanks to juicy deli meat, fresh bread, crispy bagels and warm latkes. Sliders (mini-sandwiches) are served on challah bread, an innovation that's as charming as it is tasty.

★ **27 Restaurant** FUSION $$
(Map p458; ☎786-476-7020; www.freehandhotels.com; 2727 Indian Creek Dr, Freehand Miami Hotel; mains $17-28; ⏲6:30pm-2am Mon-Sat, 11am-4pm & 6:30pm-2am Sun; ✎) Part of Freehand Miami and the very popular Broken Shaker (p468), 27 has a lovely setting – akin to dining in an old tropical cottage, with worn floorboards, candlelit tables, and various rooms slung with artwork and curious knickknacks, plus a lovely terrace. Try the braised octopus, crispy pork shoulder, kimchi fried rice and yogurt-tahini-massaged

kale. Book ahead. Brunch is also quite popular.

Downtown Miami

★Casablanca SEAFOOD $$

(Map p458; www.casablancaseafood.com; 400 N River Dr; mains $15-34; ⏲11am-10pm Sun-Thu, to 11pm Fri & Sat) Perched over the Miami River, Casablanca serves some of the best seafood in town. The setting is a big draw – with tables on a long wooden deck just above the water, and the odd seagull winging past. But the fresh fish is the real star here.

Little Havana

★Versailles CUBAN $

(Map p458; ☎305-444-0240; www.versaillesrestaurant.com; 3555 SW 8th St; mains $6-21; ⏲8am-1am Mon-Thu, to 2:30am Fri & Sat, 9am-1am Sun) Versailles (ver-*sigh*-yay) is an institution – one of the mainstays of Miami's Cuban gastronomic scene. Try the excellent black-bean soup or the fried yucca before moving onto heartier meat and seafood plates. Older Cubans and Miami's Latin political elite still love coming here, so you've got a real chance to rub elbows with Miami's most prominent Latin citizens.

Exquisito Restaurant CUBAN $

(Map p458; ☎305-643-0227; www.elexquisitomiami.com; 1510 SW 8th St; mains $9-13; ⏲7am-11pm) Great Cuban cuisine in the heart of Little Havana – the roast pork has a tangy citrus kick and the *ropa vieja* (spiced shredded beef and rice) is wonderfully rich. Even standard sides like beans and rice and roasted plantains are executed with a little more care and are extra tasty. Prices are a steal, too.

Wynwood & the Design District

Della Test Kitchen VEGAN $

(Map p458; ☎305-351-2961; www.dellabowls.com; 56 NW 29th St, Wynwood Yard; mains $11-14; ⏲noon-10pm Tue-Sun; 🌱) From a food truck parked in Wynwood Yard, this place offers delicious 'bowls' – build-your-own culinary works of art featuring ingredients such as black coconut rice, ginger tempeh, chickpeas, sweet potato and marinated kale. It's heavenly good and quite healthy. Not surprisingly, DTK has itself quite a following.

★Kyu FUSION $$

(Map p458; ☎786-577-0150; www.kyumiami.com; 251 NW 25th St; sharing plates $17-38; ⏲noon-11:30pm Mon-Sat, 11am-10:30pm Sun, bar till 1am Fri & Sat; 🌱) Kyu has been dazzling locals and food critics alike with its creative Asian-inspired dishes, most of which are cooked over the open flames of a wood-fired grill. Try the Florida red snapper, beef tenderloin and a magnificent head of cauliflower. There's also grilled octopus, soft-shell-crab steamed buns and smoked beef brisket. Book well ahead, or turn up and wait (one-hour average).

Alter MODERN AMERICAN $$$

(Map p458; ☎305-573-5996; www.altermiami.com; 223 NW 23rd St; set menu 5/7 courses $79/99; ⏲7-11pm Tue-Sun) Alter brings creative high-end cooking via its award-winning young chef Brad Kilgore. The changing menu showcases Florida's high-quality ingredients from sea and land in seasonally inspired dishes with Asian and European-flavoured haute cuisine. Expect dishes such as eggs with sea scallop foam, truffle pearls and Siberian caviar, or lamb neck, forest consommé, toasted apple miso and shaved kombu. Reserve well ahead.

Drinking & Nightlife

Miami has an intense variety of bars, ranging from grotty jazz and punk dives (with excellent music) to beautiful – and laid-back – lounges and nightclubs. There is a great live-music scene across the city. Miami's nightlife reputation for being all about wealth, good looks and phoniness is thankfully mostly isolated to the South Beach scene.

★Broken Shaker BAR

(Map p458; ☎305-531-2727; www.freehandhotels.com; 2727 Indian Creek Dr, Freehand Miami Hotel; ⏲6pm-3am Mon-Fri, 2pm-3am Sat & Sun) A single small room with a well-equipped bar produces expert cocktails, which are mostly consumed in the beautiful, softly lit garden – all of it part of the Freehand Miami hotel (p466). There's a great soundtrack at all times, and the drinks are excellent. The clientele is a mix of hotel guests (young and into partying) and hip locals.

★Sweet Liberty BAR

(Map p458; www.mysweetliberty.com; 237 20th St; ⌚4pm-5am Mon-Sat, from noon Sun) A much-loved local haunt near Collins Park, Sweet Liberty has all the right ingredients for a fun night out: friendly, easygoing bartenders who whip up excellent cocktails (try a mint julep), great happy-hour specials (including 75¢ oysters) and a relaxed, pretension-free crowd. The space is huge, with flickering candles, a long wooden bar and the odd band adding to the cheer.

Ball & Chain BAR

(Map p458; www.ballandchainmiami.com; 1513 SW 8th St; ⌚noon-midnight Mon-Wed, to 3am Thu-Sat, 2-10pm Sun) The Ball & Chain has survived several incarnations over the years. Back in 1935, when 8th St was more Jewish than Latino, it was the sort of jazz joint Billie Holiday would croon in. That iteration closed in 1957, but today's Ball & Chain is still dedicated to music and good times – specifically, Latin music and tropical cocktails.

Vagabond Pool Bar BAR

(Map p458; ☎305-400-8420; www.thevagabondhotelmiami.com; 7301 Biscayne Blvd; ⌚5-11pm Sun-Thu, to midnight Fri & Sat) Tucked behind the Vagabond Hotel, this is a great spot to start the evening, with perfectly mixed cocktails, courtesy of pro bartenders (the kind who will shake your hand and introduce themselves). The outdoor setting overlooking the palm-fringed pool and eclectic crowd pairs nicely with elixirs like the Lost in Smoke (mezcal, amaro, amaretto and orange bitters).

★Galleria CAFE

(Map p458; http://galleriadowntown.com; 69 SE 1st St; ⌚11am-4pm) Galleria is a tiny spot of beauty, with its tiled benches and coral walls. The owner, Jeremy Sapienza, makes all his own nut milks, and everything here, including the pastries, is vegan. There are also vintage ceramics on sale – if you'd like an alternative Miami souvenir.

☆ Entertainment

Miami's artistic merits are obvious, even from a distance. Could there be a better creative base? There's Southern homegrown talent, migratory snowbirds bringing the funding and attention of northeastern galleries, and immigrants from across the Americas. All that adds up to some great live music, theater and dance – with plenty of room for experimentation.

LGBTIQ+ MIAMI

In Miami, the gay scene is so integrated it can be difficult to separate it from the straight one; popular hot spots include South Beach, North Beach, and Wynwood and the Design District. Events such as the White Party and Swizzle are major dates in the North American gay calendar.

★Adrienne Arsht Center for the Performing Arts PERFORMING ARTS

(Map p458; ☎305-949-6722; www.arshtcenter.org; 1300 Biscayne Blvd; ⌚box office 10am-6pm Mon-Fri, plus 2hr before performances) This magnificent venue manages to both humble and enthrall visitors. Today the Arsht is where the biggest cultural acts in Miami come to perform; a show here is a must-see on any Miami trip. There's an Adrienne Arsht Center stop on the Metromover.

★Cubaocho LIVE PERFORMANCE

(Map p458; ☎305-285-5880; www.cubaocho.com; 1465 SW 8th St; ⌚11am-10pm Tue-Thu, to 3am Fri & Sat) Jewel of the Little Havana Art District, Cubaocho is renowned for its concerts, with excellent bands from across the Spanish-speaking world. It's also a community center, art gallery and research outpost for all things Cuban. The interior resembles an old Havana cigar bar, yet the walls are decked out in artwork that references both the classical past of Cuban art and its avant-garde future.

Colony Theater PERFORMING ARTS

(Map p460; ☎305-674-1040, box office 800-211-1414; www.colonymb.org; 1040 Lincoln Rd) The Colony was built in 1935 and was the main cinema in upper South Beach before it fell into disrepair in the mid-20th century. It was renovated and revived in 1976 and now boasts 465 seats and great acoustics. It's an absolute art-deco gem, with a classic marquee and Inca-style crenellations, and now serves as a major venue for performing arts.

New World Symphony CLASSICAL MUSIC

(NWS; Map p460; ☎305-673-3330; www.nws.edu; 500 17th St) Housed in the New World Center (p456) – a funky explosion of cubist lines and geometric curves, fresh white against the blue Miami sky – the acclaimed New World Symphony holds performances from October to May. The deservedly heralded NWS serves as a three- to four-year preparatory program for talented musicians from prestigious music schools.

Information

SAFE TRAVEL

Miami is a fairly safe city, but there are a few areas considered by locals to be dangerous:

- Liberty City, in northwest Miami; Overtown, from 14th to 20th Sts; Little Haiti and stretches of the Miami riverfront.
- South Beach, particularly along the carnival-like mayhem of Ocean Dr between 8th and 11th Sts, and deserted areas below 5th St are also dangerous at night.
- Use caution around causeways, bridges and overpasses where homeless people have set up shantytowns.

In these and other reputedly 'bad' areas you should avoid walking around alone late at night. It's best to take a taxi.

TOURIST INFORMATION

Greater Miami & the Beaches Convention & Visitors Bureau (Map p458; ☎305-539-3000; www.miamiandbeaches.com; 701 Brickell Ave, 27th fl; ⏲8:30am-6pm Mon-Fri) Offers loads of info on Miami and keeps up-to-date with the latest events and cultural offerings.

Getting There & Away

Located 6 miles west of Downtown, the busy **Miami International Airport** (MIA; Map p458; ☎305-876-7000; www.miami-airport.com; 2100 NW 42nd Ave) has three terminals and serves more than 40 million passengers each year. Around 60 airlines fly into Miami. The airport is open 24 hours and is laid out in a horseshoe design. There are left-luggage facilities on two concourses at MIA, between B and C, and on G; prices vary according to bag size.

For bus trips, **Greyhound** (www.greyhound.com) is the main long-distance operator. **Megabus** (Map p458; https://us.megabus.com; Miami International Center, 3801 NW 21st St) offers service to Tampa and Orlando.

Greyhound's **main bus terminal** (Map p458; ☎305-871-1810; 3801 NW 21st) is near the airport, though additional services also depart from the company's **Cutler Bay terminal** (Cutler Bay; ☎305-296-9072; 10801 Caribbean Blvd) and **North Miami terminal** (Map p458; ☎305-688-7277; 16000 NW 7th Ave).

If you are traveling very long distances (say, across several states), bargain airfares can sometimes undercut buses. On shorter routes, renting a car can sometimes be cheaper. Nonetheless, discounted (even half-price) long-distance bus trips are often available by purchasing tickets online seven to 14 days in advance.

The main Miami terminal of **Amtrak** (☎305-835-1222; www.amtrak.com; 8303 NW 37th Ave, West Little River), about 9 miles northwest of Downtown, connects the city with several other points in Florida (including Orlando and Jacksonville) on the Silver Service line that runs up to New York City. Travel time between New York and Miami is 27 to 31 hours. The Miami Amtrak station is connected by Tri-rail to Downtown Miami and has a left-luggage facility.

Getting Around

Bus Extensive system, though slow for long journeys.

Citi Bike Bike-sharing network in both Miami and Miami Beach. With heavy traffic, however, take care riding long distances – it can be hazardous.

Rental Car Convenient for zipping around town, but parking can be expensive.

Taxi & Ride-Sharing Services Best for getting between destinations if you don't want to drive, but can be pricey for long distances. Difficult to hail on the street; call or use an app (Lyft or Uber are the most popular) for a pick-up.

Trolley Free service with various routes in Miami Beach, Downtown, Wynwood, Coconut Grove, Coral Gables, Little Havana and other neighborhoods.

Fort Lauderdale

After years of building a reputation as *the* destination for beer-swilling college students on raucous spring breaks, Fort Lauderdale now angles for a slightly more mature and sophisticated crowd. Think martinis rather than tequila shots; jazz concerts instead of wet T-shirt contests. But don't worry, there's still plenty of carrying-on within the confines of area bars and nightclubs.

Few visitors venture far inland – except maybe to dine and shop along Las Olas Blvd; most spend the bulk of their time on the coast. It's understandable. Truly, it's hard to compete with beautiful beaches, a system of Venice-like waterways, an international yachting scene, spiffy new hotels and top-notch restaurants.

The city's Port Everglades is one of the busiest cruise-ship ports in the world, with megaships departing daily for the Caribbean, Mexico and beyond.

Sights

Fort Lauderdale Beach & Promenade BEACH
(N Atlantic Blvd;) Fort Lauderdale's promenade – a wide, brick, palm-tree-dotted pathway swooping along the beach and the A1A – is a magnet for runners, in-line skaters, walkers and cyclists.

The white-sand beach, meanwhile, is one of the nation's cleanest and best. Stretching 7 miles to Lauderdale-by-the-Sea, it has dedicated family-, gay- and dog-friendly sections.

Boating, diving, snorkeling and fishing are all extremely popular.

NSU Art Museum Fort Lauderdale MUSEUM
(954-525-5500; www.nsuartmuseum.org; 1 E Las Olas Blvd; adult/student/child $12/free; 11am-5pm Tue-Sat, from noon Sun) A curvaceous Florida standout with an interesting spilled rainbow design outside, the museum is known for its William Glackens collection (among Glackens fans) and its exhibitions on wide-ranging themes from northern European art to contemporary Cuban art, American pop art and contemporary photography.

On first Thursdays, the museum stays open to 8pm and hosts lectures, films and performances, as well as a happy hour in the museum cafe. Day courses and workshops are also available. Check the website for details.

★**Bonnet House** HISTORIC BUILDING
(954-563-5393; www.bonnethouse.org; 900 N Birch Rd; adult/child $20/16, grounds only $10; 9am-4pm Tue-Sun) This pretty plantation-style property was once the home of artists and collectors Frederic and Evelyn Bartlett. It is now open to guided tours that swing through its art-filled rooms and studios. Beyond the house, 35 acres of lush, subtropical gardens protect a pristine barrier-island ecosystem, including one of the finest orchid collections in the country.

Riverwalk LANDMARK
(www.goriverwalk.com) Curving along the New River, the meandering Riverwalk runs from Stranahan House to the Broward Center for the Performing Arts. Host to culinary tastings and other events, the walk connects a number of sights, restaurants and shops.

Museum of Discovery & Science MUSEUM
(954-467-6637; www.mods.org; 401 SW 2nd St; adult/child $17/14; 10am-5pm Mon-Sat, noon-6pm Sun;) A 52ft kinetic-energy sculpture greets you here, and fun exhibits include Gizmo City and Runways to Rockets – where it actually *is* rocket science. Plus there's an Everglades exhibit and IMAX theater. You can even have an 'Otter Encounter' for $50 per person (reservations only), where you can feed otters, participate in a training, and learn about their habits and diet.

Activities

Fort Lauderdale lies on the same reef system as the Keys. Snorkeling is a popular pastime but the real action in the water lies within a 50-minute boat ride at the site of some two-dozen wrecks. Here divers can nose around the Mercedes freighter and the Tenneco Towers artificial reef made up from an old oil platform. Soft corals bloom prolifically, and barracuda, jacks and parrotfish duck and dive between the wreckage.

Besides the underwater scenery, everything from jet-skis to parasailing to deep-sea fishing charters is available at the beach.

★**Sea Experience** BOATING, SNORKELING
(954-770-3483; www.seaxp.com; 801 Seabreeze Blvd; snorkeling adult/child $40/25, 2-tank dive $85 (not incl gear); 10:15am & 2:15pm;) Sea Experience takes guests in a 40ft glass-bottom boat along the Intracoastal and into the ocean to snorkel on a natural reef, thriving with marine life, in 10ft to 20ft of water. Tours last 2½ hours. Also offers scuba trips to multiple wreck sites.

Carrie B BOATING
(954-642-1601; www.carriebcruises.com; 440 N New River Dr E; tours adult/child $29/15; tours 11am, 1pm & 3pm, closed Tue & Wed May-Sep) Hop aboard this replica 19th-century riverboat for a narrated 90-minute 'lifestyles of the rich and famous' tour of the ginormous mansions along the Intracoastal and New River. Tours leave from Las Olas at SE 5th Ave.

★**Bar-B-Ranch** HORSEBACK RIDING
(954-424-1060; www.bar-b-ranch.com; 3500 Peaceful Ridge Rd, Davie; 60/90 min trail rides $50/60; 9am-5pm Mon-Fri, to 4:30pm Sat) With the glitter of Ft Lauderdale so close, it's hard to feel like any 'old' Florida is left,

but Davie is just 15 minutes away and at Bar-B-Ranch, a family-owned riding stable since 1969, you can truly get away from it all: on top of a horse. It offers trail and rental options, including a day and summer kids' camp.

The real magic though is just being in the saddle and seeing some of the nearby preserved woodlands and fields that once comprised most of this part of Florida. Davie has done a good job of preserving these spaces, so if the 23 acres of ranchland are too wimpy for you, there's 160-plus acres of additional countryside to explore, including live oak hammocks, wetlands, and a citrus grove.

Blue Moon Outdoor Adventures BOATING

(☎954-781-0073; www.bluemoonoutdoor.com; 1101 Bayview Dr, George English Park & Boat ramp; 1st hour kayak 1/2 person $15/25, SUP $35, then $10 per hour after; ⊙10am-sunset Thu-Sun or by appointment) Paddle the Island City Loop or go south through 'Venice of America,' Fort Lauderdale. Day, sunset, and moonlight tours are available by appointment. Tours include light refreshments.

Sleeping

The splashiest hotels are found along the beach. Of course, those places are also the priciest. Meander inland and you'll discover some wonderful inns with Old Florida charm. For more budget-friendly accommodations, check out Lauderdale-by-the-Sea.

Tranquilo MOTEL $$

(☎954-565-5790; www.tranquilofortlauderdale.com; 2909 Vistamar St; r $149-194; P ⊖ ❄ ☜ ≋) This white-on-white retro 1950s motel offers fantastic value for families. Rooms range over five buildings, each with its own pool, and some include newly refurbished kitchens along with access to outdoor grills and laundry services. No shuttle, but the beach is three blocks away. The main pool even has an accessible entry for those with mobility needs.

B Ocean Resort HOTEL $$

(☎954-524-5551; www.bhotelsandresorts.com; 1140 Seabreeze Blvd; r from $144; P ⊖ ❄ ☜ ≋) Defining the southern end of Seabreeze Blvd, this hotel straddles the uberpopular South Beach and offers breezy ocean views from the majority of its airy rooms. Built by M Tony Sherman in 1956, it looks like a giant cruise ship tethered to the sidewalk.

★ W Fort Lauderdale HOTEL $$$

(☎954-414-8200; www.wfortlauderdalehotel.com; 401 N Fort Lauderdale Beach Blvd; r $289-699; P ❄ @ ☜ ≋) With an exterior resembling two giant sails and an interior that looks like the backdrop for a J Lo video, this is where the glitterati stay – bust out your stiletto heels/skinny ties and join them. The massive lobby is built for leisure, with a silver-and-aqua lounge area, a moodily lit bar, and a deck lined with wicker chaises.

★ Lago Mar Resort RESORT $$$

(☎954-523-6511; www.lagomar.com; 1700 S Ocean Lane; r $300-700; P ⊖ ❄ @ ☜ ≋) On the south end of South Beach, this wonderfully noncorporate resort has it all: a private beach, grand lobby, massive island-style rooms, a full-service spa, on-site restaurants, a lagoon-style pool set amid tropical plantings and the personal touch of family ownership. (And no, not to be confused with President Trump's Mar-a-Lago.) A lovely fish mosaic graces the lobby floor.

Eating

Fort Lauderdale's food scene is heavily influenced by the area's large Italian American population but increasingly it's becoming known for its casual chic, farm-to-table options. Las Olas Blvd has a number of eating places, especially the stretch between 5th and 16th Aves, though these can be more touristy.

Lester's Diner DINER $

(☎954-525-5641; www.lestersdiner.com; 250 W State Rd 84; mains $6-19; ⊙24hr) Hailed endearingly as a greasy spoon, retro-since-it-was-new Lester's Diner has been keeping folks happy since the late 1960s. Everyone makes their way here at some point, from business types on cell phones to clubbers to travel writers needing pancakes at 4am.

Green Bar & Kitchen VEGAN $

(☎954-533-7507; www.greenbarkitchen.com; 1075 SE 17th St; mains $8-16; ⊙10am-9pm Mon-Sat, to 4pm Sun; P ✎) Discover bright flavors and innovative dishes at this modern, plant-based shop located in a strip mall. Get your fresh celery-juice fix, veggie voodoo shots, or non-dairy gelato. Almond milk replaces dairy in cold-pressed fruit smoothies, and the delectable cashew cup gives Reese's a run for its money.

LGBTIQ+ FORT LAUDERDALE

Sure, South Beach is a hot location for gay travelers, but Fort Lauderdale nips at the high heels of its southern neighbor. Compared to South Beach, Lauderdale is a little more rainbow-flag-oriented and a little less exclusive. And for the hordes of gay men who flock here, either to party or to settle down, therein lies the charm.

Fort Lauderdale is home to several-dozen gay bars and clubs, as many gay guesthouses, and a couple of way-gay residential areas. **Victoria Park** is the established gay hub just northeast of downtown Fort Lauderdale. A bit further north, **Wilton Manors** is a more recently gay-gentrified area boasting endless nightlife options. Look for **Rosie's** (954-563-0123; www.rosiesbng.com; 2449 Wilton Dr; 11am-11pm), a low-key neighborhood watering hole; **The Manor** (954-626-0082; www.themanorcomplex.com; 2345 Wilton Dr; cover $10-20; varies), for nationally recognized performers and an epic dance floor; and **Georgie's Alibi** (954-565-2526; www.alibiwiltonmanors.com; 2266 Wilton Dr; 11am-2am), best for its Wednesday comedy night with Cashetta, a fabulous female impersonator. Spots like Stache offer non-binary nights. There's even a leather/bear/cowboy club, **Ramrod** (954-763-8219; www.ramrodbar.com; 1508 NE 4th Ave; 3pm-2am).

Gay guesthouses are plentiful; visit www.gayftlauderdale.com. Consult the glossy weekly rag *Hot Spots* (www.hotspotsmagazine.com) to keep updated on gay nightlife. For the most insanely comprehensive list of everything gay, log on to www.jumponmarkslist.com.

★Burlock Coast INTERNATIONAL $$$
(954-302-6460; www.burlockcoast.com; Ritz Carlton, 1 N Fort Lauderdale Beach Blvd; mains $19-46; 7am-10pm) Situated in the lovely Ritz Carlton Hotel, this chic, casual spot somehow manages to be all things to all people: a cafe, bar, market and upmarket restaurant. The menu has been crafted to the mantra: local farmers and vendors. The menu changes seasonally but errs towards modern international, like pulled pork or simple fish-and-chips. The deck outside is prime for people watching.

15th Street Fisheries SEAFOOD $$$
(954-763-2777; www.15streetfisheries.com; 1900 SE 15th St; bar mains $7-16, restaurant mains $38-55; P) Tucked away in Lauderdale Marina with an open-fronted deck offering a front-row view of yachts, this place is hard to beat for waterfront dining. The wooden interior is kitted out like an Old Florida boathouse. The fine-dining restaurant is upstairs and a more informal dockside bar serves shrimp, crab and grilled mahi-mahi. You can feed the tarpon, too, which is popular with kids.

Drinking & Entertainment

Fort Lauderdale bars can stay open until 4am on weekends and 2am during the week. A handful of great bars and pubs are found in the Himmarshee Village area on SW 2nd St, while the beach offers open-air boozing.

★Stache COCKTAIL BAR
(954-449-1044; www.stacheftl.com; 109 SW 2nd Ave; 7am-5pm Mon & Thu, to 4am Fri, 8pm-4am Sat) A tall, sleek and sexy 1920s-themed drinking den serving crafted cocktails and rocking a crossover classic rock/funk/soul/R&B blend. At weekends there's live music, dancing and burlesque. Dress up; this is where the cool cats come to play. Serves coffee during the day; open late on weekends only. 'Non-binary night' is one of their themed evenings.

Revolutions Live CONCERT VENUE
(954-449-1025; www.jointherevolution.net; 100 SW 3rd Ave; varies, usually per person from $25; varies) Great event space with concerts that range from local up-and-comings to legends and household names. It's a multilevel space where up to 1300 people can rock on, and you actually have to try hard to not get a good view of the performers. No smoking is allowed.

Blue Jean Blues JAZZ
(954-306-6330; www.bjblive.com; 3320 NE 33rd St; snacks $9-17; 11am-2am Sun-Thu, to 3am Fri & Sat) Get away from the beach for a low-key evening of jazz and blues at this cool little neighborhood bar, often packed. There's live music seven nights and four afternoons a week, featuring a who's who of the southern Florida music scene. From East Sunrise Blvd

head north for 2.3 miles and then turn left onto NE 33rd Street.

Information

Greater Fort Lauderdale Convention & Visitors Bureau (954-765-4466; www.sunny.org; 101 NE 3rd Ave, Suite 100; 8:30am-5pm Mon-Fri) Has an excellent array of visitor information about the greater Fort Lauderdale region.

Getting There & Around

Fort Lauderdale is served by its own international **airport** (FLL; 866-435-9355; www.broward.org/airport; 100 Terminal Dr).

If you're driving here, I-95 and Florida's Turnpike run north–south and provide good access to Fort Lauderdale. I-595, the major east–west artery, intersects I-95, Florida's Turnpike and the Sawgrass Expwy. It also feeds into I-75, which runs to Florida's west coast.

Broward County Transit (BCT; www.broward.org/bct; single fare/day pass $2/5) operates between downtown, the beach and Port Everglades. From **Broward Central Terminal** (101 NW 1st Ave), take bus 11 to upper Fort Lauderdale Beach and Lauderdale-by-the-Sea; bus 4 to Port Everglades; and bus 40 to 17th St and the beaches.

The fun, yellow **water taxi** (954-467-6677; www.watertaxi.com; day pass adult/child $28/14) travels the canals and waterways between 17th St to the south, Atlantic Blvd/Pompano Beach to the north, the Riverwalk to the west and the Atlantic Ocean to the east. There are also services to Hollywood ($15 per person).

Palm Beach

The third-wealthiest city in America, Palm Beach, a barrier island connected by bridges to the mainland, is home to dozens of billionaires and looks every inch the playground for the rich and famous. Palatial Greco-Roman mansions line the shore; Bentleys and Porsches cruise the wide avenues of downtown; you may even see an entirely chrome Rolls Royce or two. Life here revolves around charity balls, designer shopping and cocktail-soaked lunches. Though all the bling may make you nauseated, fear not – much of Palm Beach is within the reach of all travelers. Stroll along the truly gold Gold Coast beach, ogle the massive gated compounds on A1A or window-shop in uber-ritzy Worth Ave – all for free.

Despite all the glitz, the architecture and history is nothing but fascinating, and offers some insight into how it might have been to live during the Gilded Age of late-19th-century USA.

Sights & Activities

Worth Avenue AREA

(www.worth-avenue.com) This quarter-mile, palm-tree-lined strip of more than 200 high-end brand shops is like the Rodeo Dr of the East. You can trace its history back to the 1920s when the now-gone Everglades Club staged weekly fashion shows and launched the careers of designers such as Elizabeth Arden. Even if you don't have the slightest urge to sling a swag of glossy bags over your arm, the people-watching is priceless, as is the Spanish Revival architecture.

★Flagler Museum MUSEUM

(561-655-2833; www.flaglermuseum.us; 1 Whitehall Way; adult/child $18/10; 10am-5pm Tue-Sat, from noon Sun) This museum is housed in the spectacular 1902 mansion built by Henry Flagler as a gift for his bride, Mary Lily Kenan. The beaux arts–styled Whitehall was one of the most modern houses of its era and quickly became the focus of the winter season. It was designed by John Carrère and Thomas Hastings, both students of the Ecole des Beaux-Arts in Paris and collaborators on other Gilded Age landmarks such as the New York Public Library.

★Palm Beach Lake Trail CYCLING

(Royal Palm Way, at the Intracoastal Waterway) Running along the Intracoastal Waterway, this 5-mile paved path stretches from Worth Ave (in the south) to Indian Rd (in the north). Nicknamed 'The Trail of Conspicuous Consumption,' it is sandwiched between two amazing views: Lake Worth lagoon to the west, and an unending series of mansions to the east, and it originally allowed Flagler hotel guests to check out the social scene.

Palm Beach Bicycle Trail Shop CYCLING

(561-659-4583; http://palmbeachbicycle.com; 50 Cocoanut Row, Suite 117, In the Slat House; bikes/electric bikes per day $49/89; 9am-5:30pm Mon-Sat, 10am-5pm Sun) This shop rents out bikes and electric bikes at a convenient spot for cycling. Helmets cost $5 extra.

Sleeping & Eating

Bradley Park Hotel HOTEL $$

(561-832-7050; www.bradleyparkhotel.com; 2080 Sunset Ave; r $229, ste $329-359; P ❄ ⓦ)

Though undergoing restoration at the time of research, the midrange Bradley (built in 1921) offers large rooms and will likely retain much of its previous charm. Some rooms included original features from the era and characterful furniture. It's located just a short walk from the shops and restaurants of Royal Poinciana Way. Expect that the decor may change but the grandeur will remain.

★Breakers RESORT **$$$**
(☎855-801-7057; www.thebreakers.com; 1 S County Rd; r/ste from $699/2000; P ⊖ ❄ @ ≋ ☒) Originally built by Henry Flagler (in 1904, rooms cost $4 per night, including meals), today this 538-room resort sprawls across 140 acres and boasts a staff of 2000 plus, fluent in 56 languages. Just feet from the county's best snorkeling, this palace has two 18-hole golf courses, a mile of semiprivate beach, four pools and the best brunch around.

Surfside Diner DINER, BREAKFAST **$**
(☎561-659-7495; 314 S County Rd; mains $8-13; ⊙8am-3pm) This classy remake of a classic diner serves decent breakfasts and brunch. Pancakes, chicken breakfast burritos and French toast are all tasty. For lunch there's a healthy offering of grilled cheese and tomato soup, BLTs, PB&Js and sliders.

★Būccan AMERICAN **$$$**
(☎561-833-3450; www.buccanpalmbeach.com; 350 S County Rd; mains $18-40; ⊙5pm-10pm Sun-Thu, to 11pm Fri & Sat) With its modern American menu and James Beard–nominated chef, Clay Conley, at the helm, Būccan is the 'it' place to eat in Palm Beach. Flavor-hop with a selection of small plates, including smoked chicken sliders, and move on to snapper ceviche. Reservations recommended.

The bar will stay open later if it's busy, to midnight Sunday to Thursday and to 1am on Friday and Saturday.

★Café Boulud FRENCH **$$$**
(☎561-655-6060; www.cafeboulud.com/palmbeach; 301 Australian Ave; mains $16-49, fixed-price menu $48; ⊙cafe 7am-11pm, bar to midnight) Created by renowned New York chef Daniel Boulud, the restaurant at the Brazilian Court hotel is one of the few places in Palm Beach that truly justifies the sky-high prices. The warm dining room, beautiful lit-marble bar, and terrace complements a rich menu of classic French and fusion dishes, all displaying Boulud's signature sophistication and subtlety.

Drinking & Entertainment

Leopard Lounge LOUNGE
(www.chesterfieldpb.com; 363 Cocoanut Row; ⊙7am-2:30pm & 5:30-11pm Mon-Fri, to midnight or later Sat & Sun) This gold, black and red lounge attracts a mature crowd and the occasional celeb (neither photos nor autograph hounds are allowed). The piano player and the waitstaff give off a there's-a-place-they'd-rather-be vibe, but if you want to relax with a drink or strike up a chat with someone next to you, this is the spot.

Society of the Four Arts PERFORMING ARTS
(☎561-655-7226; www.fourarts.org; 2 Four Arts Plaza) The concert series here includes cabaret, the Palm Beach Symphony, chamber orchestras, string quartets and piano performances.

Information

Chamber of Commerce (☎561-655-3282; www.palmbeachchamber.com; 400 Royal Palm Way, Suite 106; ⊙9am-5pm Mon-Fri) Excellent maps and racks of pamphlets, plus there is a dog to pat.

Getting There & Around

Palm Tran (http://discover.pbcgov.org/palmtran; per ride $2, day pass $5) bus 41 covers the bulk of the island, from Lantana Rd to Sunrise Ave; transfer to bus 1 at Publix to go north or south along Hwy 1. To get to Palm Beach International Airport (p477) in West Palm Beach, take bus 41 to the downtown transfer and hop on bus 44.

Though it's a fairly compact city, the two major downtown neighborhoods, centered on Royal Poinciana Way and Worth Ave, are a fair hike apart.

West Palm Beach

When Henry Flagler decided to develop what is now West Palm Beach, he knew precisely what it would become: a working-class community for the labor force that would support his glittering resort town across the causeway. And so the fraternal twins were born – Palm Beach, considered the fairer of the two, and West Palm Beach, a cooler work-hard-play-hard community. West Palm has a surprisingly diverse collection of restaurants, friendly inhabitants (including a strong gay community) and a gorgeous waterway that always seems to reflect the perfect amount of starlight.

Sights & Activities

★Norton Museum of Art MUSEUM

(☎561-832-5196; www.norton.org; 1451 S Olive Ave; adult/child $18/5, free on Sat; ⏰10am-5pm Mon, Tue, Thu & Sat, to 10pm Fri, from 11am Sun) This is the largest art museum in Florida and arguably the most impressive. It opened in 1941 to display the enormous art collection of industrialist Ralph Hubbard Norton and his wife Elizabeth. The Nortons' permanent collection of more than 5000 pieces (including works by Matisse, Warhol and O'Keeffe) is displayed alongside important Chinese, pre-Columbian Mexican and Southwestern USA artifacts, plus some wonderful contemporary photography and regular traveling exhibitions.

South Florida Science Center & Aquarium MUSEUM

(☎561-832-1988; www.sfsciencecenter.org; 4801 Dreher Trail North; adult/child $18/14; ⏰9am-5pm Mon-Fri, 10am-6pm Sat & Sun) A great little hands-on science center, aquarium and planetarium with weekend programs, traveling exhibits, a science trail, mini-golf and butterfly garden. On the last Friday of the month the museum stays open from 6pm to 9pm so you can view the night sky from the county's only public observatory (weather permitting). Prices change according to the exhibition.

Peanut Island ISLAND

(http://discover.pbcgov.org; $12 round-trip; ⏰11am-4pm Thu-Sun) Plopped right off the northeastern corner of West Palm, Peanut Island was created in 1918 by dredging projects. Originally named Inlet Island, the spit was renamed for a peanut-oil-shipping operation that failed in 1946. There is even a disused nuclear fallout bunker that was constructed for John F Kennedy during the days of the Cuban missile crisis (although it was closed at the time of research).

Rapids Water Park WATER PARK

(☎561-848-6272; www.rapidswaterpark.com; 6566 North Military Trail, Riviera Beach; weekday/weekend $46/52; ⏰10am-5pm mid-Mar-Dec, to 7pm or 9pm Jun-Aug) South Florida's largest water park features 30 action-packed acres of wet and wild rides. Don't let the squeals of fear and delight from the Big Thunder funnel put you off. Awesome fun. Parking costs an extra $15.

Sleeping

Hotel Biba MOTEL $

(☎561-832-0094; www.hotelbiba.com; 320 Belvedere Rd; r $149-179; P❄☜≋) With plain, white, slightly missing-a-small-something rooms, this place lacks a bit of color, but is one of the better (if only) budget options around. It's well located – only a block from the Intracoastal, and perched on the edge of the El Cid district. Suffice to say it's clean and fine if you just want a bed. Includes a simple Continental breakfast.

★Grandview Gardens B&B $$

(☎561-833-9023; www.grandview-gardens.com; 1608 Lake Ave; r $139-249; P❄☜≋) Book a room at this intimate resort and you'll feel like a local in no time. Hidden in a tropical garden on Howard Park, the enormous suites with their wrought-iron and four-poster beds access the pool patio through French doors. They're decorated to reflect the Spanish Mediterranean style that is so popular in these parts.

Eating

★Grandview Public Market MARKET $

(www.grandviewpublic.com; 1401 Clare Ave; ⏰7am-10:30pm) The Grandview Public Market is an expansive array of small shops, stalls and foodcarts with all kinds of offerings. This is by far the best option for budget travelers or a group who may want individual items. The selection ranges from Cuban sandwiches to Thai rolled ice cream and everything in between. Plenty of public seating, too!

Restoration Hardware BRASSERIE $$

(☎561-804-6826; www.restorationhardware.com; 560 Okeechobee Blvd; mains $19-27; ⏰10am-8pm Mon-Sat, 11am-7pm Sun) Both the name and the location (atop a furniture store) belie the exquisite experience that awaits those who seek out Restoration Hardware, an as-ritzy-as-it-gets rooftop dining experience with a full bar and spectacular wine room. Presentation is as lovely as the food is tasty, with beautiful salads, artfully presented burgers and snazzy lobster rolls.

Darbster VEGAN $$

(☎561-586-2622; www.darbster.com; 8020 S Dixie Hwy; mains $12-18; ⏰5-10pm Tue-Fri, 10:30am-3pm & 5-10pm Sat, to 9pm Sun) This place is out on a limb in many respects: it's 5 miles south of town in an incongruous location by the S Dixie Hwy on the Palm Beach canal;

the menu is 100% vegan; all profits go to a foundation for animal care; and it attracts everyone from Birkenstock-wearing hippies to diamond-wearing Palm Beachers.

★Table 26 Degrees AMERICAN $$$
(☎561-855-2660; www.table26palmbeach.com; 1700 S Dixie Hwy; mains $20-49; ⏲11:30am-2pm Mon-Sat, from 10:30am Sun, plus 4:30-10pm Sun-Thu, to 11pm Fri & Sat) Don't be put off by the price of this sophisticated restaurant. It is filled with locals, conversation and the clinking of glasses for good reason. They flock here for the bar (great happy hour 4:30pm to 6:30pm daily) plus the share plates and mains that are divided by water, land, field, and hands (the latter covers fried chicken and burgers).

Drinking & Entertainment

Roosters GAY
(☎561-832-9119; www.roosterswpb.com; 823 Belvedere Rd; ⏲3pm-3am Sun-Thu, to 4am Fri & Sat) A mainstay of West Palm's thriving gay community, this bar has been offering popcorn, hot dogs, bingo and hot male dancers since 1984.

★Voltaire CLUB
(☎561-408-5603; www.voltairewpb.com; 526 Clematis St; ⏲8pm-2am Sun-Wed, to 3am Thu, to 4am Fri-Sat) Part of the Subculture umbrella and next door to Respectable Street, Voltaire is the wildebeest of clubs: fresh sushi, craft cocktails and live music don't always go together, but this quirky spot is fantastic, offering great drinks, excellent maki and nigiri, and some fun, interesting bands. Spoken word, live-mic nights, and other events happen here too. Don't miss it!

Respectable Street LIVE MUSIC
(☎561-832-9999; www.respectablestreet.com; 518 Clematis St; ⏲9pm-3am Wed-Thu, to 4am Fri & Sat) Respectables has kept South Florida jamming to great bands for two decades; it also organizes October's MoonFest, the city's best block party. Great DJs, strong drinks and a breezy chill-out patio are added bonuses. See if you can find the hole that the Red Hot Chili Peppers' Anthony Kiedis punched in the wall when they played here.

International Polo Club SPECTATOR SPORT
(☎561-204-5687; www.internationalpoloclub.com; 3667 120th Ave S, Wellington; general admission $10, lawn seating from $30; ⏲Sun Jan-Apr) Between January and April the International Polo Club hosts 16 weeks of polo and glamour. As one of the finest polo facilities in the world, it not only attracts the most elite players but also the local and international glitterati who whoop it up in head-turning fashion over champagne brunches ($125, with bottle of Veuve Cliquot, $325). Why not?

Information

The *Palm Beach Post* (www.palmbeachpost.com) is the largest paper.

Discover The Palm Beaches Visitor Center (☎561-233-3000; www.thepalmbeaches.com; 2195 Southern Blvd, Suite 400; ⏲8:30am-5:30pm Mon-Fri) is a good for area information, maps and online guides.

Music lovers will want to pick up a free copy of Pure Honey (www.purehoneymagazine.com) for details of great music, live shows and other entertainment going on.

Getting There & Around

Palm Beach International Airport (PBI; ☎561-471-7420; www.pbia.org; 1000 James L Turnage Blvd) is served by most major airlines and car-rental companies. It's about a mile west of I-95 on Belvedere Rd. Palm Tran (p475) bus 44 runs between the airport, the train station and downtown ($2).

Greyhound (☎561-833-8534; www.greyhound.com; 205 S Tamarind Ave; ⏲6am-10:45pm), **Tri-Rail** (☎800-875-7245; www.tri-rail.com; 203 S Tamarind Ave) and **Amtrak** (☎800-872-7245; www.amtrak.com; 209 S Tamarind Ave) share the same building: the historic Seaboard Train Station. Palm Tran serves the station with bus 44 (from the airport).

A cute and convenient (and free!) trolley runs between Clematis St and CityPlace starting at 11am.

The Everglades

There is no wilderness in America quite like the Everglades. Called the 'River of Grass' by Native American inhabitants, this is not just a wetland, or a swamp, or a lake, or a river, or a prairie, or a grassland – it is all of those, twisted together into a series of soft horizons, long vistas, sunsets that stretch across your entire field of vision and the toothy grins of a healthy population of dinosaur-era reptiles.

The park's quiet majesty is evident when you see anhinga flexing their wings before breaking into a corkscrew dive, or the slow, rhythmic flap of a great blue heron gliding over its domain, or the shimmer of light on miles of untrammeled saw grass as the sun sets behind hunkering cypress domes. In a nation where natural beauty is measured by its capacity for drama, the Everglades subtly, contentedly flows on.

Everglades National Park

This vast **wilderness** (☎305-242-7700; www.nps.gov/ever; 40001 SR-9336, Homestead; ⏰visitor center 9am-5pm), encompassing 1.5 million acres, is one of America's great natural treasures. There's much to see and do – from spying alligators basking in the noonday sun as herons stalk patiently through nearby waters in search of prey, to going kayaking in mangrove canals and on peaceful lakes. You can also wade into murky knee-high waters among cypress domes on a rough-and-ready 'slough slog.'

There are sunrise strolls on boardwalks amid the awakening glimmers of birdsong, and moonlit glimpses of gators swimming gracefully along narrow channels in search of dinner. Backcountry camping, bicycle tours and ranger-led activities help bring the magic of this place to life. The biggest challenge is really just deciding where to begin.

There are three main entrances and three main areas of the park: one along the southeast edge near Homestead and Florida City (Ernest Coe section); at the central-north side on the Tamiami Trail (Shark Valley section); and a third at the northwest shore (Gulf Coast section), past Everglades City. The Shark Valley and Gulf Coast sections of the park come one after the other in geographic succession, but the Ernest Coe area is entirely separate.

The admission fee – $30 per vehicle, $15 per hiker and cyclist – covers the whole park, and is good for seven consecutive days. Because the Tamiami Trail is a public road, there's no admission to access national park sights along this highway, aside from Shark Valley. In the southern half of the park, one staffed checkpoint oversees access to all sights on the road between Ernest Coe down to Flamingo.

Three types of **backcountry campsites** (☎239-695-3311, 239-695-2945; www.nps.gov/ever/planyourvisit/backcamp.htm; ⏰Flamingo & Gulf Coast Visitor Centers 8am-4.30pm) are available: beach sites, on coastal shell beaches and in the 10,000 Islands; ground sites, which are basically mounds of dirt built up above the mangroves; and *chickees,* wooden platforms built above the waterline where you can pitch a freestanding (no spikes) tent. *Chickees,* which have toilets, are the most civilized – there's a serenity found in sleeping on what feels like a raft levitating above the water. Ground sites tend to be the most bug infested.

From November to April, backcountry camping permits cost $15, plus $2 per person per night; from May to October sites are free, but you must still self-register at Flamingo and Gulf Coast Visitor Centers or call ☎239-695-2945.

Warning: if you're paddling around and see an island that looks pleasant for camping but isn't a designated campsite, beware – you may end up submerged when the tides change.

Some backcountry tips:

➡ Store food in a hand-sized, raccoon-proof container (available at gear stores).

➡ Bury your waste at least 10in below ground, but keep in mind some ground sites have hard turf.

➡ Use a backcountry stove to cook. Ground fires are only permitted at beach sites, and you can only burn dead or downed wood.

Load up on provisions before you enter the park. Homestead or Florida City are your best options if going into the Southern Everglades. If heading to the Tamiami Trail, plan to stock up in Miami – or the western suburbs.

ℹ Getting There & Around

The largest subtropical wilderness in the continental USA is easily accessible from Miami. The Glades, which comprise the 80 southernmost miles of Florida, are bound by the Atlantic Ocean to the east and the Gulf of Mexico to the west. The Tamiami Trail (Hwy 41) goes east–west, parallel to the more northern (and less interesting) Alligator Alley (I-75).

You need a car to properly enter the Everglades and once you're in, wearing a good pair of walking boots is essential to penetrate the interior. Having a canoe or a kayak helps as well; these can be rented from outfits inside and outside the park, or else you can seek out guided canoe and kayak tours.

Bicycles are well suited to the flat roads of Everglades National Park, particularly in the area between Ernest Coe and Flamingo Point. Road shoulders in the park tend to be dangerously small.

Around the Everglades

Biscayne National Park

Just to the east of the Everglades is **Biscayne National Park** (☎305-230-1144, boat tours 786-335-3644; www.nps.gov/bisc; 9700 SW 328th St; boat tours adult/child $35/25; ⌚7am-5:30pm), or the 5% of it that isn't underwater. In fact, a portion of the world's third-largest reef sits here off the coast of Florida, along with mangrove forests and the northernmost Florida Keys. This is some of the best reef viewing and snorkeling you'll find in the USA, outside Hawaii and nearby Key Largo.

Biscayne requires a little extra planning, but you'll be rewarded for your effort. This unique 300-sq-mile park is easy to explore independently with a canoe, or via a boat tour. Generally summer and fall are the best times to visit the park; you'll want to snorkel when the water is calm. The offshore Keys, accessible only by boat, offer pristine opportunities for camping.

Primitive camping (www.nps.gov/bisc/planyourvisit/camping.htm; tent sites per night $25, May-Sep free) is available on Elliott and Boca Chita Keys, though you'll need a boat to get there. No-see-ums (tiny flies) are invasive, and their bites are devastating. Make sure your tent is devoid of minuscule entry points.

Information

Dante Fascell Visitor Center (☎305-230-1144; www.nps.gov/bisc; 9700 SW 328th St; ⌚9am-5pm) Located at Convoy Point, this center shows a great introductory film for an overview of the park, and has maps, information and excellent ranger activities. The grounds around the center are a popular picnic spot on weekends and holidays, especially for families from Homestead. Also showcases local artwork.

Getting There & Away

To get here, you'll have to drive about 9 miles east of Homestead (the way is pretty well signposted) on SW 328th St (North Canal Dr) into a long series of green-and-gold flat fields and marsh.

Homestead & Florida City

Homestead and neighboring Florida City, 2 miles to the south, aren't of obvious appeal upon arrival. Part of the ever-expanding subdivisions of South Miami, this bustling corridor can feel like an endless strip of big-box shopping centers, fast-food joints, car dealerships and gas stations. However, look beneath the veneer and you'll find much more than meets the eye: strange curiosities like a 'castle' built single-handedly by one lovestruck immigrant, an animal rescue center for exotic species, a winery showcasing Florida's produce (hint: it's not grapes), an up-and-coming microbrewery, and one of the best farm stands in America.

This area makes a great base for forays into the stunning Everglades National Park.

Sights & Activities

★Coral Castle CASTLE

(☎305-248-6345; www.coralcastle.com; 28655 S Dixie Hwy; adult/senior/child $18/15/8; ⌚8am-6pm Sun-Thu, to 8pm Fri & Sat) 'You will be seeing unusual accomplishment,' reads the inscription on the rough-hewn quarried wall. That's an understatement. There is no greater temple to all that is weird and wacky about South Florida. The legend goes that a Latvian man got snubbed at the altar, came to the USA and settled in Florida, and hand-carved, unseen, in the dead of night, a monument to unrequited love.

Everglades Outpost WILDLIFE RESERVE

(☎305-562-8000; www.evergladesoutpost.org; 35601 SW 192nd Ave, Homestead; adult/child $15/10; ⌚10am-5:30pm Mon, Tue & Fri-Sun, by appointment Wed & Thu) The Everglades Outpost houses, feeds and cares for wild animals that have been seized from illegal traders, abused, neglected or donated by people who could not care for them. Residents of the outpost include a lemur, wolves, a black bear, a zebra, cobras, alligators and a pair of majestic tigers (one of whom was bought by an exotic dancer who thought she could incorporate it into her act). Your money goes toward helping the outpost's mission.

Garls Coastal Kayaking Everglades KAYAKING

(www.garlscoastalkayaking.com; 19200 SW 344th St, Homestead; single/double kayak per day $40/55, half-/full-day tour $125/150) On the property of the **Robert Is Here** (☎305-246-1592; www.robertishere.com; juices $7-9; ⌚8am-7pm) fruit stand, this outfitter leads highly recommended excursions into the Everglades. A full-day outing includes hiking (more of a wet walk or slog into the lush landscape of cypress domes), followed by kayaking in both the mangroves and in Florida Bay, and, time permitting, a night walk.

Sleeping & Eating

★Hoosville Hostel HOSTEL $
(☎305-248-1122; www.hoosvillehostel.com; 20 SW 2nd Ave, Florida City; tent sites per person $18, dm $35, d $65-80, ste $149-190; P ❄ 📶 🏊) Formerly the Everglades International Hostel, the Hoosville has kept the good-value dorms, private rooms and 'semi-privates' (you have an enclosed room within the dorms and share a bathroom with dorm residents). The creatively configured backyard is the best feature. There's a small rock-cut pool with a waterfall and a gazebo.

Gator Grill AMERICAN $
(☎786-243-0620; 36650 SW 192nd Ave, Homestead; mains $9-16; ⏰11am-6:30pm) A handy pit stop before or after visiting the Everglades National Park, the Gator Grill is a white shack with picnic tables, where you can munch on all manner of alligator dishes. There are gator tacos, gator stir-fry, gator kebabs and straight-up fried alligator served in a basket.

Information

There are several info centers where you can get tips on attractions, lodging and dining.

Chamber of Commerce (☎305-247-2332; www.southdadechamber.org; 455 N Flagler Ave, Homestead; ⏰9am-5pm Mon-Fri)

Tropical Everglades Visitor Association (www.tropicaleverglades.com; 160 N 1st St, Florida City; ⏰8am-5pm Mon-Sat, 10am-2pm Sun)

Getting There & Away

Homestead runs a free weekend **trolley bus service** (☎305-224-4457; www.cityofhomestead.com; ⏰Sat & Sun Dec-Apr), which takes visitors from Losner Park (downtown Homestead) out to the **Royal Palm Visitor Center** (☎305-242-7700; www.nps.gov/ever; State Rd 9336; ⏰9am-4:15pm) in Everglades National Park. It also runs between Losner Park and Biscayne National Park (p479). Call for the latest departure times.

Tamiami Trail

Calle Ocho, in Miami's Little Havana, is the eastern end of the Tamiami Trail/Hwy 41, which cuts through the Everglades to the Gulf of Mexico. So going west along Hwy 41, you may only cross a few dozen miles but you'll feel several different worlds away – this trip leads you into the northern edges of the Everglades, past long landscapes of flooded forest, pine woods, gambling halls, swamp-buggy tours and roadside food shacks.

Airboat tours are an old-school way of seeing the Everglades (and there is something to be said for getting a tour from a raging Skynyrd fan with killer tats and better camo), but there are other ways of exploring the park as well.

Sights & Activities

★Fakahatchee Strand Preserve PARK
(☎239-695-4593; www.floridastateparks.org/parks-and-trails/fakahatchee-strand-preserve-state-park; 137 Coastline Dr, Copeland; vehicle/pedestrian/bicycle $3/2/2; ⏰8am-sunset; P 🚻) 🍃 The Fakahatchee Strand, besides having a fantastic name, also houses a 20-mile by 5-mile estuarine wetland that looks like something from the beginning of time. A 2000ft boardwalk traverses this wet and wild wonderland, where panthers still stalk their prey amid the black waters. While it's unlikely you'll spot any panthers, there's a great chance you'll see a large variety of blooming orchids, bird life and reptiles ranging in size from tiny skinks to grinning alligators.

Shark Valley Tram Tour TOURS
(☎305-221-8455; www.sharkvalleytramtours.com; adult/child under 12yr/senior $25/19/12.75; ⏰departures 9:30am, 11am, 2pm & 4pm May-Dec, 9am-4pm Jan-Apr hourly on the hour) This excellent two-hour tour runs along a 15-mile asphalt trail allowing you to see copious amounts of alligators in the winter months. Tours are narrated by knowledgeable park rangers who give a fascinating overview of the Everglades.

Information

Shark Valley Visitor Center (☎305-221-8776; www.nps.gov/ever/planyourvisit/svdirections.htm; national park entry per vehicle/bicycle/pedestrian $25/8/8; ⏰9am-5pm) A good place to pick up information about the Everglades, including trails, wildlife watching and free ranger-led activities.

Everglades City

On the edge of Chokoloskee Bay, you'll find an Old Florida fishing village of raised houses, turquoise water and scattershot emerald-green mangrove islands. 'City' is stretching

DETOUR: LOOP ROAD

The 24-mile-long Loop Rd, off Tamiami Trail (Hwy 41), offers some unique sites. One: the homes of the **Miccosukee**, some of which have been considerably expanded by gambling revenue. You'll see some traditional *chickee*-style huts and some trailers with massive add-on wings that are bigger than the original trailer – all seem to have shiny new pickup trucks parked out front. Two: great pull-offs for viewing flooded forests, where egrets that look like pterodactyls perch in the trees, and alligators lurk in the depths below. Three: houses with large Confederate flags and 'Stay off my property' signs; these homes are as much a part of the landscape as the swamp. And four: the short, pleasantly jungly **Tree Snail Hammock Nature Trail**. Though unpaved, the graded road is in good shape and fine for 2WD vehicles. True to its name, the road loops right back onto the Tamiami; expect a leisurely jaunt on the Loop to add an hour or two to your trip.

it for Everglades City – this is really a friendly fishing town where you can easily lose yourself for a day or three. You'll find some intriguing vestiges of the past here, including an excellent regional museum, as well as delicious seafood.

Hwy 29 runs south through town onto the small, peaceful residential island of Chokoloskee, which has some pretty views over the watery wilderness of the 10,000 Islands. You can arrange boating excursions from either Everglades City or Chokoloskee to explore the pristine environment here.

Sights & Activities

★Museum of the Everglades MUSEUM
(239-695-0008; www.evergladesmuseum.org; 105 W Broadway, Everglades City; 9am-4pm Mon-Sat; P) FREE For a break from the outdoors, don't miss this small museum run by volunteers who have a wealth of knowledge on the region's history. Located in the town's former laundry house, the collection delves into human settlement in the area from the early pioneers of the 1800s to the boom days of the 1920s and its tragic moments (Hurricane Donna devastated the town in 1960), and subsequent transformation into the quiet backwater of today.

10,000 Islands ISLAND
One of the best ways to experience the serenity of the Everglades – somehow desolate yet lush, tropical and forbidding – is by paddling the network of waterways that skirt the northwest portion of the park. The 10,000 Islands consist of many (but not really 10,000) tiny islands and a mangrove swamp that hugs the southwestern-most border of Florida.

Everglades Adventures CANOEING
(877-567-0679; www.evergladesadventures.com; 107 Camellia St, Everglades City; 3-4hr tours from $99, canoe/kayak rental per day from $30/50) For a real taste of the Everglades, nothing beats getting out on the water. This highly recommended outfitter offers a range of half-day kayak tours, from sunrise paddles to twilight trips through mangroves that return under a sky full of stars. Tours shuttle you to places like Chokoloskee Island, Collier-Seminole State Park, Rabbit Key or Tiger Key for excursions.

Sleeping & Eating

Outdoor Resorts of Chokoloskee MOTEL $
(239-695-2881; www.outdoorresortsofchokoloskee.com; 150 Smallwood Dr, Chokoloskee; r $119;) At the northern end of Chokoloskee Island, this good-value place is a big draw for its extensive facilities, including several swimming pools, hot tubs, tennis and shuffleboard courts, a fitness center and boat rentals. The fairly basic motel-style rooms have kitchenettes and a back deck overlooking the marina.

Everglades City Motel MOTEL $$
(239-695-4224; www.evergladescitymotel.com; 310 Collier Ave, Everglades City; r $150-250; P) With large rooms that have all the mod cons (flat-screen TVs, fridge, coffeemaker) and friendly staff who can hook you up with boat tours, this motel provides good value for those looking to spend some time near the 10,000 Islands.

★Havana Cafe LATIN AMERICAN $$
(239-695-2214; www.havanacafeoftheeverglades.com; 191 Smallwood Dr, Chokoloskee; mains lunch $10-19, dinner $22-30; 7am-3pm Mon-Thu, to 8pm Fri & Sat, closed mid-Apr–mid-Oct)

This cafe is famed far and wide for its deliciously prepared seafood served with Latin accents. Lunch favorites include stone-crab enchiladas, blackened grouper with rice and beans, and a decadent Cuban sandwich. The outdoor dining amid palm trees and vibrant bougainvillea – not to mention the incredibly friendly service – adds to the appeal.

Information

Everglades Area Chamber of Commerce (☎239-695-3941; cnr Hwys 41 & 29; ⏰9am-4pm) General information about the region is available here.

Getting There & Away

There is no public transportation out this way. If driving, it's a fairly straight 85-mile drive west from Miami. The trip takes about 1¾ hours in good traffic.

Florida Keys

If Florida is a state apart from the USA, the Keys are islands apart from Florida – in other words, it's different down here. This is a place for those escaping everyday life on the mainland. You'll find about 113 mangrove-and-sandbar islands where the white sun melts over deep green mangroves; long, soft mudflats and tidal bars; teal waters and a bunch of charming polite society castaways. Key West is still defined by its motto – One Human Family – an ideal that equals a tolerant, accepting ethos where anything goes and life is always a party (or at least a hungover day after). The color scheme: watercolor pastels cooled by breezes on a sunset-kissed Bahamian porch. Welcome to the End of the USA.

Information

The Monroe County Tourist Development Council's Florida Keys & Key West Visitors Bureau runs an excellent website (www.fla-keys.com), which is packed with information on everything the Keys has to offer.

Check www.keysnews.com for good daily online news and information about the islands.

Getting There & Away

Getting here can be half the fun – or, if you're unlucky, a whopping dose of frustration. Imagine a tropical-island hop, from one bar-studded mangrove islet to the next, via one of the most remarkable roads in the world: the Overseas Hwy (Hwy 1). On a good day, driving along the Overseas with the windows down – the wind in your face and the twin sisters of Florida Bay and the Atlantic stretching on either side – is the US road trip in tropical perfection. On a bad day, you end up sitting in gridlock behind some guy who is riding a midlife-crisis Harley.

Greyhound (www.greyhound.com) buses serve all Keys destinations along Hwy 1 and depart from Downtown Miami and Key West; you can pick up a bus along the way by standing on the Overseas Hwy and flagging one down. If you fly into Fort Lauderdale or Miami, the **Keys Shuttle** (☎888-765-9997; www.keysshuttle.com) provides door-to-door service to most of the Keys ($70/80/90 to the Upper and Middle Keys/Lower Keys/Key West). Reserve at least a day in advance.

Key Largo

We're not going to lie: Key Largo (both the name of the town and the island it's on) is slightly underwhelming at a glance. 'Under' is the key word, as its main sights are under the water – including a hotel. As you drive onto the islands, Key Largo resembles a long line of low-lying hammock and strip development. But head down a side road and duck into this warm little bar, or that converted Keys plantation house, and the island idiosyncrasies become more pronounced.

The 33-mile-long Largo, which starts at Mile Marker 106, is the longest island in the Keys, and those 33 miles have attracted a lot of marine life, all accessible from the biggest concentration of dive sites in the islands. The town of Tavernier (Mile Marker 93) is just south of the town of Key Largo.

Sights & Activities

John Pennekamp Coral Reef State Park STATE PARK
(☎305-451-6300; www.pennekamppark.com; Mile 102.6 oceanside; car with 1/2 people $4.50/9, cyclist or pedestrian $2.50; ⏰8am-sunset, aquarium to 5pm; P) John Pennekamp has the singular distinction of being the first underwater park in the USA. There's 170 acres of dry parkland here and over 48,000 acres (75 sq miles) of wet: the vast majority of the protected area is the ocean. Before you get out in that water, be sure to take in some pleasant beaches and stroll over the nature trails.

Laura Quinn Wild Bird Sanctuary WILDLIFE RESERVE
(305-852-4486; www.keepthemflying.org; 93600 Overseas Hwy, Mile 93.6; donations accepted; sunrise-sunset;) This 7-acre sanctuary serves as a protected refuge for a wide variety of injured birds. A boardwalk leads through various enclosures where you can learn a bit about some of the permanent residents – those unable to be released back in the wild. The species here include masked boobies, great horned owls, green herons, brown pelicans, double-crested cormorants and others. Keep walking along the path to reach a nice vista of Florida Bay and a wading bird pond.

African Queen BOATING
(305-451-8080; www.africanqueenflkeys.com; Key Largo Holiday Inn, 99701 Overseas Hwy; canal/dinner cruises $49/89) The steamboat used in the 1951 movie starring Humphrey Bogart and Katharine Hepburn has been restored to its former splendor. It was built in England, in 1912, and used in Africa to transport goods, missionaries and hunters, before becoming a movie star. The boat was brought to the US in 1968 and registered as a National Historic Site.

Garl's Coastal Kayaking ECOTOUR
(305-393-3223; www.garlscoastalkayaking.com; 4hr tours adult/child $75/50, single/double kayak hire per day $40/55) Garl's is an excellent ecotour operator that gets customers into the Everglades backcountry and mangrove islets of Florida Bay via kayak and canoe. It also provides reasonable equipment rentals.

Sleeping & Eating

Hilton Key Largo Resort HOTEL $$
(305-852-5553; www.keylargoresort.com; Mile 102 bayside; r/ste from $200/280;) This Hilton has a ton of character. Folks just seem to get all laid-back when lounging in clean, designer rooms outfitted in blues and greens with balconies overlooking the water. The grounds are enormous and include an artificial waterfall-fed pool and frontage to a rather large stretch of private white-sand beach. Book online for the best rates.

Jules' Undersea Lodge HOTEL $$$
(305-451-2353; www.jul.com; 51 Shoreland Dr, Mile 103.2 oceanside; s/d/tr $675/800/1050) If you fancy diving to your hotel, this place is for you. Once a research station, this module has been converted into a delightfully cheesy Keys motel, but wetter. In addition to two private guest rooms, there are common rooms, a kitchen-dining room and a wet room with hot showers and gear storage.

Telephones and an intercom connect guests with the surface.

Fish House SEAFOOD $$
(305-451-4665; www.fishhouse.com; Mile 102.4 oceanside; mains lunch $12-21, dinner $21-30; 11:30am-10pm;) The Fish House delivers on the promise of its title – very good fish, bought from local fishers and prepared fried, broiled, jerked, blackened or chargrilled. Because the Fish House only uses fresh fish, the menu changes daily based on what is available.

Islamorada

Islamorada (is-luh-murr-*ah*-da) is also known as 'The Village of Islands.' A beautiful string of pearls, or rather, six keys – Plantation, Upper and Lower Matecumbe, Shell and Lignumvitae (lignum-*vite*-ee) – shimmers as one of the prettiest stretches of the islands. The scrubby mangrove is replaced by unbroken horizons of ocean and sky, one perfect shade of blue mirroring the other. Islamorada stretches across some 20 miles, from Mile Marker 90 to Mile Marker 74.

Sights & Activities

★Florida Keys History of Diving Museum MUSEUM
(305-664-9737; www.divingmuseum.org; Mile 83; adult/child $12/6; 10am-5pm, 10am-6:45pm 3rd Wed of month;) You can't miss the diving museum – it's the building with the enormous mural of whale sharks on the side. The journey into the undersea covers 4000 years, with fascinating pieces like the 1797 Klingert's copper kettle, a whimsical room devoted to Jules Verne's Captain Nemo, massive deep-diving suits and an exquisite display of diving helmets from around the world. These imaginative galleries reflect the charming quirks of the Keys.

Windley Key Fossil Reef Geological State Site STATE PARK
(305-664-2540; www.floridastateparks.org/parks-and-trails/windley-key-fossil-reef-geological-state-park; Mile 85.5 oceanside; admission $2.50, tour $2; 8am-5pm Thu-Mon) To get

his railroad built across the islands, Henry Flagler had to quarry out some sizable chunks of the Keys. The best evidence of those efforts can be found at this former quarry-turned-state park. Windley has leftover quarry machinery scattered along an 8ft former quarry wall, with fossilized evidence of brain and staghorn coral embedded right in the rock. The wall offers a cool (and rare) public peek into the stratum of coral that forms the substrate of the Keys.

★Robbie's Marina BOATING

(305-664-8070; https://robbies.com; Mile 77.5 bayside; kayak & stand-up paddleboard rentals $45-80; 9am-8pm;) Robbie's covers all bases – it's a local flea market, tacky tourist shop, sea pen for tarpons (massive fish) and jumping-off point for fishing expeditions, all wrapped into one driftwood-laced compound. Boat-rental and tour options are also available. The best reason to visit is to escape the mayhem and hire a kayak for a peaceful paddle through nearby mangroves, hammocks and lagoons.

Sleeping & Eating

Lime Tree Bay Resort Motel MOTEL $$

(305-664-4740; www.limetreebayresort.com; Mile 68.5 bayside; r $180-360;) Hammocks and lawn chairs provide front-row seats for the spectacular sunsets at this 2.5-acre waterfront hideaway. The rooms are comfortable, airy and elegant, with wood floors and decorative rope details – the best have balconies overlooking the water. The extensive facilities include use of tennis courts, bikes, kayaks and stand-up paddleboards.

Bad Boy Burrito MEXICAN $

(305-509-7782; 103 Mastic St, Mile 81.8 bayside; mains $8-15; 10am-6pm Mon-Sat;) Tucked away in a tiny plaza among a gurgling fountain, orchids and swaying palms, Bad Boy Burrito whips up superb fish tacos and its namesake burritos – with quality ingredients (skirt steak, duck confit, zucchini and squash) and all the fixings (shaved cabbage, chipotle mayo, housemade salsa). Top it off with a hibiscus tea and some chips and guacamole.

★Lazy Days SEAFOOD $$

(305-664-5256; www.lazydaysislamorada.com; 79867 Overseas Hwy, oceanside; mains $18-34; 11am-11pm Mon-Sat, to 10pm Sun;) One of Islamorada's culinary icons, Lazy Days has a stellar reputation for its fresh seafood plates. Start off with a conch chowder topped with a little sherry (provided), before moving on to a decadent hogfish Poseidon (fish topped with shrimp, scallops and key lime butter) or a straight-up boiled seafood platter (half lobster, shrimp, catch of the day and other delicacies).

Marathon

Marathon sits right on the halfway point between Key Largo and Key West, and it's a good place to stop on a road trip across the islands. Outside Key West, it's perhaps the most 'developed' key (though that might be pushing the definition of the word 'developed') – it has large shopping centers and a population of more than 8000. It's still a place where exiles from the mainland fish, booze it up and have a good time though, so while Marathon is more family-friendly than Key West, it's maintained its wild side.

Sleeping & Eating

Seascape Motel & Marina MOTEL $$$

(305-743-6212; www.seascapemotelandmarina.com; 1075 75th St Ocean E, btwn Mile 51 & 52; r $250-550;) The understated luxury in this B&B manifests in its 12 rooms, with their minimalist and sleek decor. There is a waterfront pool, kayaks and stand-up paddleboards for guests to use, and its secluded setting will make you feel like you've gotten away from it all. Seascape also hosts afternoon wine and snacks (included).

Tranquility Bay RESORT $$$

(305-289-0667; www.tranquilitybay.com; Mile 48.5 bayside; r $340-700;) If you're serious about going upscale, you should book in here. Tranquility Bay is a massive condo-hotel resort with plush townhouses, high-thread-count sheets and all-in-white chic – the beach is just steps away from your bed. The grounds are enormous and activity-filled; they really don't want you to leave.

★Keys Fisheries SEAFOOD $$

(866-743-4353; www.keysfisheries.com; 3502 Louisa St; mains $12-27; 11am-9pm;) The lobster Reuben is the stuff of legend. Sweet, chunky, creamy – so good you'll be daydreaming about it afterward. But you can't go wrong with any of the excellent seafood here, all served with sass. Expect some seagull harassment as you dine on a working waterfront.

Lower Keys

The people of the Lower Keys vary between winter escapees and native Conchs. Some local families have been Keys castaways for generations, and there is somewhat of a more insular feel than other parts of the Overseas Hwy. The islands get at their most isolated, rural and quintessentially 'Keez-y' before opening onto (relatively) cosmopolitan, heterogeneous and free-spirited Key West.

People aside, the big draw in the lower Keys is nature. You'll find the loveliest state park in the Keys here, and one of its rarest species. For paddlers, there is a great mangrove wilderness to explore in a photogenic and pristine environment.

★Bahia Honda State Park STATE PARK
(☎305-872-3210; www.bahiahondapark.com; Mile 37; car $4-8, cyclist & pedestrian $2.50; ⊙8am-sunset; 👪) This park, with its long, white-sand (and at times seaweed-strewn) beach, named Sandspur Beach by locals, is the big attraction in these parts. As Keys beaches go, this one is probably the best natural stretch of sand in the island chain. There's also the novel experience of walking on the **old Bahia Honda Rail Bridge**, which offers nice views of the surrounding islands. Heading out on kayaking adventures (from $12/36 per hour/half day) is another great way to spend a sun-drenched afternoon.

Key West

Key West is the far frontier, edgier and more eccentric than the other Keys, and also far more captivating. At its heart, this 7-sq-mile island feels like a beautiful tropical oasis, where the moonflowers bloom at night and the classical Caribbean homes are so sad and romantic it's hard not to sigh at them.

While Key West has obvious allure, it's not without its contradictions. On one side of the road, there are literary festivals, Caribbean villas, tropical dining rooms and expensive art galleries. On the other, an S&M fetishist parade, frat boys passing out on the sidewalk and grizzly bars filled with bearded burnouts. With all that in mind, it's easy to find your groove in this setting, no matter where your interests lie.

As in other parts of the Keys, nature plays a starring role here, with some breathtaking sunsets – cause for nightly celebration down on Mallory Sq.

Sights

★Museum of Art & History at the Custom House MUSEUM
(☎305-295-6616; www.kwahs.com; 281 Front St; adult/child $10/5; ⊙9:30am-4:30pm) This excellent museum, set in a grand 1891 red-brick building that once served as the Customs House, covers Key West's history. Highlights are the archival footage from the building of the ambitious Overseas Hwy (and the hurricane that killed 400 people), a model of the ill-fated USS *Maine* (sunk during the Spanish-American War) and the Navy's role in Key West (once the largest employer), and the 'wreckers' of Key West, who scavenged sunken treasure ships.

★Mallory Square SQUARE
(www.mallorysquare.com; 👪) Take all those energies, subcultures and oddities of Keys life and focus them into one torchlit, family-friendly (but playfully edgy), sunset-enriched street party. The result of all these raucous forces is Mallory Sq, one of the greatest shows on earth that starts in the hours leading up to dusk, the sinking sun a signal to bring on the madness. Watch a dog walk a tightrope, a man swallow fire, and British acrobats tumble and sass each other.

Duval Street AREA
Key West locals have a love-hate relationship with the most famous road in Key West (if not the Keys). Duval, Old Town Key West's main strip, is a miracle mile of booze, tacky everything and awful behavior – but it's a lot of fun. The 'Duval Crawl' is one of the wildest pub crawls in the country. The mix of neon drink, drag shows, T-shirt kitsch, local theaters, art studios and boutiques is more charming and entertaining than jarring.

Hemingway House NOTABLE BUILDING
(☎305-294-1136; www.hemingwayhome.com; 907 Whitehead St; adult/child $14/6; ⊙9am-5pm) Key West's biggest darling, Ernest Hemingway, lived in this gorgeous Spanish Colonial

house from 1931 to 1940. Papa moved here in his early 1930s with his second wife, a *Vogue* fashion editor and (former) friend of his first wife (he left the house when he ran off with his third wife). *The Short Happy Life of Francis Macomber* and *The Green Hills of Africa* were produced here, as well as many cats, whose descendants basically run the grounds.

Activities

Dive Key West DIVING
(☎305-296-3823; www.divekeywest.com; 3128 N Roosevelt Blvd; snorkel/scuba from $69/95) Largest dive facility on the island, offering morning, afternoon and night dives. Wreck-diving trips cost $145 with all equipment and air provided (it's $160 with a wetsuit).

The rate for snorkelers is $69.

Tours

Old Town Trolley Tours TOURS
(☎855-623-8289; www.trolleytours.com; adult/child $43/15; ⏲tours 9am-4:30pm; 👪) These tours are a great introduction to the city, providing a good overview of Key West history. The 90-minute, hop-on, hop-off narrated tram tour starts at Mallory Sq and makes a loop around the whole city, with 12 stops along the way. Trolleys depart every 30 minutes.

Festivals & Events

Womenfest LGBTIQ+
(http://gaykeywestfl.com/womenfest; ⏲Sep) One of North America's biggest lesbian celebrations, Womenfest is four days of merrymaking, with pool parties, art shows, roller derby, drag brunches, sunset sails, flag football, and a tattoo and moustache bicycle ride.

It's great fun, with thousands descending on Key West from all corners of the USA and beyond.

★ **Fantasy Fest** CULTURAL
(https://fantasyfest.com; ⏲late Oct) Akin to New Orleans' riotous Mardi Gras revelry, Fantasy Fest is 10 days of burlesque parties, parades, street fairs, concerts and loads of costumed events. Bars and inns get competitive about decorating their properties, and everyone gets decked out in the most outrageous costumes they can cobble together (or get mostly naked with daring body paint).

Sleeping

Key West Youth Hostel & Seashell Motel HOSTEL $$
(☎305-296-5719; www.keywesthostel.com; 718 South St; dm from $55, d $120-325; P❄📶) This place isn't winning any design awards, but the staff are kind, and it's one of the only lower-priced choices on the island. The dorms and rooms have white tile floors, with the cheery paint job (yellow in dorms and blue and white in doubles) somewhat breaking up the monotony. The back patio is a fine place to meet other travelers.

Casablanca Key West GUESTHOUSE $$
(☎305-296-0815; www.keywestcasablanca.com; 900 Duval St; r $145-725; ❄📶🏊) On the quieter end of Duval St, the Casablanca is a friendly guesthouse with eight bright rooms, all with polished wood floors and comfy beds; some have small balconies. This lush, tropical and elegant inn, once a private house, was built in 1898. It has hosted a few luminaries, including Humphrey Bogart, who stayed here in 1937.

The open-sided terrace just above the street is perfect for afternoon drinks and snacks.

Saint Hotel BOUTIQUE HOTEL $$$
(☎305-294-3200; www.sainthotels.com/key-west; 417 Eaton St; r $360-700; ❄📶🏊) Despite its proximity to Duval St, the Saint feels like a world removed with its plush rooms – that play with the ideas of 'Saint' and 'Sinner' – chic minimalist lobby, photogenic pool with small cascading waterfall, and artfully designed bar. The best rooms have balconies overlooking the pool. Book well in advance.

Eating

Pierogi Polish Market EASTERN EUROPEAN $
(☎305-292-0464; www.facebook.com/PierogiPolishMarket; 1008 White St; mains $5-11; ⏲pierogi counter 11am-7pm Mon-Sat, shop 10am-8pm Mon-Sat, noon-6pm Sun; P🌶) The Keys have an enormous seasonal population of temporary workers largely drawn from Central and Eastern Europe. This is where those workers can revisit the motherland, via pierogies, dumplings, blinis and a great sandwich selection. Although it's called a Polish market, there's food here that caters to Hungarians, Czechs and Russians (among others). They do takeout and delivery, too.

Garbo's Grill FUSION $
(www.garbosgrillkw.com; 409 Caroline St; mains $10-14; ⏰11am-10pm Mon-Sat, noon-6pm Sun) Just off the beaten path, Garbo's whips up delicious tacos with creative toppings like mango ginger habanero-glazed shrimp, Korean barbecue, and fresh mahimahi with all the fixings, as well as gourmet burgers and hot dogs. It's served out of a sleek Airstream trailer, which faces onto a shaded brick patio dotted with outdoor tables.

The Café VEGETARIAN $$
(☎305-296-5515; www.thecafekw.com; 509 Southard St; mains $12-22; ⏰9am-10pm; ✍) The oldest vegetarian spot in Key West is a sunny luncheonette by day that morphs into a buzzing, low-lit eating and drinking spot by night. The cooking is outstanding, with an eclectic range of dishes: Thai curry stir-fries, Italian veggie meatball subs, pizza with shaved Brussels sprouts, and a famous veggie burger.

★**Thirsty Mermaid** SEAFOOD $$
(☎305-204-4828; www.thirstymermaidkeywest.com; 521 Fleming St; mains $12-28; ⏰11am-11:30pm; ✍) The lovely Thirsty Mermaid serves outstanding seafood in an elegant, easygoing space. The menu is a collection of sea-life culinary treasures such as an oyster bar, ceviche, middleneck clams and caviar. Among the main courses, seared diver scallops or togarashi-spiced tuna with jasmine rice are outstanding. There are also luxurious sandwiches with lobster, fried oysters or local snapper fillings.

★**Blue Heaven** AMERICAN $$$
(☎305-296-8666; www.blueheavenkw.com; 729 Thomas St; mains breakfast & lunch $10-19, dinner $22-35; ⏰8am-10:30pm; ✍) This is one of the quirkiest venues on an island of oddities – customers, together with free-ranging fowl, flock to dine in the ramshackle, tropical plant-filled garden where Hemingway once officiated boxing matches. This place gets packed with customers who come for the delectable breakfasts (blueberry pancakes) and Keys cuisine with French touches (like yellowtail snapper with citrus *beurre blanc*).

Drinking & Entertainment

★**Green Parrot** BAR
(☎305-294-6133; www.greenparrot.com; 601 Whitehead St; ⏰10am-4am) The oldest bar on an island of bars – 'A sunny place for shady people' being one of its mottos – this rogues' cantina opened in the late 19th century and keeps going. Its ramshackle interior, with local artwork on the walls and a parachute stretched across the ceiling, only adds to the atmosphere, as does the fun-loving, colorful crowd.

Captain Tony's Saloon BAR
(☎305-294-1838; www.capttonyssaloon.com; 428 Greene St; ⏰10am-2am) Propagandists would have you believe the nearby megabar complex of Sloppy Joe's was Hemingway's original bar, but the physical place where the old man famously drank was right here, the original Sloppy Joe's location (before it was moved onto Duval St and into frat-boy hell). Hemingway's third wife (a journalist sent to profile Papa) seduced him in this very bar.

Irish Kevin's BAR
(☎305-292-1262; www.irishkevins.com; 211 Duval St; ⏰10am-3:30am) One of the most popular megabars on Duval, Kevin's has a pretty good entertainment formula pinned down: nightly live acts that are a cross between a folk singer, radio shock jock and pep-rally cheerleader. The crowd consistently goes wild for acoustic covers of favorites from 1980 onward mixed with boozy, Lee Greenwoodesque patriotic exhortations.

La Te Da CABARET
(☎305-296-6706; www.lateda.com; 1125 Duval St; tickets $33; ⏰shows 8:30pm) While the outside bar is where locals gather for mellow chats over beer, you can catch high-quality drag acts – big names come here from around the country – upstairs at the fabulous Crystal Room on weekends. More low-key cabaret acts grace the downstairs lounge. The Sunday tea dance – an afternoon dance party (4pm to 7pm) by the pool – is great fun.

ℹ Information

Citizen (www.keysnews.com) A well-written, oft-amusing daily.

Key West Chamber of Commerce (☎305-294-2587; www.keywestchamber.org; 510 Greene St; ⏰9am-6pm) An excellent source of information.

Key Wester (http://thekeywester.com) Restaurant reviews and upcoming events.

ℹ Getting Around

Once you're in Key West, the best way to get around is by bicycle (rentals from the Duval St area, hotels and hostels cost from $10 a day).

For transportation within the Duval St area, the free Duval Loop shuttle (www.carfreekeywest.com/duval-loop) runs from 6pm to midnight.

Other options include **Key West Transit** (☎305-600-1455; www.kwtransit.com; day pass $4-8), with color-coded buses running about every 15 minutes; mopeds, which generally cost from $35 per day ($60 for a two-seater); or the open-sided electric tourist cars, aka 'Conch cruisers,' which travel at 35mph and cost about $140/200 for a four-/six-seater per day.

A&M Scooter Rentals (☎305-896-1921; www.amscooterskeywest.com; 523 Truman Ave; bicycle/scooter/electric car per day from $10/35/140; ⌚9am-7pm) rents out scooters and bicycles, as well as open-sided electric cars that can seat two to six people, and offers free delivery.

Parking can be tricky in town. There's a free parking lot on Fort St off Truman Ave.

ATLANTIC COAST

Florida's northern Atlantic Coast – known as the 'First Coast' thanks to its early colonization – is a land of long beaches shadowed by tall condo complexes and seaside mansions, serving as an exurb riviera for the Southern USA. Heading from south to north, you'll pass the exhaust pipes and biker bars of Daytona Beach, continue through mellow Flagler Beach, and on to historic St Augustine, where a one- or two-night sojourn is highly recommended.

An affluent series of beaches can be found just south of spread-out Jacksonville, which forms an urban break in the coastal living; many continue north from here to charming Amelia Island and the Florida–Georgia border. Along the way you'll discover a jumbled necklace of grassy barrier islands, interlaced with tidal inlets, salt marsh flats and dark clumps of maritime forest.

Space Coast

More than 40 miles of barrier-island Atlantic Coast stretch from Canaveral National Seashore south to Melbourne Beach, encompassing undeveloped stretches of endless white sand, an entrenched surf culture and pockets of Old Florida.

The Kennedy Space Center and several small museums dedicated to the history, heroes and science of the United States' space program give the Space Coast its name, and the region's tourist hub of Cocoa Beach is just south of Cape Canaveral's launching point for massive cruise ships. But beyond the 3D space movies, tiki-hut bars and surf shops, the Space Coast offers quintessential Florida wildlife for everyone from toddlers to seniors. Kayak with manatees, camp on a private island or simply stroll along miles and miles of sandy white beaches – it's easy to find a quiet spot.

Sights & Activities

★Kennedy Space Center MUSEUM
(☎866-737-5235; www.kennedyspacecenter.com; NASA Pkwy, State Rd 405, Merritt Island; adult/child 3-11yr $61/50; ⌚9am-6pm, to 8pm for special events) Whether you're mildly interested in space or a die-hard sci-fi fan, a visit to the Kennedy Space Center is awe inspiring. To get a good overview, start at the Early Space Exploration exhibit, progress to the 90-minute bus tour to the Apollo/Saturn V Center (where you'll find the best on-site cafe) and finish at the awesome *Atlantis* exhibit, where you can walk beneath the heat-scorched fuselage of a shuttle that traveled more than 126,000,000 miles through space on 33 missions.

★Merritt Island National Wildlife Refuge WILDLIFE RESERVE
(☎321-861-5601; www.fws.gov/merrittisland; Black Point Wildlife Dr, off FL 406; vehicle $10; ⌚dawn-dusk) FREE This unspoiled 140,000-acre refuge is one of the country's best birding spots, especially from October to May (early morning and after 4pm). More endangered and threatened species of wildlife inhabit the swamps, marshes and hardwood hammocks here than at any other site in the continental US. The best viewing is on **Black Point Wildlife Drive** (off FL-406; per vehicle $10; ⌚sunrise-sunset).

Canaveral National Seashore NATIONAL PARK
(☎headquarters 321-267-1110, visitors center 386-428-3384; www.nps.gov/cana; car/bike/pedestrian $15/5/5; ⌚6am-8pm Mar-Nov, to 6pm Dec-Feb) The 24 miles of pristine, windswept beaches here comprise the longest stretch of undeveloped beach on Florida's east coast. They include family-friendly **Apollo Beach** on the north end with its gentle surf, untrammeled **Klondike Beach** in the middle – a favorite of nature lovers – and **Playalinda Beach** to the south, which is surfer central and includes a nudist section near lot 13.

Sea-Turtle Nesting Tours ECOTOUR
(☎386-428-3384; adult/child 8-16yr $15/free; ⌚8pm-midnight Jun & Jul) In the summer,

rangers lead groups of up to 30 people on these nightly tours, with about a 75% chance of spotting the little guys. Reservations are required (beginning May 15 for June trips, June 15 for July trips); children under eight years are not allowed.

Sleeping

★Beach Place Guesthouses APARTMENT $$
(☎321-783-4045; www.beachplaceguesthouses.com; 1445 S Atlantic Ave; ste $199-399; P ⊖ ❄ ≋) A slice of heavenly relaxation in Cocoa Beach's partying beach scene, this laid-back two-story guesthouse has roomy suites with hammocks and a lovely deck, all just steps from the dunes and beach. Colorful art and greenery abound on the property. No pets.

Fawlty Towers MOTEL $$
(☎321-784-3870; 100 E Cocoa Beach Causeway; r $99-250; P ⊖ ❄ ≋ ≈) It's all about location, location, location. This motel is gloriously garish and extremely pink: unmissable. It has clean, non-fancy rooms with an unbeatable beachside location, a quiet pool and a BYOB tiki hut. Sometimes a decent room is what you need.

Residence Inn Cape Canaveral HOTEL $$$
(☎321-323-1100; www.marriott.com; 8959 Astronaut Blvd; r $240-300; P ❄ ≋ ≈) If you want to get away from the Cocoa Beach party scene, book into this comfortable Marriott hotel. Rooms may be corporate, but they offer acres of space, comfortable beds and kitchenettes. Staff are also extremely accommodating and there's a pretty pool area. Park-n-cruise packages are popular. The big astronaut in the lobby makes it fun for kids.

Eating

Melbourne Beach Market MARKET $
(☎321-676-5225; 302 Ocean Ave; ⊙8am-8pm Mon-Sat, to 7pm Sun) Pick up picnic essentials here, including ready-to-eat Greek and Italian meals.

★Green Room Cafe VEGETARIAN $
(☎321-868-0203; www.greenroomcafecocoabeach.com; 222 N 1st St; mains $7-13; ⊙10:30am-9pm Mon-Sat; ✎) Focusing all its energies on the 'goodness within,' this super cafe delights the health-conscious with fruit-combo acai bowls, wheat- and gluten-free sandwiches, real fruit smoothies, and homemade soups and wraps. If the 'Tower of Power' smoothie (acai, peach, strawberry, honey and apple juice) fails to lift you, the vibrant decor and friendly company will.

Those who don't surf might wonder at the name, which comes from the chamber of green water one finds when inside the barrel of a wave. Eco-minded folk will appreciate their no straws policy.

Seafood Atlantic SEAFOOD $$
(☎321-784-1963; www.seafoodatlantic.org; 520 Glen Cheek Dr, Port Canaveral; mains $8-19; ⊙11am-7pm Wed-Sun, seafood market from 10am) With deep roots in Canaveral's fishing industry, this restaurant (with outdoor deck) is one of the few places to serve locally sourced shrimp, crabs, mussels, clams, oysters and fish. If they're in, order a bucket of Florida's deep-sea golden crab, which has a deliciously moist and creamy texture. Also, bring a bag and stock up at the market next door.

If you've been missing the swampy taste of Florida gator, they have that too. Plus, you can take home recipe cards for popular items.

Information

Canaveral National Seashore Visitor Information Center (☎386-428-3384; www.nps.gov/cana; 7611 S Atlantic Ave, New Smyrna; ⊙8am-6pm Oct-Mar, to 8pm Apr-Sep) is located just south of the North District entrance gate. Alternatively, the visitor center at Merritt Island National Wildlife Refuge can also provide information.

There is a fee station at both the North and South District entrances. There is a toilet at most beach parking areas.

Note that the park can experience temporary closures around launch time. For information on launch closures, call ☎321-867-4077.

Getting There & Away

Orlando Melbourne International Airport (☎321-723-6227; www.mlbair.com; 1 Air Terminal Pkwy) is the closest airport to most destinations on the Space Coast. It is a growing airport served by Delta, American Airlines, Elite Airways, Porter Airlines and Baer, as well as all the major rental-car companies and SCAT bus 21.

Alternatively, Orlando International Airport is about 50 minutes west of Cocoa Beach, and Orlando Sanford International Airport is a little over an hour to the northwest of Cocoa Beach.

There are two ways to arrive in Cape Canaveral: traveling north on A1A from Cocoa Beach, or west on A1A across the Banana River via Merritt Island.

Cape Canaveral is served by **SCAT** (SCAT; ☎321-633-1878; www.321transit.com; per ride

$1.50, 10-ride/30-day pass $12/42; ⊙schedule varies) buses. Rte 9 connects it with Cocoa Beach and Rte 4 connects it with Cocoa Village.

Daytona Beach

Long the vacation destination of choice for leather-clad bikers, rev heads and spring breakers, Daytona Beach is most famous as the birthplace of NASCAR racing and the home of the Daytona 500.

The area's population quintuples during Speedweeks; as many as half a million bikers roar into town for **Bike Week** in March and **Biketoberfest** in October. If Confederate flags, loud motorcycles, jacked-up pickup trucks and the folks who love all of the above are your thing, you might have found your heaven on earth. If not, move on.

If you can see past the garish beachside barricade of '70s high-rise blocks, nightclubs and tourist traps (if not quite literally), you might witness the phenomena of nesting sea turtles (in season) or explore a handful of interesting and worthwhile cultural attractions.

Sights & Activities

★Daytona International Speedway STADIUM
(☎800-748-7467; www.daytonainternationalspeedway.com; 1801 W International Speedway Blvd; tours from $23; ⊙tours 9:30am-3:30pm) The Holy Grail of raceways has a diverse race schedule. Ticket prices skyrocket for good seats at big races, headlined by the **Daytona 500** in February. It's worth wandering the massive stands for free on non-race days. First-come, first-served tram tours take in the track, pits and behind-the-scenes areas, while all-access tours give you a glimpse of media rooms and pit stalls.

Southeast Museum of Photography MUSEUM
(☎386-506-3894; www.smponline.org; 1200 W International Speedway Blvd, Bldg 1200; ⊙11am-5pm Tue, Thu & Fri, to 6pm Wed, from 1pm Sat & Sun) FREE We love this hidden treasure in Daytona, a service of the Daytona State College: it's the only museum in Florida dedicated solely to photography.

This vibrant modern gallery with excellent lighting and facilities doesn't shy away from provocative subjects in its rotating exhibitions. Best of all, it's free (though donations are welcome)!

NASCAR Racing Experience DRIVING
(☎740-886-2400; www.nascarracingexperience.com; 1801 W International Speedway Blvd; from $149, discounts online; ⊙dates vary) If merely watching NASCAR drivers streak around the track isn't adrenaline-pumping enough for you, get in the car yourself via the NASCAR Racing Experience. Choose from several levels of death-defying action, from the three-lap passenger-seat Race Ride (from $149) to the intensive Advanced Experience ($4000), with multiple laps, celeb meetings, and even a certificate on completion. Dates vary; check online.

Sleeping & Eating

Hyatt Place Daytona Beach Oceanfront HOTEL $
(☎386-944-2010; www.daytonabeach.place.hyatt.com; 3161 S Atlantic Ave, Daytona Beach Shores; r from $114; P@🛜🏊) Some of Daytona's freshest, funkiest and most functional rooms can be found here. All rooms feature balconies, plush bedding, separate living and sleeping areas and a nifty panel to easily connect your laptop or phone to the 42in panel TV.

Plaza Resort & Spa RESORT $
(☎855-327-5292, 844-284-2685; www.plazaresortandspa.com; 600 N Atlantic Ave; r $109-149; P🚭❄🛜🏊) Built in 1888, Daytona's most historic resort has undergone extensive renovations in its time, but still maintains its old-world charm. If only the walls could talk... From the miles of honey-colored marble lining the lobby to the 42in plasma TVs and cloud-soft beds in the rooms, to the 15,000-sq-ft spa, this resort coos luxury.

★House of Donuts BAKERY $
(☎386-441-4066; 1350 Ocean Shore Blvd, Ormond Beach; 1/6 donuts $1.25/6; ⊙6am-2pm) Just north of Daytona in Ormond Beach is this great little donut stop, with all the flavors you'd expect plus some totally over-the-top creations, like Key Lime or Fruity Pebbles. Smores, with graham cracker cereal, chocolate and mini marshmallows, is over-the-top caloric decadence, and why not? You're in Florida, live a little!

Cracked Egg Diner BREAKFAST $
(☎386-788-6772; www.thecrackedeggdiner.com; 3280D S Atlantic Ave, Daytona Beach Shores; breakfast items $5-13; ⊙7am-3pm; P👪) Best for breakfast, this cheery joint in Daytona Beach Shores became so popular they annexed the

building next door. Brainchild of brothers Chris and Kevin, one of whom will usually greet you at the door with a smile, their mission is to deliver breakfast egg-cellence. (Sorry. It had to happen.) We think they do a fine job. Kids will have a grand time with the various meal names: the Chunky Monkey Pancakes, for instance, or the Fruity Pebble French Toast.

Aunt Catfish's on the River SOUTHERN US **$$**
(386-767-4768; www.auntcatfishontheriver.com; 4009 Halifax Dr, Port Orange; mains $9-31, brunch $18; 11:30am-9pm Mon-Sat, from 9am Sun;) Fresh-from-the-boat grouper and mahi-mahi lolling in butter or deeply and deliciously fried, as well as Southern-style Cajun-spiced catfish, make this riverside seafood establishment insanely popular with tourists: table waits can be expected. It's just outside Daytona Beach in Port Orange. A kiddie play area gives the little ones something to do while you wait.

Information

Daytona Beach Area Convention & Visitors Bureau (386-255-0415; www.daytonabeach.com; 126 E Orange Ave; 8:30am-5pm Mon-Fri) In person or online, these guys are *the* authority on all things Daytona Beach.

Getting There & Away

Daytona Beach is close to the intersection of two major interstates, I-95 and I-4. The I-95 is the quickest way to Jacksonville (about 90 miles) and Miami (260 miles), though Hwy A1A and Hwy 1 are more scenic. Beville Rd, an east–west thoroughfare south of Daytona proper, becomes I-4 after crossing I-95; it's the fastest route to Orlando (55 miles).

A cab journey from the airport to South Atlantic Ave costs $20. Ride-sharing services are also available.

Daytona Beach International Airport (386-248-8030; www.flydaytonafirst.com; 700 Catalina Dr) is just east of the Speedway; it's served by Delta and US Airways, and all major car-rental companies.

Greyhound (386-255-7076; www.greyhound.com; 138 S Ridgewood Ave) has connections to most major cities in Florida, and beyond.

St Augustine

The oldest continuously occupied European settlement in the US, St Augustine was founded by the Spanish in 1565. Today, its 144-block National Historic Landmark District is a major tourist destination. For the most part, St Augustine exudes charm and maintains its integrity, although there's no denying the presence of some tacky tourist traps: miniature theme parks, tour operators at almost every turn and horse-drawn carriages clip-clopping past townsfolk dressed in period costume.

What makes St Augustine so genuinely endearing is the accessibility of its rich history via countless top-notch museums and the authenticity of its centuries-old architecture, monuments and narrow cobbled lanes. Unlike Florida's numerous historical theme parks, St Augustine is the real deal.

You'll find a diverse array of wonderful B&Bs, cozy cafes and lamp-lit pubs, and while fine dining might not be the first thing that comes to mind at Florida's mention, it is certainly synonymous with St Augustine.

History

Timucuans settled what is now St Augustine about 1000 BCE, hunting alligators and cultivating corn and tobacco. In 1513, Spanish explorer Juan Ponce de León sighted land, came ashore and claimed La Florida (Land of Flowers) for Spain. In 1565 his compatriot Don Pedro Menéndez de Avilés arrived on the feast day of Augustine of Hippo, and accordingly christened the town San Augustín: 42 years prior to the founding of Jamestown (Virginia) and 55 years before that of Plymouth (Massachusetts).

Menéndez quickly established a military base against the French, who had established Fort Caroline near present-day Jacksonville. The French fleet did him the favor of getting stuck in a hurricane; Menéndez' men butchered the survivors. By the time Spain ceded Florida to the US in 1821, St Augustine had been sacked, looted, burned and occupied by pirates and Spanish, British, Georgian and South Carolinian forces.

Today the city's buildings, made of coquina – a DIY concrete made of sedimentary rock mixed with crushed shells – lend an enchanting quality to the slender streets. The city's long and colorful history is palpable, narrated vividly by what seems like innumerable museums, monuments and galleries.

Sights

All of St Augustine's historic district feels like a museum; there are literally dozens of attractions to choose from. Narrow little

Aviles St, the oldest European-settled street in the country, and long, pedestrian-only **St George St** are both lined with galleries, cafes, museums and pubs, and are attractions in themselves.

★Lightner Museum MUSEUM
(☎904-824-2874; www.lightnermuseum.org; 75 King St; adult/child $15/8; ⏲9am-5pm) Henry Flagler's former Hotel Alcazar is home to this wonderful museum with a little bit of everything, from ornate Gilded Age furnishings to collections of marbles and cigar-box labels. The dramatic and imposing building itself is a must-see, dating back to 1887 and designed in the Spanish Renaissance Revival style by New York City architects Carrère & Hastings.

Castillo de San Marcos National Monument FORT
(☎904-829-6506; www.nps.gov/casa; 1 S Castillo Dr; adult/child under 15yr $15/free; ⏲9am-5pm; P ♿) This photogenic fort is an atmospheric monument to longevity: it's the country's oldest masonry fort, completed by the Spanish in 1695. In its time, the fort has been besieged twice and changed hands between nations six times – from Spain to Britain to Spain Part II to the USA to the Confederate States of America to the USA again. Park rangers lead programs hourly and shoot off cannons most weekends.

Villa Zorayda Museum MUSEUM
(☎904-829-9887; www.villazorayda.com; 83 King St; adult/child $10/5; ⏲10am-5pm Mon-Sat, 11am-4pm Sun; P) Looking like a faux Spanish castle from a medieval theme park, this gray edifice was built out of a mix of concrete and local coquina shells in 1883. The structure was the fantasy (and maybe fever dream) of an eccentric millionaire who was obsessed with Spain's 12th-century Alhambra Palace. Today, it's an odd but engaging museum. The Moorish-style atrium and rooms contain quirky antiques, archaeological pieces and other artifacts: highlights being a 2400-year-old mummy's foot and an Egyptian 'Sacred Cat Rug.'

Hotel Ponce de León HISTORIC BUILDING
(☎904-823-3378; http://legacy.flagler.edu/pages/tours; 74 King St; tours adult/child $12/free; ⏲tours hourly 10am-3pm mid-May–mid-Aug, 10am & 2pm during school year) This striking former luxury hotel, built in the 1880s, is now the world's most gorgeous dormitory, belonging to Flagler College, who purchased and saved it in 1967. Guided tours are recommended to get a sense of the detail and history of this magnificent Spanish Renaissance building. At the very least, take a peek inside the lobby for free.

Colonial Quarter MUSEUM
(☎904-342-2857; www.colonialquarter.com; 43 St George St; adult/child $13/7; ⏲10am-5pm) See how they did things back in the 18th century at this re-creation of Spanish Colonial St Augustine, complete with craftspeople demonstrating blacksmithing, leather working, musket shooting and all sorts of historical stuff. A replica Spanish *caravel* (ship) is among the items. They also do canon and musket firing.

St Augustine Beach BEACH
(350 A1A Beach Blvd) This white-sand beach almost gets lost in the historical mix, but hey, it's Florida, so a visit wouldn't be complete without a little bit of sun and surf. There's a visitor information booth at the foot of **St Johns Pier**, where you can rent a rod and reel (two hours for $15). About three blocks south of the pier, the end of A St has – as Florida goes – some fine waves.

Sleeping

Jaybird's Inn MOTEL $
(☎904-342-7938; www.jaybirdsinn.com; 2700 N Ponce de Leon Blvd; r $139-159; 📶 🏊) This motel has fresh and funky decor in an aquamarine color scheme that works. Beds are big and comfy, Continental breakfast is included and free bikes will get you whizzing around in no time. There's an on-site restaurant as well.

★At Journey's End B&B $$
(☎904-829-0076; www.atjourneysend.com; 89 Cedar St; r $169-329; P 📶 🐾) Free from the granny-ish decor that haunts many St Augustine B&Bs, this pet-friendly, kids-welcome and gay-friendly spot is outfitted in a chic mix of antiques and modern furniture and is run by kind, knowledgeable hosts. Mouth-watering breakfasts and complimentary wi-fi, concierge services, and beer, wine and soda throughout your stay are some of the inclusions that set At Journey's End apart.

Eating & Drinking

Collage INTERNATIONAL $$$
(☎904-829-0055; www.collagestaug.com; 60 Hypolita St; mains $29-56; ⏲5-9pm) This upscale restaurant is renowned for its impeccable

service, intimate atmosphere and the consistency of its cuisine: the menu makes the most of St Augustine's seaside locale and nearby local farms. It's all here: artisan salads, chicken, lamb, veal and pork, lobster, scallops and grouper. A subtle mélange of global flavors enhance the natural goodness of the freshest produce.

★Odd Birds Bar COCKTAIL BAR

(☎904-679-4933; www.oddbirdsbar.com; 33 Charlotte St; ⏲5pm-2am Mon-Fri, from 1pm Sat-Sun) Odd Birds embodies just about everything one could want in a quirky, totally unique craft cocktail bar: innovative, imaginative, often playful drinks; bartenders that are serious about their art (they even invite bartender 'diplomats' from other bars to spend an evening sharing their tricks of the trade); and a casual setting that's unpretentious (even though it could be).

If you're a fan of the cocktail you'll make sure this is in your itinerary.

ℹ Information

Visitor Information Center (☎904-825-1000; www.floridashistoriccoast.com; 10 W Castillo Dr; ⏲8:30am-5:30pm) Helpful, period-dressed staff sell tour tickets and can advise you on everything St Augustinian.

ℹ Getting There & Around

Driving from the north, take I-95 exit 318 and head east past Hwy 1 to San Marcos Ave; turn right and you'll end up at the Old City Gate, just past the fort. Alternatively, you can take Hwy A1A along the beach, which intersects with San Marco Ave, or Hwy 1 south from Jacksonville. From the south, take exit 298, merge onto Hwy 1 and follow it into town.

Cars are a nightmare downtown, with one-way and pedestrian-only streets and severely limited parking; outside the city center, you'll need wheels. There's a big parking lot at the Visitor Information Center. Use it.

Northeast Florida Regional Airport (☎904-209-0090; www.flynf.com; 4900 US Hwy 1), 5 miles north of town, receives limited commercial flights. **Airport Express** (☎904-824-9400; www.airportexpresspickup.com; ⏲24hr) charges $65 to drop you downtown in a shuttle. For an additional fee, it'll take you to your hotel. Reservations required. Private services are also available.

The **Greyhound bus station** (☎904-829-6401; www.greyhound.com; 3 Cordova St) is just a few blocks north of the visitor center.

Jacksonville

At a whopping 840 sq miles, Jacksonville is the largest city by area in the contiguous United States and the most populous in Florida. The city sprawls along three meandering rivers, with sweeping bridges and twinkling city lights reflected in the water. A glut of high-rises, corporate HQs and chain hotels can make 'Jax' feel a little soulless, but patient exploration yields some interesting streets, curious characters and a Southern-fried, friendly heart.

The city's museums and restored historic districts are worth a wander if you have the time, and the Five Points and San Marco neighborhoods are charming, walkable areas lined with bistros, boutiques and bars.

The Jacksonville area beaches – a world unto themselves – are 30 to 50 minutes' drive from the city, depending on traffic and where you're coming from.

👁 Sights

★Cummer Museum of Art & Gardens MUSEUM

(www.cummermuseum.org; 829 Riverside Ave; adult/student $10/6; ⏲10am-9pm Tue, to 4pm Wed-Sat, noon-4pm Sun) This handsome museum, Jacksonville's premier cultural space, has an excellent collection of American and European paintings, Asian decorative art and antiquities. An outdoor area showcases classical English and Italian gardens, and is one of the loveliest alfresco spaces in the city.

★Museum of Contemporary Art Jacksonville MUSEUM

(MOCA; ☎904-366-6911; https://mocajacksonville.unf.edu; 333 N Laura St; adult/child $8/5; ⏲11am-5pm Tue-Sat, to 9pm Thu, from noon Sun) The focus of this ultramodern space extends beyond painting: get lost among contemporary sculpture, prints, photography and film.

Check out www.jacksonvilleartwalk.com for details of the free MOCA-run Art Walk, held on the first Wednesday of every month from 5pm to 9pm: it has more than 56 stops and is a great way to see the city.

Southbank Riverwalk WATERFRONT

This 1.2-mile boardwalk, on the south side of the St Johns River, opposite downtown and Jacksonville Landing, has excellent views of the city's expansive skyline. Most nights yield scenes that'll up your likes on social media, but the firework displays on 4 July and New Years' Eve are a real blast. The Southbank Riverwalk connects the museums flanking Museum Circle and makes a pleasant promenade.

Treaty Oak LANDMARK
(1123 Prudential Dr, Jesse Ball duPont Park) At first glance, it looks like a small forest is growing in the middle of the concrete on Jacksonville's south side. But upon closer inspection you'll see that the 'forest' is really one single enormous tree, with a trunk circumference of 25ft and a shade diameter of nearly 200ft. According to local lore, the live oak tree is the oldest thing in Jacksonville – its age is estimated to be 250 years.

Sleeping & Eating

Hotel Indigo Jacksonville HOTEL **$$**
(904-996-7199; www.hoteldeerwoodpark.com; 9840 Tapestry Park Circle; r from $150;) Lush blue color accents and airy, design-conscious rooms with hardwood floors, fluffy king beds, flat-screen TVs and a general sense of stylish yet accessible luxury define the experience at this excellent branch of the Indigo chain. The pool makes for a relaxing spot to get some sun if you're not heading for the beaches. Located about 11 miles south of downtown Jacksonville.

★**Hotel Palms** HOTEL **$$**
(904-241-7776; www.thehotelpalms.com; 28 Sherry Dr, Atlantic Beach; r $140-180, ste from $200;) An old-school courtyard motel turned into a chic little property with reclaimed headboards, concrete floors and open, airy design. Treat yourself to an outdoor shower, free beach-cruiser bicycles, an outdoor fireplace and some gorgeous rooms looking like they've been pulled straight off some fancy interior decorator's Instagram.

Beach Road Chicken Dinners SOUTHERN US **$**
(904-398-7980; www.facebook.com/BRCD1939; 4132 Atlantic Blvd; items $8-18; 11am-8:30pm Tue-Sat, to 6pm Sun) You know a place does it right if its signature meal pre-dates the Cold War, and this deliciously retro joint has been frying chicken since 1939. Tear off a chunk of tender thigh meat and wrap it up in a fluffy biscuit, and you'll understand why people line up every day at this much-loved shack.

Note the hefty sharing charge of $7!

★**Black Sheep Restaurant** AMERICAN **$$**
(904-380-3091; www.blacksheep5points.com; 1534 Oak St; mains from $14-27; 10:30am-10pm Tue-Thu, to midnight Fri, 9:30am-midnight Sat, 9:30am-10pm Sun;) A commitment to good, local ingredients, delicious food, plus a bar with a retractable rooftop and a craft cocktail menu? Sign us up! Try miso-glazed duck confit, citrus-marinated tofu, pastrami sandwiches made from in-house deli meat, or crispy skinned steelhead fish cooked in brown butter; it's all good. The cardamom pancakes and salmon on bagels served for weekend brunch are pretty fine, too.

Drinking & Entertainment

★**De Real Ting Cafe** CLUB
(904-633-9738; www.facebook.com/derealtingcafe; 125 W Adams; 11am-3pm Tue-Fri, 4-11pm Wed, 4pm-3am Fri, 8:30pm-3am Sat) This Jamaican-themed spot has decent eats, but it's the music and the vibe that people come here for: great Caribbean music, dancing, and hanging out. Hosts open-mic nights and other performers and events, too.

Birdies BAR
(904-356-4444; www.birdiesfivepoints.com; 1044 Park St; 4pm-2am Mon-Fri, from 1pm Sat & Sun) There's a lot to see at this funky spot. Local art graces the walls, there's a photo booth, and old-timers and 20-somethings will be sharing the pool tables while indie rock fills the place. It has DJs on the weekends, making for even more good vibes.

★**Florida Theatre** THEATER
(administrative office 904-355-5661, box office 904-355-2787; www.floridatheatre.com; 128 E Forsyth St) Home to Elvis' first indoor concert in 1956, which a local judge endured to ensure Presley was not overly suggestive, this opulent 1927 venue is an intimate place to catch big-name musicians, musicals and movies.

Information

There are a bunch of sources of information for Jacksonville and the surrounding areas.

Florida Times-Union (www.jacksonville.com) Conservative daily paper, in print and online; Friday's *Weekend* magazine features family-oriented events listings.

Folio Weekly (www.folioweekly.com) Free; with club, restaurant and events listings. Found all over town.

Visit Jacksonville Tourist Information Center (800-733-2668; www.visitjacksonville.com; 208 N Laura St, Suite 102; 9am-5:30pm Mon-Fri, 11am-4pm Sat & Sun) Has all there is to know about Jax and surrounds.

Getting There & Around

Jacksonville International Airport (JAX; ☎904-741-3044; www.flyjax.com; 2400 Yankee Clipper Dr; 📶), about 18 miles north of downtown on I-95, is served by major and regional airlines and car-rental companies. A cab downtown costs around $40. Otherwise, follow the signs for shuttle services: there are numerous licensed providers and reservations aren't necessary.

The **Greyhound bus station** (☎904-356-9976; www.greyhound.com; 1111 W Forsyth St) is at the west end of downtown. The **Amtrak station** (☎904-766-5110, reservations 800-872-7245; www.amtrak.com; 3570 Clifford Lane) is 5 miles northwest of downtown.

The Jacksonville Transportation Authority (www.jtafla.com) runs buses and trolleys around town and the beaches (fare $1.50), as well as a free, scenic (and underused) river-crossing Skyway (monorail).

Amelia Island

Located just 13 miles from the Georgia border, Amelia Island is a moss-draped, sun- and sand-soaked blend of the Deep South and Florida coast. It is believed the island's original inhabitants, the Timucuan tribespeople, arrived as early as 4000 years ago. Since that time, eight flags have flown here, starting with the French in 1562, followed by the Spanish, the English, the Spanish again, the Patriots, the Green Cross of Florida, the Mexican Rebels, the US, the Confederates, then the US again.

Vacationers have flocked to Amelia since the 1890s, when Henry Flagler converted a coast of salt marsh and unspoiled beaches into a vacation spot for the wealthy. The legacy of that era is evident in the central town of Fernandina Beach, 50 blocks of historic buildings, Victorian B&Bs and restaurants housed in converted fishing cottages. Dotting the rest of the island are lush parks, green fairways and miles of shoreline.

Sights & Activties

Amelia Island Museum of History MUSEUM
(☎904-261-7378; www.ameliamuseum.org; 233 S 3rd St, Fernandina Beach; adult/student $8/5; ⊙10am-4pm Mon-Sat, from 1pm Sun) Housed in the former county jail (1879–1975), this oral-history museum is tiny but has informative exhibits exploring Native American history, the Spanish Mission period, the Civil War and historic preservation. A variety of tours are available, including the eight-flags tour (11am and 2pm Monday to Saturday, and 2pm Sunday), providing lively interpretations of the island's fascinating history, as well as architecture tours, and pub crawls.

Fort Clinch State Park STATE PARK
(☎904-277-7274; www.floridastateparks.org/fortclinch; 2601 Atlantic Ave, Fernandina Beach; car/pedestrian $6/2; ⊙park 8am-sunset, fort 9am-5pm; Ⓟ) Although construction commenced in 1847, rapid technological advancements rendered Fort Clinch's masonry walls obsolete by as early as 1861, when the fort was taken easily by Confederate militia in the Civil War and later evacuated. Federal troops again occupied the fort during WWII. Today, the park offers a variety of activities, serene beaches for shelling (of the non-military kind) and 6 miles of peaceful, unpaved trails for hiking and cycling.

★**Kayak Amelia** KAYAKING
(☎904-251-0016, 904-261-5702; www.kayakamelia.com; 4 N 2nd St, Fernandina Beach; tours adult/child from $65/55, kayak rental half-day single/double from $40/55) The charms of Amelia Island are best appreciated through a quiet day on the water, with the sun glinting off the estuaries and cordgrass. That's the experience offered by Kayak Amelia, which leads paddling excursions into the watery ecosystem that ensconces the Atlantic barrier island. They also offer stand-up paddleboarding (SUP) classes and SUP yoga (both $30).

Sleeping

★**Addison** B&B $$
(☎904-277-1604; www.addisononamelia.com; 614 Ash St, Fernandina Beach; r $220-330; Ⓟ📶) Built in 1876, the Addison has modern upgrades (Jacuzzi tubs, deluge showers, Turkish-cotton towels and wi-fi) that'll trick you into thinking it was finished last week. Its white, aqua and sage color scheme is bright and totally unstuffy. Enjoy daily happy hours overlooking a delightful courtyard with some of the most accommodating innkeepers on Amelia.

Ritz Carlton HOTEL $$$
(☎904-277-1100; www.ritzcarlton.com; 4750 Amelia Island Pkwy, Fernandina Beach; r from $313; Ⓟ) The height of luxury, decadence and impeccable service awaits at this unexpectedly located Ritz Carlton. Set on 13 miles of pristine beaches, with its own private 18-hole golf course, and lavish rooms and suites furnished with casual elegance,

this is a property for those with fat wallets, accustomed to the best in life, or for that very special vacation experience.

Eating & Drinking

★Patio Place BISTRO $
(☎904-410-3717; http://patioplacebistro.com; 416 Ash St; mains $7-14; ⏰11am-8pm Wed-Thu, 8:30am-9:30pm Fri & Sat, to 2pm Sun; P) Tables named by country not numbers, international music, distressed wood, lots of outdoor seating, and pleasant service make this a joy to dine at. Known for its crepes, there are also bowls, soups, bruschettas, and daily specials. House-made sangria goes down awfully smoothly on a hot Florida day.

T-Ray's Burger Station BURGERS $
(☎904-261-6310; www.traysburgerstation.com; 202 S 8th St, Fernandina Beach; mains $4-14; ⏰7am-2:15pm Mon-Fri, 8am-1pm Sat) Inside an Exxon gas station, this high-carb, high-fat, low-pretense diner and takeout joint is worth the cholesterol spike. Revered by locals, the big breakfasts are just that, and daily specials sell out fast. Juicy burgers, chunky fries, fried shrimp and tender crab cakes all make the mouth water. Believe the hype: the line's there for a reason.

29 South SOUTHERN US $$
(☎904-277-7919; www.29southrestaurant.com; 29 S 3rd St, Fernandina Beach; mains $16-28; ⏰5:30-9:30pm daily, plus 10am-2pm Sat & Sun; P) Lobster corn dogs, sweet-tea-brined pork chops, homemade doughnut-bread pudding and mocha ice cream – we're in business. Tucked into a pale-purple cottage, this neo-Southern bistro takes culinary risks and executes them well. It's casual yet classy and full of flavor.

★Palace Saloon BAR
(www.thepalacesaloon.com; 113-117 Centre St, Fernandina Beach; ⏰noon-2am) Push through the swinging doors at the oldest continuously operated bar in Florida (since 1878), and the first thing you'll notice is the 40ft gas-lamp-lit bar. Knock back the saloon's rum-laced Pirate's Punch in dark, velvet-draped surroundings, curiously appealing to both bikers and Shakespeare buffs.

Information

Historic Downtown Visitor Center (☎904-277-0717; www.ameliaisland.com; 102 Centre St, Fernandina Beach; ⏰10am-4pm) Reams of useful information and maps in the old railroad depot. A fun stop in itself.

Shrimping Museum & Welcome Center (☎904-261-7378; 17 S Front St, Fernandina Beach; ⏰10am-4pm Mon-Sat, from 1pm Sun) This small museum on the harborfront has local maps and pamphlets.

Getting There & Away

Hwy A1A splits in two directions on Amelia Island, one heading west toward I-95 and the other following the coast; both are well marked.

To get to Amelia, the fastest route from the mainland is to take I-95 north to exit 373 and head east about 15 miles straight to the island.

Want a prettier route? Heading from Jacksonville Beach to the town of Mayport, catch the **St Johns River Ferry** (☎904-630-3100; www.jtafla.com; per pedestrian/car $1/6; ⏰from Maryport every 30min 6am-7pm Mon-Fri, 7am-8:30pm Sat & Sun; from George Island every 30min 6:15am-7:15pm Mon-Fri, 7:15am-8:45pm Sat & Sun), which runs around every 30 minutes.

SOUTHWEST FLORIDA

To drive southwest Florida's Gulf Coast is to enter an impressionistic watercolor painting: first, there is the dazzling white quartz sand of its barrier-island beaches, whose turquoise waters darken to silver-mantled indigo as the fiery sun lowers to the horizon. Later, seen from the causeways, those same islands become a phosphorescent smear beneath the inky black night sky.

The Gulf Coast's beauty is its main attraction, but variety is a close second: from Tampa to St Petersburg to Sarasota to Naples, there is urban sophistication and exquisite cuisine. There are secluded islands, family-friendly resorts and spring-break-style parties.

Here Salvador Dalí's melting canvases, Ringling's Venetian Gothic palace and Chihuly's tentacled glass sculptures fit perfectly – all are bright, bold, surreal entertainments to match wintering manatees, roseate spoonbills, open-mouthed alligators and the peacock-colored, sequined costumes of twirling trapeze artists.

Tampa

Tampa, or 'Trampa' as some locals say, is gritty in spots, but also home to a bunch of museums, parks and ambitious restaurants, many of which have popped up recently and brought the city dangerously close to becoming stylish. In the heart of downtown, the revitalized Riverwalk along the Hillsborough River glitters with contemporary architecture and scenic spaces. Plus, between the zoo, the aquarium, the children's museums and the theme parks, families have enough top-shelf entertainment to last a week. By evening Ybor City's streets transform into southwest Florida's hottest bar and nightclub scene.

Sights

Ybor (ee-bore) City is a short car or trolley ride northeast of downtown. Like the illicit love child of Key West and Miami's Little Havana, this 19th-century district is a multiethnic neighborhood that hosts the Tampa Bay area's hippest party scene. It also preserves a strong Cuban, Spanish and Italian heritage from its days as the epicenter of Tampa's cigar industry. You'll quickly find out why the rooster is Ybor's symbol: the birds are wild and proudly strutting everywhere.

★Florida Aquarium AQUARIUM
(813-273-4000; www.flaquarium.org; 701 Channelside Dr; adult/child from $28/24; 9:30am-5pm;) Tampa's excellent aquarium is among the state's best. Cleverly designed, the re-created swamp lets you walk among herons and ibis as they prowl the mangroves. Programs let you swim with the fishes (and the sharks) or take a catamaran ecotour in Tampa Bay. For better control of the crowds, tickets are priced by entry time.

Busch Gardens AMUSEMENT PARK
(813-884-4386; www.buschgardenstampabay.com; 10165 McKinley Dr; 3yr & older $105; 10am-6pm, hours vary) This theme park has 10 loosely named African zones, which flow together without much fuss. The entire park is walkable. Admission includes three types of fun: epic roller coasters and rides, animal encounters, and various shows, performances and entertainment. All are spread throughout the park, so successful days require some planning: check show schedules before arriving and plan what rides and animals to visit around the shows. Coaster lines only get longer as the day goes on. Parking costs $25.

Ybor City Museum State Park MUSEUM
(813-247-6323; www.ybormuseum.org; 1818 E 9th Ave; adult/child $4/free; 9am-5pm Wed-Sun) This dusty, old-school history museum preserves a bygone era, with cigar-worker houses (open 10am to 3pm) and wonderful photos. The museum has information on a free, self-guided, multimedia **tour** (813-505-6779; www.yborwalkingtours.com; adult/child $20/10) of Ybor City, accessible with any internet-connected device. The tour includes 21 stops and narration from prominent characters within the community.

Florida Museum of Photographic Arts MUSEUM
(FMoPA; 813-221-2222; www.fmopa.org; The Cube, 400 N Ashley Dr; adult/student $10/8; 11am-6pm Mon-Thu, to 7pm Fri, noon-5pm Sat & Sun) This small, intimate photography museum is housed on the 2nd and 3rd stories of the Cube, a five-story atrium in downtown Tampa. In addition to a permanent collection from Harold Edgerton and Len Prince, temporary exhibits have included the work of Ansel Adams, Andy Warhol and contemporary photographers such as Jerry Uelsmann. Photography courses are also offered.

Manatee Viewing Center WILDLIFE RESERVE
(813-228-4289; www.tampaelectric.com/manatee; 6990 Dickman Rd, Apollo Beach; 10am-5pm Nov–mid-Apr) FREE One of Florida's more surreal wildlife encounters is spotting manatees in the warm-water discharge canals of coal-fired power plants. Yet these placid mammals show up here so reliably from November through April that this is now a protected sanctuary. Tarpon and sharks can be spotted as well, and an interactive stingray exhibit in a 10,000-gallon tank allows up-close interaction. The latter can be touched (two fingers only!).

Sleeping

Gram's Place Hostel HOSTEL $
(813-221-0596; www.grams-inn-tampa.com; 3109 N Ola Ave, Seminole Heights; dm $32, r $63-74;) As charismatic as an aging rock star, Gram's is a small, welcoming hostel for international travelers who prefer personality over perfect linens. Dig the in-ground hot tub. Simple breakfast is included, but there are two fully serviced kitchens. Gram's Place is in Tampa Heights, 2 miles north of the Museum of Art.

Tahitian Inn HOTEL $
(813-877-6721; www.tahitianinn.com; 601 S Dale Mabry Hwy, South Tampa; r $89-155; P) The name is reminiscent of a tiki-themed motel, but this family-owned, full-service hotel offers fresh, boutique stylings on the cheap. Nice pool, and the quaint cafe offers outdoor seating by a waterfall

and pond. Also, pets are welcome and airport/cruise terminal transportation is included (guests only).

★Epicurean Hotel BOUTIQUE HOTEL $$$

(☎813-999-8700; www.epicureanhotel.com; 1207 S Howard Ave, South Tampa; r $220-450; P ❄ @ 📶 🏊) Foodies rejoice! Tampa's coolest hotel, which opened in 2014, is a food-and-drink-themed boutique Eden steeped in detailed design: a zinc bar, reclaimed woods from an 1820s railway station, oversize kitchen tools as door handles – everywhere you look, a story, usually involving **Bern's Steak House** (☎813-251-2421; www.bernssteakhouse.com; 1208 S Howard Ave; steaks for 1-2 people $37-105; ⏱5-10pm Sun-Thu, to 11pm Fri & Sat), which is a partner. The bathrooms even have rugs. Opulent to the extreme.

Eating

Tre Amici @ the Bunker CAFE $

(☎813-247-6964; www.bunkerybor.com; 1907 19th St N, Ybor City; items $4-9; ⏱7am-8pm Mon-Sat, 9am-4pm Sun) Ybor City's youth contingent wake up at this relaxed community coffeehouse, which offers a range of breakfast burritos, soups and sandwiches all day. Come evening, it hosts open mics, poetry slams and 'noise nights,' which are exactly what they sound like.

Ichicoro RAMEN $

(☎813-517-9989; www.ichicoro.com; 5229 N Florida Ave, Seminole Heights; ramen $12-16; ⏱11am-4pm daily, plus 5pm-11pm Sun-Wed, to 1am Thu-Sat) This trendy, chic ramen shop in Seminole Heights has unique options that you'd never see in Japan (like oh-so-umami mushroom broth). Also not in Japan: undercooked noodles, which waitstaff insist are *al dente* but to which we toss a well-deserved penalty card. Still, the *chāshū* (pork slabs), nearly as thick as the wooden table tops, are superb.

★Columbia Restaurant SPANISH $$

(☎813-248-4961; www.columbiarestaurant.com; 2117 E 7th Ave, Ybor City; mains lunch $12-25, dinner $23-39; ⏱11am-10pm Mon-Thu, to 11pm Fri & Sat, noon-9pm Sun) Celebrating its centennial in 2015, this Spanish Cuban restaurant is the oldest in Florida. Occupying an entire block, it consists of 15 elegant dining rooms and romantic, fountain-centered courtyards. Many of the gloved waiters have been here a lifetime, and owner Richard Gonzmart is zealous about authentic Spanish and Cuban cuisine.

★Ulele AMERICAN $$$

(☎813-999-4952; www.ulele.com; 1810 N Highland Ave; mains $19-42; ⏱11am-10pm Sun-Thu, to 11pm Fri & Sat; 📶 👪) In a pleasant Riverwalk setting, this former water-pumping station has been transformed into an enchanting restaurant and brewery whose menu harkens back to native Floridan staples made over for modern times. That means liberal use of datil peppers, sides like alligator beans and okra 'fries' (amazing!), mains like local pompano fish and desserts like guava pie.

With green lawns, walking paths, Jack & the Beanstalk statues, and goldfish ponds, this spot could involve most of the day. There's even free fish food for kids to use while the adults sip a beverage of choice outside.

Drinking & Entertainment

Independent Bar BAR

(☎813-341-4883; www.independentbartampa.com; 5016 N Florida Ave, Seminole Heights; ⏱11am-midnight Mon-Thu, 10:30am to 1am Fri-Sun) If you appreciate craft brews, roll into this converted gas station, now a low-key, hip bar in Seminole Heights. You can count on one or more local Cigar City Brews, and it serves some good pub grub.

★Skipper's Smokehouse LIVE MUSIC

(☎813-971-0666; www.skipperssmokehouse.com; 910 Skipper Rd, Village of Tampa; cover $5-25; ⏱11am-11pm Tue, to midnight Wed-Fri, noon-midnight Sat, 1-9pm Sun) Like it blew in from the Keys, Skipper's is a beloved, unpretentious open-air venue for blues, folk, reggae and gator-swamp rockabilly, beneath beautiful live oaks. It's 9 miles directly north of downtown, on a side street off N Nebraska Ave.

★Tampa Theatre CINEMA

(☎813-274-8981, box office 813-274-8286; www.tampatheatre.org; 711 N Franklin St; tickets adult/child 2-12yr $11/9) This historic 1926 theater in downtown is a gorgeous venue in which to see an independent film. The mighty Wurlitzer organ plays before most movies. Too bad showtimes are so limited, with only one or two films playing on any given day. Look for special events.

Information

Unlock Tampa Bay Visitors Center (☎813-223-2752; www.visittampabay.com; 201 N Franklin St, Ste 102; ⏱10am-5:30pm Mon-Sat, noon-5pm Sun) Good free maps and lots of information.

Ybor City Visitor Center (☎813-241-8838; www.ybor.org; 1600 E 8th Ave; ⏱10am-5pm Mon-Sat, noon-5pm Sun) Provides an excellent introduction with walking-tour maps and info.

Getting There & Around

Tampa International Airport (TPA; ☎813-870-8700; www.tampaairport.com; 4100 George J Bean Pkwy) is the region's third-busiest hub. It's 6 miles west of downtown, off Hwy 589.

HART bus 30 ($2, 25 minutes, every 30 minutes) picks up and drops off at the Red Arrival Desk on the lower level of the airport; exact change is required.

All major car agencies have desks at the airport. By car, take I-275 to N Ashley Dr, turn right and you're in downtown.

St Petersburg

Long known as little more than a bawdy spring-break party town and a retirement capital, St Petersburg is now forging a new name for itself as a culturally savvy southern city. Spurred on by awe-inspiring downtown murals, a revitalized historic district and the stunning Dalí Museum, the downtown energy is creeping up Central Ave, spawning sophisticated restaurants, craft breweries, farmers markets and artsy galleries, all of which are attracting a younger professional crowd and a new wave of culturally curious travelers.

Sights & Activities

★Salvador Dalí Museum MUSEUM
(☎727-823-3767; www.thedali.org; 1 Dali Blvd; adult/child 13-17yr/child 6-12yr $24/17/10, after 5pm Thu $10; ⏱10am-5:30pm Fri-Wed, to 8pm Thu) The theatrical exterior of the Salvador Dalí Museum speaks of great things: out of a wound in the towering white shoe box oozes a 75ft geodesic glass atrium. Even better, what unfolds inside is like a blueprint of what a modern art museum, or at least one devoted to the life, art and impact of Salvador Dalí, should be. Even those who dismiss his dripping clocks and curlicue mustache will be awed by the museum and its grand works, especially the *Hallucinogenic Toreador*.

★Weedon Island Preserve NATURE RESERVE
(☎727-453-6500; www.weedonislandpreserve.org; 1800 Weedon Dr NE; ⏱7am-sunset) Like a patchwork quilt of variegated greens tossed out over Tampa Bay, this 3700-acre preserve protects a diverse aquatic and wetland ecosystem. At the heart of the preserve is the excellent Cultural and Natural History Center (open from 11am to 4pm Thursday to Saturday) where you can browse exhibits about the natural environment and the early Weedon Island people. Sign-up also for interpretive hikes over miles of boardwalk or go it alone with the online map.

St Petersburg Museum of Fine Arts MUSEUM
(☎727-896-2667; www.mfastpete.org; 255 Beach Dr NE; adult/child 7-18yr $20/10; ⏱10am-5pm Mon-Sat, to 8pm Thu, from noon Sun) The Museum of Fine Arts' collection is as broad as the Dalí Museum's is deep, traversing the world's antiquities and following art's progression through nearly every era.

Walking Mural Tours CULTURAL
(☎727-821-7391; www.stpetemuraltour.com; adult/child $19/11; ⏱10-11:30am Sat) This excellent walking tour introduces visitors to St Pete's vibrant mural scene, which got its start when artists were given cheap gallery space downtown after the economy crashed in 2008. Now upward of 30 highly creative and one-of-a-kind murals, many with nods to the city's history and culture, grace its buildings and rival Miami's Wynwood Walls.

Sleeping

★Hollander Hotel BOUTIQUE HOTEL $
(☎727-873-7900; www.hollanderhotel.com; 421 4th Ave N; r $110-179; P ⊖ ❄ 📶 🏊) The Hollander can do no wrong with its art-deco flavor, 130ft porch, convivial Tap Room, full-service spa and Common Grounds coffee shop. Shared spaces feature gorgeous period detailing and rooms retain a hint of 1930s romance with their polished wooden floors, lazy ceiling fans and cane furniture. The pool and bar out back becomes a party scene on weekends.

Eating & Drinking

★Brick & Mortar AMERICAN $$$
(☎727-822-6540; www.facebook.com/brickandmortarkitchen; 539 Central Ave; mains $16-43; ⏱5-9pm Tue, to 10pm Wed & Thu, 4:30-11pm Fri & Sat) A husband-and-wife catering team launched this, well, brick-and-mortar establishment in 2015, and despite the fact that St Pete has been overrun with great restaurants, this New American experiment dominated. Best thing in the menu? A divine house carpaccio with leek, some goat's cheese mousse,

a touch of truffle oil and a single ravioli stuffed with deliciously runny egg yolk ($17).

Cycle Brewing BREWERY
(534 Central Ave; 3pm-midnight Mon-Thu, noon-1am Fri & Sat, noon-10pm Sun) Unique brewhouse with sidewalk seating and up to 24 rotating taps of world-class beer. The Crank IPA is a great choice.

Getting There & Around

Downtown Looper (www.loopertrolley.com; free; 7am-10pm Mon-Thu, to midnight Fri, 8am-midnight Sat, 8am-10pm Sun) Old-fashioned trolley cars run a downtown circuit every 15 to 20 minutes; great for sightseeing.

Greyhound (727-898-1496; www.greyhound.com; 180 Dr Martin Luther King Jr St N) Buses connect to Miami, Orlando and Tampa.

Pinellas Suncoast Transit Authority (PSTA; www.psta.net; adult/student $2.25/1.10) St Petersburg buses serve the barrier-island beaches and Clearwater; unlimited-ride Go Cards cost $5 per day.

Sarasota

Vacations today can be spent soaking up the sights and beaches of sophisticated Sarasota, but this city took its time becoming the culturally rich place it is today. After marauding Spanish explorers expelled the Calusa people in the 15th century, this land lay virtually empty until the Seminole Wars inspired the Armed Occupation Act (1842), which deeded 160 acres and six months' provisions to anyone who would settle here and protect their farms.

Sailing boats and steamships were the only connection to the outside world, until the Tampa railroad came in 1902. Sarasota then grew popular as a winter resort for the affluent, and the city's arts institutions followed. Finally, circus magnate John Ringling decided to relocate his circus here, building a winter residence, art museum and college, and setting the struggling town on course to become the welcoming, well-to-do bastion of the arts it is today.

Sights & Activities

★ **Ringling Museum Complex** MUSEUM
(941-359-5700; www.ringling.org; 5401 Bay Shore Rd; adult/child 6-17yr $25/5; 10am-5pm Fri-Wed, to 8pm Thu;) The 66-acre winter estate of railroad, real-estate and circus baron John Ringling and his wife, Mable, is one of the Gulf Coast's premier attractions and incorporates their personal collection of artworks in what is now Florida's state art museum. Nearby, Ringling's Circus Museum documents his theatrical successes, while their lavish Venetian Gothic home, Cà d'Zan, reveals the impresario's extravagant tastes. Don't miss the PBS-produced film on Ringling's life, which is screened in the Circus Museum.

Island Park PARK
Sarasota's marina is notable for Island Park, an attractive green space poking into the harbor: it has a great playground and play fountain, restrooms, tree-shaded benches, a restaurant and tiki bar; and kayak, jet-ski and boat rentals.

★ **Siesta Key Rum** DISTILLERY
(Drum Circle Distilling; 941-702-8143; www.drumcircledistilling.com; 2212 Industrial Blvd; 10am-5pm Mon-Sat, from noon Sun) FREE The oldest rum distillery in Florida offers an educational and intoxicating tour in its facility within an industrial park a bit outside of town. You'll learn the entire process of rum-making from the company founder Troy, who is a gifted and hilarious public speaker. Delicious free samples at the end will likely result in purchases.

Sleeping & Eating

Hotel Ranola BOUTIQUE HOTEL $$
(941-951-0111; www.hotelranola.com; 118 Indian Pl, No 6; r $129-199, ste $209-259;) This small hotel is clean, rates are a decent value, and it is convenient to the downtown area.

Mattison's City Grille GRILL $$
(941-330-0440; https://mattisons.com; 1 N Lemon Ave; mains $19-36; 11am-10pm Sun-Mon, to 11pm Tue-Thu, to midnight Fri, 9:30am-midnight Sat;) Dinners won't wow you, but healthy salads and hearty sandwiches are fine at Sarasota's central Mattison's. The outdoor dining area doubles as a bar that gets going with music, giving the place its 'party on the corner' nickname.

★ **Owen's Fish Camp** SOUTHERN US $$
(941-951-6936; www.owensfishcamp.com; 516 Burns Ct; mains $14-25; 4-9:30pm Sun-Thu, to 10:30pm Fri & Sat) The wait rarely dips below an hour at this hip, Old Florida swamp shack downtown. The menu consists of upscale Southern cuisine with an emphasis on seafood, including whatever's fresh, and solid regular dishes like scallops with braised

pork, succotash and grits. Those willing to eat in the courtyard order at the bar, which also serves wine and craft beer.

Information

Arts & Cultural Alliance (www.sarasotaarts.org) All-encompassing event info.

Sarasota Herald-Tribune (www.heraldtribune.com) The main daily newspaper.

Sarasota Visitor Information Center (941-706-1253; www.visitsarasota.org; 1945 Fruitville Rd; 10am-5pm Mon-Fri, to 2pm Sat;) Very friendly office with tons of info; sells good maps.

Getting There & Away

Sarasota is roughly 60 miles south of Tampa and about 75 miles north of Fort Myers. The main roads into town are Tamiami Trail/Hwy 41 and I-75.

Greyhound (941-342-1720; www.greyhound.com; 5951 Porter Way; 8:30-10am & 1:30-6pm) Connects Sarasota with Miami, Fort Myers and Tampa.

Sarasota-Bradenton International Airport (SRQ; 941-359-2770; www.srq-airport.com; 6000 Airport Circle) Served by many major airlines. Go north on Hwy 41, and right on University Ave.

Sanibel & Captiva Islands

By preference and by design, island life on Sanibel is informal and egalitarian, and riches are rarely flaunted. Development on Sanibel has been carefully managed: the northern half is almost entirely protected within the JN 'Ding' Darling National Wildlife Refuge. While there are hotels aplenty, the beachfront is free of commercial-and-condo blight. Plus, public beach access is limited to a handful of spread-out parking lots, so there is no crush of day-trippers in one place.

The pirate José Gaspar, who called himself Gasparilla, once roamed the Gulf Coast plundering treasure and seizing beautiful women, whom he held captive on the aptly named Captiva Island. Today the tiny village is confined to a single street, Andy Rosse Lane, and there are still no traffic lights. The preferred mode of transportation is the family-friendly bike, and life here is informal and egalitarian, with island riches rarely being flaunted. Captiva's mansions are hidden behind thick foliage and sport playful names such as 'Seas the Day.'

Sights & Activities

Captiva Beach BEACH

(14790 Captiva Dr) Besides looking directly out onto heart-melting Gulf sunsets, Captiva Beach has lovely sand and is close to several romantic restaurants.

Arrive early if you want to park in the small lot, or come by bike.

JN 'Ding' Darling National Wildlife Refuge WILDLIFE RESERVE

(239-472-1100; www.fws.gov/dingdarling; 1 Wildlife Dr; car/cyclist/pedestrian $5/1/1; 7am-sunset) Named for cartoonist Jay Norwood 'Ding' Darling, an environmentalist who helped establish more than 300 sanctuaries across the USA, this 6300-acre refuge is home to an abundance of seabirds and wildlife, including alligators, night herons, red-shouldered hawks, spotted sandpipers, roseate spoonbills, pelicans and anhingas. The refuge's 5-mile **Wildlife Drive** provides easy access, but bring binoculars; flocks sometimes sit at expansive distances. Only a few very short walks lead into the mangroves.

Captiva Cruises CRUISE

(239-472-5300; www.captivacruises.com; 11401 Andy Rosse Lane; adult/child from $30/20) Departing from **McCarthy's Marina** (239-472-5200; www.mccarthysmarina.com; 11401 Andy Rosse Lane), Captiva Cruises offers everything from dolphin and sunset cruises to various island excursions, such as Cayo Costa (adult/child $50/35), Cabbage Key ($40/25), and Boca Grande ($50/35) on Gasparilla Island.

Tarpon Bay Explorers KAYAKING

(239-472-8900; www.tarponbayexplorers.com; 900 Tarpon Bay Rd; canoe & kayak rental 2hr $25; 8am-6pm) Within the Darling refuge, this outfitter rents canoes and kayaks for easy, self-guided paddles in Tarpon Bay, a perfect place for young paddlers. Guided kayak trips (adult from $30 to $40, child from $20 to $25) are also excellent, and there's a range of other trips and deck talks. Reserve ahead or come early, as trips book up.

Sleeping & Eating

Sandpiper Inn INN $$

(239-472-1606; www.palmviewsanibel.com; 720 Donax St; r $149-229;) Set a block back from the water and in close proximity to the shops and restaurants located on

Periwinkle Way, this cheery, yellow-and-teal Old Florida inn offers good value for Sanibel.

Each of the one-bedroom units has a functional (if dated) kitchen and a spacious sitting area decked out in tropical colors.

★'Tween Waters Inn RESORT **$$$**
(☎239-472-5161; www.tween-waters.com; 15951 Captiva Dr; r $200-300, ste $285-425, cottages $265-460;) For great resort value on Captiva, choose 'Tween Waters Inn. Rooms are attractive roosts with granite counters, rainfall showerheads and bright, garish decor. All have balconies and those directly facing the Gulf are splendid. The tidy little cottages are romantic.

Families make good use of the big pool, tennis courts, full-service marina, children's pool, and spa. Multi-night discounts are attractive.

★Sweet Melissa's Cafe AMERICAN **$$$**
(☎239-472-1956; www.sweetmelissascafe.com; 1625 Periwinkle Way; tapas $9-18, mains $30-49; ⏲11:30am-2:30pm & 5pm-close Mon-Fri, 5pm-close Sat) From menu to mood, Sweet Melissa's offers well-balanced, relaxed refinement. Dishes are ever-changing, but may include things like farro fettuccine, escargot with marrow and whole crispy fish. Creative without trying too hard. Lots of small-plate options encourage experimentation.

Service is attentive and the atmosphere upbeat.

Information

Sanibel & Captiva Islands Chamber of Commerce (☎239-472-1080; www.sanibel-captiva.org; 1159 Causeway Rd; ⏲9am-5pm;) One of the more helpful visitor centers around; keeps an updated hotel-vacancy list with dedicated hotel hotline, and they even put out buckets of brochures to help after-hours visitors.

Getting There & Away

Driving is the only way to come and go. The Sanibel Causeway (Hwy 867) charges an entrance toll (cars/motorcycles $6/2). Sanibel is 12 miles long, but low speed limits and traffic makes it seem longer. The main drag is Periwinkle Way, which becomes Sanibel-Captiva Rd.

Naples

For upscale romance and the prettiest, most serene city beach in southwest Florida, come to Naples, the Gulf Coast's answer to Palm Beach. Development along the shoreline has been kept residential. The soft white sand is backed only by narrow dunes and half-hidden mansions. More than that, though, Naples is a cultured, sophisticated town, unabashedly stylish and privileged but also welcoming and fun loving. Families, teens, couture-wearing matrons, middle-aged executives and smartly dressed young couples all mix and mingle as they stroll downtown's 5th Ave on a balmy evening. Travelers sometimes complain that Naples is expensive, but you can spend just as much elsewhere on a less impressive vacation.

Sights & Activities

★Naples Botanical Gardens GARDENS
(☎239-643-7275; www.naplesgarden.org; 4820 Bayshore Dr; adult/4-14yr $20/10; ⏲9am-5pm Wed-Mon, from 8am Tue) This outstanding botanical garden styles itself as 'a place of bliss, a region of supreme delight.' And after spending some time wandering its 2½-mile trail through nine cultivated gardens you'll rapidly find your inner Zen. Children will dig the thatched-roof tree house, butterfly house and interactive fountain, while adults get dreamy-eyed contemplating landscape architect Raymond Jungles' Scott Florida garden, filled with cascades, 12ft-tall oolite rocks and legacy tree species like date palms, sycamore leaf figs and lemon ficus.

★Baker Museum MUSEUM
(☎239-597-1900; www.artisnaples.org; 5833 Pelican Bay Blvd; adult/child $10/free; ⏲10am-4pm Tue-Sat, from noon Sun) The pride of Naples, this engaging, sophisticated art museum is part of the Artis–Naples campus, which includes the fabulous Philharmonic Center next door. Devoted to 20th-century modern art, the museum's 15 galleries and glass dome conservatory host exciting temporary and permanent shows, ranging from post-modern works to photography and paper craft to glass sculpture, including a stunning Chihuly exhibition.

Naples Municipal Beach BEACH
(12th Ave S & Gulf Shore Blvd) Naples' city beach is a long, dreamy white strand that

succeeds in feeling lively but rarely overcrowded. At the end of 12th Ave S, the 1000ft pier is a symbol of civic pride, having been constructed in 1888, destroyed a few times by fire and hurricane, and reconstructed each time. Parking is spread out in small lots between 7th Ave N and 17th Ave S, each with 10 to 15 spots of mixed resident and metered parking ($1.50 per hour).

Sleeping & Eating

Inn on 5th HOTEL **$$$**
(239-403-8777; www.innonfifth.com; 699 5th Ave S; r $399, ste $599-999;) This well-polished, Mediterranean-style luxury hotel provides an unbeatable location on either side of 5th Ave. Giant red vases grace the entryway. Stylish rooms are more corporate than romantic, but who complains about pillow-top mattresses and glass-walled showers? Full-service amenities include a 2nd-floor heated pool, business and fitness centers, and an indulgent spa. Free valet parking.

★**Escalante** BOUTIQUE HOTEL **$$$**
(239-659-3466; www.hotelescalante.com; 290 5th Ave S; r $505-1285) Hidden in plain sight at 5th Ave and 3rd St, the wonderful Escalante is a boutique hotel crafted in the fashion of a Tuscan villa. Rooms and suites are nestled behind luxuriant foliage and flowering pergolas, and feature plantation-style furniture, European linens and designer bath products.

The Local AMERICAN **$$**
(239-596-3276; www.thelocalnaples.com; 5323 Airport Pulling Rd N; mains $12-29; 11am-9pm;) Aside from the irony of driving 6 miles from downtown to eat local, this strip-mall farm-to-table bistro is worth the carbon footprint for fab sustainable fare, from the Mediterranean watermelon salad to the grass-fed beef. Try the 'Not Too Effin Hot Sauce,' if you're feeling feisty. Escape tourists. Eat local.

★**Bha! Bha! Persian Bistro** IRANIAN **$$$**
(239-594-5557; www.bhabhabistro.com; 865 5th Ave S; mains $27-49; 5-9pm Sun-Thu, to 10pm Fri & Sat) This experimental, high-end establishment takes its name from the Farsi phrase for 'yum, yum,' and that turns out to be a serious understatement. Wash down the pistachio lamb meatballs ($18) with a saffron lemongrass martini, then continue on to a kebab marinated in exotic spices or the duck *fesenjune* ($38), slow braised with pomegranate and walnut sauce.

Information

Third St Concierge Kiosk (239-434-6533; www.thirdstreetsouth.com; Camargo Park, 3rd St S; 10am-6pm Mon-Wed, to 9pm Thu & Fri, from 9am Sat, noon-5pm Sun) What's in Old Naples? This friendly outdoor kiosk attendant is glad you asked.

Visitor Information Center (239-262-6376; www.napleschamber.org; 2390 Tamiami Trail N; 9am-5pm Mon-Fri) Will help with accommodations; good maps, internet access and acres of brochures.

Getting There & Away

A car is essential; ample and free downtown parking makes things easy. Naples is about 40 miles southwest of Fort Myers via I-75.

Greyhound (239-774-5660; www.greyhound.com; 3825 Tollgate Blvd) Connects Naples to Miami, Orlando and Tampa.

Southwest Florida International Airport (RSW; 239-590-4800; www.flylcpa.com; 11000 Terminal Access Rd) This is the main airport for Naples. It's about a 45-minute drive north, along I-75.

CENTRAL FLORIDA

Central Florida is like a *matryoshka*, the Russian doll that encases similar dolls of diminishing size. The region features pretty state parks, gardens and rivers, all ideal for leisurely exploration. One layer down, Central Florida then embraces Kissimmee, Celebration and the vast, sprawling area of Greater Orlando. Greater Orlando's network of multi-lane highways and overpasses leads to a huge number of theme parks, including Walt Disney World®, Universal Orlando Resort, SeaWorld and Legoland. Judging from the crowds, these parks are the reason most people visit.

But at Central Florida's core is a city: pretty, leafy downtown Orlando, whose great field-to-fork eating scene and world-class museums get overlooked by the hype, sparkle and colors of the theme parks. Many visitors never reach this kernel, the final 'doll,' and the city of Orlando tends to lie in the shadow of Cinderella and Hogwarts School of Witchcraft & Wizardry.

Orlando

It's so easy to get caught up in Greater Orlando – in the isolated, fabricated worlds of Disney or Universal Orlando (for which, let's face it, you're probably here) – that you forget all about the downtown city of Orlando itself. It has a lot to offer: lovely tree-lined neighborhoods; a rich performing arts and museum scene; several fantastic gardens and nature preserves; fabulous cuisine; great craft cocktails; and a delightfully slower pace devoid of manic crowds. So, sure, enjoy the theme parks and the sparkles, nostalgia and adrenaline-pumped fantasy there, but also take time to 'Find Orlando.' Come down off the coasters for one day to explore the quieter, gentler side of the city. You may be surprised to find that you enjoy the theme parks all that much more as a result.

Sights

★Mennello Museum of American Art MUSEUM
(407-246-4278; www.mennellomuseum.org; 900 E Princeton St, Loch Haven Park, Downtown; adult/child 6-18yr $5/1; 10:30am-4:30pm Tue-Sat, from noon Sun; Lynx 125, Florida Hospital Health Village) Tiny but excellent lakeside art museum featuring the work of Earl Cunningham, whose brightly colored images, a fusion of pop and folk art, leap off the canvas. Visiting exhibits often feature American folk art. Every four months there's a new exhibition, everything from a Smithsonian collection to a local artist. The mystical live oak in front makes even parking beautiful.

★Orlando Museum of Art MUSEUM
(407-896-4231; www.omart.org; 2416 N Mills Ave, Loch Haven Park, Downtown; adult/child $15/5; 10am-4pm Tue-Fri, from noon Sat & Sun; ; Lynx 125, Florida Hospital Health Village) Founded in 1924, Orlando's grand center for the arts boasts a fantastic collection – both permanent and temporary – and hosts an array of adult and family-friendly art events and classes. The popular First Thursday ($15), from 6pm to 9pm on the first Thursday of the month, celebrates local artists with regional work, live music and food from Orlando restaurants.

ICON Orlando AMUSEMENT PARK
(www.iconorlando.com; I-Drive 360, 8401 International Dr, International Drive; from $24; 10am-10pm Sun-Thu, to midnight Fri & Sat) Orlando has got everything else that goes up and down, so why not round and around? Opened in 2017, ICON Orlando is one of International Drive's major landmarks. Orlando is flat, but a trip in this, especially at night, affords views of theme parks and the greater area.

Check ahead as it sometimes closes for private events.

SeaWorld AMUSEMENT PARK
(407-545-5550; www.seaworldparks.com; 7007 Sea World Dr; $99, discounts online, prices vary daily; 9am-8pm; ; Lynx 8, 38, 50, 111, I-Ride Trolley Red Line Stop 28) One of Orlando's largest theme parks, SeaWorld is an aquatic-themed park filled with marine animal shows, roller coasters and up-close sea-life encounters. However, the park's biggest draw is controversial: live shows featuring trained dolphins, sea lions and killer whales. Since the release of the 2013 documentary *Blackfish,* SeaWorld's treatment of its captive orcas has come under intense scrutiny and the company has been hit by falling visitor numbers and negative PR.

Titanic: the Artifact Exhibition MUSEUM
(407-248-1166; https://titanicorlando.com; 7324 International Dr, International Drive; adult/child 6-11yr $22/16; Fri-Sat 10am-6pm, to 8pm Sun-Thu; ; Lynx 8, 38, 42, I-Ride Trolley Red Line Stop 9) Full-scale replicas of the doomed ship's interior and artifacts found at the bottom of the sea, 170 in all, including one of only two pieces of the actual ship's hull. Kids especially love the dramatic and realistic interpretation of history – each passenger receives a boarding pass, with the name of a real passenger, and at the end of the experience (once the ship has sunk) you learn your fate.

Sleeping

★Floridian Hotel & Suites HOTEL $
(407-212-3021; www.floridianhotelorlando.com; 7531 Canada Ave, International Drive; r from $75; P) A wonderful, privately owned budget hotel with similarities to a chain brand, but oh so much better in other respects: delightful front office staff, spotless rooms with fridges, and even a complimentary (if basic) breakfast, plus shuttles to various parks.

It's located near Restaurant Row and handy to International Dr.

FLORIDA ORLANDO

Hyatt Regency Grand Cypress Resort RESORT $$
(407-239-1234; www.hyattregencygrandcypress.com; 1 Grand Cypress Blvd, Lake Buena Vista; r $189-300, resort fee per day $35, self-/valet parking $22/31;) Considering the proximity to Disney's Magic Kingdom (7 miles) and Universal Resort Orlando (8 miles), plus the quality of the rooms, service, grounds and amenities, this atrium-style resort is one of the best-value options in Orlando, though it's certainly not a unique nor boutique experience.

★**Bay Hill Club and Lodge** HOTEL $$$
(407-876-2429; www.bayhill.com; 9000 Bay Hill Blvd; r $250-700;) Quiet and genteel Bay Hill feels like a time warp; as though you're walking into a TV set or your grandmother's photo album. It is reassuringly calm and simple. Handsome rooms are spread among a series of two-story buildings bordering the Arnold Palmer–designed golf course. Internet deals are frequent.

Aloft Orlando Downtown BUSINESS HOTEL $$$
(407-380-3500; www.aloftorlandodowntown.com; 500 S Orange Ave, Downtown; r from $250;) Open, streamlined and decidedly modern, although the carefully constructed minimalist decor might render the rooms oddly empty for some. The sleek little pool sits unpleasantly on the main road. But it is one of the few hotels within an easy walk to downtown Orlando's bars and restaurants.

Eating

★**P Is for Pie** BAKERY $
(407-745-4743; www.crazyforpies.com; 2806 Corrine Dr, Audubon Park; from $2; 7:30am-4:30pm Mon-Sat) Clean-lined with an artisan twist to classic pies (as in sweet tarts with a biscuit base), offering mini and specialty options.

Flavors include a sublime key lime and tiramisu. Sublime.

Graffiti Junktion American Burger Bar BURGERS $
(321-424-5800; www.graffitijunktion.com; 700 E Washington St, Thornton Park; mains $9-15; 11am-2am) This little neon, happenin' hangout, with courtyard dining and regular drink specials, is all about massive burgers with attitude. Go with a Brotherly Love (Angus beef; $11) or veggie option ($9). Happy hour is all day on Monday and from 4pm to 7pm Tuesday to Sunday.

Pho 88 VIETNAMESE $
(407-897-3488; www.pho88orlando.com; 730 N Mills Ave, Mills 50; mains $9-17; 10am-10pm;) A flagship in Orlando's thriving Vietnamese district (known as Little Saigon), just northeast of downtown in an area informally referred to as Mills 50, this authentic, no frills, *pho* (noodle soup) specialist is always packed. Big bowls of noodles are cheap and tasty, as are the popular potstickers. Many of the items are, or can be done, vegetarian.

Melting Pot EUROPEAN $$
(407-903-1100; www.meltingpot.com; 7549 W Sand Lake Rd, Restaurant Row; mains $11-48; 5-10pm Mon-Thu, to 11pm Fri, noon-11pm Sat, noon-10pm Sun;) Kids in particular love the novelty of a fondue dinner (cheese, beef, chicken, seafood and, of course, chocolate). Having said that, it's an elegant spot and a popular date-night place.

★**La Luce** ITALIAN $$$
(407-597-3675; www.laluceorlando.com; 14100 Bonnet Creek Resort Ln; mains $26-44; 6-11pm;) La Luce is a gem – whether it's a quiet corner table with a special someone or a friendly chat with folks at the bar – and feels like that place you've been going to for years even if it's your first time here. Meals are fantastic, sometimes quirky, always tasty. Duck *ragu* (meat sauce), crisp salads, melt-in-your-mouth desserts. Just a world of yum. The butterscotch pudding is so good it even has its own Facebook fan page.

Drinking & Nightlife

★**Icebar** BAR
(407-426-7555; www.icebarorlando.com; 8967 International Dr; entry at door/advance online $20/15; 5pm-midnight Sun-Wed, to 1am Thu, to 2am Fri & Sat; I-Trolley Red Line Stop 18 or Green Line Stop 10) More classic Orlando gimmicky fun. Step into the 22ºF (-5ºC) ice house, sit on the ice seat, admire the ice carvings and sip the icy drinks.

Coat and gloves are provided at the door (or upgrade to the photogenic faux fur for $10), and the fire room, bathrooms and other areas of the bar are kept at normal temperature.

Independent Bar CLUB
(407-839-0457; 70 N Orange Ave, Downtown; varies, often $10; 10pm-2:30am Sat-Thu, from

9:30pm Fri) Known to locals as simply the 'I-Bar,' it's hip, crowded and loud, with DJs spinning underground dance and alternative rock into the wee hours.

Information

Official Visitor Center (407-363-5872; www.visitorlando.com; 8102 International Dr; 8am-8pm; I-Ride Trolley Red Line 11)

Getting There & Around

Amtrak (www.amtrak.com; 1400 Sligh Blvd) offers daily trains south to Miami (from $47) and north to New York City (from $150).

Greyhound (407-292-3424; www.greyhound.com; 555 N John Young Pkwy) serves numerous cities from Orlando.

LYMMO (www.golynx.com; free; 6am-10:45pm Mon-Fri, from 10am Sat, 10am-10pm Sun) circles downtown Orlando for free with stops near Lynx Central Station, near SunRail's Church St Station, at Central and Magnolia, Jefferson and Magnolia and outside the Westin Grand Bohemian.

SunRail (www.sunrail.com), Orlando's commuter rail train, runs north–south. It doesn't stop at or near any theme parks.

In addition to the downtown station, Amtrak serves Winter Park, Kissimmee and Winter Haven (home to Legoland).

Walt Disney World® Resort

This mega-scale **resort** (407-939-5277; www.disneyworld.disney.go.com; Lake Buena Vista, outside Orlando; daily rates vary, from around $109, see website for discount packages & tickets up to 10 days;), with its own monorail, sections of eight-lane highway, and thousands of acres of rides, amusements, parks, and hotels, is larger than a good sized international airport...and about as easy to navigate. Disney World is in fact an unfenced 40-sq-mile area. But within this, although several miles apart from each other, are four contained, spotlessly sanitized theme parks: **Magic Kingdom**, **Epcot**, **Hollywood Studios** and **Animal Kingdom**.

Also within the Walt Disney World® parameters are two water parks, two shopping districts, golf courses, more than 20 Disney-owned-and-run hotels, countless places to eat, a police force, transport systems (did someone say monorail?), and kennels for the pooch.

And let's clarify something else: Walt Disney World® offers a lot more than rides. The huge number of attractions include interactive meet 'n' greets with well-known characters, including Mickey Mouse and Donald Duck, as well as more contemporary casts such as Gaston, Elsa, Anna and so on. Then there are parades, musical productions, interactive facilities, Disney promotions of the latest projects and plenty of stunt shows. And (here's the surprising part), it's not just for kids. Disney World has cleverly maintained its loyal following, resulting in hundreds of thousands of more mature visitors who just can't get enough, through programs, cuisine, cruises and behind-the-scenes tours.

Each of the four parks has its own theme, although when most people think of Walt Disney World®, they're often thinking of one of the four parks – **the Magic Kingdom**, with Cinderella Castle at its core. This is the Disney of commercials, of princesses and pirates, Tinkerbell and dreams come true; this is quintessential, old-school Disney with classic rides such as It's a Small World and Space Mountain.

Epcot is a wonderful sensory experience. The park is divided into two sections that are situated around a lake: Future World and World Showcase. **Future World** has Epcot's only two thrill rides plus several pavilions with attractions, restaurants, and character-greeting spots. **World Showcase** comprises 11 re-created nations featuring country-specific food, shopping and entertainment. This is the place to slow down a little and enjoy, where you can smell the incense in Morocco, listen to the Beatles in the UK and sip miso in Japan.

Hollywood Studios conjures the heydays of Hollywood, with a replica of Graumann's Chinese Theatre (the main focal icon), but most of the activities reflect unabashed 21st-century energy with attractions focusing on everything from *Star Wars* Jedi training to *Indiana Jones* stunt shows, from Muppet extravaganzas to the latest craze, the Frozen Sing-Along Celebration.

Set apart from the rest of Disney both in miles and in tone, **Animal Kingdom** attempts to blend theme park with zoo, carnival and African safari, all stirred together with a healthy dose of Disney characters, storytelling and transformative magic. Like the other parts, it's also divided into different sections, with wildlife experiences, rides, and musical shows at every corner, including the *The Lion King* and *Nemo*. At the time of research, Animal Kingdom was about to open another area: the much-awaited **Pandora – The World of Avatar**.

To round off the Disney experience, Walt Disney World® runs a number of accommodations, including family options and couples' luxury experiences. The advantage of staying at one of these is that most things, including meals and transportation, are arranged or easily accessible to you (but, although they make things run smoothly, especially if you have children, they're not the be all and end all; other hotels nearby also offer similar services). But they do serve up further fun and yes, even more entertainment including opportunities to dine with Disney characters. It is well designed for travelers with disabilities, with wheelchair rental, easy access and excellent arrangements for line access and the like.

In short, an experience at Walt Disney World® is extraordinary. It's an unabashed stimulation overload of music, light, sound, color, thrills and spills. It offers an other worldliness that is fully, inexplicably intoxicating, no matter your age. And that's despite the long lines, the occasional jostling and the over-priced meals. For most of the time, this is indeed the Happiest Place on Earth.

And, just when the sun has set and you think you're done for the day, there's more; each park has a nighttime fireworks show (the names of which change according to the annual program).

Daily ticket prices do vary, but the ticketing system provides for multiday tickets (one park per day over a set number of days) and Park Hopper options, which allow you to 'park hop' (note: logistically, this is time consuming and, with the exception of, say, Epcot and Hollywood Studios, not very feasible).

Sleeping & Eating

Disney resort hotels are divided according to location (Magic Kingdom, Epcot, Animal Kingdom and Disney Boardwalk). Prices vary drastically according to season, week and day.

While deluxe resorts are the best Disney has to offer, note that you're paying for Disney theming and location convenience, not luxury. Most offer multiroom suites and villas, upscale restaurants, children's programs and easy access to theme parks.

With the exception of Epcot, expect mediocre fast food, bad coffee and cafeteria cuisine at premium prices. Table-service restaurants accept 'priority seating' reservations up to 180 days in advance. Reserve through **Disney Dining** (407-939-3463; www.disneyworld.disney.go.com) or through the My Disney Experience app. Remember: while restaurants in the theme parks require theme-park admission, resort hotel restaurants do not.

Disney also offers character meals, dinner shows and specialty dining.

Getting There & Around

Disney lies 25 minutes' drive south of downtown Orlando. Take I-4 to well-signed exits 64, 65 or 67. Alamos and National car rental is available inside the Walt Disney World® Dolphin Resort.

If you're staying at a Walt Disney World® hotel and are arriving at Orlando International Airport (as opposed to Sanford), arrange in advance for complimentary luggage handling and deluxe bus transportation with **Disney's Magical Express** (866-599-0951; www.disneyworld.disney.go.com). They will send you baggage labels in advance, collect your luggage at the airport and, if during your stay you transfer from one Disney hotel to another, the resort will transfer your luggage while you're off for the day.

The Disney transportation system utilizes boats, buses, and even a monorail to shuttle visitors to hotels, theme parks and other attractions within Walt Disney World®. The Transportation & Ticket Center operates as the main hub of this system. Note that it can take an hour to get from point A to point B using the Disney transportation system, and there is not always a direct route.

Universal Orlando Resort

Pedestrian-friendly **Universal Orlando Resort** (407-363-8000; www.universalorlando.com; 1000 Universal Studios Plaza; single park 1/2 days adult $105/185, child $100/175, both parks adult/child $155/150; daily, hours vary; Lynx 21, 37 & 40, Universal) has got spunk, spirit and attitude. With fantastic rides, excellent children's attractions and entertaining shows, it's comparable to Walt Disney World®. But Universal does everything just a bit smarter, funnier, and more smoothly, as well as being smaller and easier to navigate. Universal offers pure, unabashed, adrenaline-pumped, full-speed-ahead fun for the entire family.

The Universal Orlando Resort consists of three theme parks – Islands of Adventure, with the bulk of the thrill rides, and Universal Studios, with movie-based attractions and shows (including the Wizarding World of Harry Potter). Volcano Bay is a water park of thrills and splashes and state-of-the-art rides through a 200ft volcano.

Universal's dining and entertainment district is CityWalk and it has six resort hotels. Water taxis and pleasant walking paths connect the entire resort.

Multiday and multipark tickets are available, so check online for the latest combinations and offers.

Sights

★Universal Studios AREA

(☎407-363-8000; www.universalorlando.com; 1000 Universal Studios Plaza, Universal Orlando Resort; 1 day adult $115, child $110; ⏱from 9am, closing hours vary; 🚌Lynx 21, 37 or 40, 🚐Universal) Divided geographically by region-specific architecture and ambience and fabulously themed as a Hollywood backlot, Universal Studios' simulation-heavy rides

Greater Orlando & Theme Parks

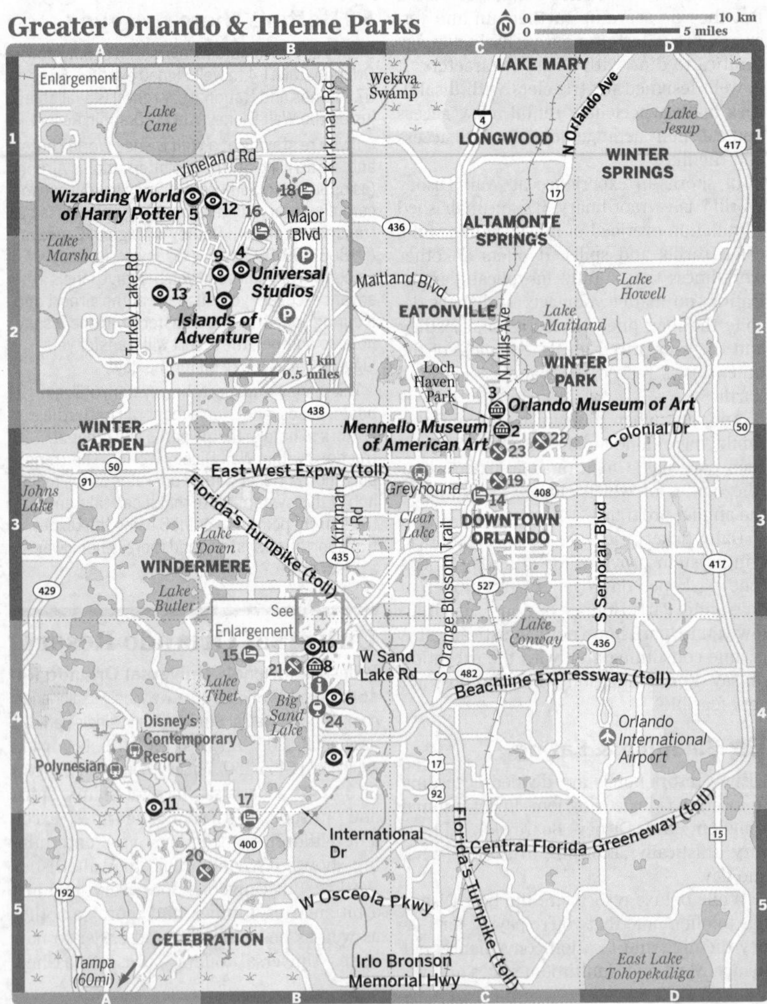

and shows are dedicated to silver screen and TV icons. Drink Duff beer, a Homer favorite, in Springville; ride the Hogwarts Express into Diagon Alley; and sidle up to Lucille Ball on Hollywood Blvd. And if you're looking for thrills, you'll find two of Orlando's best roller coasters: Revenge of the Mummy and Hollywood Rip Ride Rockit.

For some downtime, a fenced-in grassy area with shade trees, flowers and views across the lagoon sits just across from the entrance to Woody Woodpecker's Kidzone.

★Wizarding World of Harry Potter AREA

(☎407-363-8000; www.universalorlando.com; Islands of Adventure & Universal Studios; theme park admission required; ⊙from 9am (closing hours vary); 🚌Lynx 21, 37 or 40) Alan Gilmore and Stuart Craig, art director and production designer for the films, collaborated closely with the Universal Orlando Resort engineers to create what is without exception the most fantastically realized themed experience in Florida. The detail and authenticity tickle the fancy at every turn, from the screeches of the mandrakes in the shop windows to the groans of Moaning Myrtle in the bathroom.

Poke along the cobbled streets and impossibly crooked buildings of Hogsmeade, sip frothy Butterbeer, munch on Cauldron Cakes and mail a card via Owl Post, all in the shadow of Hogwarts Castle, and keep your eyes peeled for magical happenings. The Wizarding World of Harry Potter is divided into two sections, each with rides and shows: **Hogsmeade** (☎407-363-8000; www.universalorlando.com; Islands of Adventure; theme-park admission required; ⊙9am-6pm, hours vary; 🚌Lynx 21, 37 or 40) sits in Islands of Adventure and **Diagon Alley** (www.universalorlando.com; Universal Studios; theme-park admission required; ⊙from 9am; 🚌Lynx 21, 37 or 40), completed in 2014, is in Universal Studios. If you have a park-to-park ticket, hop on the Hogwarts Express from one section to the other. New to Hogsmeade is Hagrid's Magical Creatures Motorbike Adventure, where visitors buckle in and 'fly' through the Forbidden Forest.

One hour early admission is available for guests at Universal Orlando Resort hotels.

★Islands of Adventure AREA

(☎407-363-8000; www.universalorlando.com; 6000 Universal Blvd, Universal Orlando Resort; 1 day adult $115, child $110; ⊙from 9am, closing hours vary; 🚌Lynx 21, 37 or 40, ⛴Universal) Good ol' scream-it-from-the-rooftops, no-holds-barred, laugh-out-loud fun, packed with adrenaline rides and marvelous theming. Superheroes zoom by on motorcycles, roller coasters whiz overhead and plenty of rides will get you soaked. Highlights include Marvel Super Hero Island, with the Amazing Adventures of Spider-man and the Hulk Coaster; kid-friendly Seuss Landing; and, most famously of all, Hogwarts in the Wizarding World of Harry

Greater Orlando & Theme Parks

Top Sights

1 Islands of Adventure B2
2 Mennello Museum of American Art C3
3 Orlando Museum of Art C2
4 Universal Studios B2
5 Wizarding World of Harry Potter A1

Sights

6 ICON Orlando B4
7 SeaWorld B4
8 Titanic: the Artifact Exhibition B4
9 Universal Orlando Resort B2
10 Volcano Bay B4
11 Walt Disney World® Resort A4
12 Wizarding World of Harry Potter – Diagon Alley B1
13 Wizarding World of Harry Potter – Hogsmeade A2

Sleeping

14 Aloft Orlando Downtown C3
15 Bay Hill Club and Lodge B4
Floridian Hotel & Suites .... (see 8)
16 Hard Rock Hotel B1
17 Hyatt Regency Grand Cypress Resort B5
18 Loews Portofino Bay Hotel B1

Eating

19 Graffiti Junktion American Burger Bar C3
20 La Luce B5
Mama Della's Ristorante .... (see 18)
21 Melting Pot B4
22 P Is for Pie C3
23 Pho 88 .... C3

Drinking & Nightlife

24 Icebar B4
Independent Bar .... (see 14)

Potter – Hogsmeade. Multiday and multi-park tickets available.

Volcano Bay AREA

(www.universalorlando.com; 6000 Universal Blvd, Universal Resort; 1 day adult $70, child $65; ⌚ from 9am, closing hours vary) Universal Resort's third theme park – a water park – launched in 2017. Modeled on a Pacific island, the tropical oasis' main feature is a colossal volcano through and down which, you guessed it, run watery thrills and spills. Among the 18 attractions are winding rivers with family raft rides, pools and two intertwining slides, but the main attraction is the Ko'okiri Body Plunge. At a hair-raising 125ft, it's the tallest trap-door body plunge ride in North America.

It's located alongside Islands of Adventure and Universal. Hold your spot in line with a TapuTapu wristband.

Sleeping & Eating

Universal Orlando Resort is home to a number of excellent resort hotels. Staying at a resort hotel eliminates many logistical hassles: it's a pleasant gardened walk or a quiet boat ride to the parks; most offer Unlimited Express Pass access to park attractions and priority dining; several popular rides open one hour earlier for all guests. Each Universal Resort has high-quality bars and restaurants that can be enjoyed even if you're not a guest.

★Loews Portofino Bay Hotel RESORT **$$$**

(☎407-503-1000; www.loewshotels.com/portofino-bay-hotel; 5601 Universal Blvd, Universal Orlando Resort; r & ste $325-$390, self/valet parking per day $22/30; P❄@📶🏊🐾; 🚌Universal) Sumptuous and elegant, with beautiful rooms, cobblestone streets and sidewalk cafes around a central lagoon, this resort evokes the relaxing charm of seaside Italy. There's a sandy zero-entrance family pool, the secluded Hillside pool and the elegant Villa pool, as well as the Mandara Spa, evening waterside minstrel music and the excellent Mama Della's Ristorante. Rates include one-hour early entrance to the Wizarding World of Harry Potter and an Unlimited Express Pass.

Hard Rock Hotel RESORT **$$$**

(☎407-503-2000; www.hardrockhotels.com/orlando; 5800 Universal Blvd, Universal Orlando Resort; r & ste $329 to $393, self-/valet parking per day $22/30; P❄@📶🏊🐾; 🚌Universal) From the grand lawn with the massive guitar fountain at its entrance to the pumped-in, underwater music at the pool, the modern and stylized Hard Rock embodies the pure essence and energy of rock 'n' roll cool. Rates include one-hour early entrance to the Wizarding World of Harry Potter and an Unlimited Express Pass.

There's a huge zero-entry pool with a waterslide, and families mingle harmoniously alongside a young party crowd, but the loud live band that sometimes plays in the lobby and the rockin' vibe may be overkill for folk looking for a peaceful getaway. If you're looking for something more subdued, head to Portofino Bay.

★Mama Della's Ristorante ITALIAN **$$**

(☎407-503-3463; www.universalorlando.com; 5601 Universal Blvd, Loews Portofino Bay Hotel; mains $10-22; ⌚5:30-11pm; 🍷👪; 🚌Universal) Charming, cozy and friendly, with vintage wallpaper, dark wood and several rooms with romantic nooks. You really do feel like you're a welcomed guest at a private home nestled in Italy. Strolling musicians entertain tableside and the simple Italian fare is both fresh and excellent; the service is efficient but relaxed.

Good wine, old-fashioned soda in a bottle and a bowl of pasta at Mama Della's makes a very nice ending to a day at the parks, for both kids and adults.

Getting There & Around

From I-4, take exit 74B or 75A and follow the signs. From International Dr, follow the signs west onto Universal Blvd.

Lynx buses 21, 37 and 40 service the Universal Orlando Resort parking garage (40 runs directly from the downtown Orlando Amtrak station). International Dr's **I-Ride Trolley** (☎407-354-5656; www.iridetrolley.com; rides adult/child 3-9yr $2/1, passes 1/3/5/7/14 days $5/7/9/12/18; ⌚8am-10:30pm) stops at Universal Blvd, a 0.6-mile walk away.

Universal Orlando Resort – that is, Universal Orlando's resort hotels, Islands of Adventure and Universal Studios theme parks and CityWalk – are linked by pedestrian walkways. It's a 10- to 15-minute walk from the theme parks and CityWalk to the deluxe resort hotels. Cabana Bay Beach Resort is about a 25-minute walk. Several hotels outside the park are within a 20-minute walk, but it's not a very pleasant journey.

Rent strollers, wheelchairs and Electric Convenience Vehicles (ECVs) at the entrance to each park and manual wheelchairs at the Rotunda section of the parking lot. To reserve an ECV in advance, call ☎ 407-224-4233.

FLORIDA PANHANDLE

The most geographically northern end of Florida is by far its most culturally Southern side. The Panhandle – that spit of land embedded in the left shoulder of the Florida peninsula – is hemmed in by Alabama and Georgia, and in many ways the region's beaches are effectively coastal extensions of those states.

This is a coast of primal, wind-blown beauty in many places, particularly the undeveloped stretches of salt marsh and slash pine that spill east and west of Apalachee Bay. In other areas, the seashore is given to rental houses and high-rise condos.

Inland, you'll find a tangle of palmetto fans and thin pine woods interspersed with crystal springs, lazy rivers and military testing ranges – this area has one of the highest concentrations of defense facilities in the country.

In October, 2018, the area was hit by devastating Hurricane Michael, which decimated many parts of the region. Recovery was ongoing at the time of research.

Tallahassee

Florida's capital, cradled between gently rising hills and nestled beneath tree-canopied roadways, is geographically closer to Atlanta than it is to Miami. Culturally, it's far closer to the Deep South than the majority of the state it governs.

Despite its status as a government center, and the presence of two major universities (Florida State and Florida Agricultural & Mechanical University), the pace here is slower than syrup. That said, there are interesting museums and outlying attractions that will appeal to history and nature buffs and could easily detain a visitor for a day or two.

Sights & Activities

★ Tallahassee Museum MUSEUM

(☎ 850-575-8684; www.tallahasseemuseum.org; 3945 Museum Rd; adult/child $12/9; ⏰ 9am-5pm Mon-Sat, from 11am Sun; P) Occupying 52 acres of pristine manicured gardens and wilderness on the outskirts of Tallahassee, near the airport, this wonderful natural-history museum features living exhibits of Floridian flora and fauna – including the incredibly rare Floridan panther and red wolf – and has delighted visitors for more than 50 years. Be sure to check out the otters in their new home, or try ziplining above the canopy in the Tree to Tree Adventures – a variety of scenarios are available, costing $17 to $45 depending on the options.

Tallahassee Automobile & Collectibles Museum MUSEUM

(☎ 850-942-0137; www.tacm.com; 6800 Mahan Dr; adult/student/child under 10yr $18/12/8; ⏰ 8am-5pm Mon-Fri, from 10am Sat, from noon Sun; P) If you like motor vehicles, welcome to heaven! This museum houses a pristine collection of more than 165 unique and historical automobiles from around the world, including an Elvismobile. Top that with collections of boats, motorcycles, books, pianos and sports memorabilia and you've got a full day on your hands. There's even a Tie-Fighter. It is about 8 miles northeast of downtown, off I-10.

Florida State Capitol NOTABLE BUILDING

(www.floridacapitol.myflorida.com; 400 South Monroe St; ⏰ 8am-5pm Mon-Fri) FREE The stark and imposing 22-story Florida State Capitol's top-floor observation deck affords 360-degree views of the city. In session the capitol is a hive of activity, with politicians, staffers and lobby groups buzzing in and around its honeycombed corridors. There are few states that have as diverse a legislature as Florida's – in one hall, you may hear Cuban Americans from Miami brokering deals with good old boys from the Panhandle. America! Locals and tourists alike have noted that the new building, a lone shaft with rounded domes on either side, bears

WORTH A TRIP

DELAND: CRESS

Citified foodies have been known to trek to sleepy DeLand just to eat at cutting-edge **Cress** (☎ 386-734-3740; www.cressrestaurant.com; 103 W Indiana Ave; events $65-95; ⏰ ticketed reservations only), whose menu might offer such delights as local seafood *mofongo* (a classic Caribbean dish), Indonesian shrimp curry, and a salad of delicate pea tendrils with passion-fruit emulsion. It has recently switched to a ticket-only reservation system, so you must call ahead and check the website for events.

OFF THE BEATEN TRACK

APALACHICOLA NATIONAL FOREST

The largest of Florida's three national forests, the **Apalachicola National Forest** (850-523-8500, 850-643-2282; www.fs.usda.gov/main/apalachicola; entrance off FL 13, FL 67, & other locations; day-use fee $3; 8am-sunset) occupies almost 938 sq miles – more than half a million acres – of the Panhandle from just west of Tallahassee to the Apalachicola River. It's made up of lowlands, pines, cypress hammocks and oaks, and dozens of species call the area home, including mink, gray and red foxes, coyotes, six bat species, beavers, woodpeckers, alligators, Florida black bears and the elusive Florida panther. Numerous lakes and miles of trails make this one of the most diverse outdoor recreation areas in the state. Though the region was hit hard by Hurricane Michael in 2018, the natural beauty still shines through – if with a lot more broken trees.

You'll need wheels to explore the forest, either a bicycle for the exceedingly fit, or a car for the rest of us. Given that the woods cover such an enormous area, there are multiple entry points, including along SR 65 (easier if you're coming from Apalachicola) and SR 20 (good for those coming from Tallahassee).

The western half of the forest is controlled by the **Apalachicola Ranger Station** (850-643-2282; www.fs.usda.gov/apalachicola; 11152 NW SR-20, Bristol), northwest of the forest near the intersection of Hwys 12 and 20, just south of Bristol.

The eastern half of the forest is managed by the **Wakulla Ranger Station** (850-926-3561; www.fs.usda.gov/apalachicola; 57 Taff Dr, Crawfordville), just off Hwy 319 in Crawfordville.

striking resemblance to a, um, er...well, go look for yourself.

Tallahassee-St Marks Historic Railroad State Trail CYCLING
(850-487-7989; www.floridastateparks.org/tallahasseestmarks; 1358 Old Woodville Rd, Crawfordville; 8am-sunset) FREE The ultimate treat for runners, skaters and cyclists, this trail has 16 miles of smooth pavement shooting due south to the gulf-port town of St Marks and not a car or traffic light in sight. It's easy and flat for all riders, sitting on a coastal plain and shaded at many points by canopies of gracious live oaks.

Sleeping & Eating

aloft Tallahassee Downtown HOTEL $$
(850-513-0313; www.alofttallahassee.com; 200 N Monroe St; r $119-230;) This branch of the popular aloft chain boasts a prime downtown location and funky, functional rooms. Bathrooms feature counter-to-ceiling mirrors and lots of space for all the makeup in the world. Beds are uber-comfy, and free high-speed internet is included.

★**Canopy Road Cafe** CAFE $
(850-668-6600; www.canopyroadcafe.com; 1913 N Munroe; mains $8-11; 6:30am-2:15pm) Canopy Road, named for Tallahassee's beautiful canopy byways, is a modest chain, but they do everything right: great plates of good food, prices are reasonable, and service comes with a smile. Try the croissant French toast, their popular breakfast combos, or an avocado smash. Light eaters can get a half order. Wow!

Kool Beanz Café FUSION $$
(850-224-2466; www.koolbeanz-cafe.com; 921 Thomasville Rd; dinner mains $19-27; 11am-2:30pm & 5:30-10pm Mon-Fri, 5:30-10pm Sat, 10:30am-2pm Sun;) It's got a corny name but a wonderfully eclectic and homey vibe – plus great, creative fare. The menu changes daily, but you can count on finding something tasty. That can be almost anything: from hummus plates to monkfish or jerk-spiced scallops to duck in blueberry-ginger sauce. Meyer-lemon pudding was a dessert option at the time of research.

Drinking & Entertainment

Madison Social PUB
(850-894-6276; www.madisonsocial.com; 705 South Woodward Ave; mains $9-20; 11:30am-2am Sun-Thu, from 10am Fri & Sat;) Never mind the trend of flipping former transmission shops into hip, retro locales, this trendy hot spot was built to look that way from the get go. It swarms with a bold and beautiful mix of locals and FSU students, downing drinks at the stellar bar or aluminum picnic tables as the sun sets over Doak Campbell

football stadium, the largest continuous brick structure in the USA.

Bradfordville Blues Club LIVE MUSIC (☎850-906-0766; www.bradfordvilleblues.com; 7152 Moses Lane, off Bradfordville Rd; tickets $15-35; ⏲shows start 8-10pm) Down the end of a dirt road lit by tiki torches, you'll find a bonfire raging under the live oaks at this hidden-away juke joint that hosts excellent national blues acts. Event times and days vary; check online.

Information

Florida Welcome Center (☎850-488-6167; www.visitflorida.com; 400 S Munroe St; ⏲8am-5pm Mon-Fri) In the Florida State Capitol, this is a fantastic resource.

Leon County Welcome Center (☎850-606-2305; www.visittallahassee.com; 106 E Jefferson St; ⏲8am-5pm Mon-Fri) Runs the excellent visitor information center, with brochures on walking and driving tours.

Getting There & Around

Tallahassee is 98 miles from Panama City Beach, 135 miles from Jacksonville, 192 miles from Pensacola, 120 miles from Gainesville and 470 miles from Miami. The main access road is I-10; to reach the Gulf Coast, follow Hwy 319 south to Hwy 98.

Tiny **Tallahassee International Airport** (☎850-891-7800; www.talgov.com/airport; 3300 Capital Circle SW) is served by American and Delta for US domestic and international connections, and Silver Airways for direct flights to Tampa and Orlando. It's about 5 miles southwest of downtown, off Hwy 263. There's no public transportation. Some hotels have shuttles, but otherwise a taxi to downtown costs around $25; try **Yellow Cab** (☎850-999-9999; www.tallahasseeyellowcab.com).

The **Greyhound bus station** (☎850-222-4249; www.greyhound.com; 112 W Tennessee St; ⏲24hr) is at the corner of Duval, opposite the downtown **StarMetro** (☎850-891-5200; www.talgov.com/starmetro; per trip/day $1.25/3) transfer center.

Pensacola

The Alabama border is just a few miles down the road, which helps explain the vibe of Pensacola, a city that jumbles laid-back Southern syrup with Florida brashness. With lively beaches, a Spanish-style downtown, and a thrumming military culture, this is by far the most interesting city in the Panhandle.

While urban-chic trends (locavore food, craft cocktails etc) are taking root, visitors still primarily come to Pensacola for an all-American, blue-collar vacation experience: white-sand beaches, fried seafood and bars serving cheap domestic drinks. During March and April, things reach fever pitch when droves of students descend for the weeklong bacchanalia of spring break. Beware.

Downtown, centered on Palafox St, lies north of the waterfront. Across the Pensacola Bay Bridge from here is the mostly residential peninsula of Gulf Breeze. Cross one more bridge, the Bob Sikes (toll $1), to reach pretty Pensacola Beach, the ultimate destination for most visitors.

Distinctly separate from Pensacola itself, Pensacola Beach is a pretty stretch of powdery white sand, gentle, warm waters and a string of mellow beachfront hotels. The beach occupies nearly 8 miles of the 40-mile-long Santa Rosa barrier island, surrounded by the Santa Rosa Sound and the Gulf of Mexico to the north and south, and by the federally protected Gulf Islands National Seashore on either side. Though determined residents have protected much of the barrier island from development, several high-rise condos have created a bit of a Gulf Coast skyline.

The area is a major hub for local entertainment and special events, including Mardi Gras celebrations, a triathlon, wine tastings, a summer music series and parades.

Sights

★**National Naval Aviation Museum** MUSEUM (☎800-327-5002; www.navalaviationmuseum.org; 1750 Radford Blvd; ⏲9am-5pm; 👪) FREE A visit to Pensacola is not complete without a trip to this enormous collection of military aircraft muscle and artifacts. Adults and children alike will be fascinated by the range of planes on display: more than 150! That's before we even get to the high-tech stuff like flight simulators and an IMAX theater. You can watch the **Blue Angels** (☎850-452-3806; www.naspensacolaairshow.com; 390 San Carlos Rd, Suite A; ⏲8:30am Tue & Wed Mar-Nov) FREE practice their death-defying air show at 8:30am most Tuesdays and Wednesdays between March and November.

Note that the entry for non-Department of Defense identification holders is via the

WORTH A TRIP

PENSACOLA SCENIC BLUFFS HIGHWAY

This 11-mile stretch of road, which winds around the precipice of the highest point along the Gulf Coast, makes for a peaceful drive or slightly challenging bike ride. You'll see stunning views of Escambia Bay and pass a notable crumbling brick chimney – part of the steam-power plant for the Hyer-Knowles lumber mill in the 1850s – the only remnant of what was the first major industrial belt in the area.

NAS Pensacola West Gate located at 1878 South Blue Angel Parkway.

Historic Pensacola Village MUSEUM
(850-595-5985; www.historicpensacola.org; Tarragona & Church St; adult/child $8/4; 10am-4pm Tue-Sat;) Pensacola's rich colonial history spans more than 450 years. This fascinating and attractive village is a self-contained enclave of photogenic historic homes turned into museums: it's the perfect starting point for familiarizing yourself with the city. Admission is good for one week and includes a guided tour and entrance to each building.

★ **Gulf Islands National Seashore** PARK
(850-934-2600; www.nps.gov/guis; vehicle $20; sunrise-sunset;) The highlight of the Florida Panhandle, this 150-mile stretch of mostly undeveloped white-sand beach is a prime example of what the Gulf Coast looked like before human settlement (which, to be fair, can often be seen in the form of high-rises in the distance). The National Seashore is not contiguous, but you'll find portions all along the coast: long swaths of sugar-white dunes crowned with sea oats, a perfect example of pristine flatland beach.

Sleeping & Eating

Solé Inn MOTEL $
(850-470-9298; www.soleinnandsuites.com; 200 N Palafox St; r $79-199;) Just north of downtown, this motel goes for a 1960s mod look, with a black-and-white color scheme, animal-print accents and acrylic bubble lamps. The dandelion fountain in the patio is a unique touch. Rooms aren't huge, but price, location and originality make up for the lack of space. And who can complain about the self-serve happy hour between 5pm and 7pm?

Holiday Inn Resort HOTEL $$
(850-932-5331; www.holidayinnresortpensacolabeach.com; 14 Via de Luna Dr; r from $210;) This beachfront hotel has cool, inviting rooms with ultra-comfy beds, flat-screen TVs and great showers. Oceanfront rooms have spacious balconies overhanging the soft, white sands and the cool turquoise waters below. Suites and kids' suites are available, and the 'Lazy River' pool is killer. Friendly, obliging staff help seal the deal. Excellent value.

Peg Leg Pete's SEAFOOD $$
(850-932-4139; www.peglegpetes.com; 1010 Fort Pickens Rd; mains $10-22; 11am-10pm;) Ah-har, me hearties, walk ye olde plank... you get the idea, this place has a theme going. Anyways, pop into Pete's for almost-beachfront oysters, fat grouper sandwiches, crab legs and jumbo sea scallops. There's nothing fancy about the woodsy, somewhat grungy sea-shanty decor with license plates covering the walls, but the service is swift, despite how busy it gets.

★ **Iron** AMERICAN $$$
(850-476-7776; www.restaurantiron.com; 22 N Palafox St; mains $26-46; 4:30-10pm Sun-Thu, to 1am Fri & Sat;) Armed with New Orleans experience, chef Alex McPhail works his ever-changing menu magic at downtown's Iron, the best of Pensacola's line of vibrant, locally sourced, high-end culinary hotbeds. Extremely friendly mixologists know their craft; and McPhail's food – from beer-braised pork belly to Creole-seasoned catch of the day – punches above the Emerald Coast's weight class.

Drinking & Entertainment

McGuire's Irish Pub PUB
(850-433-6789; www.mcguiresirishpub.com; 600 E Gregory St; 11am-2am) This ginormous Irish theme park of a pub gets rowdy around 9pm and is super popular at dinner time: the pub grub is top-notch. Don't try to pay for your drinks with one of the thousands of dollar bills hanging from the ceiling – a local once found himself in the slammer that way!

Roundup GAY
(850-433-8482; www.theroundup.net; 560 E Heinberg St; 2pm-3am) For those who like their men manly, check out this niche-y, neighborhood hangout with a killer furry-

friendly patio. Ladies are welcome, but cowboys, tradies and bikers are always flavor of the month. There's a Facebook page (www.facebook.com/theroundupbar) that lists events.

Saenger Theatre THEATER
(☎850-595-3880; www.pensacolasaenger.com; 118 S Palafox Pl; ⊙box office 10am-4:30pm Mon-Fri) This Spanish baroque beauty was reconstructed in 1925 using bricks from the Pensacola Opera House, which was destroyed in a 1916 hurricane. It now hosts popular musicals and top-billing music acts and is home to the Pensacola Symphony Orchestra and the Pensacola Opera.

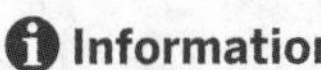

Information

Pensacola Beach Visitors Information Center (☎850-932-1500; www.visitpensacolabeach.com; 7 Casino Beach Blvd; ⊙9am-5pm Mon-Sat, 10am-3pm Sun) This is a small place with some useful maps and brochures about goings-on, road closures (due to storms) and anything else beach oriented.

Pensacola Visitors Information Center (☎800-874-1234; www.visitpensacola.com; 1401 E Gregory St; ⊙8am-5pm Mon-Fri, 9am-4pm Sat, 10am-4pm Sun) Come to the foot of the Pensacola Bay Bridge for a bounty of tourist information, knowledgeable staff and a free internet kiosk.

Getting There & Around

Pensacola Regional Airport (☎850-436-5000; www.flypensacola.com; 2430 Airport Blvd) is served by most major US airlines. Primary direct connections outside Florida include Atlanta, Charlotte, Dallas and Houston. The airport is 4 miles northeast of downtown, off 9th Ave on Airport Blvd. A taxi costs about $20 to downtown and around $35 to the beach. Try **zTrip** (☎850-433-3333; www.ztrip.com/pensacola), previously known as Yellow Cab, a convenient hybrid of the rideshare and traditional cab experiences.

The **Greyhound station** (☎850-476-4800; www.greyhound.com; 505 W Burgess Rd) is located north of the downtown area. **Escambia County Transit** (ECAT; ☎850-595-3228; www.goecat.com; rides $1.75) has a free trolley service (ECAT) connecting downtown Pensacola and the beach between Memorial Day weekend and the end of September.

I-10 is the major east–west thoroughfare used by buses, and many pass down Palafox St.

Great Lakes

Includes ➡

Illinois....517
Chicago....517
Indiana....552
Indianapolis....552
Ohio....560
Cleveland....561
Cincinnati....568
Michigan....571
Detroit....571
Wisconsin....591
Milwaukee....591
Minnesota....601
Minneapolis....602

Best Places to Eat

- Sister Pie (p576)
- Story Inn (p557)
- Hopleaf (p539)
- Birch + Butcher (p592)

Best Places to Sleep

- Shinola Hotel (p576)
- Ironworks Hotel (p554)
- Fieldhouse Jones (p535)
- Kimpton Schofield Hotel (p561)
- Lora (p609)

Why Go?

Don't be fooled by all the corn. Behind it lurks surfing beaches and Tibetan temples, car-free islands and the green-draped night lights of the aurora borealis. The Great Lakes takes its knocks for being middle-of-nowhere boring, so consider the moose-filled national parks and Hemingway, Dylan and Vonnegut sites to be its little secret.

Roll call for the region's cities starts with Chicago, which unfurls what is arguably the country's mightiest skyline. Milwaukee keeps the beer-and-Harley flame burning, while Minneapolis shines a hipster beacon out over the fields. Detroit rocks, plain and simple. The Great Lakes themselves are huge, and offer beaches, dunes, resort towns and lighthouse-dotted scenery. Dairy farms and fruit orchards blanket the region, meaning fresh pie and ice cream aplenty. And when the scenery does flatten out? There's always a goofball roadside attraction, such as the Spam Museum or the world's biggest ball of twine, to revive imaginations.

When to Go

Chicago

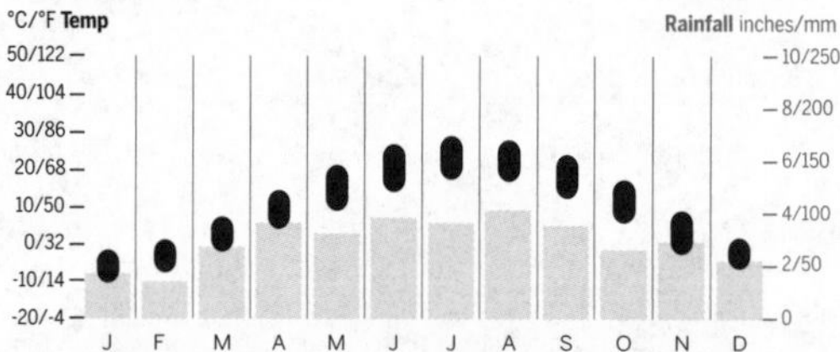

Jan & Feb Skiers and snowmobilers hit the trails.

Jul & Aug Finally, it's warm! Beer gardens hop, beaches splash, and festivals rock most weekends.

Sep & Oct Fair weather, bountiful farm and orchard harvests, and shoulder-season bargains.

History

The region's first residents included the Hopewell (around 200 BCE) and Mississippi River mound builders (around 700 CE). Both left behind mysterious piles of earth that were tombs for their leaders and possibly tributes to their deities. You can see remnants at Cahokia in southern Illinois, and Mound City in southeastern Ohio.

French voyageurs (fur traders) arrived in the early 17th century and established missions and forts. The British turned up soon after that, with the rivalry spilling over into the French and Indian Wars (Seven Years' War; 1754–61), after which Britain took control of all of the land east of the Mississippi. Following the Revolutionary War, the Great Lakes area became the new USA's Northwest Territory, which soon was divided into states and locked to the region after it developed its impressive canal and railroad network. But conflicts erupted between the newcomers and the Native Americans, including the 1811 Battle of Tippecanoe in Indiana; the bloody 1832 Black Hawk War in Wisconsin, Illinois and around, which forced indigenous people to move west of the Mississippi; and the 1862 Sioux uprising in Minnesota.

Throughout the late 19th and early 20th centuries, industries sprang up and grew quickly, fueled by resources of coal and iron, and cheap transportation on the lakes. The availability of work brought huge influxes of immigrants from Ireland, Germany, Scandinavia and southern and eastern Europe. For decades after the Civil War, a great number of African Americans also migrated to the region's urban centers from the South.

The area prospered during WWII and throughout the 1950s, but this was followed by 20 years of social turmoil and economic stagnation. Manufacturing industries declined, which walloped Rust Belt cities such as Detroit and Cleveland with high unemployment and 'white flight' (white middle-class families who fled to the suburbs).

The 1980s and '90s brought urban revitalization. The region's population increased, notably with newcomers from Asia and Mexico. Growth in the service and high-tech sectors resulted in economic balance, although manufacturing industries such as car making and steel still played a big role, meaning that when the economic crisis hit in 2008, Great Lakes towns felt the pinch first.

Some 10 years later, many of the big cities have rallied. Detroit, Cleveland, Cincinnati and Milwaukee are among those that have experienced reinvigorated cores, where businesses and residents are moving back to the downtown areas and making them shine again.

ILLINOIS

Chicago dominates the state with its sky-high architecture and superlative museums, restaurants and music clubs. But venturing further afield reveals Oak Park, Hemingway's mannerly hometown, scattered shrines to local hero Abe Lincoln, and a trail of corn dogs, pies and drive-in movie theaters down Route 66. A cypress swamp and a prehistoric World Heritage Site make appearances in Illinois too.

ℹ Information

Illinois Highway Conditions (www.gettingaroundillinois.com)
Illinois Office of Tourism (www.enjoyillinois.com)
Illinois State Park Information (www.dnr.illinois.gov) State parks are free to visit. Campsites cost $6 to $35; some accept reservations (www.reserveamerica.com; fee $5).

Chicago

Steely skyscrapers, top chefs, rocking festivals – the Windy City will blow you away with its low-key cultured awesomeness.

It's hard to know what to gawk at first. High-flying architecture is everywhere, from the stratospheric, glass-floored Willis Tower to Frank Gehry's swooping silver Pritzker Pavilion to Frank Lloyd Wright's stained-glass Robie House. Whimsical public art studs the streets; you might be walking along and wham, there's an abstract Picasso statue that's not only cool to look at, but you're allowed to go right up and climb on it. For art museums, take your pick: impressionist masterpieces at the massive Art Institute, psychedelic paintings at the midsized Museum of Mexican Art or outsider drawings at the small Intuit gallery.

History

Much of Chicago's past is downright legendary. You've probably heard about Mrs O'Leary's cow that kicked over a lantern that started the Great Fire that torched the city. And about a man named Al Capone who wielded a mean machine gun during an unsavory era of booze-fueled vice. And about

Great Lakes Highlights

❶ **Chicago** (p517) Absorbing the skyscrapers, museums, festivals and foodie bounty.

❷ **Detroit** (p571) Embracing the city's can-do spirit and partaking of its art, eateries and neighborhood bicycle rides.

❸ **Boundary Waters** (p612) Paddling deep into the piney woods and sleeping under a blanket of stars.

❹ **Ohio's Amish Country** (p565) Slowing down for clip-clopping horses and buggies.

❺ **Michigan's Western Shore** (p582) Beach lounging, dune climbing, berry eating and surfing.

❻ **Milwaukee** (p591) Polka dancing at a Friday-night fish fry and drinking lots o' beer.

❼ **Route 66** (p551) Taking the slowpoke route through Illinois, past pie-filled diners and oddball roadside attractions.

❽ **Southern Indiana** (p555) Being surprised by the Tibetan temples, phenomenal architecture and green hills.

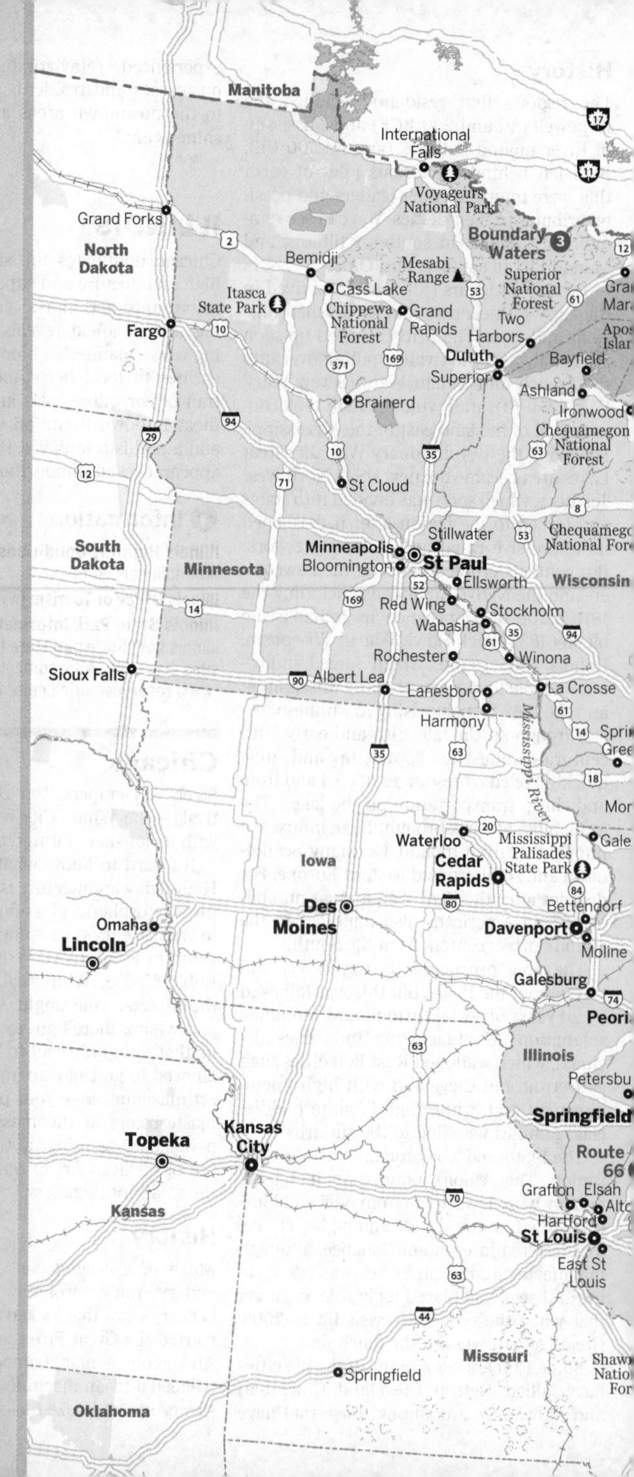

200 km
100 miles
CANADA
Ontario
Lake Superior
Isle Royale National Park
Copper Harbor
Keweenaw Peninsula
Houghton
Pictured Rocks National Lakeshore
Tahquamenon Falls
Sault Ste Marie
Marquette
Ottawa National Forest
Iron Mountain
Naubinway
St Ignace
Mackinaw City
Mackinac Island
Manitoulin Island
Georgian Bay
Lake Nipissing
Lake Michigan
Washington Island
Nicolet National Forest
Leelanau Peninsula
Petoskey
Boyne City
Charlevoix
Manitou Islands
Leland
Empire
Traverse City
Huron National Forest
Lake Huron
Lake Simcoe
Green Bay
Door Peninsula
Frankfort
Sleeping Bear Dunes National Lakeshore
Saginaw Bay
Manitowoc
Central Time Zone
Eastern Time Zone
Ludington
Toronto
Hamilton
Michigan
Muskegon
Grand Rapids
Port Huron
Milwaukee
Michigan's Western Shore
Flint
London
Lansing
Holland
Detroit
Racine
Saugatuck/ Douglas
Lake Erie
New York
Kalamazoo
Dearborn
Ann Arbor
Erie
Chicago
Middlebury
Bass Islands
Pelee Island
Kelleys Island
Madison
Gary
East Chicago
South Bend
Auburn
Toledo
Cleveland
Cuyahoga Valley National Park
Pennsylvania
Indiana Dunes National Park
Akron
Indiana
Canton
Ohio's Amish Country
Marion
Ohio
Millersburg
Lexington
Fairmount
Bloomington
Champaign
COLUMBUS
Terre Haute
Indianapolis
Dayton
Yellow Springs
Lancaster
Logan
Marietta
Chillicothe
Athens
Bloomington
Columbus
Cincinnati
Nashville
Covington
Madison
West Virginia
Southern Indiana
Vincennes
Ohio River
Huntington
Charleston
Louisville
Frankfort
New Harmony
Lexington
Harmonie State Park
Cypress Creek National Wildlife Refuge
Paducah
Kentucky
Virginia

the 'machine' that has controlled local politics for decades. Throw in the invention of the skyscraper and Ferris wheel, and you've got a whopper of a tale.

Sights

Big-ticket draws such as Millennium Park, Willis Tower and the Art Institute are downtown right in the Loop. Next door is the lakefront Museum Campus, with three popular sights including the Field Museum (p523). To the Loop's north are Navy Pier (p523) and the 360° Chicago (p527) observatory. A short distance onward Lincoln Park (p528) and Wrigley Field (p528) do their thing. All of these places are within a 6-mile span, and all are easy to reach on public transportation. Hyde Park is the one neighborhood with top sights that is further flung and requires some planning to reach.

All of the major attractions are open daily. Smaller museums are often closed on Monday and/or Tuesday.

The Loop

★Art Institute of Chicago MUSEUM

(Map p524; ☎312-443-3600; www.artic.edu; 111 S Michigan Ave; adult/child $25/free; ⏲10:30am-5pm Fri-Wed, to 8pm Thu; 👪; Ⓜ Brown, Orange, Green, Purple, Pink Line to Adams) The Art Institute is the second-largest art museum in the USA. Its collection of impressionist and post-impressionist paintings rivals those in France, and the number of surrealist works is tremendous. Download the free app for DIY audio tours; it offers several quick-hit jaunts, from highlights (including Georges Seurat's *A Sunday Afternoon on the Island of La Grande Jatte* and Edward Hopper's *Nighthawks*) to architecture and pop-art tours. Allow two hours to browse the must-sees; art buffs should allocate much longer.

More comprehensive audio guides ($7) are also available in English, Spanish, French and Mandarin. You can buy a ticket in advance online (for a $2 surcharge) but unless there's a huge exhibit on, the entrance lines move pretty quickly. Or you can skip the lines altogether with the Fast Pass ticket, available online for $10 more.

The main entrance is on Michigan Ave, but you can also enter via the dazzling Modern Wing on Monroe St. Ask at the front desk about free talks and tours once you're inside. Note that the 3rd-floor contemporary sculpture terrace is always free. It has great city views and connects to Millennium Park via the mod, pedestrian-only Nichols Bridgeway.

CHICAGO IN TWO DAYS...

Day One

You might as well dive right in with the big stuff. Take a boat or walking tour with the Chicago Architecture Foundation (p532) and ogle the most sky-scraping collection of buildings the US has to offer. Saunter over to Millennium Park to see the 'Bean' reflect the skyline and to splash under Crown Fountain's human gargoyles.

Explore the Art Institute of Chicago, the nation's second-largest art museum. It holds masterpieces aplenty, especially impressionist and post-impressionist paintings (and paperweights). Next, head over to Willis Tower, zip up to the 103rd floor and step out onto the glass-floored ledge. Yes, it is a long way down.

The West Loop parties in the evening. Haymarket Pub & Brewery (p543) pours great beers. Or down a cocktail made with the house vodka at CH Distillery (p543).

Day Two

Take a stroll on Michigan Ave – aka the Magnificent Mile (p527) – where big-name department stores ka-ching in a glittering row. Mosey over to Navy Pier (p523). Wander the half-mile promenade and take a spin on the high-in-the-sky Ferris wheel.

Spend the afternoon at the Museum Campus (p523) (the water taxi from Navy Pier is a fine way to get there). Miles of aisles of dinosaurs and gemstones stuff the Field Museum of Natural History (p523). Sharks and other fish swim in the kiddie-mobbed Shedd Aquarium (p523). Meteorites and supernovas are on view at the Adler Planetarium (p523).

Wander along Milwaukee Ave and take your pick of booming bars, indie-rock clubs and hipster shops. Quimby's (p546) shows the local spirit: the bookstore stocks zines and graphic novels, and is a linchpin of Chicago's underground culture The Hideout (p544) and Empty Bottle (p544) are sweet spots to catch a bad-ass band.

★Millennium Park PARK
(Map p524; ☎312-742-1168; www.millenniumpark.org; 201 E Randolph St; ⏲6am-11pm; 🚹; Ⓜ Brown, Orange, Green, Purple, Pink Line to Washington/Wabash) The city's showpiece is a trove of free and arty sights. It includes **Pritzker Pavilion**, Frank Gehry's swooping silver band shell, which hosts free weekly concerts in summer (6:30pm; bring a picnic and bottle of wine); Anish Kapoor's beloved silvery sculpture **Cloud Gate**, aka the 'Bean'; and Jaume Plensa's **Crown Fountain**, a de facto water park that projects video images of locals spitting water, gargoyle-style.

★Willis Tower TOWER
(Map p524; ☎312-875-9696; www.theskydeck.com; 233 S Wacker Dr; adult/child $24/16; ⏲9am-10pm Mar-Sep, 10am-8pm Oct-Feb, last entry 30min prior; Ⓜ Brown, Orange, Purple, Pink Line to Quincy) It's Chicago's tallest building, and the 103rd-floor Skydeck puts you high into the heavens. Take the ear-popping, 70-second elevator ride to the top and then step onto one of the glass-floored ledges jutting out into mid-air for a knee-buckling perspective straight down. On clear days the view sweeps over four states. The entrance is on Jackson Blvd. Queues can take up to an hour on busy days (peak times are in summer, between 11am and 4pm Friday through Sunday).

Chicago Cultural Center NOTABLE BUILDING
(Map p524; ☎312-744-6630; www.chicagoculturalcenter.org; 78 E Washington St; ⏲10am-7pm Mon-Fri, to 5pm Sat & Sun; Ⓜ Brown, Orange, Green, Purple, Pink Line to Washington/Wabash) FREE This exquisite, beaux-arts building began its life as the Chicago Public Library in 1897. Today the block-long structure houses terrific art exhibitions (especially the 4th-floor Yates Gallery), as well as classical concerts at lunchtime every Wednesday (12:15pm). It also contains the world's largest Tiffany stained-glass dome, on the 3rd floor where the library circulation desk used to be. **InstaGreeter** (Map p524; www.chicagogreeter.com/instagreeter; 77 E Randolph St; ⏲10am-3pm Fri & Sat, 11am-2pm Sun) FREE tours of the Loop depart from the Randolph St lobby, as do Millennium Park tours. And it's all free!

Chicago Architecture Center GALLERY
(CAC; Map p524; ☎312-922-3432; www.architecture.org; 111 E Wacker Dr; adult/student/child $12/8/free; ⏲9:30am-5pm; 🚌151, Ⓜ Brown, Orange, Green, Purple, Pink Line to Clark/Lake) The CAC is the premier keeper of Chicago's architectural flame. Pop in to explore its excellent galleries, which feature an interactive 3-D model of Chicago and displays on the city's architectural history, as well as giant models of and exhibits on skyscrapers around the world and the amazing technologies needed to build them, from construction to security to sustainability. You can also check out the CAC's extensive roster of boat and walking tours (p532) and make bookings here.

> ### ℹ DISCOUNT CARDS
>
> The following options let you skip the regular queues at sights.
>
> The **Go Chicago Card** (www.smartdestinations.com/chicago) allows you to visit an unlimited number of attractions for a flat fee. It's good for one, two, three or five consecutive days. The company also offers a three-, four- or five-choice **Explorer Pass** where you pick among 29 options for sights. It's valid for 30 days. Architecture cruises, the Navy Pier Ferris wheel and all major museums are among the choices.
>
> **CityPass** (www.citypass.com/chicago) gives access to five of the city's top draws, including the Art Institute, Shedd Aquarium and Willis Tower, over nine consecutive days. It's less flexible than Go Chicago's pass, but cheaper for those wanting a more leisurely pace.

Buckingham Fountain FOUNTAIN
(Map p524; 301 S Columbus Dr; Ⓜ Red Line to Harrison) Grant Park's centerpiece is one of the world's largest fountains, with a 1.5-million-gallon capacity and a 15-story-high spray. It lets loose on the hour from 9am to 11pm early May to mid-October, accompanied at night by multicolored lights and music.

Route 66 Sign HISTORIC SITE
(Map p524; E Adams St, btwn S Michigan & Wabash Aves; Ⓜ Brown, Orange, Green, Purple, Pink Line to Adams) Attention Route 66 buffs: the Mother Road begins in downtown Chicago. Look for the 'Historic 66 Begin' sign at the northwestern corner of Adams St and Michigan Ave, across from the Art Institute. (There's another sign at the end of the block, but this one is a replica of the original.) From Chicago the route traverses 2400 miles to Los Angeles, past neon signs, mom-and-pop motels and pie-and-coffee diners...but it all starts here.

Metro Chicago Area

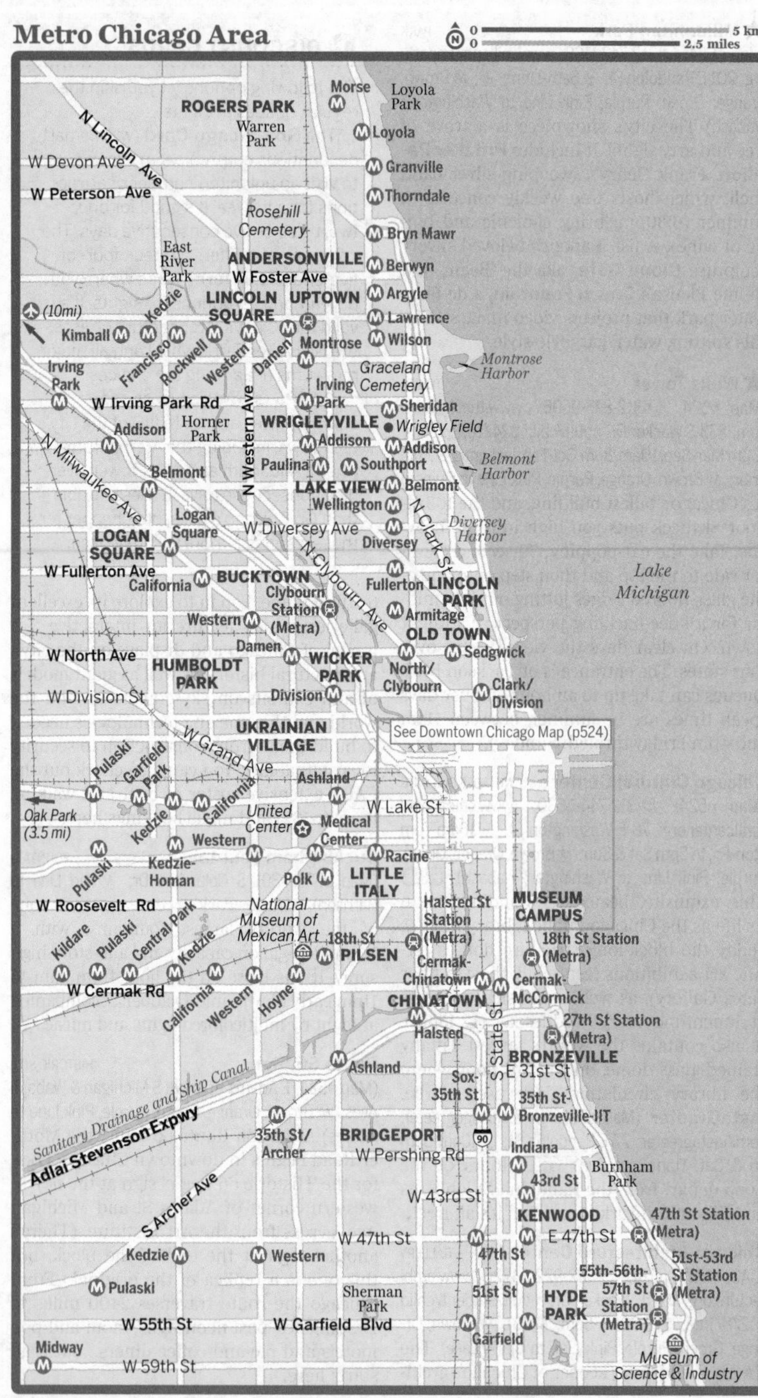

Museum of Contemporary Photography MUSEUM

(Map p524; ☎312-663-5554; www.mocp.org; 600 S Michigan Ave, Columbia College; ⏰10am-5pm Mon-Wed, Fri & Sat, to 8pm Thu, noon-5pm Sun; Ⓜ Red Line to Harrison) FREE This small museum focuses on American and international photography from the early 20th century onward, and is the only institution of its kind between the coasts. The permanent collection includes the works of Henri Cartier-Bresson, Harry Callahan, Sally Mann, Victor Skrebneski, Catherine Wagner and 500 more of the best photographers working today. Special exhibitions (also free) augment the rotating permanent collection.

Pilsen & Near South Side

★Field Museum of Natural History MUSEUM

(Map p524; ☎312-922-9410; www.fieldmuseum.org; 1400 S Lake Shore Dr, Near South Side; adult/child $24/17; ⏰9am-5pm; 👪; 🚌146, 130) The Field Museum houses some 30 million artifacts and includes everything but the kitchen sink – beetles, mummies, gemstones, Bushman the stuffed ape – all tended by a slew of PhD-wielding scientists, as the Field remains an active research institution. The collection's rock star is Sue, the largest *Tyrannosaurus rex* yet discovered. She even gets her own gift shop. Special exhibits, such as the 3-D movie, cost extra. Other highlights include **'Inside Ancient Egypt,'** a burial chamber reproduction that contains 23 real mummies; the **Hall of Gems**; and the Northwest Coast and Arctic Peoples' **totem pole collection**. The museum is vast, so get a map at the desk and make a plan of attack.

Northerly Island PARK

(1521 S Linn White Dr, Near South Side; 🚌146, 130) This prairie-grassed park has a walking and cycling trail, bird-watching, fishing and an outdoor venue for concerts. It's actually a peninsula, not an island, but the Chicago skyline views are tremendous no matter what you call it. Stop in at the field house, if it's open, for tour information. Bicycles are available at the Divvy bike-share station by the Adler Planetarium. Note that parts of the trail are closed at times due to weather damage.

★National Museum of Mexican Art MUSEUM

(Map p522; ☎312-738-1503; www.nationalmuseumofmexicanart.org; 1852 W 19th St, Pilsen; ⏰10am-5pm Tue-Sun; Ⓜ Pink Line to 18th St) FREE Founded in 1982, this vibrant museum – the largest Latinx arts institution in the US – has become one of the city's best. The vivid permanent collection sums up 1000 years of Mexican art and culture through classical paintings, shining gold altars, skeleton-rich folk art, beadwork and much more.

Adler Planetarium MUSEUM

(Map p524; ☎312-922-7827; www.adlerplanetarium.org; 1300 S Lake Shore Dr, Near South Side; adult/child $12/8; ⏰9:30am-4pm; 👪; 🚌146, 130) Space enthusiasts will get a big bang (pun!) out of the Adler. There are public telescopes to view the stars (10am to 1pm daily, by the Galileo Cafe), 3-D lectures to learn about supernovas (in the **Space Visualization Lab**), and the **Planet Explorers** exhibit where kids can 'launch' a rocket. The immersive digital films cost extra (from $13 per ticket). The Adler's front steps offer Chicago's best skyline view, so get your camera ready.

Shedd Aquarium AQUARIUM

(Map p524; ☎312-939-2438; www.sheddaquarium.org; 1200 S Lake Shore Dr, Near South Side; adult/child $40/30; ⏰9am-6pm Jun-Aug, 9am-5pm Mon-Fri, to 6pm Sat & Sun Sep-May; 👪; 🚌146, 130) Top draws at the kiddie-mobbed Shedd Aquarium include the **Wild Reef** exhibit, where there's just 5in of Plexiglas between you and two-dozen fierce-looking sharks, and the **Oceanarium**, with its rescued sea otters. Note the Oceanarium also keeps beluga whales and Pacific white-sided dolphins, a practice that's increasingly frowned upon as captivity is stressful for these sensitive creatures.

Near North & Navy Pier

★Navy Pier WATERFRONT

(Map p524; ☎312-595-7437; www.navypier.com; 600 E Grand Ave; ⏰10am-10pm Sun-Thu, to midnight Fri & Sat Jun-Aug, 10am-8pm Sun-Thu, to 10pm Fri & Sat Sep-May; 👪; 🚌65) FREE Half-mile-long Navy Pier is one of Chicago's most-visited attractions, sporting a 196ft **Ferris wheel** (adult/child $18/15) and other carnival rides ($9 to $18 each), a beer garden and lots of chain restaurants. A renovation added public plazas, performance spaces and free cultural programming. Locals still groan over its commercialization, but its lakefront view and cool breezes can't be beat. The fireworks displays on summer Wednesdays (9:30pm) and Saturdays (10:15pm) are a treat too.

Downtown Chicago

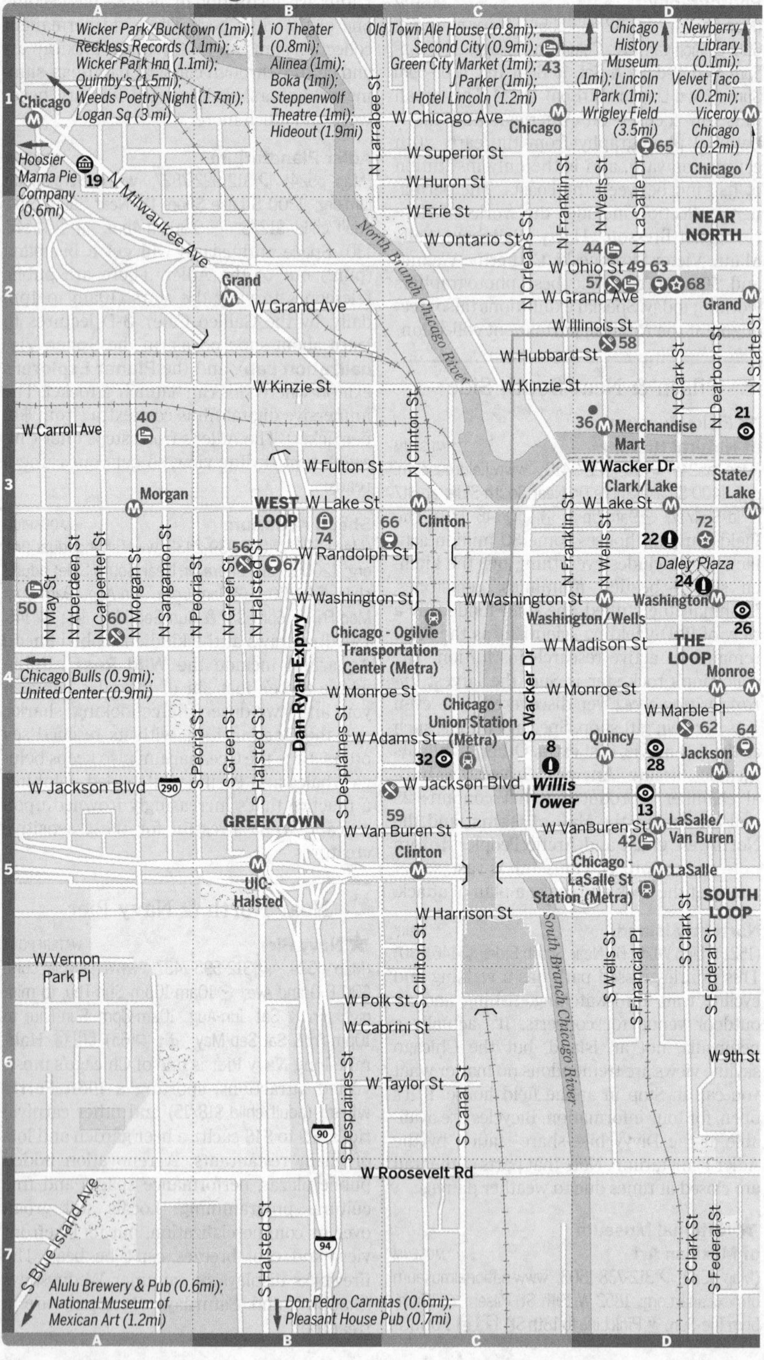

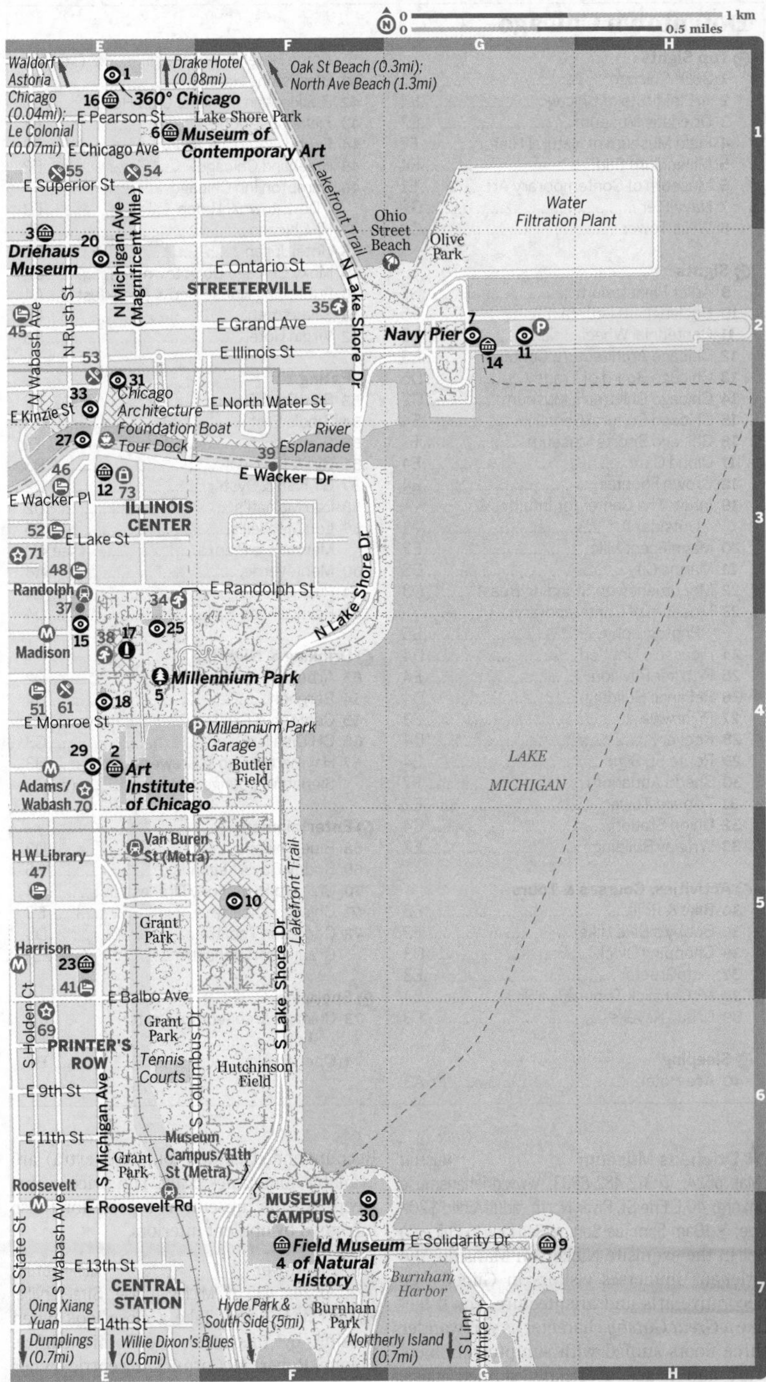

0 1 km
0 0.5 miles
E
F
G
H
1
2
3
4
5
6
7
Waldorf Astoria Chicago (0.04mi); Le Colonial (0.07mi)
Drake Hotel (0.08mi)
Oak St Beach (0.3mi); North Ave Beach (1.3mi)
1
16
360° Chicago
E Pearson St
Lake Shore Park
6
Museum of Contemporary Art
E Chicago Ave
55
54
E Superior St
Lakefront Trail
Ohio Street Beach
Olive Park
Water Filtration Plant
3
Driehaus Museum
20
N Michigan Ave (Magnificent Mile)
E Ontario St
STREETERVILLE
N Lake Shore Dr
35
45
N Wabash Ave
N Rush St
E Grand Ave
7
Navy Pier
14
11
53
E Illinois St
31
Chicago Architecture Foundation Boat Tour Dock
33
E Kinzie St
E North Water St
27
River Esplanade
39
E Wacker Dr
46
12
73
E Wacker Pl
ILLINOIS CENTER
52
E Lake St
71
48
Randolph
E Randolph St
34
37
15
38
17
25
Madison
N Lake Shore Dr
Millennium Park
5
51
61
18
E Monroe St
Millennium Park Garage
29
2
Art Institute of Chicago
Butler Field
Adams/ Wabash
70
LAKE MICHIGAN
Van Buren St (Metra)
H W Library
47
10
Grant Park
Lakefront Trail
S Lake Shore Dr
Harrison
23
41
E Balbo Ave
S Holden Ct
69
Grant Park
PRINTER'S ROW
Tennis Courts
S Columbus Dr
Hutchinson Field
E 9th St
S Michigan Ave
E 11th St
Museum Campus/11th St (Metra)
Grant Park
Roosevelt
E Roosevelt Rd
S Wabash Ave
MUSEUM CAMPUS
30
S State St
Field Museum of Natural History
4
E Solidarity Dr
9
E 13th St
CENTRAL STATION
Burnham Harbor
Qing Xiang Yuan Dumplings (0.7mi)
E 14th St
Willie Dixon's Blues (0.6mi)
Hyde Park & South Side (5mi)
Burnham Park
Northerly Island (0.7mi)
S Linn White Dr

Downtown Chicago

Top Sights
1 360° Chicago ... E1
2 Art Institute of Chicago ... E4
3 Driehaus Museum ... E2
4 Field Museum of Natural History ... F7
5 Millennium Park ... E4
6 Museum of Contemporary Art ... E1
7 Navy Pier ... G2
8 Willis Tower ... C4

Sights
9 Adler Planetarium ... G7
10 Buckingham Fountain ... F5
11 Centennial Wheel ... G2
12 Chicago Architecture Center ... E3
13 Chicago Board of Trade ... D5
14 Chicago Children's Museum ... G2
15 Chicago Cultural Center ... E4
16 Chicago Sports Museum ... E1
17 Cloud Gate ... E4
18 Crown Fountain ... E4
19 Intuit: The Center for Intuitive & Outsider Art ... A1
20 Magnificent Mile ... E2
21 Marina City ... D3
22 Monument with Standing Beast ... D3
23 Museum of Contemporary Photography ... E5
24 Picasso's Untitled ... D4
25 Pritzker Pavilion ... E4
26 Reliance Building ... D4
27 Riverwalk ... E3
28 Rookery ... D4
29 Route 66 Sign ... E4
30 Shedd Aquarium ... F7
31 Tribune Tower ... E2
32 Union Station ... C4
33 Wrigley Building ... E2

Activities, Courses & Tours
34 Bike & Roll ... E3
35 Bobby's Bike Hike ... F2
36 Chopping Block ... D3
37 InstaGreeter ... E3
38 McCormick Tribune Ice Rink ... E4
39 Urban Kayaks ... F3

Sleeping
40 Ace Hotel ... A3
Acme Hotel ... (see 45)
41 Blackstone Hotel ... E5
42 Buckingham Athletic Club Hotel ... D5
43 Fieldhouse Jones ... C1
44 Found Hotel Chicago ... D2
45 Freehand Chicago ... E2
46 Hampton Inn Chicago Downtown/N Loop ... E3
47 HI-Chicago ... E5
48 Hotel Julian ... E3
49 Moxy Chicago Downtown ... D2
50 Publishing House Bed & Breakfast ... A4
51 Silversmith ... E4
52 Virgin Hotel ... E3

Eating
53 Billy Goat Tavern ... E2
54 Gino's East ... E1
55 Giordano's ... E1
56 Girl & the Goat ... B3
57 GT Fish & Oyster ... D2
58 Lou Malnati's ... D2
59 Lou Mitchell's ... C5
Mercat a la Planxa ... (see 41)
60 Monteverde ... A4
61 Pizano's ... E4
62 Revival Food Hall ... D4

Drinking & Nightlife
63 Arbella ... D2
64 Berghoff ... D4
65 Centennial Crafted Beer & Eatery ... D1
66 CH Distillery ... C3
67 Haymarket Pub & Brewery ... B3
Signature Lounge ... (see 1)

Entertainment
68 Blue Chicago ... D2
69 Buddy Guy's Legends ... E6
70 Chicago Symphony Orchestra ... E4
71 Chicago Theatre ... E3
72 Goodman Theatre ... D3
Grant Park Orchestra ... (see 25)

Shopping
73 Chicago Architecture Center Shop ... E3
74 Open Books ... B3

★ **Driehaus Museum** MUSEUM
(Map p524; ☎312-482-8933; www.driehausmuseum.org; 40 E Erie St, River North; adult/child $20/free; ⏲10am-5pm Tue-Sun; Ⓜ Red Line to Chicago) Set in the exquisite Nickerson Mansion, the Driehaus immerses visitors in Gilded Age decorative arts and architecture. You'll feel like a *Great Gatsby* character as you wander three floors stuffed with sumptuous objets d'art and heaps of Tiffany stained glass. Recommended guided tours ($5 extra) are available four times daily. The price seems steep, but the museum is a prize for those intrigued by opulent interiors.

Tribune Tower ARCHITECTURE
(Map p524; 435 N Michigan Ave, Streeterville; Ⓜ Red Line to Grand) Take a close look when passing by this 1925 neo-Gothic edifice. Colonel Robert McCormick, eccentric owner

of the *Chicago Tribune* in the early 1900s, collected – and asked his reporters to send – rocks from famous buildings and monuments around the world. He stockpiled pieces of the Taj Mahal, Westminster Abbey, the Great Pyramid and more than 140 others, which are now embedded around the tower's base.

Marina City ARCHITECTURE

(Map p524; 300 N State St, River North; Ⓜ Brown, Orange, Green, Purple, Pink Line to State/Lake) The twin corncob towers of Marina City are an Instagram favorite for their futuristic, cartoony look. Bertrand Goldberg designed the 1964 high-rise, and it has become an iconic part of the Chicago skyline (check out the cover of the Wilco CD *Yankee Hotel Foxtrot*). And yes, there is a marina at the towers' base.

Magnificent Mile AREA

(Map p524; www.themagnificentmile.com; N Michigan Ave, Streeterville; Ⓜ Red Line to Grand) Spanning N Michigan Ave between the river and Oak St, the 'Mag Mile' is Chicago's much-touted upscale shopping strip, where Bloomingdale's, Apple, Burberry and many more will lighten your wallet. The retailers are mostly high-end chains that have stores nationwide.

Gold Coast

★360° Chicago OBSERVATORY

(Map p524; ☎888-875-8439; www.360chicago.com; 875 N Michigan Ave, 94th fl; adult/child $22/15; ⊙9am-11pm, last tickets 10:30pm; Ⓜ Red Line to Chicago) The views from the 94th-floor observatory of this iconic building (formerly known as the John Hancock Center) in many ways surpass those at the Willis Tower (p521); there are informative displays and the 'Tilt' feature (floor-to-ceiling windows you stand in as they tip out over the ground), which costs $7.20 extra and is less exciting than it sounds. Or just shoot straight up to the 96th-floor **Signature Lounge** (www.signatureroom.com; ⊙11am-12:30am Sun-Thu, to 1:30am Fri & Sat), where the view is free if you buy a drink ($10 to $18).

★Museum of Contemporary Art MUSEUM

(MCA; Map p524; ☎312-280-2660; www.mcachicago.org; 220 E Chicago Ave; adult/child $15/free; ⊙10am-9pm Tue & Fri, to 5pm Wed, Thu, Sat & Sun; Ⓜ Red Line to Chicago) Consider it the Art Institute's brash, rebellious sibling, with especially strong minimalist, surrealist and conceptual photography collections, and permanent works by René Magritte, Cindy Sherman and Andy Warhol. Covering art from the 1920s onward, the MCA's collection spans the gamut, with displays arranged to blur the boundaries between painting, sculpture, video and other media. Exhibits change regularly so you never know what you'll see, but count on it being offbeat and provocative. Illinois residents get free admission on Tuesday.

Newberry Library LIBRARY

(☎312-943-9090; www.newberry.org; 60 W Walton St; ⊙galleries 8:15am-5pm Mon, Fri & Sat, to 7:30pm Tue-Thu; Ⓜ Red Line to Chicago) FREE The Newberry's public galleries are a treat for bibliophiles: those who swoon over original Thomas Paine pamphlets about the French Revolution, or get weak-kneed seeing Thomas Jefferson's copy of the *History of the Expedition under Captains Lewis and Clark* (with margin notes!). Intriguing exhibits rotate yellowed manuscripts and tattered 1st editions from the library's extensive collection. The on-site bookstore is tops for Chicago-themed titles. Free tours of the impressive building take place at 3pm Thursday and 10:30am Saturday.

Chicago Sports Museum MUSEUM

(Map p524; ☎312-202-0500; www.chicagosportsmuseum.com; 835 N Michigan Ave, 7th fl, Water Tower Place; adult/child $10/6; ⊙11:30am-8:30pm Mon-Thu, to 9pm Fri, 11am-9pm Sat, 11am-6pm Sun; Ⓜ Red Line to Chicago) To understand Chicago's sports psyche, peruse

BLUES FANS' PILGRIMAGE

From 1957 to 1967, Chess Records was the seminal electric blues label. The building it occupied is now known as **Willie Dixon's Blues Heaven** (☎312-808-1286; www.bluesheaven.com; 2120 S Michigan Ave, Near South Side; adult/child $15/10; ⊙noon-4pm Tue-Sat; Ⓜ Green Line to Cermak-McCormick Pl), for the bassist who wrote most of Chess' hits. Staff give hour-long tours of the premises. It's pretty ramshackle, with few original artifacts on display. Still, hard-core fans will get a thrill out of hearing stories from the heady era and walking into the studio where their musical heroes recorded. Free blues concerts rock the side garden on summer Thursdays at 6pm.

the memorabilia-filled cases at this gallery attached to Harry Caray's 7th Inning Stretch restaurant. See the cleats Cubs infielder Kris Bryant wore on the winning final play of the 2016 World Series, which ended the team's 108-year championship drought. Examine Sammy Sosa's corked bat and the infamous 'Bartman ball.' The museum also enshrines relics for Da Bears, Bulls, Blackhawks and White Sox. (Admission is free if you eat or drink at the restaurant.)

Lincoln Park & Old Town

★Lincoln Park PARK

(www.chicagoparkdistrict.com; Lincoln Park; 6am-11pm; ; 22, 151, 156) The park that gave the neighborhood its name is Chicago's largest. Its 1200 acres stretch for 6 miles from North Ave north to Diversey Pkwy, where it narrows along the lake and continues on until the end of Lake Shore Dr. On sunny days locals come out to play in droves, taking advantage of the ponds, paths and playing fields or visiting the zoo and beaches. It's a fine spot to while away a morning or afternoon (or both).

Green City Market MARKET

(773-880-1266; www.greencitymarket.org; 1790 N Clark St, Lincoln Park; 7am-1pm Wed & Sat May-Oct; 22) Stands of purple cabbages, red radishes, green asparagus and other bright-hued produce sprawl through Lincoln Park at Chicago's biggest farmers market. Follow your nose to the demonstration tent, where local cooks such as *Top Chef* winner Stephanie Izard prepare dishes – say rice crepes with a mushroom *gastrique* (reduction) – using market ingredients.

Chicago History Museum MUSEUM

(312-642-4600; www.chicagohistory.org; 1601 N Clark St, Lincoln Park; adult/child $19/free; 9:30am-4:30pm Mon & Wed-Sat, to 9pm Tue, noon-5pm Sun; ; 22) Curious about Chicago's storied past? Multimedia displays at this museum cover it all, from the Great Fire to the 1968 Democratic Convention. President Lincoln's deathbed is here, as is the bell worn by Mrs O'Leary's cow. So is the chance to 'become' a Chicago hot dog covered in condiments (in the kids' area, but adults are welcome for the photo op).

Lake View & Wrigleyville

★Wrigley Field STADIUM

(Map p522; 800-843-2827; www.cubs.com; 1060 W Addison St, Wrigleyville; Red Line to Addison) Built in 1914 and named for the chewing-gum guy, Wrigley Field is the second-oldest baseball park in the major leagues. It's known for its hand-turned scoreboard, ivy-covered outfield walls and neon sign over the front entrance. The Cubs are the home team. Games are always packed. Ticket prices vary, but in general you'll be hard-pressed to get in for under $45. The area around the stadium is like a big street festival on game days.

The ballpark is filled with legendary traditions and curses, including a team that didn't win a championship for 108 years. But a 2016 World Series victory coupled with heaps of new family-friendly and foodie hot spots around the stadium have given it new life. The grassy plaza just north of the main entrance – aka **Gallagher Way** (www.gallagherway.com; 3637 N Clark St) – hosts free events including concerts, alfresco fitness classes and movie nights on the jumbo video screen.

Ninety-minute Wrigley Field tours (per person $25) are available April through September.

Wicker Park, Bucktown & Ukrainian Village

Intuit: The Center for Intuitive & Outsider Art GALLERY

(Map p524; 312-243-9088; www.art.org; 756 N Milwaukee Ave, River West; $5; 11am-6pm Tue, Wed, Fri & Sat, to 7pm Thu, noon-5pm Sun; Blue Line to Chicago) Behold this small museum's collection of naive and outsider art from Chicago artists, including rotating mixed-media exhibits and watercolors by famed local Henry Darger. In a back room the museum has re-created Darger's awesomely cluttered studio apartment, complete with balls of twine, teetering stacks of old magazines, an ancient typewriter and a Victrola phonograph. The gift shop carries groovy jewelry (such as pencil-eraser necklaces), bags and wallets made from recycled material, and art books.

Logan Square & Humboldt Park

★Galerie F GALLERY

(872-817-7067; www.galeriefchicago.com; 2415 N Milwaukee Ave, Logan Square; 11am-6pm Mon & Thu-Sun; Blue Line to California) Galerie F is exactly the type of laid-back, ubercool gallery you'd expect to find in Logan Square.

CHICAGO FOR GANGSTERS

Chicago would rather not discuss its gangster past; consequently there are no brochures or exhibits about infamous sites, so you'll need to use your imagination when visiting the following places:

Green Mill (p543) Al Capone's favorite speakeasy; the tunnels where he hid the booze are still underneath the bar.

Biograph Theater (2433 N Lincoln Ave, Lincoln Park; M Brown, Purple, Red Line to Fullerton) Where the 'lady in red' betrayed 'public enemy number one' John Dillinger.

Union Station (Map p524; ☎312-655-2385; www.chicagounionstation.com; 225 S Canal St; M Blue Line to Clinton) Fans of *The Untouchables* can see where the baby carriage bounced down the stairs..

It specializes in rock-and-roll gig posters, printmaking and street art. Walk into the bright, open space and browse – the vibe here is totally welcoming. Dip into the basement to listen to records, play chess or just linger in the sitting area.

★**Busy Beaver Button Museum** MUSEUM
(☎773-645-3359; www.buttonmuseum.org; 3407 W Armitage Ave, Logan Square; ⏲10am-4pm Mon-Fri; 🚌73) FREE Even George Washington gave out campaign buttons, though in his era they were the sew-on kind. Pin-back buttons came along in 1896. Badge-making company Busy Beaver chronicles its history in displays holding thousands of the little round mementos. They tout everything from Dale Bozzio to Bozo the clown, Cabbage Patch Kids to Big Rock Point Nuclear Plant.

Hyde Park & South Side

★**Museum of Science & Industry** MUSEUM
(Map p522; MSI; ☎773-684-1414; www.msichicago.org; 5700 S Lake Shore Dr, Hyde Park; adult/child $22/13; ⏲9:30am-5:30pm Jun-Aug, shorter hours Sep-May; 👪; 🚌6 or 10, M Metra Electric Line to 55th-56th-57th St) Geek out at the largest science museum in the Western Hemisphere. Highlights include a **WWII German U-boat** nestled in an underground display (adult/child $18/14 extra to tour it) and the **Science Storms** exhibit with a mock tornado and tsunami. Other popular exhibits include the baby chick hatchery, the minuscule furnishings in Colleen Moore's fairy castle and the life-size shaft of a coal mine (adult/child $12/9 extra to descend and tour its workings).

The museum's main building served as the Palace of Fine Arts at the landmark 1893 World's Expo, which was set in the surrounding **Jackson Park** (6401 S Stony Island Ave, Woodlawn; 🚌6, M Metra Electric Line to 59th or 63rd St). When you've had your fill of the sensory-overload sights inside, the park makes an excellent setting to recuperate.

★**Robie House** ARCHITECTURE
(☎312-994-4000; www.flwright.org; 5757 S Woodlawn Ave, Hyde Park; adult/child $18/15; ⏲10:30am-3pm Thu-Mon; 🚌6, M Metra Electric Line to 59th St) Of the numerous buildings that Frank Lloyd Wright designed around Chicago, none is more famous or influential than Robie House. Because its horizontal lines resembled the flat landscape of the Midwestern prairie, the style became known as the Prairie style. Inside are 174 stained-glass windows and doors, which you'll see on the hour-long tours (frequency varies by season, but there's usually at least one tour per hour). Advance tickets are highly recommended.

DuSable Museum of African American History MUSEUM
(☎773-947-0600; www.dusablemuseum.org; 740 E 56th Pl, Washington Park; adult/child $10/3, Tue free; ⏲10am-5pm Tue-Sat, noon-5pm Sun; 🚌6, M Metra Electric Line to 55th-56th-57th St) This was the first independent museum in the country dedicated to African American art, history and culture. The collection features African American artworks and photography, permanent exhibits that illustrate African Americans' experiences from slavery through the Civil Rights movement, and rotating exhibits that cover topics such as Chicago blues music or the Black Panther

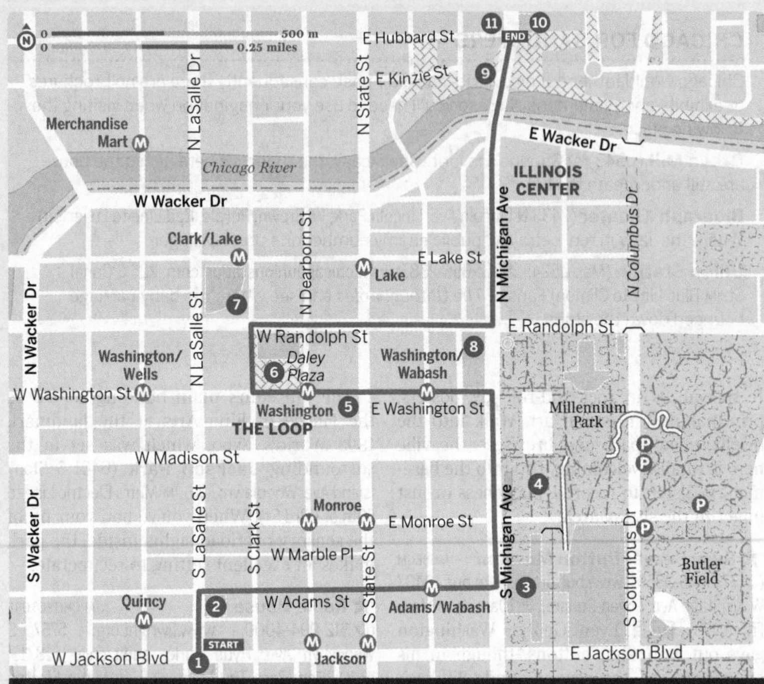

City Walk The Loop

START CHICAGO BOARD OF TRADE
FINISH BILLY GOAT TAVERN
LENGTH 3 MILES; ABOUT TWO HOURS

This tour winds through the Loop and across the Chicago River, passing some of the city's finest old buildings and notable public art.

Start at the **1 Chicago Board of Trade** (141 W Jackson Blvd), a 1930 art-deco temple of commerce. The nearby **2 Rookery** (www.flwright.org; 209 S LaSalle St) was built in 1888 by Daniel Burnham – a monumental brick building maximizing light and air with a central atrium. Frank Lloyd Wright redesigned the lobby 19 years later.

Head east on Adams to the **3 Art Institute** (p520), one of the world's finest art museums. The lion statues out front make a classic keepsake photo. Just north is **4 Millennium Park** (p521), filled with avant-garde works from world-famous names such as Frank Gehry and Anish Kapoor.

Two blocks west on Washington is the 1895 **5 Reliance Building**. Another Burnham design, it's a posh hotel today (it originally housed medical offices – Al Capone's dentist practiced in room 809).

Another block west is Pablo Picasso's **6 untitled sculpture** (50 W Washington St). He never revealed what it portrayed – popular guesses include a woman, a dog or a baboon – so interpret it however you like. Just northwest is another inscrutable sculpture, Jean Dubuffet's **7 Monument with Standing Beast** (100 W Randolph St).

Walk east on Randolph to beaux-arts beauty the **8 Chicago Cultural Center** (p521). Further famous edifices are north of the Chicago River: the gleaming-white terracotta **9 Wrigley Building** (400 N Michigan Ave) and the neo-Gothic, eye-popping **10 Tribune Tower** (p526).

Finish up at the **11 Billy Goat Tavern** (p538), a classic dive bar whose owner invoked the Cubs' famous curse in 1945 after being ejected from Wrigley Field because of his pet goat. Raise a glass to the Cubs, who broke it – and their 108-year-long World Series drought – in 2016.

movement. It's affiliated with the Smithsonian Institution.

Obama's House HOUSE

(5046 S Greenwood Ave, Kenwood; 6, Metra Electric Line to 51st-53rd St) Among the handsome manors lining S Greenwood Ave is the redbrick Georgian-style home at number 5046, where Barack Obama and his family lived from 2005 until he became president in 2008. The Obamas still own the house, though they chose to stay in Washington, DC, after his time in office. You can't go inside, and fences block the sidewalk, but you can get close enough for a photo.

Activities

Chicago offers plenty of places to get active via its city-spanning shoreline, 26 beaches and 580 parks. After a long, cold winter, everyone dashes outside to play. Top marks go to the 18-mile Lakefront Trail, prime for cycling and running. Meanwhile, Lake Michigan and the Chicago River provide loads of paddling possibilities.

On The Land

The flat, 18-mile **Lakefront Trail** is a beautiful ride along the water, though on nice days it's jam-packed. It starts at Ardmore Ave and rolls all the way south to 71st St. The path is split so cyclists and runners have separate lanes; look for signposts and markers painted on the ground to tell you what's what. The trail is most congested between Lincoln Park and the Museum Campus; it's least congested heading south from the museums.

The Active Transportation Alliance (www.activetrans.org) publishes a bike trail map. Check @activetransLFT on Twitter for updates on trail conditions; some parts close in bad weather.

★ **Bobby's Bike Hike** CYCLING

(Map p524; 312-245-9300; www.bobbysbikehike.com; 540 N Lake Shore Dr, Streeterville; per hr/day from $8/27, tours $38-70; 8:30am-8pm Mon-Fri, 8am-8pm Sat & Sun Jun-Aug, 9am-7pm Mar-May & Sep-Nov; Red Line to Grand) Locally based Bobby's earns rave reviews from riders. It rents bikes and has easy access to the Lakefront Trail. It also offers cool tours of gangster sites, the lakefront, nighttime vistas, and venues to indulge in pizza and beer. The Tike Hike caters to kids. Enter through the covered driveway to reach the shop. Call for winter hours.

> **DON'T MISS**
>
> **THE 606**
>
> Like NYC's High Line, Chicago's **606** (www.the606.org; Wicker Park/Bucktown; 6am-11pm; Blue Line to Damen) is a similar urban-cool elevated path along an old train track. Bike or stroll past factories, smokestacks, clattering L trains and locals' backyard affairs for 2.7 miles between Wicker Park and Logan Square. It's a fascinating trek through Chicago's socioeconomic strata: moneyed at the east, becoming more industrial and immigrant to the west.

Bike & Roll CYCLING

(Map p524; 312-729-1000; www.bikechicago.com; 239 E Randolph St; tours adult/child from $45/35; 9am-7pm; Brown, Orange, Green, Purple, Pink Line to Washington/Wabash) Summer guided tours (adult/child from $45/35) cover themes such as lakefront parks, breweries and historic neighborhoods, or downtown's sights and fireworks at night (highly recommended). Prices include lock, helmet and map. Operates out of the McDonald's Cycle Center in Millennium Park; there's another branch on Navy Pier. It also rents out bikes for DIY explorations (per hour/day from $12.50/35).

McCormick Tribune Ice Rink ICE SKATING

(Map p524; www.millenniumpark.org; 55 N Michigan Ave; noon-8pm Mon-Thu, to 10pm Fri, 10am-9pm Sat & Sun mid-Nov–mid-Mar; Brown, Orange, Green, Purple, Pink Line to Washington/Wabash) Millennium Park's busy rink is the city's most scenic, tucked between the reflecting Bean sculpture and the twinkling lights of Michigan Ave. Admission to the ice is free; skate rental costs $13 (Monday through Thursday) or $15 (Friday through Sunday). Free ice-skating lessons are offered an hour before the rink opens.

On The Water

Visitors often don't realize Chicago is a beach town, thanks to mammoth Lake Michigan lapping its side. There are 26 official strands of sand patrolled by lifeguards in summer. Swimming is popular, though the water is pretty freaking cold. Beaches at Montrose and North Ave have rental places offering kayaks and stand-up paddleboards. Other kayak companies have set up shop along the Chicago River.

CHICAGO FOR CHILDREN

Ferocious dinosaurs, an ark's worth of beasts, lakefront boat rides and sandy beaches are among the top choices for toddlin' times. Add in magical playgrounds, family cycling tours and lots of pizza, and it's clear Chicago is a kid's kind of town.

Chicago Children's Museum (Map p524; ☎312-527-1000; www.chicagochildrensmuseum.org; 700 E Grand Ave, Navy Pier; $15; ⏲10am-5pm, to 8pm Thu; 👪; 🚌65) is the reigning favorite, geared to kids aged 10 and under, with a slew of hands-on building, climbing and inventing exhibits. Bonus: it's located on Navy Pier.

Bring on the dinosaurs at Field Museum of Natural History (p523). The Crown Family PlayLab, on the ground floor, lets kids excavate bones and make loads of other discoveries. It's open Thursday to Monday from 10am to 3:30pm.

Families could spend a week the Museum of Science & Industry (p529) and not see it all. Staff conduct 'experiments' in various galleries throughout the day, such as dropping things off the balcony and creating mini explosions. The Idea Factory lets scientists aged 10 and under 'research' properties of light, balance and water pressure.

The **Peggy Notebaert Nature Museum** (☎773-755-5100; www.naturemuseum.org; 2430 N Cannon Dr, Lincoln Park; adult/child $9/6; ⏲9am-5pm Mon-Fri, from 10am Sat & Sun; 👪; 🚌76, 151) is somewhat overlooked, but its butterfly haven and marsh full of frogs provide gentle thrills. Bonus: it's located in Lincoln Park by the zoo.

At the Art Institute of Chicago (p520), the Ryan Learning Center provides interactive games (such as puzzles of famous works) and art-making activities.

★**Montrose Beach** BEACH
(www.cpdbeaches.com; 4400 N Lake Shore Dr, Uptown; 🚌146) One of the city's best beaches. You can rent kayaks, stand-up paddleboards and Jet Skis; sometimes you'll see surfers and kitesurfers, and anglers frequently cast here. Watch sailboats glide in the harbor over some waterside snacks or a drink at the **Dock Bar and Grill**. A wide, dog-friendly beach with a curving breakwater abuts the main beach to the north.

North Avenue Beach BEACH
(www.cpdbeaches.com; 1600 N Lake Shore Dr, Lincoln Park; ⏲6am-11pm; 👪; 🚌151) Chicago's most popular strand of sand gives off a bit of a Southern California vibe in summer. Buff teams spike volleyballs, kids build sandcastles and everyone jumps in for a swim when the weather heats up. Bands and DJs rock the steamboat-shaped beach house, which serves ice cream and margaritas in equal measure. Kayaks, Jet Skis, stand-up paddleboards, bicycles and lounge chairs are available to rent, and there are daily beach yoga classes.

Urban Kayaks KAYAKING
(Map p524; ☎312-965-0035; www.urbankayaks.com; 435 E Riverwalk S; rental per hour per person $30, tours $55; ⏲9am-6pm Mon-Fri, to 7pm Sat & Sun May-early Oct; Ⓜ Brown, Orange, Green, Purple, Pink Line to State/Lake) On the **Riverwalk** (www.chicagoriverwalk.us; Chicago River waterfront, btwn N Lake Shore Dr & W Lake St; ⏲6am-11pm), this outfitter rents out kayaks for DIY explorations and offers guided tours that glide past downtown's skyscrapers and historic sites; beginners are welcome, with a 20-minute training session starting off each tour. For extra help, try the hour-long 'intro to paddling' class ($35). Night-time tours on Wednesdays and Saturdays take in the Navy Pier summer fireworks show.

☞ Tours

★**Chicago Architecture Center Tours** BOAT TOURS
(CAC; ☎312-922-3432; www.architecture.org; 111 E Wacker Dr; tours $20-55) Gold-standard boat tours ($47) sail from the **river dock** (Map p524; Ⓜ Brown, Orange, Green, Purple, Pink Line to State/Lake) on the southeast side of the Michigan Ave Bridge. Also popular are the Historic Skyscrapers walking tours ($26) and tours exploring individual landmark buildings ($20). CAC sponsors bus, bike and L train tours, too. Buy tickets online or at the CAC's front desk; boat tickets can also be purchased at the dock.

Chicago by Foot WALKING
(☎312-612-0826; www.freetoursbyfoot.com/chicago-tours) Guides for this pay-what-you-want

walking tour offer engaging stories and historical details on different jaunts covering Loop architecture, West Loop history, Lincoln Park's gangster sites and much more. It's recommended to pay about $20 per person.

Reserve in advance to guarantee a spot; walk-up guests are welcome if space is available (chancy). Tours usually last around two hours.

Chicago Detours WALKING
(312-350-1131; www.chicagodetours.com; tours from $28) Chicago Detours offers engrossing, detail-rich tours (mostly walking, but also some by bus) that take in Chicago's architecture, history and culture. The 2½-hour Historic Bar Tour is a popular one.

Chicago Beer Experience WALKING
(312-818-2172; www.chicagobeerexperience.com; 3hr tours $67) These walking tours visit a neighborhood in order to discover its beer history along with general Chicago history. Expect to hit four bars over the course of a mile or so. Beer and a snack (such as a stuffed pizza slice or hot dog) are included. Departure points vary.

Festivals & Events

St Patrick's Day Parade CULTURAL
(www.chicagostpatricksdayparade.org; mid-Mar) The local plumbers union dyes the Chicago River shamrock-green; a big parade follows downtown in Grant Park. Held the Saturday before March 17.

Chicago Blues Festival MUSIC
(www.chicagobluesfestival.us; Jun) The biggest free blues fest in the world, with three days of the music that made Chicago famous. Held in Millennium Park.

★ **Taste of Chicago** FOOD & DRINK
(www.tasteofchicago.us; Jul) This five-day food festival in Grant Park draws hordes for a smorgasbord of ethnic, meaty, sweet and local edibles – much of it served on a stick. Several stages host free live music, including big-name bands.

Pride Parade LGBTIQ+
(http://chicagopride.gopride.com; Boystown; late Jun; M Red Line to Addison) On the last Sunday in June, colorful floats and risqué revelers pack Halsted St in Boystown. It's the LGBTIQ+ community's main event, and more than 800,000 people come to the party.

Pitchfork Music Festival MUSIC
(http://pitchforkmusicfestival.com; Union Park, Near West Side; day pass $75; mid-Jul; M Green, Pink Line to Ashland) Taste-making alternative and emerging bands strum for three days in Union Park in mid-July.

Lollapalooza MUSIC
(www.lollapalooza.com; Aug) Up to 170 bands spill off eight stages at Grant Park's four-day mega-gig.

Jazz Festival MUSIC
(www.chicagojazzfestival.us; Aug/Sep) Top names on the national jazz scene play for free over Labor Day weekend. Performances are held in Millennium Park and the Chicago Cultural Center.

Open House Chicago CULTURAL
(312-922-3432; www.openhousechicago.org; Oct) FREE Design geeks, take note: for one weekend in mid-October the Chicago Architecture Center (p521) coordinates free tours of more than 200 architectural gems around the city, many of them normally off-limits to the public.

Chicago Marathon SPORTS
(www.chicagomarathon.com; Oct) More than 45,000 runners compete on the 26-mile course through the city's heart, cheered on by a million spectators. Held on a Sunday in October (when the weather can be pleasant or freezing), it's considered one of the world's top five marathons.

Sleeping

Chicago's lodgings rise high in the sky, many in architectural landmarks. Snooze in the building that gave birth to the skyscraper, in one of Mies van der Rohe's boxy structures, or in a century-old art deco masterpiece. Huge business hotels, trendy boutique hotels and snazzy hostels blanket the cityscape too. But nothing comes cheap…

The Loop

HI-Chicago HOSTEL $
(Map p524; 312-360-0300; www.hichicago.org; 24 E Congress Pkwy; dm $35-55; M Brown, Orange, Purple, Pink Line to Library) Chicago's most stalwart hostel is immaculate, conveniently placed in the Loop, and offers bonuses such as a staffed information desk, free volunteer-led tours and discount passes to some sights. The simple dorm rooms have eight or 10 beds, and most have attached

baths; others share hallway bathrooms. Dorms are segregated by gender.

★Hampton Inn Chicago Downtown/N Loop HOTEL $$
(Map p524; 312-419-9014; www.hamptonchicago.com; 68 E Wacker Pl; r $200-290; P ❄ ; M Brown, Orange, Green, Purple, Pink Line to State/Lake) This unique property with a central location makes you feel like a road-tripper of yore. Set in the 1928 art deco Chicago Motor Club Building, the lobby sports a vintage Ford and a cool USA mural map from the era. The dark-wood-paneled rooms strike the right balance of retro vibe and modern amenities. Free wi-fi.

★Virgin Hotel HOTEL $$
(Map p524; 312-940-4400; www.virginhotels.com; 203 N Wabash Ave; r $240-380; P ❄ @ ; M Brown, Orange, Green, Purple, Pink Line to State/Lake) Billionaire Richard Branson transformed the 27-story, art deco Dearborn Bank Building into the first outpost of his cheeky new hotel chain. The airy, suite-like rooms have speedy free wi-fi, low-cost minibar items and a bed that doubles as a work desk. An app controls electronics including thermostat and TV. Guests receive earplugs, handy for dulling noise from nearby L trains.

★Hotel Julian HOTEL $$
(Map p524; 312-346-1200; www.hoteljulianchicago.com; 168 N Michigan Ave; r $200-400; P ❄ ; M Brown, Orange, Green, Purple, Pink Line to Washington/Wabash) Twelve stories in a 1912 office building now comprise one of the Loop's newest mod-luxe hotels. Large rooms are elegantly decorated with a slightly masculine retro-1930s vibe and feature king-sized captain's beds with Frette linens and leather headboards, espresso makers and 55in TVs – not to mention stunning views of Millennium Park through some of the city-view rooms.

Buckingham Athletic Club Hotel BOUTIQUE HOTEL $$
(Map p524; 312-663-8910; www.thebuckinghamclub.com; 440 S LaSalle St; r $200-280; P ❄ ; M Brown, Orange, Purple, Pink Line to LaSalle) On the 40th floor of the Chicago Stock Exchange building, this 21-room hotel isn't easy to find. The benefit if you do? It's quiet (on weekends and evenings especially) and has expansive views. Elegant rooms are so spacious they'd be considered suites elsewhere. Lots of freebies add to the excellence, including access to the namesake gym with lap pool.

Silversmith HISTORIC HOTEL $$
(Map p524; 312-372-7696; www.silversmithchicagohotel.com; 10 S Wabash Ave; r $200-350; P ❄ @ ; M Red, Blue Line to Monroe) Designed by renowned architect Daniel Burnham's firm as a place for jewelers and silversmiths to ply their trade, this 1897 building's gem-inspired theme carries over to the current, vintage-cool design. Rooms are good-sized, with pearl-colored decor and ruby and gold accents. A cushioned seat nestles in each floor-to-ceiling window, prime for city-watching.

Near North & Navy Pier

★Found Hotel Chicago HOSTEL, HOTEL $
(Map p524; 224-243-6863; www.foundhotels.com; 613 N Wells St, River North; dm $25-55, r $120-330; P ❄ ; M Brown, Purple Line to Merchandise Mart) Breezy Found Hotel joins the elevated hostel/casual-hotel brigade. The 60 rooms come in several configurations, including four-bed dorms with sturdy (and quite comfy) bunk beds, and private rooms with twin or queen beds – all with en-suite bathrooms. Rooms are small and plain, but who cares? The price is often right, and the common areas are where the fun is.

Freehand Chicago HOSTEL, HOTEL $
(Map p524; 312-940-3699; www.freehandhotels.com/chicago; 19 E Ohio St, River North; dm $35-55, r $220-310; ❄ ; M Red Line to Grand) At this super-hip hostel-hotel hybrid, travelers split evenly between the four-person, bunk-bed dorms and private rooms. All feature warm woods, bright tiles and Central American–tinged fabrics. Everyone mingles in the totem-pole-filled common area and groovy Broken Shaker bar. The Freehand works best as a hostel, its dorms spiffier than most, with en-suite bathrooms and privacy curtains around each bed.

★Acme Hotel BOUTIQUE HOTEL $$
(Map p524; 312-894-0800; www.acmehotelcompany.com; 15 E Ohio St, River North; r $170-310; P ❄ @ ; M Red Line to Grand) Urban bohemians love the Acme for its indie-cool style at (usually) affordable rates. The 130 rooms mix industrial fixtures with retro lamps, mid-century furniture and funky modern art. They're wired up with free wi-fi, good speakers, smart TVs and easy connections to stream your own music and movies. Graffiti,

GREAT LAKES IN...

One Week

Spend the first two days in Chicago (p517) stuffing your face and gawking at architecture. On your third day, make the 1½-hour trip to Milwaukee (p591) for beer, art and fierce motorcycles. Take the ferry to Michigan and spend your fourth day in Saugatuck (p583). The artsy town booms in summer thanks to its golden beaches, piney breezes, galleries and welcoming bars. Circle back via Indiana Dunes (p558) for sandy hikes and swimming, or via Indiana Amish Country (p559) for a unique cultural immersion.

Two Weeks

After two days in Chicago (p517), on day three make for Madison (p595) to chow in locavore eateries and visit the surrounding quirky sights. Spend your fourth and fifth days at the Apostle Islands (p600) boating around wind-bashed cliffs and caves. Then head into Michigan's Upper Peninsula to visit Marquette (p589) and Pictured Rocks (p588) for a few days. Both are outdoorsy places with dramatic nature at their doorstep. Follow with a visit to the towering Sleeping Bear Dunes (p584) and the foodie restaurants and wineries around Traverse City (p585). Return via the galleries, pies and beaches of Saugatuck (p583).

neon and a rock-and-roll elevator embellish the common areas.

Moxy Chicago Downtown HOTEL $$
(Map p524; ☎312-527-7200; http://moxy-hotels.marriott.com; 530 N LaSalle Dr, River North; r $224-299; P ❄ 📶 🐾; M Red Line to Grand) When a hotel's front desk doubles as a bar, you know you're in for a good time. So it goes at Moxy, where the lobby is a communal area with a 24-hour taco joint and novelty-size Jenga and Connect Four games. The wee rooms feel bigger than they are thanks to floor-to-ceiling windows and a pegboard wall to hang items.

Gold Coast

★Fieldhouse Jones HOSTEL, HOTEL $
(Map p524; ☎312-291-9922; www.fieldhousejones.com; 312 W Chestnut St; r/apt from $125/180; P ❄ 📶; M Brown, Purple Line to Chicago) This hip hotel occupies a vintage, redbrick dairy warehouse. It's great value for the Gold Coast, drawing a wide range of travelers – global backpackers, families – for its quality rooms and sociable common areas. There are standard hotel rooms, studios and one- and two-bedroom apartments, all with en-suite bathrooms, wi-fi and fun, sporty decor (dartboard wall art, old trophies etc).

Drake Hotel HISTORIC HOTEL $$
(☎312-787-2200; www.thedrakehotel.com; 140 E Walton St; r $230-360; P ❄ @ 📶; M Red Line to Chicago) Queen Elizabeth, Princess Di, the Reagans, the Bushes, the Clintons, the late, great Aretha Franklin... Who *hasn't* stayed at the Drake since its 1920 opening? The elegant, chandelier-strewn grande dame anchors the northern end of Michigan Ave, near Oak Street Beach. While the public spaces are gilded eye-poppers, the 535 rooms are more everyday yet well-sized and comfy.

★Viceroy Chicago LUXURY HOTEL $$$
(☎312-586-2000; www.viceroyhotelsandresorts.com; 1118 N State St; d $275-450, ste from $550; P ⊖ ❄ 📶 🏊; M Red Line to Clark/Division) The Gold Coast's newest luxury hotel, the Viceroy has 198 rooms and suites with art deco–inspired design elements with warm woods, gold accents and luxe furnishings. Blue-velvet curtains float across floor-to-ceiling windows with lake and skyline views; the restaurant, helmed by a Michelin-starred chef, features nautical yacht-club motifs. In summer you can use the rooftop dipping pool. Free wi-fi.

★Waldorf Astoria Chicago LUXURY HOTEL $$$
(☎312-646-1300; www.waldorfastoriachicagohotel.com; 11 E Walton St; r from $400; P ❄ @ 📶 🏊 🐾; M Red Line to Chicago) The Waldorf routinely tops the list for Chicago's best uber-luxury hotel. It models itself on 1920s Parisian glamour and, we have to admit, it delivers it in spades. Rooms are large – they have to be, to hold the fireplaces, the bars, the marble soaking tubs, the beds with 460-thread-count sheets and the fully wired work spaces and other techno gadgets.

Lincoln Park & Old Town

Hotel Lincoln BOUTIQUE HOTEL $$

(☎312-254-4700; www.jdvhotels.com; 1816 N Clark St, Lincoln Park; r $150-399; P❄@🛜; 🚌22) The boutique Lincoln is all about kitschy fun, as the lobby's 'wall of bad art' and front desk patched together from flea-market dresser drawers attest. Standard rooms are small, but vintage-cool and colorful; many have sweet views. Leafy Lincoln Park and the city's largest farmers market (p528) sprawl across the street.

The hotel's **rooftop bar** (☎312-254-4747; www.jparkerchicago.com; ⏲5pm-1am Mon-Thu, from 3pm Fri, from 11:30am Sat & Sun) offers spectacular lake views.

Lake View & Wrigleyville

★**Majestic Hotel** BOUTIQUE HOTEL $$

(☎773-404-3499; www.majestic-chicago.com; 528 W Brompton Ave, Lake View; r $159-275; P❄🛜; 🚌151) Nestled into a row of residential housing, the Majestic is walking distance to Wrigley Field and Boystown and mere steps from the lakefront. From the lobby fireplace and dark-wood furnishings to the handsome, paisley-swirled decor, the interior has the cozy feel of an English manor. Free wi-fi and continental breakfast are included.

★**Wheelhouse Hotel** BOUTIQUE HOTEL $$

(☎773-248-9001; www.wheelhousehotel.com; 3475 N Clark St, Wrigleyville; r $250-350; P❄🛜; Ⓜ Red Line to Addison) The Wheelhouse features 21 rooms in a restored greystone building not far from Wrigley Field. The smallish rooms have an earthy, urban loft feel, with exposed brick walls, cool vintage decor and bold shades of peach, yellow and blue; some even have bunk beds. The playful, baseball-tinged vibe extends to the lobby's wood-bat ceiling and scoreboard wall.

Hotel Zachary HOTEL $$

(☎773-302-2300; www.hotelzachary.com; 3630 N Clark St, Wrigleyville; r $250-425; P❄🛜🐾; Ⓜ Red Line to Addison) Gleaming Hotel Zachary – named after Zachary Taylor Davis, the architect of Wrigley Field – opened in 2018 right across the street from the celebrated ballpark. Nods to baseball are subtle in the 173 stylish, natural-light-filled rooms: ivy-green headboards, baseball-glove-colored leather chairs, gray pinstripe carpet. On game days it's a high-energy scene, and it can be noisy into the wee hours.

Wicker Park, Bucktown & Ukrainian Village

Urban Holiday Lofts HOSTEL $

(☎312-532-6949; www.urbanholidaylofts.com; 2014 W Wabansia Ave, Wicker Park; dm $25-40, r $79-115; ❄@🛜; Ⓜ Blue Line to Damen) An international crowd fills the gender-segregated dorms (with four to eight beds) and private rooms of these converted loft condos; some rooms have private bathrooms. Exposed-brick walls, hardwood floors and bunks with plump bedding feature in all 21 rooms. It's close to the L station and in the thick of Wicker Park's nightlife. Continental breakfast is included. No elevator.

Wicker Park Inn B&B $

(☎773-486-2743; www.wickerparkinn.com; 1331 N Wicker Park Ave, Wicker Park; r $180-200, apt $200-250; ❄🛜; Ⓜ Blue Line to Damen) This classic brick row house is steps away from great restaurants and nightlife. The sunny rooms aren't huge, but all have hardwood floors, small desk spaces and soothing color schemes with bright splashes of floral wallpaper. Breakfast is rich in baked goods and fruit. Across the street, three apartments with kitchens provide a self-contained experience.

Logan Square & Humboldt Park

Longman & Eagle INN $

(☎773-276-7110; www.longmanandeagle.com; 2657 N Kedzie Ave, Logan Square; r $95-250; ❄🛜; Ⓜ Blue Line to Logan Square) Check in at the tavern downstairs and then head to your wood-floored, vintage-stylish accommodations on the floor above. The six rooms aren't particularly soundproof, but after using your whiskey tokens in the bar, you probably won't care.

West Loop & Near West Side

★**Ace Hotel** HOTEL $$

(Map p524; ☎312-548-1177; www.acehotel.com/chicago; 311 N Morgan St, West Loop; r $250-400; P❄🛜; Ⓜ Green, Pink Line to Morgan) Chicago's branch of the super-hip Ace chain rises up across the street from Google's shiny office. Hints of Frank Lloyd Wright, Ludwig Mies van der Rohe and other famed local architects show up in the mod, earthy design. The 159 minimalist rooms are on the small side but have cool decor, including a turntable or Martin guitar in most.

Publishing House Bed & Breakfast B&B $$
(Map p524; ☎312-554-5857; https://publishinghousebnb.com; 108 N May St, West Loop; r $179-379; Ⓜ Green, Pink Line to Morgan) The building was indeed a publishing house more than a century ago, and it's now transformed so it looks like the stylish home of your coolest city friend. The 11 warm-toned rooms, each named for a Chicago writer, have hardwood floors, mid-century modern decor and original art on the walls. A fireplace and reading nooks fill the cozy common areas.

Hyde Park & South Side

Sophy Hyde Park BOUTIQUE HOTEL $$
(☎773-289-1003; www.sophyhotel.com; 1411 E 53rd St, Hyde Park; r $229-329; P ❄ 📶; 🚌6, Ⓜ Metra Electric Line to 51st-53rd St) Hyde Park got its first boutique hotel in 2018, and it's a design winner. The 98 rooms have an artsy-hip look that feels truly fresh. Each is a good size, with hardwood floors, a record player and albums by local blues and rock musicians, plus an 8ft, bright-hued, abstract painting (by a local artist) that anchors the space. Free wi-fi, to boot.

Eating

Chicago has become a chowhound's hot spot. For the most part, restaurants here are reasonably priced and pretension-free, serving masterful food in come-as-you-are environs. You can also fork into a superb range of international eats, especially if you break out of downtown and head for neighborhoods such as Pilsen or Uptown.

The Loop

★**Revival Food Hall** AMERICAN $
(Map p524; ☎773-999-9411; www.revivalfoodhall.com; 125 S Clark St; mains $7-12; ⏰7am-7pm Mon-Fri; 📶; Ⓜ Blue Line to Monroe) The Loop needed a forward-thinking food court, and Revival Food Hall delivered. Come lunchtime, hip office workers pack the blond-wood tables of this ground-floor modern marketplace in the historic National building.

The all-local dining concept brings 15 of Chicago's best fast-casual food outlets to the masses, from Antique Taco and Smoque BBQ to Furious Spoon ramen and HotChocolate Bakery.

Mercat a la Planxa SPANISH $$$
(Map p524; ☎312-765-0524; www.mercatchicago.com; 638 S Michigan Ave; tapas $10-18, tasting menus from $65; ⏰dinner 5-10pm Sun-Thu, to 11pm Fri & Sat, brunch 7am-3pm Sat & Sun; Ⓜ Red Line to Harrison) This Barcelona-style tapas and seafood restaurant buzzes in an enormous, convivial room where light streams in through the floor-to-ceiling windows. It cooks all the specialties of Catalonia and stokes a festive atmosphere, enhanced by copious quantities of *cava* (sparkling wine) and sangria. It's located in the beaux-arts Blackstone Hotel.

Pilsen & Near South Side

★**Don Pedro Carnitas** MEXICAN $
(1113 W 18th St, Pilsen; tacos $2.50; ⏰6am-6pm Mon-Thu, 5am-5pm Fri-Sun; Ⓜ Pink Line to 18th St) At this no-frills meat den, a man with a machete salutes you at the front counter. He awaits your command to hack off pork pieces and then wraps the thick chunks with onion and cilantro in a warm tortilla. You then devour the tacos at the tables in back. Goat stew and tripe add to the carnivorous menu.

Cash only.

Qing Xiang Yuan Dumplings DUMPLINGS $
(☎312-799-1118; www.qxydumplings.com; 2002 S Wentworth Ave, Suite 103, Chinatown; mains $9-14; ⏰11:30am-9pm; Ⓜ Red Line to Cermak-Chinatown) The name doesn't lie: it's all about dumplings in this bright room under bamboo lanterns. The dough pockets come steamed or pan-fried, in serves of 12 or 18, with fillings such as lamb and coriander, ground pork and cabbage, sea whelk and leek, and some 30 other types. Bite into one and a hot shot of flavor erupts in your mouth.

Pleasant House Pub PUB FOOD $
(☎773-523-7437; www.pleasanthousepub.com; 2119 S Halsted St, Pilsen; mains $10.50-15; ⏰10am-10pm Tue-Thu, to midnight Fri & Sat, to 10pm Sun; 📶; 🚌8) Follow your nose to Pleasant House, which bakes tall, fluffy, savory pies. Daily flavors include chicken and chutney, steak and ale, or kale and mushroom, made with produce the chefs grow themselves. The pub also serves excellent UK and local beers to accompany the food. Friday is a good day to visit, when there's a fish fry.

Near North & Navy Pier

★Billy Goat Tavern BURGERS $

(Map p524; ☎312-222-1525; www.billygoattavern.com; 430 N Michigan Ave, lower level, Streeterville; burgers $4-8; ⏰6am-1am Mon-Thu, to 2am Fri, to 3am Sat, 9am-2am Sun; Ⓜ Red Line to Grand) *Tribune* and *Sun Times* reporters have guzzled in the subterranean Billy Goat for decades. Order a 'cheezborger' and Schlitz beer, then look around at the newspapered walls to get the scoop on infamous local stories, such as the Cubs' Curse. This is a tourist magnet, but a deserving one. Follow the tavern signs leading below Michigan Ave to get here.

GT Fish & Oyster SEAFOOD $$

(Map p524; ☎312-929-3501; www.gtoyster.com; 531 N Wells St, River North; mains $17-30; ⏰5-10pm Mon-Thu, to 11pm Fri, 10am-2:30pm & 5-11pm Sat, 10am-2:30pm & 5-10pm Sun; Ⓜ Red Line to Grand) Seafood restaurants can be fusty. Not so GT Fish & Oyster. The clean-lined room bustles with date-night couples and groups of friends drinking fizzy wines and slurping mollusks. Many of the dishes are shareable, which adds to the convivial, plate-clattering ambience. The sublime clam chowder arrives in a glass jar with housemade oyster crackers and bacon.

Gold Coast

Velvet Taco TACOS $

(☎312-763-2654; www.velvettaco.com; 1110 N State St; tacos $3.50-7; ⏰11am-midnight Mon, to 2am Tue & Wed, to 3am Thu, to 5am Fri, 10am-5am Sat, 10am-midnight Sun; 🖉; 🚌36, Ⓜ Red Line to Clark/Division) An excellent late-night option for this area, Velvet Taco features hip new takes on the eminently adaptable taco: spicy chicken tikka; Nashville hot tofu with Napa slaw; shredded pork with avocado crema and grilled pineapple; Kobe bacon-burger with smoked cheddar; even shrimp and grits. Down a few accompanied by a margarita or a beer.

★Le Colonial FRENCH, VIETNAMESE $$$

(☎312-255-0088; www.lecolonialchicago.com; 937 N Rush St; mains $20-34; ⏰11:30am-3pm & 5-10pm Sun-Thu, to 11pm Fri & Sat; 🖉; Ⓜ Red Line to Chicago) Step into the dark-wood, candlelit room, where ceiling fans swirl lazily and big-leafed palms sway in the breeze, and you'd swear you were in 1920s Saigon. Staff can arrange vegetarian and gluten-free substitutions among the curries and banana-leaf-wrapped fish dishes. If you want spicy, be specific; everything typically comes out mild.

Lincoln Park & Old Town

★Sultan's Market MIDDLE EASTERN $

(☎872-253-1489; 2521 N Clark St, Lincoln Park; mains $4-10; ⏰10am-10pm Mon-Sat, to 9pm Sun; 🖉; Ⓜ Brown, Purple, Red Line to Fullerton) Neighborhood folks dig into plates heaped with falafel sandwiches, creamy hummus, lamb shawarma, spinach pies and other quality Middle Eastern fare at family-run Sultan's Market. There's a large salad bar, too. The small, homey space doesn't have many tables, but Lincoln Park is nearby for picnicking.

★Alinea GASTRONOMY $$$

(☎312-867-0110; www.alinearestaurant.com; 1723 N Halsted St, Lincoln Park; 10-/16-course menus from $205/290; ⏰5-10pm; Ⓜ Red Line to North/Clybourn) One of the world's best restaurants, the triple-Michelin-starred Alinea purveys multiple courses of molecular gastronomy. Dishes may emanate from a centrifuge or be pressed into a capsule, à la duck served with a 'pillow of lavender air.' There are no reservations; instead Alinea sells tickets two to three months in advance via its website. Check Twitter (@Alinea) for last-minute seats.

Boka MODERN AMERICAN $$$

(☎312-337-6070; www.bokachicago.com; 1729 N Halsted St, Lincoln Park; mains $21-42, small plates $14-20, 8-course menus $125; ⏰5-10pm Sun-Thu, to 11pm Fri & Sat; Ⓜ Red Line to North/Clybourn) A Michelin-starred restaurant-lounge hybrid, Boka is a pre- and post-theater stomping ground for younger Steppenwolf patrons. Order a cocktail at the bar or slip into one of the booths for small-plate dishes such as striped-jack crudo or veal sweetbreads with charred cabbage.

Lake View & Wrigleyville

★Jennivee's BAKERY $

(☎773-697-3341; www.facebook.com/jennivees; 3301 N Sheffield Ave, Lake View; items $3.25-7.50; ⏰noon-midnight Tue-Thu, to 2am Fri, 10am-2am Sat, 10am-midnight Sun; Ⓜ Red, Brown, Purple Line to Belmont) This LGBTIQ-friendly bakery mixes Filipino and American flavors. The teeny room couldn't be any cuter. Chande-

DEEP-DISH CHICAGO

Deep-dish pizza is Chicago's most famous concoction. These behemoths are nothing like the flat circular disks known as pizza in the rest of the world. Chicago's thick-crusted pie stacks up like this: a fat and crumbly crust baked in a cast-iron pan (kind of like a skillet without a handle), capped by mozzarella, then toppings and sauce. **Gino's East** (Map p524; ☎312-266-3337; www.ginoseast.com; 162 E Superior St, Streeterville; small pizzas from $18; ⊙11am-9pm Sun-Thu, to 10pm Fri & Sat; Ⓜ Red Line to Chicago), **Pizano's** (Map p524; ☎312-236-1777; www.pizanoschicago.com; 61 E Madison St; small pizzas from $16; ⊙11am-2am Sun-Fri, to 3am Sat; 📶; Ⓜ Red, Blue Line to Monroe) and **Lou Malnati's** (Map p524; ☎312-828-9800; www.loumalnatis.com; 439 N Wells St, River North; small pizzas from $13; ⊙11am-11pm Sun-Thu, to midnight Fri & Sat; Ⓜ Brown, Purple Line to Merchandise Mart) offer classic deep-dish.

An adjunct to the genre is stuffed pizza. It's like deep dish on steroids, bigger and more decadent. Basically it's dough, with cheese on top, then another layer of dough atop that, plus toppings. **Giordano's** (Map p524; ☎312-951-0747; www.giordanos.com; 730 N Rush St, River North; small pizzas from $18; ⊙11am-11pm Sun-Thu, to midnight Fri & Sat; Ⓜ Red Line to Chicago) bakes a mighty one.

Pan pizza is the third contender. It's similar to deep dish, but the crust is baked differently so it's breadier, and it has a ring of caramelized cheese that crisps in the pan. **Pequod's** (☎773-327-1512; www.pequodspizza.com; 2207 N Clybourn Ave, Lincoln Park; small pizzas from $12; ⊙11am-2am Mon-Sat, to midnight Sun; 🚌9 to Webster) sets the standard for pan deliciousness.

liers dangle from the ceiling, and a handful of French-inspired tables and chairs let you sit in dainty comfort as you dig into Jennivee's moist, creamy-frosted layer cakes and cupcakes. Specialties include purple velvet (made with purple yam) and mango cream cakes.

Gundis Kurdish Kitchen KURDISH **$$**

(☎773-904-8120; www.thegundis.com; 2909 N Clark St, Lake View; mains $17-26; ⊙9am-9pm Mon, Wed & Thu, to 10pm Fri & Sat, to 8pm Sun; Ⓜ Brown, Purple Line to Wellington) The owners, who hail from southern Turkey, prepare meals from their Kurdish homeland. Dishes include *sac tawa,* a traditional stir-fry of meat, peppers and tomatoes on a sizzling plate, and *tirsik,* a stew of eggplant, carrots and other veggies in a spicy sauce. Sunshine streams into the airy, exposed-brick room by day, while pendant lights create a romantic vibe at night.

Andersonville & Uptown

★Hopleaf EUROPEAN **$$**

(☎773-334-9851; www.hopleaf.com; 5148 N Clark St, Uptown; mains $9-32; ⊙noon-10pm Sun-Thu, to 11pm Fri & Sat; 🚌22, Ⓜ Red Line to Berwyn) A cozy, European-like tavern, Hopleaf draws crowds for its Montreal-style smoked brisket, cashew-butter-and-fig-jam sandwich, ubercreamy macaroni and Stilton cheese, and the house-specialty *frites* (fries) and beer-broth-soaked mussels. It also pours 200 types of brew (with around 60 on tap), emphasizing craft and Belgian suds. (The bar stays open several hours after the kitchen closes.)

Lincoln Square & Ravenswood

Goosefoot AMERICAN **$$$**

(☎773-942-7547; www.goosefoot.net; 2656 W Lawrence Ave, Lincoln Square; tasting menu $145; ⊙6-8:30pm Wed-Sat; Ⓜ Brown Line to Rockwell) Michelin-starred Goosefoot serves a cutting-edge, modern American tasting menu that never fails to surprise. For instance, your dessert – a vanilla-truffle-cherry-pink-peppercorn ice-cream cone – will arrive in a toy goose-foot-shaped holder surrounded by moss. Prepare for around six courses of richly textured, amazing-looking food. It's BYOB, with most people buying a bottle at Goosefoot's wine shop next door. Reservations required.

Wicker Park, Bucktown & Ukrainian Village

★Hoosier Mama Pie Company PIES **$**

(☎312-243-4846; www.hoosiermamapie.com; 1618 W Chicago Ave, East Village; slices $5-6; ⊙8am-7pm Tue-Fri, 9am-5pm Sat, 10am-4pm Sun; 🚌66, Ⓜ Blue Line to Chicago) Soothing 1950s pastels and antique pie tins set the Americana vibe at Paula Haney's celebrated pie shop, where hand-rolled, buttery-flaky crust is plumped full with fruit or creamy fillings. Favorites include sour-cream Dutch cranberry, banana cream, chocolate chess (aka 'brownie pie') and apple-blueberry-walnut. A handful of savory pies tempt, but let's not kid ourselves – we're here for the sweet stuff.

Irazu LATIN AMERICAN $

(☎773-252-5687; www.irazuchicago.com; 1865 N Milwaukee Ave, Bucktown; mains $7-16; ⏲11:30am-9:30pm Mon-Sat; ✍; Ⓜ Blue Line to Western) Chicago's lone Costa Rican eatery turns out burritos bursting with chicken, black beans and fresh avocado, and sandwiches dressed in a heavenly, spicy-sweet vegetable sauce. Wash them down with an *avena* (a slurpable milkshake in tropical-fruit flavors). For breakfast, the *arroz con huevos* (peppery eggs scrambled into rice) relieves hangovers. Irazu is BYOB with no corkage fee. Cash only.

Dove's Luncheonette TEX-MEX $$

(☎773-645-4060; www.doveschicago.com; 1545 N Damen Ave, Wicker Park; mains $13-22; ⏲9am-10pm Mon-Thu, to 11pm Fri, 8am-11pm Sat, 8am-10pm Sun; Ⓜ Blue Line to Damen) Sit at the retro counter for Tex-Mex plates of pork-shoulder posole and buttermilk fried chicken with chorizo-verde gravy. Dessert? It's pie, of course – maybe horchata, lemon cream or peach jalapeño, baked by Hoosier Mama. Soul music spins on a record player, tequila flows from the 70 bottles rattling behind the bar, and presto: all is right in the world.

Logan Square & Humboldt Park

★Spinning J BAKERY $

(☎872-829-2793; www.spinningj.com; 1000 N California Ave, Humboldt Park; mains $9-12; ⏲7am-9pm Tue-Fri, 8am-9pm Sat & Sun; 🚌52) Retro-cute as can be, little Spinning J harks back to a 1950s soda fountain, with a line of counter stools and a smattering of booths where you can sip egg creams and malts made with housemade syrups in flavors such as Thai tea and bay rum cola. Classic sandwiches, hearty soups and sweet and savory pies also please the artsy-crafty patrons.

Ground Control VEGETARIAN $

(☎773-772-9446; www.groundcontrolchicago.com; 3315 W Armitage Ave, Logan Square; mains $10-12; ⏲5-10pm Tue-Thu, 5-11pm Fri, 11am-11pm Sat, 11am-9pm Sun; ✍; 🚌73) Ground Control is an industrial, trippy mural-clad restaurant with pinball machines and craft beer on tap. That it's meat-free is incidental. The dishes play off Asian, Latin and Southern flavors, like the Nashville hot tofu, sweet-potato tacos and wasabi portobello sandwich. It's super delicious, and there's always a cool-cat crowd.

Giant AMERICAN $$$

(☎773-252-0997; www.giantrestaurant.com; 3209 W Armitage Ave, Logan Square; small plates $14-19; ⏲5-10:30pm Tue-Sat; 🚌73) This wee storefront eatery produces huge flavors in its heady comfort food. Dishes like the king-crab tagliatelle, biscuits with jalapeño butter and sweet-and-sour eggplant have wowed the foodie masses, and rightfully so. The small plate portions mean you'll need to order a few dishes to make a meal. Well-matched cocktails and wine add luster to the spread. Reserve ahead.

West Loop & Near West Side

★Lou Mitchell's BREAKFAST $

(Map p524; ☎312-939-3111; www.loumitchells.com; 565 W Jackson Blvd, West Loop; mains $9-14; ⏲5:30am-3pm Mon, to 4pm Tue-Fri, 7am-4pm Sat, to 3pm Sun; 👪; Ⓜ Blue Line to Clinton) A relic of Route 66, Lou's brings in elbow-to-elbow locals and tourists for breakfast. The old-school waitstaff deliver big fluffy omelets and thick-cut French toast with a jug of syrup. They call you 'honey' and fill your coffee cup endlessly. There's often a queue to get in, but free doughnut holes and Milk Duds help ease the wait.

Monteverde ITALIAN $$

(Map p524; ☎312-888-3041; www.monteverdechicago.com; 1020 W Madison St, West Loop; mains $18-24; ⏲5-10:30pm Tue-Fri, 11:30am-10:30pm Sat, 11:30am-9pm Sun; Ⓜ Green, Pink Line to Morgan) Housemade pastas are the specialty here. They seem simple in concept, such as the *cacio whey pepe* (small tube pasta with pecorino Romano, ricotta whey and four-peppercorn blend), but the flavors are lusciously complex. That's why the light-wood tables in the lively room are always packed. Reserve ahead, especially for weekends, or try the bar or patio for walk-in seats.

★Girl & the Goat AMERICAN $$$
(Map p524; ☎312-492-6262; www.girlandthegoat.com; 809 W Randolph St, West Loop; small plates $12-19; ⏱4:30-11pm Sun-Thu, to midnight Fri & Sat; ; Ⓜ Green, Pink Line to Morgan) Stephanie Izard's flagship restaurant rocks. The soaring ceilings, polished wood tables and cartoon-y art on the walls offer a convivial atmosphere where local beer and house-made wine hit the tables, along with unique small plates such as catfish with pickled persimmons. Reservations are difficult; try for walk-in seats before 5pm or see if anything opens up at the bar.

Hyde Park & South Side

Gorée Cuisine SENEGALESE $$
(☎773-855-8120; www.goreecuisine.com; 1126 E 47th St, Kenwood; mains $11-19; ⏱9am-10pm Mon-Wed, 8am-11pm Thu-Sun; Ⓜ Metra Electric Line to 47th St) You'll feel transported to Dakar upon entering this tidy, white-curtained cafe where spicy *yassa* chicken (marinated in lemon and onion), *bissap* (hibiscus flower drink) and a slew of other Senegalese dishes hit the tables. If you're new to the cuisine, the friendly staff will help you order. Gorée offers a terrific, authentic, reasonably priced experience that's rare to find.

Drinking & Nightlife

Chicagoans love to hang out in drinking establishments. Blame it on the long winter, when folks need to huddle together somewhere warm. Blame it on summer, when sunny days make beer gardens and sidewalk patios so splendid. Whatever the reason, drinking in the city is a widely cherished civic pastime.

The Loop

Berghoff BAR
(Map p524; ☎312-427-3170; www.theberghoff.com; 17 W Adams St; ⏱11am-9pm Mon-Fri, from 11:30am Sat; Ⓜ Blue, Red Line to Jackson) The Berghoff dates from 1898 and was the first Chicago bar to serve a legal drink after Prohibition (ask to see the liquor license stamped '#1'). Little has changed around the antique wood bar since. Belly up for mugs of local and imported beers and order sauerbraten, schnitzel and pretzels the size of your head from the adjoining German restaurant.

Pilsen & Near South Side

★Alulu Brewery & Pub MICROBREWERY
(☎312-600-9865; www.alulubrew.com; 2011 S Laflin St, Pilsen; ⏱5pm-2am Mon, Wed & Thu, 3pm-2am Fri & Sun, 3pm-3am Sat; Ⓜ Pink Line to 18th St) Pilsen's bohemians love this intimate brewpub and no wonder. Join them at the reclaimed wood tables for a flight and fancy pub grub such as poutine with *merguez*-sausage gravy. The brewers play around with styles, so anything from a watermelon sour to coffee blond, wheat beer or Mexican lager may be pouring from the 20 taps when you visit.

Near North & Navy Pier

★Arbella COCKTAIL BAR
(Map p524; ☎312-846-6654; www.arbellachicago.com; 112 W Grand Ave, River North; ⏱5pm-midnight Mon, to 2am Tue-Fri, to 3am Sat; Ⓜ Red Line to Grand) Named for a 17th-century ship full of wine-guzzling passengers, Arbella is an adventuresome cocktail bar. Booze from around the globe makes its way into the drinks, from rye to rum, pisco to mezcal. Park yourself at a dark leather banquette, under sparkly globe lights, and taste-trip the night away in one of the city's warmest, coziest rooms.

Centennial Crafted Beer & Eatery CRAFT BEER
(Map p524; ☎312-284-5353; www.centennialchicago.com; 733 N LaSalle Dr, Near North; ⏱4pm-midnight Mon-Wed, 11:30am-midnight Thu, to 2am Fri, 10:30am-3am Sat, 10:30am-midnight Sun; Ⓜ Brown, Purple Line to Chicago) Centennial hides in plain sight. It's rarely mobbed, like many of its neighborhood competitors, yet its 50 taps of carefully chosen craft beer and its cozy, candelabra-and-weathered-wood vibe are exactly what you want in a bar. Beer lovers will never want to leave. Four-beer flights are available that let you expand your hops horizon.

Lincoln Park & Old Town

★Delilah's BAR
(☎773-472-2771; www.delilahschicago.com; 2771 N Lincoln Ave, Lincoln Park; ⏱4pm-2am Sun-Fri, to 3am Sat; Ⓜ Brown Line to Diversey) A bartender rightfully referred to this hard-edged black

sheep of the neighborhood as the 'pride of Lincoln Ave': a title earned for the heavy pours and the best whiskey selection in the city – more than 860 different labels! The no-nonsense staff know their way around a beer list, too, tapping unusual domestic and international suds. Cheap Pabst longnecks are always available.

Old Town Ale House BAR
(312-944-7020; www.theoldtownalehouse.com; 219 W North Ave, Old Town; 3pm-4am Mon-Fri, noon-5am Sat, noon-4am Sun; Brown, Purple Line to Sedgwick) Located near the Second City (p545) comedy club and the scene of late-night musings since the 1960s, this unpretentious neighborhood favorite lets you mingle with beautiful people and grizzled regulars, seated pint by pint under the paintings of nude politicians (just go with it). Classic jazz on the jukebox provides the soundtrack for the jovial goings-on. Cash only.

Lake View & Wrigleyville

★Hungry Brain BAR
(773-935-2118; www.hungrybrainchicago.com; 2319 W Belmont Ave, Roscoe Village; 7pm-2am, closed Tue; 77) The owner of nearby music club Constellation also owns this off-the-beaten-path little bar. It charms with its kind bartenders and well-worn, thrift-store decor. It's a hub of the underground jazz scene; Sunday nights are the mainstay (suggested donation $10), though there are shows and literary readings other nights of the week, too. Cash only.

Ten Cat Tavern PUB
(773-935-5377; 3931 N Ashland Ave, Lake View; 3pm-2am; Brown Line to Irving Park) Pool is serious business on the two vintage tables that the pub refelts regularly with Belgian material. The ever-changing, eye-catching art comes courtesy of neighborhood artists and the furniture is a garage saler's dream. Regulars (most in their 30s) down leisurely drinks at the bar or, in warm weather, in the beer garden. The back room has a toasty fireplace.

Lincoln Square & Ravenswood

★Spiteful Brewing MICROBREWERY
(773-293-6600; www.spitefulbrewing.com; 2024 W Balmoral Ave, Ravenswood; 4-10pm Mon-Wed, to 11pm Thu, noon-midnight Fri & Sat, 11am-10pm Sun; 50) Spiteful's taproom has a rock-and-roll, DIY vibe. Two home brewers launched the brand, and they now operate out of a renovated garage. The concrete floored, exposed-ductwork place has a long bar where you can belly up for hard-hitting pale ales, IPAs and double IPAs.

Begyle Brewing MICROBREWERY
(773-661-6963; www.begylebrewing.com; 1800 W Cuyler Ave, Ravenswood; noon-9pm Mon-Thu, to 10pm Fri, 11am-10pm Sat, noon-8pm Sun; Brown Line to Irving Park) Tucked in a warehouse by the train tracks, Begyle's little taproom is a community hub. Friends play cards at one table, an old guy chills with his dog next to them, while work mates discuss business nearby. The blond and wheat ales are mainstays of the 15 beers on tap, but there are also some monster stouts and triple IPAs. They come in 5oz pours and pints, and you can bring in your own food to eat alongside them. Brewery tours ($10) take place at noon on Saturday and include generous samples.

Northman BAR
(773-935-2255; www.thenorthman.com; 4337 N Lincoln Ave, Lincoln Square; 5pm-midnight Mon, to 2am Tue-Fri, noon-3am Sat, noon-2am Sun; Brown Line to Montrose) The Northman gives the neighborhood beer scene a twist by focusing on cider. Around 20 taps flow with tart, fermented creations from the US, England, France and Spain, and there's a long list of calvados (apple or pear brandies), as well. The low-lit, dark-wood pub feels like it has been plucked from the English countryside.

Wicker Park, Bucktown & Ukrainian Village

Violet Hour COCKTAIL BAR
(773-252-1500; www.thevioletthour.com; 1520 N Damen Ave, Wicker Park; 6pm-2am Sun-Fri, to 3am Sat; Blue Line to Damen) This nouveau speakeasy isn't marked, so look for the wood-paneled building with a full mural and a yellow light over the door. Inside, high-backed booths, chandeliers and long velvet drapes provide the backdrop to elaborately engineered, award-winning seasonal cocktails with droll names.

As highbrow as it sounds, the friendly staff here make Violet Hour welcoming and accessible.

Logan Square & Humboldt Park

Metropolitan Brewing MICROBREWERY

(773-754-0494; www.metrobrewing.com; 3057 N Rockwell St, Avondale; 4-10pm Mon, to 11pm Tue-Thu, to midnight Fri, noon-midnight Sat, noon-10pm Sun; 77) An elder of the local beer scene, Metropolitan has expanded into a striking, retrofitted old tannery overlooking the Chicago River. The floor-to-ceiling windows provide water views, while the tables made of salvaged wood provide a place to put your slew of German-style lagers.

West Loop & Near West Side

CH Distillery DISTILLERY

(Map p524; 312-707-8780; www.chdistillery.com; 564 W Randolph St, West Loop; 4-10pm Mon-Thu, to midnight Fri & Sat; M Green, Pink Line to Clinton) This slick tasting room has a cool, naturalistic look with exposed concrete posts and knotty wood beams across the ceiling. Slip into a seat at the bar and watch the silver tanks behind the big glass window distilling the organic vodka and gin that go into your creative cocktail.

Haymarket Pub & Brewery BREWERY

(Map p524; 312-638-0700; www.haymarketbeer.com; 737 W Randolph St, West Loop; 11am-2am Sun-Fri, to 3am Sat; M Green, Pink Line to Clinton) An early arrival on the West Loop scene, Haymarket remains nicely low-key. It doesn't try to win you over with uberhipness like many of its neighbors. Locals hang out in the cavernous, barrel-strewn space drinking fresh-from-the-tank recipes. The focus is on classic Belgian and German styles, but saisons, IPAs and barrel-aged barley wines fill glasses, too.

Hyde Park & South Side

Marz Community Brewing MICROBREWERY

(773-579-1935; www.marzbrewing.com; 3630 S Iron St, McKinley Park; noon-11pm Tue-Thu, to midnight Fri & Sat, to 10pm Sun; 9) Marz started as a group of home brewers whose friends demanded more. The small brewery is known for its peculiar creations, such as Potion #1 (aged in absinthe barrels), Diliner Weisse (with fresh dill) and Churros Y Chocolate (milk stout brewed with cocoa nibs and cinnamon). The taproom is a gathering spot for local artists and beer buffs.

☆ Entertainment

From the evening-wear elegance of the Lyric Opera to pay-what-you-can storefront theaters and quirky magic lounges, Chicago puts on an impressive slate of performances. Improv laughs and live music spill out of muggy clubs and DIY dive bars nightly. Chicago's spectator sports might just have the most rabid fans of all.

Jazz, Blues & Folk

★ **Green Mill** JAZZ

(773-878-5552; www.greenmilljazz.com; 4802 N Broadway, Uptown; noon-4am Mon-Fri, to 5am Sat, 11am-4am Sun; M Red Line to Lawrence) The timeless – and notorious – Green Mill was Al Capone's favorite speakeasy (a trap door behind the bar accessed tunnels for running booze and escaping the feds). Sit in one of the curved booths and feel his ghost urging you on to another martini. Local and national jazz artists perform nightly; on Sunday is the nationally acclaimed **poetry slam** (cover charge $7; 7-10pm Sun). Cash only.

★ **Buddy Guy's Legends** BLUES

(Map p524; 312-427-1190; www.buddyguy.com; 700 S Wabash Ave; cover charge Sun-Thu $10, Fri & Sat $20; 5pm-2am Mon & Tue, from 11am Wed-Fri, noon-3am Sat, noon-2am Sun; M Red Line to Harrison) Top local and national acts wail on the stage of local icon Buddy Guy. The man himself usually plays a series of shows in January; tickets go on sale in October. Free, all-ages acoustic shows are staged at lunch and dinner (the place doubles as a Cajun restaurant); note that you must pay to stay on for late-evening shows.

Rosa's Lounge BLUES

(773-342-0452; www.rosaslounge.com; 3420 W Armitage Ave, Logan Square; tickets $10-20; 8pm-2am Tue-Sat; 73) Rosa's is an unadorned, real-deal blues club that brings in top local talent and dedicated fans to a somewhat derelict Logan Square block. Get ready to dance. At night a taxi or rideshare is probably the best way to get here.

★ **Constellation** LIVE MUSIC

(www.constellation-chicago.com; 3111 N Western Ave, Roscoe Village; 6pm-midnight Mon & Tue, 7pm-2am Wed, Thu & Sun, 6pm-2am Fri & Sat; 77) The producer of Pitchfork Music Festival (p533) opened this intimate club, which actually breaks down into two small venues inside. The city's hepcats come out of the woodwork for the progressive jazz and improvisational music. Many acts are free, most cost $10 to $15, and none costs more than $25.

Old Town School of Folk Music LIVE MUSIC
(☎773-728-6000; www.oldtownschool.org; 4544 N Lincoln Ave, Lincoln Square; 🚸; Ⓜ Brown Line to Western) You can hear the call of the banjos from the street outside this venerable institution, where major national and international acts such as Richard Thompson and Joan Baez play when they come to town. Old Town also hosts superb world-music shows, including every Wednesday at 8:30pm when they're free (or a $10 donation).

Blue Chicago BLUES
(Map p524; ☎312-661-0100; www.bluechicago.com; 536 N Clark St, River North; tickets $10-12; ⏲8pm-1:30am Sun-Fri, to 2:30am Sat; Ⓜ Red Line to Grand) Commanding local acts wither the mikes nightly at this mainstream blues club. It's a pretty spartan setup, with a small, narrow room that gets packed. Arrive early to get a seat.

While the crowd here and River North environs are touristy, the bands are the real deal.

Rock & World Music

★Hideout LIVE MUSIC
(☎773-227-4433; www.hideoutchicago.com; 1354 W Wabansia Ave, West Town; tickets $5-15; ⏲4pm-midnight Mon-Thu, to 2am Fri, 6pm-3am Sat, hours vary Sun; 🚌72) Hidden behind a factory past the edge of Bucktown, this two-room lodge of indie rock and alt-country is well worth seeking out. The owners have nursed an outsider, underground vibe, and the place feels like your grandma's rumpus room. Music and other events (talk shows, literary readings, comedy etc) take place nightly. On Mondays there's a great open-mike **poetry night** (www.facebook.com/WeedsPoetry; by donation; ⏲9:30pm Mon).

★Whistler LIVE MUSIC
(☎773-227-3530; www.whistlerchicago.com; 2421 N Milwaukee Ave, Logan Square; ⏲6pm-2am Mon-Thu, 5pm-2am Fri-Sun; Ⓜ Blue Line to California) Hometown indie bands, jazz combos and DJs rock this wee, arty bar most nights. There's never a cover charge, but you'd be a schmuck if you didn't order at least one of the swanky cocktails or craft beers to keep the scene going.

Whistler is also a gallery: the front window showcases local artists' work. The venue is easy to miss, as the sign on the door is discreet.

Metro LIVE MUSIC
(☎773-549-4140; www.metrochicago.com; 3730 N Clark St, Wrigleyville; ⏲box office noon-6pm Mon, to 8pm Tue-Sat; Ⓜ Red Line to Addison) For more than three decades, the Metro has been synonymous with loud rock. Sonic Youth and the Ramones in the '80s. Nirvana and Jane's Addiction in the '90s. White Stripes and the Killers in the new millennium. Each night prepare to hear noise by three or four bands who may well be teetering on the verge of stardom.

Empty Bottle LIVE MUSIC
(☎773-276-3600; www.emptybottle.com; 1035 N Western Ave, Ukrainian Village; ⏲5pm-2am Mon-Wed, from 3pm Thu & Fri, from 11am Sat & Sun; 🚌49) Chicago's music insiders fawn over the Empty Bottle, the city's scruffy, go-to club for edgy indie rock, jazz and other beats that's been a west-side institution for almost three decades. Monday's show is often a freebie by a couple of up-and-coming bands. Cheap beer, a photo booth and good graffiti-reading in the bathrooms add to the dive-bar fun.

Theater

★Steppenwolf Theatre THEATER
(☎312-335-1650; www.steppenwolf.org; 1650 N Halsted St, Lincoln Park; ⏲box office 11am-6:30pm Tue-Sat, from 1pm Sun; Ⓜ Red Line to North/Clybourn) Steppenwolf is Chicago's top stage for quality, provocative theater productions. The Hollywood-heavy ensemble includes Gary Sinise, John Malkovich, Martha Plimpton, Gary Cole, Joan Allen and Tracy Letts. A money-saving tip: the box office releases 20 tickets for $20 for each day's shows; they go on sale at 11am Tuesday to Saturday and at 1pm Sunday, and are available by phone.

Goodman Theatre THEATER
(Map p524; ☎312-443-3800; www.goodmantheatre.org; 170 N Dearborn St; Ⓜ Brown, Orange, Green, Purple, Pink, Blue Line to Clark/Lake) One of Chicago's premier drama houses, with a gorgeous Theater District facility. It specializes in new and classic American productions and has been cited several times as one of the USA's best regional theaters. Unsold tickets for the current day's performance go on sale at 10am for half-price on-

LGBTIQ+ CHICAGO

Exploring kinky artifacts in the Leather Archives & Museum, or playing a game of naughty Twister at a rollicking street fair? Shopping for gay literature, or clubbing alongside male go-go dancers? Chicago's flourishing gay and lesbian scene in party-hearty Boystown and easygoing Andersonville offers plenty of choices.

The main event on the calendar is the Pride Parade (p533), held the last Sunday in June. It winds through Boystown and attracts more than 800,000 risqué revelers. **Northalsted Market Days** (www.northalsted.com; Boystown; mid-Aug; Red Line to Addison), held in Boystown, is a steamy two-day street fair in mid-August. Crafty, incense-wafting vendors line Halsted St, but most folks come for the drag queens in feather boas, Twister games played in the street and disco divas (Gloria Gaynor!) on the main stage. The **International Mr Leather** (www.imrl.com; May) contest brings out lots of men in, well, leather in late May. Workshops and parties take place around town, with the main event happening at a downtown hotel or theater.

The following resources will assist with your explorations:

Chicago Pride (www.chicagopride.org) Events and happenings in the community.

Purple Roofs (www.purpleroofs.com) Listings for queer accommodations, travel agencies and tours.

Windy City Times (www.windycitymediagroup.com) LGBTIQ+ newspaper, published weekly. The website is the main source for events and entertainment.

line; they're also available at the box office from noon.

Chicago Theatre THEATER
(Map p524; 312-462-6300; www.thechicagotheatre.com; 175 N State St; Brown, Orange, Green, Purple, Pink Line to State/Lake) Take a gander at the illuminated six-story sign – it's an official landmark and an excellent photo op. Everyone from Duke Ellington to Dolly Parton to Prince has played here over the years (and left their signature on the famous backstage walls). The real showstopper, though, is the opulent French baroque architecture, including a lobby modeled on the Palace of Versailles.

★**Neo-Futurist Theater** THEATER
(773-878-4557; www.neofuturists.org; 5153 N Ashland Ave, Uptown; 11:30pm Fri & Sat, 7pm Sun; 50, Red Line to Berwyn) The Neo-Futurists are best known for their show *The Infinite Wrench*, in which the hyper troupe makes a manic attempt to perform 30 original plays in 60 minutes. Admission costs $10 to $15 – you pay $9 plus the roll of a six-sided die.

Comedy

★**iO Theater** COMEDY
(312-929-2401; www.ioimprov.com; 1501 N Kingsbury St, Old Town; tickets $5-16; Red Line to North/Clybourn) One of Chicago's top-tier (and original) improv houses, iO is a bit edgier (and cheaper) than its competition, with four stages hosting bawdy shows of regular and musical improv nightly. Two bars and a beer garden add to the fun. The Improvised Shakespeare Company is awesome; catch them if you can.

Second City COMEDY
(312-337-3992; www.secondcity.com; 1616 N Wells St, Lincoln Park; tickets $35-55; Brown, Purple Line to Sedgwick) Bill Murray, Stephen Colbert, Tina Fey and more honed their wit at this slick venue with nightly shows. The Mainstage and ETC stage host sketch revues (with an improv scene thrown in); they're similar in price and quality. If you turn up around 10pm Monday through Thursday (or 1am Saturday or 9pm Sunday) you can watch a free improv set.

Cinema

Music Box Theatre CINEMA
(773-871-6604; www.musicboxtheatre.com; 3733 N Southport Ave, Lake View; Brown Line to Southport) It hardly matters what's playing here; the Music Box itself is worth the visit. The restored theater dates from 1929 and looks like a Moorish palace, with clouds floating across the ceiling under twinkling stars. The art-house films are always first-rate and there's a midnight roster of cult hits such as *The Big Lebowski*. A second, smaller theater shows held-over films.

Davis Theater CINEMA

(☎773-769-3999; www.davistheater.com; 4614 N Lincoln Ave, Lincoln Square; ⏲4:30pm-1am Mon-Fri, 11am-2am Sat, 11am-1am Sun; Ⓜ Brown Line to Western) Thanks to a renovation, the century-old Davis has burnished its deco charm while adding modern amenities such as stadium seating and state-of-the-art sound.

The first-run theater also attached a bar-restaurant called Carbon Arc, named after the carbon arc lamps in old film projectors, serving fancy snacks (Thai mussels, duck-and-bean stew) and craft beers that you can take into the movie.

Performing Arts

★Grant Park Orchestra CLASSICAL MUSIC

(Map p524; ☎312-742-7638; www.grantparkmusicfestival.com; Pritzker Pavilion, Millennium Park; ⏲6:30pm Wed & Fri, 7:30pm Sat mid-Jun–mid-Aug; Ⓜ Brown, Orange, Green, Purple, Pink Line to Washington/Wabash) It's a summertime must-do. The Grant Park Orchestra – composed of top-notch musicians from symphonies worldwide – puts on free classical concerts at Millennium Park's Pritzker Pavilion (p521).

Patrons bring lawn chairs, blankets, wine and picnic fixings to set the scene as the sun dips, the skyscraper lights flicker on and glorious music fills the night air.

Chicago Symphony Orchestra CLASSICAL MUSIC

(CSO; Map p524; ☎312-294-3000; www.cso.org; 220 S Michigan Ave; Ⓜ Brown, Orange, Green, Purple, Pink Line to Adams) Riccardo Muti leads the CSO, one of America's best symphonies, known for its fervent subscribers and an untouchable brass section. Cellist Yo-Yo Ma is the creative consultant and a frequent soloist. The season runs from September to June at Symphony Center; Daniel Burnham designed the Orchestra Hall.

Shopping

From the glossy stores of the Magnificent Mile to the indie designers of Wicker Park to the brainy booksellers of Hyde Park, Chicago is a shopper's destination. It has been that way from the get-go. After all, this is the city that birthed the department store and traditions such as the money-back guarantee, bridal registry and bargain basement.

★Chicago Architecture Center Shop GIFTS & SOUVENIRS

(Map p524; ☎312-922-3432; http://shop.architecture.org; 111 E Wacker Dr; ⏲9am-5pm Mon, Wed & Fri-Sun, to 8pm Tue & Thu; 🚌151, Ⓜ Brown, Orange, Green, Purple, Pink Line to State/Lake) Browse through skyline T-shirts and posters, Frank Lloyd Wright note cards, skyscraper models and heaps of books that celebrate local architecture at this haven for anyone with an edifice complex; a children's section has books to pique the interest of budding builders. The items make excellent 'only in Chicago' souvenirs.

★Reckless Records MUSIC

(☎773-235-3727; www.reckless.com; 1379 N Milwaukee Ave, Wicker Park; ⏲10am-10pm Mon-Sat, to 8pm Sun; Ⓜ Blue Line to Damen) Chicago's best indie-rock record and CD emporium lets you listen to everything before you buy. There's plenty of elbow room in the big, sunny space, which makes for happy hunting through the new and used bins. DVDs and cassette tapes, too. Stop by for flyers and listing calendars of the local live-music and theater scene.

★Open Books BOOKS

(Map p524; ☎312-475-1355; www.open-books.org; 651 W Lake St, West Loop; ⏲9am-7pm Mon-Sat, noon-6pm Sun; 👪; Ⓜ Green, Pink Line to Clinton) Buy a used book here and you're helping to fund this volunteer-based literacy group's programs, which range from in-school reading help for grade-schoolers to book-publishing courses for teens. The jam-packed store has good-quality tomes and plenty of cushy sofas where you can sit and peruse your finds. Kids will find lots of imaginative wares. Books average around $5.

Gene's Sausage Shop FOOD & DRINKS

(☎773-728-7243; www.genessausage.com; 4750 N Lincoln Ave, Lincoln Square; ⏲9am-8pm Mon-Sat, to 4pm Sun; Ⓜ Brown Line to Western) As if the hanging sausages, ripe cheeses and flaky pastries lining the shelves at this European market weren't enough, Gene's also rocks a rooftop summer beer garden. Sit at communal picnic tables and munch hot-off-the-grill bratwursts while sipping worldly brews from the tap.

Quimby's BOOKS

(☎773-342-0910; www.quimbys.com; 1854 W North Ave, Wicker Park; ⏲noon-9pm Mon-Thu, to 10pm Fri, 11am-10pm Sat, noon-7pm Sun; Ⓜ Blue

Line to Damen) The epicenter of Chicago's comic and zine worlds, Quimby's is one of the linchpins of underground literary culture in the city. Here you can find everything from crayon-powered punk-rock manifestos to slickly produced graphic novels. It's a groovy place for cheeky literary souvenirs and bizarro readings.

Koval Distillery DRINKS
(☎312-878-7988; www.koval-distillery.com; 5121 N Ravenswood Ave, Ravenswood; ⊙2-7pm Mon-Fri, 1-6:30pm Sat, 2-5pm Sun; Ⓜ Brown Line to Damen) Koval distills organic, small-batch whiskey and gin in the shiny copper tanks that you see inside. It also makes ginger, jasmine, walnut and other unique liqueurs. The shop in front sells them; you can sample the wares before buying.

The distillery also offers hour-long tours ($10) on Wednesday, Saturday and Sunday, and weekly cocktail classes. The website has the schedule.

ℹ Information

Chicago Reader (www.chicagoreader.com) Great listings for music, arts, restaurants and film, plus news and politics.

Choose Chicago (www.choosechicago.com) Official tourism site with sightseeing and event info.

Lonely Planet (www.lonelyplanet.com/chicago) Destination information, hotel reviews and more.

ℹ Getting There & Away

AIR

Seventeen miles northwest of the Loop, **O'Hare International Airport** (ORD; ☎800-832-6352; www.flychicago.com/ohare; 10000 W O'Hare Ave) is the headquarters for United Airlines and a hub for American Airlines. Most non-US airlines and international flights use Terminal 5. The domestic terminals are 1, 2 and 3. ATMs and currency exchanges are available throughout. Wi-fi is free, but slow.

Eleven miles southwest of the Loop, **Midway International Airport** (MDW; ☎773-838-0600; www.flychicago.com/midway; 5700 S Cicero Ave, Clearing) has three concourses: A, B and C. Southwest Airlines uses B; most other airlines go out of A. There's a currency exchange in A and ATMs throughout. Wi-fi is free, but slow.

TRAIN

Grand, Doric-columned **Union Station** (www.chicagounionstation.com; 225 S Canal St; Ⓜ Blue Line to Clinton) is the city's rail hub, located at the Loop's western edge. **Amtrak** (www.amtrak.com) has more connections here than anywhere else in the country.

ℹ Getting Around

TO/FROM THE AIRPORT

O'Hare International Airport The Blue Line L train ($5) runs 24/7 and departs every 10 minutes or so. The journey to the city center takes 40 minutes. Shuttle vans cost $35, taxis around $50.

Midway International Airport The Orange Line L train ($3) runs between 4am and 1am, departing every 10 minutes or so. The journey takes 30 minutes to downtown. Shuttle vans cost $28, taxis $35 to $40.

Union Station All trains arrive here. For transportation onward, the Blue Line Clinton stop is a few blocks south (thought it's not a great option at night). The Brown, Orange, Purple and Pink Line station at Quincy is about a half-mile east. Taxis queue along Canal St outside the station entrance.

PUBLIC TRANSPORTATION

Elevated/subway trains are part of the city's public transportation system. Metra commuter trains venture out into the suburbs.

The L (a system of elevated and subway trains) is fast, frequent and will get you to most sights and neighborhoods.

Two of the eight color-coded lines – the Red Line, and the Blue Line to O'Hare airport – operate 24 hours a day. The other lines run from roughly 4am to 1am daily, departing every 10 minutes or so.

The standard fare is $3 (except from O'Hare airport, where it costs $5) and includes two transfers. Enter the turnstile using a Ventra Ticket, which is sold from vending machines at train stations.

You can also buy a Ventra Card, aka a rechargeable fare card, at stations. It has a one-time $5 fee that gets refunded once you register the card. It knocks around 75¢ off the cost of each ride.

Unlimited ride passes (one/three/seven days $10/20/28) are another handy option. Get them at train stations and drugstores.

For maps and route planning, check the website of the Chicago Transit Authority (www.transitchicago.com). The 'Trackers' section tells you when the next train or bus is due to arrive at your station.

Metra (www.metrarail.com) commuter trains traverse 12 routes serving the suburbs from four terminals ringing the Loop: LaSalle St Station, **Millennium Station** (151 N Michigan

Ave; Ⓜ Brown, Orange, Green, Purple, Pink Line to Washington/Wabash), which is below street level (look for the stairs down), Union Station (p547) and **Richard B Ogilvie Transportation Center** (OTC, Ogilvie Station; 500 W Madison St; Ⓜ Green, Pink Line to Clinton), a few blocks north of Union Station. Some train lines run daily, while others operate only during weekday rush hours. Buy tickets from agents and machines at major stations.

City buses operate from early morning until late evening. The fare is $2.25 ($2.50 if you want a transfer). You can use a Ventra Card or pay the driver with exact change. Buses are particularly useful for reaching the Museum Campus, Hyde Park and Lincoln Park's zoo.

TAXI

Taxis are plentiful in the Loop, north to Andersonville and northwest to Wicker Park/Bucktown. Hail them with a wave of the hand. Fares are meter-based and start at $3.25 when you get into the cab, then it's $2.25 per mile. The first extra passenger costs $1; extra passengers after that are 50¢ apiece. Add 10% to 15% for a tip. All major companies accept credit cards.

Reliable companies:

Checker Taxi (☎312-243-2537; www.checkertaxichicago.com)

Flash Cab (☎773-561-4444; www.flashcab.com)

The ridesharing companies **Uber** (www.uber.com), **Lyft** (www.lyft.com) and **Via** (www.ridewithvia.com) are also popular in Chicago. They can be a bit cheaper than taxis.

Around Chicago

Oak Park

This suburb next door to Chicago spawned two famous sons: novelist Ernest Hemingway was born here, and architect Frank Lloyd Wright lived and worked here for 20 years. The town's main sights revolve around the two men.

For Hemingway, a low-key museum and his birthplace provide an intriguing peek at his formative years. For Wright, the studio where he developed the Prairie style is the big draw, as is a slew of surrounding houses he designed for his neighbors. Ten of them cluster within a mile along Forest and Chicago Aves (though gawking must occur from the sidewalk since they're privately owned).

Sights

★Frank Lloyd Wright Home & Studio ARCHITECTURE
(☎312-994-4000; www.flwright.org; 951 Chicago Ave; adult/child $18/15; ⏲10am-4pm) This is where Wright lived and worked from 1889 to 1909 and it's the first home he ever designed. Tour frequency varies, from every 20 minutes on summer weekends to every hour or so in winter. The hour-long walk-through reveals a fascinating place, filled with the details that made Wright's style distinctive. The studio also offers guided neighborhood walking tours ($15) on Sundays; a self-guided audio version ($15) is available on other days.

Information

Visit Oak Park (www.visitoakpark.com) A wealth of online info, but their physical visitors center has closed.

Getting There & Away

I-290 edges the town; exit on Harlem Ave. Take Harlem north to Lake St and turn right. There's a parking garage within a few blocks.

Metra commuter trains on the Union Pacific West Line stop at Oak Park on their Chicago–western suburbs route. Green Line trains also run to/from Chicago as part of the city's public transit system. The sights are walkable from the stations.

North Shore Suburbs

Mansion-strewn real estate fringes Lake Michigan in the suburbs north of Chicago. The area became popular with the wealthy in the late 19th century.

Sights

★Illinois Holocaust Museum MUSEUM
(www.ilholocaustmuseum.org; 9603 Woods Dr, Skokie; adult/child $12/6; ⏲10am-5pm, to 8pm Thu) This is the third-largest holocaust museum in the world, after those in Jerusalem and Washington, DC. Besides its haunting Nazi-era rail car and its videos of survivors' stories from WWII, the venue contains thought-provoking art about genocides in Armenia, Rwanda, Cambodia and other countries. The special exhibitions are particularly impressive.

Getting There & Away

I-94 slices by the suburbs to the west. Sheridan Rd rambles through the towns along the lakefront to the east. Metra commuter trains on

FRANK LLOYD WRIGHT TRAILS

One of the world's most famous architects – responsible for NYC's outlandish Guggenheim Museum (1959), Tokyo's Imperial Hotel (1923), southwestern Pennsylvania's dreamy Fallingwater (1939) and heaps more – Frank Lloyd Wright (1867–1959) had deep ties to the Great Lakes region. He was born in Richland, WI. He started his career in Chicago and suburban Oak Park, IL (where he developed his famous Prairie style, so named because the buildings featured horizontal lines that resembled the flat Midwestern landscape). And he built his influential architecture school in Spring Green, WI.

Both Illinois and Wisconsin now have self-guided trails that fans can follow to see the major Wright sights. In Illinois, the route takes in 13 Wright-designed buildings. Itineraries start in Chicago and head northwest to Rockford or southwest to Springfield. See www.enjoyillinois.com/history/frank-lloyd-wright-trail for details.

Wisconsin's trail covers nine Wright-designed buildings across the southern part of the state, including Racine (p595) and Madison. See www.travelwisconsin.com/frank-lloyd-wright; there's also an app for the route.

Alas, the two states do not connect their trails.

the Union Pacific North Line stop at each North Shore community as they zip between downtown Chicago and Kenosha, WI. In Evanston, Purple Line trains also run to/from downtown Chicago as part of the Windy City's public transit system.

Galena

Wee Galena spreads across wooded hillsides near the Mississippi River, amid rolling, barn-dotted farmland. Redbrick mansions in Greek Revival, Gothic Revival and Queen Anne styles line the streets, left over from the town's heyday in the mid-1800s, when local lead mines made it rich. Even with all the touristy B&Bs, fudge and antique shops, there's no denying Galena's beauty – 85% of its structures make up the Galena Historic District, which is on the National Register of Historic Places, and its Main St is about as Pleasantville-perfect as one gets. Throw in cool kayak trips and back-road drives, and you've got a lovely, slow-paced getaway.

More than a million visitors come to the town each year; summer and fall weekends see the most action.

Sights & Activities

Ulysses S Grant Home HISTORIC SITE
(www.granthome.com; 500 Bouthillier St; adult/child $5/3; 9am-4:45pm Wed-Sun Apr-Oct, reduced hours Nov-Mar) The 1860 abode was a gift from local Republicans to the victorious general at the Civil War's end. Grant lived here until he became the country's 18th president. Docents take you through the house. Around 90% of the furnishings are original.

Sleeping & Eating

★Jail Hill Inn B&B $$$
(815-777-3000; www.jailhillgalena.com; 319 Meeker St; d $345-445; P ✱ ☎) Convicts and town drunks were locked away here until 1977, but this former jail has been lavishly converted into one of the country's best B&Bs and now you'll definitely want to spend the night in this 140-year-old Second Empire building.

Six rooms with exposed-brick ceilings clock in at a huge 800 sq ft; luxurious accoutrements include soaking tubs and fireplaces.

★Otto's Place BREAKFAST $
(www.ottosplace.com; 100 Bouthillier St; mains $3.50-13; 7am-2pm Wed-Mon) Just off Main St (read: lures in more locals), Otto constructed this historic building in 1899 and turned it into a restaurant. He and his restaurant are long gone, but new proprietors pay homage to history at this excellent breakfast stop, which serves up killer sautéed potatoes and recommended breakfast tacos, plus wildly popular sweet-potato hash and banana bread.

Information

Galena Country Welcome Center (815-776-9200; www.visitgalena.org; 123 N Commerce St; 10am-4pm) Brochures and local info.

Getting There & Away

Hwy 20 rolls into Galena. Driving is the only way to get here. The closest transportation hubs are Chicago (165 miles southeast), Madison, WI (95 miles northeast), and Dubuque, IA (16 miles northwest). There is a free **parking lot** (Bouthillier St) beside the old train depot (street parking in town is also free but limited to three hours). Most sights, shops and restaurants are walkable from here.

Central Illinois

Abraham Lincoln and Route 66 sights are sprinkled liberally throughout central Illinois, which is otherwise farmland plain, though the state capital of Springfield offers worthwhile Lincoln-themed history, a bit of architecture and a burgeoning craft-beer scene. East of Decatur, Arthur and Arcola are Amish centers.

Springfield

The small state capital has a serious obsession with Abraham Lincoln, who practiced law here from 1837 to 1861. Many of the attractions, such as the Lincoln Home National Historic Site and the Lincoln Presidential Library & Museum, are walkable downtown.

Sights

★Dana Thomas House ARCHITECTURE
(217-782-6776; www.dana-thomas.org; 300 E Lawrence Ave; adult/child $10/5; 10am-2pm Mon & Tue, 9am-5pm Wed-Sun) The third-largest home Frank Lloyd Wright ever designed, this remarkably preserved Prairie School icon dating to 1902–04 is – dare we say it – more interesting than Wright's own home in Oak Park. The 16-level abode, considered experimental from a Wright perspective, includes a duckpin bowling alley and two of the three barrel-vaulted ceilings he ever designed (the other is in Oak Park).

An astounding 90% of the furniture is original and there's exquisite, color-shifting art glass.

Lincoln Home National Historic Site HISTORIC SITE
(217-492-4150; www.nps.gov/liho; 426 S 7th St; 8:30am-5pm) FREE An entire four-block neighborhood has been preserved as part of the Lincoln Home National Historic Site. Visits begin at the National Park Service visitor center, where you must pick up a ticket to enter Lincoln's 12-room abode, located one block east.

Rangers then lead you through the house (the only home Lincoln ever owned) where Abe and Mary Lincoln lived from 1844 until they moved to the White House in 1861. A remarkable 80% of the home is original.

Lincoln Presidential Library & Museum MUSEUM
(217-558-8844; www.illinois.gov/alplm; 212 N 6th St; adult/child $15/6; 9am-5pm;) This museum contains the most complete Lincoln collection in the world. Real-deal artifacts such as Abe's shaving mirror and presidential seal join whiz-bang exhibits and Disneyesque holograms that keep the kids agog.

Sleeping

★Inn at 835 B&B $$
(217-523-4466; www.innat835.com; 835 S 2nd St; r $135-205;) This historic arts-and-crafts-style luxury apartment building from 1908 offers 11 rooms of the four-poster bed, claw-foot bathtub variety (along with two additional abodes in the adjacent Bell House). You're spoiled with nightly wine and cheese, and fresh-baked cookies delivered to your room.

Drinking & Nightlife

★Obed & Isaac's MICROBREWERY
(217-670-0627; www.obedandisaacs.com; 500 S 6th St; 11am-11:30pm) Occupying a rambling, 150-year-old mansion by Abe Lincoln's home, Obed & Isaac's offers a maze of sunny rooms to drink its wildly changing menu of ales and stouts brewed onsite. Flights let you sample freely, while the menu of elevated bar food helps soak up the alcohol.

An outdoor bar, patio and bocce courts await in summer.

Information

Springfield Visitors Center (217-789-2360; www.visitspringfieldillinois.com; 1 S Old State Capitol Plaza; 9am-5pm Mon-Fri) Produces a useful visitors' guide. The location – inside the Lincoln–Herndon Law Offices – is where Abraham Lincoln practiced law.

Getting There & Away

The downtown **Amtrak station** (800-872-7245; www.amtrak.com; 100 N 3rd St) has daily trains to/from St Louis (two hours) and Chicago (3½ hours). I-55 is the busy interstate route to Springfield. Route 66 also dawdles into town.

ROUTE 66: GET YOUR KICKS IN ILLINOIS

America's 'Mother Road' kicks off in Chicago on Adams St, just west of Michigan Ave. Before embarking, fuel up at Lou Mitchell's (p540) near Union Station. After all, it's 300 miles from here to the Missouri state line.

Sadly, most of the original Route 66 has been superseded by I-55 in Illinois, though the old road still exists in scattered sections often paralleling the interstate. Keep an eye out for brown 'Historic Route 66' signs, which pop up at crucial junctions to mark the way. Top stops include the following:

Gemini Giant (810 E Baltimore St, Wilmington) The first must-see rises from the cornfields 60 miles south of Chicago in Wilmington. Here the Gemini Giant – a 28ft fiberglass spaceman holding a rocket – stands guard outside the Launching Pad Drive In and makes a terrific photo op. To reach it, leave I-55 at exit 241, and follow Hwy 44 south a short distance to Hwy 53, which rolls into town.

Funks Grove (309-874-3360; www.funksmaplesirup.com; 5257 Old Rte 66, Shirley; 9am-5pm Mon-Sat, from 1pm Sun) FREE Drive 90 miles onward to see Funk's pretty, 19th-century maple-sirup farm (yes, that's sirup with an 'i'). It's in Shirley (exit 154 off I-55). Afterward, get on Old Route 66 – a frontage road that parallels the interstate here – and in 10 miles you'll reach...

Palms Grill Cafe (217-648-2233; www.thepalmsgrillcafe.com; 110 SW Arch St, Atlanta; mains $5-11; 10am-2pm Wed-Fri, to 3pm Sat & Sun) Pull up a chair at this diner in the throwback hamlet of Atlanta, where thick slabs of gooseberry, chocolate cream and other retro pies tempt from the glass case. Then walk across the street to snap a photo with Tall Paul, a sky-high statue of Paul Bunyan clutching a hot dog.

Cozy Dog Drive In (217-525-1992; www.cozydogdrivein.com; 2935 S 6th St; mains $2-6; 8am-8pm Mon-Sat) It's in Springfield, 50 miles down the road from Palms Grill, and it's where the cornmeal-battered, fried hot dog on a stick was born.

Ariston Cafe (217-324-2023; www.ariston-cafe.com; 413 N Old Route 66, Litchfield; mains $6-29; 11am-8pm Tue-Thu, to 9pm Fri & Sat, to 8pm Sun) Further south, a good section of Old Route 66 parallels I-55 through Litchfield, where you can fork into chicken fried steak and red velvet cake while chatting up locals at this 1924 restaurant.

Old Chain of Rocks Bridge (10820 Riverview Dr; 9am-sunset) Before driving into Missouri, detour off I-270 at exit 3. Follow Hwy 3 (aka Lewis and Clark Blvd) south, turn right at the first stoplight and drive west to the 1929 bridge. Open only to pedestrians and cyclists these days, the mile-long span over the Mississippi River has a 22-degree angled bend (the cause of many a crash, hence the ban on cars).

For more information, visit the Route 66 Association of Illinois (www.il66assoc.org) or Illinois Route 66 Scenic Byway (www.illinoisroute66.org). Detailed driving directions are at www.historic66.com/illinois.

Southern Illinois

Southern Illinois looks wildly different from the rest of the state, with rivers and rugged green hills dominating the landscape. The Mississippi River forms the western boundary, and alongside it the Great River Road unfolds. The water-hugging byway (actually a series of roads) curls by bluff-strewn scenery and forgotten towns with real-deal Main Streets. One of the knockout stretches is Hwy 100 between Grafton and Alton (near St Louis). As you slip under wind-beaten cliffs, keep an eye out for the turnoff to Elsah, a hidden hamlet of 19th-century stone cottages, wood buggy shops and farmhouses. To the south, Lewis and Clark's launch site, a prehistoric World Heritage Site and a lonely hilltop fort appear.

Inland and south, the population thins and the forested Shawnee Hills rise up, looking a lot like mini mountains. Some surprises hide around here, including an eerie swamp and a fantastic destination brewery.

Sights & Activities

Union County, near the state's southern tip, has wineries and orchards. Sample the wares on the 35-mile **Shawnee Hills Wine Trail** (www.shawneewinetrail.com), which connects 11 vineyards.

Cahokia Mounds State Historic Site HISTORIC SITE

(☎618-346-5160; www.cahokiamounds.org; Collinsville Rd, Collinsville; suggested donation adult/child $7/2; ⊙grounds 8am-dusk, visitor center 9am-5pm Wed-Sun) A surprise awaits near Collinsville, 8 miles east of East St Louis: classified as a Unesco World Heritage Site, with the likes of Stonehenge and the Egyptian pyramids, is Cahokia Mounds State Historic Site. Cahokia protects the remnants of North America's largest prehistoric city (20,000 people, with suburbs), dating from 1200 CE.

Cypress Creek National Wildlife Refuge WILDLIFE RESERVE

(☎618-634-2231; www.fws.gov/refuge/cypress_creek; Ullin) FREE You certainly don't expect to find a Southern-style swampland, complete with moss-draped cypress trees and croaking bullfrogs in Illinois. But it's here, at Cypress Creek National Wildlife Refuge. Check it out from the **Bellrose Viewing Platform** off Cache Chapel Rd. Or head to Section 8 Woods and take a short stroll on the boardwalk for a taste of the waterlogged, primeval landscape; it's near the **Cache River Wetlands Center** (☎618-657-2064; www.friendsofthecache.org; 8885 Hwy 37, Cypress; ⊙9am-4pm Wed-Sun), which also has hiking and canoeing information.

Eating & Drinking

★Firefly Grill AMERICAN $$

(☎217-342-2002; www.ffgrill.com; 1810 Ave of Mid-America, Effingham; mains $10-55; ⊙11am-9pm Mon-Thu, to 10pm Fri & Sat, 10am-8pm Sun; 📶) This fiercely sustainable, farm-to-fork destination restaurant in Effingham (of all places!) is arguably Illinois' top gastronomic haven outside of Chicago. Inside a beautiful reclaimed wooded barn, chef Niall Campbell II cooks up his proudly local creations sourced from artisan farmers, foragers and fisherman, with stunning results.

Scratch Brewing MICROBREWERY

(☎618-426-1415; www.scratchbeer.com; 264 Thompson Rd, Ava; ⊙4-10pm Fri, from noon Sat, noon-8pm Sun; 📶) You'll find this farmhouse brewery hidden away amid horse- and sheep-grazing pastures just 5 miles outside Shawnee National Forest in Ava. Twigs, bark, berries and herbs from the farm are thrown into their foraged wild ales and sours (goblets and snifters from $5), often aged in their own split-out oak trees from the property. File under: travel-worthy beer nirvana.

ℹ Getting There & Away

You'll need to drive to reach the area's far-flung sights. I-57 is the main interstate through the heart of the region. The Great River Road dawdles along the water to the west. St Louis is the nearest transportation hub.

INDIANA

The state revs up around the Indy 500 race, but otherwise it's about slow-paced pleasures in corn-stubbled Indiana: pie-eating in Amish Country, meditating in Bloomington's Tibetan temples and admiring the big architecture in small Columbus. The northwest has moody sand dunes to climb, while the south has caves to explore and rivers to canoe. Spooky labyrinths, bluegrass music shrines and a famed, lipstick-kissed gravestone also make appearances in the state.

For the record, folks have called Indianans 'Hoosiers' since the 1830s, but the word's origin is unknown. One theory is that early settlers knocking on a door were met with 'Who's here?' which soon became 'Hoosier.' It's certainly something to discuss with locals, perhaps over a traditional pork tenderloin sandwich.

Fun fact: Indiana is called 'the mother of vice presidents' for the six veeps it has spawned.

ℹ Information

Indiana Highway Conditions (https://indot.carsprogram.org)

Indiana State Park Information (☎866-622-6746; www.indianastateparks.reserveamerica.com) Park entry costs $2 per day by foot or bicycle, $7 to $12 by vehicle. Campsites cost $12 to $44; reservations accepted.

Indiana Tourism (www.visitindiana.com)

Indianapolis

Clean-cut Indy is the state capital and a perfectly pleasant place to ogle **race cars** (www.indycarfactory.com; 1201 W Main St; adult/child $10/5; ⊙10am-5pm Wed-Sat) and take a spin around the renowned speedway. The art museum and **White River State Park** (☎317-233-2434; www.whiteriverstatepark.org; 801 W Washington St; ⏰park 5am-11pm, vistors center 10am-5pm Mon-Sat, from noon Sun) have their merits, as do the Mass Ave and Broad Ripple hoods for eating and drinking. And fans of author Kurt Vonnegut are in for a treat. A swell walking and biking trail connects it all.

Sights & Activities

★Children's Museum of Indianapolis MUSEUM
(☎317-334-4000; www.childrensmuseum.org; 3000 N Meridian St; $5-35; ⏰10am-5pm, closed Mon mid-Sep–Feb;) It's the world's largest kids' museum, sprawled over five floors holding incredible exhibitions on dinosaurs, space stations and so much more. The museum is centered around a stunning 43ft sculpture by Dale Chihuly that teaches tykes to blow glass (virtually!); and the fantastic 7.5-acre Sports Legends Experience is the outdoor playground of your dreams, with numerous fields and courts dedicated to all major sports. Within the context of children's museums, this place is world-class.

★Indianapolis Motor Speedway MUSEUM
(☎317-492-6784; www.indianapolismotorspeedway.com; 4790 W 16th St; adult/child $10/8; ⏰9am-5pm Mar-Oct, 10am-4pm Nov-Feb) The Speedway, home of the Indianapolis 500 motor race, is Indy's super-sight. The Speedway Museum features some 75 racing cars (including former winners) and a 500lb Tiffany trophy. Limited availability golf-cart tours of the grounds and track ($50) are available from March to October (OK, you're not exactly burning rubber in a golf cart, but it's still fun to pretend while you take a lap!).

Newfields MUSEUM, GARDENS
(☎317-920-2660; www.discovernewfields.org; 4000 Michigan Rd; adult/child $18/10; ⏰11am-5pm Tue-Sat, to 9pm Thu, noon-5pm Sun) The 152-acre Newfields campus houses the **Indianapolis Museum of Art**, home to a terrific collection of European art (especially Turner and post-Impressionists), African tribal art, South Pacific art, Chinese works, Robert Indiana's original pop-art Love sculpture and the largest gallery dedicated to contemporary and modern design in the US.

Kurt Vonnegut Museum & Library MUSEUM
(☎317-423-0391; www.vonnegutlibrary.org; 543 Indiana Ave; ⏰11am-6pm Mon, Tue, Thu & Fri, noon-5pm Sat & Sun) FREE Author Kurt Vonnegut was born and raised in Indy, and this humble museum pays homage with displays including his Pall Mall cigarettes, droll drawings and rejection letters from publishers. The museum also replicates his office, complete with a blue Coronamatic typewriter.

You're welcome to sit at the desk and type Kurt a note; the museum tweets the musings.

Monon Trail OUTDOORS
(www.bikethemonon.com; ⏰24hr) This cycling and walking trail (no motorized vehicles allowed) plies through some of Indy's coolest districts along a 26-mile former rail path that stretches from downtown (connecting with the **Cultural Trail** (www.indyculturaltrail.org; 132 W Walnut St) at 10th and Lewis Sts) through hip Broad Ripple; Carmel, a tony North Indy suburb; and eventually on to Sheridan in central Indiana, passing bars, breweries, restaurants and attractions.

Sleeping

Indy Hostel HOSTEL $
(☎317-727-1696; www.indyhostel.us; 4903 Winthrop Ave; dm/d from $32/85, d without bath $65;) This fun hostel was completely revamped in 2019 after a drunk driver plowed through the living room. A hip and friendly couple manage the two houses, offering a six-bed female dorm, a 12-bed mixed dorm and five private rooms, as well as a new dining room, a design-forward lounge and a kitchen island.

A summer concert series draws eclectic crowds.

★Hotel Broad Ripple BOUTIQUE HOTEL $$
(☎317-787-2665; www.hotelbroadripple.com; 6520 E Westfield Blvd; d $165-250;) This Scandinavian-accented boutique hotel (the owner has Norwegian roots) is a cozy getaway in hip Broad Ripple, offering 13 spacious rooms right along the Monon Trail. A woodsy patio leads to a small bar and lounge, and modern rooms (most with outdoor decks): our

LOCAL KNOWLEDGE

GRAY BROTHERS CAFETERIA

Cafeterias are an Indiana tradition, but most have disappeared – except for **Gray Brothers Cafeteria** (www.graybroscafe.com; 555 S Indiana St, Mooresville; meals $7-10; ⌚11am-8:30pm). Enter the time-warped dining room, grab a blue tray and behold a corridor of food that seems to stretch the length of a football field. Stack on plates of pan-fried chicken, meatloaf, mac 'n' cheese and sugar cream pie, then fork in with abandon.

favorites are numbers 3, 4, 7 and 8 facing the trail.

★Ironworks Hotel BOUTIQUE HOTEL $$
(☎463-221-2200; www.ironworkshotel.com; 2721 E 86th St; d from $189; P ❄ 📶) With design touches forged from industrial parts from an abandoned Wisconsin iron foundry, this relative newcomer to Indy is a boutique gamechanger. The lobby is an Industrial Age–chic jawdropper highlighted by a massive American flag of interconnecting machinery parts by artist Jim Spelman. Steel girders, reclaimed barnwood and worn leather feature throughout, including in the 120 rooms.

Eating

★Milktooth BREAKFAST $$
(www.milktoothindy.com; 534 Virginia Ave; mains $4-17; ⌚7am-3pm; 📶) Breakfast lovers of the world unite at artsy Milktooth, a can't-miss morning hot spot set in a tchotchke-peppered garage. In 2015, Jonathan Brooks was *Food & Wine* magazine's first ever chef to win Best New Chef without serving dinner. Wondrous farm-to-fork stunners include the sourdough pearl sugar waffle with burnt honeycomb candy, parmesan, whipped citrus honey butter and raw honey.

★Tinker Street AMERICAN $$
(☎317-925-5000; www.tinkerstreetindy.com; 402 E 16th St; small plates $8-20, mains $14-28; ⌚5-10pm Tue-Sat; 🖉) Fork into seasonal dishes such as Indiana mushroom stroganoff with pappardelle, sherry, crème fraîche and parsley pistou or an incredible pork belly with housemade kimchi and sorghum-tamari glaze. Vegetarian and gluten-free options are plentiful. The industrial-meets-rustic-wood decor is just right for romantics, while the year-round patio is more casual.

Tinker Street is located in leafy Old Northside just north of downtown.

★St Elmo's STEAK $$$
(☎317-635-0636; www.stelmos.com; 127 S Illinois St; steaks $43-81; ⌚4-11pm Mon-Fri, from 3pm Sat, 4-10pm Sun; 📶) This nearly 120-year-old carnivore haunt is Indy's best – and one of its only – independent steakhouses. It receives consistent accolades for service, romance and fine dining, but it's really about woofing down the legendary shrimp cocktail ($16) and top-quality slabs of perfectly grilled beef, rubbing elbows with Colt and Pacer elite in the classic American dining room as you do.

Drinking & Nightlife

★Sun King Brewery BREWERY
(www.sunkingbrewing.com; 135 N College Ave; ⌚10am-9pm Mon-Wed, to 10pm Thu & Fri, 11am-10pm Sat, 11am-8pm Sun, reduced hours winter; 📶) You never know what'll be flowing at Sun King's unvarnished downtown taproom. Indy's young and hip pile in to find out, swilling brews from a cocoa-y Baltic porter to juice IPAs and imperial stouts. Flights (six 3oz samples) cost $8. Fridays are packed for cheap growler fills. The outdoor patio hops in summer.

All tips are given to a monthly changing charity.

Slippery Noodle Inn BAR
(www.slipperynoodle.com; 372 S Meridian St; ⌚11am-3am Mon-Fri, from noon Sat, 4pm-1am Sun) Downtown's Slippery Noodle Inn is the oldest bar in the state (slinging drinks since 1850), and has seen action as a brothel, a slaughterhouse, a gangster hangout and an Underground Railroad station; currently, it's one of the best blues clubs in the country.

There's live music nightly here; and it's cheap.

Entertainment

Chatterbox Jazz Club LIVE MUSIC
(https://chatterboxjazz.com; 435 Massachusetts Ave; ⌚4pm-midnight Mon-Thu, to 1:30am Fri-Sun) This historic bar and its grungy interior is one of Indy's best for live jazz and was one of the anchors of Mass Ave's rejuvenation.

Bankers Life Fieldhouse BASKETBALL
(☎317-917-2727; www.bankerslifefieldhouse.com; 125 S Pennsylvania St) Basketball is huge in Indiana, and Bankers Life Fieldhouse is ground zero, where the NBA's Pacers make it happen.

Lucas Oil Stadium FOOTBALL
(☎317-262-8600; www.lucasoilstadium.com; 500 S Capitol Ave) Where the NFL's Colts play football under a huge retractable roof. Tours of the stadium are available at 11am, 1pm and 3pm Monday through Friday ($10 to $15).

Information

Indianapolis has no official visitors center, but there is a a welcome center at White River State Park (p553) and a welcome desk with visitor information inside the **Artsgarden** (the glass structure over West Washington St downtown).

Indianapolis Convention & Visitors Bureau (www.visitindy.com) Download a free city guide and print out coupons for attractions and tours from the website.

Indianapolis Star (www.indystar.com) The city's daily newspaper.

Indy Rainbow Chamber (www.gayindynow.com) Provides info for gay and lesbian visitors.

Nuvo (www.nuvo.net) Free, weekly alternative paper with the arts and music lowdown.

Getting There & Around

The fancy **Indianapolis International Airport** (IND; ☎317-487-7243; www.indianapolisairport.com; 7800 Col H Weir Cook Memorial Dr) is 16 miles southwest of town. The Washington bus (8) runs between the airport and downtown ($1.75, 50 minutes); the **Go Green Airport Shuttle** (www.goexpresstravel.com/indy_express) does it quicker ($12, 20 minutes). An off-peak UberX is around $20 to $22.

Greyhound shares **Union Station** (☎800-872-7245; 350 S Illinois St) with Amtrak. Buses go frequently to Cincinnati (2½ hours) and Chicago (3½ hours). **Megabus** (www.megabus.com/us; cnr N Delaware & E Market Sts) is often cheaper. Amtrak travels these routes but takes almost twice as long.

IndyGo (www.indygo.net) runs the local buses. The fare is $1.75 (a one-day pass is $4). Bus 17 goes to Broad Ripple. Service is minimal during weekends. It's also in charge of Indy's new light-rail Red Line, which connects Broad Ripple with the University of Indianapolis.

Pacers Bikeshare (www.pacersbikeshare.org) has 250 bikes at 26 stations along the Cultural Trail downtown. A 24-hour pass costs $8, and additional charges apply for trips longer than 30 minutes.

Central Indiana

Indy Car racing is the world-recognizable draw to Indiana's Midwestern heartland, but a wealth of museums, craft breweries and James Dean remembrances all furrow into the farmland around here, where countryside basketball hoops are as as common as corn stalks.

Fairmount

Pocket-sized Fairmount is but a few streets surrounded by farmland, but it's on the international map as the hometown of 1950s actor James Dean, one of the original icons of cool (he was born 10.5 miles north in Marion), as well as *Garfield* creator Jim Davis. You may also recognize it from Morrissey's video for his 1988 debut solo single, 'Suedehead.'

Sights

Fairmount Historical Museum MUSEUM
(www.jamesdeanartifacts.com; 203 E Washington St; by donation; ⏲11am-5pm Mon, Wed & Fri-Sun May-Oct) FREE Fans of actor James Dean should head directly here to see the Hollywood icon's bongo drums and 1955 Triumph Trophy 500, among other artifacts.

James Dean Gallery MUSEUM
(☎765-948-3326; www.jamesdeangallery.com; 425 N Main St; ⏲9am-6pm) FREE The privately owned James Dean Gallery has several rooms of memorabilia (bronze busts, photos, clocks, Dean's high-school yearbooks) in an old Victorian home downtown. The owners are a font of local information and are more focused on post-death international collector's items and knickknacks.

Getting There & Away

Fairmount is 70 miles northeast from Indianapolis, the closest transportation hub. I-69 passes the town to the east.

Southern Indiana

The pretty hills, caves, bluegrass, Tibetan temples, architectural hot spots and utopian history of Southern Indiana mark it as a completely different region from the rest of the state. The farmland of the north begins to yield here to rolling hills and winding rivers that cultivate a more diverse ethos found in places from hip and liberal Bloomington to artist-driven Nashville and architecturally magnificent Columbus.

Bloomington

Lively and lovely, limestone-clad and cycling-mad, Bloomington is the home of Indiana University. The town centers on Courthouse Sq, surrounded by restaurants, bars and bookshops. Nearly everything is walkable. Also, perhaps surprisingly, there's a significant Tibetan community here too. The Dalai Lama's brother came to teach at IU in the 1960s, and Tibetan temples, monasteries and culture followed.

Sights

★Indiana University UNIVERSITY
(☎812-856-4648; www.iu.edu; 107 S Indiana Ave) Indiana University (*not* University of Indiana!) routinely ranks with the cream of the crop of America's most beautiful college campuses. Founded in 1820 and forged from locally quarried Indiana Limestone, the grounds feature cycling and walking trails, alongside numerous sculptures and historic buildings, including Old Crescent, which is listed on the National Register of Historic Places.

Tibetan Mongolian Buddhist Cultural Center BUDDHIST SITE
(☎812-336-6807; www.tmbcc.org; 3655 Snoddy Rd; ⏰sunrise-sunset) FREE Founded by the Dalai Lama's brother, this colorful, prayer-flag-covered cultural building and its traditional stupas are worth a look. A gift shop sells traditional Tibetan items, and meditation sessions open to the public take place Wednesdays and Thursday at 6pm. Check the website for other activities.

Eating & Drinking

★Cardinal Spirits AMERICAN $$
(☎812-202-6789; www.cardinalspirits.com; 922 S Morton St; mains $17-20; ⏰4-10pm Mon-Thu, noon-midnight Fri, 10am-midnight Sat, 10am-9pm Sun; 📶) Bloomington's only craft distillery makes fantastic spirits with local botanicals, but their equally interesting, seasonally changing food menu is one of the town's most innovative. Chef Dean Wirkerman sowed his culinary oats in Japan and Italy, and his menu is designed to instill feelings as well as flavors. Think porchetta benedicts for brunch, maitake mushroom and fontina cheeseburgers for dinner.

Wood Shop MICROBREWERY
(www.uplandbeer.com/locations/woodshop; 350 W 11th St; ⏰4-9pm Thu & Fri, 1-9pm Sat & Sun; 📶) Leave the more mainstream Upland Brewing Co next door to casual hopheads – it's here at Upland's all-sours brewery that the dank and funk flows among near-3000-gallon oak aging barrels.

Ten taps are devoted to sours and wild ales (collaborations with Denmark's Mikkeller and Tennessee's Blackberry Farm are not uncommon) and another 10 from Upland next door.

Information

Bloomington Visitors Center (☎812-334-8900; www.visitbloomington.com; 2855 N Walnut St; ⏰8:30am-5pm Mon-Fri, 10am-3pm Sat)

Getting There & Away

Indianapolis, 50 miles northeast, has the closest airport. Go Express Travel (www.goexpresstravel.com) runs a shuttle bus to/from the airport several times daily; it costs $23 one way. I-69 and Hwy 46 are the main roads to Bloomington.

Nashville

Nashville is the jumping-off point for **Brown County State Park** (☎812-988-6406; www.in.gov/dnr; 1801 Hwy 46 E; per car $7-9), known as the Little Smoky Mountains for its steep wooded hills and fog-cloaked ravines. Gentrified and antique-filled, the 19th-century town founded in 1872 as a pioneer artists colony is now a bustling tourist center. Nashville's bucolic landscapes – all rolling hills, pastures and picket fences, log cabins and country corrals – are busiest in fall when visitors pour in to see the area's leafy oak, hickory and birch trees burst into color.

Sleeping & Eating

Robinwood Inn CABIN $$
(☎812-988-7094; www.robinwoodinn.com; 914 Highland Ave; cabins $175-250; P ❄ 📶 🐾) Idyllically set in the woods just far enough outside Nashville to feel isolated, these wonderful one- and two-bedroom cabins feel like they're half a world away: woodsy and rustic on one hand, but wonderfully appointed and modern on another. You'll want for nothin', with various configurations boasting fireplaces, kitchens and/or vintage waterfall showers. Did we mention outdoor hot tubs?

★**Story Inn** GASTRONOMY $$$
(☎812-988-2273; www.storyinn.com; 6404 S State Rd 135, Story; mains $26-32; ⏰9am-2:30pm & 5-8pm Wed & Thu, to 9pm Fri, 8am-2:30pm & 5-9pm Sat, 8am-2:30pm & 5-8pm Sun; 📶) This former general store dating to 1851 (tin roof and metal facade still intact!) drips with countrified rustic charm, beckoning foodies for culinary getaways in the one-horse, once-abandoned town of Story 12 miles south of Nashville. Pair vintages from the *Wine Spectator*–awarded wine list with elevated Midwestern staples such as corned beef and cabbage with Smoking Goose wagyu brisket.

Information

Brown County Visitors Center (☎812-988-7303; www.browncounty.com; 211 S Van Buren St; ⏰9am-5pm Mon-Fri, from 10am Sat; 📶) Staffed facility with maps and coupons.

Getting There & Away

Nashville lies midway between Bloomington and Columbus on Hwy 46. Indianapolis, 60 miles north, is the closest big city and transportation center. Free parking is scarce in town – lots charge $5.

Columbus

When you think of the USA's great architectural cities – Chicago, New York, Washington, DC – Columbus, IN, doesn't quite leap to mind, but it should. The city is a remarkable gallery of physical design. Since the 1940s, Columbus and its leading corporation, Fortune 500 engineering company Cummins, have commissioned some of the world's best architects, including Eero Saarinen, Richard Meier and IM Pei, to create both public and private buildings.

And with the 2017 critically acclaimed film *Columbus* (a love letter to the town), folks outside of the architectural scope are now taking notice.

Sights

Architecture-gaping is the big attraction. More than 70 notable buildings and pieces of public art are spread over a wide area (car required), but about 15 diverse architectural standouts can be seen on foot downtown. The visitors center provides self-guided tour maps online and on-site. **Bus tours** (☎812-378-2622; www.columbus.in.us; 506 5th St; adult/student $25/20; ⏰10am Tue-Fri, 10am & 2pm Sat, 2:30pm Sun Apr-Nov, 10pm Fri & Sat Dec-Mar) also depart from the city center.

Miller House & Garden ARCHITECTURE
(www.discovernewfields.org/do-and-see/places-to-go/miller-house-and-garden; 2860 Washington St; $25; ⏰12:45pm & 2:45pm Tue-Sat Apr-Nov, 12:45pm & 2:45pm Fri & Sat Dec & Mar, closed Jan & Feb) A dream team is responsible for the design of the former private home of hero industrialist, architectural visionary and former Cummins President/Chairman J Irwin Miller: architect Eero Saarinen, landscape architect Dan Kiley and interior designer Alexander Girard combined their keen eyes for modernism in 1953 and churned out one of the most important – and stunning – mid-century modern residences in the US.

Sleeping & Eating

Inn at Irwin Gardens B&B $$
(☎812-376-3663; www.irwingardens.com; 608 5th St; d $205-260; P❄📶) A mighty antidote to Columbus' modernist flare, this 1864 Victorian monolith with Edwardian furnishings and Italianate gardens (inspired by Pompeii) sits steps from the architectural soul of town, but in stark contrast to its mid-century modern ethos. Chock-full of vintage furniture (some items favor form over function, but that hardly matters) and drowning in extraordinary detail, these are historic sleeps.

★**Henry Social Club** AMERICAN $$
(☎812-799-1371; www.henrysocialclub.com; 423 Washington St; mains $16-44; ⏰5-9pm Tue-Sat; 📶) Punching above its culinary class by Columbus standards, HSC's seasonally changing menu satiates local foodies (and visiting architects) and is the best bar in town for a proper cocktail (from $11). The filet and roasted cod are surefire choices, but don't discount the barley-and-wild-rice bowl with butternut-squash puree – it's a vegetarian stunner!

Information

Columbus Visitors Center (☎812-378-2622; www.columbus.in.us; 506 5th St; ⏰9am-5pm Mon-Sat, closed Sun Dec-Apr) is the place to pick up a self-guided tour map ($3) or join a two-hour bus tour to see the city's renowned architecture.

Getting There & Away

I-65 is the main highway that skirts the city. The closest airports are in Indianapolis (46 miles north) and Louisville (73 miles south). Alas, no shuttle buses connect Columbus to these cities.

Ohio River

The Ohio River marks the state's southern border. Hwys 56, 156, 62 and 66, known collectively as the Ohio River Scenic Byway, wind through a lush and hilly landscape covering 300 miles along the churning waterway. Sweet stops en route include Madison, a beautifully preserved river settlement from the mid-19th century whose genteel architecture counts as the largest contiguous National Historic Landmark District in the United States; food-focused New Albany and artsy Jeffersonville, which both hug the river across from Louisville; **Marengo Cave** (☎812-365-2705; www.marengocave.com; 400 E State Rd 64, Marengo; tours adult/child from $18/10; ⏲9am-6pm Jun-Aug, to 5pm Sep-May), with its eye-popping underground formations; and former US president Abraham Lincoln's **childhood home** (☎812-937-4541; www.nps.gov/libo; 3027 E South St, Lincoln City; ⏲8am-3pm) FREE near Dale. Canoeing, farm stays and worthwhile breweries pop up in between.

Sleeping & Eating

★Pepin Mansion B&B $$
(☎812-725-9186; www.thepepinmansion.com; 1003 E Main St, New Albany; d from $145; P ❄ ☜) Standing supremely along New Albany's historical Mansion Row, this easy-on-the-eyes 1851 Italianate abode features ornate hand-painted ceilings, original hardwood flooring and gas chandeliers among other period details. The four antique-filled but modern rooms (TVs by Roku, for example) are wildly different but equally spectacular. Our favorite, the Culbertson Suite, has a claw-foot bathtub.

Exchange AMERICAN $$
(☎812-948-6501; www.exchangeforfood.com; 118 W Main St, New Albany; mains $11-27; ⏲11am-10pm Mon-Thu, to 11pm Fri & Sat, 4-8pm Sun; ☜) All things considered, New Albany's best restaurant is a one-stop evening out. Sky-high exposed-brick walls and and true-to-their-name Big Ass Fans dominate the industrial-hip ambience. Foodwise, goat's-cheese fritters with bacon and date aioli and smoked honey woo diners to start, then spring for blueberry-brie grilled cheese, an awesome black-bean burger or far more elevated pub grub.

Information

Check out **Ohio River Scenic Byway** (www.ohioriverbyway.com) for Byway-specific info; you'll find visitors centers in **Jeffersonville** (☎812-280-5566; www.gosoin.com; 305 Southern Indiana Ave; ⏲10am-5pm Mon-Sat, from noon Sun) and **Madison** (☎812-265-2956; www.visitmadison.org; 601 W First St; ⏲9am-5pm Mon-Fri, to 4pm Sat, 11am-4pm Sun Apr–mid-Dec, 9am-5pm Mon-Fri, 10am-3pm Sat, 11am-3pm Sun mid-Dec–Mar).

Getting There & Away

Louisville and Cincinnati are the closest big-city transportation hubs. Louisville International Airport (p393) sits 8 and 13 miles south of Jeffersonville and New Albany, respectively.

In addition to the Ohio River Scenic Byway's gaggle of roads, I-64 cuts across the region. For distance reference, Madison is about 75 miles east of Marengo Cave, which is about 55 miles east of the Lincoln Boyhood National Memorial.

Northern Indiana

While much of Northern Indiana is industrial, unexpected treats rise from the flatland, too. Wild sand dunes (at one of America's newest national parks), classic cars, Amish pies and the infamous Dark Lord brewer are all within range.

Indiana Dunes

In addition to being home to one of America's newest national parks, sunny beaches, rustling grasses and woodsy campgrounds are the Indiana Dunes' claim to fame. The area is hugely popular on summer days with sunbathers from Chicago and towns throughout Northern Indiana. In addition to its beaches, the area is noted for its plant variety (more than 1100 species, including everything from cacti to pine trees, sprout here) and birds (370 species). Sweet hiking trails meander up the dunes and through the woodlands.

The Dunes can be visited on a day trip from Chicago. If you're looking to spend the night, Chesterton (the closest; popular for trainspotting) and Valparaiso (the most charming; food and drink hotbed) are both worthwhile small-town options.

INDIANA AMISH COUNTRY

The area around Shipshewana and Middlebury is the USA's third-largest Amish community. Horses and buggies clip-clop by, and long-bearded men hand-plow the tidy fields. It's not far off the interstate, but it's a whole different world.

Pick a back road between the two towns and head down it. Often you'll see families selling beeswax candles, quilts and fresh produce on their porch, which beats the often-touristy shops and restaurants on the main roads. Note that most places close on Sunday.

The Indiana Toll Rd (I-80/90) passes the region to the north. Hwy 20 comes through the area to the south, and connects Middlebury and Shipshewana (which are about 7 miles apart).

Sights & Activities

Indiana Dunes National Park NATIONAL PARK
(☎219-926-7561; www.nps.gov/indu; 1100 N Mineral Springs Rd, Porter; ⏲6am-11pm) FREE The Dunes, which became the USA's 61st national park in 2019, stretch along 15 miles of Lake Michigan shoreline. Swimming is allowed anywhere along the shore. A short walk away from the beaches, several hiking paths crisscross the dunes and woodlands. The best are the Bailly-Chellberg Trail (2.5 miles) that winds by a still-operating 1870s farm, and the Heron Rookery Trail (2 miles), where blue herons flock (though there's no actual rookery) and native wildflowers bloom.

Pedal Power CYCLING
(☎219-921-3085; www.pedalpowerrentals.com; 1215 Hwy 49; per hr/day $9/36; ⏲9am-7pm Sat & Sun late May-early Oct) This outfitter rents bicycles (including a helmet, a lock and a map) from the cul-de-sac next to the Indiana Dunes Visitor Center. From here, the 2-mile Dunes-Kankakee Trail runs to **Indiana Dunes State Park** (☎219-926-1952; www.in.gov/dnr/parklake; Chesterton; ⏲7am-11pm). Pedal Power also offers tours, such as the Beach Sunset Tour ($15 per person; Saturdays); check the website for times.

Sleeping & Eating

Riley's Railhouse B&B $
(☎219-395-9999; www.rileysrailhouse.com; 123 N 4th St, Chesterton; d $120-160; ❄📶) Occupying a decommissioned 1914 freight station in Chesterton, this railway-themed boutique B&B offers a beautiful, fireplace-warmed lounge with discerning recycled design touches, a bar and a massive open kitchen from which Richard's awesome breakfast emerges. Modern rooms – inside both the depot and the parked antique rail cars – are comfortably appointed with locomotive-themed art. Two big Labradoodles hold down the fort.

Octave Grill BURGERS $
(www.octavegrill.com; 105 S Calumet Rd, Chesterton; burgers $8.50-11.75; ⏲3-10pm Mon-Fri, noon-11pm Sat, noon-9pm Sun; 📶) Octave Grill's burgers made with grass-fed beef and piled high with gourmet goodness were voted best in Porter County. Indeed, they are cooked to perfection, just juicy and greasy enough, and are chased with a wonderful selection of five rotating craft beers.

Information

Indiana Dunes Visitor Center (☎219-395-1882; www.indianadunes.com; 1215 Hwy 49; ⏲8am-6pm Jun-Aug, 8:30am-4:30pm Sep-May) The best place to start a visit to the Dunes. Staff can provide beach details; a schedule of ranger-guided walks and activities; hiking, biking and birding maps; and general information on the area.

Getting There & Away

The Indiana Toll Rd (I-80/90), I-94, Hwy 12, Hwy 20 and Hwy 49 all skirt the lakeshore. Look for large brown signs on the roads that point the way in to the Dunes.

The **South Shore Line** (www.mysouthshoreline.com) commuter train also services the area on its Chicago–South Bend route. The stops at Dune Park and Beverly Shores put you about a 1½-mile walk from the beaches.

South Bend

You know how people in certain towns say, 'Football is a religion here'? They mean it in South Bend, home to the University of Notre Dame. Here 'Touchdown Jesus' lords over the 80,000-capacity stadium (it's a mural of the resurrected Christ with arms raised, though the pose bears a striking resemblance to a referee signaling a touchdown). The renowned campus – Indiana's second biggest tourist attraction after the Indianapolis Motor Speedway – is worth

OFF THE BEATEN TRACK

AUBURN

Classic-car connoisseurs should stop in Auburn, where the Cord Company produced the USA's favorite autos in the 1920s and '30s. Two remarkable car museums – **Auburn Cord Duesenberg Museum** (www.automobilemuseum.org; 1600 S Wayne St; adult/child $12.50/7.50; 9am-5pm) and the **National Automotive and Truck Museum** (www.natmus.org; 1000 Gordon Buehrig Pl; adult/child $10/5; 9am-5pm) – are conveniently lined up next door to one another. Round out your day with a trip to **Mad Anthony's Auburn Tap Room** (260-927-0500; www.madbrew.com/auburn; 114 N Main St, Auburn; 11am-11pm Mon-Thu, to midnight Fri & Sat, to 10pm Sun) for local brews and serviceable pub grub.

Auburn is about 50 miles southeast of Amish Country and about 25 miles north of Fort Wayne.

a pit stop, but South Bend is more than pigskin (football is only 12 days per year, after all).

Sights & Activities

Studebaker National Museum MUSEUM
(www.studebakermuseum.org; 201 S Chapin St; adult/child $10/6; 10am-5pm Mon-Sat, from noon Sun) Gaze at a gorgeous 1956 Packard and other classic beauties that used to be built in South Bend, where the Studebaker car company was based. The shiny vehicles, including vintage carriages and military tanks, spread over three floors. A local history museum shares the building. The entrance is on Thomas St.

Notre Dame Tours WALKING
(574-631-5726; www.nd.edu/visitors; 111 Eck Center) FREE Two-mile, 75-minute walking tours of the pretty university campus, with its two lakes, Gothic-style architecture and iconic Golden Dome atop the main building, start at the Eck Visitors Center. Tour times vary, but there's usually at least a 10am and 3pm jaunt Monday through Friday.

Sleeping & Eating

★Oliver Inn B&B $$
(574-232-4545; www.oliverinn.com; 630 W Washington St; d $140-220, carriage house $330;) This elegant salmon- and green-trimmed B&B occupies a gorgeous, Queen Anne–style home dating to 1886. Corner turrets, curved-glass bay windows, spindles and balustrades abound while the nine rooms ooze dignity and romance (we dig the Clem Studebaker for its spaciousness, hardwood floors and fireplace).

Chicago escapees Alice and Tom couldn't be more gracious hosts and your breakfast is candlelit.

Oh Mamma's on the Avenue DELI $
(www.facebook.com/OhMamma; 1202 Mishawaka Ave; sandwiches $6-10; 10am-6pm Tue-Fri, 9am-4pm Sat) This cute grocery store and deli features toasted sandwiches, heaps of cheeses from the region (including awesome house-made goat's-milk cheese), fresh-baked bread, cannoli and gelato. Staff are super-friendly and generous with samples. Eat in at the smattering of tables, or take away.

Information

Eck Visitors Center (www.tour.nd.edu/locations/eck-visitors-center; 100 Eck Center, Notre Dame; 8am-5pm Mon-Fri, noon-4pm Sat & Sun)

Getting There & Away

South Bend has a surprisingly large **airport** (574-282-4590; www.flysbn.com; 4477 Progress Dr) with flights to Chicago and Detroit among other destinations. The airport is also a station on the **South Shore Line** (www.mysouthshoreline.com) commuter train that goes to/from Chicago ($14.25 one way to Millennium Station). By car, the Indiana Toll Rd (I-80/90) and Hwy 20 are the primary routes to the city.

OHIO

Ohio has a split personality. The nation's seventh most populous state has big cities Cleveland, Cincinnati and Columbus that lead its urban charge, rolling out a spread of kicky eateries, IPA-loving breweries and one-of-a-kind museums. Northern Cleveland exudes a feisty, rock-and-roll vibe, while southern Cincinnati feels more languorous and European. Columbus is the polished art and tech hub that rises up in the middle. Meanwhile, Ohio's rural side is way off the grid, from the horse-and-buggy-filled roads of its enormous Amish community to the moonshine makers in its southeastern hills. It makes for an intriguing mash-up, with just a short drive between wildly different lifestyles. In between, the roadways lead to the world's fastest roller coasters, rocking party islands, beatnik towns, pie shops and a mist-draped national park.

Information

Ohio Highway Conditions (www.ohgo.com)
Ohio State Park Information Reservations to camp accepted; tent and RV sites cost $17 to $43, plus $8 booking fee. State parks are free to visit; some have free wi-fi.
Tourism Ohio (www.ohio.org)

Cleveland

Cleveland wears its Rust Belt badge with honor. While smoke-belching steel mills no longer rule the scene, the city still wafts an evocative industrial look. Railroad tracks, vertical lift bridges and stark warehouses pepper its shores on Lake Erie and the Cuyahoga River, only now stylish eateries, breweries and galleries fill the old factories, and bike trails have emerged along the waterways. Star attractions include the Rock and Roll Hall of Fame and Museum of Art, but the best action is in Cleveland's walkable neighborhoods. Meander around Ohio City, Tremont, Collinwood or Asiatown and you'll be among locals in the markets and corner taverns. Sit for a pint and hear about generations-deep businesses started by Slovenian grandparents, about epic sports team grudges and about how the city clawed its way back from financial and environmental ruin. Rust Belt realness is Cleveland's calling card.

Sights

★Rock and Roll Hall of Fame & Museum MUSEUM
(216-781-7625; www.rockhall.com; 1100 E 9th St; adult/child $24/16; 10am-5:30pm daily, to 9pm Wed & Sat Jun-Aug) Cleveland's top attraction is like an overstuffed attic bursting with groovy finds: Jimi Hendrix's Stratocaster, Keith Moon's platform shoes, John Lennon's Sgt Pepper suit and a 1966 piece of hate mail to the Rolling Stones from a cursive-writing Fijian. It's more than memorabilia, though. Multimedia exhibits trace the history and social context of rock music and the performers who created it.

★Cleveland Museum of Art MUSEUM
(216-421-7340; www.clevelandart.org; 11150 East Blvd; 10am-5pm Tue, Thu, Sat & Sun, to 9pm Wed & Fri) FREE Cleveland's whopping art museum houses an excellent collection of European paintings, as well as African, Asian and American art. Head to the 2nd floor for rock-star works from Impressionists, Picasso and surrealists. Interactive touchscreens are stationed throughout the galleries and provide fun ways to learn more. Download the free ArtLens app for additional content, including self-guided jaunts by theme. Free guided tours through the museum's highlights depart from the dazzling, light-drenched atrium at 1pm each day.

Great Lakes Science Center MUSEUM
(216-694-2000; www.greatscience.com; 601 Erieside Ave; adult/child $17/14; 10am-5pm Mon-Sat, from noon Sun, closed Mon Sep-May;) One of 10 museums in the country with a NASA affiliation, Great Lakes goes deep in space with rockets, moon stones and the 1973 Apollo capsule, as well as exhibits on the lakes' environmental problems.

The Flats WATERFRONT
The Flats, an old industrial zone turned nightlife hub on the Cuyahoga River, has had a checkered life. After years of neglect, it's on the upswing once again. The East Bank has a waterfront boardwalk, stylish restaurants, bars and outdoor concert pavilion. The West Bank is a bit edgier and further flung, with an old garage turned brewery-winery, a skateboard park and some vintage dive bars among its assets.

Sleeping

★Cleveland Hostel HOSTEL $
(216-394-0616; www.theclevelandhostel.com; 2090 W 25th St; dm/r from $26/68;) This hostel in Ohio City, steps from an RTA stop and the West Side Market, is fantastic. There are 15 rooms, a mix of dorms and private chambers. All have fluffy beds, fresh paint in soothing hues and nifty antique decor. Add in the sociable rooftop deck, coffee-roasting lobby cafe and free parking lot, and no wonder it's packed.

★Kimpton Schofield Hotel HOTEL $$
(216-357-3250; www.theschofieldhotel.com; 2000 E 9th St; r $180-270; P) Set in a rehabbed 1902 building downtown, the Schofield is for the cool cats in the crowd. Rooms are spacious and have funky artwork

(such as prints of toy cars), colorful clocks and art deco–inspired lamps and chairs. Amenities include free loaner bicycles, a free wine social hour each evening and free acoustic guitar loans for in-room jam sessions. Parking costs $36.

Metropolitan at the 9 HOTEL $$$
(☎216-239-1200; www.metropolitancleveland.com; 2017 E 9th St; r $199-319; P ❄ @ ☎ 🐾) Check in at the Metropolitan, an upscale Marriott-branded property, and perks include a seasonal rooftop lounge, indoor dog park, on-site theater for live performances and a subterranean cocktail lounge set in the building's old bank vaults. The 156 rooms are good-sized, each with a sitting area, 55in flat-screen TV and contemporary decor. Parking costs $36.

Eating

Top spots for hot-chef eats are E 4th St, Ohio City and Tremont. For global fare, Little Italy and Asiatown prevail. Goulash, stuffed cabbage and other Eastern European dishes are common around town, as Cleveland has the nation's largest concentration of Hungarians, Slovenes and Slovaks; **West Side Market** (www.westsidemarket.org; 1979 W 25th St; ⏲7am-4pm Mon & Wed, 7am-6pm Fri & Sat, 10am-4pm Sun) is a good place to explore the scene.

★Larder Delicatessen & Bakery DELI $
(☎216-912-8203; https://larderdb.com; 1455 W 29th St; sandwiches $9-12; ⏲10am-7pm Tue-Sat, to 2pm Sun) Set in a historic firehouse, Larder has an old-time vibe. Jars of pickled veggies line the wall, and the pantry sells everything from hickory nuts to dried beans and barley. The Beard Award–nominated chef stacks a mighty sandwich, maybe juicy fried chicken or schnitzel and apple slaw on thick-sliced bread. House-made root beer and chocolate sodas add to the goodness.

Nate's Deli MIDDLE EASTERN $
(☎216-696-7529; www.natesohiocity.com; 1923 W 25th St; mains $8-16; ⏲10am-5pm Mon-Fri, to 4pm Sat) Nate's small, unfussy dining room offers an unusual mix of Middle Eastern dishes and deli sandwiches, with choices from stuffed grape-leaf platters to reubens (corned beef, Swiss cheese and sauerkraut on rye), and crunchy falafel to chicken noodle soup made from scratch. It has been cooking in Ohio City for more than 30 years.

★Citizen Pie PIZZA $$
(☎216-860-1388; www.citizenpie.com; 2144 W 25th St; mains $14-17; ⏲11:30am-9pm Tue-Thu, to 10pm Fri & Sat, to 8pm Sun) Citizen Pie fires up Neapolitan-style pizzas using an oven straight from the motherland. Watch the pizza maker slide your meal into the fiery dome, and then skim it out 90 seconds later, cheese perfectly melted and crust perfectly browned. The smoked pepperoni is the meat to beat. The wee establishment has just a few counter seats and a smattering of tables.

Lola AMERICAN $$$
(☎216-621-5652; www.lolabistro.com; 2058 E 4th St; mains $30-45; ⏲5-10pm Sun-Thu, to 11pm Fri & Sat) Famous for his tattoos, Food Network TV appearances and multiple national awards, local boy Michael Symon put Cleveland on the foodie map with Lola. While the menu changes based on what's seasonal, expect dishes such as beef hanger steak with pickle sauce or braised lamb shank with mint and root vegetables. The glowy bar and open kitchen add a swanky vibe.

Drinking & Nightlife

Tremont is chockablock with chic bars, Ohio City with breweries. Downtown has the young, testosterone-fueled Warehouse District (around W 6th St) and the resurgent Flats. Most places stay open until 2am.

★Platform Beer Co BREWERY
(☎216-202-1386; www.platformbeer.co; 4125 Lorain Ave; ⏲3pm-midnight Mon-Thu, 3pm-1am Fri, 10am-2am Sat, 10am-10pm Sun) An all-ages, cool-cat crowd gathers around the silvery tanks in Platform's tasting room for $5 to $6 pints of innovative saisons, pale ales and more flowing from the 30 taps. When the weather warms, everyone heads out to the picnic table–dotted patio. The location at Ohio City's southern edge is a bit out of the way, but starting to see development.

Noble Beast Brewing Co MICROBREWERY
(☎216-417-8588; www.noblebeastbeer.com; 1470 Lakeside Ave; ⏲11am-11pm Sun & Tue-Thu, to 1am Fri & Sat) No wonder so many locals hang out at Noble Beast: it feels like home. Plants dangle from the ceiling. A skylight lets the sun shine in. The garage doors open in warm weather so a breeze blows through. From afternoon to evening, office workers and young urbanites hobnob at the tables

here over glasses of German-style ales and fruit beers.

★Millard Fillmore Presidential Library BAR

(☎216-481-9444; 15617 Waterloo Rd; ⏲4pm-2:30am Mon-Sat, to 12:30am Sun) Mention to pals that you're going to the Millard Fillmore Presidential Library, and you can tell they're impressed by your intellectual curiosity. Then they figure out it's a dive bar with craft beer in burgeoning Collinwood, and they're even more impressed. Fillmore was the USA's 13th president, and from New York incidentally. But that shouldn't hinder a great bar name.

Jerman's Cafe BAR

(☎216-361-8771; 3840 St Clair Ave NE; ⏲11am-midnight Mon-Sat) Jerman's is Cleveland's second-oldest bar. Slovenian immigrant John Jerman opened it in 1908, and his family still runs it. It's a terrific, old-school dive, with a pressed zinc ceiling, Indians baseball games flickering on the TVs and just a few beers on tap (usually a German lager). Friendly barkeeps and regulars are happy to share stories of the old days.

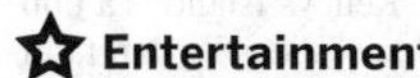

Entertainment

Check *Scene* (www.clevescene.com) and the Friday section of the local newspaper, *Plain Dealer* (www.cleveland.com), for listings.

★Happy Dog LIVE MUSIC

(☎216-651-9474; www.happydogcleveland.com; 5801 Detroit Ave; ⏲4pm-12:30am Mon-Wed, 11am-12:30am Thu & Sun, 11am-2:30am Fri & Sat) Listen to scrappy bands, DJs, storytellers or science lectures while munching on a weenie, for which you can choose from among 50 toppings, from gourmet (black truffle) to, er, less gourmet (chunky peanut butter). It's in the Gordon Sq district.

Severance Hall CLASSICAL MUSIC

(☎216-231-1111; www.clevelandorchestra.com; 11001 Euclid Ave) The acclaimed Cleveland Symphony Orchestra holds its season (August to May) at Severance Hall, a gorgeous art-deco-meets-classic building located by the University Circle museums.

Progressive Field BASEBALL

(☎216-420-4487; www.mlb.com/indians; 2401 Ontario St) The Indians (aka 'the Tribe') hit here; great sight lines make it a good park to see a game. The cheapest tickets cost $15 for standing room – and include a beer – in the rowdy District.

Rocket Mortgage Fieldhouse BASKETBALL

(☎216-420-2000; www.nba.com/cavaliers; 1 Center Ct) The Cavaliers play basketball at the Fieldhouse, which reopened in 2019 after a $185 million renovation. The revamp added a spiffy glass atrium and new public spaces. The Fieldhouse doubles as an entertainment venue for big touring acts.

WORTH A TRIP

CUYAHOGA VALLEY NATIONAL PARK

Like a great, cold snake, the Cuyahoga River worms over a forested valley, earning its Native American name of 'crooked river' (or possibly 'place of the jawbone'). Either name is evocative, and hints at the mystical beauty that Ohio's only national park engenders on a cool morning, when the mists thread the woods and all you hear is the honk of Canadian geese and the *fwup-fwup-whoosh* of a great blue heron flapping over its hunting grounds.

There was a time, early in United States history, when this was the frontier for those settlers huddled in the Eastern colonies; at the same time it was home for vast confederations of Native Americans. Today, a mere 20 miles from Cleveland and 18 miles from Akron, you can walk trails that sneak past white waterfalls and dark hollows to find the frontier still, and the traces of a great indigenous nation.

The new **Boston Mill Visitor Center** (6947 Riverview Rd; ⏲9:30am-5pm) is a good place to start your visit with helpful park rangers, interpretive displays, trail maps and info on trail closures

The park is easily accessible by car from Cleveland (20 miles) or Akron (18 miles), and lies just off of I-77.

If you'd rather go on a relaxing train ride, consider riding the rails with the **Cuyahoga Valley Scenic Railroad** (CVSR; ☎800-468-4070; www.cvsr.org; 27 Ridge St, Akron; adult $15-28, child $10-23).

Information

Cleveland Visitors Center (☎216-875-6680; 334 Euclid Ave; ⏰9am-6pm Mon-Sat) Super-friendly staff provide maps, brewery guide booklets and reservation assistance.

Cool Cleveland (www.coolcleveland.com) Arts and cultural happenings.

Destination Cleveland (www.thisiscleveland.com) Official website, chock-full for planning.

Ohio City (www.ohiocity.org) Eats and drinks in the neighborhood.

Tremont (www.experiencetremont.com) Eats, drinks and gallery hops.

Getting There & Around

Eleven miles southwest of downtown, **Cleveland Hopkins International Airport** (CLE; ☎216-265-6000; www.clevelandairport.com; 5300 Riverside Dr) is linked by the Red Line train ($2.50) that reaches the center in less than 30 minutes. A cab to downtown costs about $40. Uber and Lyft are usually a bit less.

From downtown, **Greyhound** (☎216-781-0520; www.greyhound.com; 1465 Chester Ave) offers frequent departures to Chicago ($29 to $76, 7½ hours) and New York City ($60 to $113, nine to 13 hours). **Megabus** (www.megabus.com; 2115 E 22nd St) also goes to Chicago, often for lower fares.

Amtrak (☎216-696-5115; www.amtrak.com; 200 Cleveland Memorial Shoreway) runs once daily to Chicago ($59 to $113, seven hours) and New York City ($84 to $162, 13 hours). The station has no ATM, wi-fi or lounge.

The Regional Transit Authority (www.riderta.com) operates the Red Line train that goes to both the airport and Ohio City. It also runs the HealthLine bus that motors along Euclid Ave from downtown to University Circle's museums. The fare is $2.50, or day passes are $5.50. Free trolleys also loop around downtown's core business and entertainment zones.

UH Bikes (www.uhbikes.com) is Cleveland's bike-share program, with 29 stations and 250 bikes mostly in downtown and University Circle. A 30-minute ride costs $3.50. The system is easiest to use if you download the app.

For cab service, call **Americab** (☎216-881-1111).

DON'T MISS

CEDAR POINT'S RAGING ROLLER COASTERS

One of the world's top amusement parks, **Cedar Point Amusement Park** (☎419-627-2350; www.cedarpoint.com; 1 Cedar Point Dr; adult/child $73/45; ⏰10am-10pm Jun-Aug, reduced hours May, Sep & Oct) is known for its 18 adrenaline-pumping roller coasters. Stomach-droppers include the Top Thrill Dragster, among the globe's tallest and fastest rides. It climbs 420ft into the air before plunging and whipping around at 120mph. Steel Vengeance provides 27 seconds of weightlessness, the most 'airtime' of any coaster on the planet. Meanwhile, the wing-like GateKeeper loops, corkscrews and dangles riders from the world's highest inversion.

Erie Lakeshore & Islands

In summer this good-time resort area is one of the busiest places in Ohio. Boaters come to party, daredevils come to ride roller coasters, and outdoorsy types come to bike and kayak. The season lasts from mid-May to mid-September – and then just about everything shuts down.

Kelleys Island

Peaceful and green, Kelleys Island is a popular weekend escape, especially for families. It has pretty 19th-century buildings, Native American pictographs, a good beach and glacial grooves raked through its landscape. Even its old limestone quarries are scenic.

Sights & Activities

Kelleys Islands State Park STATE PARK
(☎419-746-2546; http://parks.ohiodnr.gov/kelleysisland; Division St, Kelleys Island) FREE The park features a popular campground with 126 tent and RV sites ($17 to $39), 6 miles of hiking trails with birds flitting by and a secluded, sandy beach on the island's north side.

It's a favorite of families, especially the beach and its shallow water.

Glacial Grooves NATURAL FEATURE
(Division St, Kelleys Island; ⏰sunrise-sunset) FREE The deep scars in the limestone here – which a glacier rubbed in some 18,000 years ago – are the largest and most easily accessible grooves in the world. Look down from the walkway and stairs and behold gouges that are 400ft long, 35ft wide and up to 10ft deep.

Information

Kelleys Island Chamber of Commerce (www.kelleysislandchamber.com) Useful info on lodgings, restaurants and activities.

Getting There & Away

Kelleys Island Ferry (☎419-798-9763; www.kelleysislandferry.com; off W Main St, Marblehead) departs from the teeny village of Marblehead (one way adult/child $10/6.25, car $16). The crossing takes about 20 minutes and leaves hourly (every half-hour in summer).

Jet Express (☎800-245-1538; www.jet-express.com; 101 W Shoreline Dr) departs from Sandusky (one way adult/child $20/3, no cars); the trip takes 25 minutes. It also goes onward to Put-in-Bay on South Bass Island (one way adult/child $15/3, no cars), which takes 20 minutes. Both ferries arrive on Kelleys Island downtown (Jet Express at the foot of Division St; Kelleys Island Ferry about a half-mile east at the Seaway Marina).

Ohio Amish Country

Rural Wayne and Holmes Counties are home to the USA's largest Amish community. Visiting here is like entering a pre-industrial time warp.

Descendants of conservative Dutch-Swiss religious factions who migrated to the USA during the 18th century, the Amish continue to follow the *ordnung* (way of life), in varying degrees. Many adhere to rules prohibiting the use of electricity, telephones and motorized vehicles. They wear traditional clothing, farm the land with plow and mule, and go to church in horse-drawn buggies. Others are not so strict.

A sojourn in the region provides pleasures of a slow kind. Eat pie, buy a goat at auction, ride a horse. While parts of the bucolic area are blatantly touristy, there's always a back road to veer onto that'll take you past cow-dotted pastures and farms selling eggs, beekeeping supplies or windmill parts from their front porches. Most places are closed on Sunday.

Sights

Kidron, on Rte 52, makes a good starting point. A short distance south, **Berlin** is the area's tchotchke shop–filled core, while **Millersburg** is the region's largest town, more antique-y than Amish; US 62 connects these two 'busy' spots. To get further off the beaten path, take Rte 557 or County Rd 70, both of which twist through the countryside to little **Charm**, about 5 miles south of Berlin. **Sugarcreek**, 10 miles west, channels a slice of Switzerland with alpine-style architecture and giant cuckoo clocks.

Keep in mind the Amish typically view photographs as taboo, so don't take photos of people without permission.

> WORTH A TRIP
>
> **PELEE ISLAND**
>
> Pelee, the largest Erie island, is a ridiculously green, quiet wine-producing and bird-watching destination that belongs to Canada. The **Pelee Island Ferry** (☎800-661-2220; www.ontarioferries.com; 109 W Shoreline Dr; adult/child $13.75/6.75, per car $30) makes the 1¾-hour trip from Sandusky to Pelee, and then onward to Ontario's mainland. One-way. Check www.pelee.com for lodging and trip-planning information.

Lehman's HOMEWARES
(☎800-438-5346; www.lehmans.com; 4779 Kidron Rd, Kidron; ⊙9am-6pm Mon-Sat, to 5pm Jan-May) Lehman's is an absolute must-see. It is the Amish community's main purveyor of modern-looking products that use no electricity, housed in a 32,000-sq-ft barn. Stroll through to ogle wind-up flashlights, wood-burning stoves and hand-cranked meat grinders.

Sleeping & Eating

Inn at Honey Run INN $$$
(☎330-674-0011; www.innathoneyrun.com; 6920 County Rd 203, Millersburg; r $199-329; ❄📶) Any stress you carry eases within minutes of arriving at the inn's forested grounds. Twenty-five rooms occupy the lodge-like main building complex, while 12 'honeycomb' rooms are built right into the hillside Frank Lloyd Wright–style. All are spacious, earth-toned chambers with a cool bird feeder outside the window. Hiking trails, outdoor art installations and well-tended beehives add to the nature-loving ambience.

★Boyd & Wurthmann Restaurant AMERICAN $
(☎330-893-4000; www.boydandwurthmann.com; 4819 E Main St, Berlin; mains $7-13;

(5:30am-7:30pm Mon-Sat) Hubcap-sized pancakes, 20 pie flavors each day, fat sandwiches and Amish specialties such as country-fried steak draw locals and tourists alike. Cash only.

Information

Holmes County Chamber of Commerce (www.visitamishcountry.com)

Getting There & Around

Amish Country lies between Cleveland (80 miles north) and Columbus (100 miles southwest). I-71 and I-77 flank the area to the west and east, respectively, but you'll have to exit and drive along a series of narrow, winding back roads to reach the little towns.

Columbus

Ohio's capital city (and largest city) isn't going to wow you with a bunch of razzle-dazzle. It doesn't flaunt mega-sights, scenic splendor or wild quirks. But Columbus makes up for it with unexpected food and arts scenes. Better yet, Columbus is easy on the wallet, an influence from Ohio State University's 59,000-plus students (the campus is the nation's second largest). Entrepreneurs, tech types and artists have flocked in, drawn by low costs and a 'go ahead and try it' atmosphere. It's not in your face, but this place quietly buzzes with creativity.

Sights & Activities

Just north of downtown, the browse-worthy Short North is a redeveloped strip of High St that holds contemporary art galleries, stylish boutiques, and bars and restaurants galore.

★COSI MUSEUM

(614-228-2674; www.cosi.org; 333 W Broad St; adult/child $25/20; 10am-5pm, closed Mon & Tue in winter;) The acronym stands for Center of Science and Industry, and it ranks high in the pantheon of children's museums around the country. Of the 300-plus hands-on exhibits jammed into the building, the dinosaur gallery (with a mechanical T-rex), space gallery (with a replica space station to explore) and high-wire unicycle ride are highlights. Live science shows, Ohio's largest planetarium ($5 extra) and a 3D theater ($5 extra) are also part of the whopping spread.

Pizzuti Collection MUSEUM

(614-221-6801; www.pizzuti.columbusmuseum.org; 632 N Park St; $10; 10am-5pm Wed-Sat, from noon Sun) Curators show off the amazing collection of contemporary paintings, sculpture, film, photography and prints via exhibitions that change every three months or so. You never know what you'll see, but count on it being provocative with a focus on underrepresented voices from around the world. The lovely classical building holds three floors of works; a sculpture garden adorns the grounds. It's affiliated with the Columbus Museum of Art.

Columbus Food Tours FOOD & DRINK

(614-440-3177; www.columbusfoodadventures.com; tours $58-72) Foodie guides lead tours by neighborhood or theme (taco trucks, desserts, coffee), some by foot and others by van. Most jaunts take three to four hours. Departure points vary.

Sleeping & Eating

BrewDog DogHouse BOUTIQUE HOTEL $$

(614-908-3051; www.brewdog.com; 96 Gender Rd, Canal Winchester; r $175-200;) BrewDog – the Scottish beer maker known for its audacious, come-what-may attitude – has a huge brewing facility in Canal Winchester, about 15 miles southeast of downtown Columbus. And that facility now includes a 32-room hotel. That's right: a hotel inside the brewery, where the modern-industrial rooms each have a tap, plus a beer fridge in the shower.

Katalina's BREAKFAST $

(614-294-2233; www.katalinascafe.com; 1105 Pennsylvania Ave; mains $10-13; 8am-3pm) It seems all of Columbus gets in line at Katalina's for breakfast. Tucked in a vintage gas station where you're welcome to add to the graffitied walls and tables, the colorful cafe is famed for its pancake balls (filled with Nutella or pumpkin-apple butter), sweet and spicy bacon, breakfast tacos and pork-and-egg sandwiches.

★Skillet BREAKFAST $$

(614-443-2266; www.skilletruf.com; 410 E Whittier St; mains $14-21; 8am-2pm Wed-Sun) This teeny restaurant in German Village serves rustic, locally sourced brunch fare. The menu changes, but you might fill a plate with griddled cinnamon rolls or braised pork cheeks with gravy and grits. It's almost always crowded, and you can't make reservations. On weekends you can call ahead (30 minutes before you arrive) and put your name on the wait list.

 Drinking & Nightlife

Land-Grant Brewing Company MICROBREWERY

(☎614-427-3946; www.landgrantbrewing.com; 424 W Town St; ⏲3:30-10pm Mon-Wed, 11:30am-10pm Thu, 11:30am-midnight Fri & Sat, 11:30am-8pm Sun) Beer gurus gather around Land-Grant's communal picnic tables to discuss the finer points of hazy brut IPAs versus Baltic porters and Mexican lagers. They're all here among the 24 taps, with flights available for heady sampling. Food trucks provide the noshes, with Ray Ray's Hog Pit doing the honors barbecue-style Thursday through Sunday.

Book Loft BOOKS

(☎614-464-1774; www.bookloft.com; 631 S 3rd St; ⏲10am-11pm) Bibliophiles go gaga in this sprawling German Village bookshop occupying a block of pre–Civil War era buildings. You're guaranteed to get lost in the labyrinth of 32 rooms stacked to the rafters with best sellers, children's books, manga, memoirs and more – all new, with many at bargain rates.

Information

Columbus Convention & Visitors Bureau (☎866-397-2657; www.experiencecolumbus.com; 277 W Nationwide Blvd; ⏲8am-5pm Mon-Fri, 10am-4pm Sat, noon-5pm Sun) This visitor center in the Arena District is staffed and has a gift shop of local goods.

Getting There & Away

John Glenn Columbus International Airport (CMH; ☎614-239-4000; www.flycolumbus.com; 4600 International Gateway) is 10 miles east of town. A cab or rideshare to downtown costs about $30.

Greyhound (☎614-221-4642; www.greyhound.com; 111 E Town St) buses run at least six times daily to Cincinnati ($11 to $21, two hours) and Cleveland ($13 to $23, 2½ hours).

Yellow Springs

Artsy, beatnik little Yellow Springs was a counterculture hot spot in the 1960s and '70s, thanks to Antioch University. You can still buy a bong at the local head shop, but now galleries, craft shops and sustainable eateries cluster downtown. It's a sweet spot to hang out for a day or two. Visit the local dairy farm to milk a cow or lick an ice cream made on-site. Limestone gorges, waterfalls and canoe-able rivers fill the surrounding parkland.

> **GERMAN VILLAGE: COLUMBUS, OHIO**
>
> The remarkably large, all-brick German Village, a half-mile south of downtown, is a restored 19th-century neighborhood with beer halls, cobbled streets, arts-filled parks, and Italianate and Queen Anne architecture.

Sights

★**Young's Jersey Dairy** FARM

(☎937-325-0629; www.youngsdairy.com; 6880 Springfield-Xenia Rd; ⏲9am-11pm Jun-Aug, reduced hours Sep-May;) FREE Young's is a working dairy farm with a famous ice-cream shop, the Dairy Store, which many say whips up Ohio's best milkshakes. There are also lots of fun family activities, including mini-golf, batting cages and opportunities to feed goats and watch the cows get milked (the latter happens from 4:30pm to 5:30pm). The golf and batting cages have a fee, the animal viewings do not.

The Golden Jersey Inn restaurant is also on-site.

Sleeping & Eating

Morgan House B&B $$

(☎937-767-1761; www.arthurmorganhouse.com; 120 W Limestone St; r $145-180;) The six comfy rooms have super-soft linens and private baths. Breakfasts are organic.

It's walking distance to the main business district.

Winds Cafe AMERICAN $$$

(☎937-767-1144; www.windscafe.com; 215 Xenia Ave; mains $24-30; ⏲11:30am-2pm & 5-10pm Tue-Sat, 10am-3pm Sun) A hippie co-op 40-plus years ago, the Winds has grown up to become a sophisticated foodie favorite plating seasonal dishes such as fig-sauced asparagus crepes and rhubarb halibut. Choose from small plates, large plates, cocktails and wine.

Reservations are a good idea for the snug dining room.

Getting There & Away

Yellow Springs is about 18 miles northeast of Dayton and linked by – wait for it – Dayton–Yellow Springs Rd.

Dayton

Dayton leans hard on its 'Birthplace of Aviation' tagline, and the Wright sights deliver. It's surprisingly moving to see the cluttered workshop where Orville and Wilbur conjured their ideas and the lonely field where they tested their plane. Then there's the Air Force museum, a mind-blowing expanse for aviation buffs. The vast complex of hangars holds just about every aircraft you can think of through the ages.

Sights

★National Museum of the US Air Force MUSEUM

(☎937-255-3286; www.nationalmuseum.af.mil; 1100 Spaatz St; ⏲9am-5pm) FREE Located at Wright-Patterson Air Force Base, 6 miles northeast of Dayton, this huuuuge museum has everything from a Wright Brothers 1909 Flyer to a Sopwith Camel (WWI biplane) and the 'Little Boy' type atomic bomb (decommissioned and rendered safe for display) dropped on Hiroshima. The hangars hold miles of planes, rockets and aviation machines. Be sure to visit Building 4 for spacecraft and presidential planes (including the first Air Force One). Plan on three hours overall; aviation buffs should allocate longer.

Carillon Historical Park HISTORIC SITE

(☎937-293-2841; www.daytonhistory.org; 1000 Carillon Blvd; adult/child $10/7; ⏲9:30am-5pm Mon-Sat, from noon Sun) Highlights in this open-air heritage park include the Wright Brothers National Museum, where you'll see the 1905 Wright Flyer III biplane and a replica of the Wright workshop, and the Carillon Brewing Company, an 1850s-style brewery where you can drink the wares.

Eating & Drinking

Warped Wing Brewing Company MICROBREWERY

(☎937-222-7003; www.warpedwing.com; 26 Wyandot St; ⏲5-10pm Tue-Thu, 3pm-midnight Fri, noon-midnight Sat, noon-8pm Sun) The brewery takes its name from the Wright brothers' concept of wing-warping, which was their breakthrough idea that enabled flight. The taproom's inventions are equally awesome. Many beer fanatics have dubbed the IPAs, stouts, lagers and cucumber sour ales as the best beers in town. The housemade root beer and ginger beer are excellent, too.

Getting There & Away

Dayton has a good-sized airport north of town. Greyhound buses also serve the city, which is equidistant from Cincinnati ($13 to $25, 1½ hours, four daily) and Columbus ($13 to $25, 1½ hours, six daily).

Cincinnati

Cincinnati splashes up the Ohio River's banks. Its prettiness surprises, as do its neon troves, its European-style neighborhoods and the locals' unashamed ardor for a five-way (c'mon, that's a term for the city's famed chili). Amid all that action, don't forget to catch a soccer game, stroll the bridge-striped riverfront and visit the dummy museum.

Sights & Activities

National Underground Railroad Freedom Center MUSEUM

(☎513-333-7500; www.freedomcenter.org; 50 E Freedom Way; adult/child $15/10.50; ⏲noon-5pm Sun & Mon, 10am-5pm Tue-Sat, closed Mon Oct-Feb) Cincinnati was a prominent stop on the Underground Railroad and a hub for abolitionist activities. The center displays artifacts from the era, such as an eerie shackle-filled pen that once held slaves bound for auction. The museum also covers modern struggles for civil rights. The Rosa Parks virtual-reality exhibit ($5 extra) shows how it's done: visitors don a headset and goggles, then sit on a 'bus' to stand in Parks' shoes when she refused to give up her seat.

Cincinnati Museum Center MUSEUM

(☎513-287-7000; www.cincymuseum.org; 1301 Western Ave; adult/child $14.50/10.50; ⏲10am-5pm; 👪) This museum complex occupies the 1933 Union Terminal, an art deco jewel still used by Amtrak. The interior has fantastic murals made of local Rookwood tiles. The complex includes a nifty Museum of Natural History (with a cave and real bats inside), a children's museum, a history museum, an Omnimax theater and a special hall for traveling exhibitions. Admission includes the three museums; the theater and special exhibits cost extra. Parking costs $6.

American Sign Museum MUSEUM
(☎513-541-6366; www.americansignmuseum.org; 1330 Monmouth Ave; adult/child $15/free; ⏰10am-4pm Wed-Sat, from noon Sun) This museum stocks an awesome cache of flashing, lightbulb-studded beacons in an old parachute factory. You'll burn your retinas staring at vintage neon drive-in signs, hulking genies and the Frisch's Big Boy, among other nostalgic novelties. Guides lead hour-long tours at 11am and 2pm that also visit the on-site neon sign-making shop.

Contemporary Arts Center MUSEUM
(CAC; ☎513-345-8400; www.contemporaryartscenter.org; 44 E 6th St; ⏰10am-4pm Sat-Mon, to 9pm Wed-Fri; 👪) FREE The center displays modern art in an avant-garde building designed by star architect Zaha Hadid. The free exhibitions – say, a retrospective of fanciful paper cutouts by street artist Swoon, or the surreal multimedia sculptures of Chris Larson – change every three months or so. Kids go gaga in the interactive UnMuseum gallery on the 6th floor.

Roebling Suspension Bridge BRIDGE
(www.roeblingbridge.org) The elegant 1867 spanner was a forerunner of John Roebling's famous Brooklyn Bridge in New York. The Romanesque arches and draped cables have made it an Instagram star. It's cool to walk across while passing cars make it 'sing' around you (the sound as they drive over the grates). It links to Covington, KY.

Tours

American Legacy Tours WALKING
(www.americanlegacytours.com; 1332 Vine St; 90min tours $25) Offers a variety of historical jaunts. The best is the Queen City Underground Tour that submerges into old lagering cellars deep beneath the Over-the-Rhine district and ends at a modern brewery taproom.

Festivals & Events

Oktoberfest FOOD & DRINK
(www.oktoberfestzinzinnati.com; ⏰mid-Sep) German beer, bratwursts and mania. It's the USA's largest Oktoberfest celebration, with well over half a million revelers. It takes place on W 2nd and 3rd Sts downtown between Walnut and Elm Sts.

Sleeping

Symphony Hotel B&B $$
(☎513-721-3353; www.symphonyhotel.com; 210 W 14th St; ⏰r $139-249) Around the corner from Music Hall, the Symphony Hotel offers nine rooms in a traditional Italianate building. Each is named after a classical composer, and each is chock-full of period antique decor, such as a four-post bed or cherrywood armoire (they vary in style). Breakfast and parking are included in the rates.

★**21c Museum Hotel Cincinnati** HOTEL $$$
(☎513-578-6600; www.21cmuseumhotels.com; 609 Walnut St; r $189-379; P❄@🛜🐾) An outpost of Louisville's popular art hotel, the 21c sits next door to the Contemporary Arts Center. The modern rooms have a Nespresso machine, free wi-fi, plush bedding and, of course, original art. The lobby is a public gallery, so feel free to ogle the trippy videos and nude sculptures. The on-site restaurant and rooftop bar draw crowds. Parking costs $38.

Eating

Eli's BBQ BARBECUE $
(☎513-533-1957; www.elisbarbeque.com; 3313 Riverside Dr; mains $7-16; ⏰11am-9pm) Eli's is a wee spot that makes awesome barbecue, which is why there's always a line snaking out the door. Order at the counter, find a seat, then wait for staff to bring out your hickory-smoked ribs on a red plastic tray. The meat is tender, the sauce sweet with a smoky kick, and the jalapeño cheddar grits beyond addictive.

Drinking & Nightlife

★**Rhinegeist Brewery** BREWERY
(☎513-381-1367; www.rhinegeist.com; 1910 Elm St, 2nd fl; ⏰3pm-midnight Mon-Thu, 3pm-2am Fri, noon-2am Sat, noon-9pm Sun) Beer buffs pile in to Rhinegeist's hoppy clubhouse to knock back Truth IPA and around 20 other brews on tap. Swig at picnic tables while watching bottles roll off the production line, or play table tennis and bean-bag toss in the sprawling open warehouse. The brewery is one of Ohio's biggest. The rooftop bar offers sweet skyline views.

★ Longfellow COCKTAIL BAR
(☎513-549-0744; www.longfellowbar.com; 1233 Clay St; ⊙4pm-2am Tue-Fri, 2pm-2am Sat & Sun) Longfellow looks like a cafe you'd find in Amsterdam, all cozy and candlelit in a vintage building with creaking hardwood floors and exposed brick walls. Punk music drifts from the speakers while stylish locals hobnob over wine, craft beers and cocktails like the Spruce Goose, a deceptively strong refresher made with gin, tonic, lime and honey.

☆ Entertainment

Nippert Stadium SOCCER
(☎513-977-5425; www.fccincinnati.com; 2700 Bearcats Way; tickets $15-50) Nippert Stadium is home to FC Cincinnati, the city's Major League Soccer team. It's known for its rabid fans cloaked in orange and blue (the team colors) and their pre-game rituals that include a march with drums and flares to the venue.

Great American Ballpark BASEBALL
(☎513-765-7000; www.reds.com; 100 Main St) Home to the Reds – pro baseball's first team – Cincy is a great place to catch a game thanks to its bells-and-whistles riverside ballpark. Many of the beer stands pour top-notch local brews.

ℹ Information

Cincinnati Visitor Center (☎513-534-5877; www.cincinnatiusa.com; 511 Walnut St; ⊙11am-5pm Sep-May, 9am-6pm Jun-Aug) The visitor center on Fountain Sq has maps and info.

ℹ Getting There & Around

The **Cincinnati/Northern Kentucky International Airport** (CVG; www.cvgairport.com; 3087 Terminal Dr, Hebron) is in Kentucky, 13 miles south. To get downtown, take the TANK bus ($2), which departs from the baggage claim area's east end. A cab costs $35; Uber and Lyft are typically a bit less.

Greyhound (☎513-352-6012; www.greyhound.com; 1005 Gilbert Ave) buses travel daily to Columbus (two hours), Indianapolis (2½ hours) and Chicago (seven hours). Megabus (www.megabus.com) travels the same routes from downtown and the University of Cincinnati; check the website for curbside locations.

Amtrak choo-choos into **Union Terminal** (☎800-872-7245; 1301 Western Ave) thrice weekly en route to Chicago (9½ hours) and Washington, DC (14½ hours), departing in the middle of the night. There is no ticket window; buy tickets in advance online.

Metro (www.go-metro.com; fare $1.75) runs the local buses and links with the Transit Authority of Northern Kentucky (www.tankbus.org). Bus 1 between downtown and Mt Adams can be useful.

Red Bike (www.cincyredbike.org) has 442 bicycles at 57 stations, mostly in downtown and Over-the-Rhine. A day pass costs $8 for unlimited 60-minute rides in a 24-hour period; bikes must be docked every hour or additional charges apply. Several electric bikes are mixed in at the stations.

Cincy's **streetcar** (www.cincinnatibellconnector.com) runs on a handy, 3½-mile loop connecting the Banks, downtown and Over-the-Rhine (including Findlay Market). A day pass costs $2.

Southeastern Ohio

Ohio's southeastern corner cradles most of its forested areas, as well as the rolling foothills of the Appalachian Mountains and scattered farms. Parts are far prettier than you'd expect. The Hocking Hills region, near Logan, impresses with streams and waterfalls, sandstone cliffs and cave-like formations. Further on is Athens, a university town and the area's free-spirited hot spot. To the east, around Chillicothe, mysterious Native American mounds rise from the fields.

Athens

Athens makes a lovely base for exploring southeastern Ohio. Situated where US 50 crosses US 33, it's set among wooded hills and built around the Ohio University campus (which comprises half the town). Vintage brick buildings edge the main streets, while young, bohemian types pop in and out of the cafes and groovy shops inside.

Sleeping

Bodhi Tree Guesthouse B&B $$
(☎740-707-2050; www.bodhitreeguesthouse.com; 8950 Lavelle Rd; r $150-200) The four rooms at this serene, hippy-esque farmhouse have tasteful modern (if minimal) decor. There are no TVs, but there is wi-fi, as well as a wholesome breakfast of local cheeses, eggs, fruit and yogurt. A 4-acre organic farm surrounds the abode. The on-site studio offers yoga classes and massage. It's about a 3-mile drive from downtown Athens.

Drinking

Little Fish Brewing Co MICROBREWERY

(☎740-204-6187; www.littlefishbrewing.com; 8675 Armitage Rd; ⏲3-10pm Mon-Thu, 11am-11pm Fri & Sat, 11am-10pm Sun) Little Fish specializes in saisons and barrel-aged sour beers, though pale ales, porters and smoked lagers mix in among the taps. The brewers source the majority of their grain and some of their hops in Ohio, and their flagship beer – Saison du Poisson – is made entirely with Ohio ingredients.

Getting There & Away

The closest big city is Columbus, 75 miles northwest via US 33. **GoBus** (☎888-954-6287; www.ridegobus.com; Ohio University Baker Center, Oxbow Trail entrance) runs a few times a day to/from downtown Columbus (one way $10, two hours).

Logan

Logan is a handy headquarters for checking out the Hocking Hills area, where hiking, canoeing, camping and other activities amid dramatic gorges and grottoes are de rigueur. Hocking Hills State Park lets you immerse in the green scene by day and stargaze by night, while Logan offers local cultural quirks including a washboard museum and moonshine distillery.

Sights & Activities

Hocking Hills State Park STATE PARK

(☎740-385-6842; http://parks.ohiodnr.gov/hockinghills; 19852 Hwy 664) FREE Ohio's most popular park is splendid to explore in any season, but it's especially lovely in autumn. Thirty miles of hiking trails meander through the forest past waterfalls and gorges. Old Man's Cave is the park's hot spot, with several short paths (less than a half-mile) that deliver a scenic payoff. Nearby Cedar Falls offers a half-mile trail edged by steep rock walls that leads to a peaceful waterfall and pool. The park is 12 miles southwest of Logan.

Hocking Hills Adventures CANOEING

(☎740-385-8685; www.hockinghillscanoeing.com; 31251 Chieftain Dr; kayak/canoe trips from $23/39; ⏲Apr-Oct) Offers a variety of self-guided trips on the Hocking River, from two-hour jaunts to full-day expeditions. The monthly nighttime trip that lets you paddle by moonlight and tiki torch is festive. The outfitter also has tent and RV sites ($26 to $35) and rustic cabins ($65 to $95) on-site. Note the latter do not have bathrooms, and you must provide your own linens.

Getting There & Away

US 33 is the main road to Logan. GoBus makes a stop in town a few times a day on its route between downtown Columbus ($10, 80 minutes) and Athens ($10, 40 minutes).

MICHIGAN

More, more, more – Michigan is the Midwest state that cranks it up. It sports more beaches than the Atlantic seaboard. More than half the state is covered by forests. And more cherries and berries get shoveled into pies here than anywhere else in the USA. Plus Detroit is the Midwest's most exciting city of all, reinventing itself daily with street art and fresh architecture.

Michigan occupies prime real estate, surrounded by four of the five Great Lakes – Superior, Michigan, Huron and Erie. Islands – Mackinac, Manitou and Isle Royale – freckle its coast and make top touring destinations. Surf beaches, colored sandstone cliffs and trekkable sand dunes also woo visitors.

The state consists of two parts split by water: the larger Lower Peninsula, shaped like a mitten; and the smaller, lightly populated Upper Peninsula, shaped like a slipper. They are linked by the gasp-worthy Mackinac Bridge, which spans the Straits of Mackinac.

Information

Michigan Highway Conditions (www.michigan.gov/mdot)

Michigan State Park Information Park entry requires a vehicle permit (per day/year $9/33). Tent and RV sites cost $15 to $45; reservations accepted (www.midnrreservations.com; fee $8). Some parks have wi-fi.

Travel Michigan (www.michigan.org)

Detroit

After decades of neglect, Detroit is rolling again. It's like the whole place is caffeine-buzzed, freewheeling in ideas. Young creative types have moved to the city and transformed the glut of abandoned buildings into

WORTH A TRIP

ANCIENT MOUNDS OF OHIO

The area south of Columbus was a center for the ancient Hopewell people, who left behind huge geometric earthworks and burial mounds from around 200 BCE to 500 CE. The **Hopewell Culture National Historical Park** (740-774-1126; www.nps.gov/hocu; 16062 Hwy 104, Chillicothe; sunrise-sunset) tells their story. The visitor center (8:30am to 5pm) provides intriguing background information, but the highlight is wandering about the variously shaped ceremonial mounds spread over 13-acre Mound City, a mysterious town of the dead. It's 3 miles north of Chillicothe, next to one of Ohio's largest prisons.

Serpent Mound (937-587-2796; www.ohiohistory.org; 3850 Hwy 73, Peebles; per car $8; 9am-sunset) is perhaps the most captivating of all of the native mounds that dot southeastern Ohio. The giant, uncoiling snake stretches over a quarter of a mile and is the largest effigy mound in the world. You can walk around it or go up the observation tower for a sweeping view. The site is far flung, but cool enough to be worth the effort. It's 50 miles southwest of Chillicothe.

distilleries, cafes, galleries and chocolate shops. Downtown will pop your eyeballs, from the extraordinary art deco skyscrapers to the whimsical public parks and edgy street art. By day, intriguing sights bring Detroit's car-making history to life. By night, timeless jazz clubs show off its musical chops. Sweet bike rides and sprawling markets add to the energy.

History

French explorer Antoine de La Mothe Cadillac founded Detroit in 1701. Sweet fortune arrived in the 1920s, when Henry Ford began churning out cars. He didn't invent the automobile, as so many mistakenly believe, but he did perfect assembly-line manufacturing and mass-production techniques. The result was the Model T, the first car the USA's middle class could afford to own.

Detroit quickly became the motor capital of the world. General Motors (GM), Chrysler and Ford were all headquartered in or near Detroit (and still are). The 1950s were the city's heyday, when the population exceeded two million and Motown music hit the airwaves. But racial tensions in 1967 and Japanese car competitors in the 1970s shook the city and its industry. Detroit entered an era of deep decline, losing about two-thirds of its population.

In July 2013, Detroit filed the largest municipal bankruptcy claim in US history: $18 billion. After extreme belt-tightening, it emerged from bankruptcy in December 2014. Since then, the fortunes of downtown have been on the rise, thanks to a real-estate boom, but the tide has yet to turn for many long-term residents outside the city's core.

Sights

★Detroit Institute of Arts MUSEUM
(DIA; 313-833-7900; www.dia.org; 5200 Woodward Ave; adult/child $14/6; 9am-4pm Tue-Thu, 9am-10pm Fri, 10am-5pm Sat & Sun) The DIA holds one of the world's finest art collections. The centerpiece is Diego Rivera's mural *Detroit Industry,* which fills an entire room and reflects the city's blue-collar labor history. Beyond it are Picassos, Caravaggios, suits of armor, modern African American paintings, puppets and troves more spread through 100-plus galleries.

★Fisher Building ARCHITECTURE
(313-872-1000; www.thefisherbuilding.com; 3011 W Grand Boulevard) This 1928 masterpiece from the man who built Detroit, Albert Kahn, has an imposing art deco exterior made from Minnesota granite and Maryland marble, and an interior to rival any Italian cathedral. From the soaring vaulted ceilings, featuring an array of intricate, hand-painted patterns, to the sparkling mosaics by Hungarian artist Géza Maróti and gleaming marble on the walls, the visual inspiration here is endless.

★Eastern Market MARKET
(www.easternmarket.org; Adelaide & Russell Sts) Produce, cheese, spice and flower vendors fill the large halls on Saturday, but you also can turn up Monday through Friday to browse the specialty shops (props to the peanut roaster) and cafes that flank the halls on Russell and Market Sts. In addition, from

June through September there's a scaled-down market on Tuesdays and a Sunday craft market with food trucks. Or arrive any day for mural gaping. Eastern Market has become an internationally renowned hot spot for street art.

Campus Martius Park PARK
(www.downtowndetroitparks.com; 800 Woodward Ave;) This public space in the heart of Detroit's downtown is the perfect spot to while away a sunny afternoon. A fountain dots the middle, surrounded by umbrella-shaded tables. Beside it, a sandy beach with lounge chairs appears in warmer months; in winter, the space becomes the city's most popular ice rink. There's a stage for concerts and, in summer, a pop-up restaurant and bar. At the foot of the park is the Michigan Soldiers & Sailors Monument.

Guardian Building ARCHITECTURE
(313-963-4567; www.guardianbuilding.com; 500 Griswold St; 8:30am-6pm Mon-Sat, 11am-5pm Sun) Commissioned as a 'cathedral of finance,' this distinctive, 40-story, redbrick building with green and white accents was the world's tallest masonry structure when it opened in 1929. The interior is a colorful explosion of marble, mosaic and murals that draw from Aztec, art deco and local influences. It's certainly the prettiest Bank of America you'll ever see.

Pure Detroit (313-963-1440; www.puredetroit.com; 9:30am-6pm Mon-Sat, 11am-5pm Sun), whose flagship store is in the building, leads tours most Saturdays and Sundays.

Museum of Contemporary Art Detroit MUSEUM
(MOCAD; 313-832-6622; www.mocadetroit.org; 4454 Woodward Ave; suggested donation $5; 11am-5pm Wed, Sat & Sun, to 8pm Thu & Fri) MOCAD is set in an abandoned, graffiti-slathered auto dealership. Heat lamps hang from the ceiling over peculiar exhibits that change every few months. Music and literary events take place regularly. The on-site cafe–cocktail bar is popular.

Motown Historical Museum MUSEUM
(313-875-2264; www.motownmuseum.org; 2648 W Grand Blvd; adult/child $15/10; 10am-6pm Tue-Fri & Sun, to 8pm Sat Jun-Aug, to 6pm Tue-Sat Sep-May) In this row of modest houses Berry Gordy launched Motown Records – and the careers of Stevie Wonder, Diana Ross, Marvin Gaye and Michael Jackson – with an $800 loan in 1959. Gordy and Motown split for Los Angeles in 1972, but you can still step into humble Studio A and see where the famed names recorded their first hits.

Ford Piquette Avenue Plant MUSEUM
(313-872-8759; www.fordpiquetteplant.org; 461 Piquette Ave; adult/child $12/free; 10am-4pm Wed-Sun Apr-Oct) Henry Ford cranked out the first Model T in this landmark factory. Admission includes a detailed tour by enthusiastic docents, plus loads of shiny vehicles from 1904 onward. It's about 1 mile northeast of the Detroit Institute of Arts.

Activities

★Slow Roll CYCLING
(www.slowroll.bike; Mon late May-Oct) Up to 6000 cyclists come out for this leisurely 8-to-12-mile pedal through a different neighborhood each Monday. It's a great way to meet locals. Detroiters of all ages and fitness levels partake. Check the website for the week's location. Start time is at 6pm through early September, and then moves up to 5:30pm through October.

Riverwalk & Dequindre Cut WALKING
(www.detroitriverfront.org) The city's swell riverfront path runs for 3 miles along the churning Detroit River from Hart Plaza east to Mt Elliott St, passing several parks, outdoor theaters, riverboats and fishing spots en route. Eventually it will extend all the way to beachy Belle Isle (detour onto Jefferson Ave to get there now). About halfway along the Riverwalk, near Orleans St, the 1.5-mile Dequindre Cut Greenway path juts north, offering a convenient passageway to Eastern Market.

WORTH A TRIP

BELLE ISLE PARK

Pretty **Belle Isle Park** (www.belleisleconservancy.org; per car/bike $9/free; 5am-10pm) floats in the Detroit River. The entire expanse is parkland where kayaking, walking trails and a glass-domed conservatory await. There's a beach, zoo, aquarium and maritime museum, too. Once you pay the entry fee, the individual sights are free. The cycling here is terrific.

Detroit

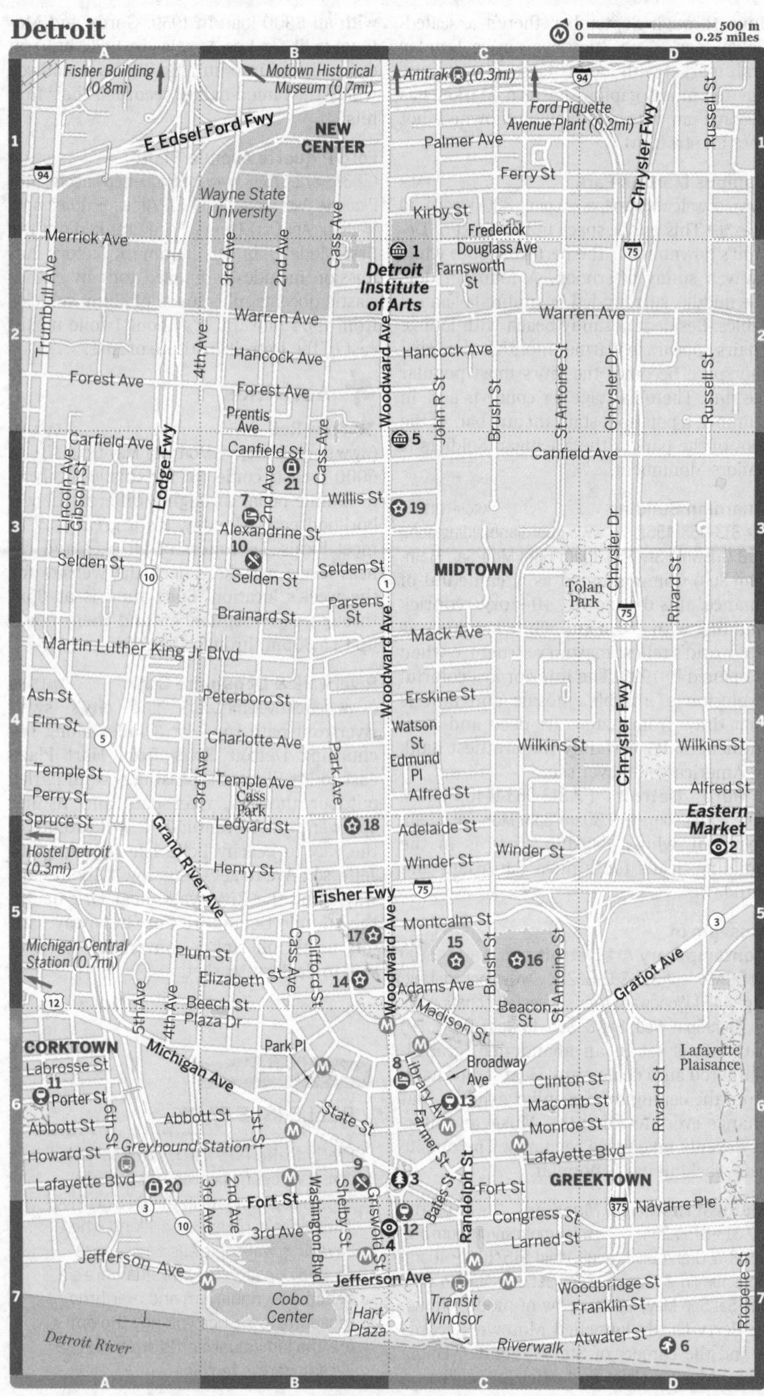
0 500 m
0 0.25 miles
Fisher Building (0.8mi)
Motown Historical Museum (0.7mi)
Amtrak (0.3mi)
Ford Piquette Avenue Plant (0.2mi)
E Edsel Ford Fwy
NEW CENTER
Palmer Ave
Ferry St
Chrysler Fwy
Russell St
Wayne State University
Kirby St
Merrick Ave
Frederick Douglass Ave
Farnsworth St
Detroit Institute of Arts
Trumbull Ave
3rd Ave
2nd Ave
Cass Ave
Warren Ave
4th Ave
Hancock Ave
Woodward Ave
Forest Ave
John R St
Brush St
St Antoine St
Chrysler Dr
Prentis Ave
Carfield Ave
Canfield St
Canfield Ave
Lodge Fwy
Lincoln Ave
Gibson St
Willis St
Alexandrine St
Selden St
MIDTOWN
Tolan Park
Parsens St
Brainard St
Rivard St
Martin Luther King Jr Blvd
Mack Ave
Ash St
Peterboro St
Erskine St
Elm St
Charlotte Ave
Watson St
Edmund Pl
Wilkins St
Temple St
Park Ave
Perry St
Temple Ave
Cass Park
Alfred St
Spruce St
Ledyard St
Adelaide St
Eastern Market
Hostel Detroit (0.3mi)
Grand River Ave
Henry St
Winder St
Fisher Fwy
Montcalm St
Michigan Central Station (0.7mi)
Plum St
Clifford St
Elizabeth St
Adams Ave
Gratiot Ave
5th Ave
4th Ave
Beech St
Plaza Dr
Madison St
Beacon St
CORKTOWN
Michigan Ave
Park Pl
Library Av
Broadway Ave
Lafayette Plaisance
Labrosse St
Porter St
Clinton St
6th St
Abbott St
State St
Farmer St
Macomb St
Monroe St
1st St
Greyhound Station
Howard St
Lafayette Blvd
Randolph St
Bates St
Fort St
GREEKTOWN
Washington Blvd
Shelby St
Griswold St
Navarre Ple
Congress St
Larned St
Jefferson Ave
Woodbridge St
Franklin St
Riopelle St
Cobo Center
Hart Plaza
Transit Windsor
Riverwalk
Atwater St
Detroit River

Tours

★Pure Detroit Tours WALKING

(☎855-874-7873; www.puredetroit.com; ⊙Sat & Sun) FREE Purveyors of locally inspired gifts, Pure Detroit also offers guided tours of some of the city's best sights, including the Fisher Building, the Guardian Building and the Packard Plant. Guides – typically local historians – are knowledgeable and friendly. Stop in at one of Pure Detroit's five locations or check the website for details.

Wheelhouse Bikes CYCLING

(☎313-656-2453; www.wheelhousedetroit.com; 1340 E Atwater St; per 2hr $17; ⊙11am-7pm Mon-Thu, 10am-8pm Fri & Sat, 10am-5pm Sun, reduced hours in winter) Cycling is a great way to explore the city. Wheelhouse rents sturdy two-wheelers (helmet and lock included) on the Riverwalk at Rivard Plaza. Themed tours ($45 including bike rental) roll by various neighborhoods, architectural sites and urban farms.

Festivals & Events

North American International Auto Show CULTURAL

(www.naias.com; 1 Washington Blvd; $14; ⊙mid-Jan) It's autos galore for two weeks at the Cobo Center.

Movement Electronic Music Festival MUSIC

(www.movement.us; cnr Jefferson & Woodward Aves; day pass $85; ⊙late May) The world's largest electronic music festival congregates in Hart Plaza over Memorial Day weekend.

Sleeping

Detroit is having a hotel boom: several design-savvy properties have opened in downtown and Midtown over the past few years, with more on the way. Myriad Airbnb rentals in these areas can be a cheaper alternative. Taxes add 9% to 15% to rates (it varies by lodging size and location).

Hostel Detroit HOSTEL $

(☎313-451-0333; www.hosteldetroit.com; 2700 Vermont St; dm $30-39, r $64-74; P❄@📶) Volunteers rehabbed this old building using recycled materials and donations for the patchwork furnishings, and painted it in vivid colors inside and out. There are two 10-bed dorms, two four-bed dorms and a handful of private rooms; everyone shares the four bathrooms and three kitchens. Bookings are taken online only (and must be done at least 24 hours in advance).

El Moore Lodge BOUTIQUE HOTEL $$

(☎313-924-4374; www.elmoore.com; 624 W Alexandrine St; r $75-170, cabins from $200; P❄📶) 🍃 A unique option in Midtown with a great friendly vibe, El Moore occupies a turreted 1898 building that has been renovated with solar panels and a geothermal heating and cooling system. Reclaimed wood and tiles feature in the interior. The 11 rooms vary widely, from basement digs with two bunk beds to chic rooftop 'cabins' with a private balcony.

Detroit

Top Sights
1 Detroit Institute of Arts C2
2 Eastern Market D5

Sights
3 Campus Martius Park C6
4 Guardian Building C7
5 Museum of Contemporary Art Detroit C3

Activities, Courses & Tours
6 Wheelhouse Bikes D7

Sleeping
7 El Moore Lodge B3
8 Shinola Hotel C6

Eating
9 Dime Store B6
10 Selden Standard B3

Drinking & Nightlife
11 Batch Brewing Company A6
12 Grand Trunk Pub C7
13 Standby C6

Entertainment
14 Cliff Bell's B5
15 Comerica Park C5
16 Ford Field C5
17 Fox Theatre B5
18 Little Caesars Arena B5
19 Magic Stick C3

Shopping
20 John K. King Used & Rare Books A6
Pure Detroit .... (see 4)
21 Third Man Records B3

LOCAL KNOWLEDGE

DETROIT'S RUINS

The derelict buildings that represent Detroit in the popular imagination aren't as prevalent as they once were – at least, not downtown, where many architectural gems have been restored and buffed to a shine, thanks to dedicated locals and private investors. National chains have also jumped on the bandwagon as the city's fortunes turn for the better, with retailers such as Madewell and Nike and hotel brands such as Element and Aloft moving in to formerly vacant commercial buildings.

You'll see construction going on everywhere in the city center. Even iconic ruins – buildings such as **Michigan Central Station** (2405 W Vernor Hwy) and the **Packard Plant** (E Grand Blvd at Concord St), thought to be entirely beyond redemption – are feeling the love. The former is getting a $350 million makeover to become Ford Motor Company's new innovation campus, while the latter is being (slowly) redeveloped into an office and entertainment complex.

Still, with 139 sq miles of city, there are plenty of vacant buildings that remain, especially outside the downtown core. But Detroit's days as the capital of 'ruin porn' (as in, people getting excited by urban decay) are dissipating as the ruins continue to vanish. Note it is illegal to enter any abandoned building.

★Shinola Hotel DESIGN HOTEL **$$$**
(☎313-356-1400; www.shinolahotel.com; 1400 Woodward Ave; r $215-325; P❄📶🐾) Shinola, Detroit's homegrown company known for its luxury crafted watches, extended the brand to this superbly stylish hotel. The 129 earth-toned rooms have hardwood floors, mid-century modern furniture, big windows letting in natural light and local beers in the minibar; some have turntables and records.

The downtown location is super-convenient near the sports arenas, QLine and shops.

Eating

Detroit's food scene is buzzing, with edgy restaurants clustered in downtown, Midtown and Corktown in particular. Two nearby suburbs also have caches of stylish eats: walkable, gay-oriented Ferndale at 9 Mile Rd and Woodward Ave, and Royal Oak just north of Ferndale between 12 and 13 Mile Rds.

★Sister Pie PIES **$**
(☎313-447-5550; www.sisterpie.com; 8066 Kercheval Ave; baked goods $1-5, pie slice $4; ⊙8am-4pm Mon-Fri, 9am-sold out Sat & Sun) Owner Lisa Ludwinski (a 2019 James Beard Award finalist) and her army of female bakers create amazing treats at this corner storefront. The milk chocolate chess, salted maple, marshmallow butterscotch and other flaky-crust pies are fabulous, and the perfectly soft peanut-butter paprika cookies will spoil your taste buds forevermore. Everything is made with seasonal ingredients and produce purchased from local farmers.

Dime Store AMERICAN **$**
(☎313-962-9106; www.eatdimestore.com; 719 Griswold St; mains $9-14; ⊙8am-3pm) Take a seat in a chunky wood swivel chair in this cozy, diner-esque eatery and chow down on a duck Reuben and truffle mayo–dipped fries, alongside a cold beer. Eggy brunch dishes are a big hit and are served all day.

★Detroit Vegan Soul VEGAN **$$**
(☎313-649-2759; www.detroitvegansoul.com; 8029 Agnes St; mains $13-17; ⊙noon-8pm Tue-Sat; 🌶) Step inside this light-wood cafe staffed by hippies and fork into splendid soul food dishes that just happen to be vegan. The soul platter, with black-eyed peas, maple-glazed yams, mac and cheese, smoked collard greens and a cornbread muffin, is the way to go. The menu also features catfish and barbecue (both tofu-based).

Selden Standard AMERICAN **$$$**
(☎313-438-5055; www.seldenstandard.com; 3921 2nd Ave; small plates $12-18; ⊙11am-2:30pm & 5-10pm Mon-Fri, 10am-2pm & 5-10pm Sat & Sun) Farm-to-table Selden Standard is the kind of place that cares enough to churn its own butter and hand-make its own pasta. The menu changes, but you'll see dishes such as fresh-caught trout and celery-root ravioli, plus creative cocktails.

Drinking & Nightlife

★Standby COCKTAIL BAR
(☎313-241-5719; www.standbydetroit.com; 225 Gratiot Ave; ⏲5pm-2am) Standby hides in the alleyway known as the Belt. Find it, and crazy-creative cocktails like Snake in the Grass (gin, lime, celery bitters and nitro-muddled mustard greens) are your reward.

The boisterous, space fills up fast on weekends; reservations are a good idea.

Batch Brewing Company MICROBREWERY
(☎313-338-8008; www.batchbrewingcompany.com; 1400 Porter St; ⏲11am-10pm Mon-Thu, 11am-midnight Fri & Sat, 10am-8pm Sun) Batch's little taproom bustles most nights of the week. Friends play board games at one table, a young couple on a date sits next to them, while workmates discuss business nearby.

German-style lagers and pale ales are mainstays of the 18 beers on tap, but there are also some monster doppelbocks and double IPAs.

Grand Trunk Pub BAR
(☎313-961-3043; www.grandtrunk.pub; 612 Woodward Ave; ⏲11am-2am Mon-Fri, from 10am Sat & Sun) Once the ticket hall for the Grand Trunk Railroad, this high-ceilinged space still buzzes, but this time patrons are content to sit and stop a while. With good reason: there's a vast beer selection and a full bar menu. The patio is an excellent spot to people-watch, thanks to the pedestrian esplanade down Woodward Ave.

Entertainment

Cliff Bell's JAZZ
(☎313-961-2543; www.cliffbells.com; 2030 Park Ave; ⏲5pm-midnight Tue-Fri, 5pm-12:30am Sat, 11am-10pm Sun) The candlelit, art deco ambience at Cliff Bell's attracts a diverse young crowd to hear local jazz bands. The elegant club, decked out in mahogany and brass, has been around since 1935. Weeknight shows typically are free, while weekend shows cost $10 to $15.

Magic Stick LIVE MUSIC
(☎313-833-9700; www.majesticdetroit.com; 4120-4140 Woodward Ave; ⏲11am-2am) The grungy Magic Stick is the place to go for rappers and rock bands on the rise. The attached Majestic Theater hosts larger shows. While the venues have lost some luster in recent years, you're still likely to see cool bands here most nights. The complex also holds a bowling alley, rooftop deck and pizza joint.

Fox Theatre PERFORMING ARTS
(☎313-471-6611; www.olympiaentertainment.com; 2211 Woodward Ave) This opulent 1928 theater, built in the Oriental style, is one of the icons of Detroit – and one of the few venues that has consistently offered entertainment during the city's ups and downs. First used to show silent films (it still has two organs), today the Fox hosts comedians, top music acts and Broadway shows.

Comerica Park BASEBALL
(☎313-962-4000; www.detroittigers.com; 2100 Woodward Ave; 👪) The Detroit Tigers play pro baseball at Comerica, one of the league's most decked-out stadiums. The park is particularly kid friendly, with a small Ferris wheel and carousel inside ($2 per ride each).

Little Caesars Arena STADIUM
(☎313-471-6606; www.olympiaentertainment.com; 2645 Woodward Ave) Opened in 2017, this is Detroit's spiffy arena for big-name concerts and sporting events. Detroit's rough-and-tumble pro hockey team the Red Wings (www.nhl.com/redwings) and pro basketball team the Pistons (www.nba.com/pistons) both play here from October through April.

Ford Field FOOTBALL
(☎877-212-8898; www.detroitlions.com; 2000 Brush St) The Lions pro football team tosses the pigskin at this indoor stadium next to Comerica Park.

Shopping

★John K. King Used & Rare Books BOOKS
(☎313-961-0622; www.johnkingbooksdetroit.com; 901 W Lafayette Blvd; ⏲9:30am-5:30pm Mon-Sat) This cluttered, multistory bookstore is a Detroit landmark sure to delight any bibliophile. Treasures await in the dusty stacks, and exploring the building is an adventure in itself.

★Third Man Records MUSIC
(☎313-209-5205; www.thirdmanrecords.com; 441 W Canfield St; ⏲10am-7pm Mon-Sat, 11am-5pm Sun) Local boy Jack White opened Third Man, and it's a super-fun browse. The store sells records (of course), turntables, T-shirts and other gear, but the coolest bits are the recording booth (where you can make your own record for $20) and the

FROM MOWTOWN TO ROCK CITY

Motown Records and soul music put Detroit on the map in the 1960s, while the thrashing punk rock of the Stooges and MC5 was the 1970s response to that smooth sound. By 1976, Detroit was dubbed 'Rock City' by a Kiss song (though – just Detroit's luck – the tune was eclipsed by its B-side, 'Beth'). In the early 2000s hard-edged garage rock pushed the city to the music-scene forefront, thanks to homegrown stars such as the White Stripes, Von Bondies and Dirtbombs, while Eminem gave Detroit its rap bona fides. And then there's techno, the electronic dance music that DJs in the city created in the mid-1980s. It went heavy on synthesizer melodies and complex machine rhythms, and became a global sensation. The world's largest electronic music festival (p575) still takes place in the city annually in honor of the style. Scope free publications such as the *Metro Times* for current show and club listings.

record pressing plant that you can peek into for free (or tour for $15 on select Saturdays).

Information

Detroit Convention & Visitors Bureau (☎800-338-7648; www.visitdetroit.com)

Getting There & Around

Detroit Metro Airport (DTW; ☎734-247-7678; www.metroairport.com; 11050 Rogell Dr), a Delta Airlines hub, is about 20 miles southwest of Detroit. Transportation options to the city are few. Taxis cost $50 or so; Lyft and Uber typically are a bit less. The 261 Fast Michigan SMART bus (fare $2) runs along Michigan Ave and takes an hour to get downtown.

Greyhound (☎313-961-8011; 1001 Howard St) runs to various cities in Michigan and beyond, including Grand Rapids ($21 to $40, 4½ hours) and Traverse City ($45 to $55, 7½ hours). Megabus (www.megabus.com/us) runs to/from Chicago ($25 to $45, 5½ hours) daily; departures are from downtown and Wayne State University. Check the website for exact locations.

Amtrak trains go three times daily to Chicago ($39 to $93, 5½ hours) from **Detroit Station** (☎313-873-3442; 11 W Baltimore Ave), located right by the QLine stop at Baltimore St. You can also head east – to New York ($95 to $223, 16½ hours) or destinations en route – but you'll first be bused to Toledo.

The **QLine streetcar** (www.qlinedetroit.com; single fare $1.50, day pass $3) provides handy transport along Woodward Ave from Congress St downtown, past the sports venues and museums of Midtown, to the Amtrak station and W Grand Blvd at the route's northern end.

MoGo (www.mogodetroit.org) is Detroit's bike-share program, with 44 stations scattered around downtown and Midtown. A 24-hour pass costs $8 for an unlimited number of 30-minute trips; additional charges apply for trips longer than 30 minutes.

Transit Windsor (☎519-944-4111; www.citywindsor.ca/transitwindsor) operates the Tunnel Bus to Windsor, Canada. It costs $5 (American or Canadian) and departs by Mariner's Church (corner of Randolph St and Jefferson Ave) near the Detroit-Windsor Tunnel entrance, as well as other spots downtown. Bring your passport.

Uber and Lyft are very popular in Detroit. For taxi service, call Checker Cab at ☎313-963-7000.

Dearborn

A stone's throw from Detroit, Dearborn is home to the Henry Ford Museum, one of the USA's finest museum complexes. It's also home to the nation's largest Arab American community, and a visit here offers a fascinating immersion into the local culture.

Sights

★**Henry Ford Museum** MUSEUM

(☎313-982-6001; www.thehenryford.org; 20900 Oakwood Blvd; adult/child $24/18; ⊙9:30am-5pm) The indoor Henry Ford Museum contains a fascinating wealth of American culture, such as the chair Lincoln was sitting in when he was assassinated, the presidential limo in which Kennedy was killed, the hot dog–shaped Oscar Mayer Wienermobile (photo op!) and the bus on which Rosa Parks refused to give up her seat. Don't worry: you'll get your vintage car fix here, too. Parking costs $6.

Greenfield Village MUSEUM

(☎313-982-6001; www.thehenryford.org; 20900 Oakwood Blvd; adult/child $28/21; ⊙9:30am-5pm daily mid-Apr–Oct, Fri-Sun Nov & Dec; 👪) Adjacent to the Henry Ford Museum (and part of its complex), outdoor Greenfield Village spreads across 80 acres and features historic buildings shipped in from all over the country, reconstructed and restored, such as Thomas Edison's laboratory from Menlo Park and the Wright Brothers' airplane workshop.

Ford Rouge Factory Tour FACTORY

(☎312-982-6001; www.thehenryford.org; adult/child $18/13.50; ⊙9:30am-3pm Mon-Sat) See F-150 trucks roll off the assembly line where Henry Ford first perfected his self-sufficient, mass-production techniques. The self-guided tours start at the Henry Ford Museum, from which a bus takes you over to the factory. Allow a couple of hours for the overall visit.

Getting There & Away

Dearborn is 10 miles west of downtown Detroit and about the same distance east of Detroit Metro Airport; a rideshare to either place costs about $20. I-94 is the primary road to town. Amtrak has a station by the Henry Ford Museum with service to Detroit ($6.50 to $17, 25 minutes, three daily).

Ann Arbor

Liberal and bookish Ann Arbor is home to the University of Michigan. The walkable downtown, which abuts the campus, is loaded with free-trade coffee shops, bookstores and brewpubs. It's also a mecca for chowhounds. Zingerman's Delicatessen led the way decades ago, but now all sorts of inventive farm-to-table and butcher-your-own-meat type places pop up in cozy spaces.

Sights

Ann Arbor Farmers Market MARKET

(☎734-794-6255; www.a2farmersmarket.org; 315 Detroit St; ⊙7am-3pm Wed & Sat May-Dec, 8am-3pm Sat Jan-Apr) Given the surrounding bounty of orchards and farms, it's no surprise this place is stuffed to the rafters with everything from spicy pickles to cider to mushroom-growing kits; located downtown near Zingerman's Delicatessen. On Sunday, an **artisan market** with jewelry, ceramics and textiles takes over from 11am to 4pm.

Sleeping & Eating

Burnt Toast Inn B&B **$$**

(☎734-395-4114; www.burnttoastinn.com; 415 W William St; r $135-225; ❄📶) The colorful house has five rooms that mix sturdy antiques with funky art. Two rooms share a bathroom; the rest have private facilities. It's an excellent location, on a leafy street walkable to downtown and the university campus. The lovely garden and big porch add to the homey vibe.

Breakfast, featuring locally made bread, milk, granola and other fare, is included here.

CLASSIC CARS IN MICHIGAN

More than sand dunes, beaches and Mackinac Island fudge, Michigan is synonymous with cars. While the connection hasn't been so positive in recent years, the state commemorates its glory days via several auto museums. The following fleets are within a few hours' drive of the Motor City.

Henry Ford Museum This Dearborn museum is loaded with vintage cars, including the first one Henry Ford ever built. In adjacent Greenfield Village, you can ride in a Model T that rolled off the assembly line in 1923.

Automotive Hall of Fame (☎313-240-4000; www.automotivehalloffame.org; 21400 Oakwood Blvd; adult/child $10/4; ⊙9am-5pm Wed-Sun May-Sep, Fri-Sun only Oct-Apr) Next door to the Henry Ford Museum, the interactive Auto Hall focuses on the people behind famed cars, such as Mr Ferdinand Porsche and Mr Soichiro Honda.

Gilmore Car Museum (☎269-671-5089; www.gilmorecarmuseum.org; 6865 Hickory Rd, Hickory Corners; adult/child $15/10; ⊙9am-5pm Mon-Fri, to 6pm Sat & Sun) North of Kalamazoo along Hwy 43, this museum complex offers some 20 buildings filled with nearly 400 vintage autos, including 15 Rolls-Royces dating back to a 1910 Silver Ghost.

RE Olds Transportation Museum (☎517-372-0529; www.reoldsmuseum.org; 240 Museum Dr, Lansing; adult/child $7/5; ⊙10am-5pm Tue-Sat year-round, noon-5pm Sun Apr-Oct) It's a whopping garage full of shiny vintage cars that date back more than 130 years.

★**Lunch Room** VEGAN $
(☎734-224-8859; www.thelunchrooma2.com; 407 N 5th Ave; mains $9-14; ⊙11am-9pm Mon-Sat, from 3pm Sun; ✍) Order at the spice jar–lined counter, and then grab one of the close-set tables to await your beet burger with tofu bacon, Korean sweet-potato noodle stir-fry, raspberry and basil grilled cheese or other wildly flavorful vegan dishes. The bar serves beer, wine and cocktails. It's located in the Kerrytown Market & Shops complex.

★**Zingerman's Delicatessen** DELI $$
(☎734-663-3354; www.zingermansdeli.com; 422 Detroit St; sandwiches $14-19; ⊙7am-9pm) The shop that launched the area's foodie frenzy, Zingerman's piles local, organic and specialty ingredients onto towering sandwiches in a sprawling downtown complex that also includes a coffee shop and bakery.

Tourist Information

Destination Ann Arbor (www.visitannarbor.org) Accommodation information and more.

Getting There & Away

Detroit's airport is 30 miles east; shuttle buses (one way $12 to $15) make the trip. Amtrak trains come through Ann Arbor three times daily to/from Detroit ($12 to $15). The train station is downtown and shared by Greyhound. Megabus serves the city, but it stops inconveniently far from its center.

Central Michigan

Michigan's heartland, plunked in the center of the Lower Peninsula, alternates between fertile farms and highway-crossed urban areas. The larger cities excel in cool art, while the entire regions shine in stellar beer making.

Lansing & East Lansing

Smallish Lansing is the state capital. A few miles east lies East Lansing, home of Michigan State University. They're worth a stop to peek into a couple of impressive museums and enjoy the simple pleasures of beer, baseball and fresh-from-the-dairy ice cream.

Sights & Activities

Broad Art Museum MUSEUM
(☎517-884-4800; www.broadmuseum.msu.edu; 547 E Circle Dr, East Lansing; ⊙noon-7pm Tue-Sun) FREE Renowned architect Zaha Hadid designed this wild-looking parallelogram of stainless steel and glass. It holds everything from Greek ceramics to Salvador Dalí paintings. Much of the space is devoted to avant-garde exhibitions.

Lansing River Trail WALKING
(www.lansingrivertrail.org) The paved, 20-mile river trail runs alongside the Grand River from the city's north edge to downtown, and then meanders east along the Red Cedar River to the university. It's popular with runners and cyclists, and the downtown portion links a number of attractions, including the RE Olds Transportation Museum, a children's museum, zoo and fish ladder.

Sleeping & Eating

Wild Goose Inn B&B $$
(☎517-333-3334; www.wildgooseinn.com; 512 Albert St, East Lansing; r $159-179; 📶) The Wild Goose Inn is a six-room B&B one block from Michigan State's campus in East Lansing. All rooms have fireplaces and most have Jacuzzis. Decor is fairly low-key – except for the Arbor room and its wild faux branches!

Drinking & Nightlife

Ellison Brewery and Spirits MICROBREWERY
(☎517-203-5498; www.ellisonbrewing.com; 4903 Dawn Ave, East Lansing; ⊙3-10pm Mon & Tue, 3-11pm Wed & Thu, noon-midnight Fri & Sat, noon-8pm Sun) Ellison hides in a no-frills warehouse in an East Lansing industrial park. Bowl up to the corrugated metal bar and order a Tiramisu coffee stout, 3 Stacks boysenberry sour ale, Relativity double IPA or any of the other 14 beers on tap, fresh from the tanks behind the bartender. Lots of locals unwind over a pint here.

Information

Greater Lansing CVB (www.lansing.org)

Getting There & Away

Amtrak stops in East Lansing on its Blue Water route; the train goes once daily to/from Chicago ($30 to $53, four hours). Greyhound has stations in both Lansing and East Lansing with service to Detroit ($10 to $28, two to three hours, four to five daily) and Grand Rapids ($14 to $23, 70 to 95 minutes, five to six daily). I-96, I-69 and Hwy 127 are the main roadways to the city.

Lansing does have a teeny airport, but Detroit (87 miles southeast) is the nearest airport for international flights.

Grand Rapids

The second-largest city in Michigan, Grand Rapids has gotten its groove on thanks to beer. Around 25 craft breweries operate in town, and suds connoisseurs have been piling in, drawn to their quality, density, proximity to each other and low prices. A foodie scene has built up around the beer makers, and new farm-to-table eateries seem to pop up weekly. Grand Rapids' big-name sculpture park and elegant manors in Heritage Hill intrigue, as well.

Sights

Frederik Meijer Gardens & Sculpture Park GARDENS
(☎616-957-1580; www.meijergardens.org; 1000 E Beltline NE; adult/child $14.50/7; ⊙9am-5pm Mon & Wed-Sat, 9am-9pm Tue, 11am-5pm Sun) The 158-acre gardens feature impressive blooms and hulking works by Auguste Rodin, Henry Moore and others. The sculpture park is star of the show, offering paths and lawns bejeweled with 50 works by artists such as Ai Weiwei, Claes Oldenburg and Anish Kapoor. The five-story glass conservatory impresses, bursting with tropical plants. The children's garden provides lots to smell, touch and dig into. The tranquil Japanese Garden is another highlight. It is 5 miles east of downtown via I-196.

Gerald R Ford Museum MUSEUM
(☎616-254-0400; www.fordlibrarymuseum.gov; 303 Pearl St NW; adult/child $10/4; ⊙9am-5pm Mon-Sat, from noon Sun) The downtown museum is dedicated to Michigan's only president. Ford stepped into the Oval Office after Richard Nixon and his vice president, Spiro Agnew, resigned in disgrace. It's a bizarre period in US history, and the museum does an excellent job of covering it, down to displaying the burglary tools used in the Watergate break-in. Ford and wife Betty are buried on the museum's grounds.

Tours

Grand Rapids Beer Tours FOOD & DRINK
(☎616-901-9719; www.grbeertours.com; 250 Grandville Ave SW; 4/6hr tours $55/75) These van tours stop at three or four breweries (depending on tour length). A guide leads you through production facilities and tastings that include four good-sized samples per venue. Pickup is in front of Grand Rapids' bus station. Tours are limited to 14 people, and they do sell out, so book ahead if possible.

Sleeping & Eating

CityFlats Hotel HOTEL $$
(☎616-608-1720; www.cityflatshotel.com; 83 Monroe Center St NW; r $175-275; ❄📶) 🌿 Rooms at this ecofriendly hotel have big windows for lots of natural light, bamboo linens, cork floors and locally made, reclaimed wood furniture. The building is gold-certified by the Leadership in Energy and Environmental Design (LEED) program. The downtown location puts you near museums, breweries and restaurants.

★Downtown Market Grand Rapids MARKET $
(☎616-805-5308; www.downtownmarketgr.com; 435 Ionia Ave SW; baked goods $2-5, mains $10-16; ⊙10am-7pm Sun-Thu, 10am-8pm Fri, 9am-8pm Sat; 📶) Chowhounds hobnob at this stylish food hall, perusing top picks such as Slows Bar BQ, Fish Lads (stellar fish and chips), Love's Ice Cream and Madcap Coffee. The main floor has tables and benches lit by floor-to-ceiling windows, or head upstairs where more tables await, along with a large, veggie-growing greenhouse.

★Green Well AMERICAN $$
(☎616-808-3566; www.thegreenwell.com; 924 Cherry St SE; mains $15-20; ⊙11am-10pm Sun-Tue, to 11pm Wed & Thu, to midnight Fri & Sat) 🌿 Burgers, green curry, and barbecue pork and polenta feature on the menu, where everything is made with sustainably farmed ingredients. Beer plays a role in many dishes, such as the beer-steamed mussels and beer cheese. The bar taps hard-to-find Michigan brews and pours Michigan wines (flights available). Plus, you can buy awesome art by local artists right off the walls.

Information

Grand Rapids CVB (www.experiencegr.com) Has maps and self-guided brewery tour information online.

Getting There & Away

Grand Rapids has a decent-sized airport with flights to many US cities. Amtrak trains chug to/from Chicago three times daily (once directly, and twice via bus transfers in Kalamazoo; $35 to $70, four hours); the station is downtown near Founders Brewing Co.

The **bus station** (☎616-456-1700; 250 Grandville Ave SW) is directly across from Founders; coaches go to Lansing ($14 to $23, 70 to 95 minutes, five to six daily) and Traverse City ($25 to $30, 4¾ hours, daily), among other destinations. I-96, I-196 and US 131 are the main roadways to the city.

Gold Coast

They don't call it the Gold Coast for nothing. Michigan's 300-mile western shoreline features seemingly endless stretches of beaches, dunes, wineries, orchards and inn-filled towns that boom during the summer – and shiver during the snow-packed winter.

Grand Haven

Grand Haven rocks the classic, old-fashioned beach-town attributes. You know the kind: a waterfront boardwalk, ice-cream shops, sand so clean it squeaks and ooh-and-aah sunsets. The bars and restaurants buzz each evening, and everyone congregates for the eye-popping show by the musical fountain once night falls. Add in the surfing, cycling and inventive breweries, and it's easy to see why Grand Haven blows up each summer.

Sights & Activities

Chinook Pier PIER

(301 N Harbor Dr) Chinook Pier has a lot going on. There's a seasonal mini-golf course (adult/child $3/2) and farmers market (8am to 1pm Wednesday and Saturday). **Wet Mitten Surf Shop** (☎616-844-3388; www.wetmittensurfshop.com; ⏰10am-8pm Mon-Sat, 12:30-7pm Sun) and other water-sports outfitters are here. But its biggest claim to fame is its charter fishing fleet. Boats head out to land king salmon and lake trout that occasionally exceed 20 pounds. It's fascinating to be here at the end of the day when the charters return and display their catch.

Musical Fountain FOUNTAIN

(www.ghfountain.com; 101 N Harbor Dr, Waterfront Stadium; ⏰sunset May-Sep) Everyone gathers for the musical fountain performance each evening in summer. It's a trippy tradition

GRAND RAPIDS BEER CITY

How did Grand Rapids – a town known for ho-hum office-furniture manufacturing – become hot Beer City? Well, as the manufacturing companies closed up shop over the years, they left behind abandoned industrial buildings – ie cheap space perfect for brewers. There was also a young, thirsty population from the dozen colleges and universities in town.

So people starting cooking up suds. It was pretty under the radar until 2012, when Grand Rapids was voted best beer city in the USA by the national Beer Examiner blog. It happened again in 2013. Then the scene boomed.

Grand Rapids now has around 25 craft breweries in the city proper, and about 20 more in nearby towns. The **Ale Trail** takes you there (download a map at www.experiencegr.com/beer). What makes the scene so popular is the breweries' density – you can walk between many makers – and the relatively low cost of drinking.

The breweries also cater to beer tourists and make it easy to taste the wares. Every taproom offers flights, where you choose the 5oz samples you want to try. Ask at any establishment for the **Brewsader Passport**, a handy little booklet that lists all the beer makers. Collect eight stamps as you make the rounds, and a free Brewsader T-shirt comes your way. You can also download the **Brewsader app** and check in at each brewery you visit.

Top picks in town include **Brewery Vivant** (☎616-719-1604; www.breweryvivant.com; 925 Cherry St SE; ⏰3-11pm Mon-Thu, 3pm-midnight Fri, 11am-midnight Sat, noon-10pm Sun) 🍃 for Belgian-style beers in an old chapel, the huge rock-and-roll–style **Founders Brewing Co** (☎616-776-1195; www.foundersbrewing.com; 235 Grandville Ave SW; ⏰11am-2am Mon-Sat, to midnight Sun; 📶), **Mitten Brewing Company** (☎616-608-5612; www.mittenbrewing.com; 527 Leonard St NW; ⏰11:30am-10pm Sun & Mon, to midnight Tue-Sat) and its wide-ranging brews in a cool old firehouse, and inventive neighborhood gem **Harmony Brewing Company** (☎616-233-0063; www.harmonybeer.com; 1551 Lake Dr SE; ⏰11am-10pm Mon, 11am-midnight Tue-Sat, noon-10pm Sun). These breweries also serve terrific food, which you'll need to stay upright through the evening.

to watch water spray high in the sky while synchronized to glowy lights and music. The 25-minute show lets loose nightly in June, July and August, and on Fridays and Saturdays in May and September. The fountain actually is on the west side of the Grand River, but spectators watch it from Waterfront Stadium's outdoor seats on the east side of the river.

Sleeping

Boyden House B&B $$
(☎616-846-3538; www.boydenhouse.com; 301 S 5th St; r $120-255; ❄📶) This rambling Victorian home with gorgeous interior woodwork offers eight rooms that mix antique and modern decor. Some have a private balcony, others have a clawfoot tub or fireplace. All have a comfy featherbed, private bathroom, flat-screen TV and wi-fi. Breakfast is a full cooked extravaganza. It's about a mile walk to the beach.

Eating & Drinking

Morning Star Café BREAKFAST $
(☎616-844-1131; 711 Washington Ave; mains $6-12; ⊙6:30am-2:30pm) This bright-hued, whimsically decorated cafe cooks the best breakfast in town. The blueberry oatmeal pancakes, pumpkin and cream-cheese crepes, and egg, bacon and cornbread scramble top the list, but there are loads of dishes to choose from, many with a Southwestern bent.

Odd Side Ales MICROBREWERY
(☎616-935-7326; www.oddsideales.com; 41 Washington Ave; ⊙11:30am-11pm Mon-Thu, to midnight Fri & Sat, to 10pm Sun) Odd Side brews some peculiar experimental suds, like the Mayan Mocha stout (with coffee, cinnamon, nutmeg and habenero chilies) and Aestas sour ale (aged in oak with sea salt, coriander, strawberry and cucumber). The convivial brewpub now has more than 40 taps delivering the goods.

Information

Grand Haven CVB (www.visitgrandhaven.com) Provides lodging, activities and events info.

Getting There & Away

You'll need a car to get to Grand Haven. US 31 is the most direct route to town and its main street, Washington Ave. The nearest cities with bus, train and plane connections are Grand Rapids (34 miles east) and Holland (23 miles south).

Saugatuck & Douglas

Saugatuck is one of the Gold Coast's most popular resort areas, known for its strong arts community, numerous B&Bs and gay-friendly vibe. Douglas is its twin city a mile or so to the south, and they've pretty much sprawled into one. It's a touristy but funky place, with ice cream–licking families, yuppie boaters and martini-drinking gay couples sharing the waterfront. Galleries and shops fill the compact downtown core. Weekends attract the masses.

Sights & Activities

Oval Beach BEACH
(Oval Beach Dr, Saugatuck; ⊙8am-10pm) Lifeguards patrol the long expanse of fine sand. There are bathrooms and concession stands, though not enough to spoil the peaceful, dune-laden scene. It costs $10 to park. Or arrive the adventurous way, via chain ferry and a trek over Mt Baldhead.

Mt Baldhead WALKING
(Saugatuck) Huff up the stairs of this 200ft-high dune for a stellar view. Then race down the other side to Oval Beach. Get here via the chain ferry; walk right (north) from the dock.

Sleeping & Eating

★ **Pines Motorlodge** MOTEL $$
(☎269-857-5211; www.thepinesmotorlodge.com; 56 Blue Star Hwy, Douglas; r $139-249; 📶) Retro-cool tiki lamps, pinewood furniture and communal lawn chairs add up to a fun, social ambience amid the firs in Douglas.

★ **Farmhouse Deli** DELI $
(☎269-455-5274; www.thefarmhousedeli.com; 100 Blue Star Hwy, Douglas; mains $8-12; ⊙9am-7pm; 🖉) 🍃 While it could coast on its looks – the shabby-chic farmhouse decor is cute as a button – the deli ups the ante with seriously top-notch food. The Cubano sandwich (pulled pork, porchetta and Gruyère), tarragon-tinged chicken salad, tangy goat cheeses, cleansing juices and house-baked croissants, cakes and cookies (try the triple ginger molasses one) dazzle.

Drinking

Virtue Cider WINERY
(☎269-722-3232; www.virtuecider.com; 2170 62nd St, Fennville; ⊙noon-7pm Mon-Wed, to 8pm

WORTH A TRIP

MUSKEGON

The western shore's largest city, Muskegon (population 37,290) features nifty architecture in its downtown district thanks to lumber barons trying to outbuild each other in the late 1800s. Hip taverns, juice bars, bistros and galleries now occupy the structures along Western Ave and its neighboring blocks. **Pigeon Hill Brewing Company** (231-375-5184; www.pigeonhillbrew.com; 500 W Western Ave; noon-10pm Mon-Thu, to midnight Fri & Sat, to 8pm Sun) shows how it's done. Locals hoist pints of eclectic stouts and IPAs in the former garage whose doors slide up to let in fresh air.

Adventure-sports enthusiasts will find action here. The **Muskegon Winter Sports Complex** (877-879-5843; www.msports.org; 462 Scenic Dr) has one of the nation's only public luge tracks. **Pere Marquette Beach** (Beach Street Rd; 6am-11pm) is a hot spot for kiteboarding and paddleboarding, and it hosts the **Great Lakes Surf Festival** (www.greatlakessurffestival.com) in mid-July.

Muskegon is also the departure point for the **Lake Express** (866-914-1010; www.lake-express.com; 1918 Lakeshore Dr; one way adult/child/car $96/39/105; May-Oct) ferry that glides to Milwaukee, WI. **Shoreline Inn** (231-727-8483; www.shorelineinn.com; 750 Terrace Point Rd; r $120-190;) provides waterfront lodging if you need a place to crash before or after your boat ride.

The city is 15 miles north of Grand Haven on US 31. See www.visitmuskegon.org for more information.

Thu-Sun) Head to Virtue's farm in Fennville and sip a pint while sheep bleat, pigs oink and chickens cluck around you. The taproom is in a barrel-strewn barn, where the Brut (crisp and dry) and Percheron (slightly sweet) star among the 13 taps. Flights are available.

Information

Saugatuck/Douglas CVB (www.saugatuck.com) Provides foodie, family and LGBTIQ-focused trip-planning info.

Getting There & Away

Most visitors drive to Saugatuck/Douglas. The I-196/US 31 whizzes by to the east, while the Blue Star Hwy goes into both towns. The closest Amtrak station is in Holland, about 12 miles north.

Sleeping Bear Dunes National Lakeshore

Eye-popping lake views from atop colossal sand dunes? Water blue enough to be in the Caribbean? Miles of unspoiled beaches? Secluded islands with mystical trees? All here at Sleeping Bear Dunes, along with lush forests, terrific day hikes and glass-clear waterways for paddling. The national park stretches from north of Frankfort to just before Leland, on the Leelanau Peninsula. Several cute little towns fringe the area.

Sights & Activities

Manitou Islands ISLAND

(per family $25) The forest-cloaked Manitou Islands provide an off-the-beaten-path adventure. They're part of Sleeping Bear Dunes National Lakeshore, hence the entrance fee. North Manitou is known for star-speckled backcountry camping, while South Manitou is terrific for wilderness-rich day trips. Kayaking and hiking are the big to-dos, especially the 7-mile trek to the Valley of the Giants, an otherworldly stand of cedar trees on South Manitou. **Manitou Island Transit** (231-256-9061; www.manitoutransit.com; 207 W River St, Leland; return adult/child $42/21) runs ferries from Leland; the trip takes 1½ hours.

Dune Climb HIKING

(Hwy 109, Glen Arbor; 24hr) The Dune Climb is the park's most popular attraction, where you trudge up a 200ft-high dune and then run or roll down. Gluttons for leg-muscle punishment can keep slogging all the way to Lake Michigan, a strenuous 1½-hour trek one way; bring water. The site, with a parking lot and bathrooms, is on Hwy 109, 5 miles north of Empire.

Sleeping Bear Heritage Trail CYCLING

(www.sleepingbeartrail.org; Empire) The 22-mile paved path goes from Empire to Bohemian Rd (aka County Rd 669), passing dreamy forested areas, quaint towns and the Dune

Climb along the way; walkers and cyclists are all over it. For the most part it rolls gently up and down, though there are some larger hills at the southern end. Trailheads with parking lots are located roughly every 3 miles; the one at Bar Lake Rd, near Empire, is a good place to embark.

Sleeping & Eating

Glen Arbor B&B B&B $$
(231-334-6789; www.glenarborlodging.com; 6548 Western Ave, Glen Arbor; r $155-290, without bath $115-160; closed mid-Nov–Apr) The owners renovated this century-old farmhouse into a sunny, French country inn with six themed rooms.

Empire Village Inn AMERICAN $
(231-326-5101; www.empirevillageinn.com; 11601 S Lacore Rd, Empire; mains $10-17; noon-10pm) Enter the low A-frame building, grab a seat at a scuffed wood table and order one of the local beers on tap while waiting for your excellent, doughy-crust pizza to arrive. Burgers and sandwiches satisfy too, along with the housemade root beer. It's a swell place to refuel after a day of hiking or biking, if you don't mind the noisy hubbub.

Drinking

Stormcloud Brewing Company MICROBREWERY
(231-352-0118; www.stormcloudbrewing.com; 303 Main St, Frankfort; 11:30am-10pm Sun-Thu, to 11pm Fri & Sat) Belgian-style beers are Stormcloud's gift to the universe. Rainmaker Ale is its medal winner (bronze at the Great American Beer Festival), and there are 15 other taps of unusual and sometimes fruity brews. They're terrific paired with the flatbread pizzas and sharable plates such as smoked whitefish spread on toast. Gluten-free and vegan options are available.

Information

Sleeping Bear Dunes National Lakeshore Visitor Center (231-326-4700; www.nps.gov; 9922 W Front St, Empire; 8am-6pm Jun-Aug, 8:30am-4pm Sep-May) The park's visitor center in Empire has information, trail maps and vehicle entry permits (week/annual $25/45).

Getting There & Away

The park is only accessible by car. US 31 is the main highway to the area. From there make your way onto Hwy 22, which is the road that goes through the park. The nearest airport is in Traverse City, about 50 miles east.

Traverse City

Michigan's 'cherry capital' is the largest city in the northern half of the Lower Peninsula. It's got a bit of urban sprawl, but it's still a happenin' base from which to see the Sleeping Bear Dunes, Mission Peninsula wineries, U-pick orchards and other area attractions. The food and arts scenes are superb, comparable to those of a much larger urban area.

Sights & Activities

Road-tripping out to the wineries is a must. Head north from Traverse City on Hwy 37 for 20 miles to the end of the grape- and cherry-planted Old Mission Peninsula. You'll be spoiled for choice. The wineries stay open all year round, with reduced hours in winter.

Brys Estate Vineyard & Winery WINERY
(231-223-9303; www.brysestate.com; 3309 Blue Water Rd; 11am-7pm Mon-Sat, to 6pm Sun late May-early Sep, reduced hours rest of year) Michigan's excellent wines taste even better on Brys Estate's sprawling deck, which

HARBOR COUNTRY

Harbor Country refers to a group of eight small, lake-hugging towns that roll out beaches, wineries, cool shops and all-round rustic charm.

New Buffalo is the largest community, home to a surf school, a busy public beach, ice-cream shops and a beer church. Three Oaks is the only Harbor community that's inland (6 miles in, via Hwy 12). Here Green Acres meets Greenwich Village in a bohemian farm-and-arts blend. Cycle backroads and browse antique stores by day, then visit the cocktail-swirling distillery and folksy theater by night. Union Pier, Lakeside, Harbert and Sawyer are some of the other cutesy towns, chock-full of historic inns, breweries and galleries. Several wineries surround the communities and offer tastings.

For information, see Harbor Country Chamber of Commerce (www.harborcountry.org).

provides stunning vineyard and bay views. Tastings from $8; cheese and charcuterie plates available.

Paddle TC WATER SPORTS

(☎231-492-0223; www.paddletc.com; 111 E Grandview Pkwy, Clinch Park; kayaks per hr from $30, tours from $45; ⏲9am-9pm May-Oct) Offers bike, kayak and stand-up-paddleboard rentals, starting at $30 per hour. Tours and lessons are available; the KaBrew tour ($69), a kayak and bike crawl of local craft breweries, is highly recommended. Call for times.

Sleeping & Eating

Sugar Beach Resort HOTEL $$

(☎231-938-0100; www.tcbeaches.com; 1773 US 31 N; r $150-250; ❄📶🏊) Sugar Beach has decent prices and it's right on the water. Rooms are nothing fancy, but they're well maintained and have small refrigerators, coffee makers and microwave ovens. Pricier rooms have a balcony and view. Continental breakfast is included. A 4% resort fee gets added to your final bill.

★**Filling Station** PIZZA $

(☎231-946-8168; www.thefillingstationmicrobrewery.com; 642 Railroad Pl; mains $10-16; ⏲11:30am-11pm Mon-Thu, 11:30am-midnight Fri & Sat, noon-10pm Sun) This family-owned business in a former railway terminal has been serving up wood-fired pizzas, fresh green salads and craft beer since 2012. Check out the specials board for seasonal items such as the Oktoberfest pizza, with brats, sauerkraut and a mustard crème fraîche. A s'mores dessert pizza is a sweet ending.

Drinking

★**Short's Production Facility Pull Barn** BREWERY

(☎231-498-2300; www.shortsbrewing.com; 211 Industrial Park Dr; ⏲noon-8pm Mon-Fri, 11am-9pm Sat & Sun late May-early Sep) Beer buffs adore Short's for its Huma Lupa Licious IPA and Juicy Brut ale, and they come en masse to this sprawling outdoor drinking yard in Elk Rapids (18 miles northeast of Traverse City) to get their fill. Folks settle in at shaded picnic tables, play bean-bag toss games and while away the afternoon gulping brews from the 15 on tap.

Information

Traverse City Tourism (www.traversecity.com)

Getting There & Away

Traverse City's small airport has several daily flights to Chicago, Detroit and Minneapolis. US 31 is the main highway to town. Indian Trails (www.indiantrails.com) runs a bus once daily to/from Grand Rapids (one way $25 to $30, 4¾ hours).

Charlevoix & Petoskey

These two towns, among the most affluent along Michigan's western shore, brim with yacht-filled marinas and fancy summer homes. They're not snooty though, and they provide a fair bit of offbeat adventure. Beachcombing, island trekking and following in the footsteps of Ernest Hemingway await those who make the trip.

Sleeping

★**Stafford's Perry Hotel** HOTEL $$

(☎231-347-4000; www.staffords.com; 100 Lewis St, Petoskey; r $169-279; ❄@📶) The Perry Hotel is a grand historic place. Hemingway once stayed here (in 1916 after a hiking and camping trip in the region).

Count on comfy beds, vintage furniture and a cozy on-site pub. Pricier rooms have bay views.

Drinking

★**Beards Brewery** MICROBREWERY

(☎231-753-2221; www.beardsbrewery.com; 215 E Lake St, Petoskey; ⏲11:30am-10pm Tue-Thu, 11:30am-11pm Fri, 10am-11pm Sat, 11;30am-9pm Sun) A couple of hairy-faced home brewers got together to open Beards, and they know their stuff, as the hoppy IPAs, tart saisons and nutty brown ales flowing from the 20 taps attest. It's a community gathering spot hosting trivia nights and local musicians. The awesome outdoor patio overlooks the bay, and a fire pit keeps you toasty on cool nights.

Getting There & Away

US 31 is the main highway to the area. It also connects Charlevoix and Petoskey, which are about 17 mile apart. The closest airport is in Traverse City.

To reach Beaver Island, hop aboard the **ferry** (☎231-547-2311; www.bibco.com; 103 Bridge Park Dr, Charlevoix; one way adult/child/car $32.50/20/105; ⏲mid-Apr–late Dec) in downtown Charlevoix. The journey takes two hours. Reserve ahead if bringing a car.

HEMMINGWAY'S HAUNTS

A number of writers have ties to northwest Michigan, but none are as famous as Ernest Hemingway, who spent the summers of his youth at his family's cottage on Walloon Lake. Hemingway buffs often tour the area to view the places that made their way into his writing.

Horton Bay General Store (231-582-7827; www.hortonbaygeneralstore.com; 5115 Boyne City Rd, Boyne City; 8am-2pm Wed & Thu, 8am-2pm & 6-9pm Fri-Sun, closed mid-Oct–mid-May) A short distance north of Charlevoix, Boyne City Rd veers off to the east. It skirts Lake Charlevoix and eventually arrives at Horton Bay. Hemingway fans will recognize the store, with its 'high false front,' from his short story 'Up in Michigan.' The old-time shop now sells groceries, souvenirs, sandwiches and ice cream, plus wine and tapas on weekend nights (reservations required for the latter).

Little Traverse History Museum (231-347-2620; www.petoskeymuseum.org; 100 Depot Ct, Petoskey; $3; 10am-4pm Mon-Sat, closed mid-Oct–late May) Further north on US 31, stop in Petoskey to see the museum's Hemingway collection, including rare first-edition books that the author autographed for a friend when he visited in 1947.

City Park Grill (231-347-0101; www.cityparkgrill.com; 432 E Lake St, Petoskey; 11:30am-10pm Sun-Thu, to 1:30am Fri & Sat) A few blocks from the museum, toss back a drink at this bar where Hemingway was a regular.

Tour Hemingway's Michigan (www.mihemingwaytour.com) provides further information for self-guided jaunts.

Straits of Mackinac

This region, between the Upper and Lower Peninsulas, features a long history of forts and fudge shops. Car-free Mackinac Island is Michigan's premier tourist draw.

One of the most spectacular sights in the area is the 5-mile-long Mackinac Bridge (known locally as 'Big Mac'), which spans the Straits of Mackinac. The $4 toll is worth every penny as the views from the bridge, which include two Great Lakes, two peninsulas and hundreds of islands, are second to none in Michigan. And remember: despite the spelling, it's pronounced *mac*-in-aw.

Mackinaw City

At the south end of Mackinac Bridge, bordering I-75, is touristy Mackinaw City. It serves mainly as a jumping-off point to Mackinac Island, but it does have a couple of intriguing historic sights.

Sights

Colonial Michilimackinac HISTORIC SITE
(231-436-5564; www.mackinacparks.com; 102 W Straits Ave; adult/child $12.50/7.25; 9am-7pm Jun-Aug, to 5pm May & Sep-early Oct;) Next to the Big Mac bridge (its visitor center is actually beneath the bridge) is Colonial Michilimackinac, a National Historic Landmark that features a reconstructed stockade first built in 1715 by the French. Costumed interpreters cook and craft here.

Getting There & Away

The main road to Mackinaw City is I-75. The docks for **Star Line** (800-638-9892; www.mackinacferry.com; 801 S Huron Ave; return adult/child/bicycle $27/15/12) and **Shepler's** (800-828-6157; www.sheplersferry.com; 556 E Central Ave; return adult/child/bicycle $27/15/11; late Apr-Oct) are a short distance off the interstate. Both send ferries to Mackinac Island. The trip takes 20 minutes; boats go at least hourly during daylight hours in spring and fall, and up to four times per hour in June, July and August. Both companies having free parking lots in which to leave your car for the day ($5 to park overnight).

Mackinac Island

From either Mackinaw City or St Ignace, you can catch a ferry to Mackinac Island. The island's location in the straits between Lake Michigan and Lake Huron made it a prized port in the North American fur trade, and a site the British and Americans battled over many times.

The most important date on this 3.8-sq-mile island was 1898 – the year cars were banned in order to encourage tourism. Today all travel is by horse or bicycle; even the police use bikes to patrol the town. The crowds of tourists – called Fudgies by the islanders – can be crushing at times, particularly during summer weekends. But when the last ferry leaves in the evening and clears out the day-trippers, Mackinac's real charm emerges and you drift back into another, slower era.

Eighty percent of the island is state parkland. Not much stays open between November and April.

Arch Rock NATURAL FEATURE

FREE This huge limestone arch curves 150ft above Lake Huron and provides dramatic photo opportunities. You can get here two ways: from stairs that lead up from the lakeshore road, or from the island's interior via Arch Rock Rd. The site crowds with tour groups around midday, so try visiting early in the morning.

Fort Mackinac HISTORIC SITE

(906-847-3328; www.mackinacparks.com; 7127 Huron Rd; adult/child $13.50/7.75; 9:30am-7pm Jun-Aug, reduced hours May & Sep–mid-Oct, closed mid-Oct–Apr;) Fort Mackinac sits atop limestone cliffs near downtown. Built by the British in 1780, it's one of the best-preserved military forts in the country. Costumed interpreters and cannon and rifle firings (every half-hour) entertain the kids.

Stop into the tearoom here for a bite and a million-dollar view of downtown and the Straits of Mackinac from the outdoor tables.

Information

Mackinac Island Visitor Center (906-847-3783; www.mackinacisland.org; 7274 Main St; 9am-5pm May-Oct) Downtown booth with maps for hiking and cycling.

Getting There & Away

Two ferry companies – **Shepler's** (800-828-6157; www.sheplersferry.com; Main St; return adult/child/bicycle $27/15/11; late Apr-Oct) and **Star Line** (800-638-9892; www.mackinacferry.com; Main St; return adult/child/bicycle $27/15/12) – operate out of Mackinaw City and St Ignace, and charge roughly the same rates. Book online and you'll save a few bucks. The ferries go at least hourly during daylight hours in spring and fall, and up to four times per hour in summer. The trip takes about 20 minutes. Both companies have parking lots to leave your car (free for the day, $5 for overnight).

Upper Peninsula

Rugged and isolated, with hardwood forests blanketing 90% of its land, the Upper Peninsula (UP) is a Midwest highlight. Only 45 miles of interstate highway slice through the trees, punctuated by a handful of cities, of which Marquette is the largest. Between the small towns lie miles of undeveloped shoreline on Lakes Huron, Michigan and Superior; scenic two-lane roads; and pasties, the local meat-and-vegetable pot pies brought over by Cornish miners 150 years ago.

You'll find it's a different world up north. Residents of the UP, aka 'Yoopers,' consider themselves distinct from the rest of the state – they've even threatened to secede in the past.

Pictured Rocks National Lakeshore

Stretching along prime Lake Superior real estate, Pictured Rocks National Lakeshore is a series of wild cliffs and caves, where blue and green minerals have streaked the red and yellow sandstone into a kaleidoscope of color. County Rd H-58 spans the park for 52 slow miles from Grand Marais in the east to Munising in the west. Either town makes a good base for exploring the area. In between you'll find lakeside hikes, kayak trips and boat tours that offer brilliant ways to take in the area's shipwrecks, waterfalls and artist's-palette geology.

Sights & Activities

Top sights (from east to west) include **Au Sable Point Lighthouse** (County Rd H-58, Grand Marais) and its shipwrecks, agate-strewn **Twelvemile Beach** (County Rd H-58, Grand Marais), hike-rich **Chapel Falls** (Chapel Rd, Munising) and view-worthy **Miners Castle** (Miners Castle Rd, Munising). Boat rides and kayak trips along the shore are an excellent way to absorb the dramatic scenery.

Pictured Rock Cruises BOATING

(906-387-2379; www.picturedrocks.com; 100 City Park Dr, Munising; 2½hr tours adult/child $38/10; mid-May–mid-Oct) Boats with both deck and enclosed seating hug the shore for 16 miles. They depart from Munising's city dock and glide along the shore to Miners Castle. The sunset cruises are particularly lovely. Advance reservations are wise.

Pictured Rocks Kayaking KAYAKING
(☎906-387-5500; www.paddlepicturedrocks.com; 1348 Commercial St, Munising; 4½hr tours adult/child $149/110; ⏲late May-Sep) This company takes you out on a 56ft passenger boat and drops you off close to the key caves and arches. A guide leads the way from there. It's good for beginners since you're only paddling for two hours or so. Tours depart at 9am and 2:30pm daily.

Getting There & Away

You'll need your own wheels to get here. Marquette, 42 miles west, offers the closest airport. Hwy 28 and Hwy 94 are the primary roads to the area. County Rd H-58 runs through Pictured Rocks; it closes in parts during winter due to snow.

The **Grand Island Ferry** (☎906-387-2600; www.grandislandup.com; N8016 Grand Island Landing Rd, Munising; return adult/child $20/15; ⏲late May–mid-Oct) makes the 15-minute trip to the island three to 10 times daily.

Marquette

Lakeside Marquette is the perfect place to stay put for a few days to explore the region. It's the Upper Peninsula's largest (and snowiest) town, known as a hot spot for outdoors enthusiasts. Forests, beaches and cliffs provide a playground spitting distance from downtown. Locals ski in winter and hit the trails with their fat-tire bikes in summer. Northern Michigan University is here, so the population skews young. Beer and good food await in the historic town center.

Sights & Activities

Da Yoopers Tourist Trap and Museum MUSEUM
(☎906-485-5595; www.dayoopers.com; 490 N Steel St; ⏲10am-6pm Mon-Fri, to 5pm Sat & Sun) FREE Behold Big Gus, the world's largest chainsaw. And Big Ernie, the world's largest rifle. Kitsch runs rampant at Da Yoopers Tourist Trap and Museum, 15 miles west of Marquette on Hwy 28/41, past Ishpeming. Browse the store for only-in-the-UP gifts such as a polyester moose tie or beer-can wind chimes.

Down Wind Sports KAYAKING
(☎906-226-7112; www.downwindsports.com; 514 N 3rd St; ⏲10am-7pm Mon-Fri, 10am-5pm Sat, 11am-3pm Sun) Rents out all kinds of gear and has the lowdown on kayaking, fly fishing, surfing, ice climbing and other adventures.

Sleeping

Landmark Inn HISTORIC HOTEL $$
(☎906-228-2580; www.thelandmarkinn.com; 230 N Front St; r $179-249; ❄📶) The elegant, six-story Landmark Inn fills a historic lakefront building and has a couple of resident ghosts.

WORTH A TRIP

SAULT STE MARIE

Founded in 1668, Sault Ste Marie (population 13,550) is Michigan's oldest city and the third oldest in the USA. Today it's a busy port and border crossing to Canada, where twin city Sault Ste Marie, Ontario, winks across the bridge. While that's all dandy, the best reason for a visit here is to see the Soo Locks raise and lower hulking freighters.

Catch the action at the **Soo Locks Visitor Center** (☎906-253-9290; Portage Ave; ⏲9am-9pm mid-May–mid-Oct) FREE. It features displays, videos and observation decks from which you can watch 1000ft-long boats leap 21ft from Lake Superior to Lake Huron. It's weirdly awesome. Afterwards head down the block to **Karl's Cuisine, Winery & Brewery** (☎906-0253-1900; www.karlscuisine.com; 447 W Portage Ave; mains $13-24; ⏲11am-9pm Wed-Sat) for pasties, Lake Superior whitefish and pasta dishes along with housemade booze.

I-75 is the main road to town, which is 59 miles north of Mackinaw City. To reach the locks, take exit 394 off the interstate and go left. To continue onward into Canada, make for the International Bridge. The border crossing is open 24/7. See www.saultstemarie.com for more information.

OFF THE BEATEN TRACK

KEWEENAW PENINSULA & ISLE ROYALE NATIONAL PARK

The Keweenaw Peninsula is the UP's northernmost bit, a wild timberland that juts by its lonesome into Lake Superior. Energetic small towns, jam-making monks and view-tastic mountain drives await adventurers who make the journey.

US 41 is the main highway on the peninsula. Take it to Houghton (population 8000), the Keweenaw's largest town. It bustles with students – Michigan Tech University is here – and it's the jump-off to **Isle Royale National Park**, with ferries and seaplanes departing in summer. **Keweenaw Brewing Company** (☎906-482-5596; www.kbc.beer; 408 Shelden Ave, Houghton; ⊙3-10pm Mon-Wed, 11am-11pm Thu-Sat, noon-8pm Sun) gives a good feel for the local scene. Grab a $3 pint and enjoy it by the fireplace.

Totally free of vehicles and roads, Isle Royale National Park – a 210-sq-mile island in Lake Superior – is certainly the place to go for peace and quiet. It gets fewer visitors in a year than Yellowstone National Park gets in a day, which means the 165 miles of hiking trails and 2000 moose roaming through the forest are all yours.

Continue north for 25 miles, veer onto Hwy 26 north, and a short distance past Eagle River you'll come to the **Jampot** (www.poorrockabbey.com; 6500 Hwy 26, Eagle Harbor; baked goods $1-3; ⊙10am-5pm Tue-Sat May–mid-Oct). Bearded, black-robed monks work in the little bakery selling jams they make from foraged berries, coffee from their house-roasted beans, and pound cake muffins that they bake.

Stay on Hwy 26 another 9 miles. Just past Lake Bailey you'll see the turnoff for the **Brockway Mountain Drive** (Eagle Harbor). The 10-mile jaunt along the spine of the eponymous crag shows off terrific views of Lake Superior. It deposits you in tiny Copper Harbor, where yet another ferry sets sail for Isle Royale. For more information, see www.copperharbor.org.

Information

Visitor Center (2201 US 41; ⊙9am-5:30pm) Stop at the log-lodge visitors center at the town's edge for brochures on local hiking trails and waterfalls.

Getting There & Away

The main roadways to town are US 41 and Hwy 28. Marquette has a small airport with flights to Detroit, Chicago and Minneapolis. Indian Trails buses (www.indiantrails.com) go daily to Milwaukee ($60 to $80, eight hours) and Hancock ($18 to $25, three hours).

Porcupine Mountains Wilderness State Park

Michigan's largest state park, with 90 miles of trails, is a wilderness winner. 'The Porkies,' as they're called, are so rugged that loggers bypassed most of the range in the early 19th century, leaving the park with the largest tract of virgin forest between the Rocky Mountains and Adirondacks. Along with 300-year-old hemlock trees, the Porkies are known for waterfalls, 20 miles of undeveloped Lake Superior shoreline, black bears lumbering about, and the view of the park's stunning Lake of the Clouds.

Sights & Activities

Lake of the Clouds LAKE

(Hwy 107, Ontonagon; per car $9) This lake is the area's most photographed sight. After stopping at the visitor center to pay the park entrance fee, continue to the end of Hwy 107 and climb 300ft via a short path for the stunning view of the shimmering water. Lengthier trails depart from the parking lot.

Porcupine Mountain Ski Area SKIING

(☎906-885-5209; www.porkiesfun.com; Hwy 107, Ontonagon; half-/full day $33/43; ⊙Dec-early Apr) Winter is a busy time here, with downhill skiing (a 787ft vertical drop) and 26 miles of cross-country trails on offer. Rentals are available for skis and snowboards ($27 each per day) and snowshoes (per day $15).

Information

Friends of the Porkies (www.porkies.org) Lowdown on local arts and events.

Porcupine Mountains and Ontonagon Area CVB (www.porcupineup.com) List of waterfalls and activities.

Porcupine Mountains Visitor Center (906-885-5275; www.michigan.gov/porkies; S Boundary Rd, Ontonagon; 8am-6pm mid-May–mid-Oct) Where you buy vehicle entry permits ($9/33 per day/year) and pick up backcountry camping permits.

Getting There & Away

You'll need a car to get here. US 45 is the main highway to the area.

WISCONSIN

Wisconsin is cheesy and proud of it. The state pumps out 2.5 billion pounds of cheddar, Gouda and other smelly goodness – a quarter of America's hunks – from its cow-speckled farmland per year. Local license plates read 'The Dairy State' with udder dignity. Folks here even refer to themselves as 'cheeseheads' and emphasize it by wearing novelty foam rubber cheese-wedge hats for special occasions (most notably during Green Bay Packers football games).

So embrace the cheese thing, because there's a good chance you'll be here for a while. Wisconsin has a ton to offer: exploring the craggy cliffs and lighthouses of Door County, kayaking through sea caves at Apostle Islands National Lakeshore, touring Green Bay's football shrine of Lambeau Field, cow chip–throwing along Hwy 12, or simply soaking up the beer, art and festivals in Milwaukee and Madison.

Information

Wisconsin B&B Association (www.wbba.org) Convenient listing of the state's B&Bs by city and region.

Wisconsin Department of Tourism (www.travelwisconsin.com) Produces tons of free guides on subjects such as biking, golf and rustic roads; also has a free app.

Wisconsin Highway Conditions (www.511wi.gov) Handy for checking winter driving conditions.

Wisconsin Milk Marketing Board (www.wisconsincheese.com) Provides a free statewide map of cheesemakers titled *A Traveler's Guide to America's Dairyland*.

Wisconsin State Park Information (608-266-2181; www.dnr.wi.gov/topic/parks) Entry requires a vehicle permit ($11/38 per day/year). Campsites cost $21 to $35; reservations accepted.

Milwaukee

Here's the thing about Milwaukee: it's cool, but for some reason it slips under the radar. The city's reputation as a working man's town of brewskis, bowling alleys and polka halls persists. But attractions such as the Calatrava-designed art museum, the badass Harley-Davidson Museum and stylish eating and shopping enclaves have turned Wisconsin's largest city into an unassumingly groovy place.

Milwaukee's enduring relationship with beer is no accident. The city was settled by Germans in the 1840s and many started breweries. A few decades later, the introduction of bulk-brewing technology turned beer production into a major industry. Milwaukee earned its 'Brew City' nickname in the 1880s when Pabst, Schlitz, Blatz, Miller and 80 other breweries made suds here. Today, only Miller remains of the national brands, though smaller brewers have made a big comeback and bars around town feature the best microbrews from Wisconsin and the region.

Sights & Activities

Lake Michigan sits to the east of the city, and is rimmed by parkland. The scenic Riverwalk path cuts through downtown along both sides of the Milwaukee River.

★**Harley-Davidson Museum** MUSEUM
(414-287-2789; www.harley-davidson.com; 400 W Canal St; adult/child $20/10; 9am-6pm Fri-Wed, 9am-8pm Thu May-Sep, 10am-6pm Fri-Wed, 10am-8pm Thu Oct-Apr) Hundreds of motorcycles show the styles through the decades, including the flashy rides of Elvis and Evel Knievel. You can sit in the saddle of various bikes (on the bottom floor, in the Experience Gallery) and take badass photos. Even nonbikers will enjoy the interactive exhibits and tough, leather-clad crowds.

★**Milwaukee Art Museum** MUSEUM
(414-224-3200; www.mam.org; 700 N Art Museum Dr; adult/child $19/free; 10am-5pm Tue, Wed & Fri-Sun, to 8pm Thu) You have to see this lakeside institution, which features a stunning winglike addition by Santiago Calatrava. It soars open and closed every day at 10am, noon and 5pm (8pm on Thursday), which is wild to watch; head to the suspension bridge outside for the best view. There are fabulous folk and outsider art galleries,

and a sizeable collection of Georgia O'Keeffe paintings. A 2015 renovation added photography and new media galleries to the trove.

American Black Holocaust Museum MUSEUM
(ABHM; www.abhmuseum.org; 411 W North Ave) This museum aims to tell the story of what it calls the 'Black Holocaust' – which includes the slave trade from Africa, slavery in the American South, the aftermath of the Civil War and the Civil Rights movement – through pictures and stories. It was founded in 1984 as a virtual museum by James Cameron, who survived a lynching as a 16-year-old boy. The museum reopened in 2022 following a redevelopment.

Miller Brewing Company BREWERY
(☎414-931-2337; www.millercoors.com; 4251 W State St; tours $10; ⏲10:30am-4:30pm Mon-Sat Jun-Aug, to 3:30pm Mon-Sat Sep-May) FREE Founded in 1855, the historic Miller facility preserves Milwaukee's beer legacy. Join the legions lined up for the free, hour-long tours. Though the mass-produced beer may not be your favorite, the factory impresses with its sheer scale: you'll visit the packaging plant where 2000 cans are filled each minute, and the warehouse where a half-million cases await shipment. And then there's the generous tasting session at the tour's end, where you can down three full-size samples. Don't forget your ID.

Festivals & Events

★Summerfest MUSIC
(www.summerfest.com; 639 E Summerfest Pl; day pass $23; ⏲late Jun-early Jul) It's dubbed 'the world's largest music festival,' and indeed hundreds of rock, blues, jazz, country and alternative bands swarm its 11 stages over 11 days. The scene totally rocks; it is held at downtown's lakefront festival grounds (aka Henry Maier Festival Park). The headline concerts cost extra.

DON'T MISS

THE BRONZE FONZ

Rumor has it the **Bronze Fonz** (east side of Riverwalk), just south of Wells St downtown, is the most photographed sight in Milwaukee. The Fonz, aka Arthur Fonzarelli, was a character from the 1970s TV show *Happy Days*, which was set in the city. What do you think – do the blue pants get an 'Aaay' or 'Whoa!'?

Sleeping

★Ambassador HOTEL $
(☎877-935-2189; www.ambassadormilwaukee.com; 2308 W Wisconsin Ave; r $119-139; P❄@📶) This renovated art deco gem, on the city's western side, near Marquette University, is an affordable central option. Architecture buffs will love all of those 'jazz age' period details, such as the polished marbled flooring in the lobby and the bronze elevator doors. The in-house restaurant exudes a 'supper club' vibe and the adjacent bar pours the perfect Wisconsin-style old-fashioned.

Brewhouse Inn & Suites HOTEL $$
(☎414-810-3350; www.brewhousesuites.com; 1215 N 10th St; r $199-249; P❄@📶) This 90-room hotel sits in the exquisitely renovated old Pabst Brewery complex. Each of the large chambers has steampunk decor, a kitchenette and free wi-fi. It's at downtown's far west edge, about a half-mile walk from sausagey Old World 3rd St and a good 2 miles from the festival grounds. Parking costs $28.

Iron Horse Hotel HOTEL $$$
(☎888-543-4766; www.theironhorsehotel.com; 500 W Florida St; r $250-360; P❄📶) The property's location, in Milwaukee's up-and-coming but still a little rough around the edges Fifth Ward, doesn't quite fit the upmarket price tag. That said, the rooms are big, and we do love the industrial post-and-beam, exposed-brick interiors. The Iron Horse is within walking distance of the Harley-Davidson Museum and some great restaurants and bars. Parking here costs $30.

Eating

Good places to scope for eats include Germanic Old World 3rd St downtown; multi-ethnic E Brady St by its intersection with N Farwell Ave; and the gastro pub–filled Third Ward, anchored along N Milwaukee St south of I-94.

★Birch + Butcher AMERICAN $$
(☎414-323-7372; www.birchandbutcher.com; 459 E Pleasant St; mains $22-34; ⏲7:30am-9pm Mon-Thu, to 10pm Fri & Sat, to 2pm Sun; 📶🖉) Birch +

LOCAL KNOWLEDGE

FISH FRIES & SUPPER CLUBS

Wisconsin has a couple of unique dining traditions that you'll likely encounter when visiting the state:

Fish Fry Friday is the hallowed day of the 'fish fry.' This communal meal of beer-battered cod, French fries and coleslaw came about years ago, providing locals with a cheap meal to socialize around and celebrate the end of the working week. The convention is still going strong at many bars and restaurants, including **Lakefront Brewery** (414-372-8800; www.lakefrontbrewery.com; 1872 N Commerce St; 45min tours $11; 11am-8pm Mon-Thu, 11am-9pm Fri, 9am-9pm Sat, 10am-5pm Sun) in Milwaukee.

Supper Club This is a type of time-warped restaurant common in the upper Midwest. Supper clubs started in the 1930s, and most retain a retro vibe. Hallmarks include a woodsy location, a radish-and-carrot-laden relish tray on the table, a surf-and-turf menu and a mile-long, unironic cocktail list. See www.wisconsinsupperclubs.net for more information. Old Fashioned (p597) in Madison is a modern take on the venue (it's named after the quintessential, brandy-laced supper-club drink).

Butcher claims to have the city's only open-fire hearth for serious searing and grilling. However it does it, we love the results. Choose from a tempting menu of grilled fish, steaks and veggies.

The weekend brunches here draw big crowds for unusual offerings like whitefish bagels and pulled-pork shoulder, served with polenta. The space is airy and casual.

Pitch's Lounge & Restaurant STEAK $$
(414-272-9313; www.pitchsribs.com; 1801 N Humboldt Ave; mains $18-26; 5-10pm Sun-Thu, 3-11pm Fri & Sat;) Steaks, chops, seafood, and the house ribs are on the menu here at this Milwaukee supper club that's been going strong since the 1940s. Walk into the hushed dining room to step back in time a few decades when an evening out always started with a brandy old-fashioned. Enjoy the traditional beer-battered cod at the Friday-night fish fry.

Ardent AMERICAN $$$
(414-897-7022; www.ardentmke.com; 1751 N Farwell St; tasting menu $95; 6-10pm Wed-Sat;) Milwaukee's foodies get weak in the knees when they sniff the Beard-nominated chef's ever-changing, farm-to-table dishes. Dinner is a lingering affair in the tiny glowing room, with two seatings each night for the 10-course tasting menu. Reserve well in advance.

Or head next door to Ardent's sibling restaurant, open 6pm to 1am Wednesday to Saturday, for slurpable bowls of ramen noodles.

Drinking & Entertainment

★Champion's BAR
(414-332-2440; www.championspub.com; 2417 N Bartlett Ave; 3pm-2am Mon-Fri, from 1pm Sat, from 11:30am Sun;) Champion's is the perfect choice if you're looking for something quiet, friendly and authentic. It has been a neighborhood fixture since the 1950s and not much has changed since. You'll find friendly locals, New Glarus' own Spotted Cow on tap and a low-key beer garden out back for relaxing summer nights.

Hi Hat COCKTAIL BAR
(414-225-9330; www.hihatlounge.com; 1701 N Arlington Place, cnr E Brady St; 4pm-2am Mon-Fri, 10am-2am Sat & Sun;) One of the city's best watering holes, Hi Hat sits along a strip of legendary bars on E Brady St on the near-north side. There's drinking on two levels, with an adjacent sports bar. The cocktails and decor have a retro vibe, and you'll occasionally catch live bands here in the evening.

★Rave LIVE MUSIC
(Eagles Club; 414-342-7283; www.therave.com; 2401 West Wisconsin Ave; concerts from $25; shows from 8pm; ;) The former Eagles Club was built in 1926 and has hosted a 'who's who' of legendary music acts, including Guy Lombardo, Glenn Miller, Buddy Holly, Bob Dylan, the Sex Pistols, all the way up to Ed Sheeran. It's still going strong, with nightly shows in one of half a dozen venues. See the website for a program and ticket info.

DON'T MISS

RACING SAUSAGES

It's common to see strange things after too many stadium beers. But a group of giant sausages sprinting around Miller Park's perimeter – is that for *real*? It is if it's the middle of the 6th inning. That's when the famous 'Racing Sausages' (actually five people in costumes) waddle onto the field to give the fans a thrill. If you don't know your encased meats, that's Brat, Polish, Italian, Hot Dog and Chorizo vying for supremacy.

★ **Miller Park** BASEBALL
(☎414-902-4400; www.brewers.com; 1 Brewers Way; ⊙box office 9am-7pm Mon-Fri, 9am-5pm Sat, 11am-5pm Sun) From April through September, the National League Milwaukee Brewers play baseball at fab Miller Park, which has a retractable roof and real grass. Buy tickets online or at the stadium box office. The stadium is about 5 miles west of downtown. The Brewers Line bus runs there on game days; pick it up along Wisconsin Ave.

Information

Milwaukee Convention & Visitors Bureau (☎800-554-1448; www.visitmilwaukee.org; 648 N Plankinton Ave; ⊙8am-5pm Mon-Fri)

Getting There & Around

General Mitchell International Airport (MKE; ☎414-747-5245; www.mitchellairport.com; 5300 S Howell Ave) is 8 miles south of downtown. Take public bus 80 ($2.25) or a cab ($35).

The **Lake Express ferry** (☎866-914-1010; www.lake-express.com; 2330 S Lincoln Memorial Dr; one way adult/child/car from $96/39/105; ⊙May-Oct) sails from downtown (the terminal is located a few miles south of the city center) to Muskegon, MI, providing easy access to Michigan's beach-lined Gold Coast.

Several bus companies use the **Milwaukee Intermodal Station** (433 St Paul Ave). Badger Bus (www.badgerbus.com) goes to Madison ($20, two hours) eight times per day. Greyhound (www.greyhound.com) and Megabus (www.megabus.com) run frequent buses to Chicago (two hours) and Minneapolis (6½ to seven hours).

Amtrak (www.amtrakhiawatha.com) runs the *Hiawatha* train seven times a day to/from Chicago ($25 to $35, 1½ hours). It also uses the Milwaukee Intermodal Station.

Central Milwaukee, including the downtown area, riverwalk and neighbouring districts such as the North Side and Third Ward, is spread out, but reasonably walkable with comfortable shoes.

South Central Wisconsin

The south-central portion of Wisconsin is often overlooked, but has some unique and surprising charms. Besides being green and largely unspoiled, the area is linked with architect Frank Lloyd Wright. Wright spent the better part of his life living and working near Spring Green and maintained a school at Taliesin. Wright's students designed several distinctive buildings in and around Spring Green.

Moving south into Green County, visitors might wonder if they need to bring along their passports, so visible are the region's connections to Switzerland. Dairies around here cut a lot of cheese. New Glarus is the place to tuck into some locally made raclette and cheese fondue, while the county seat at Monroe has its own share of limburger-loving taverns. Madison is the area's cultural jewel. A livable, walkable, cyclable state capital with a boisterous student scene and some excellent places to eat, drink and party.

Green County

This pastoral area holds the nation's greatest concentration of cheesemakers. As you're road-tripping through, you can stop at local dairy farms and shops and learn your artisanal from farmstead, Gruyere from Gouda, curd from whey. Why so cheesy here? It has to do with the limestone-rich soil. It grows distinctive grass, which makes distinctive food for cows, and that results in distinctive milk that creates distinctive cheese. Got it? Old World Europeans did, particularly the Swiss. They flocked to the region in the 1800s, bringing their cheesemaking skills with them.

Pretty New Glarus, all bedecked in Swiss flags, owing to the town's cultural and commercial roots, makes for a fun stroll. It's got plenty of cowbells and cuckoo clocks (as well as atmospheric restaurants and bars for sampling the region's wares). Monroe, the biggest town and the seat of Green County, is also stuffed with cheese history and limburger taverns.

Eating & Drinking

New Glarus Brewery BREWERY
(☎608-527-5850; www.newglarusbrewing.com; 2400 Hwy 69, New Glarus; guided tours $30; ⊙tasting room 10am-5pm Mon-Sat, from noon Sun, tours 1pm Fri;) This hilltop brewery, about a mile south of New Glarus, has won kudos around the state for its excellent Spotted Cow ale and Belgian Red (with Door County cherries). A visit here entails wandering around the brewery and then hitting the tasting room for a pint ($8 to $9.50) or three-beer sampler ($8). On Fridays, budding brewmasters are offered the possibility of a three-hour 'hard hat' guided tour ($30).

Information

Green County Tourism (www.greencounty.org) Comprehensive, well-organized website.

Traveler's Guide to America's Dairyland (www.eatwisconsincheese.com) Good map showing local dairy producers and plant tours.

Getting There & Away

Madison is the closet urban area and transportation hub. From there you'll need a car to access Green County. Hwy 69 is a main artery connecting Madison, New Glarus and Monroe. Most roads in the region are slowpoke, two-lane byways.

Madison

Madison reaps a lot of kudos – most walkable city, best road-biking city, most vegetarian-friendly, gay-friendly, environmentally friendly and just plain all-round friendliest city in the USA. Ensconced on a narrow isthmus between Mendota and Monona Lakes, it's a pretty combination of small, grassy state capital and liberal, bookish college town.

Start your exploration around Capitol Sq, where several museums are clustered. The capitol building itself and most of the attractions around town, including the museums, are free. From here, expand your horizons outward toward the lakes, where more natural sights, including an arboretum and botanical gardens, are located. This being Wisconsin, the botanical gardens are located not far from a beer garden. Madison excels at nightlife. Find the usual cluster of student bars and clubs along State St. There's an emerging dining and drinking scene northeast of the capitol along Williamson St, which the locals simply call 'Willy.'

Sights

★Dane County Farmers Market FOOD & DRINKS
(www.dcfm.org; Capitol Sq; ⊙6:15am-1:45pm Sat mid-Apr–early Nov) On Saturdays, a food

WORTH A TRIP

FRANK LLOYD WRIGHT'S RACINE

By most accounts, the southeastern city of Racine is an unremarkable industrial town, but it does have some key Frank Lloyd Wright sights that architecture fans won't want to miss. What's more, it's a prime place to sample the mega-sized state pastry known as the 'kringle.'

Wright devotees will want to start their exploration at the **SC Johnson Administration Building & Research Tower** (☎262-260-2154; www.scjohnson.com/visit; 1525 Howe St; ⊙tours 10am & 2pm Thu-Sun Mar-Dec) FREE, where the architect designed several striking buildings. Free 90-minute tours take in the 1939 Admin Building, a magnificent space with tall, flared columns in its vast Great Workroom and 43 miles worth of Pyrex glass-tube windows letting in soft, natural light. You'll also see the 1950 Research Tower – where Raid, Off and other famous products were developed – which features 15 floors of curved brick bands and more Pyrex windows.

About 5 miles north of downtown, **Wingspread** (☎262-681-3353; www.scjohnson.com/visit; 33 E Four Mile Rd; ⊙9:30am-3:30pm Wed-Fri, 11:30am-3:30pm Sat, noon-2:30pm Sun Mar-Dec) FREE is the house Frank Lloyd Wright designed for HF Johnson Jr, one of the company's leaders. It's the last and largest of Wright's Prairie-style abodes, completed in 1939. It's enormous, with 500 windows and a 30ft-high chimney. Free tours through the building take one hour, and must be booked in advance.

I-94 runs to Racine, which is 30 miles south of Milwaukee and 75 miles north of Chicago.

bazaar takes over Capitol Sq. It's one of the nation's most expansive markets, famed for its artisan cheeses and breads. Craft vendors and street musicians add to the festivities. In winter, the market moves indoors to varying locations on Wednesdays.

Olbrich Botanical Gardens GARDENS
(☎608-246-4550; www.olbrich.org; 3330 Atwood Ave; conservatory $2, garden free; ⊙conservatory 10am-4pm, garden 9am-8pm Apr-Aug, to 6pm Sep & Oct, to 4pm Nov-Mar) Roam the 16 acres of lush outdoor gardens, including an unusual gilded Thai pavilion. The Bolz Conservatory houses rare tropical plants, free-flying birds and, from mid-July to mid-August, 'blooming' butterflies.

Chazen Museum of Art MUSEUM
(☎608-263-2246; www.chazen.wisc.edu; 750 University Ave; ⊙9am-5pm Tue, Wed & Fri, 9am-9pm Thu, 11am-5pm Sat & Sun) FREE The university's art museum is huge and fabulous, and way beyond the norm for a campus collection. The 3rd floor holds most of the genre-spanning trove: everything from the Old Dutch Masters to Qing Dynasty porcelain vases, Picasso sculptures and Andy Warhol pop art. Free chamber-music concerts and art-house film showings take place on Sundays from September to mid-May.

Sleeping

Hotel Ruby Marie BOUTIQUE HOTEL $$
(☎608-327-7829; www.rubymarie.com; 524 E Wilson St; r $159-179; P@📶) This quirky central boutique began life in the 19th century as a modest railroad hotel. These days it's been retrofitted with all modern conveniences while retaining atmospheric period touches, like fireplaces and four-poster beds. Some rooms come with Jacuzzis.

The included breakfast buffet might just rate as the best in Madison.

Graduate Madison BOUTIQUE HOTEL $$
(☎608-257-4391; www.graduatehotels.com/madison; 601 Langdon St; r $139-219; P❄📶🐾) A block from campus and right off State St's action, this 72-room hotel wafts a hip academic vibe with its mod-meets-plaid decor and book-themed artwork. Rooms are on

WORTH A TRIP

ODDBALL HIGHWAY 12

Unusual sights huddle around Hwy 12 in south-central Wisconsin, all within a 55-mile span:

National Mustard Museum (☎800-438-6878; www.mustardmuseum.com; 7477 Hubbard Ave, Middleton; ⊙10am-5pm, closed Tue Jan-Mar) FREE Born of one man's ridiculously intense passion, the museum houses around 6000 mustards and kooky condiment memorabilia. Tongue-in-cheek humor abounds, especially if CMO (chief mustard officer) Barry Levenson is there to give you the shtick. It's located in Middleton, a short distance northwest of Madison.

Cow Chip Throw (www.wiscowchip.com; Grand Ave & First St, Prairie du Sac; ⊙1st weekend Sep) Prairie du Sac hosts the annual Cow Chip Throw, where 800 competitors fling dried manure patties as far as the eye can see; the record is 248ft.

Dr Evermor's Sculpture Park (☎608-219-7830; www.worldofdrevermor.com; S7703 Hwy 12, Bluffview; ⊙11am-5pm Mon & Thu-Sat, from noon Sun) FREE The doc has welded old pipes, carburetors and other salvaged metal into a hallucinatory world of futuristic birds, dragons and other bizarre structures. The crowning glory is the giant, egg-domed Forevertron, once cited by Guinness World Records as the globe's largest scrap-metal sculpture. Finding the park entrance is tricky. It is behind Delaney's Surplus on Hwy 12; look for a small road just south of Delaney's leading in. Hours can be erratic, so call to confirm it's open.

Wisconsin Dells (☎800-223-3557; www.wisdells.com; Hwy 12; 👪) The Dells is a mega-center of kitschy diversions, including 20-plus water parks, water-skiing thrill shows and epic mini-golf courses. It's a jolting contrast to the natural appeal of the area, with its scenic limestone formations carved by the Wisconsin River. To appreciate the original attraction, take a boat tour or walk the trails at nearby Mirror Lake or Devil's Lake state parks.

the small side and can be a bit noisy, but the location rocks.

Eating & Drinking

★ Old Fashioned AMERICAN $$
(☎608-310-4545; www.theoldfashioned.com; 23 N Pinckney St; mains $12-25; ⏰7am-2am Mon-Fri, 9am-2am Sat, 9am-10pm Sun; 📶🖊) With its dark, woodsy decor, the Old Fashioned evokes a supper club, a type of retro eatery common in Wisconsin. The menu is all local specialties, including walleye, cheese soup and sausages. It's hard to choose from among the 150 types of state-brewed suds in bottles, so opt for a sampler (four or eight little glasses) from the 50 Wisconsin tap beers.

L'Etoile AMERICAN $$$
(☎608-251-0500; www.letoile-restaurant.com; 1 S Pinckney St; mains $44-52, multicourse tasting menu from $150; ⏰5:30-9:30pm Tue-Thu, from 5pm Fri & Sat; 📶) 🌿 L'Etoile started doing the farm-to-table thing more than three decades ago. It's still the best in the biz, offering creative meat, fish and vegetable dishes, all sourced locally and served in a casually elegant room. Be sure to reserve in advance.

★ Memorial Union PUB
(☎608-265-3000; www.union.wisc.edu/visit/memorial-union; 800 Langdon St; ⏰7am-midnight Mon-Fri, from 8am Sat & Sun; 📶) The campus Union is Madison's gathering spot. The festive terrace, overlooking Lake Mendota, pours microbrews and hosts free live music and free Monday-night films, while the indoor ice-cream shop scoops hulking cones from the university dairy.

Information

Madison Convention & Visitors Bureau (www.visitmadison.com)

Getting There & Away

Badger Bus (www.badgerbus.com) has a street-side stop on campus at 700 Langdon St (next to the Memorial Union) for trips to/from Milwaukee ($20, two hours). Megabus (www.megabus.com) uses the same stop for trips to Chicago ($30, four hours) and Minneapolis ($50 to $60, five hours).

Western Wisconsin

Western Wisconsin brings on swooping green hills and button-cute towns with tree-shaded streets. Two-lane byways dip and curve through the region, revealing eating hot spots around many a bend.

The Mississippi River forms the southwest's border, and alongside it run some of the prettiest sections of the Great River Rd – the designated route that follows Old Man River throughout its 2300-mile flow. Top stops along the water include Stockholm (pie), Pepin (for Laura Ingalls Wilder fans), Nelson (cheese and ice cream), La Crosse (history, culture and bars) and Potosi (beer).

Road-tripping inland turns up bike trails in Sparta, organic farms and round barns in Viroqua, and a Frank Lloyd Wright sight in Richland Center. The old logging and industrial city of Eau Claire has a very good live-music scene and is busy trying to refashion itself as a miniature version of Austin or Portland.

> **WORTH A TRIP**
>
> **SPRING GREEN**
>
> Spring Green is a tiny town with big culture. **Taliesin** (☎608-588-7900; www.taliesinpreservation.org; 5607 County Rd C; ⏰9am-5:30pm May-Oct) is here, Frank Lloyd Wright's ballyhooed home and architectural school. The respected **American Players Theatre** (☎608-588-2361; www.americanplayers.org; 5950 Golf Course Rd) is also here, staging classics outdoors amid the trees (bring a picnic). And the **House on the Rock** (☎608-935-3639; www.thehouseontherock.com; 5754 Hwy 23; adult/child $15/9; ⏰9am-5pm May–mid-Oct, Thu-Mon only mid-Oct–Nov & mid-Mar–Apr, closed mid-Nov–mid-Mar) offers enough whimsy for a lifetime. Round out your art-filled day with a stay at the Prairie-style **Usonian Inn** (☎608-588-2323; www.usonianinn.com; E 5116 US 14; r $100-135; ❄📶).
>
> Spring Green is about 40 miles west of Madison on US 14.

Eastern Wisconsin

The eastern part of the state is a vacation favorite thanks to its miles of craggy shoreline for boating, swimming and fishing, its beaming lighthouses and its atmospheric maritime communities. Lonely islands, meals of fiery fish and football shrines all await, and there's always a lake or forest nearby for a nature fix.

WORTH A TRIP

EAU CLAIRE

Eau Claire (population 68,590) is basking in the glow of some favorable national publication comparisons to Austin and Portland for its aspiring hipster vibe, and city hall has begun referring to itself as the 'Indie Capital of the Midwest.' You'll still have to squint pretty hard to find a resemblance to those other cities but Eau Claire does have some great bars and restaurants, a decent live-music scene and some inspired choices for an overnight stay.

The city got its start in the middle of the 19th century and was able to leverage its position at the confluence of two important rivers, the Eau Claire and the Chippewa, to dominate the local logging industry for decades. These days, much of that industry is gone, though the riverside location continues to offer some pretty views and fun waterborne activities, such as rafting and tubing, in nice weather.

Downtown Eau Claire offers a couple of funky overnight options: the hipster-inspired **Oxbow** (715-839-0601; www.theoxbowhotel.com; 516 Galloway St; r/ste $145/185; P ❄ wifi) boutique hotel and a renovated historic **Lismore** (715-835-8888; www.doubletree3.hilton.com; 333 Gibson St; r/ste $130/220; P ❄ @ wifi), plus some very good restaurants and a bustling bar and pub scene.

For an up-to-date list of events and festivals and a nice overview of things to do, check out www.visiteauclaire.com.

Eau Claire lies astride I-94, a major east–west interstate highway. US Hwy 12, a historic motorway that crisscrosses the country, passes through downtown.

Door County, a long, slender appendage that stretches out into Lake Michigan just beyond Green Bay, is a popular summer retreat for people throughout the Midwest. People come for the coastline, camping and cycling, but mainly for that timeless summertime feel that lives on in July and August at the coastal resorts. True hermits make a beeline north to remote Washington Island, and to even more remote Rock Island. Green Bay is an unexpected treat. Fans of the NFL's Green Bay Packers will enjoy the stadium tours and football lore, while everyone else will appreciate the relaxed small-city vibe.

Green Bay

To football fans, Green Bay is synonymous with the Green Bay Packers, a legendary team in the National Football League's smallest (by far) market that's won 13 league championships, including four Super Bowls, over the past 100 years. The franchise is unique as the only community-owned nonprofit team in the NFL; perhaps pride in ownership is what makes the fans so die-hard (and also makes them wear foam-rubber cheese wedges on their heads). Indeed, football aficionados will think they died and went to heaven, with stadium tours, 'hall of fame' visits and even the chance to catch a game on the agenda.

The good news for everyone else is that Green Bay is not just football. The city has a rapidly reviving downtown, with lots of decent restaurants and authentic bars and taverns. The charming riverside port of De Pere, with its whiff of edgy chic, is just a couple of miles away.

Sights & Activities

Green Bay Packers Hall of Fame MUSEUM
(920-569-7512; www.lambeaufield.com; 1265 Lombardi Ave; adult/child $15/12; 9am-6pm Mon-Sat, 10am-5pm Sun) The two-floor Hall of Fame, located inside the atrium adjacent to Lambeau Field, is filled with Green Bay Packer memorabilia, shiny trophies and movies about the storied NFL team that'll intrigue any football fan. Buy tickets at the counter where stadium tours are offered; package deals are available for reduced rates. See the website for options and prices.

National Railroad Museum MUSEUM
(920-437-7623; www.nationalrrmuseum.org; 2285 S Broadway; adult/child $10/7.50; 9am-5pm Mon-Sat, 11am-5pm Sun, closed Mon Jan-Mar;) Forget the Packers (for just a moment), this is a must for train lovers: an enormous museum featuring some of the biggest locomotives ever to haul freight into Green Bay's vast yards. Train rides ($2) are offered in summer.

Lambeau Stadium Tours TOURS
(☎920-569-7512; www.lambeaufield.com; 1265 Lombardi Ave; classic tour adult/child $15/9; ⏲tours daily 10am, 11am, noon, 1pm, 2:30pm, 3:30pm & 4:30pm) A must for football fans of any age or stripe, Lambeau offers three tours of varying length, but most visitors will be satisfied with the hour-long 'classic' tour that takes in the luxury boxes upstairs and (the highlight) a chance to walk out onto the field. The guides are full of great stories of Packer lore.

Sleeping

Hotel Northland HOTEL $$
(☎920-393-7499; www.thehotelnorthland.com; 304 N Adams St; r from $149; P❄@📶) The landmark Northland, located in downtown Green Bay, opened in the 1920s as the biggest hotel in the state. After some lean years, it's re-emerged as part of Marriott's luxurious 'Autograph' collection. The spacious, dark-panelled lobby and public areas retain period charm, while the rooms are lighter and more contemporary. There's a good in-house restaurant on the ground floor.

Getting There & Away

Green Bay has a small airport with flights to Chicago, Minneapolis, Detroit and Atlanta.

Greyhound has a station in town. It runs regularly to Milwaukee ($20, three hours) and Chicago ($25, five hours).

For motorists, I-43 comes into Green Bay from the east. I-41 comes in from the west.

Door County

With its rocky coastline, picturesque lighthouses, cherry orchards and small 19th-century villages, you have to admit Door County is pretty darn lovely. Honeymooners, families and outdoorsy types all flock in to take advantage of the parkland that blankets the area and the clapboard hamlets packed with winsome cafes, galleries and inns.

The county spreads across a narrow peninsula jutting 75 miles into Lake Michigan. Sturgeon Bay, at the southern end, is the county seat and its only real city; it's home to some decent museums. Running north, the side of the peninsula that borders the lake proper is the more scenic 'quiet side', and home to the communities of Jacksonport and Baileys Harbor. The side that borders Green Bay is more action-oriented, where hamlets such as Egg Harbor, Fish Creek, Ephraim and Sister Bay welcome travelers.

Summer is prime time. Only about half the businesses stay open from November to April.

Sights & Activities

Cave Point County Park PARK
(☎920-746-9959; www.co.door.wi.gov; 5360 Schauer Rd; ⏲6am-11pm) FREE As you watch waves explode into the caves beneath the shoreline cliffs here, you're likely to agree, nature is pretty amazing. There are great photo opportunities for shutterbugs and hiking and biking paths take you to gorgeous vistas. The bonus? Cave Point is off the beaten path and is less visited than its state-park siblings. It's also free.

Newport State Park STATE PARK
(☎campground 888-947-2757; www.dnr.wi.gov; 475 County Rd NP; per vehicle $11; ⏲6am-11pm) Newport is one of Door County's quietest parks, tucked away at the peninsula's northern fringe. It has a beautiful beach, 30 miles of hiking trails (about half of which double as off-road bike trails) and limited year-round camping in forested seclusion (reserve in advance). It's also an excellent spot for bird-watching and star-gazing.

Bay Shore Outfitters OUTDOORS
(☎920-854-7598; www.kayakdoorcounty.com; 2457 S Bay Shore Dr, Sister Bay; ⏲10am-5pm Mon-Sat, to 4pm Sun May-Oct) Rents kayaks, stand-up paddleboards and winter gear in season, and offers a variety of kayaking tours (from $55 per two-hour trip).

Sleeping & Eating

★ **White Gull Inn** HOTEL $$$
(☎920-868-3517; www.whitegullinn.com; 4225 Main St, Fish Creek; r $270-330; P❄@📶) This gleaming, white-boarded inn, a short walk from the bay and central Fish Creek, looks as if it stepped from the pages of *Town & Country* magazine. The rooms are all floral-print wallpaper and four-poster beds. The inn is open year-round; rates drop out of season.

Bluefront Cafe AMERICAN $
(☎920-743-9218; www.thebluefrontcafe.com; 86 W Maple St, Sturgeon Bay; mains $10-13; ⏲11am-3pm Tue-Sun) Hands-down, this tiny

cafe-restaurant is the best lunch option in Sturgeon Bay. Choose from an eclectic mix of well-done dishes such as walleye sandwiches, fish tacos and homemade meatloaf as well as more far-flung choices like curried chicken, Vietnamese-style banh mi and Asian chicken wraps.

The only downside? Limited opening hours.

Information

Door County Visitor Bureau (920-743-4456; www.doorcounty.com; 1015 Green Bay Rd; 8am-5pm Mon-Fri, from 10am Sat Apr, 8am-6pm Mon-Fri, from 9am Sat & Sun May-Oct, 8am-5pm Mon-Fri, 10am-4pm Sat & Sun Nov-Mar;) The main tourist information office for the county is located just south of Sturgeon Bay. It's a good source of local information and activity maps; has brochures on art galleries, biking and lighthouses.

Egg Harbor Visitor Bureau (920-868-3717; www.doorcounty.com; 4666 Orchard Rd, Egg Harbor; 10am-5pm Mon-Sat, 10am-3pm Sun May-Sep, noon-5pm Fri, 10am-5pm Sat, 11am-2pm Sun Oct-Apr;)

Fish Creek Visitor Bureau (920-868-2316; www.doorcounty.com; 4097 Main St, Fish Creek; 10am-5pm Mon-Sat, 10am-3pm Sun May-Oct, noon-5pm Fri, 10am-5pm Sat, 11am-2pm Sun Nov-Apr;)

Sister Bay Visitor Bureau (920-854-2812; www.doorcounty.com; 2380 Gateway Dr, Sister Bay; 10am-5pm Mon-Sat, 10am-3pm Sun May-Oct;)

Sturgeon Bay Visitor Bureau (920-743-6246; www.doorcounty.com; 36 S 3rd Ave, Sturgeon Bay; 9am-5pm Mon-Fri, 9am-3pm Sat May-Oct;)

Getting There & Away

You'll need a car to get to Door County. Two small highways serve the peninsula. Hwy 57 runs beside Lake Michigan, while Hwy 42 moseys beside Green Bay (the body of water, not the city). Be prepared for heavy traffic on weekends.

Northern Wisconsin

The north is a thinly populated region of forests and lakes, where folks paddle and fish in summer, and ski and snowmobile in winter. Mountain-biking trails continue to expand and draw fat tires. Nicolet National Forest and Chequamegon National Forest protect much of the area and provide the playground for these activities. But it's the windswept Apostle Islands that really steal the show.

Apostle Islands

The National Park Service's Apostle Islands, 21 rugged pieces of rock and turf floating in Lake Superior and freckling Wisconsin's northern tip, are a state highlight. Forested and windblown, trimmed with cliffs and caves, the national park gems have no facilities. Various companies offer seasonal boat trips around the islands, and kayaking is very popular.

Jump off from Bayfield, a humming resort with hilly streets, Victorian-era buildings, apple orchards and nary a fast-food restaurant in sight.

Outside of the kayaking opportunities, people come for the leisurely hikes or bike rides, or to poke around Bayfield's sleepy shops and enjoy some good food.

Madeline Island, an Apostle Island though not part of the national park, is a popular day trip by ferry and home to a beautiful state park and campground. Beyond Bayfield, shore towns to the north and west, such as Cornucopia, can feel like a slice of heaven when visiting on a sunny July afternoon.

Sights & Activities

Kayaking in the Apostles pays off big in scenery, with stacks of dusty red-rock arches and pillars rising from the water. Caves along the mainland near Meyers Beach and the craggy shores of Devils Island and Sand Island are stars of the show. Note that much of the kayaking here is for experienced paddlers only; novices should go with a guide, as conditions can be rough and windy.

The national park publishes a *Paddling in the Apostles* brochure with information on kayak launch points and tips on how to prepare.

Popular outfitters, offering half- and full-day outings include **Lost Creek Outfitters** (715-953-2223; www.lostcreekadventures.org; 22475 Hwy 13, Cornucopia; half-/full-day tour $60/119; Jun-Sep) and **Trek & Trail** (715-779-3595; www.trek-trail.com; 7 Washington Ave, Bayfield; half-/full-day tour $60/119; Jun-Sep).

Sleeping & Eating

Camping permits (per night $15) are required for the national park islands. You must get them in advance online (www.recreation.gov; reservation fee $10).

Bayfield loads up on tidy motels, B&Bs and swanky inns. Madeline Island has a handful of inns and cottages. Book well in advance for July and August, particularly if your travels take you over a summer holiday.

★ **Old Rittenhouse Inn** B&B $$
(715-779-5111; www.rittenhouseinn.com; 301 Rittenhouse Ave, Bayfield; r $160-230; P ❄ @ ☏) This beautiful Victorian on a high hill, with a commanding view of the water, is a worthy splurge if you're looking for lace, creaky floorboards and a romantic escape. The location is ideal, within an easy walk of the port and downtown restaurants. Even if you're not staying here, get a table for breakfast, served in the stunning, period-piece dining room.

★ **Fat Radish** AMERICAN $$
(715-779-9700; www.thefatradish.weebly.com; 200 Rittenhouse Ave, Bayfield; sandwiches $7-10, mains $16-24; 9am-3pm & 5-9pm Mon-Sat, 9am-2pm Sun, closed Mon winter; ☏) The Radish uses quality, sustainable ingredients in its deli wares. It's located by the docks and handy for amassing snacks to take on boat tours. At night, the chef serves a scrumptious mix of beef and fish dishes, including to-die-for fish tacos, as well as plenty of vegan and vegetarian entrees. Book in advance.

Information

Apostle Islands National Lakeshore Visitors Center (715-779-3397; www.nps.gov/apis; 410 Washington Ave, Bayfield; 8am-4:30pm late May-Sep, closed Sat & Sun rest of year) Has camping, paddling and hiking information.

Bayfield Chamber of Commerce (715-779-3335; www.bayfield.org; 42 S Broad St, Bayfield; 6am-8pm) Good listings of lodgings and things to do in Bayfield and the surrounding towns.

Madeline Island Information Station (715-747-2051; www.madferry.com; Washington Ave, Bayfield; 9am-6pm May-Oct) Adjacent to the Madeline Island Ferry terminal in Bayfield, the first port of call for what to see and do on Madeline Island.

WORTH A TRIP

SCENIC DRIVE: HIGHWAY 13

Hwy 13 moseys through a pretty landscape between Bayfield and Superior. Toward the east it routes around the Lake Superior shore, past the Chippewa community of **Red Cliff** and the Apostle Islands' mainland segment, which has a beach.

Tiny **Cornucopia**, looking every bit like a seaside village, has great sunsets. Toward the west, the road runs through a timeless countryside of forest and farm. See www.lakesuperiorbyway.org for more.

Getting There & Away

The **Madeline Island Ferry** (715-747-2051; www.madferry.com; Washington Ave, Bayfield; return adult/child/bicycle/car $15/7/7.50/27; 7:30am-5:30pm Oct-May, to around 10pm Jun-Sep) makes the 25-minute trip from Bayfield to Madeline Island. It goes year-round, except when the water freezes (usually between January and March, when there is an ice bridge).

Apostle Islands Cruises (715-779-3925; www.apostleisland.com; 2 N Front St, Bayfield; grand tour adult/child $46/27; mid-May–mid-Oct) drops off kayakers at various islands. Experienced paddlers kayak out to some of the closer islands.

Hwy 13 is the main road into Bayfield.

MINNESOTA

Is Minnesota really the land of 10,000 lakes, as it's so often advertised? You betcha! Actually, in typically modest style, the state has undermarketed itself – there are 11,842 lakes. Which is great news for travelers. Intrepid outdoors folk can wet their paddles in the Boundary Waters, where nighttime brings a blanket of stars and the lullaby of wolf howls.

Those wanting to get further off the beaten path can journey to Voyageurs National Park, where there's more water than roadway. If that all seems too far-flung, stick to the Twin Cities of Minneapolis and St Paul, where you can't swing a moose without hitting something cool or cultural. And for those looking for middle ground – a cross between the big city and big woods – the dramatic, freighter-filled port of Duluth beckons.

Information

Minnesota Highway Conditions (www.511mn.org) Handy for checking winter road conditions before heading out.

Minnesota Office of Tourism (www.exploreminnesota.com) Official Minnesota travel portal.

Minnesota State Park Information (reservations 866-857-2757; www.dnr.state.mn.us) Park entry requires a vehicle permit (per day/year $7/35). Tent and RV sites cost $15 to $31; reservations accepted for a $7 fee online, $10 by phone.

Minneapolis

Minneapolis is the biggest and artsiest town on the prairie, with all the trimmings of progressive prosperity – swank art museums, rowdy rock clubs, organic and ethnic eateries, and edgy theaters. It's always happenin', even in winter. And here's the bonus: folks are attitude-free and the embodiment of 'Minnesota Nice.' Count how many times they tell you to 'Have a great day,' come rain, shine or snow.

The city owes its existence to the Mississippi. Water-powered sawmills along the river fueled a boom in timber in the mid-1800s. Wheat from the prairies also needed to be processed, so flour mills churned into the next big business. The population grew rapidly in the late 19th century with mass immigration, especially from Scandinavia and Germany. There has been a more recent wave of immigration in the past few decades, from places such as Vietnam and Somalia.

Sights & Activities

★Walker Art Center MUSEUM
(612-375-7600; www.walkerart.org; 1750 Hennepin Ave; adult/child $15/free; 11am-5pm Tue, Wed & Sun, to 9pm Thu, to 6pm Fri & Sat) The first-class art center has a strong permanent collection of 20th-century art and photography, including big-name US painters and great US pop art. On Monday evenings from late July to late August, the museum hosts free movies and music across the pedestrian bridge in Loring Park that are quite the to-do.

Minneapolis Sculpture Garden GARDENS
(www.walkerart.org/visit/garden; 725 Vineland Pl; 6am-midnight) FREE This 19-acre green space, studded with contemporary works such as the oft-photographed *Spoonbridge & Cherry* by Claes Oldenburg, sits beside the Walker Art Center. The Cowles Conservatory, abloom with exotic hothouse flowers, is also on the grounds. In summer (May to September) a trippy mini-golf course (adult/child $10/8) amid the sculptures adds to the fun.

★Endless Bridge OBSERVATORY
(Guthrie Theater; 818 2nd St S; 8am-8pm, to 11pm performance days) FREE Head inside the cobalt-blue Guthrie Theater and make your way up the escalator to the Endless Bridge, a far-out cantilevered walkway overlook-

MINNEAPOLIS FOR CHILDREN

Note that there are many other top sights for little ones in St Paul, at the Mall of America and Fort Snelling.

Minnesota Zoo (952-431-9500; www.mnzoo.org; 13000 Zoo Blvd; adult/child $18/12; 9am-6pm May-Sep, to 4pm Oct-Apr) You'll have to travel a way to get to the respected zoo in suburban Apple Valley, which is 20 miles south of town. It has naturalistic habitats for its 400-plus species, with an emphasis on cold-climate creatures. Parking is $7.

Valleyfair (952-445-7600; www.valleyfair.com; 1 Valleyfair Dr, Shakopee; adult/child $55/37; from 10am Jun-Aug, reduced hours May, Sep & Oct) If the rides at the Mall of America aren't enough, drive out to this full-scale amusement park 22 miles southwest in Shakopee. The animatronic dinosaur park ($5 extra) is a big hit. Save money by booking tickets online. Parking costs $12.

Children's Theatre Company (612-874-0400; www.childrenstheatre.org; 2400 3rd Ave S; shows $15-70; box office 11am-5pm Tue-Fri) This local troupe is so good it won a Tony award for 'outstanding regional theater.'

ing the Mississippi River. You don't need a theater ticket, as it's intended as a public space. The theater's 9th-floor Amber Box provides another knockout view.

★ Weisman Art Museum MUSEUM
(612-625-9494; www.wam.umn.edu; 333 E River Parkway; 10am-5pm Tue, Thu & Fri, 10am-8pm Wed, 11am-5pm Sat & Sun) FREE The Weisman, which occupies a swooping silver structure by architect Frank Gehry, is a university (and city) highlight. The airy main galleries hold cool collections of 20th-century American art, ceramics, Korean furniture and works on paper.

Minneapolis Institute of Art MUSEUM
(612-870-3000; https://new.artsmia.org; 2400 3rd Ave S; 10am-5pm Tue, Wed & Sat, 10am-9pm Thu & Fri, 11am-5pm Sun) FREE This museum is a huge trove housing a veritable history of art. The modern and contemporary collections will astonish, while the Asian galleries (2nd floor) and Decorative Arts rooms (3rd floor) are also highlights. Allot at least a few hours to visit. The museum is a mile south of downtown via 3rd Ave S.

St Anthony Falls Heritage Trail WALKING
The 1.8-mile path provides both interesting history (placards dot the route) and the city's best access to the banks of the Mississippi River. It starts at the foot of Portland Ave and goes over the car-free **Stone Arch Bridge**, from which you can view cascading St Anthony Falls.

Festivals & Events

Art-A-Whirl ART
(www.nemaa.org; mid-May) The weekend-long, rock-and-roll art-gallery crawl throughout northeastern Minneapolis heralds the arrival of spring. Held at studios across the neighborhood.

Twin Cities Pride LGBTIQ+
(www.tcpride.org; 1382 Willow St, Loring Park; mid-Jun) One of the USA's largest, the Twin Cities Pride Festival draws more than 300,000 revelers to Loring Park.

Sleeping

Aloft HOTEL $$
(612-455-8400; www.marriott.com; 900 Washington Ave S; r $159-265;) Aloft's efficiently designed, industrial-toned rooms draw a younger clientele. The clubby lobby has board games, a cocktail lounge and 24-hour snacks. There's a tiny pool, a decent fitness room and a bike-share station outside the front door. Parking costs $25.

Hewing Hotel HOTEL $$
(651-468-0400; www.hewinghotel.com; 300 Washington Ave N; r $140-260;) This North Loop stunner offers 124 rooms spread through a century-old farm-machine warehouse. The vibe is rustic and cozy. The handsome chambers feature wood-beam ceilings, exposed brick walls and distinctive outdoorsy decor, such as deer-print wallpaper and plaid wool blankets. It's within walking distance of downtown's action (plus there's a bar-restaurant on-site). Parking costs $46.

PRINCE SIGHTS

Minneapolis' most famous former resident is the late music star Prince. Even before his untimely death in 2016, visitors flocked to town to follow his trail. The city's tourism bureau has a map of Prince hot spots, including his childhood home, the house from *Purple Rain* and **Paisley Park** (www.officialpaisleypark.com; 7801 Audubon Rd, Chanhassen; tours from $38.50, service fee $7.50; Thu-Mon), his famed home and recording studio. For more, check out www.minneapolis.org/princes-minneapolis.

Eating

My Huong VIETNAMESE $
(612-702-2922; www.myhuongkitchen.com; 2718 Nicollet Ave S; mains $10-14; 11am-9pm Tue-Sat, to 6pm Sun;) A modest Vietnamese restaurant turning out authentic versions of banh mi, pho, rolls and lemongrass dishes to an appreciative 'Eat Street' public. The dining room is tiny, but don't let that dissuade you from arguably the best Vietnamese food in the area.

Safari SOMALI $
(612-353-5341; www.safarirestaurant.net; 3010 4th Avenue S; mains $12-15; 11am-midnight) Widely considered the city's best Somali restaurant, Safari is the place to dabble in chicken *suqaar*, marinated slices of meat served in a heap of spiced Somali rice, or 'Chicken Fantastic,' grilled chicken breast placed over rice and covered in a mild cream sauce.

Minneapolis

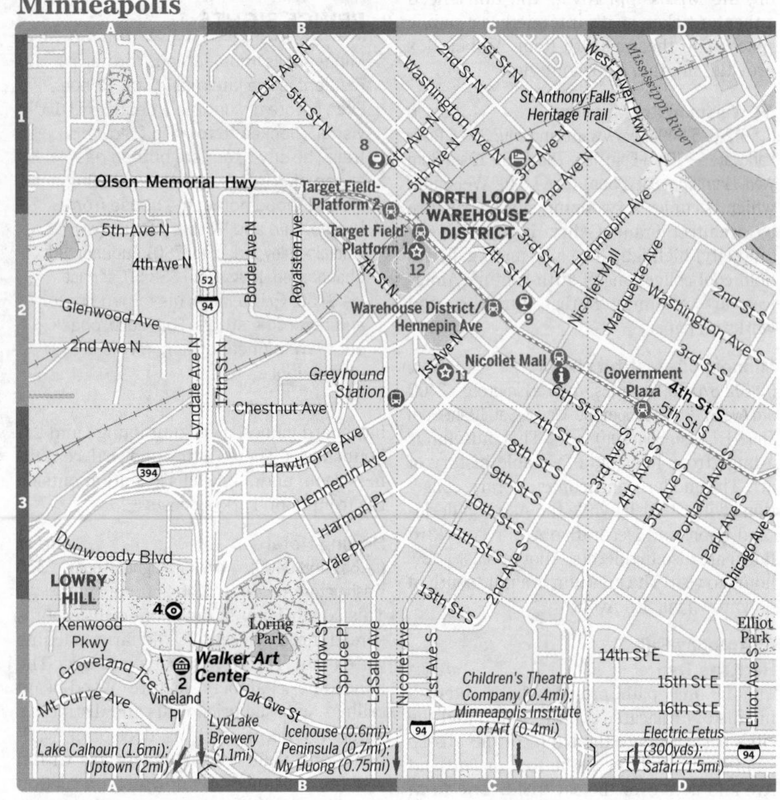

Minneapolis

Top Sights

1 Endless Bridge E2
2 Walker Art Center A4
3 Weisman Art Museum G3

Sights

4 Minneapolis Sculpture Garden A4

Activities, Courses & Tours

5 St Anthony Falls Heritage Trail E2

Sleeping

6 Aloft E3
7 Hewing Hotel C1

Drinking & Nightlife

8 Fulton Beer B1
9 Gay Nineties C2
10 Wilde Cafe E1

Entertainment

11 First Avenue & 7th St Entry C2
Guthrie Theater .... (see 1)
12 Target Field C2
13 US Bank Stadium E3

★ **Young Joni** PIZZA $$

(☎612-345-5719; www.youngjoni.com; 165 13th Ave NE; mains $14-19; ⊙4-11pm Tue-Thu, 4pm-midnight Fri, noon-midnight Sat, noon-10pm Sun) Young Joni fuses two seemingly unrelated types: pizza and Korean food. Here, you can order a wood-fired, crisp-crusted prosciutto, gruyere and ricotta pie with a side of spicy clams, kimchi and tofu. It sounds odd, but the dishes on offer here are terrific.

Bonus: the hip, industrial space has a hidden bar in back. If the red light is on, the cocktails are flowing.

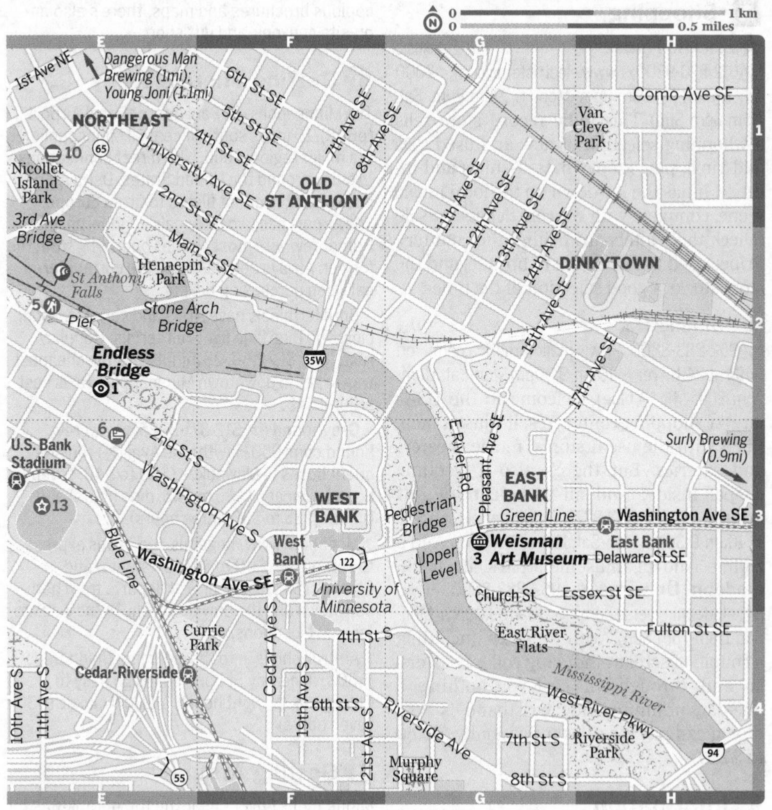

☆ Entertainment

First Avenue & 7th St Entry LIVE MUSIC

(☎612-332-1775; www.first-avenue.com; 701 1st Ave N; shows from $20) This is the longstanding bedrock of Minneapolis' music scene. First Avenue is the main room featuring national acts; smaller 7th St Entry is for up-and-comers.

Check out the exterior stars on the building: they're all bands that have graced the stage.

Buy tickets via the website.

Guthrie Theater THEATER

(☎612-377-2224; www.guthrietheater.org; 818 2nd St S; shows $30-90; ⏲box office 11am-5pm) This is Minneapolis's top-gun theater troupe, with a jumbo facility to prove it. Unsold 'rush' tickets go on sale here 30 minutes before showtime for $15 to $35 (cash only).

Download free audio tours from the website for self-guided jaunts around the funky building.

Target Field BASEBALL

(☎800-338-9467; www.mlb.com/twins; 353 N 5th St; Ⓡblue, green) This downtown stadium is home field for Major League Baseball's Minnesota Twins. The season runs from April through October (that is, if the Twins play well enough to make it into October). The stadium is notable for its beyond-the-norm, locally focused food and drink.

US Bank Stadium SPECTATOR SPORT

(☎612-338-4537; www.vikings.com; 900 5th St S; ⓦ; Ⓡblue, green) The National Football League's Minnesota Vikings play at this spiffy, glass-walled indoor arena on Sundays from September through December. See the website for a game schedule. Buy tickets online.

Shopping

★**Electric Fetus** MUSIC

(☎612-870-9300; www.electricfetus.com; 2000 4th Ave S; ⊙9am-9pm Mon-Fri, 9am-8pm Sat, 11am-6pm Sun) This indie record store sells a whopping selection of new and used CDs and vinyl, plus groovy hats, T-shirts and incense. It has the lowdown on the local music scene, complete with concert tickets for sale (check the whiteboard behind the counter). Prince used to come here to browse, and the store stocks a good selection of his tunes.

Mall of America MALL

(☎952-883-8800; www.mallofamerica.com; off I-494 at 24th Ave; ⊙10am-9:30pm Mon-Sat, 11am-7pm Sun; ; blue) Welcome to the USA's largest shopping center. Yes, it's just a mall, filled with the usual stores, movie theaters and eateries. But there's also a wedding chapel inside. And an 18-hole **mini-golf course** (☎952-883-8777; 3rd fl; per person $12; ⊙10am-9:30pm Mon-Sat, 11am-7pm Sun). And a zipline. And an amusement park, aka **Nickelodeon Universe** (☎952-883-8800; www.nickelodeonuniverse.com; ⊙10am-9:30pm Mon-Sat, 11am-7pm Sun), with 28 rides, including a couple of scream-inducing roller coasters. To walk through will cost you nothing; a one-day, unlimited-ride wristband is $37; or you can pay for rides individually ($3.60 to $7.20).

Information

Minneapolis Visitor Information (☎612-397-9278; www.minneapolis.org; 505 Nicollet Mall, Suite 100; ⊙9am-6pm Mon-Fri, to 5pm Sat, to 3pm Sun;) The staff at this downtown tourist office will bend over backwards to help you set up an itinerary, sort out transportation or find a place to eat or drink. In addition to the copious brochures and maps, there's also an on-site souvenir and gift shop.

Getting There & Away

The Minneapolis–St Paul International Airport (p608), 10 miles south of central Minneapolis, is a major regional hub, with direct connections to cities around the United States. Delta Airlines operates direct flights to/from Europe. The airport has two terminals, Lindbergh and Humphrey, with most airlines operating from the former. Always double-check the correct terminal when purchasing tickets.

Both terminals have ATMs and car-rental agencies. The Blue Line light-rail service (regular/rush-hour $2/2.50, 25 minutes) is the cheapest way to get to downtown Minneapolis. Taxis cost around $45.

Greyhound (☎612-371-3325; www.greyhound.com; 950 Hawthorne Ave;) runs frequent buses to Milwaukee ($30 to $40, seven hours), Chicago ($35 to $45, nine hours) and Duluth ($25 to $30, three hours).

Megabus (www.megabus.com) runs express to Milwaukee ($40 to $45, 6½ hours) and Chicago ($45, 8½ hours). It departs from both downtown and the university; check the website for exact locations.

Amtrak chugs in to the gleaming Union Depot (p608) in nearby St Paul. Trains go daily to Chicago ($35, eight hours) and Milwaukee ($30, seven hours).

Getting Around

Minneapolis hovers near the top of rankings for best bike city in the US. **Nice Ride** (www.niceridemn.org) is the local bike-share program, with 1800 lime-green bikes in 200 self-serve kiosks around the Twin Cities. A 30-minute ride costs $3. Insert a credit card, get your ride code, then unlock a bike. See the **Minneapolis Bicycle Program** (www.ci.minneapolis.

LGBTIQ+ MINNEAPOLIS

Minneapolis has one of the country's highest percentages of lesbian, gay, bisexual and transgender residents, and the city enjoys strong LGBTIQ+ rights. Pick up the free, biweekly magazine *Lavender* (www.lavendermagazine.com) at coffee shops around town for info on the scene. Pride Festival (p603) is one of the USA's largest, drawing more than 300,000 revelers. Top picks:

Wilde Cafe (☎612-331-4544; www.wildecafe.com; 65 Main St SE; ⊙7am-9pm Sun-Thu, to 11pm Fri & Sat;) It features amazing baked goods, riverfront digs and a Victorian ambience worthy of its namesake, Oscar Wilde; *Lavender* once ranked it 'best cafe.'

Gay Nineties (☎612-333-7755; www.gay90s.com; 408 Hennepin Ave; cover $5-10; ⊙8am-2am Mon-Sat, from 10am Sun;) This long-standing club has dancing, dining and drag shows that attract both a gay and straight clientele.

TAP ROOM BOOM

Minneapolis is all in on the local brewing trend, and most makers have taprooms. Excellent ones to try for beer fresh from the tank:

LynLake Brewery (612-224-9682; www.lynlakebrewery.com; 2934 Lyndale Ave S; 5-10pm Mon-Thu, 5pm-1am Fri, noon-1am Sat, noon-10pm Sun;) The setting is ideal: an atmospheric, rehabbed former theater with a fun rooftop terrace.

Fulton Beer (612-333-3208; www.fultonbeer.com; 414 6th Ave N; 3-10pm Tue-Thu, to 3-11pm Fri, 11am-11pm Sat, 11am-6pm Sun) There's usually a fab pale ale and blonde ale among the selection that you sip at communal picnic tables in the warehouse. It's a few blocks from the baseball stadium and fills up on game days.

Dangerous Man Brewing (612-236-4087; www.dangerousmanbrewing.com; 1304 2nd St NE; 4-10pm Tue-Thu, 3pm-midnight Fri, noon-midnight Sat, noon-8pm Sun) Pours strong, European-style beers in the happenin' Northeast. You're welcome to bring in your own food (there's a choice fish-and-chips place a block east).

Surly Brewing (763-999-4040; www.surlybrewing.com; 520 Malcolm Ave SE; 11am-11pm Sun-Thu, to midnight Fri & Sat; ; green) Surly's sprawling, mod-industrial, family-friendly beer hall is mobbed by locals who come for the rotating taps and abundant meaty snacks. It's in the Prospect Park neighborhood, next to the university and a short walk from the Prospect Park Green Line rail station.

mn.us/bicycles) for cycling information and trail maps.

Traditional rentals work better for longer recreational rides. Several companies offer rentals around town.

Wheel Fun Rentals (Kiosk at Bde Maka Ska; 612-823-5765; www.wheelfunrentals.com; 3000 Calhoun Parkway E, base of W Lake St; bike per hr/day $12/40; 9am-8:30pm late May–mid-Aug, reduced hours mid-Aug–late Oct) rents mountain bikes and tandems by the hour or day from a convenient location near Uptown.

Metro Transit (612-373-3333; www.metrotransit.org; peak/off-peak $2.50/$2) runs the handy Blue Line light rail between downtown and the Mall of America (stopping at the airport en route). The Green Line light rail connects downtown Minneapolis with Union Depot in downtown St Paul.

Machines at each station sell fare cards, including all-day passes ($6.50) that also can be used on public buses.

St Paul

St Paul, Minnesota's capital city, is smaller and quieter than its twin to the west, Minneapolis. While Minneapolis is all glitz and bustle, St Paul is more prim and proper and has managed to retain more of its historic character. St Paul's amenities are more modest as well, though the capital does excel when it comes to breweries and brew pubs.

The city is well worth a day's diversion from Minneapolis to stroll through the historic residential areas southwest of downtown, particularly along Summit Ave, or closer to the Mississippi River around Irvine Park, to gawk at the late-19th- and early-20th-century mansions. This is also F Scott Fitzgerald's old stomping grounds, and the house he was born in as well as the house where he lived when he published *This Side of Paradise* are still standing.

Sights & Activities

Landmark Center MUSEUM
(651-292-3225; www.landmarkcenter.org; 75 W 5th St; 8am-5pm Mon-Fri, 8am-8pm Thu, 10am-5pm Sat, noon-5pm Sun) Downtown's turreted 1902 Landmark Center used to be the federal courthouse, where gangsters such as Alvin 'Creepy' Karpis were tried; plaques next to the various rooms show who was brought to justice here. In addition to the city's visitor center, the building also contains a couple of small museums (one focusing on wood art, another on music).

Down In History Tours WALKING
(651-292-1220; www.wabashastreetcaves.com; 215 S Wabasha St; tours $9-10; 4pm Mon, 5pm Thu, 11am Sat & Sun May-Sep) These 45-minute tours explore St Paul's underground caves, which gangsters once used as a speakeasy. The fun ramps up on Thursday nights,

when a swing band plays in the caverns (additional $8).

Festivals & Events

St Paul Winter Carnival CULTURAL
(www.wintercarnival.com; late Jan-early Feb) Ten days of ice sculptures, ice-skating and ice fishing. Events take place at Rice Park and other venues around the city.

Sleeping & Eating

★ **Hotel 340** BOUTIQUE HOTEL $$
(651-280-4120; www.hotel340.com; 340 Cedar St; r $109-199; P ❄ @) Hotel 340 delivers old-world ambience aplenty, and it's usually a great deal to boot. The 56 rooms in the stately old building have hardwood floors and plush linens. The two-story lobby stokes a grand fireplace and a nifty little bar (the desk staff double as bartenders). Parking costs $17 per night.

Covington Inn B&B $$
(651-292-1411; www.covingtoninn.com; 100 Harriet Island Rd; r $165-250; P ❄) This four-room, Harriet Island B&B is on a tugboat floating in the Mississippi River; watch the river traffic glide by while sipping your morning coffee. The stately rooms have bright splashes of color, and each has a gas fireplace to keep you toasty in winter.

★ **Keg & Case** FOOD HALL $
(651-443-6060; www.kegandcase.com; 928 7th St W; sandwiches $12-15; 6:30am-10pm Sun-Fri, to midnight Sat;) A scrumptious food hall, with stalls serving locally sourced sandwiches, pizza, ice cream and other food items in a spiffy, remodeled brewery space. In addition to food vendors, there are stalls where you can purchase mushrooms, condiments, jellies and gifts.

It's well worth the trip south of downtown. There are plenty of vegetarian options here.

Cook AMERICAN $
(651-756-1787; www.cookstp.com; 1124 Payne Ave; mains $10-15; 7am-2pm Mon, Thu & Fri, 7am-3pm Sat & Sun) This cute, sunny spot serves creative diner dishes (gingery French toast, curried veggie burgers, braised short-rib sandwiches), including some with a spicy Korean twist. Cook also hosts Korean dinners on Friday nights. It's located in the burgeoning East Side neighborhood, where several other foodie hot spots are sprouting on Payne Ave.

Drinking & Entertainment

Summit Brewing Company BREWERY
(651-265-7800; www.summitbrewing.com; 910 Montreal Circle; 2-9pm Thu & Fri, noon-9pm Sat, noon-6pm Sun) While Summit is one of the state's largest brewers, its beer hall is welcomingly low-key. Inside it's a big open space with communal tables, large windows and around 14 beers on tap. Outside there's a patio that overlooks the river bluffs. Try the Keller pils, oatmeal stout or anything in the experimental Unchained series. Everything is really reasonably priced.

Allianz Field SPECTATOR SPORT
(www.mnufc.com; 400 Snelling Ave N) The gleaming home field of Minnesota United FC of the North American Soccer League opened its doors in 2019. See the website for a current schedule. Buy tickets online.

Fitzgerald Theater THEATER
(651-290-1200; www.thefitzgeraldtheater.com; 10 E Exchange St) This atmospheric theater hosts big-name musicians, comedians and authors in association with Minnesota Public Radio. See the website for a list of events and ticket information.

Information

Mississippi River Visitor Center (651-293-0200; www.nps.gov; 120 W Kellogg Blvd; 9:30am-5pm Sun & Tue-Thu, to 9pm Fri & Sat) Operated by the National Park Service, it occupies an alcove in the science museum lobby. Stop by to pick up trail maps and see what sort of free ranger-guided activities are going on. In summer these include short hikes to the river and bicycle rides. In winter, there are ice-fishing and snowshoeing jaunts.

St Paul Visitor Center (651-292-3225; www.visitsaintpaul.com; 75 W 5th St; 10am-4pm Mon-Sat, from noon Sun) In the Landmark Center, it makes a good first stop for maps and DIY walking-tour info.

Getting There & Around

Union Depot (651-202-2700; www.uniondepot.org; 214 E 4th St;), St Paul's grand train station, is the hub for everything: Greyhound buses, city buses, the Green Line light rail and Amtrak trains.

Minneapolis–St Paul International Airport (MSP; 612-726-5555; www.mspairport.com; 4300 Glumack Dr, St Paul; ; blue) is 15 miles southwest. Bus 54 (regular/rush-hour

$2/2.50, 25 minutes) goes downtown. A taxi costs around $35.

Metro Transit (www.metrotransit.org) operates bus service in both Minneapolis and St Paul and runs the handy Green Line light rail (regular/rush hour $2/2.50) between St Paul, starting at Union Depot, and downtown Minneapolis.

Southern Minnesota

Southern Minnesota keeps it fresh with a mix of historic river towns, Bluff Country's pastoral hamlets and oddball attractions, including the **Spam Museum** (☎507-437-5100; www.spam.com; 101 3rd Ave NE, Austin; ⏲10am-6pm Mon-Sat, 11am-5pm Sun May-Sep, 10am-5pm Mon-Sat, 11am-4pm Sun Oct-Apr) **FREE** and the **world's largest ball of twine** (1st St, Darwin; ⏲24hr) **FREE**.

Atmospheric towns on the water include Stillwater (antique laden), Red Wing (known for its Red Wing Shoes – actually more like sturdy boots – and salt glaze pottery) and Wabasha (where eagles flock). More intriguing little burgs also pop up along this stretch of the Great River Rd, the scenic thoroughfare that clasps the Mississippi River. Pull over for a slice of pie or kitschy garden-gnome shop whenever the mood strikes.

Inland and south, Bluff Country is dotted with pretty limestone cliffs and teeny villages. Lanesboro is a gem for rails-to-trails cycling. Harmony, south of Lanesboro, is the center of an Amish community and another welcoming spot.

The river towns feature inns and B&Bs in vintage, restored buildings; Stillwater has them in abundance. Bluff Country towns are also big on B&Bs, as well as campgrounds.

Old-school diners and coffee shops are common, especially along the Great River Rd. But surprisingly polished cafes also appear in what seems like the middle of nowhere.

The Great River Rd, aka Hwy 61, rolls along the Mississippi River. If you cross a bridge to the Wisconsin side, it becomes Hwy 35. Minneapolis is an hour or two by car from most hot spots in the region.

WORTH A TRIP

STILLWATER

Hilly Stillwater (population 19,400) on the lower St Croix River, is an old logging town with beautifully restored 19th-century buildings, paddle-wheel steamboats churning by and antique shops galore. It's touristy, but it's hard to deny its time-warped charm. Stillwater proudly declaims itself as the birthplace of Minnesota. It was here in 1848 where settlers from then-Wisconsin's vast northwestern territories met to petition the US Congress for statehood. They agreed on the name 'Minnesota', with the state eventually joining the union in 1858.

For a terrific boutique overnighter, try **Lora** (☎651-571-3500; www.lorahotel.com; 402 Main St S; r $160-260; P ❄ @ ᯤ).

Discover Stillwater (www.discoverstillwater.com) has good online listings of what to see and do.

To get here from Minneapolis-St Paul, follow I-694, turning off onto Hwy 36.

Northern Minnesota

Northern Minnesota is a veritable outdoor playground. The immense Boundary Waters wilderness is the main draw, and from May through September, kayaks and canoes ply the state's many fabled lakes, though the area is big enough to still feel as if you have the place to yourself. The red-cliffed Lake Superior shoreline and watery Voyageurs National Park are also popular seasonal destinations.

The north has a compelling heritage story to tell as well. For decades the region's biggest city and port, Duluth, shipped the iron ore that fueled mills throughout the Midwest. You can see the old ships and catch some of the city's revivalist spirit, this time centered around craft beer. The old mining town of Hibbing, at the heart of the Iron Range District, is home to an iron-ore mine so vast, it's referred to as Minnesota's 'Grand Canyon.'

Duluth

Duluth is a brawny shot-and-a-beer port town that offers visitors a glimpse into its storied history as a major shipping center, as well as some citified cultural, dining and drinking amenities. Duluth grew wealthy throughout most of the 20th century as a major exporter of high-quality iron ore, which was carted away on vast ships over the Great Lakes to factories and mills in Michigan, Indiana and Ohio. The port suffered in the 1970s and '80s, though, as the mills shut and the ore reserves dried up. Shipping is still a major industry, but officials have now turned to tourism to supplement the local economy. You'll find a smattering of interesting sights near the port centered on Duluth's industrial past as well as a burgeoning adventure-sports scene. The downtown is rejuvenating rapidly and there's a fun craft-beer and cider subculture developing on the formerly seedy streets, west of the downtown.

Sights & Activities

Aerial Lift Bridge BRIDGE
Duluth's main landmark raises its mighty arm to let horn-bellowing ships into port. About 1000 vessels per year glide through.

Maritime Visitor Center MUSEUM
(218-720-5260; www.lsmma.com; 600 S Lake Ave; 10am-9pm Jun-Aug, reduced hours Sep-May) FREE Located next to the Aerial Lift Bridge, the center has computer screens inside that tell what time the big ships will be sailing through. Cool model boats and exhibits on Great Lakes shipwrecks also make it a top stop in town.

Duluth Traverse BICYCLING
(www.coggs.com) A 40-mile mountain-bike trail that spans the city and surrounding area? Riders are stoked for the Duluth Traverse, a single-track path that's opening bit by bit and linking several existing trails. When it's finished, no Duluth resident will be more than a few minutes from the route. Runners, hikers and snowshoers can also commune with the pines along the way.

Duluth Experience ADVENTURE
(218-464-6337; www.theduluthexperience.com; tours from $79) This outfit offers a range of kayaking, cycling and brewery tours; gear and transportation are provided. Most jaunts depart from Fitger's.

Sleeping

Park Point Marina Inn HOTEL $$
(218-491-7111; www.parkpointmarinainn.com; 1033 Minnesota Ave; r $110-170; P ❄ @ 📶 🏊) This immaculate property is located south of the Aerial Lift Bridge on the point that juts out into Lake Superior. Don't expect luxury, but rather tidy, well-maintained rooms and public areas, and a clean pool for the kids. The attractions around Canal Park are 10 minutes' walk away, but you'll need your own wheels to get much further than that.

Fitger's Inn HOTEL $$$
(218-722-8826; www.fitgers.com; 600 E Superior St; r $185-290; P @ 📶) Fitger's created its 62 large rooms, each with slightly varied decor, from an old brewery. Located on the Lakewalk, the pricier rooms have great water views. The free shuttle to local sights is handy.

Eating

Corktown Deli & Brews DELI $
(218-606-1607; www.corktowndeli.com; 1906 W Superior St; mains $10-13; 7:45am-9pm Sun-Thu, to 10pm Fri & Sat) This lively, informal deli in the Lincoln Park Craft District is hands-down the best lunch option around. Grab a table or sit at the bar, and choose from a tantalizing list of excellent sandwiches and salads, including our new fave, the 'Lake Superior' (wild rice and smoked whitefish). There's a daily mix of craft beers on the board.

★**OMC Smokehouse** BARBECUE $$
(218-606-1611; www.omcsmokehouse.com; 1909 W Superior St; mains $15-30; 11am-9pm Sun-Thu, to 10pm Fri & Sat) The 'OMC' stands for 'Oink, Moo, Cluck,' but we'll give them a pass because of the outstanding quality of the smoked meats, as well as inventive menu items such as catfish tacos and pork 'n' grits. For drinks, there's a strong lineup of local craft brews from Bent Paddle and Castle Danger. Find it in the Lincoln Park Craft District

New Scenic Cafe AMERICAN $$$
(218-525-6274; www.newsceniccafe.com; 5461 North Shore Dr; sandwiches $15-17, mains $26-32; 11am-9pm Sun-Thu, to 10pm Fri & Sat) Foodies travel from far and near to New Scenic Cafe, 8 miles beyond Duluth on Old Hwy 61. There, in a humble wood-paneled room, they fork into rustic salmon with creamed leeks or a slice of triple berry pie, all served with a generous helping of lake views. Make reservations.

Drinking & Entertainment

Duluth Cider BAR
(218-464-1111; www.duluthcider.com; 2307 W Superior St; noon-10pm Mon-Thu, to 11pm Fri & Sat, to 8pm Sun; 📶) This cider-maker and taproom, in the Lincoln Park Craft District, was hived from an old livery for the

Duluth post office. You'll find a creative menu of apple-based hard ciders, including varieties infused with tequila-oak, orange and strawberry.

Norshor Theatre THEATER

(☎218-733-7555; www.norshortheatre.com; 211 E Superior St) Standing at the center of the city's efforts to revitalize the central business district, this landmark's offerings vary from standard theater to concert performances and screenings of classic films. Check the website.

Information

Duluth Visitors Center (☎800-438-5884; www.visitduluth.com; 21 W Superior St; ⊙8:30am-5pm Mon-Fri) Pick up a visitor guide; the website has deals and coupons.

Getting There & Away

Greyhound (☎218-722-5591; www.greyhound.com; 228 W Michigan St) has several buses daily to Minneapolis ($25 to $30, three hours).

North Shore

A trip here is dominated by water – mainly enormous, tempestuous Lake Superior – where ore-toting freighters ply the ports, little fishing fleets haul in the day's catch and wave-bashed cliffs offer awesome views if you're willing to trek. Numerous river valleys, waterfalls, hiking trails and little towns speckle the landscape as it unfurls to the Canadian border.

The highlights along the shoreline highway that leads north from Duluth include a series of state parks that offer their own unique delights. You'll find twisting gorges and dramatic waterfalls at Gooseberry Falls, Judge CR Magney and Temperance River state parks. A lonely lighthouse beckons at Split Rock, not far from Two Harbors.

The picturesque artistic retreat at Grand Marais, with its relatively 'big city' amenities such as good food and drink, caps off the drive. The town's tranquil harbor and seaside locale have been luring painters and other romantic types here for more than 70 years.

Sights & Activities

The 300-mile **Superior Hiking Trail** (www.shta.org) follows the lake-hugging ridgeline between Duluth and the Canadian border. Along the way it passes dramatic red-rock overlooks and the occasional moose and black bear. Trailheads with parking lots pop up every 5 to 10 miles, making it ideal for day hikes. The **Superior Shuttle** (☎218-834-5511; www.superiorhikingshuttle.com; from $20; ⊙Fri-Sun mid-May–mid-Oct) makes life even easier, picking up trekkers from 17 stops along the route. Overnight hikers will find 86 backcountry campsites and several lodges to cushion the body come nightfall; the trail website has details. The whole footpath is free, with no reservations or permits required.

The **trail office** (☎218-834-2700; www.superiorhiking.org; 731 7th Ave, Suite 2; ⊙10am-4:30pm Mon, Thu & Fri) in Two Harbors provides maps and planning assistance.

Split Rock Lighthouse State Park STATE PARK

(☎218-595-7625; www.dnr.state.mn.us; 3755 Split Rock Lighthouse Rd, Two Harbors; per car $7, lighthouse adult/child $10/8; ⊙10am-6pm mid-May–mid-Oct, 11am-4pm Thu-Mon mid-Oct–mid-May) This is the most visited spot on the entire North Shore. The shiner itself is a state historic site with a separate admission fee. Guided tours are available (they depart hourly), or you can explore on your own.

If you don't mind stairs, say 170 or so each way, tramp down the cliff to the beach for incredible views of the lighthouse and surrounding shore.

LOCAL KNOWLEDGE

DYLAN IN DULUTH

While the town of Hibbing and the Iron Range are most often associated with Bob Dylan, he was born in Duluth in 1941. You'll see brown-and-white signs on Superior St and London Rd for **Bob Dylan Way** (www.bobdylanway.com), pointing out places associated with the legend (like the armory where he saw Buddy Holly in concert, and decided to become a musician). But you're on your own to find **Dylan's birthplace** (519 N 3rd Ave E), up a hill a few blocks northeast of downtown. Dylan lived on the top floor until age six, when his family moved inland to Hibbing. It's a private residence (and unmarked), so all you can do is stare from the street.

Sawtooth Outfitters KAYAKING
(☎218-663-7643; www.sawtoothoutfitters.com; 7216 Hwy 61, Tofte; ⊙8am-6pm daily May-late Oct & mid-late Dec, 8am-6pm Thu-Mon Jan-early Apr) Offers guided kayaking tours (half-/full day $60/120) for all levels of paddling on the Temperance River and out on Lake Superior, as well as easier jaunts on wildlife-rich inland lakes.

Sawtooth also rents mountain bikes (from $22 per day) to pedal over the many trails in the surrounding area, including the popular **Gitchi Gami State Bike Trail** (www.ggta.org).

Sleeping & Eating

★Hungry Hippie Farm & Hostel HOSTEL $
(☎218-387-2256; www.hungryhippiehostel.com/the-farm; 410 County Rd 14; dm/r $35/60; P❄📶) If you've ever dreamt of escaping and just getting away from it all, this remote farmhouse-hostel, 8 miles east of Grand Marais, is the place to indulge those fantasies. The rooms are farmhouse chic, straight out of a design magazine. The welcome is warm.

Choose from a bunk in a six-bed dorm or your own private room.

★Northern Rail Traincar Inn HOTEL $$
(☎218-834-0955; www.northernrail.net; 1730 Hwy 3; r/ste $139/199; ❄📶) It doesn't get much cooler than 17 rooms built into renovated train boxcars. Rooms are on the small side, but quaintly furnished by theme (Victorian, golf, moose, safari). They have private bathrooms and TVs with DVD players. Wi-fi is hit or miss in the steel cars, but it's available in the lobby. Continental breakfast is included.

Naniboujou Lodge LODGE $$
(☎218-387-2688; www.naniboujou.com; 20 Naniboujou Trail; r $130-180; ⊙late May-late Oct; P❄📶) Built in the 1920s, the property was once a private club for Babe Ruth and his contemporaries, who smoked cigars in the Great Hall, warmed by the 20ft-high stone fireplace. The pièce de résistance is the hall's massive domed ceiling painted with mind-blowing, psychedelic-colored Cree Indian designs. Rooms vary in decor, but each offers an away-from-it-all experience. It's 14 miles northeast of Grand Marais.

★Gun Flint Tavern AMERICAN $$
(☎218-387-1563; www.gunflinttavern.com; 111 W Wisconsin St; mains $18-25; ⊙11am-10pm; 📶) You'll find excellent soups and sandwiches, the town's best burgers, and an array of heartier evening meals, such as steaks and walleye, at this central restaurant and tavern. A good range of seasonal and popular microbrews pour from the taps, and the adjacent Raven lounge carries on after the restaurant closes. Book in advance for dinner.

Getting There & Away

Hwy 61 is the main vein through the North Shore. The state scenic route moseys all the way to Canada. Duluth is the closest urban area with an airport. Public transport is scarce in these parts and you'll mostly need your own wheels to get around.

Boundary Waters

Legendarily remote and pristine, the Boundary Waters Canoe Area Wilderness (BWCAW) is one of the world's premier paddling regions. More than 1000 lakes and streams

SCENIC DRIVE: HIGHWAY 61

Hwy 61 conjures a headful of images. Local boy Bob Dylan mythologized it in his angry 1965 album *Highway 61 Revisited*. It's the fabled 'Blues Highway' clasping the Mississippi River en route to New Orleans. And in northern Minnesota, it evokes red-tinged cliffs and forested beaches as it follows Lake Superior's shoreline.

But let's back up and get a few things straight. The Blues Highway is actually US 61, and it starts just north of the Twin Cities. Hwy 61 is a state scenic road, and it starts in Duluth. To confuse matters more, there are two 61s between Duluth and Two Harbors: a four-lane expressway and a two-lane 'Old Hwy 61' (also called North Shore Scenic Drive). Take the latter; it morphs from London Rd in Duluth and veers off to the right just past the entrance to Brighton Beach. After Two Harbors, Hwy 61 returns to one strip of pavement – a gorgeous drive that goes all the way to the Canadian border. For more information, check the North Shore Scenic Drive at www.superiorbyways.com.

speckle the piney, 1.1-million-acre expanse. Nature lovers make the pilgrimage for the 1500 miles of canoe routes, rich wildlife and sweeping solitude. If you're willing to dig in and canoe for a while, it'll just be you and the moose, bears, wolves and loons that roam the landscape.

It's possible to glide in for the day, but most people opt for at least a night of camping. Experienced paddlers flock here, but beginners are welcome, too, and everyone can get set up with gear from local lodges and outfitters. The engaging town of Ely (pronounced *ee*-lee), northeast of the Iron Range, is the best place to start, as it has scores of accommodations, restaurants and outfitters. You can also access the Boundary Waters from coastal Grand Marais by following the Gunflint Trail (www.gunflint-trail.com), aka Hwy 12.

Canoeing is what everyone is here for May through September. In winter, Ely gets mushy – it's a renowned dogsledding town. **Ely Bike & Kicksled** (☎218-365-2453; www.elybikeandkicksled.com; 125 N Central Ave, Ely; mountain bikes per hr/day $8/40; ⏰9:30am-5pm Thu-Sat) rents bikes from May to September, and kicksleds during the winter.

You need to be prepared for a real wilderness adventure when canoeing in the Boundary Waters. The **Superior National Forest Office** (☎218-626-4395; www.fs.usda.gov/attmain/superior/specialplaces) publishes a handy BWCAW trip planning guide. It has information on what to bring and how to get the required entry permits. For camping, an overnight permit from the **National Park Service** (☎camping permits 877-444-6777; www.recreation.gov; overnight permits adult/child $16/8, plus reservation fee $6) is necessary. Day-visit permits, though free, are also required; get them at BWCAW entry-point kiosks or ranger stations. Plan ahead, as permits are quota restricted and often run out. Outfitters can help plan the logistics.

Besides remote camping, the area has loads of lodges, though these often have a minimum-stay requirement (usually three days). Downtown Ely has several midrange inns and small hotels. July and August are busy, so book ahead.

ℹ Information

Kawishiwi Ranger Station (☎218-365-7600; www.fs.usda.gov; 1393 Hwy 169, Ely; ⏰8am-4:30pm May-Sep, closed Sat & Sun Oct-Apr) Provides expert BWCAW camping and canoeing details, trip suggestions and required permits.

ℹ Getting There & Away

Hwy 169 (which becomes Sheridan St in Ely) connects the Boundary Waters to the Iron Range and its towns. Hwy 1 links the Boundary Waters to the Lake Superior shore.

Voyageurs National Park

Northern Voyageurs National Park (www.nps.gov/voya), which marks the border between the USA and Canada, is a wet wilderness of some 218,000 acres. It's almost 40% water and only accessible by hiking or motorboat – the waters are mostly too wide and too rough for canoeing. In summer, people come to boat, swim and fish in the park's five main lakes: Kabetogama, Namakan, Sand Point, Crane and Rainy Lake. In winter, people come to cross-country ski or snowmobile on specially marked trails. In addition to offering waterborne fun, the park is filled with wildlife, including large populations of deer, moose, black bears and white pelicans.

The park traces its roots to the 17th century, when French-Canadian fur traders, called voyageurs, began exploring the Great Lakes and northern rivers by canoe. Though the idea of establishing a national park here began in the early 20th century, the park was only formally founded in the 1970s.

When the boats get put away for the winter, the snowmobiles come out. Voyageurs is a hot spot for the sport, with 110 miles of staked and groomed trails slicing through the pines. Rainy Lake Visitor Center provides maps and advice. It also lends out free snowshoes and cross-country skis for local trails, including a couple that depart from outside the center. To the south, an ice road for cars spans the boat launches of the Ash River and Kabetogama Lake visitor centers. There's also a fun sledding hill near the Kabetogama center.

ℹ Information

The park's visitor centers are accessible by car and good places to begin your visit.

Ash River (☎218-374-3221; Mead Wood Rd; ⏰9am-5pm late May-late Sep) Seasonal center; staff offer occasional guided hikes around the bays and bluffs.

Destination Voyageurs National Park (www.dvnpmn.com) Has lodging and activity details for the park's gateway communities.

Kabetogama Lake (☎218-875-2111; off Hwy 53; ⊙9am-5pm late May-late Sep) Seasonal center with ranger-led programs.

Rainy Lake Visitor Center (☎218-286-5258; off Hwy 11; ⊙9am-5pm Jun-Sep, 10am-4:30pm Thu-Sun Oct-May) Eleven miles east of International Falls, just off of Hwy 11, is the main park office. Ranger-guided walks and boat tours are available here in summer, with snowshoe and ski rentals in winter.

Getting There & Away

Hwy 53 is the main highway to the region. It's about a five-hour drive from the Twin Cities (or a three-hour drive from Duluth) to Crane Lake, Ash River or Lake Kabetogama. International Falls, near the park's northwest edge, has the closest airport. It also has a busy border crossing with Canada.

Understand Eastern USA

HISTORY 616

Native Americans, colonists, revolutionaries, civil warriors, Reconstructionists, New Dealers and civil rights fighters have all shaped the region.

THE WAY OF LIFE 626

Learn about the local culture through lifestyles, immigration, religion and sports.

ARTS & ARCHITECTURE 630

Literature, film, theater, painting and architecture provide a window into the region's identity.

MUSIC 633

Blues, jazz, country, folk, rock and hip-hop morphed out of the Eastern USA, in all their beauty and dissonance.

LANDSCAPES & WILDLIFE 636

Alligators, whales, manatees and moose are among the creatures sharing the landscape.

History

With its indigenous culture beginning around 12,000 BCE, followed by its early days as an English colony in the 16th century, right through to its rise to the forefront of the world stage in the 20th, America has a history that is anything but dull. War against the British, westward expansion, slavery (and its abolishment), Civil War and Reconstruction, the Great Depression, the postwar boom and more recent conflicts in the 21st century have all played a part in shaping the nation's complicated identity.

Great History Museums

Henry Ford Museum/Greenfield Village, Detroit

Museum of the American Revolution, Philadelphia

Mississippi Civil Rights Museum, Jackson

Nantucket Whaling Museum, Massachusetts

Ellis Island Immigration Museum, New York City

First Inhabitants

Among North America's most significant prehistoric cultures were the Mound Builders, who inhabited the Ohio and Mississippi River valleys from around 3000 BCE to 1500 CE. They left behind enigmatic piles of earth that served various functions, including tombs for their leaders and possibly tributes to their gods. In Illinois, Cahokia was once a metropolis of at least 20,000 people, the largest in pre-Columbian North America. Burial or ceremonial mounds rose up throughout the Eastern USA, including several along the Natchez Trace in Mississippi.

At the time the first Europeans arrived, millions of Native Americans inhabited what is now the United States. The diverse population in the Eastern USA included groups such as the Wampanoag in New England, the Calusa in southern Florida and the Shawnee in Illinois. Two centuries later, they were all but gone. European explorers introduced diseases to which indigenous peoples had no immunity. More than any other factor – war, slavery or famine – epidemics devastated Native American populations, by anywhere from 50% to 90%.

European Claims

In 1492 Italian explorer Christopher Columbus, backed by Spain, voyaged west looking for the East Indies. He found the Bahamas. With visions of gold, Spanish explorers quickly followed: Hernando de Soto became the first European to cross the Mississippi, while Ponce de León wandered through Florida looking for the fountain of youth. Not to be left out, the

TIMELINE

7000 BCE–100 CE

'Archaic period' of nomadic hunter-gatherer lifestyles. By the end of this period, corn, beans and squash (the agricultural 'three sisters') and permanent settlements are well established.

c 1100

North America's largest city outside Mesoamerica, Cahokia (near modern St Louis), boasts a population larger than that of medieval London.

1492

Italian explorer Christopher Columbus 'discovers' America. He names the indigenous inhabitants 'Indians,' mistakenly thinking he had sailed to the East Indies.

French explored Canada and New England, while the Dutch and English cruised North America's eastern seaboard.

The first European-founded (and oldest continuously settled) city in North America was St Augustine, FL, where the Spanish set up shop in 1565. Up the coast in 1607, a group of English nobles established that country's first permanent North American settlement at Jamestown. Earlier English settlements had ended badly, and Jamestown almost did, too: the nobles chose a swamp, planted their crops late, and died from disease and starvation. Local tribes provided the settlement with enough aid to survive.

For Jamestown and America, 1619 proved a pivotal year: the colony established the House of Burgesses, a representative assembly of citizens to decide local laws, and it received its first boatload of 20 African slaves. The next year was equally momentous, as a group of radically religious Puritans pulled ashore at what would become Plymouth, MA. The Pilgrims were escaping religious persecution under the 'corrupt' Church of England, and in the New World they saw a divine opportunity to create a new society that would be a religious and moral beacon. The Pilgrims signed a 'Mayflower Compact,' one of the seminal texts of American democracy, to govern themselves by consensus.

Capitalism & Colonialism

For the next two centuries, European powers competed for position and territory in the New World, extending European politics into the Americas. As Britain's Royal Navy came to rule Atlantic seas, England increasingly profited from its colonies and eagerly consumed the fruits of their labors – tobacco from Virginia, sugar and coffee from the Caribbean. Over the 17th and 18th centuries, slavery in America was slowly legalized into a formal institution to support this plantation economy. By 1800, one out of every six persons was enslaved.

Meanwhile, Britain mostly left the American colonists to govern themselves. Town meetings and representative assemblies, in which local citizens (that is, white men with property) debated community problems and voted on laws and taxes, became common. By the end of the Seven Years' War in 1763, Britain was feeling the strains of running an empire: it had been fighting France for a century and had colonies scattered all over the world. It was time to clean up bureaucracies and share financial burdens.

The colonies, however, resented English taxes and policies. Frustrations came to a head with the Boston Tea Party in 1773, after which Britain clamped down hard, shutting Boston's harbor and increasing its military presence. In 1774 representatives from 12 colonies convened the First Continental Congress in Philadelphia's Independence Hall to air complaints and prepare for the inevitable war ahead.

Native American Sites

- *Serpent Mound (OH)*
- *National Museum of the American Indian (Washington, DC)*
- *Trail of Tears (Southeastern USA)*
- *Mashpee Wampanoag Indian Museum (MA)*
- *Emerald Mound (MI)*
- *Museum of the Cherokee Indian (NC)*
- *Cahokia Mounds (IL)*

1607

The Jamestown settlement, the first permanent English colony in North America, is founded on marshland in present-day Virginia. The first few years are hard, with many dying from sickness and starvation.

1620

The *Mayflower* lands at Plymouth with 102 English Pilgrims, who have come to the New World to escape religious persecution. The Wampanoag tribe saves them from starvation.

1675

For decades, the Pilgrims and local tribes live fairly cooperatively, but deadly conflict erupts in 1675. King Philip's War lasts 14 months and kills more than 5000 people (mostly Native Americans).

1775

Paul Revere rides from Boston to warn colonial fighters (Minutemen) that the British are coming. The next day, the 'shot heard round the world' is fired at Lexington, starting the Revolutionary War.

Revolution & the Republic

In April 1775 British troops skirmished with armed colonists in Massachusetts (who were prepared for the fight, thanks to Paul Revere's famous warning), and the Revolutionary War began. George Washington, a wealthy Virginia farmer, was chosen to lead the American army. Trouble was, Washington lacked gunpowder and money (the colonists resisted taxes even for their own military), and his troops were a motley collection of poorly armed farmers, hunters and merchants, who regularly quit and returned to their farms due to lack of pay. On the other side, the British 'Redcoats' represented the world's most powerful military. The inexperienced General Washington had to improvise constantly, sometimes wisely retreating, sometimes engaging in 'ungentlemanly' sneak attacks. During the winter of 1777–78, the American army nearly starved at Valley Forge, PA.

Meanwhile, the Second Continental Congress tried to articulate what exactly they were fighting for. In January 1776 Thomas Paine published the wildly popular *Common Sense*, which passionately argued for independence from England. Soon, independence seemed not just logical, but noble and necessary, and on July 4, 1776, the Declaration of Independence was finalized and signed. Largely written by Thomas Jefferson, it elevated the 13 colonies' particular gripes against the monarchy into a universal declaration of individual rights and republican government.

Before Jamestown or Plymouth Rock, a group of 116 British men and women set up a colony at Roanoke, NC, in the late 1580s. When a supply ship returned three years later, the settlers had disappeared. The fate of the 'Lost Colony' remains one of America's greatest mysteries.

But to succeed, General Washington needed help, not just patriotic sentiment. In 1778 Benjamin Franklin persuaded France (always eager to trouble England) to ally with the revolutionaries, and they provided the troops, material and sea power that helped win the war. The British surrendered at Yorktown, VA, in 1781, and two years later the Treaty of Paris formally recognized the 'United States of America.' At first, the nation's loose confederation of fractious, squabbling states were hardly 'united.' So the founders gathered again in Philadelphia, and in 1787 drafted a new-and-improved Constitution: the US government was given a stronger federal center, with checks and balances between its three major branches, and to guard against the abuse of centralized power, a citizen's Bill of Rights was approved in 1791.

As radical as it was, though, the Constitution also preserved the economic and social status quo. Rich landholders kept their property, which included their slaves; Native Americans were excluded from the nation; and women were excluded from politics. These blatant discrepancies and injustices, which were widely noted, were the result of pragmatic compromise (eg to get slave-dependent Southern states on board) as well as widespread beliefs in the essential rightness of things as they were.

1776

On July 4, colonies sign the Declaration of Independence. Creators of the document include John Hancock, Samuel Adams, John Adams, Benjamin Franklin and Thomas Jefferson.

1787

The Constitutional Convention in Philadelphia draws up the US Constitution. Federal power is balanced between the presidency, Congress and the judiciary.

1791

Bill of Rights is adopted as 10 constitutional amendments articulating citizens' rights, including freedom of speech, a free press and the right to bear arms.

1803–06

President Thomas Jefferson sends Meriwether Lewis and William Clark west. Guided by the Shoshone tribeswoman Sacajawea, they trailblaze from St Louis, MI, to the Pacific Ocean and back.

Louisiana Purchase & the Move West

As the 19th century dawned on the young nation, the mood was optimistic. Agriculture was industrialized, and US commerce surged. In 1803 Thomas Jefferson bought land from French leader Napoleon Bonaparte. The Louisiana Purchase included New Orleans and about 15 present-day states west of the Mississippi River. Expansion began in earnest.

Relations between the US and Britain – despite lively trade – remained tense, and in 1812 the US declared war on England again. The two-year conflict ended without much gain by either side, although the British abandoned their forts, and the US vowed to avoid Europe's 'entangling alliances.'

In the 1830s and 1840s, with growing nationalist fervor and dreams of continental expansion, many Americans came to believe it was 'Manifest Destiny' that all the land in North America should be theirs. The 1830 Indian Removal Act aimed to clear one obstacle by designating land west of the Mississippi as 'Indian territory.' Native Americans were meant to relocate themselves there, thus clearing fertile valleys in eastern states such as Georgia and Alabama for white settlement. Many tribes resisted removal, including the Seminole in Florida, but the US government cajoled, threatened and bribed Native Americans to sign treaties and cooperate; when that failed, the government used guns. An estimated 4000 Native Americans died of cold, hunger or disease as they were forced along what became known as the 'Trail of Tears.'

Meanwhile, newly built railroads cleared another hurdle, linking midwestern and western lands with East Coast markets. As new states joined the USA, a troubling question loomed: would they be slave states or free states? The nation's future depended on the answer.

Mounds built by native peoples of the Eastern USA, as recently as the 16th century, are feats of engineering as impressive as the temples and pyramids of South and Central America. Four-sided earthen platform mounds were sites of temples, dances and ceremonies, while massive effigy mounds took the shape of culturally significant animals such as serpents.

The Civil War

The US Constitution hadn't ended slavery, but it had given Congress the power to approve (or not) slavery in new states. Public debates raged constantly over the expansion of slavery, particularly since this shaped the balance of power between the industrial North and the agrarian South.

Since founding, Southern politicians had dominated government and defended slavery as 'natural and normal,' which an 1856 *New York Times* editorial called 'insanity.' The economics of slavery were undeniable. In 1860 there were more than four million slaves in the US, most held by Southern planters, who grew 75% of the world's cotton and accounted for more than half of all US exports. Thus the Southern economy supported the nation's economy, and it required slaves. The 1860 presidential election became a referendum on this issue, and the election was won by a young politician from Illinois, Abraham Lincoln, who favored limiting slavery.

1812

The War of 1812 begins with battles against the British and Native Americans in the Great Lakes region. Even after the 1815 Treaty of Ghent, fighting continues along the Gulf Coast.

1838

Having been pushed westwards by encroaching settlement, and spurned by their erstwhile ally President Andrew Jackson, the Cherokee are forcibly expelled from southeastern USA along the Trail of Tears.

1861–65

American Civil War erupts between North and South (delineated by the Mason–Dixon line). The war's end on April 9, 1865, is marred by President Lincoln's assassination five days later.

1870

Freed Black men are given the vote, but the South's segregationist 'Jim Crow' laws (which remain until the 1960s) effectively disenfranchise African Americans from every meaningful sphere of daily life.

War began in April 1861, when the Confederacy attacked Fort Sumter in Charleston, SC, and raged on for the next four years in the most gruesome combat the world had ever known until that time. By the end, more than 600,000 soldiers – nearly an entire generation of young men – were dead. Southern plantations and cities (most notably Atlanta) lay sacked and burned. The North's industrial might provided an advantage, but its victory was not preordained; it unfolded battle by bloody battle.

As fighting progressed, Lincoln recognized that if the war didn't end slavery outright, victory would be pointless. In 1863 his Emancipation Proclamation expanded the war's aims and freed all slaves. In April 1865 Confederate general Robert E Lee surrendered to Union general Ulysses S Grant in Appomattox, VA. The union had been preserved, but at a staggering cost.

The whaling industry thrived in New England in the 18th century, especially around Massachusetts. Buzzards Bay, Nantucket Island and New Bedford were all prominent centers. New Bedford eventually hosted a whaling fleet of more than 300 ships, employing 10,000 people and earning more than $12 million in profits.

The Great Depression, the New Deal & World War II

In October 1929, investors, worried over a gloomy global economy, started selling stocks; panic spread until shareholders had sold everything. The stock market crashed, and the US economy collapsed like a house of cards.

Thus began the Great Depression. Frightened banks called in their loans; people couldn't pay; and the banks folded. Millions lost their homes, farms, businesses and savings.

In 1932 Democrat Franklin D Roosevelt was elected president on the promise of a 'New Deal' to rescue the US from its crisis, which he did with resounding success. When war once again broke out in Europe in 1939, the isolationist mood in America was as strong as ever. However, the extremely popular President Roosevelt, elected to an unprecedented third term in 1940, understood that the US couldn't sit by and allow victory for fascist, totalitarian regimes. Roosevelt sent aid to Britain and persuaded a skittish Congress to go along with it.

Then, on December 7, 1941, Japan launched a surprise attack on Hawaii's Pearl Harbor, killing more than 2000 Americans and sinking several battleships. US isolationism transformed overnight into outrage, and Roosevelt suddenly had the support he needed. Germany also declared war on the US, and America joined the Allied fight against Hitler and the Axis powers.

Fighting went on for more than two years in both the Pacific and in Europe. The Allies finally dealt the fatal blow to Germany with the massive D-Day invasion of France on June 6, 1944. Germany surrendered in May 1945. Nevertheless, Japan continued fighting. Newly elected president Harry Truman – ostensibly worried that a US invasion of Japan

1880–1920

Millions of immigrants flood in from Europe and Asia, fueling the age of cities. New York, Chicago and Philadelphia swell in size, becoming global centers of industry and commerce.

1896

In *Plessy v Ferguson*, the US Supreme Court rules that 'separate but equal' public facilities for blacks and whites are legal, arguing that the Constitution addresses only political, not social, equality.

1908

The first Model T (aka 'Tin Lizzie') car is built in Detroit, MI. Assembly-line innovator Henry Ford is soon selling one million automobiles annually.

1915

African Americans begin to leave the South to pursue opportunities in northern cities. This 'great migration' of six million people over five decades shapes urban life and spurs cultural movements such as the Harlem Renaissance.

would lead to unprecedented carnage – chose to drop experimental atomic bombs, created by the government's top-secret Manhattan Project, on Hiroshima and Nagasaki in August 1945. The bombs devastated both cities, killing more than 200,000 people. Japan surrendered days later, and the nuclear age was born.

The Red Scare, Civil Rights & the Vietnam War

The US enjoyed unprecedented prosperity in the decades after WWII, but little peace. Formerly wartime allies, the communist Soviet Union and the capitalist USA soon engaged in a running competition to dominate the globe. The superpowers engaged in proxy wars – notably the Korean War (1950–53) and Vietnam War (1954–75) – with only the mutual threat of nuclear annihilation preventing direct war.

Meanwhile, with its continent unscarred and its industry bulked up by WWII, the American homeland entered an era of growing affluence. In the 1950s, a mass migration left the inner cities for the suburbs, where affordable single-family homes sprang up. Americans drove cheap cars using cheap gas over brand-new interstate highways. They relaxed with the comforts of modern technology, secured low-interest housing loans and free education through programs such as the GI Bill, and got busy, giving birth to a 'baby boom.'

Middle-class whites did, anyway. Structural racism nationwide and Jim Crow laws in the South prevented African Americans from having the same opportunities. Echoing 19th-century abolitionist Frederick Douglass, the Southern Christian Leadership Coalition (SCLC), led by African American preacher Martin Luther King Jr, aimed to end segregation and 'save America's soul': to realize color-blind justice, racial equality and economic opportunity for all.

Beginning in the 1950s, King preached and organized nonviolent resistance in the form of bus boycotts, marches and sit-ins, mainly in the South. White authorities often met these protests with water hoses and police batons, and demonstrations sometimes dissolved into riots, but with the 1964 Civil Rights Act, African Americans spurred a wave of legislation that swept away racist laws and laid the groundwork for a more just and equal society.

Meanwhile, the 1960s saw further social upheavals: rock and roll spawned a youth rebellion and drugs sent Technicolor visions spinning in their heads. President John F Kennedy was assassinated in Dallas in 1963, followed by the assassinations in 1968 of his brother, Senator Robert Kennedy, and of Martin Luther King Jr (in Memphis). Americans' faith in their leaders and government was further shocked by the

Though the town of Woodstock, NY, lent its name to the mythic 1969 music fest, the event actually took place in the nearby hamlet of Bethel, where dairy farmer Max Yasgur rented his alfalfa field to organizers. Ticket price for the bash: $18 for a three-day pass ($24 at the gate).

1917
President Woodrow Wilson enters the US into WWI. The US mobilizes 4.7 million troops, and suffers around 110,000 of the war's nine million military deaths.

1919
The temperance movement champions the 18th amendment, which bans alcohol. Prohibition leads to bootlegging and organized crime. The amendment is repealed in 1933.

1933–38
Roosevelt's New Deal establishes federal programs and legislation including Social Security, the Fair Labor Standards Act and the Civilian Conservation Corps to provide unemployment relief.

1941–45
WWII: America deploys 16 million troops and suffers 400,000 deaths. Globally, civilian deaths outpace military deaths two to one, and total 50 to 70 million people from more than 50 countries.

bombings and brutalities of the Vietnam War, seen on TV, which led to widespread student protests.

Yet Republican president Richard Nixon, elected in 1968 in part for promising an 'honorable end to the war,' instead escalated US involvement and secretly bombed Laos and Cambodia. Then in 1972 the Watergate scandal broke: a burglary at Democratic Party offices in Washington was, through dogged journalism, tied to 'Tricky Dick,' who in 1974 became the first US president to resign from office.

The tumultuous 1960s and '70s also witnessed the sexual revolution, women's liberation and other events challenging the status quo. Milestones included the 1969 Stonewall riots in Greenwich Village, NYC, which galvanized the gay rights movement when patrons of a gay bar called the Stonewall Inn fought back after a police raid, demanding equal rights and an end to persecution. A few months later, the Woodstock Festival defined the Vietnam era with its peace-love-and-flowers hippies swaying in the fields to rock music.

Civil Rights on Film

I Am Not Your Negro (2017), Raoul Peck

Hidden Figures (2016), Theodore Melfi

Selma (2014), Ava DuVernay

Ghosts of Mississippi (1996), Rob Reiner

Malcolm X (1992), Spike Lee

The Long Walk Home (1990), Richard Pearce

Mississippi Burning (1988), Alan Parker

Reagan, Clinton & the Bushes

In 1980 California's Republican governor and former actor Ronald Reagan campaigned for president by promising to make Americans feel good about America again. The affable Reagan won easily, and his election marked a pronounced shift to the right in US politics. Military spending and tax cuts created enormous federal deficits, which hampered the presidency of Reagan's successor, George HW Bush. Despite winning the first Gulf War – liberating Kuwait in 1991 after an Iraqi invasion – Bush was soundly defeated in the 1992 presidential election by Southern Democrat Bill Clinton.

On September 11, 2001, Islamic terrorists flew hijacked planes into New York's World Trade Center and the Pentagon in Washington, DC. This catastrophic attack united Americans behind their president, George W Bush, as he vowed revenge and declared a 'war on terror.' Bush soon attacked Afghanistan in an unsuccessful hunt for Al-Qaeda terrorist cells, then attacked Iraq in 2003 and toppled its anti-US dictator, Saddam Hussein. Meanwhile, Iraq descended into civil war.

The Obama Presidency

In 2008, hungry for change, Americans elected political newcomer Barack Obama, America's first African American president. He had his work cut out for him. These were, after all, unprecedented times economically, with the US in the largest financial crisis since the Great Depression. What had started as a collapse of the US housing bubble in 2007 had spread to the banking sector, with the meltdown of major financial

1948–51

The US-led Marshall Plan funnels $12 billion in material and financial aid to help Europe recover from WWII. The plan also aims to contain Soviet influence and reignite America's economy.

1954

The Supreme Court rules that segregation in public schools is 'inherently unequal' and orders desegregation 'with all deliberate speed.' The fight to integrate schools spurs the Civil Rights movement.

1963

On November 22, President John F Kennedy is publicly assassinated by Lee Harvey Oswald while riding in a motorcade through Dealey Plaza in Dallas, TX.

1964

Congress passes the Civil Rights Act, outlawing discrimination on the basis of race, color, religion, sex or national origin. First proposed by Kennedy, it was one of President Johnson's crowning achievements.

institutions. Wars in Afghanistan and Iraq, launched a decade prior, continued to simmer on the back burner of the ever-changing news cycle.

In 2011, in a subterfuge operation vetted by President Obama, Navy Seals raided Osama bin Laden's Pakistan hideout and killed the Al-Qaeda leader, bringing an end to the search for America's greatest public enemy. The economy, however, remained in bad shape, and the ambitious $800-billion stimulus package passed by Congress in 2009 hadn't borne much fruit in the eyes of many Americans – even though economists estimated that the stimulus did soften the blow of the recession. At the end of his first term, Obama's approval ratings were around 49%.

With lost jobs, overvalued mortgages and little relief in sight, millions of Americans found themselves adrift. This was not a recession they could spend their way out of, as Obama's predecessor had suggested. Flat wages contributed to the problem: the median earner was taking home 11% less than in 1999. People were upset and gathered in large numbers to voice their anger. On the left, this expressed itself as the Occupy Wall Street movement, which called out banks and corporations as having too much influence over the democratic process. On the right, it manifested as the Tea Party, a wing of politically conservative Republicans who believed that government handouts would destroy the economy and, thus, America.

Despite such unrest, Obama was reelected in 2012, though he returned to office without quite the same hope that surrounded him the first time. When Obama took the oath of office in 2013, the unemployment rate, hovering around 8%, was about what it had been during his first inauguration, though economic growth was on a more solid foundation.

On other fronts, Obama showed mixed success: he ended the US involvement in Iraq, but total civilian casualties from drone strikes during this period mounted. Government figures released in 2016 purport that drones and other airstrikes during the Obama administration killed between 64 and 116 civilians, but NGOs, such as the Bureau of Investigative Journalism, report the civilian death toll to be much higher.

His enduring legacy, the Affordable Healthcare Act (ACA), commonly known as 'Obamacare,' which became law in 2010 but wasn't effected until 2014, had a tenuous trajectory under the Trump Administration. Democrats pointed out that millions more Americans than ever before have health insurance under Obamacare, while Republicans insisted the program has been a failure from the outset, citing decreased insurance options for consumers and harsh costs for business owners.

During his campaign, Trump promised, if elected, to swiftly repeal the ACA. But when push came to shove on March 24, 2017, Trump's repeal bill failed to make it through Congress. Still, President Trump continued

US Involvement in Major Wars

Moro Revolution (14 years)

War in Afghanistan (13 years, 2 months)

War in Iraq (8 years, 9 months)

Vietnam War (8 years, 1 month)

American Civil War (4 years)

World War II (3 years, 7 months)

Korean War (3 years, 1 month)

1965–75
US involvement in the Vietnam War tears the nation apart as 58,000 Americans die, along with four million Vietnamese and 1.5 million Laotians and Cambodians.

1969
American astronauts land on the moon, culminating the 'space race' between the US and USSR. In NYC, a police raid at the Stonewall Inn, a gay bar, sparks the gay rights movement.

1973
In *Roe v Wade*, the Supreme Court legalizes abortion. Even today this decision remains controversial and socially divisive, pitting 'right to choose' advocates against the 'right to life' anti-abortion lobby.

1989
The Berlin Wall is torn down, marking the end of the Cold War between the US and the USSR (now Russia). The USA becomes the world's last remaining superpower.

to undermine the ACA through everything from rhetoric to reducing the enrollment window.

Legislation that Changed America

- *North Atlantic Treaty (1949)*
- *Civil Rights Act (1964)*
- *Immigration and Nationality Act (1965)*
- *California Proposition 13 (1978)*
- *Americans with Disabilities Act (1990)*
- *Marriage Equality Act (2015)*

The 2016 Election & the Trump Presidency

When real-estate magnate and former host of TV reality game show *The Apprentice* Donald J Trump announced he was running for president in June 2015, many around the world thought it was a publicity stunt. What ensued could be described as a media circus, with relentless coverage of the protracted campaign that pitted Trump, with no prior political experience, against Hillary Clinton, former Secretary of State (2009–13) and First Lady. Trump's pithy soundbites and no-holds-barred insults stood out in a crowded Republican primary field and made for irresistible headlines, while the primary contest on the Democratic side was winnowed to Clinton and populist candidate Bernie Sanders early on.

Once the Trump and Clinton match was announced, a contentious campaign ensued. Trump refused to follow the common practice among presidential candidates of releasing personal tax records. On October 7, *Access Hollywood* tapes leaked in which Trump admitted to assaulting women. On Clinton's side, opponents invoked the Benghazi terror attacks and her ties to Wall Street. A week before the election, FBI head James Comey stoked the conspiracy theories around Hillary Clinton by announcing in a letter to Congress that her emails, which she stored on a private server against security recommendations, were still under investigation. Nevertheless, polls gave Clinton a strong lead, and on election night, the country prepared to celebrate the election of the first female president of the United States. Clinton did win the popular vote, but the Electoral College math was not in her favor. She conceded to Donald Trump in the early hours of November 9 with an emotional speech that reminded 'all the little girls who are watching this, never doubt that you are valuable, and powerful and deserving of every chance and opportunity in the world to pursue and achieve your own dreams.'

In his victory speech, Trump declared 'I will be president for all Americans,' though many remain unsure that they are included in his definition of what an American is. Uncertainty, in fact, seems to be the defining quality of the Trump presidency. Scandal and controversy have surrounded the administration in its first term, during which the nation's democratic integrity has been challenged by conflicts of interest between public office and private enterprise. Public protest has become a key feature of the sociopolitical landscape, starting with the Women's March the day after the inauguration, the largest single-day demonstration in recorded US history with an estimated four million

1996

Atlanta hosts the Summer Olympics, only the third US city to do so. However, the Centennial Olympic Park bombing kills one and injures 111.

2001

On September 11, Al-Qaeda terrorists hijack four commercial airplanes, flying two into NYC's twin towers and one into the Pentagon (the fourth crashes in Pennsylvania); nearly 3000 people are killed.

2003

After citing evidence that Iraq possesses weapons of mass destruction, President George W Bush launches a preemptive war that will cost more than 4000 American lives and some $3 trillion.

2005

On August 29, Hurricane Katrina hits the Mississippi and Louisiana coasts, rupturing poorly maintained levees and flooding New Orleans. More than 1800 people die, and cost estimates exceed $110 billion.

participants in some 653 cities around the country. The release of the Mueller Report in 2019, which summarized the findings of a two-year investigation of Trump's connections to Russia, only muddied the waters; lacking a firm conclusion and heavily redacted, the ambiguity of the report allowed both the left and the right to argue that it supports their case. Also in 2019, the *New York Times* released 10 years of Trump's tax documents, showing that his businesses lost nearly $1 billion between 1985 and 1994.

Decency for the Win

In 2020, former Vice President Joe Biden and former US Senator from California Kamala Harris were elected to the highest offices in the country. Biden, who ran on a campaign to restore decency to the White House, won 306 electoral college votes (versus Trump's 232) and garnered seven million more votes than his rival.

The resounding loss didn't stop Trump from refusing to concede defeat. He immediately announced the election was stolen despite having no evidence to support his claim. His lieutenants, however, took up the battle cry, and engaged in antics bordering on the surreal – such as the rambling press conference hosted by Rudy Giuliani in front of the Four Seasons Total Landscaping company (not to be confused with the hotel of the same name) in an industrial neighborhood in northeast Philadelphia. More than 60 lawsuits were filed by Trump's lawyers to contest the election, the counting of votes and the certification process in states pivotal to his loss, including Arizona, Georgia, Michigan, Pennsylvania and Wisconsin. Judges, including some appointed by Trump himself, dismissed nearly all of the cases on the grounds of being 'frivolous' or 'without merit.'

Things took a turn for the worse in January, 2021, when a mob of 2000 or so Trump supporters attacked the Capitol Building and disrupted a joint session of Congress. Two rioters and one police officer died as a result of the mob violence. Months later, four responding Capitol Police officers committed suicide.

Despite unlawful efforts to overturn the election, Joe Biden was sworn in as president on schedule a few weeks after the attempted coup. After four years of chaos under Trump, millions of Americans (and the rest of the world) breathed a collective sigh of relief. Biden, who devoted his life to public service, faced daunting challenges his first year in office, namely a raging pandemic, soaring inflation, pulling troops out of Afghanistan and rebuilding America's infrastructure after years of neglect.

2008–09

Barack Obama becomes the first African American president. The stock market crashes due to mismanagement by major American financial institutions. The crisis spreads worldwide.

2011

As unemployment remains high and household income drops, activists launch Occupy Wall Street in NYC to protest economic and social inequality. The movement spreads to cities worldwide.

2015

The Supreme Court legalizes gay marriage nationwide. South Carolina removes the Confederate battle flag from its Capitol under pressure that it is a racist symbol that sparked mass murder in Charleston.

2022

In the 10 years since Colorado became the first state to legalize the sale of marijuana, 18 other states and Washington, DC, have legalized its sale and 36 states allow for medical use.

The Way of Life

The Eastern USA is a compelling mix of accents and rhythms, big-city financiers and small-town farmers, university students and sun-seeking retirees, Yankees and Southerners. A diverse range of experiences awaits all who visit, from sampling the delights of molecular gastronomy in New York to po'boy sandwiches in New Orleans; partying it up on Chicago's re-energized club circuit or at a Nashville honky-tonk; from romantic strolls through New England villages to lazy days on Florida's endless summer coastlines.

The US is home to the world's second-largest Spanish-speaking population, behind Mexico and just ahead of Spain. Latinx people make up the fastest-growing minority group in the nation. In the East, Florida, Illinois, New Jersey and New York have the largest Latinx populations.

Multiculturalism

From the get-go, cities in the East were 'melting pots,' with a long and proud heritage of welcoming newcomers from all over the world. So it's no surprise that the region is so culturally diverse.

In the Northeast, Irish and Italian communities have been well established in urban areas since the 19th century. In Chicago, Latinxs (mostly from Mexico) comprise roughly one-quarter of the population. The upper Great Lakes states are home to the nation's biggest enclaves of Somali and Hmong immigrants, a result of the area's long tradition of resettling refugees. In Florida, Cubans lead the multicultural pack; the population began arriving in Miami in the 1960s following Castro's revolution and created a politically powerful community. Nicaraguans followed in the 1980s, fleeing war in their country, and now number more than 100,000. The city's Little Haiti adds 70,000 Haitians to the mix. The South, more than any other region, is a place with a culture unto itself; more than half of all African Americans live here. These examples are just a fraction of the complex whole.

The East, like the rest of the country, can never quite decide if the continual influx of newcomers is its saving grace or what will eventually strain society to breaking point. 'Immigration reform' has been a Washington buzzword for nearly two decades. Some people believe the nation's current system deals with undocumented immigrants (there are 11.3 million) too leniently – that the government should deport immigrants who are here unlawfully and fine employers who hire them. Other Americans think those rules are too harsh – that immigrants who have been here for years working, contributing to society and abiding by the law deserve amnesty. Despite several attempts, Congress has not been able to pass a comprehensive package addressing illegal immigration, though it has put through various measures to beef up enforcement.

Religion

Separation of Church and State has been the law of the land ever since the Pilgrims came ashore in Massachusetts in the early 1600s. Their faith – Protestant Christianity – continues to predominate in the East.

Protestantism covers a wide swath of denominations. They fall under two main headings: evangelical Protestants, of which Baptists form the biggest contingent; and mainline Protestants, such as Lutherans, Methodists and Presbyterians. Evangelicals have the greater number of worshippers, and that number has grown in recent years: Baptists are their powerhouse, accounting for one-third of all Protestants and close to one-fifth of the USA's total adult population. Their numbers stack up in the South. In contrast, Lutherans (who are concentrated in Minnesota and Wisconsin, as well as the Dakotas) and other mainline denominations have experienced declining figures.

Catholicism is the East's second most practiced faith. In fact, New England is the country's most Catholic zone, and the numbers trickle down to the Mid-Atlantic states. Massachusetts is the most Catholic state, with 45% of residents of that faith. Baltimore is the country's oldest archdiocese, established in 1789. States with large Latinx populations, such as Florida and Illinois, also support big concentrations of Catholics.

Judaism has a significant presence in the Eastern USA. Jews make up roughly 12% of the population in both South Florida and the New York metro area. The latter is a major center of Orthodox Judaism and home to more Jews than anywhere outside Tel Aviv.

Also in the East: Muslim Americans cluster in the New York, Chicago and Detroit metro areas. Hindu Americans bunch in New York and New Jersey, as well as in big cities such a Chicago, Washington, DC, and Atlanta.

Americans are increasingly defining their spiritual beliefs outside of organized religion. The proportion of those who say they have 'no religion' is now around 23.1%, about the same percentage as those who identify as Catholic or Evangelical, according to the Public Religion Research Institute.

Lifestyle

In general the Eastern USA has one of the world's highest standards of living, though there are some shocking variances by region. At the top end sits Maryland, with a median household income of $78,916 (data from 2017). Mississippi dwells at the opposite end of the scale at $42,009. These figures are the high and low not just for the region, but for the nation, upholding the pattern in which households in the Northeast earn the most, while those in the South earn the least. Wages also vary by ethnicity, with African Americans and Latinxs earning less than whites and Asians ($40,232 and $50,486 respectively, versus $65,273 and $81,331 as of 2017).

About 90% of Americans are high-school graduates, while some 35% go on to graduate from college with a four-year bachelor's degree. The university lifestyle (cafes, bookshops and progressive mindsets) is especially prevalent in the Northeast, home to the eight Ivy League schools as well as the 'Little Ivies' (a self-anointed collection of a dozen elite liberal-arts colleges) and the 'Seven Sisters' (top-tier women's colleges, founded in the days when the Ivy League was still a boys-only club). More than 50 institutions of higher learning cluster around Boston alone.

If you peeked inside a house, you'd typically find a married couple with two kids occupying it. Both parents usually work, and according to the Bureau of Labor Statistics, the average adult works 42 hours per week. Divorce is common – 40% of first marriages break up – but both divorce and marriage rates have declined over the last three decades. As a result, as of 2018, 25% of US children live with only one parent.

STATES & TRAITS

Regional US stereotypes now have solid data behind them, thanks to a study of the geography of personality differences across the states. Researcher Peter Rentfrow and his colleagues processed more than a half-million personality assessments collected from individual US citizens, then looked at where certain traits stacked up on the map. Turns out 'Minnesota nice' is for real – the most 'agreeable' states cluster around the Great Lakes, Great Plains and the South. These places rank highest for friendliness and cooperation. The most neurotic states? They line up in the Northeast. But New York didn't place number one, as you might expect; that honor goes to West Virginia. Many of the most 'open' states lie out West: California, Nevada, Oregon and Washington all rate high for being receptive to new ideas – although they lag behind Washington, DC, and New York.

While many Americans hit the gym or walk, bike or jog regularly, 47% don't get the amount of daily activity recommended by the Centers for Disease Control and Prevention (CDC). Health researchers speculate that this lack of exercise and Americans' fondness for sugary and fatty foods have led to rising rates of obesity and diabetes. The South fares the worst: Mississippi, Alabama, West Virginia, Tennessee and Louisiana lead the obesity rankings, with the condition affecting one-third of residents.

About 25% of Americans volunteer their time to help others or help a cause, according to the Corporation for National and Community Service. Eco-consciousness has entered the mainstream: most big chain grocery stores – including Walmart – now sell organic foods, and many cities are pushing to go 'zero waste.' Still, only 34% of waste generated in the US is recycled, according to the Environmental Protection Agency.

StoryCorps has collected and archived more than 50,000 interviews from people across America, which it preserves in the Library of Congress. Listen to folks tell their stories of discovery, family, identity, love and much more at www.storycorps.org.

Sports

What really draws Americans together (sometimes slathered in blue body paint or with foam-rubber cheese wedges attached to their heads) is sports. In spring and summer there's baseball nearly every day; in fall and winter there's football; and through the long nights of winter there's plenty of basketball to keep the adrenaline going. In addition to the big three sports, auto racing has revved up interest, especially in the South. Major League Soccer (MLS) is attracting an ever-increasing following. Ice hockey, once favored only in northern climes, has broken into the South, drawing fans in cities such as Nashville and Atlanta. Women's basketball and soccer are also gaining traction nationwide, with multiple teams that play in pro leagues.

Baseball

Baseball may not command the same TV viewership (and subsequent advertising dollars) as football, but with 162 games over a season versus 16 for football, its ubiquity allows it to maintain its status as America's pastime.

Besides, baseball is better live than on TV: nothing beats being at the ballpark on a sunny day, sitting in the bleachers with a beer and hot dog, and indulging in the seventh-inning stretch, when the entire park erupts in a communal sing-along of 'Take Me Out to the Ballgame.' The playoffs, held every October, still deliver excitement and unexpected champions. Consistently one of America's favorite teams despite not having won a World Series in more than 100 years, the Chicago Cubs skyrocketed to legend-status when they turned that frown upside down to become the 2016 World Series Champions, defeating the Cleveland Indians in a landslide victory. The Cubs' victory parade drew almost five million people to the streets of Chicago, making it one of the largest single gatherings of people in recorded history.

Tickets to games are relatively inexpensive – seats average about $25 at most stadiums – and are easy to get for most games. Minor-league baseball games cost half as much, and can be even more fun, with lots of audience participation, stray chickens and dogs running across the field, and wild throws from the pitcher's mound. For information, see www.milb.com.

Sports Sites

Baseball: www.mlb.com

Basketball: www.nba.com

Football: www.nfl.com

Hockey: www.nhl.com

Auto racing: www.nascar.com, www.indycar.com

Hockey: www.nhl.com

Soccer: www.mlssoccer.com

Football

Football is big, physical and rolling in dough. With the shortest season and least number of games of any of the major sports, every match takes on the emotion of an epic battle, where the results matter and an unfortunate injury can deal a lethal blow to a team's playoff chances.

ICONIC SPORTING VENUES

Yankee Stadium, NYC The Bronx's fabled baseball field, steeped in history and the ghost of Babe Ruth.

Lambeau Field, Green Bay Stadium of the NFL's Packers; nicknamed 'the Frozen Tundra' for its insanely cold weather.

Fenway Park, Boston Baseball's oldest park (1912); home of the 'Green Monster' (aka the tall left-field wall).

Wrigley Field, Chicago Another vintage ballpark (1914), with ivy walls, a classic neon sign and good-time neighborhood bars all around.

Madison Square Garden, NYC Not only do the Knicks dribble at the 'mecca of basketball,' but Ali boxed here and Elvis rocked here.

Little Caesars Arena, Detroit The badass rink of pro hockey's Red Wings; witness the strange octopus-throwing custom.

Churchill Downs, Louisville Home of the Kentucky Derby: fine hats, mint juleps and the 'greatest two minutes in sports.'

Indianapolis Motor Speedway, Indianapolis Race cars scream by at 170mph at the hard-partying Indy 500.

It's also the toughest US sport, played in fall and winter in all manner of rain, sleet and snow – some of the most memorable matches have occurred at below-freezing temperatures. Green Bay Packers fans are in a class by themselves when it comes to severe weather. Their stadium in Wisconsin (Lambeau Field) was the site of the infamous Ice Bowl, a 1967 championship game against the Dallas Cowboys where the temperature plummeted to -13°F (-25°C) – mind you, that was with a wind-chill factor of -48°F (-44°C).

The rabidly popular Super Bowl is pro football's championship match, held in late January or early February. The other 'bowl' games (such as the Sugar Bowl in New Orleans and Orange Bowl in Miami) are college football's title matches, held on and around New Year's Day.

In recent years the National Football League has come under fire for failing to adjust the rules of the sport in reaction to overwhelming proof that repeated concussions (a byproduct of tackles) have a permanent effect on players. A 2017 study by Boston University of the brains of 111 NFL players showed that 110 had a degenerative brain disease, chronic traumatic encephalopathy (CTE). Though TV ratings for NFL games have taken a slight hit, the sport remains popular: 1.06 million children and teens played tackle football in 2017, according to a study by JAMA Pediatrics.

The Super Bowl costs America $800 million in lost workplace productivity as employees gossip about the game, make bets and shop for new TVs online. It's still less than the $1.9 billion estimate for March Madness, when many folks get caught up in the NCAA basketball tournament.

Basketball

The teams bringing in the most fans these days include the Chicago Bulls, the Atlanta Hawks (a promising team in a sports-mad city) and the New York Knicks (hey, you might see a celebrity!). Smaller markets can also be a great place to catch a game – the Milwaukee Hawks are filling seats thanks to up-and-coming forward Giannis Antetokounmpo.

College basketball also draws millions of fans, especially every spring when the March Madness playoffs roll around; it culminates in the Final Four, when the remaining quartet of teams competes for a spot in the championship game. The Cinderella stories and unexpected outcomes rival the pro league for excitement. The games are widely televised and bet upon – this is when Las Vegas bookies earn their keep.

Arts & Architecture

New York remains the dynamic heart of the theater and art worlds, while great literature finds its voice throughout the region. Niche media networks are making edgy, must-view TV about everything from zombies in Georgia to murderers in Minnesota. In the meantime, architects in New York and Chicago keep pushing ever higher.

Painting

In the wake of WWII, the USA developed its first truly original school of art: abstract expressionism. New York painters Jackson Pollock, Franz Kline, Mark Rothko and others explored freely created, nonrepresentational forms. Pollock, for example, made drip paintings by pouring and splattering pigments over large canvases.

Pop art followed, where artists drew inspiration from bright, cartoony consumer images; Andy Warhol was the king (or Pope of Pop, as he's sometimes called). Minimalism came next, and by the 1980s and '90s, the canvas was wide open – any and all styles could take their place at the arts table.

New York remains the red-hot center of the art world, and its make-or-break influence shapes tastes across the nation and around the globe. To get the pulse of contemporary art in the region, check out works by Jenny Holzer, Kara Walker, Chuck Close, Martin Puryear and Frank Stella.

Best Modern Art Museums

Museum of Modern Art, NYC, NY

Whitney Museum of American Art, NYC, NY

Salvador Dalí Museum, St Petersburg, FL

Andy Warhol Museum, Pittsburgh, PA

Dia:Beacon, Beacon, NY

Literature

The 'Great American Novel' has stirred the imagination for more than 150 years. Edgar Allan Poe told spooky short stories in the 1840s, and is credited with inventing the detective story, horror story and science fiction. Four decades later, Samuel Clemens, aka Mark Twain, also made a literary splash. Twain wrote in the vernacular, loved 'tall tales' and reveled in absurdity, which endeared him to everyday readers. His novel *Huckleberry Finn* (1884) became the quintessential American narrative: compelled by a primal moment of rebellion against his father, Huck embarks on a search for authenticity through which he discovers himself. The Mississippi River provides the backdrop.

The Lost Generation brought American literature into its own in the early 20th century. These writers lived as expatriates in post-WWI Europe and described a growing sense of alienation. Straight-talking Ernest Hemingway exemplified the era with his spare, stylized realism. Minnesotan F Scott Fitzgerald eviscerated East Coast society life with his fiction. Back on home turf, William Faulkner examined the South's social rifts in dense, caustic prose, and African Americans such as poet Langston Hughes and novelist Zora Neale Hurston undermined racist stereotypes during New York's Harlem Renaissance.

After WWII, American writers began depicting regional and ethnic divides, experimented with style and often bashed middle-class society's values. The 1950s Beat Generation, with Jack Kerouac, Allen Ginsberg and William S Burroughs at the center, was particularly hard-core.

Today's literature reflects an ever more diverse panoply of voices. Jacqueline Woodson, Junot Diaz and Louise Erdrich have all written bestsellers in the past decade and given voice to, respectively, African American, Dominican American and Native American issues. Titans of contemporary literature include Toni Morrison (whose most recent novel was *God Save the Child* in 2015); the prolific Joyce Carol Oates, Michael Chabon and Colson Whitehead – all Pulitzer Prize winners hailing from the Eastern USA. Whitehead's *The Underground Railroad,* a searing fictional take on one woman's journey from slavery to freedom in the 1850s, won the 2016 National Book Award and the 2017 Pulitzer Prize.

Perhaps the best-known Eastern USA author of our time was reclusive Harper Lee. Born in Monroeville, AL, Lee gained fame in 1960 when she wrote *To Kill a Mockingbird*, a staple of summer reading lists nationwide. But she shunned the spotlight and did not release another book until 2015, when *Go Set a Watchman,* a sequel of sorts, was released. The publication was controversial; many wondered whether Lee, who was 89, was capable of consenting to its release. She died less than a year later, on February 19, 2016.

Theater

Eugene O'Neill put American drama on the map with his trilogy *Mourning Becomes Electra* (1931), which sets a tragic Greek myth in post–Civil War New England. O'Neill was the first major US playwright, and is still widely considered to be the best.

After WWII, two playwrights dominated the stage: Arthur Miller, who famously married Marilyn Monroe and wrote about everything from middle-class male disillusionment (*Death of a Salesman*; 1949) to the mob mentality of the Salem witch trials (*The Crucible*; 1953); and Tennessee Williams, whose explosive works *The Glass Menagerie* (1945), *A Streetcar Named Desire* (1947) and *Cat on a Hot Tin Roof* (1955) dug deep into the Southern psyche.

Edward Albee gave the 1960s a healthy dose of absurdism, and David Mamet and Sam Shepard filled the '70s and '80s with rough-and-tough guys. These days Pulitzer Prize–winner Tracy Letts writes family dramas that are often compared to O'Neill, bringing the scene full circle.

Broadway is where shows get star treatment. The famed NYC district earns more than a billion dollars in revenue from ticket sales each year, with top shows pulling in a cool million a week. Long-running classics such as *The Lion King* and *Wicked* continue to play before sold-out houses, alongside newer hits such as the *Book of Mormon.* Meanwhile, stalwarts such as *Les Miserables* get revamped and reopen to much fanfare (as in 2014). But it's away from Broadway's bright lights, in regional theaters such as Chicago's Steppenwolf, Minneapolis' Guthrie and hundreds more, where new plays and playwrights emerge and keep the art vital.

The unlikely star of Broadway in 2016 and 2017 was a rap- and R&B-inspired musical about one of the lesser known Founding Fathers. Lin-Manuel Miranda's *Hamilton*, based on Ron Chernow's best-selling 2004 biography of Treasury Secretary Alexander Hamilton, featured a cast of nonwhite actors and an incredibly catchy soundtrack. Demand was almost unprecedented and tickets soared to astronomical prices, though it became a bit easier to score a seat after national tours launched in 2017.

Great American Novels of the 2000s

Little Fires Everywhere, Celeste Ng

Middlesex, Jeffrey Eugenides

Delicious Foods, James Hannaham

An American Marriage, Tayari Jones

Gilead, Marilynne Robinson

Film & Television

The studio system began in Manhattan, where Thomas Edison – inventor of the industry's earliest moving-picture technology – tried to create a monopoly with his patents. This drove many independents to move to a suburb of Los Angeles, where they could easily flee to Mexico in case of legal trouble – and ta-da, Hollywood was born.

While most of the movie magic still happens on the West Coast, New York retains its fair share of film and TV studios. ABC, CBS, NBC, CNN, MTV and HBO are among the Big Apple's big shots, and many visitors come expressly to see a taping of Jimmy Fallon's *Tonight Show,* Stephen Colbert's *Late Show* or other favorite talk shows. Many filmmakers and actors prefer New York to the West Coast – Robert De Niro, Spike Lee and Woody Allen most famously – so keep an eye out on local streets. Other film-friendly cities include Miami, Chicago and Atlanta, and one you wouldn't normally think of: Wilmington, NC, which hosts enough studios to earn the nickname 'Wilmywood.'

Several famous authors from the Eastern USA wrote books that have been banned at one time or another, including Indianapolis' Kurt Vonnegut *(Slaughterhouse-Five)*, New York's JD Salinger *(The Catcher in the Rye)* and Georgia-born Alice Walker *(The Color Purple)*.

As cable TV and streaming services such as Netflix, Amazon and YouTube (where users can broadcast their own channels and be their own stars) have entered the industry, mainstream networks have stuck to a formula of long-narrative serial dramas (such as *Law & Order: SVU,* which has run since 1999), as well as cheap-to-produce 'unscripted' reality TV. What started with *Survivor* in 2000, the contestants and 'actors' of *The Voice* and *The Bachelor* keep alive today, for better or for worse.

Architecture

In 1885 a group of designers in Chicago shot up the pioneering skyscraper. It didn't exactly poke the clouds, but its use of steel framing launched modern architecture.

Around the same time, another Chicago architect was doing radical things closer to the ground. Frank Lloyd Wright created a building style that abandoned historical elements and references, which had long been the tradition, and went organic. He designed buildings in relation to the landscape, which on the Great Plains meant the low-slung, horizontal lines of the surrounding prairie. An entire movement grew up around Wright's Prairie Style.

European architects absorbed Wright's ideas, and that influence bounced back when the Bauhaus school left Nazi Germany and set up in the USA. Here it became known as the International Style, an early form of modernism. Ludwig Mies van der Rohe was the main man with the plan, and his boxy, metal-and-glass behemoths rose high on urban horizons, especially in Chicago and New York City. Postmodernism followed, reintroducing color and the decorative elements of art deco, beaux art and other earlier styles to the region's sky-high designs.

Today's architects continue to break boundaries. Recent examples of visionary designs include Jeanne Gang's rippling Aqua Tower in Chicago – the world's tallest building designed by a woman. In 2013 NYC's 1776ft-high One World Trade Center rose to become the USA's loftiest building. In 2016 David Ajaye's shimmering National Museum of African American History and Culture took its place on the Mall in Washington, DC. More polarizing is the *Vessel,* Thomas Heatherwick's Escher-esque 'staircase to nowhere' at the center of New York City's Hudson Yards development. Is it a gaudy travesty or a bold new vision? Either way, since it opened in 2019, thousands of people a day have explored it for themselves.

Music

Jazz, blues, country, hip-hop and rock music were all born in the Eastern USA, and their beats permeate clubs and juke joints from north to south. Listen in and you'll hear the legacy of Muddy Waters' slide guitar, Hank Williams' yodel, John Coltrane's frenzied cascades and much more.

Blues

All US music starts with the blues. And the blues started in the South. That's where the genre developed out of the work songs, or 'shouts,' of enslaved people and out of black spiritual songs and their call-and-response pattern, both of which were adaptations of African music.

By the 1920s, Delta blues typified the sound. Musicians from Memphis to Mississippi sang passionate, plaintive melodies accompanied by a lonely slide guitar. Traveling blues musicians, and particularly female blues singers, gained fame and employment across the South. Early pioneers included Robert Johnson, WC Handy, Ma Rainey, Huddie Ledbetter (aka Lead Belly), and Bessie Smith, who some consider the best blues singer who ever lived.

At the same time, African American Christian choral music evolved into gospel. The genre's greatest singer, Mahalia Jackson came to prominence in Chicago in the 1920s, singing in the choir of the Greater Salem Baptist Church on the city's south side, where she was a faithful member until her death in 1972.

After WWII many musicians headed north to Chicago, which had become a hub for African American culture. And here the genre took a turn – it went electric. A new generation of players such as Muddy Waters, Buddy Guy, BB King and John Lee Hooker plugged in to amps, and their screaming guitars laid the groundwork for rock and roll.

Shrines for Music Lovers

- Sun Studio, Memphis, TN
- Graceland, Memphis, TN
- Country Music Hall of Fame, Nashville, TN
- Rock and Roll Hall of Fame, Cleveland, OH
- Preservation Hall, New Orleans, LA
- BB King Museum and Delta Interpretive Center, Indianola, MS

Jazz

Down in New Orleans, Congo Sq – where slaves gathered to sing and dance from the late 18th century onward – is considered the birthplace of jazz. There ex-slaves adapted the reed, horn and string instruments used by the city's multiracial Creoles – who themselves preferred formal European music – to play their own African-influenced music. This fertile cross-pollination produced a steady stream of innovative sound.

The first variation was ragtime, so-called because of its 'ragged,' syncopated African rhythms. Next came Dixieland jazz, centered on New Orleans' infamous Storyville red-light district. In 1917 Storyville shut down, and the musicians dispersed. Bandleader King Oliver moved to Chicago, and his star trumpet player, Louis Armstrong, soon followed. Armstrong's distinctive vocals and talented improvisations led to the solo becoming an integral part of jazz throughout much of the 20th century.

The 1920s and '30s are known as the Jazz Age, and New York City's Harlem was its hot spot. Swing – an urbane, big-band jazz style – swept the country, led by innovative bandleaders Duke Ellington and Count

Eastern USA Classic Playlist

'Atlantic City,' *Bruce Springsteen*

'Georgia on My Mind,' *Ray Charles*

'No Sleep till Brooklyn,' *Beastie Boys*

'Sweet Home Alabama,' *Lynyrd Skynyrd*

'Strange Fruit,' *Billie Holiday*

'Coal Miner's Daughter,' *Loretta Lynn*

Basie. Jazz singers Ella Fitzgerald and Billie Holiday combined jazz with its Southern sibling, the blues.

After WWII, bebop (aka bop) arose, reacting against the smooth melodies and confining rhythms of big-band swing. Charlie Parker, Dizzy Gillespie and Thelonious Monk led the way. In the 1950s and '60s, Miles Davis, John Coltrane and others deconstructed the sound and made up a new one that was cool, free and avant-garde. NYC, New Orleans and Chicago remain the core of the scene today.

Country

Early Scottish, Irish and English immigrants brought their own instruments and folk music to America, and what emerged over time in the secluded Appalachian Mountains was fiddle-and-banjo hillbilly, or 'country,' music. In the Southwest, steel guitars and larger bands distinguished 'western' music. In the 1920s, these styles merged into 'country and western' and Nashville became its center, especially once the Grand Ole Opry began its radio broadcasts in 1925. Classic country artists include Hank Williams, Johnny Cash, Willie Nelson, Patsy Cline, Loretta Lynn and Dolly Parton.

Something about the 'cry a tear in your beer' twanging clearly resonated with listeners, because country music is now big business. Singer-songwriters such as Blake Shelton, Tim McGraw and Eric Church have sold millions of albums. Subsequent riffs on the genre include bluegrass, rockabilly and alt-country. The South remains the genre's boot-wearin' stronghold.

Folk

The tradition of American folk music was crystallized in Woody Guthrie, who traveled the country during the Depression singing politically conscious songs. In the 1940s, New Yorker Pete Seeger emerged as a tireless preserver of America's folk heritage. Folk music experienced a revival during 1960s protest movements, but then-folkie Bob Dylan ended it almost single-handedly when he plugged in an electric guitar to shouts of 'Traitor!' at the Newport Folk Festival in 1965.

Folk has seen a resurgence in the last decade, alongside the rise of Americana. Iron & Wine's tunes channel mournful pop, blues and rock as only a Southerner can, while the Hoosier sister duo Lily and Madeleine sing ethereal, incredibly rich folk ballads.

Millennials and Gen Z are going gaga over so-called 'yacht rock,' the soft rock of the 1970s and '80s. Tribute bands such as Yacht Rock Revue play hits from Kenny Loggins, the Doobie Brothers and Christopher Cross to crowds too young to have heard them the first time around.

Rock

Most say rock and roll was born in 1954 the day Elvis Presley walked into Sam Phillips' Sun Studio in Memphis and recorded 'That's All Right.' Initially, radio stations weren't sure why a white country boy was singing 'black music,' or whether they should play him. It wasn't until 1956 that Presley scored his first big breakthrough with 'Heartbreak Hotel.'

Musically, rock was a hybrid of guitar-driven blues, black rhythm and blues (R&B), and white country-and-western music. R&B evolved in the 1940s out of swing and the blues, and was then known as 'race music.' With rock and roll, white musicians (and some African American musicians) transformed 'race music' into something that white youths could embrace freely – which they did.

Rock and roll instantly abetted a social revolution even more significant than its musical one: openly sexual as it celebrated youth and dancing freely across color lines, rock scared the nation. Authorities worked diligently to control 'juvenile delinquents' and to sanitize and suppress rock and roll, which might have withered if not for the early 1960s 'British invasion,' in which the Beatles and the Rolling Stones, emulating Chuck Berry, Little Richard and others, shocked rock and roll back to life.

The 1960s witnessed a full-blown youth rebellion, epitomized by the drug-inspired psychedelic sounds of the Grateful Dead and Jefferson Airplane, and the electric wails of Janis Joplin and Jimi Hendrix, all hailing from the West Coast. The sounds and sensibilities of the east were somewhat different to the flower children back west. Lou Reed's Velvet Underground was the most significant band to emerge from the Eastern USA in this decade.

Since then, rock has been about music and lifestyle, alternately torn between hedonism and seriousness, commercialism and authenticity. The Woodstock festival exemplified the scene in 1969, transforming a little patch of upstate New York into a legend.

Punk arrived in the late 1970s, led by the Ramones (the pride of Queens, NY), as did the working-class rock of Bruce Springsteen (the pride of New Jersey). As the counterculture became *the* culture in the 1980s, critics prematurely pronounced 'rock is dead.' Rock was saved (by Talking Heads, REM and Sonic Youth, among other Eastern US bands), as it always has been, by splintering and evolving, into the likes of new wave, heavy metal, grunge, indie rock, world beat, skate punk, hardcore, goth, emo and electronica.

Even though hip-hop has become today's outlaw sound, rock remains relevant, and it's not going anywhere. The Strokes and the Killers helped stoke a rock revival in the early 2000s. Alabama Shakes, Black Lips and Future Islands are among the bands that carry the torch currently.

Hip-Hop

From the ocean of sounds coming out of the early 1970s – funk, soul, Latin, reggae, and rock and roll – young DJs from the Bronx in NYC began to spin a groundbreaking mixture of records together in an effort to drive dance floors wild.

And so hip-hop was born. Groups such as Grandmaster Flash and the Furious Five were soon taking the party from the streets to the trendy clubs of Manhattan and mingling with punk and new wave bands including the Clash and Blondie. Break-out artists Futura 2000, Keith Haring and Jean-Michel Basquiat moved from the subways and the streets to the galleries, and soon to the worlds of fashion and advertising.

New York remained the hub into the mid-1980s. Groups such as Run-DMC, Public Enemy and the Beastie Boys sold millions. And then the sounds and styles of the growing hip-hop culture started to diversify. A rivalry developed between the East Coast groups and the West Coast 'gangsta' rappers coming out of LA. Groups such as Niggaz With Attitude (NWA) got both accolades and bad press for their daring sounds and social commentary – which critics called battle cries for violence – on racism, drugs, sex and urban poverty.

Come the turn of the millennium and what had started as kids playing their parents' funk records at illegal block parties had evolved into a multibillion-dollar business. Russell Simmons and P Diddy stood atop New York–based media empires, and stars Queen Latifah (from Jersey) and Will Smith (from Philly) were Hollywood royalty. A white rapper from Detroit, Eminem, sold millions of records.

Hip-hop is sometimes seen as a wasteland of commercial excess – glorifying consumerism, misogyny, homophobia, drug use and a host of other social ills. But just as the hedonistic days of arena rock and roll gave birth to the rebel child of punk, the evolving offspring of hip-hop and DJ culture are constantly breaking the rules to create something new and even more energizing. Today, hip-hop is the most popular music in the USA, and the genre that inspires the most creativity and innovation. Major players of the moment include Jay-Z, Drake, Nicki Minaj, Common, Kendrick Lamar and Cardi B.

Best Music Festivals

New Orleans Jazz Fest, LA; April

Movement Electronic Music Festival, Detroit, MI; May

Bonnaroo, Manchester, TN; June

Summerfest, Milwaukee, WI; June/July

Newport Folk Festival, Rhode Island; July

Lollapalooza, Chicago, IL; August

Landscapes & Wildlife

If you've come to glimpse the likes of alligators, whales, manatees or moose, the Eastern USA delivers. The region spoils for choice when it comes to wildlife spotting, whether in the lofty Appalachian Mountains or the maple forests of New England in the north, or tracing thousands of miles of estuaries and wild Atlantic coastline to the swamps and forested marshlands of the south. Scores of state and national parks, dedicated to the conservancy of the wilderness of the East, welcome you.

Landscapes

The Eastern USA is a land of temperate, deciduous forests, and contains the ancient Appalachian Mountains, a low range that parallels the Atlantic Ocean. Between the mountains and the coast lies the country's most populated, urbanized region, particularly in the corridor between Washington, DC, and Boston, MA.

To the north are the Great Lakes, which the USA shares with Canada. These five lakes, part of the Canadian Shield, are the greatest expanse of fresh water on the planet, constituting nearly 20% of the world's supply.

Going south along the East Coast, things get wetter and warmer until you reach the swamps of southern Florida and make the turn into the Gulf of Mexico, which provides the USA with a southern coastline.

West of the Appalachians are the vast interior plains, which lie flat all the way to the Rocky Mountains. The eastern plains are the nation's breadbasket, roughly divided into the northern 'corn belt' and the southern 'cotton belt.' The plains, an ancient sea bottom, are drained by the mighty Mississippi River, which together with the Missouri River forms the world's fourth-longest river system, surpassed only by the Nile, Amazon and Yangtze rivers. Beyond the East, the Rocky Mountains and Southwestern deserts eventually give way to the Pacific Ocean.

Winner of the 2015 Pulitzer Prize for nonfiction, *The Sixth Extinction* by Elizabeth Kolbert looks at why species are disappearing from the planet at an alarming rate. It examines everything from the collapse in the population of golden frogs in the Panamanian rainforest through to mass bat die-offs in Vermont, near the author's home.

Plants & Trees

Displays of spring wildflowers and colorful autumn foliage are a New England specialty. Great Smoky Mountains National Park contains all five eastern-forest types – spruce fir, hemlock, pine–oak, and northern and cove hardwood – which support more than 100 native species of trees.

In Florida, the Everglades is the last subtropical wilderness in the US. This vital, endangered habitat is a fresh- and saltwater world of marshes, sloughs and coastal prairies that supports mangroves, cypresses, sea grasses, tropical plants, pines and hardwoods.

Land Mammals

Moose

Moose nibble on shrubs throughout the northern part of the region, specifically Maine, New Hampshire, Vermont, upstate New York and the Michigan–Minnesota–Wisconsin north woods. Moose are part of the deer family but are far larger, with skinny, ballerina-like legs that support a hulking body. Males weigh up to 1200lb, all put on by a vegetarian diet of twigs and leaves. Despite their odd shape, moose can move it: they run up to 35mph, and in water they can swim as fast as two people paddling a canoe. Males grow a spectacular rack of antlers every summer, only to discard it in November.

You'll spot moose foraging near lakes and streams. They generally are not aggressive, and often will pose for photographs. They can be unpredictable, though, so don't startle them. During mating season (September) males can become belligerent, so keep your distance.

Moose have been dying at an alarming rate in many areas. Scientists think climate change may be partly to blame. In New Hampshire a longer fall with less snow has increased the number of winter ticks – parasites that prey on moose. In Minnesota it's the same story but with brain worms as the deadly parasite. In Maine, however, the population remains robust at around 70,000 moose.

Black Bears

Despite a decline in numbers, black bears prowl most parts of the region, especially in the Adirondacks, the Great Smoky Mountains and the Great Lakes' north woods. Males can stand 7ft tall and weigh 550lb – but that depends on when you encounter them. In autumn they weigh up to 30% more than when they emerge from hibernation in the spring. Although they enjoy an occasional meaty snack, black bears usually fill their bellies with berries and other vegetation. They're opportunistic, adaptable and

INFAMOUS NATURAL DISASTERS

Earthquakes, wildfires, tornadoes, hurricanes and blizzards – the Eastern USA certainly has its share of natural disasters. A few of the more infamous events that have shaped the national conscience:

Hurricane Katrina August 29, 2005, is not a day easily forgotten in New Orleans. A massive hurricane swept across the Gulf of Mexico and slammed into Louisiana. As levees failed, floods inundated more than 80% of the city. The death toll reached 1836, with more than $100 billion in estimated damages – making it America's costliest natural disaster. Heartbreaking images of the destroyed city and anger over the government's bungled response still linger.

Hurricane Irene On August 27 and 28, 2011, a mammoth storm blew over the eastern seaboard, battering 15 states from Florida through to New England and as far inland as Pennsylvania. New York City evacuated many residents and took the unprecedented step of shutting down all public transit. More than 7.4 million homes lost electrical power; rivers ran wild; and at least 45 people died. The damage has been estimated at $7 billion.

East Coast Earthquake On August 23, 2011, a rare earthquake rattled the Eastern USA. The 5.8-magnitude tremor had its epicenter in Mineral, VA, but was felt from Maine right through to South Carolina, and was the area's strongest quake since 1897. There was no serious damage, though it did crack the Washington Monument and knock three spires off the National Cathedral in Washington, DC.

Hurricane Sandy On October 29, 2012, the largest Atlantic hurricane ever recorded hit the East Coast, with storm winds spanning over 1000 miles. The Jersey Shore and low-lying areas of New York City (such as Staten Island) were hit particularly hard. More than 80 people died in the USA, and estimated damages amounted to more than $65 billion.

Louisiana Floods The worst natural disaster in the Eastern USA since Hurricane Sandy befell the state of Louisiana in August 2016, when 6 trillion, 900 billion gallons of rain fell in one week (31 inches in 15 hours in Livingstone Parish), displacing tens of thousands, causing damage in excess of $30 million and claiming 13 lives.

Hurricane Irma On September 10, 2017, Hurricane Irma made landfall in the Florida Keys. Over the next 24 hours, it swept over the state, leaving 7.7 million people without power and cutting off the Florida Keys from the mainland for days. The death toll is estimated at 84 people and the storm created more than $50 billion in damages, making it the costliest hurricane in Florida history.

EASTERN USA'S NATIONAL PARKS

PARK	STATE	FEATURES	ACTIVITIES	BEST TIME TO VISIT
Acadia National Park	ME	1530ft Cadillac Mountain, rocky coastline, islands	hiking, cycling	May-Oct
Biscayne National Park	FL	coral reefs, manatees, dolphins, sea turtles	kayaking, snorkeling, diving, glass-bottom-boat tours	mid-Dec–mid-Apr
Congaree National Park	SC	moss-draped cypresses, swamp, owls	fishing, canoeing	Apr-Jun & Sep-Nov
Cuyahoga Valley National Park	OH	rivers, waterfalls, canal tow path	hiking, cycling, scenic train ride	May-Oct
Dry Tortugas National Park	FL	remote islands, Civil War fort, 300 bird species, sea turtles	snorkeling, diving, bird-watching	Dec-Apr
Everglades National Park	FL	grasslands, swamp, alligators, panthers, manatees	cycling, canoeing, kayaking, hiking	Dec-Apr
Great Smoky Mountains National Park	NC, TN	mountains, woodlands, wildflowers, black bears, elk	hiking, horseback riding, fishing	mid-Apr–Oct
Hot Springs National Park	AK	thermal waters, historic buildings	spa soaking, hiking	Sep-Feb
Indiana Dunes National Park	IN	bogs, swamps, desert-like sand dunes	swimming, hiking, bird-watching, dune climbs	May-Oct
Isle Royale National Park	MI	huge isolated island, thick forest, lakes, moose	kayaking, hiking, backcountry camping	mid-May–Oct
Mammoth Cave National Park	KY	never-ending caves, underground rivers, bats	hiking, spelunking	year-round
Shenandoah National Park	VA	Blue Ridge Mountains, waterfalls, deer, bobcats	hiking, camping	Apr-Oct
Voyageurs National Park	MN	thick forest, islands, lakes, wolves, aurora borealis	boating, snowmobiling	May-late Sep

curious animals, and can survive on very small home ranges. As their forests diminish, they're occasionally seen traipsing through nearby populated areas.

Panthers

A remnant population of panthers licks its chops around Everglades National Park, FL. Before European contact, perhaps 1500 roamed the state. The first panther bounty ($5 a scalp) was passed in 1832, and over the next 130 years they were hunted relentlessly. Though hunting was stopped in 1958, it was too late for the panther population to rebound on its own. A captive breeding program, begun in 1991, kept the Florida panther from extinction, when an estimated 25 remained. Though they're still on the endangered species list, numbers are slowly rising: the Florida Fish & Wildlife Conservation Commission estimates there were 120 to 230 in the state as of 2017.

Wolves & Coyotes

Wolves are rare in the Eastern USA. Those that are here wander mostly in Michigan and northern Minnesota, particularly the Boundary Waters. The area's cold, boreal forest is prime territory, and is home to the International Wolf Center (www.wolf.org) in Ely, MN. The wolf can be every bit as fierce and cunning as is portrayed in fairy tales, although it rarely attacks humans. If you're out in the wilderness, you may hear them howling at the moon.

The coyote looks similar to the wolf but is about half the size, ranging from 15lb to 45lb. Coyotes are found all over the eastern region, even in cities – Chicago had one a few years ago that loped into a downtown sandwich shop during the lunchtime rush.

Deer

The white-tailed deer can be found everywhere in the region, from top to bottom. Endemic to the Florida Keys are Key deer, a 'Honey-I-Shrunk-the-Ungulate' subspecies – less than 3ft tall and lighter than a 10-year-old child, they live mostly on Big Pine Key.

Michigan's Isle Royale hosts the world's longest-running predator–prey study, of wolves and moose. While numbers have fluctuated since research began in 1958, by 2018 the wolf population had dwindled to two, while moose swelled to 1500. Disease, inbreeding and climate shifts are among the culprits. In 2018 the NPS began relocating wolves to the island; there are now about 14 wolves.

Reptiles

Alligators & Crocodiles

American alligators slither throughout the Southeast's wetlands, mostly in Florida and Louisiana. With snout, eyeballs and pebbled back so still they hardly ripple the water's surface, alligators have watched over the swamps for more than 200 million years.

Louisiana has close to two million gators, and Florida counts 1.25 million among the state's lakes, rivers and golf courses, mostly in the central and southern zones. The Everglades are perhaps the best place to catch them lurking. Alligators are alpha predators who keep the rest of the food chain in check, and their 'gator holes' become vital water cups in the dry season and during droughts, aiding the entire wetlands ecosystem. They live about 30 years, can grow up to 14ft long and weigh 1000lb. No longer officially endangered, alligators remain protected because they resemble the still-endangered American crocodile.

South Florida is home to the only North American population of American crocodiles, around 1500 of them. They prefer saltwater, and to distinguish them from gators, check their smile – a croc's snout is more tapered and its teeth stick out.

Sea Turtles

Florida is the hot spot for sea-turtle nesting in the continental US. Three main species create more than 80,000 nests annually, mostly on southern Atlantic Coast beaches, but extending to all Gulf Coast beaches, too. Loggerheads comprise the vast majority, followed by green and leatherback turtles and, historically, hawksbill and Kemp's ridley; all five species are endangered or threatened. The leatherback is the largest, bulking up to 10ft and 2000lb.

During the May–October nesting season, sea turtles deposit from 80 to 120 eggs in each nest. The eggs incubate for about two months, and then the hatchlings emerge all at once and make for the ocean. Contrary to myth, hatchlings don't need the moon to find their way.

Snakes

First, here's the bad news: there are four species of rattlesnake found east of the Mississippi – the diamondback, pygmy, canebrake and timber. At 7ft long, the diamondback is the biggest and the most aggressive. Copperheads, cottonmouths and coral snakes are other venomous types in the region. All of them slither primarily through the Mid-Atlantic and the South. Now the good news: coming across a venomous snake is uncommon. Need proof? Great Smoky Mountains National Park, with around 10 million visitors per year, has never recorded a snakebite fatality in its 80-plus-year history.

Marine Mammals & Fish

Whales & Dolphins

The Eastern USA's top spot to whale-watch is off Massachusetts' coast at Stellwagen Bank National Marine Sanctuary, a summer feeding ground for humpbacks. These awesome creatures average 49ft and 36 tons – serious heft to be launching up and out of the water for their playful breaching. They also come surprisingly close to boats, offering great photo ops. Many of the 400 remaining North Atlantic right whales, the world's most endangered leviathan, frequent the same waters. Cruises depart from Boston, Plymouth, Provincetown and Gloucester, MA.

The waters off the coast of Florida are home to several dolphin species. By far the most common species is the bottlenose dolphin, which is highly social and extremely intelligent, and frequently encountered around the entire peninsula.

In addition to its national parks, the Eastern USA holds eight national seashores (including Cape Cod, MA), three national lakeshores (including Sleeping Bear Dunes, MI) and a number of national rivers. The National Park Service (www.nps.gov) has the lowdown.

Manatees

Florida's coast is home to the unusual, gentle manatee, which moves between freshwater rivers and the ocean. Around 10ft long and weighing on average 1000lb, these agile, expressive creatures don't do much, spending most of each day resting and eating 10% of their body weight. In winter they seek out Florida's warm-water springs and power-plant discharge canals. In summer they migrate back to the ocean and can also be spotted in the coastal waters of Alabama, Georgia and South Carolina.

Manatees have been under some form of protection since 1893, and they were included in the first federal endangered species list in 1967. They were once hunted for their meat – finer than filet mignon, allegedly – but collisions with boats are now a leading cause of manatee deaths, accounting for more than 20% annually. According to the US Fish & Wildlife Service, Florida manatees number around 6300 today.

Tropical Fish

For stunning coral reefs and vibrant tropical fish, the Florida Keys is the place to go. North America's only living coral barrier reef – and the world's third-largest such reef (after the Great Barrier Reef in Australia and the Meso-American Reef in Belize) – runs for 221 miles from Key Biscayne off Miami down to Dry Tortugas National Park, 70 miles off Key West. Both the national park and John Pennekamp Coral Reef State Park (in Key Largo) are terrific places to behold the underwater world where sea fans wave and schools of blue tangs and trumpet fish dart. The reefs are home to more than 260 types of tropical fish.

Birds

The bald eagle, the USA's national symbol since 1782, is the only eagle unique to North America. Its wingspan can reach more than 6.5ft across. Good wintertime viewing sites are along the Mississippi River in Minnesota, Wisconsin and Illinois; in summer, eagles are common throughout Florida, wherever there's fish-rich water for chowing alongside tall trees for nesting. The eagle has come off the endangered species list, having made a remarkable comeback from a low of 487 breeding pairs in 1963 to almost 9800 pairs in 2006 (that's in the lower 48 states; another 30,000-plus live in Alaska). They were removed from the endangered species list in 2007.

White pelicans, which are among the region's largest birds, arrive in winter (October to April), while brown pelicans, the only kind to dive for their food, live here year-round. They're found around the Gulf Coast and throughout Florida.

Survival Guide

DIRECTORY A–Z.... 642
Accessible Travel 642
Customs Regulations ... 642
Discount Cards 643
Electricity 643
Embassies & Consulates 643
Food & Drink 643
Health 643
Insurance 644
Internet Access 644
Legal Matters 644
LGBTIQ+ Travelers 645
Money 645
Opening Hours 646
Post 646
Public Holidays 646
Responsible Travel 646
Smoking 646
Telephone 647
Time 647
Toilets 647
Tourist Information 647
Visas 648
Volunteering 648
Women Travelers 648
Work 648

TRANSPORTATION...649
GETTING THERE & AWAY 649
Entering the Country 649
Air 649
Land 650
Sea 651
GETTING AROUND 651
Air 651
Bicycle 652
Boat 652
Bus 652
Car & Motorcycle 653
Hitchhiking 655
Taxis & Ridesharing 655
Train 655

Directory A–Z

Accessible Travel

Travel in the region is relatively accommodating.

- Most public buildings are wheelchair-accessible and have appropriate restroom facilities.
- Telephone companies offer relay operators, available via teletypewriter (TTY) numbers, for the hearing impaired.
- All major airlines, Greyhound buses and Amtrak trains will assist travelers with disabilities; just describe your needs when making reservations at least 48 hours in advance.
- Some car-rental agencies, such as Budget and Hertz, offer hand-controlled vehicles and vans with wheelchair lifts at no extra charge, but you must reserve them well in advance.
- Most cities have taxi companies with at least one accessible van; you'll have to call ahead.
- Cities with underground transport have elevators for passengers needing assistance. Washington, DC, has the best network (every station has an elevator); NYC's elevators are few and far between.
- Many national and some state parks and recreation areas have wheelchair-accessible paved, graded dirt or boardwalk trails.

There are a number of organizations specializing in the needs of travelers with disabilities:

Flying Wheels Travel (www.flyingwheelstravel.com) A full-service travel agency, highly recommended for those with mobility issues or chronic illness.

Mobility International USA (www.miusa.org) Advises travelers with disabilities on mobility issues and runs educational exchange programs.

Wheelchair Getaways (www.wheelchairgetaways.com) Rents accessible vans throughout the USA.

For further information, download Lonely Planet's free Accessible Travel guides from https://shop.lonelyplanet.com/categories/accessible-travel.com

ETIQUETTE

Greetings Don't be overly physical when greeting someone. Some Americans will hug, urbanites may exchange cheek kisses, but most – especially men – shake hands.

Smoking Don't assume you can smoke – even if you're outside. Most Americans have little tolerance for smokers and have even banned smoking from many parks, boardwalks and beaches.

Punctuality Do be on time. Many folks in the US consider it rude to be kept waiting.

Politeness It's common practice to greet the staff when entering and leaving a shop ('Hello' and 'Have a nice day' will do). Americans smile a lot (often a symbol of politeness, nothing more).

Customs Regulations

For a complete list of US customs regulations, visit the official website for US Customs and Border Protection (www.cbp.gov).

Duty-free allowance per person is as follows:

- 1L of liquor (provided you are at least 21 years old)
- 100 cigars and 200 cigarettes (if you are at least 18)
- $200 worth of gifts and purchases ($800 if a returning US citizen)

If you arrive with $10,000 or more in US or foreign currency, it must be declared.

There are heavy penalties for attempting to import illegal drugs. Forbidden items include drug paraphernalia, items with fake brand names, and most goods made in Cuba, Iran, Myanmar (Burma) and Sudan. Fruit, vegetables and other food must be declared (whereby you'll undergo a time-consuming search) or left in the bins in the arrival area.

Discount Cards

The following cards can net savings (usually about 10%) on museums, accommodations and some transport (including Amtrak):

American Association of Retired Persons (www.aarp.org) For US travelers aged 50 and older.

American Automobile Association (www.aaa.com) For members of AAA or reciprocal clubs in Europe and Australia.

International Student Identity Card (www.isic.org) For students of any age and non-students under 26.

Student Advantage Card (www.studentadvantage.com) For US and foreign students 16 years and older.

Electricity

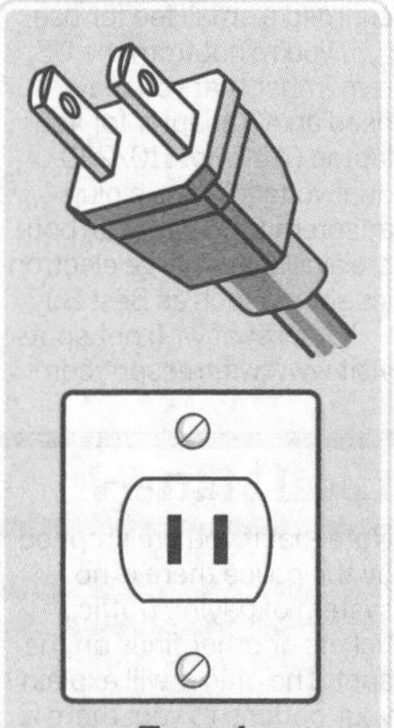

Type A
120V/60Hz

Type B
120V/60Hz

Embassies & Consulates

In addition to the embassies in Washington, DC (see www.embassy.org for a complete list), most countries have an embassy for the UN in New York City. Many countries have consulates in other large cities, such as Atlanta, Chicago, Miami and New Orleans.

Australian Embassy (☎202-797-3000; www.usa.embassy.gov.au; 1601 Massachusetts Ave NW; ⏰8:30am-5pm Mon-Fri; Ⓜ Red Line to Farragut North)

Canadian Embassy (☎202-682-1740; www.can-am.gc.ca; 501 Pennsylvania Ave NW, Penn Quarter; ⏰9am-noon Mon-Fri; Ⓜ Green, Yellow Line to Archives)

Dutch Embassy (☎202-244-5300; www.netherlandsworldwide.nl/countries/united-states; 4200 Linnean Ave NW, Forest Hills; ⏰8:30am-4:30pm Mon-Fri; Ⓜ Red Line to Van Ness-UDC)

French Embassy (☎202-944-6000; www.franceintheus.org; 4101 Reservoir Rd NW; ⏰8:45am-12:30pm & 2:30-3:30pm Mon-Fri; Ⓜ Red Line to Dupont Circle, then bus D6)

German Embassy (☎202-298-4000; www.germany.info; 4645 Reservoir Rd NW; ⏰8-11:45am & 1-2:30pm Mon-Thu, 8am-noon Fri; 🚌D6)

Irish Embassy (☎202-462-3939; www.embassyofireland.org; 2234 Massachusetts Ave NW; ⏰9am-1pm & 2-4pm Mon-Fri; Ⓜ Red Line to Dupont Circle)

Mexican Embassy (☎202-728-1600; https://embamex.sre.gob.mx/eua; 1911 Pennsylvania Ave NW; ⏰9am-6pm Mon-Fri; Ⓜ Orange, Silver, Blue Lines to Farragut West)

New Zealand Embassy (☎202-328-4800; www.mfat.govt.nz/usa; 37 Observatory Circle NW, Embassy Row; ⏰9am-4pm Mon-Fri; Ⓜ Red Line to Dupont Circle, then bus N2 or N4)

UK Embassy (☎202-588-6500; www.gov.uk/government/world/usa; 3100 Massachusetts Ave NW, Embassy Row; ⏰9am-4pm Mon-Fri; Ⓜ Red Line to Dupont Circle, then bus N2 or N4)

Food & Drink

See Eat & Drink Like a Local (p50) for everything you need to know about eating and drinking in the region.

Health

Before You Go

The eastern region, like the rest of the USA, has a high level of hygiene and tap water is safe to drink.

Bring any medications you may need in their original containers, clearly labeled. Having a signed, dated letter from your physician that describes all of your medical conditions and medications (including generic names) is also a good idea.

COVID-19

Non-US citizens are required to show proof of full vaccination from COVID-19 before entering the US. As of early 2022, all air passengers aged two or older, regardless of citizenship or vaccination status, must show a negative result of a COVID-19 viral test or documentation of recovery from COVID-19 before boarding a flight to the US.

For the most up-to-date information, see the Centers for Disease Control website (www.cdc.gov).

HEALTH INSURANCE

The US offers possibly the finest health care in the world – the problem is that it can be prohibitively expensive. It's essential to purchase travel health insurance if your home policy doesn't cover you for medical expenses abroad.

Find out in advance if your insurance plan will make payments directly to providers or reimburse you later for overseas health expenditures.

VACCINATIONS

At the time of writing, there was only one vaccination of importance concerning travel to the US: getting the double-dose and booster of the COVID-19 vaccine. It's also a good idea to get standard tetanus and polio vaccinations.

In Eastern USA

AVAILABILITY & COST OF HEALTH CARE

If you have a medical emergency, go to the emergency room of the nearest hospital.

If the problem isn't urgent, call a nearby hospital and ask for a referral to a local physician; this is usually cheaper than a trip to the emergency room.

Standalone, for-profit, urgent-care centers provide good service, but can be the most expensive option.

Pharmacies are abundantly supplied. However, some medications that are available over the counter in other countries require a prescription in the US.

If you don't have insurance to cover the cost of prescriptions, they can be shockingly expensive.

ENVIRONMENTAL HAZARDS

Cold exposure This can be a problem, especially in the northern regions. Keep all body surfaces covered, including the head and neck. Watch out for the 'Umbles' – stumbles, mumbles, fumbles and grumbles – which are signs of impending hypothermia.

Heat exhaustion Dehydration is the main contributor. Symptoms include feeling weak, headache, nausea and sweaty skin. Lay the victim flat with their legs raised; apply cool, wet cloths to the skin; and rehydrate.

INFECTIOUS DISEASES

COVID-19 aside, most infectious diseases are acquired by mosquito or tick bites or through environmental exposure.

The Centers for Disease Control and Prevention (www.cdc.gov) has further details.

Giardiasis Intestinal infection. Avoid drinking directly from lakes, ponds, streams and rivers.

Lyme Disease Occurs mostly in the Northeast. Transmitted by deer ticks in late spring and summer. Perform a tick check after you've been outdoors.

West Nile Virus Mosquito-transmitted in late summer and early fall. Prevent by keeping covered (wear long sleeves, long pants, hats and shoes rather than sandals) and apply a good insect repellent, preferably one containing DEET, to exposed skin and clothing.

Zika Of gravest concern to pregnant women, this mosquito-borne virus can cause microcephaly (when the brain does not develop fully) in utero. More than 250 locally acquired cases were reported in southern Florida in 2016–17, but as of this writing there have been no further zika outbreaks in the Eastern USA.

TAP WATER

Tap water is safe to drink everywhere in the Eastern USA, except in some state or national parks where it is expressly indicated that tap water is not 'potable' or safe to drink.

Insurance

It's expensive to get sick, crash a car or have things stolen from you in the US. Make sure you have adequate coverage before arriving. To insure yourself for items that may be stolen from your car, consult your homeowner's (or renter's) insurance policy or consider investing in travel insurance.

Internet Access

Travelers will have few problems staying connected in the tech-savvy USA.

Wi-fi (in-room, with decent speed) is common in lodgings across the price spectrum. Many properties also have an internet-connected computer for public use.

Many restaurants, bars and cafes (such as Starbucks) offer free wi-fi. Some cities have wi-fi connected parks and plazas.

If you're not traveling with a laptop or other web-accessible device, try the public library. Most have public terminals (time limits apply) and wi-fi. Occasionally out-of-state residents are charged a small fee for use.

If you're not from the US, remember that you may need an AC adapter for your laptop (if it's not 110/220 dual-voltage), plus a plug adapter for US sockets; both are available at large electronics shops, such as Best Buy.

For a list of wi-fi hot spots, visit www.wififreespot.com.

Legal Matters

Note that if you are stopped by the police there is no system of paying traffic tickets or other fines on the spot. The officer will explain your options to you; there is usually a 30-day period to pay fines by mail.

If you are arrested, never walk away from an officer. You are allowed to remain silent, and you are entitled to have access to an attorney. The legal system presumes you're innocent until proven guilty. All persons who are arrested have the right to make one phone call. If you don't have a lawyer or family member to help you, call your embassy or consulate. The police will give you the number on request.

Drugs & Alcohol

In most places it's illegal to walk with an open alcoholic drink on the street. New Orleans and Memphis' Beale St are notable exceptions.

Being 'carded' (ie asked to show photo ID to prove you're of legal drinking age, which is 21 years old) is standard practice everywhere.

Some states, especially in the South, have 'dry' counties where alcohol sales are banned altogether.

In all states, the blood alcohol limit is 0.08%. Driving under the influence of alcohol or drugs is a serious offense, subject to stiff fines and even imprisonment.

Recreational marijuana is now legal in 18 states across the US, plus Washington, DC. However, possession is still a felony in some states, so it's prudent to know the local laws.

Aside from marijuana, recreational drugs are prohibited by law. Possession of any illicit drug, including cocaine, ecstasy, LSD, heroin or hashish, is a felony potentially punishable by lengthy jail sentences. For foreigners, conviction of any drug offense is grounds for deportation.

LGBTIQ+ Travelers

In general, the Northeast is the most tolerant region in the Eastern USA, and the South the least so, though major cities in all the regions have long-standing gay communities.

Most major US cities have a visible and open LGBTIQ+ community that is easy to connect with.

However, note that the level of public acceptance varies nationwide. In some places, there is absolutely no tolerance whatsoever, and in others acceptance is predicated on LGBTIQ+ people not 'flaunting' their sexual orientation or identity. Be aware that bigotry still exists here. In rural areas and conservative enclaves, it's unwise to be openly out, as verbal abuse and even violence can sometimes occur. When in doubt, assume that locals follow a 'don't ask, don't tell' policy.

Prior to 2015, 37 states (and DC) allowed gay marriage. In 2015 the US Supreme Court declared same-sex marriage legal in all 50 states. This means that no state can ban same-sex couples from getting married.

Resources

The Queerest Places: A Guide to Gay and Lesbian Historic Sites, by Paula Martinac, is full of juicy details and history, and covers the country. Visit her blog at www.queerestplaces.com.

Further resources:

Advocate (www.advocate.com) Gay-oriented news website reports on business, politics, arts, entertainment and travel.

Gay Travel (www.gaytravel.com) Online guides to dozens of US destinations.

Gaycation (www.vice.com/en_us/topic/gaycation) VICE TV's excellent documentary series on same-sex issues in the US and beyond.

National LGBTQ Task Force (www.thetaskforce.org) National activist group's website covers news, politics and current issues.

Out Traveler (www.outtraveler.com) Gay-oriented travel articles.

Purple Roofs (www.purpleroofs.com) Lists gay-owned and gay-friendly B&Bs and hotels.

Money

ATMs & Eftpos

Most locals do not carry large amounts of cash for everyday use, relying instead on credit cards, debit cards and ATMs. Visa, MasterCard and American Express are accepted at most locations. Smaller businesses may refuse to accept bills over $20.

ATMs are available 24/7 at most banks and in shopping centers, airports, grocery stores and convenience shops. Most ATMs charge a service fee of $3 or more per transaction and your home bank may impose additional charges.

Foreign visitors should check with their bank for exact information about using its cards in stateside ATMs. The exchange rate is usually as good as you'll get anywhere.

EFTPOS is becoming more widely used but is still not common in the Eastern USA.

Credit & Debit Cards

Major credit cards are almost universally accepted. In fact, it's next to impossible to rent a car or make hotel reservations without one. Visa and MasterCard are the most widely accepted.

Foreign visitors may have to go inside to pre-pay at gas stations, since most pay-at-the-pump options require a card with a US zip code.

Note, too, that you may be asked to 'sign' for credit card purchases, or face a confused clerk or waiter when your card does not require a signature, as US credit card companies have yet to embrace the chip + PIN method available elsewhere in the world.

It's normal for restaurant servers to take your card to a pay station to process instead of allowing you to pay at the table.

Mobile pay options (Apple Pay, Google Pay) are becoming increasingly common and are a good way to bridge the technology gap.

Currency Exchange

Banks are usually the best places to exchange foreign currencies. Most large city banks offer the service, but banks in rural areas may not.

Currency-exchange counters at the airport and in tourist centers typically have the worst rates; ask about fees and surcharges first.

Travelex (www.travelex.com) is a major currency-exchange company, but American Express (www.americanexpress.com) travel offices may offer better rates.

Taxes & Refunds

Sales tax varies by state and county, and ranges from 5% to 10%. Most prices you see advertised will exclude tax, which is calculated upon purchase.

Hotel taxes vary by city and state from around 10% to 18.75%.

Tipping

Tipping is *not* optional; only withhold tips in cases of outrageously bad service.

Airport and hotel porters $2 per bag, minimum $5 per cart

Bartenders 15% to 20% per round, minimum $1 per drink

Hotel housekeepers $2 to $5 daily, left under the card provided

Restaurant servers 15% to 20%, unless a gratuity is already charged on the bill

Taxi drivers 10% to 15%, rounded up to the next dollar

Valet parking attendants At least $2 on return of keys

Opening Hours

Typical opening hours are as follows:

Banks 8:30am to 4:30pm Monday to Friday (and possibly 9am to noon Saturday)

Bars 5pm to midnight Sunday to Thursday, to 2am Friday and Saturday

Nightclubs 10pm to 3am Thursday to Saturday

Post offices 9am to 5pm Monday to Friday

Shopping malls 9am to 9pm

Stores 9am to 6pm Monday to Saturday, noon to 5pm Sunday

Supermarkets 8am to 8pm (some open 24 hours)

Post

The US Postal Service (www.usps.com) is reliable and inexpensive. The postal rates for first-class mail within the USA are 55¢ for letters weighing up to 1oz (15¢ for each additional ounce) and 35¢ for postcards.

International airmail rates are $1.15 for a 1oz letter or postcard.

For sending urgent or important letters and packages either domestically or internationally, FedEx (www.fedex.com) and UPS (www.ups.com) offer more expensive door-to-door delivery services.

Public Holidays

On the following national public holidays, banks, schools and government offices (including post offices) are closed, and transportation, museums and other services operate on a Sunday schedule. Holidays falling on a weekend are usually observed the following Monday.

New Year's Day January 1

Martin Luther King Jr Day Third Monday in January

Presidents' Day Third Monday in February

Memorial Day Last Monday in May

Independence Day July 4

Labor Day First Monday in September

Columbus Day Second Monday in October

Veterans' Day November 11

Thanksgiving Fourth Thursday in November

Christmas Day December 25

Responsible Travel

Lower your carbon footprint Opt for trains and buses rather than planes if practical. Where possible, take public transportation and explore on foot or bike rather than car.

Reduce waste Use a refillable water bottle rather than buying single-use plastic. Carry and use your own bag when making purchases.

Buy local Shop at farmers markets, seek out locally owned restaurants and buy crafts straight from the source.

Avoid overtourism Try to travel outside of peak season (generally June to August); visit major sights on weekdays rather than weekends. In state and national parks, skip the popular trails and look for quieter, less visited corners of the park.

Be kind Be sure you give greetings when entering or leaving a business. In the south, you'll be killed with kindness. Feel free to follow suit and sprinkle your speech with 'ma'am' and 'sir' when talking with others.

Smoking

➡ A little more than half the eastern states, plus Washington, DC, have enforced statewide bans on smoking in restaurants, bars and workplaces, with many municipalities enforcing controls in other states and/or in more specific ways (public areas, schools, etc).

➡ Smoking is allowed in restaurants and bars in Virginia if the smoking area is structurally separated, with a separate ventilation system, from the nonsmoking area of the restaurant. These are not commonly seen.

➡ Some southern states still have liberal attitudes towards smoking: cigarettes are inexpensive and smoking in bars and restaurants is still permitted, although sometimes smoking areas are separated.

➡ For the full list of exactly where smoking in public places is permitted, refer to the Americans for Non-smoker's Rights (ANR) website (www.no-smoke.org).

Telephone

The US phone system mixes regional service providers, competing long-distance carriers and several cell-phone companies. Overall, the system is efficient. Calls from a regular landline or cell phone are usually cheaper than a hotel phone or pay phone. Services such as Skype (www.skype.com) and Google Voice (www.google.com/hangout) can make calling quite cheap. Check the websites for details.

Cell Phones

Foreign phones operating on tri- or quad-band frequencies will work in the USA. Or purchase inexpensive cell (mobile) phones with a pay-as-you-go plan when here.

Most of the USA's cell-phone systems are incompatible with the GSM 900/1800 standard used throughout Europe and Asia (though some convertible phones will work). iPhones do work – but beware of roaming costs, especially for data. Check with your service provider about using your phone here.

It might be cheaper to buy a prepaid SIM card for the USA, such as those sold by AT&T or T-Mobile, which you can insert into your international cell phone to get a local phone number and voicemail. You can also buy inexpensive, no-contract (prepaid) phones with a local number and a set number of minutes, which can be topped up at will. Virgin Mobile, T-Mobile, AT&T and other providers offer phones starting at $30, with a package of minutes starting at around $40 for 400 minutes.

Electronics chain store Best Buy (www.bestbuy.com) sells prepaid phones, as well as international SIM cards. Online retailer Telestial (www.telestial.com) also sells SIM cards.

Rural swaths of the Eastern USA, especially in the mountains and various national parklands, don't pick up a signal. Check your provider's coverage map if you're planning to spend time outside of cities.

Long-Distance Calls & Area Codes

All phone numbers within the USA consist of a three-digit area code followed by a seven-digit local number. Typically, if you are calling a number within the same area code, you only have to dial the seven-digit number (though if it doesn't work, try adding 1 + the area code at the beginning). More information on dialing:

US country code ☎ 1

Making international calls Dial ☎ 011 + country code + area code + local number

Calling other US area codes or Canada Dial ☎ 1 + area code + seven-digit local number

Directory assistance nationwide ☎ 411

Toll-free numbers ☎ 1 + 800 (or 888, 877, 866) + seven-digit number; some toll-free numbers only work within the US

Phonecards

Prepaid phonecards are a good solution for travelers on a budget. They are available from convenience stores, supermarkets and pharmacy chains. AT&T sells a reliable phonecard that is widely available. Be sure to read the fine print, as many cards contain hidden charges such as 'activation fees' or per-call 'connection fees' in addition to the per-minute rates.

Time

The eastern region is split between Eastern and Central time zones, which are an hour apart. The demarcation line slices through Indiana, Kentucky, Tennessee and Florida. When it's noon Eastern time, it is 11am Central time (and 5pm Greenwich Mean Time).

The region, as well as most of the country, observes Daylight Saving Time (DST). On the second Sunday in March, clocks are set one hour ahead ('spring ahead'). Then, on the first Sunday of November, clocks are turned back one hour ('fall back').

The US date system is written as month/day/year. Thus, the 8th of June, 2024, becomes 6/8/24.

Toilets

Toilets are of the standard Western sit-down variety, with urinals for men common in public places. That said, public toilets aren't the most squeaky-clean of places, and toilets in national and state parks are commonly of the pit variety: take some backup toilet paper, just in case.

Tourist Information

The official tourism website of the USA (www.visittheusa.com) has links to every US state tourism office and website, plus loads of ideas for itinerary planning.

Most cities and towns have some sort of tourist center that provides local information. Typically operated by the convention and visitor bureau (CVB) or chamber of commerce, these entities tend to list only the businesses that are bureau/chamber members, so not all of the town's hotels and restaurants receive coverage – keep in mind that good, independent options may be missing.

State-run 'welcome centers,' usually placed along interstate highways, tend to have free state road maps, brochures and other travel planning materials. These offices are usually open longer hours, including weekends and holidays.

Visas

Visitors from the UK, Australia, New Zealand, Japan and many EU countries do not need visas for stays of fewer than 90 days, with ESTA approval. For other nations, see http://travel.state.gov or www.usa.gov/visas-and-visitors.

Canadians need neither a visa nor ESTA approval for stays shorter than 90 days, though they do need a passport or document approved by the Western Hemisphere Travel Initiative (www.getyouhome.gov).

Visa Waiver Program & ESTA

Admission requirements are subject to rapid change. The US State Department (www.travel.state.gov) has the latest information, or check with a US consulate in your home country.

The Visa Waiver Program (VWP) allows nationals from 40 countries and territories (including the UK, most EU countries, Japan, Australia and New Zealand) to enter the US without a visa for up to 90 days.

VWP visitors require a machine-readable passport and approval under the ESTA, the Electronic System for Travel Authorization (www.cbp.gov/esta) at least three days before arrival. There is a $14 fee for processing and authorization (payable online). Once approved, the registration is valid for two years.

In essence, ESTA requires that you register specific information online (name, address, passport info etc). You will receive one of three responses: 'Authorization Approved' (this usually comes within minutes; most applicants can expect to receive this response); 'Authorization Pending' (you'll need to check the status within the next 72 hours); or 'Travel not Authorized.' The latter means you will need to apply for a visa.

Those who need a visa (ie anyone staying longer than 90 days, or from a non-VWP country) should apply at the US consulate in their home country.

Volunteering

Volunteering opportunities abound in the Eastern USA, providing a memorable chance to interact with locals and the land.

Casual, drop-in volunteer work is plentiful in the big cities. Check weekly alternative newspapers for calendar listings or browse the free classified ads at www.craigslist.org. The public website United We Serve (www.serve.gov) and private websites Idealist (www.idealist.org) and VolunteerMatch (www.volunteermatch.org) offer free searchable databases of short- and long-term volunteer opportunities.

More formal volunteer programs typically charge a fee of $250 to $1000, depending on the length of the program and what amenities are included (eg housing, meals). None covers travel expenses.

Women Travelers

Women traveling by themselves or in a group should encounter no particular problems unique to the Eastern USA.

In bars and nightclubs solo women can attract attention, but if you don't want company, most men will respect a firm 'No, thank you.'

In the event you are assaulted, consider calling a rape-crisis hotline before calling the police, unless you are in immediate danger, in which case you should call 911. The 24-hour National Sexual Assault Hotline (800-656-4673) can help.

Community website www.journeywoman.com facilitates women exchanging travel tips, with links to resources. The Canadian government also publishes the booklet *Her Own Way*, filled with useful advice; head to www.travel.gc.ca/travelling/publications to access it.

Work

Seasonal service jobs in tourist beach towns, theme parks and ski areas are common and often easy to get, if low-paying. If you are a foreigner in the USA with a standard non-immigrant visitors visa, you are expressly forbidden to take paid work in the USA and will be deported if you're caught working illegally. In addition, employers are required to establish the bona fides of their employees or face fines. In particular, South Florida is notorious for large numbers of foreigners working illegally, and immigration officers are vigilant.

To work legally, foreigners need to apply for a work visa before leaving home. Student exchange visitors need a J1 visa, which exchange organizations will help arrange.

For nonstudent jobs, temporary or permanent, you need to be sponsored by a US employer (who will arrange an H-category visa). These are not easy to obtain.

Lonely Planet's *The Big Trip: Your Ultimate Guide to Gap Years and Overseas Adventures* has more ideas on how best to combine work and travel.

Transportation

GETTING THERE & AWAY

Entering the Country

Entering the USA is pretty straightforward, If you are flying, the first US airport that you land in is where you must go through immigration and customs, even if you are continuing on a flight to another destination.

You'll be asked to fill out the US customs declaration form, which is usually handed out on the plane. Have it completed before you approach the immigration desk. For the question 'US Street Address,' give the address where you will spend the first night (a hotel address is fine).

The immigration officer will look at your customs form and passport, and have you register with the Department of Homeland Security's Office of Biometric Identity Management. This entails having your fingerprints scanned and a digital photo taken.

The immigration officer may ask about your plans and whether you have sufficient funds. It's a good idea to list an itinerary, produce an onward or round-trip ticket and have at least one major credit card.

Travelers from some countries, ie Canada and Visa Waiver Program nations, can bypass the immigration desks and use self-service kiosks for automated passport control. Not all airports have this technology. See www.cbp.gov/travel for details on participating locations and for further eligibility requirements.

Once you go through immigration, you collect your baggage and pass through customs. If you have nothing to declare, you'll probably clear customs without a baggage search, but don't assume this. If you are continuing to another destination, you must recheck any checked bags, and you may have to go through security again – book ample time for your connection.

The Electronic System for Travel Authorization (ESTA) is now required before arrival for citizens of Visa Waiver Program countries.

Remember: your passport should be valid for at least six months longer than your intended stay in the US.

Air

➡ The Eastern USA's busiest international gateways are New York; Washington, DC; Boston; Charlotte; Atlanta and Miami. However, many other cities have direct international flights.

➡ Transportation Security Administration (TSA) and US Customs and Border Protection (CBP) checks in the USA can mean lengthy delays at airports; you may still have an hour or two to go

CLIMATE CHANGE & TRAVEL

Every form of transport that relies on carbon-based fuel generates CO_2, the main cause of human-induced climate change. Modern travel is dependent on airplanes, which might use less fuel per mile per person than most cars but travel much greater distances. The altitude at which aircraft emit gases (including CO_2) and particles also contributes to their climate change impact. Many websites offer 'carbon calculators' that allow people to estimate the carbon emissions generated by their journey and, for those who wish to do so, to offset the impact of the greenhouse gases emitted with contributions to portfolios of climate-friendly initiatives throughout the world. Lonely Planet offsets the carbon footprint of all staff and author travel.

TRAVELING TO CANADA

It's traditionally been easy to journey across the border to Canada from the Eastern USA and quite common to do so, especially at Niagara Falls. COVID-19, however, has added restrictions. See travel.gc.ca for the latest information. A few other things to keep in mind:

➡ You will have to show your passport. The exception is US citizens at land and sea borders, who have other options besides using a passport, such as an enhanced driver's license or passport card. See the Western Hemisphere Travel Initiative (www.dhs.gov/western-hemisphere-travel-initiative) for approved identification documents.

➡ Citizens of the USA, most Western European nations, Australia, New Zealand and Japan do not need a visa to enter Canada for stays of up to 180 days, but some other nationalities do. Citizenship and Immigration Canada (www.cic.gc.ca) has the details.

➡ Upon return to the USA, non-Americans will be subject to the full immigration procedure.

➡ For the lowdown on where to go, what to do and all things north of the border, check out Lonely Planet's *Canada* or *Best of Canada* guides.

before you have bags in hand and are on your way.

➡ Allow at least three hours to check in for departing international flights.

Departure Tax

Departure tax is included in the price of a ticket.

International Airports

Chicago and Atlanta trade off as the busiest airport in the region. The main international gateways in the Eastern USA:

Charlotte Douglas International (CLT; ☎704-359-4013; www.cltairport.com; 5501 Josh Birmingham Pkwy) Charlotte.

Dulles International (IAD; ☎703-572-2700, 703-572-8296; www.flydulles.com) Washington, DC.

Hartsfield-Jackson International (ATL, Atlanta; ☎800-897-1910; www.atl.com) Atlanta.

JFK International (JFK; ☎718-244-4444; www.jfkairport.com; Ⓢ A to Howard Beach, E, J/Z to Sutphin Boulevard-Archer Ave then AirTrain) New York.

Logan International (BOS; ☎800-235-6426; www.massport.com/logan-airport) Boston.

Miami International (MIA; ☎305-876-7000; www.miami-airport.com; 2100 NW 42nd Ave) Miami.

Minneapolis–St Paul International (MSP; ☎612-726-5555; www.mspairport.com; 4300 Glumack Dr, St Paul; 📶; Ⓡ blue) Minneapolis–St Paul.

O'Hare International (ORD; ☎800-832-6352; www.flychicago.com/ohare; 10000 W O'Hare Ave) Chicago.

Orlando International (MCO; ☎407-825-8463; www.orlandoairports.net; 1 Jeff Fuqua Blvd) Orlando.

Land

➡ You can enter the Eastern USA from a number of points at the US–Canada border to the north.

➡ Unless you're a permanent resident of Canada and have subscribed to the NEXUS program (www.cbsa-asfc.gc.ca), you'll need to answer a number of questions about the duration and nature of your journey when crossing the border, and Customs and Border Protection officers may search your vehicle.

➡ When entering the US by land (especially with a loaded vehicle) be sure to have conclusive proof that your intention is to leave the US within 90 days (or the terms of your visa) or you may be denied entry.

Border Crossings

The Eastern USA has more than 20 official border crossings with Canada, accessed via Maine, New Hampshire, Vermont, New York, Michigan and Minnesota. See travel.gc.ca for the latest info on COVID-19 restrictions. Crossing *back to the US* can also pose problems if you haven't brought all your documents. US Customs and Border Protection (https://bwt.cbp.gov) tracks current wait times at the main border crossings. Some borders are open 24 hours, but most are not.

In general, waits rarely exceed 30 minutes, except during peak times (ie weekends and holidays, more so in summer). Some entry points are especially busy:

➡ Detroit, MI, to Windsor, Ontario

➡ Buffalo, NY, to Niagara Falls, Ontario

➡ Calais, ME, to St Stephen, New Brunswick

As always, have your papers in order, be polite and don't make jokes or casual conversation with US border officials.

Bus

Greyhound (www.greyhound.com) operates the largest bus network in North America. There are direct connections between main cities in the USA and Canada, but you usually have to transfer to a different bus at the border (where it takes a good hour for all passengers to clear customs and immigration). Most international buses have free wi-fi on board.

Megabus (www.megabus.com) also has international routes between Toronto and eastern cities, including New York City, Philadelphia and Washington, DC.

They are often cheaper than Greyhound. Tickets are able to be purchased online only.

Car & Motorcycle

To drive across the US–Canada border, you'll need the vehicle's registration papers, proof of liability insurance and your home driver's license.

Rental cars can usually be driven across the border either way, but make sure your rental agreement says so in case you are questioned by border officials.

If your papers are in order, border crossing has traditionally been fast and easy, but occasionally the authorities of either country decided to search a car thoroughly. COVID-19 has added restrictions: see travel.gc.ca for the latest requirements for travelers.

Train

Amtrak (www.amtrak.com) and VIA Rail Canada (www.viarail.ca) run daily services between Montréal and New York (11 hours), and Toronto and New York via Niagara Falls (13 hours total). Customs inspections happen at the border, not upon boarding.

Sea

Several cities on the East Coast are cruise-ship hubs, including New York City, Boston, New Orleans and Charleston, SC. Florida's ports harbor the most ships of all, particularly Miami, followed by Port Canaveral and Port Everglades (Fort Lauderdale).

You can also travel to and from the Eastern USA on a freighter. These vessels usually carry between three and 12 passengers and, though considerably less luxurious than cruise ships, give a salty taste of life at sea.

For more information on the ever-changing routes:

Travel of America (www.travltips.com)

Maris (www.freightercruises.com)

GETTING AROUND

Air

Flying is usually more expensive than traveling by bus, train or car, but it's the way to go when you're in a hurry.

Airlines in Eastern USA

Overall, air travel in the USA is very safe (much safer than driving out on the nation's highways). For comprehensive details by carrier, check out www.airsafe.com.

The main domestic carriers:

American Airlines (www.aa.com) Nationwide service.

Delta Air Lines (www.delta.com) Nationwide service.

Frontier Airlines (www.flyfrontier.com) Denver-based airline with nationwide service.

JetBlue Airways (www.jetblue.com) Nonstop connections between eastern and western US cities, plus Florida and New Orleans.

Southwest Airlines (www.southwest.com) Service across the continental USA and to Hawaii.

Spirit Airlines (www.spiritair.com) Florida-based airline; serves many US gateway cities.

United Airlines (www.united.com) Nationwide service.

Virgin America (www.virginamerica.com) Flights between East and West Coast cities and Las Vegas.

There are also smaller regional services:

Cape Air (www.flycapeair.com) Flights to several New England destinations, including Martha's Vineyard and Nantucket.

Isle Royale Seaplanes (www.isleroyaleseaplanes.com) Flights to Rock Harbor in Isle Royale National Park from Houghton County Airport in Michigan's Upper Peninsula.

Air Passes

International travelers who plan on doing a lot of flying can consider buying a North American air pass. Passes are normally available only to non–North American citizens, and they must be purchased in conjunction with an international ticket. Conditions and cost structures can be complicated, but all passes include a certain number of domestic flights (from two to 10) that typically must be used within a 60-day period. Two of the

GREYHOUND INTERNATIONAL BUS ROUTES & FARES

Some one-way adult fares and trip times:

ROUTE	FARE ($)	TIME (HR)	FREQUENCY (PER DAY)
Boston–Montréal	75	7-10	6
Detroit–Toronto	60	5½-7½	5
New York–Montréal	75	7½-9	10

biggest airline networks offering air passes are Star Alliance (www.staralliance.com) and One World (www.oneworld.com).

Bicycle

Regional bicycle touring is popular: winding back roads and scenic coastlines make for great itineraries. Many cities (including New York City, Chicago, Minneapolis and Boston) also have designated bike routes.

Renting a bicycle is easy throughout the Eastern USA. Some things to keep in mind:

- Cyclists must follow the same rules of the road as vehicles, but don't expect drivers to always respect your right of way.
- Helmets are mandatory for cyclists in some states and towns (though there is no federal law that requires it). It usually applies to children under age 18. The Bicycle Helmet Safety Institute (www.bhsi.org/mandator.htm) has a thorough, state-by-state list of local rules.
- The Better World Club (www.betterworldclub.com) provides emergency roadside assistance for cyclists. Membership costs $40 per year, plus a $12 enrollment fee, and entitles you to two free pickups.
- The League of American Bicyclists (www.bikeleague.org) offers general tips, plus lists of local bike clubs and repair shops.

Some cities are more friendly to bicycles than others, but most have at least a few dedicated bike lanes and paths, and usually bikes can be carried on public transportation. Many big cities – New York, Chicago, Boston, Miami and Washington, DC, among them – have bike-share programs. These are also popping up in other cities such as Cincinnati, Nashville, Indianapolis and Louisville.

Transportation

If you're bringing your own wheels, call around to check oversize luggage prices and restrictions. Bikes are considered checked luggage on airplanes, but often must be boxed and fees can be high (more than $200). Amtrak trains and Greyhound buses will transport bikes within the USA, typically for much less.

Rental

Outfitters renting bicycles exist in most tourist towns. Rentals typically cost between $20 and $30 per day, including a helmet and lock. Most companies require a credit-card security deposit of $200 or so.

Buying a Bicycle

Buying a bike is easy, as is reselling it before you leave. Specialist bike shops have the best selection and advice for new bikes, but general sporting-goods stores and big-box retailers may have lower prices. Better yet, buy a used bike. To sniff out the best bargains, scour garage sales and thrift shops, or browse the free classified ads at Craigslist (www.craigslist.org).

Boat

Several ferry services provide efficient, scenic links in the East. Most ferries transport cars, but you must make reservations well in advance.

In the Northeast:

Bay State Cruise Company (www.boston-ptown.com) Ferries between Boston and Provincetown, MA.

Block Island Ferry (www.blockislandferry.com) Ferries to Block Island from Narragansett and Newport, RI.

Lake Champlain Ferries (www.ferries.com) Ferries between Burlington, VT, and Port Kent, NY.

Staten Island Ferry (www.siferry.com) Free commuter boats between Staten Island and Manhattan, NY.

Steamship Authority (www.steamshipauthority.com) Ferries to Martha's Vineyard and Nantucket from Cape Cod, MA.

In the Great Lakes:

Shepler's (☎800-828-6157; www.sheplersferry.com; Main St; return adult/child/bicycle $27/15/11; ⊙late Apr-Oct) and **Star Line** (☎800-638-9892; www.mackinacferry.com; Main St; return adult/child/bicycle $27/15/12) Passenger ferries out of Mackinaw City and St Ignace, MI, to reach Mackinac Island.

Lake Express (☎866-914-1010; www.lake-express.com; 1918 Lakeshore Dr, Muskegon; one way adult/child/car $96/39/105; ⊙May-Oct) Ferries across Lake Michigan between Milwaukee, WI, and Muskegon, MI.

SS Badger (☎800-841-4243; www.ssbadger.com; 701 Maritime Dr; one way adult/child/car $62/27/62; ⊙mid-May–mid-Oct) Ferries across Lake Michigan between Manitowoc, WI, and Ludington, MI.

In the Southern United States:

Key West Express (www.seakeywestexpress.com) Catamaran service between Fort Myers and Key West.

North Carolina Ferry System (www.ncdot.gov/travel-maps) Runs ferries throughout the Outer Banks.

Bus

Greyhound (www.greyhound.com) is the major long-distance carrier, plowing along an extensive network throughout the USA, as well as to/from Canada. As a rule, buses are reliable, clean(ish) and comfortable, with air-conditioning, barely reclining seats, on-board lavatories and a no-smoking policy. Several buses have wi-fi. While some shorter-route buses run express, most stop every 50 to 100 miles to pick up passengers, and long-

GREYHOUND DOMESTIC BUS ROUTES & FARES

Some sample standard one-way adult fares and trip times:

ROUTE	FARE ($)	TIME (HR)	FREQUENCY (PER DAY)
Boston–Philadelphia	25	7	10
Chicago–New Orleans	130	20-30	5
New York–Chicago	65	18-23	5
Washington, DC–Miami	150	25-30	4

distance buses stop for meal breaks and driver changes.

Other carriers (most with wi-fi and power outlets on board):

BestBus (www.bestbus.com) Cheap fares between the nation's capital and NYC.

Go Bus (www.gobuses.com) Serves Northeastern cities (Boston, NYC, Hartford, Providence) and the DC region.

Lucky Star Bus (www.luckystarbus.com) Cheap travel between Boston and NYC.

Megabus (www.megabus.com) The biggest Greyhound competitor, with routes between main cities in the Northeast, Great Lakes and the Southern USA. Fares can be quite low; ticket bookings online only.

Peter Pan Bus Lines (www.peterpanbus.com) Serves more than 50 destinations in the Northeast, as far north as Concord, NH, and as far south as Washington, DC.

Trailways (www.trailways.com) Services mainly the Northeast and the Great Lakes; their site also allows you to search multiple bus carriers (including Greyhound and Peter Pan) for the best price on your selected route.

Most cities and larger towns have dependable local bus systems, though they are often designed for commuters and provide limited service in the evenings and on weekends. Costs range from free to between $1 and $3 per ride.

Costs

In general, the earlier you book, the lower the fare.

On Megabus and some of the smaller companies, the first tickets sold for a route cost $1.

For lower fares on Greyhound, purchase tickets at least seven days in advance (purchasing 14 days in advance will save even more).

If you're traveling with family or friends, Greyhound's companion fares allow up to two additional travelers 50% off with a minimum three-day advance purchase.

Reservations

Greyhound tickets can be bought over the phone or online, as well as at terminals. Tickets for Megabus, Go Bus and most of the smaller companies can only be purchased online in advance. Seating is normally first-come, first-served.

Greyhound recommends that you arrive an hour before bus departure to get a seat.

Car & Motorcycle

For maximum flexibility and convenience, and to explore outside of the cities, a car is essential.

Automobile Associations

The American Automobile Association (www.aaa.com) has reciprocal membership agreements with several international auto clubs (check with AAA and bring your membership card from home). For its members, AAA offers travel insurance, tour books and a wide-ranging network of regional offices. AAA advocates politically for the auto industry.

A more ecofriendly alternative, the Better World Club (www.betterworldclub.com) donates 1% of revenue to assist environmental cleanup, offers ecologically sensitive choices for every service it provides and advocates politically for environmental causes.

For either organization, the primary member benefit is 24-hour emergency roadside assistance anywhere in the USA. Both also offer trip planning, free travel maps, travel-agency services, car insurance and a range of travel discounts (eg on hotels, car rentals and attractions).

Bring Your Own Vehicle

If you're driving from Canada, it's possible to bring your vehicle to the US as long as it remains with you for the duration of the stay permitted on your visa. Attempts to sell the vehicle in the US (if you've bought a cheap car for the trip) will usually backfire due to differing state laws on emissions control and the fact that it'll show up as a Canadian car when you attempt to transfer registration: there are lots of fees and red tape involved.

If you're moving to the USA from Canada and intend on keeping your vehicle, it will need to pass a series of tests (which vary from state to state). Fees apply.

Freighting a vehicle to the USA from anywhere else, as

an individual, is prohibitively complicated and expensive.

Driver's Licenses

Foreign visitors can legally drive a car in the USA for up to 12 months using their home driver's license. However, an International Driving Permit (IDP) will have more credibility with US traffic police, especially if your home license doesn't have a photo or isn't issued in English. Your automobile association at home can issue an IDP, valid for one year, for a small fee. Always carry your home license together with the IDP.

To drive a motorcycle in the USA, you will need either a valid US state motorcycle license or an IDP specially endorsed for motorcycles.

Fuel

Gas stations are ubiquitous and many are open 24 hours a day; however, small-town stations may open only from 7am to 8pm or 9pm. Plan on spending roughly $2.80 per US gallon. At many stations, you must pay before you pump.

Many gas stations will accept credit cards at the pump but will require the confirmation of a US zip code once you swipe: if your card isn't issued in the US, you'll need to go inside and prepay. If your car takes less fuel than you authorize payment for, the difference will be automatically refunded to the card.

Car Rental

To rent a car in the USA you generally need to be at least 25 years old, hold a valid driver's license and have a major credit card. Some companies will rent to drivers between the ages of 21 and 24 for an additional charge.

You should be able to get an economy-sized vehicle for about $30 to $75 per day. Child safety seats are compulsory (reserve them when you book) and cost about $13 per day.

Some national companies, including Avis, Budget and Hertz, offer 'green' fleets of hybrid rental cars (eg Toyota Priuses, Honda Civics), although you'll usually have to pay a lot extra to rent a more fuel-efficient vehicle.

Online, Car Rental Express (www.carrentalexpress.com) rates and compares independent agencies in US cities; it's particularly useful for searching out cheaper long-term rentals.

Major national car-rental companies:

Alamo (www.alamo.com)

Avis (www.avis.com)

Budget (www.budget.com)

Dollar (www.dollar.com)

Enterprise (www.enterprise.com)

Hertz (www.hertz.com)

National (www.nationalcar.com)

Rent-A-Wreck (www.rentawreck.com) Rents cars that may have more wear and tear than your typical rental vehicle but are actually far from wrecks.

Thrifty (www.thrifty.com)

Motorcycle & Recreational Vehicle (RV) Rental

If you dream of riding a Harley, EagleRider (www.eaglerider.com) has offices in major cities nationwide and rents other kinds of adventure vehicles, too. Beware that motorcycle rental and insurance are expensive.

Companies specializing in RV and camper rentals:

Adventures on Wheels (www.wheels9.com)

Cruise America (www.cruiseamerica.com)

Insurance

Insurance is legally required. Without it, you risk legal consequences and possible financial ruin if there's an accident.

Car-rental agencies offer liability insurance, which covers other people and property involved in an accident.

Collision Damage Waivers (CDW) reduce or eliminate the amount you'll have to reimburse the rental company if there's damage to the car itself.

Paying extra for all of this insurance increases the cost of a rental car by as much as $30 a day.

Some credit cards cover CDW for a certain rental period (usually less than 15 days), if you use the card to pay for the rental and decline the policy offered by the rental company. Always check with your card issuer to see what coverage they offer in the USA.

Road Conditions & Hazards

Road conditions are generally very good, but keep in mind:

➡ Winter travel in general can be hazardous due to heavy snow and ice, which may cause roads and bridges to close periodically. The Federal Highway Administration (www.fhwa.dot.gov/trafficinfo) provides links to road conditions and construction zones for each state.

➡ If you're driving in winter or in remote areas, make sure your vehicle is equipped with four-season radial or snow tires, and emergency supplies in case you're stranded.

➡ Where deer and other wild animals frequently appear roadside, you'll see signs with the silhouette of a leaping deer. Take these signs seriously, particularly at dusk and dawn.

Road Rules

If you're new to US roads, here are some basics:

➡ Drive on the right-hand side of the road. On highways, pass in the left-hand lane.

➡ The maximum speed limit on most interstates is 65mph or 70mph; a couple of states go up to 75mph.

Limits drop to around 55mph in urban areas. Pay attention to the posted signs. City-street speed limits vary between 15mph and 45mph.

➡ The use of seat belts is required in every state except New Hampshire. In some states, motorcyclists are required to wear helmets.

➡ The use of child safety seats and seat belts for children under 18 is required in all states.

➡ Unless signs prohibit it, you may turn right at a red light after first coming to a full stop (note that NYC is an exception, where it's illegal to turn right on a red).

➡ At four-way stop signs, the car that reaches the intersection first has right of way. In a tie, the car on the right has right of way.

➡ When emergency vehicles (ie police, fire or ambulance) approach from either direction, pull over safely and get out of the way.

➡ In many states it is illegal to talk (or text) on a handheld cell phone while driving; use a hands-free device or pull over to take your call.

➡ The blood-alcohol limit for drivers is 0.08%. Penalties are very severe for 'DUI' – Driving Under the Influence of alcohol and/or drugs.

➡ In many states it is illegal to carry 'open containers' of alcohol in a vehicle, even if they are empty.

➡ If you are pulled over by the police, do not get out of your car. Wait for the officer to approach your window – in the meantime, collect your license, proof of insurance and registration or rental agreement, and have them ready for the officer to inspect.

Hitchhiking

Hitchhiking in the USA is potentially dangerous and not recommended. Travelers who hitch should understand that they are taking a potentially serious risk. Indeed, drivers have heard so many lurid reports they tend to be just as afraid of those with their thumbs out. Hitchhiking on freeways is prohibited.

Taxis & Ridesharing

Taxis are metered, with flagfall charges of around \$2.50, plus \$2 to \$3 per mile. Extra charges apply for waiting and for handling baggage, and drivers expect a 10% to 15% tip. Taxis cruise the busiest areas in large cities; otherwise, it's easiest to phone and order one.

Rideshare companies are also well used in most cities.

Train

Amtrak (www.amtrak.com) has an extensive rail system throughout the USA, with several long-distance lines traversing the nation east to west, and even more running north to south. These link all of America's biggest cities and many of its smaller ones. In some places, Amtrak's Thruway buses provide connections to and from the rail network.

Compared with other modes of travel, trains are rarely the quickest, cheapest or most convenient option, but they turn the journey into a relaxing, social and scenic all-American experience.

Rail services are busiest in the Northeast corridor, where high-speed Acela Express trains run from Boston, MA, to Washington, DC (via NYC, Philadelphia and Baltimore).

Other busy routes include NYC to Niagara Falls, and Chicago to Milwaukee.

Free wi-fi is available on many, but not all, trains. Wi-fi speed is fine for email and web browsing, but usually not suitable for streaming videos or music.

Smoking is prohibited on all trains.

Many big cities, such as NYC, Chicago and Miami, also have their own commuter rail networks. These trains provide faster, more frequent services on shorter routes.

The largest subway systems are in NYC, Chicago, Boston, Philadelphia and Washington, DC. Other cities may have small, one- or two-line rail systems that mainly serve downtown.

Behind the Scenes

SEND US YOUR FEEDBACK

We love to hear from travelers – your comments keep us on our toes and help make our books better. Our well-traveled team reads every word on what you loved or loathed about this book. Although we cannot reply individually to your submissions, we always guarantee that your feedback goes straight to the appropriate authors, in time for the next edition. Each person who sends us information is thanked in the next edition.

Visit **lonelyplanet.com/contact** to submit your updates and suggestions or to ask for help. Our award-winning website also features inspirational travel stories and news.

Note: We may edit, reproduce and incorporate your comments in Lonely Planet products such as guidebooks, websites and digital products, so let us know if you are happy to have your name acknowledged. For a copy of our privacy policy visit **lonelyplanet.com/legal**.

WRITER THANKS

Isabel Albiston

Thanks to everyone in Massachusetts who answered my questions so patiently and treated me so kindly, especially to all the museum guides who showed me around along the way. Thanks also to Leah, Julie and Andrea for your warm hospitality and to Trisha for commissioning me for such a great project. Lastly, huge thanks to Ellie, Alan and Liz for traveling out to join me at the end of my trip.

Mark Baker

So many people came out of the woodwork to help me carry out research in Minnesota and Wisconsin. A partial list would include, in Minnesota: Monte Hanson, Alex Friedrich, Leif Pettersen, Liz Puhl, Zach Peterson, Stacey Mae McGowan Olson and Robert Olson. In Wisconsin, I'd like to thank Sarah Lewison, Richard Ryan and Joan Menefee, among many others. I'd also like to thank Trisha Ping, the Lonely Planet Destination Editor who first invited me to pitch for this project.

Amy C Balfour

For Mississippi insights, thank you Jim Foley, Eone Moore, Lake Andrews, Sarah Nobles, Kevin Webb and Erik Arnold. Team Tennessee includes Jeff and Heather Kelsey, Lauren Batte, Jim Hester, Frank Watson, Chad Graddy and David Wells. Melissa and Michael Peeler, thank you for letting me crash at your place and for escorting me to all the good restaurants, watering holes and Memphis hotspots. With a shout-out to Mary, Anna and Margie for their recommendations. And yes, Michael, I'll include Celtic Crossing! Thank you to co-writers Karla Zimmerman, Adam Karlin, and the Destination Editor team for their Nashville and Franklin hospitality and expertise!

Robert Balkovich

Thank you to my family – my mother, father and sister – and friends for their love and support. Special thanks to Michael, Raghnild, Elizabeth and Ming for their hospitality and wealth of tips, and to Matthew for your friendship on the road. And thank you to Trisha Ping for this opportunity, and many others.

Ray Bartlett

Huge thanks to Trisha and Evan, the rest of the Lonely Planet staff, and my family and friends. You rock. Met such great folks along the way, thanks for making the trip what it was: Charissa and Bret; Tara, Amber, and Shannon; Palma and Karyn; May Lee; Theresa and Jessenia; Rebeckah and Ashley; 'Cousin' Steve; Ericha and Bria; Austin (Habari!); Yimee Nguyen; Sabrina V; Michael Milgate; Kelley Luikey; birder Sara; Swanee; Jason and Sam; and, of course, Kiko the Mermaid. Can't wait to be back again soon.

Jade Bremner

Thanks to knowledgeable Destination Editor Trisha Ping for all her wisdom on the Southern States. Plus, the hardworking Georgia and North Carolina barbecue chefs for cooking all that mind-blowingly good smoky meat and sauce that fueled my entire trip around the South. Thanks to North Carolina locals Norm and Skye for their top tips and local advice. Last, but definitely not least, thanks to everyone working hard behind the scenes – Cheree Broughton, Dianne and Jane, Helen Elfer and Neill Coen.

Gregor Clark

Thanks to the many fellow Vermonters who shared their favorite spots in the Green Mountain State with me this edition – especially Shawn O'Neil, Margo Whitcomb, Victoria St John, Jim Lockridge and Joy Cohen – and to Gaen, Meigan and Chloe for a lifetime of companionship on our family adventures in this gorgeous place we call home.

Ashley Harrell

Thanks to Erin Morris for welcoming me to your state; Kourtnay King and Paul Haynes for taking me in and enabling me; Chandler Routman for getting me out of the house; Jason, Elizabeth, Iris and Loulou Ryan for being a great family; Patty Pascal for your unbridled enthusiasm; Halsey Perrin, Kim Jamieson and Ruta Fox for your help and expertise; and Chris Dorsel for still being amazing.

Adam Karlin

Thank you: Trisha for commissioning this recent edition, Evan for taking over, and my road trip friends and co-authors extraordinaire Amy and Karla. Thank you to the staff, students and faculty of the University of New Orleans CWW for helping me find my voice when it comes to writing about the South. Thank you mom and dad for all you do, and thank you my favorite traveling companions: Rachel, Sanda and Isaac.

Brian Kluepfel

To my wife and North Star, Paula Zorrilla. To Trisha at Lonely Planet, and Robert and Adam, my writing cohorts. To Marc in Atlantic City, Brooke in Montauk, and Tom K in Hoboken for local knowledge. To Joe Dawson, Laura Tafuri and Karen Ramos for cool beach recommendations. And to all the lovely toll-takers on the Garden State Parkway, some of whom I now know on a first-name basis.

Ali Lemer

Many thanks to Will Coley, Nicole Marsella, Adam Michaels, Regis St Louis and Trisha Ping, and to Professor Kenneth Jackson, who taught me more about NYC history than anyone. My work is dedicated to the memory of my father, Albert Lemer, a first-generation New Yorker who inspired my enthusiasm for international travel as much as he kindled my love of our shared hometown – the greatest city in the world.

Vesna Maric

Thanks to Trisha Ping and Evan Godt for commissioning me; to Alicia Estefania and Susana Felices; and a huge thanks to Marta Vila for her generosity. Thank you to Atena Sherry for fun times.

Virginia Maxwell

Thanks to DC locals Barbara Balman and Bob Bresnahan for their convivial company and insider tips; to Trisha Ping for giving me the gig and supplying interesting leads; to DC expert Karla Zimmerman; and to traveling companions Eveline Zoutendijk, George Grundy and Ryan Ver Berkmoes. At home in Australia, thanks and much love to Peter Handsaker, who coped with apartment-renovation chaos and didn't blame me for my absence (well, not too much).

THIS BOOK

This 6th edition of Lonely Planet's *Eastern USA* guidebook was curated by Trisha Ping, Ali Lemer, Martine Power, Charles Rawlings-Way, Regis St Louis and Mara Vorhees. It was researched and written by Trisha Ping, Ali Lemer, Regis St Louis, Mara Vorhees, Isabel Albiston, Mark Baker, Amy C Balfour, Robert Balkovich, Ray Bartlett, Jade Bremner, Gregor Clark, Ashley Harrell, Adam Karlin, Brian Kluepfel, Vesna Maric, Virginia Maxwell, Hugh McNaughtan, MaSovaida Morgan, Lorna Parkes, Kevin Raub, Simon Richmond, Benedict Walker, Greg Ward and Karla Zimmerman. This guidebook was produced by the following:

Destination Editors Evan Godt, Trisha Ping

Senior Product Editors Martine Power, Vicky Smith

Regional Senior Cartographer Alison Lyall

Product Editors Carolyn Boicos, Sasha Drew

Book Designers Gwen Cotter, Lauren Egan

Assisting Editors Sarah Bailey, James Bainbridge, Imogen Bannister, Michelle Bennett, Nigel Chin, Samantha Cook, Lucy Cowie, Andrea Dobbin, Emma Gibbs, Carly Hall, Victoria Harrison, Jennifer Hattam, Gabrielle Innes, Helen Koehne, Kellie Langdon, Lou McGregor, Rosie Nicholson, Kristin Odijk, Monique Perrin, Mani Ramaswamy, Sarah Reid, Fionnuala Twomey, Sam Wheeler

Cartographers Hunor Csutoros, Rachel Imeson

Cover Researcher Meri Blazevski

Thanks to Sain Alizada, Hannah Cartmel, Fergal Condon, Joel Cotterell, Melanie Dankel, Bruce Evans, Sonia Kapoor, Alan Newbauer, Charlotte Orr, Lars Thelen

MaSovaida Morgan

Thank you to the lovely souls in Savannah and beyond who provided tips, guidance and feedback for this project. In particular, many thanks to Chad Faries and Emily Jones, Robert Firth, and Trisha Ping for bringing me on. Special thanks and love to Ny, Ty and Haj.

Barbara Noe Kennedy

I can't thank enough the endless line of Washingtonians who always point me in the right direction, keeping me up to date with the latest and greatest happenings. But no one can surpass the tireless devotion of Kate Gibbs at Destination DC, who's always there to answer my next question or let me know about the next exhibition – thanks! I also would like to thank my husband, David Kennedy, who is always game to experience all that DC has to offer – so much fun!

Lorna Parkes

Thank you to the residents of New York for your friendliness, as well as your endearing day-to-day sidewalk and subway rage; the latter I expected, but the former not so much. Thanks to Kat and Heather who at various points joined me to rate the best cocktail mixologists and live-music dives. Thanks most of all to Austin and Lily who waited patiently for me to return home, and to Rob and my in-laws for holding family life together in my absence.

Trisha Ping

Thanks to Alicia Johnson for the sports intel, Bailey Freeman for the local edit and Martine and Sasha for signing me on!

Kevin Raub

Thanks to Trisha Ping and all my fellow partners in crime at Lonely Planet. On the road, Jordan Mazzoni, Erika Dahl, Ali Lechlitner, Anita and Kevin Welch, Jana and Bill Swigart, Tom and Alice Erlandson, Erika Dahl, Marla Cichowski, Gina Speckman, Jessica Waytenick, Jeff Berg, Luanne Mattson, Sarah Prasil, Erin Hawkins, Erin White, Tyra Miller and Morgan Snyder.

Simon Richmond

Many thanks to the following people who generously shared their time and knowledge about Philadelphia: Jerry Silverman, Lindsay Ryan, Tish Byrne, Mason Wray and Rajeev Shankar.

Regis St Louis

I am grateful to countless innkeepers, park rangers, baristas, shop owners and folks 'from away' who provided shared Maine insight. Special thanks to Brother Arnold for a fabulous meal at Sabbathday Shaker Village, Scott Cowger for the tips and barn tour in Hallowell, Jack Burke and Julie Van De Graaf for their kindness in Castine, and Gregor Clark and Diane Plauche for general Maine suggestions. Special thanks to my family, who make coming home the best part of travel.

Mara Vorhees

To the server at a Gloucester restaurant, who recommended that I spend my afternoon at a certain delightful beach (which is not in this book). Thanks for sharing your secret spot. I won't tell.

Benedict Walker

A special thanks to Cheryl Cowie and Keri Berthelot for their guidance, support and Reiki II's on the road. As always, to Trish Walker for countless hours in the prayer chair, and a big shout-out to family; Andy, Sally and P for making sure I didn't overdo the lobster! In memory of Kevin Hennessy, Ainsley Crabbe and Ben Carey, my fellow adventurers who passed away in other lands while I was researching this title. A little part of you remains in Rhode Island for me, always. You'll like it there!

Greg Ward

Thanks to the many wonderful people who helped me on the road, especially at Historic Stagville Plantation, Price's Chicken Coop, Bryson City Bicycles and the Orange County Visitor Center. Thanks too to my editor Trisha Ping for giving me this opportunity, and to my dear wife Sam for everything else.

Karla Zimmerman

Many thanks to Paula Andruss, Lisa Beran, Lisa DiChiera, Ruggero Fatica, Chuck Palmer, Keith Pandolfi and Bob Sanders for taking the time to share their favorite local spots. Thanks most to Eric Markowitz, the world's best partner-for-life and road trip companion. You top my Best List every time.

ACKNOWLEDGEMENTS

Climate map data adapted from Peel MC, Finlayson BL & McMahon TA (2007) 'Updated World Map of the Köppen-Geiger Climate Classification', *Hydrology and Earth System Sciences*, 11, 1633–44.

Cover photograph: Great Smoky Mountains; WendellandCarolyn/Getty Images ©

Illustrations pp84–5, pp260–1 by Javier Zarracina.

Index

606 531
10,000 Islands 481

A

Abingdon 320-1
Acadia National Park 15, 247-8, 331, **4-5**, **15**
accessible travel 122, 642
accommodations 26-7, 54, 55, *see also individual locations*
activities 21, 28-32, 46-9, *see also individual activities*
Adirondacks, the 136-40
air travel 649-50, 651-2
Alabama 413-19
Albany 137-8
alcohol 645, *see also* beer, bourbon
Alexandria 299-302
Alexandria Bay 140-1
Ali, Muhammad 387
alligators 639
Amelia Island 495-6
Amherst 204
Amish communities 164, 559, 565-6, **35**
amusement & water parks
  Anakeesta 385-6
  Busch Gardens 497
  Casino Pier 149
  Cedar Point Amusement Park 564
  Dinosaur Kingdom II 318
  Dollywood 385
  ICON Orlando 504
  Luna Park 87
  Rapids Water Park 476
  SeaWorld 504
  Steel Pier 150
  Trimpers Rides 290
  Universal Orlando Resort 507-11
  Universal Studios 508-9
  Valleyfair 602
  Walt Disney World® Resort 506-7
  Wisconsin Dells 596
ancient mounds 552, 572, 619
animals 636-40, *see also individual species*
Ann Arbor 579
Annapolis 286-9
Antietam National Battlefield 291-2
Apalachicola National Forest 512
Apostle Islands 600-1
Appalachian Trail 47, 316
Appomattox 314-15
aquariums
  Florida Aquarium 497
  Georgia Aquarium 395
  National Aquarium 281
  Shedd Aquarium 523
  South Carolina Aquarium 357
  South Florida Science Center & Aquarium 476
  Tennessee Aquarium 383
  Virginia Aquarium & Marine Science Center 308
architecture 632
area codes 647
Arkansas 425-32
Arlington 298-9
Arrington 377
Art Basel Miami Beach 32
art museums & galleries
  Albright-Knox Art Gallery 142
  American Visionary Art Museum 283
  Andy Warhol Museum 166
  Art Institute of Chicago 520
  Bakehouse Art Complex 462
  Baker Museum 502
  Barnes Foundation 152-3
  Bennington Museum 223-4
  Birmingham Museum of Art 414
  Broad Art Museum 580
  Carnegie Museum of Art 166
  Chazen Museum of Art 596
  Chicago Cultural Center 521
  Chrysler Museum of Art 307
  Clark Art Institute 207
  Cleveland Museum of Art 561
  Cummer Museum of Art & Gardens 493
  Currier Museum of Art 232
  Delaware Art Museum 295
  Detroit Institute of Arts 572
  Dia:Beacon 128
  District of Columbia Arts Center 266
  Dr Evermor's Sculpture Park 596
  Eric Carle Museum of Picture Book Art 205
  Farnsworth Art Museum 246
  Flagler Museum 474
  Florida Museum of Photographic Arts 497
  Frick Art & Historical Center 166
  Frick Collection 78
  Frist Center for the Visual Arts 376
  Gagosian 69
  Galerie F 528-9
  Georgia Museum of Art 406
  Gibbes Museum of Art 356
  Guggenheim Museum 78
  Harvard Art Museums 183, 185
  Herbert F Johnson Museum of Art 134-5
  High Museum of Art 395
  Hirshhorn Museum 259
  Hood Museum of Art 240
  Hunter Museum of American Art 383
  Hyde Collection Art Museum 138
  Indianapolis Museum of Art 553
  Institute of Contemporary Art (Boston) 179, 182
  Institute of Contemporary Art (Miami) 461
  Intuit: The Center for Intuitive & Outsider Art 528
  Isabella Stewart Gardner Museum 183
  Jepson Center for the Arts 408
  Lexington Art League at Loudoun House 391
  Margulies Collection at the Warehouse 462
  MASS MoCA 207
  Mennello Museum of American Art 504
  Metropolitan Museum of Art 78
  Milwaukee Art Museum 591-2
  Minneapolis Institute of Art 603
  MoMA PS1 87-8
  Museum of Contemporary Art (Chicago) 527
  Museum of Contemporary Art Detroit 573
  Museum of Contemporary Art Jacksonville 493
  Museum of Contemporary Art North Miami 463
  Museum of Contemporary Photography 523
  Museum of Fine Arts 183
  Museum of Modern Art 73
  National Gallery of Art 255
  National Museum of Mexican Art 523
  New Museum of Contemporary Art 69-70
  New Orleans Museum of Art 435, 438
  Noguchi Museum 88
  Norman Rockwell Museum 206
  North Carolina Museum of Art 343
  Norton Museum of Art 476
  NSU Art Museum Fort Lauderdale 471
  Ogden Museum of Southern Art 438-9
  Opus 40 Sculpture Park & Museum 135
  Orlando Museum of Art 504
  Parrish Art Museum 124
  Paula Cooper Gallery 69
  Pérez Art Museum Miami 457, 459
  Philadelphia Museum of Art 153
  Phillips Collection 266

Map Pages **000**
Photo Pages **000**

art museums & galleries *continued*
Pizzuti Collection 566
Portland Museum of Art 243
Provincetown Art Association & Museum 199
Renwick Gallery 264
Reynolds Center for American Art & Portraiture 265
Ringling Museum Complex 500
RISD Museum of Art 209
Rodin Museum 154
Rubin Museum of Art 68
Salvador Dalí Museum 499
SCAD Museum of Art 408
Shelburne Museum 229-30
Smith College Museum of Art 204
Southeast Museum of Photography 490
Speed Art Museum 387-8
Taubman Museum of Art 320
Torpedo Factory Art Center 301
Virginia Museum of Fine Arts 310
Void Projects 459
Wadsworth Atheneum 214-15
Walker Art Center 602
Walters Art Museum 282
Weisman Art Museum 603
Whitney Museum of American Art 67
Williams College Museum of Art 207
Wolfsonian-FIU 456
Wynwood Walls 461
Yale Center for British Art 219
Yale University Art Gallery 219
arts 630-2, *see also* *individual arts*
Asbury Park 147-8
Asheville 18, 351-4, **18**
Assateague Island 290
Athens (Georgia) 405-7
Athens (Ohio) 570
Atlanta 394-404, **396-7**
Atlanta BeltLine 404
Atlantic City 149-50
Atlantic Coast 488-96
ATMs 645

Map Pages **000**
Photo Pages **000**

Auburn 560
Aurora 136

B

B&Bs 26
Baltimore 280-6
Bar Harbor 248-9, **330**
Barataria Preserve 446
Barnegat Peninsula 148-9
baseball 628
basketball 629
Bath 245
bathrooms 647
Battle Green 192
beaches 10-11
Acadia National Park 248
Bahia Honda State Park 485
Belleayre 132
Canaveral National Seashore 488
Captiva Island 501
Chicago 532-3
Fire Island National Seashore 122-3
Folly Beach 361
Fort Lauderdale 471
Gulf Islands National Seashore 514
Hammonasset Beach 219
Kiawah Island 361
Martha's Vineyard 202
Miami 456, 457, **42**
Muskegon 584
Myrtle Beach 363-4
Naples 502-3
Ocean City 289
Ocracoke Beach 339
Ogunquit 241
Orient 127
Saugatuck 583
St Augustine 492
Virginia Beach 308
Beaufort (North Carolina) 340
Beaufort (South Carolina) 362-3
Beckley 328
Beecher Stowe, Harriet 215
beer 276, *see also* breweries
Ben & Jerry's Ice Cream Factory 228
Bennington 222-3
Berkeley Springs 324-5
Berkshires, the 205-8
Berlin 565
Bethel 249
bicycling 47, 652
Abingdon 320
Boston 185
C&O Canal National Historic Park 21, 292-3, 324, **21**
Cape Cod Rail Trail 195
Chicago 531
Cumberland 293
Detroit 573
Duluth 610
Falmouth 194
Fayetteville 329
Franconia Notch State Park 238
Indiana Dunes 559
Miami 463, 465
Minuteman Commuter Bikeway 192
New York City 88
Northampton 203
Palm Beach 474
Provincetown 199
Richmond 310
Sleeping Bear Dunes National Lakeshore 584-5
Tallahassee 512
Washington, DC 268
Biden, Joe 625
birds 640
bird-watching
Cape May 151
Grafton Notch State Park 249
Lake Martin 450
Laura Quinn Wild Bird Sanctuary 483
Merritt Island National Wildlife Refuge 488
Pea Island National Wildlife Refuge 336
Pelee Island 565
Birmingham 414-16
black bears 637-8
Block Island 212
Bloomington 556
Blowing Rock 349-50
blue crabs 288
Blue Ridge Highlands 319-22
Blue Ridge Parkway 16, 38-9, 320, 349, **16**
Bluegrass Country 390-2
bluegrass music 43, 321
blues music 13, 633, **13**
boat travel 651, 652
boat trips
Chesapeake Bay 289
Fort Lauderdale 471-2
Islamorada 484
Key Largo 483
Pictured Rocks National Lakeshore 588
Washington, DC 268
Bogue Banks 340
Boldt Castle 140-1
Bonnaroo Music & Arts Festival 30, 381
booking services 27
books 630-1, 632, 636
Boone 350-1
Boothbay Harbor 245-6
border crossings 650
Boston 174-92, **176-7**, **180-1**
accommodations 186-7
activities 185
children, travel with 179
drinking & nightlife 189-90
entertainment 190
festivals & events 186
food 187-9
itineraries 175
shopping 190-1
sights 174-85
tourist offices 191
tours 185-6
travel to/from 191
travel within 191-2
walking tour 184, **184**
Boston Tea Party 182
Boundary Waters 20, 612, **20**
bourbon 388
Brandywine Valley 295-6
Brattleboro 222
Bretton Woods 238-9
breweries, *see also* distilleries
Asheville 351, 353
Boston 189
Brew Ridge Trail 314
Burlington 231
Cape Cod 196
Charleston 360
Chicago 541, 542, 543
Cleveland 562-3
Grand Rapids 581
Mad River Valley 226-7
Milwaukee 592
Minneapolis 607
Muskegon 584
Nantucket 201-2
New York 112
Pittsburgh 168
Portland 244
Stowe 228
Washington, DC 275, 276
Bronze Fonz 592
Brooklyn Bridge 86
Brooklyn Heights Promenade 86
Brown University 209
Brunswick 411-13
budgeting 23, 26, 52, 54
Buffalo 141-3
Buffalo National River 429, 432
Burlington 229-31
bus travel 650, 652-3
bushwalking, *see* hiking
Bushwick Collective 87
business hours 646

C

Cadillac Mountain 248
Cahawba 418
Cahokia Mounds State Historic Site 552
Cajun Country 447-9
Cajun culture 433
Cajun Prairie 450-1
Cajun Wetlands 449-51
Cambridge 183, 185, 189
camping 26
Canada, travel to/from 650
Cannon Mountain 237
canoeing, *see* kayaking & canoeing
Cape Cod 11, 194-200, **197**
Cape Cod National Seashore 198
Cape Hatteras National Seashore 336
Cape May 151-2
Capital Region 250-329, **252-3**
  accommodations 250
  climate 250
  food 250
  highlights 252-3
  travel seasons 250
Capitol Hill 262-4
Captiva Island 501-2
car travel 24, 651, 653-5, *see also* scenic drives
Carrboro 345-6
cathedrals, *see* churches & cathedrals
Catskills 131-4
caves
  Blanchard Springs Caverns 430
  Luray Caverns 315
  Mammoth Cave National Park 394
  Marengo Cave 558
cell phones 22, 647
cemeteries
  Arlington National Cemetery 299
  Hollywood Cemetery 310
  Lafayette Cemetery No 1 439
  Laurel Grove Cemetery 408
Central Park 79, 84-5, **80-1**, **84-5**, **84-5**
Chapel Hill 345-6
Charleston 356-61
Charleston County Sea Islands 361-2
Charlevoix 586
Charlotte 346-8
Charlottesville 312-14
Charm 565
Chatham 196-8
Chattanooga 382-4
Chelsea Market 67-8
Chesapeake Bay 281, 288, 289
Chicago 9, 13, 517-48, **522**, **524-5**, **9**
  accommodations 533-7
  activities 531-2
  children, travel with 532
  drinking & nightlife 541-3
  entertainment 543-6
  festivals & events 533
  food 537-41
  history 517, 520
  itineraries 520
  LGBTIQ+ travelers 545
  shopping 546-7
  sights 520-31
  tours 532-3
  travel to/from 547
  travel within 547-8
  walking tour 530, **530**
children, travel with 26-7, 54-6
  Atlanta 395
  Boston 179
  Chicago 532
  Miami 463
  New Orleans 435
Chimney Rock 351
Chrysler Building 76
churches & cathedrals
  Anthony Chapel 428
  Cathedral Church of St John the Divine 83
  First Ebenezer Baptist Church 399
  Full Gospel Tabernacle Church 369
  Old North Church 178
  St Andrew's Dune Church 124
  St John's Episcopal Church 310
  St Louis Cathedral 434
  St Patrick's Cathedral 77
  Thorncrown Chapel 431
  Trinity Church (Boston) 182-3
  Trinity Church (New York City) 65
  Washington National Cathedral 267
Churchill Downs 387
Cincinnati 568-70
cinema 622
Civil Rights movement 621-2
  landmarks 417
  Martin Luther King Jr 398-9, 416
  memorials 416
  museums 367, 394-5, 414, 418, 422, 569
Civil War 301, 619-20
Clarksdale 420-1
Cleveland 561-4
climate 22, 28, 29, 30, 31, 32, *see also individual regions*
CNN Center 395
Coca-Cola 395
cold exposure 644
Columbus (Indiana) 557-8
Columbus (Ohio) 566-7
Concord 192-3
Coney Island 87
Connecticut 213-21
consulates 643
cooking classes 53
Coral Castle 479
Cornucopia 601
Corolla 333, 336
costs 26, 52, 54
country music 375, 634
coyotes 639
Crawford Notch 238-9
credit cards 645
Creole culture 433
Crisfield 281
crocodiles 639
Crooked Road 13, 321, **13**
Crystal Coast 340-1
culture 626-9
Cumberland 292
Cumberland Island National Seashore 413
currency 22
customs regulations 642-3
Cutchogue 126
cycling, *see* bicycling

D

Dahlonega 404-5
dangers, *see* safety
Daniel Boone National Forest 393-4
Dardanelle 429
Dartmouth College 240
Dayton 568
Daytona Beach 490-1
Dean, James 555
Dearborn 578-9
deer 639
DeLand 511
Delaware 293-8
Delaware Water Gap 147
Detroit 571-8, **574**
Dexter Avenue Parsonage 416
Dickinson, Emily 204-5
disabilities, travelers with 122, 642
distilleries, *see also* breweries
  Firefly Distillery 362
  Jack Daniel's Distillery 367
  Kentucky 388
  Maker's Mark 393
  Ole Smoky Moonshine 386
  Siesta Key Rum 500
  Wigle Whiskey 166
diving 48-9
  Crystal Coast 340
  Key West 486
dogsledding 613
Dolly Sods Wilderness 325
dolphins 640
Door County 599-600
Douglas 583-4
Dover 296-8
drinks 53, *see also* beer, bourbon
driving, *see* car travel, scenic drives
drugs 645
Duke University 344
Duluth 609-10
Duquesne Incline 166
Durham 344-5
Dylan, Bob 611

E

earthquakes 637
East Bay 213
East Lansing 580-1
Eastern Panhandle 323-5
Eastern Shore 289
Eastern State Penitentiary 155
Eau Claire 598
Edgar Allan Poe National Historic Site 155
Edisto Island 361
Edmund Pettus Bridge 417
electricity 643
Ellis Island 61
embassies 643
Emerald Mound 423-4
emergencies 23
Empire State Building 71-3
Empire State Plaza 137
Endless Bridge 602
Erie Islands 564-5
Essex 218-19
etiquette 53, 642
Eunice 450
Eureka Springs 431-2
events 28-32, *see also individual events, locations*
Everglades 477-8
Everglades City 480-2
Everglades National Park 20, 331, 478, **20**
exchange rates 23
Exorcist Stairs 267

F

Fairmount 555
Falmouth 194-5

family travel, *see* children, travel with
Faulkner, William 419
Fayetteville 328-9
Fenway Park 183
festivals 28-32, 50, *see also individual festivals, locations*
Fifth Avenue 77
films 622, 631-2
Finger Lakes 134-6
Fire Island National Seashore 122-3
fish 640
Flatiron Building 70
Florida 58, 452-515, **454-5**
  accommodations 452
  climate 452
  food 452
  highlights 454-5
  travel seasons 452
Florida City 479-80
Florida Hwy 1 16, 44-5, **16**, **40**
Florida Keys 482-8
Florida Panhandle 511-15
Floyd 321, **13**
Flume Gorge 238
folk music 634
food 17, 50-3, *see also individual locations*
  cooking classes 53
  costs 52
  festivals 50
  fish fry 593
  Philadelphia cheesesteak 162
  pizza 539
  seafood 17, 50-1, 288, **17**
  supper clubs 593
  vegetarian & vegan travelers 52
football 628-9
Fort Lauderdale 470-4
forts
  Castillo de San Marcos National Monument 492
  Fort Adams 211
  Fort Mackinac 588
  Fort Macon 340
Franconia Notch 237-8
Franklin 377
Frederick 291-2
Fredericksburg 302-4
Freedom Trail 184, 185
Front Royal 315
Funks Grove 551

G

Galax 322
Galena 549-50
galleries, *see* art museums & galleries
gardens, *see* parks & gardens
Gatlinburg 385-6
gay travelers, *see* LGBTIQ+ travelers
Gemini Giant 551, **18**
geography 636
Georgetown 245
Georgetown University 267
Georgia 394-413
giardiasis 644
Gold Coast 582-6
Golden Isles 411-13
Graceland 367
Grand Haven 582
Grand Rapids 581-2
Grandfather Mountain 349-50
Great Barrington 205
Great Lakes 58, 516-14, **518-19**
  accommodations 516
  climate 516
  food 51-2, 516
  highlights 518
  history 517
  itineraries 535
  travel seasons 516
Great River Road 39, 41
Great Smoky Mountains National Park 15, 331, 354-5, **14-15**
Green Bay 598-9
Green County 594
Greenbrier Valley 327-9
Greenport 126-7
Greenville 365-6
Gulf Coast 425
Gulf Islands National Seashore 11, 514, **11**
Gullah culture 358

H

Hamptons, the 123-5
hang-gliding 337, **11**
Hanover 240
Harbor Country 585
Harpers Ferry 323-4
Hartford 214-16
Harvard University 183
health 643-4
heat exhaustion 644
Hemingway, Ernest 485-6, 587
High Country 349-51
hiking 46, *see also* walks
  Abingdon 320
  Appalachian Trail 47, 316
  Big Bluff 432
  Blackwater Falls State Park 325
  Blue Ridge Pkwy 320
  Crawford Notch State Park 238
  Franconia Notch State Park 238
  Great Smoky Mountains National Park 354
  Monongahela National Forest 325
  Monument Mountain 205
  Mt Magazine State Park 429
  Mt Nebo State Park 429
  New River Gorge 327
  Petit Jean State Park 429
  Shenandoah National Park 316
  Sleeping Bear Dunes National Lakeshore 584
  Superior Hiking Trail 611
  Tamiami Trail 480-1
  Tuckerman Ravine 239
Hilton Head 362-3
hip-hop music 635
historic buildings & sites
  Audubon State Historic Site 447
  Battleship North Carolina 341
  Big Pink 135
  Biltmore Estate 351
  Breakers, the 211
  Cahokia Mounds State Historic Site 552
  Carillon Historical Park 568
  Chrysler Building 76
  Colonial Michilimackinac 587
  Dana Thomas House 550
  Dexter Avenue Parsonage 416
  Ellwood Manor 302-3
  Elms, the 211
  Embassy Row 266
  Empire State Building 71-3
  Faneuil Hall 175, 178
  Flatiron Building 70
  Fort Raleigh National Historic Site 336
  Fort Sumter National Monument 357
  Franklin D Roosevelt Home 130
  Graycliff Estate 142
  Hildene 224
  Historic RCA Studio B 376
  Independence Hall 153
  Lincoln Home National Historic Site 550
  Little Rock Central High School 426
  Martin House Complex 142
  Martin Luther King Jr Birthplace 398-9
  Martin Luther King Jr National Historic Site 19, 398, **19**
  Maryland State House 287
  Monticello 312
  Montpelier 313
  Mount Vernon 299-300
  New York State Capitol 137
  Old Exchange & Provost Dungeon 356
  Old South Meeting House 175
  Old State House 175
  Parthenon 376
  Pentagon 299
  Petersen House 265
  Pope-Leighey House 300
  Radio City Music Hall 77
  Robie House 529
  Rockefeller Center 73, 76
  Rough Point 211
  Supreme Court 263
  Ulysses S Grant Home 549
  US Capitol 262-3
  Vicksburg National Military Park 421-2
  Virginia State Capitol 310
  Washington Irving's Sunnyside 128-9
  White House 264
  Winterthur 296
  Wormsloe Historic Site 408
Historic Triangle 304-7
history 616-25, *see also* Civil Rights movement
  Boston Tea Party 182
  British colonialism 617-18
  Civil War 301, 619-20
  Great Depression 620
  Louisiana Purchase 619
  Native Americans 262, 616, 617, 619
  Obama presidency 622-4
  prehistoric cultures 616
  Revolutionary War 618
  slavery 619-20
  Trump presidency 624-5
  Vietnam War 621-2
  World War II 620-1
hitchhiking 655
Hoboken 145-6
holidays 646
Homestead 479-80
Hopewell people 572
horseback riding 391, 471
hostels 26
Hot Springs 427-8
hotels 26
Hudson Valley 127-31
Huntsville 415

Map Pages **000**
Photo Pages **000**

hurricanes 637
Hyannis 195-6

I

ice skating 89, 155, 531
Illinois 517-52
immigration 626
Independence Day 31
Indiana 552-60
Indiana Dunes 558-9
Indiana University 556
Indianapolis 552-5
inns 26
Institute Woods 146
insurance 644, 654
internet access 27, 644
internet resources 56, 628, 645
Islamorada 483-4
Isle of Palms 361
Isle Royale 639
Ithaca 134-6
itineraries 33-7, *see also individual locations*

J

Jackson 422-3
Jacksonville 493-5
James Island 361
Jamesport 126
Jamestown 305
jazz 12, 633-4, **12**
Jekyll Island 412-13
Jersey Shore 147-52
Johns Hopkins University 283

K

Kancamagus Hwy 236
kayaking & canoeing 47
- Amelia Island 495
- Apostle Islands 600
- Boundary Waters 613
- Buffalo National River 432
- Charlotte 347
- Chicago 531-2
- Clarksdale 421
- Everglades 479, 481
- Key Largo 483
- Lexington 318
- Little Rock 426
- Logan 571-2
- Ocracoke Island 339
- Pictured Rocks National Lakeshore 588
- St Simons Island 412
- Tarpon Bay 501

Kelleys Island 564-5
Kentucky 386-94
Keweenaw Peninsula 590
Key Largo 482-3
Key West 485-8
Kiawah Island 361
Kidron 565
King, BB 421
King, Martin Luther Jr 19, 255, 367, 398, 399, 416, **19**
Kinzua Bridge Skywalk 165
kiteboarding 337
Kittyhawk 336, 337
Knoxville 384-5

L

Lafayette 448-9
Lake George 138
Lake Martin 450
Lake of the Clouds 590
Lake Placid 138-40
Lake Pontchartrain 446
Lake Superior 611
Lakes Region 234
languages 22
Lansing 580-1
Leesburg 303
legal matters 644-5
lemurs 344
Lenox 206-7
lesbian travelers , *see* LGBTIQ+ travelers
Lewes 294
Lexington (Kentucky) 391-2
Lexington (New England) 192
Lexington (Shenandoah Valley) 317-19
LGBTIQ+ travelers 645
- Atlanta 403
- Boston 189
- Chicago 545
- Fort Lauderdale 473
- Miami 469
- Minneapolis 606
- New Orleans 444
- Washington, DC 277

Liberty Bell Center 154-5
libraries
- Boston Public Library 183
- Folger Shakespeare Library 264
- Latter Library 435
- Library of Congress 263
- New York Public Library 73
- Newberry Library 527
- Providence Athenaeum 209
- Woodrow Wilson Presidential Library 316-17

lighthouses
- Bodie Island Lighthouse 336
- Cape Hatteras Lighthouse 337
- Cape May Lighthouse 151
- Fire Island Lighthouse 123
- Horton Point Lighthouse 127
- Montauk Lighthouse 125
- Ocracoke Lighthouse 339
- Portland Head Light 243
- Rockland Breakwater Lighthouse 246
- Sandy Hook 150
- Saugerties Lighthouse 135
- Split Rock Lighthouse 611

Lincoln 236
Lincoln, Abraham 251, 550, 558
Lincoln Center 83
Lincoln Hwy 41-3
Lincoln Memorial 251
Litchfield Hills 216
literature 630-1, 632
Little Island 24-5
Little Rock 425-7
lobsters 17, 50-1, **17**
Logan 571-2
Long Island 121-7
Lookout Mountain 383
Louisiana 432-51
Louisiana floods 637
Louisiana Purchase 619
Louisville 387-90
Lowcountry 17, 361-3
Lower Keys 485
Luray 315-16
Lyme disease 644

M

Mackinac Island 587
Mackinaw City 587
Mad River Valley 226-7
Madison 595-6
Maine 240-9, **242**
Mammoth Cave National Park 331, 394, **330-1**
Mamou 450
Manassas National Battlefield Park 301
manatees 497-8, 640
Manchester 232-3
Manitou Islands 584
Marathon 484-5
Mardi Gras 29, 439, **12**
markets
- Ann Arbor 579
- Boston 190-1
- Burlington 229-30
- Chatham 197-8
- Chicago 528
- Detroit 572-3
- Madison 595
- New York City 67-8, 71, 100

Marquette 589
Martha's Vineyard 202-3, **197**
Martin Luther King Jr National Historic Site 19, 398, **19**
Maryland 280-93
Mashomack Nature Preserve 126-7
Massachusetts 171-208
Massachusetts Institute of Technology 185
Massachusetts State House 174
Mayflower II 194
medical services 644
memorials, *see* monuments & memorials
Memphis 366-73, **368**, **370**
Miami 453-70, **458**, **460**, **42**
- accommodations 466-7
- activities 463, 465
- children, travel with 463
- drinking & nightlife 468-9
- entertainment 469-70
- festivals & events 465-6
- food 467-8
- history 453
- itineraries 457
- LGBTIQ+ travelers 469
- safety 470
- sights 453-63
- tourist offices 470
- tours 465
- travel to/from 470
- travel within 470
- walking tour 464, **464**

Michigan 571-91
Middleburg 303
Millersburg 565
Milwaukee 591-4
Minneapolis 602-7, **604-5**
Minnesota 601-14
Minute Man National Historic Park 192
Mississippi 419-25
Mississippi Delta 420-2
Mitchell, Margaret 395
Mobile 418-19
mobile phones 22, 647
Mohonk Preserve 129
monasteries 134
money 22, 23, 26, 54, 643, 645-6
Monongahela Incline 166
Monongahela National Forest 325-7
Montauk 125-6
Montgomery 416-17
Montpelier 227-8
monuments & memorials
- African American Civil War Memorial 265-6
- Bennington Battle Monument 223
- Bunker Hill Monument 179
- Civil Rights Memorial Center 416

monuments & memorials *continued*
Fort McHenry National Monument & Historic Shrine 283
Franklin Delano Roosevelt Memorial 262
George Washington Masonic National Memorial 300-1
Jefferson Memorial 258-9
Kunta Kinte–Alex Haley Memorial 287
Lincoln Memorial 251
Lost at Sea Memorial 125-6
Martin Luther King Jr Memorial 255
Martin Luther King Jr National Historic Site 19, 398, **19**
National Memorial for Peace & Justice 416
National September 11 Memorial 65
National WWII Memorial 259
Pilgrim Monument 199
Stonewall National Monument 69
Strawberry Fields 83
Vietnam Veterans Memorial 254-5
Washington Monument (Baltimore) 282
Washington Monument (Washington, DC) 255
Wright Brothers National Memorial 336
moose 636-7, 639
Morehead City 340
Morrilton 429
motels 26
motorcycle travel 651, 653-5
Mount Desert Island 248
Mount Vernon 299-300
Mountain View 430-1
Mt Airy 291-2
Mt Baldhead 583
Mt Monadnock 233
Mt Tremper 132-3
museums, *see also* art museums & galleries, sports museums
4-H Tidelands Nature Center 412-13
Acadian Village 448
Adler Planetarium 523
Air Mobility Command Museum 297
Amazing World of Dr Seuss 204
American Black Holocaust Museum 592
American Civil War Museum – Appomattox 314
American Museum of Natural History 79, 82-3
American Revolution Museum at Yorktown 306
Art Deco Museum 456
Auburn Cord Duesenberg Museum 560
Automotive Hall of Fame 579
Backstreet Cultural Museum 434
BB King Museum & Delta Interpretive Center 421
Benjamin Franklin Museum 154
Birmingham Civil Rights Institute 414
Boston Tea Party Ships & Museum 182
Brooklyn Museum 86-7
Busy Beaver Button Museum 529
Cabildo 434
Carnegie Museum of Natural History 166
Center for Civil & Human Rights 394-5
Center for PostNatural History 166
Center for Puppetry Arts 395
Charleston Museum 357
Chatham Shark Center 196-7
Chicago Architecture Center 521
Chicago Children's Museum 532
Chicago History Museum 528
Children's Museum of Indianapolis 553
Concord Museum 193
Connecticut Science Center 215
COSI 566
Country Music Hall of Fame & Museum 375
Delta Blues Museum 420
Driehaus Museum 526
Dumbarton Oaks 266-7
DuSable Museum of African American History 529, 531
East Hampton Town Marine Museum 124
Emily Dickinson Museum 204-5
Empire State Railway Museum 132
Eudora Welty House 422
Evergreen Museum 283-4
Fernbank Museum of Natural History 395
Field Museum of Natural History 523
Florida Keys History of Diving Museum 483
Ford Piquette Avenue Plant 573
Ford Rouge Factory Tour 579
Ford's Theatre Center for Education & Leadership 265
Fort William Henry Museum 138
Frank Lloyd Wright Home & Studio 548
Franklin D Roosevelt Home 130
Freedom House Museum 300-1
Freer | Sackler 262
Gerald R Ford Museum 581
Gilmore Car Museum 579
Gold Coast Railroad Museum 463
Grand Ole Opry House 376
Graveyard of the Atlantic Museum 337
Great Lakes Science Center 561
Greenfield Village 578-9
Gulf Coast Exploreum 418
Hammond Harwood House 287
Harley-Davidson Museum 591
Harriet Beecher-Stowe Center 215
Hemingway House 485-6
Henry Ford Museum 579
Historic New Orleans Collection 434
Historic Tredegar 310
Historic Village at Allaire 148
HistoryMiami 457
Illinois Holocaust Museum 548
Immigration Museum 61
International Spy Museum 265
James Monroe Museum & Memorial Library 303
Jewish Museum 78-9
John Dickinson Plantation 297
John F Kennedy Hyannis Museum 195
Johnny Cash Museum & Store 376
Kennedy Space Center 488
Kurt Vonnegut Museum & Library 553
Landis Valley Museum 164
Levine Museum of the New South 347
Lightner Museum 492
Lincoln Presidential Library & Museum 550
Little Traverse History Museum 587
Louisiana Children's Museum 435
Lower East Side Tenement Museum 69
Lower Mississippi River Museum 422
Lowndes County Interpretive Center 417
Maine Maritime Museum 245
Margaret Mitchell House & Museum 395, 398
Mark Twain House & Museum 215
Martin Luther King Jr National Historic Site 19, 398, **19**
Maryland Historical Society 283
Maryland Science Center 282
Memphis Rock 'n' Soul Museum 367
Met Cloisters 83
Mexican Cultural Institute 266
Miami Children's Museum 463
Millyard Museum 232
Mint Museum Randolph 347
Mississippi Civil Rights Museum 422
Motown Historical Museum 573
Muhammad Ali Center 387
Museum of Art & History at the Custom House 485
Museum of Discovery & Science 471
Museum of Mississippi History 422
Museum of Science 178
Museum of Science & Industry 529
Museum of the American Revolution 153
Museum of the Bizarre 341
Museum of the Everglades 481
Mütter Museum 153-4
Mystic Seaport Museum 217
Nantucket Whaling Museum 201
National Air & Space Museum 251, 254
National Archives 264-5
National Automotive & Truck Museum 560

Map Pages **000**
Photo Pages **000**

National Civil Rights Museum 367
National Geographic Museum 266
National Great Blacks in Wax Museum 281-2
National Museum of African American History & Culture 255
National Museum of American History 258
National Museum of Civil War Medicine 292
National Museum of Natural History 255, 258
National Museum of the American Indian 262
National Museum of the US Air Force 568
National Mustard Museum 596
National Naval Aviation Museum 513-14
National Railroad Museum 598
National September 11 Memorial Museum 65
National Toy Train Museum 164
National Underground Railroad Freedom Center 568
National Women's Hall of Fame 136
National WWII Museum 439
Nauticus 307
Naval Station Norfolk 307
New York State Museum 137
North Carolina Maritime Museum 340
North Carolina Museum of History 343
North Carolina Museum of Natural Sciences 343
O. Winston Link Museum 319
Ocean City Life-Saving Station Museum 290
Old Fort Niagara 144
Old Rhinebeck Aerodrome 131
Old Slave Mart Museum 356
Osborn-Jackson House 124
Oscar Getz Museum of Whiskey History 388
Parris Island Museum 363
Patricia & Phillip Frost Museum of Science 459
Peabody Essex Museum 193
Peggy Notebaert Nature Museum 532
Penn Center 363
Plimoth Plantation 193
Poe Museum 310
Pollock-Krasner House 124
Port Discovery 282
Prairie Acadian Cultural Center 450
Railroad Museum of Pennsylvania 164
RE Olds Transportation Museum 579
Ripley's Believe it or Not! 150
River Road African American Museum 446
Rock & Roll Hall of Fame & Museum 561
Sag Harbor Whaling & Historical Museum 124
Scott & Zelda Fitzgerald Museum 416
Selma Interpretive Center 417
Shaker Village of Pleasant Hill 393
Shore Line Trolley Museum 219
Slave Haven Underground Railroad Museum/ Burkle Estate 368
Songbirds 382
South Florida Science Center & Aquarium 476
Southampton History Museum 124
Spam Museum 609
Stax Museum of American Soul Music 367
Steven F Udvar-Hazy Center 254
Strawbery Banke Museum 233
Studebaker National Museum 560
Tallahassee Automobile & Collectibles Museum 511
Tallahassee Museum 511
Telfair Academy 408
Tennessee State Museum 376
Titanic Museum 386
Titanic: the Artifact Exhibition 504
Tudor Place 267
United States Holocaust Memorial Museum 263
US Space & Rocket Center 415
USS Alabama 418
USS Constitution Museum 179
Vermilionville 448
Villa Zorayda Museum 492
Vizcaya Museum & Gardens 462
White House Visitor Center 264
William J Clinton Presidential Center 425-6
Willie Dixon's Blues Heaven 527
Willie Nelson & Friends Museum Showcase 376-7
Women's Rights National Historical Park 136
World of Coca-Cola 395
Wright Museum 235
Ybor City Museum State Park 497
music 12-13, 43, 321, 578, 633-5
Muskegon 584
Myrtle Beach 363-5
Mystic 217-18

N

Nantucket 200-2, **197**
Naples 502-3
NASCAR Racing Experience 490
Nashville (Indiana) 556-7
Nashville (Tennessee) 373-82, **374-5**
Natchez 423-4
Natchez Trace Pkwy 43-4, 424, **40**
national & state parks 25, 331, 638, *see also* parks & gardens
Acadia National Park 15, 247-8, 331, **4-5**, **15**
Appomattox Court House National Historic Park 314
Assateague State Park 290
Bahia Honda State Park 485
Berkeley Springs State Park 324
Bill Baggs Cape Florida State Park 463
Biscayne National Park 479
Blackwater Falls State Park 325
Brandywine Creek State Park 296
Canaveral National Seashore 488
C&O Canal National Historic Park 21, 292-3, 324, **21**
Cape Henlopen State Park 294
Cape May Point State Park 151
Cherry Springs State Park 165
Chicot State Park 450
Colt State Park 213
Congaree National Park 364
Crawford Notch State Park 238
Cumberland Falls State Resort Park 393
Cuyahoga Valley National Park 563
Dry Tortugas National Park 49
Everglades National Park 20, 331, 478, **20**
Fakahatchee Strand Preserve 480
Fort Adams State Park 211
Fort Clinch State Park 495
Fort Macon State Park 340
Franconia Notch State Park 237-8
Grafton Notch State Park 249
Great Smoky Mountains National Park 15, 331, 354-5, **14-15**
Hammonasset Beach State Park 219
Hawks Nest State Park 327-8
Hocking Hills State Park 571
Hopewell Culture National Historical Park 572
Hot Springs National Park 427
Hunting Island State Park 363
Indiana Dunes National Park 559
Island Beach State Park 149
Isle Royale National Park 20, 25, 590, **20**
Jamaica State Park 48
Jockey's Ridge State Park 337, **11**
John Pennekamp Coral Reef State Park 21, 482
Kelleys Islands State Park 564
Lake Dardanelle State Park 429
Leonard Harrison State Park 165
Mammoth Cave National Park 331, 394, **330-1**
Marsh-Billings-Rockefeller National Historical Park 225
Minute Man National Historic Park 192
Montauk Point State Park 125
Mt Magazine State Park 429
Mt Monadnock State Park 233
Mt Nebo State Park 429
Natural Bridge State Park 318

Natural Bridge State Resort Park 394
New River Gorge National Park 21, 327-8
Newport State Park 599
Ozark Folk Center State Park 430
Petit Jean State Park 429
Porcupine Mountains Wilderness State Park 590
Robert H Treman State Park 135
Robert Moses State Park 123
Shenandoah National Park 316, 331, **331**
Split Rock Lighthouse State Park 611
Stonewall National Monument 69
Table Rock State Park 365
Unicoi State Park 407
Vogel State Park 407
Voyageurs National Park 613-14
Whirlpool State Park 144
White River State Park 553
Windley Key Fossil Reef Geological State Site 483-4

National Archives 264-5
National Cherry Blossom Festival 29, 269, **29**
National Mall 251, 254-5, 258-62, **260-1**, **260-1**
National September 11 Memorial 65
natural disasters 637
Navy Pier 523
New England 57, 170-249, **172-3**
accommodations 170
climate 170
food 50-1, 170
highlights 172-3
history 171
travel seasons 170
New Hampshire 232-40, **223**
New Haven 219-21
New Jersey 60, 145-52, **62-3**
New London 218
New Orleans 12, 433-45, **436-7**, **12**, **13**
New Paltz 129-30
New River 327-9
New York City 9, 57, 61-121, **64**, **8**, **9**
accommodations 91-6
activities 88-9
Bronx, the 88, 112, 120
Brooklyn 86-7, 95-6, 105-7, 110-11, 119-20
Chelsea 65, 67-9, 92, 98-9, 108, 116, **74-5**
Chinatown 65, 92, 97-8, 107, 115, **66-7**
drinking & nightlife 107-12
East Village 69-70, 92, 99-100, 108, 116-17, **70-1**
entertainment 112-15
festivals & events 89, 91
Financial District 61, 91-2, 96-7, 107, 115
food 50, 96-107
Gramercy 70-1, 93, 100-1, 108-9, 117
Harlem 83, 95, 104, 110, 118
Lower East Side 69-70, 92, 99-100, 108, 116-17
Lower Manhattan 61, 91-2, 96-7, 107, 115, **66-7**
Meatpacking District 65, 67-9, 92, 98-9, 108, 116
Midtown 71-3, 76-8, 93-4, 101-2, 109, 117-18, **74-5**
Queens 87, 111, 120
safety 120
shopping 115-20
sights 61-88
SoHo 65, 92, 97-8, 107, 115
tourist offices 120
tours 89
travel to/from 120-1
travel within 121
Union Square 70-1, 93, 100-1, 108-9, 117
Upper East Side 78-9, 94, 102-3, 109, 118, **80-1**
Upper Manhattan 83, 104, 110, 118
Upper West Side 79, 82-3, 94, 103-4, 110, 118, **80-1**
walking tour 90, **90**
West Village 65, 67-9, 92, 98-9, 108, 116, **70-1**
New York State 57, 121-45, **62-3**
Newport 211-13
Niagara Falls 143-5
Norfolk 307-8
North Adams 207
North Carolina 333-55
North Carolina Mountains 348-54
North Fork 126-7
North Shore 611-12
North Woodstock 236
Northampton 203-4

O

Oak Park 548
Obama, Barack 531, 622-4
Ocean City 289-90
Ocean Grove 147-8
Ocracoke Island 339-40
Ogunquit 241
Ohio 560-71
Ohio River 558
Old Cahawba Archaeological Park 418
Old North Bridge 192-3
One World Observatory 61, 65
Opelousas 450-1
opening hours 646
Orlando 504-6, **508**
Outer Banks 11, 333, 336-9
overtourism 646
Oxford 419-20
Ozark Mountains 430-2

P

painting 630
Paisley Park 603
Palm Beach 474-7
panthers 638
Paris 429
parks & gardens, *see also* national & state parks
Airlie Gardens 341
Atlanta Botanical Garden 395
Barataria Preserve 446
Battery & White Point Garden 356
Belle Isle Park 573
Brookgreen Gardens 364
Brooklyn Botanic Garden 87
Brooklyn Bridge Park 86
Bryant Park 77
Campus Martius Park 573
Cave Point County Park 599
Central Park 79, 84-5, **80-1**, **84-5**, **84-5**
Chimney Rock Park 351
City Park 435
Coolidge Park 383
Cornell Botanic Gardens 135
Crescent Park 438
Dumbarton Oaks 266-7
Fairchild Tropical Garden 462
Forsyth Park 408
Fort Williams Park 243
Frederik Meijer Gardens & Sculpture Park 581
Garvan Woodland Gardens 428
Georgetown Waterfront Park 267
High Line 65, 67
Hudson River Park 68
Ijams Nature Center 384
Independence National Historical Park 153
Kentucky Horse Park 391
Lake Leatherwood City Park 431
LeFrak Center at Lakeside 89
Lincoln Park 528
Louis Armstrong Park 435
Madison Square Park 70-1
Mary Ann Brown Preserve 447
Máximo Gómez Park 461
Millennium Park 521
Minneapolis Sculpture Garden 602
Naples Botanical Gardens 502
National Gallery of Art Sculpture Garden 255
New York Botanical Garden 88
Northerly Island 523
Olbrich Botanical Gardens 596
Piedmont Park 398
Prospect Park 86
Public Garden 174
Rose Kennedy Greenway 175
Shelby Farms Park 369
Shofuso Japanese House & Garden 155
State Botanical Garden of Georgia 406
Tompkins Square Park 70
Vulcan Park 414
Washington Square Park 68-9
Parton, Dolly 385
passports 648, 649
Peaks of Otter 320
Peanut Island 476
Pelee Island 565
Pennsylvania 57, 152-69, **62-3**
Pennsylvania Dutch Country 163-5
Pennsylvania Wilds 165-6
Pensacola 513-15
Pentagon 299
Petoskey 586
Philadelphia 17, 152-63, **156-7**, **160**
accommodations 158-9
drinking & nightlife 161-2
entertainment 162
festivals & events 157-8
shopping 162-3
sights & activities 152-6
tourist offices 163
travel to/from 163
travel within 163
Phippsburg 245
Phoenicia 132-3
phonecards 647

Map Pages **000**
Photo Pages **000**

Pictured Rocks National Lakeshore 588
Piedmont, the 308-14
Pigeon Forge 385-6
Pinkham Notch 239-40
Pioneer Valley 203-5
Pittsburgh 165-9
planning
accommodations 26-7
activities 46-9
budgeting 23, 26, 52, 54
calendar of events 28-32
Eastern USA basics 22-3
Eastern USA's regions 57-8
family travel 54-6
food 50-3
internet resources 23
itineraries 33-7
repeat visitors 24-5
road trips 38-45
travel seasons 22, 28, 29, 30, 31, 32
plantations
Berkeley Plantation 306
Boone Hall Plantation 358
Drayton Hall 357
Historic Stagville Plantation 344
Laura Plantation 446
Magnolia Plantation 357
McLeod Plantation 361
Middleton Place 357
Monticello 312
Montpelier 313
Myrtles Plantation 447
Oakley Plantation 447
Shirley Plantation 306
Whitney Plantation 446
plants 636
Plymouth 193-4
population 626-7
Portland 241, 243-4
Portsmouth 233-4
postal services 646
Poughkeepsie 130-1
Presley, Elvis 367, 369, 634
Prince 603
Princeton 146
Princeton University 146
Providence 209-10
Provincetown 198-200, **11**
public holidays 646

Q

Quechee 225-6

R

Racine 595
Radio City Music Hall 77
rafting 47-8, 327, 328, 347, 429
railways
Cuyahoga Valley Scenic Railroad 563
Delaware & Ulster Railroad 132
Essex 218
Mt Washington Cog Railway 238
Raleigh 343-4
Red Cliff 601
Rehoboth Beach 294
religion 626-7
resorts 26
responsible travel 646
Rhinebeck 131
Rhode Island 208-13
Richmond 309-12
ridesharing 655
road trips, *see* scenic drives
Roanoke 319-20, 618
rock climbing 129, 325
rock music 634-5
Rockefeller Center 73, 76
Rockland 246-7
Rockwell, Norman 205
Route 66 18, 45, 521, 551, **18**
Rowan Oak 419
Russellville 429

S

safety 654-5
Salem 193
Sandwich 194
Sandy Hook Gateway National Recreation Area 150
Sanibel Island 501-2
Saranac Lake 140
Sarasota 500-1
Saugatuck 583-4
Saugerties 135
Sault Ste Marie 589
Savannah 408-11, **410**
scenic drives 16, 38-45, **41**
Acadia National Park 248
Blue Ridge Pkwy 16, 320, 349, **16**
Brockway Mountain Drive 590
Crooked Road 321
Florida Hwy 1 16, **16**, **40**
Foothills Pkwy 354
Highland Scenic Hwy 325-6
Hwy 13 601
Hwy 61 612
Kancamagus Hwy 236
Lincoln Hwy 41-3
Mt Magazine Scenic Byway 429
Mt Washington Auto Road 239
Natchez Trace Pkwy 43-4, 424, **40**
Pensacola Scenic Bluffs Hwy 514
Route 66 18, 45, 521, 551, **18**
Skyline Dr 316
VT 100 16, 226, **16**
Whiteface Veteran's Memorial Highway 139
sea turtles 412, 489-90, 639
seafood 17, 50-1, 288, **17**
Seaside Heights 149
Selma 417-18
Seneca Falls 136
Seneca Rocks 325
senior travelers 643
Serpent Mound 572
Shelburne Farms 229
Shelter Island 126-7
Shenandoah Valley 314-19
Singer Castle 141
skating 465
skiing 49
Belleayre Mountain 132
Hunter Mountain 133
Killington Resort 226
Mad River Glen 226
Porcupine Mountain Ski Area 590
Snowshoe Mountain Resort 326
Stowe Mountain Resort 226, **49**
Voyageurs National Park 613
Sleeping Bear Dunes National Lakeshore 584-5
Sloss Furnaces 414
Smith College 204
Smith Island 281
Smithsonian Castle 262
smoking 642, 646-7
Smugglers Notch 228
snakes 639-40
snorkeling 479
snowmobiling 613
soft drinks 53
South Bend 559-60
South Carolina 355-66
South Shore 122-3
South, the 58, 332-451, **334-5**
accommodations 332
climate 332
food 51, 332
highlights 334-5
itineraries 337
travel seasons 332
Space Coast 488-90
Sperryville 303
sports 628-9
sports museums
Carolina Basketball Museum 346
Chicago Sports Museum 527-8
College Football Hall of Fame 395
Green Bay Packers Hall of Fame 598
Indianapolis Motor Speedway 553
Kentucky Derby Museum 387
Louisville Slugger Museum & Factory 387
NASCAR Hall of Fame 347
National Sporting Museum 303
Women's Basketball Hall of Fame 384
Spring Green 597
Springfield (Illinois) 550
Springfield (Massachusetts) 204
St Augustine 19, 491-3
St Francisville 447
St Helena Island 358
St Paul 607-9
St Petersburg 499-500
St Simons Island 412
Statue of Liberty 61
Staunton 315-17
Stillwater 609
Stockbridge 205-6
Stowe 228-9, **49**
Straits of Mackinac 587-8
Sugarcreek 565
Sullivan's Island 361
Sun Studio 367, **35**
Sunken Forest 123
Super Bowl 629
surfing 48, 125, 465

T

Taliesin 597
Tallahassee 511-13
Tallulah Gorge 407
Tamiami Trail 480
Tampa 496-9
Tanglewood Music Festival 206
Tannersville 133
taxes 646
taxis 655
telephone services 647-8
Tennessee 366-86
theater 631
theme parks, *see* amusement & water parks
Thousand Islands 140-1
time 22, 647
Times Square 73
tipping 121, 646

toilets 647
Top of the Rock 77-8
tourist information 647-8
train travel 25, 651, 655
travel to/from Canada 650
travel to/from Eastern USA 649-51
travel within Eastern USA 23, 651-5
Traverse City 585
trekking, *see* hiking
Triangle, the 342-6
Tri-Peaks Region 428-30
Tuckerman Ravine 239
TV 631-2

U

Universal Orlando Resort 507-11
University of North Carolina 345
University of Virginia 312
Upcountry 365-6
Upper Peninsula 588-91
US Capitol 262-3
US Naval Academy 287
USS Constitution 179

V

vacations 646
vaccinations 644
vegetarian & vegan travelers 52
Vermont 221-31, **223**
Vicksburg 421-2
Ville Platte 450
vineyards
- Haight-Brown Vineyards 216
- Traverse City 585
- Virginia 309
- Wolf Mountain Vineyards 405

Virginia 298-322
Virginia Beach 308
Virginia Military Institute 317-18
visas 22, 648
volunteering 648
Vonnegut, Kurt 553

W

walks & walking tours, *see also* hiking
- Birmingham Civil Rights Memorial Trail 414
- Boston 184, **184**
- Chicago 530, **530**
- Cliff Walk 211
- Cotton Valley Rail Trail 235
- Miami 464, **464**
- New Orleans 440, **440**
- New River Gorge 328

Walt Disney World® Resort 506-7
Warhol, Andy 166
Washington, DC 9, 58, 251-80, **256-7**, **9**
- accommodations 269-70
- activities 268
- drinking & nightlife 275-8
- entertainment 278-9
- festivals & events 269
- food 271-5
- history 251
- itineraries 254
- LGBTIQ+ travelers 277
- sights 251-67
- tourist offices 279
- tours 268
- travel to/from 279
- travel within 279-80

Washington & Lee University 318
water, drinking 644
water parks, *see* amusement & water parks
waterfalls
- Amicalola Falls 405
- Arethusa Falls 238
- Kaaterskill Falls 133
- Niagara Falls 143-5
- Sabbaday Falls 236

WaterFire 209
weather 22, 28, 29, 30, 31, 32, *see also individual regions*
websites, *see* internet resources
Weedon Island Preserve 499
Weirs Beach 234-5
Wellfleet 198
Welty, Eudora 422
West Nile Virus 644
West Palm Beach 475-7
West Virginia 322-9
whales 199, 620, 640
White House 264
White Mountains 15, 236-40, **15**
Whiteface Mountain 139
white-water rafting 47-8
wildlife 636-40
wildlife reserves
- Bombay Hook National Wildlife Refuge 297
- Chincoteague National Wildlife Refuge 290
- Cypress Creek National Wildlife Refuge 552
- Duke Lemur Center 344
- Everglades Outpost 479
- Georgia Sea Turtle Center 412
- JN 'Ding' Darling National Wildlife Refuge 501
- Laura Quinn Wild Bird Sanctuary 483
- Louisiana Universities Marine Consortium 450
- Manatee Viewing Center 497
- Merritt Island National Wildlife Refuge 488
- Okefenokee National Wildlife Refuge 47
- Pea Island National Wildlife Refuge 336

Wildwood 150-1
Williamsburg 19, 304-5, **19**
Williamstown 207-8
Willis Tower 521
Wilmington (Delaware) 295-6
Wilmington (North Carolina) 341-2
Wingspread 595
Wisconsin 591-601
Wolfeboro 235-6
wolves 639
women travelers 648
Woodstock (New York State) 18, 133-4, **18**
Woodstock (Vermont) 225-6
Woodstock Festival 621, 622
work 648
World War II 620-1
Wright, Frank Lloyd
- architecture 300, 529, 550, 595
- homes 548, 597
- trails 549

Wrigley Field 528

Y

Yale University 219
Yankee Stadium 88
Yellow Springs 567-8
Yorktown 306-7

Z

Zika virus 644
zoos
- Bronx Zoo 88
- Central Park Zoo 79
- Jungle Island 463
- Maryland Zoo in Baltimore 282
- Minnesota Zoo 602
- Monkey Jungle 463
- Smithsonian's National Zoo 267
- Zoo Miami 463

Map Pages **000**
Photo Pages **000**

Map Legend

Sights

- Beach
- Bird Sanctuary
- Buddhist
- Castle/Palace
- Christian
- Confucian
- Hindu
- Islamic
- Jain
- Jewish
- Monument
- Museum/Gallery/Historic Building
- Ruin
- Shinto
- Sikh
- Taoist
- Winery/Vineyard
- Zoo/Wildlife Sanctuary
- Other Sight

Activities, Courses & Tours

- Bodysurfing
- Diving
- Canoeing/Kayaking
- Course/Tour
- Sento Hot Baths/Onsen
- Skiing
- Snorkeling
- Surfing
- Swimming/Pool
- Walking
- Windsurfing
- Other Activity

Sleeping

- Sleeping
- Camping
- Hut/Shelter

Eating

- Eating

Drinking & Nightlife

- Drinking & Nightlife
- Cafe

Entertainment

- Entertainment

Shopping

- Shopping

Information

- Bank
- Embassy/Consulate
- Hospital/Medical
- Internet
- Police
- Post Office
- Telephone
- Toilet
- Tourist Information
- Other Information

Geographic

- Beach
- Gate
- Hut/Shelter
- Lighthouse
- Lookout
- Mountain/Volcano
- Oasis
- Park
- Pass
- Picnic Area
- Waterfall

Population

- Capital (National)
- Capital (State/Province)
- City/Large Town
- Town/Village

Transport

- Airport
- BART station
- Border crossing
- Boston T station
- Bus
- Cable car/Funicular
- Cycling
- Ferry
- Metro/Muni station
- Monorail
- Parking
- Petrol station
- Subway/SkyTrain station
- Taxi
- Train station/Railway
- Tram
- Underground station
- Other Transport

Routes

- Tollway
- Freeway
- Primary
- Secondary
- Tertiary
- Lane
- Unsealed road
- Road under construction
- Plaza/Mall
- Steps
- Tunnel
- Pedestrian overpass
- Walking Tour
- Walking Tour detour
- Path/Walking Trail

Boundaries

- International
- State/Province
- Disputed
- Regional/Suburb
- Marine Park
- Cliff
- Wall

Hydrography

- River, Creek
- Intermittent River
- Canal
- Water
- Dry/Salt/Intermittent Lake
- Reef

Areas

- Airport/Runway
- Beach/Desert
- Cemetery (Christian)
- Cemetery (Other)
- Glacier
- Mudflat
- Park/Forest
- Sight (Building)
- Sportsground
- Swamp/Mangrove

Note: Not all symbols displayed above appear on the maps in this book

of interest – she has covered Spain, Italy, Turkey, Syria, Lebanon, Israel, Egypt, Morocco and Tunisia for Lonely Planet – but she also covers Finland, Bali, Armenia, the Netherlands, the USA and Australia. Follow her @maxwellvirginia on Instagram and Twitter.

Hugh McNaughtan
New York, New Jersey & Pennsylvania A former English lecturer, Hugh swapped grant applications for visa applications, and turned his love of travel into a full-time thing. Having done a bit of restaurant-reviewing in his home town (Melbourne) he's now eaten his way across four continents. He's never happier than when on the road with his two daughters. Except perhaps on the cricket field...

MaSovaida Morgan
The South MaSovaida is a Lonely Planet writer and multimedia storyteller whose wanderlust has taken her to more than 35 countries across six continents. Prior to freelancing, she was Lonely Planet's Destination Editor for South America for four years and worked as an editor for newspapers and NGOs in the Middle East and United Kingdom. Follow her on Instagram @MaSovaida.

Lorna Parkes
New York City Londoner by birth, Melburnian by palate and former Lonely Planet staffer in both cities, Lorna has contributed to numerous Lonely Planet books and magazines. She's discovered she writes best on planes, and is most content when researching food and booze. Wineries and the tropics (not at the same time!) are her go-to happy places, but Yorkshire will always be special to her. Follow her @Lorna_Explorer.

Kevin Raub
Great Lakes, The South Atlanta native Kevin started his career as a music journalist in New York, working for *Men's Journal* and *Rolling Stone* magazines. He ditched the rock 'n' roll lifestyle for travel writing and has written nearly 50 Lonely Planet guides, focused mainly on Brazil, Chile, Colombia, USA, India, the Caribbean and Portugal. Along the way, the confessed hophead is in constant search of wildly high IBUs in local beers. Follow him on Twitter and Instagram (@RaubOnTheRoad).

Simon Richmond
Pennsylvania Journalist and photographer Simon has specialised as a travel writer since the early 1990s, covering countries including Australia, China, India, Iran, Japan, Korea, Malaysia, Mongolia, Myanmar (Burma), Russia, Singapore, South Africa and Turkey. He has lived in the UK, Japan and Australia, and is now based back in the UK in Folkestone on the east Kent coast. His travel features have been published in newspapers and magazines around the world, including in the UK's *Independent, Guardian, Times, Daily Telegraph* and *Royal Geographical Society Magazine,* and in Australia's *Sydney Morning Herald* and *Australian* newspapers and *Australian Financial Review* magazine.

Benedict Walker
New England Born in Newcastle, Australia, Ben holds notions of the beach core to his idea of self, though he's traveled thousands of miles from the sandy shores of home to live in Leipzig, Germany. Ben was given his first Lonely Planet guide when he was 12. Two decades later, he'd write chapters for the same publication: a dream come true. A communications graduate and travel agent by trade, Ben whittled away his twenties gallivanting around the globe. He thinks the best thing about travel isn't as much where you go as who you meet: living vicariously through the stories of kind strangers enriches one's own experience. Come along for the ride on Instagram @wordsandjourneys.

Greg Ward
The South Since whetting his appetite for travel by following the hippie trail to India, and later living in northern Spain, Greg has written guides to destinations all over the world. As well as covering the USA from the Southwest to Hawaii, he has ranged on recent assignments from Corsica to the Cotswolds, and Japan to Corfu. See his website, www.gregward.info, for his favorite photos and memories.

Karla Zimmerman
Great Lakes, The South, Washington, DC Karla lives in Chicago, where she eats doughnuts and yells at the Cubs, and writes stuff for books, magazines and websites when she's not doing the first two things. She has contributed to 70-plus guidebooks and travel anthologies covering destinations in Europe, Asia, Africa, North America and the Caribbean. To learn more, follow her @karlazimmerman on Instagram and Twitter.

Other contributors
Barbara Noe Kennedy contributed to the Washington, DC section. Ben Buckner, Evan Godt, Alicia Johnson, Alexander Howard, Bailey Freeman and Sarah Stocking contributed to the Nashville section. Charles Rawlings-Way curated the Great Lakes chapter, and Martine Power curated the Florida chapter.

organisations. Find him on Instagram and Twitter @markbakerprague, and his blog at www.markbakerprague.com.

Amy C Balfour
Capital Region, New England, The South Amy practiced law in Virginia before moving to Los Angeles to try to break in as a screenwriter. After a stint as a writer's assistant on *Law & Order*, she jumped into freelance writing, focusing on travel, food and the outdoors. She has hiked, biked and paddled across Southern California and the Southwest, and recently criss-crossed the Great Plains in search of the region's best burgers and barbecue. She has written many books for Lonely Planet and her essays have appeared in the *Los Angeles Times* and *Southern Living*, and the travel anthologies *Go Your Own Way* and *The Thong Also Rises*.

Robert Balkovich
New England, New York State Robert was born and raised in Oregon, but has called New York City home for almost a decade. When he was a child and other families were going to theme parks and grandma's house, he went to Mexico City and toured Eastern Europe by train. He's now a writer and travel enthusiast seeking experiences that are ever so slightly out of the ordinary to report back on. Follow on Instagram @oh_balky.

Ray Bartlett
Florida Ray has been travel writing for nearly two decades, bringing Japan, Korea, Mexico, Tanzania, Guatemala, Indonesia, and many parts of the USA to life in rich detail for publishers, newspapers and magazines. Among other pursuits, he surfs regularly and is an accomplished Argentine tango dancer. Follow him on Instagram and Twitter @kaisoradotcom.

Jade Bremner
The South Jade has been a journalist for more than a decade. Wherever she goes she finds action sports to try, and it's no coincidence many of her favorite places have some of the best waves in the world. Jade has edited travel magazines and sections for *Time Out* and *Radio Times* and has contributed to the *Times*, CNN and the *Independent*. She feels privileged to share tales from this wonderful planet we call home and is always looking for the next adventure.

Gregor Clark
New England Gregor is a US-based writer whose love of foreign languages and curiosity about what's around the next bend have taken him to dozens of countries on five continents. Chronic wanderlust has also led him to visit all 50 states and most Canadian provinces on countless road trips through his native North America. Since 2000, Gregor has regularly contributed to Lonely Planet guides, with a focus on Europe and the Americas.

Ashley Harrell
The South After a brief stint selling day spa coupons door-to-door in South Florida, Ashley decided she'd rather be a writer. She went to journalism grad school, convinced a newspaper to hire her, and starting covering wildlife, crime and tourism, sometimes all in the same story. Fueling her zest for storytelling and the unknown, she traveled widely and moved often, from a tiny NYC apartment to a vast California ranch to a jungle cabin in Costa Rica, where she started writing for Lonely Planet.

Adam Karlin
New England, Pennsylvania, The South Adam has contributed to dozens of Lonely Planet guidebooks, covering an alphabetical spread that ranges from the Andaman Islands to the Zimbabwe border. As a journalist, he has written on travel, crime, politics, archeology and the Sri Lankan Civil War, among other topics. He has sent dispatches from every continent barring Antarctica (one day!) and his essays and articles have featured on the BBC and NPR, and in multiple non-fiction anthologies. Adam is based out of New Orleans. Learn more at http://walkonfine.com, or follow @adamwalkonfine on Instagram.

Brian Kluepfel
New England, New Jersey Brian had lived in three states and seven different residences by the time he was nine, and just kept moving, making stops in Berkeley, Bolivia, the Bronx and the 'burbs further down the line. His journalistic work across the Americas has ranged from the Copa America soccer tournament in Paraguay to an accordion festival in Québec. His titles for Lonely Planet include *Costa Rica*, *Bolivia* and *Ecuador*. He writes a blog about Venezuelan baseball players and another regarding birds of many nations called www.brianbirdwatching.blogspot.com.

Vesna Maric
Florida Vesna has been a Lonely Planet author for nearly two decades, covering places as far and wide as Bolivia, Algeria, Sicily, Cyprus, Barcelona, London and Croatia, among others. Recent work has been updating Florida, Greece and North Macedonia.

Virginia Maxwell
Washington, DC, Virginia Although based in Australia, Virginia often spends at least half of her year updating Lonely Planet destination coverage across the globe. The Mediterranean is her major area

OUR STORY

A beat-up old car, a few dollars in the pocket and a sense of adventure. In 1972 that's all Tony and Maureen Wheeler needed for the trip of a lifetime – across Europe and Asia overland to Australia. It took several months, and at the end – broke but inspired – they sat at their kitchen table writing and stapling together their first travel guide, *Across Asia on the Cheap*. Within a week they'd sold 1500 copies. Lonely Planet was born.

Today, Lonely Planet has offices in the US, Ireland and China, with a network of over 2000 contributors in every corner of the globe. We share Tony's belief that 'a great guidebook should do three things: inform, educate and amuse'.

OUR WRITERS

Trisha Ping
A year working abroad in Mulhouse, France, and a fascination with languages turned Trisha into a lifelong traveler. Over her 15-year career as a writer and editor, she spent two years as a Destination Editor at Lonely Planet and is now the publisher of BookPage. She lives in Nashville, Tennessee. Trisha researched and curated the Plan Your Trip, Understand Eastern USA and Survival Guide chapters.

Ali Lemer
New York, New Jersey & Pennsylvania Ali has been a Lonely Planet writer and editor since 2007, and has authored guidebooks and travel articles on Russia, NYC, Los Angeles, Melbourne, Bali, Hawaii, Japan and Scotland. A native New Yorker and naturalized Melburnian, Ali has also lived in Chicago, Prague and the UK, and has traveled extensively around Europe and North America.

Regis St Louis
New England, The South Regis grew up in a small town in the American Midwest – the kind of place that fuels big dreams of travel – and he developed an early fascination with foreign dialects and world cultures. He spent his formative years learning Russian and a handful of Romance languages, which served him well on journeys across much of the globe. Regis has contributed to more than 50 Lonely Planet titles, covering destinations across six continents. His travels have taken him from the mountains of Kamchatka to remote island villages in Melanesia, and to many grand urban landscapes. When not on the road, he lives in New Orleans.

Mara Vorhees
New England, Washington, DC & the Capital Region Mara writes about food, travel and family fun around the world. Her work has been published by *BBC Travel, Boston Globe, Delta Sky,* the *Vancouver Sun* and more. For Lonely Planet, she regularly writes about destinations in Central America and Eastern Europe, as well as New England, where she lives. She often travels with her twin boys in tow, earning her expertise in family travel. Follow their adventures at www.havetwinswilltravel.com.

Isabel Albiston
New England After six years working for the *Daily Telegraph* in London, Isabel left to spend more time on the road. A job as a writer for a magazine in Sydney, Australia, was followed by a four-month overland trip across Asia and five years living and working in Buenos Aires, Argentina. Isabel started writing for Lonely Planet in 2014 and has contributed to more than a dozen guidebooks. She's currently based in Ireland.

Mark Baker
Great Lakes Mark is a freelance travel writer with a penchant for offbeat stories and forgotten places. He's originally from the United States, but now makes his home in the Czech capital, Prague. He writes mainly on Eastern and Central Europe for Lonely Planet as well as other leading travel publishers, but finds real satisfaction in digging up stories in places that are too remote or quirky for the guides. Prior to becoming an author, he worked as a journalist for the *Economist*, Bloomberg News and Radio Free Europe, among other

OVER PAGE MORE WRITERS

Published by Lonely Planet Global Limited
CRN 554153
6th edition – Aug 2022
ISBN 978 1 78868 419 4

10 9 8 7 6 5 4 3 2 1
Printed in Singapore